MAKING SENSE OF LANGUAGE

MAKING SENSE OF LANGUAGE

READINGS IN CULTURE AND COMMUNICATION

SUSAN D. BLUM

The University of Notre Dame

New York   Oxford

OXFORD UNIVERSITY PRESS

2009

Oxford University Press, Inc., publishes works that further Oxford University's
objective of excellence in research, scholarship, and education.

Oxford   New York
Auckland   Cape Town   Dar es Salaam   Hong Kong   Karachi
Kuala Lumpur   Madrid   Melbourne   Mexico City   Nairobi
New Delhi   Shanghai   Taipei   Toronto

With offices in
Argentina   Austria   Brazil   Chile   Czech Republic   France   Greece
Guatemala   Hungary   Italy   Japan   Poland   Portugal   Singapore
South Korea   Switzerland   Thailand   Turkey   Ukraine   Vietnam

Copyright © 2009 by Oxford University Press, Inc.

Published by Oxford University Press, Inc.
198 Madison Avenue, New York, New York 10016

http://www.oup.com

Oxford is a registered trademark of Oxford University Press

Library of Congress Cataloging-in-Publication Data
Blum, Susan Debra.
  Making sense of language : readings in culture and communication / Susan D. Blum.
     p.   cm.
  Includes bibliographical references and index.
  ISBN 978-0-19-533638-2 (pbk.)—ISBN 978-0-19-533639-9 (hardcover)
  1. Language and languages.   I. Title.
  P107.B595 2008
  400—dc22   2008035161

Printing number: 9 8 7 6 5 4

Printed in the United States of America
on acid-free paper

CONTENTS

vi   Contents

PART III
LANGUAGE AS SOCIAL ACTION ◆ 347

UNIT 5 DISCOURSE, PERFORMANCE, AND RITUAL ◆ 349

UNIT 6 LANGUAGE IDEOLOGY ◆ 424

PREFACE

This reader grows out of my own teaching experience and my quest to find readings on language that are compelling and accessible to undergraduates, even to those who are not planning to specialize in anthropology or the study of language. Some students reading this book may never have taken a course in this field and may never take another one like it. Others may have already taken a more basic course, may be familiar with a four-field approach to anthropology, or may go on to take more advanced courses. Most of the available collections of readings in linguistic anthropology are at a higher level than is accessible to most undergraduates, and many of them focus on particular aspects of linguistic anthropology. I could not find a teaching tool that effectively reached students on various academic paths, so I decided to create one.

My own background is in both cultural and linguistic anthropology; my research focuses on issues of nationalism, identity, ethnicity, multilingualism, stereotypes, naming, truth and deception, and on general pragmatics in China. More recently I have also written about plagiarism, authorship, childhood, education, selfhood, and college culture in the United States. Since 1992 I have been teaching in four-field anthropology departments, where my students often bring me questions from their other classes, and my colleagues often talk about broad issues concerning the nature of humanity. I have become intrigued by the connections among a wide range of topics, and this experience is what I've brought to the choices I've made here.

The Readings

My intention with this book is to provide a range of topics and viewpoints on the subject of language and its relation to many aspects of being human. Some of the topics are broadly anthropological or even come from fields outside anthropology. (Unit 1 in particular, "What Is Language?," displays a generous curiosity about all things human. This topic is addressed variously by linguistic anthropologists, linguists, biologists, and others, and it is often of great interest to students with backgrounds in biological anthropology, biology, or archaeology.) Some of the readings are classics in the field, and some are contemporary. Some might be obvious choices, and some might be a bit unconventional.

No collection of readings can be all-inclusive. Thus this book does not attempt to cover the entire field of linguistic anthropology, nor does it even begin to address formal linguistics. Some instructors' favorite topics are likely to be omitted, and every academic is likely to argue about whether a particular article is the best example of a specific topic. Fair enough. This field thrives on independence of mind. My hope, though, is that this volume will provide a core set of readings that can be subtracted from or added to as each individual instructor chooses.

The readings run the gamut from many that are short and easily accessible to some that are relatively long, complex, and technical, and will be appropriate only for more advanced students. In some cases, the articles have been edited for space constraints, with a careful eye to retaining the flavor and gist of the author's original work; ellipses mark the omissions.

Many of the readings involve analysis of language in the United States, while the others are distributed (unevenly) across other cultures. This uneven distribution is not meant to imply that the United States is more important than anyplace else, nor does it mean that I assume that my audience consists entirely of students from the United States. Rather, for English-speaking students, many of the most accessible works on language have been written about English-speaking societies. Since the book does not presuppose technical linguistic knowledge, articles relying on grammatical or phonological analysis of languages other than English were overly daunting and had to be omitted.

Organization

The linear nature of a book requires that topics unfold in a given order, but sections can be taken in any order; sections do not build on one another or assume knowledge from other sections. In my own teaching, I often like to sandwich the topic "What Is Language?" around other topics, so we begin by thinking about what language is, explore it in some detail and variety, and then return to consider it again from a more informed position. Instructors may have different ideas about whether to begin with what is more familiar or more strange, with what is easy to see or with what is more challenging.

Some of the chapters could be placed into several units, because they do more than one thing. Language ideology, for example, is both a unit and a topic addressed by readings in other units. Gender, too, appears in many of the units, as well as in its own.

Chapters are not necessarily set up to provide "for" and "against" positions for most topics. Each reading is meant to open up a window, a way of looking at language. I do not necessarily agree with the arguments presented in some of the articles, but I believe that a multiplicity of perspectives is enriching and that what we gain from them is insight, if not always truth. Rarely do I find any perspective entirely, dismissively wrong.

The topics addressed here are broadly mirrored in the contents of textbooks on language and culture, and a textbook could easily complement this collection of readings. The advantage of using primary sources is that students become familiar with the complexity of actual intellectual work rather than its extract. It's a bit like getting your vitamin C from a juicy orange instead of from a tablet.

Features

The book includes features intended to be helpful for its various audiences. I've provided introductions to the three parts of the book ("The Nature of Language," "Language and Society," and "Language as Social Action" and to the six units ("What Is Language?," "Language and Thought," "Multilingualism," "Language and Identity," "Discourse, Performance, and Ritual," and "Language Ideology"). These introductions provide succinct historical and intellectual contexts for the broad topics, followed by a list of suggested further readings.

Each individual article has an introduction, giving information about the author or the context of the work, along with questions to guide student reading and discussion. There are also post-reading suggestions to help students reflect further; included here are also possible class or individual activities. Following each article is a list of key terms, whose definitions are included in the glossary at the end of the book.

The suggested further reading sections following each part introduction, unit introduction, and article point to foundational readings on each topic, alternative perspectives, or additional examples of the approach provided. Some are more difficult and technical, while others are simply additional.

Even in a reader with as many chapters as this, it is impossible to do more than point to the growing body of knowledge and wisdom regarding the many roles of language in human life. My hope is that this book will serve as an opening, an entrée, an appetizer, to lifelong fascination—whether amateur or professional—with this ubiquitous and mysterious capability that we call language.

ACKNOWLEDGMENTS

This book began when my colleague at Notre Dame, Agustín Fuentes, sent the editor of his book down the hall to see if I had any ideas for a book. I immediately told Jan Beatty, the editor at Oxford University Press, "We need a lower-level collection of readings on language and linguistic anthropology to parallel what's available in the other subfields of anthropology," and even more quickly Jan asked if I'd be interested in doing this project. Several years passed before I had time to do it, but after many more rounds of teaching related courses, many encouraging meetings with Jan at the anthropology meetings, and much helpful input from students, the book is coming to life. I'd like to thank Jan for her steady and knowledgeable guidance.

Also at Oxford were Lauren Mine, Brian Black, and Christine D'Antonio, whose work tracking down final permissions and seeing the manuscript through production were indispensable.

I extend my thanks to the following reviewers commissioned by Oxford University Press: Nobuko Adachi, Illinois State University; Jean-Paul Dumont, George Mason University; Arienne Dwyer, University of Kansas; Douglas Glick, Binghamton University; Rosalyn Howard, University of Central Florida; Janet Dixon Keller, University of Illinois; Emily McEwan-Fujita, University of Pittsburgh; Sue Meswick, Queens College of the City University of New York; John Moore, University of Florida; Susan Rasmussen, University of Houston; Robert Rotenberg, DePaul University; Emily Schultz, St. Cloud State University; H. Stephen Straight, Binghamton University; Cindi Sturtz Streetharan, California State University, Sacramento; Stephen Tyler, Rice University; and Dorothy Wills, California State Polytechnic University, Pomona. Some of their comments pushed me—hard—to define my goals for the book, and I can state without reservation that their critiques were essential in making this book live. Indeed, at least half the entries are different from those in the earlier three versions read by these reviewers. I am grateful that these colleagues read the manuscript for this book so carefully and generously.

This book has had some critical reading from a variety of students at Notre Dame (supported by funding from the College of Arts and Letters, the Department of Anthropology, and the Helen Kellogg Institute for International Studies). David "Day" Zimlich and Kaitlin Ramsey read and commented on several chapters. Kathleen Kennedy Johnson sat with me for several days just before she graduated, giving me her first, informed impression of each chapter. Former student Hillary Brass spent most of an academic year helping me track down permissions for each chapter. Tracy Jennings proofread a version of the manuscript and June Sawyers prepared the index, supported by funding from the Institute for Scholarship in the Liberal Arts, College of Arts and Letters, at the University of Notre Dame.

To these students and their many classmates at both Notre Dame and the University of Colorado Denver (where I also spent almost a decade), I express great appreciation.

My colleagues, present and past, at these two institutions and at the University of Pennsylvania—Jim Bellis, John Brett, Meredith Chesson, Kitty Corbett, Antonio Curet, Linda Curran, Greg Downey, Agustín Fuentes, Roberto Da Matta, Patrick Gaffney, Craig Janes, Satsuki Kawano, Webb Keane, Steve Koestler, Ian Kuijt, Daniel Lende, John Lucy, Joanne Mack, Cynthia Mahmood, Debra McDougall, Jim McKenna, Lisa Mitchell, Lorna Moore, Carolyn Nordstrom, Duane Quiatt, Karen Richman, Deb Rotman,

Mark Schurr, Sue Sheridan, Tammy Stone, David Tracer, Greg Urban, and Cecilia van Hollen—have made me think in broadly anthropological terms about the nature and study of language. In many ways their curiosity and (quite often) self-professed lack of expertise propelled me to locate readings that they might find worthwhile to teach. If a few of them, or their counterparts at other institutions, find this book useful, I'll consider my efforts rewarded.

The Inter-Library Loan (ILL) department of Notre Dame's Hesburgh Libraries, along with Document Delivery, were indispensable in the preparation of this book. Sometimes I requested up to a dozen—or more—articles a day for consideration. Miraculously, sometimes articles would appear on my computer within a few hours of the posting of the request. In this age of criticism of higher education, it is important to point out the bright spots, and ILL is certainly one of them.

Finally, my family great and small provided their usual encouragement and balanced perspective as I plodded through the muddy ground of pedagogy, scholarship, copyright, and economics, my shoes sometimes getting stuck. Lionel, Hannah, and Elena Jensen; Joyce and George Blum; Kathi, David, Leah, and Henry Moss; Bobby, Tracye, Natalie, Madeleine, Cameron, and Weston Blum; Linda, Ken, Veronica, and Sara Long; Barbara Blum and Daniel Friedenzohn; and Anne Jensen: To all of y'all, I say simply, "Thanks."

I welcome suggestions for improvement. Please let me know what works and what doesn't, and please feel free to suggest concrete ways to make this book a better resource. In addition to understanding the material, students should be able to apply what they learn, to become analysts and observers of life. This, I believe, is one of the most important goals of higher education. How we accomplish it is a work in progress.

SUGGESTED FURTHER READING

Here are some popular textbooks, readers, and monographs used in teaching material related to this topic.

Textbooks

Bonvillain, Nancy. 2003. *Language, Culture, and Communication: The Meaning of Messages.* 4th ed. Upper Saddle River, NJ: Prentice Hall.

Duranti, Alessandro. 1997. *Linguistic Anthropology.* Cambridge: Cambridge University Press.

Foley, William A. 1997. *Anthropological Linguistics: An Introduction.* Malden, MA: Blackwell.

Greenberg, Joseph H. 1968. *Anthropological Linguistics: An Introduction.* New York: Random House.

Hickerson, Nancy Parrott. 2000. *Linguistic Anthropology.* 2d ed. Fort Worth, TX: Harcourt.

Ohio State University Department of Linguistics. 2007. *Language Files.* 10th ed. Columbus: Ohio State University Press.

Ottenheimer, Harriet Joseph. 2006. *The Anthropology of Language: An Introduction to Linguistic Anthropology.* Belmont, CA: Thomson Higher Education. A workbook accompanies this text.

Romaine, Suzanne. 2000. *Language in Society: An Introduction to Sociolinguistics.* 2d ed. Oxford: Oxford University Press.

Saville-Troike, Muriel. 2003. *The Ethnography of Communication: An Introduction.* 3d ed. Malden, MA: Blackwell.

Salzmann, Zdenek. 1998. *Language, Culture and Society: An Introduction to Linguistic Anthropology.* 2d ed. Boulder, CO: Westview Press.

Readers

Bauman, Richard, and Joel Sherzer, eds. 1989. *Explorations in the Ethnography of Speaking.* 2d ed. Cambridge: Cambridge University Press.

Blount, Ben G., ed. 1995. *Language, Culture, and Society: A Book of Readings.* 2d ed. Prospect Heights, IL: Waveland Press.

Brenneis, Donald, and Ronald H. S. Macaulay, eds. 1996. *The Matrix of Language: Contemporary Linguistic Anthropology.* Boulder, CO: Westview Press.

Clark, Virginia P., Paul A. Eschholz, and Alfred F. Rosa, eds. 1998. *Language: Readings in Language and Culture*, 6th ed. Boston: Bedford/St. Martin's.

Duranti, Alessandro, ed. 2001. *Linguistic Anthropology: A Reader.* Malden, MA: Blackwell.

———, ed. 2004. *A Companion to Linguistic Anthropology.* Malden, MA: Blackwell.

Giglioli, Pier Paolo, comp. 1972. *Language and Social Context: Selected Readings.* Harmondsworth, UK: Penguin Books.

Gumperz, John J., and Dell Hymes, eds. 1986. *Directions in Sociolinguistics: The Ethnography of Communication.* Oxford: Blackwell.

Jaworski, Adam, and Nikolas Coupland, eds. 2006. *The Discourse Reader.* 2d ed. London and New York: Routledge.

Monographs

Basso, Keith H. 1979. *Portraits of "the Whiteman": Linguistic Play and Cultural Symbols Among the Western Apache.* Cambridge: Cambridge University Press.

Hymes, Dell. 1974. *Foundations in Sociolinguistics: An Ethnographic Approach.* Philadelphia: University of Pennsylvania Press.

Philips, Susan U. 1983. *The Invisible Culture: Communication in Classroom and Community on the Warm Springs Indian Reservation.* Prospect Heights, IL: Waveland Press.

Urciuoli, Bonnie. 1996. *Exposing Prejudice: Puerto Rican Experiences of Language, Race, and Class.* Boulder, CO: Westview Press.

Wogan, Peter. 2004. *Magical Writing in Salasaca: Literacy and Power in Highland Ecuador.* Boulder, CO: Westview Press.

Zentella, Ana Celia. 1997. *Growing Up Bilingual: Puerto Rican Children in New York.* Malden, MA: Blackwell.

INTRODUCTION

Language makes us human. Whatever other characteristics we have—bipedalism (walking on two feet), big brains, long period of dependence in infancy and childhood, "culture"—it is clear that everything we do at all times involves language. You could not read this book without language; you would have no school without language; and our technological world could not be built without language. We could not tell secrets or gossip without language; we would have no movies or songs without language. We could not create religions without language, and we would not go to war without the symbols that language enables.

Language is involved in all of our lives at all times, even when we choose silence, a choice made meaningful because of the possibility of language.

Language is far more complicated and interesting than we often think. While English teachers may be inspiring and creative, few students voluntarily seek discussions of the niceties of punctuation or grammatical parsing for fun. Yet language involves much more than learning how to write acceptable sentences.

Most of language is unconscious, and most of it operates without our knowing about it. This book aims to reveal some of the workings of language in human life.

The ways we categorize languages affect institutions such as schools. How we think of language shapes how we think of the other people we encounter, evaluating the ways they talk as a proxy for how we think about them.

Language is involved in our most intimate activities (how we talk to people we love) and in our most remote (how commerce operates at the level of international exchange). To study such a variable aspect of our lives requires a wide variety of methods and approaches.

Researchers in many fields study language, from linguistics to foreign language departments, from psychology to biology to cognitive science to anthropology, from literary theory to religious studies. This book is broadly anthropological: that is, it tries to study humans and their variations across time and space, but is also generally about linguistic anthropology, where we look at language to see how it illuminates questions about the nature of human culture and society.

This book offers a set of forty-five chapters about language, organized around six basic themes. Each chapter adds one more glimmer of understanding to what language is all about. You may not read all of them in a single semester, but whatever your instructor assigns will increase your familiarity with that most human of faculties, our language faculty.

PART I

The Nature of Language

Language may not be what you think it is. It is not mostly the perfect, well-formed grammatical sentences that your English teachers have taught you to write, though these are an aspect of language. It does not revolve around spelling and vocabulary tests, though people might analyze those too. "Language" refers to a range of communicative behavior, and the quintessential form is spoken language, though signed languages, written language, and electronic communication are also language. Many regard the sign as the principal aspect of language. Language is learned principally through interaction, not at school. It always changes, and it interacts with all other aspects of human experience.

In some sense people have been studying language for hundreds or even thousands of years. The early Sanskrit grammarians such as Panini wrote about Sanskrit grammar in the fifth century BCE; Chinese dictionaries, analyzing the phonetic and semantic (sound and meaning) aspects of words, have been written for 2000 years; Arabic and Hebrew grammarians wrote about their languages in the early Middle Ages; and the Spanish linguist Antonio de Nebrija wrote a grammar of Castillian in 1492.

The modern study of language is usually traced to the nineteenth-century encounter with the languages of "the Orient" (mostly India and China) and the discovery that the sacred Indian language Sanskrit was related to classical Greek and Latin, the treasure of European education. The stable entities that humans consider to be "a language," such as French, were understood to have evolved, in this case from varieties of Latin.

Simultaneously, revolutions in scientific thought, such as the discovery of "geological time"—measuring the earth in billions of years rather than in thousands, because of the understanding of fossils—and the Darwinian revolution in understanding humans' place among biological species, all combined to provide a new way of thinking about language. It could at least be possible that language was not entirely unique in the world. It could be analyzed in its own terms; languages could be compared; human language in general could be compared to nonhuman communication.

With the Age of Exploration leading to anthropological understanding of the nature of peoples other than the European explorers and missionaries, it was recognized that people everywhere "had language" and that their languages were just as complex and even evolved as the European and

Semitic languages. Anthropologists such as Franz Boas, himself a polyglot (one who knows many languages), tried to master and analyze the languages of Native Americans, discovering that there were hundreds of such languages, probably more than three hundred, and that they were very sophisticated.

Further advances in the study of language came from a group known as the Prague school, who set modern analytic linguistics on its way with the discovery of the *phoneme* (essentially a psychological image of a sound that had a particular pattern in a language) and other structural aspects of language.

The other major twentieth-century revolution in the study of language is associated with Noam Chomsky, who used an approach called *transformational-generative grammar* to demonstrate the primacy of syntax in the study of language. The study of language as a phenomenon reveals patterns, systems, and order that many find quite elegant and even beautiful.

Other trends in the study of language include a focus not on its structure but on the meanings and functions that emerge from *language in use* and in interaction. This has been facilitated by advances in recording technology. Early in the twentieth century, tape recorders could provide records of sound, permitting detailed transcription of natural speech. More recently, studies of interaction, including nonverbal aspects, have been enabled by video recording.

As the twentieth century unfolded, scholars began to note that since language was always changing, changes in society could be traced through the changes in language. As groups migrated to a particular location, the relations among languages might change entirely, and the language itself might even become extinct, like Hittite and Gothic. Or the languages encountering others could create a kind of blend, a "creole," using elements of the contributing languages. Languages can be born—but they also can die. Scholars estimate that of the 10,000 languages that existed a mere hundred years ago, about half are already extinct.

Efforts are made by many actors to preserve or revitalize endangered languages. Some of such efforts, such as among some groups of Navajos, are considered successful. Others, such as in Wales, are sentimental but have not yielded practical results (see Unit 3).

One of the losses an endangered language risks is the loss of the thought world accompanying it. That's because, as the great linguist and anthropologist Edward Sapir said,

> Human beings do not live in the objective world alone, nor alone in the world of social activity as ordinarily understood, but are very much at the mercy of the particular language which has become the medium of expression for their society....We see and hear and otherwise experience very largely as we do because the language habits of our community predispose certain choices of interpretation.

How this thing called language affects human thought, which is largely observed in what people say, has perplexed scholars ever since Sapir wrote of language as a "prepared road or groove" for thought.

Yet what exactly language is remains contested. There are not just one or two approaches to it, but dozens, each emphasizing some different aspect, each pointing out what the author regards as the most important thing to know about language: that it is spoken, that it is made of signs, that it enables transmission of culture, that it is similar across all languages, or that it varies greatly across languages.

In this section, we consider the nature of language, both in terms of a definition (Unit 1, "What Is Language?") and as it may or may not affect thought (Unit 2, "Language and Thought"). These are broad, foundational issues in understanding this thing so easily contained in a single, simple word, *language*.

Suggested Further Reading

Aarsleff, Hans. 1982. *From Locke to Saussure: Essays on the Study of Language and Intellectual History*. Minneapolis: University of Minnesota Press.

Harris, Roy, and Talbot J. Taylor. 1989. *The Western Tradition from Socrates to Saussure*. London and New York: Routledge.

Hymes, Dell H. 1974. *Studies in the History of Linguistics: Traditions and Paradigms*. Bloomington: Indiana University Press.

Koerner, E. F. K., and R. E. Asher, eds. 1995. *Concise History of the Language Sciences: From the Sumerians to the Cognitivists*. New York: Pergamon Press.

Lehmann, Winfred P., comp. 1967. *A Reader in Nineteenth Century Historical Indo-European Linguistics*. Bloomington: Indiana University Press.

Robins, R. H. 1990. *A Short History of Linguistics*. 3d ed. London and New York: Longman.

Seuren, Pieter A. M. 1998. *Western Linguistics: An Historical Introduction*. Oxford and Malden, MA: Blackwell.

UNIT 1

WHAT IS LANGUAGE?

All human societies have had "language" (though only some have had writing), and this is where experts often draw the boundaries between humans and other hominids. But exactly where the line between language and other communicative behavior belongs is a matter for debate. The research and debate on this topic became very lively and multifaceted beginning in the 1990s, with colorful and imaginative suggestions presented from widely differing perspectives. Many focus on the origins of language, relying on differing forms of evidence.

Some scholars regard the essence of language as symbolic behavior. Although obviously this cannot be seen, fossilized in human or other primate remains, we can see related examples of symbolic behavior in things like cave paintings, tool manufacture, and deliberate burial. Others see the essence of language as lying in what Charles Hockett calls "duality of patterning," by which small elements, themselves not meaningful, combine in meaningful ways at a higher level. This too is invisible in fossils. Some see language as lying on a continuum with other types of communicative behavior, and as stemming from humans' increased brain size (both absolute and relative) compared to our closest primate relatives, chimpanzees and other apes. For this, a deeper understanding of ape communication systems is required. This field alone has given rise to profoundly contested viewpoints.

Some see language as fundamentally spoken, in which case the anatomy of the vocal tract is of interest. Others see it as fundamentally a system of organized signs, with combinations being the most relevant piece. Sign languages may then hearken back to a gestural system of communication, and spoken languages may simply share features with these languages.

Some, such as Noam Chomsky and Steven Pinker, see language as resulting from a genetic mutation, resulting in a language facility as yet undiscovered in the physical brain but permitting all the special characteristics of language: being rule governed, being infinitely productive, employing a finite but quite large set of signifiers, and made up of many smaller "modules" governing negation, semantics, and so forth. Some emphasize the information that can be conveyed through language, and some emphasize the social relations that can be deepened through language. In recent years, scholars such as Esther Goody have pointed out that spoken language requires cooperation, since it necessarily involves conversational meanings, which emerge only through interaction. Thus the unit of evolution is not necessarily the individual organism but the social group.

Language occurs in multiple modalities, including speech, signing, and writing. Each of these is regarded as desirable or limited by some people in some circumstances, but those evaluations vary across time and space.

Debates about the nature of language can be intense. This section presents eight attempts to understand the nature of language. This selection is not meant to be exhaustive, merely to provide some outlines of the concepts that must be considered when we try to understand this most unusual faculty of language.

For those intrigued by the question of how humans developed language, it is first necessary to define language, so it can be identified in whatever data are relevant to the question. This evolving discussion involves complex information from genetics, primatology, psychology, neurobiology, paleoanthropology, linguistics, linguistic anthropology, and cultural anthropology. Some is technical and some is more discursive; all is speculative.

Suggested Further Reading

Aitchison, Jean. 2000. *The Seeds of Speech: Language Origin and Evolution*. Cambridge: Cambridge University Press.

Armstrong, David F., William C. Stokoe, and Sherman E. Wilcox. 1995. *Gesture and the Nature of Language*. Cambridge: Cambridge University Press.

Bickerton, Derek. 1980. *Language and Species*. Chicago: University of Chicago Press.

Byrne, Richard W., and Andrew Whiten, eds. 1988. *Machiavellian Intelligence: Social Expertise and the Evolution of Intellect in Monkeys, Apes and Humans*. Oxford: Clarendon Press.

Burling, Robbins. 2005. *The Talking Ape: How Language Evolved*. Oxford: Oxford University Press.

Calvin, William, and Derek Bickerton. 2000. *Lingua ex Machina: Reconciling Darwin and Chomsky with the Human Brain*. Cambridge, MA: MIT Press.

Cheney, Dorothy L., and Robert M. Seyfarth. 1990. *How Monkeys See the World: Inside the Mind of Another Species*. Chicago: University of Chicago Press.

Chomsky, Noam. 1972. *Language and Mind*. New York: Harcourt Brace Jovanovich.

Christiansen, Morten H., and Simon Kirby, eds. 2003. *Language Evolution*. Oxford: Oxford University Press.

Dessalles, Jean-Louis. 2007 [2000]. *Why We Talk: The Evolutionary Origins of Language*. Translated by James Grieve. Oxford and New York: Oxford University Press.

Dunbar, Robin. 1996. *Grooming, Gossip, and the Evolution of Language*. Cambridge, MA: Harvard University Press.

Foley, William. 1997. *Anthropological Linguistics: An Introduction*. Oxford: Blackwell.

Goody, Esther N., ed. 1995. *Social Intelligence and Interaction*. Cambridge: Cambridge University Press.

King, Barbara J., ed. 1999. *The Origins of Language: What Nonhuman Primates Can Tell Us*. Santa Fe, NM: School of American Research Press.

Lieberman, Philip. 1991. *Uniquely Human: The Evolution of Speech, Thought and Selfless Behavior*. Cambridge, MA: Harvard University Press.

———. 1998. *Eve Spoke: Human Language and Human Evolution*. New York: Norton.

Oller, D. Kimbrough, and Ulrike Griebel, eds. 2004. *Evolution of Communication Systems: A Comparative Approach*. Cambridge, MA: MIT Press.

Savage-Rumbaugh, E. Sue. 1998. *Apes, Language, and the Human Mind*. New York: Oxford University Press.

Whiten, Andrew. 1991. *Natural Theories of Mind: Evolution, Development and Simulation of Everyday Mindreading*. Oxford: Blackwell.

———, and Richard W. Byrne, eds. 1997. *Machiavellian Intelligence II: Extensions and Evaluations*. Cambridge: Cambridge University Press.

CHAPTER 1

Smiles, Winks, and Words

Robbins Burling

(2005)

Robbins Burling has written about languages in Burma and India, about how to learn a field language, and about language origins and many other aspects of language. As much anthropologist as linguist, he looks carefully at how language functions in actual human interactions in order to explain how it arose. In this chapter, excerpted from his book The Talking Ape, *he differentiates among different types of communicative signs, both verbal and gestural, but warns that "gesture" overlooks differences in the ways humans use their bodies communicatively. If we wish to understand the nature of language, it is essential to sort it out from other types of communication.*

Reading Questions

- In Burling's opening anecdote, how did he figure out that there were two fundamentally different kinds of communicative gestures?
- What does Burling mean by "language"? How is it different from signals of other types?
- How does Burling situate human communication within animal communication?
- What kinds of communication are universal and what kinds are culturally specific?
- What can we do with language that we can't do with other kinds of communication?

Human beings never run out of talk. We relate the events of the day. We gossip about our acquaintances. We speculate about people and power. Children chatter so incessantly that even their talkative parents lose patience. We explain, we cajole, we schmooze, we harangue, and we flirt, all with the help of language. To be sure, we also convey information in many other ways than by talking. We use our voices not only to speak, but to scream, sigh, laugh, hum, and cry. We show our joy with our smiles, and our anger with our scowls. We threaten by standing tall, and show submission by trying to look small. By the way we touch each other, we can show either fury or love. We even learn something from the way others smell. If we are to ask how language emerged in the human species, we need to start by understanding where it fits among the many other ways, audible, visible, olfactory, and tactile, by which humans communicate.

I had a vivid lesson about our different forms of communication when, as a young man, I landed by small boat at the little port of Marmaris on the southern coast of Turkey. Within half an hour of landing, I found myself negotiating for a room with a woman who ran a small guesthouse. She and I had no common language, but the situation made my needs obvious. We stood in a courtyard and she held out her hand, palm downward, with her fingers together and extended toward me. She then bent her hand sharply so that her fingers turned downward, while the back of her hand remained horizontal. This was clearly a stereotyped gesture, intended to convey a specific meaning to me, but I did not understand what that meaning was. I could think of two possibilities. Perhaps she wanted me to follow her or, perhaps, she wanted me to wait. I hesitated for just a moment but then decided to make a test. I deliberately took one step backward, and the woman scowled and looked a bit frustrated. I knew immediately that she wanted me to follow her, and she then led me to a room.

The woman had made two communicative gestures, and even then I was startled at how different they were. Her palm-down beckoning gesture, I would later learn, is used everywhere from Turkey through India and on to Southeast Asia, but as my previous ignorance showed, it is by no means universal. It is conventional, and it has to be learned. Her scowl, on the other hand, needed no learning at all. It was part of the heritage that the woman and I shared with every other human being. I could even use her scowl to help me define the meaning of her hand gesture.

Robbins Burling, "Smiles, Winks, and Words." In *The Talking Ape: How Language Evolved*. Oxford: Oxford University Press, 2005, pp. 23–47.

The scowl is an example of a large class of signals that are common to all humanity. These signals need little learning, and they allow us to communicate in quite subtle ways with people of all cultures. They include many of the ways in which we express ourselves with our faces, voices, hands and arms, and even with the posture and movements of our entire bodies: our laughs, screams, smiles, frowns, and shrugs. I will argue that these gestures and vocalizations, which all humans share, should be seen as forming a second kind of human communication, one that is quite different from language. I need a name for this group of signals and I will call them "gesture-calls." This is, admittedly, a somewhat contrived term, but it is useful as a way of... [describing] the similarities between these signals and the calls and communicative gestures of other mammals. The word "calls," of course, is not generally used for human signals, but only for the communicative vocalizations of animals. We do not think of human laughs and sobs as "calls" but that is only because we do not usually think of human beings as "animals"; but our laughs, sobs, sighs, and screams can be counted among the distinctive calls of the human species just as pant-hoots and long calls are among the distinctive calls of chimpanzees, and just as barks, growls, and howls are among the distinctive calls of dogs. I cannot fully justify the use of the term "gesture-calls" for human beings [here], but what matters now is to recognize that our human repertory of signals includes many that have meanings that are similar to the signals of other mammals, and that are produced with our voices, our faces, and our postures, just as theirs are.

I will use the word "language" only in its narrow sense, to refer to the system of sounds, words, and sentences to which we give names like "English," "Zulu," or "Chinese." "Body language" is something else. I will begin with an account of some characteristics of language (in this narrow sense) and of the ways in which our other forms of communication are similar to and different from language. These other forms of communication are sometimes referred to simply as our "nonverbal communication," but this expression bundles together too many different kinds of signaling to be very useful. They need to be distinguished not only from language but from one another.

[Eventually I shall conclude] that language could not have evolved from any animal-like form of communication, simply because it is so different from all other animal behavior. The headings used in the following pages identify a series of ways in which language differs from other forms of human communication and from the communication used by other species. It is the evolution of these unique characteristics of language that we must understand if we are ever to know how language originated.

DIGITAL AND ANALOG COMMUNICATION

Information can be conveyed in either analog or digital form, not only inside a computer, but in any medium at all. The steadily sweeping second hand of a clock, the swinging needle of an automobile speedometer, and a slide rule that can be manipulated into an unlimited number of positions are all analog devices. The meanings of a clock hand, speedometer needle, and slide rule vary in proportion to their positions, and in principle, there is no way to count the number of readings these instruments can give. A digital clock that bumps time abruptly from 8:45 to 8:46 but permits no compromise, presents its information with digital rather than analog signals. So does an abacus, where each bead can be positioned either up or down but can never come to rest halfway between. Digital signals have sharp boundaries. They are discrete. Digital devices can assume no more than a finite number of states. The beads of an abacus have a limited number of positions. A pocket calculator has only a finite (though huge) number of possible displays. Human beings communicate with both digital and analog signals.

The sound system of a language, its phonology, is prototypically digital. The meaningless units of our phonological systems are the phonemes that we represent, imperfectly, by the letters of our wretched spelling system. These phonemes are, as linguists say, in "contrast" with one another. This means that it is no more possible to compromise between the *p* and *b* of *pat* and *bat* than between 11:13 and 11:14 on [the] face of a digital clock. There is always a midpoint between any two positions of a speedometer needle even if the midpoints quickly become microscopic. The contrastive sounds of a language can be joined to form the many thousands of words that language users need, and the words, too, are in contrast. Contrasting words, in turn, allow sentences to be in contrast with one another. It is the digital phonological code that allows us to construct an enormous number of words and an unlimited number of sentences, and to keep them all distinct from one another.

Most of our signals, other than language, are graded rather than discrete. A giggle is not sharply distinct from a laugh, nor is a laugh clearly distinct from a guffaw. A sound that is halfway between a giggle and a laugh means something halfway between them as well. Perhaps giggles even grade into snorts, snorts into cries of objection, cries of objection into cries of anguish, and cries of anguish into sobs. This suggests a continuum that runs all the way from laughs to sobs with no sharp break at any point along the way. This is grading with a vengeance, with no boundaries in sight. The continuum may not reach quite all the way from a laugh to a sob, but human gesture-calls do show extensive grading, and this makes them utterly different from language. A halfway point between two words like *single* and *shingle* simply does not exist. A halfway point between a giggle and a laugh is perfectly real and perfectly understandable.

We can't count the number of our gesture-calls. What happens if we try? We have names for some of our gestures and for some of our calls, and these may tempt us to try to count the signals by counting the words: *laugh, snort, smile, frown, cry, sigh, squint, scream, pout, swagger*, and dozens of others. Listing the names is easy enough, but we soon run into problems. Do we count a giggle and a guffaw as different from a laugh? Or are they simply different forms of a single call? What about something halfway between a giggle and a laugh? What about a cry, a sob, and a whimper? There is an indeterminacy here that is intrinsic to an analog system. We can give names to spots or segments along the continuum, but there is no principled way to decide how many spots or segments to name, or where to draw a line between the end of one and the beginning of the next. There is no way to decide how different two signals must be in order to be counted as different.

The digital system that is provided by linguistic contrast allows human languages to be constructed according to profoundly different principles than what I am calling our "gesture-calls." To say that gesture-calls lack contrast is simply another way of saying that both in their meaning and in the manner by which they are produced, smiles, laughs, frowns, and screams vary along continuous scales. Language is digital, gesture-calls are analog.

Immediately, complications need to be acknowledged. The intonation of language, the ups and downs of pitch and emphasis, vary continuously so they form analog signals. On the other hand, the beckoning gesture of the Turkish guesthouse keeper had to be sharply distinct from her other gestures. Clearly, it would be too simple to imagine that language is uniformly digital and that everything else is analog. Examples such as these enormously complicate the description and understanding of human communication, and I will need to return to them later and put them in place. In the meantime, we can still recognize that the phonological and syntactic core of language (but not its intonation) is digital, while large parts of the rest of our communication is analog. The difference between digital and analog signals is crucial.

REFERENCE, PROPOSITIONS, AND EMOTIONS

The digital nature of the phonological code lets us distinguish thousands of words from one another. These words can be used to talk about our ideas, both our ideas about the world and ideas that are pure imagination. With language, we can tell someone where to buy fish. We can extol the virtues of a politician or an applicant for a job. We can whisper a fascinating tidbit about what Velma said to Mervin last night. We can ask questions, make requests, or give orders. We can spin yarns, tell lies, share jokes, and invent imaginary beings. Words give us names, not only for objects but also for actions, qualities, relations, sentiments, and indeed, for anything at all that we can think about. By combining words into sentences we can express propositions, and in this way convey messages about all the things that we name with our words. This kind of propositional information can be easily shared with others, so it conveys information about the state of the world, or at least, about what we imagine the state of the world to be. Our ability to form propositions even allows us to talk about language. We can use language to describe language.

Our analog cries, facial expressions, and postures are of only limited use for describing the world around us. They are much better at conveying delicate shades of emotion and intention. With frowns, smiles, shrugs, sighs, whimpers, and chuckles, we let others know how we feel, and suggest what we are likely to do next. Postures and facial expressions are likely to give a more reliable guide than words about whether to expect a kiss or slap. We use our postures, our gestures, and our facial expressions to ease relationships with others and to show that we know our place in the social world.

We convey many of our feelings more easily, more subtly, and less self-consciously with our calls and facial expressions than we do with language. Many of us dislike discussing serious or sensitive matters over the telephone, in part, at least, because we cannot read the gestures and facial expressions of the person on the other end of the line. We feel crippled by being limited to mere language. We hear one another's words, but we are left uncertain about one another's feelings. Mere language does not make up for the missing gesture-calls.

We can show our anger, our boredom, or our playfulness, with our gesture-calls. We can show others how much we love them. But we cannot tell stories. We cannot describe the difference between a pine tree and an oak, let alone the difference between an odd and even number. We cannot agree on a time and place to meet for lunch. We could easily enough invent gestures with which to plan a lunch date, but the gestures would have to refer to times, places, and events in the world, and in the very act of agreeing on them we would have to devise gestures that have more in common with language than with gesture-calls.

If we find it difficult to form true propositions about the world with our gestures and calls, we find it even more difficult to form false propositions. If we cannot tell true stories, we can hardly tell fairy tales. We cannot lie. We can, to be sure, feign, or at least we can try. The poker player must act as if his cards are different than they really are. The boxer pretends that he is about to hit from the left when he is really planning to hit from the right. We can try to pretend to a happiness we do not really feel or we can try to hide our excitement or pleasure. Feigning emotions, however, is not the same as lying, and most of us are not very good at it. The majority of human beings, who are neither con men nor skilled actors, find it much easier to lie with words than to mislead with gesture-calls.

So the most important thing about language is also the most obvious one. Language allows us, with great ease, to refer to things and events, and to say something about them. Gesture-calls are much better at expressing our emotions and intentions. Nevertheless, the association of digital language with referential messages on the one hand, and analog gestures and calls with emotional messages on the other, while high, is not perfect. Skillful poets can express emotions beautifully with words. Most of us need help from our gesture-calls. When I bite into an apple, my puckered face tells you something about its taste, and my face can also tell you whether something that I have just seen is desirable or frightening. So we can convey some information about the state of the world with our gesture-calls, and we can convey some emotions with language. More often and more easily we use digital language for facts and analog gestures and calls for emotions.

HEREDITY AND ENVIRONMENT

I need to begin this hoary subject by insisting on one thing: everything that human beings are or do (or that other animals are or do), everything about our bodies, our minds, and our behavior, comes about by the joint action of heredity and environment. Nothing could develop if the genes did not make it possible, and nothing could develop without a suitable environment. It is nonsense to ask whether heredity or environment should be credited for some human trait like stature, language, rock music, spelling, or intelligence. Both heredity and environment have a role in everything.

We find it easier to accept the interaction of inheritance and experience for physical traits like stature or complexion than for behavioral and intellectual traits like aggression, music, or a sense of humor. We feel comfortable with the idea that stature depends on both the genes we inherited from our parents and the food we ate while growing up. Skin color depends not only on how a particular set of genes has instructed a body to produce pigment, but also on how long that body has been exposed to the sun. We have more trouble recognizing that bashfulness, courting behavior, bicycle riding, spoken language, and literacy also emerge from the interaction of hereditary endowment and environmental opportunities, but our behavior is just as much the result of this interaction as is our body. The way we sit depends on both the way our genes have built our bones and the habits of the society in which we have grown up. The food we enjoy depends not only on the inherited nature of human digestion but on our idiosyncratic experiences with food. Our ability to dance, to catch fish, and to do long division, all require both inherited aptitudes and the right experiences. We ask the wrong question when we ask whether heredity or environment is responsible for a piece of our bodies or a bit of our behavior. We can be certain that both have played a role.

What makes us most uncomfortable is to attribute individual differences in behavior to heredity. We accept hereditary variability in the shape of our noses or the amount of hair on our arms, but many of us would like to believe in human perfectibility, to believe that anyone can learn to do anything if only the opportunities are right. Individual differences in inherited aptitude will not go away simply because we wish they did not exist, however, and the world would really be a much duller place if we all started life exactly alike. To make everyone average would call for a lot of dumbing down as well as smarting up, and you and I would be poorer for having no Darwins, Beethovens, and Picassos to show us what is possible.

What, then, do we do about our strong intuitions that nature is more important for some things and nurture for others? Eye color seems pretty well set by the genes. Whether we call the bottom end of our leg our *foot, pied,* or *Fuss* seems to have everything to do with experience and nothing at all to do with biology. We can deal with this intuition by asking what proportion of the variation that is found in some physical or behavioral trait is due to differences in heredity and what proportion of that variation is due to differences in experience. A trait whose variability depends on variable genes is said to be "heritable." Variability that results from experience is not. Heritability, however, is not an all-or-none matter. Different traits show different degrees of heritability. Stature depends on nutrition as well as inheritance, but it does have a high degree of heritability. The particular name that we use for the end of our leg has a very low heritability. We can legitimately ask how much of the variation that we find in some trait is due to differing kinds of experiences and how much is due to differing innate aptitude, but it is simplistic to ask whether it is one or the other.

My insistence that heredity and environment are every bit as intricately interwoven in our behavior as in our bodies, is needed because it is so terribly tempting, but also so terribly wrong, to suppose that our laughter, our cries, our frowns, and our scowls are determined by inheritance while language has to be learned. Of course we need to learn a particular language, but we could not talk at all if we had not inherited a mind that is designed for language learning. Dogs, even dogs that live in Tanzania, never learn Swahili because they have not been given the right kind of minds. Nor do Japanese very often learn Swahili, but this has nothing to do with Japanese genes or minds. To learn Swahili you need both the right kind of inheritance and the right kind of experience.

What is true for language is also true for our gesture-calls. Once past the first few weeks of life, every reasonably normal human being smiles. The magical ability of babies to smile needs both the right kind of inheritance and the environment of womb and cradle that allows a smile to develop. Short of violence or starvation, it is nearly impossible to stop a baby from smiling, but you and I would not smile under exactly the same circumstances had we grown up in a different culture. We must learn the rules laid down by our own society for the appropriate times, places, and circumstances for smiles, and for all our other gesture-calls.

Both our language and our gesture-calls, then, depend on both genes and experience, but the mixtures differ. The variation from one community to another is much greater for language than for gesture-calls, and this can only mean that language is less narrowly constrained by inheritance than are gesture-calls. Gesture-calls such as laughter are highly heritable. Whatever variability distinguishes the laughs of different individuals depends largely on inherited differences, not on variable experience. The contribution of learning is greater for language. A foreigner understands nothing of Chinese without some learning, and it takes a great deal of learning to understand or to say very much. New arrivals in China can understand much of what is conveyed by Chinese laughs and sobs, giggles and snorts, cries of anguish and all the rest of their gesture-calls, from the moment they step off the plane in Beijing. Because humans everywhere are genetically very much alike, our facial expressions, like our cries and laughs, convey much the same meanings everywhere.

Wherever you travel, a smile will suggest more friendliness than a scowl. Nowhere will you find people who habitually laugh when sad but cry in response to a joke. When anthropologists need to find their way in a new community but have not yet learned much of the language, they can easily judge the reactions of their hosts by reading their facial expressions. They do not need language to know whether people are friendly or hostile.

A half-century ago, the mind of a newborn baby was often imagined to be a "blank slate." It was supposed to contain little when it first entered the world except an ability to absorb whatever the environment offered. Language, like the rest of our behavior, was then attributed almost entirely to learning. If anything called a "mind" was even considered, it was regarded as a sort of general-purpose learning device that could learn one thing about as easily as another. The mind was thought to be pushed in one direction or another by its experiences, and learning seemed to dominate heredity. Nothing was assumed about the inherited nature of the human brain or mind.

Part of the intellectual upheaval brought about by Noam Chomsky was his challenge to this extreme behaviorism. He has always insisted that human beings come equipped with a mind and brain that are designed, in highly specific ways, for language. He has insisted that a child could not possibly master the fierce complexities of a language in a few short years if all he had to work with was a blank slate and a generalized ability to learn. Chomsky persuaded a large body of linguists that a successful language learner needs much more built in than generalized learning skills, and he shifted the focus of much of linguistics away from the differences among languages to the universal features that are presumed to arise because of the universal nature of the human mind. The mind came to be thought of as specifically designed for language.

Chomsky succeeded in pushing opinion so far away from the older behaviorism that a few linguists seem almost to have forgotten about learning. Thus, what would otherwise hardly need to be said at all, now needs to be insistently proclaimed: languages do, after all, differ. The differences among them can only result from varying experience, which is to say, from learning. Chomsky is surely right to insist that our genetic inheritance provides us with the capacity to learn a language. It is not simply a metaphor to say that we have a "language instinct." Nevertheless, a vast amount of learning is still needed in order to fulfill the potential of our inheritance. As with all other aspects of our bodies and behavior, we could never speak without both inheritance and learning. Indeed, one of the most interesting questions about human evolution is to ask how our genetic endowment managed to evolve to the point where it lets us learn so much. Our digital and propositional language requires much more learning than our analog and emotional calls and gestures.

A MASSIVE VOCABULARY AND DUALITY OF PATTERNING

Languages have tens of thousands of words. Every one of us has managed to learn a massive vocabulary. This is so utterly unlike anything found in any other communication system that it has to count as one of the most distinctive characteristics of language and, indeed, of humanity.

Our huge stock of words would not be possible without the digital phonological code. Most languages have a thousand or more possible syllables, enough to allow a million distinct two-syllable words. By some counts, to be sure, Hawaiian allows only 160 syllables, but it manages easily because most of its words have at least two syllables and many have three or more. Vocabulary size, obviously, is not limited by the phonological code. Every natural language allows its speakers to name thousands upon thousands of objects, actions, and qualities, and to make whatever subtle distinctions in meaning they need or desire. By our nature, we have the capacity to learn both a phonological code and the thousands of words that are formed with this code. Nothing remotely like this is possible with gesture-calls. These give us no names at all, and they are poorly designed to make the kinds of distinctions in meaning that come so easily with language.

It is not quite accurate to say that we have more words than gesture-calls, however. In principle, gesture-calls have infinite variability. Just as a graded slide rule allows an infinite number of positions, so graded gesture-calls allow an infinite variety of laughs. In practice, of course, we cannot discriminate so many kinds of laughter, and it is words that give us real flexibility. We cannot add new gesture-calls to our repertory in the way we can add new words to our language, and gesture-calls permit nothing like the tens of thousands of words that every adult speaker so easily controls. We ought to regard our huge vocabulary as at least as important as syntax in defining our uniqueness.

The phonological code gives language two distinct levels of organization. This has sometimes been called "double articulation" and sometimes "duality of patterning." First, we have the contrasting units of the sound system, the phonemes. These are meaningless, but they can be strung together by one set of patterns into larger chunks to which we assign meanings. These larger bits are the morphemes. They include the prefixes, suffixes, and word bases that are further organized by a different set of patterns into the words, phrases, and sentences that we toss back and forth to one another. No such dual structure characterizes our gesture-calls. Each call has a characteristic sound and each gesture has a characteristic shape and movement, but they are not constructed from smaller, meaningless parts.

ARBITRARINESS

With the phonological code of our language, we can assign a distinct sequence of sounds to every meaning for which we need a name, and we can assign the sounds to the meanings in entirely arbitrary ways. As long as everyone else calls it a "shovel," you are well advised to do so too; but if everyone agreed, the same object could just as well be called a "snurk" or a "blongsel." The form of a gesture-call such as a laugh might also be called "arbitrary." A laugh does not, in any objective sense, resemble humor, any more than the word "shovel" resembles a shovel. We can imagine a species where sobbing was a sign of humor and where laughter indicated grief, but human beings are simply not the kind of animals that can switch the meaning of these signs. The meaning and the form of laughter and sobs are narrowly set by our inheritance, with convention making only a very modest contribution. "Shovel" is conventional as well as arbitrary. The same object is called by many other names in other languages. Language is pervasively conventional as well as arbitrary.

Syntax and Productivity

For many linguists, it is the complexity of syntax that gives the most compelling evidence for the unique character of the human mind. Since gesture-calls are not organized by any sort of syntax, they seem, to these linguists, to have little in common with language. You cannot subordinate, embed, or relativize a gesture-call. It is true that two or more gesture-calls can join to convey more precise or more forceful messages than a single one could convey by itself. We can demonstrate anger by combining the right posture with the right facial expression. We can show both anger and fatigue at the same time. But our gesture-calls simply do not meld into the tight syntactic constructions that are so characteristic of all natural spoken or signed languages.

Syntax allows language to escape the limitation of a fixed number of signals. New words can be invented, but not with complete freedom. You may get through the day without hearing a single word that you had never heard before; but unless you neither speak yourself nor listen to anyone else, you will certainly hear many new sentences before you sleep. It is hardly imaginable that the sentences in this paragraph were ever before uttered or written.

Any language with tens of thousands of words that can be joined into long strings allows astronomical numbers of sentences. In fact, thanks to recursive rules, there is no limit on the number of possible sentences. Rules are called recursive if they can be used repeatedly. The most trivial recursive rule simply lets a word be repeated. We can say that something is *very very very…big* with as many *very*s as we want to toss in. A child who speculates about his *great-great-great-great-…grandmother* has discovered the joys of a recursive rule. Only slightly more complex are rules that allow sentences to be joined to one another by means of simple conjunctions: *I saw Bill, so I spoke to him, and we talked for a while, but he got tired, and….* Such a sentence could, in principle, go on for ever. Languages allow more interesting kinds of recursion than these…. [Here] we need only note that recursive rules, in principle, allow us to produce and use an infinite number of sentences. Recursion is one of the most distinctive characteristics of language.

However subtle our gestures and calls are, they are fixed in form and fixed in meaning. Only over the course of the thousands of generations that are needed for natural selection can a set of gesture-calls be expanded or elaborated. You can never use gesture-calls to say anything that is truly new. Language is open. The system of gesture-calls is closed.

Voluntary Control

We have a strong sense of having voluntary control over our language. Voluntary control over our gesture-calls is less secure. The ghastly photographs in which people pretend to smile are a tribute to the difficulty so many of us have in producing gesture-calls on demand. We don't naturally smile at inanimate objects, so it isn't easy to smile at a camera. Only something real can make us smile. On other occasions we find it just as hard not to smile, even when keeping a straight face would be more polite. The relatively involuntary nature of our smiles and of our other gesture-calls means that we are in constant danger of revealing ourselves. When people say one thing with language but send a conflicting message with their faces and bodies, they are likely to be branded as liars. It will not be their language that is believed, but their less voluntary gestures and facial expressions. Our calls and gestures sometimes convey our true emotional state considerably more faithfully than we want them to. If you want to lie, you will be well advised to stick to words and be careful to convey as little as possible with your gesture-calls. Photographers may ask us to pretend to smile, but they know better than to ask us to pretend to laugh.

Immediacy and Displacement

Gesture-calls are limited by what might be called their "immediacy." We can use them to express the present state of our emotions and intentions, but not to describe our past or future emotions. They show our reaction to our immediate surroundings but, except when used along with language, we cannot use them to convey our attitude about things that are out of sight or earshot. With language, we can easily describe things that happened long ago or at a great distance, or that never happened at all. This is sometimes described by saying that language allows "displacement," while most other forms of communication do not. Displacement is not totally absent from animal communication. Bees famously tell other bees about where nectar is to be found, but bee dancing is not likely to have much bearing on language. Only with language did human beings overcome the limitation to the immediate situation that is characteristic of all other primate communication.

Audible and Visible Mediums

Most people, everywhere, use audible languages, and our dependence on visible signals is sufficiently limited that we find it easy to talk in the dark and equally easy to adapt to a telephone. Deaf people who cannot use audible signals can develop rich and flexible visual languages, so spoken languages and sign languages each require just one medium, either audible or visible. Gesture-calls often use both. Many facial expressions are exclusively visual, but most of our audible gesture-calls can be seen as well as heard. Across a noisy room we have no trouble seeing that someone is laughing. We do not have to hear the sobs to see that a child is crying. The audible and visible parts of our gesture-call system are so similar and are so often joined closely together that I find it artificial to separate them. This is why I use the term "gesture-call." I find it helpful to be reminded that this part of our own communication includes both audible and…visible signals and that many signals are both. Languages are predominantly expressed by one medium or the other. Gesture-calls exploit both mediums more equally. Nevertheless, spoken language is regularly accompanied by waving hands and it is always accompanied by moving lips, so it cannot be said to be completely lacking a visible component. Spoken language is also accompanied by intonation, which is more like gesture-calls than most of language, both in being analog rather than digital and in being better at expressing emotion than propositional information. Waving hands, moving lips, and intonation all greatly complicate any description of human communication, and a place will eventually have to be found for each of them.

In summary up to this point: As a first approximation, language is digital and allows easy reference. Large parts of language, including its huge vocabulary, have to be learned, and this means that it can vary from one community to another. It is characterized by distinct phonological and syntactic levels of patterning. Its signals are largely arbitrary and conventional, and most languages are predominantly vocal and audible. It can be used productively to describe things distant in time and space. It is subject to a high degree of voluntary control. Our laughs, screams, groans, sobs, scowls, and smiles, like other gesture-calls, form a very different kind of communication. They are analog signals and excellent at conveying emotion. They are less subject to cultural variation than language, and they are less subject to voluntary control.

———————————

We need to consider some other forms of human communication that share features of both systems. Deaf signing is a visible language. Signs like the beckoning gesture of the Turkish guesthouse keeper are digital rather than analog. The intonation of language is analog, although most of language is digital. We need to find a place for all of these, and for several other kinds of signals by which humans communicate.

DEAF SIGNING

For most of us, language is overwhelmingly auditory and vocal. When people with normal hearing learn to read and write, they add a visible form of language to the audible language they started with; but writing is based so closely on spoken language that it needs to be seen as a secondary and specialized skill. Only in very recent times has everyone been expected to become literate, and in some parts of the world literacy is still a minority achievement. Spoken language came first in human history, and it comes first for every hearing child.

People who are deaf, however, need a visible language or they will have no language at all. Deaf people find it exceedingly difficult to learn any sort of spoken language. Without one, written language is a terrible challenge, but communities of deaf people are able to devise visible languages that use manual, instead of spoken, words. These manual languages are largely independent of the spoken languages of the wider communities in which they are used; and in the last few decades, we have come to realize that sign languages are as rich in expressive power as spoken languages.

For anyone who can hear well, spoken languages offer several practical advantages. In particular, they interfere less with other activities. We can talk and bathe the baby at the same time. Since a listener does not need to watch the speaker, a spoken language could once have been understood while checking for lions, and a spoken language can still be used while keeping one's eyes on the road. Spoken language can even be used in the dark. It is for practical reasons like these, we presume, that communities of hearing people always choose to use a spoken language rather than a manual language as their primary form of communication. Speech is simply more convenient. When the vocal channel is blocked, however, it is now clear that the human mind is every bit as capable of directing language out through the hands and in through the eyes as it is of sending it out of the mouth and in through the ears.

Sign languages share all the essential characteristics that distinguish spoken languages from our gesture-calls. Signs are as referential as spoken words, and the sentences of a sign language can express the same kinds of propositions as the sentences of spoken language. Just as the words of a spoken language contrast, so do deaf signs. The manual signs of a language such as American Sign Language are as safely distinct from one another as are the words of any spoken language, so sign languages, like spoken languages, are digital systems. Contrasting hand shapes, together with contrasting locations, orientations, and motions of the hands and arms, join to form signed words, much as the phonemes of a spoken language join to form spoken words. Like spoken languages, signed languages need to be learned, so sign languages differ from one part of the world to another, just as spoken languages do.

Sign languages can be used to convey the full range of meanings that spoken languages convey. Signers, like speakers, can agree on where to meet for lunch, discuss the qualifications of politicians, or report the latest scandal. Signers can lie as easily as speakers, and they can as easily use their language to discuss the language itself. Sign languages are as fully productive as spoken languages. New signs can be coined when new things or new ideas need to be discussed,

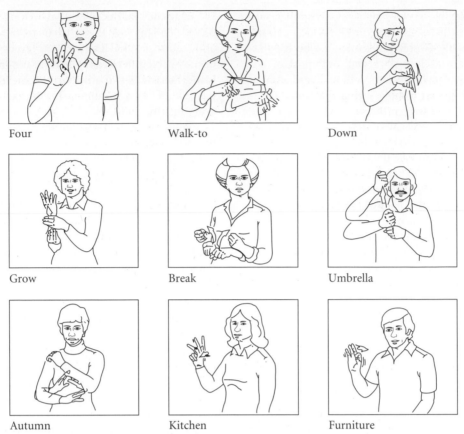

Four   Walk-to   Down

Grow   Break   Umbrella

Autumn   Kitchen   Furniture

Figure 1. *Signs of American Sign Language. Top row: Highly iconic. Middle row: Semi-iconic. Bottom row: Arbitrary. (Reprinted with permission from T. Humphries, C. Padden, and T. J. O'Rourke, A Basic Course in American Sign Language, Second Edition © 1994, T. J. Publishers Inc., Silver Spring, Maryland 20910, USA.)*

and sign languages put no more limits than spoken languages on how many new sentences can be constructed. They are just as subject to voluntary control. In all these respects, signing is utterly different from the nonverbal communication of hearing people. Sign languages are nothing like mime or a game of charades. They are complex and conventional systems that take years to master. Signing has just as much right to be called a "language" as does Chinese or Spanish.

Nevertheless, signing and spoken language are organized in somewhat different ways. Signing takes place in three-dimensional space. Unlike spoken language, it is not confined to the single temporal dimension, and this both imposes limitations and opens opportunities. Visible signs take a bit longer to produce than the average audible word; but the extra dimensions of visible space allow the signer to do several things simultaneously, and this compensates for the time needed to produce each individual sign. When signing about people or objects that are present, signers point to them. When signing about people who are not present, they often assign each person to a different location within their signing space, and then orient their signs toward these assigned spots. A sign meaning "give" can then move from one spot to another, so both the giver and the recipient are shown simultaneously with the sign for "give."

A visual medium invites a degree of iconicity that is impossible in a spoken language, and a considerable proportion of the signs of American Sign Language resemble, in some way, the object that they stand for. Figure 1 shows several ASL signs. Those in the top row are almost transparent in meaning. Those in the middle row might not be understood without an explanation, but once their meaning is known, their iconicity is clear: a branched plant growing upward, a stick being broken, an umbrella being opened. Those in the bottom row seem to be entirely arbitrary. Spoken words cannot so easily mimic the things they stand for. *Chickadee* and *bob-white* imitate the calls of birds, but the onomatopoeia of spoken languages is marginal when compared with the iconicity of sign languages, although even the languages used by the deaf have many signs that are fully arbitrary.

Because sign languages exploit the special potentials of vision and space while spoken languages exploit the potentials of sound, they are organized differently, but they share their most essential properties. Human beings can devise rich and versatile languages in either a visible or an audible medium. Sign languages show us that it is the brain, rather than the vocal organs, that has made the most important adaptations for language. The human brain can learn to produce a language with either the tongue or the hands, and it can understand with either the eyes or the ears. Which medium each of us prefers is not much more than a matter of convenience.

QUOTABLE GESTURES

We nod and shake our heads, and we use dozens of hand gestures such as the "okay circle" and the "bye-bye wave." These are meaningful signs, but they have to be learned and they are conventional, so they are very different from our laughs and sobs. These learned and stereotypic gestures have sometimes been called "emblems," but I find the term "quotable gestures" to be particularly apt. Just as we can quote a word or a sentence, so we can also quote an okay circle or a shake of the head simply by making the same sign. The palm-down beckoning gesture that I learned from the Turkish guesthouse keeper was a quotable gesture. Her scowl was not. Try quoting a scowl. You might imitate a scowl, but it is hard even to know what it would it mean to "quote" a scowl.

In both their forms and their meanings, quotable gestures are as conventional as words, and they can convey referential meanings that are as well defined as words. Like words, also, they contrast with one another. It is no more possible to compromise between two quotable gestures than between two words. In spite of the similarity of their form—fingers aimed upward—there can be no compromise, in either meaning or form, between the "finger" and a V-for-Victory sign. The conventional hand signals of a referee need to be unambiguously distinct from one another. Nothing can bridge the gap between a nod and a head shake in the way that transitional laughs bridge the gap between a giggle and a guffaw. It is their contrast that allows these gestures to be quoted, for only a contrastive system lets us know for certain whether two gestures are the same or different. We cannot know whether or not two smiles should count as the same but we do know that two head shakes mean the same thing. Quotable gestures need to be learned. Like language, they form a part of the cultural tradition of a community, and they differ from one community to another. In all these respects quotable gestures are very much like words and very different from gesture-calls. Because they are visible rather than audible, however, they cannot be incorporated into either the phonology or the syntax of spoken language.

Quotable gestures resemble the individual signs of a sign language more closely than they resemble spoken words. Everything that they share with spoken words, they also share with the signs of sign language, but in addition they are, like deaf signs, made with the hands and arms, sometimes with the assistance of facial expressions. Indeed, quotable gestures of the hearing community are sometimes incorporated into the signed languages of the deaf. The usual way to negate a sentence in American Sign Language is with a head shake. Head shakes cannot be incorporated into the audible language of a hearing community, but they can be incorporated into the grammar of sign language, and they

can be used systematically within its sentences. In that way, a head shake becomes a word, one among the thousands of other signed words of American Sign Language.

Even for those of us who use spoken languages, the clear meanings and conventionality of quotable gestures make them more like words than like gesture-calls. Although they cannot be used as a part of spoken language, they deserve to be grouped with language in any typology of human communication.

QUOTABLE VOCALIZATIONS

Everyone who uses a spoken language also uses a few expressions such as *oh-oh, tsk-tsk, m-hm*, and *uh-uh* that are meaningful vocal noises, but not really words. These expressions are difficult to spell because they don't conform to ordinary English sound patterns, but these four should be recognizable as meaning "oh dear," "shame on you," "yes," and "no." They have consistent sounds and consistent meanings, but in addition to violating the usual phonological patterns of the language, they cannot be incorporated into its syntax. They don't fit into sentences. We do not have many of these vocalizations, perhaps a dozen or so, but they are unlike any of our other communicative signals. They are discrete rather than graded, for it is no more possible to compromise between the *m-hm* that means "yes" and the *uh-uh* that means "no," than it is to compromise between *yes* and *no* or between a nod and a head shake. Their sounds and meanings are conventional and they have to be learned. All this makes them so much like quotable gestures that they deserve a parallel name, and I will call them "quotable vocalizations." Like quotable gestures, these quotable vocalizations are more like words than like gesture-calls, and they belong on the language-like side of our communication.

Since neither quotable vocalizations nor quotable gestures enter the syntactic constructions of spoken language, they cannot contribute to the kind of productivity that syntax gives to all languages. We can, however, add new quotable gestures to our repertory. We do not often do so, but the V-for-Victory sign was invented only during the Second World War. It is not difficult to learn the quotable gestures of another culture. It would also be possible to add new quotable vocalizations to our repertory, though this must be even less common than adding quotable gestures. Adding to our existing stock of gesture-calls is impossible.

We can lie with either quotable gestures or quotable vocalizations just as we can lie with language. A nod or a *m-hm* is as surely a lie as is "yes," if the nodder or vocalizer really believes the correct answer should be a head shake or an *uh-uh*. If you try to deceive by shaking your head, you lie; if you laugh at a joke that you do not find funny, you do not. Quotable vocalizations are almost words. They are subject to roughly the same degree of deliberate control as language or quotable gestures, and like words, they have to be learned by participation in the community where they are used. Since quotable vocalizations are produced with the same vocal machinery as spoken language, we usually think of them as closer to language than a shake of the head or a wink of the eye, but the two kinds of quotables are used in almost identical ways, and both exhibit full contrast. In all these respects, both quotable gestures and quotable vocalizations differ from our analog gesture-calls, and both belong with spoken and signed language on the language-like side of our communication.

GESTICULATION, INTONATION, AND INSTRUMENTAL ACTS

We communicate with several other kinds of gestures and vocalizations, including the intonations of the voice, the gesticulations of the hands, and even with instrumental gestures that are not intended to communicate at all. These [are]…introduced briefly.…

"Gesticulation" refers to the way we wave our arms and shape our hands as we speak. This hand waving is very different both from the gestural component of our gesture-call system and from quotable gestures, and it is different, also, from the manual gestures of sign language. That gives us four distinct kinds of communicative gestures, and still omits instrumental gestures which are meant for something else than communication. All this makes the word "gesture," if used alone, hopelessly ambiguous. From now on, therefore, I will avoid using "gesture" without qualification, but will, instead, use more specific terms: "gesture-calls," "quotable gestures," "gesticulation," "signing," or "instrumental gesture." Gesticulation differs from the others in its intimate association with speech. It might almost be regarded as a part of language, but its visibility and silence set it apart.

"Intonation" refers to the rhythm, stress, and ups and downs in pitch that accompany ordinary spoken language. Like gesticulation, intonation is used simultaneously with the words and sentences of language, and it is intimately related to them. Generally, we think of intonation as an integral part of language, and it is hardly conventional to set it apart, but it works so differently from the rest of the sound system that it needs special treatment.

Intonation conveys less propositional information than words and sentences generally do, but it reveals more about the attitudes and emotions of the speaker. Intonation also differs from the rest of language in being largely analog rather than digital. Both in its meaning and in its analog form, therefore, intonation is more like our gesture-calls than is the rest of language. Intonation has much in common with gesticulation. Since gesticulation is manual, it seems to be more distinct from spoken language than vocal intonation is, but intonation and gesticulation are closely linked to each other, and they have parallel kinds of involvement with language. It is even difficult to define intonation in a way that makes it a part of language without dragging in gesticulation along with it. Gesticulation and some parts of intonation have sometimes been grouped together as "paralanguage," meaning that they are used "alongside"

language. The term recognizes their close connection with language, but still sets them apart.…

Finally, we need to leave a place for instrumental acts that are not even meant to be communicative, but that can still be interpreted as meaningful by an observing individual. The business of living requires us to stand up, walk around, search for food, eat, sleep, cooperate, fight, look for mates, and engage in any number of other mundane activities. Our footsteps, our grunts, and even our breathing, can all be heard. Other people can see us and hear us as we perform these activities. These instrumental acts are meant for practical purposes, not for communication, but even if the actors would rather not be seen or heard, others may still be able to glean useful bits of information by watching and listening.

Behavior that starts instrumentally sometimes becomes conventionalized. The arms-up gesture by which babies ask to be picked up starts as an instrumental gesture that allows older hands to slip easily under the baby's arms. Children do not learn this gesture by imitation because older folks never ask a baby to pick them up, and a baby may never see another baby holding out its arms. Instead, each child conventionalizes the gesture by habit, and then exaggerates it to get attention. Adults, in turn, learn to recognize the gesture as a request. The gesture-calls of animals, such as the retracted lip that warns of a bite, also began as instrumental acts.…

Figure 2 shows our various kinds of communication in a way that is intended to highlight both their similarities and their differences. The figure has two columns, one for visible, and the other for audible, signals, but the dividing line does not extend all the way to the top. This reflects the close association of the visual and audible parts of gesture-calls. Across the middle of the figure is a horizontal line

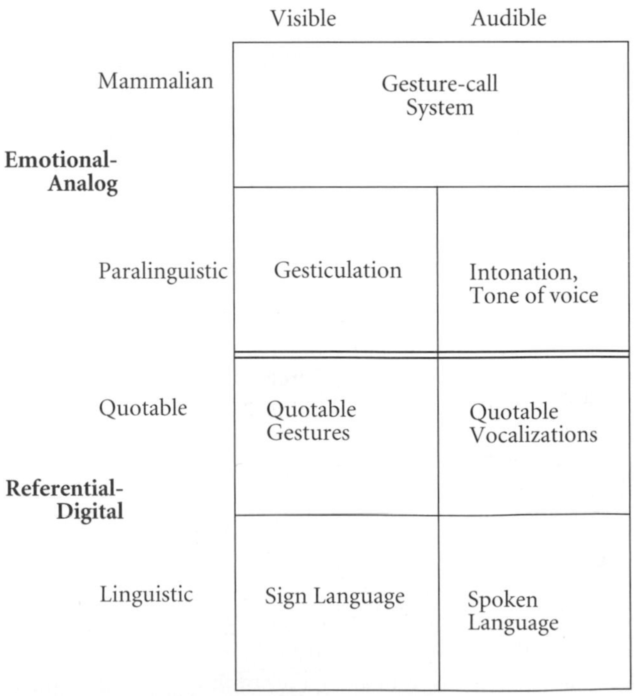

	Visible	Audible
Mammalian	Gesture-call System	
Emotional-Analog		
Paralinguistic	Gesticulation	Intonation, Tone of voice
Quotable	Quotable Gestures	Quotable Vocalizations
Referential-Digital		
Linguistic	Sign Language	Spoken Language

Figure 2. *Varieties of human communication.*

that divides the analog gesture-call-like forms that are best at conveying emotions and intentions at the top, from the language-like digital communication that is best at conveying referential meaning below. The gesture-call system at the very top is the component of our communication that is most like that of other mammals and least like language. Language, at the bottom, is the most distinctively human. Both the top and bottom halves of the figure are further divided, and the two forms just above the central line and the two just below it all share some features of both language and gesture-calls. Quotable gestures and vocalizations are very much like words, but they are not pulled into either the syntax or phonology of language. Gesticulation and intonation are both used more intimately with language than are either quotable gestures or vocalizations, but they are analog signals and thus quite different from the other parts of language. Instrumental acts are left out of the figure because they are not intended to be communicative at all.

One purpose of Figure 2 is to show how very similar to each other audible and visible communication are. Most of what we can do in one modality we can do equally well in the other. The distinctiveness of human communication lies not in our specific ability to use vocal language, but rather in our ability to use language, whether audible or visible, to convey referential and propositional meaning, and to do so by means of principles that are very different from our own gesture-calls as well as from any form of animal communication. Linguistic contrast, syntax, and a massive vocabulary are all unique to language, but they are just as characteristic of visible language as of audible language. It is our minds that changed most profoundly as our ability to use language evolved.

Post-reading Questions / Activities

- Observe friends talking for a few minutes. How do Burling's distinctions among the various components of the gesture-call system help you analyze the complexity of this (and every) interaction?
- Watch a foreign film without the sound or subtitles. Guess what is occurring. What information do you use to make your inferences? Which gestures are familiar? Are there any gestures that are unfamiliar? Now watch it again with sound or subtitles. How accurate were your guesses?

Vocabulary

analog	gesture-call	phonology
arbitrariness	heritable, heritability	productivity
behaviorism	iconicity	quotable gestures
call-system	immediacy	quotable vocalizations
digital	intonation	recursive
double articulation	manual language	sign language
duality of patterning	morpheme	syntax
gesticulation		

Suggested Further Reading

Aitchison, Jean. 2000. *The Seeds of Speech: Language Origin and Evolution.* Cambridge: Cambridge University Press.

Armstrong, David F., and Sherman E. Wilcox. 2007. *The Gestural Origin of Language.* Oxford and New York: Oxford University Press.

Bickerton, Derek. 1980. *Language and Species.* Chicago: University of Chicago Press.

Burling, Robbins. 2005. *The Talking Ape: How Language Evolved.* Oxford: Oxford University Press.

Calvin, William, and Derek Bickerton. 2000. *Lingua ex Machina: Reconciling Darwin and Chomsky with the Human Brain.* Cambridge, MA: MIT Press.

Christiansen, Morten H., and Simon Kirby, eds. 2003. *Language Evolution.* Oxford: Oxford University Press.

King, Barbara J., ed. 1999. *The Origins of Language: What Nonhuman Primates Can Tell Us.* Santa Fe, NM: School of American Research Press.

Oller, D. Kimbrough, and Ulrike Griebel, eds. 2004. *Evolution of Communication Systems: A Comparative Approach.* Cambridge, MA: MIT Press.

CHAPTER 2

The Origin of Speech

Charles Hockett

(1960)

Before scholars can begin to ask the question of how language arose, we have to know what features of language we actually seek to locate in our evolutionary past. Many such discussions end in pure speculation.

 Often known as a linguist, Charles Hockett in fact had a PhD in anthropology and considered his work importantly situated within the broadest contours of that field. His classic treatment of the "design features" puts human language on a continuum with—but in some ways distinctive from—the communicative systems of various species. He identifies 13 aspects of language, all of which apply to human language and only some of which apply to the communication systems of other animals. Most people emphasize, as did Hockett, the features of discreteness, displacement, productivity, traditional transmission, *and* duality of patterning, *which are unique to humans and hominoids. The goal of this kind of analysis is less to understand human language than to set it apart from other forms of communication. [You'll note, too, that he takes speech, with its features of* broadcast transmission *and* directional reception, rapid fading, *and the* vocal-auditory channel, *as prototypical of human language. In Chapter 43 ("Orality: Another Language Ideology"), you can see a challenge to this focus on orality.]*

Reading Questions

- What is *displacement*? How do you see it exemplified in ordinary language? Where else might you find it?
- What is *productivity*?
- What is *duality of patterning*? How is it connected to productivity? What are the ramifications of this design feature?
- How does human language differ from other animals' communication systems?
- Why is that important for any discussion of language origins?

About 50 years ago the Linguistic Society of Paris established a standing rule barring from its sessions papers on the origin of language. This action was a symptom of the times. Speculation about the origin of language had been common throughout the 19th century, but had reached no conclusive results. The whole enterprise in consequence had come to be frowned upon—as futile or crackpot—in respectable linguistic and philological circles. Yet amidst the speculations there were two well-reasoned empirical plans that deserve mention even though their results were negative.

 A century ago there were still many corners of the world that had not been visited by European travelers. It was reasonable for the European scholar to suspect that beyond the farthest frontiers there might lurk half-men or man-apes who would be "living fossils" attesting to earlier stages of human evolution. The speech (or quasi-speech) of these men (or quasi-men) might then similarly attest to earlier stages in the evolution of language. The search was vain. Nowhere in the world has there been discovered a language that can validly and meaningfully be called "primitive." Edward Sapir wrote in 1921:

> There is no more striking general fact about language than its universality. One may argue as to whether a particular tribe engages in activities that are worthy of the name of religion or of art, but we know of no people that is not possessed of a fully developed language. The lowliest South African Bushman speaks in the forms of a rich symbolic system that is in essence perfectly comparable to the speech of the cultivated Frenchman.

The other empirical hope in the 19th century rested on the comparative method of historical linguistics, the

Charles Hockett, "The Origin of Speech." *Scientific American* 203(3) (Sept 1, 1960): 88–96.

discovery of which was one of the triumphs of the period. Between two languages the resemblances are sometimes so extensive and orderly that they cannot be attributed to chance or to parallel development. The alternative explanation is that the two are divergent descendants of a single earlier language. English, Dutch, German, and the Scandinavian languages are related in just this way. The comparative method makes it possible to examine such a group of related languages and to construct, often in surprising detail, a portrayal of the common ancestor, in this case the proto-Germanic language. Direct documentary evidence of proto-Germanic does not exist, yet understanding of its workings exceeds that of many languages spoken today.

There was at first some hope that the comparative method might help determine the origin of language. This hope was rational in a day when it was thought that language might be only a few thousands or tens of thousands of years old, and when it was repeatedly being demonstrated that languages that had been thought to be unrelated were in fact related. By applying the comparative method to all the languages of the world, some earliest reconstructable horizon would be reached. This might not date back so early as the origin of language, but it might bear certain earmarks of primitiveness, and thus it would enable investigators to extrapolate toward the origin. This hope also proved vain. The earliest reconstructable stage for any language family shows all the complexities and flexibilities of the languages of today.

———

These points had become clear a half-century ago, by the time of the Paris ruling. Scholars cannot really approve of such a prohibition. But in this instance it had the useful result of channeling the energies of investigators toward the gathering of more and better information about languages, as they are today. The subsequent progress in understanding the workings of language has been truly remarkable. Various related fields have also made vast strides in the last half-century: zoologists know more about the evolutionary process, anthropologists know more about the nature of culture, and so on. In the light of these developments there need be no apology for reopening the issue of the origins of human speech.

Although the comparative method of linguistics, as has been shown, throws no light on the origin of language, the investigation may be furthered by a comparative method modeled on that of the zoologist. The frame of reference must be such that all languages look alike when viewed through it, but such that within it human language as a whole can be compared with the communicative systems of other animals, especially the other hominoids, man's closest living relatives, the gibbons and great apes. The useful items for this sort of comparison cannot be things such as the word for "sky"; languages have such words, but gibbon calls do not involve words at all. Nor can they be even the signal for "danger," which gibbons do have. Rather, they must be the basic features of design that can be present or absent in

any communicative system, whether it be a communicative system of humans, of animals, or of machines.

With this sort of comparative method it may be possible to reconstruct the communicative habits of the remote ancestors of the hominoid line, which may be called the protohominoids. The task, then, is to work out the sequence by which that ancestral system became language as the hominids—the man-apes and ancient men—became man.

———

A set of 13 design-features is presented in [this section]. There is solid empirical justification for the belief that all the languages of the world share every one of them. At first sight some appear so trivial that no one looking just at language would bother to note them. They become worthy of mention only when it is realized that certain animal systems—and certain human systems other than language—lack them.

The first design-feature—the "vocal-auditory channel"—is perhaps the most obvious. There are systems of communication that use other channels: for example, gesture, the dancing of bees, or the courtship ritual of the stickleback. The vocal-auditory channel has the advantage—at least for primates—that it leaves much of the body free for other activities that can be carried on at the same time.

The next two design-features—"rapid fading" and "broadcast transmission and directional reception," stemming from the physics of sound—are almost unavoidable consequences of the first. A linguistic signal can be heard by any auditory system within earshot, and the source can normally be localized by binaural direction-finding. The rapid fading of such a signal means that it does not linger for reception at the hearer's convenience. Animal tracks and spoors, on the other hand, persist for a while; so of course do written records, a product of man's extremely recent cultural evolution.

The significance of "interchangeability" and "total feedback" for language becomes clear upon comparison with other systems. In general a speaker of a language can reproduce any linguistic message he can understand, whereas the characteristic courtship motions of the male and female stickleback are different, and neither can act out those appropriate to the other. For that matter in the communication of a human mother and infant neither is apt to transmit the characteristic signals or to manifest the typical responses of the other. Again, the speaker of a language hears, by total feedback, everything of linguistic relevance in what he himself says. In contrast, the male stickleback does not see the colors of his own eye and belly that are crucial in stimulating the female. Feedback is important, since it makes possible the so-called internalization of communicative behavior that constitutes at least a major portion of "thinking."

The sixth design-feature, "specialization," refers to the fact that the bodily effort and spreading sound waves of speech serve no function except as signals. A dog, panting with his tongue hanging out, is performing a biologically essential activity, since this is how dogs cool themselves off and maintain the proper body temperature. The panting dog incidentally produces sound, and thereby may inform other dogs (or humans) as to where he is and how he feels. But this transmission of information is strictly a side effect. Nor does the dog's panting exhibit the design-feature of "semanticity." It is not a signal meaning that the dog is hot; it is part of being hot. In language, however, a message triggers the particular result it does because there are relatively fixed associations between elements in messages (e.g., words) and recurrent features or situations of the world around us. For example, the English word "salt" means salt, not sugar or pepper. The calls of gibbons also possess semanticity. The gibbon has a danger call, for example, and it does not in principle matter that the meaning of the call is a great deal broader and more vague than, say, the cry of "Fire!"

In a semantic communicative system the ties between meaningful message-elements and their meanings can be arbitrary or nonarbitrary. In language the ties are arbitrary. The word "salt" is not salty nor granular; "dog" is not "canine"; "whale" is a small word for a large object; "microorganism" is the reverse. A picture, on the other hand, looks like what it is a picture of. A bee dances faster if the source of nectar she is reporting is closer, and slower if it is farther away. The design-feature of "arbitrariness" has the disadvantage of being arbitrary, but the great advantage that there is no limit to what can be communicated about.

Human vocal organs can produce a huge variety of sound. But in any one language only a relatively small set of ranges of sound is used, and the differences between these ranges are functionally absolute. The English words "pin" and "bin" are different to the ear only at one point. If a speaker produces a syllable that deviates from the normal pronunciation of "pin" in the direction of that of "bin," he is not producing still a third word, but just saying "pin" (or perhaps "bin") in a noisy way. The hearer compensates if he can, on the basis of context, or else fails to understand. This feature of "discreteness" in the elementary signaling units of a language contrasts with the use of sound effects by way of vocal gesture. There is an effectively continuous scale of degrees to which one may raise his voice as in anger, or lower it to signal confidentiality. Bee-dancing also is continuous rather than discrete.

Man is apparently almost unique in being able to talk about things that are remote in space or time (or both) from where the talking goes on. This feature—"displacement"—seems to be definitely lacking in the vocal signaling of man's closest relatives, though it does occur in bee-dancing.

One of the most important design-features of language is "productivity"; that is, the capacity to say things that have never been said or heard before and yet to be understood by other speakers of the language. If a gibbon makes any vocal sound at all, it is one or another of a small finite repertory of familiar calls. The gibbon call system can be characterized as closed. Language is open, or "productive," in the sense that one can coin new utterances by putting together pieces familiar from old utterances, assembling them by patterns of arrangement also familiar in old utterances.

Human genes carry the capacity to acquire a language, and probably also a strong drive toward such acquisition, but the detailed conventions of any one language are transmitted extragenetically by learning and teaching. To what extent such "traditional transmission" plays a part in gibbon calls or for other mammalian systems of vocal signals is not known, though in some instances the uniformity of the sounds made by a species, wherever the species is found over the world, is so great that genetics must be responsible.

The meaningful elements in any language—"words" in everyday parlance, "morphemes" to the linguist—constitute an enormous stock. Yet they are represented by small arrangements of a relatively very small stock of distinguishable sounds which are in themselves wholly meaningless. This "duality of patterning" is illustrated by the English words "tack," "cat," and "act." They are totally distinct as to meaning, and yet are composed of just three basic meaningless sounds in different permutations. Few animal communicative systems share this design-feature of language—none among the other hominoids, and perhaps none at all.

———————

It should be noted that some of these 13 design-features are not independent. In particular, a system cannot be either arbitrary or nonarbitrary unless it is semantic, and it cannot have duality of patterning unless it is semantic. It should also be noted that the listing does not attempt to include all the features that might be discovered in the communicative behavior of this or that species, but only those that are clearly important for language.

It is probably safe to assume that nine of the 13 features were already present in the vocal-auditory communication of the protohominoids—just the nine that are securely attested for the gibbons and humans of today. That is, there were a dozen or so distinct calls, each the appropriate vocal response (or vocal part of the whole response) to a recurrent and biologically important type of situation: the discovery of food, the detection of a predator, sexual interest, need for maternal care, and so on. The problem of the origin of human speech, then, is that of trying to determine how such a system could have developed the four additional properties of displacement, productivity and full-blown traditional transmission. Of course the full story involves a great deal more than communicative behavior alone. The development must be visualized as occurring in the context of the evolution of the primate horde into the primitive society of food-gatherers and hunters, an integral part, but a part, of the total evolution of behavior.

It is possible to imagine a closed system developing some degree of productivity, even in the absence of the other three features. Human speech exhibits a phenomenon that could have this effect, the phenomenon of "blending." Sometimes a speaker will hesitate between two words or phrases, both reasonably appropriate for the situation in which he is speaking, and actually say something that is neither wholly one nor wholly the other, but a combination of parts of each. Hesitating between "Don't shout so loud" and "Don't yell so loud," he might come out with "Don't shell so loud." Blending is almost always involved in slips of the tongue, but it may also be the regular mechanism by which a speaker of a language says something that he has not said before. Anything a speaker says must be either an exact repetition of an utterance he has heard before, or else some blended product of two or more such familiar utterances. Thus even such a smooth and normal sentence as "I tried to get there, but the car broke down" might be produced as a blend, say, of "I tried to get there but couldn't" and "While I was driving down Main Street the car broke down."

Children acquiring the language of their community pass through a stage that is closed in just the way gibbon calls are. A child may have a repertory of several dozen sentences, each of which, in adult terms, has an internal structure, and yet for the child each may be an indivisible whole. He may also learn new whole utterances from surrounding adults. The child takes the crucial step, however, when he first says something that he has not learned from others. The only way in which the child can possibly do this is by blending two of the whole utterances that he already knows.

———————

In the case of the closed call-system of the gibbons or the protohominoids, there is no source for the addition of new unitary calls to the repertory except perhaps by occasional imitation of the calls and cries of other species. Even this would not render the system productive, but would merely enlarge it. But blending might occur. Let AB represent the food call and CD the danger call, each a fairly complex phonetic pattern. Suppose a protohominoid encountered food and caught sight of a predator at the same time. If the two stimuli were balanced just right, he might emit the calls ABCD or CDAB in quick sequence, or might even produce AD or CB. Any of these would be a blend. AD, for example, would mean "both food and danger." By virtue of this, AB and CD would acquire new meanings, respectively "food without danger" and "danger without food." And all three of these calls—AB, CD, and AD—would now be composite rather than unitary, built out of smaller elements with their own individual meanings: A would mean "food"; B, "no danger"; C, "no food"; and D, "danger."

But this is only part of the story. The generation of a blend can have no effect unless it is understood. Human beings are so good at understanding blends that it is hard to tell a blend from a rote repetition, except in the case of slips of the tongue and some of the earliest and most tentative blends used by children. Such powers of understanding cannot be ascribed to man's prehuman ancestors. It must be supposed, therefore, that occasional blends occurred over many tens of thousands of years (perhaps, indeed, they still may occur from time to time among gibbons or the great apes), with rarely any appropriate communicative impact on hearers, before the understanding of blends became speedy enough to reinforce their production. However, once that did happen, the earlier closed system had become open and productive.

It is also possible to see how faint traces of displacement might develop in a call system even in the absence of productivity, duality, and thoroughgoing traditional transmission. Suppose an early hominid, a man-ape say, caught sight of a predator without himself being seen. Suppose that for whatever reason—perhaps through fear—he sneaked silently back toward others of his band and only a bit later gave forth the danger call. This might give the whole band a better chance to escape the predator, thus bestowing at least slight survival value on whatever factor was responsible for the delay.

Something akin to communicative displacement is involved in lugging a stick or a stone around—it is like talking today about what one should do tomorrow. Of course it is not to be supposed that the first tool-carrying was purposeful, any more than that the first displaced communication was a discussion of plans. Caught in a cul-de-sac by a predator, however, the early hominid might strike out in terror with his stick or stone and by chance disable or drive off his enemy. In other words, the first tool-carrying had a consequence but not a purpose. Because the outcome was fortunate, it tended to reinforce whatever factor, genetic or traditional, prompted the behavior and made the outcome possible. In the end such events do lead to purposive behavior.

Although elements of displacement might arise in this fashion, on the whole it seems likely that some degree of productivity preceded any great proliferation of communicative displacement as well as any significant capacity for traditional transmission. A productive system requires the young to catch on to the ways in which whole signals are built out of smaller meaningful elements, some of which may never occur as whole signals in isolation. The young can do this only in the way that human children learn their language: by learning some utterances as whole units, in due time testing various blends based on that repertory, and finally adjusting their patterns of blending until the bulk of what they say matches what adults would say and is therefore understood. Part of this learning process is bound to take place away from the precise situations for which the responses are basically appropriate, and this means the promotion of displacement. Learning and teaching, moreover, call on any capacity for traditional transmission that the band may have. Insofar as the communicative system itself has survival value, all this bestows survival value also on the capacity for traditional transmission and for displacement. But these in turn increase the survival value of the communicative system. A child can be taught how to avoid certain dangers before he actually encounters them.

———————

These developments are also necessarily related to the appearance of large and convoluted brains, which are better storage units for the conventions of a complex communicative system and for other traditionally transmitted skills and practices. Hence the adaptive value of the behavior serves to select genetically for the change in structure. A lengthened period of childhood helplessness is also a longer period of plasticity for learning. There is therefore selection for prolonged childhood and, with it, later maturity and longer life. With more for the young to learn, and with male as well as female tasks to be taught, fathers become more domesticated. The increase of displacement promotes retention and foresight; a male can protect his mate and guard her jealously from other males even when he does not at the moment hunger for her.

There is excellent reason to believe that duality of patterning was the last property to be developed, because one can find little if any reason why a communicative system should have this property unless it is highly complicated. If a vocal-auditory system comes to have a larger and larger number of distinct meaningful elements, those elements inevitably come to be more and more similar to one another in sound. There is a practical limit, for any species or any machine, to the number of distinct stimuli that can be discriminated, especially when the discriminations typically have to be made in noisy conditions. Suppose that Samuel F. B. Morse, in devising his telegraph code, had proposed a signal .1 second long for "A," .2 second long for "B," and so on up to 2.6 seconds for "Z." Operators would have enormous difficulty learning and using any such system. What Morse actually did was to incorporate the principle of duality of patterning. The telegraph operator has to learn to discriminate, in the first instance, only two lengths of pulse and about three lengths of pause. Each letter is coded into a different arrangement of these elementary meaningless units. The arrangements are easily kept apart because the few meaningless units are plainly distinguishable.

The analogy explains why it was advantageous for the forerunner of language, as it was becoming increasingly complex, to acquire duality of patterning. However it occurred, this was a major breakthrough; without it language could not possibly have achieved the efficiency and flexibility it has.

One of the basic principles of evolutionary theory holds that the initial survival value of any innovation is conservative in that it makes possible the maintenance of a largely traditional way of life in the face of changed circumstances. There was nothing in the makeup of the protohominoids that destined their descendants to become human. Some of them, indeed, did not. They made their way to ecological niches where food was plentiful and predators sufficiently avoidable, and where the development of primitive varieties of language and culture would have bestowed no advantage. They survive still, with various sorts of specialization, as the gibbons and the great apes.

———

Man's own remote ancestors, then, must have come to live in circumstances where a slightly more flexible system of communication, the incipient carrying and shaping of tools, and a slight increase in the capacity for traditional transmission made just the difference between surviving—largely, be it noted, by the good old protohominoid way of life— and dying out. There are various possibilities. If predators become more numerous and dangerous, any nonce use of a tool as a weapon, any co-operative mode of escape or attack might restore the balance. If food became scarcer, any technique for cracking harder nuts, for foraging over a wider territory, for sharing food so gathered or storing it when it was plentiful might promote survival of the band. Only after a very long period of such small adjustments to tiny changes of living conditions could the factors involved—incipient language, incipient tool-carrying and toolmaking, incipient culture—have started leading the way to a new pattern of life, of the kind called human.

Post-reading Questions / Activities

- How has "traditional transmission" played a role in the development of human society? Where does it come into play in your life?
- After reading this chapter, has your view of the relationship between human language and nonhuman communication changed? How?

Vocabulary

arbitrariness	duality of patterning	primate
blending	extragenetic	productivity
closed-call system	hominid	proto
comparative method	morpheme	Proto-Indo-European
(of historical linguistics)	philology, philological	semanticity
design features	plasticity	traditional transmission
discrete, discreteness		
displacement		

Suggested Further Reading

Oller, D. Kimbrough, and Ulrike Griebel, eds. 2004. *Evolution of Communication Systems: A Comparative Approach*. Cambridge, MA: MIT Press.

CHAPTER 3

Nature of the Linguistic Sign

Ferdinand de Saussure
(1907–1911)

Ferdinand de Saussure was a linguist working right around the turn of the twentieth century. He is credited with pointing out many important aspects of language, such as that it can be looked at not only historically (diachronically), as most linguists including himself were doing at the time, but also at any given moment in time (which he called synchronically). Language forms a system, *an orderly set of rules and words related to each other.*

But words are more than just items in a list. One of the important things to note is that they are a kind of sign—*a linguistic sign, though there could be other kinds of sign. Linguistic signs have certain properties, most important of which are that they have two aspects and that the two aspects are bonded in an arbitrary way.*

The writings we attribute to Saussure were actually compiled from his students' lecture notes after his death. His influence, however, has been unprecedented in the study of language and other cultural phenomena. He proposed a general science of signs, which he termed semiology. *It did not exist at the time, but it does exist now, more commonly as* semiotics. *This science can be used to analyze film, literature, clothing, food, and any other aspect of human behavior.*

Reading Questions

- What is the linguistic sign unit?
- What are the two aspects of a linguistic sign?
- How can looking across languages emphasize that fact?
- What does Saussure mean by "the arbitrary nature of the sign"?

SIGN, SIGNIFIED, SIGNIFIER

Some people regard language, when reduced to its elements, as a naming-process only—a list of words, each corresponding to the thing that it names. For example:

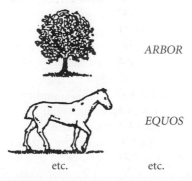

ARBOR

EQUOS

etc.   etc.

Ferdinand de Saussure, "Nature of the Linguistic Sign," pp. 65–70. Reprinted by permission of McGraw-Hill, New York, from *Course in General Linguistics* by Ferdinand de Saussure, edited by Charles Bally and Albert Sechehaye, translated by Wade Baskin, copyright © 1959 by McGraw-Hill and by permission of The Philosophical Library, New York.

This conception is open to criticism at several points. It assumes that ready-made ideas exist before words…; it does not tell us whether a name is vocal or psychological in nature (*arbor*, for instance, can be considered from either viewpoint); finally, it lets us assume that the linking of a name and a thing is a very simple operation—an assumption that is anything but true. But this rather naive approach can bring us near the truth by showing us that the linguistic unit is a double entity, one formed by the associating of two terms.

We have seen [elsewhere] in considering the speaking-circuit that both terms involved in the linguistic sign are psychological and are united in the brain by an associative bond. This point must be emphasized.

The linguistic sign unites, not a thing and a name, but a concept and a sound-image.[1] The latter is not the material sound, a purely physical thing, but the psychological imprint of the sound, the impression that it makes on our senses. The sound-image is sensory, and if I happen to call it "material," it is only in that sense, and by way of opposing it to the other term of the association, the concept, which is generally more abstract.

The psychological character of our sound-images becomes apparent when we observe our own speech. Without moving our lips or tongue, we can talk to ourselves or recite mentally a selection of verse. Because we regard the words of our language as sound-images, we must avoid speaking of the "phonemes" that make up the words. This term, which suggests vocal activity, is applicable to the spoken word only, to the realization of the inner image in discourse. We can avoid that misunderstanding by speaking of the *sounds* and *syllables* of a word provided we remember that the names refer to the sound-image.

The linguistic sign is then a two-sided psychological entity that can be represented by the drawing:

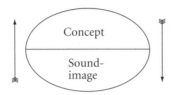

The two elements are intimately united, and each recalls the other. Whether we try to find the meaning of the Latin word *arbor* or the word that Latin uses to designate the concept "tree," it is clear that only the associations sanctioned by that language appear to us to conform to reality, and we disregard whatever others might be imagined.

Our definition of the linguistic sign poses an important question of terminology. I call the combination of a concept and a sound-image a *sign*, but in current usage the term generally designates only a sound-image, a word, for example (*arbor*, etc.). One tends to forget that *arbor* is called a sign only because it carries the concept "tree," with the result that the idea of the sensory part implies the idea of the whole.

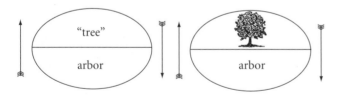

Ambiguity would disappear if the three notions involved here were designated by three names, each suggesting and opposing the others. I propose to retain the word *sign* [*signe*] to designate the whole and to replace *concept* and *sound-image*, respectively, by *signified* [*signifié*] and *signifier* [*signifiant*]; the last two terms have the advantage of indicating the opposition that separates them from each other and from the whole of which they are parts. As regards *sign*, if I am satisfied with it, this is simply because I do not know of any word to replace it, the ordinary language suggesting no other.

The linguistic sign, as defined, has two primordial characteristics. In enunciating them I am also positing the basic principles of any study of this type.

PRINCIPLE I: THE ARBITRARY NATURE OF THE SIGN

The bond between the signifier and the signified is arbitrary. Since I mean by sign the whole that results from the associating of the signifier with the signified, I can simply say: *the linguistic sign is arbitrary*.

The idea of "sister" is not linked by any inner relationship to the succession of sounds *s ö-r*, which serves as its signifier in French; that it could be represented equally by just any other sequence is proved by differences among languages and by the very existence of different languages: the signified "ox" has as its signifier *b-ö-f* on one side of the border and *o-k-s* (*Ochs*) on the other.

No one disputes the principle of the arbitrary nature of the sign, but it is often easier to discover a truth than to assign to it its proper place. Principle I dominates all the linguistics of language; its consequences are numberless. It is true that not all of them are equally obvious at first glance; only after many detours does one discover them, and with them the primordial importance of the principle.

One remark in passing: when semiology becomes organized as a science, the question will arise whether or not it properly includes modes of expression based on completely natural signs, such as pantomime. Supposing that the new science welcomes them, its main concern will still be the whole group of systems grounded on the arbitrariness of the sign. In fact, every means of expression used in society is based, in principle, on collective behavior or—what amounts to the same thing—on convention. Polite formulas, for instance, though often imbued with a certain natural expressiveness (as in the case of a Chinese who greets his emperor by bowing down to the ground nine times), are nonetheless fixed by rule; it is this rule and not the intrinsic value of the gestures that obliges one to use them. Signs that are wholly arbitrary realize better than the others the ideal of the semiological process; that is why language, the most complex and universal of all systems of expression, is also the most characteristic; in this sense linguistics can become the master-pattern for all branches of semiology although language is only one particular semiological system.

The word *symbol* has been used to designate the linguistic sign, or more specifically, what is here called the signifier. Principle I in particular weighs against the use of this term. One characteristic of the symbol is that it is never wholly arbitrary; it is not empty, for there is the rudiment of a natural bond between the signifier and the signified. The symbol of justice, a pair of scales, could not be replaced by just any other symbol, such as a chariot.

The word *arbitrary* also calls for comment. The term should not imply that the choice of the signifier is left entirely to the speaker ([since] the individual does not have the power to change a sign in any way once it has become established in the linguistic community); I mean that it is unmotivated, i.e., arbitrary, in that it actually has no natural connection with the signified.

In concluding let us consider two objections that might be raised to the establishment of Principle I:

1. *Onomatopoeia* might be used to prove that the choice of the signifier is not always arbitrary. But onomatopoeic formations are never organic elements of a linguistic system. Besides, their number is much smaller than is generally supposed. Words like French *fouet* "whip" or *glas* "knell" may strike certain ears with suggestive sonority, but to see that they have not always had this property we need only examine their Latin forms (*fouet* is derived from *fāgus* "beech-tree", *glas* from *classicum* "sound of a trumpet"). The quality of their present sounds, or rather the quality that is attributed to them, is a fortuitous result of phonetic evolution.

   As for authentic onomatopoeic words (e.g., *glug-glug, tick-tock*, etc.), not only are they limited in number, but also they are chosen somewhat arbitrarily, for they are only approximate and more or less conventional imitations of certain sounds (cf. English *bow-bow* and French *ouaoua*). In addition, once these words have been introduced into the language, they are to a certain extent subjected to the same evolution—phonetic, morphological, etc.—that other words undergo (cf. *pigeon*, ultimately from Vulgar Latin *pīpiō*, derived in turn from an onomatopoeic formation): obvious proof that they lose something of their original character in order to assume that of the linguistic sign in general, which is unmotivated.

2. *Interjections*, closely related to onomatopoeia, can be attacked on the same grounds and come no closer to refuting our thesis. One is tempted to see in them spontaneous expressions of reality dictated, so to speak, by natural forces. But for most interjections we can show that there is no fixed bond between their signified and their signifier. We need only compare two languages on this point to see how much such expressions differ from one language to the next (e.g., the English equivalent of French *aïe!* is *ouch!*). We know, moreover, that many interjections were once words with specific meanings (cf. French *diable!* "darn"! *mordieu!* "golly"! from *mort Dieu* "God's death", etc.).[2]

Onomatopoeic formations and interjections are of secondary importance, and their symbolic origin is in part open to dispute.

PRINCIPLE II: THE LINEAR NATURE OF THE SIGNIFIER

The signifier, being auditory, is unfolded solely in time from which it gets the following characteristics: (a) it represents a span, and (b) the span is measurable in a single dimension; it is a line.

While Principle II is obvious, apparently linguists have always neglected to state it, doubtless because they found it too simple; nevertheless, it is fundamental, and its consequences are incalculable. Its importance equals that of Principle I; the whole mechanism of language depends upon it. In contrast to visual signifiers (nautical signals, etc.), which can offer simultaneous groupings in several dimensions, auditory signifiers have at their command only the dimension of time. Their elements are presented in succession; they form a chain. This feature becomes readily apparent when they are represented in writing and the spatial line of graphic marks is substituted for succession in time.

Sometimes the linear nature of the signifier is not obvious. When I accent a syllable, for instance, it seems that I am concentrating more than one significant element on the same point. But this is an illusion; the syllable and its accent constitute only one phonational act. There is no duality within the act but only different oppositions to what precedes and what follows.

Notes

1. The term sound-image may seem to be too restricted inasmuch as beside the representation of the sounds of a word there is also that of its articulation, the muscular image of the phonational act. But for F. de Saussure language is essentially a depository, a thing received from without. The sound-image is par excellence the natural representation of the word as a fact of potential language, outside any actual use of it in speaking. The motor side is thus implied or, in any event, occupies only a subordinate role with respect to the sound-image. [Ed. (Bally and Sechehaye)]

2. Cf. English *goodness!* and *zounds!* (from *God's wounds*). [Tr.]

Post-reading Questions / Activities

- Why was it important for Saussure to show that the relationship between sign and signifier is arbitrary? Can you think of an (unmentioned) argument that he is refuting?
- Why does he argue that onomatopoeia and interjections are not central parts of language? What do they have to do with his claims about arbitrariness?
- Pick an aspect of human behavior (clothing, food, art, film, etc.) and see how you might begin to look at it as a set of signs.

Vocabulary

arbitrary   sign
diachronic   signified
semiology   signifier
semiotics   synchronic

Suggested Further Reading

Barthes, Roland. 1982. *The Empire of Signs*. Translated by Richard Howard. New York: Hill & Wang.

Bignell, Jonathan. 2002. *Media Semiotics: An Introduction*. 2d ed. Manchester and New York: Manchester University Press.

Cobley, Paul, ed. 2001. *The Routledge Companion to Semiotics and Linguistics*. London and New York: Routledge.

Saussure, Ferdinand de. 1959. *Course in General Linguistics*. Translated by Wade Baskin. New York: Philosophical Society.

CHAPTER 4

How Language Works

Steven Pinker

(1994)

Psychologist Steven Pinker has been interpreting and building on the ideas of linguist Noam Chomsky since the 1990s. This chapter comes from his book The Language Instinct, *which introduces the notion of generative grammar. Chomsky showed in the 1950s and 1960s that language cannot be learned simply through imitation and repetition; children make errors they have never heard. Further, the words in a sentence are not simply equivalent. They form clusters that are regular components, such as the prepositional phrase* up the creek. *These components move as units.*

One of the most important properties of language, according to this viewpoint, is its potential for infinitely new sentences, for productivity, for generating novelty. This novelty, however, is nonetheless intelligible.

For Pinker, and Chomsky, language is innate, and it is mental. Though there are clearly physical dimensions to speech, its interesting and important properties are entirely in the mind.

Though Chomsky's work relied on analysis of English, he claimed that all languages really embody the single principles of Universal Grammar.

Reading Questions

- What are the two "tricks" that allow humans to understand language? Which of Hockett's design features (Chapter 2) are these?
- Why does Pinker say it is important that humans can produce and understand a huge number of sentences? How does he explain this?
- Why is what he calls a "word-chain device" not an adequate model for how human language works?
- What are the "trees" that Pinker introduces? How are they related to ambiguous sentences (sentences with more than one meaning)?

Journalists say that when a dog bites a man that is not news, but when a man bites a dog that is news. This is the essence of the language instinct: language conveys news. The streams of words called "sentences" are not just memory prods, reminding you of man and man's best friend and letting you fill in the rest; they tell you who in fact did what to whom. Thus we get more from most stretches of language than Woody Allen got from *War and Peace*, which he read in two hours after taking speed-reading lessons: "It was about some Russians." Language allows us to know how octopuses make love and how to remove cherry stains and

why Tad was heartbroken, and whether the Red Sox will win the World Series without a good relief pitcher and how to build an atom bomb in your basement and how Catherine the Great died, among other things.

When scientists see some apparent magic trick in nature, like bats homing in on insects in pitch blackness or salmon returning to breed in their natal stream, they look for the engineering principles behind it. For bats, the trick turned out to be sonar; for salmon, it was locking in to a faint scent trail. What is the trick behind the ability of *Homo sapiens* to convey that man bites dog?

In fact there is not one trick but two, and they are associated with the names of two European scholars who wrote in the nineteenth century. The first principle, articulated by the Swiss linguist Ferdinand de Saussure, is "the arbitrariness of the sign," the wholly conventional pairing of a sound

Steven Pinker, "How Language Works." *The Language Instinct: How the Mind Creates Language*. New York: HarperCollins, 1994, pp. 83–105, 120–125. Reprinted by permission of HarperCollins Publishers, William Morrow.

with a meaning. The word *dog* does not look like a dog, walk like a dog, or woof like a dog, but it means "dog" just the same. It does so because every English speaker has undergone an identical act of rote learning in childhood that links the sound to the meaning. For the price of this standardized memorization, the members of a language community receive an enormous benefit: the ability to convey a concept from mind to mind virtually instantaneously. Sometimes the gunshot marriage between sound and meaning can be amusing. As Richard Lederer points out in *Crazy English,* we drive on a parkway but park in a driveway, there is no ham in hamburger or bread in sweetbreads, and blueberries are blue but cranberries are not cran. But think about the "sane" alternative of depicting a concept so that receivers can apprehend the meaning in the form. The process is so challenging to the ingenuity, so comically unreliable, that we have made it into party games like Pictionary and charades.

The second trick behind the language instinct is captured in a phrase from Wilhelm Von Humboldt that presaged Chomsky: language "makes infinite use of finite media." We know the difference between the forgettable *Dog bites man* and the newsworthy *Man bites dog* because of the order in which *dog, man,* and *bites* are combined. That is, we use a code to translate between orders of words and combinations of thoughts. That code, or set of rules, is called a generative grammar; . . . it should not be confused with the pedagogical and stylistic grammars we encountered in school.

The principle underlying grammar is unusual in the natural world. A grammar is an example of a "discrete combinatorial system." A finite number of discrete elements (in this case, words) are sampled, combined, and permuted to create larger structures (in this case, sentences) with properties that are quite distinct from those of their elements. For example, the meaning of *Man bites dog* is different from the meaning of any of the three words inside it, and different from the meaning of the same words combined in the reverse order. In a discrete combinatorial system like language, there can be an unlimited number of completely distinct combinations with an infinite range of properties. Another noteworthy discrete combinatorial system in the natural world is the genetic code in DNA, where four kinds of nucleotides are combined into sixty-four kinds of codons, and the codons can be strung into an unlimited number of different genes. Many biologists have capitalized on the close parallel between the principles of grammatical combination and the principles of genetic combination. In the technical language of genetics, sequences of DNA are said to contain "letters" and "punctuation"; may be "palindromic," "meaningless," or "synonymous"; are "transcribed" and "translated"; and are even stored in "libraries." The immunologist Niels Jerne entitled his Nobel Prize address "The Generative Grammar of the Immune System."

Most of the complicated systems we see in the world, in contrast, are *blending systems,* like geology, paint mixing, cooking, sound, light, and weather. In a blending system the properties of the combination lie *between* the properties of its elements, and the properties of the elements are lost in the average or mixture. For example, combining red paint and white paint results in pink paint. Thus the range of properties that can be found in a blending system are highly circumscribed, and the only way to differentiate large numbers of combinations is to discriminate tinier and tinier differences. It may not be a coincidence that the two systems in the universe that most impress us with their open-ended complex design—life and mind—are based on discrete combinatorial systems. Many biologists believe that if inheritance were not discrete, evolution as we know it could not have taken place.

The way language works, then, is that each person's brain contains a lexicon of words and the concepts they stand for (a mental dictionary) and a set of rules that combine the words to convey relationships among concepts (a mental grammar). We will [discuss] the design of grammar.

The fact that grammar is a discrete combinatorial system has two important consequences. The first is the sheer vastness of language. Go into the Library of Congress and pick a sentence at random from any volume, and chances are you would fail to find an exact repetition no matter how long you continued to search. Estimates of the number of sentences that an ordinary person is capable of producing are breathtaking. If a speaker is interrupted at a random point in a sentence, there are on average about ten different words that could be inserted at that point to continue the sentence in a grammatical and meaningful way. (At some points in a sentence, only one word can be inserted, and at others, there is a choice from among thousands; ten is the average.) Let's assume that a person is capable of producing sentences up to twenty words long. Therefore the number of sentences that a speaker can deal with in principle is at least 10^{20} (a one with twenty zeros after it, or a hundred million trillion). At a rate of five seconds a sentence, a person would need a childhood of about a hundred trillion years (with no time for eating or sleeping) to memorize them all. In fact, a twenty-word limitation is far too severe. The following comprehensible sentence from George Bernard Shaw, for example, is 110 words long:

> Stranger still, though Jacques-Dalcroze, like all these great teachers, is the completest of tyrants, knowing what is right and that he must and will have the lesson just so or else break his heart (not somebody else's, observe), yet his school is so fascinating that every woman who sees it exclaims: "Oh why was I not taught like this!" and elderly gentlemen excitedly enroll themselves as students and distract classes of infants by their desperate endeavours to beat two in a bar with one hand and three with the other, and start off on earnest walks around the room, taking two steps backward whenever M. Dalcroze calls out "Hop!"

Indeed, if you put aside the fact that the days of our age are threescore and ten, each of us is capable of uttering an *infinite* number of different sentences. By the same logic that shows that there are an infinite number of integers—if you ever think you have the largest integer, just add 1 to it and you will have another—there must be an infinite number of sentences. The *Guinness Book of World Records* once claimed to recognize the longest English sentence: a 1,300-word stretch in William Faulkner's novel *Absalom, Absalom!* that begins:

> They both bore it as though in deliberate flagellant exaltation…

I am tempted to achieve immortality by submitting the following record-breaker:

> Faulkner wrote, "They both bore it as though in deliberate flagellant exaltation…"

But it would be only the proverbial fifteen minutes of fame, for soon I could be bested by:

> Pinker wrote that Faulkner wrote, "They both bore it as though in deliberate flagellant exaltation…"

And that record, too, would fall when someone submitted:

> Who cares that Pinker wrote that Faulkner wrote, "They both bore it as though in deliberate flagellant exaltation…"?

And so on, ad infinitum. The infinite use of finite media distinguishes the human brain from virtually all the artificial language devices we commonly come across, like pull-string dolls, cars that nag you to close the door, and cheery voice-mail instructions ("Press the pound key for more options"), all of which use a fixed list of prefabricated sentences.

The second consequence of the design of grammar is that it is a code that is *autonomous* from cognition. A grammar specifies how words may combine to express meanings; that specification is independent of the particular meanings we typically convey or expect others to convey to us. Thus we all sense that some strings of words that can be given common-sense interpretations do not conform to the grammatical code of English. Here are some strings that we can easily interpret but that we sense are not properly formed:

> Welcome to Chinese Restaurant. Please try your Nice Chinese Food with Chopsticks: the traditional and typical of Chinese glorious history and cultual.
> It's a flying finches, they are.
> The child seems sleeping.
> Is raining.
> Sally poured the glass with water.
> Who did a book about impress you?
>
> Skid crash hospital.
> Drum vapor worker cigarette flick boom.
>
> This sentence no verb.
> This sentence has contains two verbs.
> This sentence has cabbage six words.
> This is not a complete. This either.

These sentences are "ungrammatical," not in the sense of split infinitives, dangling participles, and the other hobgoblins of the schoolmarm, but in the sense that every

ordinary speaker of the casual vernacular has a gut feeling that something is wrong with them, despite their interpretability. Ungrammaticality is simply a consequence of our having a fixed code for interpreting sentences. For some strings a meaning can be guessed, but we lack confidence that the speaker has used the same code in producing the sentence as we used in interpreting it. For similar reasons, computers, which are less forgiving of ungrammatical input than human listeners, express their displeasure in all-too-familiar dialogues like this one:

```
> PRINT (x + 1
*****SYNTAX ERROR*****
```

The opposite can happen as well. Sentences can make no sense but can still be recognized as grammatical. The classic example is a sentence from Chomsky, his only entry in *Bartlett's Familiar Quotations*:

> Colorless green ideas sleep furiously.

The sentence was contrived to show that syntax and sense can be independent of each other, but the point was made long before Chomsky; the genre of nonsense verse and prose, popular in the nineteenth century, depends on it. Here is an example from Edward Lear, the acknowledged master of nonsense:

> It's a fact the whole world knows,
> That Pobbles are happier without their toes.

Mark Twain once parodied the romantic description of nature written more for its mellifluousness than its content:

> It was a crisp and spicy morning in early October. The lilacs and laburnums, lit with the glory-fires of autumn, hung burning and flashing in the upper air, a fairy bridge provided by kind Nature for the wingless wild things that have their homes in the tree-tops and would visit together; the larch and the pomegranate flung their purple and yellow flames in brilliant broad splashes along the slanting sweep of the woodland; the sensuous fragrance of innumerable deciduous flowers rose upon the swooning atmosphere; far in the empty sky a solitary esophagus slept upon motionless wing; everywhere brooded stillness, serenity, and the peace of God.

And almost everyone knows the poem in Lewis Carroll's *Through the Looking-Glass* that ends:

> And, as in uffish thought he stood,
>   The Jabberwock, with eyes of flame,
> Came whiffling through the tulgey wood,
>   And burbled as it came!
>
> One, two! One, two! And through and through
>   The vorpal blade went snicker-snack!
> He left it dead, and with its head
>   He went galumphing back.
>
> "And hast thou slain the Jabberwock?
>   Come to my arms, my beamish boy!

O frabjous day! Callooh! Callay!"
    He chortled in his joy.

'Twas brillig, and the slithy toves
    Did gyre and gimble in the wabe:
All mimsy were the borogoves,
    And the mome raths outgrabe.

As Alice said, "Somehow it seems to fill my head with ideas—only I don't exactly know what they are!" But though common sense and common knowledge are of no help in understanding these passages, English speakers recognize that they are grammatical, and their mental rules allow them to extract precise, though abstract, frameworks of meaning. Alice deduced, "*Somebody* killed *something*: that's clear, at any rate—." And after reading Chomsky's entry in *Bartlett's*, anyone can answer questions like "What slept? How? Did one thing sleep, or several? What kind of ideas were they?"

How might the combinatorial grammar underlying human language work? The most straightforward way to combine words in order is explained in Michael Frayn's novel *The Tin Men*. The protagonist, Goldwasser, is an engineer working at an institute for automation. He must devise a computer system that generates the standard kinds of stories found in the daily papers, like "Paralyzed Girl Determined to Dance Again." Here he is hand-testing a program that composes stories about royal occasions:

He opened the filing cabinet and picked out the first card in the set. *Traditionally*, it read. Now there was a random choice between cards reading *coronations, engagements, funerals, weddings, comings of age, births, deaths*, or *the churching of women*. The day before he had picked *funerals*, and been directed on to a card reading with simple perfection *are occasions for mourning*. Today he closed his eyes, drew *weddings*, and was signposted on to *are occasions for rejoicing*.

The wedding of X and Y followed in logical sequence, and brought him a choice between *is no exception* and *is a case in point*. Either way there followed *indeed*. Indeed, whichever occasion one had started off with, whether coronations, deaths, or births, Goldwasser saw with intense mathematical pleasure, one now reached this same elegant bottleneck. He paused on *indeed*, then drew in quick succession *it is a particularly happy occasion, rarely*, and *can there have been a more popular young couple*.

From the next selection, Goldwasser drew *X has won himself/herself a special place in the nation's affections*, which forced him to go on to *and the British people have clearly taken Y to their hearts already*.

Goldwasser was surprised, and a little disturbed, to realise that the word "fitting" had still not come up. But he drew it with the next card—*it is especially fitting that*.

This gave him *the bride/bridegroom should be*, and an open choice between *of such a noble and illustrious*

line, a commoner in these democratic times, from a nation with which this country has long enjoyed a particularly close and cordial relationship*, and *from a nation with which this country's relations have not in the past been always happy*.

Feeling that he had done particularly well with "fitting" last time, Goldwasser now deliberately selected it again. *It is also fitting that*, read the card, to be quickly followed by *we should remember*, and *X and Y are not merely symbols—they are a lively young man and a very lovely young woman*.

Goldwasser shut his eyes to draw the next card. It turned out to read *in these days when*. He pondered whether to select *it is fashionable to scoff at the traditional morality of marriage and family life* or *it is no longer fashionable to scoff at the traditional morality of marriage and family life*. The latter had more of the form's authentic baroque splendour, he decided.

Let's call this a word-chain device (the technical name is a "finite-state" or "Markov" model). A word-chain device is a bunch of lists of words (or prefabricated phrases) and a set of directions for going from list to list. A processor builds a sentence by selecting a word from one list, then a word from another list, and so on. (To recognize a sentence spoken by another person, one just checks the words against each list in order.) Word-chain systems are commonly used in satires like Frayn's, usually as do-it-yourself recipes for composing examples of a kind of verbiage. For example, here is a Social Science Jargon Generator, which the reader may operate by picking a word at random from the first column, then a word from the second, then one from the third, and stringing them together to form an impressive-sounding term like *inductive aggregating interdependence*:

dialectical	participatory	interdependence
defunctionalized	degenerative	diffusion
positivistic	aggregating	periodicity
predicative	appropriative	synthesis
multilateral	simulated	sufficiency
quantitative	homogeneous	equivalence
divergent	transfigurative	expectancy
synchronous	diversifying	plasticity
differentiated	cooperative	epigenesis
inductive	progressive	constructivism
integrated	complementary	deformation
distributive	eliminative	solidification

Recently I saw a word-chain device that generates breathless book jacket blurbs, and another for Bob Dylan song lyrics.

A word-chain device (see below) is the simplest example of a discrete combinatorial system, since it is capable of creating an unlimited number of distinct combinations from a finite set of elements. Parodies notwithstanding, a word-chain device can generate infinite sets of grammatical English sentences. For example, the extremely simple scheme assembles many sentences, such as *A girl eats ice cream* and *The happy dog eats candy*. It can assemble an infinite number because of the loop at the top that can take the device from the *happy* list back to itself any number of times: *The happy dog eats ice cream, The happy happy dog eats ice cream*, and so on.

When an engineer has to build a system to combine words in particular orders, a word-chain device is the first thing that comes to mind. The recorded voice that gives you a phone number when you dial directory assistance is a good example. A human speaker is recorded uttering the ten digits, each in seven different sing-song patterns (one for the first position in a phone number, one for the second position, and so on). With just these seventy recordings, ten million phone numbers can be assembled; with another thirty recordings for three-digit area codes, ten billion numbers are possible (in practice, many are never used because of restrictions like the absence of 0 and 1 from the beginning of a phone number). In fact there have been serious efforts to model the English language as a very large word chain. To make it as realistic as possible, the transitions from one word list to another can reflect the actual probabilities that those kinds of words follow one another in English (for example, the word *that* is much more likely to be followed by *is* than by *indicates*). Huge databases of these "transition probabilities" have been compiled by having a computer analyze bodies of English text or by asking volunteers to name the words that first come to mind after a given word or series of words. Some psychologists have suggested that human language is based on a huge word chain stored in the brain. The idea is congenial to stimulus-response theories: a stimulus elicits a spoken word as a response, then the speaker perceives his or her own response, which serves as the next stimulus, eliciting one out of several words as the next response, and so on.

But the fact that word-chain devices seem ready-made for parodies like Frayn's raises suspicions. The point of the various parodies is that the genre being satirized is so mindless and cliché-ridden that a simple mechanical method can churn out an unlimited number of examples that can almost pass for the real thing. The humor works because of the discrepancy between the two: we all assume that people, even sociologists and reporters, are not really word-chain devices; they only seem that way.

The modern study of grammar began when Chomsky showed that word-chain devices are not just a bit suspicious; they are deeply, fundamentally, the wrong way to think about how human language works. They are discrete combinatorial systems, but they are the wrong kind. There are three problems, and each one illuminates some aspect of how language really does work.

First, a sentence of English is a completely different thing from a string of words chained together according to the transition probabilities of English. Remember Chomsky's sentence *Colorless green ideas sleep furiously*. He contrived it not only to show that nonsense can be grammatical but also to show that improbable word sequences can be grammatical. In English texts the probability that the word *colorless* is followed by the word *green* is surely zero. So is the probability that *green* is followed by *ideas, ideas* by *sleep*, and *sleep* by *furiously*. Nonetheless, the string is a well-formed sentence of English. Conversely, when one actually assembles word chains using probability tables, the resulting word strings are very far from being well-formed sentences. For example, say you take estimates of the set of words most likely to come after every four-word sequence, and use those estimates to grow a string word by word, always looking at the four most recent words to determine the next one. The string will be eerily Englishy, but not English, like *House to ask for is to earn our living by working towards a goal for his team in old New-York was a wonderful place wasn't it even pleasant to talk about and laugh hard when he tells lies he should not tell me the reason why you are is evident*.

The discrepancy between English sentences and Englishy word chains has two lessons. When people learn a language, they are learning how to put words in order, but not by recording which word follows which other word. They do it by recording which word *category*—noun, verb, and so on—follows which other category. That is, we can recognize *colorless green ideas* because it has the same order of adjectives and nouns that we learned from more familiar sequences like *strapless black dresses*. The second lesson is that the nouns and verbs and adjectives are not just hitched end to end in one long chain; there is some overarching blueprint or plan for the sentence that puts each word in a specific slot.

If a word-chain device is designed with sufficient cleverness, it can deal with these problems. But Chomsky had a definitive refutation of the very idea that a human language is a word chain. He proved that certain sets of English sentences could not, even in principle, be produced by a word-chain device, no matter how big or how faithful to probability tables the device is. Consider sentences like the following:

Either the girl eats ice cream, or the girl eats candy.
If the girl eats ice cream, then the boy eats hot dogs.

At first glance it seems easy to accommodate these sentences:

But the device does not work. *Either* must be followed later in a sentence by *or*; no one says *Either the girl eats ice cream, then the girl likes candy*. Similarly, *if* requires *then*; no one says *If the girl eats ice cream, or the girl likes candy*. But to

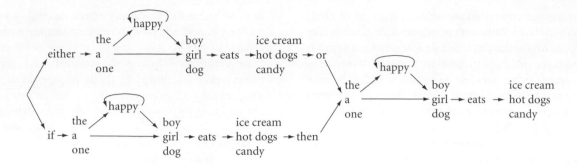

satisfy the desire of a word early in a sentence for some other word late in the sentence, the device has to remember the early word while it is churning out all the words in between. And that is the problem: a word-chain device is an amnesiac, remembering only which word list it has just chosen from, nothing earlier. By the time it reaches the *or/then* list, it has no means of remembering whether it said *if* or *either* way back at the beginning. From our vantage point, peering down at the entire road map, we can remember which choice the device made at the first fork in the road, but the device itself, creeping antlike from list to list, has no way of remembering.

Now, you might think it would be a simple matter to redesign the device so that it does not have to remember early choices at late points in the sentence. For example, one could join up *either* and *or* and all the possible word sequences in between into one giant sequence, and *if* and *then* and all the sequences in between as a second giant sequence, before returning to a third copy of the sequence—yielding a chain so long I have to print it [across two columns]. There is something immediately disturbing about this solution: there are three identical subnetworks. Clearly, whatever people can say between an *either* and an *or*, they can say between an *if* and a *then*, and also after the *or* or the *then*. But this ability should come naturally out of the design of whatever the device is in people's heads that allows them to speak. It shouldn't depend on the designer's carefully writing down three identical sets of instructions (or, more plausibly, on the child's having to learn the structure of the English sentence three different times, once between *if* and *then*, once between *either* and *or*, and once after a *then* or an *or*).

But Chomsky showed that the problem is even deeper. Each of these sentences can be embedded in any of the others, including itself:

> If either the girl eats ice cream or the girl eats candy, then the boy eats hot dogs.
> Either if the girl eats ice cream then the boy eats ice cream, or if the girl eats ice cream then the boy eats candy.

For the first sentence, the device has to remember *if* and *either* so that it can continue later with *or* and *then*, in that order. For the second sentence, it has to remember *either* and *if* so that it can complete the sentence with *then* and *or*. And so on. Since there's no limit in principle to the number

of *if*'s and *either*'s that can begin a sentence, each requiring its own order of *then*'s and *or*'s to complete it, it does no good to spell out each memory sequence as its own chain of lists; you'd need an infinite number of chains, which won't fit inside a finite brain.

This argument may strike you as scholastic. No real person ever begins a sentence with *Either either if either if if*, so who cares whether a putative model of that person can complete it with *then...then...or...then...or...or*? But Chomsky was just adopting the esthetic of the mathematician, using the interaction between *either-or* and *if-then* as the simplest possible example of a property of language—its use of "long-distance dependencies" between an early word and a later one—to prove mathematically that word-chain devices cannot handle these dependencies.

The dependencies, in fact, abound in languages, and mere mortals use them all the time, over long distances, often handling several at once—just what a word-chain device cannot do. For example, there is an old grammarian's saw about how a sentence can end in five prepositions. Daddy trudges upstairs to Junior's bedroom to read him a bedtime story. Junior spots the book, scowls, and asks, "Daddy, what did you bring that book that I don't want to be read to out of up for?" By the point at which he utters *read*, Junior has committed himself to holding four dependencies in mind: *to be read* demands *to, that book that* requires *out of, bring* requires *up*, and *what* requires *for*. An even better, real-life example comes from a letter to *TV Guide*:

> How Ann Salisbury can claim that Pam Dawber's anger at not receiving her fair share of acclaim for *Mork and Mindy*'s success derives from a fragile ego escapes me.

At the point just after the word *not*, the letter-writer had to keep four grammatical commitments in mind: (1) *not* requires *-ing* (her anger at *not* receiv*ing* acclaim); (2) *at* requires some kind of noun or gerund (her anger *at* not *receiving acclaim*); (3) the singular subject *Pam Dawber's anger* requires the verb fourteen words downstream to agree with it in number (Dawber's *anger...derives* from); (4) the singular subject beginning with *How* requires the verb twenty-seven words downstream to agree with it in number (*How...escapes* me). Similarly, a reader must keep these dependencies in mind while interpreting the sentence. Now, technically speaking, one could rig up a word-chain model to handle even these sentences, as long as there is some actual limit on the number of dependencies that the speaker need keep in mind (four, say). But the degree of redundancy in the device would be absurd; for each of the thousands of *combinations* of dependencies, an identical chain must be duplicated inside the device. In trying to fit such a super-chain in a person's memory, one quickly runs out of brain.

The difference between the artificial combinatorial system we see in word-chain devices and the natural one we see in the human brain is summed up in a line from the Joyce Kilmer poem: "Only God can make a tree." A sentence is not a chain but a tree. In a human grammar, words are grouped into phrases, like twigs joined in a branch. The phrase is given a name—a mental symbol—and little phrases can be joined into bigger ones.

Take the sentence *The happy boy eats ice cream*. It begins with three words that hang together as a unit, the noun phrase *the happy boy*. In English a noun phrase (NP) is composed of a noun (N), sometimes preceded by an article or "determiner" (abbreviated "det") and any number of adjectives (A). All this can be captured in a rule that defines what English noun phrases look like in general. In the standard notation of linguistics, an arrow means "consists of," parentheses mean "optional," and an asterisk means "as many of them as you want," but I provide the rule just to show that all of its information can be captured precisely in a few symbols; you can ignore the notation and just look at the translation into ordinary words below it:

NP → (det) A* N
"A noun phrase consists of an optional determiner, followed by any number of adjectives, followed by a noun."

The rule defines an upside-down tree branch:

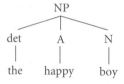

Here are two other rules, one defining the English sentence (S), the other defining the predicate or verb phrase (VP); both use the NP symbol as an ingredient:

S → NP VP
"A sentence consists of a noun phrase followed by a verb phrase."

VP → V NP
"A verb phrase consists of a verb followed by a noun phrase."

We now need a mental dictionary that specifies which words belong to which part-of-speech categories (noun, verb, adjective, preposition, determiner):

N → boy, girl, dog, cat, ice cream, candy, hot dogs
"Nouns may be drawn from the following list: *boy, girl,…*"

V → eats, likes, bites
"Verbs may be drawn from the following list: *eats, likes, bites.*"

A → happy, lucky, tall
"Adjectives may be drawn from the following list: *happy, lucky, tall.*"

det → a, the, one
"Determiners may be drawn from the following list: *a, the, one.*"

A set of rules like the ones I have listed—a "phrase structure grammar"—defines a sentence by linking the words to branches on an inverted tree:

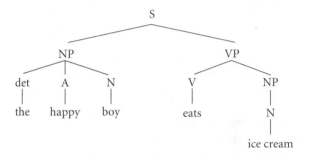

The invisible superstructure holding the words in place is a powerful invention that eliminates the problems of word-chain devices. The key insight is that a tree is *modular*, like telephone jacks or garden hose couplers. A symbol like "NP" is like a connector or fitting of a certain shape. It allows one component (a phrase) to snap into any of several positions inside other components (larger phrases). Once a kind of phrase is defined by a rule and given its connector symbol, it never has to be defined again; the phrase can be plugged in anywhere there is a corresponding socket. For example, in the little grammar I have listed, the symbol "NP" is used both as the subject of a sentence (S → NP VP) and as the object of a verb phrase (VP → V NP). In a more realistic grammar, it would also be used as the object of a preposition (*near the boy*), in a possessor phrase (*the boy's hat*), as an indirect object (*give the boy a cookie*), and in several other positions. This plug-and-socket arrangement explains how people can use the same kind of phrase in many different positions in a sentence, including:

[The happy happy boy] eats ice cream.
I like [the happy happy boy].
I gave [the happy happy boy] a cookie.
[The happy happy boy]'s cat eats ice cream.

There is no need to learn that the adjective precedes the noun (rather than vice versa) for the subject, and then have to learn the same thing for the object, and again for the indirect object, and yet again for the possessor.

Note, too, that the promiscuous coupling of any phrase with any slot makes grammar autonomous from our common-sense expectations involving the meanings of the words. It thus explains why we can write and appreciate grammatical nonsense. Our little grammar defines all kinds of colorless green sentences, like *The happy happy candy likes the tall ice cream,* as well as conveying such newsworthy events as *The girl bites the dog.*

Most interestingly, the labeled branches of a phrase structure tree act as an overarching memory or plan for the whole sentence. This allows nested long-distance dependencies, like *if…then* and *either…or,* to be handled with ease. All you need is a rule defining a phrase that contains a copy of the very same kind of phrase, such as:

S → either S or S
"A sentence can consist of the word *either,* followed by a sentence, followed by the word *or,* followed by another sentence."

S → if S then S
"A sentence can consist of the word *if,* followed by a sentence, followed by the word *then,* followed by another sentence."

These rules embed one instance of a symbol inside another instance of the same symbol (here, a sentence inside a sentence), a neat trick—logicians call it "recursion"—for generating an infinite number of structures. The pieces of the bigger sentence are held together, in order, as a set of branches growing out of a common node. That node holds together each *either* with its *or,* each *if* with its *then,* as in the following diagram (the triangles are abbreviations for lots of underbrush that would only entangle us if shown in full):

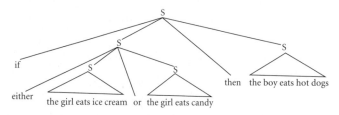

There is another reason to believe that a sentence is held together by a mental tree. So far I have been talking about stringing words into a grammatical order, ignoring what they mean. But grouping words into phrases is also necessary to connect grammatical sentences with their proper meanings, chunks of mentalese. We know that the sentence shown above is about a girl, not a boy, eating ice cream, and a boy, not a girl, eating hot dogs, and we know that the boy's snack is contingent on the girl's, not vice versa. That is because *girl* and *ice cream* are connected inside their own phrase, as are *boy* and *hot dogs,* as are the two sentences involving the girl. With a chaining device it's just one damn word after another, but with a phrase structure grammar the connectedness of words in the tree reflects the relatedness of ideas in mentalese. Phrase structure, then, is one solution to the engineering problem of

taking an interconnected web of thoughts in the mind and encoding them as a string of words that must be uttered, one at a time, by the mouth.

One way to see how invisible phrase structure determines meaning is to recall one of the reasons…that language and thought have to be different: a particular stretch of language can correspond to two distinct thoughts. [In] examples like *Child's Stool Is Great for Use in Garden,* the single word *stool* has two meanings, corresponding to two entries in the mental dictionary. But sometimes a whole sentence has two meanings, even if each individual word has only one meaning. In the movie *Animal Crackers,* Groucho Marx says, "I once shot an elephant in my pajamas. How he got into my pajamas I'll never know." Here are some similar ambiguities that accidentally appeared in newspapers:

> Yoko Ono will talk about her husband John Lennon who was killed in an interview with Barbara Walters.
>
> Two cars were reported stolen by the Groveton police yesterday.
>
> The license fee for altered dogs with a certificate will be $3 and for pets owned by senior citizens who have not been altered the fee will be $1.50.
>
> Tonight's program discusses stress, exercise, nutrition, and sex with Celtic forward Scott Wedman, Dr. Ruth Westheimer, and Dick Cavett.
>
> We will sell gasoline to anyone in a glass container.
>
> For sale: Mixing bowl set designed to please a cook with round bottom for efficient beating.

The two meanings in each sentence come from the different ways in which the words can be joined up in a tree. For example, in *discuss sex with Dick Cavett,* the writer put the words together according to the tree at the left ("PP" means prepositional phrase): sex is what is to be discussed, and it is to be discussed with Dick Cavett.

The alternative meaning comes from our analyzing the words according to the tree at the right: the words *sex with Dick Cavett* form a single branch of the tree, and sex with Dick Cavett is what is to be discussed.

Phrase structure, clearly, is the kind of stuff language is made of. But what I have shown you is just a toy. [Now] I will try to explain the modern Chomskyan theory of how language works. Chomsky's writings are "classics" in Mark

Twain's sense: something that everybody wants to have read and nobody wants to read. When I come across one of the countless popular books on mind, language, and human nature that refer to "Chomsky's deep structure of meaning common to all human languages" (wrong in two ways, we shall see), I know that Chomsky's books of the last twenty-five years are sitting on a high shelf in the author's study, their spines uncracked, their folios uncut. Many people want to have a go at speculating about the mind but have the same impatience about mastering the details of how language works that Eliza Doolittle showed to Henry Higgins in *Pygmalion* when she complained, "I don't want to talk grammar. I want to talk like a lady in a flower shop."

For nonspecialists the reaction is even more extreme. In Shakespeare's *The Second Part of King Henry VI*, the rebel Dick the Butcher speaks the well-known line "The first thing we do, let's kill all the lawyers." Less well known is the second thing Dick suggests they do: behead Lord Say. Why? Here is the indictment presented by the mob's leader, Jack Cade:

> Thou hast most traitorously corrupted the youth of the realm in erecting a grammar school.... It will be proved to thy face that thou hast men about thee that usually talk of a noun and a verb, and such abominable words as no Christian ear can endure to hear.

And who can blame the grammarphobe, when a typical passage from one of Chomsky's technical works reads as follows?

> To summarize, we have been led to the following conclusions, on the assumption that the trace of a zero-level category must be properly governed. 1. VP is α-marked by I. 2. Only lexical categories are L-markers, so that VP is not L-marked by I. 3. α-government is restricted to sisterhood without the qualification (35). 4. Only the terminus of an X^0-chain can α-mark or Case-mark. 5. Head-to-head movement forms an A-chain. 6. SPEC-head agreement and chains involve the same indexing. 7. Chain coindexing holds of the links of an extended chain. 8. There is no accidental coindexing of I. 9. I-V coindexing is a form of head-head agreement; if it is restricted to aspectual verbs, then base-generated structures of the form (174) count as adjunction structures. 10. Possibly, a verb does not properly govern its α-marked complement.

All this is unfortunate. People, especially those who hold forth on the nature of mind, should be just plain curious about the code that the human species uses to speak and understand. In return, the scholars who study language for a living should see that such curiosity can be satisfied. Chomsky's theory need not be treated by either group as a set of cabalistic incantations that only the initiated can mutter. It is a set of discoveries about the design of language that can be appreciated intuitively if one first understands the problems to which the theory provides solutions. In fact, grasping grammatical theory provides an intellectual pleasure that is rare in the social sciences. When I entered high school in the late 1960s and electives were chosen for their

"relevance," Latin underwent a steep decline in popularity (thanks to students like me, I confess). Our Latin teacher Mrs. Rillie, whose merry birthday parties for Rome failed to slow the decline, tried to persuade us that Latin grammar honed the mind with its demands for precision, logic, and consistency. (Nowadays, such arguments are more likely to come from the computer programming teachers.) Mrs. Rillie had a point, but Latin declensional paradigms are not the best way to convey the inherent beauty of grammar. The insights behind Universal Grammar are much more interesting, not only because they are more general and elegant but because they are about living minds rather than dead tongues....

Anyone who goes to cocktail parties knows that one of Chomsky's main contributions to intellectual life is the concept of "deep structure," together with the "transformations" that map it onto "surface structure." When Chomsky introduced the terms in the behaviorist climate of the early 1960s, the reaction was sensational. Deep structure came to refer to everything that was hidden, profound, universal, or meaningful, and before long there was talk of the deep structure of visual perception, stories, myths, poems, paintings, musical compositions, and so on. Anticlimactically, I must now divulge that "deep structure" is a prosaic technical gadget in grammatical theory. It is not the meaning of a sentence, nor is it what is universal across all human languages. Though universal grammar and abstract phrase structures seem to be permanent features of grammatical theory, many linguists—including, in his most recent writings, Chomsky himself—think one can do without deep structure per se. To discourage all the hype incited by the word "deep," linguists now usually refer to it as "d-structure." The concept is actually quite simple.

Recall that for a sentence to be well formed, the verb must get what it wants: all the roles listed in the verb's dictionary entry must appear in their designated positions. But in many sentences, the verb does not seem to be getting what it wants. Remember that *put* requires a subject, an object, and a prepositional phrase; *He put the car* and *He put in the garage* sound incomplete. How, then, do we account for the following perfectly good sentences?

> The car was put in the garage.
> What did he put in the garage?
> Where did he put the car?

In the first sentence, *put* seems to be doing fine without an object, which is out of character. Indeed, now it rejects one: *The car was put the Toyota in the garage* is awful. In the second sentence, *put* also appears in public objectless. In the third, its obligatory prepositional phrase is missing. Does this mean we need to add new dictionary entries for *put*, allowing it to appear in some places without its object or its prepositional phrase? Obviously not, or *He put the car* and *He put in the garage* would slip back in.

In some sense, of course, the required phrases really are there—they're just not where we expect them. In the first sentence, a passive construction, the NP *the car*, playing the role of "thing put" which ordinarily would be the object, shows up in the subject position instead. In the second sentence, a *wh*-question (that is, a question formed with *who, what, where, when,* or *why*), the "thing put" role is expressed by the word *what* and shows up at the beginning. In the third sentence, the "place" role also shows up at the beginning instead of after the object, where it ordinarily belongs.

A simple way to account for the entire pattern is to say that every sentence has two phrase structures. The phrase structure we have been talking about so far, the one defined by the super-rules, is the deep structure. Deep structure is the interface between the mental dictionary and phrase structure. In the deep structure, all the role-players for *put* appear in their expected places. Then a transformational operation can "move" a phrase to a previously unfilled slot elsewhere in the tree. That is where we find the phrase in the actual sentence. This new tree is the surface structure (now called "s-structure," because as a mere "surface" representation it never used to get proper respect). Here are the deep structure and surface structure of a passive sentence:

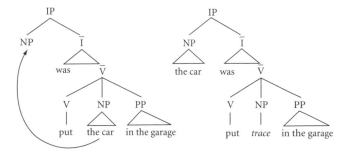

In the deep structure on the left, *the car* is where the verb wanted it; in the surface structure on the right, it is where we actually hear it. In the surface structure, the position from which the phrase was moved contains an inaudible symbol that was left behind by the movement transformation, called a "trace." The trace serves as a reminder of the role that the moved phrase is playing. It tells us that to find out what *the car* is doing in the putting event, we should look up the "object" slot in the entry for the verb *put*; that slot says "thing put." Thanks to the trace, the surface structure contains the information needed to recover the meaning of the sentence; the original deep structure, which was used only to plug in the right sets of words from the lexicon, plays no role.

Why do languages bother with separate deep structures and surface structures? Because it takes more than just keeping the verb happy—what deep structure does—to have a usable sentence. A given concept often has to play one kind of role, defined by the verb in the verb phrase, and simultaneously a separate role, independent of the verb, defined by some other layer of the tree. Consider the difference between *Beavers build dams* and its passive, *Dams are built by beavers.* Down in the verb phrase—the level of who did what to whom—the nouns are playing the same

roles in both sentences. Beavers do the building, dams get built. But up at the sentence (IP) level—the level of subject-predicate relations, of what is being asserted to be true of what—they are playing different roles. The active sentence is saying something about beavers in general, and happens to be true; the passive sentence is saying something about dams in general, and happens to be false (since some dams, like the Grand Coulee Dam, are not built by beavers). The surface structure, which puts *dams* in the sentence's subject position but links it to a trace of its original verb phrase position, allows the cake to be both eaten and had.

The ability to move phrases around while still retaining their roles also gives the speaker of a rigid-word-order language like English a bit of wiggle room. For example, phrases that are ordinarily buried deep in the tree can be moved to early in the sentence, where they can hook up with material fresh in the listener's mind. For example, if a play-by-play announcer has been describing Nevin Markwart's progression down the ice, he could say *Markwart spears Gretzky!!!* But if it was Wayne Gretzky the announcer had been describing, he would say *Gretzky is speared by Markwart!!!!* Moreover, because a passive participle has the option of leaving the doer role, ordinarily the subject, unfilled in deep structure, it is useful when one wants to avoid mentioning that role altogether, as in Ronald Reagan's evasive concession *Mistakes were made.*

Hooking up players with different roles in different scenarios is something that grammar excels at. In a *wh*-question like

What did he put [*trace*] in the garage?

the noun phrase *what* gets to live a double life. Down in the who-did-what-to-whom realm of the verb phrase, the position of the trace indicates that the entity has the role of the thing being put; up in the what-is-being-asserted-of-what realm of the sentence, the word *what* indicates that the point of the sentence is to ask the listener to provide the identity of something. If a logician were to express the meaning behind the sentence, it would be something like "For which x, John put x in the garage." When these movement operations are combined with other components of syntax, as in *She was told by Bob to be examined by a doctor* or *Who did he say that Barry tried to convince to leave?* or *Tex is fun for anyone to tease*, the components interact to determine the meaning of the sentence in chains of deduction as intricate and precise as the workings of a fine Swiss watch.

———

Now that I have dissected syntax in front of you, I hope your reaction is more favorable than Eliza Doolittle's or Jack Cade's. At the very least I hope you are impressed at how syntax is a Darwinian "organ of extreme perfection and complication." Syntax is complex, but the complexity is there for a reason. For our thoughts are surely even more complex, and we are limited by a mouth that can pronounce a single word at a time. Science has begun to crack the beautifully designed code that our brains use to convey complex thoughts as words and their orderings.

The workings of syntax are important for another reason. Grammar offers a clear refutation of the empiricist doctrine that there is nothing in the mind that was not first in the senses. Traces, cases, X-bars, and the other paraphernalia of syntax are colorless, odorless, and tasteless, but they, or something like them, must be a part of our unconscious mental life. This should not be surprising to a thoughtful computer scientist. There is no way one can write a halfway intelligent program without defining variables and data structures that do not directly correspond to anything in the input or output. For example, a graphics program that had to store an image of a triangle inside a circle would not store the actual keystrokes that the user typed to draw the shapes, because the same shapes could have been drawn in a different order or with a different device like a mouse or a light pen. Nor would it store the list of dots that have to be lit up to display the shapes on a video screen, because the user might later want to move the circle around and leave the triangle in place, or make the circle bigger or smaller, and one long list of dots would not allow the program to know which dots belong to the circle and which to the triangle. Instead, the shapes would be stored in some more abstract format (like the coordinates of a few defining points for each shape), a format that mirrors neither the inputs nor the outputs to the program but that can be translated to and from them when the need arises.

Grammar, a form of mental software, must have evolved under similar design specifications. Though psychologists under the influence of empiricism often suggest that grammar mirrors commands to the speech muscles, melodies in speech sounds, or mental scripts for the ways that people and things tend to interact, I think all these suggestions miss the mark. Grammar is a protocol that has to interconnect the ear, the mouth, and the mind, three very different kinds of machine. It cannot be tailored to any of them but must have an abstract logic of its own.

The idea that the human mind is designed to use abstract variables and data structures used to be, and in some circles still is, a shocking and revolutionary claim, because the structures have no direct counterpart in the child's experience. Some of the organization of grammar would have to be there from the start, part of the language-learning mechanism that allows children to make sense out of the noises they hear from their parents. The details of syntax have figured prominently in the history of psychology, because they are a case where complexity in the mind is not caused by learning; learning is caused by complexity in the mind. And that was real news.

Post-reading Questions / Activities

- How does Pinker's (and Chomsky's) view of language differ from other accounts of language and communication?
- Discuss the ramifications of this theory for the topic of the origin of language. What in other animal communicative systems resembles this view of language?

Vocabulary

arbitrariness	grammar	
autonomous	lexicon	recursion
blending systems	modular	syntax
generative grammar	phrase structure	

Suggested Further Reading

Bickerton, Derek. 1980. *Language and Species.* Chicago: University of Chicago Press.

Calvin, William, and Derek Bickerton. 2000. *Lingua ex Machina: Reconciling Darwin and Chomsky with the Human Brain.* Cambridge, MA: MIT Press.

Chomsky, Noam. 1972. *Language and Mind.* New York: Harcourt Brace Jovanovich.

Pinker, Steven. 1994. *The Language Instinct: How the Mind Creates Language.* New York: HarperCollins.

———. 1997. *How the Mind Works.* New York: Norton.

———. 1999. *Words and Rules: The Ingredients of Language.* New York: Basic Books.

———. 2002. *The Blank Slate: The Modern Denial of Human Nature.* New York: Viking.

———. 2007. *The Stuff of Thought: Language as a Window into Human Nature.* New York: Viking.

CHAPTER 5

Signing and Speaking
Competitors, Alternatives, or Incompatibles?

William C. Stokoe
(1991)

William Stokoe, a pioneer in the study of sign languages, points out that in our quest to understand the origins of language, we should not assume that it was spoken and heard. Thus studies focusing on the vocal tract structures in early hominids and other ancestors of Homo sapiens, *including Neanderthals [Neandertals in his usage], would miss facets of language that may have been present. He reminds us that sign languages are true languages, that there are different types of signed language, that people in different cultures use a combination of signed and spoken languages, and "that human cultures vary widely and unpredictably." He accepts that language is necessary for humanity, but denies that the crucial feature is vocal. This is a warning that we should not assume that our own ways of regarding language are universal; that holds true as much for our scientific theories as for our daily interactions.*

Reading Questions

- What kind of language did Neanderthals likely possess?
- What are some examples of signed languages? What are the two types of sign language that Stokoe proposes?
- Why do some societies seem to use spoken language alone and others a combination of spoken and signed language?
- How have supposedly scientific theories been used to support ideas of education for deaf children?

The search for the origins and evolution of language may be frustrated at the outset by shortsightedness of two kinds in the searchers: first, the earliest human languages may not have been spoken and heard and so the earliest evidence of vocal and auditory specialization may be later than the origin of systematic symbolic signalling; second, even when the brain and not the vocal and auditory apparatus is recognized as the language center, we must look beyond biology to culture.

Of course no serious investigation can ignore biology. Human structure differs in significant ways from that of our closest primate relatives. But function as well as structure plays a role: even a single fossil bone may prove whether its owner walked and stood erect or not and had more or less human character. Function alone cannot be trusted:

William C. Stokoe, "Signing and Speaking: Competitors, Alternatives, or Incompatibles?" *Studies in Language Origins* vol. 2, edited by Jan Wind. Amsterdam: John Benjamins, 1991, pp. 115–121. With kind permission by John Benjamins Publishing Company, Amsterdam/Philadelphia. www.benjamins.com.

bats fly like birds and cetaceans swim like fish, but when Neandertalers buried the dead and put artifacts into their graves, we have evidence of a culture fully human, not only because such objects are not made by other animals but also because they unmistakably imply a culture that transcends the material, a culture that includes some notions of a life after death.

The question is, how could Neandertal man have lacked the physiology for speech, as Lieberman has suggested he did (1972, 1975), and yet possessed a fully human culture complete with language? Responses to the dilemma Lieberman's experiments pose have either been objections to the methods he used to reconstruct vocal tracts from skulls, or taken the form of denials that a two-tube superlaryngeal vocal tract is needed for language. The objectors reason somewhat as follows:

1. Evidence of Neandertal culture implies a human culture;
2. Such a culture requires language;

3. Therefore Neandertal man could speak and understand; and
4. Lieberman's conclusions must be false.

This train of language origin logic misses two important stations:

A. Whatever the physiology of the Neandertal superlaryngeal vocal tract, these people had other human attributes, among them true bipedalism, human hands with unpongid thumb placement, convergent binocular vision, human faces....
B. Despite its one-thousand-to-one distribution in the human population of the earth, spoken language is not the only form of human language.

Taking the logical train over this route, one reaches the conclusion that Neandertalers had a fully human language exactly as the surviving cultural evidence implies. This language may not have been exclusively vocal, but it had to be a complete language, produced by actions of the (human) body and perceived by human vision. This implies that Neandertalers had hands and faces more human than pongid. The binocular vision of the primate order would seem to have evolved with an arboreal way of life—swinging and catching and leaping require a precise perception of distances. But the higher primates use the face for more than a range finder mounting. Close observers can read chimpanzee and gorilla faces accurately and determine, as Darwin made clear (1873), the emotion signified and so communicated. But that is not all that ape faces express. Head turning and lip pointing indicate directions or things worth others' attention, and can be observed not just to signify the pointer's intention but also to communicate it to others.

When the primate range of behavioral patterns is expanded to include some of the behavior and ideation found in human cultures, it is safe to infer that the mobility of the face and the range of what it could express were increased by a quantum leap. Even without anything like a full spoken language, Neandertal man could have possessed a viable language that made use of the potential in the human face and body, and in the information gathering capability of the visual sensory system (Gibson, 1966). How this may have come about is a major question for archaeology and anthropology, but presumably the creatures branching off the primate line lived differently. That is to say they must have expanded the rudimentary toolmaking ability and weapon wielding behavior we can see in chimpanzees. In doing so they would have had to remember past actions, objects other than the one in present attention, to make comparisons and choices, and in short to develop with hand and eye and brain the cognitive base for language.

There are limits, however, to how far one can go with implications, speculation, and bits of physical evidence in reconstructing the past. It does seem certain that Neandertalers had a language, and with or without laryngeal limitations, could have had a language largely if not exclusively read by eye from just those physical changes and actions that characterize the hominid increments to the pongid physiology and capabilities.

On the present scene, sign languages of deaf people have been recognized as true languages since the late nineteen fifties, and for the last three decades the amount and precision of knowledge about them has been on the increase. The impact of knowledge about sign languages on questions of language origins has been various. Some of us see it as strong support for a gestural origin theory; others perceive so much difference between sound and sight that they doubt whether a sign language could have duality of patterning; and a few perhaps object that we have not the slightest reason to suppose any of the language-using, language-originating ancestors of the race were deaf.

Quite so. No such implication is intended. The inability to hear at all and to speak unless long and laboriously trained has resulted in deaf people's use of fully articulated sign languages. The study of sign languages used by deaf people, at the very least, provides us with evidence that languages produced gesturally and understood visually are languages. These sign languages also make it quite clear that speech and hearing are not, as many have supposed, essential to language. It is this last point that has been too often overlooked, not only in the search for language origins but in linguistics generally, and in the education and social integration of deaf persons.

A very recent addition to the growing science of signed languages is the work by Adam Kendon, *Sign Language of Aboriginal Australia* (1988). It complements other sign language studies in an important way. Kendon begins by taking note of a very crucial cultural difference: some signed languages are used by groups of persons as their major or sole language; other signed languages are used by persons who also have at their disposal a spoken language, or more than one. The two kinds he calls, respectively, primary sign languages and alternate sign languages. The importance is that this difference lies more in culture than in language. Primary sign languages are used in most instances by persons whose hearing acuity makes it impossible for them to acquire true spoken language competence—often despite heroic efforts on their part and teachers' to learn to speak and to understand speech by looking at speakers' faces. Although deafness may seem to take away freedom of choice, in fact, many deaf or partially deaf users of primary sign languages have chosen to sign and not to speak in most of their interactions with others.

Alternate sign languages have a more complex relation to culture. Most Americans are aware of the alternate sign language used by the Indian tribes of the plains and learned by mountain men, buffalo hunters, cavalry officers, and their scouts during the era of westward expansion. They may assume, perhaps correctly, that the term "language" may have been misbestowed on a gestural system used only for certain limited purposes when disparate cultures and languages were in constant confrontation. Mallery's work suggests (1880), and some later scholarship agrees, that the practice of gesturally communicating messages commonly spoken may have had a much earlier origin on the North

American continent. Be that as it may, Kendon's work shows conclusively that among the aboriginal tribes of Australia the use of signing instead of speech is common practice, that its use is determined by culture not by physical necessity, and that it is not limited to special domains but can be and is used as speech is used, for normal conversation.

Kendon's work shows that signing and speaking are not incompatible. Aboriginal culture not merely permits but strictly requires signing to be substituted for speaking under certain circumstances. Cultural—not physical nor universal psycholinguistic—determinants impose signing; yet no one in that culture feels imposed upon. On the contrary, as Kendon points out, among the older women of the Warlpiri and Warramungu, signing is the preferred medium for prolonged conversational sessions.

We who like to consider the possible origins of language need to give greater heed to cultural differences. In Western cultures sign language is largely confined to deaf persons and those who communicate with them, and until very recently even that evidence of signing was kept away from hearing eyes. Plain signing survives now mainly as a form of intercultural entertainment. Everyone, it is alleged, spoke sign language on Martha's Vineyard (Groce, 1985). Washabaugh (1985) and others have found that deaf signers and their sign language are not despised by hearing people in Caribbean island communities. Hubert Smith has shown on film (in the Smithsonian Film Archives) Yucatec hearing and deaf villagers communicating fluently in sign language. And Du Bois has reported (Lecture Gallaudet College, 1980) that in Yucatan teenagers mix signed words with spoken words in their everyday discourse and so when there are deaf people in a village there they are easily brought into full communication with the hearing because of the alternate sign language (some of whose lexicon Du Bois traces to Mayan carvings).

The indications are plain; human cultures vary widely and unpredictably. The belief that to communicate by speaking is human and communicate by gesturing is subhuman cannot be upheld. It is a belief, in fact, peculiar to recent Western cultures and arose in part from a particular phase of the enlightenment, the oralist-manualist controversy between Heinicke and de l'Épée over the proper way to instruct those born deaf—more generally, over the nature of language itself, whether it is essentially hearing and speech as Heinicke held, or essentially intellectual and indifferent to the particular mode of expression as Épée insisted. (See Garnett in Heinicke, de L'Épée, and Garnett, 1968; Lane, 1984.)

To read onto all cultures the norms and suppositions of one's own is to pervert anthropological science, and yet precisely that is done when the use of a primary sign language is banned from the education of deaf children. Even when signing is permitted, to insist that the signs be manual only (without the facial and other components of natural sign language), and must reproduce as exactly as possible the grammatical structure of the teachers' spoken language—this too does more than retard education and deal unfairly with deaf persons who cannot learn to use speech. It also blinds investigators to the truth that language can operate equally well,

for those who have competence, in the gestural-visual channel as in the vocal-auditory channel. This is true not only because language is based more deeply in human anatomy than the vocal folds and the cochlea but also because language is as much determined by culture as by physiology.

More research must be directed to the actual communication of those peoples with the least urbanized cultures, but we already have strong evidence that in such cultures there is no tendency to equate talking with language and mental competence and to equate signing with mental incompetence and lack of language. I believe that much of our own culture's readiness to make such equations is simply ethnocentrism. Once this prejudice natural to a literate, print-oriented culture is overcome and real knowledge about signed languages both primary and alternate is more widely diffused, it may be possible to look more closely at gesture and vision as precursors of vocal noise and hearing and the beginnings of human mentality and culture. As James J. Gibson made remarkably clear, vision for primates, especially humans, is the master perceptual system (1966). Current anthropology tells us that the chief physical difference between man and the other apes is that man walks erect. Thus more than other animals, hominids had forearms and hands not only for fighting and foraging but also for signifying and communicating. Still more obvious is the common expression of emotions in man and animals so thoroughly explored by Darwin (1873). But more than emotions will have shown on faces and body postures when members of the new erect walking primate branch began to develop cognitively and culturally by using their vision, forelimb capability, and deep-seated ability to read meaning in each others' actions by watching.

There is nothing to keep us from supposing that, along with this increased use of vision and visible action to signify and communicate the increased complexity of their lives, these folk did not also exploit voice. Quite the reverse; sounds as well as visible signs of what is going on are common to the communication of most mammals and especially important in primate life. However, it is important to note that once there was sufficient hominid ability to adapt to new territory and conditions, a culture could have developed that required the use of a silent language—or the reverse, a vocal language—when one or the other was appropriate to conditions.

I conclude that signing and speaking did not compete in the earliest stages of hominid differentiation; they do not now, unless cultural values and social forces make them (in schools for deaf children). I conclude too that signing and speaking are and always were compatible. Not only do the Aboriginal tribes of Australia use them both, but also there is growing evidence that among un-urbanized societies, signing and speaking (or the use of gestures for more than embellishment) can be and are used in close cooperation. And even among users of primary sign languages there are bilinguals. Some severely deaf persons can and do use speech and lipreading with some success; and many become bilingual, not only reading and writing the language the surrounding community speaks, but also transmitting and receiving it with manual signs representing words or letters. Finally, I conclude that signing and speaking are true alternatives, in the sense of being equally effective input-output devices for the central processor of language. Despite the thousand-to-one disproportion of speaking to signing in primary language use today, the natures of language, physiology, and culture argue that signing is more likely than speaking to have been the means by which language was first transmitted and acquired.

References

Darwin, C. 1873. *The Expression of Emotion in Man and Animals.* New York: Appleton.

Gibson, J. J. 1966. *The Senses Considered as Perceptual Systems.* New York: Houghton Mifflin.

Groce, N. E. 1985. *Everyone Here Spoke Sign Language.* Cambridge, MA: Harvard University Press.

Heinicke, Samuel, Charles-Michel de L'Epée, and Christopher Browne Garnett. 1968. *The Exchange of Letters Between Samuel Heinicke and Abbe Charles Michel de L'Epee; A Monograph on the Oralist and Manualist Methods of Instructing the Deaf in the Eighteenth Century, Including the Reproduction in English of Salient Portions of Each Letter.* New York: Vantage Press.

Kendon, A. 1988. *Sign Language of Aboriginal Australia.* London: Cambridge University Press.

Lane, H. 1984. *When the Mind Hears: A History of the Deaf.* New York: Random House.

Lieberman, P. 1975. *On the Origins of Language.* New York: Macmillan.

———, E. S. Crelin, and D. H. Klatt. 1972. Phonetic ability and related anatomy of the newborn adult human, Neanderthal man, and the chimpanzee. *American Anthropologist* 7, 287–307.

Mallery, G. 1880. *Introduction to the Study of Sign Language Among the North American Indians.* Washington, DC: Government Printing Office.

Washabaugh, W. 1985. *Five Fingers for Survival.* Ann Arbor, MI: Karoma Press.

Post-reading Questions / Activities

- If language does not have to be spoken to be genuine language, what *is* required for that identification? How would we observe this in the fossil record?
- How does the prejudice against signed languages come into play in the insistence that deaf children learn a "pure" signed language without even facial expressions?
- How does Stokoe's discussion of sign languages challenge conventional theories of language origins?

Vocabulary

aboriginal	duality of patterning	primary sign language
alternate sign languages	manual	sign languages
binocular	Neanderthal	superlaryngeal vocal tract
bipedalism	pongid	

Suggested Further Reading

Armstrong, David F., William C. Stokoe, and Sherman E. Wilcox. 1995. *Gesture and the Nature of Language.* Cambridge: Cambridge University Press.

Farnell, Brenda M. 1995. *Do You See What I Mean? Plains Indian Sign Talk and the Embodiment of Action.* Austin: University of Texas Press.

King, Barbara J., ed. 1999. *The Origins of Language: What Nonhuman Primates Can Tell Us.* Santa Fe, NM: School of American Research Press.

Klima, Edward S., and Ursula Bellugi. 1979. *The Signs of Language.* Cambridge, MA: Harvard University Press.

Lieberman, Philip. 1991. *Uniquely Human: The Evolution of Speech, Thought and Selfless Behavior.* Cambridge, MA: Harvard University Press.

———. 1998. *Eve Spoke: Human Language and Human Evolution.* New York: Norton.

Meier, Richard P., Kearsy Cormier, and David Quinto-Pozos, eds., with the assistance of Adrianne Cheek, Heather Knapp, and Christian Rathmann. 2002. *Modality and Structure in Signed and Spoken Languages.* Cambridge and New York: Cambridge University Press.

Monaghan, Leila Frances. 2007. *Many Ways to Be Deaf: International Variation in Deaf Communities.* Washington, DC: Gallaudet University Press.

CHAPTER 6

Why Gossip Is Good for You

Robin Dunbar
(1992)

Robin Dunbar is trying to figure out why humans have such large brains, relative to our size. Brains are metabolically expensive for organisms to maintain, so there must be an evolutionary advantage that outweighs the costs. (He is assuming that evolutionary details can be explained by a kind of cost-benefit analysis.) His conclusion, that humans evolved to live in groups of approximately 150 people, necessitating a transformation from physical to social grooming, has received much attention. Thus gossip is the equivalent of physical grooming. So instead of dismissing the tabloids as cheap fluff, he sees them as satisfying a profound human need!

Dunbar does not see the essence of language as vocal, mental, or gestural. He sees it rather as fundamentally social (though of course supported by a biological framework).

Reading Questions

- How are primate societies structured? Why does this matter?
- Dunbar sees a correlation between group size and the relative size of the neocortex as critically important. But how does he explain the enormous size of contemporary human societies, such as nation-states? How does he use information from anthropologists about hunter-gatherers?
- How is gossip like grooming?

Humans are fascinated by what other people get up to. The success of the tabloid dailies is ample proof of that. But why should we find tittle-tattle about the private lives of minor celebrities, royalty, and politicians of such overwhelming interest that it can drive the starving children of Somalia and the war-ravaged cities of former Yugoslavia off the front pages of even the most sedate of newspapers? The answer seems to lie in the evolutionary roots of our large brains.

As far as absolute brain size goes, humans don't have the largest brains in the animal kingdom; that privilege goes to whales. But, relative to body size, primates have much larger brains than any other animals, and we humans, not surprisingly, have the biggest brains of all—about six times larger than you would expect for a mammal of our size.

So why do primates have such big brains? There are two general kinds of theories. The more conventional one is that they need big brains to help them to find their way about the world and solve problems in their daily search for food. The alternative type of theory is that the complex social world in which primates live has provided the impetus for the evolution of large brains. The main version of the social

intelligence theory, sometimes known as the Machiavellian intelligence hypothesis, has the merit of identifying the thing that sets primates apart from all other animals—the complexity of their social relationships.

Primate societies seem to differ from those of other animals in two key respects. The first is the dependence on intense social bonds between individuals, which gives primate groups a highly structured appearance. Primates cannot join and leave these groups as easily as animals in the relatively amorphous herds of migrating antelope or the swarms of many insects. Other species may have groups that are highly structured in this way—elephants and prairie dogs are two obvious examples—but these animals differ from primates in a second respect. This is that the primates use their knowledge about the social world in which they live to form more complex alliances with each other than do other animals.

KEEPING TRACK OF RELATIONSHIPS

This social intelligence hypothesis is supported by a strong correlation between the size of the group, and hence complexity of the social world, and the relative size of the neocortex—the outer surface layer of the brain that is mainly

Robin Dunbar, "Why Gossip Is Good for You." *New Scientist* 136 (1848) (Nov. 21, 1992), pp. 28–31.

responsible for conscious thinking—in various species of nonhuman primates. This result seems to reflect a limitation on the number (and/or quality) of relationships that an animal of a given species can keep track of simultaneously. Just as a computer's ability to handle complex tasks is limited by the size of its memory and processor, so the brain's ability to manipulate information about the constantly changing social domain may be limited by the size of its neocortex.

In evolutionary terms, [my data suggest] that it was the need to live in larger groups that has driven the evolution of large brains in primates. After all, group size is flexible, and often variable, within a given population but increases in brain size would only come about if they offered an evolutionary advantage to a species. There are several reasons why particular species might want to live in larger groups, not least protection against predators. And it is conspicuous that the primates which both live in the largest groups and have the biggest neocortices are species such as baboons, macaques, and chimpanzees that spend most of their time on the ground and live either in relatively open habitats, such as savannah woodlands, or on the forest edge where they are exposed to much higher risk from predators than most forest-dwelling species.

This relationship between neocortex and group size in the nonhuman primates begs an obvious question. What size of group would we predict for humans, given our unusually large neocortex? Extrapolating from [our data] gives a size of 148. But is there any evidence to suggest that groups of this size actually occur in humans?

On the face of it, things do not look promising. After all, in the modern world, we live in huge nation-states containing tens of millions of individuals. However, we have to be a little more subtle: the relationship for nonhuman primates [we developed] is concerned with the number of individuals with whom an animal can maintain a coherent relationship over time. It is quite obvious that those of us living in, for example, Britain do not have personal relationships with every one of the other 55 million inhabitants. Indeed, the vast majority of these people are born, live, and die without ever knowing each other's names, let alone meeting. The existence of such large groupings is certainly something we have to explain, but they are something quite different to the natural groupings we see in primates.

One place we might look for evidence of "natural" human group sizes is among pre-industrial societies, and in particular among hunter-gatherers. Most hunter-gatherers live in complex societies that operate at a number of levels. The smallest groupings occur at temporary night camps and have between 30 and 50 individuals. These are relatively unstable, however, with individuals or families constantly joining and leaving as they move between different foraging areas or water holes. The largest grouping is normally the tribe itself, usually a linguistic grouping that defines itself rather strictly in terms of its cultural identity. Tribal groupings typically number between 500 and 2,500 men, women, and children. These two layers of traditional societies are widely recognised in anthropology. In between these two layers, however, is a third group often discussed, but seldom enumerated. Sometimes, it takes the form of "clans" that have ritual significance, such as the periodic celebration of coming-of-age ceremonies. Sometimes, the clan is based on common ownership of a hunting area or a set of water holes.

FINDING THE RIGHT GROUPS

For the few cases where census data are available, these clan groups turn out to have a mean size of about 153. [I have collated data from the literature on traditional hunter-gatherers, as well as] settled hunter-gatherers and simple horticultural societies living in villages. The sizes of all but one of the village and clan-like groupings for these societies fall between 100 and 230, which is within the range of variation that, statistically, we would expect from the prediction of 148. In contrast, the mean sizes of overnight camps and tribal groupings all fall outside these statistical limits.

But what about our own societies? Is there anything to suggest that the figure of 150 might be a relevant social unit? The answer is yes. Once you start to look for them, groups of about this size turn up everywhere. In most modern armies, for example, the smallest independent unit is the company, which normally consists of three fighting platoons of 30 to 40 men each plus the commander's staff, making a total of 130–150 men. Even the basic fighting unit of the Roman army during the Republic was of similar size, containing exactly 130 men.

The same figure turns up in businesses. A rule of thumb commonly used by managers is that companies smaller than 150 work fine on a person-to-person basis, but once they grow larger than this they need a formal hierarchy if they are to work efficiently. Sociologists have known since the 1950s that there is a critical threshold in the region of 150 to 200, with larger companies suffering a disproportionate amount of absenteeism and sickness. In 1989, Tony Becher of the education department of the University of Sussex published a survey of 12 disciplines in both the sciences and the humanities. He found that the number of researchers whose work an individual was likely to pay attention to was between 100 and 200. Once a discipline becomes larger than this, it seems that it fragments into two or more subdisciplines.

There are other interesting examples. Neolithic villages from the Middle East around 6000 B.C. typically seem to have contained 120 to 150 people, judging by the number of dwellings. The Hutterites, a group of contemporary North American religious fundamentalists who live and farm communally, regard 150 as the maximum size for their communities. What is interesting is the reason they give for splitting communities at this size. They find that when there are more than about 150 individuals, they cannot control the behaviour of the members by peer pressure alone.

CEMENTING RELATIONSHIPS

These are just a few of the examples from a great deal of sociological and anthropological evidence which suggest that "natural" groupings of about 150 individuals do occur in human societies, and that it is possible for individuals within such groups to maintain a coherent set of relationships through time by direct contact between individuals.

The fact that the "natural" human group might be as large as 150 raises some interesting questions about how such large groups are kept together. Among primates in general, and the Old World monkeys and apes in particular, social grooming is the main mechanism used to cement relationships between individuals. Moreover, the amount of time devoted to grooming other individuals is proportional to group size, at least within the Old World monkeys and apes. Those living in large groups of about 55 animals (essentially baboons and chimpanzees) spend up to 20 per cent of their day in this activity. Extrapolating from these data, we find that the amount of time required to maintain cohesion within a group of 150 would be something in the region of 35 to 45 per cent. It is doubtful whether any species that has to search for food daily could afford to spend almost half its day in social interaction. How then could the ancestral humans have ensured the proper degree of bonding within such large groups?

COST OF GROOMING

The main problem with social grooming is that it is costly in terms of time. A monkey can only groom one individual at a time, and grooming cannot easily be combined with eating, travelling between feeding sites, or other essential activities. The baboons and chimpanzees, for whom grooming consumes 20 per cent of their time, are probably already operating at the limits of their capacity. Any increase in group size can only come through a shift in gear in the mechanism used for social bonding.

For humans, that shift in gear may have come in the form of language. Language has two interesting properties compared to grooming: you can talk to several people at once and you can talk while travelling, eating, or working in the fields. Conventional wisdom has always supposed that language evolved to enable humans to exchange information about food sources and to aid cooperation during hunting. But it is difficult to see why humans should be any more in need of this than other primates or, if hunting is the issue, the social carnivores such as lions and wolves. A more plausible suggestion is that language evolved to enable humans to integrate a larger number of individuals into their social groups.

Some evidence to support this comes from the number of people it is possible to have a conversation with. If language really is just a form of vocal grooming designed to service a larger number of relationships, then its efficiency relative to grooming should mirror the ratio of the size of human groups to the largest found among primates—55 in chimpanzees and baboons. If human groups are typically about 148, then speech should be 148/55 times more efficient than grooming as a bonding mechanism. Given that grooming is limited to a one-to-one relationship, this should mean that language should make a [ratio of 1:2 to

1:7] possible. In other words, while monkeys are limited to grooming in pairs, human conversation groups should consist of an average of 3–7 individuals (one speaker and 2–6 listeners). And indeed they do.

The sizes of conversation groups in a student refectory, for example, consist of an average of 3–4 individuals, with a striking tendency for groups larger than four to fragment into two or more smaller conversation subgroups. Interestingly, there turns out to be an acoustical limit on conversation group sizes. Measurements of the sound level of speech over distance indicate an upper group size for conversation of about five people. If the group gets larger than this, individuals are forced to stand in too large a circle to be able to hear everyone clearly. Thus, the characteristics of speech seem to be closely tied to the size of the interaction group required to maintain cohesion.

IMPORTANCE OF A GOOD GOSSIP

There is, of course, another way in which language allows us to integrate a large number of social relationships, and that is by allowing us to exchange information about other individuals who are not present. In other words, by talking to one person, we can find out a great deal about how other individuals are likely to behave, how we should react to them when we actually meet them, and what kinds of relationships they have with third parties. All these things allow us to coordinate our social relationships within a group more effectively. And this is likely to be especially important in the dispersed groups that are characteristic of humans.

This would explain our fascination for social gossip in the newspapers, and why gossip about relationships accounts for an overwhelming proportion of human conversations. Even conversations in such august places as university coffee rooms tend to swing back and forth between academic issues and gossip about individuals. To get some idea of how important gossip is, we monitored conversations in a university refectory, scoring the topic at 30-second intervals. Social relationships and personal experiences accounted for about 70 per cent of conversation time. About half of this was devoted to the relationships or experiences of third parties (people not present). Males, however, tended to talk more about their own relationships and experiences whereas females tended to talk most about other people's.

This is interesting because it can be interpreted as suggesting that language evolved in the context of social bonding between females. Most anthropologists have assumed that it evolved in the context of male-male relationships, during hunting for example. The suggestion that female-female bonding, based on knowledge of the relationships of other individuals, was more important fits much better with views about the structure of nonhuman primate societies where relationships between females are all-important.

That conversations allow us to exchange information about people who are not present is vitally important. It allows us to teach others how to relate to individuals they have never seen before. Combined with the fact that language also makes it easy to categorise people into types, we can learn how to relate to classes of individuals rather than being restricted to single individuals as primates are in grooming. For example, we can give types of individuals special markers, such as dog collars, white lab coats, or large blue helmets, which allow us to behave appropriately towards them even though we have never met before. Without that knowledge, it would take us days to work out the basis of a relationship. Classifications and social conventions allow us to broaden the network of social relationships by making networks of networks, and this in turn allows us to create very large groups indeed. Of course, the level of the relationship is necessarily rather crude but at least it allows us to avoid major social faux pas at the more superficial levels of interaction when we first meet someone. Significantly, when it comes to really intense relationships that are especially important to us, we invariably abandon language and revert to that old-fashioned primate form of direct interaction—mutual mauling.

What we seem to have here, then, is a new theory for the evolution of language that also seems to account for a number of other facets of human behaviour. The theory explains why gossip about other people is so fascinating; it explains why human societies are so often hierarchies; it predicts the small size of conversation groups; it meshes well with our general understanding of why primates have larger brains than other mammals; and it agrees with the general view that language only evolved with the appearance of *Homo sapiens*. What it does not explain, of course, is why our ancestors should have needed to live in groups of about 150. It is unlikely that this has anything to do with defence against predators (the main reason why most non-human primates live in groups) because human groups far exceed the sizes of all other primate groups. But it might have something to do with the management or defence of resources, particularly dispersed resources such as water holes that nomadic hunter-gatherers might have had to depend on at certain times of the year.

Post-reading Questions/Activities

- Why is it so important that, to explain the big brains of humans, Dunbar is using a "social intelligence" theory (also called the "Machiavellian intelligence hypothesis") instead of a theory focusing on the search for food and survival? What evidence does he provide in support of his contention? How would the human needs for social intelligence differ from those of apes?
- Dunbar dismisses the primary function of language as permitting exchange of information about food sources and to facilitate hunting. What fundamentally different view of humans does this suggest?
- How does gender intersect with this view? What evidence does Dunbar muster for his claims about language and gender?
- Observe the topics of conversation over the next 24 hours. How much of your conversation could be seen as gossip?

Vocabulary

Machiavellian intelligence hypothesis   social intelligence theory

Suggested Further Reading

Aitchison, Jean. 2000. *The Seeds of Speech: Language Origin and Evolution*. Cambridge: Cambridge University Press.

Byrne, Richard W., and Andrew Whiten, eds. 1988. *Machiavellian Intelligence: Social Expertise and the Evolution of Intellect in Monkeys, Apes and Humans*. Oxford: Clarendon Press.

Burling, Robbins. 2005. *The Talking Ape: How Language Evolved*. Oxford: Oxford University Press.

Calvin, William, and Derek Bickerton. 2000. *Lingua ex Machina: Reconciling Darwin and Chomsky with the Human Brain*. Cambridge, MA: MIT Press.

Cheney, Dorothy L., and Robert M. Seyfarth. 1990. *How Monkeys See the World: Inside the Mind of Another Species*. Chicago: University of Chicago Press.

Christiansen, Morten H., and Simon Kirby, eds. 2003. *Language Evolution*. Oxford: Oxford University Press.

Dessalles, Jean-Louis. 2007 [2000]. *Why We Talk: The Evolutionary Origins of Language*. Translated by James Grieve. Oxford and New York: Oxford University Press.

Dunbar, Robin. 1996. *Grooming, Gossip, and the Evolution of Language.* Cambridge, MA: Harvard University Press.

Foley, William. 1997. *Anthropological Linguistics: An Introduction.* Oxford: Blackwell.

Goody, Esther N., ed. 1995. *Social Intelligence and Interaction.* Cambridge: Cambridge University Press.

King, Barbara J., ed. 1999. *The Origins of Language: What Nonhuman Primates Can Tell Us.* Santa Fe, NM: School of American Research Press.

Oller, D. Kimbrough, and Ulrike Griebel, eds. 2004. *Evolution of Communication Systems: A Comparative Approach.* Cambridge, MA: MIT Press.

Savage-Rumbaugh, E. Sue. 1998. *Apes, Language, and the Human Mind.* New York: Oxford University Press.

Whiten, Andrew. 1991. *Natural Theories of Mind: Evolution, Development and Simulation of Everyday Mindreading.* Oxford: Blackwell.

——, and Richard W. Byrne, eds. 1997. *Machiavellian Intelligence II: Extensions and Evaluations.* Cambridge: Cambridge University Press.

CHAPTER 7

The Orality of Language

Walter J. Ong

(1982)

Language occurs in many modalities: oral, manual, written, electronic, visual. Each carries with it implications about how humans live in the world.

The influential Jesuit scholar Walter Ong wrote prolifically about interactions among technologies (including writing), communication, visuality/orality/aurality, belief, and human consciousness. His work on orality has been especially well known.

In this short chapter he conveys how thoroughly transformed are people who have been raised to be literate, so much so that they cannot entirely conceive of a society in which language is primarily oral. Though his concern is with what is now more commonly termed "verbal art" (and he protests the term "oral literature" because of the associations between literature *and* literae *'letters [of the alphabet]'), he more broadly reminds us that literacy and writing have been a very recent introduction in human terms, and that most societies for most of human history have been principally oral.*

Reading Questions

- How does Ong support his claim that humans have been primarily oral for most of our history?
- Why, according to Ong, had the study of language focused on written rather than oral sources, given the dominance of oral expression?
- How do people in "primary oral cultures" learn? How do they remember things?
- Why does Ong object to the terms "oral literature," "preliterate," and "text"? Why does it matter how we choose words to discuss concepts? Can we just define them, or are they forever bound to their origins?

THE LITERATE MIND AND THE ORAL PAST

In the past few decades the scholarly world has newly awakened to the oral character of language and to some of the deeper implications of the contrasts between orality and writing. Anthropologists and sociologists and psychologists have reported on fieldwork in oral societies. Cultural historians have delved more and more into prehistory, that is, human existence before writing made verbalized records possible. Ferdinand de Saussure (1857–1913), the father of modern linguistics, had called attention to the primacy of oral speech, which underpins all verbal communication, as well as to the persistent tendency, even among scholars, to

From Walter J. Ong, "The Orality of Language." In *Orality and Literacy: The Technologizing of the Word*. London and New York: Methuen, 1982, pp. 5–15. Reproduced by permission of Taylor & Francis Books UK.

think of writing as the basic form of language. Writing, he noted, has simultaneously "usefulness, shortcomings and dangers" (1959, pp. 23–4). Still he thought of writing as a kind of complement to oral speech, not as a transformer of verbalization (Saussure 1959, pp. 23–4).

Since Saussure, linguistics has developed highly sophisticated studies of phonemics, the way language is nested in sound. Saussure's contemporary, the Englishman Henry Sweet (1845–1912), had early insisted that words are made up not of letters but of functional sound units or phonemes. But, for all their attention to the sounds of speech, modern schools of linguistics until very recently have attended only incidentally, if at all, to ways in which primary orality, the orality of cultures untouched by literacy, contrasts with literacy (Sampson 1980). Structuralists have analyzed oral tradition in detail, but for the most part without explicitly contrasting it with written compositions (Maranda and Maranda 1971). There is a sizable literature on differences between written and spoken language which compares the written and spoken language of persons who can read and write (Gumperz, Kaltmann and O'Connor 1984). These are not the differences that the present study is centrally concerned with. The orality centrally treated here is primary orality, that of persons totally unfamiliar with writing.

Recently, however, applied linguistics and sociolinguistics have been comparing more and more the dynamics of primary oral verbalization and those of written verbalization. Jack Goody's…book, *The Domestication of the Savage Mind* (1977), and his earlier collection of his own and others' work, *Literacy in Traditional Societies* (1968), provide invaluable descriptions and analyses of changes in mental and social structures incident to the use of writing. Chaytor very early (1945), Ong (1958, 1967), McLuhan (1962), Haugen (1966), Chafe (1982), Tannen (1980) and others provide further linguistic and cultural data and analyses. Foley's expertly focused survey (1980) includes an extensive bibliography.

The greatest awakening to the contrast between oral modes of thought and expression and written modes took place not in linguistics, descriptive or cultural, but in literary studies, beginning clearly with the work of Milman Parry (1902–1935) on the text of the *Iliad* and the *Odyssey*, brought to completion after Parry's untimely death by Albert B. Lord, and supplemented by later work of Eric A. Havelock and others. Publications in applied linguistics and sociolinguistics dealing with orality–literacy contrasts, theoretically or in fieldwork, regularly cite these and related works (Parry 1971; Lord 1960; Havelock 1963; McLuhan 1962; Okpewho 1979; etc.).

Before taking up Parry's discoveries in detail, it will be well to set the stage here by asking why the scholarly world had to reawaken to the oral character of language. It would seem inescapably obvious that language is an oral phenomenon. Human beings communicate in countless ways, making use of all their senses, touch, taste, smell, and especially sight, as well as hearing (Ong 1967b, pp. 1–9). Some non-oral communication is exceedingly rich—gesture, for example. Yet in a deep sense language, articulated sound, is paramount. Not only communication, but thought itself relates in an altogether special way to sound. We have all heard it said that one picture is worth a thousand words. Yet, if this statement is true, why does it have to be a saying? Because a picture is worth a thousand words only under special conditions—which commonly include a context of words in which the picture is set.

Wherever human beings exist they have a language, and in every instance a language that exists basically as spoken and heard, in the world of sound (Siertsema 1955). Despite the richness of gesture, elaborated sign languages are substitutes for speech and dependent on oral speech systems, even when used by the congenitally deaf (Kroeber 1972; Mallery 1972; Stokoe 1972). Indeed, language is so overwhelmingly oral that of all the many thousands of languages—possibly tens of thousands—spoken in the course of human history, only around 106 have ever been committed to writing to a degree sufficient to have produced literature, and most have never been written at all. Of the some 3,000 languages spoken

that exist today only some 78 have a literature (Edmonson 1971, pp. 323,332). There is as yet no way to calculate how many languages have disappeared or been transmuted into other languages before writing came along. Even now hundreds of languages in active use are never written at all: no one has worked out an effective way to write them. The basic orality of language is permanent.

We are not here concerned with so-called computer "languages," which resemble human languages (English, Sanskrit, Malayalam, Mandarin Chinese, Twi, or Shoshone, etc.) in some ways but are forever totally unlike human languages in that they do not grow out of the unconscious but directly out of consciousness. Computer language rules ("grammar") are stated first and thereafter used. The "rules" of grammar in natural human languages are used first and can be abstracted from usage and stated explicitly in words only with difficulty and never completely.

Writing, commitment of the word to space, enlarges the potentiality of language almost beyond measure, restructures thought, and in the process converts a certain few dialects into "grapholects" (Haugen 1966; Hirsh 1977, pp. 43–48). A grapholect is a transdialectal language formed by deep commitment to writing. Writing gives a grapholect a power far exceeding that of any purely oral dialect. The grapholect known as standard English has accessible for use a recorded vocabulary of at least a million and a half words, of which not only the present meanings but also hundreds of thousands of past meanings are known. A simply oral dialect will commonly have resources of only a few thousand words, and its users will have virtually no knowledge of the real semantic history of any of these words.

But, in all the wonderful worlds that writing opens, the spoken word still resides and lives. Written texts all have to be related somehow, directly or indirectly, to the world of sound, the natural habitat of language, to yield their meanings. "Reading" a text means converting it to sound, aloud or in the imagination, syllable-by-syllable in slow reading or sketchily in the rapid reading common to high-technology cultures. Writing can never dispense with orality. Adapting a term used for slightly different purposes by Jurij Lotman (1977, pp. 21, 48–61; see also Champagne 1977–8), we can style writing a "secondary modeling system," dependent on a prior primary system, spoken language. Oral expression can exist and mostly has existed without any writing at all, writing never without orality.

Yet, despite the oral roots of all verbalization, the scientific and literary study of language and literature has for centuries, until quite recent years, shied away from orality. Texts have clamored for attention so peremptorily that oral creations have tended to be regarded generally as variants of written productions or, if not this, as beneath serious scholarly attention. Only recently have we become impatient with our obtuseness here (Finnegan 1977, pp. 1–7).

Language study in all but recent decades has focused on written texts rather than on orality for a readily assignable reason: the relationship of study itself to writing. All thought, including that in primary oral cultures, is to some degree analytic: it breaks its materials into various components. But abstractly sequential, classificatory, explanatory examination of phenomena or of stated truths is impossible without writing and reading. Human beings in primary oral cultures, those untouched by writing in any form, learn a great deal and possess and practice great wisdom, but they do not "study."

They learn by apprenticeship—hunting with experienced hunters, for example—by discipleship, which is a kind of apprenticeship, by listening, by repeating what they hear, by mastering proverbs and ways of combining and recombining them, by assimilating other formulary materials, by participation in a kind of corporate retrospection—not by study in the strict sense.

When study in the strict sense of extended sequential analysis becomes possible with the interiorization of writing, one of the first things that literates often study is language itself and its uses. Speech is inseparable from our consciousness, and it has fascinated human beings, elicited serious reflection about itself, from the very early stages of consciousness, long before writing came into existence. Proverbs from all over the world are rich with observations about this overwhelmingly human phenomenon of speech in its native oral form, about its powers, its beauties, its dangers. The same fascination with oral speech continues unabated for centuries after writing comes into use.

In the West among the ancient Greeks, the fascination showed in the elaboration of the vast, meticulously worked-out art of rhetoric, the most comprehensive academic subject in all Western culture for two thousand years. In its Greek original, *technē rhētorikē*, "speech art" (commonly abridged to just *rhētorikē*) referred essentially to oral speaking, even though as a reflective, organized "art" or science—for example, in Aristotle's *Art of Rhetoric*—rhetoric was and had to be a product of writing. *Rhētorikē*, or rhetoric, basically meant public speaking or oratory, which for centuries even in literate and typographic cultures remained unreflexively pretty much the paradigm of all discourse, including that of writing (Ong 1967b, pp. 58–63; Ong 1971, pp. 27–8). Thus writing from the beginning did not reduce orality but enhanced it, making it possible to organize the "principles" or constituents of oratory into a scientific "art," a sequentially ordered body of explanation that showed how and why oratory achieved and could be made to achieve its various specific effects.

But the speeches—or any other oral performances—that were studied as part of rhetoric could hardly be speeches as these were being orally delivered. After the speech was delivered, nothing of it remained to work over. What you used for "study" had to be the text of speeches that had been written down—commonly after delivery and often long after (in antiquity it was not common practice for any but disgracefully incompetent orators to speak from a text prepared verbatim in advance—Ong 1967b, pp. 56–8). In this way, even orally composed speeches were studied not as speeches but as written texts.

Moreover, besides transcription of oral performances such as orations, writing eventually produced strictly written compositions, designed for assimilation directly from the written surface. Such written compositions enforced attention to texts even more, for truly written compositions came into being as texts only, even though many of them were commonly listened to rather than silently read, from Livy's histories to Dante's *Commedia* and beyond (Nelson 1976–7; Bäuml 1980; Goldin 1973; Cormier 1974; Ahern 1981).

DID YOU SAY "ORAL LITERATURE"?

The scholarly focus on texts had ideological consequences. With their attention directed to texts, scholars often went on to assume, often without reflection, that oral verbalization was essentially the same as the written verbalization they normally dealt with, and that oral art forms were to all intents and purposes simply texts, except for the fact that they were not written down. The impression grew that, apart from the oration (governed by written rhetorical rules), oral art forms were essentially unskillful and not worth serious study.

Not all, however, lived by these assumptions. From the mid-sixteenth century on, a sense of the complex relationships of writing and speech grew stronger (Cohen 1977). But the relentless dominance of textuality in the scholarly mind is shown by the fact that to this day no concepts have yet been formed for effectively, let alone gracefully, conceiving of oral art as such without reference, conscious or unconscious, to writing. This is so even though the oral art forms which developed during the tens of thousands of years before writing obviously had no connection with writing at all. We have the term "literature," which essentially means "writings" (Latin *literatura*, from *litera*, letter of the alphabet), to cover a given body of written materials—English literature, children's literature—but no comparably satisfactory term or concept to refer to a purely oral heritage, such as the traditional oral stories, proverbs, prayers, formulaic expressions (Chadwick 1932–40, *passim*), or other oral productions of, say, the Lakota Sioux in North America or the Mande in West Africa or of the Homeric Greeks.

As noted above, I style the orality of a culture totally untouched by any knowledge of writing or print, "primary orality." It is "primary" by contrast with the "secondary orality" of present-day high-technology culture, in which a new orality is sustained by telephone, radio, television, and other electronic devices that depend for their existence and functioning on writing and print. Today primary oral culture in the strict sense hardly exists, since every culture knows of writing and has some experience of its effects. Still, to varying degrees many cultures and subcultures, even in a high-technology ambiance, preserve much of the mind-set of primary orality.

The purely oral tradition or primary orality is not easy to conceive of accurately and meaningfully. Writing makes "words" appear similar to things because we think of words as the visible marks signaling words to decoders: we can see and touch such inscribed "words" in texts and books.

Written words are residue. Oral tradition has no such residue or deposit. When an often-told oral story is not actually being told, all that exists of it is the potential in certain human beings to tell it. We (those who read texts such as this) are for the most part so resolutely literate that we seldom feel comfortable with a situation in which verbalization is so little thing-like as it is in oral tradition. As a result—though at a slightly reduced frequency now—scholarship in the past has generated such monstrous concepts as "oral literature." This strictly preposterous term remains in circulation today even among scholars now more and more acutely aware how embarrassingly it reveals our inability to represent to our own minds a heritage of verbally organized materials except as some variant of writing, even when they have nothing to do with writing at all. The title of the great Milman Parry Collection of Oral Literature at Harvard University monumentalizes the state of awareness of an earlier generation of scholars rather than that of its recent curators.

One might argue (as does Finnegan 1977, p. 16) that the term "literature," though devised primarily for works in writing, has simply been extended to include related phenomena such as traditional oral narrative in cultures untouched by writing. Many originally specific terms have been so generalized in this way. But concepts have a way of carrying their etymologies with them forever. The elements out of which a term is originally built usually, and probably always, linger somehow in subsequent meanings, perhaps obscurely but often powerfully and even irreducibly. Writing, moreover, as will be seen later in detail, is a particularly pre-emptive and imperialist activity that tends to assimilate other things to itself even without the aid of etymologies.

Though words are grounded in oral speech, writing tyrannically locks them into a visual field forever. A literate person, asked to think of the word "nevertheless," will normally (and I strongly suspect always) have some image, at least vague, of the spelled-out word and be quite unable ever to think of the word "nevertheless" for, let us say, 60 seconds without adverting to any lettering but *only* to the sound. This is to say, a literate person cannot fully recover a sense of what the word is to purely oral people. In view of this pre-emptiveness of literacy, it appears quite impossible to use the term "literature" to include oral tradition and performance without subtly but irremediably reducing these somehow to variants of writing.

Thinking of oral tradition or a heritage of oral performance, genres, and styles as "oral literature" is rather like thinking of horses as automobiles without wheels. You can, of course, undertake to do this. Imagine writing a treatise on horses (for people who have never seen a horse) which starts with the concept not of horse but of "automobile," built on the readers' direct experience of automobiles. It proceeds to discourse on horses by always referring to them as "wheelless automobiles," explaining to highly automobilized readers who have never seen a horse all the points of difference in an effort to excise all idea of "automobile" out of the concept "wheelless automobile" so as to invest the term with a purely equine meaning. Instead of wheels, the

wheelless automobiles have enlarged toenails called hooves; instead of headlights or perhaps rear-vision mirrors, eyes; instead of a coat of lacquer, something called hair; instead of gasoline for fuel, hay, and so on. In the end, horses are only what they are not. No matter how accurate and thorough such apophatic description, automobile-driving readers who have never seen a horse and who hear only of "wheelless automobiles" would be sure to come away with a strange concept of a horse. The same is true of those who deal in terms of "oral literature," that is, "oral writing." You cannot without serious and disabling distortion describe a primary phenomenon by starting with a subsequent secondary phenomenon and paring away the differences. Indeed, starting backwards in this way—putting the car before the horse—you can never become aware of the real differences at all.

Although the term "preliterate" itself is useful and at times necessary, if used unreflectively it also presents problems which are the same as those presented by the term "oral literature," if not quite so assertive. "Preliterate" presents orality—the "primary modeling system"—as an anachronistic deviant from the "secondary modeling system" that followed it.

In concert with the terms "oral literature" and "preliterate," we hear mention also of the "text" of an oral utterance. "Text," from a root meaning "to weave," is, in absolute terms, more compatible etymologically with oral utterance than is "literature," which refers to letters etymologically/(*literae*) of the alphabet. Oral discourse has commonly been thought of even in oral milieus as weaving or stitching—*rhapsōidein*, to "rhapsodize," basically means in Greek "to stitch songs together." But in fact, when literates today use the term "text" to refer to oral performance, they are thinking of it by analogy with writing. In the literate's vocabulary, the "text" of a narrative by a person from a primary oral culture represents a back-formation: the horse as an automobile without wheels again.

Given the vast difference between speech and writing, what can be done to devise an alternative for the anachronistic and self-contradictory term "oral literature"? Adapting a proposal made by Northrop Frye for epic poetry in *The Anatomy of Criticism* (1957, pp. 248–50, 293–303), we might refer to all purely oral art as "epos," which has the same Proto-Indo-European root, *wekw-*, as the Latin word *vox*, and its English equivalent "voice," and thus is grounded firmly in the vocal, the oral. Oral performances would thus be felt as "voicings," which is what they are. But the more usual meaning of the term epos, (oral) epic poetry (see Bynum 1967), would somewhat interfere with an assigned generic meaning referring to all oral creations. "Voicings" seems to have too many competing associations, though if anyone thinks the term buoyant enough to launch, I will certainly aid efforts to keep it afloat. But we would still be without a more generic term to include both purely oral art and literature. Here I shall continue a practice common among informed persons and resort, as necessary, to self-explanatory circumlocutions—"purely oral art forms," "verbal art forms" (which would include both oral forms and those composed in writing, and everything in between), and the like.

At present the term "oral literature" is, fortunately, losing ground, but it may well be that any battle to eliminate it totally will never be completely won. For most literates, to think of words as totally dissociated from writing is simply too arduous a task to undertake, even when specialized linguistic or anthropological work may demand it. The words keep coming to you in writing, no matter what you do. Moreover, to dissociate words from writing is psychologically threatening, for literates' sense of control over language is closely tied to the visual transformations of language: without dictionaries, written grammar rules, punctuation, and all the rest of the apparatus that makes words into something you can "look" up, how can literates live? Literate users of a grapholect such as standard English have access to vocabularies hundreds of times larger than any oral language can manage. In such a linguistic world dictionaries are essential. It is demoralizing to remind oneself that there is no dictionary in the mind, that lexicographical apparatus is a very late accretion to language as language, that all languages have elaborate grammars and have developed their elaborations with no help from writing at all, and that outside of relatively high-technology cultures most users of languages have always got along pretty well without any visual transformations whatsoever of vocal sound.

Oral cultures indeed produce powerful and beautiful verbal performances of high artistic and human worth, which are no longer even possible once writing has taken possession of the psyche. Nevertheless, without writing, human consciousness cannot achieve its fuller potentials, cannot produce other beautiful and powerful creations. In this sense, orality needs to produce and is destined to produce writing. Literacy…is absolutely necessary for the development not only of science but also of history, philosophy, explicative understanding of literature and of any art, and indeed for the explanation of language (including oral speech) itself. There is hardly an oral culture or a predominantly oral culture left in the world today that is not somehow aware of the vast complex of powers forever inaccessible without literacy. This awareness is agony for persons rooted in primary orality, who want literacy passionately but who also know very well that moving into the exciting world of literacy means leaving behind much that is exciting and deeply loved in the earlier oral world. We have to die to continue living.

Fortunately, literacy, though it consumes its own oral antecedents and, unless it is carefully monitored, even destroys their memory, is also infinitely adaptable. It can restore their memory, too. Literacy can be used to reconstruct for ourselves the pristine human consciousness which was not literate at all—at least to reconstruct this consciousness pretty well, though not perfectly (we can never forget enough of our familiar present to reconstitute in our minds any past in its full integrity). Such reconstruction can bring a better understanding of what literacy itself has meant in shaping man's consciousness toward and in high-technology cultures. Such understanding of both orality and literacy is what [I, in what of necessity is] a literate work and not an oral performance, [attempt] in some degree to achieve.

References

Abrahams, Roger D. (1968). 'Introductory remarks to a rhetorical theory of folklore, *Journal of American Folklore*, 81, 143–58.

—— (1972). 'The training of the man of words in talking sweet', *Language in Society*, 1, 15–29.

Ahern, John (1981). Singing the book: orality in the reception of Dante's *Comedy*', *Annals of Scholarship*, 2, 17–40.

Bäuml, Franz H. (1980). 'Varieties and consequences of medieval literacy and illiteracy', *Speculum*, 55, 237–65. Highly informed and informative. Medieval culture was basically literate in its leaders, but the access of many to the written text was not necessarily direct: many knew the text only because they had someone who knew how to read it to them. Medieval literacy and illiteracy were more 'determinants of different types of communication' than simply personal attributes' of individuals.

Bynum, David E. (1967). 'The generic nature of oral epic poetry, *Genre*, 2 (3) (September 1967), 236–58. Reprinted in Dan Ben-Amos (ed.), *Folklore Genres* (Austin and London: University of Texas Press, 1976), 35–58.

Chadwick, H[ector] Munro, and Chadwick, N[ora] Kershaw (1932–40). *The Growth of Literature*, 3 vols. (Cambridge, England: Cambridge University Press).

Chafe, Wallace L. (1982). 'Integration and involvement in speaking, writing, and oral literature', in Deborah Tannen (ed.), *Spoken and Written Language: Exploring Orality and Literacy* (Norwood, NJ: Ablex), 35–54.

Champagne, Roland A. (1977–8). 'A grammar of the languages of culture: literary theory and Yury M. Lotman's semiotics', *New Literary History*, IX, 205–10.

Chaytor, H[enry] J[ohn] (1945). *From Script to Print: An Introduction to Medieval Literature* (Cambridge, England: Cambridge University Press).

Cohen, Murray (1977). *Sensible Words: Linguistic Practice in England 1640–1785* (Baltimore and London: Johns Hopkins University Press).

Cormier, Raymond J. (1974). 'The problem of anachronism: recent scholarship on the French medieval romances of antiquity', *Philological Quarterly*, LIII (2) (Spring 1974), 145–57. Only in part do the widely accepted features of preliterate society fit the new, precocious, emerging audience of romance. It would be most tempting to posit illiteracy as a cause for the anachronisms in the romances of antiquity and elsewhere. Only *in part*, I would submit, do the widely recognized features of non-literate society, orality, dynamism, polemicism, and externalized schizoid behavior, characterize that of the mid-twelfth century.

Edmonson, Munro E. (1971). *Lore: An Introduction to the Science of Folklore and Literature* (New York: Holt, Rinehart & Winston).

Finnegan, Ruth (1977). *Oral Poetry: Its Nature, Significance, and Social Context* (Cambridge, England: Cambridge University Press).

Foley, John Miles (1980). 'Oral literature: premises and problems', *Choice*, 18, 487–96. Expertly focused article, with invaluable bibliography including a list of sound recordings.

Frye, Northrop (1957). *Anatomy of Criticism* (Princeton, NJ: Princeton University Press).

Goldin, Frederick (ed.) (1973). *Lyrics of the Troubadours and Trouvères: An Anthology and a History*, trans. and introduction by Frederick Goldin (Garden City, NY: Anchor Books).

Goody, Jack [John Rankin] (ed.) (1968a). *Literacy in Traditional Societies*, introduction by Jack Goody (Cambridge, England: Cambridge University Press).

—— (1968b). 'Restricted literacy in Northern Ghana', in Jack Goody (ed.), *Literacy in Traditional Societies* (Cambridge, England: Cambridge University Press), 198–264.

—— (1977). *The Domestication of the Savage Mind* (Cambridge, England: Cambridge University Press).

Gumperz, John J., Kaltmann, Hannah, and O'Connor, Catherine (1984). 'Cohesion in spoken and written discourse: Ethnic style and the transition to literacy' in Deborah Tannen (ed.), *Coherence in Spoken and Written Discourse* (Norwood, NJ: Ablex), 3–19. This paper was presented at a pre-conference session of the thirty-second annual Georgetown University Round Table on Languages and Linguistics, March 19–21, 1981. Manuscript received from authors.

Haugen, Einar (1966). 'Linguistics and language planning', in William Bright (ed.), *Sociolinguistics: Proceedings of the UCLA Sociolinguistics Conference 1964* (The Hague: Mouton), 50–71.

Havelock, Eric A. (1963). *Preface to Plato* (Cambridge, MA: Belknap Press of Harvard University Press).

Hirsch, E. D., Jr. (1977). *The Philosophy of Composition* (Chicago and London: University of Chicago Press).

Kroeber, A. L. (1972). 'Sign language inquiry', in Garrick Mallery (ed.), *Sign Language among North American Indians* (The Hague: Mouton). Reprinted Washington, DC, 1981.

Lord, Albert B. (1960). *The Singer of Tales*, Harvard Studies in Comparative Literature, 24 (Cambridge, MA: Harvard University Press).

Lotman, Jurij (1977). *The Structure of the Artistic Text*, trans. by Ronald Vroon, Michigan Slavic Contributions, 7 (Ann Arbor, MI: University of Michigan).

McLuhan, Marshall (1962). *The Gutenberg Galaxy: The Making of Typographic Man* (Toronto: University of Toronto Press).

Mallery, Garrick (1972). *Sign Language among North American Indians compared with That among Other Peoples and Deaf-Mutes* with articles by A. L. Kroeber and C. F. Voegelin, Approaches to Semiotics, 14 (The Hague: Mouton). Reprint of a monograph published in 1881 in the first Report of the Bureau of Ethnology.

Maranda, Pierre, and Maranda, Elli Köngäs (eds.) (1971). *Structural Analysis of Oral Tradition* (Philadelphia: University of Pennsylvania Press). Studies by Claude Lévi-Strauss, Edmund R. Leach, Dell Hymes, A. Julien Greimas, Victor Turner, James L. Peacock, Alan Dundes, Elli Köngäs Maranda, Alan Lomax and Joan Halifax, Roberto DaMatta, and David Maybury-Lewis.

Nelson, William (1976–7). 'From "Listen, Lordings" to "Dear Reader"', *University of Toronto Quarterly*, 46, 111–24.

Okpewho, Isidore (1979). *The Epic in Africa: Toward a Poetics of the Oral Performance* (New York: Columbia University Press).

Ong, Walter J. (1958). *Ramus, Method, and the Decay of Dialogue* (Cambridge, MA: Harvard University Press).

—— (1967). *The Presence of the Word* (New Haven and London: Yale University Press).

—— (1971). *Rhetoric, Romance, and Technology* (Ithaca and London: Cornell University Press).

Parry, Milman (1971). *The Making of Homeric Verse: The Collected Papers of Milman Parry*, ed. [his son] Adam Parry (Oxford: Clarendon Press).

Sampson, Geoffrey (1980). *Schools of Linguistics* (Stanford, CA: Stanford University Press).

Saussure, Ferdinand de (1959). *Course in General Linguistics*, trans. by Wade Baskin, ed. by Charles Bally and Albert Sechehaye, in collaboration with Albert Reidlinger (New York: Philosophical Library). Originally published in French (1916). This, the most important of Saussure's works, was compiled and edited from students' notes from his course in general linguistics given at Geneva in 1906–7, 1908–9, and 1910–11. Saussure left no text of his lectures.

Tannen, Deborah (1980). 'A comparative analysis of oral narrative strategies: Athenian Greek and American English', in Wallace L. Chafe (ed.), *The Pear Stories: Cultural, Cognitive, and Linguistic Aspects of Narrative Production* (Norwood, NJ: Ablex), 51–87.

Post-reading Questions / Activities

- Why can literate people never "fully recover a sense of what [a] word is to purely oral people"? Do you think something is lost by this total eclipse of the oral?

- What do you do during your daily activities that are primarily involved with literacy? With orality? Observe a fraction of a day in the life of a person in a culture with "secondary orality." How much time is spent with oral and how much with written communication?

Vocabulary

grapholect	rhetoric
orality	secondary orality
primary orality	

Suggested Further Reading

Goody, Jack. 1987. *The Interface Between the Written and the Oral*. Cambridge: Cambridge University Press.

Harris, Roy. 1986. *The Origin of Writing*. London: Duckworth.

Lord, Albert B. 1960. *The Singer of Tales*. Cambridge, MA: Harvard University Press.

Parry, Milman. 1971. *The Making of Homeric Verse: The Collected Papers of Milman Parry*. Edited by Adam Parry. Oxford: Clarendon Press.

Scribner, Sylvia, and Michael Cole. 1981. *The Psychology of Literacy*. Cambridge, MA: Harvard University Press.

CHAPTER 8

Aspects of Literacy

Brian V. Street and Niko Besnier

(1994)

What are reading and writing? They are natural to all engaged in higher education, but they are relatively recent introductions in human history—at the most about 6,000 years old. Early language scholars such as Saussure emphasized that orality was the dominant condition for human beings, and for about 70 or 80 years most of the study of language focused on spoken language. In the 1970s and 1980s, however, researchers began to inquire about writing itself, discovering that it too was complex and interesting. Literacy is a matter of psychological, educational, sociological, linguistic, technological, political, economic, and anthropological importance.

In this summary article, Brian Street and Niko Besnier, two anthropologists who have written extensively about literacies, introduce the major issues in understanding literacy.

Reading Questions

- How do Street and Besnier summarize the history of writing? What were its functions?
- What types of writing systems exist?
- Why do Street and Besnier reject an evolutionary model of writing systems?
- What is the "autonomous" or "Great Divide" model of literacy? What is the "ideological model" of literacy?
- Why do they argue that it is best to consider that there are a variety of literacies rather than a single type of literacy?
- What are some of the ways writing has been used around the world (past and present)?

Until the early part of the twentieth century, the ability to read and write was commonly thought to be the crucial factor distinguishing "civilized" from "primitive" peoples, history from prehistory. While contemporary anthropology has for the most part eschewed such overarching determinism, traces of it remain in much anthropological work on literacy and its consequences for society and the individual. What follows is a critical examination of current thought about literacy, its role in society, and its place in sociopolitical life.

Literacy has been viewed alternatively as a technology and as a social phenomenon. First, it is a system of secondary signs, in that written signs refer to another semiotic system consisting of the signs of spoken language. The encoding and decoding of this secondary

From Brian V. Street and Niko Besnier, "Aspects of Literacy." In *Companion Encyclopedia of Anthropology*, ed. by Tim Ingold. London and New York: Routledge, 1994, pp. 527–562. Reproduced by permission of Taylor & Francis Books UK.

semiotic system require certain cognitive skills akin to the skills associated with various technologies. Second, using literacy in normative ways presupposes certain kinds of sociocultural knowledge: constructing written texts; knowing when, where, and how to consume them; and understanding the associations of literacy with other aspects of the life of the group are all essential for a person to function as a literate member of society. In exploring these various aspects of literacy, we here opt for a strategy that differs from more traditional accounts in at least two ways. Rather than seeking broad generalizations regarding the impact of literacy on society, culture, and the human mind, we demonstrate that literacy is a varied phenomenon, and that an investigation of this variety must take priority over the search for a priori, universalist generalizations. Further, we argue that technological and social aspects of literacy are so intricately interwoven that it may be counterproductive to address them through separate analytic approaches. In particular, both aspects are heavily constrained, even probably determined, by culturally constructed ideologies.

LITERACY AS TECHNOLOGY

In this section we present a brief overview of the historical development of writing systems, and of their diversity as technologies. For more detailed discussion of both topics, the reader is referred to Diringer (1968), Gaur (1984), and Gelb (1963); works more specifically concerned with the origin of writing are Harris (1986) and Senner (1989); on writing systems, see Coulmas (1989), DeFrancis (1989), and Sampson (1985).

The Origin of Writing

It is generally agreed that writing is semiotically different from pictographic representation, or "pre-writing," and this difference is commonly used to define writing operationally in opposition to other semiotic systems. Graphic representations of objects, ideas, and notions (e.g., road signs, maps, drawings) differ from writing in that they are iconic signs with non-linguistic (notional) referents, while written signs are symbols, which refer to (spoken) linguistic units.

Little is known for sure about the antiquity and purposes of the earliest literacies, and of the processes which led up to their invention. Commonly thought to have been first invented in the third or fourth millennium B.C. in Sumerian Mesopotamia, writing appeared in various parts of the world shortly after that date: in Egypt around 3000 B.C., in the Indus Valley around 2500 B.C., and in China around 2000 B.C. Everywhere, there seems at first to have been a strong connection between early literacy and religious practices; the uses of reading and writing diversified only slowly over the course of their history. In Sumeria, this connection was probably mediated by economic needs, like record keeping in economic transactions, but these clearly fell under the jurisdiction of religious officialdom. In Mesoamerica, more than a dozen literacy traditions flourished between the third century A.D. and the Spanish Conquest. There again, writing arose as a religious practice, particularly in connection with extremely complex calendrical systems, and remained an elite art until its disappearance (Lounsbury 1989). While some archaic writing systems may have been the result of diffusion, particularly in the Middle East, writing was invented independently in at least Sumeria, the Far East, and Mesoamerica. (However, the later spread of literacy in the Mediterranean region, throughout South and South-east Asia, in the Far East, and elsewhere was certainly due to diffusional processes.) In each case, writing was developed from pictograms through a shift from iconicity to symbolization, and from non-linguistic to linguistic reference, accompanied by a trend toward greater stylization of the signs. All evidence underscores the gradual and complex nature of this process. For many centuries, graphic representations consisted of an amalgam of pictographs and different writing systems.

Types of Writing Systems

Three major types of writing systems are commonly recognized. The type usually taken to be the earliest is *logographic* (or *ideographic*) writing, a system in which each symbol represents a word. In *syllabic* writing, by contrast, individual symbols refer to syllables, and in *alphabetic* writing they refer to contrastive sound units, or phonemes. A *consonantal* alphabet provides symbols exclusively for consonants, a *phonemic* alphabet includes symbols for both consonants and vowels, while the symbols of a *featural* alphabet are made up of graphic elements that refer to the phonological characteristics of sounds. Commonly invoked as illustrations of each of these types are Chinese characters, early Egyptian hieroglyphics, and Mayan hieroglyphics for logographic writing; Japanese *katakana* and late Assyrian cuneiform for syllabic writing; the systems used for Hebrew and Arabic for consonantal alphabets; the Greek, Roman, and Cyrillic systems for phonemic alphabetic writing; and the Korean writing system for featural alphabets.

The three systems, according to the orthodox view (e.g. Goody 1977, 1986, 1987, Goody and Watt 1963, Ong 1982), follow an evolutionary order. According to this view, logographic systems were the first to arise in history, are the closest in nature to pictographic representations, and constitute the most "primitive," cumbersome, and inefficient technology of literacy, in that knowledge of many symbols is required to represent even simple utterances. Gradually, logographic symbols became more stylized and came to represent syllables (i.e., sequences of sounds) rather than whole words. At the same time, the inventory of symbols needed to represent a comprehensive range of linguistic meanings decreased radically. Eventually, syllabic symbols came to represent single sounds, their inventory again decreased radically, and the system reached maximal technological efficiency.

But a closer look at the writing systems that are attested today or reconstructed from historical records demonstrates that none fits these prototypes. For example, the system used for writing Chinese does not exhibit the sort of one-to-one correspondence between written symbol and word (or even morpheme) associated with prototypical logography. Most words in spoken Mandarin Chinese are compounds of two or three morpheme-like monosyllabic elements, the meanings of which frequently do not add up straightforwardly to the meaning of the whole, and each of these elements is written with a separate character:

語
yŭ 'discourse'

語法
yŭfă 'grammar'

法
fă 'rule'

語言
yŭyén 'language'

言
yén 'utterance'

言語
yényŭ 'speech'

Thus many lexical units can be written by combining a small number of characters in various configurations. In contrast, the many homophones in spoken Chinese are represented with different characters, all of which are read in the same manner:

jīn 'catty'   jīn 'gold'   jīn 'ford'   jīn 'tendon'   jīn 'lapel'

Furthermore, many Chinese characters contain elements which provide visual cues to the phonological shape of the words they represent. For example, the characters in the following series share a common visual element, which indexes the homophony or near-homophony of the words they represent (which are semantically unrelated):

shī 'poetry'   shí 'time'   shì 'wait on'   shì 'rely upon'

Thus the Chinese writing system is neither the vast, complex, and unsystematic inventory that it is often depicted to be (e.g., Goody and Watt 1963), nor is it devoid of references to the sound system of the language it represents. Rather, Chinese writing is adapted to the structure of the language, as well as to the sociolinguistic context of its use. The Chinese-speaking area is fragmented into regions in which are spoken numerous mutually unintelligible varieties, but all dialects that are commonly written share a basic stock of characters. While in practice literate speakers of one dialect cannot easily read a text written in a more distant dialect, the system still provides homogeneity in a highly fragmented linguistic situation. (The structural and sociolinguistic features of Chinese writing are treated at length in Coulmas 1989, Norman 1988, and Sampson 1985.)

The trichotomy between logographic, syllabic, and alphabetic writing, which may be of some use as a theoretical model based on largely unattested prototypicality, is inadequate as a descriptive device. Furthermore, evolutionary models of writing systems, which are frequently based more on enduring stereotypes than on empirical observations, often fail to recognize that writing systems are used in particular contexts. It is particularly sobering to note that these evolutionary accounts identify the historical "perfectioning" of writing with the rise of Western civilization in the Mediterranean region. But even in Middle Eastern and Greek antiquity, the development of writing from logographs to the alphabet via syllabic systems was by no means a straight road: in the course of the history of many writing systems, logographic elements were discarded and then reintroduced, because they were viewed as more efficient representations of linguistic units in written texts (Davies 1986). Rather than ranking all writing systems in a single order from the most unwieldy and cumbersome to the most efficient and learnable, a comparative perspective should approach the question as a problem of *adaptation* (Barton 1988). For example, the very complex character of a writing system may serve specific social functions, as Crump (1988) argues for Japanese writing, and "complexity" itself is very

difficult to define precisely. Writing systems are adapted to the structural characteristics of the linguistic code and the macrosociolinguistic context. Situations in which different writing systems compete or coexist, and situations of transition from one writing system to another (e.g., the change from a Sinitic-derived syllabary to the Roman alphabet in Vietnam between the seventeenth and nineteenth centuries) offer fruitful grounds for investigating the different adaptive dimensions of writing systems. The physical characteristics of writing systems also bear the imprint of the technological and social practices surrounding literacy. For example, incisions made with a stylus in clay, as practised in ancient Sumeria, necessarily have a very different shape from hand-brushed classical Chinese characters on paper and from Mayan hieroglyphics carved on stone monuments.

A particularly rich illustration of the way in which a writing system refracts broader technological and social dynamics is provided by the Hanunóo of Mindoro island (Philippines). The Hanunóo Sanskritic-derived syllabary is most commonly carved on green bamboo stalks (but also tattooed on human arms), and both the shape of the characters and their usual bottom-to-top directionality are a direct consequence of the position of the carver with respect to the bamboo stalk and of the nature of the tools involved. But the patterns go further. Norms governing Hanunóo writing are remarkably flexible: for example, the symbols can be written in mirror-image fashion and in any direction besides the standard one (thus easing the task for left-handed individuals); certain phonemic contrasts in the language are indicated in writing by some individuals, but not by others. The systemic laxness of the writing system can only be understood in its broader social context, as a token of the non-directive and egalitarian ethos which the Hanunóo value. The Hanunóo case illustrates that many aspects of writing systems can only be understood in relation to their technological and social contexts.

LITERACY AS A SOCIOCULTURAL CONSTRUCT

Much has been written on the relationship, on the one hand, between literacy and its converse, orality, and on the other hand, between social and cultural institutions and the intellectual makeup of individuals. In this section, two broad schools of thought are first contrasted critically; two case studies are then presented; and the question of the impact of literacy on language is broached.

Literacy and Its Consequences

Anthropological interest in literacy is deeply embedded in the history of anthropological thought and that of related disciplines. Early in the development of social-scientific thinking, literacy was implicated, more or less explicitly, as a determinant of differences between "primitive" and "civilized" thought and action (Tylor), collective and individualistic consciousness (Durkheim, Mauss), prelogical and logical mentalities (Lévy-Bruhl, Luria), closed and open systems (Popper), *pensée sauvage* and *pensée domestiquée* (Lévi-Strauss), mythopoeic and scientific thinking (Lévi-Strauss, Cassirer), and context-bound and context-free cognitive processes (Vygotsky). The view that literacy plays a pivotal role in bringing about fundamental changes in the individual and society has been most clearly articulated by Goody (in increasingly mitigated terms, in Goody and Watt 1963, Goody 1977, 1986, 1987; also Havelock 1976, Illich and Sanders 1988, Innis 1972, McLuhan 1962, Parsons 1966). This work, represented in what has come to be referred to as the "autonomous" or "Great Divide" model of literacy, takes to task earlier dichotomies for their lack of an explanatory dimension, and proposes that "many of the valid aspects of these somewhat vague dichotomies can be related to changes in the mode of communication, especially the introduction of various forms of writing" (Goody 1977: 16).

According to the autonomous model, literacy, particularly alphabetic literacy, causes (or, in more recent versions, facilitates) basic changes in the makeup of both society and the individual because of its inherent properties. For example, writing leads to permanent records which can be subjected to critical scrutiny, and as a result it gives rise to historical and scientific verifiability and concomitant social designs. Similarly, bureaucratic institutions and complex state structures depend crucially on the types of long-distance communication that literacy makes possible. The individual's psychological functions are also altered by literacy: a written text, particularly if written in an alphabetic script, is in some sense more abstract and less context-dependent than a comparable spoken text, and the ability to produce and process written texts presupposes and brings about context-free thinking (Olson 1977). Further, literacy affects memory in significant ways, making possible rigorous recall of lengthy texts, compared with the imprecise, pattern-driven memory of preliterate individuals (Hunter 1985).

The premises and claims of the autonomous model have been subjected to severe critical scrutiny by researchers in a variety of fields, including social anthropology (Street 1984), sociolinguistics (Heath 1983), psychology (Scribner and Cole 1981), rhetoric (Pattison 1982), folklore (Finnegan 1988), and history (Clanchy 1979, Graff 1979, Harris 1989). For most critics, literacy should be viewed not as a monolithic phenomenon but as a multi-faceted one, whose meaning, including any consequences it may have for the individual and society, depends crucially on the social practices surrounding it and on the ideological system in which it is embedded. Proponents of an "ideological model" view literacy as a sociocultural construct, and propose that literacy cannot be studied independently of the social, political, and historical forces which shape it (Street 1984). They point out, for example, that literacy is found in many societies of the world without the social and cognitive characteristics which the autonomous model predicts should accompany it.

To meet these objections, advocates of the autonomous model have proposed that there exist various situations of so-called *restricted literacy* (Goody 1977), in which constraints on the scope of literacy have inhibited the full realization of its expected social and cognitive potentials. Thus literacy is said to be *socially* restricted when it is available only to a political or intellectual (usually male) elite, which uses it as a tool for control; it is said to be *functionally* restricted when it is used by many people, but for a narrow range of purposes; and it is said to be *intellectually* restricted when, for some reason, it has failed to trigger the intellectual changes that are engendered in "fully" literate individuals and groups. Advocates of the ideological perspective view with suspicion the assumptions underlying these qualifications, which more or less explicitly equate non-restricted literacy with Western middle-class standards, and they ask whether any society is in fact "fully" literate in this sense. For example, the use of literacy and associated institutions by the political and intellectual elites of Western societies, in order to control access to symbolic capital (Bourdieu 1984), fits the description of a socially restricted literacy. By contrast, in sixteenth-century insular South-east Asia, literacy was deeply ingrained in the everyday life of every social stratum, particularly among women (Reid 1988). Even though this situation clearly does not fit the definition of restricted literacy, it did not give rise to Western-style history, science, political structures, or even schooling.

The ideological reaction to autonomous approaches to literacy represents a retreat from generalization, a call back to the ethnographic drawing board, which some have criticized for its sociological reductionism (Cole and Nicolopoulou 1992). Underlying the ideological view is the belief that generalizations are much more likely to be discovered in the relationship between literacy and its sociocultural, political, and ideological context than in the inherent properties of literacy itself (Besnier 1991). In fact, these very properties are frequently the subject of contention. Compare, for example, the premise that "speech is transient, writing is permanent" (Crystal and Davy 1969: 69) with the contradictory premise that "speech, once uttered, can rarely be revised, no matter how much we might struggle to unsay something we wish we had not said. But writing can be reflected upon, and even erased at will" (Smith 1983: 82). Clearly, what is represented in these two statements is the articulation of two different ideologies, or perhaps two facets of the same ideology.

Literacy and Literacies

The diversity of literacy experiences, which the ideological model takes as the object of its inquiry, is illustrated here with two case studies: Scribner and Cole's (1981) work on literacy among the Vai of Liberia, and Heath's (1983) analysis of literacy in three rural Appalachian communities in the United States. These now classic studies complement one another in several ways: while Scribner and Cole examine the cognitive consequences that the autonomous model ascribes to literacy, Heath is concerned with the social and cultural correlates of literacy; the former demonstrates the intrinsic variety of literacy experiences within a single group, whereas the latter illustrates variety across social groups in a complex society; both studies demonstrate how ethnographically informed work in two different disciplines, psychology and sociolinguistics respectively, leads to congruent conclusions on the meaning of literacy; and they illustrate how an ideological approach can inform work on the role of literacy in both "traditional" and Western societies. In both works, a common theme will emerge, which will be taken up later . . . : the complex intertwining of literacy and schooling.

Among the Vai of Liberia, three different types of literacies are attested, each being associated with different languages, institutions, and social activities: Vai literacy, which exploits a locally devised syllabary and is used to write letters and keep records of economic transactions; Koranic literacy, which is learnt in religious schools and used to read Muslim scriptures; and English literacy, learnt in school and used in transactions with the outside world. In this ideal comparative laboratory, Scribner and Cole (1981) set out to test two claims put forward in "autonomous" approaches: that significant cognitive consequences can be ascribed to literacy; and that alphabetic writing in particular fosters analytic thought. They administered a battery of psychological tests adapted to the Vai situation, such as syllogistic problems, memory tasks, and rebus games. The results demonstrated that literacy itself is not a good predictor of cognitive skills. Rather, the cognitive performance of different Vai subpopulations is best explained in terms of the psychological and social accompaniments of each literacy tradition, particularly those that are given salience during apprenticeship in literacy. For example, Koranic literates perform well on incremental recall tests, a reflection of the importance of memory work in Koranic schools. Subjects literate in the Vai syllabary perform well in rebus-solving tests, because using the Vai syllabary involves rebus-like problems. Vai subjects literate in English, who all attend Western-style schools, do well on tests that resemble school activities, like syllogisms. Thus the pedagogical practices that characterize each literacy experience, rather than literacy itself, shape the individual's cognitive makeup: "particular practices promote particular skills" (Scribner and Cole 1981: 258).

Learning how to read and write is not simply a process of developing cognitive skills associated with these activities, but also of learning how these skills are to be used in their social context. Heath (1983) investigates the implications of this proposition in three communities of the rural American South: Maintown, a white middle-class community; Roadville, a white working-class town; and Trackton, a black working-class community. She found strikingly divergent patterns in how children are socialized in these three groups with respect to such language-related activities as story-telling and reading books. In Maintown, pre-school children are taught to pay attention to books from an early age. Bedtime stories are accompanied by pedagogical practices like question–answer and "initiation–reply–evaluation" sequences. In particular, questions like "What did you like about the story?" resemble the sort of analytic questions that children are expected to answer early on in school contexts. Similarly, Maintown children learn turn-taking mechanisms (i.e., when to be silent, when to speak) and fictionalization skills that are valued in schools. In contrast, Roadville children learn to find connections between literacy and "truth." Christian Roadville parents use literacy for instruction and moral improvement, and explicitly value the "real" over the "fictional." Reading to children in Roadville is an uncommon performance in which children are passive participants, and written materials are not connected to everyday life. Finally, Trackton children learn early in life how to defend themselves orally and to engage in verbal play. Young children receive attention from adults if they can offer a good verbal performance. Adult Trackton residents are not literacy-oriented, and do not read to children. Children are not asked pedagogical questions about their surroundings; Trackton adults assume that they will learn through their own efforts and observations of adults. In these three communities, children are thus exposed to different pedagogical practices, and learn very different associations with literacy in pre-school years, which will accompany them to school and in large part determine their performance in such middle-class-dominated institutions.

The two case studies summarized here demonstrate the pronounced heterogeneity of literacy experiences both within and across social groups. Literacy is deeply embedded in, and derives its meaning from, the social practices which are most clearly articulated in pedagogical contexts. Both case studies demonstrate that it is futile to try to arrive at a decontextualized characterization of the cognitive and social consequences of literacy, and they provide an alternative route: a focus on the *activities* and *events* in which literacy plays a central role (Basso 1974, Szwed 1981).

Spoken and Written Language

The important question of the impact of literacy on language is one which has received little attention until recently. Here again, one finds in the evolution of the problem a history of a priori overgeneralizations followed by a return to "thicker" descriptive approaches.

Ever since de Saussure, Bloomfield, and Sapir, arguably the founders of modern linguistics, emphasized that the primary goal of linguistics was the study of spoken language, few scholars in that field had paid much attention to literacy. In the late 1970s and early 1980s, two subfields of linguistics, sociolinguistics and discourse analysis, witnessed a surge of interest in the study of written language. Primarily motivated by questions of structural comparison between spoken and written language, studies of this sort would typically take particular linguistic structures (e.g., complex-sentence structures) and analyse their distribution across various types of spoken and written texts (for a comprehensive overview of this research, see Chafe and Tannen 1987). The resulting correlations would then be explained in terms of what the researcher perceives as the "natural" adaptation of language users to various communicative environments. This leads on to discussion of various oral and literate "strategies," viewed as the overall patterns of language users' structural and stylistic "choices" in adapting to such factors as the presence or absence of an immediate audience, and the degree of personal "involvement" or "detachment" that the language producer experiences vis-à-vis the text (Tannen 1985).

Work in this vein recognizes that spoken and written communication are neither structurally nor functionally opposed, but lie on a continuum from most literate-like (e.g., academic writing) to most oral-like (e.g., informal conversation); most registers, or situational varieties of language use, fall between these two extremes. Thus the pitfalls of the "Great Divide" approach are to a certain extent overcome. But problems remain. For example, in order for there to be a continuum, there must be well-defined extremes, the most literate-like of which is pretheoretically associated with such features as the effacement of the authorial voice, structural complexity, and informational "repleteness" (for the text to be amenable to processing with little knowledge of the extratextual context). Furthermore, the responses of communicators to different communicative contexts along this continuum, which are evident in the structural characteristics of the texts they produce, are explained in cognitive terms; in this respect, this tradition of work does not differ from other areas of mainstream linguistics, which defines its task as a search for universal cognitive explanations for language (of course, there are many different accounts of what "cognition" consists of). In addition, there is evidence that a uni-dimensional continuum is inadequate to accommodate the variations in linguistic behaviour across contexts of oral and written communication (Biber 1988).

Sociolinguistic investigations of literacy can be better contextualized in the perspective of broader sociocultural issues. Most work to date suffers from the virtual lack of a cross-cultural and cross-social perspective, being largely based on the speaking and writing activities of the Western middle-class academic elite. This has led researchers to confuse cognitive behaviour and sociocultural norms which have become, in the process of a long sociohistorical evolution, "naturalized" (i.e., made to appear as if they were the only valid way to communicate through the medium of literacy). As we go on to show, this naturalization is a powerful device in controlling access to such institutions as schooling, and is thus pivotal in the maintenance of sociocultural hegemony.

THE SPREAD OF LITERACY

...

Tensions Between Preliteracy and Literacy

Literacy is commonly introduced to preliterate groups in conjunction with many other technologies, institutions, and practices, among which religion figures prominently. While historically, literacy had accompanied the spread of Islam, Buddhism, and Hinduism, since the nineteenth century Christian missionization has provided the most common

vehicle and rationale for the spread of literacy, and this has frequently been underscored by a First-World–Third-World dichotomy. Since the middle of the twentieth century, many agents of proselytization have legitimized their existence by invoking their literacy-promoting campaigns, in tune with Western middle-class ideology which views literacy, and in particular essayist literacy, as an essential tool for "progress," "happiness," and integration into the post-modern world. The explicitness with which literacy, religious conversion, and political economy are intermeshed in missionizing discourse clearly calls for an analytic stance that recognizes the complexity of these relationships.

The reactions of target groups to the introduction of literacy depend on many different factors, among which figure the relationship between the group and the introducing agents, attitudes toward sociocultural elements concurrently being introduced to the group, and the social and political associations of literacy (Spolsky et al. 1983). Frequently, where literacy is initially viewed as a means of gaining access to the economic or symbolic capital associated with the agents of introduction, it is readily incorporated into the communicative repertoire of the target group. Witness, for example, nineteenth-century missionary reports of the enthusiastic acceptance of literacy in various parts of the insular Pacific (cf. Parsonson 1967, Jackson 1975)....

A group's reaction to literacy can also function as an idiom of resistance: among many post-contact Native American groups, one witnesses a basic suspicion towards literacy, which is viewed as yet another element of sociocultural hegemony and an encroachment from the outside, associated with the American government's Bureau of Indian Affairs, Christian proselytizers, and other institutions of the dominant culture (Leap 1991, Philips 1975, Spolsky and Irvine 1982; but see McLaughlin 1989). Comparable disinterest is encountered in contemporary Papua New Guinea, the theatre of many missionizing and literacizing onslaughts (Schieffelin and Cochran-Smith 1984). The acceptance or rejection of literacy technologies and practices can thus play a symbolic role in defining a group's stance towards powerful outsiders, and the nature of its involvement in sociopolitical and ideological dynamics imposed from without the group. In all cases, it is important to view the group to which literacy is being introduced as actively "taking hold" of literacy, rather than remaining a passive participant in the process (Kulick and Stroud 1990).

The spread of literacy can be accompanied by various types of engineering efforts on the part either of the group introducing literacy or of those on the receiving end. Outside agents may devise orthographies for the language of the newly literate group, translate texts, and set up pedagogical institutions, as many contemporary missionizing agencies do. There are even cases where the party introducing literacy has devised new writing systems; such systems were invented for Cree, Kutchin Athapaskan, and Inuit in Northern and Western Canada, where they are still in use (Scollon and Scollon 1981, Walker 1981). On the other hand, agents of introduction may provide no more than training in literacy consumption, in an attempt to restrict their trainees' access to writing; such is the case of nineteenth-century missionaries in much of Polynesia, who brought printing presses with them, printed catechisms and other religious literature, but left the islanders to fend for themselves when it came to writing. The spread of literacy from literate to preliterate groups often accompanies the introduction (sometimes the imposition) of a new language, be it a "major" language like English or Arabic or a locally based lingua franca, often a creole (e.g., Tok Pisin in Papua New Guinea). Even when it is the policy of the introducing agent to base literacy on local languages, a lingua franca generally looms not far behind. In contemporary Mexico, education policy-makers advocate the use of Mesoamerican languages as a medium for instruction in literacy for Native American minorities, but view it only as a bridge to literacy in Spanish (King 1994)....

At the "receiving" end, many aspects of literacy undergo redefinition, in that the literacy practices developed by newly literate groups frequently differ from those of introducing agents. For example, in the later half of the nineteenth century, the Diyari of central Australia were taught to read and write by Lutheran missionaries for the purpose of reading the Scriptures. They co-operated in the process because schooling gave them access to food and other economic resources. But soon, empowering the technology, they began to write letters and keep records, neither of which was encouraged by the missionaries. Thus literacy acquired a very different cultural meaning from the one it had had for the agents of introduction (Ferguson 1987). Similarly, on Nukulaelae Atoll in the Central Pacific, letter writing developed very soon after the introduction of literacy in the 1860s, even though literacy was first brought there, again, to turn Nukulaelae Islanders into consumers of Christian Scriptures. Letter writing quickly became well integrated into the secular life of the community, in which it fulfilled specific functions, such as the expression of certain types of affect (Besnier 1989). Literacy can also become a new vessel for communicative practices already extant in the oral mode. Among the Gapun of Papua New Guinea, face-to-face interaction frequently involves tension between two conflicting aspects of the Gapun self, individualism and other-centredness, and the very same conflict can be witnessed in the Gapun's literate activities (Kulick and Stroud 1990).

The diversity of initial literacy experiences illustrated here leads one to hypothesize that newly literate groups do not necessarily perceive literacy as a homogeneous, monolithic phenomenon, but rather as a set of diverse communicative possibilities, defined in part with the contextual background to the introduction of literacy technologies and ideologies, and in part by the communicative dynamics already in place (Street 1993). Situations where preliteracy and literacy come into contact are often extremely complex, and commonly occur together with great social and cultural upheavals, which are usually brought about by the very same agents introducing literacy.

"Invented" Literacies

One of the most remarkable feats of literacy engineering since the invention of the technology itself was the creation of new writing systems, usually syllabaries, by preliterate individuals. Several cases are known to have occurred in the course of the nineteenth and twentieth centuries, in various parts of West Africa (among the Mende and the Vai, for example), in Native North America, among the Apache and the Cherokee, and in South-east Asia (Smalley, Vang, and Yang 1990). The best-known case is that of Sequoyah, a preliterate Cherokee who spent several years in the 1810s and 1820s devising a functional 85-symbol syllabary for his native language, using symbols from the Roman alphabet and probably the Greek and Cyrillic alphabets, supplemented by symbols of Sequoyah's invention (Walker 1981). The system was first viewed with much suspicion (its inventor was even tried for witchcraft), but within a few years literacy was widespread, and an active tradition of print literacy was established, principally in the form of newspapers. The currency of the writing system subsequently declined owing to the forced relocation of the Cherokee from the Southeastern United States to Oklahoma in 1839 along the infamous Trail of Tears, and to subsequent efforts by the American government to "integrate" the Cherokee, which culminated in their confiscation of the Cherokee newspaper press in 1909. Today, Sequoyah's syllabary is used for a limited range of purposes: for reading the Christian Bible, and for recording and reading curing formulae for traditional medical practices.

Most invented literacies were developed to answer the needs of an economically and politically disadvantaged group, dominated by a literate society in which literacy was associated with power. This association was evident to Sequoyah, who was reputedly obsessed with the idea that the Cherokee should learn to communicate in the written mode if they were to ensure their survival in the face of Anglo-American encroachment. Thus the very invention of the syllabary was motivated by aspects of the dominant group's ideology regarding literacy. The extent to which Cherokee literacy practices were influenced by Anglo-American literacy practices is unclear. But invented literacies obviously arose from more or less extensive contact with the pre-existing literacy of the dominant group (Harbsmeier 1988). However, they differed from other contexts in which the technology spread from a dominant to a subordinate group in that they arose with no encouragement from the former. In fact, in the Cherokee case, literacy existed against the wishes of the dominant group.

Tensions Between Literacy Practices

The basic diversity in literacy experiences around the world leads to literacy practices with differing historical and sociocultural associations coming into contact with one another. First, different literacy practices may be associated with different social groups. Heath's (1983) work on three

Appalachian communities, reviewed above, demonstrates how tensions between the literacy practices of middle-class, white working-class, and black working-class groups both reflect and reinforce inequality, oppression, and hegemony.

Second, distinct literacy practices may be associated with different contexts of use, and may thus play divergent roles in the lives of members of a society. In a rural community in pre-revolutionary Iran, three sets of literacy practices have been described, which Street (1984) calls "*maktab*" literacy, "commercial" literacy, and "school" literacy. Before state schools were introduced into the rural areas, villagers learnt reading and writing in Koranic schools, or *maktabs*. While these have been denigrated by many Western commentators and educationalists as involving only rote learning and repetition, in this case the literacy learnt in that context was transferred to other contexts. During the boom years of the early 1970s, there was a growing demand from urban areas for village produce, and villagers developed entrepreneurial skills in marketing and distributing their fruit that required an ability to write, make out bills, mark boxes, use cheque-books, etc. These literate skills were particularly evident among those who had been to the *maktab* and had continued their Koranic learning in their homes; they were able to transfer literacy skills from one context to another, at the same time extending both their content and their function. School literacy remained relatively one-dimensional from this point of view, and did not provide an entry into commercial literacy. It did however provide a novel social and economic route to urban professional employment, notably through entry to urban schools. The three literacies belonged to different social domains, although a single individual might learn more than one of them.

Third, situations abound in which different literacy practices compete for the same or for closely related intellectual and social spaces in the lives of members of a group. In Seal Bay, an Aleut village in Alaska, one finds two sets of literacy practices, having different historical antecedents, and conflicting social and symbolic associations: a "village" literacy, associated with the Russian Orthodox church and conducted in Aleut (written in Cyrillic); and "outside" literacy, which is associated with English, schooling, economic transactions, and Baptist missionaries (Reder and Green 1983). These two literacies, which until recently remained functionally separate, have begun to compete in certain contexts. Characteristically, the competition between literacies is both a reflection and an enactment of conflicts between "tradition" and "intrusion," between different economic systems, and between competing religious ideologies....

LITERACY AND SOCIOPOLITICAL PROCESSES

The emphasis on social rather than cognitive processes in the study of literacy practices has opened up new and fruitful areas of inquiry for social anthropology. We now examine four connected themes in the light of the concepts and approaches outlined in the earlier sections: the relationship between literacy and nationalism; literacy and gender relations; literacy and education; and literacy and development.

Literacy and Nationalism

A number of recent studies of the emergence and persistence of nationalism have attributed a significant role in these processes to literacy. Those who argue that nationalism is a relatively modern phenomenon ground a great deal of their case on the supposed nature of literacy. Gellner (1983), for instance, sees the homogeneity required by the modern state as being made possible only through a common national literacy, unavailable in previous "agro-literate" stages of social development. The literacy of these agro-literate societies was of what Goody (1977) calls the "restricted" kind. In the modern state, on the other hand, literacy has to be available to the mass of the population and not simply to an elite: indeed, in Gellner's view, it is the development of such mass literacy that explains the rise of the modern nation state itself. Modern industry requires a mobile, literate, technologically equipped population and the nation state, Gellner claims, is the only agency capable of providing such a work force, through its support for a mass, public, compulsory, and standardized education system.

The literacy being referred to here is that of the "autonomous" model. A single, nationally sanctioned literacy supposedly rises above the claims of the different ethnic communities that may constitute the state. The education system, according to Gellner, genuinely provides a neutral means of authenticating knowledge through reasonably impartial centres of learning, which issue certificates "on the basis of honest, impartially administered examination." Scholars who have focused upon the concept of a plurality of literacies, rather than a single autonomous literacy, are less inclined to take these claims at face value: while they are evidently part of the rhetoric of nationalism, they do not necessarily correspond to the social reality, in which it is much more usual to find a variety of different literacy practices. Accounts of the uses of literacy to express identity among youth groups in urban situations (Shuman 1986, Weinstein 1993, Camitta 1993), of mode-switching as well as code-switching in the Moroccan community in London (Baynham 1993), of mother-tongue literacy among Latin American migrants in Toronto (Klassen 1991), and of "community" literacy in Lancaster, England (Barton and Ivanič 1991), challenge the view of the modern world as consisting of homogeneous nations each with a single, homogenizing literacy.

Likewise, scholars who stress the symbolic and cultural dimensions of ethnic ties and nations focus upon the variety of routes to nationalism and put less weight on the claims made for literacy in its emergence (Smith 1986, 1994). The account of the growth and persistence of modern nationalism requires analysis not only of the exigencies of modern technology and economy but also of the ideological and cultural aspects of literacy practices in nationalism's "prehistory." Recent studies of medieval and early modern Europe have thrown into question the extent to which literacy was the preserve simply of an elite, and describe a range of different literacies there too (Houston 1988, Graff 1987). McKitterick (1990) argues that literacy in eighth- and ninth-century Carolingian France and Germany was not confined to a clerical elite, but was dispersed in lay society and used for government and administration as well as for ordinary legal transactions among the people of the Frankish kingdom. Clanchy (1979) describes the shift to a "literate mentality" in the centuries following the Norman Conquest in England, where the growth of a bureaucratic centralized system was associated with the colonizers' claims for legitimacy and was resisted over a long period through counter-claims for orality and for indigenous language and literacy. Thomas (1986) describes the association of literacy with religious beliefs and teaching, such that terms like "primer" referred not so much to an aid in the process of learning to read and write as to one in the process of learning to pray.

A similar story of variation in the uses and meanings of literacy in the pre-modern period and subsequently is emerging with regard to other parts of the world. In Southeast Asia, literacy was widespread in the era preceding Western impact. This was a matter neither of elite nor of commercial interests but of a variety of local customs and practices. Writing in the Philippines in the sixteenth century, for instance, served no religious, judicial, or historical purposes, but was used only for notes and letters. Elsewhere women actively used writing for exchanging notes and recording debts, while in southern Sumatra as late as 1930 a large proportion of the population employed literacy for poetic courting contests (Reid 1988). The arrival of Islam and Christianity had the effect of *reducing* literacy rates, particularly among women, by restricting writing to the male, sacral, and monastic domains. In the Philippines knowledge of the traditional scripts disappeared within a century of Christianization and a similar fate befell pre-Islamic scripts in Malaya and parts of Sumatra. The Indic-based script used by the Hanunóo, as described above, represents perhaps one of the few modern survivals of these local literacies. The variety and complexity of social and ideological uses of literacies in the pre-modern era suggest that simple accounts of "agro-literate" society, as divided between a literate elite and an illiterate peasantry, may have to be revised. Theories of the rise of nationalism founded on such assumptions are consequently being subjected to serious critique....

These questions have yet to be investigated in any depth with regard to the role of literacy, although recent studies on literacy campaigns in Mexico (King 1994), on the persistence of oral speech conventions in Somalia despite a mass literacy campaign there in the 1970s (Lewis 1986), and on the significance of "politicized ethnicity" in the Nicaraguan Literacy Crusade (Bourgois 1986) suggest that a more complex pattern is emerging than that suggested either by Fishman (1986), in terms of the concept of diglossia, or by Gellner, in his proposed linkage of modern nationalism with autonomous literacy.

Literacy Practices and the Construction of Gender

The example of widespread literacy in South-east Asia, prior to Western expansion there, raises novel questions about the relative participation of men and women in literacy, and about the uses made of it. Since literacy was not taught in any formal institution and had no vocational or religious value, its transmission tended to be mainly a domestic matter, largely the responsibility of mothers and older siblings. The social context in which literacy practices were learned probably facilitated their uses by women, who employed them not only in the poetic courting contests mentioned above but also for exchanging notes, recording debts, and other commercial matters which were in the female domain (Reid 1988). As a result, literacy rates for women were at least as high as those for men, and some travellers found them even higher (Reid 1988: 219). The advent of Westerners, with their male-oriented religious institutions, shifted the balance towards male literacy and formal schooling. Such imbalance characterizes many accounts of gendered literacy practices in the contemporary world.

Until recently, statistical and quantitative surveys of the gender imbalance in schooling have dominated the agenda in studies of literacy, gender, and development (Kelly 1987, Stromquist 1989). Bown, for instance, writes: "In the Third World countries of Africa, Asia and Latin America, women's enrolment in schools lags behind that of men...fewer girls go to schools than boys, and they remain in schools for a shorter time than boys" (Bown 1990). Where researchers have attended to literacy, statistics invariably demonstrate that rural women are the least likely to be literate, while urban men have retained the command of the secular and bureaucratic literacy of the state that they had previously held in religions of the book (Kaneko 1987).

Recently, researchers have begun to ask the subjects themselves for their opinions, studying for instance adult women's motivations in coming forward for literacy programmes (Opiyo 1981, Saraswathi and Ravindram 1982). The balance between economic and "personal" motives is frequently cited, government agencies tending to focus on the former while women themselves, when given the opportunity, frequently express the latter (MacCaffery 1988, MacKeracher 1989), although Saraswathi and Ravindram (1982) put women's interest in "economic and gender justice" above their concern for literacy. A project undertaken by the Council for Social Development of India (1972, 1975) highlights the extent to which groups may differentiate between male and female models of literacy. Local women assumed that literacy was associated with male, white-collar, urban labour and saw no reason for attending classes. The project team's model was likewise male-oriented, but focused on the role of women as wives and mothers, directing literacy to them as a means of improving their health management. It thus ignored the significance of the major economic role played by women in family and village life, and the role of structural poverty in explaining their children's poor health. It assumed that literacy was associated with cognitive advance, whereas oral skills were presumed to be "weak" when it came to acquiring new knowledge. Literacy itself would improve "general skills for efficient functioning." These classic assumptions of the autonomous model of literacy were undermined by the outcome of the project: those classes that involved practical health-care support and oral instruction, but no literacy, were successful by the project's criteria, while classes that involved only functional literacy, but lacked practical backup, registered the highest drop-out rates. The message was that it is not women's lack of literacy that leads to poor nutrition and high infant mortality, but the structural problems of poverty, employment, and gender relations....

A number of other studies have focused on meaning rather than function and have introduced an anthropological perspective into the complex relations of women and men to writing processes. In counter-balancing the dominant accounts of male literacy, they have provided evidence of what women in different places and times actually do with literacy and what it means to them. For instance, Ko (1989) describes how, in seventeenth-century China, educated middle-class women wrote poetry as a means of constructing a private female culture, against the homogenizing male character of late Imperial Chinese culture; and Mikulecky (1985) records the uses by fifteenth-century English women of the literacy skills being developed by the rising gentry to write letters concerning the "business affairs of the family, personal intrigues, duty and death" (Mikulecky 1985: 2).

Rockhill (1987a, b) attempts to provide a theoretical framework for the study of how literacy is gendered. She points out how literacy practices are significant in constructing different identities for women and men. For Hispanic women in Los Angeles, among whom she conducted life history interviews, literacy practices are defined and ruled by the men in their lives, and resistance involves considerable personal and political strain. Women do the literacy work of the household, purchasing goods, paying bills, transacting with social services, and dealing with children's schooling. These forms of literacy remain invisible, as do many of women's contributions to the household. The women are labelled by men as "illiterate" while the men, who acquire and use more spoken English to obtain jobs in the "public" domain, consider themselves "literate."...

"Literacy practices," then, help to position women and men in relation to authority and submission, to the public and private domains, and to personal identity (Cameron 1985, Moore 1988). Models of literacy are differentiated by gender as well as by class and ethnicity. Research has only begun in this field, but it is evident that it will have to be informed by insights from the "New Literacy Studies" (Street 1993) of multiple and socially varied literacies, on the one hand, and by feminist writing on multiple and socially varied constructions of gender, on the other.

Literacy and Development

The shifts in approaches to literacy practices evident in many of the publications of the 1980s have considerable implications for policy on literacy and development. The theory and findings of the new literacy studies should have made it harder for development and literacy agencies to persist with a single, dominant, and frequently ethnocentric view of literacy. But in many cases the assumptions of earlier times have persisted. Wagner asserts that while "specialists have been developing a much more complete understanding of literacy and the kinds of skills required in the coming millennium...the transfers of information between researchers and policymakers are fragile at best" (1989). In the post-war era it was assumed that "development" for Third World countries meant following in the footsteps of the "West" (Rogers 1992). With regard to education and literacy, this meant providing institutions and procedures that would enable Western literacy to be disseminated throughout a population. Literacy was seen as a causal factor in development.

Anderson, for instance, links a 40 per cent "literacy threshold" to the attainment of "economic take off," a principle to be found in many agency accounts (Anderson and Bowman 1965). Development workers interested in education also tended to associate cognitive change with the acquisition of literacy (Oxenham 1980). For Lerner (1958), literacy would effect the change from a "traditional" to a "modern" mentality, the latter characterized by "empathy," flexibility, adaptability, willingness to accept change, and an entrepreneurial and confidently outgoing spirit. Traditional societies were seen to embody the negation of all of these qualities: they were perceived to be ignorant, narrow-minded, and, from the evidence of early development campaigns, to be intransigent to "modern" ideas. As a catalyst of the transition to modernity, literacy was supposed to be "functional," a term that, being sufficiently ambiguous to embrace the political interests of the many different governments and agencies involved in literacy work, came to dominate the field. UNESCO, for instance, adopted in 1965 a programme of "Work-Oriented Functional Literacy Campaigns" that targeted social groups which, once literate, would be expected to contribute to the functioning of the modern economy in their country (Furter 1973, UNESCO 1973). The programme failed, among other reasons, because of the lack of attention to local uses and meanings of literacy, and because of the narrow, Western interpretation of "functionality" it employed (UNESCO 1976, Berggren and Berggren 1975, Lankshear and Lawler 1987)....

With regard to the role of literacy in formal schooling and development, some research has begun to take account of the kinds of questions regarding knowledge and meaning familiar to anthropological inquiry. Schooling, like literacy, has been seen as far more uniform than it really is. We need to ask what actually is being communicated in processes of instruction, if we want to know what carries over from school experience into social and economic "effects." Drawing on experimental and ethnographic data from the Mswambeni region of coastal Kenya, Eisomon (1988) examines ways in which the school experience is transformed into school effects. It was not literacy itself, he concludes, nor simply the experience of school, that enabled students to interpret written material, but rather "prior knowledge" and "procedural skills": schools, however, often fail to make this kind of knowledge explicit or to help students organize it. How to make inferences from particular written texts, and how to apply the scientific principles that the texts assume, need as much attention as the technical skills of reading and writing and the mere attendance at school that appear to remain the aims of many development programmes.

Studies such as Eisomon's highlight the possibility both of linking theory and practice, and of extending anthropological perspectives in the field of education and development (Roberts and Akinsaya 1976, Vulliamy et al. 1990, Fetterman and Pitman 1986). The many ethnographies of literacy produced [since the mid-1980s] and summarized above have suggested the kinds of questions that need to be asked in the context of development programmes, whether formal or informal: what literacy actually means, why it is being imparted, for whom and by whom; which literacies are developed in which contexts, how they relate to the literacies that were there before the campaign; and what complex relations are set up between oral and written language uses in these situations (Wagner 1987, Street 1984, 1987, Schieffelin and Gilmore 1986, Bledsoe and Robey 1986, Finnegan 1988, Fingeret 1983). There is also considerable scope for ethnographies of the literacy campaigns themselves. Who engages in the campaign as organizers, animateurs, and teachers, and why? How do ethnic variations within a country affect the content and form of a literacy campaign (King 1994, Sjostrom and Sjostrom 1983)? These questions have not traditionally been on the agendas of either development workers or anthropologists, but shifts in approaches to literacy of the kind outlined in this chapter, and recent shifts in anthropological approaches to development (Grillo and Rew 1985), suggest that they may become considerably more prominent in future research.

Literacy and Education

Since the time of Boas and Mead, social and cultural anthropologists in the United States have been concerned with issues of education and society (Erikson and Bekker 1986), whereas in Britain the level of interest in this field has remained fairly low. However, with the development of new directions in literacy studies, particular aspects of the education process are being opened up to anthropological analysis in both American and British traditions.

From a sociological and educational perspective, the major questions have focused on the underperformance in school of children from specific, "disadvantaged" backgrounds, whether defined in class or in ethnic terms.

Anthropological insights have suggested both a broadening and a narrowing of this focus. They are broadening in the sense that they lead to the study of educational institutions and processes themselves as social phenomena rather than allowing the institutions and processes of education to remain as the sole arbiters of what is to be regarded as problematic. Anthropologists have been interested in questions of socialization (Spindler 1974, Hanson 1979), social reproduction (Bourdieu and Passeron 1977, Collins 1986, 1988), and the ritual and symbolic aspects of schooling (McLaren 1986, Turner 1982). Anthropological perspectives have also narrowed the focus in the sense that they suggest ethnographies of the school (Willis 1977, Everhardt 1983, Schieffelin and Gilmore 1986), of the classroom (Cazden 1978, Michaels and Cazden 1986), and of the home (McDermott et al. 1982, Taylor 1985). Thus the minutiae of daily literacy and education-related behaviours such as "homework" are analysed as social and cultural processes and not simply in terms of their educational objectives and success. Bloome (1989), for instance, has criticized the emphasis, in studies of schooling, on efficiency and access and has called for analysis of the nature of classroom communities as social groups, while micro-studies of the language of the classroom (Erikson 1982, 1984, Collins 1986) have linked local ethnography, including family literacy, to wider political and economic currents in the culture.

The continuities and discontinuities between home and school culture have remained an axis of attention, with anthropologists demonstrating how in many non-Western societies schooling tends to be more closely integrated with everyday social life, at least until Western forms of schooling develop (Fishman 1991, Bloch 1993, King 1994). Literacy practices provide a rich ethnographic focus for such inquiry, and the development of ethnographies of literacy in the community and the home (Philips 1975, Varenne and McDermott 1986, Barton and Ivanič 1991) is beginning to undermine still further assumptions regarding the natural dominance of schooled literacy.

In much of the educational literature, the increasingly recognized divergence between home and community literacies was, for a long time, defined as a "problem": home literacies were seen as "deficient," requiring to be overcome by the intervention of educational institutions bearing proper, schooled literacy. Thus Heath's (1983) account of the varieties of literacy in three communities in the American South reviewed earlier...(p. 55), far from being taken as evidence of rich learning outside of school on which educational institutions might build—as Heath herself intended and worked to implement practically—has been interpreted as providing evidence of the failure of home culture. Where Heath recognized that children were learning complex oral and literacy skills that tended to be ignored when they arrived at school, many educationalists pointed to what they saw as the inadequacies of mothers who did not read bedtime stories or "scaffold" their children's "emergent literacy" towards school achievement (Teale and Sulzby 1986). Nevertheless, even in middle-class America there are variations in the uses and meanings of literacy that suggest discontinuity between home and school, as well as intra-class and intra-ethnic variation, so much so that heterogeneity rather than homogeneity now appears to be the norm. This raises the question of how it is that the model of a single literacy is sustained: how, amidst this variation, does the model of "schooled" literacy (Cook-Gumperz 1986) come to be taken as the standard and indeed as the "natural" form of literacy, thus marginalizing other literacy practices?...

Many of these changes stemmed from the work of educationalists such as James Britton, whose classic accounts of how children learn, and notably of the importance of speech in classroom interaction, led to greater attention being paid to the processes of language and literacy acquisition and their implications for pedagogy. Willinsky's summary of the "new literacy" in the United States, and the focus of Meek and fellow educationalists in Britain on children's own uses of reading and writing from an early age, shifted attention from product to process and from teacher to student (Meek 1991, Willinsky 1990, Kimberley et al. 1992). Czerniewska, for instance, documents the National Writing Project in Britain that attempted to build the writing curriculum on the insight that children brought into the classroom from their homes, and communities, rich knowledge of literacy practices (Czerniewska 1992). The apparent scribbles and badly spelled texts that children passed among themselves were evidence of early understanding of the uses and meanings of literacy, to be built upon rather than rejected and denigrated as in traditional schooling. "Correct" spelling and grammar could be taught once children had a motivation for writing in the first place. They were to be encouraged, for instance, to write reflectively in journals about their experience, and teachers would respond in the same journals, thus making the writing process genuine communicative interaction rather than a dry classroom exercise. Or children would be given the opportunity to read "real books" in "book covers" in the classroom, designed as supportive and comfortable environments for enjoying reading, so that reading would no longer seem like a chore, or be undertaken solely in order to pass administered tests.

In the field of adult literacy a similar qualitative movement is under way, both in research and in teaching. The traditional view of adults with literacy needs in modern industrial society has shifted from the confident post-war assumption that the whole society was literate, to the discovery of "illiteracy," a concept associated on the one hand with metaphors of "disease" as something to be eradicated as a danger to public health, and on the other with courageous but disadvantaged individuals bravely managing but basically inadequate. More recently, the focus of research, particularly with an ethnographic aspect, has turned attention to more complex analyses of the social and cultural correlates of the many different literacies to be found in different communities and cultural contexts (Levine 1986, Mace 1979, 1992, Hunter and Harman 1979, Barton and Hamilton 1990). Fingeret (1983), for example, investigates the reciprocity associated with literacy and other skills in urban American communities: a person may exchange his or her skills as a mechanic for the literacy skills of a fellow community member, who will help fill in forms and transact with the institutions of the state that lean heavily on writing. Immigrants may get by in similar ways, one member of the community learning standard literacy and acting as a "cultural broker" for others (Weinstein 1993, Klassen 1991, Grillo 1990)....

While the relationship between literacy and education remains a focus for much of this research, the introduction of anthropological perspectives has provided a recognition, not always apparent in the educational literature, of the extent to which literacy exists in social contexts independent of educational institutions. Where literacy *is* associated with education, anthropological research has drawn attention to the social and cultural nature of schooling, of the classroom environment, and of the conceptualizations of knowledge and learning on which they are based. But historical and cross-cultural evidence shows that literacy practices are to be found in many contexts other than those of education, formal learning, and essayist conceptions of reading and writing. This has implications both for the model of literacy purveyed in educational settings and for the relationship of school literacy to the literacies of the home and the community. The heterogeneity and complexity of literacy practices, evident in studies of the relations between literacy and nationalism, gender, and development, are coming to be recognized as equally central to our understanding of the relationship between literacy and education.

Note

We are indebted to David Barton for his comments on this chapter, to Harold Conklin for providing us with details on Hanunóo literacy, and to Helen Siu for her help with the Chinese data presented here. The characters on pp. 52–53 were drawn by Ye Ding.

References

Anderson, C. A. and Bowman, M. (eds.) (1965). *Education and Economic Development,* London: Frank Cass.

Barton, D. (1988). *Problems with an Evolutionary Account of Literacy,* Lancaster Papers in Linguistics no. 49, Department of Linguistics, University of Lancaster.

Barton, D. and Hamilton, M. (1990). *Researching Literacy in Industrialized Countries: Trends and Prospects*, Hamburg: UNESCO Institute for Education.

Barton, D. and Ivanič, R. (1991). *Writing in the Community*, London: Sage.

Basso, K. H. (1974). "The ethnography of writing," in R. Bauman and J. Sherzer (eds.) *Explorations in the Ethnography of Speaking*, Cambridge: Cambridge University Press.

Basso, K. H. and Anderson, N. (1977). "A Western Apache writing system: the symbols of Silas John," in B. G. Blount and M. Sanches (eds.) *Sociocultural Dimensions of Language Change*, New York: Academic Press.

Baynham, M. (1993). "Code switching and mode switching: community interpreters and mediators of literacy," in B. Street (ed.) *Cross-Cultural Approaches to Literacy*, Cambridge: Cambridge University Press.

Berggren, C. and Berggren, L. (1975). *The Literacy Process: Domestication or Liberation?* London: Writers and Readers Publishers' Cooperative.

Besnier, N. (1989). "Literacy and feelings: the encoding of affect in Nukulaelae letters," *Text* 9: 69–92.

—— (1991). "Literacy and the notion of person on Nukulaelae atoll," *American Anthropologist* 93: 570–87.

Biber, D. (1988). *Variation Across Speech and Writing*, Cambridge: Cambridge University Press.

Bledsoe, C. and Robey, K. (1986). "Arabic literacy and secrecy among the Mende of Sierra Leone," *Man* (NS) 21: 202–26.

Bloch, M. (1993). "The uses of schooling and literacy in a Zafimaniry village," in B. Street (ed.) *Cross-Cultural Approaches to Literacy*, Cambridge: Cambridge University Press.

Bloome, D. (ed.) (1989). *Classrooms and Literacy*, Norwood, NJ: Ablex.

Bourdieu, P. (1984). *Homo Academicus*, Paris: Éditions de Minuit.

Bourdieu, P. and Passeron, J-C. (1977). *Reproduction in Education, Society and Culture*, London: Sage.

Bourgois, P. (1986). "The Miskitu of Nicaragua: politicized ethnicity," *Anthropology Today* 2(2): 4–9.

Bown, L. (1990). "Women, literacy and development," Action Aid Development Report, No. 4, London.

Cameron, D. (1985). *Feminism and Linguistic Theory*, London: Macmillan.

Camitta, M. (1993). "Vernacular writing: varieties of literacy among Philadelphia high school students," in B. Street (ed.) *Cross-Cultural Approaches to Literacy*, Cambridge: Cambridge University Press.

Cazden, C. (1978). "Learning to read in classroom interaction," in L. Resnick and P. Weaver (eds.), *Theory and Practice in Early Reading*, Hillsdale, NJ: Lawrence Erlbaum.

Chafe, W. L. and Tannen, D. (1987). "The relation between written and spoken language," *Annual Review of Anthropology* 16: 383–407.

Clanchy, M. T. (1979). *From Memory to Written Record: England 1066–1307*, London: Edward Arnold.

Cole, M. and Nicolopoulou, A. (1992). "Literacy: intellectual consequences," in W. Bright (ed.), *International Encyclopaedia of Linguistics*, vol. 2, New York and Oxford: Oxford University Press.

Collins, J. (1986). "Differential treatment and reading instruction," in J. Cook-Gumperz (ed.), *The Social Construction of Literacy*, Cambridge: Cambridge University Press.

—— (1988). "Language and class in minority education," *Anthropology and Education Quarterly* 19(4): 299–326.

Cook-Gumperz, J. (ed.) (1986). *The Social Construction of Literacy*, Cambridge: Cambridge University Press.

Coulmas, F. (1989). *The Writing Systems of the World*, Oxford: Blackwell.

Council for Social Development (1972). *An Experimental Non-formal Education Project for Rural Women to Promote the Development of the Young Child: Project Design*, New Delhi: Council for Social Development.

—— (1975). *An Experimental Non-formal Education Project for Rural Women to Promote the Development of the Young Child: Final Report*, New Delhi: Council for Social Development.

Crump, T. (1988). "Alternative meanings of literacy in Japan and the West," *Human Organization* 47: 138–45.

Crystal, D. and Davy, D. (1969). *Investigating English Style*, London: Longmans.

Czerniewska, P. (1992). *Learning About Writing*, Oxford: Blackwell.

Davies, A. M. (1986). "Forms of writing in the ancient Mediterranean world," in G. Baumann (ed.) *The Written Word: Literacy in Transition*, Oxford: Clarendon Press.

DeFrancis, J. (1989). *Visible Speech: The Diverse Oneness of Writing Systems*, Honolulu: University of Hawaii Press.

Diringer, D. (1968). *The Alphabet: A Key to the History of Mankind*, 3d ed., London: Hutchinson.

Eisomon, T. (1988). *Benefitting from Basic Education, School Quality and Functional Literacy in Kenya*, Oxford: Pergamon.

Erikson, F. (1982). "Classroom discourse as improvisation: relationships between academic task structure and social participation structure in lessons," in L. C. Wilkinson (ed.) *Communication in the Classroom*, New York: Academic Press.

—— (1984). "School literacy, reasoning and civility: an anthropologist's perspective," *Review of Educational Research* 54(4): 525–46.

—— (1985). "Qualitative methods in research on teaching," in W. Hrock (ed.) *Handbook of Research on Teaching*, New York: Macmillan.

Erikson, F. and Bekker, G. (1986). "On anthropology," in J. Hannaway and M. Lockheed (eds.) *The Contributions of the Social Sciences to Educational Policy and Practice: 1965–1985*, Berkeley: McCutchan.

Everhardt, R. (1983). *Reading, Writing and Resistance: Adolescence and Labour in a Junior High School*, London: Routledge & Kegan Paul.

Ferguson, C. A. (1987). "Literacy in a hunting-gathering society: the case of the Diyari," *Journal of Anthropological Research* 43: 223–37.

Fetterman, D. and Pitman, M. (eds.) (1986). *Educational Evaluation: Ethnography in Theory, Practice and Politics*, Beverly Hills: Sage.

Fingeret, A. (1983). "Social network: a new perspective on independence and illiterate adults," *Adult Education Quarterly* 33(3): 133–46.

Finnegan, R. (1988). *Literacy and Orality: Studies in the Technology of Communication*, Oxford: Blackwell.

Fishman, A. (1991). "'Because this is who we are': writing in the Amish community," in D. Barton and R. Ivanič (eds.) *Writing in the Community*, London: Sage.

Fishman, J. (1986). "Nationality-nationalism and nation-nationism," in J. Fishman, C. Ferguson, and J. Das Gupta (eds.) *Language Problems of Developing Nations*, New York: John Wiley.

Freedman, S., Dyson, A., Flower, I., and Chafe, W. (1987). *Research in Writing: Past, Present and Future*, technical report no. 1, Center for the Study of Writing. Pittsburgh, PA: Carnegie Mellon University.

Furter, P. (1973). *Possibilities and Limitations of Functional Literacy: The Iranian Experiment*, Paris: UNESCO.

Gaur, A. (1984). *A History of Writing*, London: British Library.

Gelb, I. J. (1963). *A Study of Writing*, 2d ed., Chicago: University of Chicago Press.

Gellner, E. (1983). *Nations and Nationalism*, Oxford: Blackwell.

Goody, J. (ed.) (1968). *Literacy in Traditional Societies*, Cambridge: Cambridge University Press.

—— (1977). *The Domestication of the Savage Mind*, Cambridge: Cambridge University Press.

—— (1986). *The Logic of Writing and the Organization of Society*, Cambridge: Cambridge University Press.

—— (1987). *The Interface Between the Written and the Oral*, Cambridge: Cambridge University Press.

Goody, J. and Watt, I. (1963). "The consequences of literacy," *Comparative Studies in Society and History* 5: 304–45.

Graff, H. J. (1979). *The Literacy Myth: Literacy and Social Structure in the Nineteenth Century*, New York: Academic Press.

—— (1987). *The Legacies of Literacy: Continuities and Contradictions in Western Culture and Society*, Bloomington: Indiana University Press.

Grillo, R. (1990). *Social Anthropology and the Politics of Language*, London: Routledge.

Grillo, R. and Rew, A. (eds.) (1985). *Social Anthropology and Development Policy*, ASA Monograph 23, London: Tavistock.

Hanson, J. (1979). *Sociocultural Perspectives on Human Learning: An Introduction to Educational Anthropology*, Englewood Cliffs, NJ: Prentice-Hall.

Harbsmeier, M. (1988). "Inventions of writing," in J. Gledhill, B. Bender, and M. T. Larsen (eds.) *The Emergence and Development of Social Hierarchy and Political Centralization*, One World Archaeology 4, London: Unwin Hyman.

Harris, R. (1986). *The Origin of Writing*, London: Duckworth.

Harris, W. V. (1989). *Ancient Literacy*, Cambridge, MA: Harvard University Press.

Havelock, E. (1976). *Origins of Western Literacy*, Toronto: Ontario Institute of Education.

Heath, S. B. (1983). *Ways with Words: Language, Life, and Work in Communities and Classrooms*, Cambridge: Cambridge University Press.

Houston, R. (1988). *Literacy in Early Modern Europe: Culture and Education 1500–1800*, London: Longman.

Hunter, C. and Harman, D. (1979). *Adult Illiteracy in the United States*, New York: McGraw-Hill.

Hunter, I. M. L. (1985). "Lengthy verbal recall: the role of text," in A. Ellis (ed.) *Progress in the Psychology of Language*, vol. 1, London: Lawrence Erlbaum.

Illich, I. and Sanders, B. (1988). *ABC: The Alphabetization of the Popular Mind*, San Francisco: North Point Press.

Innis, H. A. (1972). *Empire and Communications*, 2d ed., Toronto: University of Toronto Press.

Jackson, M. (1975). "Literacy, communications, and social change: a study of the meaning and effect of literacy in early nineteenth century Maori society," in I. H. Kawheru (ed.) *Conflict and Compromise: Essays on the Maori Since Colonization*, Wellington: A. H. & A. W. Reed.

Kaneko, M. (1987). *The Educational Composition of the World's Population: A Data Base*, Washington, DC: World Bank.

Kay, P. (1977). "Language evolution and speech style," in B. G. Blount and M. Sanches (eds.) *Sociocultural Dimensions of Language Change*, New York: Academic Press.

Kelly, G. (1987). "Setting state policy on women's education in the Third World: perspectives from comparative research," *Comparative Education* 23(1): 95–102.

Kimberley, K., Meek, M., and Miller, J. (1992). *New Readings: Contributions to an Understanding of Literacy*, London: A. & C. Black.

King, L. (1994). *Roots of Identity: Language and Literacy in Mexico*, Stanford, CA: Stanford University Press.

Klassen, C. (1991). "Bilingual literacy: the adult immigrant's account," in D. Barton and R. Ivanič (eds.) *Writing in the Community*, London: Sage.

Ko, Y.-Y. D. (1989). "Toward a social history of women in seventeenth century China," PhD thesis, Stanford University.

Kulick, D. and Stroud, C. (1990). "Christianity, cargo and ideas of self: patterns of literacy in a Papua New Guinea village," *Man* (NS) 25: 286–304.

Lankshear, C. and Lawler, M. (1987). *Literacy, Schooling and Revolution*, Brighton: Falmer Press.

Leap, W. L. (1991). "Pathways and barriers to Indian language literacy-building on the Northern Ute reservation," *Anthropology and Education Quarterly* 22: 21–41.

Lerner, D. (1958). *The Passing of Traditional Society*, Edinburgh: Glencoe Free Press.

Levine, K. (1986). *The Social Context of Literacy*, London: Routledge & Kegan Paul.

Lewis, I. M. (1986). "Literacy and cultural identity in the Horn of Africa: the Somali case," in G. Baumann (ed.) *The Written Word: Literacy in Transition*, Oxford: Clarendon Press.

Lounsbury, F. G. (1989). "The ancient writing of Middle America," in W. Senner (ed.) *The Origins of Writing*, Lincoln: University of Nebraska Press.

MacCaffery, J. (1988). "Combining research and practice," in J. MacCaffery and B. Street (eds.) *Literacy Research in the UK: Adult and School Perspectives*, Lancaster: Research and Practice in Adult Literacy.

Mace, J. (1979). *Working with Words,* London: Chameleon.

—— (1992). *Talking About Literacy,* London: Routledge.

MacKeracher, D. (1989). "Women and literacy," in M. Taylor and J. Draper (eds.) *Adult Literacy Perspectives,* Toronto: Culture Concepts.

McDermott, R., Varenne, H., and Buglione, V. (1982). *"I teach him everything he learns in school": The Acquisition of Literacy for Learning in Working Class Families,* New York: Teachers' College, Columbia University.

McKitterick, R. (1990). *The Carolingians and the Written Word,* Cambridge: Cambridge University Press.

McLaren, P. (1986). *Schooling as a Ritual Performance,* London: Routledge & Kegan Paul.

—— (1988). "Culture or canon? Critical pedagogy and the politics of literacy," *Harvard Educational Review* 58(2): 213–34.

McLaughlin, D. (1989). "The sociolinguistics of Navajo literacy," *Anthropology and Education Quarterly* 20: 275–90.

McLuhan, M. (1962). *The Gutenberg Galaxy,* Toronto: University of Toronto Press.

Meek, M. (1991). *On Being Literate,* London: Bodley Head.

Michaels, S. and Cazden, C. (1986). "Teacher/child collaboration as oral preparation for literacy," in B. Schieffelin and P. Gilmore (eds.) *The Acquisition of Literacy: Ethnographic Perspectives,* Norwood, NJ: Ablex.

Mikulecky, B. (1985). "The Paston letters: an example of literacy in the fifteenth century," unpublished MS.

Moore, H. (1988). *Feminism and Anthropology,* Oxford: Polity.

Norman, J. (1988). *Chinese* (Cambridge Language Surveys), Cambridge: Cambridge University Press.

Olson, D. R. (1977). "From utterance to text: the bias of language in speech and writing," *Harvard Educational Review* 47: 257–81.

Ong, W. J. (1982). *Orality and Literacy: The Technologizing of the Word,* London and New York: Methuen.

Opiyo, M. (1981). "Kenya case study on women's literacy and development projects," *Adult Education and Development* 16: 73–82, Bonn: German Adult Education Association.

Oxenham, J. (1980). *Literacy: Writing, Reading and Social Organization,* London: Routledge & Kegan Paul.

Parsons, T. (1966). *Societies: Evolutionary and Comparative Perspectives,* Englewood Cliffs, NJ: Prentice-Hall.

Parsonson, G. S. (1967). "The literate revolution in Polynesia," *Journal of Pacific History* 2: 169–90.

Pattison, R. (1982). *On Literacy: The Politics of the Word from Homer to the Age of Rock,* New York and Oxford: Oxford University Press.

Philips, S. U. (1975). "Literacy as a mode of communication on the Warm Springs Indian reservation," in E. H. Lenneberg and E. Lenneberg (eds.) *Foundations of Language Development: A Multidisciplinary Approach,* vol. 2, New York: Academic Press.

Reder, S. and Green, K. R. (1983). "Contrasting patterns of literacy in an Alaskan fishing village," *International Journal of the Sociology of Language* 42: 9–39.

Reid, A. (1988). *Southeast Asia in the Age of Commerce: 1450–1680,* New Haven, CT: Yale University Press.

Roberts, J. and Akinsaya, S. (eds.) (1976). *Schooling in the Cultural Context: Anthropological Studies of Education,* New York: David McKay.

Rockhill, K. (1987a). "Gender, language and the politics of literacy," *British Journal of the Sociology of Education* 8(2): 153–67.

—— (1987b). "Literacy as Threat/Desire: longing to be SOMEBODY," in J. S. Gaskell and A. McLaren (eds.) *Women and Education: A Canadian Perspective,* Calgary: Detselig.

Rogers, A. (1992). *Adults Learning for Development,* London: Cassel.

Sampson, G. (1985). *Writing Systems: A Linguistic Introduction,* Stanford, CA: Stanford University Press.

Saraswathi, L. S. and Ravindram, D. J. (1982). "The hidden dreams: the new literates speak," *Adult Education and Development,* 19: 183–88, Bonn: German Adult Education Association.

Schieffelin, B. and Cochran-Smith, M. (1984). "Learning to read culturally: literacy before schooling," in H. Goelman, A. Oberg, and F. Smith (eds.) *Awakening to Literacy,* Exeter, NH: Heinemann.

Schieffelin, B. and Gilmore, P. (eds.) (1986). *The Acquisition of Literacy: Ethnographic Perspectives,* Norwood, NJ: Ablex.

Scollon, R. and Scollon, S. B. K. (1981). *Narrative, Literacy, and Face in Interethnic Communication* (Advances in Discourse Processes series, 7), Norwood, NJ: Ablex.

Scribner, S. and Cole, M. (1981). *The Psychology of Literacy,* Cambridge, MA: Harvard University Press.

Senner, W. (ed.) (1989). *The Origins of Writing,* Lincoln: University of Nebraska Press.

Shuman, A. (1986). *Storytelling Rights: The Uses of Oral and Written Texts by Urban Adolescents,* Cambridge: Cambridge University Press.

Sjostrom, M. and Sjostrom, R. (1983). *How Do You Spell Development?,* Uppsala: Scandinavian Institute of African Studies.

Smalley, W. A., Vang, C. K., and Yang, G. Y. (1990). *Mother of Writing: The Origin and Development of a Hmong Messianic Script,* Chicago: University of Chicago Press.

Smith, A. D. (1986). *The Ethnic Origins of Nations,* Oxford: Blackwell.

——. 1994. "The politics of culture: ethnicity and nationalism," in T. Ingold (ed.) *Companion Encyclopedia of Anthropology,* New York: Routledge, pp. 706–33.

Smith, F. (1983). *Essays into Literacy,* Exeter, NH: Heinemann.

Spindler, G. (1974). *Educational and Cultural Process: Toward an Anthropology of Education,* New York: Holt, Rinehart & Winston.

Spolsky, B., Engelbrecht, G., and Ortiz, L. (1983). "Religious, political, and educational factors in the development of biliteracy in the Kingdom of Tonga,"

Journal of Multilingual and Multicultural Development 4: 459–69.

Spolsky, B. and Irvine, P. (1982). "Sociolinguistic aspects of the acceptance of literacy in the vernacular," in F. Barkin, E. A. Brandt, and J. Ornstein-Galicia (eds.) *Bilingualism and Language Contact: Spanish, English, and Native American Languages*, New York: Teachers' College Press.

Street, B. V. (1984). *Literacy in Theory and Practice*, Cambridge: Cambridge University Press.

—— (1987). "Literacy and social change: the significance of social context in the development of literacy programmes," in D. Wagner (ed.) *The Future of Literacy in a Changing World*, Oxford: Pergamon Press.

—— (ed.) (1993). *Cross-Cultural Approaches to Literacy*, Cambridge: Cambridge University Press.

Stromquist, N. (1989). "Recent developments in women's education: closer to a better social order?" in R. Gallin et al. (eds.) *The Women and International Development Annual*, vol. 1, Boulder, CO: Westview Press.

Szwed, J. F. (1981). "The ethnography of literacy," in M. F. Whiteman (ed.) *Writing: The Nature, Development, and Teaching of Written Communication*, vol. 1, Hillsdale, NJ: Lawrence Erlbaum.

Tannen, D. (1985). "Relative focus on involvement in oral and written discourse," in D. R. Olson, N. Torrance, and A. Hildyard (eds.) *Literacy, Language, and Learning: The Nature and Consequences of Reading and Writing*, Cambridge: Cambridge University Press.

Taylor, D. (1985). *Family Literacy*, London: Heinemann.

Teale, W. H. and Sulzby, E. (eds.) (1986). *Emergent Literacy: Writing and Reading*, Norwood, NJ: Ablex.

Turner, V. (ed.) (1982). *From Ritual to Theatre: the Human Seriousness of Play*, New York: Performing Arts Journal Publications.

Thomas, K. (1986). "The meaning of literacy in early modern England," in G. Baumann (ed.), *The Written Word: Literacy in Transition*, Oxford: Clarendon Press.

UNESCO (1973). *Experimental World Literacy Programme: Practical Guide to Functional Literacy*, Paris: UNESCO.

—— (1976). *The Experimental World Literacy Programme: A Critical Assessment*, Paris: UNESCO.

Varenne, H. and McDermott, R. (1986). "'Why' Sheila can read: structure and indeterminacy in the reproduction of familial literacy," in B. Schieffelin and P. Gilmore (eds.) *The Acquisition of Literacy: Ethnographic Perspectives*, Norwood, NJ: Ablex.

Vulliamy, G., Lewin, K., and Stephens, D. (eds.) (1990). *Doing Educational Research in Developing Countries*, Brighton: Falmer Press.

Wagner, D. (ed.) (1987). *The Future of Literacy in a Changing World*, Oxford: Pergamon Press.

—— (1989). "Literacy campaigns: past, present, and future," *Comparative Educational Review* 33(2): 256–60.

Walker, W. (1981). "Native American writing systems," in C. A. Ferguson and S. B. Heath (eds.) *Language in the USA*, Cambridge: Cambridge University Press.

Weinstein, G. (1993). "Literacy and social process: a community in transition," in B. Street (ed.) *Cross-Cultural Approaches to Literacy*, Cambridge: Cambridge University Press.

Willinsky, J. (1990). *The New Literacy: Redefining Reading and Writing in the Schools*, London: Routledge.

Willis, P. (1977). *Learning to Labour*, Farnborough: Saxon House.

Further Reading

Barton, D. and Ivanič, R. (eds.) (1991). *Writing in the Community*, Newbury Park, CA: Sage.

Coulmas, F. (1989). *The Writing Systems of the World*, Oxford: Blackwell.

Finnegan, R. (1988). *Literacy and Orality: Studies in the Technology of Communication*, Oxford: Blackwell.

Goody, J. (1977). *The Domestication of the Savage Mind*, Cambridge: Cambridge University Press.

—— (ed.) (1968). *Literacy in Traditional Societies*, Cambridge: Cambridge University Press.

Graff, H. J. (1987). *The Legacies of Literacy*, Bloomington: Indiana University Press.

Harris, R. (1986). *The Origin of Writing*, London: Duckworth.

Heath, S. B. (1983). *Ways with Words: Language, Life, and Work in Communities and Classrooms*, Cambridge: Cambridge University Press.

Kimberly, K., Meek, M., and Miller, J. (1992). *New Readings: Contributions to an Understanding of Literacy*, London: A. & C. Black.

Kintgen, E. R., Kroll, B. M., and Rose, M. (eds.) (1988). *Perspectives on Literacy*, Carbondale: Southern Illinois University Press.

Mace, J. (1992). *Talking About Literacy*, London: Routledge.

Meek, M. (1991). *On Being Literate*, London: Bodley Head.

Mercer, N. (ed.) (1988). *Language and Literacy from an Educational Perspective: A Reader*, 2 vols, Milton Keynes: Open University Press.

Säljö, R. (ed.) (1988). *The Written World: Studies in Literate Thought and Action*, Springer Series in Language and Communication no. 23, Berlin and New York: Springer.

Schieffelin, B. and Gilmore, P. (eds.) (1986). *The Acquisition of Literacy: Ethnographic Perspectives*, Advances in Discourse Processes no. 21, Norwood, NJ: Ablex.

Scribner, S. and Cole, M. (1981). *The Psychology of Literacy*, Cambridge, MA: Harvard University Press.

Street, B. V. (1984). *Literacy in Theory and Practice*, Cambridge Studies in Oral and Literate Cultures no. 9, Cambridge: Cambridge University Press.

—— (ed.) (1993). *Cross-Cultural Approaches to Literacy*, Cambridge Studies in Oral and Literate Cultures, Cambridge: Cambridge University Press.

Stubbs, M. (1980). *Language and Literacy: The Sociolinguistics of Reading and Writing*, London and Boston: Routledge & Kegan Paul.

Wagner, D. A. (ed.) (1983). "Literacy and Ethnicity," *International Journal of the Sociology of Language* 42, Berlin: Mouton.

Wagner, D. A. and Puchner, L. D. (1992). *World Literacy in the Year 2000*, Annals of the American Academy of Political and Social Science 520, Newbury Park, CA: Sage.

Willinsky, J. (1990). *The New Literacy: Redefining Reading and Writing in the Schools*, New York: Routledge.

Post-reading Questions / Activities

- Discuss how literacy has been introduced to various societies and how unequal relations might play a role in that introduction.
- Focus on one of the four themes introduced in the second half of the chapter (literacy and nationalism; literacy practices and the construction of gender; literacy and development; or literacy and education) and investigate thoroughly one of the cases mentioned.
- Interview people about their views of literacy. How do the views you collect compare to the models presented by Street and Besnier?
- Given this account of literacy, how do you think we should interpret statistics about the "literacy rate" in various countries? What are they, in fact, measuring?

Vocabulary

alphabetic writing	lingua franca	rebus
consonantal writing system	literacy	register
creole	logographic writing	secondary sign
diglossia	monosyllabic	semiotic
discourse analysis	morpheme	Sinitic
ethnography	orthography	sociolinguistics
featural writing system	phonemic	syllabary
homophones	phonemic writing	syllabic writing
iconic signs	phonological	
ideographic writing	pictographic	

Suggested Further Reading*

Barton, David, Mary Hamilton, and Roz Ivanic, eds. 2000. *Situated Literacies: Reading and Writing in Context.* London and New York: Routledge.

Besnier, Niko. 1995. *Literacy, Emotion, and Authority: Reading and Writing on a Polynesian Atoll.* Cambridge: Cambridge University Press.

Coe, Michael D. 1992. *Breaking the Maya Code.* New York: Thames & Hudson.

DeFrancis, John. 1989. *Visible Speech: The Diverse Oneness of Writing Systems.* Honolulu: University of Hawai'i Press.

Gaur, Albertine. 1984. *A History of Writing.* London: British Library.

Goody, Jack. 1987. *The Interface Between the Written and the Oral.* Cambridge: Cambridge University Press.

Harris, Roy. 1986. *The Origin of Writing.* London: Duckworth.

Heath, Shirley Brice, and Brian V. Street. 2007. "On Ethnography: Approaches to Language and Literacy Research," National Conference on Research in Language and Literacy; Teachers College Columbia.

Hornberger, Nancy, ed. 1996. *Indigenous Literacies in the Americas: Language Planning from the Bottom Up.* Berlin and New York: Mouton de Gruyter.

Kalman, Judy. 1999. *Writing on the Plaza: Mediated Literacy Practice Among Scribes and Clients in Mexico City.* Cresskill NJ: Hampton Press.

Larson, Joanne, ed. 2007. *Literacy as Snake Oil: Beyond the Quick Fix.* New York: Peter Lang. See especially the articles by Gee, Larson, and Coles.

---

*With contributions from Brian Street and Niko Besnier.

Robinson-Pant, Anna, ed. 2004. *Women, Literacy and Development: Alternative Perspectives*. London and New York: Routledge.

Rogers, Alan, ed. 2005. *Urban Literacy: Communication, Identity, and Learning in Development Contexts*. Hamburg, Germany: UNESCO Institute for Education.

Pahl, Kate, and Jennifer Rowsell, eds. 2006. *Travel Notes from the New Literacy Studies: Instances of Practice*. Clevedon: Multilingual Matters.

Sampson, Geoffrey. 1985. *Writing Systems: A Linguistic Approach*. London: Hutchinson.

Saussure, Ferdinand de. 1959. *Course in General Linguistics*. Translated by Wade Baskin. New York: Philosophical Society.

Schmandt-Besserat, Denise. 1992. *Before Writing*. Austin: University of Texas Press.

———. 1996. *How Writing Came About*. Austin: University of Texas Press.

Scribner, Sylvia, and Michael Cole. 1981. *The Psychology of Literacy*. Cambridge, MA: Harvard University Press.

Street, Brian V., ed. 2001. *Literacy and Development: Ethnographic Perspectives*. London and New York: Routledge.

———, ed. 2005. *Literacies Across Educational Contexts: Mediating Learning and Teaching*. Philadelphia: Caslon Publishing.

———, and Adam Lefstein. 2007. *Literacy: An Advanced Resource Book*. London and New York: Routledge.

UNIT 2

LANGUAGE AND THOUGHT

The topic of the relationship between language and thought has captivated writers and readers for centuries. With many precursors, some trace this idea to the nineteenth-century German thinker Humboldt. But the topic is most often associated with the writings of Benjamin Lee Whorf and Edward Sapir. Sometimes the idea that "language determines thought" or its milder form, "language shapes habitual thought," is called the Sapir-Whorf hypothesis, from the two men who wrote sympathetically and foundationally of this view, and sometimes the *linguistic relativity hypothesis.*

Whorf noted, in his paying work as an insurance inspector, that the ways barrels were labeled—"empty" or "full"—affected the ways workers acted around them, despite the fact that barrels "empty" of gasoline were more flammable than full ones. He also studied Mayan and Hopi languages, and noted ways of discussing the world quite disparate from those expressed in the European languages with which he was familiar. Edward Sapir had similarly noted that people's habitual thought tends to follow the "grooves" established by their languages.

This suggestion was traced in work by Brent Berlin and Paul Kay, among others, on color terms, which had sometimes been taken to refute Whorf's claims about the power of language to shape thought. However, since the 1980s new, empirical studies of Whorf's ideas have generated excitement about and refinement of the original concept. John Lucy in particular has attempted to spell out exactly what it would take to confirm or disprove the "hypothesis" that Whorf never quite elucidated, and has then carried out such research. Other recent scholarship, such as that of Stephen Levinson at the Max Planck Institute for Psycholinguistics, has been creative in developing empirical methods for testing this hypothesis.

Suggested Further Reading

Berlin, Brent, and Paul Kay. 1969. *Basic Color Terms: Their Universality and Evolution.* Berkeley: University of California Press.

Bloom, Albert H. 1981. *The Linguistic Shaping of Thought: A Study in the Impact of Language on Thinking in China and the West.* Hillsdale, NJ: Erlbaum.

Boas, Franz. 1966 [1911]. Introduction. In *Handbook of American Indian Languages*, edited by Franz Boas, pp. 1–79. Reprint editor, P. Holder. Lincoln: University of Nebraska Press.

Brown, Penelope, and Stephen C. Levinson. 1993. "'Uphill' and 'Downhill' in Tzeltal." *Journal of Linguistic Anthropology* 3(1): 46–74.

Friedrich, Paul. 1986. *The Language Parallax: Linguistic Relativism and Poetic Indeterminacy.* Austin: University of Texas Press.

Gentner, Dedre, and Susan Goldin-Meadow, eds. 2003. *Language in Mind: Advances in the Study of Language and Thought.* Cambridge, MA: MIT Press.

Gumperz, John J., and Stephen C. Levinson, eds. 1996. *Rethinking Linguistic Relativity.* Cambridge: Cambridge University Press.

Hill, Jane H. 1985. "The Grammar of Consciousness and the Consciousness of Grammar." *American Ethnologist* 12: 725–737.

Hill, Jane H., and Bruce Mannheim. 1992. "Language and World View." *Annual Review of Anthropology* 21: 381–406.

Kay, Paul, and W. Kempton. 1984. "What Is the Sapir-Whorf Hypothesis?" *American Anthropologist* 86: 65–79.

Koerner, E. F. Konrad. 1992. "The Sapir-Whorf Hypothesis: A Preliminary History and a Bibliographic Essay." *Journal of Linguistic Anthropology* 2: 173–198.

Lakoff, George. 1987. *Women, Fire, and Dangerous Things: What Categories Reveal About the Mind.* Chicago: University of Chicago Press. Especially the chapter "Whorf and Relativism."

——, and Mark Johnson. 1980. *Metaphors We Live By.* Chicago: University of Chicago Press.

Levinson, Stephen C. 1996. "Language and Space." *Annual Review of Anthropology* 25: 353–382.

Lucy, John A. 1985. "Whorf's View of the Linguistic Mediation of Thought." In *Semiotic Mediation: Sociocultural and Psychological Perspectives*, edited by E. Mertz and R. J. Parmentier, pp. 73–97. Orlando, FL: Academic Press.

——. 1992a. *Language Diversity and Thought: A Reformulation of the Linguistic Relativity Hypothesis.* Cambridge: Cambridge University Press.

———. 1992b. *Grammatical Categories and Cognition: A Case Study of the Linguistic Relativity Hypothesis.* Cambridge: Cambridge University Press.

———. 1997. "Linguistic Relativity." *Annual Review of Anthropology* 26: 291–312.

———, and Richard A. Shweder. 1979. "Whorf and His Critics: Linguistic and Nonlinguistic Influences on Color Memory." *American Anthropologist* 81: 581–615.

Martin, Laura. 1986. Eskimo Words for Snow. *American Anthropologist* 88, no. 2 (June): 418–423.

Sapir, Edward. 1964 [1931]. "Conceptual Categories in Primitive Languages." In *Language in Culture and Society: A Reader in Linguistics and Anthropology*, edited by Dell H. Hymes. New York: Harper & Row.

Whorf, Benjamin Lee. 1956. *Language, Thought, and Reality: Selected Writings of Benjamin Lee Whorf*, edited by John B. Carroll. Cambridge, MA: MIT Press.

CHAPTER 9

The Relation of Habitual Thought and Behavior to Language

Benjamin Lee Whorf
(1939)

For his entire working life, Benjamin Lee Whorf was an insurance inspector, attempting to discover the causes of industrial accidents and ways of preventing them. (He worked at the very same company, the Hartford Insurance Company in Hartford, Connecticut, where poet Wallace Stevens worked for his complete paying career.) Whorf was a most unusual character. Not only did he have an active intellectual life completely apart from the work that provided his salary, but he was a Theosophist with belief in ESP and other mystical concepts; he also rejected evolution and held deep religious convictions about the literal truth of the Bible. To reconcile the Bible and science, he attempted to learn the original language of the Bible, on the hunch that problems of consistency stemmed from poor translations. In the process of learning ancient languages, he became more and more interested in language for its own sake. This led him to study Maya, Aztec, and Hopi on his own, and finally to Yale, where he studied with Edward Sapir. Though he was offered an academic position, he turned it down.

This chapter presents the classic piece in which Benjamin Lee Whorf makes his suggestion that different languages give rise to different types of "habitual thought," quoting liberally from his teacher, Edward Sapir. Note that he is not saying that it is not possible to understand things in ways different from what our language predisposes us to—in fact it would be impossible for him to understand the Hopi if that were the case—but that in our ordinary, habitual ways of thinking and acting, we tend to follow the patterns established by our language. He is less interested in single words that label objects or activities than in the powerful, fundamental organizing aspects of language (grammar) such as tense or number. Every time we speak (or sign) we must make use of the grammatical categories of our languages. English speakers, for instance, cannot avoid differentiating singular and plural every time they use a noun or verb, which is to say essentially every time they speak (with trivial exceptions). Chinese speakers, in contrast, because of the way their language works, may explicitly label a noun as singular or plural but are not forced by the grammar to do so.

Whorf's ideas have been regarded variously as obvious and trivial, as completely wrong, as partially correct, as essentially correct, or as untestable. More recent attempts to sort these positions out by actually testing his claims have been proliferating. John Lucy has been especially prominent in teasing out what Whorf meant. You are likely to read more about this in the future.

Reading Questions

- How does Whorf explain the risky behavior that people exhibited around "empty" gasoline drums, "spun limestone," kettles of varnish, and other aspects of industrial life? What conclusion does he draw about language and thought from these real-life incidents?

Benjamin Lee Whorf, "The Relation of Habitual Thought and Behavior to Language." In *Language, Thought, and Reality*, ed. by John B. Carroll. Cambridge, MA: MIT Press, 1956, pp. 134–159.

- What are some of the ways that concepts of "time" and "matter" vary between SAE and Hopi? What cultural accompaniments to the linguistic differences does Whorf point to?

Human beings do not live in the objective world alone, nor alone in the world of social activity as ordinarily understood, but are very much at the mercy of the particular language which has become the medium of expression for their society. It is quite an illusion to imagine that one adjusts to reality essentially without the use of language and that language is merely an incidental means of solving specific problems of communication or reflection. The fact of the matter is that the "real world" is to a large extent unconsciously built up on the language habits of the group. . . . We see and hear and otherwise experience very largely as we do because the language habits of our community predispose certain choices of interpretation.   —EDWARD SAPIR

There will probably be general assent to the proposition that an accepted pattern of using words is often prior to certain lines of thinking and forms of behavior, but he who assents often sees in such a statement nothing more than a platitudinous recognition of the hypnotic power of philosophical and learned terminology on the one hand or of catchwords, slogans, and rallying cries on the other. To see only thus far is to miss the point of one of the important interconnections which Sapir saw between language, culture, and psychology, and succinctly expressed in the introductory quotation. It is not so much in these special uses of language as in its constant ways of arranging data and its most ordinary everyday analysis of phenomena that we need to recognize the influence it has on other activities, cultural and personal.

THE NAME OF THE SITUATION AS AFFECTING BEHAVIOR

I came in touch with an aspect of this problem before I had studied under Dr. Sapir, and in a field usually considered remote from linguistics. It was in the course of my professional work for a fire insurance company, in which I undertook the task of analyzing many hundreds of reports of circumstances surrounding the start of fires, and in some cases, of explosions. My analysis was directed toward purely physical conditions, such as defective wiring, presence or lack of air spaces between metal flues and woodwork, etc., and the results were presented in these terms. Indeed it was undertaken with no thought that any other significances would or could be revealed. But in due course it became evident that not only a physical situation *qua* physics, but the meaning of that situation to people, was sometimes a factor, through the behavior of the people, in the start of the fire. And this factor of meaning was clearest when it was a LINGUISTIC MEANING, residing in the name or the linguistic description commonly applied to the situation. Thus, around a storage of what are called "gasoline drums," behavior will tend to a certain type, that is, great care will be exercised; while around a storage of what are called "empty gasoline drums," it will tend to be different—careless, with little repression of smoking or of tossing cigarette stubs about. Yet the "empty" drums are perhaps the more

dangerous, since they contain explosive vapor. Physically the situation is hazardous, but the linguistic analysis according to regular analogy must employ the word 'empty,' which inevitably suggests lack of hazard. The word 'empty' is used in two linguistic patterns: (1) as a virtual synonym for 'null and void, negative, inert,' (2) applied in analysis of physical situations without regard to, e.g., vapor, liquid vestiges, or stray rubbish, in the container. The situation is named in one pattern (2) and the name is then "acted out" or "lived up to" in another (1), this being a general formula for the linguistic conditioning of behavior into hazardous forms.

In a wood distillation plant the metal stills were insulated with a composition prepared from limestone and called at the plant "spun limestone." No attempt was made to protect this covering from excessive heat or the contact of flame. After a period of use, the fire below one of the stills spread to the "limestone," which to everyone's great surprise burned vigorously. Exposure to acetic acid fumes from the stills had converted part of the limestone (calcium carbonate) to calcium acetate. This when heated in a fire decomposes, forming inflammable acetone. Behavior that tolerated fire close to the covering was induced by use of the name "limestone," which because it ends in "-stone" implies non-combustibility.

A huge iron kettle of boiling varnish was observed to be overheated, nearing the temperature at which it would ignite. The operator moved it off the fire and ran it on its wheels to a distance, but did not cover it. In a minute or so the varnish ignited. Here the linguistic influence is more complex; it is due to the metaphorical objectifying (of which more later) of "cause" as contact or the spatial juxtaposition of "things"—to analyzing the situation as 'on' versus 'off' the fire. In reality, the stage when the external fire was the main factor had passed; the overheating was now an internal process of convection in the varnish from the intensely heated kettle, and still continued when 'off' the fire.

An electric glow heater on the wall was little used, and for one workman had the meaning of a convenient coathanger. At night a watchman entered and snapped a switch, which action he verbalized as 'turning on the light'. No light appeared, and this result he verbalized as 'light is burned out'. He could not see the glow of the heater because of the old coat hung on it. Soon the heater ignited the coat, which set fire to the building.

Because of the language used on warning signs, people were not as careful as they should have been.

Study the culture to use the language!

A tannery discharged waste water containing animal matter into an outdoor settling basin partly roofed with wood and partly open. This situation is one that ordinarily would be verbalized as 'pool of water'. A workman had occasion to light a blowtorch near by, and threw his match into the water. But the decomposing waste matter was evolving gas under the wood cover, so that the setup was the reverse of 'watery'. An instant flare of flame ignited the woodwork, and the fire quickly spread into the adjoining building.

A drying room for hides was arranged with a blower at one end to make a current of air along the room and thence outdoors through a vent at the other end. Fire started at a hot bearing on the blower, which blew the flames directly into the hides and fanned them along the room, destroying the entire stock. This hazardous setup followed naturally from the term 'blower' with its linguistic equivalence to 'that which blows', implying that its function necessarily is to 'blow'. Also its function is verbalized as 'blowing air for drying', overlooking that it can blow other things, e.g., flames and sparks. In reality, a blower simply makes a current of air and can exhaust as well as blow. It should have been installed at the vent end to DRAW the air over the hides, then through the hazard (its own casing and bearings), and thence outdoors.

Beside a coal-fired melting pot for lead reclaiming was dumped a pile of "scrap lead"—a misleading verbalization, for it consisted of the lead sheets of old radio condensers, which still had paraffin paper between them. Soon the paraffin blazed up and fired the roof, half of which was burned off.

Such examples, which could be greatly multiplied, will suffice to show how the cue to a certain line of behavior is often given by the analogies of the linguistic formula in which the situation is spoken of, and by which to some degree it is analyzed, classified, and allotted its place in that world which is "to a large extent unconsciously built up on the language habits of the group." And we always assume that the linguistic analysis made by our group reflects reality better than it does.

GRAMMATICAL PATTERNS AS INTERPRETATIONS OF EXPERIENCE

The linguistic material in the above examples is limited to single words, phrases, and patterns of limited range. One cannot study the behavioral compulsiveness of such material without suspecting a much more far-reaching compulsion from large-scale patterning of grammatical categories, such as plurality, gender and similar classifications (animate, inanimate, etc.), tenses, voices, and other verb forms, classifications of the type of "parts of speech," and the matter of whether a given experience is denoted by a unit morpheme, an inflected word, or a syntactical combination. A category such as number (singular vs. plural) is an attempted interpretation of a whole large order of experience, virtually of the world or of nature; it attempts to say how experience is to be segmented, what experience is to be called "one" and what "several." But the difficulty of appraising such a far-reaching influence is great because of its background character, because of the difficulty of standing

aside from our own language, which is a habit and a cultural *non est disputandum*, and scrutinizing it objectively. And if we take a very dissimilar language, this language becomes a part of nature, and we even do to it what we have already done to nature. We tend to think in our own language in order to examine the exotic language. Or we find the task of unraveling the purely morphological intricacies so gigantic that it seems to absorb all else. Yet the problem, though difficult, is feasible; and the best approach is through an exotic language, for in its study we are at long last pushed willy-nilly out of our ruts. Then we find that the exotic language is a mirror held up to our own.

In my study of the Hopi language, what I now see as an opportunity to work on this problem was first thrust upon me before I was clearly aware of the problem. The seemingly endless task of describing the morphology did finally end. Yet it was evident, especially in the light of Sapir's lectures on Navaho, that the description of the LANGUAGE was far from complete. I knew for example the morphological formation of plurals, but not how to use plurals. It was evident that the category of plural in Hopi was not the same thing as in English, French, or German. Certain things that were plural in these languages were singular in Hopi. The phase of investigation which now began consumed nearly two more years.

The work began to assume the character of a comparison between Hopi and western European languages. It also became evident that even the grammar of Hopi bore a relation to Hopi culture, and the grammar of European tongues to our own "Western" or "European" culture. And it appeared that the interrelation brought in those large subsummations of experience by language, such as our own terms 'time', 'space', 'substance', and 'matter'. Since, with respect to the traits compared, there is little difference between English, French, German, or other European languages with the POSSIBLE (but doubtful) exception of Balto-Slavic and non-Indo-European, I have lumped these languages into one group called SAE, or "Standard Average European."

That portion of the whole investigation here to be reported may be summed up in two questions: (1) Are our own concepts of 'time', 'space', and 'matter' given in substantially the same form by experience to all men, or are they in part conditioned by the structure of particular languages? (2) Are there traceable affinities between (a) cultural and behavioral norms and (b) large-scale linguistic patterns? (I should be the last to pretend that there is anything so definite as "a correlation" between culture and language, and especially between ethnological rubrics such as 'agricultural, hunting', etc., and linguistic ones like 'inflected', 'synthetic', or 'isolating'.) When I began the study, the problem was by no means so clearly formulated, and I had little notion that the answers would turn out as they did.

PLURALITY AND NUMERATION IN SAE AND HOPI

In our language, that is SAE, plurality and cardinal numbers are applied in two ways: to real plurals and imaginary plurals.

The same rules for pluralization apply to both things we can objectively experience as plurals and those that are metaphorical.

CHAPTER 9 The Relation of Habitual Thought and Behavior to Language   75

Or more exactly if less tersely: perceptible spatial aggregates and metaphorical aggregates. We say 'ten men' and also 'ten days'. Ten men either are or could be objectively perceived as ten, ten in one group perception[2]—ten men on a street corner, for instance. But 'ten days' cannot be objectively experienced. We experience only one day, today; the other nine (or even all ten) are something conjured up from memory or imagination. If 'ten days' be regarded as a group, it must be as an "imaginary," mentally constructed group. Whence comes this mental pattern? Just as in the case of the fire-causing errors, from the fact that our language confuses the two different situations, has but one pattern for both. When we speak of 'ten steps forward, ten strokes on a bell', or any similarly described cyclic sequence, "times" of any sort, we are doing the same thing as with 'days'. CYCLICITY brings the response of imaginary plurals. But a likeness of cyclicity to aggregates is not unmistakably given by experience prior to language, or it would be found in all languages, and it is not.

Our AWARENESS of time and cyclicity does contain something immediate and subjective—the basic sense of "becoming later and later." But, in the habitual thought of us SAE people, this is covered under something quite different, which though mental should not be called subjective. I call it OBJECTIFIED, or imaginary, because it is patterned on the OUTER world. It is this that reflects our linguistic usage. Our tongue makes no distinction between numbers counted on discrete entities and numbers that are simply "counting itself." Habitual thought then assumes that in the latter the numbers are just as much counted on "something" as in the former. This is objectification. Concepts of time lose contact with the subjective experience of "becoming later" and are objectified as counted QUANTITIES, especially as lengths, made up of units as a length can be visibly marked off into inches. A 'length of time' is envisioned as a row of similar units, like a row of bottles.

In Hopi there is a different linguistic situation. Plurals and cardinals are used only for entities that form or can form an objective group. There are no imaginary plurals, but instead ordinals used with singulars. Such an expression as 'ten days' is not used. The equivalent statement is an operational one that reaches one day by a suitable count. 'They stayed ten days' becomes 'they stayed until the eleventh day' or 'they left after the tenth day'. 'Ten days is greater than nine days' becomes 'the tenth day is later than the ninth'. Our "length of time" is not regarded as a length but as a relation between two events in lateness. Instead of our linguistically promoted objectification of that datum of consciousness we call 'time', the Hopi language has not laid down any pattern that would cloak the subjective "becoming later" that is the essence of time.

Time = 2 events in the past, not quantities

NOUNS OF PHYSICAL QUANTITY IN SAE AND HOPI

We have two kinds of nouns denoting physical things: individual nouns, and mass nouns (e.g., 'water, milk, wood, granite, sand, flour, meat'). Individual nouns denote bodies with definite outlines: 'a tree, a stick, a man, a hill'. Mass nouns denote homogeneous continua without implied boundar-

ies. The distinction is marked by linguistic form; e.g., mass nouns lack plurals,[3] in English drop articles, and in French take the partitive article *du, de la, des*. The distinction is more widespread in language than in the observable appearance of things. Rather few natural occurrences present themselves as unbounded extents; 'air' of course, and often 'water, rain, snow, sand, rock, dirt, grass'. We do not encounter 'butter, meat, cloth, iron, glass', or most "materials" in such kind of manifestation, but in bodies small or large with definite outlines. The distinction is somewhat forced upon our description of events by an unavoidable pattern in language. It is so inconvenient in a great many cases that we need some way of individualizing the mass noun by further linguistic devices. This is partly done by names of body-types: 'stick of wood, piece of cloth, pane of glass, cake of soap'; also, and even more, by introducing names of containers though their contents be the real issue: 'glass of water, cup of coffee, dish of food, bag of flour, bottle of beer'. These very common container formulas, in which 'of' has an obvious, visually perceptible meaning ("contents"), influence our feeling about the less obvious type-body formulas: 'stick of wood, lump of dough,' etc. The formulas are very similar: individual noun plus a similar relator (English 'of'). In the obvious case this relator denotes contents. In the inobvious one it "suggests" contents. Hence the 'lumps, chunks, blocks, pieces', etc., seem to contain something, a "stuff," "substance," or "matter" that answers to the 'water', 'coffee', or 'flour' in the container formulas. So with SAE people the philosophic "substance" and "matter" are also the naïve idea; they are instantly acceptable, "common sense." It is so through linguistic habit. Our language patterns often require us to name a physical thing by a binomial that splits the reference into a formless item plus a form.

Hopi is again different. It has a formally distinguished class of nouns. But this class contains no formal subclass of mass nouns. All nouns have an individual sense and both singular and plural forms. Nouns translating most nearly our mass nouns still refer to vague bodies or vaguely bounded extents. They imply indefiniteness, but not lack, of outline and size. In specific statements, 'water' means one certain mass or quantity of water, not what we call "the substance water." Generality of statement is conveyed through the verb or predicator, not the noun. Since nouns are individual already, they are not individualized by either type-bodies or names of containers, if there is no special need to emphasize shape or container. The noun itself implies a suitable type-body or container. One says, not 'a glass of water' but *kə·yi* 'a water', not 'a pool of water' but *pa·hə*,[4] not 'a dish of cornflour' but *ŋəmni* 'a (quantity of) cornflour', not 'a piece of meat' but *sikʷi* 'a meat'. The language has neither need for nor analogies on which to build the concept of existence as a duality of formless item and form. It deals with formlessness through other symbols than nouns.

PHASES OF CYCLES IN SAE AND HOPI

Such terms as 'summer, winter, September, morning, noon, sunset' are with us nouns, and have little formal linguistic difference from other nouns. They can be subjects or objects,

substance - Glass of water.

Matter. Chunk of cheese.

all nouns are definite; verbs indicate "vague body."

and we say 'at sunset' or 'in winter' just as we say 'at a corner' or 'in an orchard'.[5] They are pluralized and numerated like nouns of physical objects, as we have seen. Our thought about the referents of such words hence becomes objectified. Without objectification, it would be a subjective experience of real time, i.e., of the consciousness of "becoming later and later"—simply a cyclic phase similar to an earlier phase in that ever-later-becoming duration. Only by imagination can such a cyclic phase be set beside another and another in the manner of a spatial (i.e., visually perceived) configuration. But such is the power of linguistic analogy that we do so objectify cyclic phasing. We do it even by saying 'a phase' and 'phases' instead of, e.g., 'phasing'. And the pattern of individual and mass nouns, with the resulting binomial formula of formless item plus form, is so general that it is implicit for all nouns, and hence our very generalized formless items like 'substance, matter', by which we can fill out the binomial for an enormously wide range of nouns. But even these are not quite generalized enough to take in our phase nouns. So for the phase nouns we have made a formless item, 'time'. We have made it by using 'a time', i.e., an occasion or a phase, in the pattern of a mass noun, just as from 'a summer' we make 'summer' in the pattern of a mass noun. Thus with our binomial formula we can say and think 'a moment of time, a second of time, a year of time'. Let me again point out that the pattern is simply that of 'a bottle of milk' or 'a piece of cheese'. Thus we are assisted to imagine that 'a summer' actually contains or consists of such-and-such a quantity of 'time'.

In Hopi however all phase terms, like 'summer, morning', etc., are not nouns but a kind of adverb, to use the nearest SAE analogy. They are a formal part of speech by themselves, distinct from nouns, verbs, and even other Hopi "adverbs." Such a word is not a case form or a locative pattern, like 'des Abends' or 'in the morning'. It contains no morpheme like one of 'in the house' or 'at the tree'.[6] It means 'when it is morning' or 'while morning-phase is occurring'. These "temporals" are not used as subjects or objects, or at all like nouns. One does not say 'it's a hot summer' or 'summer is hot'; summer is not hot, summer is only WHEN conditions are hot, WHEN heat occurs. One does not say 'THIS summer', but 'summer now' or 'summer recently'. There is no objectification, as a region, an extent, a quantity, of the subjective duration-feeling. Nothing is suggested about time except the perpetual "getting later" of it. And so there is no basis here for a formless item answering to our 'time'.

TEMPORAL FORMS OF VERBS IN SAE AND HOPI

The three-tense system of SAE verbs colors all our thinking about time. This system is amalgamated with that larger scheme of objectification of the subjective experience of duration already noted in other patterns—in the binomial formula applicable to nouns in general, in temporal nouns, in plurality and numeration. This objectification enables us in imagination to "stand time units in a row." Imagination

of time as like a row harmonizes with a system of THREE tenses; whereas a system of TWO, an earlier and a later, would seem to correspond better to the feeling of duration as it is experienced. For if we inspect consciousness we find no past, present, future, but a unity embracing complexity. EVERYTHING IS in consciousness, and everything in consciousness IS, and is together. There is in it a sensuous and a nonsensuous. We may call the sensuous—what we are seeing, hearing, touching—the 'present' while in the nonsensuous the vast image-world of memory is being labeled 'the past' and another realm of belief, intuition, and uncertainty 'the future'; yet sensation, memory, foresight, all are in consciousness together—one is not "yet to be" nor another "once but no more." Where real time comes in is that all this in consciousness is "getting later," changing certain relations in an irreversible manner. In this "latering" or "durating" there seems to me to be a paramount contrast between the newest, latest instant at the focus of attention and the rest—the earlier. Languages by the score get along well with two tenselike forms answering to this paramount relation of "later" to "earlier." We can of course CONSTRUCT AND CONTEMPLATE IN THOUGHT a system of past, present, future, in the objectified configuration of points on a line. This is what our general objectification tendency leads us to do and our tense system confirms.

In English the present tense seems the one least in harmony with the paramount temporal relation. It is as if pressed into various and not wholly congruous duties. One duty is to stand as objectified middle term between objectified past and objectified future, in narration, discussion, argument, logic, philosophy. Another is to denote inclusion in the sensuous field: 'I SEE him.' Another is for nomic, i.e., customarily or generally valid, statements: 'We SEE with our eyes.' These varied uses introduce confusions of thought, of which for the most part we are unaware.

Hopi, as we might expect, is different here too. Verbs have no "tenses" like ours, but have validity-forms ("assertions"), aspects, and clause-linkage forms (modes), that yield even greater precision of speech. The validity-forms denote that the speaker (not the subject) reports the situation (answering to our past and present) or that he expects it (answering to our future)[7] or that he makes a nomic statement (answering to our nomic present). The aspects denote different degrees of duration and different kinds of tendency "during duration." As yet we have noted nothing to indicate whether an event is sooner or later than another when both are REPORTED. But need for this does not arise until we have two verbs: i.e., two clauses. In that case the "modes" denote relations between the clauses, including relations of later to earlier and of simultaneity. Then there are many detached words that express similar relations, supplementing the modes and aspects. The duties of our three-tense system and its tripartite linear objectified "time" are distributed among various verb categories, all different from our tenses; and there is no more basis for an objectified time in Hopi verbs than in other Hopi patterns; although this does not in the least hinder the verb forms and other patterns from being closely adjusted to the pertinent realities of actual situations.

Duration, Intensity, and Tendency in SAE and Hopi

To fit discourse to manifold actual situations, all languages need to express durations, intensities, and tendencies. It is characteristic of SAE and perhaps of many other language types to express them metaphorically. The metaphors are those of spatial extension, i.e., of size, number (plurality), position, shape, and motion. We express duration by 'long, short, great, much, quick, slow', etc.; intensity by 'large, great, much, heavy, light, high, low, sharp, faint', etc.; tendency by 'more, increase, grow, turn, get, approach, go, come, rise, fall, stop, smooth, even, rapid, slow'; and so on through an almost inexhaustible list of metaphors that we hardly recognize as such, since they are virtually the only linguistic media available. The nonmetaphorical terms in this field, like 'early, late, soon, lasting, intense, very, tending', are a mere handful, quite inadequate to the needs.

It is clear how this condition "fits in." It is part of our whole scheme of OBJECTIFYING—imaginatively spatializing qualities and potentials that are quite nonspatial (so far as any spatially perceptive senses can tell us). Noun-meaning (with us) proceeds from physical bodies to referents of far other sort. Since physical bodies and their outlines in PERCEIVED SPACE are denoted by size and shape terms and reckoned by cardinal numbers and plurals, these patterns of denotation and reckoning extend to the symbols of nonspatial meanings, and so suggest an IMAGINARY SPACE. Physical shapes 'move, stop, rise, sink, approach', etc., in perceived space; why not these other referents in their imaginary space? This has gone so far that we can hardly refer to the simplest nonspatial situation without constant resort to physical metaphors. I "grasp" the "thread" of another's arguments, but if its "level" is "over my head" my attention may "wander" and "lose touch" with the "drift" of it, so that when he "comes" to his "point" we differ "widely," our "views" being indeed so "far apart" that the "things" he says "appear" "much" too arbitrary, or even "a lot" of nonsense!

The absence of such metaphor from Hopi speech is striking. Use of space terms when there is no space involved is NOT THERE—as if on it had been laid the taboo teetotal! The reason is clear when we know that Hopi has abundant conjugational and lexical means of expressing duration, intensity, and tendency directly as such, and that major grammatical patterns do not, as with us, provide analogies for an imaginary space. The many verb "aspects" express duration and tendency of manifestations, while some of the "voices" express intensity, tendency, and duration of causes or forces producing manifestations. Then a special part of speech, the "tensors," a huge class of words, denotes only intensity, tendency, duration, and sequence. The function of the tensors is to express intensities, "strengths," and how they continue or vary, their rate of change; so that the broad concept of intensity, when considered as necessarily always varying and/or continuing, includes also tendency and duration. Tensors convey distinctions of degree, rate, constancy, repetition, increase and decrease of intensity, immediate sequence, interruption or sequence after an interval, etc., also QUALITIES of strengths, such as we should express metaphorically as smooth, even, hard, rough. A striking feature is their lack of resemblance to the terms of real space and movement that to us "mean the same." There is not even more than a trace of apparent derivation from space terms.[8] So, while Hopi in its nouns seems highly concrete, here in the tensors it becomes abstract almost beyond our power to follow.

Habitual Thought in SAE and Hopi

The comparison now to be made between the habitual thought worlds of SAE and Hopi speakers is of course incomplete. It is possible only to touch upon certain dominant contrasts that appear to stem from the linguistic differences already noted. By "habitual thought" and "thought world" I mean more than simply language, i.e., than the linguistic patterns themselves. I include all the analogical and suggestive value of the patterns (e.g., our "imaginary space" and its distant implications), and all the give-and-take between language and the culture as a whole, wherein is a vast amount that is not linguistic but yet shows the shaping influence of language. In brief, this "thought world" is the microcosm that each man carries about within himself, by which he measures and understands what he can of the macrocosm.

The SAE microcosm has analyzed reality largely in terms of what it calls "things" (bodies and quasibodies) plus modes of extensional but formless existence that it calls "substances" or "matter." It tends to see existence through a binomial formula that expresses any existent as a spatial form plus a spatial formless continuum related to the form, as contents is related to the outlines of its container. Nonspatial existents are imaginatively spatialized and charged with similar implications of form and continuum.

The Hopi microcosm seems to have analyzed reality largely in terms of EVENTS (or better "eventing"), referred to in two ways, objective and subjective. Objectively, and only if perceptible physical experience, events are expressed mainly as outlines, colors, movements, and other perceptive reports. Subjectively, for both the physical and nonphysical, events are considered the expression of invisible intensity factors, on which depend their stability and persistence, or their fugitiveness and proclivities. It implies that existents do not "become later and later" all in the same way; but some do so by growing like plants, some by diffusing and vanishing, some by a procession of metamorphoses, some by enduring in one shape till affected by violent forces. In the nature of each existent able to manifest as a definite whole is the power of its own mode of duration: its growth, decline, stability, cyclicity, or creativeness. Everything is thus already "prepared" for the way it now manifests by earlier phases, and what it will be later, partly has been, and partly is in act of being so "prepared." An emphasis and importance rests on this preparing or being prepared aspect of the world that may to the Hopi correspond to that "quality of reality" that 'matter' or 'stuff' has for us.

HABITUAL BEHAVIOR FEATURES OF HOPI CULTURE

Our behavior, and that of Hopi, can be seen to be coordinated in many ways to the linguistically conditioned microcosm. As in my fire casebook, people act about situations in ways which are like the ways they talk about them. A characteristic of Hopi behavior is the emphasis on preparation. This includes announcing and getting ready for events well beforehand, elaborate precautions to insure persistence of desired conditions, and stress on good will as the preparer of right results. Consider the analogies of the day-counting pattern alone. Time is mainly reckoned "by day" (taLk, -tala) or "by night" (tok), which words are not nouns but tensors, the first formed on a root "light, day," the second on a root "sleep." The count is by ORDINALS. This is not the pattern of counting a number of different men or things, even though they appear successively, for, even then, they COULD gather into an assemblage. It is the pattern of counting successive reappearances of the SAME man or thing, incapable of forming an assemblage. The analogy is not to behave about day-cyclicity as to several men ("several days"), which is what WE tend to do, but to behave as to the successive visits of the SAME MAN. One does not alter several men by working upon just one, but one can prepare and so alter the later visits of the same man by working to affect the visit he is making now. This is the way the Hopi deal with the future—by working within a present situation which is expected to carry impresses, both obvious and occult, forward into the future event of interest. One might say that Hopi society understands our proverb 'Well begun is half done,' but not our 'Tomorrow is another day.' This may explain much in Hopi character.

This Hopi preparing behavior may be roughly divided into announcing, outer preparing, inner preparing, covert participation, and persistence. Announcing, or preparative publicity, is an important function in the hands of a special official, the Crier Chief. Outer preparing is preparation involving much visible activity, not all necessarily directly useful within our understanding. It includes ordinary practicing, rehearsing, getting ready, introductory formalities, preparing of special food, etc. (all of these to a degree that may seem overelaborate to us), intensive sustained muscular activity like running, racing, dancing, which is thought to increase the intensity of development of events (such as growth of crops), mimetic and other magic, preparations based on esoteric theory involving perhaps occult instruments like prayer sticks, prayer feathers, and prayer meal, and finally the great cyclic ceremonies and dances, which have the significance of preparing rain and crops. From one of the verbs meaning "prepare" is derived the noun for "harvest" or "crop": *na'twani* 'the prepared' or the 'in preparation.'[9]

Inner preparing is use of prayer and meditation, and at lesser intensity good wishes and good will, to further desired results. Hopi attitudes stress the power of desire and thought. With their "microcosm" it is utterly natural that they should. Desire and thought are the earliest, and therefore the most important, most critical and crucial, stage of preparing. Moreover, to the Hopi, one's desires and thoughts influence not only his own actions, but all nature as well. This too is wholly natural. Consciousness itself is aware of work, of the feel of effort and energy, in desire and thinking. Experience more basic than language tells us that, if energy is expended, effects are produced. WE tend to believe that our bodies can stop up this energy, prevent it from affecting other things until we will our BODIES to overt action. But this may be so only because we have our own linguistic basis for a theory that formless items like "matter" are things in themselves, malleable only by similar things, by more matter, and hence insulated from the powers of life and thought. It is no more unnatural to think that thought contacts everything and pervades the universe than to think, as we all do, that light kindled outdoors does this. And it is not unnatural to suppose that thought, like any other force, leaves everywhere traces of effect. Now, when WE think of a certain actual rosebush, we do not suppose that our thought goes to that actual bush, and engages with it, like a searchlight turned upon it. What then do we suppose our consciousness is dealing with when we are thinking of that rosebush? Probably we think it is dealing with a "mental image" which is not the rosebush but a mental surrogate of it. But why should it be NATURAL to think that our thought deals with a surrogate and not with the real rosebush? Quite possibly because we are dimly aware that we carry about with us a whole imaginary space, full of mental surrogates. To us, mental surrogates are old familiar fare. Along with the images of imaginary space, which we perhaps secretly know to be only imaginary, we tuck the thought-of actually existing rosebush, which may be quite another story, perhaps just because we have that very convenient "place" for it. The Hopi thought-world has no imaginary space. The corollary to this is that it may not locate thought dealing with real space anywhere but in real space, nor insulate real space from the effects of thought. A Hopi would naturally suppose that his thought (or he himself) traffics with the actual rosebush—or more likely, corn plant—that he is thinking about. The thought then should leave some trace of itself with the plant in the field. If it is a good thought, one about health and growth, it is good for the plant; if a bad thought, the reverse.

The Hopi emphasize the intensity-factor of thought. Thought to be most effective should be vivid in consciousness, definite, steady, sustained, charged with strongly felt good intentions. They render the idea in English as 'concentrating, holding it in your heart, putting your mind on it, earnestly hoping.' Thought power is the force behind ceremonies, prayer sticks, ritual smoking, etc. The prayer pipe is regarded as an aid to "concentrating" (so said my informant). Its name, *na'twanpi,* means 'instrument of preparing.'

Covert participation is mental collaboration from people who do not take part in the actual affair, be it a job of work, hunt, race, or ceremony, but direct their thought and good will toward the affair's success. Announcements often seek to enlist the support of such mental helpers as well as of overt participants, and contain exhortations to the people to aid with their active good will.[10] A similarity to our concepts of a sympathetic audience or the cheering section at a football game should not obscure the fact that it is primarily the power of directed thought, and not merely sympathy or encouragement, that is expected of covert participants. In fact these latter get in their deadliest work before, not during, the game! A corollary to the power of thought is the power of wrong thought for evil; hence one purpose of covert participation is to obtain the mass force of many good wishers to offset the harmful thought of ill wishers. Such attitudes greatly favor cooperation and community spirit. Not that the Hopi community is not full of rivalries and colliding interests. Against the tendency to social disintegration in such a small, isolated group, the theory of "preparing" by the power of thought, logically leading to the great power of the combined, intensified, and harmonized thought of the whole community, must help vastly toward the rather remarkable degree of cooperation that, in spite of much private bickering, the Hopi village displays in all the important cultural activities.

Hopi "preparing" activities again show a result of their linguistic thought background in an emphasis on persistence and constant insistent repetition. A sense of the cumulative value of innumerable small momenta is dulled by an objectified, spatialized view of time like ours, enhanced by a way of thinking close to the subjective awareness of duration, of the ceaseless "latering" of events. To us, for whom time is a motion on a space, unvarying repetition seems to scatter its force along a row of units of that space, and be wasted. To the Hopi, for whom time is not a motion but a "getting later" of everything that has ever been done, unvarying repetition is not wasted but accumulated. It is storing up an invisible change that holds over into later events.[11] As we have seen, it is as if the return of the day were felt as the return of the same person, a little older but with all the impresses of yesterday, not as "another day," i.e., like an entirely different person. This principle joined with that of thought-power and with traits of general Pueblo culture is expressed in the theory of the Hopi ceremonial dance for furthering rain and crops, as well as in its short, piston-like tread, repeated thousands of times, hour after hour.

SOME IMPRESSES OF LINGUISTIC HABIT IN WESTERN CIVILIZATION

It is harder to do justice in few words to the linguistically conditioned features of our own culture than in the case of the Hopi, because of both vast scope and difficulty of objectivity—because of our deeply ingrained familiarity with the attitudes to be analyzed. I wish merely to sketch certain characteristics adjusted to our linguistic binomialism of form plus formless item or "substance," to our metaphoricalness, our imaginary space, and our objectified time. These, as we have seen, are linguistic.

From the form-plus-substance dichotomy the philosophical views most traditionally characteristic of the "Western world" have derived huge support. Here belong materialism, psychophysical parallelism, physics—at least in its traditional Newtonian form—and dualistic views of the universe in general. Indeed here belongs almost everything that is "hard, practical common sense." Monistic, holistic, and relativistic views of reality appeal to philosophers and some scientists, but they are badly handicapped in appealing to the "common sense" of the Western average man—not because Nature herself refutes them (if she did, philosophers could have discovered this much), but because they must be talked about in what amounts to a new language. "Common sense," as its name shows, and "practicality" as its name does not show, are largely matters of talking so that one is readily understood. It is sometimes stated that Newtonian space, time, and matter are sensed by everyone intuitively, whereupon relativity is cited as showing how mathematical analysis can prove intuition wrong. This, besides being unfair to intuition, is an attempt to answer offhand question (1) put at the outset of this [discussion], to answer which this research was undertaken. Presentation of the findings now nears its end, and I think the answer is clear. The offhand answer, laying the blame upon intuition for our slowness in discovering mysteries of the Cosmos, such as relativity, is the wrong one. The right answer is: Newtonian space, time, and matter are no intuitions. They are recepts from culture and language. That is where Newton got them.

Our objectified view of time is, however, favorable to historicity and to everything connected with the keeping of records, while the Hopi view is unfavorable thereto. The latter is too subtle, complex, and ever-developing, supplying no ready-made answer to the question of when "one" event ends and "another" begins. When it is implicit that everything that ever happened still is, but is in a necessarily different form from what memory or record reports, there is less incentive to study the past. As for the present, the incentive would be not to record it but to treat it as "preparing." But OUR objectified time puts before imagination something like a ribbon or scroll marked off into equal blank spaces, suggesting that each be filled with an entry. Writing has no doubt helped toward our linguistic treatment of time, even as the linguistic treatment has guided the uses of writing. Through this give-and-take between language and the whole culture we get, for instance:

1. Records, diaries, bookkeeping, accounting, mathematics stimulated by accounting.
2. Interest in exact sequence, dating, calendars, chronology, clocks, time wages, time graphs, time as used in physics.
3. Annals, histories, the historical attitude, interest in the past, archaeology, attitudes of introjection toward past periods, e.g., classicism, romanticism.

Just as we conceive our objectified time as extending in the future in the same way that it extends in the past, so we set down our estimates of the future in the same shape as our records of the past, producing programs, schedules, budgets. The formal equality of the spacelike units by which we measure and conceive time leads us to consider the "formless item" or "substance" of time to be homogeneous and in ratio to the number of units. Hence our prorata allocation of value to time, lending itself to the building up of a commercial structure based on time-prorata values: time wages (time work constantly supersedes piece work), rent, credit, interest, depreciation charges, and insurance premiums. No doubt this vast system, once built, would continue to run under any sort of linguistic treatment of time; but that it should have been built at all, reaching the magnitude and particular form it has in the Western world, is a fact decidedly in consonance with the patterns of the SAE languages. Whether such a civilization as ours would be possible with widely different linguistic handling of time is a large question—in our civilization, our linguistic patterns and the fitting of our behavior to the temporal order are what they are, and they are in accord. We are of course stimulated to use calendars, clocks, and watches, and to try to measure time ever more precisely; this aids science, and science in turn, following these well-worn cultural grooves, gives back to culture an ever-growing store of applications, habits, and values, with which culture again directs science. But what lies outside this spiral? Science is beginning to find that there is something in the Cosmos that is not in accord with the concepts we have formed in mounting the spiral. It is trying to frame a NEW LANGUAGE by which to adjust itself to a wider universe.

It is clear how the emphasis on "saving time" which goes with all the above and is very obvious objectification of time, leads to a high valuation of "speed," which shows itself a great deal in our behavior.

Still another behavioral effect is that the character of monotony and regularity possessed by our image of time as an evenly scaled limitless tape measure persuades us to behave as if that monotony were more true of events than it really is. That is, it helps to routinize us. We tend to select and favor whatever bears out this view, to "play up to" the routine aspects of existence. One phase of this is behavior evincing a false sense of security or an assumption that all will always go smoothly, and a lack in foreseeing and protecting ourselves against hazards. Our technique of harnessing energy does well in routine performance, and it is along routine lines that we chiefly strive to improve it—we are, for example, relatively uninterested in stopping the energy from causing accidents, fires, and explosions, which it is doing constantly and on a wide scale. Such indifference to the unexpectedness of life would be disastrous to a society as small, isolated, and precariously poised as the Hopi society is, or rather once was.

Thus our linguistically determined thought world not only collaborates with our cultural idols and ideals, but engages even our unconscious personal reactions in its patterns and gives them certain typical characters. One such character, as we have seen, is CARELESSNESS, as in reckless driving or throwing cigarette stubs into waste paper. Another of a different sort is GESTURING when we talk. Very

many of the gestures made by English-speaking people at least, and probably by all SAE speakers, serve to illustrate, by a movement in space, not a real spatial reference but one of the nonspatial references that our language handles by metaphors of imaginary space. That is, we are more apt to make a grasping gesture when we speak of grasping an elusive idea than when we speak of grasping a doorknob. The gesture seeks to make a metaphorical and hence somewhat unclear reference more clear. But, if a language refers to nonspatials without implying a spatial analogy, the reference is not made any clearer by gesture. The Hopi gesture very little, perhaps not at all in the sense we understand as gesture.

It would seem as if kinesthesia, or the sensing of muscular movement, though arising before language, should be made more highly conscious by linguistic use of imaginary space and metaphorical images of motion. Kinesthesia is marked in two facets of European culture: art and sport. European sculpture, an art in which Europe excels, is strongly kinesthetic, conveying great sense of the body's motions; European painting likewise. The dance in our culture expresses delight in motion rather than symbolism or ceremonial, and our music is greatly influenced by our dance forms. Our sports are strongly imbued with this element of the "poetry of motion." Hopi races and games seem to emphasize rather the virtues of endurance and sustained intensity. Hopi dancing is highly symbolic and is performed with great intensity and earnestness, but has not much movement or swing.

Synesthesia, or suggestion by certain sense receptions of characters belonging to another sense, as of light and color by sounds and vice versa, should be made more conscious by a linguistic metaphorical system that refers to nonspatial experiences by terms for spatial ones, though undoubtedly it arises from a deeper source. Probably in the first instance metaphor arises from synesthesia and not the reverse; yet metaphor need not become firmly rooted in linguistic pattern, as Hopi shows. Nonspatial experience has one well-organized sense, HEARING—for smell and taste are but little organized. Nonspatial consciousness is a realm chiefly of thought, feeling, and SOUND. Spatial consciousness is a realm of light, color, sight, and touch, and presents shapes and dimensions. Our metaphorical system, by naming nonspatial experiences after spatial ones, imputes to sounds, smells, tastes, emotions, and thoughts qualities like the colors, luminosities, shapes, angles, textures, and motions of spatial experience. And to some extent the reverse transference occurs; for, after much talking about tones as high, low, sharp, dull, heavy, brilliant, slow, the talker finds it easy to think of some factors in spatial experience as like factors of tone. Thus we speak of "tones" of color, a gray "monotone," a "loud" necktie, a "taste" in dress: all spatial metaphor in reverse. Now European art is distinctive in the way it seeks deliberately to play with synesthesia. Music tries to suggest scenes, color, movement, geometric design; painting and sculpture are often consciously guided by the analogies of music's rhythm; colors are conjoined with feeling for the analogy to concords and discords. The European theater and opera seek a synthesis of many arts. It may be that in this way our metaphorical language that is in some sense a confusion of thought is producing, through art, a result of far-reaching value—a deeper esthetic sense leading toward a more direct apprehension of underlying unity behind the phenomena so variously reported by our sense channels.

HISTORICAL IMPLICATIONS

How does such a network of language, culture, and behavior come about historically? Which was first: the language patterns or the cultural norms? In main they have grown up together, constantly influencing each other. But in this partnership the nature of the language is the factor that limits free plasticity and rigidifies channels of development in the more autocratic way. This is so because a language is a system, not just an assemblage of norms. Large systematic outlines can change to something really new only very slowly, while many other cultural innovations are made with comparative quickness. Language thus represents the mass mind; it is affected by inventions and innovations, but affected little and slowly, whereas TO inventors and innovators it legislates with the decree immediate.

The growth of the SAE language-culture complex dates from ancient times. Much of its metaphorical reference to the nonspatial by the spatial was already fixed in the ancient tongues, and more especially in Latin. It is indeed a marked trait of Latin. If we compare, say Hebrew, we find that, while Hebrew has some allusion to not-space as space, Latin has more. Latin terms for nonspatials, like *educo, religio, principia, comprehendo*, are usually metaphorized physical references: lead out, tying back, etc. This is not true of all languages—it is quite untrue of Hopi. The fact that in Latin the direction of development happened to be from spatial to nonspatial (partly because of secondary stimulation to abstract thinking when the intellectually crude Romans encountered Greek culture) and that later tongues were strongly stimulated to mimic Latin, seems a likely reason for a belief, which still lingers on among linguists, that this is the natural direction of semantic change in all languages, and for the persistent notion in Western learned circles (in strong contrast to Eastern ones) that objective experience is prior to subjective. Philosophies make out a weighty case for the reverse, and certainly the direction of development is sometimes the reverse. Thus the Hopi word for "heart" can be shown to be a late formation within Hopi from a root meaning think or remember. Or consider what has happened to the word "radio" in such a sentence as "he bought a new radio," as compared to its prior meaning "science of wireless telephony."

In the Middle Ages the patterns already formed in Latin began to interweave with the increased mechanical invention, industry, trade, and scholastic and scientific thought. The need for measurement in industry and trade, the stores and bulks of "stuffs" in various containers, the type-bodies in which various goods were handled, standardizing of measure and weight units, invention of clocks and measurement of "time," keeping of records, accounts, chronicles, histories, growth of mathematics and the partnership of mathematics

and science, all cooperated to bring our thought and language world into its present form.

In Hopi history, could we read it, we should find a different type of language and a different set of cultural and environmental influences working together. A peaceful agricultural society isolated by geographic features and nomad enemies in a land of scanty rainfall, arid agriculture that could be made successful only by the utmost perseverance (hence the value of persistence and repetition), necessity for collaboration (hence emphasis on the psychology of teamwork and on mental factors in general), corn and rain as primary criteria of value, need of extensive PREPARATIONS and precautions to assure crops in the poor soil and precarious climate, keen realization of dependence upon nature favoring prayer and a religious attitude toward the forces of nature, especially prayer and religion directed toward the ever-needed blessing, rain—these things interacted with Hopi linguistic patterns to mold them, to be molded again by them, and so little by little to shape the Hopi world-outlook.

To sum up the matter, our first question asked in the beginning (p. 72) is answered thus: Concepts of "time" and "matter" are not given in substantially the same form by experience to all men but depend upon the nature of the language or languages through the use of which they have been developed. They do not depend so much upon ANY ONE SYSTEM (e.g., tense, or nouns) within the grammar as upon the ways of analyzing and reporting experience which have become fixed in the language as integrated "fashions of speaking" and which cut across the typical grammatical classifications, so that such a "fashion" may include lexical, morphological, syntactic, and otherwise systemically diverse means coordinated in a certain frame of consistency. Our own "time" differs markedly from Hopi "duration." It is conceived as like a space of strictly limited dimensions, or sometimes as like a motion upon such a space, and employed as an intellectual tool accordingly. Hopi "duration" seems to be inconceivable in terms of space or motion, being the mode in which life differs from form, and consciousness *in toto* from the spatial elements of consciousness. Certain ideas born of our own time-concept, such as that of absolute simultaneity, would be either very difficult to express or impossible and devoid of meaning under the Hopi conception, and would be replaced by operational concepts. Our "matter" is the physical subtype of "substance" or "stuff," which is conceived as the formless extensional item that must be joined with form before there can be real existence. In Hopi there seems to be nothing corresponding to it; there are no formless extensional items; existence may or may not have form, but what it also has, with or without form, is intensity and duration, these being nonextensional and at bottom the same.

But what about our concept of "space," which was also included in our first question? There is no such striking difference between Hopi and SAE about space as about time, and probably the apprehension of space is given in substantially the same form by experience irrespective of language. The experiments of the Gestalt psychologists with visual perception appear to establish this as a fact. But the CONCEPT OF SPACE will vary somewhat with language, because, as an intellectual tool,[12] it is so closely linked with the concomitant employment of other intellectual tools, of the order of "time" and "matter," which are linguistically conditioned. We see things with our eyes in the same space forms as the Hopi, but our idea of space has also the property of acting as a surrogate of nonspatial relationships like time, intensity, tendency, and as a void to be filled with imagined formless items, one of which may even be called 'space.' Space as sensed by the Hopi would not be connected mentally with such surrogates, but would be comparatively "pure," unmixed with extraneous notions.

As for our second question (p. 72): There are connections but not correlations or diagnostic correspondences between cultural norms and linguistic patterns. Although it would be impossible to infer the existence of Crier Chiefs from the lack of tenses in Hopi, or vice versa, there is a relation between a language and the rest of the culture of the society which uses it. There are cases where the "fashions of speaking" are closely integrated with the whole general culture, whether or not this be universally true, and there are connections within this integration, between the kind of linguistic analyses employed and various behavioral reactions and also the shapes taken by various cultural developments. Thus the importance of Crier Chiefs does have a connection, not with tenselessness itself, but with a system of thought in which categories different from our tenses are natural. These connections are to be found not so much by focusing attention on the typical rubrics of linguistic, ethnographic, or sociological description as by examining the culture and the language (always and only when the two have been together historically for a considerable time) as a whole in which concatenations that run across these departmental lines may be expected to exist, and, if they do exist, eventually to be discoverable by study.

Notes

1. We have plenty of evidence that this is not the case. Consider only the Hopi and the Ute, with languages that on the overt morphological and lexical level are as similar as, say, English and German. The idea of "correlation" between language and culture, in the generally accepted sense of correlation, is certainly a mistaken one.

2. As we say, 'ten at the SAME TIME', showing that in our language and thought we restate the fact of group perception in terms of a concept 'time', the large linguistic component of which will appear in the course of this [discussion].

3. It is no exception to this rule of lacking a plural that a mass noun may sometimes coincide in lexeme with an individual noun that of course has a plural; e.g., 'stone' (no pl.) with 'a stone' (pl. 'stones'). The plural form denoting varieties, e.g., 'wines' is of course a different sort of thing from the true plural; it is a curious outgrowth from the SAE mass nouns, leading to still another sort of imaginary aggregates, which will have to be omitted from this [discussion].

4. Hopi has two words for water quantities; *kə·yi* and *pa·hə*. The difference is something like that between 'stone' and 'rock' in English, *pa·hə* implying greater size and "wildness"; flowing water, whether or not outdoors or in nature, is *pa·hə*; so is

'moisture'. But, unlike 'stone' and 'rock', the difference is essential, not pertaining to a connotative margin, and the two can hardly ever be interchanged.

5. To be sure, there are a few minor differences from other nouns, in English for instance in the use of the articles.

6. 'Year' and certain combinations of 'year' with name of season, rarely season names alone, can occur with a locative morpheme 'at', but this is exceptional. It appears like historical detritus of an earlier different patterning, or the effect of English analogy, or both.

7. The expective and reportive assertions contrast according to the "paramount relation." The expective expresses anticipation existing EARLIER than objective fact, and coinciding with objective fact LATER than the status quo of the speaker, this status quo, including all the subsummation of the past therein, being expressed by the reportive. Our notion "future" seems to represent at once the earlier (anticipation) and the later (afterwards, what will be), as Hopi shows. This paradox may hint of how elusive the mystery of real time is, and how artificially it is expressed by a linear relation of past–present–future.

8. One such trace is that the tensor 'long in duration', while quite different from the adjective 'long' of space, seems to contain the same root as the adjective 'large' of space. Another is that 'somewhere' of space used with certain tensors means 'at some indefinite time.' Possibly however this is not the case and it is only the tensor that gives the time element, so that 'somewhere' still refers to space and that under these conditions indefinite space means simply general applicability, regardless of either time or space. Another trace is that in the temporal (cycle word) 'afternoon' the element meaning 'after' is derived from the verb 'to separate'. There are other such traces, but they are few and exceptional, and obviously not like our own spatial metaphorizing.

9. The Hopi verbs of preparing naturally do not correspond neatly to our "prepare"; so that *na'twani* could also be rendered 'the practiced-upon, the tried-for,' and otherwise.

10. See, e.g., Ernest Beaglehole, *Notes on Hopi economic life* (Yale University Publications in Anthropology, no. 15, 1937), especially the reference to the announcement of a rabbit hunt, and on p. 30, description of the activities in connection with the cleaning of Toreva Spring—announcing, various preparing activities, and finally, preparing the continuity of the good results already obtained and the continued flow of the spring.

11. This notion of storing up power, which seems implied by much Hopi behavior, has an analog in physics: acceleration. It might be said that the linguistic background of Hopi thought equips it to recognize naturally that force manifests not as motion or velocity, but as cumulation or acceleration. Our linguistic background tends to hinder in us this same recognition, for having legitimately conceived force to be that which produces change, we then think of change by our linguistic metaphorical analog, motion, instead of by a pure motionless changingness concept, i.e., accumulation or acceleration. Hence it comes to our naïve feeling as a shock to find from physical experiments that it is not possible to define force by motion, that motion and speed, as also "being at rest," are wholly relative, and that force can be measured only by acceleration.

12. Here belong "Newtonian" and "Euclidean" space, etc.

Post-reading Questions / Activities

- Can you try to understand the Hopi examples that Whorf gives of, for instance, differentiating real and imaginary plurals? Is this easy or hard? Why do you think this is the case?
- Think about time. What images come to mind? Do these line up with what Whorf says about SAE time? Can you think of time without the words to do so?
- Why does Whorf emphasize that "language is a system, not just an assemblage of norms"? How well does an observer have to know a language and culture to be able to see its systematicity?
- Identify someone who is a native speaker of a non-Indo-European language. Ask her or him about learning English and where the difficulties lie. Does the answer support or refute Whorf's thesis?

Vocabulary

animate	inflection	ordinals
aspect	isolating	plurality
cardinal numbers	metaphor	SAE
gender	morpheme	synthetic
inanimate	morphology	tense
inflected	number	voice

Suggested Further Reading

Bloom, Albert H. 1981. *The Linguistic Shaping of Thought: A Study in the Impact of Language on Thinking in China and the West*. Hillsdale, NJ: Erlbaum.

Boas, Franz. 1966 [1911]. Introduction. In *Handbook of American Indian Languages*, edited by Franz Boas, pp. 1–79. Reprint editor, P. Holder. Lincoln: University of Nebraska Press.

Brown, Penelope, and Stephen C. Levinson. 1993. "'Uphill' and 'Downhill' in Tzeltal." *Journal of Linguistic Anthropology* 3(1): 46–74.

Friedrich, Paul. 1986. *The Language Parallax: Linguistic Relativism and Poetic Indeterminacy*. Austin: University of Texas Press.

Gentner, Dedre, and Susan Goldin-Meadow, eds. 2003. *Language in Mind: Advances in the Study of Language and Thought*. Cambridge, MA: MIT Press.

Gumperz, John J., and Stephen C. Levinson, eds. 1996. *Rethinking Linguistic Relativity*. Cambridge: Cambridge University Press.

Lavery, David. N.d. The Benjamin Lee Whorf WWW. Website. http://mtsu32.mtsu.edu:11072/Whorf/.

Lucy, John A. 1985. "Whorf's View of the Linguistic Mediation of Thought." In *Semiotic Mediation: Sociocultural and Psychological Perspectives*, edited by E. Mertz and R. J. Parmentier, pp. 73–97. Orlando, FL: Academic Press.

———. 1992a. *Language Diversity and Thought: A Reformulation of the Linguistic Relativity Hypothesis*. Cambridge: Cambridge University Press.

———. 1992b. *Grammatical Categories and Cognition: A Case Study of the Linguistic Relativity Hypothesis*. Cambridge: Cambridge University Press.

———. 1997. "Linguistic Relativity." *Annual Review of Anthropology*. 26: 291–312.

———, and Richard A. Shweder. 1979. "Whorf and His Critics: Linguistic and Nonlinguistic Influences on Color Memory." *American Anthropologist* 81: 581–615.

Ridington, Robin. 1987. "Models of the Universe: The Poetic Paradigm of Benjamin Lee Whorf." *Anthropology and Humanism Quarterly* 12(1): 16–24.

Sapir, Edward. 1964 [1931]. "Conceptual Categories in Primitive Languages." In *Language in Culture and Society: A Reader in Linguistics and Anthropology*, edited by Dell H. Hymes. New York: Harper & Row.

Witherspoon, Gary. 1977. *Language and Art in the Navaho Universe*. Ann Arbor: University of Michigan Press.

CHAPTER 10

Codifications of Reality
Lineal and Nonlineal

Dorothy Lee
(1950)

Dorothy Lee was a creative, humanistic, and philosophical anthropologist who wrote about the Wintu, Hopi, Trobriand Island, Dakota, Greek, and other cultures. She taught at Vassar College and at the Merrill-Palmer School of Motherhood—she was an unconventional scholar—from which she also derived anthropological ideas about motherhood. Writing at approximately the same time as Whorf, she came up independently with her ideas about the experiencing of reality through language and other patterned behavior.

Reading Questions

- What do the Ontong Javanese terms *ave* and *kainga* really mean? Why is it so difficult for English speakers to figure this out? Why is simple one-to-one translation inadequate for understanding the meanings even of words?
- What does Lee mean when she says that English speakers and Wintu Indians of California "classify on a different basis"?
- What are the implications of Trobriand words being, as Lee describes it, "self-contained concepts," without adjectives or the term *to be*? How is this related to the lack of tenses and the lack of causality?
- What is "the line" or "linearity" in Lee's text? Where does she see evidence of this?

The people of the Trobriand Islands codify, and probably apprehend reality, nonlineally in contrast to our own lineal phrasing. Basic to my investigation of the codification of reality on these two societies, is the assumption that a member of a given society not only codifies experienced reality through the use of the specific language and other patterned behavior characteristics of his culture, but that he actually grasps reality only as it is presented to him in this code. The assumption is not that reality itself is relative; rather, that it is differently punctuated and categorized, or that different aspects of it are noticed by, or presented to the participants of different cultures. If reality itself were not absolute, then true communication of course would be impossible. My own position is that there is an absolute reality, and that communication is possible. If, then, that which the different codes refer to is ultimately the same, a careful study and analysis of a different code and of the culture to which it

Dorothy Lee, "Codifications of Reality: Lineal and Nonlineal." In *Freedom and Culture*. Englewood Cliffs, NJ: Prentice-Hall, 1959, pp. 105–20. Reprinted with the permission of Simon & Schuster Adult Publishing Group, from *Freedom and Culture* by Dorothy Lee. Copyright © 1959 by Dorothy Lee. All rights reserved.

belongs, should lead us to concepts which are ultimately comprehensible, when translated into our own code. It may even, eventually, lead us to aspects of reality from which our own code excludes us.

It is a corollary of this assumption that the specific phrasing of reality can be discovered through intensive and detailed analysis of any aspect of culture. My own study was begun with an analysis of linguistic formulation, only because it is in language that I happen to be best able to discover my clues. To show how these clues can be discovered and used as guides to the apprehension of reality, as well as to show what I mean by codification, I shall present at first concrete material from the field of language.

That a word is not the reality, not the thing which it represents, has long been a commonplace to all of us. The thing which I hold in my hand as I write, *is* not a pencil; I *call* it a pencil. And it remains the same whether I call it *pencil, molyvi, Bleistift,* or *siwiqoq*. These words are different sound-complexes applied to the same reality; but is the difference merely one of sound-complex? Do they refer to the same *perceived* reality? *Pencil* originally meant little tail; it delimited and named the reality according to form. *Molyvi* means lead and refers to the writing element. *Bleistift* refers both to the form and to the writing element. *Siwiqoq* means painting-stick and refers to observed function and form. Each culture has phrased the reality differently. To say that *pencil*, for example, applies primarily to form is no idle etymologic statement. When we use this word metaphorically, we refer neither to writing element nor to function, but to form alone; we speak of a pencil of light, or a styptic pencil.

When I used the four words for this object, we all knew what reality was referred to; we knew the meaning of the word. We could visualize the object in my hand, and the words all delimited it in the same way; for example, none of them implied that it was a continuation of my fist. But the student of ethnography often has to deal with words which punctuate reality into different phrasings from the ones with which he is familiar. Let us take, for instance, the words for "brother" and "sister." We go to the islands of Ontong Java to study the kinship system. We ask our informant what he calls his sister and he says *ave*; he calls his brother *kainga*. So we equate *ave* with "sister" and *kainga* with "brother." By way of checking our information we ask the sister what she calls her brother; it turns out that for her, *ave* is "brother," not "sister" as we were led to expect; and that it is her sister whom she calls *kainga*.

The same reality, the same actual kinship is present there as with us; but we have chosen a different aspect for naming. We are prepared to account for this; we say that both cultures name according to what we would call a certain type of blood relationship; but whereas we make reference to absolute sex, they refer to relative sex. Further inquiry, however, discloses that in this, also, we are wrong. Because in our own culture we name relatives according to formal definition and biologic relationship, we have thought that this formulation represents reality; and we have tried to understand the Ontong Javanese relationship terms according to these distinctions which, we believe, are given in nature. But the Ontong Javanese classifies relatives according to a different aspect of reality, differently punctuated. And because of this, he applies *kainga* as well to a wife's sister and a husband's brother; to a man's brother's wife and a woman's sister's husband, as well as to a number of other individuals.

Neither sex nor blood relationship, then, can be basic to this term. The Ontong Javanese name according to their everyday behavior and experience, not according to formal definition. A man shares the ordinary details of his living with his brothers and their wives for a large part of the year; he sleeps in the same large room, he eats with them, he jokes and works around the house with them; the rest of the year he spends with his wife's sisters and their husbands, in the same easy companionship. All these individuals are *kainga* to one another. The *ave*, on the other hand, names a behavior of great strain and propriety; it is based originally upon the relative sex of siblings, yes, but it does not signify biologic fact alone. It names a social relationship, a behavior, an emotional tone. *Ave* can never spend their adult life together, except on rare and temporary occasions. They can never be under the same roof alone together, cannot chat at ease together, cannot refer even distantly to sex in the presence of each other, not even to one's sweetheart or spouse; more than that, everyone else must be circumspect when the *ave* of someone of the group is present. The *ave* relationship also carries special obligations toward a female *ave* and her children. *Kainga* means a relationship of ease, full of shared living, of informality, gaiety; *ave* names one of formality, prohibition, strain.

These two cultures, theirs and our own, have phrased and formulated social reality in completely different ways, and have given their formulation different names. The word is merely the name of this specific cultural phrasing. From this one instance we might formulate the hypothesis—a very tentative one—that among the Ontong Javanese names describe emotive experiences, not observed forms or functions. But we cannot accept this as fact, unless further investigation shows it to be implicit in the rest of their patterned behavior, in their vocabulary and the morphology of their language, in their ritual and their other organized activity.

One more instance, this time from the language of the Wintu Indians of California, will deal with the varying aspect or segmentation of experience which is used as a basis of classification. To begin with, we take the stem *muk*. On the basis of this stem we form the word *mukeda*, which means: "I turned the basket bottom up"; we form *mukuhara*, which means: "The turtle is moving along"; and we form *mukurumas*, which means: "automobile." Upon what conceivable principle can an automobile be put in the same category as a turtle and a basket? There is such a principle, however, and it operates also when the Wintu calls the activity of laundering, *to make foam continuously*. According to this principle, he uses only one stem, (puq or poq) to form words for all of the following:

puqeda: I just pushed a peg into the ground.
olpuqal: He is sitting on one haunch.
poqorahara: Birds are hopping along.
olpoqoyabe: There are mushrooms growing.
tunpoqoypoqoya: You walk shortskirted,
              stifflegged ahead of me.

It is difficult for us to discover the common denominator in the different formations from this one stem, or even to believe that there can be one. Yet, when we discover the principle underlying the classification, the categories themselves are understandable. Basic to the classification is the Wintu view of himself as observer; he stays outside the event. He passes no judgment on essence, and where we would have used kinesthetic or participatory experience as the basis of naming, he names as an observer only, for the shape of the activity or the object. The turtle and the automobile can thus naturally be grouped together with the inverted baskets. The mushroom standing on its stem, the fist grasping a peg against the ground, the stiff leg topped by a short skirt or by the body of a bird or of a man resting on a haunch, obviously all belong together in one category. But the progress of a grasshopper cannot be categorized with that of a hopping bird. We, who classify on a different basis, apprehend the hop of the two kinesthetically and see it as basically the same in both cases; but the Wintu see the difference in recurrent shape, which is all-important to them, and so name the two by means of completely different stems. Again, when we discover this principle, it is easy to see that from the observer's point of view laundering is the making of a lot of foam; and to see why, when beer was introduced to the Wintu, it was named *laundry*.

I have discussed at length the diversity of codification of reality in general, because it is the foundation of the specific study which I am about to present. I shall speak of the formulation of experienced reality among the Trobriand Islanders in comparison to our own; I shall speak of the nature of expectancy, of motivation, of satisfaction, as based upon a reality which is differently apprehended and experienced in two different societies; which is, in fact, for each, a different reality. The Trobriand Islanders were studied by the late Bronislaw Malinowski, who has given us the rich and circumstantial material about them which has made this study possible. I have given a detailed presentation of some implications of their language elsewhere; but since it was in their language that I first noticed the absence of lineality, which led me to this study, I shall give here a summary of the implications of the language.

A Trobriand word refers to a self-contained concept. What we consider an attribute of a predicate, is to the Trobriander an ingredient. Where I would say, for example, "A good gardener," or "The gardener is good," the Trobriand word would include both "gardener" and "goodness"; if the gardener loses the goodness, he has lost a defining ingredient, he is something else, and he is named by means of a completely different word. A taytu (a species of yam) contains a certain degree of ripeness, bigness, roundedness, etc.; without one of these defining ingredients, it is something else, perhaps a *bwanawa* or a *yowana*. There are no adjectives in the language; the rare words dealing with qualities are substantivized. The term *to be* does not occur; it is used neither attributively nor existentially, since existence itself is contained; it is an ingredient of being.

Events and objects are self-contained points in another respect; there is a series of beings, but no becoming. There is no temporal connection between objects. The taytu always remains itself; it does not *become* over-ripe; over-ripeness is an ingredient of another, a different being. At some point, the taytu *turns into a yowana,* which contains over-ripeness. And the yowana, over-ripe as it is, does not put forth shoots, does not *become* a sprouting yowana. When sprouts appear, it ceases to be itself; in its place appears a *silasata*. Neither is there a temporal connection made—or, according to our own premises, perceived—between events; in fact, temporality is meaningless. There are no tenses, no linguistic distinction between past or present. There is no arrangement of activities or events into means and ends, no causal or teleologic relationships. What we consider a causal relationship in a sequence of connected events, is to the Trobriander

an ingredient of a patterned whole. He names this ingredient *u'ula.*

There is no automatic relating of any kind in the language. Except for the rarely used verbal it-differents and it-sames, there are no terms of comparison whatever. And we find in an analysis of behavior that the standard for behavior and of evaluation is non-comparative.

These implications of the linguistic material suggest to my mind an absence of axiomatic lineal connection between events or objects in the Trobriand apprehension of reality, and this implication, as I shall attempt to show below, is reinforced in their definition of activity. In our own culture, the line is so basic, that we take it for granted, as given in reality. We see it in visible nature, between material points, and we see it between metaphorical points such as days or acts. It underlies not only our thinking, but also our aesthetic apprehension of the given; it is basic to the emotional climax which has so much value for us, and, in fact, to the meaning of life itself. In our thinking about personality and character, we have taken for granted the presence of the line.

In our academic work, we are constantly acting in terms of an implied line. When we speak of *applying* an *at*tribute, for example, we visualize the process as lineal, coming from the outside. If I make a picture of an apple on the board, and want to show that one side is green and the other red I connect these attributes with the pictured apple by means of lines, as a matter of course; how else would I do it? When I organize my data, I *draw* conclusions *from* them. I *trace* a relationship between my facts. I describe a pattern as a *web* of relationships. Look at a lecturer who makes use of gestures; he is constantly making lineal connections in the air. And a teacher with chalk in hand will be drawing lines on the board whether he be a psychologist, a historian, or a paleontologist.

Preoccupation with social facts merely as self-contained facts is mere antiquarianism. In my field, a student of this sort would be an amateur or a dilettante, not an anthropologist. To be an anthropologist, he can arrange his facts in an upward slanting line, in a *unilinear* or *multilinear course* of development; or in *parallel lines* or *converging lines.* Or he may arrange them geographically, with *lines* of diffusion connecting them; or schematically, using *concentric circles.* Or at least, he must indicate what his study *leads to,* what new insights we can *draw from* it. To be accorded status, he must use the guiding line as basic.

The line is found or presupposed in most of our scientific work. It is present in the *induction* and the *deduction* of science and logic. It is present in the philosopher's phrasing of means and ends as lineally connected. Our statistical facts are presented lineally as a *graph* or reduced to a normal *curve.* And all of us, I think, would be lost without our *diagrams.* We *trace* a historical development; we *follow the course* of history and evolution *down* to the present and *up from* the ape; and it is interesting to note, in passing, that whereas both evolution and history are lineal, the first goes up the blackboard, the second goes down.

Our psychologists picture motivation as external, connected with the act through a line, or, more recently, entering the organism through a lineal channel and emerging transformed, again lineally, as response. I have seen lineal pictures of nervous impulses and heartbeats, and with them I have seen pictured lineally a second of time. These were photographs, you will say, of existing fact, of reality; a proof that the line is present in reality. But I am not convinced, perhaps due to my ignorance of mechanics, that we have not created our recording instruments in such a way that they have to picture time and motion, light and sound, heartbeats and nerve impulses lineally, on the unquestioned assumption of the line as axiomatic. The line is omnipresent and inescapable, and so we are incapable of questioning the reality of its presence.

When we see a *line* of trees, or a *circle* of stones, we assume the presence of a connecting line which is not actually visible. And we assume it metaphorically when we follow a *line* of thought, a *course* of action or the *direction* of an argument; when we *bridge* a gap in the conversation, or speak of the *span* of life or of teaching a *course*, or lament our *interrupted career*. We make children's embroidery cards and puzzle cards on this assumption; our performance tests and even our tests for sanity often assume that the line is present in nature and, at most, to be discovered or given visual existence.

But is the line present in reality? Malinowski, writing for members of our culture and using idiom which would be comprehensible to them, described the Trobriand village as follows: "Concentrically with the circular row of yam houses there runs a ring of dwelling huts." He saw, or at any rate, he represented the village as two circles. But in the texts which he recorded, we find that the Trobrianders at no time mention circles or rings or even rows when they refer to their villages. Any word which they use to refer to a village, such as *a* or *this*, is prefixed by the substantival element *kway* which means *bump* or *aggregate of bumps*. This is the element which they use when they refer to a pimple or a bulky rash; or to canoes loaded with yams. In their terms, a village is an aggregate of bumps; are they blind to the circles? Or did Malinowski create the circles himself, out of his cultural axiom?

Again, for us as well as in Malinowski's description of the Trobrianders, which was written necessarily in terms meaningful to us, all effective activity is certainly not a haphazard aggregate of acts, but a lineally planned series of acts leading to an envisioned end. Their gardening with all its specialized activities, both technical and magical, leading to a rich harvest; their *kula* involving the cutting down of trees, the communal dragging of the tree to the beach, the rebuilding or building of large sea-worthy canoes, the provisioning, the magical and ceremonial activities involved—surely all these can be carried through only if they are lineally conceived.

But the Trobrianders do not describe their activity lineally; they do no dynamic relating of acts; they do not use even so innocuous a connective as *and*. Here is part of a description of the planting of coconut: "Thou-approach-there coconut thou-bring-here-we-plant-coconut thou-go thou-plant our coconut. This-here it-emerge sprout.

We-push-away this we-push-away this-other coconut-husk-fiber together sprout it-sit together root." We who are accustomed to seek lineal continuity, cannot help supplying it as we read this; but the continuity is not given in the Trobriand text; and all Trobriand speech, according to Malinowski, is "jerky," given in points, not in connecting lines. The only connective I know of in Trobriand is the *pela*[,] . . . a kind of preposition which also means "to jump."

I am not maintaining here that the Trobrianders cannot see continuity; rather that lineal connection is not automatically made by them, as a matter of course. At Malinowski's persistent questioning, for example, they did attempt to explain their activities in terms of cause or motivation, by stating possible "results" of uncooperative action. But Malinowski found their answers confused, self-contradictory, inconsistent; their preferred answer was, "It was ordained of old"—pointing to an ingredient value of the act instead of giving an explanation based on lineal connection.

And when they were not trying to find answers to leading questions, the Trobrianders made no such connection in their speech. They assumed, for example, that the validity of a magical spell lay, not in its results, not in proof, but in its very being; in the appropriateness of its inheritance, in its place within the patterned activity, in its being performed by the appropriate person, in its realization of its mythical basis. To seek validity through proof was foreign to their thinking, yet they attempted to do so at the ethnographer's request. I should add here that their names for constellations imply that here they do see lineal figures; I cannot investigate the significance of this, as I have no contextual material. At any rate, I would like to emphasize that, even if the Trobriander does occasionally supply connecting lines between points, his perception and experience do not automatically fall into a lineal framework.

The fact remains that Trobrianders embark on, what is certainly for us, a series of acts which "must require" planning and purposiveness. They engage in acts of gift-giving and gift-receiving which we can certainly see as an exchange of gifts if we want to. When we plot their journeys, we find that they do go from point to point, they do navigate a course, whether they say so or not. Do they merely refrain from giving linguistic expression to something which they actually recognize in nature? On the nonlinguistic level, do they act on an assumption of a lineality which is given no place in their linguistic formulation?

I believe that, where valued activity is concerned, the Trobrianders do not act on an assumption of lineality at any level. There is organization or rather coherence in their acts because Trobriand activity is patterned activity. One act within this pattern brings into existence a pre-ordained cluster of acts. Perhaps one might find a parallel in our culture in the making of a sweater. When I embark on knitting one, the ribbing at the bottom does not *cause* the making of the neckline, nor of the sleeves or the armholes; and it is not part of a lineal series of acts. Rather it is an indispensable part of a patterned activity which includes all these other acts. Again, when I choose a dress pattern, the acts involved in the making of the dress are already present for me. They are embedded in the pattern which I have chosen.

In this same way, I believe, can be seen the Trobriand insistence that though intercourse is a necessary preliminary to conception, it is not the cause of conception. There are a number of acts in the pattern of procreating; one is intercourse, another the entrance of the spirit of a dead Trobriander into the womb. However, there is a further point here. The Trobrianders, when pressed by the ethnographer or teased by the neighboring Dobuans, showed signs of intense embarrassment, giving the impression that they were trying to maintain unquestioningly a stand in which they had to believe. This, I think, is because pattern is truth and value for them; in fact, acts and being derive value from the embedding pattern.

So the question of the perception of a line remains. It is because they find value in pattern that the Trobrianders act according to nonlineal pattern; not because they cannot perceive lineality.

But all Trobriand activity does not contain value; and when it does not, it assumes lineality, and is utterly despicable. For example, the pattern of sexual intercourse includes the giving of a gift from the boy to the girl; but if a boy gives a gift so as to win the girl's favor, he is despised. Again, the kula pattern includes the eventual reception of a gift from the original recipient; the pattern is such that it keeps the acts physically and temporally completely disparate. In spite of this, however, some men are accused of giving gifts as an inducement to their kula partner to give them a specially good kula gift. Such men are labeled with the vile phrase: he barters. But this means that, unvalued and despised, lineal behavior does exist. In fact, there are villages in the interior whose inhabitants live mainly by bartering manufactured articles for yams. The inhabitants of Omarakana, about whom Malinowski's work and this study are mainly concerned, will barter with them, but consider them pariahs.

This is to say that it is probable that the Trobrianders experience reality in nonlineal pattern because this is the valued reality; and that they are capable of experiencing lineally, when value is absent or destroyed. It is not to say, however, that this in itself means that lineality is given, is present in nature, and that pattern is not. Our own insistence on the line, such as lineal causality, for example, is also often based on unquestioned belief or value. To return to the subject of procreation, the husband in our culture, who has long hoped, and tried in vain, to beget children, will nevertheless maintain that intercourse causes conception; perhaps with the same stubbornness and embarrassment which the Trobrianders exhibited when maintaining the opposite.

The line in our culture not only connects, but it moves. And as we think of a line as moving from point to point, connecting one to the other, so we conceive of roads as *running from* locality *to* locality. A Trobriander does not speak of roads either as connecting two points, or as *running from*

point *to* point. His paths are self-contained, named as independent units; they are not *to* and *from*, they are *at*. And he himself is *at*; he has no equivalent for our *to* or *from*. There is, for instance, the myth of Tudava, who goes—in our view—from village to village and from island to island planting and offering yams. The Trobriand text puts it this way: "Kitava it-shine village already (i.e., completed) he-is-over. 'I-sail I-go Iwa'; Iwa he-anchor he-go ashore…He-sail Digumenu…They-drive (him off)…he-go Kwaywata." Point after point is enumerated, but his sailing from and to is given as a discrete event. In our view, he is actually following a southeasterly course, more or less; but this is not given as course or line, and no directions are even mentioned. In fact, in the several texts referring to journeyings in the Archipelago, no words occur for the cardinal directions. In sailing, the "following" winds are named according to where they are *at*, the place where they strike the canoe, such as wind-striking-the-outrigger-beam; not according to where they *come from*. Otherwise, we find names for the southwest wind (youyo), and the northwest wind (bombatu), but these are merely substantival names which have nothing to do with direction; names for kinds of wind.

When a member of our society gives an unemotional description of a person, he follows an imaginary line, usually downward: from head to foot, from tip to toe, from hair to chin. The Navaho do the opposite, following a line upward. The Trobriander follows no line, at least none that I can see. "My head boils," says a kula spell; and it goes on to enumerate the parts of the head as follows: nose, occiput, tongue, larynx, speech, mouth. Another spell casting a protective fog, runs as follows: "I befog the hand, I befog the foot, I befog the head, I befog the shoulders…." There is a magic formula where we do recognize a line, but it is one which Malinowski did not record verbatim at the time, but which he put down later from memory; and it is not improbable that his memory edited the formula according to the lineality of his culture.

When the Trobriander enumerates the parts of a canoe, he does not follow any recognizable lineal order: "Mist…surround me my mast…the nose of my canoe…my sail…my steering oar…my canoe-gunwale…my canoe-bottom…my prow…my rib…my threading-stick…my prow-board…my transverse stick…my canoe-side."

Malinowski diagrams the garden site as a square piece of land subdivided into squares; the Trobrianders refer to it in the same terms as those which they use in referring to a village—a bulky object or an aggregate of bumps. When the plots in the garden site are apportioned to the gardeners, the named plots are assigned by name, the others by location along each named side of the garden. After this, the inner plots, the "belly" of the garden, are apportioned. Following along a physical rim is a procedure which we find elsewhere also. In a spell naming villages on the main island, there is a long list of villages whch lie along the coast northward, then westward around the island, then south. To us, of course, this is lineal order. But we have no indication that the Trobrianders see other than geographical location, point after point, as they move over a physically continuous area; the line as a guide to procedure is not necessarily implied. No terms are used here which might be taken as an implication of continuity; no "along the coast" or "around" or "northward."

———————

When we in our culture deal with events or experiences of the self, we use the line as guide for various reasons, two of which I shall take up here. First, we feel we must arrange events chronologically in a lineal order; how else could our historians discover the causes of a war or a revolution or a defeat? Among the Trobrianders, what corresponds to our history is an aggregate of anecdotes, that is, unconnected points, told without respect to chronological sequence, or development, or causal relationship; with no grammatical distinction made between words referring to past events, or to present or contemplated ones. And in telling an anecdote, they take no care that a temporal sequence should be followed. For instance, they said to Malinowski, "They-eat-taro, they-spew-taro, they-disgusted-taro"; but if time, as we believe, is a moving line, then the revulsion came first in time, the vomiting was the result, coming afterward. Again, they say, "This-here…ripes…falls-down truly gives-birth…sits seed in belly-his"; but certainly the seed is there first, and the birth follows in time, if time is lineal.

Secondly, we arrange events and objects in a sequence which is climactic, in size and intensity, in emotional meaning, or according to some other principle. We often arrange events from earlier to later, not because we are interested in historical causation, but because the present is the climax of our history. But when the Trobriander relates happenings, there is no developmental arrangement, no building up of emotional tone. His stories have no plot, no lineal development, no climax. And when he repeats his garden spell, his list is neither climactic, nor anticlimactic; it sounds merely untidy to us:

The	belly	of	my	garden	lifts
The	belly	of	my	garden	rises
The	belly	of	my	garden	reclines
The	belly	of	my	garden	is-a-bushhen's-nest-in-lifting
The	belly	of	my	garden	is-an-anthill
The	belly	of	my	garden	lifts-bends
The	belly	of	my	garden	is-an-ironwood-tree-in-lifting
The	belly	of	my	garden	lies-down
The	belly	of	my	garden	burgeons.

When the Trobrianders set out on their great ceremonial kula expedition, they follow a pre-established order. First comes the canoe of the Tolab wage, an obscure sub-clan. Next come the canoes of the great chiefs. But this is not climactic; after the great chiefs come the commoners. The order derives meaning not from lineal sequence, but from correspondence with a present, experienced, meaningful pattern, which is the recreation or realization of the mythical pattern; that which has been ordained of old and is forever. Its meaning does not lie in an item-to-item relationship, but in fitness, in the repetition of an established unit.

An ordering of this sort gives members of our society a certain esthetic dysphoria except when, through deliberate training, we learn to go beyond our cultural expectation; or, when we are too young to have taken on the phrasings of our culture. When we manipulate objects naively, we arrange them on some climactic lineal principle. Think of a college commencement, with the faculty arranged in order of rank or length of tenure or other mark of importance; with the students arranged according to increasing physical height, from shortest to tallest, actually the one absolutely irrelevant principle as regards the completion of their college education, which is the occasion for the celebration. Even when the sophisticated avoid this principle, they are not unconscious of it; they are deliberately avoiding something which is there.

And our arrangement of history, when we ourselves are personally involved, is mainly climactic. My great grandmother sewed by candle light, my grandmother used a kerosene lamp, my mother did her studying by gaslight, I did it by a naked electric ceiling light, and my children have diffused fluorescent lighting. This is progress; this is the meaningful sequence. To the Trobriander, climax in history is abominable, a denial of all good, since it would imply not only the presence of change, but also that change increases the good; but to him value lies in sameness, in repeated pattern, in the incorporation of all time within the same point. What is good in life is exact identity with all past Trobriand experience, and all mythical experience.

There is no boundary between past Trobriand existence and the present; he can indicate that an action is completed, but this does not mean that the action is past; it may be completed and present or timeless. Where we would say "Many years ago" and use the past tense, the Trobriander will say, "In my father's childhood" and use non-temporal verbs; he places the event situationally, not temporally. Past, present, and future are presented linguistically as the same, are present in his existence, and sameness with what we call the past and with myth, represents value to the Trobriander. Where we see a developmental line, the Trobriander sees a point, at most a swelling in value. Where we find pleasure and satisfaction in moving away from the point, in change as variety or progress, the Trobriander finds it in the repetition of the known, in maintaining the point; that is, in what we call monotony.

Esthetic validity, dignity, and value come to the Trobriander not through arrangement into a climactic line, but rather in the undisturbed incorporation of the events within their original, nonlineal order. The only history which has meaning for him is that which evokes the value of the point, or which, in the repetition, swells the value of the point. For example, every occasion in which a kula object participates becomes an ingredient of its being and swells its value; all these occasions are enumerated with great satisfaction, but the lineal course of the traveling kula object is not important.

As we see our history climactically, so do we plan future experiences climactically, leading up to future satisfaction or meaning. Who but a very young child would think of starting a meal with strawberry shortcake and ending it with spinach? We have come to identify the end of the meal with the height of satisfaction, and we identify semantically the words dessert and reward, only because of the similarity of their position in a climactic line. The Trobriand meal has no dessert, no line, no climax. The special bit, the relish, is eaten *with* the staple food; it is not something to "look *forward to*," while disposing of a meaningless staple.

None of the Trobriand activities is fitted into a climactic line. There is no job, no labor, no drudgery which finds its reward outside the act. All work contains its own satisfaction. We cannot speak of S–R here, as all action contains its own immanent "stimulus." The present is not a means to future satisfaction, but good in itself, as the future is also good in itself; neither better nor worse, neither climactic nor anticlimactic, in fact, not lineally connected nor removed.

It follows that the present is not evaluated in terms of its place within a course of action leading upward to a worthy end. In our culture, we can rarely evaluate the present in itself. I tell you that Sally is selling notions at Woolworth's, but this in itself means nothing. It acquires some meaning when I add that she has recently graduated from Vassar. However, I go on to tell you that she has been assistant editor of *Vogue*, next a nursemaid, a charwoman, a public school teacher. But this is a mere jumble; it makes no sense and has no meaning, because the series leads to nothing. You cannot relate one job to another, and you are unable to see them discretely simply as part of her being. However, I now add that she is gathering material for a book on the working mother. Now all this falls in line, it makes sense in terms of a career. Now her job is good and it makes her happy, because it is part of a planned climactic line leading to more pay, increased recognition, higher rank. There was a story in a magazine about the college girl who fell in love with the milkman one summer; the reader felt tense until it was discovered that this was just a summer job, that it was only a means for the continuation of the man's education in the Columbia Law School. Our evaluation of happiness and unhappiness is bound with this motion along an envisioned line leading to a desired end. In the fulfillment of this course or career—not in the fulfillment of the self as point—do we find value. Our conception of freedom rests on the principle of non-interference with this moving line, non-interruption of the intended course of action.

It is difficult to tell whether climax is given in experience at all, or whether it is always imposed on the given. At a time when progress and evolution were assumed to be implicit in nature, our musicians and writers gave us climactic works. Nowadays, our more reflective art does not present experience climactically. Then, is emotion itself climactic? Climax, for us, evokes "thrill" or "drama." But we have cultures, like the Tikopia, where life is lived, to our perception, on an even emotive plane without thrill or climax. Experiences which "we know to be" climactic, are described without climax by them. For example, they, as well as the Trobrianders, described intercourse as an aggregate of pleasurable experiences. But Malinowski is disturbed by this; he cannot place the erotic kiss in Trobriand experience, since it has no climactic function.

In our culture, childbearing is climactic. Pregnancy is represented by the usual obstetrician as an uncomfortable means to a dramatic end. For most women, all intensity of natural physical experience is nowadays removed from the actual birth itself; but the approach of birth nevertheless is a period of mounting tension, and drama is supplied by the intensive social recognition of the event, the dramatic accumulation of gifts, flowers, telegrams. A pregnancy is not formally announced since, if it does not eventuate in birth, it has failed to achieve its end; and failure to reach the climax brings shame. In its later stages it may be marked with a shower; but the shower looks forward to the birth, it does not celebrate the pregnancy itself. Among the Trobrianders, pregnancy has meaning in itself, as a state of being. At a first pregnancy, there is a long ceremonial involving "preparatory" work on the part of many people, which merely celebrates the pregnancy. It does not anchor the baby, it does not *have as its purpose* a more comfortable time during the pregnancy, it does not *lead to* an easier birth or a healthy baby. It makes the woman's skin white, and makes her be at her most beautiful; yet this *leads to* nothing, since she must not attract men, not even her own husband.

Are we then right in accepting without question the presence of a line in reality? Are we in a position to say with assurance that the Trobrianders are wrong and we are right? Much of our present-day thinking, and much of our evaluation, are based on the premise of the line and of the line as good. Students have been refused admittance to college because the autobiographic sketch accompanying their application showed absence of the line; they lacked purposefulness and ability to plan; they were inadequate as to character as well as intellectually. Our conception of personality formation, our stress on the significance of success and failure and of frustration in general, is based on the axiomatically postulated line. Yet can there be blocking without presupposed lineal motion or effort? If I walk along a path because I like the country, or if it is not important to get to a particular point at a particular time, then the insuperable puddle from the morning's shower is not frustrating; I throw stones into it and watch the ripples, and then choose another path. If the undertaking is of value in itself, a point good in itself, and not because it leads to something, then failure has no symbolic meaning; it merely results in no cake for supper, or less money in the family budget; it is not personally destructive. But failure is devastating in our culture, because it is not failure of the undertaking alone; it is the moving, becoming, lineally conceived self which has failed.

Ethnographers have occasionally remarked that the people whom they studied showed no annoyance when interrupted. Is this an indication of mild temper, or might it be the case that they were not interrupted at all, as there was no expectation of lineal continuity? Such questions are new in anthropology and most ethnographers therefore never thought of recording material which would answer them. However, we do have enough material to make us question the line as basic to all experience; whether it is actually present in given reality or not, it is not always present in experienced reality. We cannot even take it for granted as existing among those members of our society who are not completely or naively steeped in their culture, such as many of our artists, for example. And we should be very careful, in studying other cultures, to avoid the unexamined assumption that their actions are based on the predication of a lineal reality.

References

Lee, Dorothy. *Being and Value in a Primitive Culture.* Journal of Philosophy 46: 401–415 (1949) [and references therein].

Post-reading Questions / Activities

- Lee claims that she believes in an absolute reality but also that "reality…is differently apprehended and experienced in two different societies" and "is, in fact, for each, a different reality." What does she mean? Do you see reality in these two different ways, as well?
- When Lee generalizes about "our culture" or how "we see linearity," to whom is she referring? Is this a reasonable generalization, in contrasting with Trobriand or other cultures? Would anyone speaking American English or participating in North American culture dispute her account of linearity?
- Read or listen to accounts of an event. Do they follow the linear progression, leading to a climax, as Lee says? How might a Trobriander recount the same event? Would it, in fact, be "the same"?

Vocabulary

kula   Trobriand Islands

Suggested Further Reading

Lee, Dorothy. 1987 [1959]. *Freedom and Culture.* Prospect Heights, IL: Waveland Press.

CHAPTER 11

Metaphors We Live By

George Lakoff and Mark Johnson
(1980)

George Lakoff and Mark Johnson's book, Metaphors We Live By, *sparked a lively conversation when it was published in 1980. The authors pointed out that all language was metaphoric; that there is no such thing as pure, transparent language; and that the metaphors work together in systematic ways. In this short excerpt from their book, you are introduced to the basic idea of conceptual metaphors.*

Reading Questions

- Where do Lakoff and Johnson see evidence of metaphor in everyday life? What claims do they make about "our ordinary conceptual system"?
- Why is it important that they claim that human thought processes are largely metaphorical?
- Consider their claims about TIME IS MONEY. Do you experience time this way? Can you think of it any other way? Have you ever read about a culture in which time is conceived of differently? What do you think would happen if people from cultures with two different concepts of time encountered each other?

Metaphor is for most people a device of the poetic imagination and the rhetorical flourish—a matter of extraordinary rather than ordinary language. Moreover, metaphor is typically viewed as characteristic of language alone, a matter of words rather than thought or action. For this reason, most people think they can get along perfectly well without metaphor. We have found, on the contrary, that metaphor is pervasive in everyday life, not just in language but in thought and action. Our ordinary conceptual system, in terms of which we both think and act, is fundamentally metaphorical in nature.

The concepts that govern our thought are not just matters of the intellect. They also govern our everyday functioning, down to the most mundane details. Our concepts structure what we perceive, how we get around in the world, and how we relate to other people. Our conceptual system thus plays a central role in defining our everyday realities. If we are right in suggesting that our conceptual system is largely metaphorical, then the way we think, what we experience, and what we do every day is very much a matter of metaphor.

But our conceptual system is not something we are normally aware of. In most of the little things we do every day, we simply think and act more or less automatically along certain lines. Just what these lines are is by no means obvious. One way to find out is by looking at language. Since

communication is based on the same conceptual system that we use in thinking and acting, language is an important source of evidence for what that system is like.

Primarily on the basis of linguistic evidence, we have found that most of our ordinary conceptual system is metaphorical in nature. And we have found a way to begin to identify in detail just what the metaphors are that structure how we perceive, how we think, and what we do.

To give some idea of what it could mean for a concept to be metaphorical and for such a concept to structure an everyday activity, let us start with the concept ARGUMENT and the conceptual metaphor ARGUMENT IS WAR. This metaphor is reflected in our everyday language by a wide variety of expressions:

ARGUMENT IS WAR

> Your claims are *indefensible.*
> He *attacked every weak point* in my argument.
> His criticisms were *right on target.*
> I *demolished* his argument.
> I've never *won* an argument with him.
> You disagree? Okay, *shoot!*
> If you use that *strategy,* he'll *wipe you out.*
> He *shot down* all of my arguments.

It is important to see that we don't just *talk* about arguments in terms of war. We can actually win or lose arguments.

George Lakoff and Mark Johnson, "Metaphors We Live By" "and the systematicity of Metaphorical Concepts." In *Metaphors We Live By.* Chicago and London: University of Chicago Press, 1980, pp. 3–9.

We see the person we are arguing with as an opponent. We attack his positions and we defend our own. We gain and lose ground. We plan and use strategies. If we find a position indefensible, we can abandon it and take a new line of attack. Many of the things we *do* in arguing are partially structured by the concept of war. Though there is no physical battle, there is a verbal battle, and the structure of an argument—attack, defense, counterattack, etc.—reflects this. It is in this sense that the ARGUMENT IS WAR metaphor is one that we live by in this culture; it structures the actions we perform in arguing.

Try to imagine a culture where arguments are not viewed in terms of war, where no one wins or loses, where there is no sense of attacking or defending, gaining or losing ground. Imagine a culture where an argument is viewed as a dance, the participants are seen as performers, and the goal is to perform in a balanced and aesthetically pleasing way. In such a culture, people would view arguments differently, experience them differently, carry them out differently, and talk about them differently. But *we* would probably not view them as arguing at all: they would simply be doing something different. It would seem strange even to call what they were doing "arguing." Perhaps the most neutral way of describing this difference between their culture and ours would be to say that we have a discourse form structured in terms of battle and they have one structured in terms of dance.

This is an example of what it means for a metaphorical concept, namely, ARGUMENT IS WAR, to structure (at least in part) what we do and how we understand what we are doing when we argue. *The essence of metaphor is understanding and experiencing one kind of thing in terms of another.* It is not that arguments are a subspecies of war. Arguments and wars are different kinds of things—verbal discourse and armed conflict—and the actions performed are different kinds of actions. But ARGUMENT is partially structured, understood, performed, and talked about in terms of WAR. The concept is metaphorically structured, the activity is metaphorically structured, and, consequently, the language is metaphorically structured.

Moreover, this is the *ordinary* way of having an argument and talking about one. The normal way for us to talk about attacking a position is to use the words "attack a position." Our conventional ways of talking about arguments presuppose a metaphor we are hardly ever conscious of. The metaphor is not merely in the words we use—it is in our very concept of an argument. The language of argument is not poetic, fanciful, or rhetorical; it is literal. We talk about arguments that way because we conceive of them that way—and we act according to the way we conceive of things.

The most important claim we have made so far is that metaphor is not just a matter of language, that is, of mere words. We shall argue that, on the contrary, human *thought processes* are largely metaphorical. This is what we mean when we say that the human conceptual system is metaphorically structured and defined. Metaphors as linguistic expressions are possible precisely because there are metaphors in a person's conceptual system. Therefore, whenever . . . we speak of metaphors, such as ARGUMENT IS WAR, it should be understood that *metaphor* means *metaphorical concept.*

Arguments usually follow patterns; that is, there are certain things we typically do and do not do in arguing. The fact that we in part conceptualize arguments in terms of battle systematically influences the shape arguments take and the way we talk about what we do in arguing. Because the metaphorical concept is systematic, the language we use to talk about that aspect of the concept is systematic.

We saw in the ARGUMENT IS WAR metaphor that expressions from the vocabulary of war, e.g., *attack a position, indefensible, strategy, new line of attack, win, gain ground,* etc., form a systematic way of talking about the battling aspects of arguing. It is no accident that these expressions mean what they mean when we use them to talk about arguments. A portion of the conceptual network of battle partially characterizes the concept of an argument, and the language follows suit. Since metaphorical expressions in our language are tied to metaphorical concepts in a systematic way, we can use metaphorical linguistic expressions to study the nature of metaphorical concepts and to gain an understanding of the metaphorical nature of our activities.

To get an idea of how metaphorical expressions in everyday language can give us insight into the metaphorical nature of the concepts that structure our everyday activities, let us consider the metaphorical concept TIME IS MONEY as it is reflected in contemporary English.

TIME IS MONEY

> You're *wasting* my time.
> This gadget will *save* you hours.
> I don't *have* the time to *give* you.
> How do you *spend* your time these days?
> That flat tire *cost* me an hour.
> I've *invested* a lot of time in her.
> I don't *have enough* time to *spare* for that.
> You're *running out* of time.
> You need to *budget* your time.
> *Put aside* some time for ping pong.
> Is that *worth your while?*
> Do you *have* much time *left?*
> He's living on *borrowed* time.
> You don't *use* your time *profitably.*
> I *lost* a lot of time when I got sick.
> *Thank you for* your time.

Time in our culture is a valuable commodity. It is a limited resource that we use to accomplish our goals. Because of the way that the concept of work has developed in modern Western culture, where work is typically associated with the time it takes and time is precisely quantified, it has become customary to pay people by the hour, week, or year. In our culture TIME IS MONEY in many ways: telephone message units, hourly wages, hotel room rates, yearly budgets, interest on loans, and paying your debt to society by "serving time." These practices are relatively new in the history of the human race, and by no means do they exist in all cultures. They have arisen in modern industrialized societies and structure our basic everyday activities in a very profound way. Corresponding to the fact that we *act* as if time is a valuable commodity—a limited resource, even money—we *conceive of* time that way. Thus we understand and experience time as the kind of thing that can be spent, wasted, budgeted, invested wisely or poorly, saved, or squandered.

TIME IS MONEY, TIME IS A LIMITED RESOURCE, and TIME IS A VALUABLE COMMODITY are all metaphorical concepts. They are metaphorical since we are using our everyday experiences with money, limited resources, and valuable commodities to conceptualize time. This isn't a necessary way for human beings to conceptualize time; it is tied to our culture. There are cultures where time is none of these things.

The metaphorical concepts TIME IS MONEY, TIME IS A RESOURCE, and TIME IS A VALUABLE COMMODITY form a single system based on subcategorization, since in our society money is a limited resource and limited resources are valuable commodities. These subcategorization relationships characterize entailment relationships between the metaphors. TIME IS MONEY entails that TIME IS A LIMITED RESOURCE, which entails that TIME IS A VALUABLE COMMODITY.

We are adopting the practice of using the most specific metaphorical concept, in this case TIME IS MONEY, to characterize the entire system. Of the expressions listed under the TIME IS MONEY metaphor, some refer specifically to money (*spend, invest, budget, profitably, cost*), others to limited resources (*use, use up, have enough of, run out of*), and still others to valuable commodities (*have, give, lose, thank you for*). This is an example of the way in which metaphorical entailments can characterize a coherent system of metaphorical concepts and a corresponding coherent system of metaphorical expressions for those concepts.

Post-reading Questions / Activities

- Why do you think we tend to be unaware of the systematic metaphors that Lakoff and Johnson point out? How aware are we, in general, of the way our language works?
- Analyze a text, looking for conceptual metaphors. What metaphors do you find? Could the concepts be expressed without the metaphors?
- For native speakers of languages other than English: do you have equivalents in your language to the English metaphors mentioned by Lakoff and Johnson? Are there other metaphors that English does not have?
- What is the relationship between reality, our concepts, and our metaphorical linguistic expressions? Do humans who speak different languages live in the same reality?

Vocabulary

metaphor   metaphorical concept

Suggested Further Reading

Black, Max. 1962. *Models and Metaphors: Studies in Language and Philosophy*. Ithaca, NY: Cornell University Press.

Fernandez, James W. 1991. *Beyond Metaphor: The Theory of Tropes in Anthropology*. Stanford, CA: Stanford University Press.

Holland, Dorothy C., and Naomi Quinn, eds. 1987. *Cultural Models in Language and Thought*. Cambridge and New York: Cambridge University Press.

Kittay, Eva Feder. 1987. *Metaphor: Its Cognitive Force and Linguistic Structure*. Oxford: Clarendon Press.

Kuhn, Thomas S. 1970. *The Structure of Scientific Revolutions*. Chicago: University of Chicago Press.

Lakoff, George. 1987. *Women, Fire, and Dangerous Things: What Categories Reveal About the Mind*. Chicago: University of Chicago Press.

———. 2004. *Don't Think of an Elephant! Know Your Values and Frame the Debate: The Essential Guide for Progressives*. White River Junction, VT: Chelsea Green.

———, and Mark Johnson. 1980. *Metaphors We Live By*. Chicago and London: University of Chicago Press.

Ortony, Andrew, ed. 1979. *Metaphor and Thought*. Cambridge and New York: Cambridge University Press.

Pepper, Stephen C. 1942. *World Hypotheses: A Study in Evidence*. Berkeley and Los Angeles: University of California Press.

Sacks, Sheldon, ed. 1979 [1978]. *On Metaphor*. Chicago: University of Chicago Press.

CHAPTER 12

Language and Mind
Let's Get the Issues Straight!

Stephen C. Levinson
(2003)

Stephen Levinson has been very much involved in the revival and empirical assessment of the linguistic relativity hypothesis since the 1990s. He has worked at the Max Planck Institute for Psycholinguistics in the Netherlands since 1991, serving as director for many years. Psycholinguistics is the study of the relationship between language and thought, including the neurobiological dimensions of cognition. Much of this research is very technologically sophisticated and laboratory based, but some of it relies on in-depth ethnographic studies of people, their language, and their behavior, especially in its cross-cultural dimension.

Levinson's work on this topic has been especially focused on the relationship between language and space, comparing the ways different languages discuss space, whether in locating something relative to something else (to the left of the house) *or in absolute terms* (north of the house), *or in discussing the proximity and relationship of various objects* (in the box, on the shelf). *These systems vary quite prominently across languages, and Levinson has shown that there are cognitive consequences of these linguistic differences. In other words, we think the way our language prepares us. One of the most striking findings is that people with absolute spatial systems are many times better at finding their location than people with relative spatial systems. (English has both, but the relative system is more widespread and powerful.)*

Levinson argues for the principle of "coevolution" (biology and culture [and language]), and against the doctrine of "simple nativism," which holds that the essence of human language is syntax and that language is innate, and that the world's thousands of languages simply apply different labels to the same shared concepts (see Pinker, Chapter 4). Levinson sees the great diversity among languages as more than simple "noise," but rather as providing evidence about something profound. Further, he emphasizes that humans have evolved to have culture, but also to have a specific, not a general human, culture.

Reading Questions

- Levinson summarizes a body of research that has shown that children's first task is to figure out the sounds of the particular language into which they are born. By 18 months, they have sorted this out quite thoroughly. How does this support Levinson's broader point?
- What evidence does Levinson provide to dispute Li and Gleitman's claim that "the grammars and lexicons of all languages are broadly similar"?
- What sorts of things vary across languages? Why does Levinson regard this as "*the fundamentally interesting thing about language*"?

Stephen C. Levinson, "Language and Mind: Let's Get the Issues Straight!" In *Language in Mind: Advances in the Study of Language and Thought*. Edited by Dedre Gentner and Susan Goldin-Meadow. Cambridge, MA., and London: MIT Press, 2003, pp. 25–46.

- What are linguistic universals? Are there any specific ones? What conclusion does Levinson draw from this? How does he interpret the implications of Berlin and Kay's studies of color?

Current discourse on the topic of language and mind is at about the intellectual level of a chat show on the merits of democracy. Ideological nonsense, issued by famous scholars, fills the air, even the scientific journals. Serious scholars tend to leave well enough alone, since such exchanges reveal a banal underlying lack of analysis. It is as if the topic of "Whorfianism" is a domain where anybody can let off steam, go on mental holiday, or pounce upon an ideological enemy. This is a pity, because the issues are deeply relevant to understanding our place in nature, and how we should understand our unique language capacity. Further, the issues are entirely open to careful analysis and empirical investigation, using the normal methods of the linguistic and psychological sciences.

In this chapter, I try to spell out in the simplest terms what the underlying issues are (but see Levinson 1996, 1997a, 2000, 2001, 2003, for deeper discussion). We have to establish some kind of sensible mode of discourse before empirical results can be appreciated for what they are. As I outline at the end of the chapter, there is an accumulated body of such results, but first we had better try to establish the foundations for rational discourse.

THE DOCTRINE OF SIMPLE NATIVISM AND ITS COEVOLUTIONARY ALTERNATIVE

There is a widespread presumption in the cognitive sciences that language is essentially innate. All the other species have innate communication systems, so why not humans too? Of course, languages don't all sound alike, but that's a matter of superficial clothing. Underneath, it's the very same flesh and blood. There are two basic tenets to the doctrine. The first holds that the syntax of language is fundamentally universal and innate, a view of course associated with Chomsky. The second (of central interest to this chapter) holds that the semantics is given by an innate "language of thought," a view ably defended by Fodor (1975). Put them together and one has the widespread presumption, which I will dub *Simple Nativism*, which curiously enough is not generally associated with any adaptational or evolutionary argument for language (see Levinson 2000). The central property of Simple Nativism is the claim that all the major properties of language, the object of study, are dictated by inbuilt mental apparatus. The observable variation is simply "noise," and nothing much can be learned from it. Protagonists of this view can be found across the cognitive sciences, including linguists like Jackendoff (see Landau and Jackendoff 1993), cognitive psychologists like Pinker (1994) or Gleitman (see, e.g., Li and Gleitman 2002), and the so-called evolutionary psychologists like Tooby and Cosmides (1992).

Despite its prominence, this doctrine is peculiar. First, it is impossible to reconcile with the facts of variation across languages. Second, it is a theory of innate (thus biological) endowment outside biology. There is no biological mechanism that could be responsible for providing us with all the meanings of all possible words in all possible languages—there are only 30,000 genes after all (about the number of the most basic words in just one language), and brain tissue is not functionally specific at remotely that kind of level. Third, it misses the most fundamental biological specialization of our species: the species has coevolved with culture—we cannot survive without it, but with it we have evolved a method of adapting to new ecological niches with much greater rapidity than our genome.

This last point is worth developing a little further. Human evolution has been shaped by the development of two distinct types of information transfer across generations, genetic and cultural, with systematic interactions between them (Durham 1991). Just look at the evolution of our hands and the progression of the tools to be found in the archaeological record. Language is an obvious central part of this gene-culture coevolution—it is culture, responding to its particular ecological niche, that provides the bulk of the conceptual packages that are coded in any particular language. The contents of language, and much of its form, are thus largely the products of cultural tradition—but at the same time those cultural elements are constrained in many different ways by the biological nature of the organism, particularly its learning capacity. Rather precise information about this kind of interaction has now been provided by the study of infant speech perception. Infants are highly sensitive to the initial speech sounds around them, and they seem to have an innate fine-grained categorical system of perception shared with monkeys and other mammals. But by six months after birth infants have done something no monkey can do: they have warped this system of categories into line with the local language they are hearing around them. In that short time, they have acquired a cultural acoustic landscape. It is hard to escape the conclusion that human infants are "built" to expect linguistic diversity and have special mechanisms for "tuning in" to the local variety (Kuhl and Meltzoff 1996, 1997). We can expect to find exactly the same sort of interaction between prelinguistic perceptual distinctions and linguistically variable semantic distinctions. Thus, Choi et al. (2000; see also McDonough, Choi, and Mandler, 2003; Bowerman and Choi, 2003) have shown that 9-month-old infants have equal facility to make, for example, English versus Korean spatial distinctions, while by 18 months they are tuned into the local language-specific distinctions. By the time we reach adulthood, just as we find alien language distinctions hard to hear, so English-speaking adults have lost the ability to make Korean distinctions even in nonlinguistic implicit categorization. Infants, unlike monkeys, are preadapted for cultural variation, for discovering the local system and specializing in it.

This alternative coevolutionary account, with psychology and cultural variation locked in mutual adaptation, is much better suited than Simple Nativism to understanding linguistic and cultural variation. It makes us think differently about what the biological endowment for language must be like. Instead of expecting that endowment to predict all the interesting properties of observable languages, we need rather to think about it as a learning mechanism wonderfully adapted to discerning the variability of culturally distinctive systems—a mechanism that simultaneously puts limits on the variation that those systems can throw at it. On this account, the essential properties of language are divided between two inheritance systems, biological and cultural, and the long-term interactions between them.

Simple Nativism has blocked sensible and informed discussion of the relation between language and thought for decades. Once the facts about linguistic diversity are properly appreciated, it will be clear that Simple Nativism ceases to be of any real interest.

Linguistic Variation

Simple Nativists hold that linguistic categories are a direct projection of universal concepts that are native to the species:

> Knowing a language, then, is knowing how to translate mentalese into strings of words and vice versa. People without a language would still have mentalese, and babies and many nonhuman animals presumably have simpler dialects. (Pinker 1994, 82)

Learning a language is on this view simply a matter of learning the local projection, that is, finding the local phonetic clothing for the preexisting concepts. Or as Li and Gleitman (2002, 266) put it:

> Language has means for making reference to the objects, relations, properties, and events that populate our everyday world. It is possible to suppose that these linguistic categories and structures are more or less straightforward mappings from a preexisting conceptual space, programmed into our biological nature: Humans invent words that label their concepts.

Hence, they hold, "the grammars and lexicons of all languages are broadly similar."

The view just sketched is simply ill informed. There is no sense of "broad" under which "the grammars and lexicons of all languages are broadly similar." If there were, linguists could produce a huge range of absolute linguistic universals—but they cannot do so. As Greenberg (1986, 14) has put it, either language universals are trivial ("All spoken languages have vowels"), or they are conditional generalizations with statistical generality. It is fundamentally important to cognitive science that the true range of human language variation is not lost sight of.

It may be useful to review some of the fundamental parameters of variation. Natural languages may or may not be in the vocal-auditory channel—they can be shifted to the visual-manual one, as in sign languages. When they are broadcast in an acoustic medium, they may have as few as 11 or as many as 141 distinctive sounds or phonemes (Maddieson 1984). Languages may or may not have morphology, that is, inflection or derivation. Languages may or may not use constituent structure (as in the familiar tree-diagrams) to encode fundamental grammatical relations (Austin and Bresnan 1996; Levinson 1987). Thus, they may or may not have syntactic constraints on word or phrase order. Languages may or may not make use of such basic word class distinctions as adjective, adverb, or even, arguably, noun and verb (Mithun 1999, 60–67). If they do, the kind of denotation assigned to each may be alien from an English point of view. Languages force quite different sets of conceptual distinctions in almost every sentence: some languages express aspect, others don't; some have seven tenses, some have none; some force marking of visibility or honorific status of each noun phrase in a sentence, others don't; and so on and so forth. Linguists talk so often about universals that nonlinguists may be forgiven for thinking that they have a huge list of absolute universals in the bag; but in fact they have hardly any that have even been tested against all of the 5%–10% of languages for which we have good descriptions. Almost every new language that is studied falsifies some existing generalization—the serious comparative study of languages, and especially their semantic structures, is unfortunately still in its infancy.

I emphasize the range of linguistic variation because *that's the fundamentally interesting thing* about language from a comparative point of view. We are the only known species whose communication system is profoundly variable in both form and content (thus setting aside, e.g., minor dialects in bird song form; Hauser 1997, 275–276). So we can't have the same kind of theory for human communication that we have for bee or even monkey communication; fixed innate schemas are not going to give us a full explanation of language. Of course, the human innate system must be superbly equipped to expect and deal with the variation—and so it is. This is what Kuhl (1991) has so nicely shown in the realm of speech sounds, as noted above: infants, unlike monkeys, are built to specialize early in the local sound-system.

Let us now pursue the subject of special interest to this chapter: semantic variation across languages. Take the spatial domain. On first principles, this is a conceptual domain where we would least expect major semantic variation; after all, every higher animal has to be able to find its way home, and mammals share a great many specialized anatomical and neurophysiological systems dedicated to telling them where they are and where things are with respect to them. So if the Fodor, Pinker, or Gleitman story is correct anywhere, it should be so here: spatial categories in language should be direct projections of shared innate conceptual categories. But it turns out that there is not the slightest bit of evidence for this.

We may take a few simple examples of spatial concepts where universal agreement on spatial categories has been expected. Let us start with deixis, often presumed universal in all essentials. It has been supposed that all languages have demonstratives that make at least a contrast between 'this' and 'that', but even spoken German seems to falsify that (some German dialects arguably have no demonstratives at all, but only articles). And for languages that do have two demonstratives, it turns out that there are at least four semantic types; more generally, research shows almost as many semantic distinctions in demonstratives as languages investigated (Dunn and Meira, in preparation). Likewise, it has been supposed that all languages make a basic distinction between 'come' and 'go' verbs. But in fact not all languages handle this distinction in lexical verbs (instead, e.g., using 'hither', 'thither' particles), and, when they do, there is tremendous variation in exactly what is coded. Typically, but not always, 'go' has no deictic coding, merely pragmatically contrasting with 'come', and the 'come' verb may or may not entail arrival at the deictic center, and may or may not allow motion continued beyond this center (Wilkins and Hill 1995).

Next, let us turn to the subdomain of so-called topological spatial relations. These are relations of contact or propinquity (like English *on, at, in, near*), which, following Piaget and Inhelder (1956), have been taken to be the simplest kind of spatial relation. Landau and Jackendoff (1993) have suggested that closed-class spatial expressions in languages are highly restricted in conceptual type, referring only to "the very gross geometry of the coarsest level of representation of an object—whether it is a container or a surface" (p. 227). On the basis of English prepositions, they confidently make universal claims of the following sort: no language will have spatial relators expressing specific volumetric shapes of ground objects—for example, there will be no preposition or closed-class spatial relator *sprough* meaning 'through a cigar-shaped object' (p. 226). But the Californian language Karuk has precisely such a spatial prefix, *-vara* 'in through a tubular space' (Mithun 1999, 142)! The whole set of claims is based on woeful ignorance of the crosslinguistic facts.

Still, however rich the rest of the semantic distinctions, it could be that every language encodes a notion precisely like English *on* and *in*. Not so: many languages fractionate these notions and indeed have much more specific notions, like 'in a hemispherical container' versus 'in a cylindrical container.' Tzeltal makes many such distinctions in spatial predicates (Brown 1994). But perhaps we simply need to qualify the claim: if a language encodes spatial relations in prepositions (or postpositions), then every such language encodes a notion precisely like English *on* or *in*. This is not remotely true either. In current work, Sergio Meira and I have mapped the adpositions (prepositions or postpositions) of a dozen languages of different stocks onto exactly the same set of 70 spatial scenes, each scene depicting a subtype of a topological relation.[1] What emerges quite clearly is that there is no basic agreement on what constitutes an 'in' scene, a spatial relation of containment, or any other

basic topological relation. It is simply an empirical matter that spatial categories are almost never the same across languages, even when they are as closely related as English and Dutch.

Finally, we have also surveyed a wide sample of languages for the kinds of coordinate systems or frames of reference they use for describing the location of objects widely separated from a reference object (Levinson, 2003). In these situations, some kind of angular specification on the horizontal plane is called for—as in 'The ball is behind the tree'. It turns out that although languages vary greatly in the detailed geometry employed, there are three main families of solutions: an egocentric (or more accurately viewpoint-dependent) *relative* system (as in 'The ball is left of the tree'), a geocentric *absolute* system (as in 'The ball is north of the tree'), and an object-centered *intrinsic* system (as in 'The ball is at the front of the truck'). These three are all polar coordinate systems and constitute the best claim for universals in the spatial domain. But there are some important caveats. First, not all languages use all three systems. Rather, they form an inventory from which languages must choose at least one—all combinations are possible, except that a relative system entails an intrinsic system. That means there are languages without words for 'left' or 'right' directions, but where all spatial directions must be specified in terms of cardinal directions like 'east' (so one has to say things like 'Pass the northern cup', 'There's a fly on your northern leg', etc.). Second, as mentioned, the local instantiation of any one system may be of a unique kind. Consider for example relative systems, which if fully developed involve a 'left', 'right', 'front', 'back' set of distinctions. Now, these distinctions are very variously mapped. They involve a projection of viewer-centered coordinates onto a landmark object, so that, for example, the ball can be said to be behind the tree. In English, this projection involves a reflection of the viewer's own left-right-front-back coordinates onto (in this case) the tree, so the tree's *front* is the side facing us, and its *back* is the side away from us, but its *left* and *right* are on the same side as the viewer's. In Hausa and many other languages, this projection involves translation, so 'left' and 'right' remain as in English, but 'front' and 'back' are reversed ('The ball is behind the tree' means it is between the viewer and the tree). In some dialects of Tamil, the projection involves rotation, so 'front' and 'back' are like in English, but 'left' and 'right' are reversed. And so on and so forth—there is plenty of semantic variation. Although the choices between different frames of reference are limited, they are quite sufficient to induce the very strongest "Whorfian" effects, as described below (and see Levinson 1996; Pederson et al. 1998).

To sum up: the Simple Nativist idea (as voiced by Pinker and Gleitman) that universal concepts are directly mapped onto natural language words and morphemes, so that all a child-learner has to do is find the local name as it were, is simply false. There are vanishingly few universal notions, if any, that every language denotes with a simple expression. Even the renowned case of the color words only substantiates this fact: languages vary substantially in the number of color words they have, and what they actually denote (Kay and McDaniel 1978; Kay, Berlin, and Merrifield 1991). A term glossed as 'red' may—according to the standard theory—actually include brown, yellow, and related hues, and 'black' may include blue and green. But some languages have at best only incipient color words (Levinson 2000), and this has required substantial weakening of the standard theory (Kay and Maffi 1999). There is really no excuse for continued existence of the myth of a rich set of lexically packaged semantic universals. Removing that myth opens the way for entertaining seriously a heretical idea.

THE VERY THOUGHT: COULD THE LANGUAGE WE SPEAK INFLUENCE THE WAY WE THINK?

There is an ideological overtone to Simple Nativism: the independence of thought from language opens up to us the freedom of will and action ("[S]ince mental life goes on independently of particular languages, concepts of freedom and equality will be thinkable even if they are nameless" Pinker 1994, 82). So Whorfianism and linguistic determinism *have* to be impossible! This moral imperative is beside the point, not only because we are not in the preaching business, but also because, despite some incautious language, no one, not even Whorf, ever held that our thought was in the infernal grip of our language. Whorf's own idea was that certain grammatical patterns, through making obligatory semantic distinctions, might induce corresponding categories in habitual or nonreflective thought in just the relevant domains (see Lucy 1992b for careful exposition). Now that idea, generalized also to lexical patterns, seems neither anti-American nor necessarily false. More generally still, it seems fairly self-evident that the language one happens to speak affords, or conversely makes less accessible, certain complex concepts. There are languages with no or very few number words, and without a generative system of numerals—it seems unlikely that the speakers of such a language would ever entertain the notion 'seventy-three', let alone that of a logarithm, and certainly their fellows would never know if they did. As mentioned, there are languages that only use cardinal direction terms for spatial directions, where one must constantly be able to unerringly locate the center of a quadrant at, say, 15 degrees east of north—speakers of such languages can be shown to have a developed sense of direction of a different order of magnitude from speakers of languages that lack such constant reference to geocentric coordinates (Levinson, 2003). If they didn't have such competence, they couldn't communicate; the language affords, even requires, certain underlying computations (see "The Issues in the Light of Empirical Evidence," below). In this sort of way, languages can differentially impede, facilitate, or require underlying mental operations.

In this section, I want to show that the web of theoretical commitments we already have in the linguistic and psychological sciences seem to converge on the presumption that speaking specific languages does indeed have cognitive consequences for the speakers of those languages.

First, take the simple question "Do we think the same way that we speak?" Making various classical assumptions (e.g., accepting the notion of a *representation*), this question can reasonably be rendered as the more specific "Are the representations we use in serious nonlinguistic thinking and reasoning the very same representations that underlie linguistic meanings?" The answer, I have shown (Levinson 1997a), has to be no. The reasons are various, but conclusive: semantic representations have to be decoupled from conceptual representations to allow for various properties of linguistic meaning like deixis, anaphora, very limited lexica, linearization, and so on, which are clearly not properties of conceptual representations. Besides, there are many different kinds of conceptual representation, from the imagistic to the propositional. But there are also quite persuasive arguments to the effect that though linguistic and nonlinguistic representations are distinct, there must be at least one level of conceptual representation that is closely aligned to a semantic level; otherwise, we couldn't transform the one into the other with the facility we have, as shown by the speed of language encoding and comprehension. Further, any semantic distinctions must be supported by the underlying conceptual distinctions and processes that are necessary to compute them (if you have a lexical concept 'seven'—and not all languages do—you had better be able to count to 7 if you are going to use it correctly). So, overall, that level of conceptual representation is close to, but not identical to, a level of semantic representation.

Our next simple question is, "Do all humans think alike?" Given that there are multiple representation systems (for vision, touch, smell, etc.), many of them specialized to the sensory modalities, and given that many human sensory experiences are basically similar (given the world we all inhabit), there is no doubt that there is a broad base of "psychic unity" in the species. But we are interested in the more abstract representations in which we think and reason, which are closest to language. We can transform the basic question then into the more specific "Is the conceptual representation system closest to semantic representation universal in character?" The answer to that question is—perhaps surprisingly—almost certainly no. The answer can be derived from both first principles and empirical investigation. Here I concentrate on the reasoning from first principles, postponing the empirical arguments to the following section.

Why must the conceptual representations closest to semantic representations be nonuniversal? Because languages vary in their semantic structure, as we saw [earlier: "Linguistic Variation"]. Simply put, the fact is that there are few if any lexical concepts that universally occur in all the languages of the world; not all languages have a word (or other expression) for 'red' or 'father' or 'in' or 'come' or even 'if'. Now the consequences of that basic fact are easily enough appreciated. Let us pursue a *reductio*. We have established that semantic representations map fairly directly, but not exactly, onto the closest level of conceptual representation (CR). Assume now that CR is universal. Then, allowing for some slippage, semantic representations (SR) must be roughly universal too. But they are not. Therefore, we must abandon the assumption that CR is universal.

Approaching the problem from the other direction, we know that languages code different concepts at the lexical level. Now assume—as Fodor and many psychologists do—that corresponding to a lexical item is a single holistic concept (Fodor, Fodor, and Garrett 1975). Further assume, as they do, that SR and CR are coextensive. Then, since we think in CR, users of different languages think differently. So, it follows that "nondecompositionalists" (i.e., those who do not think that lexical concepts decompose into subconcepts) are implicit Whorfians—a fact that they do not seem to have appreciated.[2]

Linguists tend to be decompositionalists—they tend to think that lexical concepts are complex, composed out of atomic concepts. Naturally, they are not always so naive about semantic variation as the psychologists. But they think they can escape the immediate Whorfian consequence: languages encode different concepts at the lexical level, but they "compose" those semantical concepts from a universal inventory of atomic concepts. Even assuming that SR and CR are closely related, as seems to be the case, it no longer seems to follow that different languages require different conceptual relations, or that speaking a language would induce different ways of thinking: both SR and CR could be universal at the level of conceptual primes or primitives. So we can cook our varied semantic cakes out of the same old universal flour and sugar.

Though I am sympathetic with the decompositional move, it is hardly the intellectual triumph that it may seem. Suppose I hypothesize a universal inventory of 20 or 100 primes, and now I come across a language that has words that won't decompose into those primes. What will I do? Add to the universal inventory the features we need for that language, of course. So what makes them universal? At least one language uses them! How would you falsify such a theory? There isn't any way to falsify a theory of universals that consists in an augmentable list of features that any one language may freely select from. It's the weakest possible kind of theory—it would need to be supplemented with a theory that tells us why *just those features* and no others are in the inventory, and we are in no position to do that because we have as yet no idea of the real extent of semantic variation.

But there's another problem with decomposition. Psycholinguistic evidence shows that when words are activated, the concept as a whole is activated, not little bits of it. And the psychologists have compelling evidence that we don't think at that atomic level—we think at the macrolevel of conceptual wholes, the level reflected in lexical concepts. The reasons for this lie partly in properties of short-term memory, the major bottleneck in our computing system. For short-term memory is limited to, say, five chunks at a time, while not caring a jot about how complex the underlying chunks are—or, put another way, what they can be decomposed into

(Miller 1956; Cowan 2001). We don't have to think about a *hundred* as 'ten tens' when doing mental arithmetic, or *aunt* as 'mother's sister, or father's sister, or father's brother's wife, or mother's brother's wife' when greeting Aunt Mathilda. Composing complex concepts gives enormous power to our mental computations, and most of those complex concepts are inherited from the language we happen to speak. So the linguists are wrong to think that lexical decomposition will let them off the Whorfian hook. Sure, it allows them to hold a remoter level of universal concepts, and it might help to explain how we can learn complex cultural concepts, but the conceptual level closest to the semantic representations, and the level in which we compute, seems likely to be heavily culture specific.

So, given the facts of semantic variation, and what we know about mental computation, it is hard to escape the conclusion that, yes, the ways we speak—the kinds of concepts lexically or grammatically encoded in a specific language—are bound to have an effect on the ways we think. And this conclusion is going to be general over all the different kinds of theory scholars are likely to espouse: noncompositional or compositional representational theories, and equally of course connectionist theories, where activation patterns are a direct reflection of input patterns.

THE ISSUES IN THE LIGHT OF EMPIRICAL EVIDENCE

So now at last we might be prepared to accept the idea that it is worth empirically investigating the kinds of influence a specific language might have on our mental coding of scenes and events, our nonlinguistic memory and inference. In fact, there is already a quite impressive body of evidence that demonstrates significant effects here. I will review a few examples, concentrating on our own work.

Curiously enough, the color work in the tradition of Berlin and Kay (1969), which has been taken to indicate simple universals of lexical coding, has also yielded evidence for the impact of linguistic categories on memory and perceptual discriminations. As noted above, the lexical universals are of a conditional sort; for example, if a language has just three color words, one will cover the "cool" range (black, green, blue), another the "warm" range (red, yellow, orange), and another the "bright" range (white, pink, pale blue, etc.) (see Kay and McDaniel 1978). So it is easy to find languages that differ in their color coding. Lenneberg and Roberts (1956) had earlier shown that having specific terms for, say, 'yellow' versus 'orange', helped English speakers memorize colors, compared to Zuni speakers who have no such lexical discrimination. Lucy (1981) showed similar effects for Yucatec versus Spanish versus English speakers, and Davidoff, Davies, and Roberson (1999) did the same for English versus Berinmo. Kay and Kempton (1984) explored the effects of linguistic coding on perceptual discriminability and found that if a language like English discriminates 'blue' and 'green', while another like Tarahumara does not, English speakers but not Tarahumara speakers will exaggerate the perceptual differences on the boundary. This suggests that our visual perception may be biased by linguistic categorization just as our auditory perception clearly is by the specific phonemes in a language (which is why of course late second language learners have difficulty perceiving and producing the alien speech sounds).

Turning to our own work, in a large-scale, long-term collaborative enterprise involving two score researchers, we have researched linguistic differences in the spatial domain. Our goals have been first, to understand the linguistic differences here, and second, to then explore the relation of those linguistic differences to nonlinguistic cognition. I have already outlined above some of the quite surprising linguistic differences to be found across languages; in general, it is hard to find any pair of spatial descriptors with the same denotation across languages (see, e.g., Levinson and Wilkins 2006). In the subdomain of frames of reference, we have pursued the nonlinguistic correlates in detail. The following is a synopsis of much detailed work (see Levinson 1996, 1997b, 2003; Pederson et al. 1998; and references therein).

As mentioned above, languages make different use of the three basic frames of reference. Some languages, like English or other European languages, employ the relative frame of reference (involving left/right/front/back terms projected from a viewpoint) along with the intrinsic (involving properties of the landmark or reference object, e.g., its intrinsic top, back, sides, etc.). Other languages, like Tzeltal or Arrernte, use no relative frame of reference, but instead supplement an intrinsic system with an absolute one—that is, a cardinal-direction type system. In languages like these, speakers can't say 'Pass me the cup to your left', or 'Take the first right', or 'He's hiding behind the tree'—the relevant spatial expressions simply don't exist. Instead, they have to say 'Pass me the cup to the west', or 'Take the first turn to the south', or 'He's hiding east of the tree', as appropriate. Such cardinal-direction systems are actually quite diverse (e.g., they may have arbitrary directions unrelated to the earth's poles) and are always different from the English speaker's use of map coordinates (e.g., in the English system there is no linguistic convention about how many degrees on either side of grid-north still constitutes 'north', and English speakers only use this system on a geographic scale).

We made the following predictions. First, speakers of languages with absolute coordinates should have a better sense of direction than speakers of relative languages: they not only have to know where, say, 'south' is at any one moment (otherwise they couldn't speak the language), but they also need to know, for example, that place B is south of A, because they may have a verb 'go-south' properly used for any motion from A to B. We transported people from three absolute communities to novel locations and got them to point to a range of other locations at varying distances. They can do this with remarkable accuracy, but speakers of relative languages cannot (Levinson 2003). We have also examined unreflective gesture while speaking: for absolute speakers, gestures to places are geographically accurate; for

relative speakers, are not. Second, we supposed that speakers of absolute languages would have to maintain internal representations of space in terms of fixed bearings, rather than egocentric coordinates. That is because if memories were coded in egocentric coordinates, there would be no way to describe them in the relevant language: there is no translation algorithm from egocentric coordinates to geocentric ones, or vice versa (you can't get from the description 'The knife was north of the fork' to the description 'The knife was left of the fork', or vice versa). Since one might want to talk about any observed situation, it had better be memorized in coordinates appropriate to the language. To test this, we invented a rotation paradigm, with which it is possible to distinguish nonlinguistic mental coding in any of the frames of reference. For example, subjects see an arrow on a table pointing to their left, or south. They are now rotated 180 degrees and are asked to place the arrow on another table so it is just as before. If they point it to their left, they thought about it in terms of egocentric coordinates; if to their right (i.e., south), in geocentric coordinates. This paradigm allows examination of different psychological capacities, and we designed a battery of tests exploring recognition memory, recall, and inference of different kinds, all conducted under rotation. The tasks were carried out in four relative and six absolute language communities. The results are quite startling: overwhelmingly, subjects follow the coding pattern in their language when performing these entirely nonlinguistic tasks (Levinson 1996, 2003).

We find these results to be convincing evidence that linguistic coding is both a facilitator of a specific cognitive style and a bottleneck, constraining mental representations in line with the output modality. It seems that preferred frames of reference in language deeply affect our mental life. They affect the kind of mental coding of spatial relations in memory, and the way in which we reason about space, since the different frames of reference have different logical properties (see Levinson 1996). They affect the kinds of mental maps we maintain (as shown by the navigation experiments mentioned above), even the kind of mental imagery we use when we gesture. These are anything but superficial correlates of a mode of linguistic coding.

In a recent paper, Li and Gleitman (2002) try to resist these conclusions and reassert a Simple Nativist perspective. They carried out one simplified version of one of our tasks with an American student population and claimed that they could induce absolute or relative coding by manipulating the conditions of the task. First, the task yielded a relative result indoors, but a mixed relative/absolute result outdoors. Second, by placing salient landmarks or spatial cues at alternate ends of the stimulus and response tables, subjects could be made to construct the response in line with the landmark cue. Li and Gleitman conclude that we all think equally in relative or absolute frames of reference; it just depends on the conditions under which one coding system or another becomes more appropriate. Unfortunately, their results are either not replicable (the outdoors condition) or betray a misunderstanding of the nature of the three frames of reference (the landmark cues condition). When they used salient spatial cues on the stimulus and response tables, what they were actually doing was invoking a response in the intrinsic frame of reference, not the absolute one. We showed this by reproducing their experiment and introducing a new condition: subjects were now rotated 90 degrees instead of 180 degrees (Levinson et al. 2002). If you see a row of animals headed leftward, or south, on table 1 toward a jug, and are then rotated to face table 2 at 90 degrees, and are asked to place the animals just as they were (with an emphasis on remembering which animals were in which order), a response that preserves them heading left or heading south or heading toward the jug can easily be distinguished. English- or Dutch-speaking subjects will place the animals so they are heading either left (relative) or toward the jug (intrinsic), not south (absolute). That's because English and Dutch offer both the relative and intrinsic frames of reference—although the relative is dominant, as can be shown by increasing the memory load (e.g., by adding to the number of animals), whereupon the relative is selected over the intrinsic. In short, pace Li and Gleitman, the evidence remains that the frames of reference used in people's language match those used in their nonlinguistic cognition.

There are many other results that support the idea that linguistic coding has an effect on nonlinguistic cognition. Special mention should be made of the work of John Lucy (1992a; see also Lucy and Gaskins, 2003), which demonstrates that the original ideas of Whorf can be verified—namely, the idea that grammatical patterning with semantic correlates may have an especially powerful effect on implicit categorization. English has obligatory number marking (singular vs. plural) on countable nominals, while Yucatec has only optional number marking, mostly only on animates. Following the hypothesis that this insistent number marking in English might have nonlinguistic effects, Lucy showed that English speakers are better at remembering number in nonlinguistic stimuli. In work with Suzanne Gaskins, he has gone on to show that this lack of number marking in Yucatec is associated with nominals whose semantics are unspecified for quantificational unit (Lucy and Gaskins 2001). They tend to denote not bounded units, but essence or "stuff"; thus, the term used for 'banana' actually denotes any entity made of banana-essence (e.g., the tree or the leaf or the fruit). On sorting tasks, Yucatec speakers behave differently than English speakers: English speakers tend to sort by shape or function, Yucatec speakers by the material out of which things are made. The suggestion is that the pattern in the grammar has far-reaching correlations with implicit mental categories.

Conclusion

Where are we? I have tried to establish that (1) languages vary in their semantics just as they do in their form, (2) semantic differences are bound to engender cognitive differences, (3) these cognitive correlates of semantic differences can be empirically found on a widespread basis. As a conse-

quence, the semantic version of Simple Nativism ought to be as dead as a dodo. But it isn't.

Why not? One reason is that its proponents think they have an argument that it *just has to be right,* so no negative evidence will be seriously entertained! The argument of course is a learnability argument. Consider what the poor child has to do: find the meaning corresponding to some acoustic signal—the child must segment the signal, find the word forms, and then hypothesize the meanings. Suppose, as Fodor, Pinker, and Gleitman hold, that the child is already provided with the relevant conceptual bundles; then all she has to do is map strings of phonemes to ready-made conceptual bundles. This is already difficult, since there are lots of those bundles. Now, suppose the picture was radically different, and the child had to construct the bundles—not a chance! Even worse, suppose that the child has not only to construct the possible meanings for words, but even to figure out how the adults *think,* since they think differently in different cultures. Now the child first has to learn the local cognitive style, and then construct the relevant meanings in line with the cognitive style, before finally being in a position to map the acoustics onto the meanings. The picture is hopeless—Simple Nativism just has to be right!

We can disarm this argument (but see Levinson 2001 for the full counterargument). First, the Fodorean picture doesn't really help. If languages only label antecedently existing concepts, the set of those concepts must include every possible concept lexicalizable in every possible language—a billion or more to be sure. So how will knowing that the needle is already in the haystack help the child find the one correct concept to match to a particular acoustic wave? Second, the picture of the child thumbing through her innate lexicon to find the right antecedently existing concept is surely absurd in the first place; once the lexicon gets to any size at all, it will be much easier to construct the concept than to find it. What the child is going to do is try and figure out what those peculiar adults or elder siblings are really preoccupied with. She will use every clue provided to her, and there are plenty. And some of the most valuable clues will be provided in many different ways by the fact that the adults *think* in a way tightly consistent with the semantics of the language they speak. For example, suppose the adults speak a language where the relative frame of reference predominates. Every aspect of the environment will reflect that fact—the way doors or books open, the arrangement of things (knife always to the right of the fork, socks in the left drawer), the nature of gesture (pointing to the side the referent was on when they were looking at it, not where it actually is from here now), the preferred side of the sidewalk they choose to walk on. In contrast, suppose the adults speak a language where the absolute frame of reference predominates. Now they won't care about preserving egocentric constancies; they will only care that one sleeps with one's head always to the north, builds windbreaks to the east, and, when pointing, points in the veridical direction. A thousand little details of the built environment and, more importantly, the conduct of interaction (see Tomasello 2003) will inform the discerning toddler again and again till she gets the message. It is just *because* we think in line with how we speak, that the clues are not all in the language but are distributed throughout the context of language learning. This new picture doesn't banish the puzzles of how children perform the incredible feat of learning a language, but one thing is certain: it doesn't make it any *more* of an impossible feat than it was on the old picture given to us by the Simple Nativists.

So the overall message is that Simple Nativism has outlived its utility; it blocks a proper understanding of the biological roots of language, it introduces incoherence into our theory, it blinds us to the reality of linguistic variation and discourages interesting research on the language-cognition interface. As far as its semantic tenets go, it is simply false—semantic variation across languages is rich in every detail. We don't map words onto antecedently existing concepts, we build them according to need. That's why cognitive development in children exists, and why the history of science shows progress. The reason we have a developed vocabulary (instead of the limited repertoire of other animals) is that we have found it helps us to *think*. How it does that is explained by that foundational cornerstone of cognitive psychology, Miller's (1956) theory of recoding as a method of increasing computational power by getting around the bottleneck of short-term memory (see Cowan 2001 for an update). Linguistically motivated concepts are food for thought.

Notes

1. The scenes were devised by Melissa Bowerman, with additions by Eric Pederson, and are available as the stimulus set Topological Relations Picture Series of the Max Planck Institute for Psycholinguistics, Nijmegen. For a preliminary report, see the Annual Report 2001, Max Planck Institute for Psycholinguistics (<http://www.mpi.nl>).

2. Fodor himself adopts the only way out of this dilemma, which is to say that every lexical concept in every language that ever has been and ever will be is already sitting there in our heads. So Cro-Magnon man already had the notions 'neutrino' and 'piano', but probably hadn't gotten around to giving them phonetic form!

References

Austin, P., and Bresnan, J. (1996). Non-configurationality in Australian Aboriginal languages. *Natural Language and Linguistic Theory, 14*, 215–268.

Berlin, B., and Kay, P. (1969). *Basic color terms: Their universality and evolution.* Berkeley and Los Angeles: University of California Press.

Bowerman, M., and Choi, S. (2003). Space under construction: Language-specific spatial categorization in first language acquisition. In D. Gentner and S. Goldin-Meadow (Eds.), *Language in mind: Advances in the study of language and thought* (pp. 387–427). Cambridge, MA, and London: MIT Press.

Bowerman, M., and Levinson, S. C. (Eds.). (2001). *Language acquisition and conceptual development.* Cambridge: Cambridge University Press.

Brown, P. (1994). The INs and ONs of Tzeltal locative expressions: The semantics of static descriptions of location. *Linguistics, 32*, 743–790.

Choi, S., McDonough, L., Mandler, J., and Bowerman, M. (2000, May). *Development of language-specific semantic categories of spatial relations: From prelinguistic to linguistic stage.* Paper presented at the workshop "Finding the Words." Stanford University.

Cowan, N. (2001). The magical number 4 in short-term memory: A reconsideration of mental storage capacity. *Behavioral and Brain Sciences, 24*, 87–114.

Davidoff, J., Davies, I., and Roberson, D. (1999). Colour in a Stone-Age tribe. *Nature, 398*, 203–204.

Dunn, M., and Meira, S. In preparation. *Demonstratives in use.*

Durham, W. (1991). *Coevolution.* Stanford, CA: Stanford University Press.

Fodor, A. J. (1975). *The language of thought.* New York: Crowell.

Fodor, J. D., Fodor, J. A., and Garrett, M. F. (1975). The unreality of semantic representations. *Linguistic Inquiry, 6*, 515–531.

Greenberg, J. (1986). On being a linguistic anthropologist. *Annual Review of Anthropology, 15*, 1–24.

Hauser, M. (1997). *The evolution of communication.* Cambridge, MA: MIT Press.

Kay, P., Berlin, B., and Merrifield, W. (1991). Biocultural implications of systems of color naming. *Journal of Linguistic Anthropology, 1*, 12–25.

Kay, P., and Kempton, W. (1984). What is the Sapir-Whorf hypothesis? *American Anthropologist, 86*, 65–79.

Kay, P., and Maffi, L. (1999). Color appearance and the emergence and evolution of basic color lexicons. *American Anthropologist, 101*, 743–760.

Kay, P., and McDaniel, C. K. (1978). The linguistic significance of the meanings of basic color terms. *Language, 54*, 610–646.

Kuhl, P. (1991). Perception, cognition and the ontogenetic and phylogenetic emergence of human speech. In S. E. Brauth, W. S. Hall, and R. J. Dooling (Eds.), *Plasticity of development* (pp. 73–106). Cambridge, MA: MIT Press.

Kuhl, P., and Meltzoff, A. N. (1996). Infant vocalizations in response to speech: Vocal imitation and developmental change. *Journal of the Acoustical Society of America, 100*, 2425–2438.

Kuhl, P. K., and Meltzoff, A. N. (1997). Evolution, nativism and learning in the development of language and speech. In M. Gopnik (Ed.), *The inheritance and innateness of grammars* (pp. 7–44). New York: Oxford University Press.

Landau, B., and Jackendoff, R. (1993). "What" and "where" in spatial language and spatial cognition. *Behavioral and Brain Sciences, 16*, 217–238.

Lenneberg, E., and Roberts, J. (1956). *The language of experience: A study in methodology.* Memoir 13. Indiana University Publications in Anthropology and Linguistics. Baltimore, MD: Waverly Press.

Levinson, S. C. (1987). Pragmatics and the grammar of anaphora. *Journal of Linguistics, 23,* 379–434.

Levinson, S. C. (1996). Frames of reference and Molyneux's question: Cross-linguistic evidence. In P. Bloom, M. Peterson, L. Nadel, and M. Garrett (Eds.), *Language and space* (pp. 109–169). Cambridge, MA: MIT Press.

Levinson, S. C. (1997a). From outer to inner space: Linguistic categories and non-linguistic thinking. In J. Nuyts and E. Pederson (Eds.), *Language and conceptualization* (pp. 13–45). Cambridge: Cambridge University Press.

Levinson, S. C. (1997b). Language and cognition: The cognitive consequences of spatial description in Guugu Yimithirr. *Journal of Linguistic Anthropology, 7,* 98–131.

Levinson, S. C. (2000). Language as nature and language as art. In R. Hide, J. Mittelstrass, and W. Singer (Eds.), *Changing concepts of nature and the turn of the millennium* (pp. 257–287). Vatican City: Pontifical Academy of Science.

Levinson, S. C. (2001). Covariation between spatial language and cognition, and its implications for language learning. In M. Bowerman and S. C. Levinson (Eds.), *Language acquisition and conceptual development* (pp. 566–588). Cambridge: Cambridge University Press.

Levinson, S. C. (2003). *Space in language and cognition: Explorations in cognitive diversity.* Cambridge: Cambridge University Press.

Levinson, S. C., Kita, S., Haun, D., and Rasch, B. (2002). Returning the tables: Language affects spatial reasoning. *Cognition, 84,* 155–188.

Levinson, S. C., and Wilkins, D. (Eds.). (2006). *Grammars of space.* Cambridge: Cambridge University Press.

Li, P., and Gleitman, L. (2002). Turning the tables: Language and spatial reasoning. *Cognition, 83,* 265–294.

Lucy, J. (1981). Cultural factors in memory for color: The problem of language usage. Paper presented at AAA.

Lucy, J. (1992a). *Grammatical categories and cognition: A case study of the linguistic relativity hypothesis.* Cambridge: Cambridge University Press.

Lucy, J. (1992b). *Language diversity and thought: A reformulation of the linguistic relativity hypothesis.* Cambridge: Cambridge University Press.

Lucy, J., and Gaskins, S. (2001). Grammatical categories and the development of classification preferences: A comparative approach. In M. Bowerman and S. C. Levinson (Eds.), *Language acquisition and conceptual development* (pp. 257–283). Cambridge: Cambridge University Press.

Lucy, J., and Gaskins, S. (2003). Interaction of language type and referent type in the development of nonverbal classification preferences. In D. Gentner and S. Goldin-Meadow (Eds.), *Language in mind: Advances in the study of language and thought* (pp. 465–492). Cambridge, MA, and London: MIT Press.

Maddieson, I. (1984). *Patterns of sounds.* Cambridge: Cambridge University Press.

McDonough, L., Choi, S., and Mandler, J. (2003). Understanding spatial relations: Flexible infants, lexical adults. *Cognitive Psychology, 46(3),* 229–259.

Miller, G. A. (1956). The magical number seven, plus or minus two: Some limits on our capacity for processing information. *Psychological Review, 63,* 81–97.

Mithun, M. (1999). *The languages of Native North America.* Cambridge: Cambridge University Press.

Pederson, E., Danziger, E., Wilkins, D., Levinson, S., Kita, S., and Senft, G. (1998). Semantic typology and spatial conceptualization. *Language, 74,* 557–589.

Piaget, J., and Inhelder, B. (1956). [1948] *The child's conception of space.* London: Routledge and Kegan Paul.

Pinker, S. (1994). *The language instinct.* New York: Morrow.

Tomasello, M. (2003). The key is social cognition. In D. Gentner and S. Goldin-Meadow (Eds.), *Language in mind: Advances in the study of language and thought* (pp. 47–57). Cambridge, MA, and London: MIT Press.

Tooby, J., and Cosmides, L. (1992). The psychological foundations of culture. In J. H. Barkow, L. Cosmides, and J. Tooby (Eds.), *The adapted mind* (pp. 19–136). Oxford: Oxford University Press.

Wilkins, D., and Hill, D. (1995). When 'GO' means 'COME': Questioning the basicness of basic motion verbs. *Cognitive Linguistics, 6,* 209–259.

Post-reading Questions / Activities

- Consider the two primary approaches to the study of language origins that Levinson outlines: simple nativism and the coevolutionary account. Be sure you understand how they differ, especially with regard to language universals and diversity. How does each approach explain linguistic and cultural diversity? Is biological evolution an appropriate analogy for language? Compare the two approaches to the various views of the nature of language in Unit 1.
- What did Levinson's own work with frames of reference show?
- Try to carry out one of Levinson's experiments. Compare your results to his claims.

Vocabulary

absolute coordinate system	intrinsic coordinate system	"Simple Nativism"
aspect	linguistic determinism	syntax
cognitive sciences	morphology	visual-manual
constituent structure	nativism	vocal-auditory
deixis	phoneme	Whorfianism
innate	relative coordinate system	

Suggested Further Reading

Berlin, Brent, and Paul Kay. 1969. *Basic Color Terms: Their Universality and Evolution.* Berkeley: University of California Press.

Bloom, Albert H. 1981. *The Linguistic Shaping of Thought: A Study in the Impact of Language on Thinking in China and the West.* Hillsdale, NJ: Erlbaum.

Brown, Penelope, and Stephen C. Levinson. 1993. "'Uphill' and 'Downhill' in Tzeltal." *Journal of Linguistic Anthropology* 3(1): 46–74.

Friedrich, Paul. 1986. *The Language Parallax: Linguistic Relativism and Poetic Indeterminacy.* Austin: University of Texas Press.

Gentner, Dedre, and Susan Goldin-Meadow, eds. 2003. *Language in Mind: Advances in the Study of Language and Thought.* Cambridge, MA: MIT Press.

Gumperz, John J., and Stephen C. Levinson, eds. 1996. *Rethinking Linguistic Relativity.* Cambridge: Cambridge University Press.

Hill, Jane H. 1985. "The Grammar of Consciousness and the Consciousness of Grammar." *American Ethnologist* 12: 725–737.

———, and Bruce Mannheim. 1992. "Language and World View." *Annual Review of Anthropology* 21: 381–406.

Kay, Paul, and W. Kempton. 1984. "What Is the Sapir-Whorf Hypothesis?" *American Anthropologist* 86: 65–79.

Koerner, E. F. Konrad. 1992. "The Sapir-Whorf Hypothesis: A Preliminary History and a Bibliographic Essay." *Journal of Linguistic Anthropology* 2: 173–198.

Levinson, Stephen C. 1996. "Language and Space." *Annual Review of Anthropology* 25: 353–382.

Lucy, John A. 1985. "Whorf's View of the Linguistic Mediation of Thought." In *Semiotic Mediation: Sociocultural and Psychological Perspectives,* edited by E. Mertz and R. J. Parmentier, pp. 73–97. Orlando, FL: Academic Press.

———. 1992a. *Language Diversity and Thought: A Reformulation of the Linguistic Relativity Hypothesis.* Cambridge: Cambridge University Press.

———. 1992b. *Grammatical Categories and Cognition: A Case Study of the Linguistic Relativity Hypothesis.* Cambridge: Cambridge University Press.

———. 1997. "Linguistic Relativity." *Annual Review of Anthropology* 26: 291–312.

———, and Richard A. Shweder. 1979. "Whorf and His Critics: Linguistic and Nonlinguistic Influences on Color Memory." *American Anthropologist* 81: 581–615.

Martin, Laura. 1986. "Eskimo Words for Snow." *American Anthropologist* 88, no. 2 (June): 418–423.

Sapir, Edward. 1964 [1931]. "Conceptual Categories in Primitive Languages." In *Language in Culture and Society: A Reader in Linguistics and Anthropology,* edited by Dell H. Hymes. New York: Harper & Row.

Whorf, Benjamin Lee. 1956. *Language, Thought, and Reality: Selected Writings of Benjamin Lee Whorf,* edited by John B. Carroll. Cambridge, MA: MIT Press.

PART II

Language and Society

If you are reading this, you are a user of English. You may be a native speaker of English, or you may have learned English well after you learned another language. You may have learned English as a young child along with another language or two. You may know English from residing in the United States, but you could just as easily have learned it by growing up and becoming educated in Singapore, the Philippines, India, South Africa, Australia, Canada, England, the Netherlands, or Thailand. (If I haven't included your home, that just reinforces my point about English being available in multiple locations.) English dominates the communicative interactions in today's world, much as French, Dutch, or Latin did in the past. We don't really know how long its hegemony will last; some predict that Chinese will overtake English as a world language.

But we do know that it is possible for a world language to be used for some purposes while another or several other language varieties are used for other purposes. That is the basic insight that governs this part of the book, "Language and Society."

It is tempting to ask "How many languages are there in the world?" That seems like a basic enough starting point if we wish to explore relations of language and society. But it turns out the question is very complicated, and forces us to ask more questions, such as "How do we define *a language*?" and "How do people in any speech community use the multiple linguistic resources around them?"

Language is not simply a tool to be had, but is a tool used by somebody, and by somebodies as members of groups, not simply as individuals. Humans are social by nature, and we signal our social identities largely through the ways we speak. Language is intimately involved in all social interactions, from the largest entities such as nation-states to the smallest and most intimate interactions such as those among friends or family. The study of language and society is rich and multifaceted, and moves outward to a range of topics from education to stereotypes. When we look at the social meanings of language, we learn about the nature of identity and society as they affect all humans.

There are, by most estimates, approximately 6,000 languages still extant in the world. Languages have always been born and have died through the movement and change of their speakers.

But to speak of "a language" is far too simple. If we count "English" with its billion speakers as a single language, and also count the Hezhe language with its 4,000 speakers as a single language, and conclude that there are "two languages," we have overlooked a great deal of the complexity in the world. For, English has uncountable varieties, from the upper-class variety spoken by the educated in England to the Rastafarian English spoken in Jamaica, from African American Vernacular English spoken in the urban United States, to the Appalachian English spoken in rural Kentucky. There are also *Englishes* spoken in Malaysia, India, Africa, and so on.

Many people are speakers of more than one language variety. They acquire multiple languages in complex ways and use them for subtle communicative purposes. Sometimes languages used by decreasing numbers of speakers become endangered and efforts must be made to maintain or revive them if they are to survive.

So simply trying to account for the question "How many languages are there in the world?" requires attention to the realities of how language is used and how it varies within and across societies. It is not simply the case that "The French speak French"; there are multiple varieties of French spoken by people within France and in Francophone Africa and the Caribbean, and there are multiple languages spoken within the boundaries of each country besides just the *official language*.

Beyond even the nameable language varieties such as Malaysian Chinese, there are variations in how exactly language is used, variations that index speakers' identities. These may be social identities, such as social class or gender, or they could be regional identities, or religious identities. Speakers have multiple facets to their identities, and can draw on varying resources as they interact in different spheres.

If we think ecologically, that is, within a system (though a system without clear boundaries), we can look at language varieties and variants as resources that are called upon for particular purposes in particular circumstances.

This sounds like something people might do in a very calculating way: "use resources for a purpose" almost as if one were manufacturing a machine; but of course one of the mysteries of language is that we can do all this without ever having to think about it consciously.

Some people do think about it, though, especially when they are charged with *language planning* or *language revitalization*.

This section takes as its basic premises that (1) multilingualism is the norm, (2) societies and individuals use and value their diverse languages in a variety of ways, (3) languages change and their relative power and value change, (4) identities are enacted at least in large part through language, and (5) status and solidarity are two poles of a continuum.

Vocabulary

language planning
language revitalization
official language

UNIT 3

Multilingualism

Is it a blessing or a curse that most societies everywhere are multilingual? It is the case that for most of human history, all groups interacted with other groups. Attitudes about this differ; sometimes this diversity and divergence are celebrated, sometimes they are ignored, and sometimes they are repressed. Many societies, such as Judeo-Christian societies, have creation myths explaining such linguistic diversity (as in the Tower of Babel story, in which it was deplored).

The term *multilingualism* encompasses a range of behavior from *bilingualism* and *diglossia* (a special kind of bilingualism in which often-related languages such as Arabic and the vernaculars are divided by function) to tri- and quadrilingualism and more. Further, we might distinguish between *societal multilingualism*, in which the society as a whole permits the use of two or more official languages, and *individualism multilingualism*, in which a particular person commands two or more languages.

Some nation-states specify in their constitutions an official or national language, and sometimes also what linguistic rights minority groups retain. India's constitution, for instance, specifies Hindi as the official language, stating that English was to be the medium for official purposes for a limited time, and naming a variety of other national languages, for a total of 22 officially recognized languages. In China, minority groups are allowed by law to have an education and to publish in their own languages and scripts. (These rights are not always granted in fact.) Canada is officially bilingual, but the province of Quebec is monolingual (French only). The United States has no official statement on language, but several states have since the 1980s passed legislation making English the official language.

Language planning and standardization involve the determination of which language can be recognized for official purposes, such as government communication and education.

Some nations, such as most famously France and Spain, have academies (the *Académie française* was founded in 1635, and the French language has been identified with the French nation in the classical case) that determine not only which language is official but specifics about how that language should change or be prevented from changing. The Real Academia Española, founded in 1713, has a modern website that permits users to ascertain which forms are proper in Spanish.

However societies and individuals resolve the issue of multilingualism, it is a fact of human life everywhere.

Individuals can also be multilingual. They can switch from one language to another in appropriate settings, as when they move to a new country or speak to a different person. Or they can switch mid-utterance, for emphasis or to convey a different feeling or because different languages are used for different functions. Hearers also make inferences about speakers' use of their various languages.

Increasingly, languages with fewer speakers and those with less power are being abandoned in favor of more powerful languages and those associated with greater educational or economic opportunities. Estimates of language endangerment and even language death are alarming. Some efforts are being made, however, to resist this trend.

Suggested Further Reading

Edwards, John R. 1994. *Multilingualism*. London and New York: Routledge.

Ferguson, Charles. 1972 [1959] "Diglossia." In *Language and Social Context*, edited by Pier Paolo Giglioli, pp. 232–251. Middlesex, UK: Penguin Books.

Fishman, Joshua A. 1991. *Reversing Language Shift: Theoretical and Empirical Foundations of Assistance to Threatened Languages*. Clevedon and Philadelphia: Multilingual Matters.

Gal, Susan. 1979. *Language Shift: Social Determinants of Linguistic Change in Bilingual Austria*. New York: Academic Press.

Grosjean, François. 1982. *Life with Two Languages: An Introduction to Bilingualism*. Cambridge, MA: Harvard University Press.

Gumperz, John J. 1982. *Discourse Strategies*. Cambridge: Cambridge University Press.

Heller, Monica, ed. 1988. *Codeswitching: Anthropological and Sociolinguistic Perspectives*. Berlin and New York: Mouton de Gruyter.

Myers-Scotton, Carol. 1988. "Codeswitching as Indexical of Social Negotiations." In *Codeswitching: Anthropological and Sociolinguistic Perspectives*, edited by Monica Heller, pp. 151–186. Berlin and New York: Mouton de Gruyter.

Ramaswamy, Sumathi. 1997. *Passions of the Tongue: Language Devotion in Tamil India, 1891–1970.* Berkeley: University of California Press.

Romaine, Suzanne. 1989. *Bilingualism.* New York: Blackwell.

Schiffman, Harold F. 1996. *Linguistic Culture and Language Policy.* London and New York: Routledge.

Terralingua. http://www.terralingua.org/. This website is devoted to maintenance and restoration of biological, cultural, and linguistic diversity.

———. http://www.terralingua.org/TLUNLetterLHR.htm. This provides Terralingua's presentation to the United Nations about linguistic rights.

UNESCO. http://www.unesco.org/most/ln2pol.htm. MOST Clearing House on Linguistic Rights.

Woolard, Kathryn. 1985. *Double Talk: Bilingualism and the Politics of Ethnicity in Catalonia.* Stanford, CA: Stanford University Press.

Zentella, Ana Celia. 1997. *Growing Up Bilingual: Children in El Barrio.* Malden, MA: Blackwell.

CHAPTER 13

Chinese, English, Spanish—and the Rest

Tom McArthur

(2005)

When empires were ruled by European nations, the question of language was often pressing: How could the colonial rulers communicate with the local people? How could the various local peoples, speaking a wide range of languages, communicate efficiently and trade effectively? One solution was to develop a lingua franca, a language like Latin, that would serve as a shared medium of expression, even if it was a second (or third) language for most of its speakers. The choice of which variety to select as a lingua franca involved understanding of local power relations, history, and a good dose of chance.

In recent times, we can see a different dynamic at work. For example, Melayu (a variety of Malay) was deliberately developed as a lingua franca in what was later to become the new nation of Indonesia (and Melayu became the national language, Indonesian). The Dutch who ruled the Dutch East Indies selected it for a variety of reasons.

At various times in the past, certain languages rose to dominance because of the widespread economic and political power of their speakers. Though many have tried to explain this dominance in terms of some intrinsic virtue of the language itself (French as nuanced and appropriate for diplomacy, English as having a wide vocabulary), it is clear that empires took their languages with them and imposed them on the populations they ruled.

Tom McArthur, editor of the journal English Today, *categorizes the languages of the world in the twenty-first century, singling out English as a unique language (actually as a set of languages collected as "Englishes"). Though it is not the first language of the majority of the world's speakers, it is the language used for many affairs of the world, constituting a "world language." People who speak English, perhaps quite well, nonetheless frequently speak a number of other languages in addition. Native speakers of English are the least likely to feel obliged to learn other languages.*

McArthur's seven levels of languages help make sense of the varying breadth and power of the languages in the world, with the largest number of speakers focused in the top three levels and the largest number of languages focused in the bottom four levels. As many of the authors in Unit 3 do implicitly, McArthur writes explicitly of an "ecology" of languages.

Reading Questions

- What are the characteristics of a "world language"? Which languages have had that designation in the past? What are the reasons for English having become one recently?
- Why does McArthur write of the "English language complex" rather than simply the "English language"?
- What is the difficulty in determining the difference between *language* and *dialect*?
- Look carefully at the evidence by which McArthur singles out English from, say, Spanish and Chinese. Does this make sense to you? What other evidence might you amass?

The second edition of the *Oxford Dictionary of English* (2003) defines *ecology* as "the branch of biology that deals with the relations of organisms to one another and to their physical surroundings." I would, however, like to extend this definition here to include an "ecology of communication," covering the nature and evolution of language, the media, and such technologies as radio, telephony, television, and

Tom McArthur, "Chinese, English, Spanish—and the Rest." *English Today* 83 (vol. 21, no. 3), July 2005: 55–61.

the net/web. This discussion will not, however, deal with an ecology of communication at large, but five particular, related matters: English and the rest of the world's languages; the idea of a "world language"; the interaction of the world's languages and communicative technologies; the millions of people who use English and at least one other language; and the size, security, and health of our global linguistic inheritance.

THE ENGLISH LANGUAGE COMPLEX

English is a paradox. In traditional terms it is a single language, but in recent centuries it has become so large and varied that it has taken on the features of a family of languages: like the *Semitic languages* (origin, West Asia) or the *Romance languages* (which might more properly be called the *Latin languages*: cf. Wright 2004). Anyone concerned after the 1980s with *world* or *international* or *global* English also knows (and may use) the form *Englishes*, promoted with marked success by the Indian American linguist Braj B. Kachru. However, although phrases like *the Englishes* and *world Englishes* imply a family, Kachru has not (to my best recollection) explicitly proposed that any of the Englishes are, or might become, distinct languages. One wonders, therefore, whether his "Englishes" constitute a single complex entity or a family of entities.

Since bringing out *The English Languages* in 1998 I have continued to hold the plural view expressed there. However, I have also felt the need for a further phrase: *the English language complex,* which retains the tradition of *English* as a single entity, while allowing for both *the Englishes* and *the English languages* as terms for handling a multiplicity that includes *African English, African-American English, American English, British English, China English, Indian English,* and *Nigerian English.* Yet wherever one looks there are semantic complications. For example:

- The label *British English* can be ambiguous if not overtly clarified: it may mean upper- and middle-class British usage with an RP accent (as conventionally on offer in ELT textbooks and dictionaries) <u>or</u> all English as used in England alone <u>or</u> all English as used in England, Scotland, Wales, and Northern Ireland.
- The label *Indian English* has a range of sub-divisions that includes *Anglo-Indian English, Bengali English,* and is at the same time (uncontentiously) part of *Asian English,* yet we do not usually say that *British English* is part of *European English,* although oddly enough (since there are now many such entities as *Dutch English* and *Swedish English*) this is the case. To complicate matters further, people now talk (often disparagingly) of a European Union kind of English, used especially in Brussels, that is often called *Euro-English,* but explicitly *not* what either the British or the Irish use.

Containing by definition these and other (often confusing) *varieties,* the English language complex is, as it were, a system of systems whose membership is unclear, because commentators can always find another English to add to the list: for example, *Afghan English* or *United Nations English.* One cannot predict or apparently exhaust the number of such terms, whether they are geographic, educational, professional, social, or a mix of these, as with *British English* (as above), *Business English, British Business English, American Business English, Anglo-American Business English* (note: much more likely than *British-American Business English),* *Californian English, Californian Media English, China English,* and *Chinese English* (delicately contrasted in recent issues of *ET*), *Jamaican English Creole,* and indeed that really difficult pair, *X Standard English* and *Standard X English* (where we can replace the *X* with whatever nation, region, ethnicity, business, or other activity we wish) ad infinitum et nauseam.

We *can* say, however, that for some time there have been two universally agreed nation-based standards of English, one cent<u>red</u> on the UK, the other cent<u>ered</u> on the US. It has become increasingly clear, however, over the last half-century, that these are no longer alone. Most Australians, Canadians, and New Zealanders now assume that they too have standard varieties, and there are dictionaries to demonstrate the fact. And indeed, the Irish Republic, South Africa, India, and Singapore can arguably be added to this list (with or without national dictionaries).

In a major everyday sense, however, English remains a language among languages. Yet, even so, many would agree that, since at least the mid-twentieth century, it has not been a language in the way that Danish, Hungarian, Korean, Maori, or Nahuatl are languages, for at least *six* reasons: its scale, its distribution, the number and range of its varieties, its technical and professional applications, and the number of its users and would-be users, whether as a mother tongue or an other tongue. One reason for calling it a *complex* is that many of its varieties are *not,* and never have been, dialects. No one talks of an *Indian dialect of English,* or sub-dialects within Indian English. They do, however, talk about *Punjabi English, Bengali English,* and such like, as (sub)varieties of *Indian English,* each of them influenced by at least one major regional language and/or the vagaries of regional life, and *not* by isolation from the mother source, as was the case for example with the usage of Newfoundland and the Falkland Islands.

In traditional terms, dialects are seldom sharply separated, but are areas within continua: that is, Dialects A and B do not usually "meet" at a boundary line: rather, an area of A shades into an area of B, until A-ness becomes B-ness. In certain politico-cultural instances, however, one area in such a continuum acquires prestige and a script in which records can be kept, orders issued, and books written, becoming because of this the primary and perhaps sole official tool for national record-keeping, news, policy, and officially-received culture, as with *le bon français* or the *King's English.* When a speech form becomes like that, linguists call it an *acrolect* (Greek: "high dialect") and the rest become *basilects* ("low dialects"), maybe with an intermediate layer or two, the *mesolects* ("middle dialects"). Such names make commentary more clinical, but *acro* and *basi* are just Greek elements in English that mean "high" and "low"—verging (dare I say it?) on a cosmetic exercise. The distance between Standard English and the vernacular Englishes, between Mandarin Chinese [Putonghua] and the Han dialects, or Classical Arabic and the vernacular Arabics remains great however the scale is calibrated.

STANDARD, DIALECT, VARIETY, ACCENT, PIDGIN, CREOLE

By and large, the standard and near-standard forms of British and American English are mutually intelligible (especially in print): in effect "the same language" while differing in ways which do not invoke questions about which is a dialect of the other. Many British people have of course insisted that US usage is derivative and therefore secondary, but an overwhelming reversal of global roles in the course of the twentieth century has gravely damaged that particular argument. Linguists, however, agree that neither is a lect of the other and each has lects of its own—and that, in any case, the US is vastly larger and more populous, and carries a bigger stick.

After 1945, there was no reason for Americans to feel secondary to anyone in any aspect of their lives, even if some might defer to British niceties. The rest of the twentieth century simply affirmed a state of affairs that seems likely to last well into the twenty-first. But by and large none of this affected other kinds of English elsewhere, including entities far more exotic than traditional dialects and mildly different standard varieties. English-based pidgins and creoles have sometimes been called "dialects", but usually they have been described not just as "barbarous" or "uncouth" (as dialects have often been described) but as "broken" and "debased": not real English but bastard offshoots to be regretted, and kept at arm's length.

In such a world climate the term *variety* has been immensely reassuring (but at times a copout) for linguists and language teachers. Although I find the term invaluable, I worry about its catch-all blandness: any distinctive spoken, written, printed, electronic or other aspect of a language, and especially English, can be a "variety." And the term has not helped much in avoiding the original problem: In everyday life, *variety* is not much used for talking about language, and the term *dialect* is far more likely to be applied to mesolects and basilects than to acrolects (which are or become the "standard" language that is blessed with orthography and print). Meanwhile, the term *pidgin* remains low, often negative, and at best neutral (despite having been adopted by linguists as a technical term), and *creole* is hardly known outside the Caribbean, Louisiana, and linguistics libraries.

There is more, however. In addition to dialects, pidgins, and creoles, English in all its varieties has long been mixing with other languages, producing a range of, as it were, *Anglo-hybrids*. Such entities may seem chaotic to an outsider meeting them for the first time, but blends of this kind are inevitable in locales where two or more avowed languages are in wide daily contact. Such outcomes as *franglais* and *Spanglish* are not, however, chaotic to their users but are pragmatic blends in which the most immediately recalled and relevant material takes pride of place. Many social commentators deplore such hybridization, but deploring it has never put an end to it, any more than it has put an end to dialect.

When people of different backgrounds within "the same" language come together, the amount of adjustment needed for adequate communication may range from minimal to massive, but by and large exposure to such media as TV and films/movies and news services such as BBC World and CNN appears to have made encounters with variation easier than in the past. Even so, however, remoteness from the world's main travel routes and lack of exposure to the media may make some varieties of a language like English as exotic as the flora and fauna of their locale, as, say, with *Caribbean Creole* and *Tok Pisin* in Papua New Guinea.

SEVEN LEVELS

English is a vast language, whereas Scottish Gaelic now has about 70,000 speakers left. A thousand years ago Gaelic was the primary language of Scotland, accumulating a strong tradition of orature and literature that only a few can now access. I was born into a family whose last Gaelic speaker died in the 1930s. My children know only a few words (such as *slainte* "health," and also a toast which few know, and *glen*, which many know because it became an English word). Both my father and I wanted to acquire it, but life got in the way. However, all three of my children know English, and also French, from living in Quebec; my older daughter is fluent in Japanese, and my son is competent in Italian. Alas, however, none speaks Persian, their mother's language, because she chose not to use it with them. Crucially, however, neither set of grandparents when young could have predicted the languages their grandchildren would know, and this seems increasingly to be the way of the world.

The following is a seven-level model that seeks to represent the world's languages in terms of size and "clout" (if any). The first five levels "contain" the largest and safest languages, and here I spend more time on them (alas), while the lowest two levels contain the many languages worldwide suffering diminution and facing extinction (cf. Crystal 2000).

Level 1: English

A vast, unevenly but widely distributed language complex with two globalized national varieties (American and British), each with a standard form, three further major national varieties (Australian, Canadian, New Zealand), and many varieties worldwide. Around a billion people use it, as a first, second, or other language, and its standard varieties are taught to further millions. It can be heard or read almost everywhere, and is the world's primary vehicle for the media, commerce, technology, science, medicine, education, popular and youth culture, travel, trade in armaments, and United Nations peace-keeping. In terms of its widest reach it is often called *World, International,* or *Global English,* and there is a multitude of regional and other *Englishes,* known more or less formally as, say, *South African English* and *Japanese English,* or informally and often facetiously as, say, *Japlish* and *Taglish* (English mixed with Tagalog, in the Philippines).

Level 2: Chinese, Spanish, Hindi-Urdu

Three language complexes covering hundreds of millions of people. *Chinese,* the largest, has over a billion users, the vast majority in the People's Republic of China, Hong Kong, and Taiwan. *Spanish* is widely disseminated in the Americas, with a limited role in Europe (its continent of origin, as with English). Despite the prestige of Castilian usage in Spain, the language has no single strong centre, like Chinese, or centres, like English. Its geopolitical focus, like English, is the western hemisphere, from Argentina to the US. It is also spoken in Morocco and Equatorial Guinea in Africa and the Philippines in Asia. The vast majority of users of *Hindi-Urdu* are in northern India and Pakistan, with diaspora populations elsewhere. Hindi-Urdu is more or less one entity in speech but not in sociocultural terms. Its Hindi component is the official language of India, uses the Devanagari script, and is largely a medium for northern (not southern) Hindus. Its Urdu component uses the Perso-Arabic script and is primarily a medium for Muslims in India and Pakistan. All three complexes are world-regional, with little (though increasing) wider diffusion.

Level 3: Arabic, French, German, Japanese, Malay

The *Arabic* complex is used across North Africa and in much of the Middle East, throughout which it is the primary medium of ethnic Arabs. In addition, from Europe and North Africa to the Philippines it is the historic vehicle of Islam. It has both a Classical form and a range of colloquial, and not necessarily mutually intelligible, forms in Bahrain, Dubai, Egypt, the Emirates, Iraq, Jordan, Kuwait, Lebanon, Morocco, Qatar, Saudi Arabia, Sudan, Syria, and Yemen. *French* has traditionally been in cultural competition with English, German, and Italian, and until the mid-twentieth century was the elite language of diplomacy. After the Second World War, it lost ground to *les anglo-saxons* (the Americans and British viewed as a unity in which the British formerly dominated and the Americans now dominate). The community of *le français mondial* ("World French") is known as *La Francophonie* ("the French-speaking world"). *German,* formerly strong in Europe and some African colonies, and in academic-cum-scientific writing, lost influence as a consequence of the defeat of Germany and Austria in two world wars, but retains strength in business and technology. *Japanese* has never had a world role, despite Japan's global commercial success. *Malay,* however, has begun to develop a higher profile in Asia because of its role in Malaysia, Indonesia, Brunei, Singapore, and southern Thailand.

Level 4: Significant Nationally and/or Regionally

This level includes such flourishing strong regional languages as Ashanti, Hausa, Ibo, and Yoruba in West Africa; Amharic, Swahili, Somali, and Kikuyu in East Africa; Dutch, Hungarian, Polish, Romanian, and Swedish in Europe; Portuguese in Brazil, Portugal, Angola, Mozambique, East Timor, and Macao; Turkish and Persian in Western and Central Asia; Bengali, Gujarati, Kannada, Konkani, Marathi, Oriya, Punjabi, Tamil, Telugu, and Malayalam in India: all used in communities with large populations, complex social histories, and thriving cultures. Most of the languages at this level are robustly healthy, and many have diaspora communities.

Level 5: Locally and Socially Strong

Languages within one or more nations or territories, such as Berber in Morocco, Catalan in Spain and France, Danish in Denmark, Finnish in Finland, Maya in Mexico and Central America, Guarani in Paraguay, Tagalog and Ilocano in the Philippines, Nahuatl in Mexico, Quechua in Peru, and, as an exceptional case, the vibrant small language Icelandic. Some languages at this level are secure in national terms (as with Danish and Finnish, although English is in use for professional, higher-educational, and international purposes), while others occupy a mid-position in their local hierarchy (as with Catalan and Ilocano), and others have large numbers of users but little or no international prominence (as with Berber, Maya, and Quechua).

Level 6: Small and (Perhaps) Managing

Hundreds of languages used mainly in politically or geographically non-metropolitan areas, or among migrant workers, whose speakers number in the low millions, hundreds of thousands, or less. They may or may not be well-situated nationally, regionally, continentally, socioculturally, or in educational terms, and in many cases have been depleted by social change, including emigration of speakers and immigration of non-speakers. They may, however, be sustaining themselves, sometimes in secure situations, such as Faroese in Denmark's Faroe Islands, sometimes in situations less negative than formerly, as with Maori in New Zealand, sometimes under politically neutral conditions, such as Welsh in Wales (within the UK), Gallego in Spain, and more secure Amerindian languages such as Navajo.

Level 7: Extremely Small and Endangered

Some thousands of languages in the Americas, Asia, Africa, Australasia, Europe, and the Pacific whose speakers number in the thousands, hundreds, or tens and less, often in communities that are shrinking for various reasons (including migration and intermarriage) or disrupted and sometimes demoralized, within and ranging across the boundaries of nation-states, and therefore semi-assimilated into more socially and economically powerful societies. Some manage to sustain themselves, as with Lapp in northern Scandinavia, while others have for many years been in dire straits, particularly the remaining Aboriginal languages of Australia, the "heritage languages" of Canada's "Native Peoples," such as Ojibwa and Inuit; and comparable "American Indian" languages in the US, such as Cherokee and Mohawk. Some may be dichotomous, where for example Irish Gaelic (or Irish) is somewhat sustained by government effort and a national education policy in the Irish Republic, but Scottish Gaelic has no official role or protection, and dwindles despite efforts to promote it (including through internet lessons). Some groups are stable and fairly secure but many are socially disrupted, the numbers of active speakers dwindling, and many probably will not survive the next half-century.

Discussion of the languages in Categories 1 and 2 of this list is difficult without bringing in the languages of 3 to 7, because in many instances multilingual individuals and communities use both large languages alongside their own local-cum-ethnic languages, or have given up a local tongue, or are using it less, or see the next generation giving it up in favour of one or more languages offering better prospects. Significantly, for our purposes here, if users of a language at the sixth or seventh level are not only learning and using a language of wider local distribution but also learning English at school or using it in their work, then *two* kinds of pressure are being exerted on small languages that may not yet be endangered, but could become so in, say, fifty years' time.

Millions of busy people worldwide *can* and *do* become successful trilinguals. In India this is often the norm: mother tongue, other Indian tongue, and English ("the window on the world"). Many native-speakers of English, however, do not use any other language beyond, say, school-days French. It is often therefore difficult for them to imagine or take seriously competition among languages *inside* a nation-state. I don't have Gaelic because local work and migration patterns meant that Highlanders and Islanders moved to the Lowland cities, where they acquired Lowland Scots as the language of work and their children learned Scottish English in school while using versions of Scots vernacular in the street and playground. Nothing simple there, nor anything simple elsewhere. Language ecologies are like bio-ecologies: they normally function well enough, but can be thrown off balance. I don't speak Gaelic, but I *do* know Scots and English natively, plus French and Persian non-natively. Maybe two out of three isn't too bad. And probably Lowland Scots will survive, partly because many people don't accept that it's a language. It may therefore manage to sneak around for quite some time, heavily disguised as bad English.

MEANWHILE, AT THE BIG END OF THE SCALE

The spread since 1945 of "world" or "international" or "global English" has been remarkable, which is why it has Category 1 to itself. Yet even if I'd put Levels 1 and 2 of 7 levels together as 1 of 6 levels, it would have made no difference

to language reality. I didn't do this because the distributions are so different: Spanish, Chinese, and Hindi-Urdu massively concentrated in particular regions, with limited impact elsewhere, and Hindi-Urdu not well known as a single entity, even in India. As a result, this vast complex removes itself from the world discussion, despite its scale and significance. The following three factors apply to it, but in global terms relate more to Chinese, Spanish, and English:

1. Far more users of Chinese and Spanish are learning English than there are users of English learning Spanish and Chinese.
2. Far more users of Chinese and Spanish are learning English than are learning one another's language.
3. Far more users of other languages are learning English than are learning Chinese and Spanish.

However, we can note that Spanish occupies a unique role as the only language currently making inroads into the English-speaking world, and in its most powerful locale, the United States. The demographic and linguistic advance of Latino migrants into the US (from Mexico and further south) has been so marked in recent times that alarmed US linguistic conservatives campaign for English to be made the official federal language (as if this would make much difference). Ironically, in the most powerful fortress of English, enough people have been nervous enough to band together to protect the one language on the planet that is least in need of protection.

The Chinese complex is vast, but the majority of its speakers are Han (ethnic Chinese) living in the People's Republic of China. The vast majority of the world's non-native learners of Chinese are non-Han citizens of the PRC, with however a small but growing number of learners in neighbouring East Asia, their eyes on trade. Like Hindi-Urdu and Spanish, therefore, Chinese is (despite its size) a world-regional language, whereas English (with all its built-in spelling and other hurdles) is the closest we have come to universality in the use of a language, and so, even if English has nearly destroyed Gaelic and long ago upstaged Scots (which was my mother's tongue), I have learned to live with it, and, like my revered English teacher Miss Frances Anderson, at Woodside Senior Secondary School in Glasgow, love it as much as I love Scots. Not to forget French, Latin, Greek, and Persian.

In *The Future of English?* (1997), David Graddol suggests three options for English as a lingua franca in Asia: that it might keep this role indefinitely; that it might be supplanted by Mandarin; or that there might not in future be any Asian lingua franca. A few years further on, in 2005, it would seem that English will sustain its transnational role in Asia, as illustrated by recent developments in the Association of South East Asian Nations (ASEAN), which since its formation in 1967 has used English as its common medium. One must suppose that, when ASEAN members meet such prospective regional trading partners as China and India, English will continue in its current role. In that role, however, it will not be operating as an Atlantic language, but as an Asian lingua franca. And when in the nearish future ASEAN will be dealing with both India and China, English will be the broker language, working together with Hindi-Urdu, Chinese, and Malay as key languages in South and East Asia.

One might call this *English Plus*. In the Americas it will be English plus Spanish (plus Portuguese for Brazil, and French for Quebec). In North and West Africa, it will be English plus Arabic (plus French). In West Asia, it will be Arabic plus English. In South Asia, it will be English plus Hindi-Urdu (South Indians preferring English to Hindi; Pakistanis comfortable with Urdu and English; Sri Lankans opting for English). In parts of Eastern Europe and Central Asia, it will be English plus Russian (with French in the wings in Romania, and German in the Balkans). In western Europe, however, it looks as though English will be the lingua franca (even for the French). That is, English will be everywhere, but often in partnership with other large languages. Not much help (alas) for the languages in Level 7, but less monolithic than some may fear. And maybe an ecology in which people from traditionally multilingual backgrounds can work towards reducing the downward drift.

References and Related Reading

Crystal, David. 1997 (2nd ed., 2003). *English as a Global Language*. Cambridge: Cambridge University Press.

———. 2000. *Language Death*. Cambridge: Cambridge University Press.

Graddol, David. 1997. *The Future of English?* London: The British Council.

Kachru, Braj B. 1982. *The Other Tongue: English Across Cultures*. Urbana: University of Illinois Press.

———. 1992. *The Other Tongue: English Across Cultures*. [new collection]. Urbana & Chicago: University of Illinois Press.

———. 2005. *Asian Englishes: Beyond the Canon*. Hong Kong: Hong Kong University Press.

McArthur, Tom. 1998. *The English Languages*. Cambridge: Cambridge University Press.

———. 2002. *Oxford Guide to World English*. Oxford: Oxford University Press.

Wright, Roger. 2004. "Latin and English as world languages." In *English Today* 80 (20:4).

Post-reading Questions / Activities

- Have you studied a foreign language? Which level does that language occupy? Have you learned about the force and power of the nations associated with that language? Could *every* language be portrayed as important and significant? In what sense?
- How can you account for the languages taught in schools in your country? On what basis are they selected? Have those languages changed since your parents were students? Would you expect the next generation to be learning the same or different languages? What languages do you think *should* be taught? Why?
- What is the role of the media in determining which languages have world dominance?

Vocabulary

accent	Diaspora	standard
creole	mutually intelligible	variety
dialect	pidgin	

Suggested Further Reading

Edwards, John R. 1994. *Multilingualism*. London and New York: Routledge.

Romaine, Suzanne. 1989. *Bilingualism*. New York: Blackwell.

Schiffman, Harold F. 1996. *Linguistic Culture and Language Policy*. London and New York: Routledge.

CHAPTER 14

Triglossia
African Privilege or Necessity?

Rajmund Ohly
(2004)

It is often surprising that African countries threw off the burden of colonialism, only to select the former colonial languages as their national or official language. The late Polish expert on African languages and cultures, Rajmund Ohly, explains this by comparing the different ways various African nations engaged in language planning. He challenges a ready comparison to Charles Ferguson's idea of diglossia, *with the official language the H (high) language and the L (low) language the vernacular. This is incorrect, he argues.*

All African states are richly multilingual. For example, in Nigeria's Middle Belt, there are approximately 400 distinct minority languages; of these, at least 180 have fewer than 400 speakers. Many are unstudied, unwritten, and unknown to outsiders. Some have as many as one million speakers, but none are addressed in government policy.

In the words of the United Nations Educational, Scientific, and Cultural Organization (UNESCO), people have a right to "mother tongue education," but many African countries cannot provide it to all people. Some groups such as the Khoesan in Botswana wish for assimilation, by learning the dominant language (Setswana).

Africans have largely been characterized by trilingualism, which has been the norm, making Africans accept the need for languages with varying spheres of use (a vernacular language, or mother tongue; a contact language used for local relations; and a lingua franca for regional communication). In most African countries, the lingua franca is now an imported language—sometimes transformed into a creole.

Language planning includes the need to determine which languages will serve as the medium of education and government. In Nigeria, for instance, language planners accept that additive multilingualism is desirable and incorporate this into the curriculum. Outside languages such as English, French, Portuguese, and Spanish were retained as a means of neutralizing conflict among various ethnic groups, but in the end those who master them have become a new elite.

Languages have to serve many functions: to express identity and solidarity, to communicate practical information, to educate children, to provide a medium for technical knowledge, and to facilitate political and governmental exchange. Though it is an item of faith among linguists that any language can express any thought—granted that some vocabulary may not exist in some languages in some domains—in fact languages have been used for varying purposes and bring with them varying functions. The intermediate languages have been found to be lacking in technical terminology, for instance, which makes them less valuable as lingua francas. Thus other languages pick up that purpose.

Reading Questions

- Why are African nations multilingual?
- What policies does Ohly describe regarding minority languages?
- What languages are used in schools?

Rajmund Ohly, "Triglossia: African Privilege or Necessity?" In *Globalisation and African Languages: Risks and Benefits,* edited by Katrin Bromber and Birgit Smieja. Berlin and New York: Mouton de Gruyter, 2004, pp. 103–116.

- How do you think the expectation of multilingualism affects the way Africans encounter new languages? How would this differ from the expectation of monolingualism?

The multilingual environment, typical of the African continent, demanded the emergence of sophisticated, sociolinguistically motivated, systems of communication. In general, systems developed either as a result of formal, i.e., authoritative initiatives (*contrat*-oppression), or informal proceedings (*lutte*-repression) arising from different social strata.

In 1979, Bernd Heine presented a typology still valid today, classifying African states according to the language policy conducted by the given government. In general, nations[1] have been divided into endoglossic and exoglossic units. Endoglossic states, employing a native language as a medium of nationwide communication, are further arranged into

(a) states conducting an active endoglossic policy such as Egypt with Arabic, Somalia with Somali or Tanzania with Kiswahili, and

(b) states without an active endoglossic policy such as Botswana with Setswana, Lesotho with Sesotho or Rwanda with Kinyarwanda.

In all the cases in the (a) category, African languages fulfil official administrative functions and are spoken by most of the population. For example, in Tanzania (see later herein), English still occupies a complementary position in the communication system. States in the (b) category, on the other hand, utilise the former colonial languages in administration, education, and the mass media although the bulk of their population communicates through the dominant African languages, called national languages. Their survival depends on their ethoglossia.

States conducting an exoglossic policy employ no African languages in official functions. Heine (1979) recognises four types in this regard:

(a) states in which a national language is spoken by the majority and serves as the ordinary means of communication (e.g., Bambara in Mali and Wolof in Senegal), but where a language not spoken by the majority as a mother tongue is the sole official language (e.g., French in those two countries), or Siswati in Swaziland and Kiswahili in Kenya, while English is the official language in those two countries;

(b) states with one dominant national language, where the domination is numerical in character. In Angola, for example, 31% of the population speak Umbundu, and 48% speak Hausa in Niger. However, the official languages, respectively, are Portuguese and French in those two countries;

(c) states with several dominant languages. In this situation, the African languages are in a dominant position as a result of the numerical force of their speakers or their official regional function. For example, Hausa, Igbo, and Yoruba serve as regional official languages and lingua francas in Nigeria, but nationwide, English is the only official language of the state. In Zimbabwe, Chishona and Isindebele serve as official regional languages, while English is the sole official language of the state; and

(d) states without dominant languages, such as Cameroon, where 286 languages/dialects are in use while only some speech-forms have been recognised as languages par excellence, cf. Bamileke (12% speakers countrywide) and Duala (7%). French and English are in official use.

The presentation of Heine's typology has been necessary to show the emergence of an apparent diglossia conditioned by the language policy of a state authority. Furthermore, the presence of an imported language seems to be vital—even imperative. Consequently, according to the social allocation of functions in most cases, the given imported language represents a H(igh) variety confronted by an African language that constitutes the L(ow) variety. However, such an observation would be wrong. With Cobarrubias (1983), quoting Fishman, H might be a different language with or without a corresponding nexus with L, which in turn may be another language used by a linguistically different community. L would stand in a non-competitive complementary relationship to the H language (Cobarrubias: 57), cf. below. Heine's (1979) typology suggests that verbal efficiency in communication demands bilingualism from an African, i.e., to have mastered an imported language and to be able to apply the given African language with competence. Therefore, it does not mean that the African language in question is linguistically on an L level.

African language surveys[2] visualise the multitude of languages spreading across the continent. This raises the question of what is happening to tens or even hundreds of languages used daily in an African country, confronted by a bilingual system. Alexandre (in Heine 1979: 27), taking into consideration linguistically heterogeneous states, proposed their division into countries (a) with *langues immédiatement utilisables* (languages with directly usable applications) and (b) those without. He also assigned to the given state mostly one African language, e.g., Bemba in Zambia fell into the (a) category, while Wolof in Senegal was categorised as (b). The affiliation of the states in question to the anglophone and francophone zones was taken for granted.

Meanwhile, indigenous African languages in their majority are either involved in a rationalisation process or are following natural courses of sociolinguistic events. Rationalisation is realised through language planning. This means that every state is empowered to control some language functions according to promotion-oriented rights on the use of a language by public authorities at national, provincial, or municipal level (Cobarrubias 1983: 76). At national level, almost all African countries have clung to the ideology of internationalisation, i.e., the establishment of the former colonial language (LWC) as official language. As a result, African languages have been excluded from achieving such a prominent status. Even in the rare case of vernacularisation, i.e., the adoption of an indigenous language as the official language, e.g., Setswana in Botswana (but cf. below) or Kiswahili in Tanzania, an imported language still functions as co-official language.

As a form of rationalisation, exclusion manifests itself especially in educational planning. The linguistic pluralism applied is only partial in character. For instance, a project under the acronym PROPELCA has been implemented in Cameroon, which is—as already mentioned—one of those highly multilingual countries with over 200 languages in a total population of about 12 million people. In 1981, the project set out to conduct initial literacy in the mother tongue, followed by partial use of the mother tongue as a medium of instruction at school. Of the seven languages selected for the project, four (Duala, Ewondo, Fe'efé'é, and Nso) are already being used. The time allocation in respect of these African languages is 70% in the first year, gradually decreasing to 30% by the third year. At present the generalisation phase makes use of 12 languages in education at the primary and, in some cases, secondary school level (Bamgbose 2000: 51f.). However, most Cameroonian languages have either been marginalised or ignored.

Although the Organisation of African Unity (OAU) often called for the implementation of the United Nations Educational, Scientific, and Cultural Organisation (UNESCO) resolution on the value of mother tongue education, most African countries still justify the exclusion of smaller languages by using economic arguments. The lifeboat theory serves as a paraphrase: the available places are limited.

African states generally constitute a conglomeration of ethnic groups which form either minorities or non-minorities;[3] all of them have at least toleration-oriented language rights. Most endangered are the minoritised languages of minorities,[4] i.e., those that are simply ignored by state authorities and totally exposed to their sociolinguistic environment and its rules. For example, there are approximately 400 distinct minority languages spoken in Nigeria's Middle Belt. Of these, at least 180 have less than 400 speakers, and the majority of these languages remain completely undescribed. The speakers of the remaining languages range between 200 and ca. 1 million. There is no government policy towards these languages at all (Brenzinger 1998a: 203).

A specific role plays the push factor—which aims at enforcing language shift from outside, and the pull factor—which tries to incite assimilation wishes among an ethnic group (Tosco 1998: 129). For instance, Setswana is threatening most of the Khoesan languages spoken in Botswana. At the same time, the Khoesan minorities expose a negative attitude towards their own languages and express the wish that their children should be integrated into the Tswana "state culture" of Botswana (Batibo 1998: 10).

Language shift may occur as a mixture of radical and gradual death in an obsolescent speech community: a unilingual situation with a dominant L_1 may, under the influence of an L_2, turn into bilingualism and later towards a unilingual situation for L_2 or dominance in L_2 (Dimmendaal 1998: 71). Language shift has been observed especially among members of the younger generation of Nigeria, where Owon Afra-speakers enter the Yoruba option, for example, while Holma become part of the Fulfulde speech community (1998: 82).

Minorities whose languages are minoritised undergo external administrative pressure. Suppression of such languages by a state authority is the result of national language planning. In Tanzania, in Kiswahili's process of vernacularisation, it was declared the sole national medium. By implication, other indigenous languages were considered non-existent (Batibo 1995: 72). In this way, the other 120 ethnic languages become endangered. Language shift towards Kiswahili has involved coastal languages, e.g., Bondei and Zaramo, while Nyamwezi, Shambaa, and Sukuma have successfully resisted assimilation attempts. Nevertheless, the education authorities suggest that parents use Kiswahili in the home. In effect, this will accelerate the death of local languages (Brenzinger 1998b: 79).

The languages of promotion-oriented minorities can also be minoritised. A good example is provided by Namibia. As in most African countries, the use and non-use of African languages as media of instruction depended largely on historical antecedents. In Namibia, in compliance with the ruling party's language policy, English was established as the sole official language while Afrikaans was deprived of its former official position and reduced to the status of a local language. However, the Namibian government preserved the use of ten African languages as media of instruction in functional literacy and in Grades 1–3 in lower primary education. After that, most of the African languages are offered as subjects in the higher grades of formal education. Oshindonga, Oshikwanyama, Otjiherero, Rukwangali, and Silozi are taught up to Grade 12.

Some Namibian languages in education were taken over from the former South African administration after Namibia's independence in 1990. However, the Namibian Languages Bill of 1995, which stipulated that all Namibian languages should be official and that the language spoken by the majority in a particular region should accompany English in schools, business, and government – was rejected by the Ministries of Higher Education[5] and Basic Education,[6] respectively. At the same time, the implementation of corpus planning activities in order to modernise the African languages in use was not systematically initiated. In this way the latter are losing ground lexically compared with English, in the domains of professional skills, know-how, and expertise (Legère 1996b: 55f.; Ohly 1987).

A non-minority whose language has been minoritised can be found in Senegal, for instance. The Wolof ethnic group constitutes 44% of the population, while 72% speak Wolof countrywide. Wolof is spreading at the expense of both French (the only official language) and other indigenous languages, e.g., Bambara, Diola, or Peul, which are increasingly confined to the periphery of the country and then to rural areas as Wolof takes over towns. At present, 20 small ethnic groups are linguistically endangered. Nevertheless, 40 years after independence, French is still the sole educational language of instruction—without any didactic connections with African languages, i.e., the mother tongue of 90% of the learners (Bichler 2000: 62).

To summarise, most African languages belong to the category of deprived languages, i.e., not being used for important social functions, while hundreds of them are being threatened by extinction.

According to Ali and Alamin Mazrui (1998), Africans are already well known for their strong tendency towards multilingualism. Throughout history, they have been talented linguists in the pragmatic sense of the word. Unlike much of Europe, monolingualism has never been the norm. The forces of functional complementarity definitely encourage multilingualism (1998: 81). For example, many members of the black community in South Africa are already multilingual in up to five languages (Bamgbose 2000: 40).

According to Mazrui and Mazrui (1998: 78f.), most sociolinguistic studies in Africa recognise a three-way distinction between

(a) vernacular languages that serve as media of intra-ethnic communication and solidarity,
(b) vehicular languages of inter-ethnic communication and integration, and
(c) official languages of administration and national communication.

Trilingualism forms a part of Africa's triple linguistic heritage. That is, generally speaking, an effective social order of communication in the past consisted first of the mother tongue, being the very carrier of ethnic culture and identity (e.g., Nyamwezi); then a contact language, which was needed to establish relations with neighbours and the local market (e.g., Sukuma in the case of the Nyamwezi population); and finally, a lingua franca (e.g., Kiswahili) to enable regional communication.

Early African states such as 13th-century Mali proved that an African language—in this case Manding—was able to fulfil all the administrative tasks of an empire. Manding became the language of power and influence: during the height of Mali's power all official exchanges were carried out in Manding. Even in its diplomatic relations with the King of Morocco and the Sultan of Egypt, it seems that Manding was used on a regular basis (Mansour 1993: 37).

Indispensable in the African communication system today are the mother tongue, the vehicular language, and the imported language. The functions of the imported language—either English, French, Portuguese, or Spanish—have become entrenched in almost all out-group social domains. Moreover, English, for example, has stultified and

weakened indigenous languages by marginalising most of them in the education system in particular and in the life of the nation in general (Mazrui and Mazrui 1998: 79). It has been observed (e.g. Legère 1996b: 66) that attitudes towards someone who knows only African languages are to regard him/her as a useless and foolish person in society.

On the other hand, imported languages have also undergone "nationalisation" with the creation of Cameroon Pidgin English, Crioulu in Guinea Bissau, Krio in the Gambia and in Sierra Leone, Liberian English, Morisyen on Mauritius, Nigerian Pidgin English, South African English, and West African Pidgin French (Maho 2000: 30).

The modern elite in any African nation, i.e., politicians and those that assumed former colonial offices in the civil service, maintains the imported languages. They staff institutions of higher education and create the mass media, and they comprise the middle management in the still mainly foreign-owned business corporations. This elite cuts across traditional ethnic boundaries and has little or no formal organisation—thus creating elite closure.

Nevertheless, the elite typically knows indigenous languages that are also spoken by the masses (Myers-Scotton 1990: 29). Consequently, African vehicular languages become significant. English, French, or Portuguese play a less pervasive role in the daily lives of people than elsewhere, thereby leaving room for patterns of stable multilingualism rather than resulting in diglossia (Brenzinger 1998a). Hence, there has been a tendency for some dominant African languages to gain in popularity and spread countrywide at the cost of numerous minority languages. In this respect Kiswahili and Hausa are often called "killer" or "oppressing" languages that purposely threaten other languages. However, most members of speech communities in fact abandon their own language voluntarily, recognising another language as being superior and more useful (Brenzinger 1998a: 15). In the Namibian context, for example, speakers of minority languages are normally competent in regional lingua francas such as Silozi or Rukwangali as well (Legère 1996b: 51). In Zambia, 2.7 million people speak a second African language besides an imported.

African languages that facilitate the process whereby the elite successfully penetrates the masses and whereby the masses have adequate access to the elite are a definite advantage in the quest for vertical integration. As regards fostering horizontal integration at lower levels, lingua francas like Hausa and Mandingo in West Africa, Kiswahili in East Africa and Lingala in Central Africa are especially important. Horizontal integration concerns the degree to which the masses are in contact with each other and are able to establish a linguistic basis for sustained interaction. African lingua francas can, therefore, also be said to be involved in the process of socioeconomic consolidation (Mazrui and Mazrui 1998: 103).

The mother tongue is treated as an inborn trait. Consequently, parents often assume that there is no need to teach home languages at school since children speak them anyway. Meanwhile, an indigenous language assembles cultural specificities, the Little and Great Tradition, comprising the treasury of the given ethnic group, the cultural wealth which is bequeathed to posterity. G. Aisha Bichler (2000) indicated in her work quoted above the connection between the acquisition of the Wolof language and knowledge of the Wolofs' cultural background—which is indispensable in proper communication. Only the decoding process, which uses cultural keywords, makes it possible to avoid anisomorphism. Sedar L. Senghor proposed embedding Serere code-terms into French expressions in order to highlight and spread their unique sophistication and folk philosophy through a world language.

Taking into consideration the social advantages of functional multilingualism, Nigerian educational planners recognised five categories of languages that are gradually introduced into the school curriculum (Bamgbose 2000: 69f.):

   (a) the mother tongue
   (b) the language of the immediate community
   (c) a major Nigerian language (Hausa, Igbo, Yoruba)
   (d) English, and
   (e) a foreign language (i.e., Arabic or French).

Revised language planning in Botswana now provides for a third language in addition to English and Setswana to be taken as an optional subject, i.e., dominant local language favourably (Legère 1996b: 112).

The South African Constitution anchors nine indigenous languages, as well as English and Afrikaans, as official languages, according to a pluralistic linguistic ideology. Additive multilingualism is to be introduced in schools, leading to a situation where one's home language is retained throughout one's schooling and is supported by other languages. The selected languages should find implementation in the public service as economic resource and community languages. A trifocal policy is promoted in terms of which each South African should be encouraged (by means of incentives where necessary) to know their mother tongue or home language besides English and another regionally important language (LANTAG 1996: 42).

The [preceding] has consideration have led to the assumption that a trilingual communication scheme is easy to access in African conditions, although the components of such a scheme may have several serious shortcomings. For instance, by following the modernisation theory, governments propagated the belief that there would be a homogenisation and harmonisation of society by introducing English as a "neutral" language. However, instead of a reclassing of society, the effect of introducing this extraglossic language was merely to restratify society. Thus, a new elite has been formed, whose knowledge of English determines their position of economic and political power (Beck 1995: 257). In Namibia, for example, 25% of the total number of children have a rudimentary exposure to English at best; therefore, they are automatically disqualified from any activity requiring a knowledge of the official language (Legère 1996b: 62). Laitin (1992: 54) argues, as

do Mazrui and Mazrui (1998), that data based on socio-economic indicators from 40 African countries demonstrate no obvious statistical relationship between language diversity and economic growth. Even African literature in English constitutes a major contribution to contemporary literature in English only.

Lingua francas are criticised chiefly on the grounds of their underdeveloped terminology. In several science subjects at secondary school level, they are still unable to replace English, for example. Even more important is the slow technicalisation of vehicular languages, since they have to play a central role in the development of the whole community and should be viewed as an integrated part of the community's intellectual life (Webb 1995: 87). They also contribute to the decay of smaller language groups. For instance, some critics even insisted that Kiswahili had become a scapegoat for the declining standards of education: from the language of hope it turned to a language of empty promises (Ngonyani 2001: 256).

The position of minority languages depends on their ethoglossia—the communicative character of a language or variety. It is the expressive power of the language, i.e., its communicative strength, determined by the number of functions it performs and the quality of such functions relative to the social structure of the speech community. The speakers may choose to use the language for reasons of ethnic identity, economic power, or the social organisation of the speech community. It is assumed that the environment does not endanger ethnic groups that are numerically strong. In Botswana, for example, Setswana is spoken by about 80% of the population of 1.3 million. It is also Botswana's national language. In South Africa a further 3.6 million people speak it. However, learners' attitudes towards Setswana are negative because it does not contribute to their career advancement (Legère 1996a: 120f.). At the same time, there is no interest in the development of Setswana literature, and literary activity is low.

On the other hand, in Nigeria for example, literature in Yoruba (10–12 million speakers) is well established. It reflects a creative strategy that makes art amenable to popular dissemination media like television, radio, and newspapers, which now accommodate poems and short stories (Bodunde 2001: 10). Yoruba is also taught as a subject from the beginning of primary education while the other subjects (e.g., mathematics, science) are taught in Yoruba in the experimental classes for a six-year duration. Nevertheless, in South Africa for example, Zulu and all the other African languages spoken there—which have more speakers than either English or Afrikaans—fall into the category of dominated languages.

It may be assumed that, in African societies, trilingual, quadrilingual, and even multilingual communication is common. However, regardless of the circumstances, bilingualism creates a problematic situation. The acquisition of a second language might lead from an incipient stage of bilingualism to a progressive stage, an integral stage, a regressive stage, and a residual bilingualism in relation to L_1 (Sommer 1995: 24).

Thus, as Legère (1996a: 68) observes, a two-language policy which does not implement additive bilingualism is geared towards subtractive bilingualism, i.e., the given African language would become a second-class language, inferior to English, good only for informal communication.

At present since the official (LWC) language, the lingua franca, and local language cannot compete with each other, they should form a complementary environment in a functional multilingual situation. Therefore, a triglossic occurrence has to be recognised. The lingua franca plays the most important role because downward accommodation, i.e., vertical integration, seems to be the rule in much of Africa. In East Africa and the eastern Democratic Republic of Congo, the elite learns enough Kiswahili to communicate with the masses. Along the West African coast, a pidginised or creolised form is used to communicate across groups; and in other countries, an indigenous vehicular language such as Dyula in the Ivory Coast is used for this purpose (Myers-Scotton 1990: 39). As already mentioned, African languages which facilitate the process by which the elite successfully penetrates the masses and the masses have adequate access to the elite are a definite advantage in the quest for vertical integration. In performing horizontally integrative functions at the lower level, African vehicular languages serve as the main languages of trade unionism and organised labour (Mazrui and Mazrui 1998: 103).

Minority languages are often exposed to the ethnicisation of politics in a pluralistic society. That is, different political parties often tend to derive popular support from specific ethnic groups. SWAPO of Namibia, the ruling party in that country, provides a good example of popular support deriving chiefly from an ethnic group—in this case the Ovambo. On the other hand, governments often try to activate defensive minorities, for instance, through folklorisation that enhances the cultural performance of such minorities. Meanwhile, self-contained strong minorities employ cultural and linguistic islandisation, thus avoiding language shift or any predominant influence from the outside.

A triglossic situation may emerge by sociolinguistic necessity. For example, according to official sources, English in the Caprivi Region in Namibia functions as the official language, Silozi functions as a semi-official language and accepted lingua franca, while Sifwe and Cisubiya serve as local or national languages, although only in colloquial use. Therefore, in the Official Language Model, English forms the upper layer, Silozi the middle layer, and Sifwe/Cisubiya the lower layer. In language practice the position of the given language is variable. For instance, in the Cisubiya Discourse Model, in almost all speech situations (with one exception—"amongst good friends") Silozi occupies the lowest place of preference, with Cisubiya reigning supreme in all speech situations and English serving in second place (Ohly 1994). Thus, arguments such as those quoted by Batibo (1995: 73) to the effect that a triglossia model (English–Kiswahili–local languages) is not realistic in the case of Tanzania—because the vehicular function of Kiswahili is not stable and, at the same time, English and the local languages would be deemed to be progressively redundant and not complementary as an ideal triglossia situation would demand—seem to reflect a misunderstanding.

Triglossia, taking into consideration the African's inborn gift for language acquisition, is therefore a privilege within each African's reach. On the other hand, the sociolinguistic request for nationwide communication under existing conditions makes the implementation of triglossia a necessary step towards communication at the national level in order to achieve national integration and national development.

Notes

1. The term "nation" denotes all of the citizens or people of the given country.

2. See, e.g., Jouni Maho (2000). *African Languages Country by Country. A Reference Guide.* Gothenburg University. Also J. F. Maho and B. Sands (2002). *The Languages of Tanzania. A Bibliography.* Acta Universitatis Gothoburgensis.

3. Classification according to J. Cobarrubias (1987). Models of language planning for minority languages, *Bulletin of the Canadian Association of Applied Linguistics,* 47–70.

4. A language is described as "minoritised" if it lacks certain fundamental language functions or if some of its functions are restricted.

5. In full, the Ministry of Higher Education, Training, and Employment Creation.

6. In full, the Ministry of Basic Education, Sport, and Culture.

References

Bamgbose, Ayo (2000). *Language and Exclusion: The Consequences of Language Policies in Africa.* Hamburg: LIT.

Batibo, Herman M. (1995). The growth of Kiswahili as language of education and administration in Tanzania. In: Pütz, M. (ed.)[1995], 57–82.

———. (1998). The fate of the Khoesan languages of Botswana. In: Brenzinger, M. (ed.) [1998a], 267–281.

Beck, Anke (1995). Language and nation in Namibia: the fallacies of modernization theory. In: Pütz, M. (ed.)[1995], 207–222.

Bichler, Aisha G. (2000). Bejo, Curay and Bin-Bimm. Eine soziolinguistische Studie. PhD Thesis, University of Vienna.

Bodunde, Charles (2001). Aesthetics, media, and political currents in Yoruba literature. In: Bodunde, C. (ed.), *African Languages and Literature in the Political Context of the 1990s,* 9–12. Bayreuth: Bayreuth University.

Brenzinger, Matthias (ed.) (1998a). *Endangered Languages in Africa.* Cologne: Rüdiger Köppe.

Brenzinger, Matthias (ed.) (1998b). *Sprachwechsel afrikanischer Minoritäten aus soziolinguistischer Sicht.* Cologne: Institut für Afrikanistik, University of Cologne.

Cobarrubias, Juan (1983). Ethical issues in status planning. In: Cobarrubias, J. and J. A. Fishman (eds.), *Progress in Language Planning,* 41–85. The Hague: Mouton.

Dimmendaal, Gerrit J. (1998). Language contraction versus other types of contact-induced change. In: Brenzinger, M. (ed.) [1998a], 71–118.

Heine, Bernd. (1979). *Sprache, Gesellschaft und Kommunikation in Afrika: zum Problem der Verständigung und sozio-ökonomischen Entwicklung im sub-saharischen Afrika*. München: Weltforum Verlag.

Laitin, David (1992). *Language Repertoire and State Construction in Africa*. Cambridge: Cambridge University Press.

LANTAG (1996). *Towards a National Language Plan for South Africa. Final Report of LANTAG*. Pretoria: Department of Arts, Culture, Science and Technology.

Legère, Karsten (ed.) (1996a). *African Languages in Basic Education*. Windhoek: Gamsberg Macmillan.

——. (1996b). *Cross-border Languages*. Windhoek: Gamsberg Macmillan.

Maho, Jouni F. (2000). *African Languages Country by Country*. Gothenburg: Gothenburg University.

Mansour, Gerda (1993). *Multilingualism and Nation Building*. Clevedon: Multilingual Matters.

Mazrui, Ali A. and Alamin M. Mazrui (1998). *The Tower of Babel: Languages and Governance in the African Experience*. Oxford: James Currey.

Myers-Scotton, Carol (1990). Elite closure as boundary maintenance: The evidence from Africa. In: Weinstein, B. (ed.), *Language Policy and Political Development*, 25–41. Norwood, NJ: Ablex.

Ngonyani, Deo (2001). The changing fortunes of Kiswahili in Tanzania. *South African Journal of African Languages* 21 (3): 244–258.

Ohly, Rajmund (1987). *The Destabilization of the Herero Language*. Windhoek: The Academy.

——. (1994). The position of the Subiya language in Caprivi. *Afrika und Übersee* 77: 105–127.

——. (2001). Śmierć języka w Afryce. *Afryka* 13, PTAfr.: 17–33.

Pütz, Martin (ed.) (1995). *Discrimination Through Language in Africa? Perspectives on the Namibian Experience*. Berlin and New York: Mouton de Gruyter.

Sommer, Gabriele (1995). *Ethnographie des Sprachwechsels*. Cologne: Rüdiger Köppe.

Tosco, Mauro (1998). People who aren't the language they speak; on language shift without language decay in East Africa. In: Brenzinger, M. (ed.) [1998a], 119–143.

Webb, Victor (1995). The technilization of the autochthonous languages of South Africa: constraints from a present day perspective. In: Pütz, M. (ed.), 83–100.

Post-reading Questions / Activities

- Investigate the specific educational and linguistic policies of one of the African nations Ohly mentions. What are the costs of implementing such a complex policy? What are the arguments produced about it? What are the educational goals and actual attainments in that country?
- What language policies exist outside Africa? Consider looking into the official, national, minority, and regional languages recognized in India, Switzerland, Canada, Mexico, and China.
- Interview people from other countries about their language capabilities: What languages do they know? How did they learn each one? What was each one used for?

Vocabulary

additive multilingualism	Francophone	official language
Anglophone	Kiswahili	triglossia
colonial language	language planning	vehicular languages
creole	language policy	vernacular languages
diglossia	language shift	vernacularization
endoglossic	lingua franca	
exoglossic	mother tongue	

Suggested Further Reading

Edwards, John R. 1994. *Multilingualism*. London and New York: Routledge.

Ferguson, Charles. 1972 [1959]. "Diglossia." In *Language and Social Context,* edited by Pier Paolo Giglioli, pp. 232–251. Middlesex, UK: Penguin.

Grosjean, François. 1982. *Life with Two Languages: An Introduction to Bilingualism*. Cambridge, MA: Harvard University Press.

Heller, Monica, ed. 1988. *Codeswitching: Anthropological and Sociolinguistic Perspectives*. Berlin and New York: Mouton de Gruyter.

Myers-Scotton, Carol. 1988. "Codeswitching as Indexical of Social Negotiations." In *Codeswitching: Anthropological and Sociolinguistic Perspectives,* edited by Monica Heller, pp. 151–186. Berlin and New York: Mouton de Gruyter.

Ramaswamy, Sumathi. 1997. *Passions of the Tongue: Language Devotion in Tamil India, 1891–1970.* Berkeley: University of California Press.

Romaine, Suzanne. 1989. *Bilingualism.* New York: Blackwell.

Schiffman, Harold F. 1996. *Linguistic Culture and Language Policy.* London and New York: Routledge.

Woolard, Kathryn. 1985. *Double Talk: Bilingualism and the Politics of Ethnicity in Catalonia.* Stanford, CA: Stanford University Press.

CHAPTER 15

Bad Language—Bad Citizens

Edwin L. Battistella

(2005)

Is some language better than other language? Most people in most places feel that the answer is obviously "Yes," while anthropologists and linguists see the answer as "No." Edwin Battistella looks at different kinds of language that tend to be evaluated negatively in his book Bad Language: Are Some Words Better than Others? *He considers bad writing, bad grammar, bad words, bad citizens, and bad accents. All five of these could be regarded as arbitrary; they are socially determined, and they vary across time and space. But people within any given society see their judgments as natural, inevitable, and* right.

Linguists often distinguish between prescriptive *and* descriptive *grammar. Prescriptive grammar is what we learn in school, telling us what we should say or write: "Don't say* Him and me *went; the proper form is* He and I*." "Make sure the items in a list are parallel." Descriptive grammar, by contrast, analyzes what people actually say.*

In many places in the world, multilingualism gives rise to formulas and policies that have value judgments attached to them, giving preferential treatment to one language or another. Some nations have officially designated languages while others—including the United States—do not. The Académie Française in France and the Real Academia Española in Spain offer pronouncements about how to protect, preserve, and improve their languages. In some countries, such as China, minority language rights are recognized in the constitution. In some countries, such as India, the officially recognized national languages are enumerated in the constitution. Some countries, such as Israel, recognize several official languages (Hebrew, Standard Arabic, English).

There are clear decisions that must be made when institutions such as government or education are involved: Which language(s) should be used? What are the positions of other languages? Should efforts be made to protect minority languages? Are national efforts primarily directed toward assimilation or toward diversity and pluralism?

How linguistic diversity is regarded depends on a number of underlying principles, and in many countries these change over time, along with other historical factors. In this chapter, Battistella chronicles some of the ways multilingualism has been regarded in the United States.

Reading Questions

- What were the dominant concerns of the founders of the United States with regard to language?
- What attitudes did pre-twentieth-century Americans display toward linguistic diversity? What attitudes did they hold toward assimilation or cultural pluralism?

Edwin L. Battistella, "Bad Citizens." *Bad Language: Are Some Words Better than Others?* Oxford and New York: Oxford University Press, 2005, pp. 101–123.

- What seems to account for waves of concern about an official language?
- What are the similarities and differences among attitudes toward foreign language learning, deaf manualism, Native American language, bilingual education, and English-only legislation?

———————————————●———————————————

In a 1917 speech, Theodore Roosevelt famously made the link between speaking the English language and good American citizenship, saying that

> We must have one flag. We must also have one language.…The greatness of this nation depends on the swift assimilation of the aliens she welcomes to her shores. Any force which attempts to retard that assimilative process is a force hostile to the highest interests of our country.[1]

For Roosevelt, language was both a symbol of national unity, like the flag, and a means of creating that unity, by swift assimilation of immigrants to American language, customs, and values. For many, the foreign languages of immigrants, to the extent that they were maintained rather than given up, were a form of bad language that got in the way of their adoption of American speech and values.

[Elsewhere] I have examined how differences of grammar and vocabulary lead to judgments about speakers. The same is true of retention of foreign languages, which has often been seen as unpatriotic, uneducated, or separatist. [Here] I focus on American attitudes toward languages other than English, beginning with some history and case studies and moving forward to contemporary issues of English-only and bilingual education. In looking at the urge to assimilate other languages, my aim is to explore why some see foreign languages as making bad citizens.

BIRTH OF A NATION

The United States began as a developing nation. Much early American discussion of language issues focused on the relative merits of American versus British usage and whether British English should continue to be the standard in the United States. Writers like Benjamin Franklin, who helped to set standards for American prose style—and who were successful writers in part because their prose style satisfied English critics—argued for British standards. As historian Daniel Boorstin notes, Franklin wrote to his friend David Hume in 1760 that he hoped that "we in America make the best English of this Island our standard."[2] John Pickering likewise argued that attention to English standards was necessary for literary appreciation, scientific communication, and international respect. Pickering cited English criticisms of American usage and remarked that, while the American language had changed less than might have been expected, "it has in so many instances departed from the English standard, that our scholars should lose no time in endeavoring to restore it to its purity, and to prevent further corruption."[3]

On the other hand, writers like Thomas Jefferson and Noah Webster were proponents of an American language. Jefferson argued that language planning should look to the future by expanding the vocabulary so that English would be an appropriate vehicle for new knowledge. In a letter of 1813 stressing usage and innovation over grammar and tradition, Jefferson suggested that the new United States would require a certain amount of new vocabulary and that language, like government, ought to follow the will of the people.[4] Jefferson's own writing was criticized for using novel words and, in an 1820 letter to John Adams, Jefferson wrote, "I am a friend to neology. It is the only way to give a language copiousness and euphony," adding that "Dictionaries are but the depositories of words legitimated by usage."[5]

Noah Webster had a businessman's interest in creating an independent American economy. He also had a revolutionary's interest in creating a unified and independent American culture and language.[6] He wrote that "Custom, habits, and *language*, as well as government, should be national. America should have her *own* language distinct from all the world."[7] In addition, Webster saw American usage as reflecting a conservatism that had been given up by British grammarians. In his view, the best speech was that of the American gentleman farmers, whom he saw as different from the English peasants—as better educated, landowning, and independent.

Webster also feared that copying British manners would mean carrying over British linguistic vices to the new American nation. As literary scholar David Simpson emphasizes, Webster saw the establishment of an American language as a way to recapture the former purity of the English language before its corruption by the London court and the English theater.[8] This view arose in part from Webster's Puritan suspicion of ornamentation, though disdain for the language of the court was also characteristic of reformers like Bishop Lowth. Webster's distaste was particularly aimed at the language of writers like Samuel Johnson, which he viewed as pompous and antiquated. He believed that freed of British vices, educated usage in America would reflect principles of rational analogy and would preserve a uniformity of American speech against both literary affectation and dialect variation. And he hoped that adopting such a version of English, together with access to land and an egalitarian commercial environment, would preserve the social and moral health of America. As Simpson explains, Webster worried that Americans who adopted contemporary British speech habits would create disharmony in their own communities by introducing the class distinctions of England. Historian Kenneth Cmiel notes that such attitudes were common— many expressed a "fear of aristocratic overrefinement, of using civil forms solely to maintain social distinctions."[9] But fears of refinement were balanced by a sense that eloquence was necessary for participation in political affairs. Cmiel notes that "even radicals understood that entrance to public life demanded verbal felicity."[10]

The dispersion of the population in America and the distance from British cultural standards also raised concerns that linguistic corruption would follow from the lack of a cultural center. Standardization of usage was a concern to some of the political founders of the United States. One solution entertained was the establishment of a legal authority to govern language, with John Adams advocating that Congress establish a national academy to standardize usage and pronunciation. Adams feared a natural degeneration of English and saw a national academy promoting the study of English (and other languages) as key to diplomatic goals.[11] Adams, who was often characterized as a monarchist, was careful to stress the democratic effect of a common standard. In 1780 he wrote that, with a public standard in place, "eloquence will become the instrument for recommending men to their fellow citizens, and the principal means of advancement through the various ranks and offices of society."[12] Adams also stressed that he was not advocating a new American language. He wrote that "[w]e have not made war against the English Language, any more than against the old English character," and he suggested that an academy would be an American accomplishment of something that England had not succeeded in doing.[13] The Continental Congress, however, did not place a high priority on a national academy, and the proposal never emerged from the committee studying it. While an official English Academy was never established, there does not seem to have been much doubt that English was intended as the de facto standard language. As John Jay noted in the *Federalist Papers:* "Providence has been pleased to give this one connected country to one united people—a people descended from the same ancestors, speaking the same language, professing the same religion, attached to the same principles of government."[14]

In colonial and post-Revolution discussions of language, we find the familiar theme of choosing a standard. Here the choice was between British and American styles and involved considerations of simplicity, commonness, and refinement. The discussion of an American language was embedded in larger discussions of American and British culture, and language played an important role in defining an American identity that could be linked to the best of English values and culture yet remain separate from perceived English vices. A separate American language was seen as a means of representing and maintaining international status and of accommodating new knowledge and situations.

NATIVE AMERICAN LANGUAGES

The founders of America understood the need to accommodate various European linguistic groups, as a means of fostering support for the revolution and as a means of encouraging settlement. While many of the founders were sympathetic toward the learning of other languages, broader public attitudes toward foreign and minority languages have often been indifferent or hostile. In this section and the next, I look at two case studies of attempts at assimilation—Native American languages and the sign language of the deaf. While these cases are very different, what stands out is the way that language differences are seen as a social problem.

From colonial times, European settlers' attitudes toward Native Americans often focused on civilizing and Christianizing, in part by forcing Native Americans to speak English. From the early 1800s, Congress provided funds for missionary Indian schools that promulgated official government views about land holding and resettlement. By the late 1800s, as the military was more capable of policy enforcement in the West, the government became much more directive toward Native Americans. As John Reyhner notes, when Congress ended treaty making in 1871, policy shifted from relocation to assimilation, and the government became involved in the operation of Indian schools.[15] A report of the Commissioner for Indian Affairs in 1878 advocated removal of children from the influence of reservation life (and from parents) and proposed the creation of boarding schools. Prototype schools were developed in 1878 at the Hampton Institute in Virginia and in 1879 at the Carlisle Indian School in Pennsylvania, a converted army barracks. By 1902 almost 10,000 children had been relocated to twenty-five Indian boarding schools where English-only rules were enforced by corporal punishment. Also during this period, mission schools that had been instructing students in Bible studies using their native languages were forced to conduct instruction only in English in order to retain federal funds.

Federal policy of the late 1800s was exemplified by the views of J. D. C. Atkins, Commissioner of Indian Affairs. In his 1887 annual report, Atkins cited the report of a commission on Indian conditions the previous year, which advocated that "barbarous dialects should be blotted out, and the English language substituted." The report also linked assimilation of language to assimilation of thought and behavior, in language that foreshadows Orwell's theme of language as a mechanism of conformity and social control:

> Through sameness of language is produced sameness of sentiment, and thought; customs, and habits are moulded and assimilated in the same way, and thus in process of time the differences producing trouble would have been gradually eliminated.[16]

Adopting the majority language, in his view, would assimilate Indians to the majority perspective. Atkins went on to say that Indians "must be taught the language which they must use in transacting business with the people of this country. No unity or community of feeling can be established among different peoples unless they are brought to speak the same language."[17]

Assimilationism remained the main policy direction in Indian affairs well into the twentieth century, though a shift away from the assimilationist perspective did occur in the 1930s. The Meriam Report of 1928, an extensive survey of social and economic conditions sponsored by the Institute of Government Research, criticized the practice of breaking up Native American families and the practices of the boarding schools. The report led to such federal legislation as the Indian Reorganization Act of 1934, which promoted self-determination and cultural pluralism. Federally sponsored day schools were also established to provide English training with less disruption of the family and community. During World War II, however, funding was reallocated to the war effort. After the war, assimilationism reemerged as a way of encouraging Native American urbanization, and a policy of terminating reservations emerged in the 1950s.

During the New Frontier and Great Society era, termination efforts were challenged and policy again shifted to ways of combining federal assistance with self-determination. President Lyndon Johnson called for the end to termination efforts in his March 1968 Special Message to Congress, "The Forgotten American," and won passage of the Indian Civil Rights Act of 1968. The Nixon administration continued efforts to support self-determination, with the Indian Education Act of 1972 strengthening Indian control of education in their communities. In addition, the tribal college movement begun in the 1960s expanded Native American higher education. Most recently, the 1990 Native American Languages Act made it policy to "preserve, protect, and promote the rights and freedom of Native Americans to use, practice, and develop Native American languages."[18] Among other things, the act encouraged Native American language survival and recognized the rights of tribes to use Native American languages as a medium of instruction in federally funded schools.

The support for Native American languages is a case in which the policy of assimilation and termination was recognized as counterproductive in a variety of ways—socially, educationally, and culturally. Earlier policies of relocation to boarding schools, restraint of language traditions, and termination of reservations have been supplanted by perspectives that give communities more voice in how schools educate youth and that encourage the use of native languages and cultures to strengthen educational opportunities for Native American students.

MANUALISM VERSUS ORALISM

Education of the deaf in the United States provides an interesting parallel to the assimilationist theme apparent in attitudes toward Native American languages. As historian Douglas Baynton points out in *Forbidden Signs: American Culture and the Campaign against Sign Language*, attitudes toward sign language changed dramatically at the end of the nineteenth century. Deafness had been viewed as an affliction that isolated the deaf from religion and prayer. But after the Civil War period, it came to be seen as a social condition, isolating groups from the nation as a whole.[19] Baynton remarks that "the ardent nationalism that followed the Civil War—the sense that the divisions or particularisms within the nation were dangerous and ought to be suppressed—

provided most of the initial impetus for a new concern about what came to be called the 'clannishness' of deaf people."[20] The deaf were treated essentially as immigrant communities and sign was referred to as a foreign language by Alexander Graham Bell and others. Bell in fact warned of the dangers of intermarriage of deaf adults creating a separatist race of deaf people.

The sentiment that deafness was a social problem as well as an individual affliction was reflected in a shift in the methods of teaching the deaf from manualism to oralism. Manualism, the use of sign language as a means of communication, had arisen from the work of reformers like Thomas Gallaudet, an evangelical minister who founded the American Asylum for the Deaf and Dumb in Hartford, Connecticut, in 1817. Gallaudet and others believed that the deaf could not acquire moral understanding without taking part in group religious exercises, which sign made possible. Gallaudet's manualism reflected a somewhat romantic view of the deaf as in need of salvation, but at the same time it acknowledged that the deaf were a cohesive community. By contrast, oralists tended to see community among the deaf as a danger and viewed sign as encouraging the deaf to communicate primarily among themselves. As Baynton notes, the focus of oralism was not on the individual but, as with the assimilation of Native Americans, on "national unity and social order through homogeneity in language and culture."[21]

Oralism focused instruction on the goal of speaking. It drew support from popular ideas from the emerging theory of evolution: sign language was seen as reflecting lower orders of communication and oral language as one of evolution's higher achievements. In fact, the view that oral language had arisen from gesture was taken as evidence that sign represented an evolutionary step back.[22] With its apparent progressive flavor and with advocates like Alexander Graham Bell, the oralist position took hold in the education system. According to Baynton, by 1899 sign was prohibited in about 40 percent of schools for the deaf and by 1920, in about 80 percent, establishing a pattern that held for the first half of the twentieth century.[23]

During the twentieth century, advocates of oralism also stressed pedagogical and psychological factors. Alexander and Ethel Ewing's 1964 *Teaching Deaf Children to Talk*, for example, argued that "the highest priority for deaf children is learning to talk, this not only in terms of speech as a means of communication, but because the spoken language is a prime factor in social development (from its very beginning with the mother-child relationship) in thought-patterning and the development of intelligence."[24] And as Marc Marschark notes, until the late 1960s many hearing people still saw sign as "a relatively primitive communication system that lacked extensive vocabulary and the means to express subtle or abstract concepts."[25]

Like Native American languages, sign has enjoyed a resurgence in the last forty years. One factor in this was a critical mass of studies in the 1960s and 1970s confirming that oralism had failed. Education researcher Herbert Kohl, for example, in his 1966 study *Language and Education of the Deaf*, described deaf education as dismal. Kohl drew on government statistics showing that of the 1,104 sixteen-year-old students leaving deaf schools in 1961–1962, 501 graduated (with a mean grade level of 7.9) and 603 left without graduating (at a mean grade level of 4.7). He characterized the deaf child as isolated from the start of life, likely to show "outbursts of anger, rage, and frustration" in school, and to be "further frustrated by their failure in language" due to oral instruction.[26]

There may be other factors as well in the renewed viability of sign. Marschark notes that the number of deaf children experienced a tremendous growth in the 1960s due to the rubella epidemic of 1962–1965, which left close to 40,000 infants born deaf. This undoubtedly focused attention on improving deaf education. In addition, linguistic researchers from the 1970s on have emphasized the affinities of sign with spoken language. And members of the deaf community themselves have become very effective at making the case for sign language and deaf culture and at pointing out the failures of oralism.[27] Federal legislation has also benefited sign users: the Rehabilitation Act of 1973 required programs receiving federal aid to provide access to individuals with disabilities, with sign interpretation as a possible way of doing this for the deaf. And the 1990 Americans with Disabilities Act required comparable access in all state and local government schools, regardless of whether or not the schools get federal assistance.[28] For a variety of reasons, sign language has survived the assimilationist efforts of the oralist movement. Sign is accepted by many universities as meeting a second language requirement and major sign research centers exist at the Rochester Institute of Technology, the Salk Institute, and of course Gallaudet University. As with Native American languages, issues of access, education, and culture have reversed an earlier trend toward assimilating language communities.

Restrictions on Foreign Languages

So far we have seen how late-nineteenth-century thinking reflected the assimilationist ideology of "one nation–one language." The national language impetus of colonial times evolved so that minority languages such as sign language and Native American languages came to be treated as diversity problems—as barriers to efficiency, national unity, and civic participation. The tension between assimilation and pluralism also provides a context from which to consider language issues that arise from immigration and settlement. In the early twentieth century, concerns about assimilation reached a fever pitch after the influx of immigration that lasted from 1880 to 1919. Some reactions, such as literacy tests and proposals for the deportation of immigrants who failed to learn English, were clearly exclusionary.[29] Other initiatives, such as those that focused on Americanization, were motivated by concern for the newcomers' welfare, as well as for promoting American ideas.

During this period public schools increasingly focused on Americanization and civics, and civics instruction included fostering certain attitudes toward language. There was an increased pressure to ensure that English was the language of the classroom by restricting foreign language instruction. The most famous incident of this sort is the case of *Meyer v. Nebraska*.[30] The *Meyer* case arose in the context of anti-German sentiment following World War I. Several states adopted laws that restricted the use of foreign languages in public, that prohibited foreign language parochial schools, and that proscribed the teaching of modern foreign languages to young children. Nervous about its state's German-speaking population, the Nebraska legislature passed two laws restricting foreign languages. In 1919 legislators passed an open meeting law which required that meetings concerning "political or non-political subjects of general interest…be conducted in the English language exclusively." The other law, known as the Siman Law after its legislative sponsor, prohibited the teaching of any foreign language before the completion of the eighth grade and provided for a fine of up to $100 and a jail sentence of up to 30 days.[31]

The Siman Law was challenged when parochial school teacher Robert Meyer was fined for teaching German during the school's lunch hour. Meyer, who had been reading a Bible story in German to a student, claimed that he was merely providing religious instruction outside of normal school hours. While extracurricular religious instruction was allowable under the law, state prosecutors noted that the school had extended its lunch recess specifically to permit the lunchtime study of German. The Nebraska Supreme Court, voting 4–2, ruled that the school curriculum was within the state's jurisdiction and took the view that the teaching of foreign languages was harmful to the country and to young children. The Nebraska Court wrote:

> To allow the children of foreigners, who had emigrated here, to be taught from early childhood the language of the country of their parents was to rear them with that language as their mother tongue. It was to educate them so that they must always think in that language, and, as a consequence, naturally inculcate in them the ideas and sentiments foreign to the best interests of this country.[32]

The case was appealed to the United States Supreme Court, which ruled in 1923 that the restrictions on foreign language instruction were unconstitutional abridgements of liberty. Justice James McReynolds wrote the majority opinion voiding the Siman Law on the basis of the Fourteenth Amendment. McReynolds wrote that "the protection of the Constitution extends to all—to those who speak other languages as well as to those born with English on the tongue."[33] He agreed that all citizens needed to be literate in English, writing that the Court appreciated "the desire of the legislature to foster a homogeneous people with American ideals, prepared readily to understand current discussions of civic matters." But he maintained that English literacy could not be promoted through an unconstitutional ban on foreign language instruction. McReynolds argued in addition that the state could not interfere with parents' natural duty to provide for the education of their children. The decision was not unanimous, however. Justice Oliver Wendell Holmes, Jr., dissented in the concurrent case of *Nebraska District of Evangelical Lutheran Synod v. McKelvie*, drawing on the idea that childhood is a critical time in establishing language skills:

> Youth is the time when familiarity with a language is established and if there are sections in the State where a child would only hear Polish or French or German spoken at home I am not prepared to say that it is unreasonable to provide that in his early years he shall hear and speak only English at school. But if it is reasonable it is not an undue restriction of the liberty of either of teacher or scholar.

Meyer v. Nebraska provides a good illustration of the way in which foreign language issues were seen by policy makers in the first quarter of the twentieth century. Foreign languages were seen as promoting a heterogeneity at odds with good citizenship. Even as it accepted the rights of parents to have foreign languages taught to children, the Court asserted the desire of the majority for English literacy and for, in McReynolds's words, "a homogeneous people."

BILINGUAL EDUCATION

Just as earlier controversies about the teaching of foreign languages prefigure some of today's English-only debates, the issue of bilingualism and bilingual education has an interesting history as well. Though some of us may associate debates over bilingualism with issues arising in the last forty years, it has actually been a policy concern since the founding of the nation. In fact, the eighteenth-century and early nineteenth-century discussions of the role of German in Pennsylvania are similar to discussions heard today regarding Spanish. Benjamin Franklin worried about the third of the state's population who were German-speaking, fearing that Pennsylvania would become a German-dominated colony. Fears of political and cultural domination—and of possible sedition—led to proposals for Americanization of German areas and for English requirements for public discourse. But some early policy makers also advocated bilingual education as a means to assimilate the German population to English political and religious ideas, while at the same time providing them with an education in a language they could understand. Bilingualism came to be an important issue in the Pennsylvania Constitutional Convention of 1837–1838, at which Charles Ingersoll proposed that schools provide education in both English and German. According to linguist Dennis Baron, objections to Ingersoll's proposal included the fear that other languages would need similar provisions. Concerns were also expressed that bilingual teachers were generally less qualified and that bilingual education would corrupt schoolroom English. Some delegates also argued that there was little need for bilingual education because most Germans had been already assimilated to English and that educated Germans themselves favored assimilation. The Pennsylvania Constitutional Convention rejected

Ingersoll's bilingualism proposal by fewer than ten votes.[34] As we will see, similar objections recur today in debates about bilingual education and English-only legislation.

The impetus for modern bilingual education efforts came from studies in the 1960s showing that schools were ignoring the language barrier between Spanish-speaking children and English-speaking teachers, and in some cases even punishing children for speaking Spanish. The 1968 Bilingual Education Act, sponsored by Senator Ralph Yarborough of Texas, was originally proposed as part of President Lyndon Johnson's Great Society programs aimed at improving school success and economic opportunity. In his January 1967 speech introducing the act, Senator Yarborough spoke of the disparities in the education of Mexican-American children in the Southwest in language echoing that of the Supreme Court's 1954 *Brown v. Board of Education* decision outlawing school segregation:

> Little children, many of whom enter school knowing no English and speaking only Spanish, are denied the use of their language. Spanish is forbidden to them, and they are required to struggle along as best they can in English, a language understood dimly by most and not at all by many.
>
> Thus the Mexican American child is wrongly led to believe from the first day of school that there is something wrong with him, because of his language. This misbelief soon spreads to the image he has of his culture, of the history of his people, and of his people themselves. This is a subtle and cruel form of discrimination because it imprints upon the consciousness of young children an attitude which they will carry with them all the days of their lives.[35]

The 1968 Bilingual Education Act established federal jurisdiction over bilingual education and provided financial assistance for new programs, though without specifically defining what bilingual education was. Later amendments to the act, in 1974 and 1978, emphasized assimilation but also promoted language maintenance as well. Equally important in determining educational policy was Title VI of the 1964 Civil Rights Act, which prohibited discrimination on the basis of race or national origin in federally funded programs.

The view that equal treatment alone did not address the needs of students with limited English proficiency led to lawsuits such as *Lau v. Nichols* in 1974. In the Lau case, parents of about 3,000 students in San Francisco filed a class-action suit that argued that the city of San Francisco had not provided sufficient supplementary instruction in English to students whose primary language was Chinese. The U.S. Supreme Court ultimately reversed a Federal District Court ruling that having access to the same curriculum entailed lack of discrimination.[36] However, the Supreme Court's opinion did not provide a specific remedy; it only required that the Board of Education solve the problem. The Lau decision was extended to all public schools as part of the 1974 Equal Educational Opportunity Act but again without identifying solutions. In 1975, the Department of Health, Education, and Welfare began outlining so-called Lau remedies, which included a requirement that students' native languages be used in instruction and that native cultures be taken into account as well. Compliance to the Lau ruling was monitored by the U.S. Office of Civil Rights. But as many states adopted bilingual education measures, school systems often were compelled to develop bilingual programs whether or not they had any expertise in doing so. As linguist Lily Wong Fillmore has noted, many programs that arose this way were perfunctory and understaffed, leading to poor results.[37]

As English language education became more central to the work of schools, various types of programs developed. English as a second language instruction is typically geared to classes that are made up of students from many different languages and often focuses specifically on English skills. By contrast, transitional bilingual education programs involve classes of students who share the same second language. In such cases, instruction in school subjects takes place in the native language but time is also spent on English. English immersion approaches are ones in which instruction is entirely in English (often simplified) and which focus both on English skills and on other academic subjects. Still another approach is dual-immersion (or two-way bilingual education), where instruction is given in two languages. Here classes include native speakers of two languages, for example, English and Spanish, with the goal being dual proficiency.

Transitional bilingual education came under increasing attack in the 1980s as Hispanic and Asian immigration increased and as social programs lost federal funding. Such critics as Education Secretary William Bennett argued that there was no evidence that bilingual education programs helped students learn English. In 1980, an English-only Lau remedy had been approved in Virginia because the number of language groups made bilingual education less feasible than intensive English instruction. Soon Congressional amendments began to focus on the possibility of adding English-only immersion methods to Lau remedies, and a 1988 reauthorization designated up to 25 percent of the federal funding for immersion methods. Amendments to the Bilingual Education Act in 1994 increased emphasis on bilingual education, bilingual proficiency, and language maintenance, but funding was then cut by over 30 percent in 1996.

The broad policy goal of bilingual education programs remains educational opportunity and assimilation of minorities to English. Opponents of bilingual education often see it as unnecessarily delaying the learning of English and as unrealistically assuming that minority children can be comfortable in both cultures. Arguments are often focused on the effectiveness of bilingual programs and the claim that they are costly diversions from English instruction that reduce incentives to learn English. Opponents also argue that bilingual education serves more as a means of preserving ethnic cultures than of assimilating speakers to English and American culture. Bilingual education has been characterized by some as a cultural program for minorities rather than an educational program aimed at fluency in English. In a 1985 opinion piece in the *New York Times*, writer Richard Rodriguez argued that bilingual education efforts, despite the outward focus on learning English, reflect ethnic identity movements that romanticize dual culture. In Rodriguez's view, the cost of bilingual efforts is the embarrassment and silence of working-class immigrant children who do not succeed in mastering English.[38]

In June of 1998, 61 percent of California voters approved Proposition 227 (*English Language in the Public Schools*), which required that students from non-English backgrounds be taught in intensive immersion classes rather than bilingual programs. The initiative was part of a broader "English for the Children" campaign initiated by California activist Ron Unz. As a result, California law now requires that schools place children with limited English skills in an English immersion program for at least a year. As the name of Unz's campaign suggests, the rationale is that early literacy in English is fostered by rapid exposure to native speakers of English in mainstream classrooms. In 2002 Massachusetts voters followed, overwhelmingly rejecting bilingual education in favor of English immersion classes. Massachusetts had been the first state to enact bilingual education in 1971, but 70 percent of voters approved ballot Question 2, funded by Unz.[39] Like the California measure, Question 2 called for placing most non-English-speaking students in English immersion classes for a year. Under the Massachusetts bilingual education plan that had existed, about 30,000 non-English-speaking students took subjects like math or science in their native languages, easing into English over time. In California, bilingual programs served about 30 percent of that state's 1.3 million limited-English-proficiency students. Critics of these measures have expressed concern about inflexible, state-mandated curricula and about the potential difficulty of obtaining waivers for parents who choose not to have their children participate in immersion. Educators have concerns as well. One is the effect that mainstreaming limited English speakers after just one year of English instruction might have on the broader learning environment. Another is the consequence of grouping students by English proficiency rather than age.

Proponents of transitional bilingual education often view sink-or-swim approaches as ineffective and unfair, arguing that non-English-speaking children fall behind in early learning and cognitive development when they are unable to comprehend classroom language. Supporters of bilingual education may also argue that rejection of the home language in English-only immersion affects children's self-perception, as Senator Ralph Yarborough did in introducing the act. In addition, proponents often stress bilingual education as a positive factor in developing a workforce competent in languages other than English, and see support for bilingualism in childhood as a way to foster adult second-language proficiency.

Does bilingual education work? Is it better or worse than immersion programs? A review commissioned by the

National Research Council and the Institute of Medicine assessed the success of various types of bilingual and second-language learning efforts. Chaired by Stanford University psychologist Kenji Hakuta and directed by Diane August of the National Research Council, the study was unable to answer the question of what type of program was best. Hakuta and August found beneficial effects to both bilingual programs and structured immersion programs, and noted that successful bilingual and immersion programs had elements in common. They concluded that questions of effectiveness needed to be community based. Equally significant, the study condemned the "extreme politicization" of the research process by advocates, noting that "most consumers of the research are not researchers who want to know the truth, but advocates who are convinced of the absolute correctness of their positions."[40]

ENGLISH-ONLY

In the background of the debate over bilingual education and immersion is the recent campaign to make English the official language of many states. The origins of this English-only effort began with California Senator S. I. Hayakawa's unsuccessful English Language Amendment to the U.S. Constitution. In the early 1980s, Hayakawa and others believed such an amendment was necessary to prevent language differences from becoming divisive. Following the defeat of that amendment, Hayakawa and John Tanton of the Federation for American Immigration Reform founded the group U.S. English in 1983.[41] This group saw a number of political successes including initiatives that made English the official language of various states (in Virginia, Indiana, Kentucky, Missouri, Alaska, Tennessee, California, Georgia, Arkansas, Mississippi, North Dakota, North Carolina, South Carolina, Arizona, Colorado, Florida, Alabama, New Hampshire, Montana, Utah, South Dakota, Iowa, and Wyoming). Some of these initiatives were characterized by proponents as merely symbolic. Others, however, were intended to curtail demands for bilingual services. As linguist Geoffrey Nunberg reports, English-only advocates have petitioned for limits on the number of licenses for foreign-language radio stations and have attempted to halt the publication of such resources as the *Hispanic Yellow Pages*.[42]

While the U.S. English group has been successful in promoting English-only legislation at the state level, restrictive legislation has been challenged in courts. Arizona's 1988 English-only amendment, for example, was struck down in 1990 because it required the use of English by state employees on the job. Judge Paul Rosenblatt ruled that by prohibiting state legislators from speaking to their constituents in languages other than English, the state amendment abridged First Amendment rights. Judge Rosenblatt noted that while the government may regulate the speech of public employees in the interests of efficiency, "a state may not apply stricter standards to its legislators than it may to private citizens,…nor may a state require that its officers and employees relinquish rights guaranteed them by the

First Amendment as a condition of public employment."[43] Rosenblatt stopped short, however, of ruling that the plaintiff had a First Amendment right to speak Spanish at work.

The arguments of English-only proponents draw on the idea of English as having an economic and civic value, but also on fears about linguistic diversity.[44] English-only rhetoric casts English as the bond that unites us as a nation and sees that unity as threatened by bilingual services, foreign-language mass media, and the preservation of heritage languages. Such services and efforts are seen as a disincentive to the transition to English and as serving the interests of separatist ethnic leaders. For example, a U.S. English fund-raising brochure from the mid-1980s describes English as being "under attack" and raises fears of "institutionalized language segregation and a gradual loss of national unity."[45] The brochure also refers disapprovingly to "new civil rights assertions" such as bilingual ballots and voting instructions, to "record immigration…reinforcing language segregation and retarding language assimilation," and to the availability of foreign-language electronic media as providing "a new disincentive to the learning of English." In addition to the English-only constitutional amendment, the brochure called for elimination of bilingual ballots, curtailment of bilingual education, enforcement of English language requirements for naturalization, and the expansion of opportunities for learning English.[46]

English-only rhetoric also draws on the fears of the kind of violence and fragmentation that have affected Canada. In the 1960s the Canadian province of Quebec became the focus of militant efforts to establish a separate French-speaking nation. Beginning in 1969, a series of riots and terrorist acts, including the kidnapping and murder of Quebec's minister of labor and immigration, led the Canadian government to temporarily suspend civil liberties in 1970. After a political accommodation was reached, French became the official language of Quebec in 1974. In 1976 Quebec separatists won the provincial election and soon passed a charter that restricted education in English-language schools, changed English place-names, and established French as the language of government and public institutions. While Quebec voters rejected referenda to make the province an independent country in 1980 and again in 1995, the earlier pattern of violence, legislation, and separatism has made many Americans nervous about heritage language retention, especially in the Southwest where there are large numbers of Hispanic speakers.

English-only rhetoric incorrectly assumes that today's immigrants refuse to learn English and that official status is an effective means of fostering identification with the majority culture. Sociologist Carol Schmid has summarized a number of surveys of immigrant attitudes which suggest that there is little danger of English losing its desirability for nonnative speakers, and which dispel the fallacy that Spanish speakers don't want to learn English.[47] She notes that surveys of Hispanics find that they overwhelmingly support the idea that speaking and understanding English is necessary for citizenship and economic success, a fact that is also supported by the robustness of advertisements for English training on Spanish-language television. And there is also evidence that speakers of other languages shift to English over time. Schmid cites the well-known study by Calvin Veltman which found that about three-quarters of Spanish-speaking immigrants were speaking English regularly after about fifteen years of residence.[48] She also emphasizes that language loyalty rates of Spanish speakers in the Southwest actually declined between 1970 and 1990. The idea that English is in danger from Spanish is not supported by such data.

The English-only movement of the 1980s and 1990s has been counterbalanced to some extent by the work of groups such as the English Plus Clearinghouse and the English Plus Coalition, both of which were established in 1986. These groups see the learning of languages as a resource and argue that English-only restrictions are counterproductive both economically and politically. They have also argued that English-only laws are unnecessary as a means of fostering assimilation. As linguist Robert King has emphasized, linguistic diversity does not necessarily entail political violence.[49] The English-only rhetoric ignores the many linguistically heterogeneous nations that lack the separatist violence that has existed in Belgium, Sri Lanka, and Canada. Switzerland, for example, has a long tradition of language rights, decentralization, and power sharing among groups, and the Swiss very successfully accommodate multilingualism. Schmid sees the Swiss adaptation to multilingualism as an instructive model for both the United States and Canada.[50] Switzerland arose from a military confederacy of German states dating from 1291, which gradually added French, Italian, and Romansch allies. Though German remained the alliance's official language until 1798, there was little linguistic conflict among the various cantons, and a tradition of local autonomy and diversity was an important factor in attracting new groups to the confederation. An 1848 constitution established the equality of French, German, and Italian in the Swiss confederation by making them all national languages. And while today's French-speaking minority in Switzerland has a strong linguistic identity, the intensity of that identity is attenuated by Swiss national pride and the allegiance of French and German speakers to a common civic culture. There are also important differences between the language situations in the United States and in Canada which suggest that the Canadian experience is not likely to be repeated in the United States. Schmid emphasizes that the dominance of English has historically been much stronger in the United States than in Canada, and she notes the strong interest that nonnative speakers in the United States have had in learning English. She attributes the interest in separatism in Canada to French-Canadians' worries over assimilation, to optimism about the sustainability of a separate existence, and to the failure of Canadian political institutions to accommodate the collective identity of a French-speaking region. These different conditions suggest that the United States is in no danger of being overcome by linguistic separatism.

ONE FLAG, ONE LANGUAGE

The ideology of language assimilation arises from several factors. It is motivated by the belief that a common language is necessary for national unity and for economic productivity. It is also motivated by the assumption that a common language resolves social differences and builds understanding among those of different backgrounds. And it is motivated by the fear that language diversity will lead to political disunity and potential violence. In the United States there have also been sustained periods in which foreign and minority languages have been stigmatized, suppressed, and seen as problems to be overcome rather than resources to be fostered. As a result, foreign languages and minority languages have been the focus of social engineering that often attempts to legislate a process of assimilation already underway and to dictate its nature as monolingual rather than bilingual. The acceptance of sign language and the preservation and revitalization of Native American language are areas where progress has been seen. But the perception of foreign languages seems to have changed little since Theodore Roosevelt's 1917 statement extolling language as the symbol of national unity.

Notes

1. Theodore Roosevelt's "Children of the Crucible" speech is reprinted in *Language Loyalties: A Source Book on the Official English Controversy,* ed. James Crawford (Chicago: University of Chicago Press, 1992), 84–85.

2. Daniel J. Boorstin's *The Americans: The Colonial Experience* (New York: Vintage, 1958), chs. 41 and 42, is the source for background on colonial attitudes and for the citation to Franklin's 1760 letter to Hume (278); for Boorstin's views on descriptive linguistics, see *The Americans: The Democratic Experience* (New York: Vintage, 1973), pp. 452–62.

3. The quote from John Pickering's "Essay on the Present State of the English Language in the United States" is excerpted in C. Merton Babcock's *The Ordeal of American English* (Boston: Houghton Mifflin, 1961), 30.

4. David Simpson's *The Politics of American English, 1776–1850* (New York: Oxford University Press, 1988), p. 32, is the source for the citation to Jefferson's 1813 letter. Writers such as John Witherspoon also advocated an American style. Witherspoon saw the issue as a contest between the more cultured nature of British speech and the potential for uniformity that an American language might foster, particularly in light of the mobility of Americans. He saw the common speech in America as less parochial than the common speech of England, but nevertheless cautioned against too common a style, arguing for a language that expressed neither "bombast and empty swelling" nor "low sentiments and vulgar terms." See the excerpts of *The Druid,* no. 5, collected in Babcock's *The Ordeal of American English,* 74.

5. See Adrienne Koch, *The Philosophy of Thomas Jefferson* (Gloucester, MA: Peter Smith, 1957), 109, for the citation to Jefferson's 1820 letter to Adams. As Julie Tetel Andressen notes in her *Linguistics in America, 1769–1924: A Critical History* (London: Routledge, 1990), pp. 57–62, Jefferson also advocated spelling reform and the resurrection of provincial archaisms.

6. Webster is most famous for his spelling reforms, and as a publisher he was sometimes accused of self-interest for these since he would profit from Americanized editions of books. Webster saw spelling reform as a means to reduce the gap between speaking and writing and to foster communication and opportunities for unified political action. Webster's own reforms were largely unsuccessful in his lifetime, and his greatest influence may have been the association of correct language with American values, which ensured the success of his competitors Murray, Brown, and Kirkham.

7. Webster, quoted in Simpson, 65.

8. Simpson, *The Politics of American English, 1776–1850,* 52–72, is the source for the summary of Noah Webster's views. Both Webster and Jefferson were influenced by the revival of interest in Anglo-Saxon as a source of English political and linguistic traditions. Webster, in particular, was influenced by the Saxonist speculations of John Horne Tooke. See Simpson, 81–90.

9. Kenneth Cmiel, *Democratic Eloquence* (New York: William Morrow, 1990), 45.

10. Cmiel, 47.

11. As Shirley Brice Heath notes, antimonarchists in the United States were skeptical of a centralized authority setting cultural norms, so proponents focused the debate on the role of language in education and law. See Shirley Brice Heath, "A National Language Academy? Debate in the New Nation," *Linguistics* 10.189 (1977), 9–43.

12. Simpson (30) is the source for this quote from John Adams.

13. Heath (21) is the source for this quote from Adams and for information generally on the language academy issue.

14. The quote from John Jay is cited in Carol Schmid's *The Politics of Language: Conflict, Identity, and Cultural Pluralism in Comparative Perspective* (New York: Oxford University Press, 2001), 18.

15. The sketch of Native American language policy draws on John Reyhner's "Policies toward American Indian Languages: A Historical Sketch," in *Language Loyalties: A Source Book on the Official English Controversy,* ed. James Crawford (Chicago: University of Chicago Press, 1992), 41–47, and William Leap's "American Indian Languages," in *Language in the USA,* ed. Charles Ferguson and Shirley Brice Heath (Cambridge: Cambridge University Press, 1981), 116–44.

16. The report of the 1868 commission on Indian conditions is cited by Atkins (48).

17. J. D. C. Atkins, Annual Report [of the Federal Commissioner of Indian Affairs] (excerpted as "Barbarous Dialects Should Be Blotted Out" in Crawford, *Language Loyalties,* 50).

18. The Native American Languages Act is Public Law 101–477 (Oct. 30, 1990). For a report on the Native American educational experience, see *Indian Nations at Risk: An Educational Strategy for Action* (Washington, DC: U.S. Department of Education, 1991, ERIC Document Reproduction Service No. ED339587).

19. See Douglas Baynton, *Forbidden Signs: American Culture and the Campaign against Sign Language* (Chicago: University of Chicago Press, 1996), pp. 15–26. Baynton's book was a key source for many of the facts in this section: Alexander Graham Bell's views (30–31), Thomas Gallaudet's beliefs (17–20, 113–14), John Tyler's comments (36–38), the influence of evolution (38–44), and teacher statistics (25).

20. Baynton, 29.

21. Baynton, 16. The impetus for assimilation in the post–Civil War period reform mentality was also connected to "widespread fears of unchecked immigration and expanding, multiethnic cities."

22. Baynton cites an 1899 keynote address by John Tyler to the American Association to Promote the Teaching of Speech to the Deaf, which characterized sign language as brutish and advocated education based on the characteristics that evolution had promoted, namely speech. Baynton notes also that religious advocates of sign interpreted the origin of language differently, some seeing sign as closer to creation and thus representing a morally superior state.

23. In his 1943 book *Deafness and the Deaf in the United States* (New York: Macmillan, 524), Harry Best notes that opponents of sign continued to stress the social dangers of separatism.

24. Alexander Ewing and Ethel Ewing, *Teaching Deaf Children to Talk* (Manchester: Manchester University Press, 1964), viii.

25. Marc Marschark, *Raising and Educating a Deaf Child* (New York: Oxford University Press, 1997), 54.

26. Herbert Kohl's observations are from his *Language and Education of the Deaf* (New York: Center for Urban Education, 1966), 4–5; for citations to other summaries of the research on sign language and oralism, see Baynton 166, n.11.

27. Baynton (155) suggests that another factor in changing attitudes toward sign was a cultural shift in the 1960s in the way people viewed physicality. He notes that this included "such things as new and more sensuous forms of dance, a greater openness concerning sexuality, and an expanded tolerance for nudity and the celebration of the body,... [a] renewed fascination with "body language" generally,... more open expressions of passion and personal feelings,... [and] the popularity of new psychotherapies."

28. Earlier, the Bilingual Education Act of 1988 had included sign language for the first time.

29. The 1917 Immigration Act, passed over Woodrow Wilson's veto, excluded immigrants over the age of sixteen who were physically capable of reading but could not. Earlier literacy restrictions had been vetoed by Grover Cleveland and William Howard Taft.

30. Jack Rodgers's review of the "The Foreign Language Issue in Nebraska" (*Nebraska History,* 39.1 [1958], 1–22) was a source for the facts of *Meyer v. Nebraska.*

31. The relevant statues can be found in *Nebraska Laws* 1919, chapter 234 (Nebraska's open meeting law) and chapter 249 (the Siman Law).

32. The 1922 Nebraska Supreme Court ruling can be found at 187 *Northwestern Reporter* 100, 1922.

33. The Supreme Court's *Meyer v. Nebraska* ruling may be found at 262 U.S. 390 (1923) and its *Nebraska District of Evangelical Lutheran Synod v. McKelvie* ruling may be found at 262 U.S. 404 (1923).

34. Dennis Baron's *The English-Only Question: An Official Language for Americans* (64–83) was a valuable source for background on

Post-reading Questions / Activities

- Is maintenance of a language—as for Native Americans—necessary for cultural survival?
- Contrast the outcomes, motives, and contexts of the French Canadian and English-only movements.
- What is the difference between bilingual education and English-immersion education? What are the arguments in favor of each? How could their effectiveness be measured? Why do you think advocates and opponents are so passionate?
- Research English-only, English-plus, bilingual education, and the Unz amendment. What kinds of arguments is each group using (moral, psychological, pedagogical, etc.)? Are they addressing the same issues? How could someone decide between their positions? What are the participants' assumptions about the relationship between linguistic diversity and national unity? Do they use evidence from other societies to support their position? How do they evaluate individual and collective needs and rights?

Vocabulary

bilingual education	language maintenance	prescriptive grammar
descriptive grammar	manual language	standard language
English-immersion	oralism	

Suggested Further Reading

Center for Applied Linguistics. http://www.cal.org/.

Crawford, James, ed. 1992. *Language Loyalties: A Source Book on the Official English Controversy*. Chicago: University of Chicago Press.

Edwards, John R. 1994. *Multilingualism*. London and New York: Routledge.

Ethnologue: Languages of the World. http://www.ethnologue.com/web.asp.

Schmid, Carol. 2001. *The Politics of Language*. New York: Oxford University Press.

CHAPTER 16

A Linguistic Odyssey
One Family's Experience with Language
Shift and Cultural Identity
in Germany and France

David Antal
(1998)

Tolstoy claimed that each unhappy family is unhappy in its own way. The same could be said of multilingual people: each one is multilingual—though not unhappy!—in his or her own way. Even within the same family, the particular details of biography greatly affect each individual's relationship to languages: age of contact with the language, classroom situation, parents' and other relatives' (including siblings') languages, other caregivers' languages, relationships to classmates and friends, and so forth.

David Antal gives a very detailed account of his family's multilingualism and multiliteracy (literacy in multiple languages), showing why his three children have different attitudes toward their English, German, and French.

Though the family described here is relatively privileged, with high levels of excellent education, all multilingual families have similarly particular relationships with their languages (see Chapter 17). School plays a part, but so do many accidental encounters in children's lifetimes. Adults can also add languages throughout their lives, but it is much less common than it is for children to learn new languages.

Reading Questions

- What attitudes do the author and his wife hold about multilingualism? How did this result in their choice to remain in Europe for 20 years? What languages did they bring to their European residency, and how had they learned them?
- What language did the parents speak with each of their three children, and why? What were their goals for making those choices? Did the children's later language use bear out the parents' expectations?
- Which languages, in what order, does each child favor, and why?
- What is the relationship between language and identification with a nation or culture, for each child?

In a continuing bid to maintain the interest and curiosity of her students, my teacher of intermediate French once handed our international adult class an article popularizing the diversity of Europe's "little habits and ways" (*ses petites manies et ses bonnes manières*). We were amused to learn that a nod of the head meant 'no' among the Greeks and the Turks but 'yes' everywhere else. Sweeping from Cyprus to Iceland and from Portugal to the Ukraine, the author cited similar engaging differences in several facets of life. Informative, entertaining, and full of useful vocabulary, the article admirably succeeded for the purposes of our class's language unit and, no doubt, those of the general-interest magazine in which it had appeared.

To compatriots who have not had long-term interaction with other peoples, languages, and cultures, the details that emerged from that text may cast expatriate life as exotic. Not surprisingly, however, it could only begin to scratch the

David Antal, "A Linguistic Odyssey: One Family's Experience with Language Shift and Cultural Identity in Germany and France." *International Journal of the Sociology of Language* 133 (1998): 143–168. Notes have been renumbered and edited.

surface of what my wife, I, and our three children have lived as residents of Berlin, Germany, and Haute Savoie (Upper Savoy), France. Representing only the tip of the iceberg, the author's instructive observations inevitably leave uncharted the bulk of the underlying dimensions that often remove daily expatriate existence from the realm of the exalted.

Take relations with the family "back home," for example. Upon coming to Germany from the United States just after marrying in 1975, Ariane and I had initially planned to remain in Europe only about two years. But, as with several similarly intentioned fellow North Americans whom we have met during the two decades since our own arrival in Europe, we wound up striking roots and staying. We have come to know how distance and time can gradually limit the scope for sharing with our families. (E-mail has proven to be a welcome, speedy, efficient remedy to the vague sense of alienation that frequently seems to accompany international telephone calls, letter-writing, and transcontinental reunion travel, but its advent and relatively wide, spontaneous use has been only fairly recent.) There was little casual chatting to keep abreast of the doings of other family members, no celebrating or grieving immediately beside our parents or siblings, no question of mutual aid in the situations that mold the lives of most families.

With the birth of each child, the cost of family trips between Europe and the US West Coast has increased. Such travel became even more complicated when the children of our families on opposite sides of the Atlantic entered school, for the opportunities for cross-continental visits were narrowed by the virtual impossibility of internationally synchronizing school vacation schedules, not to mention the vacation schedules of working parents. As a result, our journeys to California and our Californian families' visits to Europe have become ever fewer and further between. Under these circumstances interaction with relatives abroad can become sporadic as daily local realities and routines take over.

Of course, this process does not require bona fide foreign residence. It can claim family members living within the same country or region, even within the same city. But moving abroad arguably reinforces the dynamics involved. And if that second home is set in a different language and culture, lengthy separation from one's original home lends an added dimension to the key questions of whether and how much to assimilate to that new setting. Given the issues of personal, linguistic, and cultural identity that are entailed, why should such an odyssey have ever begun, or continued?

ORIGINS OF A QUEST

The traditional utilitarian arguments for bilingualism or multilingualism are familiar: enhanced social life, more enjoyable travel, superior academic and professional performance and opportunities, edification and insights through foreign literature to which one gains access, and improved chances for economic rewards from a world economy on whose markets multilinguals are often more competitive

than monolinguals (see Merrill 1984: 1–2). As powerful as such incentives may be, however, they have not been primary goals in themselves for us. The evolution of our current existence in Europe had different origins. Ariane had received the gift of bilingualism from her parents as a child. Sheer curiosity and fascination with foreign language and with European history and culture had led me to my study of German literature and Germany. Those early foundations, the energy of youth, our feeling of adventure and independence as newlyweds establishing themselves on their own, a desire for new horizons, a purely practical search for work, and the attendant challenges originally brought us to central Europe.

What has kept us here for more than 20 years has grown along the way. The aforementioned advantages of maintaining and using more than one language have been simply potential outcomes of a commitment to something else: we want to live—and want our children to grow up—as "citizens of the world" (Merrill 1984: 1), not just as US citizens. We wish to be "in touch with the world as it really is" (Merrill 1984: xii), and the second and third languages in our lives impress upon us the vast diversity, interdependence, and complexity of that world. We do not seek to assimilate as in a melting pot but to integrate, coordinate, and, most important, to understand other cultures. We cannot deny or belie any of our linguistic or cultural backgrounds, anyway:

> Because each individual has only one life and one identity, the notion that the same person can be entirely German in Germany with Germans and entirely French with French people is somewhat unrealistic. On the whole, people whose lives are shared between two communities exhibit various combinations of two distinct cultures. (Harding and Riley 1986: 43)

Setting Out

Few cities in the 1970s offered a context more diverse, interdependent, and complex than Berlin (see Katona 1997 for an enlightening personal depiction), in whose western half we arrived in September 1975. Greater Berlin at that time was still an occupied city divided into a western part (in which the American, British, and French Allied military sectors were located) and an eastern part (the Soviet military sector). The Wall separated West Berlin from both East Berlin and the surrounding territory of the German Democratic Republic. As a cosmopolitan arena of intense competition between the values and performance of two major ideologies, West Berlin depended on the Western world for sheer survival as much as the Western world claimed to depend on West Berlin for the credibility of capitalism and democracy. Postwar complications had enshrouded the city as a whole in a labyrinthine web of international law, Four-Power military regulations, and prerogatives of largely restored German self-government. For all these reasons, the atmosphere in West Berlin's cultural, economic, historical, and political spheres was charged with immediacy and excitement.

Having no affiliation with the US Departments of Defense or State in any official capacity, Ariane and I had no access to any of the extensive housing, shopping, travel, and recreational facilities that were provided in the city for American military and diplomatic personnel and dependents, who lived mainly on or near the American base in Zehlendorf and Dahlem, two southwestern districts of West Berlin. Instead, we lived "on the economy" (for another example, see Smith in Varro 1998a), meaning within the German infrastructure, finding work after a five-week search during which we faced major initial disadvantages on the labor market. First, the American bachelor-of-arts degrees we held were not recognized as certification of completed postsecondary education, so we were considered unqualified for many kinds of jobs. (Still today, it is only at the master's level and above that US and German academic degrees are recognized as equivalent by German authorities.) Second, we held only US citizenship, which did not permit us to compete with German citizens for the other, nonspecialized jobs available.

It was the activation of Ariane's French citizenship that enabled employers to hire us as members (or spouse of a member) of the European Community (EC), who enjoyed free movement of labor within its territory. At that point Ariane was allowed to take a job in an international social science research institute funded by the West German federal and state governments, and she went on to build her career there. After working in the press section of a small German bookstore in a nationwide chain, I took a position as a film and record librarian at a television and radio station staffed primarily by Germans and Americans. By the end of the decade Ariane and I had both earned our master's degrees (international relations and education, respectively), we had been granted permanent and unrestricted residence and work permits, I had been able to launch myself as a self-employed translator and editor in addition to teaching part-time at the Free University, and we were expecting our first child. Germany, specifically West Berlin, had been (and still is) good to us.

The Social Milieu

For the first $2\frac{1}{4}$ years of our stay, we made our home in the Kreuzberg district. Located on the eastern fringe of West Berlin, and in some areas at that time still a showcase of the ravages of World War II and the Cold War (the Wall constituted the district's eastern and northern borders, which included Checkpoint Charlie), Kreuzberg had the advantage of relatively inexpensive housing and was the hub of the city's artist and alternative scene. Its population had the highest percentage of both working-class residents (approximately 70%, as compared to just under 25% from the middle class) and foreign nationals (nearly 25%) of any district in West Berlin (Baedeker 1977: 13). Our reception in West Berlin was open and friendly. The German neighbors with whom we had contact (a bank clerk and a seamstress whose eldest son soon hoped to begin apprenticeship as an electrician) were friendly and supportive, inviting us over for visits while we were settling in. They gave us advice

about shopping, transport, and city attractions and even lent us furniture from their cellar.

In the subways and stores and on the streets and squares of Kreuzberg and other parts of West Berlin, however, relations between the local German residents and some "ethnic" groups were not always as understanding as what we had enjoyed. The difference soon made us aware that there were various levels of foreigners present in the city. The largest one, the foreign workers (later officially referred to as *Gastarbeiter*, or 'guest workers'), consisted of those enlisted by the West German government to help rebuild West Berlin and its economy. Totaling 18,754 in 1968, their numbers in Berlin had been doubling annually since then, with the overall foreign population surging even further when the families of those workers joined them (on the dynamics of this demographic development, see Ribbe 1987: 1114–1116). An especially high percentage of the foreign workers in Berlin at that time came not from member countries of the EC or other parts of Western Europe but from Turkey and what was then Yugoslavia, so their cultural and religious differences from the native German population were felt more than those of other groups in this category (mainly Greek, Italian, and Spanish). With housing scarce throughout West Berlin, waves of foreign workers and their families had gravitated to Kreuzberg and two other districts in that part of town (Neukölln and Wedding), where ghettos formed in areas of substandard accommodation that most German citizens did not wish to live in. The sheer scale and rapid increase of this influx, along with the vicissitudes of living in an isolated and occupied city at the often grinding interface of two opposing ideologies and social systems, tended to foster a sense of estrangement.

In this sense, Ariane and I as French and American citizens enjoyed a somewhat higher status than that accorded many other foreign nationals in Germany (see Varro and Boyd 1998). Neither appearance nor "accent" instantly distinguishes us as foreign, and neither the type nor the setting of our work has exposed us to the kind of discriminatory acts that guest workers sometimes endure. Nevertheless, we have felt the insult every time we witness other foreigners being verbally abused while using public transportation, shopping in stores, or trying to manage their affairs with the foreign police (in encounters with whom many aliens must cope with rudeness, lack of information, frustration, and tension). In all fairness, Berlin has arguably been one of Germany's most tolerant cities (see Zimmermann 1996; for an earlier period in Berlin's history, see Escher 1987: 357–359, 364–367), yet we, too, are reminded today of the conditional nature of our place in Germany when reading of incessant right-wing extremist attacks on immigrants and foreigners in our very region (see Jansen 1996; Wendler 1996). Differences that German citizens had with Americans (and presumably British and French), whether as members of the occupying powers or as private persons independent of the military and diplomatic presence in the city, were largely political rather than "ethnic" or religious. When, for example, the Reagan administration pressed ahead with the NATO two-track decision in the early 1980s, US government installations in Berlin became sites for clashes between left-wing German protestors and police. (This decision established NATO's strategy of continuing disarmament negotiations with the Soviet Union while preparing for war by installing Pershing missiles on West German soil.) A less threatening, but no less indicative, example of attitudes toward US policy was a demonstration during the Gulf War in early 1991. On that occasion, German social science researchers from Ariane's institute publicly protested US actions in the Middle East but pointedly failed to speak out against a specific kind of violence much closer to home: the attacks that right-wing extremists had mounted against buildings housing asylum seekers in the German towns of Hoyerswerda and Rostock. The intense discussion Ariane had with her colleagues about this discrepancy after they returned to the office led nowhere, and their frustrating inability to see it has remained a poignant memory for her.

In any case, sources of outright physical threat to US nationals and property in Berlin lay further away. When American fighter jets attacked targets in Libya in 1986, the US command in Berlin ordered combat-ready motorized units to escort the local American military school buses in order to help thwart terrorist retaliation against the children riding in them. During the 1991 Gulf crisis, the two main schools attended by American children closed altogether for one week for the same reason. One precautionary suggestion that circulated at that time was that Americans should speak German, if they could, rather than English on Berlin's public transportation in order to avoid identifying themselves as Americans unnecessarily.

Getting Oriented

Such have been some of the broad patterns of our lives as expatriates in Berlin. As noted above, however, it is the daily local realities, details, and routines that tend to take precedence in one's experience, and they offered a rich setting for interaction. By 1979 our day-to-day work brought us into frequent contact with people (primarily academics, students, office workers, and people from the liberal professions) from a variety of cultures (though mostly German and American). We lived and worked in the German community and participated solely in the German economy, but we observed both German and American festival days and customs. All along we have embraced Berlin as our home and source of livelihood but have not desired or tried to shed our American (and in the case of Ariane and the children, also French) backgrounds, nor have we sought to assume German identity. This relation with the culture, language, and people of Germany, specifically Berlin, has always been an act of integrating, coordinating, and understanding the sometimes disparate elements of this environment.

That sort of integration does not always come easily. Multilinguals are just as susceptible as anyone to the surprising, even disconcerting and sometimes frustrating differences between the values, attitudes, behavior, and orientations encountered when moving from one cultural context to another (see Adler 1997: 14–32). The signs and symbols of communication go far beyond verbal language to include body language (eye contact, smiling, hand and facial gestures, mien, and posture) and other nonverbal cues intended to convey (or disguise) thoughts and feelings (Harding and Riley 1986). Further still, they grow out of and express the entire culture, or "the way of life of the society in which one grows up, its habits, customs, the way one dresses or eats, one's beliefs and values, ideas and feelings, the notions of politeness and beauty" (Harding and Riley 1986: 42). One might also add the humor, etiquette, traditions, history, and technologies of that social environment. In short, just speaking a second or third language is evidently not all there is to comprehending a culture other than one's own.

Personal language shift, that is, situations in which an individual changes from using one language to using another (Harding and Riley 1986: 34; on the distinction between language shift and such strategies of code-switching as borrowing and language choice, see 1986: 56–57), thus entails more than switching back and forth from one linguistic system to another, as when translating. Something else moves, too—one's entire cultural identity, or the degree to which one embraces a given society's patterns of the dimensions cited in the paragraph above. Ultimately, identity revolves around a perennial question: "Who am I?" At various levels of human organization (e.g., states, associations, cities, business organizations, and churches), it has long been bound up with such issues as citizenship, nationality, consent, loyalty, or migration (see Bauböck 1992, 1994). At the more personal level being explored [here], however, the five of us can at least partly understand the question through specific experiences we have had in our two countries of residence. What has it been like navigating the passages through the realities of individual language shift and cultural identity?

A LINGUISTIC TRIPTYCH

As noted above, our family's collective experience in Europe has been rooted primarily in the continent's three major languages: English, French, and German. I was raised in English in southern California, a second-generation American of Hungarian and German descent. When 12 years old, I opted to begin learning German at school and over the subsequent ten years went on to earn a college degree in German literature. Ariane grew up in France, Great Britain, and the United States, was educated in English, and spoke both French and English at home. She began studying German (among other languages) at college and quickly became fluent in it after starting her job in the research institute about five weeks after we arrived in West Berlin. From the beginning of our relationship, we have always preferred to speak and write English to each other, using German in our separate worlds of work and, as a couple, for social reasons when the occasion has demanded.

In the months before our first baby was born, the question arose as to which language(s) we would use with our future children. In the process of exploring that issue, we saw how trilingualism can work well in a family as modeled by close friends of ours, a German–Hungarian–American couple and their two daughters aged 9 and 14 years. On the strength of their example, we, too, decided to adopt a trilingual pattern of language use. With our three children (Soscha, Rachelle, and Ian), I have therefore always spoken English. Because I did not know French, Ariane at first felt strange about speaking it to Soscha. As Ariane kept telling herself, Soscha was, after all, my child, too. But with sincere encouragement from me, she overcame her initial reaction and went on to establish her relationship with all our children strictly in French, the main language of her own early childhood. They also heard German because I use it with clients in my translating and editing office at home and, like Ariane, for daily business on the telephone and in the surrounding community. Before the age of 18 months each of the children began hearing German for 20 to 30 hours a week in a monolingual German daycare setting as well, a situation that continued until they entered school. With neither English nor French being the dominant language of Berlin or Germany, our linguistic setting can be described as the first of Mackey's nine combinations of relations between the language(s) used in and outside the home (1972: 162): neither the language of the area nor the national language is that of the home.[1]

For each child in turn, however, the social and institutional structure of language acquisition differed in significant ways during the first five years of life. Not surprisingly, so did each one's linguistic development.

Pattern 1: Soscha

Initially cared for at home, Soscha (born in 1979) thus heard predominantly English from me and French from Ariane. She had little active contact with either German or other infants until about 1½ years of age, at which time she joined the German daycare group noted above. The initial group consisted of five children (including a German–Sri Lankan girl) and met each weekday in the home of the German woman running it, a warm, soft-spoken registered nurse who was studying medicine for a further career as a doctor. We did not socialize with the various sets of parents outside the framework of the daycare group, though on the occasions that one or both of us did come together with them (the daycare group's seasonal celebrations, the dropping off and picking up of the children, scheduled parent meetings with those in charge of the group, and so on), we got along smoothly.

Soscha responded well to her peers there. She quickly became dominant in German and clearly felt herself to be a member of that linguistic group. In addition to 'Mama' and 'Papa', which are common to German, French, and English, her first words were German: *bitte* 'please', *nein* 'no', *auf* 'open', 'on', and *Puppi* 'dolly'. By the age of 2¼ years, she used German pretty freely whenever she wanted to say something, especially when talking to herself or to her dolls. By 2¾ years, Soscha would also "ring up" her German

playmates on her toy telephone and give detailed descriptions in German about our latest family trip or weekend activities. By then, Soscha was able to ask for a variety of foods in French and English, the two languages she was especially keen on using when seeking to charm us into letting her have a bit of chocolate. She could also use French and English to say the words for a variety of actions or things and to give or pass on orders around the house (sometimes even repeating them in both languages just to make sure I got the message), but by no stretch of the imagination did she habitually speak either of our native languages even with us. Soscha simply felt more comfortable speaking German, and she knew we understood it, too. To adapt a term referred to in Harding and Riley (1986: 34), the three of us were thus practicing receptive trilingualism, with each using the language that came most naturally. To help Soscha keep her nascent English, French, and German separate, Ariane and I consciously strove to associate each language with a different native-speaking person or group: English with me (and other Americans we periodically had contact with), French with Ariane, and German with the outside community.

As multilingual home settings go, this arrangement is common. More important, Soscha was happy and communicative. When she did go to the trouble of speaking English or French, her utterances often contained German vocabulary or syntax. We simply recognized and accepted the amusing results for what has been called interference, "those deviations from the norms of either language which occur in the speech of bilinguals as a result of their familiarity with more than one language" (Weinreich, quoted in Harding and Riley 1986: 32; but see also 1986: 50). It is not at all uncommon in young multilinguals, and we never really worried about it. Ariane's experience with languages; my own language learning, related readings, and study of bilingualism (Antal and Eyth 1978); and our mutual observations of multilingual individuals and families had familiarized us with what we could reasonably expect and had convinced us that bilingualism need not hinder development. Our matching of a language with a person was not totally expected to prevent language mixing and the potentially annoying, unnecessary obstacles it can pose during encounters with persons not familiar with both of the languages involved. Indeed, at play, leisure, work, and school, multilinguals habitually draw on the expressive resources offered by all the languages available to them.

More realistically, we have always tried to *model* the practice of keeping the languages apart, confident that the children would thereby eventually learn to do the same. When instances of language mixing have occurred within our fivesome, we have called attention to the fact and gone to the effort of reformulating the message in one language or the other. As the children steadily progress in language, we continue suggesting and discussing alternative words and meanings in the relevant language(s), written or spoken, so that the desired expressions are available when needed. Of course, interpolations of this kind are sometimes met with impatience when they are unsolicited, but mutual annoyance can be avoided if they are offered positively and judiciously.

Thus far, our family's trilingual interaction has confirmed Dodson's observation about *bi*lingual development:

> The bilingual, if born without gross mental deficiencies, gradually learns to separate his two languages in his own time and of his own accord, especially if his family, friends and others around him do not mix up the languages in normal speech. (Dodson 1983: 407)

Soscha did not begin volunteering to speak English with us regularly until she had to be registered for elementary school. To choose an appropriate one, we took her in the spring of 1984, when she was 4¾ years old, to visit a bilingually taught kindergarten class (*Vorschulklasse*) at a publicly funded and publicly regulated school for Germans and Americans, Berlin's John F. Kennedy School (JFKS).[2] Soscha was so captivated by what she saw and heard there that day that she immediately decided she wanted to attend the school. As a child of US rather than German passport holders, however, she was eligible to enter only the American contingent and had to be able to speak American English. Attracted by the social setting and activities she had just witnessed, and realizing she had to leave her familiar social milieu in the daycare group in any case, she quickly changed her attitude toward English. From that point on, she began trying to talk only in English with us. Soscha found it difficult at first. She would forgetfully revert to German or falter in English, particularly when she was tired. Practice at home and with family and friends during a four-week visit to the United States that summer reinforced both her progress and her intrinsic motivation. By the time school started in late August, our shy five-year-old spoke and understood about on par for her age in both languages, and she was admitted to the JFKS.

German has never regained its primacy with Soscha. Though her teachers and her circle of friends included both German and American nationals over the years, and though the JFKS elementary school program devotes nearly equal attention to the cultures of both Germany and the United States, Soscha's preference for English and her preoccupation with things American intensified deeply. In addition to the strong desire to be a part of the JFKS program, she seemed to draw newly discovered inspiration from the old facts that she had close relatives in the United States and that English was spoken as one of the two home languages. Perhaps also buoyed by the prestige imputed to English through the enthusiasm with which many non-American JFKS students eventually embrace the language and American popular culture, Soscha succeeded in her efforts to acquire an American accent in English. In addition, she had adopted the two daughters of our German–Hungarian–American friends, whom we saw regularly on weekends, as older sisters and had found a role model in the English-speaking side of their trilingualism.

Progressing through the JFKS curriculum from kindergarten through the first semester of eighth grade, Soscha became biliterate in English and German but showed an early predilection for books in English. One likely reason for these leanings is that she may well have simply found it easier to read English primary books than German ones, for the JFKS pursues the policy of firmly establishing the student's declared mother tongue in all four language skills. And whereas she and I had often listened to German (and American) children's songs together at home and had sung them during the years we walked to and from her daycare group, I had only rarely read to her in German. Not being intimately familiar with German children's literature, Ariane and I followed our natural inclination to share with Soscha the American stories we had grown up with. (For the same reasons, Ariane read to her in French as well.) As for writing, most of Soscha's letters were to her American grandparents and cousins, who know only English, and to former American classmates who had moved back to the United States. Because Soscha was in the JFKS's *English mother-tongue program*, most of her written school assignments were in English as well. Moreover, we owned no television in those years, so *our home continued to constitute a predominantly English-language sphere within a German-language community*. When Soscha began attending the rough equivalent of eighth grade (*quatrième*) at a rural French private school in Haute Savoie (see below), German as a reference point for Soscha was eclipsed altogether (but certainly not forgotten).

We had, in other words, been witnessing a case of wholesale individual language shift, and for Soscha it was not the last instance of it, either. Her strong focus on English and the United States was itself gradually supplanted in a partial, second shift in language allegiance. The family's temporary move to France, due to a change in Ariane's job, meant immersion in French society—its language, customs, and perspectives. At school, Soscha heard, spoke, wrote, and read only French; at home, she spoke English and, increasingly, French. After a time Soscha (and Rachelle) responded more to things French than to things German; preferred reading French to reading German; chose to watch French films, particularly comedies, rather than German films; and simply understood both the French language and French humor more readily than German and German humor. When Soscha returned to the Berlin school system 2¾ years later in the fall of 1995, she chose to complete her schooling in the French system rather than switch back to the German–American program of the JFKS. She still feels that her greatest facility is in English, but French has become and has remained a rather close second, supported as it is by the school and new French friends in Berlin, by former classmates as pen pals back in Haute Savoie, and, as always, by Ariane at home.

Pattern 2: Rachelle

The pattern of Rachelle's linguistic development differed somewhat from Soscha's. Rachelle (born in 1981) joined Soscha's daycare group at about eight months of age, so contact with German came significantly earlier in her life than it had in Soscha's. As the second child in the family, Rachelle benefited from another major factor when it came to language acquisition: the constant close contact with an elder sibling at home. Like Soscha, Rachelle first began speaking in German. By the age of 26 months, she had an active vocabulary of about 15 words, including *meins* 'mine', *nein* 'no', *danke* 'thank you', *ja* 'yes', and *Schuhe* 'shoes'. The desire to keep up with and be like Soscha and the need to assert herself within the group meant that German went on to become Rachelle's language of daily peer communication (playing, requesting, informing, teasing, quarreling, and so on). The two girls maintained this dyadic language relationship at home as well.

Up to the age of two years, Rachelle had thus heard and had begun speaking more German in and outside the home than Soscha had as an only child at that age. By habit, German remained the dominant language between the girls after Soscha entered kindergarten in August 1984, but with Soscha's shift from German to English in full swing by then, English began creeping in, especially during the four-week US vacation. After our return, Rachelle's German continued developing through her monolingual German interaction within a different daycare group to which we transferred her. But in 1985, in the long wake of Soscha's conversion to English, Rachelle, too, made her first decided attempts to speak English to me at home. In what seemed to be an increasingly conscious person–language association, she also began trying out French with Ariane more regularly than had been the case up to that point.

Unlike Soscha, however, Rachelle mixed her three languages a great deal, at least at home, until she was about 6½ years old. Preferring to make up what seemed to be her own rules, she would invent novel conjugations of German verbs and combine them in a single sentence with equally idiosyncratic pronunciations of English and French words. The result was what we came to call "Rachellian," her highly personalized system oriented just to getting a message out with whatever words happened to be most convenient at the moment. This approach to the use of language began to taper off with her as she became surer of her English.

Having begun tentative vocalization in English with me in 1985, Rachelle made great strides the following year in voluntarily speaking the language. The grammar was often faulty, but she good-naturedly repeated the correct formulation after me. The decisive change in attitude seemed to come in August 1986, when this fiercely competitive little soul had to be told that she might not be admitted to Soscha's school the next year if she did not speak English as well as her sister. She became determined to master the task. By April 1987, 4½ months before the commencement of kindergarten classes at the JFKS, she was speaking English habitually with me and, increasingly, with Soscha but tended to revert to German when groggy, tired, or very moody. In June Rachelle's capability in English was developing rapidly, but she was still mixing English, German, and French in the same sentence. Then, after her first day at school in August, she returned home so excited and bubbly that she could hardly contain herself. In that frame of mind, she told me all about her day—in English. Never before had Rachelle spoken so much English so rapidly for five minutes straight. By December, her English vocabulary and grammar had progressed to the point that she was participating in class as easily in German as in English, and she consistently spoke English with me at home. By fourth grade (1991–1992), Rachelle's free blending of German and English, which may be charming for a preschooler, had long since ceased in situations where it could have jeopardized assessments of her work in school. She was scoring well on vocabulary tests, dictations, and writing assignments in both languages and, according to her homeroom teacher, was equally at ease in American, German, and mixed German-American groups. In the estimation of the German partner-tongue teacher at that time, Rachelle was a natural candidate for the JFKS's *double mother-tongue program,* in which students are taught and graded at mother-tongue level in both their English and German language classes.

Rachelle's facility in the two languages by the time she began school in 1987 was aided by an additional factor, age. Born in late November, Rachelle was well past the cutoff line for admittance in the year she turned five. When she did enter the JFKS's bilingually taught kindergarten program, she was 8½ months older than Soscha had been upon commencing. Rachelle had also been speaking at least some English at home for a longer period than Soscha had by the time formal schooling began. The effect of an older sibling had therefore been advantageous for Rachelle's English as well as her German. Rachelle was as comfortable in one language as in the other. According to her bilingual teacher, Rachelle and a few others like her quickly came to function as a kind of hinge between the German and American monolinguals in the class, mediating and clarifying as the situation and their own comprehension allowed. Her ability with the two languages seemed to help establish her both socially and academically in her new institutional environment, and she remained a happy, industrious, and well-adjusted bilingual. Rachelle and Soscha continued to use English and German rather freely with each other, often in the same sentence, but rarely, if ever, did so with people they knew could not speak both. As their schooling continued, communication between them took place more and more in English.

Pattern 3: Ian

Ian (born in 1988) also had a major language-learning context outside the home early in life. Like the one described for Soscha and Rachelle, it revolved around a monolingual German daycare mother (albeit a different one), to whom he began going at the age of 14 months. The setting offered him less contact with children his own age than Soscha and Rachelle had had, but equally warm and direct contact with his caretaker. The main difference between Ian's early exposure to languages and that which his two older sisters had experienced lay within our home, where, by 1990, Soscha and Rachelle were speaking almost solely in English (and slightly increasing their production of French with Ariane).

Their input, combined with my own and that of a Welsh au pair who joined us when Ian was 14 months old, meant that he heard English for the most part. At the age of 22 months, he was producing words in both languages ('book' and 'happy' being his first two), and he was fond of standing up at the dinner table to deliver long, solemn pronouncements in a kind of protolanguage, complete with dramatic intonation and expressive gestures before taking his seat again with a satisfied smile. His spoken vocabulary of approximately 20 words at about 25 months of age also included 'Mama', 'Papa', 'hug', 'kiss', 'cup', 'buggy', 'push chair' (British English for 'stroller'), and 'money'. At three years, Ian understood English, German, and French, did not mix the first two much, spoke more French with Ariane than either Soscha or Rachelle ever had at that age, and was dominant in English.

In mid-August 1991, Ian was transferred from his daycare mother to the larger, half-day, monolingual German daycare program that Rachelle had once attended. After these morning sessions, he remained with his English-speaking au pair. Given Rachelle's relatively smooth transition from her first daycare group to this second one years earlier, we had few reservations about Ian's move.

But Ian responded surprisingly. After about two weeks, the educators running the group reported that he was not speaking. He appeared, they said, to understand part of what was going on but remained silent. As Rachelle had also initially done in her day, Ian preferred to observe the other children and their activities from the perimeter. The behavior persisted for weeks, which invited some bullying from one or two of the more assertive children in the group. One of the daycare professionals, who was monolingual, began speculating that Ian's trilingual background was retarding his development and suggested that three languages "was too much to ask" of a child. We counseled patience, confident that Ian's development was neither inexplicable nor entirely abnormal given his nature and his switch into an utterly new, large, and highly regulated setting. More days passed with hardly a word from Ian in the group.

At home, however, we noticed a major leap in Ian's English. In about late September, he began expressing himself in nothing but complete sentences and accurately parroted even sophisticated words. Like most multilinguals, he also experimented with his languages, inadvertently treating us to new, and very appropriate, hybrid words to fit a given situation. For a time, he was apt to combine the English verb 'to laugh' and the German adjective *lustig* 'funny' into an adjective pronounced *laf'-tik*. He usually used it in the negative while scolding one of us when anything happened that he did not consider at all funny: *Das ist nicht laftig!*

The concern of the daycare professional heightened as October wore on. Around the beginning of November, however, Ian suddenly erupted in German not just with individual words or snatches of phrases and clauses but, as in English, with complete, even complex, sentences, formulating requests, explanations, and descriptions as well as defending himself verbally against perceived inroads on his

psychological space. The "problem" had been solved, and Ian quickly found his place in the group.

A New Environment

For all three children, resettlement in January 1993 proved traumatic when the family moved to Haute Savoie, France, across the Swiss border near Geneva. Their difficulty was not due to the radical change in living conditions. Indeed, we all loved going from the center of a city of nearly four million inhabitants in the flat plains of northern Germany to a rural village of just a few hundred surrounded by fields, farm animals, and mountains (the Jura to the west and Salève to the east, not to mention the foothills of the French Alps). Not even the loss of independent mobility (urban public transportation) bothered Rachelle and Soscha, at least not initially. Nor was there any hint at all of discrimination in the population. The local public officials, teachers, clerks, shopkeepers, and mechanics in the village and neighboring towns were friendly, patient, and receptive, especially our resident landlords, a French and British–Swiss couple. It is true that the issue of foreign immigrants was almost as heated in France as it had become in Germany since the fall of the Berlin Wall in November 1989. However, the main pockets of support for right-wing, antiforeigner politicians such as Le Pen lay outside Haute Savoie—along parts of the southern coast where the influx of French-speaking immigrants from Algeria, Tunisia, and other former French colonies was greatest, and in or near Paris, where these residents tended to concentrate in certain districts. As in Berlin, we were not seen as belonging to the same category.

The adjustment problem the children encountered was their immersion in French. True, they had since birth heard French consistently and directly from one parent, had used it on family summer vacations with relatives and friends in France, and had sometimes spoken it around the house in Berlin. But using a language in those capacities is quite different from using it for monolingual instruction in school. This reality was especially stark for Rachelle and Soscha, for the contexts in which adolescents (and adults) interact with native speakers of the target language tend to require responses that are more sophisticated than those usually expected of very young language learners. The academic burden of the new linguistic environment was compounded by the complications of the social dimension, to which Soscha and Rachelle, by then 14 and 12 years old, were keenly sensitive. Not surprisingly, culture shock—the "frustration and confusion that result from being bombarded by uninterpretable cues" (Adler 1997: 237)—deepened, with the depths of its cycle being plumbed by both girls from the fourth through about the sixth month after arrival in France (see Adler 1997: 238). This cumulative culture shock led to cultural fatigue, or what can be called "the lack of energy or emotional projection for social relations" (Darrow and Palmquist 1977: 147). Early one evening after a hard day at school and a minor accident on the stairs at home, Soscha all but disintegrated and retreated to her room, sobbing,

"I just want to go back to Berlin!" And that even from a tri-lingual child of proven resilience and flexibility. It appears that no amount of preparation can ultimately preclude all symptoms of culture shock and cultural fatigue. The nadir had been reached.

Once again, role models figured critically in the learning process. Two particular examples of successful survival in the transition to life and schooling in a different culture served the girls well. One was the experience shared with us a few years earlier by an American woman whom the girls knew and highly respected and who is today a career diplomat. She had suffered through, and had surmounted, the same problems of contextual uncertainty and unpredict-ability when she had been immersed into a Russian school as a child. The second example was the author Judith Kerr, one of whose books Soscha had read in German translation while in 8th grade. As if foreshadowing Soscha's own experi-ence, Kerr described how difficult the adjustment to French schools had been for her when she and her family arrived in France after fleeing from her native Berlin in the 1930s.

Soscha and Rachelle do not recollect any single critical event in their deliverance from the depths of culture shock. It seemed gradual. They did have occasional setbacks even after they emerged from it, of course, but the impacts were never again either as enduring or as threatening as they had been during the first six months of the stay in Savoie. From then on, the girls rapidly gained in their confidence that they, too, could not only survive but also go on to meet the school's demands on them as well as their own. As Kerr (1980) put it,

> Es war wie ein Wunder....Es war, als hätte sie plötzlich herausgefunden, daß sie fliegen konnte,... Am Ende der Woche betrachtete Mama sie voller Erstaunen.
>
> "Ich habe noch nie bei einem Menschen eine solche Veränderung erlebt," sagte sie, "vor ein paar Tagen sahst du noch blaß und elend aus. Jetzt ist es, als wärest du fünf Zentimeter gewachsen, und du hast ganz rosige Wangen. Was ist nur mit dir geschehen?"
>
> "Ich glaube, ich kann jetzt französisch sprechen," sagte Anna[3] (Kerr 1980: 141–142).

Ian's adjustment was equally painful. Arriving in the middle of the school year, after the other children in his group had already established friendships, he was an outsider at first. Having spoken French only with an adult up to that point, he was further ostracized by his inability to speak at the same level as his classmates. Although the linguistic demands upon preschool and kindergarten children are not as great as those upon older children and adults, the academic and social expectations of Ian (e.g., pressure to conform, defend oneself, and engage with others) were no less real. Never having mixed his languages much before this point, Ian, at least when tired, began producing such sentences as *Me nicht dormir* 'I don't want to go to sleep'. Recalling the way in which Rachelle had created trilingual blends years ear-lier, we dubbed Ian's private language "Ianesque" and figured that it would eventually disappear as he got things sorted

out. Fortunately, he soon caught up in French, and within three months his language (as well as his accent) was virtu-ally indistinguishable from that of his Savoyard playmates and classmates. His language mixing also declined.

By the end of the 1993–1994 school year, all three chil-dren had a circle of monolingual French-speaking friends, above-average grade reports, and fluent French. Even at home, French, at least temporarily, became the dominant language of the children. They each simply found it easier to tell the rest of us about the school day by using the language in which they had gone through it. Their narratives, ban-ter, and jokes tended to lose all spontaneity when translated into English, so it was up to me to continue improving my French. Reveling in their newly achieved facility, the chil-dren had thus switched their language allegiance largely to French and were identifying with their respective friends at a social level.

LANGUAGE, CULTURE, AND IDENTITY

Two aspects seem to have been at play in the language shifts described in the previous section. They are pointed out by Lambert (1972), whose comments about bilingual language learning appear equally applicable to our children's trilin-gual experience:

> [The language student's] motivation to learn is thought to be determined by both his attitudes and by the type of orientation he has toward learning a second language. The orientation is *instrumental* in form if, for example, the purposes of language study reflect the more utilitar-ian value of linguistic achievement, such as getting ahead in one's occupation, and is *integrative* if, for example, the student is oriented to learn more about the other cultural community, as if he desired to become a potential mem-ber of the other group. It is also argued that some may be anxious to learn another language as a means of being accepted in another cultural group because of dissatis-factions experienced in their own culture while other individuals may be as much interested in another culture as they are in their own. In either case, the more profi-cient one becomes in a second language the more he may find that his place in his original membership group is modified at the same time as the other linguistic–cultural group becomes something more than a reference group for him. It may, in fact, become a second membership group for him (Lambert 1972: 395–396).

As stated at the outset, we feel the integrative element more than the instrumental one in the linguistic odyssey we have experienced. Viewing that journey as a search for the answer to the question of who we are, I venture to add a third dimension as well, one that seems to underlie both the motivations that Lambert points out for learning a language and the culture it conveys: personal origins. Personal origins help people identify themselves. It is natural to seek one's identity in part through the language, culture, and heritage from which one springs. That sense of identity can even outlast the language itself, at least for a time. At the microcosmic level of my own family, for instance, Hungarian was not passed on to my generation, only the second after my grandfather immigrated to the United States from Budapest in 1912. (On my mother's side, German had "died out" long before.) The general mobility of American society, the melting-pot mentality that prevailed during my father's and grandfather's eras, marriage outside the Hungarian-speaking community, and issues of sheer practicality seemed to discourage my father and his brother from using the language after they grew up. But I still feel and claim my Hungarian background (see also Varro 1998b).

Nonetheless, without the language of the culture and heritage, "ethnic" groups eventually struggle to survive, and it is fortunate for our family that English, French, and German, the active languages of our known background, are not likely to suffer worldwide demise anytime soon. The vibrant context in which we have lived in Europe has animated the quest for our identities and has shown how much it can expand the minds of young people who have direct parental, scholastic, and community contact with the language(s) of their own culture(s). For instance, learning European history and literature from the French, German, and American perspectives has given Soscha insights into her heritage and the human condition that are broader than would have been likely from just one national viewpoint. In that context she has come to take pride in the grandeur, influence, and leadership of France and yet also knows enough to smile at exaggerated claims of French predominance in all walks of life. She learned early in classes with American, French, and German teachers that history is not just a series of dates but a story told differently depending on the perspectives of each country.

Why is that learning so important? It is because identity and identity shift are closely related to a person's acceptance as one of the members of the target-language community. That acceptance, in turn, depends partly on the degree of common knowledge that one shares with the "natives." As Harding and Riley (1986: 17) point out, the bilingual

> speaks the language but, because he has been living abroad, does not know many of the things which people who speak that language usually know. He may well have problems understanding what people mean which have nothing to do with the language as such, but with the way of life which is unfamiliar to him. Precisely because he speaks the language so well, people will take it for granted that he knows things that he does not know but which they would expect to have to explain to a foreigner.

Stretching the horizons of a young person's mind does not end in the history class. In Soscha's respective language classes this semester, the students have read and discussed Immanuel Kant's *Was ist Aufklärung?* [What Is Enlightenment?], Jean Paul Sartre's *Huis Clos* [No Exit], William Golding's *Lord of the Flies,* and Tennessee Williams's *A Streetcar Named Desire.* Rooted in different systems of knowledge and beliefs about the way the world works and the role of individuals in the system, the authors of this literature address a wide spectrum of world views, aspirations, hopes, fears, themes, and problems from four cultural spheres. The issue is not which of those systems Soscha favors at the expense of the others, but to what degree she can draw on all of them in the inevitable search for her own self. Recognition of that difference is what we understood Soscha to be expressing when, shortly after the family returned to Berlin after 2½ years in Haute Savoie, she summed up her experience, "Mama, I'm glad we went to live in France. It is there that I found part of my identity."

Each child's development of facility in the three languages has differed. Rachelle speaks German less readily than Soscha; Ian, less readily than Rachelle. Ian's English dominance from speaking age on was greater than Soscha's during the same period because he had two older siblings communicating with him in English. Soscha did not. His peers were more English speakers than German speakers. In their early years, Rachelle and Soscha used to play and argue mostly in German. Ian preferred English. As we have found, neither the trilingualism of the individual nor the pattern of trilingualism established within the family is static; it is not fixed once and for all.

And so it is with the cultural identity that goes with a language. Just how relative cultural identity can be is indicated anecdotally by the additional responses of Rachelle and Ian, who, like Soscha, also have claim to French citizenship through Ariane. When asked about which country she identified more with—France, Germany, or the United States— Rachelle shrugged her shoulders, saying that, if anything, she felt somewhat more oriented to the United States at this time. After all, we have family and friends in California with whom she has enjoyed long visits; she is attracted to the West Coast, as are many Europeans; and none of us have claim to German citizenship in any case, for German nationality is currently still based on *jus sanguinis* rather than on *jus soli.* Her generally positive attitude toward the United States and English, and the high status commonly accorded both English and California in Europe and other parts of the world, seem to bear out an observation by Dodson:

> The welter of evidence now available shows that the languages of bilinguals do not affect their development. What does affect it, however, is *what we think of those languages, how highly we regard them, how we deal with the child learning them and, as a consequence, the self-image the child develops in the process of acquiring two languages.* (Dodson 1983: 405; emphasis in original)

Ian has been more volatile than his sisters in his personal identification with language and culture. During a family tour of Belgium in September 1994, we visited the fields outside the town of Waterloo, where Napoleon and his imperial French army fought their final battle in June 1815. Hearing that the beleaguered buildings at the center of the Allied lines had eventually fallen to Napoleon's troops during their ferocious eight-hour attack, six-year-old Ian got confused. Feeling "very French," he thought at first that the French had won. But reality soon hit home: "The French didn't win the battle, only a farm!" he noted. "Why would anyone want to win a farm?" We then gently broke the news to him that the French had, in the end, actually lost to the British and Prussians. Ian, evidently serious about being on the victorious side, gave the matter deep thought, for a few hours later he broached the subject again:

"Mama, we speak English, don't we?"

"Yes."

"Well, then we're English, so we also won that battle."

Indeed, cultural identity may depend on immediate social constellations and on the inclination to establish one's individuality in one's own mind. Despite eventual integration into French social and scholastic life in Haute Savoie, for example, Soscha reported feeling "more American" at her school there than she had at the JFKS because when she was in France with her French peers, she was "not as French" as they.

As deliberate as her statement sounds, it strongly suggests that the cultural identity of an individual is not defined by that person alone but by others as well, and the result may be a good deal less conscious than one might be aware of. For instance, Soscha and Rachelle have never stated that they feel German or German–American, despite living in Germany and despite their intense, early contact with the German language and German playmates and classmates, but their 12- and 13-year-old American cousins who recently visited quickly detected that our daughters have a gait different from that of native Californians. To the cousins, Soscha and Rachelle seem at least "European" in that regard. Soscha and Rachelle choose not to speak German with me or Ariane (unless politeness toward others dictates otherwise, of course), thus confirming our own sense that it feels artificial for us to use anything but our native language with them under normal circumstances, but grammatical idiosyncrasies of their speech and writing clearly reflect the German experience the girls have had (e.g., 'If I would be' instead of 'If I were', 'I have been home since three hours' instead of 'I have been home for three hours'). For reasons such as these, their grandmother in California often affectionately calls or introduces the girls as "our Berliners."

Negative stereotypes constitute a third aspect defining one's cultural identity. Who, for example, wants to be the "ugly American," the "ugly German," or the "arrogant French"? To Soscha (and perhaps to others), her cultural and legal status as French-American, which she feels sometimes excludes her from full acceptance among French and German students at Berlin's French *lycée,* can also afford her partial exemption from criticism that members of one national group at the school occasionally feel cause to voice about the behavior of the other national group. The motto: "I'm only half French, so how the French kids act only half concerns me."

As pointed out earlier, however, the fact that one is also "half-American" is not necessarily an asset at all times, either. The United States, because of its prominence in the world, is not universally admired or loved, and American citizens at home and abroad may reap antagonism as a result (see Varro and Boyd 1998). The country has emerged from the Cold War as the only one able to project vast power quickly to virtually any place on the globe. In Europe, American popular culture has dominated both the record and film industries for decades. The US economy is still the fulcrum of the world economy in many respects. For better or worse, American diplomacy is a leading factor in much of the world, notably in Eastern and Western Europe, the Near and Far East, and Central America. For a nation with so great a global presence, mutual acceptance and cultural understanding become integral to long-term effectiveness. Yet these very qualities are sometimes felt to be wanting in US engagement in the world. For lack of interest in or contact with other peoples, some Americans might still prefer to ignore such issues. In occupied Berlin this outlook seemed to be epitomized by the self-contained infrastructural facilities that enabled personnel and dependents of the US forces to live in a world apart from the surrounding community.

But such circumstances have now vanished in Berlin and have become increasingly rare for US citizens elsewhere in the world. Global interdependence and mobility are making it ever less desirable, or even possible, to avoid mingling with and trying to understand other peoples, cultures, languages, customs, and ways of viewing life. The question of loyalties is being recast. Indeed, traditional concepts of nation, nationality, citizenship, and allegiance may well be gradually redefined or possibly even rendered obsolete (see Herzog 1996), though perhaps not in the near future. In that process, the orientations described by people like Soscha, Rachelle, and Ian may have profound implications for the concept of cultural identity. For the five of us, multilingual and multicultural identity is constantly on the move, propelled, shaped, and guided by role models, age, expectations, motivations, social context, acceptance by others, travel, relationships with family members, and schools as an instrument not only of cultural survival but of cultural *partnership.* Trilingualism and multiculturalism are the *modus vivendi* that prompts us to seek out opportunities to challenge, explore, and expand our shared knowledge and beliefs. It is this way of life that constitutes that "source of interest and achievement" to which Harding and Riley (1986: 2) refer and that provides us with the resources we need for improving our comprehension of daily modern realities.

Notes

1. Mackey's other combinations are

> 2)…the language of the home but not that of the area is the national tongue. 3) Conversely, the language of the area and not of the nation may be that of the home. 4) Both area and national language may be that of the home. 5) The national language may not be that of the home[,] but the area may be bilingual with both the home and national languages being used. 6) Conversely, the country may be bilingual and the area unilingual. 7) Both the area and the country may be bilingual. 8) The

area may be bilingual and the national language may be that of the home. 9) Finally, the country may be bilingual and the area language that of the home. (Mackey 1972: 162–163)

2. The JFKS is a

dual-medium equal-maintenance (DEM) type [of single school] with a number of nontypical divergences due to the fact that the type of bilingualism practiced is free rather than formalized alternation of the two languages" (Mackey 1972: xviii)....."[I]t is a school in which native German children may receive their instruction or part of their instruction in...a language which is not one of the official or area languages of the country....As a special language school, the [JFKS] has the added advantage of interaction from native speakers of English [in the same classroom]....[In terms of the] customs, rules, and patterns of interpersonal relations [in this bilingual community], the leading one, which lends the school its particular character, may be stated thus: USE EITHER LANGUAGE AND UNDERSTAND BOTH" (Mackey 1972: 8–9)....."[A]ll students, both German and American, may come in at the kindergarten level and stay on until the end of Grade 13. In other words, a complete bilingual and bicultural primary and secondary program is offered" (Mackay 1972: 28; see also JFKS 1996).

In a special law of 26 October 1964 (GVB1 1964: 1154)—*das Gesetz über die John F. Kennedy Schule (Deutsch-Amerikanische Gemeinschaftsschule)*, referred to in English as the Kennedy School Law—the Berlin state (*Land*) government declared the JFKS to be a "school with a special pedagogical character" (*eine Schule mit besonderer pädagogischer Prägung*; §1, par. 2). The JFKS is subject to the educational regulations and standards applied to the schools of Berlin (§2), but the Kennedy School Law provides for certain procedures (§3, §4), committees (§5–8), and programs (§1, par. 3) that are unique to this school in the German public educational system. As an accredited US primary and secondary educational institution, for example, the JFKS has a K-through-12 program that prepares students in English for graduation with a high school diploma recognized throughout the United States.

Admission of German applicants at the kindergarten level is decided by lottery (§3, par. 2), and the waiting lists are long. Students can be admitted at higher grades upon recommendation by the relevant principal and approval of the Educational Directorate, the JFKS's unique elective and appointive body that serves in a capacity somewhat similar to that of a school board in the United States. Admission of students for the American contingent is based on space available, nationality (passport), mother-tongue English proficiency, and, if the student is in high school, the courses taken and the grades received.

At various times in the school's development, the proportions of the nationalities represented in the student body have varied, and the school has usually had a small number of students who were neither German nor American nationals. In practice, the relation from the early 1970s through the early 1980s was approximately 50 percent German nationals, 40 percent American nationals, and 10 percent third nationals, especially at the high-school level. From the early 1980s through late September 1994, that is, before US military personnel and their dependants were withdrawn from Berlin in the process of Germany's postwar unification, the relation was 50 percent German nationals and

50 percent American nationals. Since the withdrawal, the resulting reduction in the number of American students attending the JFKS has been at least partially offset by the admission of English-speaking students who are not US citizens. The languages and cultural backgrounds of the school's student body—and of the faculty—thus currently lend the JFKS a measure of the international dimension encountered at international schools.

3.   It was like a miracle....It was as though she had suddenly found that she could fly,...

    By the end of the week Mama looked at her in amazement.

    "I've never seen such a change in anyone," she said. "A few days ago you looked green and miserable. Now it's as though you'd grown 5 centimeters and you look quite pink. What's happened to you?"

    "I think I can speak French now," said Anna. (Kerr 1971: 154)

References

Adler, Nancy J. (1997). *International Dimensions of Organizational Behavior,* 3rd ed. Cincinnati: Southwestern College.

Antal, David; and Eyth, Dagmar (1978). A study of bilingualism and bilingual reading performance. Unpublished master's thesis, University of Southern California, Los Angeles.

Baedeker, Karl (1977). *Baedekers Berlin-Kreuzberg.* Freiburg: Baedeker.

Bauböck, Rainer (1992). Immigration and the boundaries of citizenship. *Monographs in Ethnic Relations* 4 (n.s.).

——— . (1994). *Transnational Citizenship: Membership and Rights in International Migration.* Aldershot: Elgar.

Darrow, Ken; and Palmquist, Brad (1977). *Transcultural Study Guide,* 2nd ed. Stanford: Volunteers in Asia.

Dodson, C.J. (1983). Living with two languages. *Journal of Multilingual and Multicultural Development* 4, 401–414.

Escher, Felix (1987). Die brandenburgisch-preußische Residenz und Hauptstadt Berlin im 17. und 18. Jahrhundert [The Brandenburg-Prussian residence and capital of Berlin in the 17th and 18th centuries]. In *Geschichte Berlins von der Frühgeschichte bis zur Gegenwart,* vol. 1: *Von der Frühgeschichte bis zur Industrialisierung,* W. Ribbe (ed.), 343–403. Munich: Beck.

Harding, Edith; and Riley, Philip (1986). *The Bilingual Family.* Cambridge: Cambridge University Press.

Herzog (1996). Der Nationalstaat hat sich überlebt [Herzog: The nation-state has had its day]. *Der Tagesspiegel* (Berlin), 18 September, 4.

Jansen, Frank (1996). Keine Welle! Keine Welle? [Not a ripple! Not a ripple?] *Der Tagesspiegel* (Berlin), 11 November, 1.

JFKS (1996). *Thirty-five Years: The John F. Kennedy Schule, 1960–1995 (Festschrift).* Berlin: John F. Kennedy School.

Katona, Marianna S. (1997). *Tales from the Berlin Wall.* London: Minerva Press.

Kerr, Judith (1980). *Als Hitler das rosa Kaninchen stahl* [When Hitler stole pink rabbit], A. Böll (trans.). Ravensburg: Otto Maier. (First published 1971. London: Collins.)

Lambert, Wallace E. (1972). A social psychology of bilingualism. In *Teaching English as a Second Language,* 2nd ed., H. B. Allen and R. N. Campbell (eds.), 385–430. New York: McGraw-Hill.

Mackey, William F. (1972). *Bilingual Education in a Binational School: A Study of Equal Language Maintenance Through Free Alternation.* Rowley, MA: Newbury House.

Merrill, Jane (1984). *Bringing Up Baby Bilingual.* New York: Facts on File.

Ribbe, Wolfgang (1987). Berlin zwischen Ost und West (1945 bis zur Gegenwart) [Berlin between East and West (1945 to the present)]. In *Geschichte Berlins von der Frühgeschichte bis zur Gegenwart,* vol. 2: *Von der Märzrevolution bis zur Gegenwart,* W. Ribbe (ed.), 1025–1124. Munich: Beck.

Varro, Gabrielle. 1998a. The Absentee American: Repatriate's Perspectives on America. Review of Carolyn D. Smith. *International Journal of the Sociology of Language* 133: 177–187.

———. 1998b. Does Bilingualism Survive the Second Generation? Three Generations of French-American Families in France. *International Journal of the Sociology of Language* 133: 105–128.

———, and Sally Boyd. 1998. Introduction: Probing the Background. *International Journal of the Sociology of Language* 133: 1–30.

Wendler, Simone (1996). Ausländer meiden die Stadt [Foreigners Avoid the Town]. *Der Tagesspiegel* (Berlin), 18 September, 3.

Zimmermann, Monika (1996). Tolerantes Berlin [Tolerant Berlin]. *Der Tagesspiegel* (Berlin), 2 December, 1.

Post-reading Questions / Activities

- What are the general patterns Antal identifies for his children? Could these be generalized to other cases and situations?
- Antal points out that English, German, and French are strong languages, each with educational and literary uses. How might this story be different if the languages were "smaller" or ethnic or minority languages?
- Conduct a language life history for one multilingual individual, tracing earliest relationships and the languages in which those relationships were conducted, movements, education, and other life events. How have these experiences shaped the way that person uses her or his languages today?

Vocabulary

code switching	language shift
interference	receptive trilingualism (multilingualism)
language mixing	

Suggested Further Reading

Fishman, Joshua A. 1991. *Reversing Language Shift: Theoretical and Empirical Foundations of Assistance to Threatened Languages.* Clevedon and Philadelphia: Multilingual Matters.

Gal, Susan. 1979. *Language Shift: Social Determinants of Linguistic Change in Bilingual Austria.* New York: Academic Press.

Grosjean, François. 1982. *Life with Two Languages: An Introduction to Bilingualism.* Cambridge, MA: Harvard University Press.

Wei, Li. 1994. *Three Generations, Two Languages, One Family: Language Choice and Language Shift in a Chinese Community in Britain.* Clevedon: Multilingual Matters.

CHAPTER 17

Bilingualism *en casa*

Ana Celia Zentella

(1997)

Bilingualism is a special case of multilingualism, which is the norm around the world. Like multilingual people, bilingual individuals employ two languages in very subtle ways. They know in which situations to use one language or the other, or with fellow bilinguals which topics, or which aspects of which topics, call for a specific language. This knowledge is gained very young, as they move from setting to setting and interact with others.

Ana Celia Zentella conducted a careful study of a Puerto Rican community in New York City, looking at patterns of language use among not just "English" and "Spanish" in a neighborhood in Spanish Harlem (East Harlem). She identified three different varieties of Spanish (Popular Puerto Rican Spanish, Standard Puerto Rican Spanish, and English-dominant Spanish) and four different varieties of English (Puerto Rican English, African American Vernacular English, Hispanized English, and Standard New York City English), as well as "Spanglish." For a period of about eighteen months she interacted with and observed numerous families and their children, using participant-observation and interviews to get to know intimately how people used language.

What is clear from the complexity of Zentella's account in this chapter is that bilinguals do not simply throw in random phrases or words from one language or another, but that they must master a subtle set of patterns and rules for gauging the linguistic capacities and identities of the people with whom they converse. As in many settings where bilingualism is the result of migration, children are more learned in the language of the new society (English, in this case) than their elders. While their caregivers might address them in Spanish (as is common), children might respond in either Spanish or English, and they frequently speak English among themselves. Gender, level of involvement in the outside English-speaking world, type of employment, age, and many other factors are involved in people's mastery and use of various codes.

An old view of bilinguals is that they often suffered cognitive deficiency as a result of their bilingualism, but it is evident from more recent data that navigating this complex world calls for very detailed social and linguistic knowledge.

It is not only impersonal rules that govern which language should be employed at any given moment, but also speakers' individual preferences. Some people are directed inwardly, toward el bloque, *while others spend more time and attention at activities in the English-dominant world.*

The term code switching *(also written as* codeswitching *or* code-switching*) refers to the movement from one language ("code") to another, whether in different situations or even within the same sentence ("intrasentential code switches"). (See Chapter 18.) Scholars accounting for the switches have observed many important things about this phenomenon, including the fact that it follows precise grammatical rules and that it gives evidence of the speaker's attitude toward what is said.*

Reading Questions

- Why do some siblings differ in their linguistic preferences?
- How does gender play a role in determining which language is most likely to be used?

Ana Celia Zentella, "Bilingualism *en casa." Growing Up Bilingual: Puerto Rican Children in New York.* Malden, MA: Blackwell, 1997, pp. 56–79.

- What rules of politeness come into play when people are deciding which language to use with a new conversational partner?
- What educational experiences do you see described in this chapter?
- Zentella writes of Lolita's "meta-linguistic awareness." What is this? Why does she have it? How might this be channeled into academic success more broadly for other bilingual children?

A knock on the door of any of the apartments that housed the families of *el bloque* was greeted by "WHO?" or "*¿Quién es?*" ("Who is it?"), or both. The lone English interrogative was most popular, even with Spanish-dominant occupants. Children greeted me in English because they knew that I was a teacher, but they ran to call an adult in Spanish. Inside the door, residents addressed visitors predominantly in English or Spanish, in a consistent pattern. The bilingual-multidialectal repertoire of the home approximated that of the block, with some limitations: standard and non-standard Puerto Rican Spanish (SPRS/NSPRS), Hispanized English (HE), and Puerto Rican English (PRE) predominated. The vernacular of African Americans (AAVE) was heard less frequently than on the street, and no one spoke standard English consistently at home. PRS, PRE, and alternating between them, constituted the basic verbal repertoire for the four communication dyads at home:

1 the language(s) that caretakers spoke to each other
2 the language(s) that caretakers spoke to children
3 the language(s) that children spoke to caretakers
4 the language(s) that children spoke to each other

Theoretically, a large number of patterns was possible, since each dyad could be realized by one of nine combinations:

Span-Eng	Span-Span	Span-Both
Eng-Eng	Eng-Span	Eng-Both
Both-Eng	Both-Span	Both-Both

In practice, the 20 homes of *el bloque's* families fell under six major language configurations (see Table 1).

The major patterns at home can be described as follows:

1. Caregivers spoke Spanish among themselves and addressed children in Spanish. Children answered adults in Spanish but spoke English and Spanish to each other.
2. Caregivers were fluent in both English and Spanish. They spoke both languages among themselves (except single mothers, #s 2 and 8) and to children. Children responded predominantly in English, and favored English among themselves.
3. Caregivers spoke Spanish to each other. One spoke to the children in Spanish and the other spoke Spanish and English. The children talked Spanish and English to their caregivers and among themselves.
4. All communication among caregivers and children was carried out in Spanish, but the children were too young to speak more than a few words.
5. Caregivers communicated in English with each other and the males spoke English to the children, but mothers talked to them in Spanish and English. The children in 5a in Table 1 spoke English to their parents and to each other, but

Table 1 Language Dyads Within *el bloque's* Families

Caregiver(s) to Each Other	Caregiver(s) to Child(ren)	Child(ren) to Caregiver(s)	Children to Each Other
1 Families #4, 5, 7, 9, 10, 11 Spanish	Spanish	Spanish	English and Spanish
2 Families #2, 8, 17, 18, 19 English and Spanish	English and Spanish	English	English
3 Families #12, 13, 15 Spanish	One = Spanish, One = Spanish and English	Spanish and English	English and Spanish
4 Families #3, 14 Spanish	Spanish	Spanish	Spanish
5a Family #16 English	One = English One = Spanish and English	English	English
5b Family #20 English (Anglo male)	Anglo = English only Mother, Spanish and English	English to Anglo Spanish and English to mother	Spanish and English
6a Family #6 (mother alone)	Spanish	Spanish and English	English
6b Family #1 (mother alone)	Spanish and English	Spanish and English	(only child)

those in 5b distinguished between their caregivers by interacting with the Anglo male in English and with the mother in Spanish and English. They talked both languages to each other.

6. The mothers were single and Spanish dominant. One mother (#6) spoke Spanish to her children but the other (#1) spoke Spanish and English to her child. Children in both families talked to their mothers in Spanish and English, but they preferred English with their siblings and/or friends.

This overview necessarily obscures many differences among and within families; ultimately there were almost as many language patterns as families because of the unique configurations of several variables, including the number of caregivers and children, and differences in language proficiency, education, bilingual literacy skills, years in the US, gender and age of each speaker. Even if every caregiver-caregiver, caregiver-child, and child-child communication dyad were specified, other crucial input in the linguistic development of the children would be missing. The following profiles of three families, representative of categories 1, 3, and 5 in Table 1, respectively, bring to life the multiple, contrasting, and ever changing linguistic demands that were made on the children of *el bloque* at home.

PROFILE I   PACA AND HERMAN AT HOME WITH MAGDA

The ideal Puerto Rican family includes at least one *parejita* ("couple"), a boy and a girl, born in that order approximately two or more years apart. Very few women wanted more than two or three children, but some who bore only males or females continued to have children until a girl or a boy was born. Magda was fortunate; two years after she had Herman at age 20, her daughter Paca was born. In 1979, Magda was living apart from her husband, Paca was six years old and had just completed one year of half-day kindergarten in the local public school, and eight-year-old Herman had completed third grade in the same school's bilingual program. During the following year, a number of changes in their home and school lives produced contrasting language experiences which alternately strengthened their English and weakened their Spanish, and vice versa.

Paca and Herman were the only children on the first floor of the building sandwiched between one of the *bodegas* and the pinball storefront.... Their two-bedroom apartment was at the end of the hall—a dangerous location because their windows faced the back alley—but advantageous in other respects. They did not have to climb stairs, and all who went up or down the five flights were forced to pass their door, so they knew everyone's whereabouts. Also, children played in the hall all year long; its narrow passageway was ideal for a junior version of baseball, learning how to maneuver a bicycle, and racing battery-operated toys. No traditional Puerto Rican games were known to the children,

and all play was carried on without adult participation, in English with some Spanish code switches.

The next door neighbors were elderly Spanish speakers, whom Paca and Herman greeted with short Spanish phrases. When the children were drafted to help carry groceries or strollers, those interactions occurred in Spanish and English. On errands to the *bodega*, they repeated the adult's Spanish request. The different language backgrounds of the people Paca and Herman encountered in the hall, the *bodega*, and on the street required constant code switching in accordance with the addressee's dominant language.

Because Paca and Herman had excellent access to the main areas for congregating, they spent a good deal of time with other children. In fair weather they were often outside until 9 P.M. after Magda returned from work and on weekends. Herman was allowed to go around the corner to the pizza shop, because he was older and because he was a boy, although he was supposed to ask permission to do so. As the year progressed, Herman roller skated and rode his bicycle further distances on forays away from *el bloque*. On one occasion Paca petulantly pointed out that her brother was not restricted as she was, but her older cousin Dylcia said, "*Déjalo, él es macho*" ("Let him, he's a male"). Paca usually was with a female adult; Herman often was nowhere in sight.

Paca and Herman underwent dramatic changes in their daily routine in the course of one year. They changed apartments three times, they changed baby sitters twice, and Paca changed schools. One person remained constant—their mother Magda. Due to her efforts, their schooling proceeded with few interruptions. Their daily routine began at 7 A.M.: Magda woke, fed, and dressed them as the Spanish radio warned her of the fleeting time at five-minute intervals. Magda dropped Paca off at school on her way to her job as housekeeper for a shut-in who lived ten blocks away. Paca was picked up from school at 3 o'clock by her baby sitter, with whom she stayed until about 6 or 7 P.M. when her mother called for her. Herman walked the three blocks to another school in the morning with children from the block. He was in a bilingual class and attended an after-school program conducted in English. Magda picked him up on her way home from work at 5.30 P.M. Paca's baby sitter also looked after Herman during the summer and on all school holidays.

When the study began, the household also included Magda's 23-year-old niece Dylcia, who had migrated from Puerto Rico with her 12-month-old daughter Jennie seven months earlier. Dylcia, a high school graduate, was three months pregnant, spoke no English, and had no job or income. She helped her aunt with the chores and the children, and in turn Paca and Herman helped with Jennie. Dylcia could not be counted on as a permanent baby sitter because her future plans were up in the air. Four months later she moved into an empty apartment on the fifth floor with Luís, the college student who had introduced me to *el bloque*.

For five years, Paca and Herman were looked after by one of the block's most beloved residents, Dolores, a good-natured woman in her forties who had raised six children of her own and 13 others over a period of 20 years on the block. Dolores was credited with having nursed Paca to health after doctors had given her slim chances for survival shortly after birth. Magda trusted and loved Dolores as if she were an older sister, and she lavished the best gifts on her that her limited salary allowed. To Paca and many other children Dolores was *Mamá.* The children she helped raise dropped by regularly and three of her former charges came from Puerto Rico to spend their summer vacation with her. During the years when she was taking care of Paca and Herman, Dolores' apartment—really two apartments with a wall broken through to connect them—was constantly full with some of the 22 members of her family who were part of *el bloque*. Participation in this setting demanded rapid alternation of Spanish and English. Paca and Herman learned the intra-sentential code switching that was common among the second generation, but they also got practice in speaking Spanish to Dolores.

When the city began a limited housekeeping service for indigent shut-ins, Dolores began to clean and cook for some of *El Barrio*'s senior citizens, a paying job which could be performed in Spanish. Dolores had worked at home raising others' children along with her own, but she did not always charge for her services. Magda, for example, had not been able to pay her a regular salary because she could not find a steady job. She had completed three years of high school in Puerto Rico and had lived in NYC for eight years, but like Dolores, Magda had never carried on a conversation in English. Stable employment was out of her reach until the housekeeping program hired her upon Dolores' recommendation. When Dolores and Magda found jobs, Paca and Herman had to be left with a new baby sitter, one who was trustworthy, available, and nearby. One of Dolores' daughters in law, 20-year-old Vicky, fulfilled the prerequisites. She lived in the same building with Dolores' son, Güiso, and was known to take good care of their three-year-old boy, Eddie. Vicky was unable to work outside of the home because she was expecting another baby.

Several aspects of the new baby sitting arrangement were different. Paca and Herman were no longer immersed in an extended Spanish-English family; Vicky and Güiso, both US born, spoke English to each other and to their toddler (see Profile III). Afternoons and school vacations were spent playing with Eddie in English, watching English television programs, and singing along with the radio's English lyrics. The importance of Spanish in their lives diminished further when Dolores' long-standing application for public housing was granted, and she moved seven blocks away. Paca and Herman no longer saw her every day, although they spent some weekends with her. Eight months later, a fire set by a disturbed alcoholic left many apartments uninhabitable. Magda and her children were relocated in a hotel across town, and then they moved three more times: to another hotel, to the father's basement apartment, and to Dolores' project apartment. Traveling was expensive, time-consuming, and painful in the cold, but they made daily trips

to the block to watch over their belongings in their burned out home. After three months, the city began to repair the building, and Magda, Paca, and Herman returned to the block. During this period of upheaval, the children missed several days of school despite Magda's strenuous efforts to get them to class every day and to get to her own job. Vicky took care of them after school. Paca became Vicky's little helper, carefully dressing and feeding the boys. She was gentle and patient with demanding Eddie, who at three years of age weighed more than Paca and tended to grab and punch a lot. Herman and Paca always spoke to the boys in English, and their English vocabulary and syntax increased notably over the year. As the school year progressed, Paca and Herman spoke more English than Spanish to each other.

After six years of predominantly Spanish-filled days, Paca participated in a full school day in English in the local Catholic school's first grade. She stayed with Vicky until Magda completed her errands after work, and did her homework under Vicky's supervision in English. When winter darkness and cold set in, Paca and Herman spent more time indoors, playing with separate groups of friends or alone, but rarely with each other. Paca went to bed by 9 P.M. but Herman stayed up late watching television in English. When his mother had visitors, he played with toys or watched television, never participating in the conversations. Dylcia dubbed him "*el rey de la casa*" ("the king of the house") because he had few responsibilities and generally determined his own schedule.

Magda's day began at 6 A.M. and often ended after midnight. After work, she shopped, cooked, swept, washed and ironed clothes. Paca and Herman always were smartly and neatly dressed in the latest fashions, which—along with baby sitting fees—ate up a good part of her salary. Her cramped two-bedroom apartment had no closets, little furniture or decorations, many leaks, cracks, and roaches, and her chores took most of her free time. She rarely sat, except to see a *novela*. She was interested in many topics, but was a quiet woman who listened more than she spoke, perhaps because of a speech impediment. Neighbors who dropped by stood in the kitchen doorway while she went on with tasks similar to the ones she did all day for an invalid.

The tiny kitchen had no table, so each child was given a plate of food and ate in the living room, often at different times. Paca was a poor eater, and received weekly injections for anemia; the refrigerator door was full of her medicines. Magda usually fed her frail daughter to make sure she ate, and those feedings included mother-daughter chats in Spanish. When visitors came, Paca often sat and listened to the women talk. Magda spent blocks of time with her children only on weekends. She never played with them, but she took them to visit Dolores or their father, and on shopping trips downtown. She also sought out organized excursions and was the only parent who ever joined my outings to zoos, beaches, puppet shows, and parks. On those trips she was constantly concerned for their welfare and safety getting on and off subways or crossing the street. She did not take on a "teacher" role, that is, expounding, explaining, comparing, or asking questions meant to instruct, and she depended on Herman to interpret for her. A good reader, he read signs, asked questions and directions, made purchases and explained procedures to his mother. Magda was left out of the conversation when the children competed for my hand and attention with constant questions in English. Whenever Paca and Herman played with other children, they spoke in English, and she did not understand what they were talking about. They spoke Spanish only when addressing her, usually for short comments or requests. Magda was a concerned, responsible, and hardworking mother whose Spanish monolingualism left her at the periphery of most of her children's activities; she was more a provider and a watchdog than a participant.

Magda chose Catholic school for her daughter because Herman had been in several fights in the public school, and after looking into [the incidents] she characterized the school as lacking in discipline. Fearing that the diminutive Paca would not be well-protected there, she sacrificed to pay for Catholic school. Paca cried often during the first three weeks in her English-only classroom, and said she had no friends there. By October she seemed to have adjusted, although Catholic school did not turn out to be a totally safe environment. There were schoolyard incidents in which others took advantage of her slight build, but she defended herself and claimed victory in at least one instance. Those narratives were vividly reported in Spanish to her mother and in English to her playmates. She was getting so accustomed to English that she even called to her mother in English one day, asking her to corroborate her age; "I'm six [said five times], Mami, right I'm six?" No one commented on the fact the Paca had addressed her mother in English, and I never heard her do it again.

The nuns sent Paca home with a preliminary progress report which indicated she was about average in most areas, although she had not kept up with all homework assignments. The report became the only wall adornment in the apartment; it was taped near the entrance and visitors commented on it. Paca's given name was written at the top—Ivón. A few months later Paca said she preferred Yvonne /ivan/, i.e., the English spelling and pronunciation. On the block, everyone continued to call her by her nickname, Paca, with its Spanish pronunciation. Once a friend jokingly used exaggerated English phonology (/pha:kha:/); Paca looked amazed and repeated it in a disbelieving tone. Still, she continued to prefer the English /ivan/ over the Spanish /ibon/, just like her friends Lolita, Isabel, Blanca, and Elli preferred the English pronunciations of their names. Toward the end of the year Paca also commented on Puerto Rican nicknames: "*¿Por qué la gente en español tiene* funny names?" ("Why do people in Spanish have funny names?"). Her code switching was increasing along with her awareness of dominant cultural norms, and her distancing from those of the home culture. During the first months of taping, Paca rated herself a better Spanish than English speaker, "or both a little." She used to greet me and other bilingual adults in Spanish, and adhered to the community norm by responding in Spanish

if she was addressed in it. By the summer of the following year, she greeted us in English and she did not always switch to Spanish if it was directed at her, unless the addressee was a monolingual Spanish speaker.

A house guest from Puerto Rico, Magda's sister, offset the English avalanche. The older woman often played with her young niece, and she was an articulate speaker with captivating narratives about family incidents and superstitions in their home town. Paca was an eager listener, and she asked about topics or words unknown to her, for example, "*¿Qué son 'leyendas'?*" ("What are 'legends'?"), "*¿Qué es 'cariño'?*" ("What is 'affection'?"), and "*¿Qué es 'relación'?*" ("What is 'relationship'?"). Paca made developmental errors, for example, "*juegaba*" and "*sueñé*" instead of *jugaba* ("I used to play") and *soñé* ("I dreamt"), which went uncorrected. A few of her errors caused laughter, for example when Magda told the group: "*A Herman le gusta més Puerto Rico porque quiere que le compre un caballo.*" ("Herman likes Puerto Rico better because he wants me to buy him a horse"), Paca piped up with: "*Uy mami! ¿Tú me puedes comprar una caballa?*" ("Oh mommy! Can you buy me a horse-feminine?") Her aunt laughingly commented "*porque es femenina*" ("because it's/she's? feminine"), but no one explained the joke to Paca, and she did not ask why everyone had laughed.

When Paca sat in on the conversations of her Spanish-speaking elders, she behaved according to appropriate Puerto Rican norms for children. She did not break into the conversation precipitously, often waiting up to six turns, tentatively attempting to speak at turn exchange points with "*y-y-y*" ("and-and-and"), softly calling the names of the speakers, and asking permission, e.g., "*con permiso*" ("excuse me"). Despite her increasing preference for English with me, Paca honored the language of adult Spanish conversations by addressing me in Spanish when she intended to participate in such a discussion. Switching languages for parts of sentences was rare in either her Spanish or English contributions in that setting. Her short exchanges in English either were not related to the adult topic or were asides meant specifically for someone who was English-dominant.

Paca's turn-taking behavior and the pitch of her voice during the Spanish discussions contrasted sharply with her English contributions in group settings. The latter were often high-pitched or shrill, and competitive; she interrupted others in a loud demanding tone. Since most of the English conversations in which she participated were with children (because she was not exposed to similar gatherings of monolingual English-speaking adults), we can assume that her more aggressive linguistic behavior in English was a function of what Philips (1972) called the "participant structures," that is, Paca learned that interacting with female adults required not only Spanish but certain respectful behaviors regarding the way Spanish was spoken, but she talked with peers in English and in a more contentious manner.

Herman always referred to himself with the English version of his name and spoke more fluent English than Paca, but he too had the opportunity to strengthen his command of Spanish during 1979–80. He was in a bilingual class, and he had Spanish monolingual friends for a while when three boys emigrated from Puerto Rico, with whom he communicated easily. After four months, however, two of the families returned to Puerto Rico, and the father of the remaining boy severely curtailed his son's activities. Herman resumed hanging out with long-time block residents who spoke more English than Spanish. By the end of the year, Herman, like Paca but even more so, initiated Spanish and responded in it only when he had to talk with a diminishing number of Spanish monolinguals. Nevertheless, Herman's mother was proud of the fact that he could read and write Spanish and English, skills learned in the bilingual program. He read the Spanish newspapers and cards and letters that arrived from Puerto Rico. His English reading ability was at grade level in school, and he read comic books, game instructions, subway signs, and Monopoly Community Chest cards with ease. Herman himself claimed he spoke both languages equally well, and this appeared to be the case; he was a more balanced bilingual than Paca. After observing them for two years, I thought that both Herman and Paca would grow up to be English-dominant bilinguals, but that Paca's skills in Spanish would be better than Herman's as he became more disconnected from the family and *el bloque* and Paca became more immersed in the Spanish-dominant female networks....

No Spanish-speaking adult ever stopped Herman and Paca from speaking English to each other, and only rarely did they ask for translations of what was said in that language. The implicit rule seemed to be that if the children had anything to say that concerned the adults, they would say it in Spanish. English was another "channel" for children and their activities. This acceptance of English at home contradicted Magda's response to a question concerning the appropriate domains for Spanish and English. When she was asked whether there were any times or places when the children should speak only Spanish or only English, she answered that they should speak Spanish at home and English outside whenever there was anyone around who did not understand Spanish. In fact, Magda never insisted that the children speak only Spanish at home, but they were expected to speak it to her and to their relatives from Puerto Rico. Most of the parents expressed a greater concern for accommodating English speakers who could not understand Spanish than for accommodating Spanish monolinguals. This imbalance may be interpreted as an indication that the need to speak Spanish was a given, especially *en casa*, but the repeated concern for the predicament of English monolinguals pointed to the symbolic dominance exerted by English. It paralleled the frequent refrain that "It is important to know English" or "Everybody should know English"; similar expressions about the importance of knowing Spanish were rarer. Paca's family spoke positively about being bilingual, but they referred to it in terms of adding English to one's linguistic repertoire, not in terms of adding Spanish.

PROFILE II   LOLITA AND MARTA AT HOME WITH ARMANDO AND LOURDES

Lolita, eight years old, was born and raised on the block and lived with her 16-year-old sister Marta, her mother Lourdes (36), and her father Armando (40). Armando had lived there for several years before his 17-year marriage and was one of the best-known members of the community. He was a high school graduate, had some college credits, had been an army officer, and was a skilled electrician, but because of the massive layoffs that occurred when the city almost declared bankruptcy in the mid-seventies, he had been unemployed for four years when we met. His problems with alcohol worsened as the years went by. Armando spent most of his time with Spanish-speaking men in the *bodega* network, but he was fluent in English and was the only block resident who spoke of extensive contacts with Black residents of the projects across the street.[1]

Lolita's father was recognized as a good speaker of standard Spanish and he held strong opinions about language; for example, he was very vocal about the value of being bilingual: "*Son dos personas en una.*" ("They are two people in one.") His pride in his own fluency in both languages, and that of his children, was stated often. Armando reproached Puerto Ricans for a lack of linguistic ability and language consciousness, claiming that Puerto Ricans did not speak real Spanish ("*el español verdadero*"), and that they did not prepare for tomorrow's world. He laid special blame at the feet of Puerto Rican parents; if their children did not speak Spanish, parents should stress it: "*Los padres no hacen énfasis.*" ("The parents don't emphasize it.") Armando reported that he required Spanish at home, and that he corrected his daughters often. As for the disparity in the girls' abilities ("*Marta mata el español, ésta no. Esta lo lee, lo escribe, todo bien.*" ... "Marta kills Spanish, but not this one [Lolita]. She reads it, writes it, all well."), he credited the difference to school programs. Lolita had learned her skills in three years of bilingual classes, but Marta had never been in a bilingual program and was now in a public high school outside of El Barrio. She spent her free time off the block, and her language abilities and preferences reflected her position outward, toward the external, English-dominant, world. Lolita's activities and networks were confined to *el bloque*.

Armando exerted a tight rein on his daughters' movements and behavior. Lolita requested his permission to go anywhere, visit anyone, do anything—even to put on the television in the morning if he was listening to a Spanish radio station. She was on constant alert for his distinctive whistle; it meant that she had to leave whatever she was doing and run to his side. When she spoke in his presence, her father corrected her for how she carried herself more than for what she said. He was concerned about her posture ("*Párate bien.*" ... "Stand up right."), her mouth ("*Cierra la boca.*" ... "Close your mouth."), her attentiveness ("*Te están hablando.*" ... "They're talking to you."), and her grimaces ("*Los monos están en el circo.*" ... "Monkeys are in the zoo.").

In contrast, he did not correct her when she alternated Spanish and English ten times in one half-hour tape, although Marta reported that her father disapproved of code switching and insisted that she speak one language or the other.

In his own speech, Armando usually kept both codes strictly apart despite frequent switching for interlocutors who spoke Spanish or English. Only three intra-sentential code switches by him were recorded throughout the study—all directed at his daughters:

1. *Tú* share *con los demás.* ("You share with the rest.")
2. *Tráeme un* flashlight. ("Bring me a flashlight.")
3. *No me gusta ese* neighborhood. ("I don't like that neighborhood.")

In these sentences the switches to English were for single words, not the larger constituents or whole phrases that characterized the switching of the second generation [see Zentella (1997), Chapter 5, Honoring the Syntactic Hierarchy]. Armando usually spoke to his children in standard Spanish, but he addressed them in English too. The girls heard their father speak English most often when he talked with the Anglo male who lived on the block.

The girls spent less time with their virtually monolingual mother because of her long day, first at a factory in New Jersey and then at beauty school in the Bronx. A baby sitter picked Lolita up after school and took her to the block where she played within earshot of her father until her mother returned. In cold weather, Lolita went home with the baby sitter and played with her daughter in English, but she spoke Spanish with the child's mother, as she normally did with her own mother.

Lourdes had remained Spanish-dominant despite having lived for 17 years in NYC because her daily activities did not provide opportunities to participate in English conversations. She knew enough English to buy what she needed, as recordings of two exchanges with monolingual English-speaking merchants revealed, but otherwise she never initiated speaking it on her own. Unlike her husband, she had never been in a job or a classroom that developed her proficiency and her self-confidence in English. For the previous 14 years, her factory job in New Jersey, where her co-workers were Spanish speakers, required her to leave the block before 7 A.M. and return at 5.30 P.M. Three nights a week and on Saturdays she travelled to a Beautician's Academy in the Bronx where classes were conducted in Spanish. Her time on the block was spent cooking, washing clothes, and shopping for food, clothes, and school supplies for the girls. She was a quiet person and rarely had time for standing around with the other women, but they all expressed admiration for her as a hard worker, a loyal wife, and a devoted mother. Everyone could see that Lourdes' relationship with her children was close and warm, despite the fact that her obligations restricted her time with them.

Lourdes, like her husband, produced a few examples of the community-wide practice of code switching:

1. *¿Costó* dollar seventy two? ("It cost dollar seventy two?")
2. *Allí,* across the street. ("Over there, across the street.")

Switches by Spanish-dominant but long-term residents of *el bloque* like Lourdes and Armando reflected the influence that constant interaction with code-switching children had on their parents' language behavior.

Lolita and Marta spoke to their mother in Spanish, often followed up with English. [However], Lolita and her mother communicated in Spanish on occasion, but they were more likely to engage in non-reciprocal language dyads. Lolita understood everything her mother said in Spanish and Lourdes understood what her daughters said in English, but each preferred to respond in her stronger language. Lourdes did not insist that the girls speak to her in Spanish; she concentrated on the content instead of the form of their messages. In contrast to her husband, she never held forth on the importance of Spanish, but she was a more consistent source of uninterrupted Spanish in their lives than he was. Also, because of her close ties to her siblings and mother in Puerto Rico and the fact that she was the one who accompanied the girls on visits to the island, Lourdes embodied her children's most intense link between Spanish and Puerto Rico. That connection did not necessarily translate into an overt expression of Puerto Rican identity for Lolita and Marta when they were young.

Lolita's very first words to me reflected the identity conflict faced by second and third generation Puerto Ricans that has been the subject of some research and much debate (Seda Bonilla 1975; Fitzpatrick 1971). When I told Armando (with Lolita at his side) that I was interested in observing his daughters and other children in order "to understand how Puerto Rican children learn to speak two languages," Lolita's reaction was, "But I'm not Puerto Rican, I'm American." Her statement reflected the popular notion that Puerto Ricans are those born on the island of Puerto Rico, but those born in the United States are "Americans." Lolita identified herself as a US American, but her environment and behavior, linguistic and otherwise, would not have been deemed characteristic of the "typical American child" by anyone who subscribed to the "Leave it to Beaver" or "Family Ties" television models. The extent to which Lolita was representative of eight-year-old, island-born-and-raised Puerto Rican girls cannot be ascertained because of the lack of contemporary ethnographies of children's socialization in Puerto Rico. I once visited with Lolita and her cousins in Puerto Rico and did not note any dramatic differences, but prolonged observation undoubtedly would have revealed behaviors in addition to language that distinguished her from her island cousins. Lolita was, after all, a product of both worlds—her parents' Puerto Rico and her *bloque* in NYC—and both were reflected in her ways of speaking and everyday activities.

Lolita was attractive, outgoing, bright, talented, and respectful, and she was selected for activities which marked her as special both in and out of school and which expanded her bilingual/multidialectal repertoire. Her third grade bilingual class at the local public school was labeled IGC—for Intellectually Gifted Children. A prestigious African American dance company had selected her for its weekly classes, and Lolita's petite frame was also in the front line of her school's baton twirling troupe. Her tiny stature and her dependence on her parents made her seem younger than her years. Still, she was not anemic like Paca, and she danced, sang, and partook in many physical games. Her linguistic abilities were among her principal accomplishments; she was proud of and confident in her ability to speak, read, and write both English and Spanish. My observations and taping corroborated that she was adept at the following:

1. switching rapidly from one language to another;
2. describing the language dyads in all the block families, that is, she knew who spoke what to whom;
3. determining whether a stranger was bilingual or not;
4. correcting the English and Spanish of peers;
5. knowing the linguistic limitations of others and translating to meet them;
6. meeting a variety of reading and writing demands for herself and her friends;
7. combining the morphological and phonological systems of both languages for comic effect.

Lolita, a quick and accurate judge of the linguistic abilities of those who addressed her, generally accommodated others by speaking to them in their dominant language, especially if their English was noticeably weak. She spoke Spanish to her father's friends, the older women, and the infant children of Spanish-dominant parents. Conversations with her sister, peers, the block teenagers, and the infant children of English-oriented parents, were in English. The ability to shift from one language to the other developed as a natural consequence of constant interaction with members of different networks, which demanded rapid alternation between English and Spanish, as in the following episode:

[Context: Lolita (L) was in the *bodega* with another eight-year-old, Corinne (C), who barely spoke and understood Spanish. The two-year-old daughter of a recent migrant, Jennie (J), followed them into the store. The *bodeguero* (B) belonged to her father's network of Spanish-dominant men.]

C to L:	Buy those.
L to C:	No, I buy those better.
L to *bodeguero*:	*Toma la quora.* ("Take the quarter.")
L to C:	What's she doing here? [referring to Jennie]
L to J:	*Vete pa(-ra) dentro.* ("Go inside.")

The three switches in rapid succession in this excerpt accommodated the linguistic abilities of three different addressees. Lolita spoke to her nearly monolingual English friend in English, to the Spanish-dominant male in Spanish, and to the child of a recent immigrant in Spanish. Her control of the

pronunciation, grammar, and vocabulary of each segment was native, that is, she sounded like a native PRS speaker in Spanish and like a native PRE speaker in English. Switching without hesitation from one language to another when they interacted with members of different networks became a mark of in-group community membership. Ultimately, the switches were not limited to accommodating addressees who had distinct levels of linguistic proficiency; bilinguals switched with other bilinguals in the same conversation or sentence to accomplish a variety of discourse strategies [see Zentella (1997), Chapter 5, Conversational Strategies]. Toddlers like Jennie who were exposed to this bilingual style from infancy could be expected to acquire the same ability.

Lolita knew what every member of *el bloque* spoke because she had been a part of it all her life, but she also deduced which language newcomers were most comfortable with. Like a "junior ethnographer" (Fantini 1985), she determined how to address them guided by three observables:

1. Physical features: Spanish for Latinos and English for others.
2. Gender: Spanish for women and English for men.
3. Age: Spanish for infants and the elderly, English for others.

Because these factors determined who spoke what to whom on the block, all older Latinas were expected to speak Spanish, and young African American or Anglo-looking men were expected to know English.

Lolita seemed incredulous of those for whom this process of deduction was not second nature. Doris, a nine-year-old who, like Lolita, was born and raised in *el bloque*, listened to my description, in English, of my interest in bilingual children and asked:

D to ACZ:	You talk two languages?
L to D:	Of course she does!
D to L	Some people don't. [said defensively]
L to D:	I know, like this girl in my class....

Whereas Doris hesitated to assume that I was bilingual, Lolita was surprised that Doris could not tell that I spoke Spanish—given my gender, looks, and age—just as she was surprised that a Puerto Rican classmate of hers, in a bilingual class, was not bilingual. Lolita was very sure of herself, albeit not very clear, when she told me another way she could tell if someone was not bilingual:

ACZ:	How do you know if somebody doesn't talk two languages?
L:	By the looks sometimes.
ACZ:	How come?
L:	Because sometimes English people don't look like they were um—like if they were too glad to talk—if they wasn't glad—if they ain't glad because they won't talk Spanish. That's one way. And every time we go to Spanish in class, they say that Spanish is cancelled. And everybody says "Yeaa, that's good!" because they don't like Spanish.

ACZ: Who?

L: The children in my class. And my teacher says that you should be proud because like that if you go to Puerto Rico and you don't know Spanish you won't be able to talk their language, and to other places.

ACZ: How come the children don't like it?

L: Because they got mean teachers. I got Ms.—, she's meean! She pulls hair, and pulls ears too.

Despite Lolita's difficulty with the verb ("if they were too glad," "if they wasn't glad," "if they ain't glad"), her first point is that "English people" do not like to be addressed in Spanish. Her second point is that the other third graders in her bilingual class did not enjoy Spanish, presumably because of the teacher's harsh methods. She went on, however, to disassociate herself from their negative attitudes: "But I like Spanish because sometimes she tells us stories, about what she used to do in Cuba."

Lolita not only reported on the attitudes of schoolmates toward English and Spanish, she also described the abilities and attitudes of most of the members of *el bloque*. While Paca was mulling over what language she spoke to whom, Lolita anticipated her answers and, in one instance, corrected her:

ACZ to Paca: *¿Qué me hablas a mi?* ("What do you speak to me?")

P to ACZ: To you? In Spanish.

L to P: And in English.

P to L: No, in Spanish.

L to P: You just spoke to her in English!

Lolita's meta-linguistic awareness, which exceeded that of her friends, was heightened by her father's preoccupation with language standards and her participation in a bilingual class; both made explicit references to language and bilingualism that she adopted.

Lolita had a special mentor-like relationship with her two closest friends, and language caregiving was part of it. She spent most of her time with Isabel, who was her age but who had been left back and spoke both languages with nonstandard and unique forms [see Zentella (1997), Chapter 6, Standards, Constraints, and Transfers]. Lolita often translated for Isabel; she tended to interpret anybody's "What?" or questioning look in response to a statement by Isabel as a request for a translation. She helped Isabel with her homework, and took over most of her reading and writing tasks. When I gave each child some pictures of our trip to the zoo and suggested they write the date and comments on the back, Lolita realized that Isabel was not up to the task. Immediately, she offered to write whatever Isabel wanted to say on another paper, from which Isabel could copy onto her pictures. Isabel spoke, Lolita wrote down, and Isabel copied: "It was fun. We saw lots of animals. Ana was the one who took me." For Valentine's Day, Isabel's valentine to a friend was written with Lolita's help. In March, Isabel's birthday party invitations were filled in by Lolita and another girl; Isabel signed them. When we

play-acted a visit to the doctor, Lolita wrote out the diagnosis ("ulcers"), the prescription ("mylanta"), and the appointment slips for "Dr. Isabel." She added a note from "Walfar" [Welfare] for me, the patient: "Ana is too poor to pay. So don't acks for money." It was unclear whether Isabel's literacy was aided by her friend's efforts as much as Lolita's own literacy was.

Lolita's translations for Isabel were most often from English into Spanish, while Corinne required translations from Spanish into English. For example, Lolita translated the quoted price of a mango for Corinne because "sometimes she doesn't understand numbers." In deference to Corinne's limitations, Lolita's code switching was curtailed whenever Corinne joined the otherwise bilingual group of children. In contrast, Lolita was more likely to initiate Spanish with Isabel; for example, in one tape, the only Spanish utterance she initiated (total $n = 169$) was directed at Isabel. It took the form of a solicitous *¿No quieres?* ("Don't you want any?") after Isabel turned down her offer of candy, made in English. Switching to Spanish for the purpose of mothering exemplified one of the role-changing strategies that the children accomplished by alternating languages with the same speaker [see Zentella (1997), Chapter 5, Footing].

Lolita met school and community literacy demands in both languages confidently. She beamed when she reported a fifth grade reading score in Spanish at the end of the third grade, and 3.9 in English. On the block, she read everything that came her way, including record album covers, greeting cards, advertisements, and prayer cards in Spanish, and joke books, birthday invitations, game instructions, report cards, product labels in English. On one occasion she switched phonology with ease when she read a bilingual announcement aloud despite words such as "hospital," which often trip up bilingual readers because they are spelled alike in English and Spanish but pronounced differently.

Never hesitant about writing in either language, Lolita frequently asked for paper and pencil when she wanted to entertain herself, and she took on little writing projects such as labeling my tapes with the date, time, and names of speakers. On Christmas and Valentine's Day she made her own impromptu cards, and she wrote out my *bloque* Christmas card list including name, address, and apartment number of each family. Occasions to write Spanish arose less frequently, but they presented no problems when they did. When I described—in Spanish—the pattern for a blouse with the aid of folded pieces of paper, Lolita wrote *manga* ("sleeve"), *frente* ("front"), and *espalda* ("back") on the papers with no help.

Lolita was the only child in the study who played with Spanish and English for special effects. She comically exaggerated a request that her friends not grab a package of candy she was about to open by imitating a US American speaking Spanish: "No touch-ey, Es-pear-uh-tay" (*No toque. Espérate.* "Don't touch. Wait."). On another occasion, she demonstrated that she was attuned to the role of Spanish phonology in expressing politeness. The *bodeguero* made an elaborate gesture to take Lolita's money for a purchase, and carefully enunciated "*GraciaS*" ("Thank you"). In keeping with his exaggerated formality—obvious because of his emphasis on the syllable-final -s—Lolita's response was "*De nadaS,*" that is, she added and stressed a final -s in a phrase that does not have one (*De nada.* "You're welcome."). Puerto Rican jokes often derive their humor from the same hypercorrection that Lolita captured with "*de nadaS*"; the juxtaposition of formal and informal styles for comic effect is part of every native speaker's knowledge of the sociolinguistic rules of his/her language.

It appeared that Lolita would continue to develop her proficiency in English and Spanish for several reasons. She was promoted to the fourth grade bilingual class for gifted children and looked forward to three more years in a school with many bilingual teachers and pupils, she spent two weeks in Puerto Rico after six years of not visiting and her family planned to return on a yearly basis, and life on the block continued to require both languages. By the end of 1980, however, her future bilingual development was in question. Lolita's mother astonished *el bloque* by leaving her husband unexpectedly. Lolita left *El Barrio*, its bilingual school, and her lifelong friends, and she was not allowed to reveal her new address or have visitors. Her new neighborhood, school, friends, and baby sitter were predominantly English-speaking. Asked whether her ability in Spanish was Excellent, Good, Fair, or Poor, she chose Fair; 15 months earlier she had rated it as Good....

PROFILE III   EDDIE AND DAVEY AT HOME WITH VICKY AND GÜISO

Vicky and Güiso, both 20 years old, were the youngest couple with children. They had lived together for four years and had two boys: three-year-old Eddie, and Davey, born three months into the study. Güiso said he wanted to have two more children but Vicky was reluctant, although both of them longed for a girl. Each came from a large family: Vicky was one of five children and Güiso had one older brother and four younger sisters, all of whom had been born in *el bloque* and had never been to Puerto Rico. Until his mother Dolores moved to the projects and a fire forced out two married sisters, most of Güiso's family lived in his building. Even after the fire, he could count on various kin among his neighbors, and whenever his mother or his sisters visited, the clan gathered in his apartment. These gatherings were characterized by conversations that alternated rapidly between English and Spanish, especially among the younger women. One sister accurately observed that the girls often spoke Spanish to each other and to their mother, but that the boys "stuck to English."

Güiso spoke English to all his siblings; when he spoke to his mother, he struggled with his limited Spanish. Dolores gave this version of her son's attempt to explain what he would do if he were to have a third child and it did not turn out to be a girl:

> *Me estaba hablando en español. El habla mucho español pero algunas palabras se le—que él cogía una nena y que la adoptaba. Ve, entonces cuando me dijo así, que si iba a tener otro nene, otro, y si le salía nene cogía* "girls *y lo* adopt," *tú sabe(-s), eso me lo metió en inglés.*

("He was talking to me in Spanish. He talks a lot of Spanish but some words [escape] him—that he would take a little girl and adopt her. See, when he told me that, that if he was going to have another baby, another, and if it came out a little boy he was going to get 'girls and adopt it [masculine singular]', you know, that part he stuck in in English.")

Güiso was insecure about his Spanish, and reported that as a child he stuttered and "wouldn't talk at all." It is unclear to what extent his problems were normal, or whether they contributed to the acting-out behavior that led to his removal from the fourth grade. After a few years in one of the notorious 600 schools for discipline problems, he dropped out when he was 15.

In addition to extended family, Güiso had lifelong friends on the block, especially among the young dudes who whiled away most summer evenings and winter weekends discussing and playing sports, drinking, and listening to *salsa* music until the wee hours. Güiso's newfound sense of responsibility as a father did not allow him to "break night" anymore, but he still socialized with his *panas* ("buddies") for long hours. Their conversations were always in English—either PRE or AAVE.

Ironically, Güiso rated himself a poor speaker of Spanish but it was his ability to speak Spanish that landed him his job, guarding the wares at a local Korean-owned market and serving as interpreter. The job helped reinforce positive attitudes nurtured as an adolescent when he had longed to "rap to the beautiful Spanish-speaking girls," mainly recent immigrants. As an adult, he defended the benefits of bilingualism to his African American friends: "This is a Spanish-speaking community, you need both." Güiso and Vicky, both dark-skinned Puerto Ricans, identified with the racial concerns of their African American friends, but they identified with Puerto Ricans culturally. Consequently, Güiso was trying to learn to speak better Spanish, and he practiced reading bilingual advertisements and palm cards. Despite proclaiming that his children would be bilingual and that "it's up to the parents," all of his conversations with his wife and children were in English.

Vicky shared Güiso's confidence in their children's bilingual future, but she too helped maintain the English-speaking atmosphere of their household. Her television was always on English channels, as was her radio. She spoke English to Güiso, the old girl friends who visited, her two sons, and her baby sitting charges. Vicky reported that she spoke Spanish to the children most often when she was angry, and observations bore her out. Most of her Spanish comments to the children were commands or threats that followed the English version and served to underscore them, as in the following example:

> *V to Eddie:* See that chair over there, go squash your seat in it. Go sit down, go.
> *¡Deja eso y sién-ta-te!*
> ("Leave that and sit down!")

Most often she addressed her sons in English only.

Outside her home, Vicky had many occasions to speak Spanish, for example, when she picked up or dropped off

Paca, when she visited Güiso's mother, aunt, or cousin, when she stopped to chat on the stoop with the first-generation women, or when she made a new friend of a recent arrival from Puerto Rico. Vicky's first language as a child had been Spanish, but she had learned English quickly from her brothers and sisters because she was the youngest of the brood. She still spoke Spanish to her parents, but English to her brothers and sisters. Unlike her husband, she had close relationships with several Spanish monolinguals, including two of her seven *comadres*. As a result, although Vicky's Spanish included non-standard forms and she asked help for unknown words, she was a much more confident Spanish speaker than Güiso. But she could not read or write Spanish because she had dropped out of school at 16 and had never had a job that required literacy skills in any language. A year after we met, she replaced her husband at the vegetable stand while he recuperated from a lingering foot ailment; that job increased her oral proficiency in Spanish, but made few demands on literacy in Spanish or English.

With their father in charge, Eddie and Davey heard almost no Spanish at home, and very little was directed to them outside of their home; everyone on the block knew them to be English speakers. Nonetheless, their parents overrated the children's language abilities and were optimistic about their future as bilinguals. Vicky was counting on the school's bilingual program, unaware that its classes were off limits to English monolinguals. Her claim that Eddie understood Spanish and that he spoke to Güiso's aunts and mother in Spanish conflicted with my observations: I never heard him speak it and he looked blank whenever someone addressed him in Spanish. In fact, much of what Eddie spoke was garbled until he was four years old. Paca translated for Eddie when she understood him. Vicky did not express alarm over her son's speech, perhaps because of her own pronounced lisp and her husband's similar language history, but her concern surfaced in her unwillingness to interfere in his choice of language. She was the only parent who felt that there were no situations which should require that her child speak only English or only Spanish:

> "It's really up to him. I can't tell him just speak to this person in Spanish, this person in English. That's really up to him. The language that he understands best, that's the one he should speak."

Vicky and Güiso were the first of *el bloque's* parents to favor English at home with each other and their children, although they voiced a strong belief in the importance of being bilingual and were convinced that their children would be able to speak, read, and write both Spanish and English. Because the principal settings, social networks, and activities in which the children participated were dominated by English, their parents' aspirations seemed unrealistic. Still, it was possible that the boys' lives might change in ways that would bring them into closer contact with Spanish monolinguals, or otherwise expand their limited knowledge of Spanish. That, after all, had been the case with their parents, whose ability to speak Spanish strengthened as they took on parental roles and jobs in *El Barrio*....

CONCLUSION

The larger socio-political context in which bilingualism *en casa* was enmeshed pitted the children's strong, intimate links with Puerto Rico, Puerto Ricans, and Spanish-speaking elders against the ever expanding and authority-laden role of English. Given the "symbolic domination" (Bourdieu and Passeron 1977) of English, English became the language not only of the children's channel, it also seeped into their parents' formerly monolingual Spanish channel. Together, old and new generations forged a joint way of speaking that "spoke to" the experiences of both. Like the push-pull forces that propel the NYC-Puerto Rico circulatory migration pattern, the increasing power of English in the homes of *el bloque* is a statement about the economic, social, and political forces propelling children towards English.

At the beginning of the 1980s, *el bloque* was between stages five and six on Fishman's (1991) eight-level measure of community language shift, the Graded Intergenerational Disruption Scale (GIDS), and there were signs that it was moving in the direction of greater language loss (at GIDS eight, only a few old speakers are left). Principal among these were the reluctance of parents to insist that they be addressed in Spanish, and the widespread use of English in all children's activities. Even when second–generation parents resurrected their childhood Spanish via participation in adult networks, they used it more for communicating with their elders than with their siblings or children. If Fishman (1991: 91) is right that, for language maintenance, nothing "can substitute for the re-establishment of young families of child-bearing age in which Xish [Spanish in this case] is the normal medium or co-medium of communication and/or of other culturally appropriate home, family, neighborhood, and community intergenerational vernacular activity," then the likelihood of maintaining Spanish beyond the second generation in the NYPR community looks bleak. Ethnography provided a complex portrait of the factors that made parents and children favor English or Spanish.

In *el bloque*, six principal communication patterns existed among the 20 families with children; they differed in terms of the language(s) that parents spoke to each other, the language(s) parents spoke to children and vice versa, and the language(s) children spoke among themselves. The presence of Spanish was related to the migration history of the caretakers, as follows:

1. In the majority of families (12/20 in Table 1), children heard their parents speak Spanish at home to each other and were always spoken to in Spanish by at least one parent. Those parents had migrated to the United States after spending their youth, including early adolescence, in Puerto Rico.
2. When one or more parents was Puerto Rican born but had migrated before late adolescence, Spanish and English were alternated in the home. This occurred in six families which included 14 children.

3. English was the predominant language among parents and children in two families, with two children each: in one there was an Anglo male who could not speak Spanish and in the other both parents, Vicky and Güiso, had been born and raised in *El Barrio* and had never been to Puerto Rico.

Children's English increased in proportion to the amount of English understood and spoken by their parents. Parents who had migrated to the US as adolescents or young adults continued to speak to their siblings in Spanish. This held true even for sisters and brothers who had lived more years in NYC than in Puerto Rico, so that many of those who had arrived at 14 and 16 years old still spoke Spanish to each other at 42 and 44, at 62 and 64. When they spoke to their children, however, some used English and those who did not allowed their children to respond in English as they came to understand it more. As a result, children's comprehension skills in Spanish and parents' comprehension skills in English outdistanced their ability to speak, read, or write their second language. Every adult knew some survival English, but there was already one child who did not understand enough Spanish to participate fully in the life of the community.

Schooling was the most important promoter of English dominance, whether children were in an all–English class or in a bilingual program. After one year in school, young children spoke to each other increasingly in English, even when their primary caretakers had not made any visible improvement in their knowledge of English. The children in bilingual programs had one major advantage: they were the only ones who learned to read and write in Spanish as well as English, skills that were valued and useful in the community.

Despite the impact of family migration histories and schooling, children from the same type of background could differ markedly in their ability to speak, read, and/or write Spanish or English. Some visited Puerto Rico more frequently or for longer stays than others, some were enrolled in a bilingual program or in an English-only class, some were allowed to spend many hours out on the block whereas others were confined to their apartment and female networks, some identified more with African Americans than with Puerto Ricans, some participated in religious activities that required literacy in English or Spanish, etc. As the pro-files of three families proved, specifying the language dyads, or who speaks what to whom in each family, as listed in Table 1, provides a limited view of children's linguistic input. *El bloque's* children were not raised behind closed doors in nuclear families isolated from their neighbors. It is incorrect to assume that children with monolingual Spanish parents did not speak English with adults, or that those whose parents spoke only English heard no Spanish conversations. The presence of overlapping networks guaranteed constant visiting, sharing, and exposure to both languages. Children could emerge from any number of apartment doors, behind which they might have been taking part in English, Spanish, or Spanish and English conversations.

More than anything else in their lives, the frequent interspersal of sentences and words from both languages was the primary symbol of membership in *el bloque* and reflected the children's dual cultural identification....

Note

1 Only "Black" was heard in the community; I use "African American" when I am not quoting community members.

References

Bourdieu, P. and Passeron, J. C. 1977: *Reproduction in Education, Society, and Culture.* Beverly Hills, CA: Sage.

Fantini, A. 1985: *Language Acquisition of a Bilingual Child: A sociolinguistic perspective.* San Diego: College Hill Press.

Fishman, J. A. 1991: *Reversing Language Shift.* Clevedon: Multilingual Matters.

Fitzpatrick, J. 1971: *Puerto Rican Americans: The meaning of migration to the mainland.* Englewood Cliffs, NJ: Prentice Hall.

Philips, S. U. 1972: Participant structures and communicative competence: Warm Springs children in community and classroom. In C. B. Cazden, D. H. Hymes, and V. John (eds.), *Functions of Language in the Classroom,* New York: Teachers' College Press, 370–94.

Seda Bonilla, E. 1975: Qué somos: puertorriqueños, neorriqueños, o niuyorriqueños? *The Rican: Journal of contemporary Puerto Rican thought,* 2(2–3), 81–107.

Zentella, A. C. 1997. *Growing up Bilingual: Puerto Rican Children in New York.* Malden, MA: Blackwell.

Post-reading Questions / Activities

- Why does Zentella focus on families rather than individuals? How are linguistic practices known by a researcher?
- Zentella herself is bilingual, having grown up in a New York Puerto Rican community. Do you think that a person without this membership could have learned what she did? Why or why not? She writes that being a member of the group under investigation brings with it both assets and liabilities. What kinds of liabilities do you think this would have?
- Zentella identifies six principal communication patterns among the 20 families with children that she knew best. List the factors that make people more likely to use Spanish, and those that make people more likely to use English.

- Interview someone who is bilingual and try to figure out what the uses of each language are (as reported by the speaker). How does your subject feel about his or her languages?

Vocabulary

AAVE	intrasentential code switching	PRE
HE	NSPRS	SPRS

Suggested Further Reading

Dewaele, Jean-Marc, Alex Housen, Li Wei, and Hugo Baetens Beardsmore, eds. 2003. *Bilingualism: Beyond Basic Principles*. Clevedon and Buffalo: Multilingual Matters.

Edwards, John R. 1994. *Multilingualism*. London and New York: Routledge.

Grosjean, François. 1982. *Life with Two Languages: An Introduction to Bilingualism*. Cambridge, MA: Harvard University Press.

Gumperz, John J. 1982. *Discourse Strategies*. Cambridge: Cambridge University Press.

Heller, Monica, ed. 1988. *Codeswitching: Anthropological and Sociolinguistic Perspectives*. Berlin and New York: Mouton de Gruyter.

Myers-Scotton, Carol. 1988. "Codeswitching as Indexical of Social Negotiations." In *Codeswitching: Anthropological and Sociolinguistic Perspectives*, edited by Monica Heller, pp. 151–186. Berlin and New York: Mouton de Gruyter.

Romaine, Suzanne. 1989. *Bilingualism*. New York: Blackwell.

Stavans, Ilan. 2003. *Spanglish: The Making of a New American Language*. New York: Rayo.

Urciuoli, Bonnie. 1996. *Exposing Prejudice: Puerto Rican Experiences of Language, Race, and Class*. Boulder, CO: Westview Press.

Woolard, Kathryn. 1985. *Double Talk: Bilingualism and the Politics of Ethnicity in Catalonia*. Stanford, CA: Stanford University Press.

Zentella, Ana Celia. 1997. *Growing Up Bilingual: Children in El Barrio*. Malden, MA: Blackwell.

CHAPTER 18

Conversational Code Switching

John J. Gumperz
(1982)

Individuals who are multilingual regard their languages as resources that can be used for a variety of purposes in a variety of settings, but they often do so unconsciously. Asking them about their language use can reveal only a fraction of the interesting factors involved in actual behavior. This is best assessed by observing (and recording). In this chapter, the eminent sociolinguist John Gumperz explains what he observed in recording the natural conversation of bilingual individuals, in a variety of languages and cultures.

Mixing of different "codes" (or linguistic varieties) is often seen as lazy or improper, and speakers often deny that they do it, despite clear evidence that they mix codes liberally when speaking with other bilinguals. Yet recorded behavior shows clear patterns and sophisticated judgment.

Code switching has been studied in many contexts since Gumperz's initial work on it. It always involves detailed delving into the actual conversation of particular people in particular contexts, which can sometimes seem technical. But in those very details—where in a sentence a switch occurs, which terms are repeated in a second language—are found the meanings and uses of code switching.

Reading Questions

- Where is code switching most likely to be found?
- What are some of the reasons usually given for conversational code switching? How does Gumperz evaluate these reasons?
- Why do people code switch?
- How does Gumperz show that code switching is meaningful and patterned rather than random and idiosyncratic?

Conversational code switching can be defined as the juxtaposition within the same speech exchange of passages of speech belonging to two different grammatical systems or subsystems. Most frequently the alternation takes the form of two subsequent sentences, as when a speaker uses a second language either to reiterate his message or to reply to someone else's statement. The following examples are taken from natural talk recorded in bilingual communities. The language pairs in question are Spanish and English (*Sp*–E), Hindi and English (*H*–E), and Slovenian and German (*Sl*–G); where appropriate, English translations are given in parentheses. Speakers are fluent in both languages and regularly use both in the course of their daily routines.

(1) Chicano professionals in California, exchanging goodbyes (*Sp*–E).
    A. Well, I'm glad I met you.
    B. *Andale pues* (O.K. swell).
(2) A college student in India, telling an anecdote (*H*–E):
    Mai gəya jodhpur mẽ (I went to Jodhpur). There is one professor of Hindi there, he is a phonetician. *To us-ne pronauns kiya əpne vais-se* (so he pronounced it in his own voice).
(3) Family conversation in a Slovenian village in Austria talking about a visiting peddler (*Sl*–G):
    A. *Totə kuarbcə yə mewa* (she had such baskets).
    B. *Nɔ na jinyan* (no I don't believe it).
    C. Ya ya di mit di kɛrbalan (the one with the baskets).
    A. *Vinarca yə βoa* (she was Viennese).
    B. Na (no)! Di mit di kɛrbalan (the one with the baskets)?

John J. Gumperz, "Conversational Code Switching." Adapted from *Discourse Strategies*, Cambridge: Cambridge University Press, 1982, pp. 59–99. Reprinted with the permission of Cambridge University Press.

Each of the above exchanges forms a single unitary interactional whole. Speakers communicate fluently, maintaining an even flow of talk. No hesitation pauses, changes in sentence rhythm, pitch level, or intonation contour mark the shift in code. There is nothing in the exchange as a whole to indicate that speakers don't understand each other. Apart from the alternation itself, the passages have all the earmarks of ordinary conversations in a single language.

Often code switching also takes place within a single sentence as in the next set of examples:

(4) Go and get my coat *aus dem Schrank da* (out of the closet there). (E–*G*)

(5) *Uzeymas ti kafe* (will you take coffee)? Oder te (or tea)? (*Sl*–G)

(6) *Jo wo ɔccha tičər hota* (Anyone who is a good teacher) he'll come straight to Delhi. (*H*–E)

(7) That has nothing to do *con que hagan ese* (with the fact that they're doing this). (E–*S*)

(8) Those are friends from Mexico *que tienen chamaquitos* (who have little children). (E–*S*)

Here phrases with the internal characteristics of two distinct grammatical systems enter into sentence level syntactic constructions of the topic–comment, noun–noun complement, predicate–predicate complement type. They combine to form one message, the interpretation of which depends on understanding both parts.

METAPHORICAL AND CONVERSATIONAL USAGE

The conversational switching described here clearly differs both linguistically and socially from what has been characterized as diglossia in the sociolinguistic literature on bilingualism (Ferguson 1964). In diglossia, code alternation is largely of the situational type (Blom & Gumperz 1972). Distinct varieties are employed in certain settings (such as home, school, work) that are associated with separate, bounded kinds of activities (public speaking, formal negotiations, special ceremonials, verbal games, etc.) or spoken with different categories of speakers (friends, family members, strangers, social inferiors, government officials, etc.). Although speakers in diglossia situations must know more than one grammatical system to carry on their daily affairs, only one code is employed at any one time.

To be sure there are some cases of situational alternation, where passages in the two varieties may follow one upon the other within a relatively brief timespan. In the old Catholic mass, for example, Latin was interspersed with the local languages. Or in some tribal societies the etiquette of public address may require that something said in one language be translated and repeated in another. Yet the alternation always corresponds to structurally identifiable stages or episodes of a speech event. Both conversationalists and linguists agree in assigning each sentence or group of sentences to one code or another. There is a simple, almost one-to-one, relationship between language usage and social context, so

that each variety can be seen as having a distinct place or function within the local speech repertoire.

Where such compartmentalization of language use occurs, norms of code selection tend to be relatively stable. The rules of etiquette that govern their use are often explicitly taught and breaches may evoke overt comment. There may be some justification in these cases for dealing with code selection in traditional sociological terms, as a matter of conformance or nonconformance to contextually or situationally determined norms or usage rules (Fishman 1972). Information on such norms can be elicited through questionnaire surveys, language usage diaries, or similar self-report methods and compared to frequency counts of code incidence in actual texts.

In conversational code switching, on the other hand, where (as in our example) the items in question form part of the same minimal speech act, and message elements are tied by syntactic and semantic relations equivalent to those that join passages in a single language, the relationship of language usage to social context is much more complex. While linguists, concerned with grammatical description as such, see the code alternation as highly salient, participants immersed in the interaction itself are often quite unaware which code is used at any one time. Their main concern is with the communicative effect of what they are saying. Selection among linguistic alternants is automatic, not readily subject to conscious recall. The social norms or rules which govern language usage here, at first glance at least, seem to function much like grammatical rules. They form part of the underlying knowledge which speakers use to convey meaning. Rather than claiming that speakers use language in response to a fixed, predetermined set of prescriptions, it seems more reasonable to assume that they build on their own and their audience's abstract understanding of situational norms, to communicate metaphoric information about how they intend their words to be understood (Gumperz & Hernandez-Chavez 1971; Blom & Gumperz 1972).

LANGUAGE USAGE AND PARTICIPANTS' REPORTS

To ask a bilingual to report directly on the incidence of particular switched forms in a conversational passage is in fact equivalent to and perhaps no more effective than asking an English speaking monolingual to record his use of—for example—future tense forms in messages referring to something that is about to take place. Attempts to elicit such self-report information on bilingual usage regularly show significant discrepancies between speakers' descriptions of their own usage and empirical studies of tape recorded texts.

When residents of a small North Norwegian town were asked to recall which of two speech varieties isolated through linguistic analysis they had used in an informal tape recorded conversation, they categorically claimed that they had spoken only the local dialect and not used standard

Norwegian, since as they said "everyone in our town speaks only village dialect, except in school, church or in some formal meetings." Yet when tape recordings were examined sentence by sentence, they revealed frequent conversational switching into standard Norwegian. On further questioning, participants referred to their own metaphorical switching as lapses of attention, or failures to live up to village norms, and 'promised' that only the village dialect would be used in subsequent discussion sessions. Yet tape recordings of these later sessions showed no significant decrease in the amount of switching. In the same vein, some Spanish–English bilinguals living in a Puerto Rican neighborhood in Jersey City consistently claim that they speak only Spanish at home and mainly English at work. Yet tapes of their informal conversations showed a great deal of metaphorical switching. In interview sessions where conversational code switching is discussed, speakers tend to express widely differing attitudes. Some characterize it as an extreme form of language mixing or linguistic borrowing attributable to lack of education, bad manners, or improper control of the two grammars. Others see it as a legitimate style of informal talk. For the most part participants have no readily available words or descriptive terms to characterize the process of switching as such. Whatever words exist take the form of stereotypical labels which vary in meaning with changing attitudes.

In Texas and throughout the American Southwest, where code switching is common among Mexican Americans, the derogative term 'Tex-Mex' is widely used. In French Canada the word *joual* has similar stigmatizing connotations. Montreal buses some time ago carried the slogan *Bien parler est bien penser* (to speak right is to think right) reflecting official attitudes which, according to local linguists, are by no means shared by all sectors of the population.

Until quite recently pejorative attitudes to code switching were also found among many students of folk culture. Barbara Kirschenblatt-Gimblett, in an article on narrative performances among Jews in Canada, analyzes several instances of dialect humor in which the juxtaposition of Yiddish and English phrases serves to create humorous effect. Yet she notes that many folklorists refuse to recognize this type of material as a legitimate form of Yiddish. She quotes Nathan Ausubel, author of the well-known *A Treasury of Jewish Folklore* (1948), who refers to such materials as part of the "large body of Jewish dialect jokes which are not Jewish at all but which are the confections of antisemites who delight in ridiculing the Jews" (Kirschenblatt-Gimblett 1971:41).

When political ideology changes, attitudes to code switching may change also. In California and elsewhere in the Southwest *pocho* or *caló* served as a pejorative term for the Spanish of local Chicanos. But with the awakening of ethnic consciousness and the growing pride in local folk traditions, these speech styles and the code switching they imply have become symbolic of Chicano ethnic values. *Pocho* or *caló* is now increasingly and quite effectively used in the modern Chicano poetry and prose which seeks to depict the California experience. In bilingual groups as

in other human communities the relationship of language usage to language ideology is a complex one which cannot be taken for granted.

In the linguistic literature on bilingualism, conversational code switching tended until quite recently to be treated primarily as a marginal or transitory phenomenon, as if it were a form of linguistic interference which accompanies the learning of a new grammatical system. Existing studies are for the most part concerned either with language change or second language acquisition and tend to concentrate on identification of the type of structures that can be exchanged and on the linguistic and extralinguistic factors that 'trigger' the switch (Haugen 1973). That code switching serves to convey semantically significant information in verbal interaction has not been systematically explored. The purpose of the present chapter is to focus on these communicative aspects of code switching; to show how speakers and listeners utilize subconsciously internalized social and grammatical knowledge in interpreting bilingual conversations.

SOME SOCIAL USES OF CONVERSATIONAL CODE SWITCHING

In spite of the prevailing stereotypes, existing descriptive and historical information on bilingualism provides little support for the contention that code switching is unusual and either historically transitory or a mere matter of individual preference. A recent survey by Timm (1975), which reviews much of the recent literature on the subject, cites evidence going back to the early middle ages. During the last few centuries the practice has been noticed throughout the world in many situations of language and culture contact. Literary histories of seventeenth-century Germany, nineteenth-century Russia, and Edwardian England describe the speech habits of upper class speakers whose German, Russian or English is interspersed with French phrases. In our own time many urban residents of the ex-colonial countries of Asia and Africa freely alternate between their own tongue and the language of the colonizing power.

Code switching is perhaps most frequently found in the informal speech of those members of cohesive minority groups in modern urbanizing regions who speak the native tongue at home, while using the majority language at work and when dealing with members of groups other than their own. The individuals concerned live in situations of rapid transition where traditional intergroup barriers are breaking down and norms of interaction are changing. Eventually such situations lead to the displacement of one language variety by the other. Yet…bilingualism in any one population often persists for several generations. Furthermore, as old populations assimilate, new groups of foreign language speakers move in and other types of bilingualism arise. Thus there is little indication that code switching is merely a deviation from monolingual norms that will soon disappear. On the contrary, with the increasing displacement of formerly stable populations and the growing ethnic diversification of metropolitan centers, the communicative uses of code switching are more likely to increase than to decrease.

The bilingual exchanges we have examined furthermore show that code switching does not necessarily indicate imperfect knowledge of the grammatical systems in question. Only in relatively few passages is code alternation motivated by speakers' inability to find words to express what they want to say in one or the other code. In many cases, the code-switched information could equally well be expressed in either language. Something may be said in one code and reiterated without pause in the other, or an expression in one code may be repeated in the other code elsewhere in the same conversation. Considerations of intelligibility, lucidity, or ease of expression, important as they are in some instances, can therefore not be the main determining reasons. Nor is educational inferiority an important factor.

Two of the three situations discussed here involve examples from the everyday talk of urbanized professionals, students, and other educated speakers, who know both languages well. The individuals in question live in ethnically and culturally diverse settings and spend much of their day interacting with others of different linguistic backgrounds. To be effective at work or in business, they must have near native control of the majority language. Yet at the same time they also actively participate in functioning, ethnically based, peer, friendship, or kinship networks, which stress separate values, beliefs, communicative norms, and conventions.

It is this overtly marked separation between in- and out-group standards which perhaps best characterizes the bilingual experience. The problem is not merely one of cultural differentiation such as one finds among geographically separated societies. What distinguishes bilinguals from their monolingual neighbors is the juxtaposition of cultural forms: the awareness that their own mode of behavior is only one of several possible modes, that style of communication affects the interpretation of what a speaker intends to communicate, and that there are others with different communicative conventions and standards of evaluation that must not only be taken into account but that can also be imitated or mimicked for special communicative effect. This juxtaposition of cultural standards is most evident in in-group activities where participants are bilingual. While in relation with outsiders, of necessity, only the majority style prevails, in bilingual situations the participants' awareness of alternative communicative conventions becomes a resource, which can be built on to lend subtlety to what is said. Rhetorical strategies employed in such settings, as Mitchell-Kernan (1971) points out, tend to be marked by explicit or implicit allusions to what the others do or think.

THE EMPIRICAL STUDY OF CONVERSATIONAL SWITCHING

At the most general level it can be said that grammatical distinctions which mark the bilinguals' two codes directly reflect or signal the contrasting cultural styles and standards of evaluation which they encounter in daily interaction. The tendency is for the ethnically specific, minority language to be regarded as the 'we code' and become associated with in-group and informal activities, and for the majority language to serve as the 'they code' associated with the more formal, stiffer, and less personal out-group relations. But it must be emphasized that, in situations such as those discussed here, this association between communicative style and group identity is a symbolic one: it does not directly predict actual usage. There is no necessary direct relationship between the occurrence of a particular set of linguistic forms and extralinguistic context. Only in relatively few interaction situations, such as for example in contacts with older monolinguals, when talking to very small children, or for certain highly ritualized activities, is only one code appropriate. Elsewhere a variety of options occur, and as with conversations in general, interpretation of messages is in large part a matter of discourse context, social presuppositions, and speakers' background knowledge.

Because of this, there are a number of empirical difficulties which the analyst must face in describing members' perceptions of what count as instances of 'we' and 'they' codes. To begin with, code switching must be separated from loan word usage or borrowings. Borrowing can be defined as the introduction of single words or short, frozen, idiomatic phrases from one variety into the other. The items in question are incorporated into the grammatical system of the borrowing language. They are treated as part of its lexicon, take on its morphological characteristics, and enter into its syntactic structures. Code switching, by contrast, relies on the meaningful juxtaposition of what speakers must consciously or subconsciously process as strings formed according to the internal rules of *two distinct grammatical systems*.

If we rely on purely linguistic criteria the problem of distinguishing borrowings from code switching can sometimes be a complex one. Linguists who have developed methods for the identification of loans have done so primarily from the perspective of language change. Their primary criterion is etymological origin. By this criterion, strictly applied, most words in most modern world languages would count as borrowed. Some scholars therefore make a further distinction between established loans and more recent introductions, which either because of their newness or because they retain some salient non-native characteristics are often seen as foreign. Thus items such as the English *nice* (from Latin *nescius*) *veal, beef, mutton,* and many other early borrowings can for all intents and purposes be regarded as part of the native vocabulary. Others, on the other hand, continue to count as foreign, either because they are recent in origin or because they are seen as having some perceivable non-native characteristics. The word *tičər* (teacher) in (6) above, for instance, has a recognizably English phonological shape. Many native speakers when considering it in isolation will class it as an English word. Yet in this example it is used as a Hindi item since it obeys Hindi number and gender concord rules. Some other seemingly marginal cases are:

(9) Er hat das *gefixt* (he fixed it). (G)
(10) Usne *fix* kiya (he fixed it). (H)
(11) Yes gren *mit* (I go along). (Sl)
(12) Hice *kliam* (he climbed). (Sp)
(13) Na *hiyō-mē*, na *šiyō-mē* tha (he was neither with the men nor the women). (H)

These examples show that both grammatical features and lexical roots can be borrowed. In (9) the italicized borrowed verb stem takes on German prefixes and suffixes, while in (10) the same English stem *fix* forms a compound verb with the Hindi *kiya* serving as the inflected auxiliary. Example (13) seems even odder. Here the English pronouns he and she are borrowed and become Hindi nouns. Regular Hindi case endings (personal communication from L. Khubchandani, 1974) are used and the English gender distinction becomes part of the semantic features of the noun. In (11) and (12) loan items participate in what itself is a borrowed syntactic construction. But such borrowed separable prefix constructions can also occur with native lexical items (Reyes 1974).

In general, loans of all kinds tend to follow the grammatical rules of the new language. Where grammatical features are borrowed these are lower order items which are then integrated into higher order rules. Moreover borrowing affects only one level of linguistic signalling at a time. New lexical and grammatical items assimilate phonetically and rhythmically so that the total conversational effect is that of an utterance as spoken in a single variety.

There are some marginal cases where phonologically unassimilated items from a high prestige foreign language are inserted as marked expressions into an otherwise monolingual passage. Examples are: "She is a *grande dame*"; "He has great *savoir faire*." Here speakers may pronounce *grande* with French-like nasalization or emphasize the fricative *r* in *savoir* and thus by conscious use of foreign sounds suggest refinement or ridicule. The semantic effect here is similar to that of code switching. For the most part, however, these are isolated cases. They occur most frequently in formulaic expressions and this is quite different from the constant alternation which marks code switching in bilingual communities.

Whereas borrowing is a word and clause level phenomenon, code switching is ultimately a matter of conversational interpretation, so that the relevant inferential processes are strongly affected by contextual and social presuppositions. This raises a further problem since, as our discussion of attitudes to language usage suggests, norms of appropriateness with respect to both borrowings and code switching vary greatly. Bilingual speech is highly receptive to loans. Many items in general use in bilingual communities are unknown or unacceptable in the monolingual home regions. Even among bilinguals [themselves] norms of appropriateness vary. In a relatively small Puerto Rican neighborhood in New Jersey, some members freely used code switching styles and extreme forms of borrowing both in everyday casual talk and in more formal gatherings. Other local residents were careful to speak only Spanish with a minimum of loans on formal occasions, reserving code switching styles for informal talk. Others again spoke mainly English using Spanish or code switching styles only with small children or with neighbors.

Depending on such factors as region of origin, local residence, social class, and occupational niche, each communicating subgroup tends to establish its own conventions with respect to both borrowing and code switching. To judge a bilingual by any a priori standards of grammaticality can therefore hardly be satisfactory. The best that can be done is to establish a range of interpretable alternatives or communicative options and thus to distinguish between meaningful discourse and errors due to lack of grammatical knowledge. Rules of productive control within such a range of options are always context bound so that generalization becomes difficult. Acceptable usage is learned through constant practice by living in a group and varies just as control of lexicon and style varies in monolingual groups.

There is evidence to show that most bilinguals have at least a comprehension knowledge of usage norms other than their own, and that they can use this knowledge to judge speakers' social background and attitudes in much the same way that monolinguals use pronunciation and lexical knowledge in assessments of social status. Residents of such large Spanish–English speaking communities as San Francisco or New York, which include immigrants from many Latin American regions, in fact claim that they can tell much about a person's family background and politics from the way that person code switches and uses borrowings. What the outsider sees as almost unpredictable variation, becomes a communicative resource for members. Since bilingual usage rules must be learned by living in a group, ability to speak appropriately is a strong indication of shared background assumptions. Bilinguals, in fact, ordinarily do not use code switching styles in their contact with other bilinguals before they know something about the listener's background and attitudes. To do otherwise would be to risk serious misunderstanding.

CONVERSATIONAL CODE SWITCHING AS A SOCIOLINGUISTIC PHENOMENON

Code alternation among bilinguals shows some similarity to alternation among dialect variables in the urban speech community studied in recent sociolinguistic surveys. In both situations selection of variants is in large part due to subconscious processes, so that when participants are asked to evaluate utterances or report on their own usage, their reports often differ systematically from actual usage (Trudgill 1972). It seems that in both cases social and ideological considerations outweigh actual usage as predictors of message form.

Yet there are some significant differences between the two types of problems. Variable distribution rules are statistical abstractions relating the incidence of certain items of surface form in the speech of significant samples of speakers to independently determined sociological categories, such as social class, ethnic identity, education, and the like. With bilingual groups which are deeply divided with respect to code switching rules these macro-categories are not necessarily relevant.

In fact Labov (1971), who first formalized the notion of variable rule, explicitly cites the following Spanish–English passage as an instance of non–rule governed variation. (In the transcription English passages are in roman type and Spanish passages are italicized; English translations are in parentheses.)

(14) ...*por eso* (therefore) you know it's nothing to be proud of *porque yo no estoy* (because I am not) proud of it as a matter of fact I hate it. *Pero viene viernes y sabado yo estoy...tu me ve haci a mi sola* (but comes Friday and Saturday I am...you see me here by myself alone)...*aqui solite a veces que Frankie me deja* (here alone sometimes Frankie leaves me) you know a stick or something *y yo aqui solita queces Judy no sabe y yo* (and I am here alone perhaps Judy does not know and I) but I rather...*y cuando yo estoy con gente yo me borracha porque me siento mas* happy *mas* free (and when I am with people I get drunk because I feel happier freer) you know *perso si yo estoy con mucha gente yo no estoy* (but if I am with many people I am not), you know high more or less...I couldn't get along with anybody.

Labov describes the switching in this passage as idiosyncratic behavior, not covered by the regularities which determine the occurrences of sociolinguistic variables. His argument hinges on his implicit definition of the term social as limited to phenomena that show statistically predictable distributions within extralinguistically defined human groups. Labov does not attempt to account for listeners' ability to assign speakers to social categories, i.e., to use knowledge of variability to place speakers within the spectrum of known social categories and to assess shared social background. If we extend our definition to these latter phenomena, which clearly fall within the scope of sociological role theory, then code switching cannot be dismissed as merely a matter of idiosyncratic behavior. To be sure, code switching occurs in conditions of change, where group boundaries are diffuse, norms and standards of evaluation vary, and where speakers' ethnic identities and social backgrounds are not matters of common agreement. Yet, if it is true that code switching styles serve as functioning communicative systems, if members can agree on interpretations of switching in context and on categorizing others on the basis of their switching, there must be some regularities and shared perceptions on which these judgements can be based.

Perhaps a more fruitful way to visualize the issue of social regularities in code alternation is to set aside the assumption that speakers either do or do not conform to one or another set of extralinguistically defined and presumably stable norms and to consider speaker participation in various networks of relationship. Network analysis focuses directly on the social ties that actors establish in the course of their regular routines and...makes possible the empirical examination of the relationship of ethnic group membership to everyday behavior.

A number of scholars have noted that the speech of closed network groups is marked by an unusually large number of truncated, idiomatic stock phrases and context bound deictic expressions (Sapir 1921, Bernstein 1971). Although some tend to see this as evidence for socially based differences in language ability, it is more reasonable and more in line with modern linguistic and social theory to assume that exclusive interaction with individuals of similar background leads to reliance on unverbalized and context bound presuppositions in communication, and that the formulaic nature of closed network group talk reflects this fact. When these presuppositions are shared this speeds up communication. Yet speakers who have little experience to the contrary often fail to account for the fact that others who do not share their communicative experience may also not have the background knowledge to interpret their speech as they themselves do.

Open network situations, by contrast, are marked both by diversity of norms and attitudes and by diversity of communicative conventions. To be effective here speakers must be aware of differences in interpretation processes. They cannot expect that the unspoken communicative conventions of their own peer group are understood by others, and thus they learn to be flexible with respect to speech style.

Note that network position is only partly a matter of ethnic identity as such. It is a function of actual communicative experience and also varies with education, occupation, generational cohort, political values, and individual aspiration for mobility. Accordingly, members of the same family and neighborhood background group may show different language usage practices.

The bilingual speakers we have described show the social and attitudinal characteristics of open network situations. One would expect their language usage practices to reflect this also. Yet because of its reliance on unverbalized shared understandings, code switching is typical of the communicative conventions of closed network situations. Our observation that switching strategies serve to probe for shared background knowledge suggests an explanation for this apparent contradiction. Since usage conventions can be learned only through actual communicative experience, if in a situation of social diversity a speaker can appropriately employ these strategies as part of the give and take of a longer conversational exchange, this is in itself socially significant. Regardless of the attitudes participants may express elsewhere, regardless of how an individual would rate on conventional social scales, control of the relevant communicative strategies is prima facie evidence for the existence of shared underlying assumptions which differentiate those who know from others who cannot use these strategies.

It is not necessary therefore to turn to larger samples of text or extralinguistic indices in order to determine whether bilingual alternation is more than idiosyncratic behavior.

What we need are detailed investigations of speakers' use of code switching strategies, in actual conversational exchanges, to show that they exhibit some form of linguistic patterning, that they contribute to the interpretation of constituent messages, and that participants in the interaction agree in evaluating what is intended.

Even a casual examination of (14) in these terms reveals a number of regularities in the speaker's use of the two codes. Many of the seemingly English items clearly count as borrowings in terms of our criteria. Examples are: *happy* in "me siento mas happy"; *free* in "mas free." *Proud of it* in "yo no estoy proud of it" is marginal, but probably also a borrowing because of its position within the Spanish phrase.

If we disregard the initial sentence, which is incomplete, the rest of the passage is mainly in Spanish. The speaker describes her loneliness at home while her husband is away. The code switched phrases consist largely of interjections, dependent clauses, or verb complement phrases. English serves mainly to amplify or to qualify information already introduced. This is not random language mixture, yet motivation for code switching seems to be stylistic and metaphorical rather than grammatical. The process by which meaning is conveyed must be studied in terms of the stylistic interrelationship of sentences or phrases within the passage as a whole, not in terms of the internal structure of particular sentences.

CODE SWITCHING IN THREE LANGUAGE SITUATIONS

To explore the mechanisms by which code switching conveys meaning and their relationship to grammar and speaker's and listener's social presuppositions in more detail, code switched passages (isolated from a number of conversational exchanges) were examined. Examples derive from three linguistically and socially distinct situations.

The first is [an] Austrian–Yugoslavian border village of farmers and laborers.... The population here has a history of 150–200 years of bilingualism. Speakers use Slovenian at home but they are educated in German and live in close proximity to German speaking villages and shopping centers. German is the exclusive language of most business and work relations. The second situation involves Indian college students from urban Delhi. All students are native speakers of Hindi who have had all their secondary education in English. Some members of the group are teachers of English, some have published poems and short stories in Hindi. In situation three participants are members of a group of Chicano college students and urban professionals who were born in the United States and are largely from economically deprived backgrounds. They speak Chicano Spanish especially at home with their elders, but speak English in many of their work and friendship relations. The conversations studied were recorded for the most part by participants themselves and interpretations of meanings in each case were checked with participants and with others of similar social and linguistic background.

Knowledge of cultural values and social factors affecting language use are a necessary starting point for any study of code switching but, as we have argued above, this information is only one of the factors which enter into the speaker's interpretation process. When interviewed about their language usage, speakers in all three situations readily identify Slovenian, Hindi, and Spanish respectively as the 'we' code, suitable with kin and close friends. German and English serve as 'they' codes to be used with outsiders or for special types of formal discourse. Beyond this, however, opinions about language usage norms vary and can be interpreted and understood only in relation to the background conditions that shape each language situation.

The Austrian situation [is not] described [here]. In urban North India, English has since the nineteenth century been the main symbol of urbanization and Western technology. Until quite recently secondary and higher education were almost entirely in English. Hindi is a literary language with a written tradition going back to the middle ages. Hindi literature has flourished during the last decades; poetry, novels, and short stories are widely read since Indian independence. Furthermore, Hindi has become the official language of administration and has replaced English as an important medium for business in much of North India. There has been a great deal of effort by language reformers and government planners to replace English altogether. Yet English continues to be widely used especially in those metropolitan centers where large sectors of the population come from non–Hindi speaking areas.

By the time they go to college most students in these larger cities have a functional reading and speaking knowledge of English and use it along with Hindi. The use of English in informal conversations is deplored by many critics, who see the tendency to use foreign loan words and to 'mix languages' as a threat to the purity of Hindi and a threat to the preservation of traditional values. Yet among students and young intellectuals of the type recorded here, knowledge of English serves as a mark of sophistication. The individuals in question pride themselves on their knowledge of modern Hindi literature and on their sense of Hindi literary style, but they see no conflict between this attachment to Hindi and their use of English in everyday talk.

Speakers of Chicano Spanish in California are in part descendants of Mexican immigrants to the Southwestern United States who came as farm laborers or industrial workers and in part descendants of indigenous Spanish speaking populations. They tend to live in ethnically segregated Spanish neighborhoods where Spanish speaking natives of the United States intermingle with recently arrived monolinguals. Until quite recently they ranked lowest among Californian ethnic minorities in income or education. Middle class occupations were not open to those individuals who retained obvious signs of ethnic distinctness. Spanish speakers who entered the middle class felt obliged to assimilate to middle class American culture and this meant giving up ties with their Spanish speaking home background.

As elsewhere in the case of minority language settlements, residents of Spanish speaking neighborhoods have developed their own dialect of Spanish. This language has many features in common with the dialects of Mexican farmers. It has also incorporated some of the features of *caló*, the slang of urban youth groups, and incorporates large numbers of borrowings from English. Residents of Mexico tend to use the term *pocho* to refer both to the Americans of Mexican descent and—in a derogatory sense—to the urban dialect the latter speak. As we pointed out before, with the recent awakening of ethnic consciousness the terms *pocho, caló,* and *Chicano* have been adopted as symbols of the newly asserted values. Urban professionals and intellectuals consciously affirm their tie to their low income ethnic brothers and symbolize this by deliberate adoption of *pocho* speech along with English and literary Spanish.

The Conversational Functions of Code Switching

The three situations we have described all reflect conditions of change marked by diversity of values, norms of language usage, and standards of grammaticality that cut across commonly recognized ethnic boundaries. We have pointed out that in such situations expressed attitudes tend to conflict with the observed facts of behavior and that the usual methods of sociolinguistic analysis which begin by isolating patterning at the level of linguistic form and then rely on generalizations about social structure to infer relationships run into serious difficulty. Since speakers do understand each other and can agree on what is being accomplished in particular settings, there must be some sharing of codes and principles of interpretation, but this takes the form of taken for granted, tacit presuppositions which are best recovered through indirect conversational analysis.

As an initial step in our discussion we rely on discourse analysis to isolate the conversational functions of code switching. Illustrative brief exchanges, just long enough to provide a basis for context bound interpretation, were extracted from tape recorded conversations in all three situations. These indicate that switching serves roughly similar functions in all three situations, so that a single preliminary typology can be set up which holds across language situations. We will then go on to point out some of the limitations of this approach and suggest other approaches which more adequately account for members' interpretive strategies.

Quotations

In many instances the code switched passages are clearly identifiable either as direct quotations or as reported speech. Some examples follow (Slovenian, Hindi, and Spanish sequences are italicized and followed by translations in parentheses; German is not italicized but is also translated in parentheses):

(15) *Slovenian–German.* From an informal business discussion among neighboring farmers, called to discuss the sharing of farm machinery. The speaker is reporting on a conversation with a German speaking businessman:
    Pa prawe (then he said) wen er si nit cɔlt gib i si nit (if he does not pay for it, I will not give it).

(16) Elsewhere in the same discussion a speaker reports on what a fellow villager, who is a potential participant to the sharing arrangement, has said:
    Pa vaguta jə tudi reku mənə učera (and Vaguta has also said to me yesterday): also a hektar hob i gel (so I have about a hectare) also i bin gewilt (so I am willing).

(17) *Slovenian–German.* Village woman talking with neighbors about her conversation with the German speaking doctor:
    Tədei yə viu…tolə tudi tolə yə (then there was also…there was)…*prou vaudə yə mou* (he actually had wrinkles) *pa yɔs sn varaua rainaryə yɔs sn reakua* (and I asked (Dr) Rainer, I said) is etwas kešvolən (is something swollen). *Praba* (he says): nain er is gut ernert er hɔt kain vɔsar unt guar niks (no he is well nourished he has no water or anything).

(18) *Hindi–English.* From a conversation among young Hindi speaking college teachers. The speaker is talking about his visit to the doctor:
    He says: *ye hi medsin kɔntinyu kəro bhai* (continue taking this medicine friend).

(19) *Hindi–English.* From a conversation among Hindi speaking college students and writers in Delhi:
    I went to Agra, *to maine əpne bhaiko bola ki* (then I said to my brother that), if you come to Delhi you must buy some lunch.

(20) *Spanish–English.* From a conversation among two Chicano professionals. The speaker is talking about her baby-sitter.
    She doesn't speak English, so, *dice que la reganan: "Si se les va olvidar el idioma a las criaturas"* (she says that they would scold her: "the children are surely going to forget their language").

(21) *Spanish–English.* Later in the above situation, the speaker is reporting on what her father said about her children's inability to speak Spanish:
    To this day he says that…uh…it's a shame that they don't speak…uh…Spanish. *Estan como burros. Les abla uno y* (they are like donkeys. someone talks to them and): "What he say, what's he saying."

Addressee Specification

In a second set of examples the switch serves to direct the message to one of several possible addressees. This occurred very frequently in the Austrian village when a speaker turned to someone standing aside from a group of conversationalists:

(22) *Slovenian–German.* Informal conversation about the weather in a village home (a strong wind is blowing and there is a danger of rain and of the fruit being blown off the trees):

    A: [speaking to B] *Nčeabə prišu, vɔ ki šu vaitar* (it will not come, it will pass by).

    B: [speaking to A] *Ya ki təkə naβásan zapkamə pa yə žiə ciu štəm yə pastranə* (it is so overloaded with apples and the entire tree is bent already).

    B: [continues turning to C sitting apart] *Regən vert so ain vint is drausən* (it will rain it is so windy outside).

(23) A group of Hindi speaking graduate students are discussing the subject of Hindi–English code switching:

    A: Sometimes you get excited and then you speak in Hindi, then again you go on to English.

    B: No nonsense, it depends on your command of English.

    B: [shortly thereafter turning to a third participant, who has just returned from answering the doorbell] *Kɔn hai bai* (who is it)? [Note the discrepancy here between actual usage and *talk about* usage.]

(24) A Hindi speaking student couple is talking to a Hindi speaking visitor in their home:

    Wife: *Pipəlmint piyēŋgi ap* (will you have some peoplemint)?

    Visitor: *Piyengi* (drink)?

    Wife: *Pinekihi čiz hai* (that is what it's for, drinking).

    Visitor: *Ye kaise piya jata hai* (how can I drink it)?

    Husband: But she doubts us, *ki isme kuč əlcohol to nəhī* (there might be some alcohol in it).

    Husband: [turning to his wife] Put it in a glass for her.

Interjections

In other cases the code switch serves to mark an interjection or sentence filler. Example (1) at the beginning of this chapter is a good example of this phenomenon. The exchange is reproduced more fully in (25):

(25) *Spanish–English.* Chicano professionals saying goodbye, and after having been introduced by a third participant, talking briefly:

    A: Well, I'm glad I met you.

    B: *Andale pues* (O.K. swell). And do come again. Mm?

(26) *Spanish–English.* A is talking to someone else later on in the same situation. Here the main message is in Spanish and the switch to English:

    Pero como (but how) you know *la Estella y la Sandi relistas en el telefon* (Stella and Sandi are very precocious on the phone).

(27) *Slovenian–German.* Austrian village conversation. B replies to A prior to continuing in Slovenian:

    A: *Grta yətə* (go there).

    B: Ya so ist das.

Reiteration

Frequently a message in one code is repeated in the other code, either literally or in somewhat modified form. In some cases such repetitions may serve to clarify what is said, but often they simply amplify or emphasize a message.

(28) *Spanish–English.* Chicano professionals:

    A: The three old ones spoke nothing but Spanish. Nothing but Spanish. *No hablaban ingles* (they did not speak English).

(29) *Spanish–English.* Later in the same conversation:

    A: I was…I got to thinking *vacilando el punto ese* (mulling over that point) you know? I got to thinking well this and that reason…

(30) *Hindi–English.* Father in India calling to his son, who was learning to swim in a swimming pool:

    Baju-me jao beṭa, andar mat (go to the side son, not inside). Keep to the side.

(31) *English–Hindi.* Father calling his small son while walking through a train compartment:

    Keep straight. *Sidha jao* [louder] (keep straight)

(32) *Spanish–English.* Puerto Rican mother in New York calling to her children who are playing on the street:

    Ven acá (come here). *Ven acá* (come here). Come here, you.

(33) *Slovenian–German.* Austrian village family conversation about a woman peddler who had come by some time ago:

    Father: *Tota kə yə uanə mewa kuarbcə* (the one who last year had baskets).

    Daughter: *Kə yə ušə mewa* (the one who had lice).

    Father: *Koi yɔ mewa* (what did she have)?

    Daughter: *Təšə kuarbcə pa ušə yə mewa* (such baskets and she had lice).

    Father: *Nɔ na žinian* (no I don't believe it).

    Mother: Ya ya di mit kerbəlan (yes yes the one with the baskets).

    Father: *Vinarca yə woa* (she was from Vienna).

    Mother: Na di mit di kerbəlan (no the one with the baskets).

    Father: *Ya vinarca* (yes from Vienna).

    Daughter: *Ya* (yes).

    Mother: Fon vin vɔr si (from Vienna she was)?

Father here is using Slovenian to talk about a peddler who had come to the house to sell baskets. Daughter replies in Slovenian that this peddler had lice. Father disputes her claim still in Slovenian. Mother then shifts to German in breaking in to support her daughter. When Father retorts with additional information in Slovenian, Mother repeats her own assertions once more in German. Father then uses

Slovenian to reiterate his words, whereupon Mother questions what he says in German. Whereas in the preceding examples speakers code switch in reiterating their own words, here a second speaker switches and a first speaker refuses to follow suit. The matter is complex and requires further discussion, but the failure to follow another participant's lead in code choice here is clearly significant.

Message Qualification

Another large group of switches consist of qualifying constructions such as sentence and verb complements or predicates following a copula. Examples (6), (7), and (8) above illustrate this. Other examples are:

(34) *English–Spanish.*
   We've got all…all these kids here right now. *Los que estan ya criados aquí, no los que estan recien venidos de México* (those that have been born here, not the ones that have just arrived from Mexico). They all understood English.

(35) *English–Spanish.*
   The oldest one, *la grande la de once años* (the big one who is eleven years old).

(36) *Hindi–English.* College student conversation:
   A: *Bina veṭ kiye ap a gəe* (without waiting you came)?
   B: *Nəhī* (no), I came to the bus stop *nau bis pəččis pər* (about nine twenty-five).

(37) *Hindi–English.*
   Nəhī, aegi zərur (no, she will certainly come) because she said *ki yədi maī nəhī aūgi to* (if I should not come then) I'll ring you up and she hasn't rung me up.

In (34) and (35) the main message is in English and Spanish is used to qualify this message. In (36) and (37) the Hindi conveys the main message.

Personalization Versus Objectivization

In this last, relatively large group of instances function is somewhat more difficult to specify in purely descriptive terms. The code contrast here seems to relate to such things as: the distinction between talk about action and talk as action, the degree of speaker involvement in, or distance from, a message, whether a statement reflects personal opinion or knowledge, whether it refers to specific instances or has the authority of generally known fact. Perhaps the best way to illustrate this is through more detailed discussion of examples.

(38) *Slovenian–German.* Austrian village farmers making plans for sharing machinery and dealing with problems that might come up:
   A: *Alə mormaya təkə nadritə* (O.K. let us do it like this) dann vɔn etwas is, nɔ guət (then if something happens, O.K. fine). *Pa tolə gax wikɔlna* (if sometimes the motor must be rewound) kost sibn

ɔxthundert šiling (it costs seven or eight hundred shillings).
   B: *Ja ja payə dənar tau* (O.K., O.K. then the money is there) [later in the same discussion:]
   A: *Yəs sak leta diən oli ntər* (I put in oil every year). Kost virzen šiling (it costs fourteen shillings).

A begins with a personalized statement, suggesting what the group should do. He shifts to German upon mentioning a possible problem with the arrangement, as if to imply that such things may happen without anyone being at fault. Later on the cost of the repair is given in German, as is the cost of the oil in the last statement. Perhaps the shift to German gives the air of objective factuality to the cost figures quoted.

(39) Same situation as above. The discussion now concerns the origin of a certain type of wheat:
   A: *Vigələ ma yə sa america* (Wigele got them from America).
   B: *Kanada pridə* (it comes from Canada).
   A: Kanada mus i sɔgn nit (I would not say Canada).

Here B disputes A's statement and A counters in German, as if to lend his statement more authority.

(40) *Hindi–English.* College student conversation:
   A: *Vaišna ai* (did Vaishna come)?
   B: She was supposed to see me at nine-thirty at Karol Bag.
   A: Karol Bag?
   B: *ɔr maī nɔ bəje ghərse nikla* (and I left the house at nine).

B's English response to A's Hindi question here treats the appointment as an objective fact. B shifts back to Hindi in explaining his own actions.

(41) *Hindi–English.* College girls talking about what a male friend said:
   A: *Tera nam liya, lipa ka nam liɣa* (he mentioned you, he mentioned Lipa).
   B: *əha kya kəkne* (ah what should I say) she'll be flattered. *Aj maī leke a rəhi thi na* (today I was going to bring her see).

Here B's shift to English in talking about Lipa's feelings suggests that the statement is a casual one, not implying personal involvement. B shifts back to Hindi in talking about what she personally intended to do.

(42) *Spanish–English.* Chicano professionals. A talks about her attempt to cut down on smoking:
   A: …I'd smoke the rest of the pack myself in the other two weeks.
   B: That's all you smoke?
   A: That's all I smoked.
   B: And how about now?
   A: *Estos…me los halle…estos Pall Malls me los hallaron* (these…I found these Pall Malls they…these were found for me). No I mean that's

all the cigarettes…that's all. They're the ones I buy.

Later in the same conversation:

A: …they tell me "How did you quit Mary?" I don't quit I…I just stopped. I mean it wasn't an effort that I made *que voy a dejar de fumar por que me hace daño o* (that I'm going to stop smoking because it's harmful to me or) this or that uh-uh. It's just that I used to pull butts out of the waste paper basket yeah. I used to go look in the…*se me acababan los cigarros en la noche* (my cigarettes would run out on me at night). I'd get desperate *y ahi voy al basarero a buscar, a sacar* (and there I go to the wastebasket to look for some, to get some), you know.

Note how the code contrast symbolizes varying degrees of speaker involvement in the message. Spanish statements are personalized while English reflects more distance. The speaker seems to alternate between *talking about* her problem in English and *acting out* her problem through words in Spanish.

The above list, although by no means exhaustive, illustrates some of the most common uses of code switching. The range of interpretations that results is much greater than one would expect from speakers' descriptions of language usage in terms of the simple 'we' and 'they' dichotomy. What is conveyed varies greatly with context and discourse content. Yet the same kinds of uses or functions tend to recur in what on both linguistic and social grounds are quite distinct situations.

The fact that it is possible to isolate conversational functions such as those listed here constitutes a convenient first step in our analysis of code switching. It opens up the possibility of examining code switching functions directly and provides a set of categories that can be employed in discussing the relevant problems of interpretation with participants who ordinarily have no words of their own for referring to the phenomenon. If participants agree on an interpretation of a code switched passage, one can assume that this agreement is based on similar linguistic perceptions and then proceed to investigate code switching as part of the contextualization cues which give rise to these perceptions.

Yet a list of functions cannot by itself explain what the linguistic bases of listeners' perceptions are and how they affect the interpretation process. It is always possible to postulate extralinguistic social factors or items of background knowledge which affect the incidence of switching. This is done in a number of recent sociolinguistically oriented discourse studies (Ervin-Tripp & Mitchell-Kernan 1977). Yet to attempt to set up language usage rules which predict or reliably account for the incidence of code switching proves to be a highly difficult task.

Consider the problem of quoted or reported speech. It is clear that not all speakers are quoted in the language they normally use. In (15) a Slovenian bilingual quotes a German monolingual in German, but in (16) a Slovenian speaker quotes a Slovenian speaking neighbor's remarks in German. One might attempt to formulate a rule such as the following: A message is quoted in the code in which it was

said. Examples (15), (16), (17), and (18) might support this rule. Example (21) where a speaker reports on a conversation in English and shifts to Spanish for the direct quote, would seem to illustrate the signalling value of the rule. But note that in (21) Spanish is used both for reported speech and for the direct quote. In (19), moreover, the speaker tells about his trip to Agra in the 'they' code, switching to the 'we' code to state that he talked to his brother and switching back to the 'they' code for the quote. It might be said that this last example reflects the actual language used, but this does not explain why the 'we' code was chosen to introduce the quotation.

A detailed examination of the conversation from which example (18) was excerpted reveals some further difficulties.

(43) Speaker A begins with a Hindi question:

Aur kya bola doktər ne (and what did the doctor say)?

B replies, starting in English and shifting to Hindi for the quote:

He says: *ye hi medsin kɔntinyu kəro bhai* (continue taking this medicine friend).

B then goes on in English:

He'll see me on Monday. But he told me: You continue with this medicine.

A then counters in Hindi:

Injekšən usne ləga da (did he give an injection)?

Whatever patterning there is in this type of code switching cannot be explained by generalized rules relating conversational functions to instances of code use.

Difficulties with the notion of function increase as we go from quotation and addressee specification to reiteration, qualification, and personalization. In (30) a Hindi message is repeated in English; in (31) the shift is reversed. This reversal clearly does not relate to train travel and swimming. Example (33) shows Father and Daughter arguing in Slovenian. Mother comes in, shifting to German in supporting her daughter. The fact that Father both sticks to his opinion and does not follow Mother's code choice lends the exchange an air of enhanced disagreement. The effect is created by the exchange itself rather than any other contextual factors.

Note moreover that whereas our other functional categories refer to observable sequential or syntactic features of the interaction, personalization and objectification are merely rough labels for a large class of stylistic and semantic phenomena. As we will attempt to show later, in examples (38)–(42), participants are likely to interpret 'we' code passages as personalized or reflecting speaker involvement and 'they' code passages as indicating objectification or speaker distance. But this does not mean that all 'we' code passages are clearly identifiable as personalized on the basis of overt content or discourse context alone. In many of these cases it is *the choice of code itself in a particular conversational context* which forces this interpretation. Thus, rather than attempting to refine our classification of functions, so as to be able to predict code occurrence, it seems more useful to take a more semantic approach to code switching and to examine how code switching constrains the processes of inference by which we assess communicative intent.

...

THE SITUATED INTERPRETATION OF SWITCHED PASSAGES

While our examples show that code switching contributes to meaning through juxtaposition of message elements, this demonstration alone does not explain what semantic processes are at work and how situated interpretations relate to the identification of the two varieties as 'we' and 'they' codes. Exchanges where the same message is said first in one and then reiterated in the other code throw some light on this issue. Consider once more the items cited in (30)–(32):

(44) a. Father talking to his five year old son, who is walking ahead of him through a train compartment and wavering from side to side:
  Keep straight. *Sidha jao* (keep straight).
  b. Adult talking to a ten year old boy who is practicing in the swimming pool:
  Baju-me jao beṭa, andar mat (go to the side son, not inside). Keep to the side!

The two sequences were reversed so that (44a) starts with the 'we' code, Hindi, and (44b) with the 'they' code, English. Both sets of sequences were played and members were asked if the reversal in direction of the code switch changed the meaning of the message. There was general agreement that the reversal *normally does make a difference*. The shift to the 'we' code was seen as signifying more of a personal appeal, paraphrasable as "won't you please," whereas the reverse shift suggests more of a warning or mild threat.

(45) A Spanish–English sequence taken from a mother's call to children:
  Ven acá (come here). *Ven acá* (come here). Come here, you.

This was similarly interpreted as a warning by Spanish-English bilinguals whereas the reverse:

  Come here. Come here. *Ven acá.*

was seen as a personal appeal.

Interpretation processes were analyzed in somewhat more detail with college student English-Hindi conversations. The procedure followed was to isolate key passages, change the English switches back to Hindi, and ask members familiar with the relevant rhetorical strategies to judge the two versions. When the Hindiized versions were judged to be inappropriate, or semantically different from the original versions, judges were asked for more detailed explanations of exactly what they thought speakers intended to convey in each case. These descriptions served as the basis for constructing alternative paraphrases

or verbal expansions for each of the possible interpretations. The conversations were then presented to a second group of judges who were asked to choose an appropriate paraphrase. Our predictions of what choices would be made proved right in all cases.

In the following example a conversationalist who has recently applied for a job is asked to tell about his job interview. The preceding conversation is in Hindi.

(46) *Apka intərvyu kaisa huwa* (how did your interview go)?
  After a hardly noticeable pause, when there is no immediate answer the same speaker repeats his question:
  How did your interview go?

Two possible interpretations for the second question are: (a) tell me frankly, how did the interview affect you; (b) give me a general impersonal account of what went on. Members agreed on the second alternative. In other words they interpreted the shift to English as signalling that what was wanted was a neutral, factual reply rather than an indication of personal feelings.

In another case a speaker reports on a missed appointment with a female acquaintance, who was to have accompanied him on a trip to town. Talking in Hindi, he says that she had called him to say she would meet him at the bus stop, but when he arrived she was not there. He goes on as follows:

(47) *Timarpur ki bəs samne khəri thi* (the Timarpur bus was standing before me). Then I thought I might as well take it.

Here both the all Hindi and the Hindi–English version were judged as potentially appropriate, but their meaning was seen as quite distinct. The English version was interpreted as implying that the appointment in question was a casual one, that there was no personal involvement. The Hindi version on the other hand is seen as suggesting that the appointment was more in the nature of a date and that he was annoyed at his friend's not turning up.

In a final example a speaker is attempting to persuade his friends to change their college program. He begins with a personalized statement:

(48) *Tu aplae kər de* (you should apply). *Mai bhi aplae kər dū.* (I will also apply). *Aie es next year-mē baith rəha hū* (I will take the I.A.S. exam next year).
  Shifting to English he then continues.
  Tell Rupa that Ashok is I.A.S. officer next year in any case.

The shift from Hindi to English was seen as indicating that the last sentence reflects a generally known fact and not just personal opinion. The semantic effect here is quite similar to that illustrated in examples (39) and (42).

Code switching is thus more than simply a way of contrastively emphasizing part of a message. It does not merely set off a sequence from preceding and following ones. The direction of the shift may also have semantic value. In a sense the oppositions warning/personal appeal; casual remark/personal feeling; decision based on convenience/decision based on annoyance; personal opinion/generally known fact can be seen as metaphoric extensions of the 'we'/'they' code opposition.

Perhaps the closest analogue to this view of what code switching does can be found in Paul Grice's discussion of conversational implicature. Grice is concerned with the inability of current formal semantic theory to account for problems that arise in the analysis of so-called logical operators such as *and*, *or,* and *if.* He argues that the difficulties encountered in these cases are not matters of ambiguity or fuzziness inherent in the logical operators themselves, but derive from the nature of the conversational processes in which they are used. Conversation, he points out, is a cooperative activity where the participants, in order to infer what is intended, must reconcile what they hear with what they understand the immediate purpose of the activity to be. What is conveyed in any one circumstance therefore is a function of (a) literal meaning in the sense in which that term is understood by semanticists and (b) a series of indirect inferences based on what he calls the cooperative principle. He formulates this principle as follows: "Make your contribution such as is required at the stage at which it occurs by the accepted purpose or direction of the talk exchange in which you are engaged" (1975: 67).

Grice uses the term conversational implicature to refer to the assumptions a hearer must make to reinterpret messages so as to accord with the presumption that this conversational principle is observed. He lists four subcategories and related maxims in terms of which the cooperative principle is articulated in particular instances: quantity—make your contribution as informative as necessary; quality—be truthful; relation—be relevant with reference to what is being talked about; manner—avoid obscurity and ambiguity and obey proper form. These maxims function as general guidelines or evaluative criteria which when apparently violated give rise to the implicatures or chains of reasoning by means of which we reinterpret what is said in such a way as to fit the situation.

We assume that this is the type of explanation that accounts for the interpretations we elicited in connection with (44)–(48). For example, by repeating his own words in (44), the speaker violates the principle of quantity. Hence we infer that what he actually intended to convey was something like: "I note that you didn't pay attention to what I said. Listen carefully, I said…" The second code repetition violates both quantity and manner. Here a likely argument would go as follows: The speaker has repeated himself once more and in addition has shifted from a style of speaking which we associate with the public 'they' situation we are in at the moment, to a 'we' style which we associate with home and family bonds. I assume that by doing this he intends to convey something like: "I'm your father and it is in your own best interest to listen." This explains our informants' feeling that the direction of the shift affects the interpretation of intent.

To argue that code switching can be analyzed in terms of conversational implicature, is to assume that the usage conventions by which two speech varieties are categorized as 'we' and 'they' codes and become associated with in- and out-group experiences have conversational functions that are equivalent to the relationship of words and referents. This implies that both message form and message content play a role in implicature. The parallel is of course only approximate. Basic referential meanings are shared by all speakers of a language regardless of social background. They are stable over time and can be preserved in dictionaries. Code usage, on the other hand, reflects conventions created through networks of interpersonal relationships subject to change with changing power relationships and socio-ecological environments, so that sharing of basic conventions cannot be taken for granted. This accounts for the fact that listeners in code switching situations may understand the literal meaning of an utterance but differ in their interpretations of communicative intent.

In most everyday situations, however, variability of usage conventions presents no serious problems since the range of available options is limited by syntactic and pragmatic constraints. Interactions among speakers who don't know each other well generally begin with a set of introductory probing moves, where the basic ground rules to be applied later are negotiated. Participants' ability to respond to the tacit presuppositions reflected in these moves is in itself a measure of shared background knowledge. Although Grice did not go on to explore the broader implications of his distinction between lexico-grammatical phenomena and conversational processes relying on inferences not recoverable from isolated utterances, the concept of implicature has been highly influential in linguistics. Linguists, however, have for the most part tended to assume that implicature is purely a matter of abstract semantics, a way of relating what is said to an individual's knowledge of the world. Our analysis of code switching suggests that while basic conversational principles are universal and apply to verbal exchanges of all kinds, the way they are articulated in situ is culturally and subculturally specific. The term implicature is here used to refer to a sociolinguistic process by which communicative experience is retrieved to supply information not shared by listeners of different backgrounds. Symbols that at the macro-societal level count as markers of ethnic identity here serve to signal information on communicative intent. When seen from this perspective, sociolinguistic norms become more than just simply rules to be obeyed or violated. They are an integral part of what a speaker has to know to be effective in face to face communication.

To say that code switching conveys information, however, does not mean that a switch can be assigned a single meaning in any one case. What is signalled are guidelines to suggest lines of reasoning for retrieving other knowledge. The actual judgements of intent are situated, i.e., negotiated, as part of the interactive process and subject to change as more information is brought in.

Examples (33)–(42) illustrate these points. In each instance the main portion, the part that conveys what the message is about, is in one code while certain sequences are set off by shifts into the other code. We assume that participants (a) recognize the shift as potentially meaningful, (b) identify its syntactic function in relation to other discourse signals and (c) search their memory for an explanation which accords with what the contrast signifies in each circumstance. In (33) the mother by using village German to say "the one with the baskets" repeats information which the father had first introduced in Slovenian. In the exchange that follows the father stays with Slovenian while the mother keeps replying in German. Father's failure to respond to the other's lead here enhances the sense of disagreement conveyed in the lexical content. In (39) A's "I would not say Canada" denies the previous speaker's statement, but the fact that this denial is made in a code which is commonly associated with official pronouncements suggests that the speaker intends to convey a sense of authoritativeness. In (34) the English sentence "we've got all these kids here" is followed by Spanish, which can be taken to suggest that the individuals referred to are of the 'we' group, i.e., Chicanos. In (42) speaker B challenges A's claim that she has cut down on smoking by asking about the pack of cigarettes she has with her. The Spanish reply here suggests personal involvement, so that the subsequent English segment then comes to signify personal distance. Continued switching throughout the rest of the passage can be seen as maintaining the contrast between personalized and generalized utterances, although this does not mean that every English segment reflects distance and every Spanish segment reflects involvement.

As a signalling mechanism then code switching contributes to interpretation by signalling information about what the direction of the argument is to be. The resulting inferences are not unambiguous in the sense that they can be confirmed or disconfirmed through direct questions about what something means in isolation. But indirect eliciting methods like those illustrated here, which ask participants to select among interpretations that according to our analysis reflect alternative lines of reasoning, can provide insights into underlying inferential processes. Knowledge of what these processes are does not guarantee agreement on how a message is to be interpreted, but it sets up the conditions for possible understanding. Since the tacit conventions involved can be learned only through actual communicative experience, those who share that experience will find it easier to interact than those who don't.

CONCLUSION

The view that code switching is a discourse phenomenon in which speakers rely on juxtaposition of grammatically distinct subsystems to generate conversational inferences has important implications for our understanding of how verbal signs function in human interaction and for our understanding of the role of speech variation in human society. The scope of linguistic analysis has been extended greatly in the last decade and many earlier notions on what are linguistic and nonlinguistic phenomena have been abandoned. It is now generally agreed that social presuppositions play an important part in understanding. Yet the assumption that meaning is conveyed through signs that count as emic in terms of the grammatical system of a single language, dialect, or speech variety and that discourse coherence is primarily a matter of abstract semantic relations remains.

In bilingual situations such as those we have illustrated neither grammatical nor ethnic boundaries necessarily prevent contact. On the contrary, they constitute a resource in as much as they enable us to convey messages that only those who share our background and are thus likely to be sympathetic can understand. They allow us to suggest inferences without actually putting ourself on record and risking loss of face (Brown & Levinson 1978). To deal with such issues, theories of discourse process will have to be modified to allow for the possibility that such aspects of sentence form as code choice in bilingual situations contribute to interpretation.

Code switching signals contextual information equivalent to what in monolingual settings is conveyed through prosody or other syntactic or lexical processes. It generates the presuppositions in terms of which the content of what is said is decoded. But these presuppositions operate at several levels of generality. In situational switching, where a code or speech style is regularly associated with a certain class of activities, it comes to signify or connote them, so that its very use can signal the enactment of these activities even in the absence of other clear contextual cues. Component messages are then interpreted in terms of the norms and symbolic associations that apply to the signalled activity.

The case of metaphorical usage is much more complex. The signalling mechanism involved is a shift in contextualization cues, which is not accompanied by a shift in topic and in other extralinguistic context markers that characterize the situation. This partial violation of co-occurrence expectations then gives rise to the inference that some aspects of the connotations, which elsewhere apply to the activity as a whole, are here to be treated as affecting only the illocutionary force and the quality of the speech act in question. The distinction between the two types of alternation is however not a qualitative one. The level of generality of the signal is in itself determined by what happens in the interactive situation.

The fact that metaphorical switching presupposes the ability to identify code distinctions has important bearings on the discussion concerning Saussure's concepts of *langue* (language) and *parole* (speech). Although there is general agreement about the usefulness of the distinction, what is meant by the two terms (especially by the second, *langue*) continues to be highly controversial. Theoretical linguists tend to see *langue* as a highly abstract set of rules, while other more socially oriented scholars see it in Durkheimian terms as the aggregate or perhaps vector sum of the processes of change in a statistically significant sample of speakers (Labov 1973).

In both views language is regarded as a separate system, independent of overt individual behavior, at any one time. The study of code switching exchanges leads to the conclusion that members have their own socially defined notions of code or grammatical system. Although such notions are often substantially different from those derived through linguistic analysis or taught in standard grammars, it is nevertheless clear that in situations such as we have discussed, effective speaking presupposes sociolinguistically based inferences about where systemic boundaries lie. Speakers rely on these notions to categorize and lump together sets of grammatical rules at various levels of structure, to relate speech to nonlinguistic environment and to generate indirect conversational inferences.

In addition to its linguistic significance, code switching provides evidence for the existence of underlying, unverbalized assumptions about social categories, which differ systematically from overtly expressed values or attitudes. It suggests empirical methods for studying the working of such symbols and the role they play in persuasion and rhetorical effectiveness. More detailed studies of conversational processes along these lines might bridge the gap between macro- and micro-analysis by providing insights into the functioning of broader social concepts in interpersonal relations.

Note

This analysis was completed in 1976. Since that time, a number of detailed empirical studies focusing on the syntactic constraints and on the stylistic significance of code switching have been completed, particularly for Latino Spanish-American discourse. These are discussed in detail in Duran (1981). Although a number of exceptions to the regularities reported here were noted, the basic finding that code switching is governed by grammatical rules and that it often does reflect interspeaker attitudes has been confirmed (Poplak 1981, Valdes 1981). The acquisition of code switching skills, moreover, seems to be governed by developmental constraints which are quite similar to those observed in the acquisition of the first language (Genishi 1981, McClure 1981).

References

Ausubel, N. 1948. *A Treasury of Jewish Folklore*. New York: Crown.

Bernstein, B. 1971. *Class, Codes and Control*. London: Routledge and Kegan Paul.

Blom, J. P. & Gumperz, J. J. 1972. Social meaning in linguistic structures. In *Directions in Sociolinguistics*, ed. J. J. Gumperz & D. Hymes. New York: Holt, Rinehart and Winston.

Brown, P. & Levinson, S. L. 1978. Universals in language usage: politeness phenomena. In *Questions and polite-ness*, ed. E. N. Goody. Cambridge: Cambridge University Press.

Duran, R.P. (ed.) 1981. *Latino Language and Communicative Behavior*. Norwood, NJ: Ablex.

Ervin-Tripp, S. & Mitchell-Kernan, C. 1977. *Child Discourse*. New York: Academic Press.

Ferguson, C. A. 1964. Diglossia. In *Language in Culture and Society*, ed. D. Hymes. New York: Harper and Row.

Fishman, J. 1972. *Language and Sociocultural Change*. Stanford, CA Stanford University Press.

Genishi, C. 1981. Codeswitching in Chicano six-year-olds. In *Latino Language and Communicative Behaviour*, ed. R. P. Duran. Norwood, NJ: Ablex.

Grice, P. 1975. Logic and conversation. In *Syntax and Semantics*, vol. 3, ed. P. Cole & J. Morgan. New York: Academic Press.

Gumperz, J. J. & Hernandez-Chavez, E. 1971. Bilingualism, bidialectalism and class-room interaction. In *The Functions of Language in the Class-Room*, ed. C. Cazden, V. John & D. Hymes. New York: Teachers College Press.

Haugen, E. 1973. Bilingualism, language contact and immigrant languages in the United States. In *Current Trends in Linguistics*, vol. 10, ed. T. Sebeok. The Hague: Mouton.

Kirschenblatt-Gimblett, B. 1971. Multilingualism and immigrant narrative. Ms.

Labov, W. 1971. The notion of "system" in Creole languages. In *Pidginization and Creolization of Languages*, ed. D. Hymes. Cambridge: Cambridge University Press.

Labov, W. 1973. *Language in the Inner City*. Philadelphia: University of Pennsylvania Press.

McClure, E. 1981. Formal and functional aspects of the codeswitched discourse of bilingual children. In *Latino Language and Communicative Behavior*, ed. R. P. Duran. Norwood, NJ: Ablex.

Poplak, S. 1981. Syntactic structure and social function of code-switching. In *Latino Language and Communicative Behavior*, ed. R. P. Duran. Norwood, NJ: Ablex.

Reyes, R. 1974. Studies in Chicano Spanish. Ms.

Sapir, E. 1921. *Language*. New York: Harcourt, Brace.

Timm, L. A. 1975. Spanish–English code switching: el porque y how-not-to. *Romance Philology*.

Trudgill, P. 1972. Sex, covert prestige and linguistic change. *Language in Society* 1(2): 179–96.

Valdes, G. 1981. Codeswitching as deliberate verbal strategy: a microanalysis of direct and indirect requests among bilingual Chicano speakers. In *Latino Language and Communicative Behavior*, ed. R. P. Duran. Norwood, NJ: Ablex.

Post-reading Questions / Activities

- Is code switching evidence of imperfect language mastery? Why does the answer to this question matter?
- How does the relative prestige of the two languages being considered affect how they are used? Are there regular patterns that can be discerned in terms of more local or more widespread languages?
- What does Gumperz mean when he says that "the direction of the shift may also have semantic value"?
- Observe and record bilinguals talking among themselves. What triggers code switching? Is it the same as or different from what Gumperz reports?

Vocabulary

bidialectalism	deictic	network analysis
borrowing	discourse analysis	pragmatic
code switching	loan word	semantic
conversational implicature	metaphorical code switching	situational code switching

Suggested Further Reading

Edwards, John R. 1994. *Multilingualism*. London and New York: Routledge.

Ferguson, Charles. 1972 [1959]. "Diglossia." In *Language and Social Context*, edited by Pier Paolo Giglioli, pp. 232–251. Middlesex, UK: Penguin Books.

Grosjean, François. 1982. *Life with Two Languages: An Introduction to Bilingualism*. Cambridge, MA: Harvard University Press.

Gumperz, John J. 1982. *Discourse Strategies*. Cambridge: Cambridge University Press.

Heller, Monica, ed. 1988. *Codeswitching: Anthropological and Sociolinguistic Perspectives*. Berlin and New York: Mouton de Gruyter.

Myers-Scotton, Carol. 1988. "Codeswitching as Indexical of Social Negotiations." In *Codeswitching: Anthropological and Sociolinguistic Perspectives*, edited by Monica Heller, pp. 151–186. Berlin and New York: Mouton de Gruyter.

Romaine, Suzanne. 1989. *Bilingualism*. New York: Blackwell.

Woolard, Kathryn. 1985. *Double Talk: Bilingualism and the Politics of Ethnicity in Catalonia*. Stanford, CA: Stanford University Press.

Zentella, Ana Celia. 1997. *Growing Up Bilingual: Children in El Barrio*. Malden, MA: Blackwell.

CHAPTER 19

Language Choice, Religion, and Identity in the Banarsi Community

Beth Simon

(1993)

India, the largest nation in the South Asian subcontinent, is characterized by a swirl of languages and cultures. Its precolonial linguistic situation was full of multilingualism; it was normal for individuals to know many languages, and to know how to switch from one to the other for a variety of functions and in a variety of situations. The official language of India is Hindi, but English is also widely used as a language of education, technology, business, and government (a legacy of colonialism). Twenty-two other languages are recognized as national languages in the constitution of India. Some states, further, recognize other languages as official languages.

Hindi is a descendant language of Sanskrit, the sacred language of India and the language in which Indian religious texts are written. It is an Indo-European language. (Not all languages in India are Indo-European.) Despite its status as the official language, not everybody can speak it. There is a standard variety of Hindi, but many speakers speak variants of it. Still, it holds a certain ideological importance.

Beyond officially recognized languages, however, there are many varieties that are used regularly even if they have no official status. (Charles Ferguson, in his seminal article "Diglossia," found that the Arabic vernaculars were so unofficial that people denied using them, even when he had taped them doing so!) Many have not been studied, and most are probably named, simply, the language of such-and-such a place.

In this selection, Beth Simon provides a snapshot of the complexity of the linguistic situation in the famous holy city of Banaras (also spelled Benares and Benaras, and now more frequently called Varanasi) located on the banks of the Ganges (Ganga) River. It is here, among the many colorful temples, that many people come to send off the dead, and Banaras is the frequent destination of pilgrims and tourists.

Language choice is connected to ethnic and regional identity, something brought with them when Indians move from one region to another. Banarsis, the long-time residents of Banaras, speak a local language, Banarsi Boli.

Religion also plays a role in ethnic identity; Hindus and Muslims have long lived side by side in India. Since partition of India into India and Pakistan in 1947, however, Indian Muslims have increasingly identified with the official language spoken in Pakistan—Urdu—though it is essentially identical to Hindi (the two "languages" are written with different scripts, however). But in people's understanding of the language they speak and their identity, Hindi and Urdu have differing roles.

One thing is perfectly clear from this account: it is impossible to know how many people speak a given language. The census relies on people's responses to questions, which are

Beth Simon, "Language Choice, Religion, and Identity in the Banarsi Community." In *Living Banaras: Hindu Religion in Cultural Context*, edited by Bradley R. Hertel and Cynthia Ann Humes. Buffalo: State University of New York Press, 1993, pp. 245–268. Reprinted by permission from *Living Banaras: Hindu Religion in Cultural Context*, edited by Bradley R. Hertel and Cynthia Ann Humes, the State University of New York Press © 1993, State University of New York. All rights reserved.

interpreted in wildly varying ways. Experts change their categories (sometimes treating sepa-rately and sometimes together "dialects" of major languages), and respondents have varying interpretations of what "mother tongue" means.

Simon gives an account of the many social features of language and how people think and talk about their multiple linguistic resources. Having lived among a variety of people for a period of time, she tells stories of how these people actually used their multiple languages, often switching within a single interaction, and sometimes within a sentence. Relying on the notion of "code switching" as introduced by John Gumperz (see Chapter 18) and Suzanne Romaine, Simon ends with examples of code switching among Banarsis, both conscious and uncon-scious, showing the identities and attitudes associated with each linguistic code. The switch from one code to another brings with it moral, religious, and social meaning.

Reading Questions

- What languages are spoken by Banarsi Hindus? Banarsi Muslims?
- What is Bhojpuri? Who speaks it? What is its relationship to Banarsi Boli?
- What are some views of Hindi? Why would Hindus want to emphasize that they speak it?
- What is the relationship between educational level and dominant language? How does this vary between men and women?

The language in common use [in Banaras] is Bihaarii which is spoken by 90% of the population, while Western Hindi (chiefly Hindustani) is spoken by 7%.

—(*Imperial Gazetteer, Varanasi District, 1908*)

Varanasi is a polyglot city, but the majority of the…population of the district speaks Bhoj-puri, and even the educated people speak it in their homes. The number of such persons is included in the figure of Hindi-speaking people which, calculated on the basis of the census of 1951, is 87.5 percent.

—(*Uttar Pradesh Census, District Gazetteer of Varanasi, 1965*)

THE COMPLEXITY OF BANARAS

Banaras has always been a city of language. Some of the oldest continuously inhabited urban sites on earth, even today, the original areas of Banaras are composed of "pock-ets of ethnicity" (Sinha and Saraswati, 1978), concentra-tions of people with antecedents from regions or ethnic groups throughout South Asia. Demographically, most of original Banaras is divided into neighborhoods (*muhal-las*) known informally by linguistic or ethnic labels asso-ciated with the origin of the residents. Streets and alleys often define regional or ethnic borders.[1] A walk through the older areas of Banaras may take one from a Nepali-speaking area to a Gujarati enclave centered around a temple, or from the Tamil neighborhood fragrant with roasting coffee beans into the substantial and influential Bengali section.[2]

Banaras has its own community of native Banarsis, who live in neighborhoods infacing those of outside lan-guage groups. Like the others, this community too has its own local language, Banarsi Boli. In this study, a family was considered "Banarsi" if it had been based in Banaras for at least three generations and had a sense that Banaras was its home place.[3] This means that the Banarsi community is both

Hindu and Muslim, and hence is demographically divided within itself along religious lines.

THE BANARSI COMMUNITY AND BANARSI BOLI, THE SPEECH OF BANARAS

Traditionally, Banarsis, both Hindus and Muslims, have been the people who provide the services and produce the goods that are basic to the socioeconomic foundation of the city as a Hindu pilgrimage site, as a center for ritual and practice, and as a tourist draw. Banarsis make their living from "sacred" Banaras by performing rituals, poling boats on the Ganga for tourists and pilgrims, performing classical and semi-classical music, and fashioning objects from the materials traditionally associated with Banaras, for instance, the silk brocades and brass.[4]

A common language, Banarsi Boli, and a common eco-nomic ground make a Banarsi community distinct from other linguistic or ethnic groups in Banaras. Banarsis talk to each other, within and across religious lines, in Banarsi Boli. Banarsis are identified by others in Banaras by their lan-guage, and most Banarsis claim their speech as part of who they are. Banarsi Hindus claim to speak Hindi, and many do use regional standard Hindi. Increasingly, Banarsi Muslims claim Urdu, and again, because of education being allowed or provided in Urdu, many are Urdu speakers. Nonetheless, whatever other speech they use, Banarsi Hindus and Muslims are related in the same way that they differ from the others, including the Hindi and Urdu speakers, around them.[5] Banarsis use language to identify themselves, and alternate between languages to structure discourse and to convey differences between themselves.

The presence and influence of Hindi and Urdu means that Banarsis are a bilingual group. There has been stable bilingualism within the Banarsi community over an extended period of time. Because much of Banaras economic life is still largely based on pilgrimage, ritual performances, and tourism, most Banarsis who are employed outside their immediate neighborhoods, especially in any service capacity, are actively bilingual in regional Hindi. Although not all Banarsis speak Hindi with grammatical accuracy, "street" fluency is common, and most are able to interact appropriately in situations where Hindi is the dominant language.[6] One participates in Hindi situations by inserting formulaic and idiomatic phrases. Adept Banarsi monolinguals "Hindi-ize" their speech (just as local Hindi speakers "Banarsi-ize" their speech) by substituting better-known parallel features of one language for the other.

The following anecdote demonstrates nicely how, especially for some Hindus, being part of the Banarsi speech community can result in an interesting dynamic between Banarsi Hindu identity and Hindi language association. A Hindu male friend invited to me to sit with his father, a brahmin astrologer[7] and a man of standing in his neighborhood. Several mornings a week, neighbors and friends would come to their front room, where the astrologer would recite verses, direct conversation, make charts, provide refreshment, and offer insights. Earlier, my friend had stressed that his father, a "true" (*pakka*) Banarsi, spoke only "pure" (*shuud*) Hindi, but since I seemed to be taping everyone else they knew, his father had decided I should tape him as well.

On the morning in question, we sat at the front of the room, closely observed by a group of neighbors. We began in Hindi. I offered my standard opening, "When did your family first come to Banaras?" and he replied

Ham log to banaaras aaye kariib DeRh sau varsh.
(we [plural morph] then came to Banaras about a hundred and fifty years ago)

HunDreD phiphTi iyars baek ham log aaye the.
(hundred fifty years back we [plural morph] came.)

"As for us, we came to Banaras about a hundred and fifty years ago. A hundred and fifty years back, we came here."

His reply, code-switching between Hindi and English, both with Banarsi Boli phonology, was an efficient social statement. He indicated that he knew English, that I knew Hindi, and that he was a true Banarsi. He continued speaking in

Hindi for over an hour, commenting on neighborhood *Ramlilas*, and explaining how illness and death have been defeated in Banaras. He brought each topic to touch on religious practice or ethics, and he adorned his conversation with appropriate verses from *shastras* (Hindu law books) and Tulsidas. Several times the room echoed with "Wah! Wah!" when a verse was particularly fitting and the diction beautiful. Finally, he inquired whether there was anything else I wanted to know, and I asked why he hadn't spoken in Banarsi Boli. The following was said in Hindi.

"Banarsi Boli, what is that?"
"Isn't it the speech (*bhasha*) of Banaras?"
"The bhasha of Kashi is Hindi."
Giggles in the room. I'm nonplused. His son is my field worker, so he knows quite well what I'm talking about.
"But, isn't there another bhasha people use around here?"
Long pause, then: "Do you mean Bhojpuri?"
"Yes, exactly, the Banaras style of Bhojpuri." And in Banarsi Boli he says: "Bhojpuri is the language of Bihar. Here we don't speak Bhojpuri. We don't even understand it." Everybody laughs and then we all have tea.

Bhojpuri is an Indo-Aryan language with five main variants.[8] The *Linguistic Survey of India* (*LSI*; Grierson, 1901, 1903, 1904) recognized Banarsi Boli as a distinct dialect of Western Bhojpuri,[9] particular to "Banaras City." Later official publications confirm the *LSI* recognition, although some change the language label. The 1908 *Imperial Gazetteer* calls it "Bihaarii,"[10] and the 1965 *District Gazetteer* calls it "Banarsi Boli," reiterating that it is a "western counterpart of Bhojpuri." The 1965 *Gazetteer* states that (Banarsi) Bhojpuri is the first language, or home/neighborhood variety, or "mother tongue" of the Banaras community. (See opening quotes.)

To the west, the Banaras district is contiguous with a variety of Eastern Hindi known as Awadhi.[11] In all other directions Banaras district conjoins areas of the other Bhojpuri dialects. More important than geography, however, is the fact that Banaras lies within the historical and political purview of what has become regional standard Hindi. Banarsi Boli has, over time, come to exhibit phonological and grammatical features similar to regional standard Hindi,[12] and thus it has become increasingly unlike other Bhojpuri varieties. These linguistic changes are a product of ongoing complex language contact, and the noticeable points of similarity between Hindi and Banarsi Boli have encouraged a sense that Banarsi Boli is "a kind of Hindi."

Historically, Banaras has been a center for Sanskrit preservation and learning.[13] Beginning early in [the twentieth] century, Banaras became a base for the Hindi national language movement.[14] The lexicon for this consciously developed Hindi was derived, directly or indirectly, from Sanskrit. Today, modern standardized Hindi is more than a partially engineered linguistic variety. It is a sociopolitical entity, one with which many local Banarsi Hindus identify.[15] For a Hindu, identification with regional standard Hindi may mean self-identification as a Hindi speaker and a perception of Banaras as part of the Hindi regional language area. There is strong motivation for this view. Such identification carries with it potential political and economic benefits that do not follow from being a Banarsi Boli speaker.

The converse association has occurred as well in Banaras. Because Sanskrit is a hallmark of Hinduism, and Hindi is associated with Sanskrit, Hindi has come to be associated with Hindu, particularly educated Hindu, identity. Finally, there has been a third effect, less obvious but pervasive nonetheless. Insofar as Banarsi Hindus identify themselves with Hindi, Banarsi Boli is then identified with Banarsi Hindus.[16]

LANGUAGE, RELIGION, BILINGUALISM, AND THE CENSUS

For a number of reasons, the Census of India has never been a reliable source for language data. Documentation of mother tongue claims or of multiple language use has often been vitiated by political and bureaucratic definitions of "language." These definitions change from one decade to the next.

Until the 1961 census, in Banaras as elsewhere in India, all "Urdu" responses were merged with "Hindustani" or "Hindi," and consequently any correlation between Urdu and Muslims was obscured. Beginning with the 1961 census, Urdu responses were recorded separately. Since 1961, the number of recorded Urdu speakers has steadily increased, and identification of Banarsi Muslims with Urdu language has become much more explicit.[17] The 1971 census count for mother tongue in Banaras showed a 300 percent increase in reported Urdu speakers.

On the other hand, while the number of reported Urdu speakers has become more accurate, the number of individuals who speak languages not listed in Schedule VIII of the Constitution of India, and the number of bilingual or multilingual speakers reported, is now far less accurate than previously. This loss is due to changes in language definitions. The *Census of India* for 1981 (*Varanasi District Handbook*, 1987: 1.1) expanded the parameters of Schedule VIII languages such that twenty-eight speech varieties previously considered separate were included within, and hence not named or counted separately from, the official languages. For instance, the 1981 census called "Hindi" what had been eighteen other varieties. Bhojpuri was one of the eighteen languages now called "Hindi." Bhojpuri was considered to have anywhere from sixty to seventy million speakers.[18] As of the 1981 census, any response naming Bhojpuri, including Banarsi Boli, was officially counted as "Hindi." These new definitions provide for a radical decrease in the number of mother tongue labels recorded, and ultimately in the number of bilinguals.

The Banaras Urdu returns of 1981 were recorded separately, but here too, there were still potential problems. The instructions were not clear as to whether "Urdu" was recorded only when the respondent was Muslim but not when Hindu. Again, if a Muslim responded with a variety other than "Urdu" but included under "Hindi," the census taker may well have recorded "Hindi."

The 1981 census created millions of monolingual mother tongue Hindi speakers. In Banaras this meant that a fairly representative number of Muslims returned themselves as Urdu speakers, and all others, by and large, were returned as Hindi speakers.

Since most other languages in which a Banarsi might be bilingual were officially considered Hindi, almost no one was returned as bilingual.[19] In fact, though, whatever the census instructions, few individuals reported themselves as bilingual. In 1951, census takers were specifically instructed to ask about multiple language use. The data show that only 1.2 percent of the urban population reported themselves as bilingual. Of those who did, almost 98 percent claimed "Hindi/Hindustani/Urdu" as the second language. The censuses of 1961 and of 1971 each show "Bhojpuri" responses increasing, but the absolute number was still very small.

Coincidentally, what the census recorded for Banarsis may reflect their own view. Most Banarsis simply do not see themselves as either monolingual Banarsi Boli or Bhojpuri speakers. Nor do they see themselves as bilinguals. Although most Banarsis have Banarsi Boli either as their first language or alternate language, few Banarsis, Hindu or Muslim, female or male, give "language" status to Banarsi Boli. Almost no one associates himself or herself with "Bhojpuri." This denial is interesting, because it is of language label and language status, not of that individual's actual use or association with use.

GENDER, RELIGION, AND LINGUISTIC IDENTITY

Language label and status are sociocultural considerations, and among Banarsis, as elsewhere, formal affirmation of them appears to be influenced by gender, and hence, education level. In urban Banaras overall literacy rates are higher than in the rest of the district (and are very high compared with the rest of Uttar Pradesh), but literacy rates for Banarsi females are well under those for males. The 1981 census showed not only substantially lower literacy rates for urban Banaras females than males, but also a far lower number of females educated past the primary levels.

Throughout Uttar Pradesh, public education from primary level on is provided in Hindi,[20] and at the secondary level Hindi is either the only medium of instruction or is a compulsory offering as a language along with English.[21] One can assume, then, that an individual's level of formal education is a good indicator of access to and identification with standardized Hindi. Since the number of Banarsi females educated past the primary level is far below that of males,[22] uneducated Banarsi females tend to be monolingual Banarsi Boli speakers, and to see themselves as speakers of a lesser, nonstandardized localized dialect.[23] I spent an afternoon recording a group of Banarsi Boli–speaking women of a low-caste group geographically isolated within Banaras.

They told me repeatedly that they didn't know "good" or "real" Hindi, and that their own speech did not have a formal name because it was particular to their group. When I asked whether they thought their speech and Hindi were related, they said that what they spoke was "like Hindi" but different, and that it was not what most people speak. These women were typical of most of the Hindu women with whom I spent time. Most said the language they spoke was Banarsi Boli.[24]

The Hindu males with whom I had contact represented themselves quite differently. No matter how accurately or frequently they spoke Hindi, most of the adult Hindu males whom I knew identified themselves as Hindi speakers. Those who claimed a second "language" usually named English, not Banarsi Boli or Urdu as that language. Of interest here is that almost every Hindu male said that, at least part of the time, Banarsi Boli was used at home. Every Hindu male I asked said that Muslims spoke Urdu (although several who made this statement had no close, informal contact with Muslims).

Most Banarsi males are educated beyond primary level. Since second language education begins at secondary level, most Banarsi males receive formal education both in Hindi and in a second language.[25] Education beyond primary level, a male domain, is both *in* Hindi and *of* Hindi. Hence, there is a strong institutionalized basis for Hindu males to identify with Hindi. Among my own acquaintances, most of the Hindu males said they spoke Banarsi Boli, but few claimed to be Banarsi Boli speakers. They said Banarsi Boli was a "dear" or "special" or "home" speech they used with loved ones, at the tea stalls, with close friends, among Banarsis.

MUSLIMS, BANARSI IDENTITY, AND BANARSI BOLI

There are those who assert a strong association with Banaras, but not with "Banarsi" identity. I was acquainted with a Muslim tailor (*darzi*). He spoke his language and I spoke my university Hindi-Urdu which I adapted with Banarsi Boli verb endings, lexical items, and phonology. One day without my asking, he invited me to his house, saying that his family had lived in Banaras for several generations and I should tape them. I was complimented but surprised, and said that I hadn't realized he was a "true" (*pakka*) Banarsi. After a silence he said, "I am not a pakka Banarsi. I am a Muslim. Pakka Banarsis," he said enunciating clearly, "are milkmen and thieves."

His response was a sophisticated and complex insult to Hindus. Because the products of the cow are sacred, dairy people in Banaras are a particular caste, and, as most Banaras residents know, some dairy people water the milk. According to the Muslim's insult, milkmen are Banarsis, and milkmen are thieves. Since milkmen are Hindus, Hindus are Banarsis, and Hindus are thieves.

The tailor made another point with this insult. In daily life, this man spoke the same language as his neighbors, Muslim or Hindu. He and his family were not Banarsis, however; they were Muslims. This suggests that within the local Muslim community it is the Hindus of Banaras who are the recognized Banarsis.

HINDI AND BANARSI BOLI: ALTERNATE LANGUAGES

Diglossia

Going around public Banaras—at the bazaars, in shops, around temples, on ghats—one commonly hears Banarsi Boli and Hindi used in alternation; that is, people alternate between languages depending on the participants, topic, and function. This pattern of language alternation is called "diglossia."

Diglossia names a situation in which two languages coexist with an almost symmetrical relation between each language and the function or social context in which that language is used. This type of functional or contextual specialization is related to the status of each language.

Throughout the plains of northern India east of Bengal, Hindi is the major regional language; it is standardized and has a fairly extensive, recognized body of written literature. It also has a higher explicit social prestige. Hindi is the language medium of public school. Finally, Hindi is, with English, the official national language. It is the language of public life, public education, and public politics.[26]

In Banaras, it stands in contrast to Banarsi Boli, which is not standardized, has little formal literary tradition, and has a lower explicit social value (see Ferguson, 1972).

Expanding the concept of diglossia to include stylistic register means that in Banaras Hindi is the language choice for formal or official public events and for nonlocally based workplaces such as civil service and quasi-government offices. Because it is the regional lingua franca, Hindi can serve as the neutral choice for interchanges between new acquaintances, for people who are not members of the same first language group, or for those who are socially unequal and meeting in formal situations.

Language alternation between Hindi and Banarsi Boli expresses language-function relations specific to Banaras. I was invited to the home of a Banaras Sanskrit University–educated Brahmin whose family had held controlling interest in one of the most important temples in Banaras. Beside fulfilling his priestly duties, he also performed at home as a Tantric. When I arrived he was seated on the floor conversing in Banarsi Boli with a mother and daughter from whom an object had been stolen.[27]

The mother requested the Tantric to use his power to discover the thieves and restore the object, and the daughter made an offering of coconut and sweets. The Tantric began his *puja* (worship), reciting in Sanskrit and in Hindi with Sanskrit case endings. Then he became possessed. Rocking and calling, he invited his goddess, praised her, propitiated her, and commanded her, all in Banarsi Boli. Finally, snatching up the coconut and smashing it on the floor, he ceased being possessed. He reported the goddess's judgment and distributed *prasad* (food blessed by the deity), and his clients left. We two then sat on chairs, and with great courtesy he told me his life story in flowing regional standard Hindi.

Banarsi Boli and Hindi Within the Hindu Family

Especially in educated or higher-caste Hindu families, both Banarsi Boli and Hindi are part of a shared family speech repertoire, each used to signal subtle notes of intimacy, respect, and hierarchy. In these households, intrafamily relations are incorporated and expressed partially through language alternation. For instance, Banarsi Boli will be used between grandson and grandmother, and Hindi between the same boy and his father. If the family includes daughters-in-law originating from outside Banaras and their mother-in-law is a Banarsi Boli speaker, then the incoming females learn Banarsi Boli and in turn pass it to their children. Within the household, adult males use Banarsi Boli with females but Hindi with nonadult males, particularly once they reach school age. Thus, Banarsi Boli is maintained in the family while at the same time Hindi is confirmed as the language of educated males. My impression is that in educated and upper-caste Hindu families Banarsi Boli is maintained across generations through female use.

Code-Switching with Banarsi Boli and Hindi

Among Banarsi bilinguals, one finds not only diglossia but also "code-switching," and these are different in important ways (see Romaine, 1989:111). In Banaras, Hindi of one sort or another has been used on an everyday basis both by outsiders and by Banarsi Boli speakers for at least two centuries. The result is that the speech repertoire of most Banarsi Boli Hindus includes a Hindi end of the verbal spectrum. This is evidenced in code-switching between Hindi and Banarsi Boli.

Code-switching is "the juxtaposition within the same speech exchange of passages of speech belonging to two different grammatical systems or subsystems" (Gumperz, 1982:59). Romaine expands on how code-switching works. "In code-switched discourse, the items in question form part of the same speech act. They are tied together prosodically as well as by semantic and syntactic relations equivalent to those that join passages in a single speech act" (Romaine, 1989:111). Code-switching, then, is a linguistic phenomenon and is structurally different from diglossia, a social phenomenon. Both have become means of passing, incorporating, and expressing community and religious identity.

In Banaras, code-switching is common. One type of code-switching is "intrasentential." In this type, a speaker switches between Hindi and Banarsi Boli within a sentence boundary. Intrasentential code-switching is evidence that functional specialization, a hallmark of diglossia, has been naturalized into a unified Banarsi speech repertoire. For many bilingual Banarsis, Hindi and Banarsi Boli exist in a

linguistic continuum and language choice is a matter of stylistics and discourse functions conditioned by shared social norms.

Code-Switching in a Stable Multilingual Community

Bilingual Banarsis have open to them more strategies for conversational interactions than do monolinguals. Each language choice can be a device for structuring discourse, controlling focus, and guiding interpretation and response. Unconscious, spontaneous code-switching is a natural expression of who one is. Conscious, controlled code-switching is a ready means for exploiting shared group background. Gumperz makes the point that dialect differences can "serve both as reflections of indices of social identity and as symbols of shared cultural background…[S]uch symbols serve as effective carriers of information and powerful means of persuasion" (Gumperz, 1978:401). It is in the daily acts of dual language use, and of code-switching in particular, that we see how both Hindi and Banarsi Boli are "effective carriers of" social and cultural "information" for Banarsis. "If conversational inference depends on shared social presuppositions, and if conversational continuity is a function of the success of such inferences, then the mere fact that two speakers can sustain an interaction over time is evidence for the existence of at least some common level of social knowledge and agreement on interpretation" (Gumperz, 1978:401)

In order to investigate just how Banarsi Boli and Hindi function together, the rest of this chapter will examine two acts of code-switching. These two examples are typical of daily, informal conversation among Banarsi bilinguals. They have the same primary situational features: Hindu males who have a long-standing relation with each other. The first case provides a typical example of bilingual behavior in a community where multiple language use is common and unremarkable. The second case differs primarily because the person controlling the discourse uses code-switching to focus attention on languages and cultural features associated with them. By consciously code-switching, the speaker controls participant response in order to draw a relation between religious identity and Banarsi identity.

Hindu Males Pass the Time of Day: Unmarked Code-Switching

In Banaras, Hindi and Banarsi Boli are used in rapid alternation within a sentence boundary. This intrasentential code-switching occurs within the body of the sentence itself, or between the main part and the "tag"—phrases such as "isn't it," "and then," and so on. Code-switching at these points is typical of informal, spontaneous conversation. In the first conversation, intrasentential code-switching separates what the participants know as "facts" from what the speaker says about those facts. The code-switching itself differentiates these discourse functions, and each speech variety is assigned a function.[28]

The conversation is between two Brahmin males, twenty-four and thirty, educated beyond secondary level, and married. These men are friends, neighbors, and cousins. The immediate topic is the convalescence of a popular and wealthy film star, Amitabh Bacchan, who has suffered extensive injuries in a motorcycle accident. In this portion, one man speculates on the star's medical treatment.

Banarsi Boli
    aitnaa siriiyas rahal, na, u ta, sunaat rahal
(It was so serious, wasn't it then I heard)

    "It [=the accident] was so serious, that I heard"

Hindi
    ki agar yahaã nahĩ hogaa, to
(that if it [=the operation] doesn't happen here, then)

    "that if the operation can't be done here, then"

    londan jaayegaa, ruus jaayegaa.
he will [may] go to London, he will [may] go to Russia)

    "he'll go to London, he'll go to Russia."

Banarsi Boli
    u, ta, prashan hau ki, paisa hau
(he, then, this is the question, he has money)

    "The point is—he's got the money!"

    ta, kahĩ bhii ja sakelaa, ar-e
(then, wherever ! he is able to go, EXCLAMATION)

    "He can go wherever he damn well wants!"

The following is mixed, with expressive, noncontent words in Banarsi Boli, and content words in Hindi.

    u ta jitna kharch lagii
(that then however much it costs [treatment and recuperation])

    "Whatever the costs are,"

    utna ta aik sinemaa mẽ u khaam karke nikaal lagii."
(that much comes out of the work in one film)

    "that much is what comes out of making just one film."

The commentary is in Banarsi Boli, for example: "It [=the accident] was so serious [*siriiyas*—occurs as a naturalized item]" and "Here's the point: money. He can go anywhere [with a Banarsi exclamation *ar-e*]." Naming actual locations and details about the actor's income, what pass here for facts, are in Hindi: "He will/could go to London, He will/could go to Russia." The speaker puts the point or "moral" of the story in Hindi with Banarsi Boli demonstrative adjectives and fillers: "Whatever it costs, he makes that much from working in one film."

Here are two Banarsis, passing the time of day. They talk movies, they talk politics, they talk weddings and prices, and the way they do it involves unself-conscious code-switching.[29] Neither participant is explicitly demonstrating or asserting anything about himself to the other. The above speaker code-switches because it is part of who he is: a fluent, unself-conscious bilingual. The code-switch-

ing pattern demonstrates that both Hindi and Banarsi Boli are deeply embedded in the social speech repertoire of these two participants.[30] It is an essential part of the unconscious knowledge that bilingual Banarsi community members share about how to talk with each other.[31]

Romaine holds that intrasentential code-switching involves "the greatest syntactic risk, and may be avoided by all but the most fluent bilinguals" (1989:113). The frequency with which intrasentential code-switching occurs in the informal conversation between Banarsi bilinguals is strong evidence that bilingualism itself is common, accepted. It is a basic characteristic of Banarsi identity.[32] It is natural, unself-conscious code-switching which occurs as a part of natural, unself-conscious speech acts. Such code-switching appears to be a stable feature of conversational interaction among Banarsis, and as such it is indicative of the positive (albeit often covert) value of Banarsi identity.[33]

Marked Code-Switching: A Performed Narrative in Ordinary Conversation

Another type of code-switching is the intentional shifting of languages within conversation for strategic purposes. Structurally, this type of code-switching occurs at sentence or clause boundaries; this is called "intersentential" code-switching. Such switches assume fluency in separate linguistic codes *as* separate codes. Intersentential code-switching seems to be more conscious and can be used to manipulate conversation and focus participants on a particular issue or point of view. What underlies significant code-switching in a close social group is a deep agreement, a commonality, in the way participants use language to signal "cultural presuppositions." Given that agreement, known differences can be exploited. The different languages the group shares are marked for sociocultural differences and thus can be used as reminders of in-group membership and its consequent obligations. Hindi–Banarsi Boli code-switching stands out among bilingual Banarsis when code-switches point to a pertinent shared social norm. Group interaction utilizing language differences depends on this deep agreement.

In this second example, the speaker's confidence in his use of code-switching depends on sharing the same speech repertoire with his audience, one in which Banarsi Boli and Hindi stand not as separate languages per se but as symbols of social norms. The following is part of a long conversation that took place on a weekday morning in a side street in an old Banarsi neighborhood near the ghats. In this piece, the two verbally active participants are Hindu males. Both are mother tongue Banarsi Boli speakers. The dominant speaker is an older man. He is the launderer (*dhobi*) for most of the present group. The other is upper caste, in his mid-twenties, and employed in a government office. The younger man comes from a household in which both Banarsi Boli and Hindi are the home speech. He has been educated through college in a Hindi-language medium. The launderer, without any formal education, knows Hindi in the same way that most uneducated Banarsi males in service occupations know it. These two participants directly address only each other.

In this portion, the launderer complains to his audience about the vicissitudes in his business caused by the growing popularity of polyester blend fabrics. The launderer then tells about his stay in Delhi. He says that he lived in Delhi for one year, and he worked for a Muslim employer in a dry-cleaning establishment.

The Lead-in: The Economic Situation. The laundryman tells his audience how things have changed in the laundry business over the years.

> Earlier, everyone, like your family [=the younger man's], had dhobis take care of their clothes. Nowadays of course we're in great demand during the festival season. Everyone gets new clothes, they want their clothes pressed, and we have a lot of work. I'm very busy right now, but later, well, you understand, I don't know. Will there be work later? Well, brother, I don't know.

The other man asks what has changed. The launderer says that these days, people buy much more terrycot.[34] Worse, people now do more of their own daily washing. It is only at festival time that all the old clients, "like you brother, come looking for me. At festival times, you understand," but not, it is implied, at other times.

The Lead-in: Employment in Delhi. The launderer says that ten years earlier he had gone to Delhi. He points to his iron, a heavy brass implement, and gives a local equivalent for "have brass iron, will travel." In Delhi, he says, the traditional social and economic relationships based on kinship and caste are missing. Everyone is a stranger, without kin. One is on one's own. The launderer says:

> I worked for a Muslim employer, you know; he was a Muslim, a Muslim, in a Muslim neighborhood. He paid me 300 rupees, this employer a Muslim you understand.[35]

In Banaras, by contrast, laundry charges are a set amount per piece of clothing. The younger man asks about this 300 rupees. Wasn't the launderer paid by the piece?

Launderer: No, brother, this [wage arrangement] was for time. I worked from eight in the morning until six in the evening.

The younger man suggests that those hours aren't so good.

Launderer: Understand that at twelve [noon] there was a two-hour break, you know two to three hours.
Younger man: I understand, you were at the employer's for two to three hours a day, and you were someplace else for two to three hours.
Launderer: Yes.

Younger man: Given that much *break*,[36] well, doing ironing here, do you get more money or less?
Launderer: No, you can't explain it like that. Here, there's housekeeping, I have children, things cost. There, I was alone. There I had 300 rupees, from this employer, a Muslim you understand. Here, I set up in that park across the way, and I send my little girls around [to pick up and drop off the clothes]. They don't go to school, they can't read. *We're* not literate people you know.
Younger man: Okay fine. But what I mean is, if you worked for about four hours here, then how much can you make?
Launderer: Okay, let's say I do ironing for about four hours. Then, brother, understand, that I've gotten maybe 10 rupees.
Younger man: By that account, you earned less *there*, right?
Launderer: All right, maybe, but look, that was ten years ago. And that doesn't tell the story. At that time, 300 rupees was adequate (or serviceable).
Younger man: Yet, you left?

The Story

Launderer: Well, I got a letter. They [=the family] asked me to come back. I had this letter. I returned to Banaras, to here. I have a household you understand, I have children.
Younger man: You mean, the work there was finished.
Launderer: No, the work wasn't finished. There was work there. But my household was here. The [Delhi] employer didn't want to permit me to return here.

The launderer then reconstructs the final conversation between himself, a Banarsi Hindu, and his employer, a Delhi Muslim. The launderer presents the narrative framing utterances ("then I said to the employer," "then the employer said") in Banarsi Boli. The signal for the shift from frame to direct speech is the transitional conjunction *ki*, "that." The launderer gives the Delhi employer's speech within the body of the narrative in Hindi.

The Launderer Performs His Narrative

Banarsi Boli—launderer
   bahut jabrii kailii maalik se ki hame ek haptaa me cal aiib
   "I said very firmly to the employer, 'in one week I will leave.' "
Banarsi Boli
   Ta u kahe,

"Then the employer said,"

Hindi—Delhi employer
Nahīī, mat jaao Ihaa kaam kaun karegaa?
'No, don't go. Who will do the work here?'

Banarsi Boli—launderer
Ham kahilii, Ham ruukbe na karab.
"I said, 'I won't stay.'"

Hindi—Delhi employer
Nahīī, mat jaao. Ihaa kaam hau.[37]
'No, don't go. There is work here.'

Banarsi Boli—launderer
Ta bahut jabrii maalik se kahalii, Cal aiib.
"Then I said quite firmly to the employer, 'I will go.'"

At this point the launderer returns to indirect speech and finishes his story in Banarsi Boli.

> Then the employer said a lot of things to me. Then he allowed me to leave. Later, I got a letter from him. You know, he asked me to come back.

What Does the Launderer Accomplish? As represented by the launderer, the Delhi Muslim's pleas, given in the simplest Hindi, are notably repetitious within the dialogue itself, and some are nearly identical to the launderer's direct interchange with the younger man, for instance, "there is work here"—"there was work there." The employer is presented as the alien because he appears to speak Hindi, and the repetitions then mark his speech as significant.

Earlier the launderer had reminded the younger man that they have a long-standing relation, one that has never been strictly that of employer-employee. He notes his own obligations, mentioning specifically his young children. As a Hindu husband and father, in a group of Hindu husbands and fathers, there is no need to mention the rest of the extended family. This juxtaposition of topics—changes in laundry patterns against his children's illiteracy—should prod the younger man into agreeing that he too has certain *moral* obligations which in the past have been fulfilled by giving the launderer work. No one challenges the launderer's inference: in Delhi, work was plentiful, money was easy, and he had a choice many of them never have had. The launderer uses his performed narrative to articulate his personal grievance with the younger man and to extend it to include the others.

The launderer's switch from Banarsi Boli to Hindi helps move the discourse from conversation to drama. The status quo is no longer identified with Banarsi Boli. In the story, it is *outside* the community, *away* from Banarsis, that the launderer is treated as he should have been at home. By presenting the Delhi dialogue as direct speech, in "Hindi," the launderer uses code-switches to signal identities based on religion as social grouping. He can then make a moral point, to the detriment of the entire audience.

The insertion of Hindi into a Banarsi Boli conversation lets the launderer call upon an attitude regarding Hindi: a Hindi speaker is not a Banarsi. A Banarsi speaks Banarsi Boli. Therefore the Hindi speaker must be the outsider.

Yet it is the outsider, someone without social or cultural or traditional or familial ties to the narrator, who offers a fair, generous arrangement. This is the pivot upon which the narrator turns the moral of his story. The means by which he establishes his moral superiority is language alternation in a performance. The launderer makes his audience watch while he once again chooses family over personal independence, group over individual, Banaras over Delhi, Hindu over Muslim. He does this when he performs the Muslim outsider in Hindi, and himself—the Hindu, the home, the family, "Banaras"—in Banarsi Boli.[38]

For Banarsis, Banarsi Boli and Hindi are available as flexible metaphors. The potential for such use is present in the Banarsi bilingual situation. The launderer calls on shared cultural knowledge that Banarsi Boli and Hindi can be "marked" as symbols of a fundamental division in Indian culture: Hindu and Muslim. In this instance, Banarsi Boli and Hindi function as metaphors for belonging and otherness. The launderer uses code-switching to insist on the interdependency of Banarsi Hindus and the responsibility such interdependency implies.

THE SIGNIFICANCE OF LANGUAGE CHOICE AMONG BANARSI-BOLI SPEAKERS

These two examples demonstrate different aspects of the bilingual situation in the Banarsi community. In both instances, code-switching is used as a structuring device. In the second case, however, it allows the speaker to assert a set of rights and obligations that, he implies, are particularly Hindu. This suggests three things. First, there is a defined set of relations between linguistic choices in the shared speech repertoire and the outer, social manifestations of these choices. Second, speakers "know" this. Third, this knowledge can be used by virtue of the equation between religious identity and social group.

The very commonness of code-switching in this bilingual community indicates that the relation between language choice and language function is integral to the norms for language use. Code-switching structures spontaneous, informal conversation. Therefore, we must assume that it is embedded in a deep cultural knowledge.

Notes

The research upon which this article is based was conducted in Banaras (Varanasi) between 1981 and 1982 and was funded by the American Institute for Indian Studies and the National Science Foundation. The data were collected by tape-recording largely unstructured, spontaneous conversation. When I was a participant, I occasionally asked such questions as "When did your family first come to Banaras?" or "What changes have you seen here?" Otherwise no particular topic, style, features, or setting was disallowed. I did not use prepared questionnaires or survey instruments. At the time of the recording, participants were asked if I could tape them. I recorded in two types of situations. The first consisted of small groups of people (two to six) who normally got together, and they were taped at such a gathering—having tea, during the long afternoon hours on a street, in the courtyard. Participants were connected by kinship or marriage, friendship, or long-term work-related activity. There were forty-one participants, all over eighteen years old: twenty-two men and nineteen women. Thirteen men were over forty years old; nine were Hindi educated, one was Urdu educated; the others had primary level or less education. Only four of the twenty-two were not active in both Hindi or Urdu and Banarsi Boli. Eight of the nineteen women were over forty; two were Hindi educated, both under forty. Seven women were at least minimally active in Hindi as well as Banarsi Boli; six of those were under forty years old.

The author gratefully acknowledges all assistance given by the American Institute for Indian Studies and the individuals staffing the offices in Delhi and Ramnagar, particularly that of Mr. Pradeep Mehendiratta.

The author also wishes to acknowledge and thank her advisor, Professor Manindra K. Verma, for his interest, guidance, and patience. She would also like to thank Professor Sheela Verma, without whom she would not know Hindi.

All errors and faults in this article are the sole responsibility of the author.

1. This type of urban spatial isolation is conducive to maintenance over several generations of the residents' original language and culture. Simultaneously, because of proximity, shared markets, and so on, there is impetus to develop some facility with the languages of other neighborhoods. Neighborhoods, although fairly discrete, often interface.

2. The *Linguistic Survey of India* (Grierson, 1903:270) gives the following description of the languages in use by nonnative Banarsis.

   The city is, of course, largely inhabited by people from other parts of India, who speak corrupted forms of their mother-tongues, Panjabi, Gujarati, Marathi, Bengali. The influence is felt by the native inhabitants, and the true Benares language is every year becoming more and more uniform. Rather than being due to the influence of all the outside languages, it is much more likely that the increasing uniformity in Banarsi Boli noticed by the *Survey* is, even at that time, due to the influence of Hindi in the form of long-term and complex patterns Banarsis have had with Hindi speakers—both Awadhi dialect speakers and regional standard Hindi speakers.

3. Not all Banarsi families have been based in Banaras for more than three generations, and in many cases this geographic (re)location does not sever a family's ties with their earlier regional base. Banarsi families I knew had strong feeling for two home places: Banaras *as well as* their region of origin—Rajasthan, for instance—where members of the extended family still reside, and where the Banaras branch of the family may look for suitable marriage candidates.

4. More recently the children, especially males, from Banarsi families have gotten university-level degrees and gone into government and professional careers. But at the time of this research, most of the Banarsi families with whom I was acquainted still identified themselves in terms of caste, historical place of origin, religious considerations, and occupation.

5. I have tapes of interactions between Muslim and Hindu males who have known each other over time in a work situation. In each of these interactions, participants spoke Banarsi Boli. The data from those tapes show interesting differences in verb forms between the Hindu and the Muslim speakers, but I have no data that allow for correlation between speech and religious identity. This is not to say such evidence is not there. My method of finding participants for my research depended on getting to know a person who would then introduce me to another. Because my first contacts were with Hindus, I have far more material from Hindus than from Muslims. Furthermore, all Muslim participants were male.

6. See Dorian (1982). Anyone who has attended a Hindi-language film in an audience for whom Hindi is not the first language knows that almost everyone is following the story quite well. In Banaras and elsewhere in northern India, it is "filmy Hindi" rather than the regional standard Hindi of public education that appears in the local idiom.

7. He mentioned to me several times that he had never worked for money and he wanted me to remember that.

8. Bhojpuri, with Assamese, Bengali, Magahi, Maithili, and Oriya, are part of a language family labeled the "Eastern group" (Grierson, 1901) or "Magadhan group" (Chatterji, 1926) of the greater Indo-Aryan language grouping. Of these six, Bhojpuri is geographically the western-most language, and linguistically the most dissimilar to the others.

   The *LSI* divides Bhojpuri into "three main varieties,—the Standard [subdivided into Northern Standard and Southern Standard], the Western, and Nagpuria. It has also a border sub-dialect called Madhesi, and a broken form called Tharu…Western Bhojpuri is spoken in…Fyzabad, Azamgargh, Jaunpur, Benares, the western half of Ghazipur, and South-Gangetic Mirzapur" (Grierson, 1903:42, 44).

   Most of the people I asked in Banaras identified Bhojpuri as the language of Bihar. In one group, I was told that Bhojpuri was not spoken in Banaras, although everybody agreed that what they spoke at home was not Hindi.

9. Banarsi Boli is also known as Banarsi Bhojpuri, a more informative and technically accurate label. In this article I have chosen to use the term *Banarsi Boli* rather than *Banarsi Bhojpuri* because the former is the term used often by native Banarsi Boli speakers.

10. Grierson, 1903:264: "The dialect spoken in the District of Benares [*sic*] is Western Bhojpuri, the same as that of Azamgarh. It is locally known as Banarsi." Ibid., 270: "The language spoken by the natives of Benares City varies considerably according to the castes of the speakers." Ibid., 273 (Following a transliteration of a "middle class" reading of the Parable of the Prodigal Son): "The dialect of the lowest dregs of the populace has many marked peculiarities and has occupied more than one native scholar."

11. Banarsi Boli exhibits certain morphophonemic similarities with Awadhi, particularly in the pronominal and verbal systems. These similarities are part of what distinguish Banarsi Boli from other dialects of Western Bhojpuri (Simon, 1986).

12. The *LSI* notes that Banarsi Boli differs from other varieties of Western Bhojpuri. Tiwari attributes these linguistic differences to contact with Awadhi. My data show that where Banarsi Boli differs from other dialects of Western Bhojpuri, it matches either Awadhi or regional standard Hindi. I suggest that the

morphosyntactic parallels between Banarsi Boli and Hindi are due to the immersion of Banarsi Boli speakers in Hindi-language situations in most of the important aspects of Banarsi social and economic life.

13. In 1965, Banaras housed over eighty-four Sanskrit *pathshalas* (traditional schools where Sanskrit is taught by memorization and repetition), many of which are over 150 years old.

14. As early as 1917, Gandhi argued that Hindi should be the national language. Among other reasons, he said that it would be easy for "the whole country" to learn Hindi, and that it was "the speech of the majority of the inhabitants of India." "Thus Hindi has already established itself as the national language of India. We have been using it as such for a long time…The birth of Urdu is due to this fact" (Gandhi, "Hindi Swaraj," in Gopal, 1966:90).

15. The influence of Hindi in the Banaras area is remarked, for instance, in the *Uttar Pradesh District Gazetteer* of 1965: "Linguistically, the district of Varanasi is a Bhojpuri-speaking area, the social development of which, from the cultural and literary points of view, has been intimately related to the Hindi speaking regions of the State."

16. In general, Muslims feel they have not quite gotten their due in Banaras. Over the centuries, the population in Banaras has been between a quarter to a third Muslim, but usually among the poorer segment. Muslims are often employed by Hindus in the labor-intensive, low-wage occupations such as silk production, much of which is used for elaborate brocades purchased by wealthier Hindus for weddings. The same attitude toward cross-religion employment is implied to different purpose in the laundryman's story in the section on marked code-switching.

17. Until recently, only well-educated but politically naive Banarsi natives would return themselves as first language or mother tongue Bhojpuri speakers. Between 1961 and 1971, however, the number of "nonstandard" or nonregional language returns has increased because of several factors, among which is the change in instructions regarding recording responses as given.

18. "Variants have been grouped in some cases under the relevant languages [languages named in Schedule VIII to the Constitution of India]. This has been done on the basis of linguistic information readily available or in light of studies already made. These identifiable variants which returned 10,000 or more speakers each at all-India level…are…*Hindi*—Awadhi; Bhojpuri; Braj Bhasha, Bundeli/Bundelkhandi, Chhattisgarhi, Garhwali; Haryanvi; Jaunsari, Kangri, Khariboli, Kumauni; Magadhi/Magahi; Maithili; Marwari; Nagpuria, Nimadi, Pahari; Rajasthani" (*Census of India, 1981*:5).

19. For each census where the individual's response was to be recorded as given, the census taker was allowed to record only two languages, and to do so in the order given. Even here, the census taker determines whether the variety named is a "language." "Banarsi Boli" would not have been included. Thus, in Banaras, an individual returning Hindi and Banarsi Boli is counted as a monolingual Hindi speaker. An individual claiming three languages—Urdu, Hindi, and Bhojpuri—is recorded as bilingual in Urdu and Hindi, and Bhojpuri is not counted at all.

Predictably, most Banaras natives, and almost all Banaras Hindus, have always been returned as Hindi speakers. In 1951, for instance, no "Bhojpuri" responses were recorded, although over 6,500 people claimed areas of western Bihar as "place of birth."

20. When the language medium for education is determined, the regional language is taken as the "first language" in most states. This means that although each state is required to provide education through the primary level in whatever mother tongue is requested (within certain student minima), the number of "mother tongues" is considerably reduced by using the *regional language* label as an umbrella for any number of mother tongues within the state.

As of 1961 at the primary level, Uttar Pradesh provided education in Hindi, as well as in Bengali, English, Marathi, Punjabi, Sindhi, and Urdu. (Neither Uttar Pradesh, nor Bihar—with a substantial Bhojpuri-speaking population—officially provided education in Bhojpuri.) (Goel and Saini, 1972:41.)

In practice, as Pattanayak has pointed out (1981), when teachers and students are from the same locality, the language medium is often the speech of that locality, although it is often given the regional language label and is often perceived *to be* the regional language.

21. At the university level, Banaras Hindu University offers English, Hindi, Sanskrit, Bengali, Pali, and Urdu; the classroom language medium is officially Hindi. At Varanasi Sanskrit Vishvavidyalaya, the language offered is, of course, Sanskrit; those language media are Sanskrit and Hindi. Kashi Vidyapith offers Hindi and Sanskrit; the official medium is Hindi (Goel and Saini, 1972:49–55).

22. The District Varanasi *Primary Census Abstract* gives the number of *literates* ("a person who can both read and write with understanding") for urban Banaras in 1981 as 376,410: females number 128,770 and males 247,640. The literacy rate for urban Varanasi is nearly 46 percent, compared to 27 percent for Uttar Pradesh in general. The rate for females of the whole Varanasi *tahsil* (subdivision of a district) is somewhat higher than for the rest of the state (16.25 percent against 14 percent). With regard to the relation between gender, literacy (at least via public education), and language identity, the literacy rate for Varanasi tahsil males, compared with that of both the rest of the males in the state and with the females of Varanasi, is particularly revealing. Literacy rates for Varanasi tahsil males compared with those for females show 46 percent against 16.25 percent. (Males of Varanasi tahsil show a literacy rate of nearly 46 percent against about 39 percent for all males throughout Uttar Pradesh.)

23. See Humes [1993] for a discussion of how female participation in religious activities is in part determined by education and access to the "higher" language of Sanskrit. Women worshiping with the Khatri female guru use a new form of devotional singing of a Sanskrit text in their mother tongue of Punjabi.

24. Among the Hindu women I knew, it was the poorest and least educated, and hence most isolated, who identified Banarsi Boli as some form of Hindi. Those with more outside contact distinguished between Banarsi Boli and Hindi, and between their own speech and that of the males in the household. I was not studying this type of valuation, however, and the

remarks from these participants may not be at all representative.

25. Government records on education show that the second language is usually English or Sanskrit for Hindus.

26. Diglossia is present to some degree in the urban areas of most of the northern Indian plains, which constitute the Hindi regional language area. In this area, Hindi coexists with a given local speech variety.

27. I thought I was barging in, but he was insistent that I not only stay, but also tape the proceedings.

28. Ferguson (1972:236) has suggested typical language situations in which speech varieties are function specific, and notes that there is little overlap. For instance, in a situation where bilinguals are fluent in both speech varieties, speakers may read from the newspaper in the "high" variety and then discuss what was just read in the "low."

29. That is, no individual code-switch can be "attributed to stylistic or discourse functions" (Poplack, 1988).

30. Neither man commented on his code-switching during the conversation, nor seemed to notice it later when listening to the tape.

31. This type of code-switching is frequent. Very few conversations did not include Banarsi Boli-Hindi code-switching at some point. However, my data do not show it to be the predominant stylistic or discourse strategy: that is, no single speaker whom I recorded used intrasentential code-switching throughout a whole conversation.

32. Several—for instance, Poplack (1988), Scotton (1988)—see this overall pattern of unmarked, intrasentential code-switching as analogous to monolingual discourse.

33. Within the Banarsi Boli–speaking community, intrasentential code-switching is, in itself, unremarkable. As is common in Chicano Spanish-English, or Puerto Rican Spanish-English bilinguals in the United States, or French-English bilinguals in Canada, the speaker and the other participants may be unaware of code-switching.

    The frequency of unmarked intrasentential code-switching among Banarsis supports the current hypothesis that such code-switching "is only frequent when both varieties are indexical of identities which are positively evaluated for the specific exchange type" (Scotton, 1988:166).

34. This is a loan, a blend of terry and cotton, which has been naturalized with retroflex initial and final [T] and the mid-back rounded open. Terrycot is a polyester blend that is not only substantially more expensive than cotton, but also one that lasts longer and requires little pressing.

35. Among Hindus in Banaras, Muslims are reputed not to pay very good wages, especially to Hindus.

36. Again, an English loan, naturalized with a retroflex [R].

37. *Ihaa* has the Banarsi Boli vowel rather than the Hindi semivowel; *hau* has a Banarsi Boli diphthong.

38. It is, of course, unlikely that the actual conversation of ten years earlier took place in this pattern of language alternation.

References

Census of India. 1951, 1961, 1971, 1981 *Uttar Pradesh: District Census Handbook—Varanasi District*.

Chatterji, S.K. 1926 *The Origin and Development of the Bengali Language*. Vol. 1. London: Allen and Unwin.

Dorian, Nancy. 1982 "Defining the Speech Community to Include Its Working Margins." In Suzanne Romaine (ed.), *Sociolinguistic Variation in Speech Communities*. London: Edward Arnold.

Ferguson, Charles. 1972 "Diglossia." pp. 232–252 in P. Gigliolo (ed.), *Language and Social Context*. New York: Penguin.

Goel, B. S., and S. K. Saini. 1972 *Mother Tongue and Equality of Opportunity in Education*. New Delhi: National Council of Educational Research and Training.

Gopal, Ram. 1966 *Linguistic Affairs of India*. Bombay: Asia Publishing House.

Grierson, Sir George A. 1901 *Seven Grammars of the Dialects and Subdialects of the Bihari Language*. Varanasi: Motilal Banarsidass.

———. [1903] 1968 *Linguistic Survey of India*, Vol. 5. *Indo-Aryan Family, Eastern Group*, Part 2. Varanasi: Motilal Banarsidass.

———. 1904 *Linguistic Survey of India*, Vol 6. *Indo-Aryan Family, Mediate Group*. Calcutta: Office of the Superintendent of Government Printing.

Gumperz, John. 1978 "Dialect and Conversational Inference in Urban Communication." *Language in Society* 7:393–409.

———. 1982 "Conversational Code-switching." pp. 59–99 in his *Discourse Strategies*. Cambridge: Cambridge University Press. [Reprinted as Chapter 18, this volume.]

Humes, Cynthia Ann. 1993. "The Goddess of the Vindhyas in Banaras." pp. 181–204 in Bradley R. Hertel and Cynthia Ann Humes (eds.), *Living Banaras: Hindu Religion in Cultural Context*. Albany: State University of New York Press.

Imperial Gazetteer. 1908 *Imperial Gazetteer—Varanasi*. Vol. 7. Oxford: Clarendon Press.

Pattanayak, D.P. 1981 *Multilingualism and Mother-Tongue Education*. Delhi: Oxford Press.

Poplack, Shana. 1988 "Contrasting Patterns of Code-switching in Two Communities." pp. 215–244 in Monica Heller (ed.), *Codeswitching*. Berlin: Mouton de Gruyter.

Romaine, Suzanne. 1989 *Bilingualism*. Oxford: Basil Blackwell.

Scotton, Carol Myers. 1988 "Codeswitching as Indexical of Social Negotiations." In Monica Heller (ed.), *Codeswitching*. Berlin: Mouton de Gruyter.

Simon, Beth Lee. 1986 "Bilingualism and Language Maintenance in Banaras." Ph.D. thesis, University of Michigan microfilm.

Sinha, Surajit, and Baidyanath Saraswati. 1978 *The Ascetics of Kashi: An Anthropological Exploration*. Varanasi: N.K. Bose Memorial Foundation.

Post-reading Questions / Activities

- Why did Simon's friend's father appear to deny knowledge of Banarsi Boli? Can you think of a situation where someone you know might do such a thing? What are the pressures to admit or conceal use of a particular linguistic variety?
- Why is it impossible to rely on census information about the languages people speak? How else might this information be gained?
- What are the contexts in which Banarsi Boli and Hindi are spoken? What kinds of code switching did Simon describe? Why do people code switch? Why did the launderer use Banarsi Boli and Hindi in each case?

Vocabulary

caste
code switching
diglossia
intersentential code switching
intrasentential code switching

language contact
lingua franca
mother tongue
phonology
register

stable bilingualism
stable multilingualism
standard, standard language,
  standardization

Suggested Further Reading

Edwards, John R. 1994. *Multilingualism*. London and New York: Routledge.

Ferguson, Charles. 1972 [1959]. "Diglossia." In *Language and Social Context*, edited by Pier Paolo Giglioli, pp. 232–251. Middlesex, UK: Penguin Books.

Gumperz, John J. 1958. "Dialect Differences and Social Stratification in a North Indian Village." *American Anthropologist,* new series, 60 (4): 668–682.

——. 1982. *Discourse Strategies*. Cambridge: Cambridge University Press.

Heller, Monica, ed. 1988. *Codeswitching: Anthropological and Sociolinguistic Perspectives*. Berlin and New York: Mouton de Gruyter.

Myers-Scotton, Carol. 1988. "Codeswitching as Indexical of Social Negotiations." In *Codeswitching: Anthropological and Sociolinguistic Perspectives*, edited by Monica Heller, pp. 151–186. Berlin and New York: Mouton de Gruyter.

Romaine, Suzanne. 1989. *Bilingualism*. New York: Blackwell.

CHAPTER 20

Most of the World's Languages Went Extinct

John H. McWhorter

(2001)

Since human language began, perhaps 100,000 to 150,000 years ago, new languages have formed and old languages have "died." Humans have migrated as part of our species heritage, until we began to settle down following the Neolithic revolution—the invention/discovery of agriculture (at different times in different parts of the world)—and with that movement has come increasing language loss. Migrants may learn the language of groups they encounter, or the two languages may form a hybrid form (a creole). People may add more languages to those they already know, or they may delete old ones as they learn new ones. When small groups speak an isolated language, its fate is intertwined with their biological and cultural fate; if they die off, the language dies with them.

Experts speculate that prior to the advent of agriculture, humans spoke a vastly greater number of different languages, perhaps as many as 100,000! Now that number is down to about 6,000, but many of them are spoken only by very small numbers of people.

Of course, "language death" is a metaphor, but it is the one commonly used to discuss this phenomenon. Language death begins with multilingualism, followed by "language shift," when people begin to move to another language for many of their communicative needs.

Using the analogy of biological evolution, in this chapter John McWhorter discusses the tragedy of linguistic extinction. He adds that linguistic extinction is even more complete than biological extinction, because languages have left no trace at all, while organisms have had the chance to remain as fossils or as genetic constructs from offspring DNA.

McWhorter begins with a discussion of the reasons one language may give way to another over a brief period of time. He details many cases of languages known to have died both in the remote past and in very recent time. Moreover, even when languages have not completely disappeared, the vast majority of the people in the world—96 percent—speak just 20 powerful languages (maybe along with an indigenous language). But he argues that with the growth of cities and of national cultures, it is unrealistic to expect anything like the 6,000 currently spoken languages to endure, sad though that prospect is.

McWhorter pleads the case that what is lost when a language dies is not so much the cultural knowledge associated with that language but rather the specifics of the language, *the details of its structure, the delicate, elaborate rules. So he urges linguists and others who love language at the very least to record dying languages so that in the future at least we can know what they were.*

Reading Questions

- What is the general pattern of language death?
- What evidence do we have of earlier languages that have died?

"Most of the World's Languages Went Extinct." In *The Power of Babel: A Natural History of Languages* by John H. McWhorter (New York: Times Books, 2001, pp. 253–286). Reprinted by permission of Henry Holt and Company, H.C.

- What causes languages to die? How can this be resisted, if it can? What cases have been successful?
- How have the specifics of industrialization and urbanization contributed to language death? What is the future likely to hold in terms of linguistic diversity?

[This discussion is part of a larger work] dedicated to an analogy between biological evolution and human language. Like animals and plants, languages change, split into subvarieties, hybridize, revivify, evolve functionless features, and can even be genetically altered. The analogy continues in that languages, like animals and plants, can go extinct.

As animals and plants drive one another to extinction by nosing one another out of ecological niches in competition for sustenance, in the past languages have usually gone extinct when one group conquers another or when a group opts for a language that it perceives as affording it greater access to resources it perceives as necessary to survival. Typically, a generation of speakers of a language becomes bilingual in one spoken by a group that is politically dominant or endowed with valuable goods or access to same. This bilingual situation can persist across several generations, but as often as not, the inevitable tendency for languages to be indexed to social evaluations takes its toll. Usually, through time new generations come to associate the outside language with status and upward mobility and the indigenous one with "backwardness." This is especially the case when the dominant language is a First World "tall building" language associated with money, technology, and enshrinement in the media while the indigenous one is an obscure tongue spoken only in villages.

A point arrives when one generation speaks the outside language better than the indigenous language, largely using the latter to speak with older relatives and in ritual functions. As such, these people do not speak the indigenous language much better than many Americans might speak French or Spanish after a few years of lessons in high school. One is unlikely to speak to one's child in a language one is not fully comfortable in and does not consider an expression of oneself. It is here that a language dies, because a language can only be passed on intact as a mother tongue to children. Once it is spoken only by adults and is no longer being passed on to children, even though it will be "spoken" in the strict sense for another several decades, it will die with its last fluent speakers.

Our natural sense is to suppose that, as long as the language has been written down or codified in a grammar, then it need not be dead forever. However, grammar writing is a relatively recent practice, and in the absence of a grammar, a dead language's full apparatus is only evident when there is a considerable volume of writings. This is in turn only the case for a small number of "big actors" such as Latin. Because writing itself is a relatively recent invention—as it has been put, if humans had existed for just one day, then writing would have been invented about 11:00 P.M.—obviously even these potential paths of rescue have been unavailable to human language for most of its existence. Until 11:00 P.M., once a language went extinct, it was gone forever.

An extinct language before the advent of writing is even more unrecoverable than an extinct life form. Life forms may leave their impressions as fossils, and technology gets ever closer to allowing us to someday at least partially resurrect ancient life forms through remains of their DNA. However, a language could not leave an "imprint" before writing existed, because an individual language is not encoded in a person's genes. If the ability to speak is genetically encoded, we can be quite sure that this inheritance is a generalized one allowing someone to speak any language on earth. The particular word shapes, grammatical configurations, and various irregularities that characterize any one language are the result of largely random accretions through the millennia, no more reproducible from basic human materials than the form of an individual snowflake is from the water droplets that it began as.

And even when a language is preserved in writing, there is a long trip indeed between the tales, recipes, battle accounts, and poetry preserved on the page and the language being used daily by living, breathing human beings as an expression of their souls. Many of us can attest to this from our exposure to Latin—no matter how good you may have gotten at those declensions, conjugations, and ablative absolutes, even this was a long way from speaking the language fluently, and what life conditions can we even imagine, outside of the clergy, where fluent Latin would be natural or necessary? Languages die when others take their place—we don't *need* Latin or any dead language, because we've got languages of our own. As often as not, a revived language hovers in the realm of the "undead"—part of the revivification effort entails gamely making space for the language in lives already quite full without it and sometimes even vaguely discomfited by its return.

WORLD HISTORY: A TREADMILL TO LINGUISTIC OBLIVION?

It Was Ever Thus—To an Extent

Like biological extinctions, language death has been a regular and unsung occurrence throughout human history. We have records of Indo-European languages now no longer spoken, such as Hittite from present-day Turkey and Syria, and Tocharian, spoken by Europeans who penetrated as far east as present-day China. There was once a Romance language spoken on the Adriatic shores called Dalmatian, a kind of transition between Italian and Romanian, whose last speaker died in 1898.[1] The Romance languages in general spread in a continuous patch from Portugal eastward until a break after Italy, turning up again only in Romania, with the exception of some dots of odd Romanian dialects spoken in the interim. As was Dalmatian, these dots are remnants of what once were many other Romance languages filling in today's gap—languages that died in the face of encroaching Slavic varieties now spoken in the former Yugoslavia. A Slavic language called Sorbian (or Wendish) is spoken within German borders and, predictably, has lost in the competition with German and is now only spoken by a few elderly people. King Arthur represented the Celtic peoples who once inhabited all of the British Isles and significant swaths of Iberia and present-day France. The onslaught of the Romans and then the Vikings pushed the languages they spoke to the margins. Gaelic hangs on tenuously in Ireland, as does an offshoot variety in Scotland; Welsh does so in Wales; and Breton is fighting for life in northwestern France. But the Gaulish that the *Asterix* characters are supposed to be speaking has not been heard from since about A.D. 500, the last full speaker of Cornish of Cornwall died in 1777, and Manx of the Isle of Man died in 1974.

In other cases, language deaths in the past are only reconstructable by inference. In Africa, where languages often change from one small region to another, the Maa language is relatively unusual in being spoken across a belt of territory incorporating two countries, stretching from the top of Kenya to the middle of Tanzania. Peculiarities among various groups of its speakers attest to Maa having "killed" local languages in its spread, the Maa being a traditionally successful pastoral people who migrated widely in the past in search of grazing lands.

In northern Kenya, there are Maa speakers who stand out in being hunter-gatherers instead of pastoralists. These Dorobo peoples assist the Maa of the area in their herding, and the Maa's oral tradition mentions having met hunter-gatherers in the past. Presumably before the meeting, the Dorobo spoke their own language, this made even more likely by the cultural distinctiveness they retain today. Southward there are other Maa speakers whose cultural distinctiveness tips us off to language death in days of yore. The Camus people on Lake Baringo of Kenya farm and fish, traits alien to and even looked down on by traditional Maa peoples; the Arusa of Tanzania also remain farmers, though speaking Maa. In other cases, the death of languages in the face of Maa is concretely visible as speakers remain who speak a shredded version of the original language: the Elmolo, Yaaku, and Omotik languages are now only spoken by the very old, their communities having opted for Maa in connection with the benefits of the pastoral life style.

It was ever thus, then. No more ammonites, *Pteranodon*, or eighteen-foot-tall rhinoceroses;[2] no more Hittite, Dalmatian, or Elmolo. There is a sense in which we cannot help but regret the demise of any of the endlessly marvelous permutations of life or language, and surely the demise of each creature or language is in the strict sense a tale of marginalization and erasure. Animals and plants have vanished as often in catastrophic grand extinctions as through gradual outnumbering by more successful competitors, and

languages have often died as the result of violent conquest, enslavement, and oppression. However, under ordinary conditions, we could perhaps congratulate ourselves that naked conquest of this sort is no longer officially sanctioned by the world community (even if, sadly, conditions too often leave such events to be allowed passively to proceed, especially when the people in question are not perceived as commercially important) and that our enlightened awareness of the value of diversity combined with the availability of writing will further help ensure that languages will no longer disappear at nearly the rate that they used to.

This, however, is an understandable but mistaken view. Our parallel with animals and plants unfortunately extends to the fact that, today, languages are in fact disappearing at a rate as alarmingly rapid as that of flora and fauna. The same geopolitical forces that are raping the global environment are also vaporizing not just the occasional obscure tongue spoken in remote regions, but most of the world's six thousand languages. Today, a subset of the "top twenty" languages (Chinese, English, Spanish, Hindi, Arabic, Bengali, Russian, Portuguese, Japanese, German, French, Punjabi, Javanese, Bihari, Italian, Korean, Telugu, Tamil, Marathi, and Vietnamese)[3] are imposed as languages of education and wider commerce throughout the world. The result is that ninety-six percent of the world's population speaks one or more of these top twenty; that is, these people speak one of these languages in addition to an indigenous one, and there is a threat that succeeding generations will learn only the dominant one and let the indigenous one die. This means that only *four percent* of the world's population is living and dying speaking *only* an indigenous language.

This imbalance of power leads to some rather gruesome predictions. By one reasonable estimate, ninety percent of the world's languages will be dead by 2100—that is, about fifty-five hundred full, living languages will no longer be spoken about 1,125 months from when you are reading this. As David Crystal puts it, this means that a language is dying roughly every two weeks.

Many of the languages we are most exposed to are among the top twenty or will be among the five-hundred-odd "medium" languages that will likely survive the impending mass extinction (Catalan, Finnish, Wolof, Thai, Tagalog, etc.), and all of these languages have been so richly documented in writing and in recordings that, even if they lost all of their native speakers, their revival, or at least maintenance on life support, would be at least technically feasible. Thus it can be difficult to appreciate the massive loss that more widespread language death will entail.

The Native American situation is illustrative. Before the arrival of Europeans, there were about three hundred separate languages spoken by Native Americans in what is today the continental United States. Today, a third of those languages are no longer spoken, whereas all but a handful of the rest are spoken only by the very old and will surely be extinct within a decade or so. The current situation is as if, in Europe, Albanian, Frisian, Romanian, Basque, Catalan, Occitan, Welsh, Lithuanian, Latvian, and Irish and Scottish

Gaelic were no longer spoken, and meanwhile only English, German, and Russian were still being passed on to children, with Swedish, Norwegian, Danish, Icelandic, Dutch, French, Spanish, Italian, Portuguese, Serbo-Croatian, Macedonian, Polish, Bulgarian, Finnish, Estonian, and Hungarian only spoken by very old people, viewed as "quaint" and backward by young people jetting around in sports cars.

Each of these Native American languages was an astoundingly complex and remarkably beautiful conglomeration, presenting the glorious kinds of baroquenesses we [might see] in Cree. Europe is covered mostly by languages of one family such that all are based on a common general "game plan," but the Native American languages spoken north of Mexico constituted at the very least two dozen families, with a range of variation across the continent as broad as that on the entire Eurasian landmass, taking in Indo-European, Chinese, Japanese, Arabic, and others.

The First Crack in the Dam: The Neolithic Revolution

The trend toward a decrease in the number of the world's languages is, in large view, not an isolated phenomenon but one symptom of general trends in human development in the past several millennia. Until just about eleven thousand years ago, humanity worldwide consisted of relatively small groups of hunter-gatherers. This life style was not inherently geared toward population increase and spread, and thus the world was feasibly shareable by large numbers of such groups, with minimum occasion for one group to exterminate another one along with its language. We can be sure such things happened but generally on a very local scale, counterbalanced by the birth of new languages as groups that reached a certain size spawned offshoot groups who moved away from the original group, their speech eventually developing into a new language. It has been estimated that this world could have harbored as many as one hundred thousand languages, and the scenario has been termed *linguistic equilibrium*.

Large-scale language death began with the development of agriculture in many societies, starting in about 9000 B.C. Agriculture required large expanses of land, and its greater yield of food led to hitherto unknown population growth. Cultivation allows the amassing of food surpluses, which, freeing certain classes of people from hand-to-mouth subsistence, is the basis of the development of hierarchies of specialization that breed technological advances. Armed with these, and in constant need of extra space as their populations burgeoned, agricultural societies quickly began overrunning hunter-gatherer groups worldwide.

Even the way in which the world's language families are distributed today makes it clear that language death has been a regular part of human existence for several millennia. In India, roughly speaking, the languages spoken in the top half are Indo-European languages such as Hindi, Bengali, and Marathi, whereas in the bottom half, languages of another family called Dravidian are spoken, including Tamil,

Kannada, Telugu, and Malayalam. However, the subdivision of space is not perfect: there is the occasional Dravidian language spoken way up in northern India or even as far northwest as present-day Pakistan. What are those people doing way up there? From our present-day perspective, it looks as if certain Dravidian speakers decided at some point to pack up and move thousands of miles away from their homelands. Much more likely, and supported archaeologically, is that Indo-European speakers slowly moved southward, with formerly spoken Dravidian languages dying along the way as their speakers were incorporated into the invaders' societies for generations and gave up their original languages. Life is never tidy, and naturally some pockets remain that the invaders never happened to get to. Thus the Dravidian "outliers" are remnants of a once greater variety of Dravidian languages spoken in southern Asia.

A similar case is the Dahalo language of Kenya, unusual in having the clicks otherwise found only way down in the south of Africa, among a small group of languages called Khoi-San and a few Bantu languages spoken near them such as Xhosa and Zulu. It is easy to see why the Bantu languages have the clicks—language contact long ago with Khoi-San speakers. However, what are clicks doing way up in Kenya? Clicks are so extremely rare cross-linguistically—otherwise found only in one Australian language, and even there, only in a special "secret" variety of that language—that it is unlikely that the clicks developed in Kenya merely by chance. Most likely, Khoi-San "click" languages were once spoken more widely in Africa, and Dahalo is one of the only remnants of that situation. What this means is that untold numbers of click languages must have died as Bantu and other peoples spread into what began as click-language territory. Again, archaeological evidence supports this scenario: skulls of people of the ethnicity who today speak Khoi-San languages have been found as far north as Zambia, and the Bantu takeover apparently occurred within a mere few centuries' time after 1000 B.C.

In the New World and Australia, Europeans similarly overwhelmed Native American and Aboriginal languages, assisted by the germs that living among livestock had immunized them to but that quite often decimated indigenous hunter-gatherer populations on impact.

Situation Critical: The Downsides of the Global Economy

Thus even today's six thousand languages constitute a vast decrease in the number of languages that existed before the Neolithic revolution. Today, however, a second revolution, which some leftist political commentators term the imperialist one, is having an even starker effect on how many languages are spoken in the world.

During the Neolithic revolution, when a language spread across an area, it generally did so relatively slowly such that, by the time the spread was complete, the language had already developed into several new ones, which continued to spawn new ones in turn. For example, by the time

Latin was disseminated throughout the Roman Empire, its progenitor Proto-Indo-European had elsewhere in Europe already split into several branches such as Germanic, Slavic, Celtic, Hellenic (Greek). Then Latin itself developed into more than a dozen new languages, the Romance languages, while at the same time Proto-Slavic was developing into several new tongues. Thus, though Europe was once covered by languages now lost forever, this original diversity was replaced at least partly by new diversity. Furthermore, until recently, Europeans were unable to physically take over tropical and subtropical regions, where farming methods developed for temperate climates were ineffective and diseases Europeans had no immunity to tended to kill them, just as their own diseases tended to kill Native Americans and Australian Aborigines.

However, in the past few hundred years, the development of capitalism and the Industrial Revolution, and its resultant technological advances and encouragement of strongly centralized nationalist governments, have led a certain handful of languages to begin gradually elbowing not just many but *most* of the world's remaining languages out of existence. The urgencies of capitalism require governments to exact as much work and allegiance from their populations as possible, and the imposition of a single language has traditionally been seen as critical to this goal, especially within the nationalist models that have ruled since the 1700s. [Relevent is] the active hostility of the French government to the Occitan dialects and other "patois" of France, in favor of a scenario under which everyone in France spoke French.

In our era, climatological boundaries present few barriers to the onslaught. Today, language death is often caused less by physical conquest than by gradually yoking indigenous peoples into a centralized cash economy. This is often done by transforming their traditional life styles on site according to what their local topography can bear, with the aid of advances in agricultural technology. In other cases, the dominant power renders much of the population migrant laborers, spending half of their lives working in cities, this facilitated by modern transportation technology (assembling part-time work forces drawn from afar was more difficult before the invention of trains, for example). In the past few centuries, a great many human societies have been drawn from independent subsistence on the land into dependent relationships with capitalist superstructures, with traditional ways of life often actively discouraged in favor of new practices geared toward supplying the central government with salable resources.

A SKELETON OF ITS FORMER SELF: A LANGUAGE WITHERS AWAY

What happens to a language as it dies? Generally, the last generation of fluent speakers has learned it only partly, never truly living in the language, using it only in the corners of their lives. As a result, the language is slightly pidginized. However, whereas in many cases a pidgin has been a temporary "setback" on the way to its expansion into a new language, the moribund variety of a dying language is a step along the way to permanent demise.

"I Wish I Had the Words": Atrophied Vocabulary

Just as pidgins such as early Tok Pisin had restricted vocabularies, dying languages' vocabularies are constricted, with many single words pinch-hitting for concepts that were expressed by several more specific ones in the living language. Cayuga is a Native American language originally spoken in New York State. Under the Jackson Administration in the 1830s, as *you was* popped up in letters written by white clerks in New York City, many Native Americans were relocated to Oklahoma, intended as a delineated Indian Territory, and Cayugas were among them. By 1980, only a few elderly people spoke any Cayuga but had been thoroughly English-dominant all of their lives, and their Cayuga was seriously frayed around the edges as a result. The Oklahoma Cayuga had a word for *leg* but none for *thigh*, a word for *foot* but none for *ankle* or *toe*, words for *face* and *eye* but none for *cheek* or *eyebrow*. Where full Cayuga had a word specifically meaning *enter*, these old people substituted the more general word *go*, such that *Come into the house* was rendered as *Go into the house*. The nuance of where the speaker was in relation to the house—determining whether one would say from the porch **Come** in or say from a hill up yonder **Go** in—was left to context.

The Genericization of a Language: The Demise of the "Hard Stuff"

Just as pidgins strip away aspects of language not necessary to basic communication, dying languages are marked by a tendency to let drop many of the accreted "frills" languages drift into developing through time. In a language that one uses little, the first thing to start wearing away in the grammar is, predictably, the "hard stuff" that takes lifelong daily practice to learn and retain.

The Death of Inflections One "frill" in a language is the inflectional prefix or suffix, which quite a few languages do without. Inflections arise accidentally through time from what begin usually as separate words, which as inflections become one of the challenging aspects of language to learn, entailing lists of arbitrarily shaped bits of stuff signaling concepts such as gender, person, and number that are in any case either clear from context or unnecessary to communication. People who use an inflected language day in and day out learn the inflections with ease and have no trouble retaining them throughout their lives; they become as ingrained as walking. But in dying languages speakers have often never mastered the inflections fully or have lost control of them in time, and thus to them the inflections become "hard," just as they would be to a foreigner learner.

Thus speakers of a dying inflected language often avoid using inflections in favor of more immediately transparent constructions, just as an English speaker feels as if he has gotten a kind of break when finding out that, in Spanish, instead of *hablaré* "I will speak" he can also say *Voy a hablar*, which allows him to get around calling up the ending in favor of using a form of the verb *go* that he has already learned. In traditional forms of Pipil, spoken in Guatemala and El Salvador, there were future inflections, such that *I will pass* was:

Ni-panu-**s**
I- pass- will

But today we mostly see this in old texts; elderly living speakers might cough it up for money, but in the Pipil they speak, stripped down in comparison with the living language of yore, the future is expressed with a "going to" construction. *I'm going to do it* is:

Ni-yu ni-k-chiwa
I- go I- it-do

Thus Pipil has moved in the direction of pidginhood, paralleling the tendency in pidgins to express the future with "going" expressions (although many old languages happen to express the future this way as well).

The Soul of Celtic Melts Away   In Welsh,…the first consonant of a noun often changes, depending on which possessive word comes before. The word for *cat* is *cath*, but the word takes on a different form as used with the word for *my*:

eu cath   "their cat"
fy **nghath**   "my cat"

The *his* and *her* case is particularly interesting because the same word is used for both: only the change in the consonant shows whether *his* or *her* is intended in the meaning:

ei **gath**   "his cat"
ei **chath**   "her cat"

In Welsh's relative Gaelic—namely, the Scottish variety spoken in Sutherland County—speakers in their forties were the last generation of fluent speakers left in the early 1970s. Gaelic has the same kinds of consonant changes as Welsh does, and one sign of the decay of the Sutherland speakers' Gaelic was the gradual breakdown of these rules. To say *She was kept in* in living Scottish Gaelic, laid as all Celtic languages are on a basic foundation quite different from English's, one says literally "Was she on her keeping in":

Bha i   air a   cùmail.
was she on her keeping-in

This is a little challenging to wrap our heads around, but for our purposes concentrate on the last two words:

Bha i   air   **a**   **cùmail**.
was she on   **her** **keeping-in**

To say *He was kept in*—that is, "Was he on his keeping in"— one uses the same word as for *her*, but the consonant in the following verb changes:

Bha e   air a   **ch**ùmail.
was he on   his keeping-in

And to say *They were kept in*, there is a different consonant change:

Bha iad   air   an   **g**ùmail.
was they on   their keeping-in

In the moribund Scottish Gaelic of Sutherland County, however, as often as not, in all three cases the form **ch**ùmail, properly used with *his*, was used for all three:

Bha i   air a   **ch**ùmail.   "She was kept in."
Bha e   air a   **ch**ùmail.   "He was kept in."
Bha iad   air an   **ch**ùmail.   "They were kept in."

These speakers have a general sense that there is some consonant change after possessive words but have not mastered the particular changes that each possessive pronoun requires or does not require. Thus just as we might do in trying to learn to speak Scottish Gaelic, these speakers simply generalized one kind of change to all persons.

There's Speaking and There's Speaking   The last generation to speak a language is often incapable of being *articulate* in it as well, a crucial indication that the language is no longer capable of expressing full humanity.

There are scattered examples in English of concepts that are expressed as a single word incorporating both the object and the verb together: *He sat the baby for her* is more often rendered as *He babysat for her*. In many Native American languages, however, this process is central to basic expression, usable for just about any commonly occurring verb–object combination. In Cayuga, to say *She has a big house*, one might say "It house-bigs her," in the sense of "Things have it that she has a big house." Moreover, all of this is one word: *Koṇǫhsowá:neh*. When to use expressions like this and when not to are central to manipulating language artfully in these cultures, in the same vein as word choice and relative clauses are for us.

Of course, as we in particular know, a language can do just fine without this sort of thing, which evolves accidentally in certain languages through time—[elsewhere I show] it having done so just in the past century with "camp-sat" in Ngan'gityemerri in Australia. It's an extra and, as such, one of the first things to start wearing away as a language containing it dies. In living Cayuga, to render *She has a big onion* within a narrative, one would likely say "It onion-bigs her." In dying Cayuga, however, speakers are more likely to just say something like *The onion is big* or *Her onion is big*.

When a language is dying, then, its last speakers typically render it in the very way that we or another foreigner might, taking the easy ways out, avoiding the kinky stuff, reducing complexities to one-size-fits-all. The moribund version of a language is like one of those 1920s 78 rpm records of a symphony orchestra playing, recorded acoustically rather than electrically. You get the basics, but no matter how carefully we enhance the recording with modern techniques, it's nothing like having been at the performance.

All of this is to say that, when a language dies, one of the thousands of offshoots of the first language simply grinds to a halt, after having thrived and morphed and mixed with abandon for 150,000 years.

How Do You Solve a Problem Like Revival?

Language Revival Meets the Realities of Language in Time and Space

In response to all of this, there are attempts proceeding worldwide to halt the death of minority languages, with a particularly concerted effort by many linguists in the past ten years to call worldwide attention to the problem. The effort serving as a primary inspiration is the example of Hebrew, which by the late 1800s had essentially been used only in writing and for liturgical purposes for more than two thousand years—Hebrew was an archaic-looking language encountered in weighty books, not something you had dinner in. The movement to make it the official language of Israel was so successful that today it is spoken natively by a nation of six million people. There are movements to similarly resuscitate threatened languages such as Irish Gaelic, which in many areas is taught, and taught in, in schools, with radio and television time set aside for broadcasts in the language and various activities in the language encouraged for young people. There are similar movements for Breton, Occitan, Maori, Hawaiian, and other languages. Yet these efforts, laudable as they are, face many imposing obstacles, posed in large part by the realities of how languages live in the world as we know it.

For one, . . . most "languages" are actually clusters of dialects. The form of a dying language taught in school is often a single, standardized variety, which can be quite different from the various dialects that constitute the "language" as it actually exists. If there is still a healthy population of people speaking the language natively and well, this "school" variety that children learn may sound rather sanitized and even imposed from without. This is a special problem in communities where the impending death of the language is a symptom of historical oppression by a surrounding power, as has been the case in Brittany with Breton. France's former policy was to discourage the use of Breton in favor of French, treating Breton as a primitive "patois" only suitable for talking to livestock. The Breton nationalist movement in response has occasionally been a violent one, and to its partisans, the alien air of "school" Breton often suffers by association with the martinet French educational tradition that has been so hostile to the language rights of Breton peoples.

[It is also important to see] how languages mix, often when speakers are shifting from one language to another one through time. Typically, speakers leave footprints from their old language in their version of the new one (the peculiarities of Irish English come largely from Gaelic) while at the same time, during the twilight of their old language, they speak it with heavy influence from the new one. This means that, in many cases, the dying language we encounter is no longer its true self, having been tinted by the one its speakers are now dominant in.

Gros Ventre was a Native American language of Montana. When its last speakers were interviewed in the 1960s, their Gros Ventre showed evidence of remodeling on an English template. In the living language, there was no way to express the word for a body part in isolation. One could not simply say *eye*; one had to say *my eye, your eye, his eye*. The closest you could come to just *eye* was "someone's eye." Thus, to express the root *síitheh* "eye" alone would be pidgin Gros Ventre; one would have to at least say **bi**-*síitheh* "someone's eye." In true Gros Ventre, *my eye* was **nesíitheh**. In dying Gros Ventre, however, it was **ne**-**bi**-*síitheh*, where the speaker tacked the prefix for *my* onto the word meaning "someone's eye." To this speaker, more comfortable with English, in which we can say just *eye*, **bi**-*síitheh* had come to mean simply *eye* rather than "someone's eye," such that it felt natural to him to render *my eye* as **ne**-**bi**-*síitheh*, although to a tribal elder this would have meant the nonsensical "my someone's eye."[4]

Because it is harder for adults to learn new languages well than it is for children, when adults are forced to learn a new language quickly, the result is often various degrees of pidginization, utilizing just the bare bones of a language. This becomes a problem in revival efforts because, even when adults of a given nationality desire strongly to have their ethnic language restored to them, the mundane realities of a busy life can make it difficult to get beyond a pidgin-level competence in the language.

This is especially crucial in the language-revival case, because the languages in most immediate danger of death tend to be those spoken by previously isolated groups—for example, the peoples who were isolated enough by geography that Europeans could not transform their lands into plantation colonies in the middle of the past millennium. As we have seen, languages spoken by such groups, having had millennia to complexify without intermediation by large numbers of second-language speakers to keep the overgrowth in check, tend to be more imposingly complex than the "big dude" languages.

To the English speaker, Spanish presents its challenges with its gender marking, conjugations, and occasional quirks like *Me gusta el libro* instead of the "Yo gusto el libro" that would feel "normal" to us. But in general, one senses oneself as "still in Kansas"—there are plenty of similar word shapes, and how thoughts are put together is generally akin to how we do so in English. Go to languages beyond familiar ones like this and things get rockier. Someone I know who emigrated from Romania at fourteen speaks English perfectly (with a lovely hint of accent), and learning French was no problem for her. But during a stay in the Czech Republic, she ultimately decided that it was hopeless trying to pick up any Czech because, as she put it, there was simply nothing familiar: word shapes are usually unlike anything we are used to in Germanic or Romance (remember Romanian is a Romance, not Slavic, language); there is a sound or two that one essentially has to be born hearing to render properly; the nouns are declined as fiercely as the verbs are conjugated; and then there are the notorious Slavic verb pairs, where each verb takes arbitrarily different prefixes or suffixes or even changes its root according to whether actions are continuous or abrupt.

And my Romanian friend was still within Indo-European. With Native American languages, for example, one is confronted not simply with learning extremely unfamiliar word shapes, but with ways of putting words together to render even the most basic of thoughts that an English speaker might barely believe humans could spontaneously resort to in running speech. *She has a big house* in Spanish translates almost word for word: *Ella tiene una casa grande.* In Czech, it is similar; typically of Slavic languages, no word for *a*, but that's not hard to get used to: *Ona má velký dům.* In general Czech "puts" things in ways that make intuitive sense to an English speaker. But then recall Cayuga's "It house-bigs her"—that's just off the scale, and remember that this is not just one wrinkle but a general way of phrasing things throughout the grammar. "Someone's eye" instead of just "eye"; having to specify just how you broke something—these are the sorts of things that confront the now English-dominant Native Americans seeking to reacquire the language of their ancestors. Here is Mohawk for *Suddenly, she heard someone give a yell from across the street:*

> *Tha'kié:ro'k iá:ken' ísi' na'oháhati iakothón:te'
> ónhka'k khe tontahohén:rehte'.*

Literally translated, with an attempt to make this sound the *least* needlessly "exotified," what this comes out as is "Suddenly, by what you could hear, there, it's beyond the street, the ear went to who just then made-shouted back toward her."

It's not impossible to learn a Native American language after childhood, and one can gradually wrap one's head around such ways of putting things. The language makes its own sense once one masters various general principles distinguishing such languages from ours. There are success stories of young Native Americans acquiring competence in their tribe's language from tutelage by elders, as in a long-term project directed by Leanne Hinton at the linguistics department of the University of California, Berkeley, pairing Native Americans with elders in an attempt to save as many Californian indigenous languages as possible. But learning one of these languages or an Australian Aboriginal language is hard work for someone raised in English or a related language, much harder work than picking up Spanish, and quite a job to expect of whole communities of people.

This difficulty relates to the fact that living languages are developed far beyond the strict necessities of communication and that incomplete learning guarantees that some of these baubles will be stripped away. Children learning an indigenous language in school but more comfortable in a dominant one such as English typically speak a rather simplified variety, just as do American students who learn French or Spanish in school. There is a perhaps universal tendency for elders to view youngsters as insufficiently mindful of tradition, which is heightened when the youngsters in question are assimilating to a dominant culture. This area of tension extends into children's version of a threatened language, when older fluent speakers often disparage the new version as "not real X," sometimes putting a damper on enthusiasm for the revival itself.

One of the notorious "Dammits" in Polynesian languages such as Maori and Hawaiian, for example, is the often arbitrary classification of nouns as taking either an *o* or an *a* possessive marker, and young speakers are often unsure which class a given noun belongs to. To a fluent Maori or Hawaiian speaker, this sounds like "bad" speech, just as saying *speaked* or *squoze* sounds to an English speaker. One can only imagine what schoolchildren's version of an immensely elaborated language such as Fula would sound like. The truth is that a revived language, if it "takes" and is passed on to children, will almost certainly be a considerably simplified version of the language as it was once spoken.

Finally, just as writing tends to give a language an air of "legitimacy," the converse also is true—a language that has not been traditionally written is often considered "less of a language" even by its speakers if they have been reared in a written, standardized "top twenty" language. Whereas to the scholar or social services worker, the indigenous language appears, quite properly, an exotic treasure to be cherished, to a person for whom the language is a mundane aspect of daily life, sociological realities intrude and often stamp the language as a lowly vehicle, associated with the elderly, parochialism, and a world many consider—for better or worse—a lesser option than the world of tall buildings.

Scholars have not always been immune to shades of this view. Before cultural pluralism was as overtly valued in mainstream educated discourse in America, even a linguist might describe Occitan in this fashion, this passage being from a generally masterful 1944 book on the world's languages (or the pipe-smoking Western professor of the period's conception thereof, with a Eurocentric bias focusing on standardized languages): "This *Provençal* has a flourishing culture of romantic poetry greatly influenced by Moorish culture. Its modern relatives are hayseed dialects."

If this was the best even some scholars could do until recently, then certainly lay speakers traditionally tend toward the same equation of "written" with "real." The very sound of the indigenous language immediately conveys a social context considered orthogonal to prestige, just as, no matter how Politically Correct we are and no matter what race we happen to be, we would be hard pressed to see the Declaration of Independence written in inner-city Black English as a document equal in gravity to the one Thomas Jefferson wrote. Such judgments are thoroughly arbitrary but noisomely deeply ingrained, and many communities resist efforts to revive their dying languages out of a sense that the languages are incompatible with the upward mobility they seek.

Language versus Prosperity

And this brings us to a very important matter regarding language death: why people give up their languages.

To be sure, indigenous languages have often been actively discouraged, by school policies calling for corporal punishment on any Native American student heard conversing in his home language, a practice especially common in the United States until the middle of the twentieth century, and by governmental positions declaring minority languages antithetical to national unity (witness France in the 1700s). My first office at Berkeley looked out on a courtyard called Ishi Court, named after a man who found himself the last living speaker of his native language, Yahi, after all of the other Yahis had been massacred. Many Native Americans died after similar massacres carried out by presidential administrations in the nineteenth century and depicted so placidly in the history books. Dozens of these languages expired under the watch of the Millard Fillmores and Chester Alan Arthurs by extermination or when groups were forced to live among others or to scatter, thus making it impossible to pass their languages on to enough children to keep them alive.

It is not difficult to make a case that people must not have their languages forcibly taken from them or beaten out of them. But in reality, just as often the reason groups abandon their traditional languages is ultimately a desire for resources that their native communities do not offer. Sometimes this occurs "naturally," as with the groups who now speak Maa in Kenya and Tanzania, a by no means unusual case that Western linguists would be unlikely to decry as an injustice. But more often today, it happens as a result of the pervasive effects of First World imperialism: the language of the dominant power—written, spoken by the wealthy, and broadcast constantly on radio and television—quite often comes to be associated with legitimacy, the cosmopolitan, and success. Almost inevitably, the home language is recast as, basically, *not* that—and thus antithetical to survival under the best possible conditions. This judgment is ultimately as unrelated to the stuff of the language itself as our evaluation of nonstandard dialects as "backward" is. But that's something only linguists know, for the most part, and in the meantime, many languages of Papua New Guinea, for instance, are gradually being replaced by Tok Pisin within their own largely self-subsisting villages, not through active outside imposition but because the villagers themselves have come to see this language and the access to the outside world that it offers as "cool."

Urbanization: Linguistic Slurry   The trend toward urban migration that this cultural co-optation encourages is particularly lethal for language diversity. There is a short step from spending half of one's life working in a city to relocating there permanently in search of larger opportunities,

especially when the degradation by large-scale logging, mining, monoculture, and other resource extractions destroys the environment a group formerly inhabited. For better or for worse, the modern geopolitical trend is toward general population intermixture in multiethnic polities. This could be termed "diversity," and indeed one potential aim might be that peoples speaking different languages will coexist within large cities, maintaining their native languages at home while using the dominant top twenty languages as utilitarian lingua francas in the realms of education, politics, and the workplace. This is the goal stated by many language revivalists, who certainly do not wish to bar indigenous peoples from the world economy.

This vision seems unobjectionable enough on its face but in reality simply could not support six thousand distinct languages. Certainly there are cities and countries where two or more languages coexist, such as English and French in Canada, Spanish and Catalan in the Catalonian region of Spain, or even more than a dozen in India. However, it is impossible, by the dictates of sheer logic, that *six thousand* languages, or anything even close, could thrive and be passed on generation after generation within the world's cities.

This is because if a city is to contain ethnic groups in a state of harmony—and presumably this is the ideal—then a phenomenon inherent to harmony is intermarriage. Love knows no boundaries, and world history eloquently demonstrates that intermarriage can only be prevented under conditions of virulent enmity between groups or, at the very least, stringent caste relations such as those in India, designating certain groups as unsuitable for intimate contact with others. The problem is that, if a couple speaking different native languages but both fluent in the dominant lingua franca marry and have children, then the children almost inevitably become more competent and comfortable in the lingua franca than in the language spoken by either parent. This is partly because the parents are more likely to speak the lingua franca to each other. Furthermore, even if the parents dutifully make sure to speak to the children only in their respective native languages, once the children are exposed to the lingua franca in school and in the world outside of the home, social evaluations kick in. Young children are exquisitely sensitive to such metrics, and quite commonly, as the child gets older, he or she begins to reject the parents' home languages in favor of the "cool" language, the one spoken by playmates, heard incessantly on television, and in general the marker of success and acceptance in the only society they have ever known. Many are the people we know who say that they spoke their parents' native language or languages when they were young but have since forgotten most of it—even when they still live with the parents and hear the language constantly. Social evaluations play a crucial role in a child's receptivity to linguistic input and orientation toward it.

Finally, even in rare cases when parents are diligent enough to maintain their child's fluency in the home language or languages, when that child himself marries, the chances of his marrying someone who speaks the same language (or certainly languages) are slim, and hence the chances that *their* children will speak a language they hear only occasionally from one parent and otherwise only when grandparents visit is nil.

The Grass Is Always Greener: The Mundane Realities of the "Exotic" What this means is that a world where all six thousand of today's languages thrived would be, properly speaking, one where a great many peoples remained rooted to isolated hunter-gatherer, pastoral, or small-scale cultivational existences, untouched by the First World. There is perhaps a certain romance in that idea: we are trained to emphasize the downsides of our First World existences, which are certainly many, such that a picture of a globe peopled by smallish groups living on the land may seem "the way things should be." Yet for all of the pernicious injustices and psychological dislocation inherent to Western life, there is perhaps a danger in romanticizing Third World cultures as well. The rain forest–dwelling Amazonians whose cultures and languages are dying at an alarming rate are, after all, also societies where life expectancy is often brief, diseases easily cured in the West are often rampant and lethal, there is a high infant mortality rate, and the treatment of women would be unthinkable to anyone reared in a "modern" society, especially since the 1970s. It is not accidental that it is often women in rural and indigenous societies who are in the vanguard of opting out of the native language in favor of the linguistic key to success in the surrounding culture, where women have more freedom of choice about child rearing and more control over their relationships with men.

In the conclusion of a much-discussed article in academic linguistics' signature journal *Language*, the eminent linguist Peter Ladefoged described a Dahalo-speaking father who was proud that his son now spoke only Swahili, because this was an index of his having moved beyond the confines of village life into material success beyond. "Who am I to say that he was wrong?" writes Ladefoged. Certainly we cannot prefer that the son opt for poverty; he was most likely moving away from a context in which few Westerners, language revivalists or not, could even conceive of living if other options were available. This last point is crucial: even if the Dahalo speaker was seduced by attractions of city life and the cash economy that in our eyes are of superficial value, we put ourselves in a tenuous position when we argue that the son should resist the very life style that none of us, downsides fully acknowledged, would even consider giving up.

The possible objection that it would be preferable for his son to move to a city but be bilingual in Dahalo and Swahili would most likely be a stopgap solution: dozens of languages are spoken in Tanzania, and the chances that the son will marry a fellow Dahalo speaker in the city are slim. In response, Nancy Dorian, who spearheaded the study of language death with seminal work on the demise of Scottish Gaelic, answered Ladefoged by noting that the generations sired by the one that let its language go often come to resent their parents for not passing on such a precious inheritance. But the sad question is whether their having tried to pass the language on would have been effective in a context where those very children would have been lapping up the dominant language as eagerly as all children do—and if they had, would the children have been able to pass the language on to *their* children?

Practical Solutions

Cognizant of these problems and paradoxes, Daniel Nettle and Suzanne Romaine argue in *Vanishing Voices*, the most deeply thought of the various book-length treatments of the language-death matter, that any realistic worldwide language-revival effort must take place within a general initiative allowing indigenous groups to continue living on their lands within their own cultures. Nettle and Romaine view language death as a symptom of the larger process of the rape of the world's landscapes and the destruction of the cultures that once thrived within them, driven by the insatiable capitalist thirst for natural resources and the often brutally centralized control necessary to ensure its continual slaking. By no means so utopian as to require that native groups not acquire top twenty languages in order to participate to some extent in the world economy, Nettle and Romaine propose that such groups be ushered into a diglossic use of dominant languages and their native ones. Their point is that only if such groups are encouraged and allowed to stay in their traditional settings will such diglossia not be a mere stopgap along the way to the abandonment of the "low" language forever in favor of the "high."

Nettle and Romaine's message is as depressing as it is sensible, because at its heart is the belief that the preservation of any significant number of the world's languages will require a significant transformation in the global economy, which is driven largely by governments for whom such notions as cultural diversity have been anathema at worst and of low priority at best. The sad fact is that Western scholars' earnest musings on the value of linguistic diversity are ultimately a luxury of the prosperity created by the very destructive policies at the heart of the extinctions in question. It is not accidental, for example, that to date almost all of the seminal books and anthologies on language death have been published by Cambridge University Press, an entity representing and founded on an institution made possible only through the wealth generated by what was once one of the world's most nakedly imperialist, exploitative powers.

Developing countries, constrained by limited budgets, pressing poverty, and poor educational systems, and too frequently run by despotic dictatorships as little concerned with minority rights as the monarchies that created today's First World countries, generally only pay lip service to European calls that they preserve their lands and indigenous cultures. After all, the very European countries urging "multiculturalism" on, say, an Indonesia only developed their own broad-horizoned intelligentsia on the basis of resources derived from deforesting and polluting their own countries, as well as others, and often exterminating other cultures in the process.

This is not to say that we coddled Western intellectuals are wrong in our exhortations. It is clear to many that cultural relativism has its limits, and I believe that we can assert that the preservation of environments and indigenous cultures is a desirable pathway for humankind without censuring ourselves for imposing "ethnocentric" conceptions. I for one can quite confidently reject the notion that the erasure of the entire Amazonian rain forest be treated as a legitimate expression of a "different culture." I would love to see Nettle and Romaine's articulate exhortation and its general frame of reference serve as the foundation of increased efforts to prevent most of the world's peoples from being subsumed into a slurry of multiethnic urban misery and exploitation voiced in just a couple of dozen big fat languages.

WHAT WILL HAPPEN TO THE FIRST LANGUAGE'S CHILDREN?

Yet it is clear in view of modern realities that a great many languages now technically alive will not be saved. A sober yet progressive assessment of the situation might be that today's endangered languages constitute three main sets having potential viability.

Many Will Either Survive or Become Thriving "Taught" Languages

In the relatively successful language revivals of Irish, Breton, Maori, Welsh, and Hawaiian, large numbers of children are learning the languages in school, the media have joined the effort, and there are increasing amounts of printed materials available in the languages. However, it is also true that these languages remain very much the second languages of most of the learners, not much spoken at home or in casual situations. Whether these languages will survive as natively spoken ones is at this writing essentially a question mark.

Hebrew was indeed revived from the page at the founding of Israel—but the fact that today this case remains the only one commonly referred to as a success story signifies that it was unusual. The revival of Hebrew was favored by its occurrence within a new country where the language was explicitly designated as the intended official one, with the government expressly committed to the effort rather than setting aside occasional funds for the use of Hebrew "alongside" another language. Furthermore, the original immigrants to Israel spoke various languages and thus there was a motivation for a new language to express the new national identity, in contrast with Welsh, Irish, Hawaiian, or Maori people who, for better or for worse, can only adopt the indigenous language as an "add-on," English having long been their primary language. Finally, the adoption of Hebrew was assisted by its link to a religious tradition, virtually a covenant: even though Hebrew was declared the official language of Israel from on high, the success of the

movement was determined by a powerful sentiment within the families themselves that the use of this language was critical to the establishment of a Jewish state. It has been said that the revival would not have succeeded without this crucial element—a sense of learning Hebrew as an imperative of, again, one's very soul, not just as a kind of party trick or "local custom."

Conditions in Ireland, Wales, New Zealand, or Hawaii only approximate the spiritual ones that reanimated Hebrew. The indigenous languages are not connected to religions still alive and deeply felt by most, nor are the revival efforts taking place among a people committed so starkly and universally to cultural sovereignty as to relocate to a brand-new nation or be allowed by sociohistorical serendipity to found one. Yet many of the people learning these languages feel that they are not fully expressing their souls without speaking the indigenous language. This is a hopeful sign. In all of these places, increasing numbers of homes are passing the language on to their children as a first one.

Yet even if these success stories remain too scattered to revive the languages generally, their situation is not quite as hopeless as is claimed by various commentators who have declared the Irish revival movement a failure because of the unlikelihood that significant numbers of families will pass the language on to children as a mother tongue. It is a central tenet of the language-revival movement that a language is only truly alive when it is regularly passed on to children, but this is not necessarily true. More properly, throughout human history thus far, this has been the case. Yet it is conceivable that languages such as Irish, Welsh, Maori, and Hawaiian could be passed on as second languages, taught in school and spoken nonnatively but proficiently, *in perpetuo.* Under such conditions, the languages could persist as cultural indicators, the very learning of the language in school itself constituting a hallmark of cultural identity. As such, the population would surely speak the language with varying degrees of proficiency, some excellently, others only controlling the basics (as do many Americans in California who "speak Spanish" as the result of a few years of classes in school followed by constant exposure to the language from the large Latino population), and many people falling somewhere between these poles.

This is, after all, the case with many lingua francas in Third World countries, with more speakers having learned the languages as teenagers or later than having learned them natively; Swahili has long been an example. Many languages born as pidgins have been spoken as nonnative languages for centuries, learned mostly by men in work contexts and quickly expanding through constant use of this kind into creoles, suitable for precise and modulated expression. It is perhaps something of a Western conceit to suppose that a language is not "a language" unless it is spoken from the cradle. This requirement, after all, would imply that clergy speaking Latin or Sanskrit are not really "speaking the language," because they did not learn the language as infants, a claim that would ultimately seem to be rather arbitrary. Similarly, Africans typically "speak" many languages that were not spoken to them until adolescence or later; even if a speaker's version of a language constitutes only, say, seventy-five percent of what a natively transmitted version consists of, it is unclear that this African "does not speak" the language.

For better or for worse, the cultural conditions are present to preserve, for example, Irish within what could be considered a domain for minority languages commensurate with new world conditions: a living *taught* language. The invention of writing, which has threatened minority languages in tending to anoint the dominant languages chosen to write in as "legitimate," can ironically be of assistance here, in allowing the transcription and dissemination of language-teaching materials.

Many Will Likely Survive Only as Living "Taught" Languages

Then there are the languages concentrated in tropical regions that are threatened by the encroachments of global capitalism—the Dahalos of the world, such as the Ugong language that Thai is edging away, and the more than eight hundred fabulously complex and variegated languages of Papua New Guinea. In these cases, the glass-half-full perspective suggests hope that national governments can be persuaded to assist in preserving the cultures speaking these languages, because only this will allow them to continue to be spoken natively. On the other hand, a constructive response to the glass-half-empty perspective, conceding that brutal realities make it likely that such attempts will not be able to save anything approaching all of these languages, would be to adopt the "taught language" perspective, providing for a time when descendants of today's native speakers will at least be able to acquire some proficiency in their languages through schooling, to the extent that the descendants remain a coherent enough entity to ensure a suitable demand.

A Historically Unprecedented Number Will Die

On the other hand, almost all of the indigenous languages of North America and Australia would appear to be lost forever as living languages. All but a handful are spoken only by the very elderly, as foreign and imposing to many of their English-dominant children and grandchildren as they are to us. In most cases, surviving descendants of a given group are too few and too geographically scattered for there to be significant demand for revival of any kind in the future.

A Really Good Chinese Restaurant in San Francisco

In general it would appear that the linguistic landscape of the future will be a less diverse and somewhat blander one than has existed until now. Many of the languages that survive as natively spoken will be mostly geopolitically dominant ones, and such languages, by the very nature of having through the ages been learned by large numbers of adults

and as often as not used as secondary rather than primary languages, are often somewhat "streamlined" in regard to grammatical elaborations. This means that a certain "vanilla" quotient will be overrepresented among the surviving languages—. . . Swahili is somewhat watered down in complexity as Bantu languages go; it has even been argued that the Romance languages, representing Latin learned as a second language by subjugated populations, are slightly "pidginized" in comparison with other Indo-European languages. Note also that Wolof, in becoming the lingua franca of Senegal, is probably on the way to seeing its array of noun class markers severely reduced as a "price" to pay for its new broadened sway—power corrupts! Meanwhile, a substantial number of minority languages will persist in use as "taught" languages—but then in this guise these languages will be somewhat less elaborated than they were when spoken natively.

One might analogize the linguistic landscape of the future to a world where the dazzling variety and subtlety of native Chinese cuisines, the product of thousands of years of accumulated skills, evolutions, branchings, and mixture, are represented only by Chinese food as available in the United States. Certainly, a great deal of excellent Chinese food is available here, but not in the protean richness available in China, and a great deal of what Americans are accustomed to eating as "Chinese" food is actually better described as Chinese ingredients adapted to a beef-stew palate. Yet just as this is surely better than nothing (there was no won ton soup, sushi, coconut milk soup, or even spaghetti and meatballs served on the *Titanic* in 1912), the admittedly blanched language palate that even our most dedicated language-revival efforts will most likely leave behind is certainly better than what would remain if we did nothing.

The Task Ahead and Why It Must Be Done

It is therefore urgent that we record as many languages as possible before they no longer exist so that, even if they are not actively spoken anymore, we have their essences preserved for posterity for the benefit of descendants of speakers who want to make contact with their heritage by learning some of the language; for research; and for sheer wonder.

It is here that linguists, the people most qualified to carry out this task, will be crucial, but only if there is a fundamental recasting of current attitudes in the discipline. People often suppose that linguists are either professional polyglots or arbiters of "proper grammar." Neither is the case; in fact, precisely what most linguists are engaged in would surprise many people by virtue of the extremely specific nature of the enterprise, focused on a particular issue barely perceptible at all to the layperson.

The linguistics discipline as it is today configured is centered on identifying through elegant induction the precise structure of our innate neurological endowment for language, sparked by a paradigm founded by Noam Chomsky in the late 1950s. There are many other branches of linguistics and a great many linguists with no serious interest in the Chomskyan approach. However, the paradigm looms over the field with a sociological "capital" analogous to the domination of the music composition field decades ago by atonalists despite their never having been a numerical majority.

One's basic training focuses on the Chomskyan framework, and there is a tacit but powerful sense in the field that this subarea is not only the "sexiest," but also the most intellectually substantial. For example, there are some departments where students are trained in nothing but the Chomskyan paradigm, but none where students are grounded entirely in any other subfield—the other subfields are ultimately regarded as "other," the icing rather than the cake. Regardless of the caliber of his work in another subfield, the linguist who does not display at least token interest in the Chomskyan endeavor is not considered "a *linguist* linguist" in the back of the minds of a great many in the field, and the most general respect is accorded the linguist in an "icing" subfield who is invested in showing the implications of his work for the latest developments in the Chomsky bailiwick. For example, it is safe to say that to most modern linguists in America the phenomena I [cover many of my books] are perhaps "interesting" in a passing way, but generally not considered "real linguistics."

To be sure, Chomskyan linguistics is a thoroughly fascinating investigation. Steven Pinker's book *The Language Instinct* should in my opinion, along with Jared Diamond's *Guns, Germs, and Steel* (a rare example of a book that tells us what we want to hear and is empirically correct in the bargain), be required reading for all thinking people. It is not for nothing that the Chomskyan paradigm took our field by storm to such an extent in the 1960s and has obsessed so many fine minds since. Properly, however, illuminating the possibility that we possess a neural mechanism calibrated to produce basic sentences is but one of dozens of ways that one might study the multifarious thing known as human language. In our moment, as linguist R. M. W. Dixon eloquently calls for in his book *The Rise and Fall of Languages*, linguists should be trained to go out and document at least one dying language before it disappears forever from the earth—I myself will be embarking on such work as soon as I finish this book. This is particularly appropriate given that the study of such a language inestimably enriches the study of the possibility of an innate language competence, often furnishing a career's worth of relevant data. (Notice my sense of obligation to say that, so powerful is the sense of "Chomsky—smart/other—also-ran" in modern academic linguistics in the United States.)

It is often said that we must preserve the world's languages because each one reflects a particular culture. Although this is true in itself, I have always felt that to elevate this as a guiding motivation for preserving languages is based on an oversimplified conception of the relationship between language and culture. It is true that when a group loses its language millennia of accumulated knowledge regarding the medicinal properties of plants, the subtleties of managing crops, the life cycles of fishes, and other phenomena are lost. However, in the strict sense, the linkage of language revival with cultures seems to imply that once researchers recorded the cultural aspects of language for posterity, then it would no longer be important whether or not the language as a whole continued to be spoken.

And in any case, as I have noted previously, most of a given language has evolved less on the basis of culture than through the structured randomness of an evolution bounded only by human physiognomy and cognitive requirements. All but a few pages of any written grammar of a language is taken up with elaborate rules, lists, and exceptions that no more reveal anything specific to the culture that uses them than a pattern of spilled milk reveals anything specific about the bottle it came from.

Linguists are quite aware of this, and in fact most linguists' scholarship on languages has little to do with charting links between grammars and cultures. It is safe to say that most, although not all, linguists largely cherish languages because of the sheer marvel of their various architectures, elegantly combining structure and chaos in six thousand different ways. I surmise that the emphasis on culture among linguists active in the language-revival movement stems from a sense that the purely linguistic wonder of human speech is less accessible to the general public than arguments founded on more easily perceived concepts such as culture.

Yet…I have hoped to usher the reader into the very awareness animating linguists that human speech is a truly wondrous thing in itself. In this vein, it pays to note that the Dahalo language that Peter Ladefoged referred to is the one with clicks spoken far from the territory where the other click languages are spoken—the language the farmer thinks of as a sign of backwardness is, with all due respect to his justifiable relationship to his immediate circumstances, a language with a wondrous sound system. A great many of the Native American languages dying before our eyes were so complex that children were not fully competent in them until they were ten years old. It is truly sad that world history cannot allow all of these languages to continue to be spoken, transform themselves into new ones, overgrow, and mix with one another. But at the very least we can make sure that as many of them as possible are written down as thoroughly as possible before their demise as living systems and that at least a healthy number of lucky ones can be passed along as secondary but essential languages across generations.

Let's take a look at one last descendant of the world's first language. Because prefixes and suffixes generally evolve in a language from what begin as full, separate words, the first language can be assumed to have had no prefixes or suffixes at all (or tones or a great many other complications of a grammar that only arise through gradual reinterpretations of material). Yet 150,000 years later, gradual evolution produced a remarkable array of prefixes in the Central Pomo language of California. English speakers associate prefixes with relatively basic meanings such as repetition (*re-*) and opposition (*un-, in-, mis-*). But in Central Pomo, prefixes carry much more robust and specific meanings:

ba-	orally
s-	by sucking
š-	with a handle
ča-	by slicing
čʰ-	pertaining to vegetative growth
da-	by pushing with the palm
h-	by poking
m-	with heat
qa-	by biting
ša-	by shaking
'-	by fine hand action, such as using the fingers

The root *yól* means "to mix." Each of its combinations with these eleven prefixes yields a particularly useful word:

bayól	to insert words suddenly while humming; that is, mix orally
syól	to wash down cookies or doughnuts with coffee; that is, to mix by sucking
šyól	to stir with a spoon; that is, to mix with a "handle"
čayól	to chop up several things together, such as celery and onions for stew
čʰyól	to plant things close together
dayól	to fold in dry ingredients while baking
hyól	to add salt or pepper (I guess they "poke" it in)
myól	to throw various ingredients into a pot; that is, to mix by heating
qayól	to eat several things together, such as meat and potatoes; that is, to mix by biting
šayól	to sift dry ingredients
'yól	to throw ingredients into a bowl with the fingers

Of course, the prefixes create new words with each verb; *'ól*, with a glottal stop as its first consonant, means "to summon," and here are some of its prefixed versions:

ba'ól	to call; that is, to summon orally
š'ól	to set a fishing line; that is, to summon by manipulating a handle
čʰ'ól	to comb hair; that is, to summon vegetative growth (by analogy with the flowing motion of some vegetation)
da'ól	to dig for; that is, to summon by pushing with the palm
h'ól	to probe for a creature with a stick; that is, to summon by poking

It is this kind of thing, then, that we are losing when languages die—the last known fluent speakers of Central Pomo have died since these data were collected. Just as we would be inestimably poorer to be denied the opportunity to see giraffes, roses, bombardier beetles, tulips, and little black house cats with white spots on their chests that sit on our laps as we write, we lose one of the true wonders of the world every time one of these glorious variations on a theme set by the first language slips away unrecorded for posterity. We will never encounter a stegosaur, but we can be thankful that fossils allow us to know what it was like. In the same way, if we cannot enjoy all six thousand of the world's languages alive for much longer, let us at least make sure to afford them high-quality preservation.

In the Central Pomo case, certainly the loss of the language entailed the loss of a vehicle of cultural expression. But surely all of us value sucking, poking, and shaking as much as the Central Pomo speakers did: it's just that our languages chose not to index such things with prefixes. Most likely the reader's native language chose instead to genuflect to marking each noun as definite or indefinite. Both the Central Pomo prefixes and the European languages' articles are fascinating in their own right as alternate methods of packaging information in order to talk about this thing called living, and both are only the tip of the iceberg in regard to the endless ways in which humans can express themselves in speech.

Each variant of the first language is festooned with gloriously random remnants of things caught in the cracks in the course of transformations long forgotten, and most of them exist in an array of subvariants on the theme related to one another rather like Barbara Cartland's hundreds of romance novelettes. All carry mementoes of past liaisons with other dialects of other languages; some of them once rose from the ashes; most of them developed as far beyond the call of duty as the Cathedral of Notre Dame. A select few even sit swathed in a Dorian Gray complex as a by-product of the invention of the printing press. The world's riffs on basic materials that emerged in East Africa around 148,000 B.C. represent six thousand ways of being human.

Notes

1. Unfortunately he died toothless, rendering the data elicited from him somewhat fuzzy around the edges—particularly awkward because he was the only source of the language ever recorded.

2. Yes, there *were!* Just imagine that.

3. Notice that India is so populous that languages many of us have never heard of are spoken by more people than almost any others in the world (Bihari, Telugu, Marathi).

4. Which in itself sounds like a song cut from *The Music Man* on the road to New York.

Post-reading Questions / Activities

- Do you agree that it is tragic to lose a language? Why? What is lost with it?
- Analogies help us think about unfamiliar things in terms of something more familiar, which provides advantages. At the same time, they may urge us to overlook differences. Discuss the advantages and disadvantages of using biological evolution as an analogy for human language.
- Poll the students in your class. How many generations back did their forebears speak languages other than English? How many languages were spoken? How many languages can your classmates speak, and how well? Are any of their ancestors' languages endangered?
- What does it mean for a language to be genuinely spoken?
- Research an endangered language and the activities being done to combat its loss.

Vocabulary

diglossia	lingua franca
language revival	pidgin

Suggested Further Reading

Abley, Mark. 2003. *Spoken Here: Travels Among Threatened Languages.* Boston and New York: Houghton Mifflin.

Dorian, Nancy C. 1981. *Language Death: The Life Cycle of a Scottish Gaelic Dialect.* Philadelphia: University of Pennsylvania Press.

———, ed. 1989. *Investigating Obsolescence: Studies in Language Contraction and Death.* Cambridge: Cambridge University Press.

McWhorter, John H. 2001. *The Power of Babel: A Natural History of Language.* New York: Times Books.

Nettle, Daniel, and Suzanne Romaine. 2000. *Vanishing Voices: The Extinction of the World's Languages.* Oxford: Oxford University Press.

Walsh, Michael. 2005. "Will Indigenous Languages Survive?" *Annual Review of Anthropology* 34: 293–315.

CHAPTER 21

The Future of Native Languages

Lindsay J. Whaley

(2003)

Experts tend to repeat the estimate that 90% of the world's 6,000 languages are likely to be extinct within two hundred years. While Lindsay Whaley deplores the likely extinction of many languages, he examines the premises underlying this estimate with great care.

"Globalization" is a broad term often used to explain homogenization of the world's cultures. Scholars disagree about the completeness of that process and about what it means in particular cases. Whether smaller minority languages will disappear in the future at the same rate as we believe they have in the past depends on social, political, economic, cultural, and technological processes. Their great complexity means that predicting the future is a never-ending enterprise with little agreement.

Reading Questions

- What are the typical predictions about the vitality of languages, worldwide, in the future? How and why does Whaley dispute these predictions?
- On what is the common estimate of 90% language extinction based?
- What are the important differences between the linguistic situations in North America, Australia, and Russia, on the one hand, and Papua New Guinea, Indonesia, Nigeria, India, and Cameroon, on the other?
- What variables have to be considered in understanding the vitality of a particular language?

We are in the midst of a massive demographic transformation on our planet—a shift from linguistic and cultural diversity toward linguistic and cultural homogeneity. Such a shift, it seems, is not without precedent; the steady dispersal of agricultural societies that occurred 10,000 years ago likely involved the disappearance of a large number of cultures and languages. However, what makes the current demographic shift distinctive is the astonishing rapidity at which it is happening. Of course, phenomena such as languages and cultures prove difficult to objectify, and our knowledge about many languages/cultures is limited. Both factors make them difficult to enumerate for statistical purposes, but credible attempts to measure the contemporary magnitude of decline in linguo-cultural diversity are startling. For example, widely accepted estimates point to the loss of a language at every 2 weeks on average over the next century [4], where 'loss' means the complete absence of any fluent speaker.

The decline in overall numbers of languages (and presumably a significant number of cultures) has been going on for several centuries, yet because the shift is of global proportion and is discernable only in the passing of several generations, its trajectory has gone unexamined until relatively recently. Certainly, the academic community was slow to make it a topic of inquiry. It was only in the first half of the 20th century that comments on the immanent loss of indigenous languages began to appear with any degree of frequency, both in the writings of scholars of international renown, such as Franz Boas and Edward Sapir, and in publications of missionaries and explorers (as just one example, see Ref. [10]). Not until the end of the 20th century had discussion over the leveling of linguistic and cultural variation matured to the point where we might be justified in speaking of a corpus of literature on the issue. Looking just to work on language endangerment, one finds good general accounts [4,32], as well as case studies too numerous to cite here. There are efforts to capture the core causes of language loss [7,40], regional studies (see most of the papers in Ref. [34]), and efforts to establish comparative accounts of language loss situations [12]. The effects of language loss both

Lindsay J. Whaley, "The Future of Native Languages." *Futures* 35 (2003): 961–973.

on the structure of language [3,17,18] and on individual self-identity [5,22] have been investigated. Most recently, we find work exploring the relation of language loss to biodiversity [15,16,32] and the question of where language use fits into the slate of basic human rights [36].

One lacuna in this important body of research is the attempt to be more precise in predicting how many languages are, in fact, *likely* to disappear in the next century or so versus how many are *at risk* of disappearing....I would like to clarify this distinction and point out why it is of key significance in understanding the future of languages on the planet. Before doing so, two caveats are in order. First, while I will argue that from both a theoretical and empirical perspective not all languages at risk of dying will actual die, this in no way diminishes the profound global reformation that is occurring due to the loss of languages. Whether 50 or 55 or even 90% of the existing languages become extinct, the fact remains that a remarkable demographic event would have taken place. Second, while this [work] is grounded in the conviction that a more precise forecast of the future of languages is desirable and possible, I will not accomplish any precision in numbers here. The goal is, rather, to underscore a few of the variables that need to be considered in developing a more reliable and specific account of how many languages will die in the coming 100–200 years.

WHAT IS AN 'ENDANGERED' LANGUAGE?

Even a quick survey of writing on endangered languages, both in the popular press and in scholarly publications, will reveal a ubiquitous statistic about language vitality: 50–90% of languages could die in the next 200 years. Here is a representative statement: "Some prominent linguists predict that half of roughly 6000 world languages will be silenced by the end of this century, and that 80–90% will die off within the next 200 years" (*Newsweek International*, June 19, 2000). As is typical, the statistics here are attributed to unnamed authorities on the topic, though it is almost certain that they are ultimately derived from the seminal research of Michael Krauss. He may be one of the most cited linguists in the world, yet often does not receive his due credit. The published version of this research [24] remains, to the best of my knowledge, the most explicit attempt to predict the rate of language loss in the imminent future.

Among other contributions in this work, Krauss makes a four-way classification of language vitality: (1) Extinct languages are those that are no longer spoken; (2) Moribund languages are those that are no longer being learned by children as a mother-tongue; (3) Safe languages are those that will continue to be spoken into the indefinite future due to large numbers of speakers and/or official state support; and (4) Endangered languages are those languages which do not fall into the other three categories and "will—if the present conditions continue—cease to be learned by children during the coming century" (p. 6). That is, these languages will become moribund, and in all but exceptional cases, will eventually become extinct.

Taking 6000 languages as a reasonable estimate for the number of languages being spoken in the world, Krauss places 600 in his safe category, 3000 in the moribund category and the remainder in the endangered category. On this basis a range of 50–90% of languages dying out is obtained. Moribund languages (50%), since they are no longer being transmitted, are doomed and set the lower mark for language death. Add the endangered languages (i.e., 40% of the world's languages), and one sees the foundation to Krauss' dire conclusion: "Therefore, I consider it a plausible calculation that—at the rate things are going—the [21st] century will see either the death or the doom of 90% of mankind's languages" (p. 7).

For present purposes, two basic, as well as related, objections must be raised in connection with this conclusion. First, although Krauss' negative definition of an 'endangered language', i.e., a language that is not 'safe' nor 'moribund', poses no difficulty per se, his monolithic understanding of what is going to happen to the vitality of these languages is at least debatable, if not misleading. Consider the following: Shoshone, an Uto-Aztecan language of the US, and Foi, a Papuan language of Papua New Guinea, both have roughly 2500 speakers and would both be considered endangered under Krauss' taxonomy. However, the social contexts in which one finds these languages could not be more different. For well-known historical reasons, Shoshone speakers have been under pressure to switch to English for over a century. They live in a country where stable bilingualism is discouraged and where they are surrounded by English-speaking people—not to mention an English-based pop culture that is marketed with great effect. Most people of Shoshone heritage do not speak the language. Short of a Herculean effort on the part of Shoshone communities, the language will become moribund in the coming decades. But what about Foi? The speakers of this language dwell in a country with a long history of multilingualism. They are surrounded by speakers of several other languages (e.g., Kewa and Samberigi), but these languages are not encroaching on Foi. The infrastructure of the country is such that the development of this area is not an imminent possibility. Almost everyone of Foi ethnicity speaks the language. In this case, the future vitality of the language is much harder to predict. Certainly, because Foi has a small number of overall speakers, it is at risk. Disease or environmental catastrophe could wipe out the population or cause migration. The government of Papua New Guinea could instigate a massive campaign to spread Tok Pisin or English at the expense of countless indigenous languages. A neighboring speech community might achieve a regional prestige that leads speakers of Foi to learn this language in place of their own. All these occurrences are possible, but they do not seem likely, at least not in the near future.

Therefore, a more accurate prediction about language loss must involve a more nuanced treatment of endangered languages. Indeed, this is precisely the tack taken by other linguists [41], especially those who have examined language vitality on regional levels rather than a global scale, for example, Kinkade [23] in Canada and Krauss himself [25] in the circumpolar countries. Minimally, we must recognize a distinction between two subsets of endangered languages, languages that are likely to disappear (typically because they are already on a recognizable path to moribundity) versus languages that are currently viable but are at risk of becoming moribund because they are not 'safe' in Krauss' sense. Ideally, this latter subset should involve further discriminations depending on the nature of the risk, a point to which I return later.

The second objection to treating Krauss' statistics as a reliable forecast to the future of language use is that his estimate for current moribundity is probably too high. Krauss arrives at his number of 50% in the following manner. He begins by noting that his primary source for language vitality data, *Ethnologue* [13], has 50% of the world's languages being sufficiently viable to warrant Bible translations, 10% not being viable enough, and 40% not being classifiable due to lack of information. Krauss grants that a good many of the "unknown 40% may be viable" (p. 6) but contends that the compilers of *Ethnologue* "might agree that as many as 20% of the world's languages are already moribund" (p. 6). Why, then, does Krauss raise this number to 50%? Two reasons. First, he indicates that two other (unfortunately unnamed) experts had arrived at a number more along the lines of 50%. Second, he asserts that the conditions which are known to have led to high language mortality seems to hold sway in countries with the highest levels of language diversity. Though his argument is not explicit, the logic appear to be that since language moribundity is known to be around 90% in well-surveyed parts of the world—North America, Australia, and the northern region of the former Soviet Union—then moribundity is probably also around 90% in other areas of high linguistic diversity. Therefore, many of the unknown languages in the *Ethnologue* are probably moribund, as perhaps are some of those that the *Ethnologue* implies are viable. If so, 50% is a reasonable mark to set for the current level for moribundity in the world's languages.

However, the presupposition behind Krauss' logic is dubious. While some points of commonality can be identified for at-risk languages around the world, there are also important variations in circumstances in some regions, and significantly, the widest points of variation are found in many countries that have high linguistic diversity. Take just the five countries that have the most languages spoken within their borders. According to Krauss, these are: Papua New Guinea (850 languages), Indonesia (670), Nigeria (410), India (380), and Cameroon (270). Taken together, the languages of these five countries constitute roughly 43% of the overall global total. Although these countries were all colonized to a degree, they are also unlike the Americas, Australia, and Russia in that the majority of the colonizing population ultimately left, and native populations remained. As a result, the colonial languages of these countries are not the primary threat to at-risk languages, at least in the short run. Indeed, one is hard pressed to identify any indigenous languages that have become moribund due to the spread of the language of the colonizers, e.g., English in Nigeria and India, or French in Cameroon. Rather the typical pattern in these countries is for widely spoken indigenous languages to pose the largest immediate threat to smaller languages.

When the literature on endangered languages in these countries is examined, it does not focus on widespread moribundity of languages; rather it highlights the very real threats which might cause languages to become moribund (e.g., the excellent overview of the language situation in Papua New Guinea by Nettle and Romaine [32]), accounts for the current absence of widespread moribundity (cf. Annamalai [2], who says about India: "The reasons for the general *lack* of loss and shift [of Indian languages] can be found in the social, economic and political structure of the country,"), or identifies the beginnings of a language shift (a recent example from Nigeria is provided by Adegbija [1], who looks at the use of Oko in urban areas, but writes "Oko seems to be doing quite well in its own village hinterland").

The point here is decidedly not to say that small indigenous languages spoken in sub-Saharan Africa, South Asia, and areas of the Pacific are all thriving and that concerns about their future vitality are misplaced. On the contrary, many of these languages continue to be passed on to children only due to a tenuous set of circumstances that might well change due to war, destruction of local environments, disease, surrounding social or economic assimilatory pressures, government policies unfavorable to ethnic minorities or their languages, and so on. And many of the speech communities where these languages are spoken have already begun a shift such that a smaller percentage of children are learning them than in the past. While avoiding a false optimism, I suggest that Krauss' guess at the percentage of the present level of moribund languages is inflated by as much as 20%.

CATEGORIZING THREATENED LANGUAGES

When it comes to forecasting the future of languages, both in terms of whether they are likely to disappear and when, it is imperative to make a sufficient number of distinctions among language vitality types. The prospects for a moribund language are bleak; this is less obviously true for a currently viable language, say one spoken in a rural part of Cameroon, even if the language is the mother tongue of only a few thousand people. At the least, a six-way scheme is required to categorize languages: safe, at risk, disappearing, moribund, nearly extinct, and extinct.[1] This classification subdivides two of Krauss' categories. First, I make a distinction between moribund languages, i.e., those which are not being learned by children as a mother-tongue versus nearly extinct languages, which are those that, properly speaking, lack a speech community. That is, they are not being used by anyone on a regular basis. For most nearly extinct languages, there are only a handful of native speakers left, where in some cases a moribund language may still have a sizable number of speakers. This is the case, for example, with Oroqen, a Northwestern Tungusic language in China, which is moribund. There are roughly 2000 native speakers, and in at least a couple of villages, there are adults who will use the language on a daily basis. The language could conceivably survive if there were a substantial shift in attitudes about the desirability of transmitting the language to children. For nearly extinct languages, however, long-term survival is almost inconceivable.

I also subdivide Krauss' 'endangered languages' category into 'at risk' and 'disappearing'. By a disappearing language, I mean one for which there is an observable shift to another language in most or all of the communities where it is spoken. This does not mean that children are not learning the language, but only that an increasingly smaller percentage of children do. Such languages are on a path to moribundity, but we cannot simply assume that they will eventually enter into that state without first looking at the specific variables which affect the likelihood of long-term use.

When prognosticating on what the global picture of language diversity will look like in 100 years (or 50 or 200 years for that matter), the most careful attention must be given to languages that fall in the at-risk or disappearing category, and to a lesser extent moribund languages that still have a significant number of fluent speakers. Whereas cataclysmic changes in the world, for example large-scale nuclear war, might mean the loss of a safe language, and an extraordinary set of circumstances might vivify an extinct language (such as Hebrew) or revitalize a nearly extinct language (such as seems to be happening with Manx), such occurrences are truly atypical. Similarly, since the long-term success rate in reversing language shift for highly moribund languages is unknown, we must identify their survival only as a hopeful, yet remote possibility. For other types of languages, however, the future prospects are much harder to state with certainty, and we should make categorical statements with utmost reserve.

What makes the future of at-risk languages and disappearing languages uncertain is the fact that a complex matrix of political, social, economic, environmental, and educational variables influence the ongoing use of these languages. Some of the variables are purely localized, but others are more regional, national, or transnational in character (see Grenoble and Whaley's work [12] for a discussion on how such variables relate). Furthermore, the variables are dynamic, which is to say that what was true of the situation facing, say Oroqen, Shoshone, or Oko, in the past 200 years is not the same today with respect to certain variables, nor will it be true 200 years from now. The task, then, for understanding how a language will fare in the future is the task of identifying the important variables that are buttressing or sapping the strength of a language and predicting whether and how these variables will change.

FLUCTUATING VARIABLES OF LANGUAGE VITALITY

For any given language community, there are a large number of variables that are relevant to understanding the vitality of the primary language, including such things as the spheres of language use, the degree of multilingualism, educational practices, scale and type of local economy, levels of exogamy, and so on. Any time that one or more variables change, the possibility arises that the vitality of the language can be affected, for better or for worse. The premise behind this view of assessing language use is that every community must ultimately be studied in its own right because no two language communities ever share precisely the same combination of variables. Even so, it is clear that there are persistent patterns across language communities that make generalizations possible. For example, Krauss [24] accurately recognizes the official status of a language and a large number of speakers as dominant variables that allow us to predict the long-term survival of a language.

There are many variables whose values are currently in flux for speech communities all over the world because of social, political, and economic trends of a global scale. In the present context, such variables are of particular interest because they underscore some difficulties that arise in making predictions for the future of languages. The trajectory for language endangerment will shift depending on what happens in the domains described by these variables, which means that the already rapid rate of languages moving into moribundity could accelerate, or to the contrary, could slow. I describe a set of these variables here to exemplify the point.

Revitalization and Maintenance Programs

A recent phenomenon around the world is the appearance of programs designed to preserve threatened languages. These programs are diverse in their design and in their aims. Some are geared at developing immersion education, others at expanding the social domains in which a particular language is spoken, and still others in actively developing the vocabulary of a language to provide standard terms for new technologies. Some of these programs are proactive, attempting to stay language decline before it begins or is in its early stages. Others are trying to recoup the losses in numbers of speakers that have occurred. In some instances of extreme moribundity or near extinction, the goal of language revitalization programs is to ensure that at least a reasonable degree of fluency is being passed on to younger speakers so that the language does not die (see Hinton [19] for a good survey).

Because most of these programs are relatively new, few longitudinal studies are available to assess their impact on language vitality. Certainly, one need not look hard in order to find any number of failed or flailing efforts, yet other programs have had some measure of success, most famously the Maori and Hawaiian 'language nests', yet there are encouraging reports from elsewhere. For example, the Kahnawà:ke community in Quebec has seen an increase in the number of children learning Mohawk due to an immersion school [21]. The number of Welsh speakers has shown an increase for the first time in almost a century due to educational efforts, changes in language policy, and the presence of Welsh on the radio and television [29]. There is renewed interest in Ainu, a language spoken in Japan that is occasionally described as extinct or on the brink of extinction, such that the language is beginning to see an increase in the number of young people with an ability to converse in Ainu [28].

Of course, the achievements recorded for these revitalization efforts may be short term. It is fully possible that they are futile attempts to stop the inevitable march toward language moribundity and death. The polar opposite possibility must also be considered, however. One might argue that a new political openness in some parts of the world to the teaching and promotion of small minority languages, combined with the growing desire by small speech communities to preserve their linguistic heritage and higher sophistication in knowing how to design effective maintenance programs makes it more and more likely that at-risk and disappearing languages will not become moribund. Perhaps, more remarkably, many moribund languages may shift back to vitality.

The Information Age and Technology

In research on language endangerment and death, we find an emerging consensus regarding a set of distinct eras of human (pre-)history that have variably affected linguistic diversity. The emerging story goes something like this [27,32]. The earliest human societies were small bands of hunter-gatherers. They began to spread out and populate the earth, each new migration into a previously uninhabited region, giving rise to the potentiality, if not the actuality, of a new linguistic community. Borrowing terminology of Dixon [6], who in turn borrowed it from Eldridge and Gould [8], we might call this a period of punctuation. That is, it is a time with rapid diversification of languages, the birth of many new languages, branches, and families. At some point, the expansion levels off, and we enter a state of equilibrium, again borrowing the application of the term from Dixon. Estimates of the linguistic diversity of the time range from 8000 to 20,000 languages.

Roughly 10,000 years ago, the story continues, agriculture appears in scattered locations around the globe, and in a least a few areas it catches on as the mode of subsistence du jour, and we see three massive waves of agricultural advance, one out of Mesopotamia into Eurasia, one spreading across sub-Saharan Africa, and one engulfing east Asia. We have entered another period of punctuation. The spreading peoples bring their languages with them, and as the wave presses forward, linguistic diversification follows in its wake. During this punctuation, however, the spreading languages are replacing the languages of indigenous hunter-gathering tongues. We have the first great instance of rapid language death. Therefore, although there is localized punctuation and certain language families such as Niger-Congo, Sino-Tibetan, and Indo-European are rapidly diversifying, there is actually a decrease in overall linguistic diversity on the planet because the diversification cannot keep up with the language death.

We then again enter a period of equilibrium where the amount of language diversification is small, but neither are there social transformations that lead to much language death. In the 16th century, we enter the next great phase of language death. European colonization, followed by industrialization and the birth of the nation-state, once again redefine the nature of human society, and in this redefinition certain peoples, cultures, and languages come to dominate. The linguistic consequence is that scores of smaller languages simply disappear. We now sit at the end of this wave of advance, observing its consequences first hand.

This is the context in which most projections about the future of endangered languages are cast. The expectation is that the measurable decline of linguistic diversity brought about by the colonial age will continue unabated in the postcolonial age. If so, we can expect the decline to continue at the current pace, or more likely, at an accelerated pace. However, if some futurists (notably Toffler [38]) are correct, then we have begun a third great wave of social transformation, the information age, which will so transform the dynamics of our lives, that we will no longer be able to make the same assumptions about how language users make their choices about language loyalties.

The social patterns of the proposed information age are themselves a matter of conjecture, which makes language forecasting in light of them all the more problematic. Least controversially, the technology of the information age itself raises some fascinating possibilities for bolstering at-risk and disappearing languages. There now exists the potential of locally produced educational materials, web sites dedicated to the promotion of endangered languages, phone and computer connections between related language communities in remote regions, and so on. All of this places the practical ability to promote language use more in the hands of local communities and less in the hands of regional or national authorities [14]. However, the influence of the information age could very well be more dramatic than this. As geography becomes less important, demographic phenomena such as urbanization, which have been detrimental to endangered languages, may become less prominent or may cease altogether. The work place and the home may become less distinct (which could be a boon or a hindrance to the use of local languages). On the clearly negative side, the information age brings with it an unprecedented ability to spread mass consumerism and pop culture, both of which are regularly identified as agents that undermine the value and social structures of other cultures [39], which are essential to the continued use of many heritage languages.

The New World Order

The notion of an incipient 'information age' operates part and parcel with other sorts of global trends most often grouped together under the rubric of 'globalization'. The term is rarely employed with much precision, and as a consequence it is often difficult to get a handle on just what people mean by it. Loosely speaking, globalization is a process of increasing international integration of economic life. The integration demands certain adjustments of national political structures (often described as an adoption of 'neoliberalism', though at this point probably better taken as a move in the direction of neoliberalism rather than a wholesale implementation). Beyond this, there is a lack of consensus on the ultimate effects of globalization, indeed even whether it is a desirable or deleterious process, especially for developing regions of the world. But few deny that globalization has at least some attendant influence on culture.

Very little attention has been given to the question of what globalization might mean for endangered languages. On the one hand, if globalization is taken to be an "intensification of world-wide social relations which link distant localities in such a way that local happenings are shaped by events occurring many miles away" [11], and the influence exerted is asymmetrical in favor of more powerful economic entities, then the effect on small communities might be profound. Certainly, the pressure to assimilate economically could, and probably would, extend to linguistic and cultural assimilation, which would lead to language loss unless countered by other variables (e.g., pride in one's cultural differences). When Fukuyama [9] identifies liberal democracy and the type of capitalism it produces as the "end of history," he is in effect suggesting the inevitability of global homogenization. Given the dominance of the US in the world today, this vision of the new world order all but obliges us to see the spread of English to all regions of the world. Even the safe languages will not stay safe indefinitely.

Not all agree with this vision, however. Huntington [20], for example, predicts that American hegemony will be placed in check by the emergence of increasingly powerful alliances of nations. The conglomerations will be based on shared cultural traits such as religion, social philosophies, and ethnicity (which, of course, is typically tied to language). This perspective on the future, like Fukuyama's, takes the diminishment of the nation-state to be inevitable, but that eventuality does not correlate with a cultural homogenizing of the planet (see also Ref. [31]); on the contrary, Huntington (p. 64) argues with respect to language that as "power diffuses Babelization spreads," i.e., there will be a push towards linguistic heterogeneity. What is not clear under this view is whether the Babelization will be true of most languages or solely of large languages (i.e., safe languages). Huntington's view is predicated on the emergence of eight 'civilizations', which will dominate and determine the geopolitical future of the world. Within each civilization, there might be extreme pressure to assimilate culturally, religiously, and linguistically (In fact this is a fairly accurate picture of what is currently going on.).

One last mitigating circumstance in these economic and political shifts is the emergence of increasingly effective movements for indigenous political rights, which include linguistic rights. As Skutnabb-Kangas [35] so incisively puts it: "The linguistic human rights of both indigenous peoples and linguistic minorities, especially educational language rights, play a decisive role in maintaining and revitalizing languages." Certainly, one needs to look only to Europe (as in the case of Welsh and Manx, mentioned above, but also many other at-risk/moribund languages) and Canada [33] to find impressive gains in linguistic rights that have had an amelioratory effect on the use of heritage languages. The key issue in this regard is what the long-term impact of linguistic rights will be. The political right to speak and learn one's native language makes long-term viability more possible, but it is no guarantee of vitality. Economic and cultural forces (for instance, the seemingly irresistible lure of pop culture for teens around the globe) may prove to dominate in determining language use.

The Environment

Increasingly, scholars, activists, and members of minority communities have raised the issue of links among language, culture, and the environment. For example, Mace and Pagel [26] point out that both diversity of languages and diversity of species are greatest near the equator and decrease as one moves away from it. The correlation has only begun to be adequately explored, though some [30,32] take it to signal an inherent link between environment and languages. Hence, Nettle and Romaine state (p. 46): "The evidence we have presented in this chapter also allows us to understand why the same amount of habitat destruction in the tropics *would lead* to many more biolinguistic extinctions than would occur in the higher latitudes" (emphasis mine). If the link between language and environment is this direct, then habitat destruction becomes an important indicator of language use in the future.

Not all research has borne out a strong correlation between bio- and linguistic diversity [37], and a core assumption of much work on this issue, namely that the knowledge about a local environment is inextricably connected to the local language spoken there, is not likely to gain wide acceptance without better empirical justification. But even a more indirect association between language and environment would need to be factored into predictions about long-term language use. Since this variable has hitherto been ignored in estimates on language diversity in the coming centuries, there is a need for it to receive far greater attention.

CONCLUSION

The underlying point of this [discussion] has been a negative one. We do not currently have a good estimate for how many current languages will survive indefinitely. The reasons for this fact are multiple. Basic information about the social, political, and economic circumstances of a large number of languages is unavailable. Moreover, since no one seriously doubts that a significant portion of current languages will die or become moribund in the next century, research on endangered languages has properly made other areas of investigation a priority such as understanding the causes of language loss and identifying ways to slow or stop language shift. Both of these are practical realities. There are also methodological issues that have interfered with understanding the future of languages, and these have been of more concern than the above. There has been a lack of critical examination of certain assumptions that lie behind previous estimates, and there has been a tendency to apply a straightforward analogy with the past as the primary tool for predicting future linguistic diversity rather than tempering this analogy with observations about how the world is making a break with the past.

Such observations cover a wide range of disciplines. No individual can hope to master the range of research necessary to make plausible predictions about coming changes to the political, economic, and social structures that be. And so a positive contribution of this [discussion] is to advocate a continued and increased interdisciplinary dialogue on the issue of linguistic/cultural diversity. As should have been evident throughout, such dialogue does exist, particularly in matters relating to environmental destruction and the legal rights of cultural minorities, but it still noticeably lacks much input from political scientists, sociologists, and economists, among others.

A second positive contribution of this [discussion] is that it raises hopes, not falsely I think, that language and culture moribundity is not as inevitable as it is often depicted in print. This is not to say that the linguistic future is rosy for at-risk and disappearing languages. On the contrary, I am not optimistic. Rather, it is to say that the future is not yet decided against the continued use of thousands of languages.

Note

1. The categorization that I am suggesting is similar in spirit to the five-way system of Kinkade [23], but differs in two respects. First, Kinkade groups disappearing and moribund languages together (labeled 'endangered languages'). Second, Kinkade's equivalent to my 'at-risk' category is reserved only for languages with a small number of people spoken in an isolated community.

References

[1] E. Adegbija, Saving threatened languages in Africa: A case study of Oko, in: J. A. Fishman (Ed.), Can Threatened Languages Be Saved?, Multilingual Matters, Clevedon, 2001, p. 284.

[2] E. Annamalai, Language survival in India: Challenges and responses, in: K. Matsumura (Ed.), Studies in Endangered Languages, Hituzi Syobo, Tokyo, 1998, p. 24 (Papers from the International Symposium on Endangered Languages, Tokyo, 18–20 November 1995).

[3] L. Campbell, M. C. Muntzel, The structural consequences of language death, in: N. C. Dorian (Ed.), Investigating Obsolescence, Cambridge University Press, Cambridge, 1989, pp. 197–210.

[4] D. Crystal, in: Language Death, Cambridge University Press, Cambridge, 2000, p. 9.

[5] N. M. Dauenhauer, R. Dauenhauer, Technical, emotional, and ideological issues in reversing language shift: examples from southeast Alaska, in: L. A. Grenoble, L. J. Whaley (Eds.), Endangered Languages: Current Issues and Future Prospects, Cambridge University Press, Cambridge, 1998, pp. 57–98.

[6] R. M. W. Dixon, The Rise and Fall of Languages, Cambridge University Press, Cambridge, 1997.

[7] N. C. Dorian, Western language ideologies and small-language prospects, in: L. A. Grenoble, L. J. Whaley (Eds.), Endangered Languages: Current Issues and Future Prospects, Cambridge University Press, Cambridge, 1998, pp. 1–25.

[8] N. Eldridge, S. J. Gould, Punctuated equilibria: An alternative to phyletic gradualism, in: J. M. Schopf (Ed.), Models in Paleobiology, San Francisco, Freeman, Cooper, 1972, pp. 82–115.

[9] F. Fukuyama, The end of history, The National Interest 16 (Summer) (1989) 1–18.

[10] C. W. Furlong, The Haush and the Onas, primitive tribes of Tierra del Fuego, in: Proceedings of the Nineteenth International Congress of Americanists, Washington DC, 1917, pp. 432–444.

[11] A. Giddens, in: The Consequences of Modernity, Stanford University Press, Stanford, CA, 1990, p. 64.

[12] L. A. Grenoble, L. J. Whaley, Toward a typology of language endangerment, in: L. A. Grenoble, L. J. Whaley (Eds.), Endangered Languages: Current Issues and Future Prospects, Cambridge University Press, Cambridge, 1998, pp. 22–54.

[13] B. F. Grimes (Ed.), Ethnologue: Languages of the World, Summer Institute of Linguistics, Arlington, TX, 1992.

[14] K. Hale, Strict locality in local language media, in: L. Hinton, K. Hale (Eds.), The Greenbook of Language Revitalization, Academic Press, San Diego and London, 2001, pp. 277–282.

[15] D. Harmon, Losing species, losing languages: Connections between biological and linguistic diversity, Southwest Journal of Linguistics (15) (1996) 89–108.

[16] D. Harmon, Sameness and silence: language extinctions and the dawning of a biocultural approach to diversity, Global Biodiversity (8) (1998) 2–10.

[17] J. H. Hill, Language death, language contact, and language function, in: S. Wurm, W. McCormack (Eds.), Approaches to Language, Mouton, The Hague, 1979, pp. 44–78.

[18] J. H. Hill, Dimensions of attrition in language death, in: L. Maffi (Ed.), On Biocultural Diversity: Linking Language, Knowledge and the Environment, Smithsonian Institution, Washington, DC, and London, 2001, pp. 175–189.

[19] L. Hinton, Language revitalization: An overview, in: L. Hinton, K. Hale (Eds.), The Greenbook of

Language Revitalization, Academic Press, San Diego and London, 2001, pp. 3–18.

[20] S. P. Huntington, The Clash of Civilizations, Simon & Schuster, New York, 1996.

[21] A. Jacobs, A chronology of Mohawk language instruction at Kahnawà:ke, in: L. A. Grenoble, L. J. Whaley (Eds.), Endangered Languages: Current Issues and Future Prospects, Cambridge University Press, Cambridge, 1998, pp. 117–123.

[22] C. Jocks, Living words and cartoon translations: Longhouse "texts" and the limitations of English, in: L. A. Grenoble, L. J. Whaley (Eds.), Endangered Languages: Current Issues and Future Prospects, Cambridge University Press, Cambridge, 1998, pp. 217–233.

[23] M. D. Kinkade, The decline of languages in Canada, in: R. H. Robins, E. M. Uhlenbeck (Eds.), Endangered Languages, Berg, Oxford, 1991, pp. 157–176.

[24] M. Krauss, The world's languages in crisis, Language (68) (1992) 4–10.

[25] M. Krauss, Status of northern languages. Paper presented at the Dartmouth Conference on Endangered Languages, Dartmouth College, Hanover, NH, 1995.

[26] R. Mace, M. Pagel, A latitudinal gradient in the density of human languages in North America, Proceedings of the Royal Society of London (261) (1995) 117–121.

[27] L. Maffi, Introduction: On the interdependence of biological and cultural diversity, in: L. Maffi (Ed.), On Biocultural Diversity: Linking Language, Knowledge and the Environment, Smithsonian Institution, Washington, DC, and London, 2001, pp. 1–50.

[28] J. C. Maher, Akor Itak—our language, your language: Ainu in Japan, in: J. A. Fishman (Ed.), Can Threatened Languages Be Saved? Multilingual Matters, Clevedon, 2001, pp. 323–349.

[29] G. Morgan, Welsh: A European case of language maintenance, in: L. Hinton, K. Hale (Eds.), The Greenbook of Language Revitalization, Academic Press, San Diego and London, 2001, pp. 107–113.

[30] P. Mühlhäusler, Ecolinguistics, linguistic diversity, ecological diversity, in: L. Maffi (Ed.), On Biocultural Diversity: Linking Language, Knowledge and the Environment, Smithsonian Institution, Washington, DC, and London, 2001, pp. 133–144.

[31] J. Nederveen Pieterse, Globalization and human integration: We are all migrants, Futures (32) (2000) 385–398.

[32] D. Nettle, S. Romaine, Vanishing Voices: The Extinction of the World's Languages, Oxford University Press, Oxford, 2000.

[33] D. Patrick, Language, power and ethnicity in an Arctic Quebec community. Unpublished PhD dissertation, University of Toronto, 1988.

[34] R. H. Robins, E. M. Uhlenbeck (Eds.), Endangered Languages, Berg, Oxford, 1991.

[35] T. Skutnabb-Kangas, Linguistic human rights in education for language maintenance, in: L. Maffi (Ed.), On Biocultural Diversity: Linking Language, Knowledge and the Environment, Smithsonian Institution, Washington, DC, and London, 2001, p. 399.

[36] T. Skutnabb-Kangas, R. Phillipson (Eds.), Linguistic Human Rights: Overcoming Linguistic Discrimination, Mouton de Gruyter, Berlin and New York, 1998.

[37] E. A. Smith, On the coevolution of cultural, linguistic and biological diversity, in: L. Maffi (Ed.), On Biocultural Diversity: Linking Language, Knowledge and the Environment, Smithsonian Institution, Washington, DC, and London, 2001, pp. 95–117.

[38] A. Toffler, The Third Wave, Morrow, New York, 1980.

[39] W. Van Dusen Wishard, Globalization: Humanity's great experiment, The Futurist 33 (8) (1999) 60–61.

[40] S. Wurm, Language death and disappearance: causes and circumstances, in: R. H. Robins, E. M. Uhlenbeck (Eds.), Endangered Languages, Berg, Oxford, 1991, pp. 1–18.

[41] S. Wurm, Methods of language maintenance and revival, with selected cases of language endangerment in the world, in: K. Matsumura (Ed.), Studies in Endangered Languages, Hituzi Syobo, Tokyo, 1998, pp. 191–211 (Papers from the International Symposium on Endangered Languages, Tokyo, 18–20 November 1995).

Post-reading Questions / Activities

- What are the social, political, and economic factors that have affected the fates of languages in the past 200 years? Do you think these factors are likely to remain the same? Why?
- In what ways is it difficult to make predictions about the future survival of languages?
- How have new technologies both contributed to and resisted language endangerment?
- Are you optimistic or pessimistic (or something else) about the long-term prospects of linguistic diversity? Why?
- Research one of the languages mentioned in this chapter. What efforts are being made on behalf of language revitalization or maintenance? How successful have those efforts been? What are the factors involved in this case? What do you think its prospects are?

Vocabulary

endangered language	language loss	moribund language
exogamy	language revitalization	speech community
language endangerment	language shift	

Suggested Further Reading

Abley, Mark. *Spoken Here: Travels Among Threatened Languages.* Boston and New York: Houghton Mifflin.

Dixon, Robert M. W. 1997. *The Rise and Fall of Languages.* Cambridge and New York: Cambridge University Press.

Dorian, Nancy C. 1981. *Language Death: The Life Cycle of a Scottish Gaelic Dialect.* Philadelphia: University of Pennsylvania Press.

——, ed. 1989. *Investigating Obsolescence: Studies in Language Contraction and Death.* Cambridge: Cambridge University Press.

Krauss, Michael. 1992. "The World's Languages in Crisis." *Language* 68: 4–10.

Nettle, Daniel, and Suzanne Romaine. 2000. *Vanishing Voices: The Extinction of the World's Languages.* Oxford: Oxford University Press.

Walsh, Michael. 2005. "Will Indigenous Languages Survive?" *Annual Review of Anthropology* 34: 293–315.

CHAPTER 22

Language Loss and Revitalization in California
Overview

Leanne Hinton
(1998)

However counted, most of the world's languages are endangered. Scholars estimate that about half of the languages have been lost in the last several hundred years and that more than half of those remaining will become extinct in the next several hundred years (see Chapters 20 and 21). Most of those likely to become extinct are smaller languages, spoken by minority groups or indigenous groups. This will happen because, to participate in the wider world, it is necessary for people to speak languages of wider communication. Such communicative mastery can be accomplished through additive multilingualism; but when languages are vastly unequal, this multilingualism is not likely to endure for many generations. When that happens, succeeding generations gradually shift their primary communication toward the more powerful languages. Eventually, the original language ceases to have much hold, and in time it is no longer learned as a mother tongue.

Efforts are under way throughout the world, however, to intervene actively in this process of language loss.

A catalog of such revitalization efforts would be very long, but would have to include at minimum Maori in New Zealand, Irish, Hawaiian, and Navajo. Most of the effort has originated among indigenous people rather than from officials or scholars. Since the fate of a language is determined in part by how its speakers regard it, the fact that many indigenous activists have turned their attention to revitalizing their languages means that these languages cannot be dismissed as extinct.

The only unqualified success story of language revitalization is Hebrew, which was revived as a vernacular language at the time of the birth of the state of Israel, but the particular circumstances surrounding this cannot be replicated.

Still, it is possible to observe significant creative efforts worldwide in the teaching and maintenance of endangered languages. Sometimes single individuals take on this task and sometimes it is a community effort.

A wide variety of activities surrounding language revitalization is occurring among American Indian languages, especially in California. Leanne Hinton is one of the primary scholars and practitioners of language revitalization activities, having worked for several decades with speakers of various California Indian languages.

Prior to European colonization of the Americas, linguists estimate, there were approximately three hundred languages in use on these continents. Hinton believes that 98 of them were spoken in what is now the state of California. But of these rich and varied languages, none are spoken daily as a principal form of communication. However, revitalization efforts are being undertaken by natives of a number of tribes, and only time will tell how successful they will be.

Leanne Hinton, "Language Loss and Revitalization in California: Overview." *International Journal of the Sociology of Language* 132 (1998): 83–93.

Reading Questions

- What conditions led to the decline of California Indian languages? What conditions have created a more hospitable climate since the second half of the twentieth century?
- What has led many Native Californians to seek to achieve language revitalization?
- What is the Master–Apprentice Language Learning Program? How does it work? How successful has it been? What other programs have been implemented to revitalize California Indian languages?

California, one of the most linguistically diverse places in the world, is rapidly losing its rich heritage of indigenous languages. Of at least 98 languages[1] originally spoken in what are now the political confines of this state, 45 (or more) have no fluent speakers left at all, 17 have only one to five speakers left, and the remaining 36 have only elderly speakers.[2] Not a single California Indian language is being used now as the language of daily communication. The elders do not in actuality speak their language—rather, they remember how to speak their language.

However, as [we] will show, there is a rapidly growing movement among California Indians to save their languages: to learn them as second languages, and to develop programs to bring their languages back into daily use. The intense dedication that they have to their cause brings new promise to the future of California Indian languages.

LINGUISTIC DIVERSITY AND DECLINE

Table 1 gives a list of the languages of California and their classification. Starred languages have no known fluent native speakers (although some of them have semispeakers). Languages with five or fewer speakers are marked "(<5)."

Linguistic decline in California is of course directly the result of European contact. During the mission era and the subsequent Gold Rush and annexation of California to the United States, an estimated 310,000 population declined to about 20,000 (Cook 1978), a loss of over 90 percent. This was due partly to introduced diseases, which often decimated the Indians at missions, but later, the continued population decline was due also to outright annihilation by miners and farmers, especially in the decade of 1845–1855 (Cook 1978: 93). Furthermore, the legalized practice of kidnapping and

Table 1. California Languages and Their Classification (adapted from Hinton 1994: 83–85)

Stock	Family/Branch	Languages in California
Hokan[3]		Chimariko*
		Esselen*
		Karuk
		Salinan*
		Washo
	Shastan	Shasta,* New River Shasta,* Okwanuchu,* Konomihu*
	Palaihnihan	Achumawi (Pit River), Atsugewi (Hat Creek) (<5)
	Yanan	Northern Yana,* Central Yana,* Southern Yana,* Yahi*
	Pomoan	Northern (<5), Northeastern,* Eastern (<5), Central, Southeastern (<5), Southern (<5), Kashaya Pomo
	Yuman	Quechan, Mojave, Cocopa, Kumeyaay, Ipai, Tipai
	Chumashan	Obispeño,* Barbareño,* Ventureño,* Purisimeño,* Ynezeño,* Island*
Penutian	Costanoan (Ohlone)	Karkin,* Chochenyo,* Tamyen,* Ramaytush,* Awaswas,* Chalon,* Rumsen,* Mutsun*
	Wintun	Wintu, Nomlaki,* Patwin (<5)
	Maiduan	Maidu (<5), Konkow (<5), Nisenan (<5)
	Miwokan[4]	Lake Miwok (<5), Coast Miwok (<5), Bay Miwok,* Saclan,* Plains Miwok (<5), Northern Sierra Miwok, East Central Sierra Miwok, West Central Sierra Miwok, Southern Sierra Miwok
	Yokutsan	Choynumni, Chukchansi, Dumna (<5), Tachi (<5), Wukchumi, Yowlumni, Gashowu (<5) (at least 6 other extinct Yokutsan major dialects or languages)*[5]
	Klamath-Modoc	Klamath, Modoc (<5)
Algic		Yurok
		Wiyot*
Na-Dené	Athabascan	Tolowa (<5), Hupa, Mattole,* Wailaki-Nongatl-Lassik-Sinkyone-Cahto* (a group of related dialects, all without known speakers)
Uto-Aztecan	Numic	Mono, Owens Valley Paiute, Northern Paiute, Southern Paiute, Shoshoni, Kawaiisu, Chemehuevi
	Takic	Serrano, Cahuilla, Cupeño (<5), Luiseño, Ajachemem* (Juaneño), Tongva* (Gabrielino), Tataviam,* San Nicolas,* Kitanemuk,* Vanyume* Tubatulabal
Yukian		Yuki,* Wappo

enslavement of Indian children and young women removed many survivors from their families and cultures forever. During this period, some reservations were established, but Indians found little protection there, due to the corruption of the government agents (Castillo 1978). It was not until the 1870s that the atrocities began to decline enough for Indian survivors to begin establishing settled families again, and by the end of the century their population was growing once more.

But even then, it was a rare family that was in a position to do anything to retain traditional culture. Despite the establishment of some reservations and rancherias, the vast majority of California Indians had no land base and were not even recognized by the federal government through treaty; while about 80 treaties were drawn up by federal agents in the 1880s, they were sealed and never ratified by Congress. Also, beginning in the 1880s, boarding schools were established, resulting in the forced separation of children from their families. This practice continued well into the twentieth century. And up to the present, even Indians whose tribes are recognized and landed have difficulty staying with their communities due to the lack of economic opportunities, and are likely to leave for years or a lifetime to pursue a living. Modern technology and communications, especially radio and television, exacerbate the present condition of constant exposure to English. Thus California Indians are now immersed in English. There is little or no space in the present-day way of life for the use of indigenous languages.

Given this long history of abuse, it is no wonder that California Indian languages have declined. The fact that there are still languages with any speakers at all is a testimony to the resourcefulness of speakers and their loyalty to their heritage.

The last remaining native speakers of languages today are people who as children had an unusual degree of exposure to their languages, through such events as being kept home from boarding school, or living with grandparents who spoke no English (Sims 1998). They themselves usually could not pass on the language to their own children—often their spouses don't know the language, and there was simply no one left in the world for the speakers to talk to in their language of heritage. After years of discrimination and abuse in the schools for speaking their language of heritage, some people consciously chose not to put their children through the same agony by teaching them the language—but given the lack of context, the loss of function, and the omnipresence of English, even had they chosen to try to pass on their language it would have been exceedingly difficult to do so. Linguists and anthropologists, envisioning the complete loss of the California Indian languages, worked hard throughout the twentieth century to document them; and for the languages that now have no speakers, those records are all that remain.

LINGUISTIC REVITALIZATION

Events over the last few decades have led to a friendlier environment for linguistic diversity. The increasing ethnic diversity of the United States, America's recognition and exploration of racism, the Civil Rights movement led by African-Americans, and legislation such as the Bilingual Education Act and Native American Languages Act involving minority rights and especially minority language rights have all combined to create a very different atmosphere than existed in the first half of this century. In this new atmosphere, California Indians have been able to ponder their past and make their own decisions (rather than having decisions forced on them) about the degree to which they value their heritage and what they want to do about it. California Indians with no land base and no federal recognition are now forming tribal organizations, going through the complex process of seeking federal recognition, and buying back patches of traditional lands, thus creating communities that could potentially form a protected environment in which an indigenous language might be spoken. Traditional ceremonials are being practiced with a new vigor and vastly growing participation, and more and more Native Californians are becoming proficient at native arts and cultural practices such as the gathering and preparation of wild native foods. Experience in school bilingual/bicultural education programs in the 1970s and 1980s led a number of people in those communities to develop a sense of appreciation for their linguistic heritage. While in most California Indian communities the passion for language is an individual matter rather than tribal policy, nevertheless the number of individuals seeking to achieve language revitalization is growing rapidly.

In many California Indian communities there have been diverse efforts at language revival for several decades. Some of these are individual efforts by people making a conscious effort to reach fluency in their language as adults, or giving their children as much exposure to the language as possible. Some efforts are institutional, such as the 20 years of Indian bilingual education that have taken place in Humboldt County. In the last decade, there has been increasing opportunity for native language enthusiasts from different tribes to have contact with each other, and this contact has resulted in a great flowering of energy and ideas.

Funding

In the late 1970s, funding for bilingual education became the first wave of financial support for Native American language programs. Due to the small and scattered state of California Indian groups, and the degree to which language loss had occurred, there were not very many California tribes able to develop bilingual programs. However, some California Indian communities were able to develop such programs; and although in the 1980s funding for bilingual education steadily diminished, some programs, especially in Humboldt County, were maintained over the long run and are still in existence. In the 1990s, a whole new wave of funding has become available, partly from government agencies, especially the Administration for Native Americans (ANA), which oversees federal funds for the Native American Languages Act, and partly from a number of private foundations that have become interested in minority language issues. Availability of funding has been a very important component of language revitalization in California, but there are also many people doing language-revitalization work with no funding at all.

News from Native California

In 1987, Malcolm Margolin of Heyday Books established a new journal called *News from Native California*. He envisioned it as a newsletter for and by California Indians and their friends and associates, which would include a calendar of upcoming events (such as meetings, ceremonies, and exhibits), as well as news about traditional cultural practices, relevant legislation, and educational programs. Language issues soon became an important part of the journal, and it became a source of information for people interested in language revitalization to draw from, and a way for people to know who else is working on these issues around the state.

The Native California Network

In 1992, the Native California Network (NCN) was formed under the directorship of Mary Bates Abbott. NCN provides funding for California Indian individuals and communities developing projects related to traditional culture. The organization quickly came to see language as one of the most important aspects of traditional culture and organized a series of events and programs relating to language revitalization.

Conferences and Workshops

The first language event organized by NCN was a conference attended by some 60 California Indians interested in language (cosponsored by Heyday Books and with participation based on the mailing list for *News from Native California*). At the conference, a number of ideas were generated for language programs, and a committee was formed called Advocates for Indigenous California Language Survival (AICLS), consisting of seven California Indians who would oversee the development and implementation of language programs and advise NCN about language issues. The conference was also the first time most California language activists had met each other, and this direct contact allowed mutual encouragement and idea sharing that was extremely helpful to many. The conference has since become a biannual event. Besides having Californians share information with each other about their language work, representatives from successful language programs elsewhere in the United States have been invited to be presenters at these gatherings.

Workshops have also been set up. In 1995, the "Circle of Voices" workshop was held by and for California Indians to help them learn to document their language and culture as told by the elders, through videotape. In 1996, the "Breath of Life, Silent No More" California Native Language Restoration Workshop was held at the University of California at Berkeley, where 20 California Indians were shown the archives of linguistic fieldnotes and tapes, taught phonetic reading and basic linguistic analysis, and shown how to extract useful language from the materials that can be used for language revitalization.

Master–Apprentice Program

The most ambitious language program to be set up has been the Master–Apprentice Language Learning Program, administered by AICLS. Speakers of California Indian languages, paired with younger members of the tribes who want to learn their language of heritage, are given training in a unique system of common-sense immersion-style language teaching and learning with the goal of making the apprentice fluent (see Hinton 1997 for a complete description of the Master–Apprentice Program). Now in its fourth year, the program has supported one or more teams from each of 15 languages: Chemehuevi, Hupa, Karuk, Mojave, Northern Pomo, Patwin, Paiute, Tubatulabal, Washo, Western Mono, Wintu, Wukchumni, Yowlumne, Yurok, and Kiliwa (from Baja California). The program has been quite successful, producing a number of young fluent speakers, as well as functioning to implement increased usage of the languages by the native speakers. It has also served as a model for tribes elsewhere in the United States.

NCN has recently obtained funding for a five-year plan to expand the various programs discussed above and is also working with one tribe to set up an immersion preschool, modeled on preschools and grade schools successfully established in New Zealand, and in the US for Hawaiian, Blackfeet, and Mohawk, among others. Several California tribes are aiming toward the development of immersion preschools in their communities within the next few years.

Other Community Efforts

NCN has had a major influence on the design and implementation of language programs in California communities. However, the NCN programs are always only one aspect of what Indian people are doing to work toward the goal of language revitalization. Other projects being taken on in various communities include the following:

Development of Practical Writing Systems. Several communities have official standardized writing systems, including the Hupa, Karuk, and Mojave, among others; and many other communities are working now on the design of writing systems. Often, people use an individualized "folk writing" approach (to use a term coined by Wally Chafe [personal communication]), where they write using English spelling rules; a number of materials around the state have been designed this way. Again, such efforts are usually individual ones; but it has been a common practice that once a good system is designed, the designer presents it to the tribal council and the system may be officially adopted.

Development of Written and Recorded Materials.
California Indians have worked with linguists over the past few decades to develop practical dictionaries and pedagogical grammars. In locales that have bilingual-education programs in the schools, various language curricula and reading materials have also been developed. Increasingly, Indians are becoming the directors of written projects, hiring linguists as consultants or else working on their own. One of the recent genres of written products is the "phrase book," a pocket-sized book of useful phrases and vocabularies; the first one, entitled *Now You're Talking—Karuk!* (Richardson and Burcell 1993), was designed by the Center for Indian Community Development at Humboldt State University. *Now You're Speaking—Hupa!* (Hupa Indian Language Classes et al. 1994) is also out now, and similar phrase-books for other languages are in progress.

Besides the tape recordings that many individuals have made in most California Indian communities, there are also now audiotaped and videotaped lessons in some communities. The Hupas have a fine series of videotaped language lessons, and several communities have produced audiotapes along with pedagogical materials for community use. There are also computerized pedagogical materials in some communities, such as the Miwok computerized lessons developed by Brian Bibby.

Language Classes. Language classes have been given in various Indian communities for a long time now, at least since the mid-1970s. Some take place in the schools or in after-school programs; others are more informal classes held in the evenings for adults. Native speakers are usually the main instructors, but they are often assisted by a semi-speaking learner or a linguist. Recently, the application of state-of-the-art language-teaching models learned through the Master–Apprentice Program and the California Foreign Language Project, a statewide organization dedicated to training language teachers in modern approaches, has been functioning to increase the classes' effectiveness.

Language Gatherings. Communities have begun having gatherings where language use is stressed. These are often potluck dinners, such as the Washo "Language Circle." Native speakers are honored guests, and language issues are discussed, programs are planned, and the language is practiced.

Immersion Camps. The language "immersion camps" of California were probably first developed by the Karuks about five years ago and have been practiced by an increasing number of tribes. These are sometimes family camps and sometimes children's camps, sometimes formally organized in detail and sometimes informal and improvised; but they always stress using the language for all activities as much as possible. Members of the community go to a camping area, hopefully part of their own traditional lands, and are free from the interruptions of modern life and the English language. Various cultural activities such as traditional food preparation or basket-making are featured, along with recreation and relaxation. People use as much of their language as they know how, and learn to use more during the camp events.

General Usage. Most of all, people are simply trying to use the language again in any way they can. In the Wiyot tribal council, for example, the chair has instructed the members to vote "yes" or "no" in Wiyot, not English. In gatherings around the state, such as the annual basketmakers' gatherings, people try to introduce themselves first in their language, not English. Elders are asked to give blessings in their language. People try to greet each other in their language. Word by word, phrase by phrase, an increasing number of California Indians are trying to bring their languages back into daily use.

LANGUAGE CHANGE

As is to be expected, the languages of California are not being spoken by learners in exactly the same way as they are spoken by the old native speakers. Learners have an accent and exhibit many grammatical simplifications and influences from English, their dominant language. Learners are conscious of the differences and are always striving to bring their language closer to the language of the native speakers; but at the same time, a number of them have expressed a willingness to tolerate linguistic change. Given the urgency of the situation, coupled with the difficulty of obtaining the linguistic input necessary for complete language learning, the philosophy expressed most often at language conferences and training sessions can be summed up as this: "Strive for improvement, but use what you have." It is the present generation of language learners who will characterize the language in the future, as the last native speakers pass on. The learners are already the main teachers of children in communities where children's language programs exist. The learners are aware of their position of responsibility for the language, but see that insistence on complete perfection in language learning would actually lead to complete linguistic paralysis. A number of learners have expressed the notion that even if the future of their language takes on a pidginized form, the social value of using their language far exceeds the detriments of the change. It will be of great interest to observe the ways in which the California languages change during this significant period of revival.

CONCLUSION

Sims (1998) presents a detailed study of one California Indian community, showing how language revitalization is taking place. In languages so close to extinction, and with tribal councils and most members of any community still not committed to language revitalization, the process is still individualistic and scattered. But it is a movement with gathering momentum. The passion and dedication of those who are working with their languages is obvious and inspiring to others. It is a healthy movement, a movement toward recovery from the devastating social and cultural wounds inflicted by the European incursion into California.

Notes

1. The fluctuation seen in the literature on the estimate of numbers of languages is due partly to the difficulty of determining what counts as separate languages vs. what should be classified as dialects of a single language. My number 98 is based on the research leading to Table 1..., but fluctuating interpretation of the fine lines of language differentiation will continue.

2. Actually, three of these languages still have some children learning, but while the original territory of the languages included bits of California, the active communities are in adjoining states (see discussion in Hinton 1994).

3. This is not the place to argue classification, but it should be noted here that both Hokan and Penutian are hypothesized deep-time groupings whose membership and validity as genetic units is still being actively debated by researchers.

4. The Miwokan and Costanoan families are demonstrably related and are classified together as the "Utian" branch of Penutian (Callaghan 1967).

5. Shipley (1978: 83) says, "There were 40 to 50 small tribes in this area, each with a distinctive dialect..., a state of affairs unlike any other in California. Kroeber [1963] classified these dialects into 12 groups belonging to two divisions; his arrangement was based on lexical material collected for 21 of the dialects. These facts make it very difficult to say how many Yokutsan languages there were."

References

Callaghan, Catherine A. (1967). Miwok-Costanoan as a subfamily of Penutian. *International Journal of American Linguistics* 33, 224–227.

Castillo, Edward D. (1978). The impact of Euro-American exploration and settlement. In *Handbook of North American Indians*, vol. 8: *California*, Robert F. Heizer (ed.), 99–127. Washington, DC: Smithsonian Institution.

Cook, Sherbourne (1978). Historical demography. In *Handbook of North American Indians*, vol. 8: *California*, Robert F. Heizer (ed.), 91–98. Washington, D.C: Smithsonian Institution.

Hinton, Leanne (1994). *Flutes of Fire: Essays on California Indian Languages*. Berkeley: Heyday.

———. (1997). Survival of endangered languages: The California Master–Apprentice Program. *International Journal of the Sociology of Language* 123, 177–191.

Hupa Indian Language Classes, et al. (1994). *Now You're Speaking—Hupa!* Hupa Valley, CA: Hupa Valley Tribal Council.

Kroeber, Alfred L. (1963). Yokuts dialect survey. *University of California Anthropological Records* 11, 177–251.

Richardson, Nancy; and Burcell, Suzanne (1993). *Now You're Talking—Karuk!* Arcata, CA: Humboldt State University Center for Indian Community Development.

Shipley, William F. (1978). Native Languages of California. *Handbook of North American Indians*, vol. 8: *California*, Robert F. Heizer (ed.), 80–90. Washington, DC: Smithsonian Institution.

Sims, Christine. (1998). Community-based efforts to preserve native languages: A descriptive study of the Karuk tribe of northern California. *International Journal of the Sociology of Language* 132, 95–113.

Post-reading Questions / Activities

- What role do indigenous activists play in language revitalization? What role do outside linguists and anthropologists play?
- Some of the efforts described here involve using words from an indigenous language in limited situations, rather than insisting that the language be used completely, for all communication, or not at all. In some cases, the language learned is a simplified, or pidginized, version of the original language. Discuss the benefits and disadvantages of using an endangered language only partially.
- Select one group mentioned by Hinton and conduct research into its most recent situation: Have language revitalization efforts borne fruit? What activities have continued? What activities have been dropped or added? Have the prospects for this language improved or declined? What factors have contributed to this fate?

Vocabulary

language loss   language revitalization

Suggested Further Reading

Bradley, David, and Maya Bradley, eds. 2002. *Language Endangerment and Language Maintenance*. London and New York: RoutledgeCurzon.

Fishman, Joshua. 1991. *Reversing Language Shift: Theoretical and Empirical Foundations of Assistance to Threatened Languages.* Clevedon: Multilingual Matters.

Hinton, Leanne. 1994. *Flutes of Fire: Essays on California Indian Languages.* Berkeley: Heyday Books.

———, and Kenneth L. Hale, eds. 2001. *The Green Book of Language Revitalization in Practice.* San Diego: Academic Press.

Nettle, Daniel, and Suzanne Romaine. 2000. *Vanishing Voices: The Extinction of the World's Languages.* Oxford: Oxford University Press.

Walsh, Michael. 2005. "Will Indigenous Languages Survive?" *Annual Review of Anthropology* 34: 293–315.

UNIT 4

LANGUAGE AND IDENTITY

Since we speak every time we interact, and since language varies, the ways we speak are evident and available to everybody. They advertise our origins and our identifications, whether we are proud or ashamed of them. All people reveal many aspects of identity with each word and sentence they utter: which nation they are identifying with (in terms of broader linguistic variety), which region, which social class, which ethnic group, which gender, and each speaker's age.

When sociolinguists first discovered the regularities of linguistic variation, and could demonstrate a correlation between linguistic variation and social segment, there was a heady sense of explanatory power. In recent years, a number of critiques of this approach have pointed out that all people have a number of different aspects of their gender; that we are not so easily compartmentalized; and that we do not stay in statistical boxes very readily. A new approach to the study of sociolinguistic variation relies on the notion of "communities of practice," a little like old-fashioned network theory. It suggests that any kind of identity is *accomplished in interaction* rather than existing in some abstract way prior to any action (see, e.g., Fought 2004, Schilling-Estes 2004). Further, people can play with their identities, consciously, in what Ben Rampton has so vividly described as "crossing." Rather than speak of static linguistic *style*, as was the foundational sociolinguistic custom, Rampton has suggested we thinking of *styling*, an active strategic activity.

REGION

Just as there is no intrinsic linguistic reason for a particular linguistic variety to become a world language, so there is no inherent feature of a language that causes it to become "standard." That is purely a matter of history and the power that certain speakers end up having because of economic and political conditions. The speech of certain areas of the United States, like regions elsewhere, derives from their precise history: who settled there when, where they came from, what other groups moved in and what the relations were among various groups, and any number of other social factors.

But regional language is often given a kind of social meaning and value, so that it is possible for outsiders to develop stereotypes about the speech—and speakers—of a particular region. There is a tendency to applaud one's own language variety and to denigrate that of others. Regional linguistic differences are the subject of humor, of friends' conversation, and of scholarly inquiry.

CLASS

Though Americans don't typically name or acknowledge their social classes, there is no doubt that such classes exist. Classes are stratified (layered) by means of income, education, occupation, and general "cultural capital." Language is one of the enduring aspects of a person's class identity, and it is changed only with difficulty. Language correlates with social class everywhere it has been studied in the world, with some linguistic features seen as marking identification with one class or another.

There is no intrinsic superiority of the linguistic features associated with "superior" social classes, only their association with a particular social group. For instance, the presence of postvocalic (r) (as in the word *fourth*) in postwar New York City, as you will see described in Chapter 24, is associated with higher social status while before World War II it was associated with lower social status. Thus, any study of the relations among status and language must be done with deep knowledge of social setting and context.

"RACE" AND ETHNICITY

Ethnicity is the identity that comes from belonging to a group, often with a sense of shared background or descent, shared cultural practices, and shared social situation. In the United States, we have ethnic groups on the basis of "race" (African Americans), national heritage (Asian Americans, Irish Americans), language ("Hispanics," to use the government category), and religion (Jews). Generally these ethnic categories are meaningful only in contrast and in relation to other groups.

The term "race" is put in scare quotes because as a biological entity there is no such phenomenon. It does exist, powerfully and consequentially, however, as a social phenomenon.

All countries in the world are multiethnic, even those that have an ideology of homogeneity, such as Japan and Korea. Some celebrate their multiethnicity, like Brazil and, maybe, the United States. Some attempt to eradicate all ethnic differences, as in the "ethnic cleansing" campaigns of Bosnia in the 1990s and former Yugoslavia, and Darfur. (There are usually significant cultural and economic strains leading to this "solution" to social problems.) For many, the ideology of nationalism requires a homogeneous populace, though in reality none has ever existed.

The role of language in the construction of ethnicity can vary quite significantly, from ethnicity based on language (Hispanics in the United States) to language having almost no role (Irish Americans, Jews). It is often stereotyped, in the Ebonics jokes of the 1990s and what Jane Hill calls "Mock Spanish," and pejorative views of speakers with ethnic features are often found throughout the world.

GENDER

The study of language and gender got its major boost with the publication of Robin Tolmach Lakoff's *Language and Woman's Place* in 1975. Though researchers had written about this topic before, Lakoff's clear style and the feminist movements in the air at the time combined to create a research agenda that has been pursued avidly ever since. Though "gender" meant primarily "women" at the time, it is understood now that the speech of both women and men must be studied; there is no nongendered speech (which is not to say that women's speech is essentially and entirely distinct from men's, and vice versa).

Two principal approaches to the study of language and gender are that (1) women are essentially different from men (though this can be culturally shaped) and (2) women are seen as generally less powerful than men and, thus, they use speech that corresponds to the less powerful party in an interaction.

Some researchers set out to demonstrate absolute differences between women's and men's language, while others showed more of a continuum or more strategic choices dependent on the particular context of use. We could consider the first category *essentialist* and the second *social constructionist*. The latter have built on the idea of "communities of practice," in which speakers' specific choices stem from interactions in particular groups, which may yield language associated stereotypically with their gender—but may not.

Gender interacts with many other aspects of identity, including class, ethnicity, and age. In many ways, the topic of gender has been fully integrated into the study of language in society, as you can see from the many chapters in this book that touch on gender, but are placed in different units. The chapters in this unit focus specifically and centrally on language and gender.

Though I have divided this unit into components of region, class, ethnicity, and gender, in fact these (and there are more aspects, as well) are all entirely intersecting. At all times we reveal all these facets of our identity.

Suggested Further Reading

SOCIOLINGUISTIC VARIATION AND THEORY

Eckert, Penelope, and John R. Rickford, eds. 2001. *Style and Sociolinguistic Variation*. Cambridge: Cambridge University Press.

Fought, Carmen, ed. 2004. *Sociolinguistic Variation: Critical Reflections*. Oxford and New York: Oxford University Press.

Hansen, Alan D. 2005. "A Practical Task: Ethnicity as a Resource in Social Interaction." *Research on Language and Social Interaction* 38 (1): 63–104.

Labov, William. 1972. *Sociolinguistic Patterns*. Philadelphia: University of Pennsylvania Press.

Rampton, Ben. 1995. *Crossing: Language and Ethnicity Among Adolescents*. London and New York: Longman.

Schilling-Estes, Natalie. 2004. "Constructing Ethnicity in Interaction." *Journal of Sociolinguistics* 8/2: 163–195.

REGION

Blount, Roy. 2007. *Long Time Leaving: Dispatches from Up South*. New York: Knopf.

Carver, Craig M. 1987. *American Regional Dialects: A Word Geography*. Ann Arbor: University of Michigan Press.

Cassidy, Frederic G. (editor-in-chief). 1985. *Dictionary of American Regional English*, vol. 1, A–C. Cambridge, MA: Harvard University Press, Belknap.

———, and Joan Houston Hall, eds. 1991. *Dictionary of American Regional English*, vol. 2, D–H. Cambridge, MA: Harvard University Press, Belknap.

———. 1996. *Dictionary of American Regional English*, vol. 3, I–O. Cambridge, MA: Harvard University Press, Belknap.

Francis, Nelson. 1983. *Dialectology: An Introduction*. New York: Longman.

———, and Hall, Joan Houston (editor-in-chief). 2002. *Dictionary of American Regional English*, vol. 4, P–Sk. Cambridge, MA: Harvard University Press, Belknap.

Labov, William, Sharon Ash, and Charles Boberg. 2006. *The Atlas of North American English: Phonetics, Phonology, and Sound Change*. Berlin: Mouton de Gruyter.

MacNeil, Robert, and William Cran, eds. 2005. *Do You Speak American?* New York: Doubleday.

Milroy, James. 1992. *Linguistic Variation and Change: On the Historical Sociolinguistics of English*. Oxford: Blackwell.

Trudgill, Peter. 1983. *On Dialect: Social and Geographical Perspectives*. New York: New York University Press.

———. 1990. *The Dialects of England*. Cambridge, MA: Blackwell.

Wolfram, Walt. 1991. *Dialects and American English*. Englewood Cliffs, NJ: Prentice Hall.

———, and Natalie Schilling-Estes. 2006 [1998]. *American English: Dialects and Variation*. 2d ed. Malden, MA: Blackwell.

———, and Ben Ward, eds. 2006. *American Voices: How Dialects Differ from Coast to Coast*. Malden, MA: Blackwell.

CLASS

Corfield, Penelope J., ed. 1991. *Language, History, and Class*. Oxford: Blackwell.

Edwards, John. 1994. *Multilingualism*. London: Routledge.

Fasold, Ralph. 1984. *The Sociolinguistics of Society*. Oxford: Blackwell.

Fasold, Ralph, 1990. *The Sociolinguistics of Language*. Oxford: Blackwell.

Giglioli, Pier Paolo, ed. 1972. *Language and Social Context*. Harmondsworth: Penguin Books.

Grillo, Ralph D. 1989. *Dominant Languages: Language and Hierarchy in Britain and France*. Cambridge: Cambridge University Press.

Labov, William. 1996. *The Social Stratification of English in New York City*. Washington, DC: Center for Applied Linguistics.

———. 1972. *Sociolinguistic Patterns*. Philadelphia: University of Pennsylvania Press.

Macaulay, R. K. S. 1977. *Language, Social Class, and Education: A Glasgow Study*. Edinburgh: University of Edinburgh Press.

Milroy, James. 1991. *Linguistic Variation and Change: On the Historical Sociolinguistics of English*. Oxford: Blackwell.

———, and Lesley Milroy. 1985. *Authority in Language: Investigating Language Prescription and Standardization*. London: Routledge & Kegan Paul.

Mugglestone, Lynda. 1995. *"Talking Proper": The Rise of Accent as a Social Symbol*. Oxford: Oxford University Press.

Romaine, Suzanne, ed. 1982. *Sociolinguistic Variation in Speech Communities*. London: Edward Arnold.

———. 2000. *Language in Society: An Introduction to Sociolinguistics*. 2d ed. Oxford: Oxford University Press.

Trudgill, Peter. 1974. *The Social Differentiation of English in Norwich*. Cambridge: Cambridge University Press.

"Race" and Ethnicity

Abrahams, R. D. 1974. "Black Talking on the Street." In *Explorations in the Ethnography of Speaking*, edited by Richard Bauman and Joel Sherzer, pp. 240–262. Cambridge: Cambridge University Press.

American Anthropological Association. "Race: Are We So Different?" http://www.understandingrace.org/home.html.

Baugh, John. 1983. *Black Street Speech: Its History, Structure, and Survival*. Austin: University of Texas Press.

———. 1999. *Out of the Mouth of Slaves: African American Language and Educational Malpractice*. Austin: University of Texas Press.

Fought, Carmen. 2003. *Chicano English in Context*. New York and Basingstoke: Palgrave Macmillan.

Gumperz, John J. 1982. *Discourse Strategies*. Cambridge: Cambridge University Press.

Hansen, Alan D. 2005. "A Practical Task: Ethnicity as a Resource in Social Interaction." *Research on Language and Social Interaction* 38(1): 63–104.

Herskovitz, Melville J. 1958. *The Myth of the Negro Past*. Boston: Beacon Press.

Hill, Jane H. 1998. "Language, Race, and White Public Space." *American Anthropologist* 100: 680–689.

Labov, William. 1972. *Language in the Inner City: Studies in the Black English Vernacular*. Philadelphia: University of Pennsylvania Press.

Leap, William L. 1993. *American Indian English*. Salt Lake City: University of Utah Press.

Morgan, Marcyeliena. 2002. *Language, Discourse, and Power in African American Culture*. Cambridge: Cambridge University Press.

Rampton, Ben. 1995. *Crossing: Language and Ethnicity Among Adolescents*. London and New York: Longman.

Rickford, John R., and Russell J. Rickford. 2000. *Spoken Soul: The Story of Black English*. New York: Wiley.

Schilling-Estes, Natalie. 2004. "Constructing Ethnicity in Interaction." *Journal of Sociolinguistics* 8/2: 163–195.

Smitherman, Geneva. 1977. *Talkin and Testifyin: The Language of Black America*. Boston: Houghton Mifflin.

———. 1994. *Black Talk: Words and Phrases from the Hood to the Amen Corner*. Boston: Houghton Mifflin.

Urciuoli, Bonnie. 1996. *Exposing Prejudice: Puerto Rican Experiences of Language, Race, and Class*. Boulder, CO: Westview Press.

Wolfram, Walt, and Erik R. Thomas. 2002. *The Development of African American English*. Malden, MA: Blackwell.

Gender

Bucholtz, Mary, A. C. Liang, and Laurel A. Sutton, eds. 1999. *Reinventing Identities: The Gendered Self in Discourse*. New York: Oxford University Press.

Cameron, Deborah. 1992. *Feminism and Linguistic Theory*. 2d ed. London: Routledge.

———, and Jennifer Coates, eds. 1988. *Women in Their Speech Communities: New Perspectives on Language and Sex*. London: Longman.

Coates, Jennifer, ed. 1998. *Language and Gender: A Reader*. Malden, MA: Blackwell.

Eckert, Penelope, and Sally McConnell-Ginet. 1992. "Think Practically and Look Locally: Language and Gender as Community-Based Practice." *Annual Review of Anthropology* 21: 461–490.

———, and ———. 2003. *Language and Gender*. Cambridge: Cambridge University Press.

Goodwin, Marjorie Harness. 1990. *He Said–She Said: Talk as Social Organization Among Black Children*. Bloomington: Indiana University Press.

Graddol, David, and Joan Swann. 1989. *Gender Voices*. Oxford: Blackwell.

Hall, Kira, and Mary Bucholtz, eds. 1995. *Gender Articulated: Language and the Socially Constructed Self*. New York and London: Oxford University Press.

Holmes, Janet. 1995. *Women, Men, and Politeness*. London and New York: Longman.

Ide, Sachiko, and Naomi Hanaska McGloin, eds. 1990. *Aspects of Japanese Women's Language*. Tokyo: Kurosio Publishers.

Inoue, Miyako. 2006. *Vicarious Language: Gender and Linguistic Modernity in Japan*. Berkeley and Los Angeles: University of California Press.

Irvine, Judith T. 1979. "Formality and Informality in Communicative Events." *American Anthropologist* 81 (4): 773–790.

Johnson, Sally, and Ulrike Hanna Meinhof, eds. 1997. *Language and Masculinity*. Oxford: Blackwell.

Lakoff, Robin Tolmach. 1975. *Language and Woman's Place*. New York: Harper & Row.

———. 2004. *Language and Woman's Place: Text and Commentaries*. Revised and expanded edition, edited by Mary Bucholtz. Oxford and New York: Oxford University Press.

Livia, Anna, and Kira Hall, eds. 1997. *Queerly Phrased: Language, Gender, and Sexuality*. Oxford and New York: Oxford University Press.

Mehl, Matthias R., et al. 2007. "Are Women Really More Talkative Than Men?" *Science* 317 (July 6): 82.

Mori, Kyoko. 1997. *Polite Lies: On Being a Woman Caught Between Cultures*. New York: Henry Holt.

Ochs, Elinor. 1991. "Indexing Gender." In *Rethinking Context*, edited by Alessandro Duranti and Charles Goodwin, pp. 335–358. Cambridge: Cambridge University Press.

Philips, Susan U., Susan Steele, and Christine Tanz, eds. 1987. *Language, Gender, and Sex in Comparative Perspective*. Cambridge: Cambridge University Press.

Romaine, Suzanne. 1999. *Communicating Gender*. Mahwah, NJ: Erlbaum.

Smith, Janet Shibamoto. 1985. *Japanese Women's Language*. New York: Academic Press.

Spender, Dale. 1980. *Man Made Language*. London: Routledge & Kegan Paul.

Tannen, Deborah. 1990. *You Just Don't Understand: Women and Men in Conversation*. New York: Ballantine Books.

Thorne, Barrie, and Nancy Henley, eds. 1975. *Language and Sex: Difference and Dominance*. Rowley, MA: Newbury House.

———, Cheris Kramarae, and Nancy Henley, eds. 1983. *Language, Gender, and Society*. Rowley, MA: Newbury House.

CHAPTER 23

They Speak Really Bad English Down South and in New York City

Dennis R. Preston

(1998)

In the United States, though there is no officially defined "standard" variety of our language (unlike Britain, which has "Received Pronunciation" or the "Queen's English"), many speakers believe they can identify some language that is standard or more proper. Most people prefer the language of their own region. The two most stigmatized varieties of American English are the language of the South and of New York City. As you can see, however, even the language of the South is not timeless and changeless.

Dennis Preston has studied people's "language attitudes," the way they regard other people's (and their own) ways of speaking. His method set consultants at ease; they seemed quite willing to convey their forceful views of others—views that are not usually complimentary.

Reading Questions

- What attitudes do people have about their own speech? About the speech of others? How is the speech of the South and of New York City seen?
- What does Preston mean when he asks respondents to identify "correct English"? What about "pleasant English"? Are these the same thing? Where do you think these ideas come from?

Imagine this. You have persistent bad headaches. Aspirin and other miracle products don't make them go away. Your family doctor decides it's time to have a specialist's opinion. He hasn't said the words, but you turn the terrible possibility over in your mind—"Brain tumor!"

You appear at the New York City office of Dr N. V. Cramden, Brain Surgeon; you sign in and await the beginning of the process that will reveal your fate. Cramden approaches and speaks:

> Hey, how's it goin'? Rotten break, huh? Ya got a pain in da noggin'. Don't sweat it; I'm gonna fix ya up. Hey, nois! Ovuh heah! Bring me dat whatchamacallit. How da hell am I gonna take care of my patient heah if you don't hand me dem tools? Dat's a goil.

You still have your clothes on (it's a brain surgeon's office, right?), so you just head for the door, stopping at the front desk and tell the receptionist that someone in the examining room is posing as Dr Cramden. Maybe you never return to your trusted family doctor, since he or she has sent you to a quack. Whatever your decision, you do not continue under the care of Dr Cramden.

Linguists know that language variety does not correlate with intelligence or competence, so Dr Cramden could well be one of the best brain surgeons in town. Nevertheless, popular associations of certain varieties of English with professional and intellectual competence run so deep that Dr Cramden will not get to crack many crania unless he learns to sound very different.

A primary linguistic myth, one nearly universally attached to minorities, rural people, and the less well educated, extends in the United States even to well-educated speakers of some regional varieties. That myth, of course, is that some varieties of a language are not as good as others.

Professional linguists are happy with the idea that some varieties of a language are more standard than others; that is a product of social facts. Higher-status groups impose their behaviors (including language) on others, claiming theirs are the standard ones. Whether you approve of that or not, the standard variety is selected through purely social

Dennis R. Preston, "They Speak Really Bad English Down South and in New York City." In *Language Myths*, ed. Laurie Bauer and Peter Trudgill. London: Penguin, 1998, pp. 139–149.

processes and has not one whit more logic, historical consistency, communicative expressivity, or internal complexity or systematicity than any other variety. Since every region has its own social stratification, every area also has a share of both standard and nonstandard speakers.

I admit to a little cheating above. I made Dr Cramden a little more of a tough kid from the streets than I should have. The truth is, I need not have done so. Although linguists believe that every region has its own standard variety, there is widespread belief in the US that some regional varieties are more standard than others and, indeed, that some regional varieties are far from the standard—particularly those of the South and New York City (NYC).

Please understand the intensity of this myth, for it is not a weakly expressed preference; in the US it runs deep, strong, and true, and evidence for it comes from what real people (not professional linguists) believe about language variety. First, consider what northern US (Michigan) speakers have to say about the South:

> (Mimics Southern speech) As y'all know, I came up from Texas when I was about twenty-one. And I talked like this. Probably not so bad, but I talked like this; you know I said "thiyus" ["this"] and "thayut" ["that"] and all those things. And I had to learn to learn reeeal [elongated vowel] fast how to talk like a Northerner. 'Cause if I talked like this people'd think I'm the dumbest shit around.
>
> Because of TV, though, I think there's a kind of standard English that's evolving. And the kind of thing you hear on the TV is something that's broadcast across the country, so most people are aware of that, but there are definite accents in the South.

Next, consider NYC, which fares no better, even in self-evaluation, as the American sociolinguist William Labov has shown. Here are some opinions he collected in the mid 1960s:

> I'll tell you, you see, my son is always correcting me. He speaks very well—the one that went to [two years of] college. And I'm glad that he corrects me—because it shows me that there are many times when I don't pronounce my words correctly.

> Bill's college alumni group—we have a party once a month in Philadelphia. Well, now I know them about two years and every time we're there—at a wedding, at a party, a shower—they say, if someone new is in the group: "Listen to Jo Ann talk!" I sit there and I babble on, and they say, "Doesn't she have a ridiculous accent!" and "It's so New Yorkerish and all!"

Such anecdotal evidence could fill many pages and includes even outsider imitations of the varieties, such as mock partings for Southerners—"Y'all come back and see us sometime now, ya heah?"—and the following putative NYC poem which plays on the substitution of t- and d-like for th-sounds and the loss of the r-sound (and modification of the vowel) in such words as "bird":

> T'ree little boids sittin' on a coib,
> Eatin' doity woims and sayin' doity woids.

These informal assessments are bolstered by quantitative studies. Nearly 150 people from southeastern Michigan (of European-American ethnicity, of both sexes, and of all ages and social classes) rated (on a scale of one to ten) the degree of "correctness" of English spoken in the fifty states, Washington, DC, and NYC. Figure 1 shows the average scores for this task.

These responses immediately confirm what every American knows—the lowest ratings are for the South and NYC (and nearby New Jersey, infected by its proximity to the NYC metropolitan area). Only these areas score averages below 5; Alabama, the heart of the horrible South, scores in the 3 range.

Although it is not the major focus here, it is also clear that the Michiganders doing these ratings think pretty well of themselves; they give their home state a ranking in the 8 range, the only area so rewarded. Linguists call such local hubris "linguistic security." It is not hard to determine why: Michiganders believe another interesting myth—that they do not speak a dialect at all (although, as any linguist will assert, if you speak a human language, you must speak some dialect of it, even if it is a bland Michigan one). When Michigan respondents carry out another task, which asks them to draw on a blank map of the US where they think the various dialect areas are and label them, results such as Figure 2 emerge, confirming their local linguistic pride.

The respondent who drew Figure 2 places only Michigan in the "normal" area and, as we would expect from the rankings of Figure 1, impolite things are said about the South (although not NYC). If one studies a large number of such hand-drawn maps, it is possible to produce a generalized map such as Figure 3. This map shows not only where Michigan respondents draw lines for the areas of the US but also how many respondents drew a boundary around each one. The most important thing to note about Figure 3 is the number of Michigan respondents who drew a South—138 out of 147 (94 percent). Even the home area (which houses the uniquely correct Michigan speech) is registered as a separate speech region by only 90 respondents (61 percent). The third most frequently drawn area is, not surprisingly, the area which contains NYC (80; 54 percent).

These Michiganders seem, therefore, to hear dialect differences not as linguists do—on the basis of objective differences in the language system—but on the basis of their evaluation of the correctness of areas. The linguistic South, the area perceived most consistently as incorrect, quite simply exists for these respondents more than any other area.

Michiganders are not unique; in other areas where this work has been done, a South is always drawn by the highest percentage of respondents—South Carolina 94 percent, NYC 92 percent, western New York 100 percent, southern Indiana 86 percent, and Oregon 92 percent. Only Hawai'ians recognize another area (their own) more frequently, and only marginally (97 percent Hawai'i; 94 percent South).

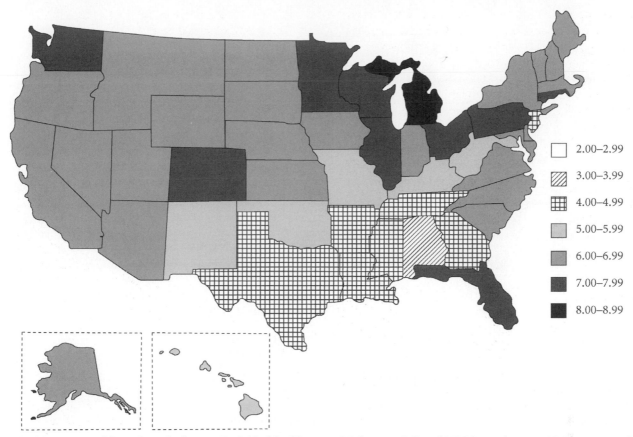

Figure 1. *Mean scores of the rankings for "correct English" of the fifty states, Washington, DC, and NYC by southeastern Michigan respondents (1 = "worst English"; 10 = "best English").*

Figure 2. *Hand-drawn map of a Michigan respondent's idea of the dialect areas of the US.*

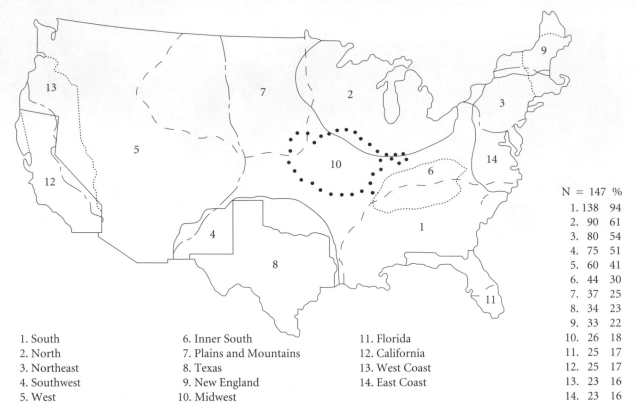

N = 147 %
1. 138 94
2. 90 61
3. 80 54
4. 75 51
5. 60 41
6. 44 30
7. 37 25
8. 34 23
9. 33 22
10. 26 18
11. 25 17
12. 25 17
13. 23 16
14. 23 16

1. South
2. North
3. Northeast
4. Southwest
5. West

6. Inner South
7. Plains and Mountains
8. Texas
9. New England
10. Midwest

11. Florida
12. California
13. West Coast
14. East Coast

Figure 3. *Generalized map of 147 Michigan respondents' idea of the dialect areas of the US.*

Also important to these respondents is the other place where they believe bad English is spoken. A "Northeast" [region] (a small area with a focus in NYC) or NYC itself figures very high in the percentages—South Carolina 46 percent, NYC itself 64 percent, western New York 45 percent, southern Indiana 51 percent, Oregon 75 percent, and Hawai'i 57 percent, nearly all of these second-place scores (after the South).

A study of labels on hand-drawn maps, such as the one shown in Figure 2, by fifty respondents each from southeastern Michigan, southern Indiana, South Carolina, and Oregon further confirms these stereotypes. The intensity of recognition of the South and NYC as separate speech areas parallels the idea that they are the regions where the most incorrect English is spoken. Of the labels assigned to Southern speech by Michigan respondents 22 percent are negative; 36 percent by Indiana respondents are negative; 31 percent by Oregon respondents and even 20 percent by South Carolina respondents. Similarly, the "Northeast" area (which contains NYC) fares poorly: 15 percent negative labels by Michigan respondents; 18 percent by Indiana; 24 percent by Oregon and a whopping 65 percent by South Carolina.

Negative labels assigned to speech areas overall were low (13 percent for Michigan respondents; 22 percent for Indiana, 18 percent for Oregon—but 32 percent for South Carolina, a reflection of their evaluation of much non-Southern territory for the entire US, e.g., 33 percent for California and 30 percent for the Midwest). One South Carolina respondent identifies everything north of the

Mason-Dixon line with the notation "Them—The Bad Guys" in contrast to the label for the entire South: "Us—The Good Guys." Other Southerners note that Northern speech is "mean" or "rude," and one calls it "scratch and claw." A common caricature of NYC speech refers to its "nasal" quality and its rate (fast).

There are labels for Southerners, like "Hillbillies" and "Hicks," but there are far more "linguistic" designations— "drawl," "twang," "Rebel slang," and many references to speed (slow).

Finally, what about a quantitative analysis of Southerners' views of the correctness issue? Figure 4 shows the ratings by thirty-six Auburn University students (principally from Alabama, a few from Georgia and South Carolina).

NYC fares even worse here than in the Michigan ratings; it is the only area to fall in the 3 range. Antipathy to NYC from the South is obvious. Other ratings for correctness, however, show none of the strength and certainty of the Michigan opinions seen in Figure 1. Michigan respondents consider their speech the best and steadily assign lower ratings the farther South a state is. Imagine a Michigander's disdain for an evaluation of correct English which, as Figure 4 shows, rates the territory from Michigan to Alabama as an undifferentiated 5!

These "eastern" Southern respondents, however, also find parts of the South especially lacking in correct English, namely the Mississippi, Louisiana, and Texas areas just to the west of them, which they put in the 4 range. Their own areas (rated in the 5 and 6 ranges) are neither fish nor fowl,

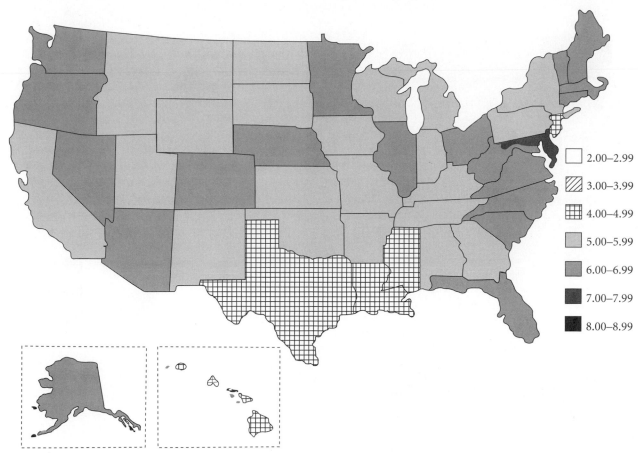

Figure 4. *Mean scores of the rankings of the fifty states, Washington, DC, and NYC for "correct English" by Auburn University (Alabama) students (ratings as in Figure 1).*

and they reserve the best ratings (only one step up at 7) for Maryland and the national capital, Washington, DC, both areas within a more general southern speech region.

Southerners pretty clearly suffer from what linguists would call "linguistic insecurity," but they manage to deflect the disdain of Northerners to adjacent areas rather than suffer the principal shame locally. They do not rate themselves at the top of the heap (as Michiganders do), and they appear to associate "correct English" with some official or national status (Washington, DC).

If Southerners don't find their own speech correct, can they find anything redeeming about it? Figure 5 shows what these same Southerners believe about language "pleasantness."

Here is the neat reversal of Figure 1 which did not emerge in Figure 4. Just as Michiganders found their variety "most correct" (8), these principally Alabama students find theirs "most pleasant" (also 8). As one moves north, a steady disapproval of the "friendly" aspects of speech (what linguists like to call the "solidarity" aspects) emerges, leaving Michigan part of a pretty unhospitable northern area, itself a 4.

There is one thing, however, that Michiganders and Alabamians agree on. NYC (and its partner in linguistic "grime," nearby New Jersey) are at the bottom of the scale for both "correctness" and "pleasantness." (In fact, the 2 in

Figure 5 for New Jersey is the lowest average rating for any area ever assigned in these tests.)

In summary, respondents from all over the US confirm the myth that some regions speak better English than others, and they do not hesitate to indicate that NYC and the South are on the bottom of that pile.

Students of US culture will have little difficulty in understanding the sources of the details of this myth. The South is thought to be rural, backward, and uneducated; its dialect is quite simply associated with the features assigned its residents. NYC fares little better. As one of Labov's respondents told him in the mid-1960s, "They think we're all murderers." Just as US popular culture has kept alive the barefoot, moonshine-making and drinking, intermarrying, racist Southerner, so has it continued to contribute to the perception of the brash, boorish, criminal, violent New Yorker. Small wonder that the varieties of English associated with these areas have these characteristics attributed to them.

Like all groups who are prejudiced against, Southerners (and New Yorkers) fight back by making their despised language variety a solidarity symbol, but there is no doubt they suffer linguistic insecurity in spite of this defensive maneuver.

Since you now understand that a belief in the superiority or inferiority of regional varieties is simply a US language

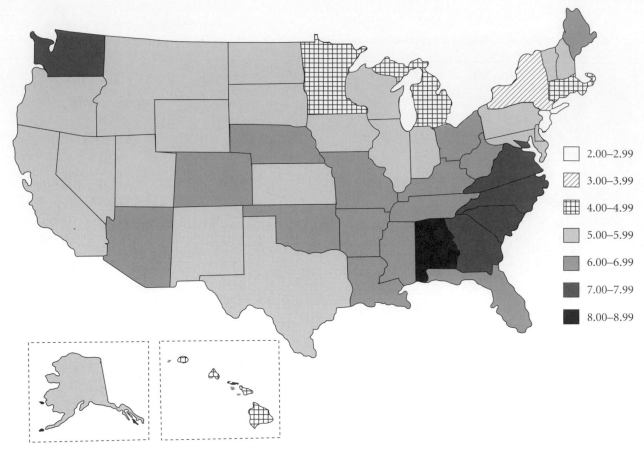

Figure 5. *Mean scores of the rankings for "pleasant English" by Auburn University (Alabama) students (1 = "least pleasant English"; 10 = "most pleasant English").*

myth, you can apologetically approach your good old family doctor about the headache problem again. Of course, you are too embarrassed to return to Cramden's office, so you ask for another referral and are sent to Dr B. J. ("Jimmy") Peaseblossom. You are relieved to hear his dulcet tones as he approaches:

> Bubba, haw's it hangin'? Cain't buy no luck, kin yuh? Yore hay-ud ailin' yuh? Don't git all flustrated; I'm gonna fix yew up good. Sweetheart! Looka hyeah! Bring me that thayngamabob, wouldja? How kin Ah take keer of ol' Bubba without mah thayngs? Thank yuh honey!

Your headaches turn out to be hangovers.

SOURCES AND FURTHER READING

The maps and data are taken from my collections. Readers who want an introduction to the folk perceptions of regional speech in the United States may consult my *Perceptual Dialectology* (Dordrecht: Foris, 1989). A current survey of recent and earlier work in this area (including research from the Netherlands, Japan, Germany, Wales, Turkey, and France) appears under my editorship as *A Handbook of Perceptual Dialectology* (Beverly Hills, CA: Sage, 1997). The quotations from New Yorkers are taken from William Labov's seminal work on NYC speech, *The Social Stratification of English in New York City* (Arlington, VA: The Center for Applied Linguistics, 1966). The work on Oregon has been carried out by Laura Hartley and is reported in *Oregonian Perceptions of American Regional Speech* (East Lansing, MI: MA thesis, Department of Linguistics and Languages, Michigan State University, 1996).

A quantitative method for calculating linguistic insecurity is first introduced in Labov's work cited above but refined and extended to gender in Peter Trudgill's "Sex, covert prestige and linguistic change in the urban British English of Norwich" in *Language in Society* 1 (1972), pp. 179–95. A good introduction to the techniques and principal findings of the study of language attitudes (and to the functions of language for "status" and "solidarity") may be found in Ellen Bouchard Ryan and Howard Giles (eds.), *Attitudes Towards Language Variation* (London: Arnold, 1982).

Post-reading Questions / Activities

- How are people from the South and New York City represented in the media and in popular culture? Is there a tendency to stereotype them? In what way?
- Is there harm in holding stereotypes about the ways people talk?
- Survey your class or your hallway or some other group that you frequently interact with. Where are people from? Are there any words or sounds that they are aware of that they say differently from others?

Vocabulary

linguistic insecurity   standard
linguistic security

Suggested Further Reading

Blount, Roy. 2007. *Long Time Leaving: Dispatches from Up South.* New York: Knopf.

Carver, Craig M. 1987. *American Regional Dialects: A Word Geography.* Ann Arbor: University of Michigan Press.

Cassidy, Frederic G. (editor-in-chief). 1985. *Dictionary of American Regional English,* vol. 1, A–C. Cambridge, MA: Harvard University Press, Belknap.

———, and Joan Houston Hall, eds. 1991. *Dictionary of American Regional English,* vol. 2, D–H. Cambridge, MA: Harvard University Press, Belknap.

———, and ———. 1996. *Dictionary of American Regional English,* vol. 3, I–O. Cambridge, MA: Harvard University Press, Belknap.

Francis, Nelson. 1983. *Dialectology: An Introduction.* New York: Longman.

Hall, Joan Houston. (editor-in-chief). 2002. *Dictionary of American Regional English,* vol. 4, P–Sk. Cambridge, MA: Harvard University Press, Belknap.

Labov, William, Sharon Ash, and Charles Boberg. 2006. *The Atlas of North American English: Phonetics, Phonology, and Sound Change.* Berlin: Mouton de Gruyter.

MacNeil, Robert, and William Cran, eds. 2005. *Do You Speak American?* New York: Doubleday.

Milroy, James. 1992. *Linguistic Variation and Change: On the Historical Sociolinguistics of English.* Oxford: Blackwell.

Trudgill, Peter. 1983. *On Dialect: Social and Geographical Perspectives.* New York: New York University Press.

———. 1990. *The Dialects of England.* Cambridge, MA: Blackwell.

Wolfram, Walt. 1991. *Dialects and American English.* Englewood Cliffs, NJ: Prentice Hall.

———, and Natalie Schilling-Estes. 2006 [1998]. *American English: Dialects and Variation.* 2d ed. Malden, MA: Blackwell.

———, and Ben Ward, eds. 2006. *American Voices: How Dialects Differ from Coast to Coast.* Malden, MA: Blackwell.

CHAPTER 24

Social Stratification of (r) in New York City Department Stores

William Labov

1972 [1966]

William Labov's classic study of New York City Department Stores—elegant, inexpensive, clear—showed that people who worked in these stores tended to have the speech corresponding to that of their social class (working class, middle class, upper-middle class) but that this speech lay on a continuum. Further, their speech showed greater similarity to "standard" American English in formal contexts—such as when they had to repeat something—than in casual contexts.

Labov's findings are considered to be "robust." They have been replicated in a wide range of societies and languages, from various areas in England to Belgium, France, and elsewhere. What was especially novel in his account was the observation that the variation in even a given speaker's speech was not random and unpredictable; on the contrary it could be quantified, predicted, and explained.

Labov is well known for both his methodological care and his decades-long attention to dialects, especially in Philadelphia, where it is said he can identify speakers' origins to the block or neighborhood. A recent outgrowth of this work is his editing of the Atlas of North American English *(with Ash and Boberg). He was one of the first prominent researchers to point out what he called the "logic" of African American English, having developed more appropriate methods of studying the speech of young black men than interviewing them one by one in a formal office. Labov has testified about Black English in several prominent legal cases, helping win recognition that African American Vernacular English, or Black English Vernacular, as it was formerly called, is a genuine, distinct variety of English. He has worked on the question of narrative, which grew out of his attempt to set speakers at ease so he could study their most natural ways of speaking. Finally, he has been working for quite some time on the question of how best to reduce the reading gap for African American children.*

Reading Questions

- What exactly was Labov trying to find out in the three department stores? Why did he choose the particular phonological variable he did?
- How does (r) differ among the three stores, and why?
- What pattern is revealed by the differences in age and their respective differences in r-less speech?
- How has (r) changed over time?

"As this letter is but a jar of the tongue,...it is the most imperfect of all the consonants."
JOHN WALKER, *Principles of English Pronunciation. 1791*

William Labov, "The Social Stratification of (r) in New York City Department Stores." In *Sociolinguistic Patterns*. Philadelphia: University of Pennsylvania Press, 1972. pp. 43–69. Notes have been renumbered and edited. Reprinted with permission of the University of Pennsylvania Press.

Anyone who begins to study language in its social context immediately encounters the classic methodological problem: the means used to gather the data interfere with the data to be gathered. The primary means of obtaining a large body of reliable data on the speech of one person is the individual tape-recorded interview. Interview speech is formal speech—not by any absolute measure, but by comparison with the vernacular of everyday life. On the whole, the interview is public speech—monitored and controlled in response to the presence of an outside observer. But even within that definition, the investigator may wonder if the responses in a tape-recorded interview are not a special product of the interaction between the interviewer and the subject. One way of controlling for this is to study the subject in his own natural social context—interacting with his family or peer group (Labov, Cohen, Robins, and Lewis 1968). Another way is to observe the public use of language in everyday life apart from any interview situation—to see how people use language in context when there is no explicit observation. This chapter is an account of the systematic use of rapid and anonymous observations in a study of the sociolinguistic structure of the speech community.

This chapter is the first of a series of six which deal primarily with the sociolinguistic study of New York City. The main base for that study (Labov 1966) was a secondary random sample of the Lower East Side.... But before the systematic study was carried out, there was an extensive series of preliminary investigations. These included 70 individual interviews and a great many anonymous observations in public places. These preliminary studies led to the definition of the major phonological variables which were to be studied, including (r): the presence or absence of consonantal [r] in postvocalic position in *car, card, four, fourth*, etc. This particular variable appeared to be extraordinarily sensitive to any measure of social or stylistic stratification. On the basis of the exploratory interviews, it seemed possible to carry out an empirical test of two general notions: first, that the linguistic variable (r) is a social differentiator in all levels of New York City speech, and second, that rapid and anonymous speech events could be used as the basis for a systematic study of language. The study of (r) in New York City department stores which I will report here was conducted in November 1962 as a test of these ideas.

We can hardly consider the social distribution of language in New York City without encountering the pattern of social stratification which pervades the life of the city. This concept is analyzed in some detail in the major study of the Lower East Side; here we may briefly consider the definition given by Bernard Barber: social stratification is the product of social differentiation and social evaluation (1957:1–3). The use of this term does not imply any specific type of class or caste, but simply that the normal workings of society have produced systematic differences between certain institutions or people, and that these differentiated forms have been ranked in status or prestige by general agreement.

We begin with the general hypothesis suggested by exploratory interviews: *if any two subgroups of New York City speakers are ranked in a scale of social stratification, then they will be ranked in the same order by their differential use of (r).*

It would be easy to test this hypothesis by comparing occupational groups, which are among the most important indexes of social stratification. We could, for example, take a group of lawyers, a group of file clerks, and a group of janitors. But this would hardly go beyond the indications of the exploratory interviews, and such an extreme example of differentiation would not provide a very exacting test of the hypothesis. It should be possible to show that the hypothesis is so general, and the differential use of (r) pervades New York City so thoroughly, that fine social differences will be reflected in the index as well as gross ones.

It therefore seemed best to construct a very severe test by finding a subtle case of stratification within a single occupational group: in this case, the sales people of large department stores in Manhattan. If we select three large department stores, from the top, middle, and bottom of the price and fashion scale, we can expect that the customers will be socially stratified. Would we expect the sales people to show a comparable stratification? Such a position would depend upon two correlations: between the status ranking of the stores and the ranking of parallel jobs in the three stores; and between the jobs and the behavior of the persons who hold those jobs. These are not unreasonable assumptions. C. Wright Mills points out that salesgirls in large department stores tend to borrow prestige from their customers, or at least make an effort in that direction.[1] It appears that a person's own occupation is more closely correlated with his linguistic behavior—for those working actively—than any other single social characteristic. The evidence presented here indicates that the stores are objectively differentiated in a fixed order, and that jobs in these stores are evaluated by employees in that order. Since the product of social differentiation and evaluation, no matter how minor, is social stratification of the employees in the three stores, the hypothesis will predict the following result: salespeople in the highest-ranked store will have the highest values of (r); those in the middle-ranked store will have intermediate values of (r); and those in the lowest-ranked store will show the lowest values. If this result holds true, the hypothesis will have received confirmation in proportion to the severity of the test.

The three stores which were selected are Saks Fifth Avenue, Macy's, and S. Klein. The differential ranking of these stores may be illustrated in many ways. Their locations are one important point:

Highest-ranking: Saks Fifth Avenue
    at 50th St. and Fifth Ave., near the center of the high-fashion shopping district, along with other high-prestige stores such as Bonwit Teller, Henri Bendel, Lord and Taylor

Middle-ranking: Macy's
> Herald Square, 34th St. and Sixth Ave., near the garment district, along with Gimbels and Saks-34th St., other middle-range stores in price and prestige

Lowest-ranking: S. Klein
> Union Square, 14th St. and Broadway, not far from the Lower East Side

The advertising and price policies of the stores are very clearly stratified. Perhaps no other element of class behavior is so sharply differentiated in New York City as that of the newspaper which people read; many surveys have shown that the *Daily News* is the paper read first and foremost by working-class people, while the *New York Times* draws its readership from the middle class.[2] These two newspapers were examined for the advertising copy in October 24–27, 1962: Saks and Macy's advertised in the *New York Times*, where Kleins was represented only by a very small item; in the *News*, however, Saks does not appear at all, while both Macy's and Kleins are heavy advertisers.

No. of pages of advertising October 24–27, 1962

	NY Times	Daily News
Saks	2	0
Macy's	6	15
S. Klein	¼	10

We may also consider the prices of the goods advertised during those four days. Since Saks usually does not list prices, we can only compare prices for all three stores on one item: women's coats. Saks: $90.00, Macy's: $79.95, Kleins: $23.00. On four items, we can compare Kleins and Macy's:

	Macy's	S. Klein
Dresses	$14.95	$5.00
Girls' coats	16.99	12.00
Stockings	0.89	0.45
Men's suits	49.95–64.95	26.00–66.00

The emphasis on prices is also different. Saks either does not mention prices, or buries the figure in small type at the foot of the page. Macy's features the prices in large type, but often adds the slogan, "You get more than low prices." Kleins, on the other hand, is often content to let the prices speak for themselves. The form of the prices is also different: Saks gives prices in round figures, such as $120; Macy's always shows a few cents off the dollar: $49.95; Kleins usually prices its goods in round numbers, and adds the retail price which is always much higher, and shown in Macy's style: "$23.00, marked down from $49.95."

The physical plant of the stores also serves to differentiate them. Saks is the most spacious, especially on the upper floors, with the least amount of goods displayed. Many of the floors are carpeted, and on some of them, a receptionist is stationed to greet the customers. Kleins, at the other extreme, is a maze of annexes, sloping concrete floors, low ceilings; it has the maximum amount of goods displayed at the least possible expense.

The principal stratifying effect upon the employees is the prestige of the store, and the working conditions. Wages do not stratify the employees in the same order. On the contrary, there is every indication that high-prestige stores such as Saks pay lower wages than Macy's.

Saks is a nonunion store, and the general wage structure is not a matter of public record. However, conversations with a number of men and women who have worked in New York department stores, including Saks and Macy's, show general agreement on the direction of the wage differential.[3] Some of the incidents reflect a willingness of sales people to accept much lower wages from the store with greater prestige. The executives of the prestige stores pay a great deal of attention to employee relations, and take many unusual measures to ensure that the sales people feel that they share in the general prestige of the store.[4] One of the Lower East Side informants who worked at Saks was chiefly impressed with the fact that she could buy Saks clothes at a 25 percent discount. A similar concession from a lower-prestige store would have been of little interest to her.

From the point of view of Macy's employees, a job in Kleins is well below the horizon. Working conditions and wages are generally considered to be worse, and the prestige of Kleins is very low indeed. As we will see, the ethnic composition of the store employees reflects these differences quite accurately.

A socioeconomic index which ranked New Yorkers on occupation would show the employees of the three stores at the same level; an income scale would probably find Macy's employees somewhat higher than the others; education is the only objective scale which might differentiate the groups in the same order as the prestige of the stores, though there is no evidence on this point. However, the working conditions of sales jobs in the three stores stratify them in the order: Saks, Macy's, Kleins; the prestige of the stores leads to a social evaluation of these jobs in the same order. Thus the two aspects of social stratification—differentiation and evaluation—are to be seen in the relations of the three stores and their employees.

The normal approach to a survey of department store employees requires that one enumerate the sales people of each store, draw random samples in each store, make appointments to speak with each employee at home, interview the respondents, then segregate the native New Yorkers, analyze and resample the nonrespondents, and so on. This is an expensive and time-consuming procedure, but for most purposes there is no short cut which will give accurate and reliable results. In this case, a simpler method which relies upon the extreme generality of the linguistic behavior of the subjects was used to gather a very limited type of data. This method is dependent upon the systematic sampling of casual and anonymous speech events. Applied in a poorly defined environment, such a method is open to many biases and it would be difficult to say what population had been studied. In this case, our population is well defined as the sales people (or more generally, any employee whose speech might be heard by a customer) in three specific stores at a specific time. The result will be a view of the role that speech would play in the overall social imprint of the employees upon the customer. It is surprising that this simple and economical approach achieves results with a high degree of consistency and regularity, and allows us to test the original hypothesis in a number of subtle ways.

The Method

The application of the study of casual and anonymous speech events to the department-store situation was relatively simple. The interviewer approached the informant in the role of a customer asking for directions to a particular department. The department was one which was located on the fourth floor. When the interviewer asked, "Excuse me, where are the women's shoes?" the answer would normally be, "Fourth floor."

The interviewer then leaned forward and said, "Excuse me?" He would usually then obtain another utterance, "*Fourth floor*," spoken in careful style under emphatic stress.[5]

The interviewer would then move along the aisle of the store to a point immediately beyond the informant's view, and make a written note of the data. The following independent variables were included:

the store
floor within the store[6]
sex
age (estimated in units of five years)
occupation (floorwalker, sales, cashier, stockboy)
race
foreign or regional accent, if any

The dependent variable is the use of (r) in four occurrences:

casual: fou<u>r</u>th floo<u>r</u>
emphatic: *fou<u>r</u>th floo<u>r</u>*

Thus we have preconsonantal and final position, in both casual and emphatic styles of speech. In addition, all other uses of (r) by the informant were noted, from remarks overheard or contained in the interview. For each plainly constricted value of the variable, (r-1) was entered; for unconstricted schwa, lengthened vowel, or no representation, (r-0) was entered. Doubtful cases or partial constriction were symbolized *d* and were not used in the final tabulation.

Also noted were instances of affricates or stops used in the word *fourth* for the final consonant, and any other examples of nonstandard (th) variants used by the speaker.

This method of interviewing was applied in each aisle on the floor as many times as possible before the spacing of the informants became so close that it was noticed that the same question had been asked before. Each floor of the store was investigated in the same way. On the fourth floor, the form of the question was necessarily different:

"Excuse me, what floor is this?"

Following this method, 68 interviews were obtained in Saks, 125 in Macy's, and 71 in Kleins. Total interviewing time for the 264 subjects was approximately 6.5 hours.

At this point, we might consider the nature of these 264 interviews in more general terms. They were speech events which had entirely different social significance for the two participants. As far as the informant was concerned, the exchange was a normal salesman-customer interaction, almost below the level of conscious attention, in which relations of the speakers were so casual and anonymous that they may hardly have been said to have met. This tenuous relationship was the minimum intrusion upon the behavior of the subject; language and the use of language never appeared at all.

From the point of view of the interviewer, the exchange was a systematic elicitation of the exact forms required, in the desired context, the desired order, and with the desired contrast of style.

Overall Stratification of (r)

The results of the study showed clear and consistent stratification of (r) in the three stores. In Figure 1, the use of (r) by employees of Saks, Macy's, and Kleins is compared by means of a bar graph. Since the data for most informants consist of only four items, we will not use a continuous numerical index for (r), but rather divide all informants into three categories.

all (r-1): those whose records show only (r-1) and no (r-0)
some (r-1): those whose records show at least one (r-1) and one (r-0)
no (r-1): those whose records show only (r-0)

From Figure 1 we see that a total of 62 percent of Saks employees, 51 percent of Macy's, and 20 percent of Kleins used all or some (r-1). The stratification is even sharper for the percentages of all (r-1). As the hypothesis predicted, the groups are ranked by their differential use of (r-1) in the same order as their stratification by extralinguistic factors.

Next, we may wish to examine the distribution of (r) in each of the four standard positions. Figure 2 shows this type of display, where once again, the stores are differentiated in

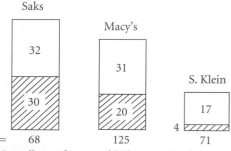

Figure 1. *Overall stratification of (r) by store. Shaded area = % all (r-1); unshaded area = % some (r-1); % no (r-1) not shown; N = total number of cases.*

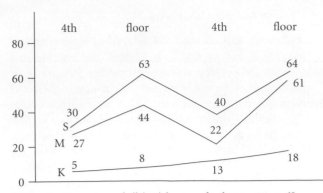

Figure 2. *Percentage of all (r-1) by store for four positions (S = Saks, M = Macy's, K = Kleins).*

the same order, and for each position. There is a considerable difference between Macy's and Kleins at each position, but the difference between Macy's and Saks varies. In emphatic pronunciation of the final (r), Macy's employees come very close to the mark set by Saks. It would seem that *r*-pronunciation is the norm at which a majority of Macy's employees aim, yet not the one they use most often. In Saks, we see a shift between casual and emphatic pronunciation, but it is much less marked. In other words, Saks employees have more *security* in a linguistic sense.[7]

The fact that the figures for (r-1) at Kleins are low should not obscure the fact that Kleins employees also participate in the same pattern of stylistic variation of (r) as the other stores. The percentage of *r*-pronunciation rises at Kleins from 5 to 18 percent as the context becomes more emphatic: a much greater rise in percentage than in the other stores, and a more regular increase as well. It will be important to bear in mind that this attitude—that (r-1) is the most appropriate pronunciation for emphatic speech—is shared by at least some speakers in all three stores.

Table 1 shows the data in detail, with the number of instances obtained for each of the four positions of (r), for each store. It may be noted that the number of occurrences in the second pronunciation of *four* is considerably reduced, primarily as a result of some speakers' tendency to answer a second time, "Fourth."

Table 1. Detailed Distribution of (r) by Store and Word Position

(r)	Saks				Macy's				S. Klein			
	Casual		Emphatic		Casual		Emphatic		Casual		Emphatic	
	4th	floor	4th	floor	4th	floor	4th	floor	4th	floor	4th	floor
(r-1)	17	31	16	21	33	48	13	31	3	5	6	7
(r-0)	39	18	24	12	81	62	48	20	63	59	40	33
d	4	5	4	4	0	3	1	0	1	1	3	3
No data*	8	14	24	31	11	12	63	74	4	6	22	28
Total no.	68	68	68	68	125	125	125	125	71	71	71	71

* The "no data" category for Macy's shows relatively high values under the emphatic category. This discrepancy is due to the fact that the procedure for requesting repetition was not standardized in the investigation of the ground floor at Macy's, and values for emphatic response were not regularly obtained. The effects of this loss are checked in Table 2, where only complete responses are compared.

Table 2. Distribution of (r) for Complete Responses

		% of Total responses in		
	(r)	Saks	Macy's	S. Klein
All (r-1)	1 1 1 1	24	22	6
Some (r-1)	0 1 1 1	46	37	12
	0 0 1 1			
	0 1 0 1 etc.			
No (r-1)	0 0 0 0	30	41	82
		100	100	100
N =		33	48	34

Since the numbers in the fourth position are somewhat smaller than the second, it might be suspected that those who use [r] in Saks and Macy's tend to give fuller responses, thus giving rise to a spurious impression of increase in (r) values in those positions. We can check this point by comparing only those who gave a complete response. Their responses can be symbolized by a four-digit number, representing the pronunciation in each of the four positions respectively (see Table 2).

Thus we see that the pattern of differential ranking in the use of (r) is preserved in this subgroup of complete responses, and omission of the final "floor" by some respondents was not a factor in this pattern.

THE EFFECT OF OTHER INDEPENDENT VARIABLES

Other factors, besides the stratification of the stores, may explain the regular pattern of *r*-pronunciation seen above, or this effect may be the contribution of a particular group in the population, rather than the behavior of the sales people as a whole. The other independent variables recorded in the interviews enable us to check such possibilities.

Race

There are many more black employees in the Kleins sample than in Macy's, and more in Macy's than in Saks. Table 3 shows the percentages of black informants and their responses. When we compare these figures with those of Figure 1, for the entire population, it is evident that the presence of many black informants will contribute to a lower use of (r-1). The black subjects at Macy's used less (r-1) than the white informants, though only to a slight extent; the black subjects at Kleins were considerably more biased in the *r*-less direction.

The higher percentage of black sales people in the lower-ranking stores is consistent with the general pattern of social stratification, since in general, black workers have been assigned less desirable jobs. Therefore the contribution of black speakers to the overall pattern is consistent with the hypothesis.

Table 3. Distribution of (r) for Black Employees

(r)	% of Responses in		
	Saks	Macy's	S. Klein
All (r-1)	50	12	0
Some (r-1)	0	35	6
No (r-1)	<u>50</u>	<u>53</u>	<u>94</u>
	100	100	100
N =	2	17	18
% of black informants:	03	14	25

Occupation

There are other differences in the populations of the stores. The types of occupations among the employees who are accessible to customers are quite different. In Macy's, the employees who were interviewed could be identified as floorwalkers (by red and white carnations), sales people, cashiers, stockboys, and elevator operators. In Saks, the cashiers are not accessible to the customer, working behind the sales counters, and stockboys are not seen. The working operation of the store goes on behind the scenes, and does not intrude upon the customer's notice. On the other hand, at Kleins, all of the employees seem to be operating on the same level: it is difficult to tell the difference between sales people, managers, and stockboys.

Here again, the extralinguistic stratification of the stores is reinforced by objective observations in the course of the interview. We can question if these differences are not responsible for at least a part of the stratification of (r). For the strongest possible result, it would be desirable to show that the stratification of (r) is a property of the most homogeneous subgroup in the three stores: native New York, white sales women. Setting aside the male employees, all occupations besides selling itself, the black and Puerto Rican employees, and all those with a foreign accent,[8] there are still a total of 141 informants to study.

Figure 3 shows the percentages of (r-1) used by the native white sales women of the three stores, with the same type of graph as in Figure 1. The stratification is essentially

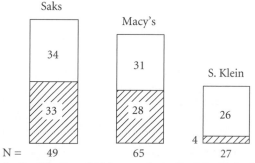

Figure 3. *Stratification of (r) by store for native New York white sales women. Shaded area = % all (r-1); unshaded area = % some (r-1); % no (r-1) not shown; N = total number of cases.*

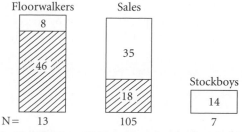

Figure 4. *Stratification of (r) by occupational groups in Macy's. Shaded area = % all (r-1); unshaded area = % some (r-1); % no (r-1) not shown. N = total number of cases.*

the same in direction and outline, though somewhat smaller in magnitude. The greatly reduced Kleins sample still shows by far the lowest use of (r-1), and Saks is ahead of Macy's in this respect. We can therefore conclude that the stratification of (r) is a process which affects every section of the sample.

We can now turn the heterogeneous nature of the Macy's sample to advantage. Figure 4 shows the stratification of (r) according to occupational groups in Macy's: in line with our initial hypothesis, this is much sharper than the stratification of the employees in general. The total percentage of those who use all or some (r-1) is almost the same for the floorwalkers and the sales people but a much higher percentage of floorwalkers consistently use (r-1).

Another interesting comparison may be made at Saks, where there is a great discrepancy between the ground floor and the upper floors. The ground floor of Saks looks very much like Macy's: many crowded counters, salesgirls leaning over the counters, almost elbow to elbow, and a great deal of merchandise displayed. But the upper floors of Saks are far more spacious; there are long vistas of empty carpeting, and on the floors devoted to high fashion, there are models who display the individual garments to the customers. Receptionists are stationed at strategic points to screen out the casual spectators from the serious buyers.

It would seem logical then, to compare the ground floor of Saks with the upper floors. By the hypothesis, we should find a differential use of (r-1). Table 4 shows that this is the case.

In the course of the interview, information was also collected on the (th) variable, particularly as it occurred in the word *fourth*. This is one of the major variables used in the study of social stratification in New York (Labov 1966) and elsewhere (Wolfram 1969; Anshen 1969). The most strongly stigmatized variant is the use of the stop [t]

Table 4. Distribution of (r) by Floor in Saks

(r)	Ground floor	Upper floors
% all (r-1)	23	34
% some (r-1)	23	40
% no (r-1)	<u>54</u>	<u>26</u>
	100	100
N =	30	38

in *fourth, through, think*, etc. The percentage of speakers who used stops in this position was fully in accord with the other measures of social stratification which we have seen:

Saks   00%
Macy's   04
S. Klein   15

Thus the hypothesis has received a number of semi-independent confirmations. Considering the economy with which the information was obtained, the survey appears to yield rich results. It is true that we do not know a great deal about the informants that we would like to know: their birthplace, language history, education, participation in New York culture, and so on. Nevertheless, the regularities of the underlying pattern are strong enough to overcome this lack of precision in the selection and identification of informants.

DIFFERENTIATION BY AGE OF THE INFORMANTS

The age of the informants was estimated within five-year intervals, and these figures cannot be considered reliable for any but the simplest kind of comparison. However, it should be possible to break down the age groups into three units, and detect any overall direction of change.

If, as we have indicated, (r-1) is one of the chief characteristics of a new prestige pattern which is being superimposed upon the native New York City pattern, we would expect to see a rise in *r*-pronunciation among the younger

Table 5. Distribution of (r) by Estimated Age

(r)	Age Groups		
	15–30	35–50	55–70
% all (r-1)	24	20	20
% some (r-1)	21	28	22
% no (r-1)	55	52	58

sales people. The overall distribution by age shows no evidence of change, however, in Table 5.

This lack of direction is surprising, in the light of other evidence that the use of (r-1) as a prestige variant is increasing among younger people in New York City. There is clear-cut evidence for the absence of (r-1) in New York City in the 1930s (Kurath and McDavid 1951) and a subsequent increase in the records of Hubbell (1950) and Bronstein (1962). When we examine the distributions for the individual stores, we find that the even distribution through age levels disappears. Figure 5 shows that the expected inverse correlation with age appears in Saks, but not in Macy's or Kleins. Instead, Macy's shows the reverse direction at a lower level, with older subjects using more (r-1), and Kleins no particular correlation with age. This complex pattern is even more puzzling, and one is tempted to dismiss it as the absence of any pattern. But although the numbers of the subgroups may appear to be small, they are larger than many of the subgroups used in the discussions of previous pages, and as we will see, it is not possible to discount the results.

The conundrum represented by Figure 5 is one of the most significant results of the procedures that have been followed to this point. Where all other findings confirm the

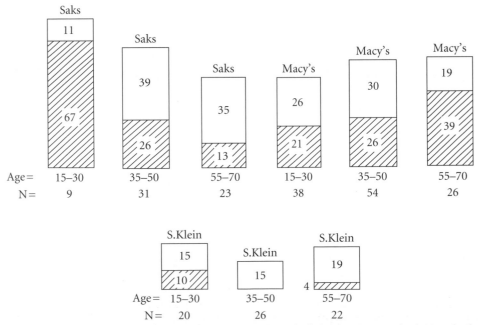

Figure 5. *Stratification of (r) by store and age level. Shaded area = % all (r-1); unshaded area = % some (r-1); % no (r-1) not shown; N = total number of cases.*

original hypothesis, a single result which does not fit the expected pattern may turn our attention in new and profitable directions. From the data in the department store survey alone, it was not possible to account for Figure 5 except in speculative terms. In the original report on the department store survey, written shortly after the work was completed, we commented:

> How can we account for the differences between Saks and Macy's? I think we can say this: the shift from the influence of the New England prestige pattern (r-less) to the Midwestern prestige pattern (r-ful) is felt most completely at Saks. The younger people at Saks are under the influence of the r-pronouncing pattern, and the older ones are not. At Macy's, there is less sensitivity to the effect among a large number of younger speakers who are completely immersed in the New York City linguistic tradition. The stockboys, the young salesgirls, are not as yet fully aware of the prestige attached to r-pronunciation. On the other hand, the older people at Macy's tend to adopt this pronunciation: very few of them rely upon the older pattern of prestige pronunciation which supports the r-less tendency of older Saks sales people. This is a rather complicated argument, which would certainly have to be tested very thoroughly by longer interviews in both stores before it could be accepted.

The complex pattern of Figure 5 offered a considerable challenge for interpretation and explanation, but one possibility that always had to be considered was that it was the product of the many sources of error inherent in rapid and anonymous surveys. To confirm and explain the results of the department store survey it will be necessary to [anticipate] the results of [our] systematic interviewing program (Labov 1972b, Chs. 3–7). When the results of [our] major study of the Lower East Side were analyzed, it became clear that Figure 5 was not an artifact of the method but reflected real social patterns (Labov 1966: 342 ff). The Lower East Side data most comparable to the department store study are the distribution of (r) by age and class in Style B—the relatively careful speech which is the main bulk of the individual interview.... To Saks, Macy's, and Kleins, we can compare upper middle class, lower middle class, and working class as a whole. The age ranges which are most comparable to the department store ranges are 20–29, 30–39, and 40–. (Since

the department store estimates are quite rough, there would be no gain in trying to match the figures exactly.) Figure 6 is then the age and class display for the Lower East Side use of (r) most comparable to Figure 5. Again, we see that the highest-status group shows the inverse correlation of (r-1) with age: younger speakers use more (r-1); the second-highest-status group shows (r) at a lower level and the reverse correlation with age; and the working-class groups at a still lower level with no particular correlation with age.

This is a very striking confirmation, since the two studies have quite complementary sources of error. The Lower East Side survey was a secondary random sample, based on a Mobilization for Youth survey, with complete demographic information on each informant. The interviews were tape-recorded, and a great deal of data on (r) was obtained from each speaker in a wide variety of styles. On the other hand, the department store study involved a much greater likelihood of error on a number of counts: the small amount of data per informant, the method of notation, the absence of tape recording and reliance on short-term memory, the method of sampling, the estimation of age of the informant, and the lack of background data on the informants. Most of these sources of error are inherent in the method. To compensate for them, we had the uniformity of the interview procedure, the location of the informants in their primary role as employees, the larger number of cases within a single cell, the simplicity of the data, and above all the absence of the biasing effect of the formal linguistic interview. The Lower East Side [LES] survey was weak in just those areas where the department store [DS] study was strong, and strong where it was weak. The methodological differences are summed up in the table below.

	Lower East Side Survey	Department Store Study
LES > DS		
Sampling	Random	Informants available at specific locations
Recording of data	Tape-recorded	Short-term memory and notes
Demographic data	Complete	Minimal: by inspection and inference
Amount of data	Large	Small
Stylistic range	Wide	Narrow

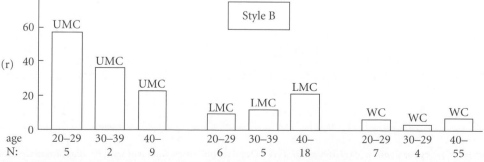

Figure 6. *Classification of (r) by age and class on the Lower East Side: in style B, careful speech.*

DS > LES

Size of sample	Moderate	Large
Location	Home, alone	At work, with others
Social context	Interview	Request for information
Effect of observation	Maximal	Minimal
Total time per subject (location and interview)	4–8 hours	5 minutes

The convergence of the Lower East Side survey and the department store survey therefore represents the ideal solution to the Observer's Paradox [Labov 1972b, Ch. 8]: that our goal is to observe the way people use language when they are not being observed. All of our methods involve an approximation to this goal: when we approach from two different directions, and get the same result, we can feel confident that we have reached past the Observer's Paradox to the structure that exists independently of the analyst.

Given the pattern of Figure 5 as a social fact, how can we explain it? The suggestions advanced in our preliminary note seem to be moving in the right direction, but at that time we had not isolated the hypercorrect pattern of the lower middle class nor identified the crossover pattern characteristic of change in progress. We must draw more material from the later research to solve this problem.

Figures 5 and 6 are truncated views of the three-dimensional distribution of the new *r*-pronouncing norm by age, style, and social class. Figure 7 shows two of the stylistic cross sections from the more detailed study of the Lower East Side population, with four subdivisions by age. The [dashed] line shows us how the highest-status group (Class 9) introduces the new *r*-pronouncing norm in casual speech. In Style A only upper-middle-class speakers under 40 show any sizable amount of (r-1). None of the younger speakers in the other social groups show any response to this norm in Style A, though some effect can be seen in the middle-aged subjects, especially in the second-highest-status group (Class 6–8, lower middle class). In Style B, this imitative effect is exaggerated, with the middle-aged lower-middle-class group coming very close to the upper-middle-class norm. In more formal styles, not shown here, this subgroup shows an even sharper increase in *r*-pronunciation, going beyond the upper-middle-class norm in the "hypercorrect" pattern that has appeared for this group in other studies (see Levine and Crockett 1966; Shuy, Wolfram, and Riley 1967;) [Labov 1972b, Ch. 5]). Figure 7 is not a case of the reversal of the age distribution of (r-1); rather it is a one-generation lag in the peak of response to the new norm. The second-highest status group responds to the new norm with a weaker form of imitation in connected speech, with middle-aged speakers adopting the new norm of the younger high-status speakers; Figure 8 shows this schematically. Our studies do not give the exact profile of the use of (r) among younger upper-middle-class

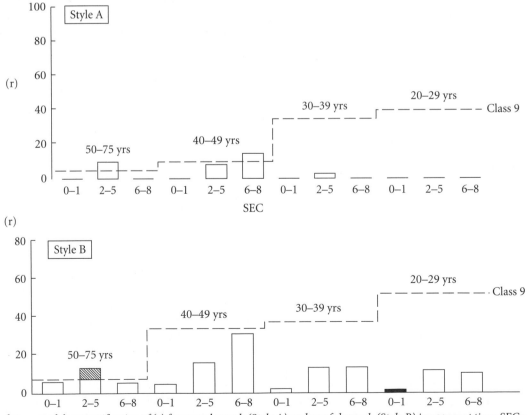

Figure 7. *Development of class stratification of (r) for casual speech (Style A) and careful speech (Style B) in apparent time; SEC = socioeconomic class scale.*

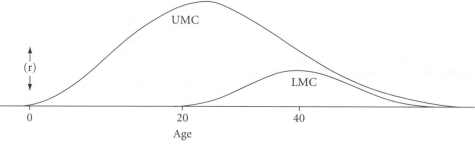

Figure 8. *Hypothetical distribution of (r) as an incoming prestige feature.*

speakers, since we did not focus on that age range. In later observations, I have met some upper-middle-class youth who use 100 percent (r-1), but in most families, (r-1) is still a superposed pronunciation in adolescence and Figure 8 reflects this. If we wish to express the (r-1) distribution in a single function, we can say that it is inversely correlated with distance from the highest-status group (taking Class 9 as 1, Classes 6–8 as 2, Classes 2–5 as 3, and Classes 0–1 as 4). It is also directly correlated with the formality of style and the amount of attention paid to speech (taking casual speech, Style A, as 0, careful speech, Style B, as 1, etc.). The slope of style shifting is modified by a function which may be called the "Index of Linguistic Insecurity" (ILI), which is maximized for the second-highest-status group.... The age distribution must be shown as greatest for the upper middle class at age 20 and at age 40 for the lower middle class. We can formalize these observations by writing

(r-1) = −a (Class) + b (Style)(ILI) − c|(Class) · 20 − (Age)| + d

The third term is minimized for the upper middle class at age 20, for the lower middle class at age 40, the working class at age 60, etc. Figure 7 supports this semiquantitative expression of a wave effect, which still has a number of unspecified constants.

There is a considerable difference between the behavior of the highest-status group and the others. The upper middle class develops the use of (r-1) early in life—as a variable expression of relative formality to be found at all stylistic levels. For the other groups in New York City, there is no solid basis for (r-1) in the vernacular style of casual speech; for them, (r-1) is a form which requires some attention paid to speech if it is realized at all. As in so many other formal marks of style-shifting, the lower middle class overdoes the process of correction. This is a process learned late in life. When speakers who are now 40–50 were growing up, the prestige norm was not (r-1) but (r-0). Before World War II, the New York City schools were dominated by an Anglophile tradition which taught that (r-1) was a provincial feature, an incorrect inversion of the consonant, and that the correct pronunciation of orthographic *r* in *car* was (r-0), [*ka* ·], in accordance with "international English."[9] No adjustment in the pronunciation of this consonant was then necessary for New Yorkers who

were trying to use the prestige norm—it was only vowel quality which had to be corrected. This *r*-less norm can be seen in the formal speech of upper-middle-class speakers over 40, and lower-middle-class speakers over 50. It also appears in subjective-reaction tests for older speakers. The lower-middle-class speakers who now shift to (r-1) in formal styles have abandoned their prestige norm and are responding to the form used by the younger high-status speakers that they come into contact with. On the other hand, many upper-middle-class speakers adhere to their original norm, in defiance of the prevailing trend. The pattern which we have observed in the department store survey is therefore a reflection of the linguistic insecurity of the lower middle class, which has led the older generation to adopt the most recent norm of (r-1) in preference to the older norm. The process of linguistic socialization is slower for lower-middle-class groups who do not go to college than for upper-middle-class speakers, who begin adjusting to the new norm in the upper class tracks of the academic high schools. For those who do not follow this path, it takes 10 or 20 years to reach maximum sensitivity to the hierarchical organization of formal language in their community.

SOME METHODOLOGICAL DIRECTIONS

The most important conclusion of the department store study is that rapid and anonymous studies can be a valuable source of information on the sociolinguistic structure of a speech community. There are a number of directions in which we can extend and improve such methods. While some sources of error are inherent in the method, others can be eliminated with sufficient attention.

In the department store survey, the approach to sampling might have been more systematic. It would have been preferable to select every *nth* sales person, or to use some other method that would avoid the bias of selecting the most available subject in a given area. As long as such a method does not interfere with the unobtrusive character of the speech event, it would reduce sampling bias without decreasing efficiency. Another limitation is that the data were not tape-recorded. The transcriber, myself, knew what the object of the test was, and it is always possible that an unconscious bias in transcription would lead to some doubtful cases being recorded as (r-1) in Saks, and as (r-0) in Kleins.[10] A third limitation is in the method used to elicit emphatic speech. Figure 2 indicates that the effect of stylistic variation may be slight as compared to the internal phonological constraint of preconsonantal vs. final position. The total percentages for all three stores bear this out.

% of All (r-1) for Each Position			
Casual		**Emphatic**	
fourth	*floor*	*fourth*	*floor*
23	39	24	48

A simple request for repetition has only a limited effect in inducing more formal speech. The use of reading passages, word lists, and minimal pairs in the Lower East Side study gave a wider range of styles. It might be possible to enlarge the stylistic range in rapid and anonymous studies by emphasizing the difficulty in hearing by one technique or another.

The sources of error in the department store study are offset by the comparability of the three subsections, the size of the sample, and the availability of the population for rechecking. Though the individual speakers cannot be relocated, the representative population can easily be reexamined for longitudinal studies of change in progress. There are limitations of such a "pseudopanel" as compared to a true panel study of the same individuals; but the advantages in cost and efficiency are overwhelming.

With such promising results in hand, it should be possible to refine and improve the methods used, and apply them in a wider range of contexts. In large cities it is reasonable to select single large institutions like department stores, but there is no reason to limit rapid and anonymous surveys to sales people or to institutions of this character. We can turn to any large body of individuals located at fixed "social addresses" and accessible to interaction with the public: policemen, postal clerks, secretaries, ushers, guides, bus drivers, taxi drivers, street peddlers and demonstrators, beggars, construction workers, etc. The public groups which are most clearly identified tend to be concentrated towards the lower end of the social scale, with sales people at the upper end. But we can reach a more general public by considering shoppers, spectators at sports events, parades, or construction sites, amateur gardeners, park strollers, and passersby in general; here the general character of the residential area can serve the same differentiating function as the three department stores mentioned above. Many professionals of relatively high social standing are available for public interaction: particularly teachers, doctors, and lawyers. Such public events as courtroom trials and public hearings allow us to monitor the speech of a wide range of socially located and highly differentiated individuals.[11]

There is in all such methods a bias towards those populations that are available to public interaction, and against those which are so located as to insure privacy: business and social leaders, or those engaged in aesthetic, scholarly, scientific, or illegal activities. Any of these groups can be studied with sufficient ingenuity: sociolinguistic research should certainly rise to the challenge to develop rapid and anonymous studies that will escape the limitations of convenience. But it should be emphasized that since those who are most available to public interaction may have the most direct effect upon linguistic change and the sociolinguistic system, the bias through missing the more extreme and obscure ends of the social spectrum is not as great as it may first appear.

Since the department store survey was carried out in Manhattan, several parallel studies have been made. In Suffolk County, Long Island, rapid and anonymous observations of the use of (r) were made by Patricia Allen (1968). In three stratified stores, 156 employees were observed. In the highest-status store (Macy's), only 27 percent of the subjects used no (r-1); in the intermediate store (Grant City), 40 percent; and in the low-status store (Floyd's), 60 percent. We see that the general New York City pattern has moved outward from the city, producing a comparable stratification of (r) in three stores of a somewhat narrower range than those studied in Manhattan. Our own analysis of the New York City situation shows that rapid and anonymous surveys of this kind cannot be interpreted fully without detailed knowledge of the dialect history of the area, and a more systematic study of the distribution of linguistic variables and subjective norms.[12] In this case, rapid and anonymous surveys should be considered a supplement or preliminary to other methods, not substitutions for them. Yet there are cases where rapid methods can give solutions to problems that have never been circumnavigated by conventional techniques. We have used observations of the speech of telephone operators to construct a national map of the merger of the low back vowels in *hock* and *hawk*, and the merger of *i* and *e* before nasals in *pin* and *pen*. In our recent study of the Puerto Rican speech community in New York City, we utilized such natural experimentation to find out what percentage of those heard speaking Spanish on the street were raised in the United States, and what percentage were born in Puerto Rico (Labov and Pedraza 1971).

Future studies of language in its social context should rely more heavily on rapid and anonymous studies, as part of a general program of utilizing unobtrusive measures to control the interactive effect of the observer (Webb et al. 1966). But our rapid and anonymous studies are not passive indices of social use, like observations of wear and tear in public places. They represent a form of nonreactive experimentation in which we avoid the bias of the experimental context and the irregular interference of prestige norms but still control the behavior of subjects. We are just beginning to study speech events like *asking for directions,* isolating the invariant rules which govern them, and on this basis develop the ability to control a large body of socially located public speech in a natural setting. We see rapid and anonymous observations as the most important experimental method in a linguistic program which takes as its primary object the language used by ordinary people in their everyday affairs.

Notes

This chapter is based upon Chs. 3 and 9 of *The Social Stratification of English in New York City* (1966), revised in the light of further work with rapid and anonymous observations. I am indebted to Frank Anshen and Maverick Marvin Harris for reference to illuminating replications of this study (Allen 1968, Harris 1969).

1. C. Wright Mills, *White Collar* (New York: Oxford University Press, 1956), p. 173. See also p. 243: "The tendency of white-collar people to borrow status from higher elements is so strong that it has carried over to all social contacts and features of the work-place. Salespeople in department stores…frequently attempt, although often unsuccessfully, to borrow prestige from their contact with customers, and to cash it in among work colleagues as well as friends off the job. In the big city the girl who works on 34th Street cannot successfully claim as much prestige as the one who works on Fifth Avenue or 57th Street."

2. This statement is fully confirmed by answers to a question on newspaper readership in the Mobilization for Youth Survey of the Lower East Side. The readership of the *Daily News* and *Daily Mirror* (now defunct) on the one hand, and the *New York Times* and *Herald Tribune* (now defunct) on the other hand, is almost complementary in distribution by social class.

3. Macy's sales employees are represented by a strong labor union, while Saks is not unionized. One former Macy's employee considered it a matter of common knowledge that Saks wages were lower than Macy's, and that the prestige of the store helped to maintain its nonunion position. Bonuses and other increments are said to enter into the picture. It appears that it is more difficult for a young girl to get a job at Saks than at Macy's. Thus Saks has more leeway in hiring policies, and the tendency of the store officials to select girls who speak in a certain way will play a part in the stratification of language, as well as the adjustment made by the employees to their situation. Both influences converge to produce stratification.

4. A former Macy's employee told me of an incident that occurred shortly before Christmas several years ago. As she was shopping in Lord and Taylor's, she saw the president of the company making the rounds of every aisle and shaking hands with every employee. When she told her fellow employees at Macy's about this scene, the most common remark was, "How else do you get someone to work for that kind of money?" One can say that not only do the employees of higher-status stores borrow prestige from their employer—it is also deliberately loaned to them.

5. The interviewer in all cases was myself. I was dressed in middle-class style, with jacket, white shirt, and tie, and used my normal pronunciation as a college-educated native of New Jersey (*r*-pronouncing).

6. Notes were also made on the department in which the employee was located, but the numbers for individual departments are not large enough to allow comparison.

7. The extreme style shifting of the second-highest status group appears throughout the New York City pattern, and is associated with an extreme sensitivity to the norms of an exterior reference group [. When the number of items in which a speaker distinguishes between his own pronunciation of a word and the correct pronunciation was given, the second-highest group had the highest scores on our metric, the Index of Linguistic Insecurity.] We find parallel phenomena in Shuy, Wolfram, and Riley 1967, Wolfram 1969, and Levine and Crockett 1966, who found in their study of Hillsboro, North Carolina, that the second-highest group on the basis of education showed the most extreme stylistic shift of (r).

8. In the sample as a whole, 17 informants with distinct foreign accents were found, and one with regional characteristics which were clearly not of New York City origin. The foreign language speakers in Saks had French, or other western European accents, while those in Kleins had Jewish and other eastern European accents. There were three Puerto Rican employees in the Kleins sample, one in Macy's, none in Saks. There were 70 men and 194 women. Men showed the following small differences from women in percentages of (r-1) usage:

	Men	Women
all (r-1)	22	30
some (r-1)	22	17
no (r-1)	57	54

9. See for example *Voice and Speech Problems*, a text written for New York City schools in 1940 by Raubicheck, Davis, and Carll (1940:336):

> There are many people who feel that an effort should be made to make the pronunciation conform to the spelling, and for some strange reason, they are particularly concerned with *r*. We all pronounce *calm, psalm, almond, know, eight, night*, and *there* without worrying…Yet people who would not dream of saying kniː or psai'kplədʒi insist on attempting to sound the *r* in words like paˑ'k or faðə just because an *r* marks the spot where our ancestors used a trill.…More often than not, people do not really say a third sound in a word like paˑ'k but merely say the vowel *a:* with the tongue tip curled back toward the throat. This type of vowel production is known as "Inversion."

Letitia Raubicheck was the head of the speech program in the New York City schools for many years and exerted a powerful influence on the teaching of English there. The norm of "international English" was maintained by William Tilly of Columbia and followed by Raubicheck and many others in the 1930s and 1940s. As far as I know, this norm has lost entirely its dominant position in the school system: a detailed study of its disappearance from the radio networks and the school system in the 1940s would tell us a great deal about the mechanism of such shifts in the prestige form.

10. When the phonetic transcriptions were first made, doubtful cases were marked as *d* and were not included in the tabulations made later. There is however room for interviewer bias in the decision between (r-0) and *d* and between *d* and (r-1).

11. Hearings of the New York City Board of Education were recorded during the study of New York City, and preliminary analysis of the data shows that the pattern of social and stylistic stratification of (r) can easily be recovered from the wide variety of speakers who appear in these hearings. Courtroom proceedings at the New York Court of General Sessions are a natural focus for such studies, but speakers often lower their voices to

the point that spectators cannot hear them clearly. Only a small beginning has been made on the systematic study of passersby. Plakins (1969) approached a wide variety of pedestrians in a Connecticut town with requests for directions to an incomprehensible place, phrased at three levels of politeness. She found systematic differences in mode of response according to dress (as an index of socioeconomic position) and mode of inquiry; there were no "rude" responses [huh?] to polite inquiries.

12. Allen's tables resemble the New York City patterns but with one major difference; the number of speakers who use all (r-1) is roughly constant in all three stores: 27 percent in Floyd's, 27 percent in Grant City, 32 percent in Macy's. Examination of the distribution in apparent time showed that this phenomenon was due to the presence of a bimodal split in the lower-store adults (over 30 years old). Eighty percent used no (r-1) and 20 percent used a consistent all (r-1): there were none who varied. On the other hand, 50 percent of the adults were showing variable (r) in the two other stores. This points to the presence of an older *r*-pronouncing vernacular which is now dominated by the *r*-less New York City pattern (Kurath and McDavid 1961), but survives among working-class speakers. The disengagement of such bimodal patterns is a challenging problem (Levine and Crockett 1966), and certainly requires a more systematic survey. Similar complexity is suggested in the results of rapid and anonymous survey of stores in Austin, Texas, by M. M. Harris (1969). In this basically *r*-pronouncing area, the prestige norms among whites appear to be a weak constricted [r], with a strongly retroflex consonant gaining ground among younger speakers. But for the few blacks and Mexican-Americans encountered, this strong [r] seems to be the norm aimed at in careful articulation. Although these results are only suggestive, they are the kind of preliminary work which is required to orient a more systematic investigation towards the crucial variables of the sociolinguistic structure of that community.

References

Allen, P. 1968. /r/ variable in the speech of New Yorkers in department stores. Unpublished research paper SUNY, Stony Brook.

Anshen, F. 1969. Speech variation among Negroes in a small Southern community. Unpublished dissertation, New York University.

Barber, Bernard. 1957. *Social stratification*. New York: Harcourt, Brace.

Bronstein, A. 1962. Let's take another look at New York City speech. *American Speech* 37:13–26.

Harris, M. M. 1969. The retroflexion of postvocalic /r/ in Austin. *American Speech* 44: 263–271.

Hubbell, A. F. 1950. *The pronunciation of English in New York City*. New York: Columbia University Press.

Kurath, H., and R. McDavid. 1961. *The pronunciation of English in the Atlantic states*. Ann Arbor: University of Michigan Press.

Labov, W. 1966. *The social stratification of English in New York City*. Washington, DC: Center for Applied Linguistics.

———. 1972a. *Language in the inner city: studies in the black English vernacular*. Philadelphia: University of Pennsylvania Press.

———, 1972b. *Sociolinguistic patterns*. Philadelphia: University of Pennsylvania Press.

———, P. Cohen, C. Robins, and J. Lewis. 1968. A study of the non-standard English of Negro and Puerto Rican speakers in New York City. Final report, Cooperative Research Project 3288. 2 vols. Philadelphia: U.S. Regional Survey, 204 N. 35th St., Philadelphia 19104.

———, and P. Pedraza. 1971. *A Study of the Puerto Rican speech community in New York City*. Report to the Urban Center of Columbia University.

Levine, L., and H. J. Crockett, Jr. 1966. Speech variation in a piedmont community: postvocalic r. *In* S. Lieberson, *Explorations in Sociolinguistics*. Special issue of *Sociologies Inquiry* 36(2).

Shuy, R., W. Wolfram, and W. K. Riley. 1967. *A study of social dialects in Detroit*. Final report, Project 6–1347. Washington, DC: Office of Education.

Webb, Eugene J., et al. 1966. *Unobtrusive measures: non-reactive research in the social sciences*. Chicago: Rand McNally.

Wolfram, W. 1969. Linguistic correlates of social stratification in the speech of Detroit Negroes. Unpublished thesis, Hartford Seminary Foundation.

Post-reading Questions / Activities

- Why is it important that Labov chose not to tape-record speech for this article? Are his methods reliable? Why? What does he mean by saying that "our goal is to observe the way people use language when they are not being observed"? What can researchers do?
- If speakers are aware that their speech may be stigmatized, why do they not simply use the standard form?
- Identify a sociolinguistic variable in your area (with an independent and dependent variable). Devise a "rapid, anonymous" study like Labov's. What did you find? How did your method work?

Vocabulary

affricate	postvocalic	stop
linguistic insecurity	preconsonantal	UMC
MC	schwa	WC
orthographic	SEC	
phonological variables	social stratification	

Suggested Further Reading

Corfield, Penelope J., ed. 1991. *Language, History, and Class*. Oxford: Blackwell.

Edwards, John. 1994. *Multilingualism*. London: Routledge.

Fasold, Ralph. 1984. *The Sociolinguistics of Society*. Oxford: Blackwell.

———. 1990. *The Sociolinguistics of Language*. Oxford: Blackwell.

Giglioli, Pier Paolo, ed. 1972. *Language and Social Context*. Harmondsworth, UK: Penguin Books.

Grillo, Ralph D. 1989. *Dominant Languages: Language and Hierarchy in Britain and France*. Cambridge: Cambridge University Press.

Labov, William. 1996. *The Social Stratification of English in New York City*. Washington, DC: Center for Applied Linguistics.

———. 1972. *Sociolinguistic Patterns*. Philadelphia: University of Pennsylvania Press.

Macaulay, R. K. S. 1977. *Language, Social Class, and Education: A Glasgow Study*. Edinburgh: University of Edinburgh Press.

Milroy, James. 1991. *Linguistic Variation and Change: On the Historical Sociolinguistics of English*. Oxford: Blackwell.

———, and Lesley Milroy. 1985. *Authority in Language: Investigating Language Prescription and Standardization*. London: Routledge & Kegan Paul.

Mugglestone, Lynda. 1995. *"Talking Proper": The Rise of Accent as a Social Symbol*. Oxford: Oxford University Press.

Romaine, Suzanne, ed. 1982. *Sociolinguistic Variation in Speech Communities*. London: Edward Arnold.

———. 2000. *Language in Society: An Introduction to Sociolinguistics*. 2d ed. Oxford: Oxford University Press.

Trudgill, Peter. 1974. *The Social Differentiation of English in Norwich*. Cambridge: Cambridge University Press.

CHAPTER 25

New York Jewish Conversational Style

Deborah Tannen
(1981)

There are some stereotypes about regional linguistic varieties that have a basis in actual practice. One of them is that of the "pushy New York Jews." Though most people could not provide a detailed technical description of what that consists of, they can talk animatedly about its features: people talk fast, they "crowd" out others, they talk about themselves.... Americans also have a sense of "Midwestern reserve" and its concomitant politeness. Much of this involves judgment and evaluation.

Deborah Tannen stumbled upon this phenomenon accidentally as she went to analyze a tape-recorded Thanksgiving dinner conversation that included half New York Jews and half Midwesterners (or Californians). Herself a New Yorker, she was startled to find that there was not a single interchange in which New Yorkers did not take part. How to describe and explain this?

This chapter uses two important approaches to the study of language: the study of politeness, based largely on the work of Erving Goffman, Robin Lakoff, Penelope Brown, and Stephen Levinson, and the detailed study of conversation, called conversational analysis (a subfield of discourse analysis), inspired by sociologists/ethnomethodologists Harvey Sacks, Emanuel Schegloff, and others. In this kind of analysis, transcripts are made that show not only the words people uttered but their relationship to one another, almost like a musical score, showing when each person entered the talk, when they speak together (overlap), and something about the volume and other paralinguistic features of their talk.

Reading Questions

- What are the three rules of politeness (or, rules of rapport)? Which one do people usually associate with "politeness"?
- What are positive face and negative face?
- How does cross-stylistic interchange, as in the first long example with Peter, David, and Tannen, prove disconcerting? What happens in co-stylistic interchange, as in the second long example with Peter and Tannen?
- What does Tannen mean by saying "People tend to take their conversational habits as self-evident and draw conclusions not about others' linguistic devices but about their intentions or personalities"? Do you think this is true? Have you ever had this experience?

A pause in the wrong place, an intonation misunderstood, and a whole conversation went awry.   —E.M. FORSTER, *A Passage to India*

Conversation, New York's biggest cottage industry, doesn't exist in San Francisco in the sense of sustained discourse and friendly contentiousness.   —EDMUND WHITE, *States of Desire*[1]

Deborah Tannen, "New York Jewish Conversational Style." *International Journal of the Sociology of Language* 30 (1981): 133–149.

Take, for example, the following conversation.[2]

F: How often does your acting group work?
M: Do you mean how often we rehearse or how often we perform.⌐
F: ⌊Both.
M: [Laughs uneasily.]
F: Why are you laughing?
M: Because of the way you said that. It was like a bullet. Is that why your marriage broke up?
F: What?
M: Because of your aggressiveness.

Of the many observations that could be made based on this interchange, I would like to focus on two: the general tendency to extrapolate personality from conversational style, and the specific attribution of aggressiveness to a speaker who uses fast pacing in conversation. In the discussion that follows, I will suggest that the stereotype of the "pushy New York Jew" may result in part from discourse conventions practiced by some native New Yorkers of East European Jewish background. After examining some evidence for the existence of such a stereotype, I will (1) briefly present my notion of conversational style, (2) outline the linguistic and paralinguistic features that make up New York Jewish style, and (3) demonstrate their use in cross-stylistic and co-stylistic interaction. In conclusion, I will (4) discuss the personal and social uses of conversational style.

THE NEGATIVE STEREOTYPE

Evidence abounds of the negative stereotype of New York speech in general and New York Jewish speech in particular. The most widely recognized component of this speech is, of course, phonology. An Associated Press release (Boyer, 1979) reports on California therapists who help cure New York accents. One such therapist is quoted: "It's really a drag listening to people from New York talk. It upsets me when I hear a New York accent.... We're here to offer a service to newcomers to this area, especially to New Yorkers.... When they open their mouths, they alienate everyone. We're here to help them adjust to life in Marin County."

A third-grade teacher in Brooklyn wrote to Ann Landers complaining of native-born children who say, for example, "Vot's the kvestion?," "It's vorm ottside," and "heppy as a boid." Ann Landers advised the teacher, "With consistent effort, bad speech habits can be unlearned. I hope you will have the patience to work with these students. It's a real challenge."

Teachers in New York City have been rising to the challenge for a long time. Not so long ago one of the requirements for a license to teach in the New York City public schools was passing a speech exam, which entailed proving that one did not speak with the indigenous "accent." I myself recall being given a shockingly low midterm grade by a speech teacher in a Manhattan high school who promised that it would not be raised until I stopped "dentalizing." I am not aware of any

other group whose members feel that their pronunciation is wrong, even when they are comfortably surrounded by others from the same group and have never lived anywhere else. Labov (1970) has documented the hypercorrection that results from the linguistic insecurity of middle-class Jewish New York women. I confronted this myself each time I recognized a fellow New Yorker in California by her or his accent. The most common response was, "Oh is it THAT obvious?" or "Gee, I thought I'd gotten rid of that."

Unfortunately, moreover, evaluations of "accent" are not applied merely to the speech itself but form the basis of personality judgments. In an attempt to evaluate the effect of Southern-accented speech on judgments of employability, Van Antwerp and Maxwell (1982) serendipitously tapped the negative valence of New York speech. One of their sample non-Southern speakers happened to be a woman from northern New Jersey whose speech approximated the dialect of New York City. Commentators from the Washington, D.C., area evaluated her employability negatively, attributing to her such characteristics as "inability to articulate," "disorganized and dull," "seemed educated but not very together," "a little too energetic, sort of in a hurry to get it over with," "didn't seem to have things straight in her head before she spoke," "sounded aggressive." These findings demonstrate the possible consequences of negative evaluations based on speech style when cross-stylistic interaction takes place in "gatekeeping" (Erickson, 1975) situations.

BACKGROUND OF THE STUDY

My own findings on New York Jewish conversational style were in a way serendipitous as well. I had begun with the goal of discovering the features that made up the styles of each participant in two-and-a-half hours of naturally occurring conversation at dinner on Thanksgiving 1978. Analysis revealed, however, that three of the participants, all natives of New York of East European Jewish background, shared many stylistic features which could be seen to have a positive effect when used with each other and a negative effect when used with the three others. Moreover, the evening's interaction was later characterized by three of the participants (independently) as "New York Jewish" or "New York." Finally, whereas the tapes contained many examples of interchanges between two or three of the New Yorkers, it had no examples of talk among non–New Yorkers in which the New Yorkers did not participate. Thus, what began as a general study of conversational style ended by becoming an analysis of New York Jewish conversational style (Tannen, 1979).

The dinner at which this conversation was taped took place in the home of Kurt, a native New Yorker living in Oakland, California. The guests, who were also New Yorkers living in California, were Kurt's brother, Peter, and myself.[3] The three other guests were Kurt's friend David, a native of Los Angeles of Irish, Scotch, and English parents from Iowa and North Dakota; David's friend Chad, a native and resident of Los Angeles whose father was of Scotch/English extraction and whose mother was from New York, of Italian background; and Sally, born and raised in England, of a Jewish father and American mother.[4] Complex as these ethnic backgrounds are, the group split into two when looked at on the basis of conversational style.

THEORETICAL BACKGROUND

My notion of conversational style grows out of R. Lakoff's (1973; 1979) work on communicative style and Gumperz's (1977; 1982) on conversational inference. "Style" is not something extra, added on like frosting on a cake. It is the stuff of which the linguistic cake is made: pitch, amplitude, intonation, voice quality, lexical and syntactic choice, rate of speech and turntaking, as well as what is said and how discourse cohesion is achieved. In other words, style refers to all the ways speakers encode meaning in language and convey how they intend their talk to be understood. Insofar as speakers from similar speech communities share such linguistic conventions, style is a social phenomenon. Insofar as speakers use particular features in particular combinations and in various settings, to that extent style is an individual phenomenon. (See Gumperz and Tannen, 1979, for a discussion of individual vs. social differences.)

Lakoff (1973) observes that speakers regularly avoid saying precisely what they mean in the interest of social goals which they pursue by adhering to one of three *rules of politeness*, later renamed *rules of rapport* (Lakoff, 1979). Each rule is associated with a communicative style growing out of habitual application of that rule:

1. Don't impose (distance).
2. Give options (deference).
3. Be friendly (camaraderie).

To illustrate (with my own examples), if a guest responds to an offer of something to drink by saying, "No thank you; I'm not thirsty," s/he is applying R1. If s/he says, "Oh, I'll have whatever you're having," s/he is applying R2. If s/he marches into the kitchen, throws open the refrigerator, and says, "I'm thirsty. Got any juice?" s/he is applying R3. Individuals differ with regard to which sense of politeness they tend to observe, and cultural differences are reflected by the tendency of members of a group to observe one or the other sense of politeness in conventionalized ways.

These differing senses of politeness are associated as well with two goals of indirectness: *defensiveness* and *rapport*. Defensiveness, associated with R1 "don't impose," is the desire to be able to renege, to say, "I never said that," or "That's not what I meant." Rapport, associated with R3 "be friendly," refers to the fine feeling of being "on the same wavelength," which accrues when one gets what one wants without asking for it or feels understood without having explained.

Another deeply related strand of research in sociology is brilliantly elaborated by Goffman, building on the work of Durkheim. Durkheim (1915) distinguishes between negative and positive religious rites. Negative rites are "a system of abstentions" which prepares one for "access to the positive cult." Goffman (1967: 72–73) builds upon this dichotomy in his notion of *deference*, "the appreciation an individual shows of another to that other, whether through avoidance rituals or presentational rituals." Presentational rituals include "salutations, invitations, compliments, and minor services. Through all of these the recipient is told that he is not an island unto himself and that others are, or seek to be, involved with him…" Avoidance rituals "lead the actor to keep at a distance from the recipient" (Goffman 1967: 62) and include "rules regarding privacy and separateness" (Goffman 1967: 67). Following Lakoff and Goffman, Brown and Levinson (1978) refer to two overriding goals motivating linguistic forms of politeness: negative face, "the want of every adult member that his actions be unimpeded by others," and positive face, "the want of every adult member that his actions be desirable to at least some others."

All these schemata for understanding human interaction recognize two basic but conflicting needs: to be involved with others and to be left alone. Linguistic systems, like other cultural systems, represent conventionalized ways of honoring these needs. I would like to suggest that the conversational style of the New Yorkers at Thanksgiving dinner can be seen as conventionalized strategies serving the need for involvement, whereas the non–New York participants expected strategies serving the need for independence.

FEATURES OF NEW YORK JEWISH CONVERSATIONAL STYLE

Following are the main features found in the talk of three of the six Thanksgiving celebrants. (More detailed discussion of these can be found in Tannen, 1979; 1980a; 1981; 1987.)

1. *Topic* (a) prefer personal topics, (b) shift topics abruptly, (c) introduce topics without hesitance, (d) persistence (if a new topic is not immediately picked up, reintroduce it, repeatedly if necessary).
2. *Genre* (a) tell more stories, (b) tell stories in rounds, (c) internal evaluation (Labov, 1972) is preferred over external (i.e., the point of a story is dramatized rather than lexicalized), (d) preferred point of a story is teller's emotional experience.
3. *Pacing* (a) faster rate of speech, (b) inter-turn pauses avoided (silence is evidence of lack of rapport), (c) faster turntaking, (d) cooperative overlap and participatory listenership.
4. *Expressive paralinguistics* (a) expressive phonology, (b) pitch and amplitude shifts, (c) marked voice quality, (d) strategic within-turn pauses.

All of these features were combined to create linguistic devices which enhanced conversational flow when used among the New Yorkers, but they had an obstructive effect on conversation with those who were not from New York. Comments by all participants upon listening to the tape indicated that they misunderstood the intentions of members of the other group.

Perhaps the most easily perceived and characteristic feature of this style is the fast rate of speech and tendency to overlap (speak simultaneously) and latch (Sacks' term for allowing no pause before turntaking). I have demonstrated at length elsewhere (Tannen, 1979; 1980a) that overlap is used cooperatively by the New Yorkers, as a way of showing enthusiasm and interest, but it is interpreted by non–New Yorkers as just the opposite: evidence of lack of attention. The tendency to use fast pace and overlap often combines, moreover, with preference for personal topics, focusing attention on another in a personal way. Both the pacing and the personal focus can be seen repeatedly to cause Sally, Chad, and David to become more hesitant in their speech as they respond in classic complementary schismogenetic fashion (Bateson, 1972). That is, the verbal devices used by one group cause speakers of the other group to react by intensifying the opposing behavior, and vice versa.

CROSS-STYLISTIC INTERCHANGE

The following conversation illustrates how both Peter and I use fast pacing and personal focus to show interest in David's discourse, with the result that he feels "caught off guard" and "on the spot." (This is only one of many such examples.) David, a professional sign interpreter, has been talking about American Sign Language.

(1) D So: and thís is the one that's Bèrkeley. This is the Bérkeley…sign for..for ⌈ Christmas
  p

(2) T   ⌊ Do yòu figure oút those..
  f

 those um correspòndences?
 Or do? when you learn the signs, /does/ somebody télls you.

(3) D Oh you mean ⌈ watching it? like

(4) T   ⌊ Cause I can imagine knówing that sígn,…and not..figuring out that it had anything to do with the decorátions.
  ….

(5) D No. Y you knów that it has to do with the decorátions. ⌉

(6) T   ⌊ Cause somebody télls you? Or you figure ⌉ it oút.
  D: ⌊No ⌋

(7) D Oh…. You you talking about mé, or a deàf person. ⌉

(8) T   ⌊ Yeah. ⌋   ⌊ You. You.

(9) D Me? uh: Someone télls me, ùsually…. But a lót of em I can tèll. I mean they're óbvious ….. The bétter I get the mòre I can tell. The lónger I do it the mòre I can tell what they're talking about.

….. Withoút knowing what the sign is. ⌉

(10) T ⌊ Huh. ⌋   ⌊ That's interesting. ⌋

(11) P   ⌊ But how do you learn a new sign.
  ….

(12) D How do I learn a new sign? ⌉

(13) P   ⌊ Yeah. I mean supposing…Víctor's talking and all of a sudden he uses a sign for Thanksgíving, and you've never séen it before.

My questions (2) (4) and (6) and Peter's questions (11) and (13) overlap or latch onto David's preceding comments. In contrast, David's comments follow our questions after "normal" or even noticeable (5, 12) pauses.

My question (2) about how David learns about the symbolism behind signs not only is latched onto David's fading comment (1) but is spoken loudly and shifts the focus from a general discourse about signs to focus on David personally. The abrupt question catches him off guard, and he hesitates by rephrasing the question. I then interrupt David's rephrasing to supply more information (4), interpreting his hesitation as indication that I had been unclear. The real trouble, however, was the suddenness of my question and its shift from general to personal. Thus, I hoped to make David comfortable by acknowledging the fault had been mine and rectifying the matter by supplying more information right away, but the second interruption could only make him more uncomfortable; hence, the pause.

David answers my question (4) by commenting (5) "You know that it has to do with the decorations," but he avoids the more personal focus of my question (2) about *how* he knows. I therefore become more specific (6) and again latch my question. David stalls again, this time by asking (7) for clarification. His question comes after a filler, a pause, a slight stutter: "Oh…. You you talking about me…." He expresses his surprise at the shift in focus. Yet again, I clarify in machine-gun fashion: (8) "Yeah. You. You." David then answers the question and my response (10) overlaps his answer.

Just as this interchange between David and me is settled, Peter uses precisely the strategy that I was using, with the same results. Latching onto David's answer (9), Peter asks another question focusing on David (11); David hesitates by rephrasing the question after a pause (12); Peter barely waits for the rephrasing to finish before he makes his question more specific (13).

The rhythm of this segment is most peculiar. Normally, a question–answer are seen as an "adjacency pair" (Sacks, Schegloff, and Jefferson, 1974), and in a smooth conversation they are rhythmically paired as well. The differences in David's pacing on the one hand and Peter's and mine on the other, however, create pauses between our questions and his delayed answers, so that the resultant rhythmic pairs are made up of an answer and the next question. This is typical of how stylistic differences obstruct conversational rhythm. While participants in this conversation were friends and disposed to think well of each other, the operation of such differences in other settings can leave participants with the conviction that the other was uncooperative or odd.

Co-stylistic Interchange

In the previous example, Peter and I directed similar questions to David, with unexpected results. The following segment shows how the same device serves to enhance conversational flow when used with each other. This segment begins when I turn to Peter suddenly and address a question to him.

(1) T Do you réad?
  ....
(2) P Do I ˈréad?
  ...
(3) T Do you reàd things just for fún?
  ....
(4) P Yeah.....Right now I'm reading Norma Jean the Térmite Queen. [Laughs]
(5) T ⌈Whàt's thát?....Norma Jean like uh:....Marilyn Monˈróe?
(6) P It's.. ˈNo:. It's a book about......a housewife /??/
  dec
(7) T Is it a ⌈nóvel or whàt.
(8) P ˈIt's a ⌊nóvel.
(9) T ˈYeah?
(10) P Before that...I read the French Lieutenant's Woman?
  ⌈Have you ⌈read that?
(11) T ⌊Oh yeah? No. Whó wrote that?
(12) P John Fowles.
(13) T Yeah I've heárd that he's good.
(14) P ˈHe's a ⌊gréat writer. ˈÍ think he's one of the ⌊bést writers.
  T: hm
(15) T /?/
(16) P ˈHe's really ⌊goòd.
(17) T /?/
  ....
(18) P But Í get very bùsy..... ⌈Yknow?
(19) T   ⌊Yeah. I ?.. hardly éver read.
  ....
(20) P What I've been dòing is cutting down on my sléep.
(21) T Oy!⌉ [sighs]
(22) P   ⌊And I've been   .....and I⌈ s
                  [K laughs]
(23) T   ⌊Í do that tòo but it's páinful.⌉
(24) P   ⌊Yeah. Fi:ve, six hours a ˈníght, and⌉
(25) T   ⌊Oh
  Gód, hòw can you dó it. You survíve?
  ....
(26) P Yeah làte afternoon méetings are hàrd.....But
                              T: mmm
  outside of thát I can keep gòing ⌈pretty well.
(27) T   ⌊Not sleeping

enough is térrible.....I'd múch rather not eàt than not sleèp.
  ᵖ
  [S laughs]
(28) P I próbably should not eàt so much, it would..it would uh...sáve a lot of tìme.
(29) T If I'm /like really/ busy I don't I don't I don't eat. I don't yeah I just don't eat but⌈I
(30) P   ⌊I?I tend to spend a lòt of time eáting and prepáring and ⌈ /?/
(31) T   ⌊Oh: I néver
  prepare foòd.......I eat whatéver I can get my hánds on.⌉
(32) P   ⌊Yeah.

This interchange exhibits many features of New York Jewish conversational style. In addition to the characteristic use of overlap, fast pacing, and personal focus, it exhibits devices I have called (Tannen, 1979) persistence, mutual revelation, and expressive paralinguistics.

Both Peter and I use overlap and latching in this segment: Peter's (22) (24) and (30) and my (19) (23) (25) (27) and (31). The interchange begins with a sudden focus of attention on him by my question (1). Like David, Peter is initially "caught off guard," so he repeats the question after a pause. But then he not only answers the question but supplies specific information (4) about the book he is reading. A common feature of participatory listenership is seen in (5) and (6). While (6) is ostensibly an answer to my question (5), it is clear that Peter would have gone on to give that information in any case. He begins, "It's...," has to stop in order to answer my question with "No," and then repeats the beginning and continues, "It's a book about a housewife."

Persistence refers to the pattern by which speakers continue trying to say something despite lack of attention or interruption. In this example it can be seen in (22) and (24), in which Peter makes three attempts to say that he sleeps only five or six hours a night. Persistence is a necessary concomitant to overlap. It reflects a conversational economy in which it is not the business of a listener to make room for another speaker to speak. Rather, it is the business of the listener to show enthusiasm; the speaker, in this system, can be counted on to find room to speak. The conversational burden, in other words, is to serve the need for involvement at the risk of violating independence.

The mutual revelation device can be seen in the series of observations Peter and I make about our own habits. In (19) I state that I hardly ever read as a way of showing understanding of Peter's tight schedule (18). (23) is a similar response to his statement that he cuts down on sleep. (27) is a statement of my preference to balance his statement (26) about sleeping. In (28) Peter makes a statement about his eating habits; in (29) I describe mine; in (30) he reiterates his, and in (31) I reiterate mine. It might seem to some observers that we are not "communicating" at all, since we both talk only about ourselves. But the juxtaposition of comments and the relationship of topics constitutes thematic cohesion and establishes rapport. In this system, the offer of personal information is encouragement to the other to volunteer the same, and volunteered information is highly valued.

Throughout the Thanksgiving conversation, Peter, Kurt, and I use exaggerated phonological and paralinguistic cues. For example, my question (5) "What's that?" is loud and high pitched. When any of the New Yorkers uses such features with Chad or David, the result is that they stop talking in surprise, wondering what caused the outburst. When used in talk among the New Yorkers, introduction of exaggerated paralinguistics spurs the others to follow suit, in a mutually escalating way such as Bateson (1972) has characterized as symmetrical. In the present segment, many of the words and phrases are uttered with extra high or low pitch as well as heavily colored voice quality.

It seems likely that my use of high pitch on "What's that?" as well as on the last syllable of "Monroe" in (5) was triggered by Peter's laughter while uttering the book title. In any case, Peter's response (6) uses sharp contrasts in pitch and pacing to signal the message, "I know this is a silly book." The pitch on "No" is very low, the vowel is drawn out, the sentence is uttered slowly, and it contains a very long pause before the key word "housewife" is uttered. Similar sharp shifts from high to low pitch can be seen repeatedly.

(8) P |It's a |novel.
(14) P |He's a ⌊great writer. I think he's one of the ⌊best writers.
(16) P |He's really |good.

These pitch shifts, together with voice quality, signal in (8) denigration of the book discussed and in (14) and (16) great earnestness.

Exaggerated paralinguistics can be seen as well in my expressions of concern for Peter's loss of sleep in (23) (25) and (27). These are all uttered with marked stress and breathy voice quality that demonstrate exaggerated and stylized concern.

Yet another stylized response to Peter's assertion that he doesn't sleep enough is a Yiddish nonverbal "response cry" (Goffman 1978), "Oy!" This utterance is rapport-building in a number of ways. Obviously, the choice of a Yiddish expression signals our shared ethnic background. At the same time, the exaggerated nature of my response—the utterance of a great sigh along with "oy"—is a way of mocking my own usage, making the exclamation ironic in much the way Peter was mocking his own reading material while telling about it. (In a similar way, Kurt often mocks his own hosting behavior by offering food in an exaggerated Yiddish accent.) Finally, I utter this cry as if it were an expression of my own feeling, thus taking Peter's point of view as a show of empathy.

The interchange between Peter and me ends with another cooperative use of overlap and repetition. The conversation has turned to dating, and it has continued to be

characterized by the features seen in the earlier segment. It ends this way:

(1) P And you just cán't get to know....ten people really well.
　　　　　　　　　　[breathy]
(2) T ⌈ You can't dó it.
　　　⌊ Yeah right. Y'have to there's no? Yeah there's
(3) P ⌈no tíme.
　　 ⌊There's not tíme.
(4) T Yeah....'strue.

Peter's statements (1) and (3) flow in a continuous stream, ending with "You can't do it. There's not time." However the last phrase echoes my words in (2). The end of the talk is signaled by a quieting down of voices as well as the pattern of blended voices and phrases.

THE OPACITY OF STYLE

To those unfamiliar with the workings of particular stylistic strategies, their use seems like evidence of lack of communication—which is simply to say they don't see how they work. More often than not the features used have meaning in the speech habits of the different group, so conclusions are drawn based on what the signals would mean if the hearer had used them. To those who do not expect overlap to be used cooperatively, and would not use it in that way themselves, another's overlap will be interpreted as lack of attention. Thus an article in *New West* magazine (Esterly, 1979) tells of the work of a UCLA psychologist, Gerald Goodman, who believes that fast talkers are a conversational menace. Calling them "crowders," he eloquently articulates the effect they have on those unaccustomed to this style:

> There's a dehumanizing aspect to being crowded; there's a lack of respect involved. Interrupting arises from a variety of factors—anxiety, a desire to dominate, boredom, the need to express freshly stimulated thoughts.... People walk away from conversations with crowders feeling upset or dissatisfied or incompetent, though they may not understand why. (p. 68)

Clearly, this is the interpretation of fast pacing made by David, Chad, and Sally during Thanksgiving, at least at times. It is the feeling of being imposed upon, in violation of Brown and Levinson's (1978) negative politeness. However, the "dehumanizing aspect," the vague feeling of dissatisfaction and incompetence, is not a response to others' use of specific linguistic features but rather to their use of such features in an unexpected way. It is the lack of sharedness of style that is disconcerting. Fast talkers walk away from those same conversations feeling similar discomfort, most likely having interpreted the slower pacing as a failure of positive politeness.

Style is often invisible. People tend to take their conversational habits as self-evident and draw conclusions not about others' linguistic devices but about their intentions or personalities.

Moreover, few speakers are aware of ways in which others' linguistic behavior may be a reaction to their own.

THE COHERENCE OF CONVERSATIONAL STYLE

As Reisman (1974: 110) points out, "The conventions which order speech interaction are meaningful not only in that they order and mediate verbal expression, but in that they participate in and express larger meanings in the society which uses them." Becker (1979a: 18) explains, "The figure a sentence makes is a strategy of interpretation" which "helps the people it is used by understand and feel coherent in their worlds." The structure and habits of language which seem self-evidently natural, serve not only as a way to communicate meaning but also to reestablish and ratify one's way of being in the world. In another paper, Becker (1979b: 241) explains:

> The universal source of language pathology is that people appear to say one thing and "mean" another. It drives people mad (the closer it gets to home). An aesthetic response is quite simply the opposite of this pathology.... Schizophrenia, foreign language learning, and artistic expression in language all operate under the same set of linguistic variables—constraints on coherence, invention, intentionality, and reference. The difference is that in madness (and in the temporary madness of learning a new language or a new text) these constraints are misunderstood and often appear contradictory, while in an aesthetic response they are understood as a coherent integrated whole.... The integration of communication (art) is, hence, as essential to a sane community as clean air, good food, and, to cure errors, medicine.

The emotional/aesthetic experience of a perfectly tuned conversation is as ecstatic as an artistic experience. The satisfaction of having communicated successfully goes beyond the pleasure of being understood in the narrow sense. It is a ratification of one's place in the world and one's way of being human. It is, as Becker calls a well-performed shadow play, "a vision of sanity."

To some extent there is for everyone a discontinuity between the private code, i.e., communicative habits learned at home and on the block (or in the fields) around one's home, and the public code, i.e., the form of language used in formal settings. Hence the anxiety most people feel about communicating with strangers. But the degree of discontinuity may be greater or lesser. Those who learned and have reinforced at home norms of interaction which are relatively similar to those which are widely accepted in society at large have a certainty about their linguistic convictions. If they proclaim that it is rude to interrupt or that one ought to state the point of a story outright, it is without ambivalence. But those who have grown up hearing and using norms of interaction which differ significantly from more widely accepted ones may feel ambivalent about their own styles. Thus New Yorkers of Jewish background cannot complain "Why don't you interrupt?" On hearing a tape recording of a conversa-

tion they thoroughly enjoyed in the process, they often feel critical of themselves and slightly embarrassed. They, too, believe that it is rude to interrupt, to talk loudly, to talk too much. The "interruption" may actually be the creation of the interlocutor who stopped when s/he was expected to continue talking over the overlap, but the cooperative overlapper is no more likely to realize this than the overlap-resistant speaker.

The greater the discontinuity between ingroup style and public expectations, the more difficult it is for one to feel sane in both worlds. Hence it is not surprising that many speakers reject one or the other style, and New York Jews who have moved away from New York may be heard to proclaim that they hate New York accents, hate to go back to New York, or hate to go home, because "no one listens to anyone else" or "it's so loud" or "people are so rude." There are probably few speakers of this background who have not at times felt uncomfortable upon seeing through public eyes someone from their own background talking in a way that is attracting attention in an alien setting, just as American travelers may feel embarrassed on seeing another American tourist who fits too neatly the stereotype of the ugly American abroad. In contrast, the comfort of interaction in a setting in which one's home style predominates goes far to explain what often appears as clannishness—the preference for the company of those of similar ethnic background. The coherence principles (to borrow a term from Becker) that create conversational style operate on every level of discourse and contribute to, at the same time that they grow out of, people's attempts to achieve coherence in the world.

AFTERWORD ON ACCOUNTABILITY

Perhaps a word is in order on the validity of the case-study method. How generalizable are findings based on close observation and interviews with six speakers? The most reassuring confirmation is a phenomenon I have called "the aha factor" (Tannen, 1979). When I explain these style differences in public or private forums, a cry of relief goes up from many of my hearers—especially from intermarried couples, of whom only one partner is Jewish and from New York City. They invariably report that these style differences have been the cause of complaints; the non–New York spouse chronically complains of being interrupted, not listened to, not given a chance to talk, while the New York–bred partner feels unjustly accused and in turn complains that the other partner is unaccountably withholding. If the family does not live in New York City, the misunderstanding often extends as well to children who complain that the New York parent does not listen to them and overreacts to their talk.

In a recent column in *The Washington Post*, Judith Martin, assuming the persona of an etiquette expert named Miss Manners, addressed the question of conversational norms. A disgruntled reader wrote to complain that she is "a good listener," but "there are so many people in this world who will just talk right over me. Sometimes I'm halfway into a sentence or an idea when they burst in with their own."

Miss Manners responded in the spirit of cooperative overlap and participatory listenership:

> If you are, in fact, a practiced "good listener," you have not been traveling through life in silence. You have been asking questions, inserting relevant information and providing commentary on what the chief talkers to whom you have been listening are saying. A good listener is not someone who has to be checked every now and then by the speaker to see if he or she is awake....Once in the driver's seat, you should try to be a good talker. That is to say, you must allow proper interruptions that are in the tradition of good listening, and even encourage them....

Surprised to find such linguistic values articulated in the popular press, I contacted the writer and was not surprised to learn that Martin is Jewish.

This raises the question of the extent to which the linguistic conventions I have discussed are "New York" and/or "Jewish." My hypothesis is that the style (i.e., the combination of linguistic devices used in the way described) I have discussed represents a prototype of a kind of conversation that is familiar to most New York Jews and unfamiliar to most midwestern and western Americans of non-Jewish background. My impression is that New Yorkers of non-Jewish background and Jews not from New York City use many of the devices I have described and that there are New York Jews who use few of them. I suspect that the existence of this style represents the influence of conversational norms of East European Jewish immigrants and that similar norms are probably general to the Levant.[5] I have not encountered evidence to indicate that Jews of German background necessarily share this style.

The precise distribution of these and related linguistic devices, like the distribution of dialect features, can only be determined by the painstaking research of many workers in many settings, if there turn out to be enough researchers who find this a thing worth doing. In any case, there is no doubt that the acquisition, maintenance, and accomodation of conversational style is a crucial linguistic and social process.

Notes

1. My thanks to Stephen Murray for this reference.

2. This conversation was reconstructed from memory. Others presented are transcribed from tape recordings. The following transcription conventions are used, as gleaned from Schenkein (1978) and from those developed at the University of California, Berkeley, by Gumperz and Chafe and their respective collaborators.

...	half second pause. Each extra dot represents another half-second of pause.
/	marks primary stress
\	marks secondary stress
underline	indicates emphatic stress
ˈ	marks high pitch on word
ˈ	marks high pitch on phrase, continuing until punctuation
ˌ	marks low pitch on word

.	sentence-final falling intonation
,	clause-final intonation (more to come)
?	yes/no question rising intonation
ʔ	glottal stop
:	lengthened vowel sound
p	spoken softly (piano)
f	spoken loudly (forte)
dec	spoken slowly
/?/	inaudible segment

⎡ Brackets connecting lines show overlapping speech.
⎣ Two people talking at the same time.

Brackets with reversed flaps ⎤
⎦ indicate latching (no intraturn pause)

3. Thus I was both perpetrator and object of my analysis, making me not a participant observer (an observer who becomes a participant) but a participant who is also an observer. At the time of taping, I was in the habit of taping many interactions and had not decided to use this one, let alone what I would look for in analysis. Nonetheless there is a problem of objectivity which I have tried to correct for by painstaking review of the analysis with participants as well as others. I believe that the loss of objectivity is a disadvantage outweighed by the advantage of insight into what was going on which is impossible for a nonparticipant to recover, and that only by taping an event in which one is a natural participant can one gather data not distorted by the presence of an alien observer.

4. With the exception of my own, names have been changed. Now, as always, I want to express my gratitude to these friends who became my data, for their willingness and insight during taping and later during playback. The transcripts will reflect initials of these pseudonyms, except for my own, which is rendered "T" to avoid confusion with "D" (David).

5. The use of cooperative overlap has been reported among American blacks, throughout the West Indies (see in particular Reisman, 1974), and the Middle and Near East.

References

Bateson, Gregory (1972). *Steps to an Ecology of Mind.* New York: Ballantine.

Becker, Alton (1979a). The figure a sentence makes. In *Discourse and Syntax*, T. Givon (ed.). New York: Academic Press.

———. (1979b). Text-building, epistemology, and aesthetics in Javanese Shadow Theatre. In *The Imagination of Reality: Essays in Southeast Asian Coherence Systems*, A. L. Becker and A. A. Yengoyan (eds.). Norwood, NJ: Ablex.

Boyer, Peter J. (1979). Therapists cure New York accents. *The Tribune*, Sunday February 4, 6E.

Brown, Penelope, and Levinson, Stephen (1978). Universals in language usage: Politeness phenomena. In *Questions and Politeness*, E. Goody (ed.), 56–289. Cambridge: Cambridge University Press.

Durkheim, Émile (1915). *The Elementary Forms of the Religious Life.* New York: The Free Press.

Erickson, Frederick (1975). Gatekeeping and the melting pot: Interaction in counseling interviews. *Harvard Education Review* 45(1), 44–70.

Esterly, Glenn (1979). Slow talking in the big city. *New West*, 4(11) (May 21, 1979), 67–72.

Forster, E. M. (1924). *A Passage to India*. New York: Harcourt Brace Jovanovich.

Goffman, Erving (1967). *Interaction Ritual: Essays on Face-to-Face Behavior*. Garden City, NY: Doubleday.

———. (1978). Response cries. *Language* 54(4), 787–815.

Gumperz, John (1977). Sociocultural knowledge in conversational inference. In *Georgetown University Round Table on Languages and Linguistics 1977*, M. Saville-Troike (ed.), 191–211. Washington, DC: Georgetown University.

———. (1982). *Discourse Strategies*. Cambridge and New York: Cambridge University Press.

———, and Tannen, Deborah (1979). Individual and social differences in language use. In *Individual Differences in Language Ability and Language Behavior*, C. J. Fillmore, D. Kempler, and W. S.-Y. Wang (eds.). New York: Academic Press.

Labov, William (1970). The study of language in its social context. *Studium Generale* 23, 30–87.

———. (1972). *Language in the Inner City*. Philadelphia: University of Pennsylvania Press.

Lakoff, Robin (1973). The logic of politeness; or, minding your p's and q's. *Papers from the Ninth Regional Meeting of the Chicago Linguistics Society*. Chicago: University of Chicago Department of Linguistics.

———. (1979). Stylistic strategies within a grammar of style. In *Language, Sex, and Gender*, J. Orasanu, M. Slater, and L. Adler (eds.), 327. Annals of the New York Academy of Sciences.

Reisman, Karl (1974). Contrapuntal conversations in an Antiguan village. In *Explorations in the Ethnography of Speaking*, R. Bauman and J. Sherzer (eds.), 110–124. Cambridge: Cambridge University Press.

Sacks, Harvey, Schegloff, Emanuel, and Jefferson, Gail (1974). A simplest systematics for the organization of turn-taking for conversation. *Language* 50(4), 696–735.

Schenkein, Jim (1978). *Studies in the Organization of Conversational Interaction*. New York: Academic Press.

Tannen, Deborah (1979). Processes and consequences of conversational style. Unpublished thesis, University of California, Berkeley.

———. (1980a). When is an overlap not an interruption? *First Delaware Symposium on Languages and Linguistics*. Newark: University of Delaware Press.

———. (1981). The machine-gun question: An example of conversational style. *Journal of Pragmatics* V(5): 383–397.

———. (1987). Conversation style. In *Psycholinguistic Models of Production*, H. Dechert and M. Raupach (eds.). Hillsboro, NJ: Erlbaum.

Van Antwerp, Caroline, and Maxwell, Monica (1982). Speaker sex, regional dialect, and employability: A study in language attitudes. In *Linguistics and the Professions*, R. DiPietro (ed.). Norwood, NJ: Ablex.

White, Edmund (1980). *States of Desire: Travels in Gay America*. New York: Dutton.

Post-reading Questions / Activities

- Do you consider your own speech preferences as more like the New Yorkers, or more like the Californians, (to take two iconic cases)? Have you had experience talking with people who tend to use the other style? What happens?
- What is "good listening"? Might rules for this vary across cultures? Ask classmates about the norms in their home settings.
- Why are some people proud of and others embarrassed about their own speech styles? In the latter case, why don't people simply abandon the "embarrassing" styles?
- Assign parts and read aloud the transcripts as if they are the script of a play. Be sure to overlap and interrupt when appropriate. How does this kind of reading change your understanding of this topic? Is it difficult for some speakers to read some parts? Why?

Vocabulary

adjacency pair	overlap	style, conversational
deference	paralinguistic	topic
genre	phonology	turn taking
latch	politeness	
negative face	positive face	

Suggested Further Reading

Brown, Penelope, and Stephen C. Levinson. 1978. "Universals in Language Usage: Politeness Phenomena." In *Questions and Politeness: Strategies in Social Interaction*, edited by Esther N. Goody. Cambridge: Cambridge University Press.

Goffman, Erving. 1959. *The Presentation of Self in Everyday Life*. Garden City, NY: Doubleday.

———. 1967. *Interaction Ritual: Essays on Face-to-Face Behavior*. Garden City, NY: Doubleday.

Lakoff, Robin Tolmach, and Sachiko Ide, eds. 2005. *Broadening the Horizon of Linguistic Politeness*. Amsterdam and Philadelphia: John Benjamins.

Ochs, Elinor, Emanuel A. Schegloff, and Sandra A. Thompson, eds. 1996. *Interaction and Grammar*. Cambridge and New York: Cambridge University Press.

Sacks, Harvey. 1995. *Lectures on Conversation*. Edited by Gail Jefferson. Oxford and Cambridge, MA: Blackwell.

Schegloff, Emanuel A. 2007. *Sequence Organization in Interaction: A Primer in Conversational Analysis*, vol. I. Cambridge and New York: Cambridge University Press.

CHAPTER 26

Suite for Ebony and Phonics

John R. Rickford
(1997)

In late 1996, the Oakland School Board in California declared that "Ebonics"—a newly coined term combining "ebony" and "phonics"—was the native language of most of its students, almost all African American. As speakers of a distinct language, students attempting to learn Standard English were in effect learning a second language, and thus would be entitled to funding to help them in this.

Oakland had some of the worst-performing schools in the country. What could be the cause of this? It seemed that language might play a role in students' inability to test well. It was worth a try; most other efforts had failed. They wanted to teach the systematic differences between the two languages rather than continue to reprimand students for using their home language, since decades of reprimanding had not succeeded in teaching minority students to use Standard English consistently.

But the political storm that followed this mild cloud was thunderous: the effort was dismissed as racist, defeatist, wrong-headed, and many other things. When linguists weighed in, however, they tended to side with the school board, though they wished to correct some of the misconceptions that accompanied the initial proclamation, making sure to point out that there was no necessary biological connection between "race" and language spoken.

This was not the first time school boards had tried to connect African American English and achievement in school; among other cases, in 1979 the case of Martin Luther King Junior Elementary School Children, et al., v. Ann Arbor School District Board *included testimony from linguists such as William Labov about the regular differences between Black English and Standard English. But public understanding of language issues has not substantially improved.*

John Rickford has been writing about language, especially African American Vernacular English and creole languages, since the early 1980s. This widely circulated article explains not just the Ebonics issue but also discusses relationships among different types of related languages, often called "dialects" or "slang." At the same time, Rickford shows very clearly some of the distinctiveness of African American Vernacular English (Ebonics), supporting the school board's claims that it is a separate "language" from Standard English.

Reading Questions

- What are the three basic principles that linguists agree on in studying the Ebonics controversy?
- What are some of the distinct features of Ebonics in contrasting with Standard English?

John R. Rickford, "Suite for Ebony and Phonics." http://www.stanford.edu/~rickford/papers/SuiteForEbonyAndPhonics.html. Published in *Discover* magazine, December 1997. Reproduced by permission of John R. Rickford.

- What are the three common accounts of the origins of African American Vernacular English?
- What practical educational solutions were offered to help improve the educations of speakers of Ebonics (and other minority "dialects")?

———————————————————

To James Baldwin, writing in 1979, it was "this passion, this skill,... this incredible music." Toni Morrison, two years later, was impressed by its "five present tenses," and felt that "The worst of all possible things that could happen would be to lose that language." What these African American novelists were talking about was Ebonics, the vernacular or informal speech of many African Americans, which rocketed to public attention after the Oakland school board approved a resolution in December 1996 recognizing it as the primary language of African American students.

The reaction of most people across the country—in the media, at holiday gatherings, and on electronic bulletin boards—was overwhelmingly negative. In the flash-flood of email on America Online, Ebonics was variously described as "lazy English," "bastardized English," "poor grammar," and "fractured slang." Oakland's decision to recognize Ebonics and use it to facilitate mastery of Standard English [SE] also elicited superlatives of negativity: "ridiculous, ludicrous," "VERY, VERY STUPID," "a terrible mistake." Linguists—the scientists who carefully study the sounds, words, and grammars of languages and dialects—were less rhapsodic about Ebonics than the novelists, but much more positive than most of the media and the general public. At their January 1997 annual meeting, members of the Linguistic Society of America [LSA] unanimously approved a resolution describing Ebonics as "systematic and rule-governed like all natural speech varieties," and referring to the Oakland resolution as "linguistically and pedagogically sound." In order to understand how linguists could have had such a different take on the Ebonics issue, we need to understand how linguists study language and what their studies of Ebonics over the past thirty years have led them to agree on (and what [they have] not).

Although linguists approach the study of language from different perspectives—some are keener on language change, for instance, while others are more interested in language as a formal system, in what language tells us about human cognition, or how language reflects social divisions—we agree on a number of general principles. One of these is that linguistics is descriptive rather than prescriptive, our goal being to describe how language works rather than to prescribe how people should or shouldn't speak. A second principle is that all languages have dialects—regional or social varieties which develop when people are separated by geographical or social barriers and their languages change along different lines, as they develop their own pronunciations, for instance, or their own ways of referring to things. When linguists speak of "dialects" they don't do so in the pejorative way that many non-linguists do. A dialect is just a variety of a language; everyone speaks at least one. A third principle, vital for understanding linguists' reactions to the Ebonics controversy, is that all languages and dialects are systematic and rule-governed. To

some extent, this is a theoretical assumption—for if individuals made up their own sounds and words and did NOT follow a common set of rules for putting them together to express meaning, they would be unable to communicate with each other, and children would have a hard time acquiring the "language" of their community. But it is also an empirical finding. Every human language and dialect which we have studied to date—and we have studied thousands—has been found to be fundamentally regular, although its rules may differ from those of other varieties.

Now is Ebonics just "slang," as so many people have characterized it? Well, no, because slang refers just to the vocabulary of a language or dialect, and even so, just to the small set of new and (usually) short-lived words like *chillin* ("relaxing") or *homey* ("close friend") which are used primarily by young people in informal contexts. Ebonics includes non-slang words like *ashy* (referring to the appearance of dry skin, especially in winter) which have been around for a while, and are used by people of all age groups. Ebonics also includes distinctive patterns of pronunciation and grammar, the elements of language on which linguists tend to concentrate because they are more systematic and deep-rooted.

But is Ebonics a different language from English or a different dialect of English? Linguists tend to sidestep questions like these, noting, as the 1997 LSA resolution did, that the answers often depend on sociohistorical and political considerations rather than on linguistic ones. For instance, spoken Cantonese and Mandarin are mutually unintelligible, but they are usually regarded as "dialects" of Chinese because their speakers use the same writing system and see themselves as part of a common Chinese tradition. By contrast, although Norwegian and Swedish share many words and their speakers can generally understand each other, they are usually regarded as different languages because they are the autonomous varieties of different political entities (Norway, Sweden). Despite this, most linguists might agree that Ebonics is more of a dialect of English than a separate language, insofar as it shares most of its vocabulary and many other features with other informal varietes of American English, and insofar as its speakers can understand and be understood by speakers of most other American English dialects.

At the same time, Ebonics is one of the most distinctive varieties of American English, differing from Standard English [SE]—the educated standard—in several ways. Consider, for instance, its verb tenses and aspects. ("Tense" refers to WHEN an event occurs, e.g., present or past, and "aspect" to HOW it occurs, e.g., habitually or not.) When Toni Morrison referred to the "five present tenses" of Ebonics, she didn't give examples, but it is probably usages like these—each one different from SE—which she had in mind:

1. Present progressive: He Ø runnin (=SE "He is running" or "He's running").
2. Present habitual progressive: He be runnin (=SE "He is usually running").
3. Present intensive habitual progressive: He be steady runnin (=SE "He is usually running in an intensive, sustained manner").
4. Present perfect progressive: He bin runnin (=SE "He has been running").
5. Present perfect progressive with remote inception: He BIN runnin (=SE "He has been running for a long time, and still is").

The distinction between events which are non-habitual or habitual, represented in 1 and 2 respectively by the non-use or use of an invariant *be* form, can only be expressed in SE with adverbs like "usually." Of course, SE can use simple present tense forms (e.g., "He runs") for habitual events, but then the meaning of an ongoing or progressive action signalled by the "-ing" suffix is lost. Note too that *bin* in 4 is unstressed, while *BIN* in 5 is stressed. The former can usually be understood by non-Ebonics speakers as equivalent to "has been" with the "has" deleted, but the stressed BIN form can be badly misunderstood. Years ago, I presented the Ebonics sentence "She BIN married" to twenty-five Whites and twenty-five Blacks from various parts of the US, and asked them, individually, if they understood the speaker to be still married or not. While almost all the Blacks (23, or 92%) said "Yes," only a third of the whites (8, or 32%) gave this correct answer. In real life, a misconstrual of this type could be disastrous!

OK, so it's not just slang, but an English dialect, sharing a lot with other English varieties, but with some pretty distinctive features of its own. What of characterizations of Ebonics as "lazy" English, as though it were the result of snoozing in a hammock on a Sunday afternoon, or the consequences of not knowing or caring about the rules of "proper" English? Well, if you remember the linguistics principle that all languages are rule-governed, you'll probably be ready to reject these characterizations as a matter of general principle, but you can also challenge them on specific grounds.

One problem with statements like these is that they fail to recognize that most of the "rules" we follow in using language are below the level of consciousness, unlike the rules that we're taught in grammar books or at school. Take for instance, English plurals. Although grammar books tell us that you add "s" to a word to form a regular English plural, as in "cats" and "dogs," that's only true for writing. (Let's ignore words that end in s-like sounds, like "boss," which add "-es," and irregular plurals like "children.") In speech, what we actually add in the case of "cat" is an [s] sound, and in the case of "dog" we add [z]. (Linguists use square brackets to represent how words are pronounced rather than how they are spelled.) The difference is that [s] is voiceless, with the vocal cords in the larynx or voice box in our throats (the Adams apple) spread apart, and that [z] is voiced, with the vocal cords held closely together and noisily vibrating.

You can hear the difference quite dramatically if you put your fingers in your ears and produce a "ssss" sequence followed by a "zzzz" sequence followed by a "ssss" sequence: sssszzzzssss. Every time you switch to "zzzz" your voice box switches on (voiced), and every time you switch to "ssss" your voice box switches off (voiceless). Now, how do you know whether to add [s] or [z] to form a plural when you're speaking? Easy. If the word ends in a voiceless consonant, like "t," add voiceless [s]. If the word ends in a voiced consonant, like "g," add voiced [z]. Since all vowels are voiced, if the word ends in a vowel, like "tree," add [z]. Because we spell both plural endings with "s," we're not aware that English speakers make this systematic difference every day, and I'll bet your English teacher never told you about "voiced" [z] and "voiceless" [s]. But you follow the "rules" for using them anyway, and anyone who didn't—for instance, someone who said "book[z]"—would strike an English speaker as sounding funny.

One reason people might regard Ebonics as "lazy English" is its tendency to omit word-final consonants, especially if they come after another consonant, as in "tes(t)" and "han(d)." But if one were just being lazy or cussed or both, why not also leave out the final consonant in a word like "pant"? This is NOT permitted in Ebonics, and the reason (building on your newly acquired knowledge about voicing) is that Ebonics does not allow the deletion of the second consonant in a word-final sequence unless both consonants are either voiceless, as with "st," or voiced, as with "nd." In the case of "pant," the final "t" is voiceless, but the preceding "n" is voiced. Not only is Ebonics systematic in following this rule, but even its exceptions to the rule—negative forms like "ain'" and "don'"—are non-random. In short, Ebonics is no more lazy English than Italian is lazy Latin. To see the (expected) regularity in both we need to see each in its own terms, appreciating the complex rules that native speakers follow effortlessly and unconsciously in their daily lives.

Talking about native speakers naturally brings up the question of who speaks Ebonics. If we made a list of all the ways in which the pronunciation or grammar of Ebonics differs from that of SE, we probably couldn't find anyone who uses all of them 100% of the time. There is certainly no gene that predisposes one to speak Ebonics, so while its features are found most commonly among African American speakers ("Ebonics" is itself derived from "Ebony" and "phonics," meaning "Black sounds"), not all African Americans speak it. Ebonics features, especially distinctive tense-aspect forms like those in examples 1–5 above, are more common among working class than among middle class speakers, among adolescents than among the middle aged, and in informal contexts (a conversation in the street) rather than formal ones (a sermon at church) or writing. These differences are partly the result of differences in environment and social network (recall our point about geographical and social conditions forging dialects), and partly the result of differences in identification. Lawyers and doctors and their families have more contact than blue collar workers and the unemployed do with Standard English speakers, in their schooling, their work environments, and their neighborhoods. Moreover, working class speakers, and adolescents in particular, often embrace Ebonics features as markers of Black identity, while middle class speakers (in public at least), tend to eschew them.

What about Whites and other ethnic groups? Some Ebonics pronunciations and grammatical features are also found among other vernacular varieties of English, especially Southern White dialects, many of which have been significantly influenced by the heavy concentration of African Americans in the South. But other Ebonics features, including copula absence, habitual *be*, and remote *BIN* are rarer or non-existent in White vernaculars. When it comes to vocabulary, the situation is different. Partly through the influence of rap and hip-hop music, a lot of African American slang has "crossed over" to whites and other ethnic groups, particularly among the young and the "hip" (derived from Wolof *hipi* "be aware"). Expressions like *givin five* ("slapping palms in agreement or congratulation") and *Whassup?* are so widespread in American discourse that many people don't realize they originated in the African American community. This is also true of older, non-slang words like *tote* ("carry," derived from Kongo *-tota*, Swahili *-tuta*).

By this point, some readers…might be fuming. It's one thing to talk about the distinctiveness and regularity of Ebonics and its value as a marker of Black identity and hipness, you might say, but don't linguists realize that nonstandard dialects are stigmatized in the larger society, and that Ebonics speakers who cannot shift to SE are less likely to do well in school and on the job front? Well, yes. As the January 1997 LSA resolution emphasized, "there are benefits in acquiring Standard English." But there is experimental evidence both from the United States and Europe that the goal of mastering the standard language might be better achieved by approaches that take students' vernaculars into account and teach them explicitly to bridge the gap to the standard than by conventional approaches which ignore the vernacular altogether. (Most conventional approaches show a shockingly poor success rate, I should add.) To give only one example: at Aurora University, outside Chicago, African American inner-city students taught by a contrastive analysis approach in which SE and Ebonics features were systematically contrasted through explicit instruction and drills showed a 59% REDUCTION in their use of Ebonics features in their SE writing after eleven weeks, while a control group taught by conventional methods showed an 8.5% INCREASE in such features. Despite ambiguities in their original wording, what the Oakland school board essentially wanted to do is help their students increase their mastery of SE and do better in school through an extension of the Standard English Proficiency program, a contrastive analysis approach widely used in California and already in use in some Oakland schools. It was considerations like these that led the Linguistic Society of America to endorse the Oakland proposal as "linguistically and pedagogically sound."

Let us turn now to the issue of the origins of Ebonics, on which there is much less agreement among linguists. The Oakland resolution referred to the influence of West African languages as the source of Ebonics' distinctive features, and as one reason for its recognition. The African ancestors of today's African Americans came to America mostly as slaves, and mostly between 1619 and 1808, when the [British] slave trade officially ended. Like the forebears of many other Americans, these waves of African "immigrants" spoke languages other than English. Their languages were from the Niger-Congo language family, especially the West Atlantic, Mande and Kwa subgroups spoken from Senegal and Gambia to the Cameroons (e.g., Wolof, Mandingo, Twi, Ewe, Yoruba, Igbo), and the Bantu subgroup spoken further South (e.g., Kimbundu, Umbundu, Kongo). Arriving in an American milieu in which English was dominant, the slaves learned English. But how quickly and completely they did so, and with how much influence from their African languages, are matters of dispute.

One view, the Afrocentric or ethnolinguistic view, is that most of the distinctive pronunciation and grammatical features of Ebonics represent transfers or continuities from Africa, since West Africans acquiring English as slaves restructured it according to the patterns of Niger-Congo languages. On this view, Ebonics simplifies word final consonant clusters ("pas'") and omits linking verbs like *is* and *are* ("He Ø happy") because these features are generally absent from Niger-Congo languages, and Ebonics creates verbal forms like habitual *be* and remote *BIN* because these tense-aspect categories are present in Niger-Congo languages. However, most Afrocentrists don't specify the particular West African languages and examples which support their argument, and given the wide array of languages in the Niger-Congo family, some historically significant Niger-Congo languages don't support them. For instance, while Yoruba does indeed lack a linking verb like *is* for some adjectival constructions, it has another linking verb *rí* for other adjectives, and SIX other linking verbs for non-adjectival constructions where English would use *is* or *are*. Moreover, features like consonant cluster simplification are also found among other English vernaculars (for instance, in England) which had little or no West African influence, and this weakens the Afrocentric argument. Many linguists acknowledge continuing African influences in some Ebonics and American English words (direct loans like *hip* and *tote* were cited earlier, and we can add to these loan-translations of West African concepts into English words, as with *cut-eye* "a glance of derision or disgust"). But when it comes to Ebonics pronunciation and grammar, they want more specific proof.

A second view, the Eurocentric or dialectologist view, is that African slaves learned English from White settlers, and that they did so relatively quickly and successfully, with little continuing influence from their African linguistic heritage. Vernacular or non-SE features of Ebonics, including consonant cluster simplification and habitual *be*, are seen as transfers from vernacular dialects spoken by colonial English, Irish, or Scotch Irish settlers, many of whom were indentured servants, or as features which developed in the 20th century, after African Americans became more isolated in urban ghettoes. (Habitual *be* appears to be commoner in urban than in rural areas.) However, as with Afrocentric arguments, we still don't have enough details of the putative source features in British and settler English varieties, and crucial Ebonics features like the absence of linking *is* appear to be rare or non-existent in them, so they're unlikely to have been the source. Moreover, even with relatively low proportions of Blacks to Whites in the early colonial period, and the fact that they worked alongside each other in households and fields, particularly in the North, the assumption that slaves rapidly and successfully acquired the dialects of the Whites around them requires a rosier view of their social relations and interactions than the historical record and contemporary evidence suggest.

A third view, the creolist view, is that many African slaves, in acquiring English, developed a simplified fusion of English and African languages which linguists call a pidgin or creole, and that this influenced the subsequent development of Ebonics. A *pidgin* is a contact vernacular, used to facilitate communication between speakers of two or more languages. Native to none of its speakers, a pidgin is a mixed language, incorporating elements of its users' native languages, and it also has a less complex grammar and a smaller vocabulary than its input languages. A *creole*, as traditionally defined, is a pidgin which has become the primary or native language of its users (e.g., the children of pidgin speakers), expanding its vocabulary and grammatical machinery in the process, but still remaining simpler than the original language inputs in some respects. Most creoles, for instance, don't use inflectional suffixes to mark tense ("he walk*ed*"), plurality ("boy*s*"), or possession ("John'*s* house").

Where are creoles common? All over the world, but particularly on the islands of the Caribbean and the Pacific, where large plantations brought together huge groups of slaves or indentured laborers, speaking various ethnic languages, and smaller groups of colonizers and settlers whose European languages (English, French, Dutch) the former had to learn. Under such conditions, with minimal access to European speakers, new restructured varieties like Haitian Creole French and Jamaican Creole English arose. These do show African influence, as the Afrocentric theory would predict, but where the patterns of various African languages were conflicting, the creolist theory would provide for elimination or simplification of more complex alternatives, like the seven linking verbs of Yoruba referred to above. Within the United States, one well-established English creole is Gullah, spoken on the Sea Islands off the coast of South Carolina and Georgia, where Blacks constituted 80% to 90% of the local population in places. When I did research on one of the South Carolina Sea Islands some years ago, I recorded the following creole sentences, much like what one would hear in Caribbean Creole English today:

6. E.M. *run an gone* to *Suzie* house (=SE "E.M. went running to Suzie's house").
7. But I *does* go to see people when they Ø sick (=SE "But I usually go to see people when they are sick").
8. De mill *bin* to Bluffton *dem time* (=SE "The mill was in Bluffton in those days").

Note the characteristically creole absence of past tense and possessive inflections in 6, the absence of linking verb *are* and the presence of unstressed habitual *does* in 7, and the use of unstressed *bin* for past and *dem time* (without *s*, but with pluralizing *dem*) in 8.

What about creole origins for Ebonics? One way in which creole speech might have been introduced to many of the American colonies is through the large numbers of slaves who were imported in the 17th and 18th centuries from Caribbean colonies like Jamaica and Barbados where creoles definitely did develop. Some of those who came directly from Africa may also have brought with them pidgins or creoles which developed around West African trading forts. Moreover, some creole varieties—apart from well-known cases like Gullah—might have developed on American soil. While the percentages of Blacks in the local population might have been too low in 18th-century New England and Middle Colonies for creoles to develop (3% and 7% respectively, compared with 50% to 90% in the early Caribbean), they were higher in the South (40% overall, 61% in South Carolina), where the bulk of the Black population in America was concentrated. There are also observations from travelers and commentators through the centuries to Black speech being different from White speech (contra the Eurocentric scenario), and repeated textual attestations of Black speech with creole-like features. Even today, certain features of Ebonics, like the absence of linking *is* and *are*, are widespread in Gullah and Caribbean English creoles, while rare or non-existent in British dialects.

My own view, perhaps evident from the preceding, is that the creolist hypothesis most neatly incorporates the strengths of the other hypotheses, while avoiding their weaknesses. But there is no current consensus among linguists on the origins issue, and research from these competing perspectives is proceeding at fever pitch. One of the spinoffs of this kind of research is the light it sheds on aspects of American history which we might not otherwise consider. Whatever the final resolution of the origins issue, we should not forget that linguists from virtually all points of view agree on the systematicity of Ebonics, and on the potential value of taking it into account in teaching Ebonics speakers to read and write. That position may strike non-linguists as unorthodox, but that is where our science leads us.

Post-reading Questions / Activities

- Why is it important to show that African American Vernacular English has consistent grammatical patterns?
- Why do you think traditional teaching methods have failed to teach Standard English to speakers of minority "dialects"?
- Investigate the contrastive analysis approach (sometimes called the bridge method) of teaching Standard English to speakers of nonstandard varieties of English. How does it work? How effective has it been? How has it fared politically?

Vocabulary

aspect	dialect	tense
copula	pidgin	vernacular
creole	prescriptive	voiced
descriptive	slang	voiceless

Suggested Further Reading

Abrahams, R. D. 1974. "Black Talking on the Street." In *Explorations in the Ethnography of Speaking*, edited by Richard Bauman and Joel Sherzer, pp. 240–262. Cambridge: Cambridge University Press.

Baugh, John. 1983. *Black Street Speech: Its History, Structure, and Survival*. Austin: University of Texas Press.

———. 1999. *Out of the Mouth of Slaves: African American Language and Educational Malpractice*. Austin: University of Texas Press.

Herskovitz, Melville J. 1958. *The Myth of the Negro Past*. Boston: Beacon Press.

Labov, William. 1972. *Language in the Inner City: Studies in the Black English Vernacular*. Philadelphia: University of Pennsylvania Press.

Linguistics Society of America (LSA). 1997. Linguistics Society of America (LSA) Resolution on the Oakland "Ebonics" Issue. http://www.stanford.edu/~rickford/ebonics/LSAResolution.html.

Morgan, Marcyeliena. 2002. *Language, Discourse, and Power in African American Culture*. Cambridge: Cambridge University Press.

Rickford, John R., and Russell J. Rickford. 2000. *Spoken Soul: The Story of Black English*. New York: Wiley.

Schilling-Estes, Natalie. 2004. "Constructing Ethnicity in Interaction." *Journal of Sociolinguistics* 8/2: 163–195.

Smitherman, Geneva. 1977. *Talkin and Testifyin: The Language of Black America*. Boston: Houghton Mifflin.

———. 1994. *Black Talk: Words and Phrases from the Hood to the Amen Corner*. Boston: Houghton Mifflin.

Wolfram, Walt, and Erik R. Thomas. 2002. *The Development of African American English*. Malden, MA: Blackwell.

CHAPTER 27

"Nuthin' but a G Thang": Grammar and Language Ideology in Hip Hop Identity

Marcyliena Morgan

(2001)

African American English (AAE) has been much studied since William Labov first dem-onstrated that what he called "Black English Vernacular" had logic and was not simply a degraded form of standard English, as popular opinion had it. Many scholars have shown the grammatical features of AAVE, providing subtle categories that distinguish, for example, between ongoing activities and those that occur once (see Chapter 26). Grammarians term this a distinction between habitual *and* punctual *events. In Standard American English, it can be explained: "I usually go to the store on Fridays" and "I am going to the store right after I finish this pie." In AAE, in contrast, this can be expressed more simply, as in* I be going to the store (on Fridays) *and* I going to the store (now). *This feature—termed* aspect—*exists in many of the world's languages, including many West African languages, but does not exist as an obligatory grammatical category in standard English, or what Morgan calls "General American English" (GAE).*

There are many other well-documented features of AAE, from sound patterns through lexicon through grammar and all the way to discourse features, that differ from GAE.

All language choice carries with it social meaning, both for the speaker and the listener. Those who use AAE—usually but not only African Americans, and not all African Americans—attach social and personal meaning to it, just as listeners attach meaning to it (sometimes negative).

Marcyliena Morgan, who has contributed generously to the study of African American English, here focuses on the music genre now typically styled hip-hop and its contribution to a particular identity. What Morgan calls Hip Hop invokes not merely the songs and their verbal and musical styles but a number of institutional forms and institutional practices. Translating a fast-paced ironic genre of popular culture into careful academic analysis may seem surprising, but it reminds us that close examination of human meanings—of speech, of song, of social interaction—is the core of anthropology, and that it can illuminate any human activity.

Reading Questions

- What is the Hip-Hop nation? How unified is it? What divisions, if any, exist in it?
- What are the ways "keeping it real" is exemplified in hip-hop practices? What gives hip-hop "authenticity"?
- How does the core audience interact with hip-hop artists? What are "crews"? How do they build on other African American networks?

Marcyliena Morgan, "'Nothin' but a G Thang': Grammar and Language Ideology in Hip Hop Identity." In *Sociocultural and Historical Contexts of African American English*, ed. Sonja L. Lanehart. Amsterdam and Philadelphia: John Benjamins, 2001, pp. 187–209. Notes have been renumbered. With kind permission by John Benjamins Publishing Company, Amsterdam/Philadelphia. www.benjamins.com.

- What are "semantic extension" and "semantic inversion"? Give an example of each. How does hip-hop use the AAE tendency to shift grammatical classes and meanings? What other ways does hip-hop innovate, linguistically?

BACKGROUND: "DON'T TRY TO FADE THIS"[1]

If one were to believe the current news media hype, Hip Hop music has only recently become the favored music of youth throughout the U.S. and indeed the world. In fact, Hip Hop began in the late 1970s and has been a significant presence in urban African American communities since the late 1980s (Fab 5 Freddy 1992; Jones 1994; Toop 1991). With the introduction of the Hip Hop salutations "Word!" and "Word Up!" the Hip Hop nation has emerged as a cultural, social, and political force, constituted and instantiated through language style, often illustrated in the rap itself. Hip Hop arose as a youth response to the political ideology of the Reagan–Bush era and its promotion of the social and civic abandonment of urban schools and communities in the U.S. The music, sounds, and lyrics from some of Hip Hop's most talented writers and performers has resulted in what has undeniably become the one cultural institution that urban youth rely on for representation, honesty—*keeping it real*—and leadership.

In 1996, there were 19 million young people aged 10–14 years old and 18.4 million aged 15–19 years old living in the U.S. (Chadwick/Heaton 1996). According to a national Gallup poll of adolescents aged 13–17 (Bezilla 1993), by 1992 rap music had become the preferred music of youth (26%), followed closely by rock (25%). Though Hip Hop artists often rap about adolescent confusion, desire, and angst, at Hip Hop's core is the commitment and vision of youth who are agitated, motivated, and willing to confront complex and powerful institutions and practices to improve their world.

This chapter is part of a larger work on Hip Hop culture and language. It explores the social organization and some of the language practices that both constitute and mediate the Hip Hop community/nation and converge around African American urban youth culture and identity. In some respects, Hip Hop's influence on the larger urban speech community is surprising. Because of its homogeneity across regions (e.g., Baugh 1983; Labov 1972; Smitherman 1977), the African American speech community is often thought to be impervious to most political, social, historical, and geographical divisions and policies that normally lead to significant language change toward the dominant culture. In many respects the introduction of Hip Hop cultural beliefs and values has resulted in a significant reclamation and restructuring of African American language practices by youth who have, for the first time in urban African American communities, intentionally highlighted and re-constructed regional and local urban language norms. These norms and values essentially apportion the urban community, thereby constantly marking people—young African Americans—as cultural insiders or outsiders.

Hip Hop's language ideology is consciously and often defiantly based on urban African American norms, values, and popular culture constructed against dominant cultural and linguistic norms. It thus relies on the study, knowledge, and use of African American English (AAE) and General American English (GAE)[2] linguistic features and principles of grammaticalization. This language ideology has been operating since the late 1970s and did not have sweeping consequences until the middle 1980s. At that time, technology shifted and intimate friendship networks, families, and crews based on Hip Hop artists became prominent outside of the East Coast. This resulted in new speech community formations and a drive to distinguish and articulate linguistic characteristics to represent major cities and regions on the East and West Coasts. This drive initially resulted in the marginalization of the Southern U.S. and the Midwest. But as Hip Hop cultural norms of local representation stabilized, the South's "Third Coast" and "Dirty South" contingent found permanent recognition. Hip Hop urban language ideology has also resulted in an increase of widespread yet locally marked lexicon and an awareness of the importance of phonology (mainly working class)—especially the contrasts between vowel length, consonant deletion, and syllabic stress—in representing urban cultural space.

This discussion is based on an ongoing study of fifteen years of research that incorporates observations of young people at play, in underground venues, open-mic sessions, concerts, and rap contests. It also includes ethnographic interviews and analyses of conversations; letters and interviews in Hip Hop magazines and rap sheets; radio and video call-in shows; and play lists. Besides the researcher, those participating in fieldwork and/or contributing to this analysis include groups of 12–16 year olds and groups in their late teens to early twenties. The U.S. cities include Los Angeles, New York, Chicago, and Atlanta. Researchers also work in other parts of the Southern U.S., including Mobile, Alabama, and parts of Mississippi.

HIP HOP CULTURE: "YOU WOULDN'T UNDERSTAND THE GHETTO"

In many respects, Hip Hop has done more to crystallize a young, urban African American identity than any other historic and political change since the late 1970s. While the Civil Rights Movement and Black Power struggles of the 1950s, 1960s, and 1970s may have introduced the promise of a united, culturally, politically, and linguistically homogeneous African American community, Hip Hop members boldly and brazenly argue for the "real" in relation to regional and local identities. Referring to Hip Hop as a Black urban cultural institution may seem an overstatement, but its role in addressing modern issues of morality, injustice, representation, and responsibility cannot be denied. The frequent depiction of Hip Hop as nihilistic (De Genova 1995; West 1993) and some sort of postmodern glitch (Gilroy 1993a, 1993b) results from a focus on aggressive (*gangsta*) raps and particular Hip Hop productions and artists. While a focus on salacious and aggressive content may be a common criticism of Hip Hop, it provides only a rudimentary view of the complex and interactive workings of the Hip Hop community. In fact, there are a variety of Hip Hop styles, including old school, hard core, gangster, social and political consciousness, smooth, and others. The choice of style is associated with how artists construct themselves or the type of message in the rap. Both men and women use all styles, though some artists are strongly associated with one type of rap.

Unlike rock and other musical genres, Hip Hop is based on the co-authorship of artists and urban youth communities. When one considers that Hip Hop is represented by radio and video programs, hundreds of web sites, several national magazines, underground clubs, neighborhood record stores, concerts, newsletters, and community organizations, it is obvious there are complex organizational and institutional structures and activities that support the philosophy of rap culture. It is the preferred music for 67% of Black and 55% of all non-White youth (Bezilla 1993) and is steadily becoming a staple of rock performances and recordings.[3] In the process, what has taken place is a new form of youth socialization that explicitly addresses racism, sexism, capitalism, and morality in ways that simultaneously expose, exploit, and critique these practices. Rappers from Afrika Baambaata of the Zulu Nation[4] and the next group or person to be lauded as the Hip Hop "flavor of the month" all refer to the Hip Hop nation in terms of its vitality and as an alternative for urban youth who face a bleak and often difficult passage into adulthood.

In Hip Hop culture, language is not simply a means of communication. Rather, language use is viewed as a series of choices that represent beliefs and have consequences. As with any case of language socialization (Schieffelin/Ochs 1986), participants in Hip Hop must learn the appropriate language for particular social contexts. In a sense, Hip Hop is constructed around the exploitation and subversion of the following tenets of language philosophy and theory:

1. all sounds and objects have specific meanings in culture;
2. all languages have system;
3. all leaks in grammar can be exploited;
4. a society's reference system or indexicality is often political; and
5. meaning is co-constructed and co-authored.

Artistic success in Hip Hop is often defined in terms of its relevance to the urban community irrespective of its popularity with the non–African American community. Consequently, performers always run the risk of appearing outdated and being removed from the public sphere

by more vibrant and real rappers. The tension and conflicting value systems between the two results in a creative tension to "keep it real." Membership in the community is instantiated and mediated through audience corroboration and collaboration. The audience demonstrates loyalty to Hip Hop culture by vigilantly critiquing the language as well as cultural and public representations of Hip Hop. The right to represent the Hip Hop nation is substantiated by members'

1. purchase of recordings,
2. memorization of rap lyrics,
3. freestyle practice (spontaneous, improvised, and/or re-stylized) performance,
4. loyalty to crews and/or individuals, and, recently,
5. publication of lyrics and artists' biographies on rap web sites.

The core of the Hip Hop nation is adolescent males and females between 12 and 17 years old who exclusively listen to and memorize raps (Wheeler 1992); dress the current Hip Hop style; keep up with the current dances; and often tag or at least practice writing raps. This younger group also practices freestyle rapping and competes with each other over the best rap, delivery, style, etc.

While the core purchases the most recordings and is essential to Hip Hop's stability as an artistic form, the most influential segment of the Hip Hop nation is in its late teens to middle twenties. These long-term (LT) members also practice freestyle, participate in local and underground open-mic performances and competitions, and identify with particular rap genres or crews. This segment of Hip Hop often writes letters of praise or complaint to various Hip Hop publications or rap sheets to give *props* ('respect') to artists. They also disclose which performer is *wack* ('outdated or unacceptable') or who *drops phat tracks* ('very good recordings'). Long-term members also serve as nation builders and often offer political and historical commentary and context to current Hip Hop styles and artists. They have the power to influence artists because they can attend most Hip Hop venues at clubs and concerts and monitor the authenticity of the audience and artist. If LTs designate that an artist has sold out, that artist generally cannot perform without reprisals anywhere that Hip Hop members congregate in the African American community. Most members of the Hip Hop nation argue that there are at least two versions to every Hip Hop record released in a record store: the one that goes to all audiences and the "real" version that is sold at concerts, clubs, and on the street.

Achievement in Hip Hop is related to creative and relevant writing, style, and delivery that resonates with the audience. How one gains financial success is not a serious issue unless the community perceives that the artist ignored the core Hip Hop audience in order to achieve it. Clearly, youth outside of urban areas are attracted to Hip Hop for the same reasons as its primary audience. If the core audience rejects the artist because the words, referents, experiences, and symbols evoked do not reflect the reality of the streets, suburbia also rejects him or her. In this regard, Adler's famous quotation that Hip Hop "... is adored by millions in the streets and reviled by hundreds in the suites" (Adler 1991) is, at best, a limited view of the real relationship between the streets and suites. Few artists can navigate the scrutiny and pressure of a crossover hit since this form of success results in the LTs' intense re-evaluation of the artist for urban authenticity. Suburbia's uncritical acceptance might signify that the artist is a *perpetrator*, a term that is the equivalent of a spy and the antithesis of what Hip Hop symbolizes.

THE HIP HOP CREW: "GET IN WHERE YOU FIT IN"

Though the Hip Hop speech community has always been comprised of DJs mixing sounds, artists rapping and writing lyrics, graffiti writers, dancers, and dress styles, the focus on each element can vary. In its early stages, Hip Hop lyrics were largely related to the beat, sound, and rhythm generated by DJs. As MCs became more of a focus, Hip Hop began to identify local membership and describe and name neighborhoods, public transportation systems, highways, etc. Since the East Coast (or East Side) was the birthplace of Hip Hop, its urban terrain became common knowledge among Hip Hop members and the center of African American urban culture. Not only did members learn about the Bronx, Bedford Stuyvesant (Bedstuy), and Harlem, but also Hollis, New Jersey, Jamaica, Queens, and avenues and streets like Houston, along with their local pronunciations. Through Hip Hop artistry, the local descriptions of East Coast areas were like a demographer and cartographer's dream.

But on the West Side of the U.S., artists' frustration and simmering desire for regional recognition and respect as major contributors and innovators erupted. While the 1987 release of Ice T's debut album *Rhyme Pays* introduced Hip Hop audiences to Los Angeles' youth gang world view, it only hinted at things to come. After all, Los Angeles, having unseated Chicago and been crowned the second most populated U.S. city by the 1990 census, was also experiencing an unprecedented Black exodus to suburbs and other parts of the U.S. In a city where cultural variation and bilingualism are mainstays of working-class communities, the construction and exhibition of Los Angeles symbols and metaphors guaranteed an ebullient, and sometimes menacing, youthful African American presence. The ultimate emergence of the West as not simply imitators and students of East Coast Hip Hop, but innovators with a message and style, introduced a new development in Hip Hop culture. The nature and extent of the change was not clear until 1989 when N.W.A. introduced their album *Straight Outta Compton*, effectively placing California, and Southern California in particular, on the Hip Hop map. Suddenly, Northern California cities like Oakland and those in Southern California like Los Angeles, Compton, Inglewood, Long Beach, and El Segundo found their place on the Hip Hop landscape. Along with the cities came street

names that defined the terrain of African American communities such as Slauson, Rosecrans, and Crenshaw.

With the establishment of place, the West Coast arose as distinct from the East Coast in terms of geographical references, sounds, and social and cultural influences. For the first time, the Hip Hop community had to consciously address whether the emergence of different regional styles constituted a split in the Hip Hop nation. Young audiences and LTs aligned around artistic styles and regional loyalties. The extremes that artists and their followers were willing to go to in order to demonstrate East Coast and West Coast loyalties culminated in the deaths of two of Hip Hop's most gifted performers, Tupac Shakur and Notorious B. I. G. As both coasts asserted the right to define Hip Hop, distinct identities and performance style shifts began to emerge that further instantiated regional difference. These shifts included music sampling (Rose 1994) and conscious language style choices. Yet instead of becoming more vulnerable in the midst of rap battles and negative media hype, the Hip Hop world became stronger through the dominance of family and crew affiliation.

SHOUT OUTS—AND "A LITTLE FLAVAH IN YOUR EAR"

The Hip Hop world is comprised of a range of artists who are often grouped according to performance style, family (e.g., the Shaolin Family), crew and house affiliation (e.g., Wu-Tang Clan), and by whether they reside on the East or West Coast of the U.S. Style in Hip Hop may refer to the content of the rap (hard core, gangsta, socially conscious, sex), how the message is delivered (speed, quality of pitch or tone across syllables, phrasing, etc.), and the audience or speech community for whom the message is intended. Membership in a crew enables audiences to quickly understand the artist's role and status within Hip Hop culture. The heads of most crews are influential artists and/or producers in Hip Hop. Crews insure that all members are employed and they offer artists support in terms of production as well as protection from unscrupulous record companies and other crews who compete within the same market. Members are expected to be loyal and to protect and "represent" each other.

The importance of relationship and performance ties in Hip Hop creates and reflects a speech community that highlights region, ideology, and language style. The solidification of the Hip Hop crew as a family/business unit ushered in an era of artistic and cultural stability in the Hip Hop community. Crews are constructed within an African American cultural system based on extended kinship ties and loyalties that are economical, emotional, and social. If there is a failure to represent his or her crew and audience, there is a crisis in the "family" that must be resolved. Many artistic crews have neighborhood crews and friendship networks that emulate them. These crews operate as close social networks, offering support and critique that is based on loyalty and respect.

The recognition of influences—*giving props, representin', recognizin'*—as well as exposing artists who do not acknowledge the source of their materials is accomplished by directly stating the name of a person or group during a rap and/or using the words or phrases of another artist who belongs to the same crew.[5] This often includes the use of simile and metaphor, which requires "local" Hip Hop knowledge in order to be understood. Local knowledge includes lived experiences as well as familiarity with popular culture. For instance, the use of the word "CREAM" indicates both respect for the group who popularized the term (the Wu-Tang Clan) and its meaning (*Cash Rules Everything Around Me*). Stephen DeBerry (1995) suggests there are three functions accomplished through simile in props. First, it indexes an artist as a member of the urban community and/or a crew. Secondly, it serves as a mechanism to display a rapper's wit and/or lyrical ability, especially in freestyle sessions. Finally, it can be used to exhibit levels of pedantic knowledge unparalleled by competitors (DeBerry 1995). All artistic styles are influenced by the distinction between the East and West Coasts, or "Sides," of the country. Artistic styles are constructed within a basic language ideology that can be loosely described as:

1. regularize General American English features,
2. highlight AAE and working class regional features, and
3. cast lexical havoc.

Because of a crew's close affiliation and need to represent a particular group of people, it is the smallest speech community unit in Hip Hop. Originally, crews were mainly based on childhood and family ties (e.g., Public Enemy, Flavor Unit, and Boogie Down Productions); the type of music and sounds sampled; and dress and rap styles. When N. W. A. introduced West Coast gangsta rap, membership was also based on a notion of street-gang loyalty to the group. Any failure to *represent* was seen as an attack on the group and was responded to accordingly. The gangsta approach to family meant that no one could collaborate with another artist without agreement. Artists had little or no say in compensation and often adhered to a style orthodoxy that stifled artistic creativity. Though other artists began to reverse this trend—especially Ice Cube on the West Coast—the success of the Wu-Tang Clan (Table 1) proved that family support could lead to group stability, artistic freedom, and economic success.

Because members of the Wu-Tang Clan had experienced unscrupulous producers and record deals early in their careers, their reorganization within the Shaolin Family was based on the desire to work as a group and to pursue individual artistic freedom. Wu-Tang and the Shaolin Family fought for the right to have control over their own group as well as the right to perform outside of the group without being disowned.

Besides focusing on performance skills and loyalty, Wu-Tang members were very concerned with keeping as much of the revenue from their work as possible (CREAM). Their philosophy meant that members could succeed as individuals and as members. Shaolin's sixteen members could appear under at least twenty names and under different labels. Urban youth who looked to the Hip Hop community for

Table 1. The Shaolin Family*

Groups	Members
Wu-Tang Clan	Prince Rakeem The Rza
	The Method Man
	U-God
	Rebel Ins
	Shallah Raekwon
	Ghostface Killah
	Dirty
	The Genius—Tha Gza
	Inspectah Deck
	Masta Killa (his part of Wu-Tang Clan)
N-Tyce	N-Tyce
Shyheim	Shyheim
Gravediggaz	Prince Paul
	Prince Rakeem The Rza
	Frukwan
	Poetic
Method Man	The Method Man
The Genius	The Genius—Tha Gza
Dirty	Dirty
King Just	King Just
Genius/Gza	The Genius—Tha Gza
Raekwon	Shallah Raekwon
	Ghostface Killah
Ghostface Killah	Ghostface Killah
Cappadonna	Cappadonna

* From www.onebadrap.com. The Shaolin Family has included other members over time.

leadership began emulating a family that supported members and encouraged individual goals. New groups like The Fugees, fissures created in crews like The Family (Puff Daddy) and Da Lench Mob (Ice Cube), and the maturing of rappers like LL Cool J, Ice Cube, MC Lyte, and others, contributed to the new definition of the Hip Hop community. Thus family protection evolved and new members were introduced as guests on artist's recordings with the expectation that the crew would help with a solo career. Though there had always been female rappers (especially MC Lyte, Queen Latifah, and YoYo), this system opened the door for a women's chorus (Missy Elliott, Lil' Kim, Da Brat, and Foxy Brown) to take center stage.

THE LANGUAGE OF HIP HOP: "THE SURE SHOT"

I'm outspoken, my language is broken into a slang
But it's just a dialect I select when I hang. (Special Ed 1989)

I'll damage ya, I'm not an amateur
But a professional, unquestionable, without a doubt superb
So full of action, my name should be a verb.
(Big Daddy Kane 1988)

This section analyzes the language use on artists' recordings and on radio, television, and personal interviews. I asked fifty urban African American LTs between the ages of 16 and 25 to identify their top five favorite Hip Hop artists and crews. Six male artists and groups were selected who released recordings during 1997–8 and represented a range

Table 2. Artists and Recordings

Artist	Album	Region	Year	No. of Songs	No. Coded	%
Aceyalone	*A Book of Human Language*	West	1998	17	16	94
	All Balls Don't Bounce		1995	15	13	87
Common	*One Day It'll All Make Sense*	Midwest	1997	17	13	76
	Resurrection		1994	15	12	80
	Can I Borrow a Dollar?		1992	13	6	46
Goodie Mob	*Still Standing*	South	1998	15	15	100
	Soul Food		1995	19	19	100
Ice Cube	*Lethal Injection*	West	1993	12	10	83
	The Predator		1992	16	12	75
	Death Certificate		1991	20	15	75
	Amerikkka's Most Wanted		1990	16	14	88
Jay-Z	*Streets Is Watching*	East	1998	12	7	58
	Vol. 2 Hard Knock Life		1998	14	14	100
	Vol. 1 In My Lifetime		1997	14	14	100
	Reasonable Doubt		1996	14	14	100
KRS-One	*I Got Next*	East	1997	20	13	65
	KRS-One		1995	14	8	57
	Return of the Boom Bap		1993	14	9	64
Totals			18	254	224	

of Hip Hop styles and regions. In order to be included in the analysis, each artist had to appear among the top three favorite artists on a person's list. Women are not included in this analysis because, though individual women artists were listed as favorites (especially MC Lyte and Queen Latifah), they were not among the top three of any individual's list.[6] Draft transcripts were taken from web site lyrics like www. Ohhla.com (a Hip Hop archive web site) and from lyrics available on album jackets.[7] They were then compared to the recording used for analysis and changed accordingly.

Table 2 lists the artists and albums included in the analysis. Aceyalone (pronounced "AC alone") is a well-known freestyle artist in the Los Angeles area. He has been rapping professionally since the late 1980s and is a member of Freestyle Fellowship. Common (formerly Common Sense) is an artist from Chicago. The Goodie Mob is a group from the South. Ice Cube is from Los Angeles and was originally with N. W. A. Jay-Z is from New York and KRS-One is from the Bronx. KRS-One is considered a significant figure in Hip Hop and East Coast Hip Hop in particular. Jay-Z's 1998 recordings are actually two related versions of one recording. Though many of the albums generated remixes, they were not included in the overall analysis.

While family crew and East Coast and West Coast differences have emerged as major components of Hip Hop, there is a specific language ideology which informs all language practices. All participants incorporate American regional urban Spanish styles in their pronunciation of vowels and in some aspects of their syllable stress.[8] Thus the West is more likely to show pronunciation influence from Chicano English and Spanish phonology while the East has a strong Caribbean Spanish language influence. However, perhaps due to the territorial nature of Los Angeles West Coast rap, only a few African American rap artists have

directly addressed their Spanish bilingual audience (e.g., Ice T). In contrast, East Coast artists like Raekwon, Nas, KRS-One, Master Ace, and Method Man intersperse their raps with East Coast urban Spanish and popular Spanish expressions.

SEMANTIC EXTENSION AND INVERSION[9]

Hip Hop artists constantly change word classes and meanings resulting in a sense of chaos, movement, and urgency. The value of lexical items rises and falls for reasons that range from poor artistic and musical expression to uncritical appropriation by suburban youth. This turmoil is often accomplished through semantic inversion, extension, and the reclamation of GAE and AAE forms. Semantic extension emphasizes one aspect of an English word definition and extends or changes the focus of the word's meaning. Thus, the word *wack*, which means 'unbelievably inept, inadequate, and deficient' (Smitherman 1994), is from the adjective *wacky*, which means 'absurd or irrational'. In cases of semantic inversion (Holt 1972; Smitherman 1994), an AAE word means the opposite of at least one definition of the word in the dominant culture. For example, the word *down* can have a positive meaning of support in the sentence "I want to be down with you." It can also be used as part of a locative with "low" to mean 'secretive' as in "Keep it on the down low." In the early 1990s, stressed *STUpid* meant 'good', though its usage is archaic in Hip Hop today.

The process of extension has evolved in Hip Hop so that a word can be extended from GAE and then inverted once it has stabilized as a Hip Hop word. For example, the Hip Hop word *ill* has been grammaticalized to include verbal usage (Stavsky/Mozeson/Mozeson 1995; Atoon 1992–99) and can also mean 'extremely positive', though initially its meaning was categorically negative (e.g., Fab 5 Freddy 1992).[10] Adjectival examples are in (1–3) and predicate examples are in (4–7).

(1) Get ill if you wanna ill, smoke if you wanna smoke (Jay-Z and Memphis Bleak).
(2) Who's the illest shorty alive, I confess (Jay-Z and Memphis Bleak).
(3) Some of the realest, illest, chillest cats you may see (Common).
(4) I be illin', parental discretion is advised still (KRS One).
(5) And bust and rushed and illed and peeled the cap (Ice Cube).
(6) For chillin, illin', willin' to do what I got to do (Goodie Mob).
(7) Big up Grand Wizard Theodore, gettin' ill (KRS One).

Finally in AAE, a *player* was defined as someone who exploited people (especially women), but now it is a person who has extreme and enviable success (Major 1994; Smitherman 1994). This meaning has led to *player hater*, a term that refers to envious people who criticize others' success. Now in Hip Hop, a Ph.D. is an insult suggesting envy and refers to *Player Hater Degree*.

Working Grammar

In conversation, performances, and recordings, Hip Hop members use multiple applications of AAE features. For example, grammatical classes and meaning are routinely shifted so that the verb *fly* also functions as an adjective in Hip Hop that embellishes the noun as in: "Those boots sure are fly" and "Jennifer Lopez was one of the fly girls on the television program *In Living Color*." The verb *floss* (e.g., "Do you want to floss with us?") has an extremely positive meaning that incorporates coolness and focuses on the attitude

and intentionality of the subject. It follows the norms of action verbs (e.g. *floss/flossed/flossing*). Artists also form new words by changing affixes (bound morphemes) into independent lexical items. Thus the bound prefix *dis-* becomes a free form with a negative meaning similar to its use in words like *disrespect, dispose, disdain*, etc. It also exists as a verb that marks tense and aspect (*diss/dissed/dissing*). Another striking aspect of Hip Hop language style is the regularization of verbs. For example, the verb *converse* has been replaced with the verb *conversate*, including its non-finite form *conversating* (e.g. *conversate/conversated/conversating*): "They just be conversating with me all the time" (Smitherman 1994).

In addition to the grammatical norms described above, American working-class phonological features, like consonant cluster simplification and vowel length, are used to distinguish regional differences. Thus, the shortening of vowels, the increase in glottal stops, and the reduction of consonants mark the East Coast. In contrast, vowel lengthening marks the West Coast. The different use of vowels in the West and consonants in the East is related to musical influences as well as social-class allegiances. Thus, the words *didn't* and *ghetto* are often pronounced /dɪʔn/ and /gɛʔo/ on the East Coast and /diːn/ and /gɛːdo/ on the West. Both the East and West Coasts are heavily influenced by a variety of musical styles, though fast-paced Jamaican Dance Hall music is central to East Coast rap and funk rhythms are central to the West Coast.

Fantasizing and Grammaticalizing: "Got you all in check"

This analysis explores the type of innovation in terms of source of word and grammatical category. Table 3 reveals the source of words used in the 18 recordings I analyzed. In order for an item to be counted as a Hip Hop word (not new word), it had to

① Take a regular word and change its part of speech and meaning

② Allow affixes to stand alone.

③ Regularization of verbs.

Table 3. New Words [NW]

Artist	Album	No. of diff. NWs	% of NWs which are Adjs.	Verbs	Nouns
Aceyalone	*A Book of Human Language*	8	12	0	88
	All Balls Don't Bounce	15	0	19	81
Common	*One Day It'll All Make Sense*	3	33	0	67
	Resurrection	9	11	11	78
	Can I Borrow a Dollar?	12	33	17	50
Goodie Mob	*Still Standing*	17	12	29	59
	Soul Food	15	33	27	40
Ice Cube	*Lethal Injection*	9	22	11	67
	The Predator	9	0	100	0
	Death Certificate	7	17	0	83
	Amerikkka's Most Wanted	5	0	60	40
Jay-Z	*Streets Is Watching*	8	78	0	22
	Vol. 2 Hard Knock Life	24	46	8	46
	Vol. 1 In My Lifetime	20	25	5	70
	Reasonable Doubt	28	35	10	55
KRS-One	*I Got Next*	9	33	11	56
	KRS-One	16	50	12	38
	Return of the Boom Bap	8	24	38	38

meet at least two of three usage criteria. First, a word had to be used by other artists in recordings, interviews, or conversations in other Hip Hop venues. These artists could be members of the same crew. Secondly, the terminology had to be used by youth and LTs. The final criterion focuses on new inventions that may not be directly derived from existing words. Rather, it recognizes words that focus on language ideology and that explore stylistic phrasing, syllabification, compounding, and/or morphophonemics that could also be applied to other similar words. For the purpose of this discussion, there is a distinction between new words within Hip Hop and Hip Hop language ideology.

New words refer to words that are not directly derived from free morphemes. They may also reflect a change in meaning, usage, and/or grammatical category of a word previously occurring in GAE or AAE.[11] For example, *dis* (discussed above) is not only a bound morpheme but a new word that means 'to reject, ignore, and embarrass' (see also Smitherman 1994). Hip Hop language ideology also favors adding bound morphemes (prefixes and suffixes) to highlight an already established meaning or change in meaning. Other favored bound morphemes include *-est*, *-ous/-ious*, *-er*, *-ic*, and *un-/in-*. Thus, the words *mack* and *mack daddy*, though fitting within Hip Hop language style, would not be counted as new words since they have existed in AAE with the same meaning of 'someone who exploits or hustles for sexual favors' (Major 1994; Smitherman 1994). Likewise though *I got my mack on* suggests new usage, it is not a new word but a Hip Hop word since the grammatical category remains a noun and the meaning of 'hustler' is retained. However, *mackadocious* and *mackness* would be considered new words since they have strictly adjectival functions, are used to refer to having power to control rather than just hustling for sex, and were repeated by LTs during the time of its circulation. Using these criteria, *beautifullest* is considered a Hip Hop word, though not a new one, since it retains its GAE meaning. The adjectival category is the same as 'beautiful', the addition of the suffix fits Hip Hop language ideology, and the imitation among LTs is in reference to suffixation (e.g., *He's the most particularest, realest, thoroughest, wickedest*).

Aceyalone, in his recording *All Balls Don't Bounce*, demonstrates the importance of bound morphemes on "Arhythamaticulas"[12] in (8):

(8) oh yes welcome to hiphology please open up your work-
    books to page
    and break out your pads and pens and your calculators
    for the first lesson of today is—
    arhythamatic, arhythamaticulas
    this rhythm is sick this rhythm's ridiculous.
    arhythamatic arhythamaticulas
    this rhythm is sick this rhythm's ridiculous (Aceyalone
    1995).

In "Arhythamaticulas," Aceyalone compounds and rhymes using variations on the following formula: a+rhythm+(atic/culas/culous/culas). Innovations occur at all levels and include:

1. reclaimed words (RCW) that have archaic
    English usage or were previously used in AAE;

2. a change of word class (CWC) where a word is used as a different category than in GAE grammar;

3. a reduced word (RW) to indicate when the term is being simplified by loss of a consonant, syllable, or vowel; and

4. reduced words (RWS) when more than one word has been put together and simplified in terms of a consonant, syllable, or vowel.

SPELLING IDEOLOGY[13]

Though each category is important unto itself, it is the relationship between categories that makes words significant within urban Hip Hop youth culture. New spellings follow English CVCV format and are an important signifier in Hip Hop wording. New spellings often accompany a change in word meaning and reflect AAE and Hip Hop pronunciation as well as knowledge of subversion of GAE spelling rules and alphabet symbol ideology. For instance, when writing about America's negative treatment of urban youth, it is common to find it spelled *Amerikkka*, using the initials for the White supremacist group the Ku Klux Klan (KKK). New spellings also focus on English irregular spelling rules. So, to give a compliment about an activity or object, one might say that it is *phat* (pronounced "fat"). Virtually every word that exceeds two syllables and ends with the suffix *-er* is vocalized and spelled *-a*, *-uh*, or *-ah*, as in *brothah* ('brother') and *sucka* ('sucker'). Similarly, words ending in *-ing* are written as *-in* or *-un*, as in *sumthin* ('something') and *thumpun* ('thumping'). Spelling also reflects syllable reduction and vowel assimilation with rhotics and semi-vowels. Thus, "all right" is spelled *aight*. Table 4 reveals the total number of new words and their grammatical categories.

Reclaimed Words account for the smallest category of Hip Hop words and the single most used words are *mack* and *gat*.[14] The main exception is *gaffled* used by Ice Cube: "I was hassled and gaffled in the back seat." According to The Rap Dictionary (Atoon 1992–99) at www.rapdict.org, *gaffle* refers to 'harassment by the police' while its earlier usage was in reference to an ordeal.

A **Change of Word Class** often reflects potential grammaticalized forms of words that have a high frequency of usage. As with *ill* described above, many words listed share more than one grammatical category in GAE but are used in one category in Hip Hop. Though one may say "I ain't mad at ya," it is also common during rhymes to hear an emcee say "I drop *madd* rhymes," where "madd" is both a quantifier and an adjective that means 'crazy and extreme'. This is also true of the Hip Hop word *loc*. Smitherman (1994) and Atoon (1992–9) include the following meanings and grammatical categories for this term.

1. (n) Term used for local person.
2. (n) Lock or locks, as in Jheri-curls, but always pronounced with the long o as in "go."
3. (adj) Crazy one, from the Spanish *loco*, often used for friends or locals in a positive way (usually pronounced 'loke').

Table 4. Frequency of Occurrence of the Lex/Morph Category (for abbreviations, see above)

Artist	Album	RCW	CWC	RW	RWS
Aceyalone	*A Book of Human Language*	0	3	65	19
	All Balls Don't Bounce	0	8	73	23
Common	*One Day It'll All Make Sense*	0	4	33	23
	Resurrection	1	2	54	18
	Can I Borrow a Dollar?	0	0	39	17
Goodie Mob	*Still Standing*	2	2	105	44
	Soul Food	1	2	115	28
Ice Cube	*Lethal Injection*	1	0	83	12
	The Predator	1	0	166	39
	Death Certificate	4	5	129	24
	Amerikkka's Most Wanted	1	3	89	8
Jay-Z	*Streets Is Watching*	1	14	39	15
	Vol. 2 Hard Knock Life	2	24	105	70
	Vol. 1 In My Lifetime	4	6	112	47
	Reasonable Doubt	0	5	66	43
KRS-One	*I Got Next*	1	2	58	15
	KRS-One	0	1	39	16
	Return of the Boom Bap	0	1	32	6
Total	18		19	82	1,402	467

4. (adj) To get high. "We was in the park getting' loc'ed."

5. (v) To "go loc" means to get ready for a drive-by or to shoot someone. This means putting on dark glasses, skullies, caps, and generally getting hard to identify.

Thus Jay-Z and Memphis Bleak rhyme:

> Bounce if you wanna bounce, ball if you wanna ball
> Play if you wanna play, floss if you wanna floss
> Get ill if you wanna ill, smoke if you wanna smoke
> Get ill if you wanna ill, smoke if you wanna smoke
> Kill if you wanna kill, loc if you wanna loc.[15]

The single **Reduced Word**, as in (9) and (10) [see below], is separated from multiple **Reduced Words**, as in (11–14), to determine whether the reductions occur within previously described AAE categories or haphazardly. These words are not viewed as consonant cluster simplification as in most AAE studies because, in many cases, there is an awareness of GAE pronunciation that is being ignored or exploited. Unsurprisingly, the most common reductions (also recognized in spelling) are morphophonemic and focus on the suffix *-ing*, as in (9) and contracted negation. Thus, "didn't" is written *didin* or *did'n* to represent the voicing of stops before nasals (West Coast) and the glottalization of voiceless stops before nasals (East Coast). As reported in Rickford (1999) and elsewhere, "I'm gonna"/"I'm going to" is written as *Ima*, as in (11) and (12), reflecting the reduction of "gonna"/"going to" to "a". Finally, *gots*, as in (13) and (14), is frequently used in place of "got"/"have" in order to highlight urgency, unfairness, power, and, at times, necessity.

Examples of Reduced Words:

(9) Figg murder, crosses burnin' in my front yard
KKK throwin' up rallies but not no more in these parts (Goodie Mob).
'(We) figure murder, crosses burning in my front yard. Klu Klux Klan having rallies but no more in these parts'.

(10) Steada treated, we get tricked
Steada kisses, we get kicked
It's the hard knock life!! (Jay-Z).
'Instead of being treated, we get tricked. Instead of getting kisses, we get kicked'.

(11) I'ma try my best, and if you real like I real (Jay-Z)

(12) I don't know, but I'ma be on, for eons, and eons (Aceyalone).

(13) I just gots to say that, actin large I don't play that (KRS One).

(14) I gots to live (Ice Cube).

CONCLUSION

> Ain't nothin' but a G thang, baaaaabay!
> Two loc'ed out G's so we're craaaaazay!
> Death Row is the label that paaaaays me!
> Unfadable, so please don't try to fade this (Hell yeah)
> (DR. DRE FEATURING SNOOP DOGGY DOGG 1992).

In Hip Hop, the *Word* is both the bible and the law; a source of worship and competition. Through both commercial and underground media, the music and words of Hip Hop transcend language, neighborhoods, cities, and national boundaries resulting in international varieties where marginalized groups and political parties appropriate Hip Hop as a symbol of resistance (e.g., Italy, Spain, and Japan).[16] Irrespective of its popularity, and whether one is introduced to rap through radio, dance clubs, videos, cassette tapes, compact discs, news reports, congressional hearings, documentaries, or talk shows, Hip Hop artists must constantly work to maintain the notion that they are *real* and *true to the streets*.

Unlike the music, rhythm, and sounds of Hip Hop, the particular linguistic ideology of the cultural and speech community—the ideology of the *Word*—is the one aspect which, by definition, remains particularly urban African American.[17] It is the core of the Hip Hop nation, the power, trope, message, and market all in one. The representation of African American culture, popular culture, language, and history as well as social, economic, and political life mediate Hip Hop's notions of reality. Thus, urban African American life is not simply represented in relation to in-group intersubjectivities, but through cultural symbols and sounds, especially linguistic symbols, which signify membership, role, and status so that, as Rossi-Landi (1983: 49) argues, "…words, expressions, messages circulate as commodities." In this respect, the *Word* in Hip Hop is at once the realization of Foucault's *The Discourse on Language* (1972), Bakhtin's *Dialogic Imagination* (1981), and Labov's *Language in the Inner City* (1972).

Hip Hop uses language rules to mediate and construct a present which considers the social and historicized moment as both a transitory and stable place. It produces a frenetic dialectic by interspersing and juxtaposing AAE and GAE conventions and norms (Morgan 1996, 1998). It is this particular energy which attracts new generations of youth who study the history of Hip Hop and *recognize* by interpreting and giving props through crew affiliations, using metaphors, etc. The constant re-working of language style provides a canvas on which youth can experiment with each new generation of members. Thus, unlike much of American throwaway popular culture, Hip Hop celebrates memory and the moment. In so doing, it offers a political and social analysis that, though too often simplistic, maintains a youth consciousness that cries out to the dominant society and the world.

Notes

This study would not have been possible without the assistance and comments from several research assistants at UCLA and Harvard and youth working in various cities. They include: Uma Thambiaya, Sumeeya Chishty Mujahid, Lauren Ferguson, Danielle Beurteaux, Jenigh Garret, Jessica Norwood, Stephen DeBerry, Tarek Captan, and Dionne Bennett. Ben Caldwell, Geneva Smitherman, John Rickford, and John Baugh have provided valuable comments on this project. Funding has been provided by the Humanities Institute of the University of California, Ford Foundation, and Harvard University Graduate School of Education.

1. Most section headings are accompanied by Hip Hop expressions and phrases found in Hip Hop culture.

2. The distinction here is similar to William Labov's 1998 comparison of African American (AA) and General English (GE) components. The main difference is that AAE includes usage across class and other interactions and discourses where speakers use both dialects. GAE refers to middle-class varieties of American English unless otherwise noted.

3. The August 22, 1999, Sunday *New York Times* ran two different columns on the increasing popularity of Hip Hop—one focusing on White youth's avaricious consumption of Hip Hop (Neil Strauss) and the other on the necessity that it maintains its Black focus (Touré).

4. Afrika Baambaata of the Zulu Nation is one of the originators of Hip Hop and often works to maintain unity between artists.

5. Until recently, the music sampled as background to raps was used without permission or credit on Hip Hop recordings (Rose 1994; Wheeler 1992). In contrast, sanctions have always been placed on performers who used words—raps or phrases—without recognizing or acknowledging the author. Consequently, artists usually mention other performers and those who influence them in their raps.

6. The women included in other studies were Queen Latifah, MC Lyte, Yo Yo, Da Brat, and Missy Elliott.

7. Fans of artists submit lyrics and update various versions of a song on www.Ohhla.com. I consider this site the most important since it represents what the audience actually believes an artist is saying and it represents loyalty from the audience or crews that relate to particular artists.

8. American regional urban Spanish refers to Spanish spoken by youth in urban areas. This form of Spanish often includes some English words (e.g., Spanglish). The point here is that youth from Spanish language–identified communities incorporate their language practices within the general urban youth experience.

9. "Semantics" is the term widely used to refer to this phenomenon, though it is actually based on pragmatic relationships.

10. Its Hip Hop meaning has evolved and it has been inverted as illustrated by Chris Rock's excited promotion of his comedy special, "It's gon be ill y'all!" The evolution to predicate adjective occurred with the inverted positive meaning of the word, though in many cases the focus is ambiguous. There are also forms such as *illified* (Stavsky et al. 1995) and *Illtown* which refer to Orange, New Jersey.

11. Several dictionaries are consulted in this process. Those referring to AAE include Major (1994) and Smitherman (1994). Those referring to Hip Hop include "The Unofficial Rap Dictionary" and several earlier sources (e.g., Fab 5 Freddy's Rap Dictionary, *The Source* magazine glossary) though the most common method for current usage was to ask LTs and observe usage in context.

12. Spelling symbol is discussed below. Aceyalone uses *culas* as a bound morpheme though the spelling may be derived from *calculus* as part of a word play on *arithmetic*.

13. The regularizing of spelling conventions is impressive considering the various literacy histories of some of the writers. There is often a move toward iconicity in spelling, though, except in cases like *Amerikkka*, in-depth local knowledge is necessary to locate the sound-letter-symbol relationship.

14. Reclaimed words also include archaic racial insults like *jiggaboo, handkerchief head*, and so on.

15. *Bounce* means 'leave' and *ball* is in reference to someone who has an enviable life.

16. There are now web sites that focus on rap in nearly every language or nation, especially Europe and Asia.

17. By this I mean African American linguistic ideology, which assumes that each locality relies on local knowledge and its own method of representation of life for youth.

References

Adler, B. 1991. *Rap: Portraits and Lyrics of a Generation of Black Rockers.* New York: St. Martin's Press.

Atoon, P. 1992–99. The Rap Dictionary. www.rapdict.org.

Bakhtin, Mikhail M. 1981. *The Dialogic Imagination: Four Essays.* Michael Holquist, ed.; Caryl Emerson & Michael Holquist, trans. Austin: University of Texas Press.

Baugh, John. 1983. *Black Street Speech: Its History, Structure, and Survival.* Austin: University of Texas Press.

Bezilla, Robert, ed. 1993. *America's Youth in the 1990s.* Princeton, NJ: George H. Gallup International Institute.

Chadwick, Bruce A. & Tim B. Heaton. 1996. *Statistical Handbook on Adolescents in America.* Phoenix, AZ: Oryx Press.

De Genova, Nick. 1995. "Gangster rap and nihilism in Black America." *Social Text 43:* 89–132.

DeBerry, Stephen. 1995. *Gender Noise: Community Formation, Identity, and Gender Analysis in Rap Music.* Unpublished manuscript.

Duranti, Alessandro & Donald Brenneis. 1986. "The audience as co-author: An introduction." *Text Special Issue* 6(3): 239–347.

Fab 5 Freddy (Fred Braithwaite). 1992. *Fresh Fly Flavor: Words and Phrases of the Hip-Hop Generation.* Stamford, CT: Longmeadow Press.

Foucault, Michel. 1972. *The Archaeology of Knowledge and the Discourse on Language.* New York: Pantheon Books.

Gilroy, Paul. 1993a. *Small Acts: Thoughts on the Politics of Black Cultures.* London: Serpent's Tail.

———. 1993b. *The Black Atlantic: Modernity and Double Consciousness.* Cambridge, MA: Harvard University Press.

Holt, Grace Sims. 1972. "'Inversion' in Black communication." In Thomas Kochman, ed. *Rappin' and Stylin' Out: Communication in Urban Black America.* Urbana: University of Illinois Press, 152–9.

Jones, K. Maurice. 1994. *The Story of Rap Music.* Brookfield, CT: Millbrook Press.

Labov, William. 1972. *Language in the Inner City: Studies in the Black English Vernacular.* Philadelphia: University of Pennsylvania Press.

Major, Clarence. 1994. *Juba to Jive: A Dictionary of African-American Slang.* New York: Penguin Books.

Morgan, Marcyliena. 1996. "Conversational signifying: Grammar and indirectness among African American women." In Elinor Ochs, Emmanuel Schegloff, & Sandra Thompson, eds. *Interaction and Grammar.* Cambridge: Cambridge University Press, 405–34.

———. 1998. "More than a mood or an attitude: Discourse and verbal genres in African-American culture." In Salikoko S. Mufwene, John R. Rickford, Guy Bailey, & John Baugh, eds. *African-American English: Structure, History, and Use.* London: Routledge, 251–81.

Rickford, John. 1999. *African American Vernacular English: Features, Evolution, Educational Implications.* Oxford: Blackwell.

Rose, Tricia. 1994. *Black Noise: Rap Music and Black Culture in Contemporary America.* Hanover, NH: Wesleyan University Press.

Rossi-Landi, Ferruccio. 1983. *Language as Work and Trade: A Semiotic Homology for Linguistics and Economics.* South Hadley, MA: Bergin & Garvey.

Schieffelin, Bambi & Elinor Ochs. 1986. *Language Socialization Across Cultures.* Cambridge: Cambridge University Press.

Smitherman, Geneva. 1977. *Talkin and Testifyin: The Language of Black America.* Boston: Houghton Mifflin.

———. 1994. *Black Talk: Words and Phrases from the Hood to the Amen Corner.* New York: Houghton Mifflin.

Stavsky, Lois, I. E. Mozeson, & Dani Reyes Mozeson. 1995. *A2Z: The Book of Rap & Hip-Hop Slang.* New York: Boulevard Books.

Toop, David. 1991. *Rap Attack 2: African Rap to Global Hip Hop.* London: Pluto Press.

West, Cornell. 1993. *Race Matters.* Boston: Beacon Press.

Wheeler, Elizabeth. 1992. "'Most of my heroes don't appear on no stamps': The dialogics of rap music." *Black Music Research Journal* 11(2): 193–216.

Discography

Aceyalone. 1995. *All Balls Don't Bounce.* Capitol. 30023.

———. 1998. *A Book of Human Language.* Project Blowed Records. PBRCD002.

Big Daddy Kane. 1988. R.A.W. Cold Chillin'. Music Publishing ASCAP.

Common. 1992. *Can I Borrow a Dollar?* Relativity Records. XE4K0249899.

———. 1994. *Resurrection.* Relativity Records. ZK91017.

———. 1997. *One Day It'll All Make Sense.* Relativity Records. EK91118.

Dr. Dre. 1992. *The Chronic.* Interscope Records. P257128.

Goodie Mob. 1995. *Soul Food.* LaFace Records. 73008-26018-2.

———. 1998. *Still Standing.* LaFace Records. 73008-26147-2.

Ice Cube. 1990. *Amerikkka's Most Wanted.* Fourth and Broadway Records. CDL 57120.

———. 1991. *Death Certificate.* Fourth and Broadway Records. CDL 57055.

———. 1992. *The Predator.* Priority Records. P257185.

———. 1993. *Lethal Injection.* Priority Records. P253876.

Jay-Z. 1996. *Reasonable Doubt.* Priority Records/Freeze Records/Rock-A-Fella Records. PRR50402.

———. 1997. *Vol. 1 My Lifetime.* BMG Music/Roc-A-Fella Records. 3145363922.

———. 1998. *Vol. 2 Hard Knock Life.* Def Jam Recordings/Roc-A-Fella Records. 314558902-2.

———. 1998. *Streets Is Watching.* Roc-A-Fella Records. 3145581322.

KRS-One. 1993. *Return of the Boom Bap*. Jive Records/ Zomba Recording Corp. 01241-41517-2.

———. 1995. *KRS-One*. Jive Records/Zomba Recording Corp. 01241-44073-2.

———. 1997. *I Got Next*. Jive Records/Zomba Recording Corp. 01241-41601-2.

Special Ed. 1989. *Youngest in Charge*. Profile Records. 1280.

Post-reading Questions / Activities

- Why is hip-hop especially associated with adolescents or youth?
- Despite an ideology that sets hip-hop against GAE, much of its language does follow the rules of GAE. How consciously do you think hip-hop artists seek to differentiate their language from GAE? What is the social significance of this difference?
- How might you use Morgan's approach to analyze other forms of popular culture? Select a genre and carry out your analysis. Besides a look at the artistic products themselves, what other information must you include?

Vocabulary

AAE	GAE	rhotics
affix	language ideology	semantic extension
aspect	lexical item	semantic inversion
bound morpheme	lexicon	speech community
CVCV	morphophonemic	tense
free morpheme	phonology	

Suggested Further Reading

Abrahams, R. D. 1974. "Black Talking on the Street." In *Explorations in the Ethnography of Speaking*, edited by Richard Bauman and Joel Sherzer, pp. 240–262. Cambridge: Cambridge University Press.

Baugh, John. 1983. *Black Street Speech: Its History, Structure, and Survival*. Austin: University of Texas Press.

———. 1999. *Out of the Mouth of Slaves: African American Language and Educational Malpractice*. Austin: University of Texas Press.

Chang, Jeff. 2005. *Can't Stop, Won't Stop: A History of the Hip-Hop Generation*. New York: St. Martin's Press.

Herskovitz, Melville J. 1958. *The Myth of the Negro Past*. Boston: Beacon Press.

Labov, William. 1972. *Language in the Inner City: Studies in the Black English Vernacular*. Philadelphia: University of Pennsylvania Press.

Morgan, Marcyeliena. 2002. *Language, Discourse, and Power in African American Culture*. Cambridge: Cambridge University Press.

Rampton, Ben. 1995. *Crossing: Language and Ethnicity Among Adolescents*. London and New York: Longman.

Rickford, John R., and Russell J. Rickford. 2000. *Spoken Soul: The Story of Black English*. New York: Wiley.

Schilling-Estes, Natalie. 2004. "Constructing Ethnicity in Interaction." *Journal of Sociolinguistics* 8/2: 163–195.

Smith, Marc Kelly, and Mark Eleveld. 2003. *The Spoken Word Revolution: Slam, Hip-Hop, and the Poetry of a New Generation*. Naperville, IL: Sourcebooks MediaFusion.

Smitherman, Geneva. 1977. *Talkin and Testifyin: The Language of Black America*. Boston: Houghton Mifflin.

———. 1994. *Black Talk: Words and Phrases from the Hood to the Amen Corner*. Boston: Houghton Mifflin.

Watkins, S. Craig. 2005. *Hip Hop Matters: Politics, Pop Culture, and the Struggle for the Soul of a Movement*. Boston: Beacon Press.

Wolfram, Walt, and Erik R. Thomas. 2002. *The Development of African American English*. Malden, MA: Blackwell.

CHAPTER 28

The Whiteness of Nerds
Superstandard English
and Racial Markedness

Mary Bucholtz
(2001)

Although the United States has no officially recognized "standard" language, many speakers—especially from economically advantaged groups—believe their own variety to be standard.

Adolescents frequently play with language, trying on and discarding identities as they make their way into the world. It is common for teenagers to incorporate role models and activities from popular culture, which in the contemporary United States borrows heavily from African American and Latino culture. Mary Bucholtz studied a group of self-identified "nerd" teenagers who rejected that cultural borrowing, insisting rather that their own language be "superstandard" and thus denuded of features associated with African American speech.

This "whiteness" contrasts notably with the more mainstream "coolness" of other teenage groups, and is demonstrated in the careful pronunciation, the elevated vocabulary, and the standard grammar of the speech of these nerds, even in casual situations where one might expect more casual speech.

"Markedness" is an approach to culture and language that points out that certain practices or categories are considered default, normal, expected, unmarked. Examples of this include men, as opposed to women (it is not necessary to specify "a male business owner" but it is common to mention "a female business owner"), whites instead of blacks ("a college student" may be understood as white, with a need to specify as marked "a black college student"). In the 1990s the study of whiteness was very energetic, as researchers realized that the unmarked category had essentially been neglected. Bucholtz's study grows out of this wave of research.

Reading Questions

- What are nerds? How have the nerds in Bucholtz's study embraced their identity?
- Do all European Americans operate in the "white" culture? Why or why not?
- What does Bucholtz mean when she writes that she provides an example of a white identity "that is nonnormative, nonhegemonic, and highly marked in the local racial economy"?
- Who are the cultural trendsetters in this context? What is "coolness"?
- What is Standard English, and how does "superstandard" English differ from it?
- How do nerds set themselves apart, linguistically, from their peers?

As the explosion of the study of whiteness throughout the past decade continues with little sign of abatement, a corresponding set of critiques about the field's foundational assumptions has also begun to emerge. Perhaps the most cogent of these

From Mary Bucholtz, "The Whiteness of Nerds: Superstandard English and Racial Markedness." *Journal of Linguistic Anthropology* 11(1) (2001): 84–100. Notes have been renumbered and edited. Reproduced by permission of Blackwell Publishing Ltd.

critiques is the concern that in viewing whiteness as a normative, hegemonic, and unmarked racial position, scholars may be unwittingly reifying a singular and static version of whiteness. It is not the concept of racial unmarkedness itself that creates the problem but rather the common scholarly misperception that the unmarked status of whiteness is impervious to history, culture, or other local conditions. On the contrary, markedness theory, which can be traced back to its origins in linguistic theory (Trubetzkoy 1969), has been

whites marked against blacks → also against other whites

usefully extended to a broader semiotic context to provide a model of cultural ideologies, including racial ideologies.

Anthropology offers a perspective on markedness that is more sensitive to the instability of racial marking, as demonstrated most recently and thoroughly by the work of John Hartigan (1999). Through a close ethnographic examination of the intraracial as well as interracial distinctions that shape whiteness in Detroit, Hartigan shows that certain white identities, such as "hillbillies," are racially marked because their class orientation and cultural style separate them from the middle-class white norm. Crucially, interracial ties between hillbillies and African Americans also contribute to the view that hillbillies display a "degraded form of whiteness" (Hartigan 1999:90). Thus while all whites are racially marked vis-à-vis blacks in inner-city Detroit insofar as their race is visible and salient, hillbillies are also racially marked vis-à-vis other whites insofar as their version of whiteness is both recognized and problematized as a racial subject position.

Hartigan's work suggests that there may be other styles of whiteness that are racially marked due to their lack of compliance with local ideologies of racial appropriateness. In particular, it raises the question of whether it is possible for white identities to be racially marked not for transgressing racial boundaries but for maintaining such boundaries too assiduously—that is, for being "too white." [I address] this question by offering an example of a white identity that is nonnormative, nonhegemonic, and highly marked in the local racial economy. This identity, the nerd, is racially marked precisely because individuals refuse to engage in cultural practices that originate across racialized lines and instead construct their identities by cleaving closely to the symbolic resources of an extreme whiteness, especially the resources of language.[1]

Nerds are members of a stigmatized social category who are stereotypically cast as intellectual overachievers and social underachievers. From the Columbine High School killers to Microsoft monopolist Bill Gates, the label *nerd* clearly has negative associations in American culture (especially when, as in these cases, it is used to explain highly antisocial behaviors). It is also, as such examples suggest, a cultural category that is both ideologically gendered (male) and racialized (white), although these dimensions are not always contextually foregrounded. Despite such cultural images, to be a nerd is not an inevitable social death sentence but instead is often a purposeful choice that allows those who embrace this identity to reject locally dominant social norms. In U.S. high schools, where such norms usually center on participation in youth culture, nerds stand out for their resistance to current trends, and more generally for their rejection of coolness as a desirable social goal.[2] As the basic value of youth culture, coolness may be defined as engagement with and participation in the trends and practices of youth culture; it frequently involves a stance of affectlessness as well. In rejecting coolness, students who consider themselves nerds signal their distance from both the practices and the stances of trendier youth. Instead, they embrace the values of nerdiness, primarily intelligence. But

in so doing, especially in contexts of racial diversity, the oppositional identity of the nerd becomes as salient for its racialized position as for its subcultural orientation.

YOUTH CULTURE AND RACIAL APPROPRIATION

One such context is Bay City High School, a large urban high school in the San Francisco Bay Area where I conducted a year of fieldwork in 1995–96.[3] In spite of the school's tremendous racial and ethnic diversity, resulting in the visibility of whiteness as a racial category, white students at Bay City High frequently operated according to an ideological dichotomy between African Americans and European Americans, the two largest racialized groups at the school. This binary put many European American students into a double bind: on the one hand, they were often monitored by their white peers for incursions of blackness into their cultural styles, but on the other hand, many of the practices of European American youth cultures, including linguistic practices, are borrowed from African American teenagers. To remain both culturally and racially acceptable, white students had to maintain a delicate balance between embracing coolness and avoiding cultural practices that were racialized as black by their European American peers.

The black origins of many elements of youth culture in the United States have been well documented; trends in music, dance, fashion, sports, and language in a variety of youth subcultures are often traceable to an African American source (e.g., Kiesling 2001; Lhamon 1990; Rose 1994). This connection is often obscured, however, for as increasing numbers of European American teenagers embrace particular black cultural practices, these practices become detached from blackness—they become *deracialized*, or racially unmarked, at least in the eyes of the white youths who participate in them. At the same time, such practices often lose their urban associations and become normalized in suburban and rural settings as well (witness the expansion of rap in the past decades). Even the concept of coolness itself stems from African American traditions (Morgan 1998). *Blacks are cool by definition*

As a result of their status as cultural innovators and trendsetters, black students at Bay City High, as elsewhere around the country (Solomon 1988), were often viewed by their white counterparts as cool almost by definition. Yet for European American teenagers to adopt elements of African American youth culture before the deracializing process was well under way was to risk being marked by their peers as racially problematic; this was the situation for many white hip-hop fans at the school. Conversely, for white teenagers to refuse to participate in youth culture in any form was likewise problematic, not only culturally but racially. It may be said that appropriate whiteness requires the appropriation of blackness, but only via those black styles that are becoming deracialized and hence no longer inevitably confer racial markedness on those who take them up.

White nerds disrupted this ideological arrangement by refusing to strive for coolness. The linguistic and other social practices that they engaged in indexed an uncool stance that was both culturally and racially marked: to be uncool in the context of the white racial visibility at Bay City High was to be racialized as hyperwhite, "too white." Consequently, the production of nerdiness via the rejection of coolness and the overt display of intelligence was often simultaneously (though not necessarily intentionally) the production of an extreme version of whiteness. Unlike the styles of cool European American students, in nerdiness African American culture and language did not play even a covert role. This is not to say that individuals who were not white never engaged in nerdy practices, but that when they did they could be culturally understood as aligned with whiteness. This phenomenon is illustrated by the fact that, in U.S. culture generally, Asian Americans are ideologically positioned as the "model minority"—that is, the racialized group that most closely approaches "honorary" whiteness—in part because they are ideologically positioned as the nerdy minority, skilled in scientific and technical fields but utterly uncool (see Chun 2001 for research that challenges this ideology). In general, then, white nerds were identifying not against blackness but against trendy whiteness, yet any dissociation from white youth trends entailed a dissociation from the black cultural forms from which those trends largely derive.

Membership in the nerd category, for purposes of this study, was not assigned by me but reported by students themselves, both nerds and non-nerds. Nerdiness is not an essence, of course, but a set of practices, engagements, and stances, and individuals oriented to nerdiness to a greater or lesser degree in their actions. Central to nerdy practice, as I have argued elsewhere (Bucholtz 1998, 1999a), is a particular emphasis on language as a resource for the production of an intelligent and nonconformist identity. I focus on a linguistic practice that simultaneously indexed such identities and marked speakers as non-normatively white: the use of superstandard English.

Language Ideology and Superstandard English

...[I]deologies of race are also ideologies of language, an unsurprising convergence given the long-standing association between ethnoracial and linguistic differentiation promoted both in early linguistic theorizing and in (other) nationalist projects (Bauman and Briggs 2000). The ideology of racial markedness therefore has as a corollary an ideology of linguistic markedness. In particular, the difficulty (which afflicts only white people) in seeing whites as racialized is matched by the difficulty (again, only for whites) in hearing white speakers' language as racialized: as specifically white rather than neutral or normative—or standard. In such an arrangement, unmarked status confers power by allowing whiteness to move through the social world ghostlike, unseen and unheard, evident only in its effects. Likewise, the notion of a linguistic "standard," which in the U.S. context is closely bound up with whiteness (Lippi-Green

1997), implies both unmarkedness (standard as ordinary) and power (standard as regulative).

Although there are numerous sociolinguistic treatments of Standard English from a variety of perspectives (e.g., Crowley 1989; Milroy and Milroy 1999; Silverstein 1996), scholarly opinion is remarkably unanimous. In nearly every discussion Standard English is located in opposition to nonstandard English (and sometimes to other languages); many commentators point out that Standard English, as it is usually defined, is not spoken at all but is a particular register of written language; and a number of authors note that Standard English does not, properly speaking, exist but rather is a prescriptive ideal. Such analyses, valuable as they are for correcting misapprehensions about the nature of sociolinguistic variation, do not always carefully distinguish between the notion of an idealized prescriptive standard, usually based on formal written language, and the spoken vernacular believed most closely to approximate it. This spoken Standard English, as a primarily informal or colloquial variety, differs from formal written Standard English (Carter 1999; Cheshire 1999) but is still granted ideological authority as "the standard." Thus spoken Standard English is positioned in relation not only to nonstandard English but also to what I call *superstandard English*.[4] A linguistic superstandard is a variety that surpasses the prescriptive norm established by the standard. While available to some standard and nonstandard speakers as a special formal—and often written—register, when used as a social rather than situational variety the superstandard is restricted neither to formal contexts nor to written language. For some speakers, the superstandard may be the everyday, "unmarked" variety for ordinary interaction.

Superstandard English contrasts linguistically with Standard English in its greater use of "supercorrect" linguistic variables: lexical formality, carefully articulated phonological forms, and prescriptively standard grammar. It may also go beyond traditional norms of prescriptive correctness, to the point of occasionally over-applying prescriptive rules and producing hypercorrect forms. But the recognition of such difference is at least as ideologically as linguistically motivated. It is precisely because of the robustness of the ideology of Standard English in the United States that those linguistic varieties generally classified as nonstandard—African American Vernacular English foremost among them—are regularly held up as divergent from the standard despite considerable overlap in grammar, phonology, and the lexicon. By the same token, the superstandard need not deviate substantively from the colloquial standard in order to be considered distinctive; because it is marked with respect to Standard English forms, even relatively slight use of supercorrection and hypercorrection can call attention to itself. Superstandard English is therefore a marked variety that may contrast ideologically both with the unmarked colloquial standard and with marked nonstandard English. However, because it draws on the prescriptive standard, it also contributes to the linguistic ideologies that elevate one linguistic variety

Most see whiteness as unmarked linguistically, because whites use standard English.

They almost want to brag about not knowing slang.

over others. How these varieties come to be associated with particular racial positions—that is, how they become racialized styles—is likewise the work of ideology....

NERDS AND SLANG

In their use of superstandard English to set themselves apart from cool students, nerds at Bay City High showed an awareness of some of these ideological dimensions. One characteristic of superstandard English is its lack of current slang. By avoiding particular linguistic forms, speakers can separate themselves from the social category indexically associated with such forms; thus the absence of slang in nerds' speech symbolically distanced them from their cooler peers. When I asked nerdy students to discuss current slang, which other students usually found the most enjoyable part of the interviews I conducted, most expressed dismay at the task and professed unfamiliarity with the terms (one of the rare instances when the nerdy teenagers I spoke to were willing to admit to ignorance). They also removed themselves from the slang terms they did know in various ways, such as providing literal, nonslang definitions for the slang terms I presented to them on slips of paper (Example 1) or offering nonslang terms that convey the same meaning (Example 2).

In Example 1, Bob, Conqueror of the Universe, announces to her friends the slang word (*blood*), an affiliative address term, which is printed on the slip of paper she has selected:[5]

1. Bob: [blːəd]. B-L. O-O-D. The word is [blʌd].... That's the stuff which is inside of your veins. That's the stuff that—I don't know. I haven't gotten to that chapter yet.

Bob turns the task of defining slang terms into a quasi-academic activity by humorously invoking the format of a spelling bee (state the word, spell it, restate it). This academic orientation continues in her formal, literal definition of the term and her allusion to one of her textbooks where the answer can be found. Through such strategies Bob repeatedly distances herself from the use of slang while simultaneously invoking discourse genres and topics associated with intelligence.

Where Bob emphasizes her unfamiliarity with this slang term (even as she reveals her awareness of it through a marked, "black," pronunciation, as discussed below), Erich asserts that the absence of slang in his lexicon is a matter of preference. As with other people, I asked Erich to comment on which of the printed slang terms he uses. In response, Erich rejects slang as a whole while making clear that some of the activities that the words refer to are relevant to his life:

2. Erich: The idea behind the term fits but the term itself doesn't-isn't the way I prefer it to be. Like "kick back." I just prefer something-some normal term.... Like "to relax."... Something like that.

Erich's view of slang involves a process of iconization that brings youthful trendiness into the pragmatic orbit of such lexical items. Just as slang is trendy (not "normal"), so too are its speakers. Erich avoids slang not because of its referential meaning but because of the semiotic meaning that iconization assigns to it. *To avoid seeming trendy*

Of course, students who described themselves as nerds did use some slang, particularly older terms. But these items were often marked in some way in their speech, as when Claire explained why she does not like many people:

3. Claire: When it seems to me that people are really young <i.e., immature>, it's like their emotional response to different things just seems [dʒʌst simz] really w-(.) wacked.

Claire's utterance of the slang term *wack(ed)* is preceded by a false start and a brief pause, both signals of some kind of production difficulty. Whether her hesitance is due to uncertainty about the term or simply its appropriateness in front of me, it highlights the word as unusual for Claire, at least in this context. Supporting this interpretation is her formal, careful language elsewhere in her turn (such as *emotional response* and the full articulation of *just seems*) and the standardized form of the slang term itself, which more usually occurred as *wack*. In adding a Standard English past participial marker to a word popularized by African American students, then, Claire reveals that she is not quite as cool as her use of the term might imply. (At the time of the study, Claire was deliberately trying to become cooler, mainly by smoking marijuana, while retaining her commitment to nerdy ideals like intelligence.) What is more, her standardization of African American Vernacular English grammar is not racially neutral: through fractal recursivity, the two variants Claire chooses between are linked to racial categories. Hence the supercorrect *wacked* is not only more standard but also whiter than the original term.

THE PHONOLOGY OF SUPERSTANDARD ENGLISH

The recursivity seen in Example 3 participates in a widespread racialized language ideology. Among European American students at Bay City High School, a three-way ideological division of English corresponded to similarly ideologically based social divisions: most students of color were thought to speak nonstandard English, most white students were thought to speak colloquial Standard English, and nerds, who did not always incorporate colloquial forms into their speech, were heard to speak an exaggeratedly formal version of Standard English; that is, superstandard English. Superstandard English, unlike Standard English, was a marked linguistic variety among European American students at Bay City High School. Evoking the registers of scholarship and science, nerds' use of superstandard English produced a very different kind of identity than did the colloquial Standard English used by cooler students. And as noted above, because of the ideological force of Standard English, even the slightest use of marked linguistic forms could be sufficient to produce a semiotic distinction. Thus, in nerds' speech, colloquial forms were juxtaposed with superstandard varieties (a violation of Ervin-Tripp's [1973] "co-occurrence rules"). As with most linguistic variables, the use of superstandard features was not categorical.

One linguistic strategy that nerds used to make their speech distinctive was to imbue it with a measured quality, which lent a certain gravitas to their words, particularly as a result of resistance to phonological processes characteristic of colloquial speech, such as consonant-cluster simplification and the phonological reduction of unstressed vowels. Claire's pronunciation in Example 3 above illustrates the former pattern; Example 4 exemplifies the latter. In 4a, Erich describes his difficulties with another student in the school's computer club; in 4b he talks about construction problems in his neighborhood.

4a. He made up all these rules that he sort o- we sort of voted on and I didn't vote on them [ðɛm] because I wasn't there that day, and I have to abide by them [ðɛm].

4b. They're going to [goɪŋ tu] have to [hæv tu] change-close off streets…

Erich's careful pronunciation in these examples is all the more remarkable given that the items in Example 4 occur in linguistic contexts that favor the phonological reduction of these words to 'em, goin' or gonna, and hafta. The lack of stress on both tokens of *them* in 4a, the nasal of *on* preceding the first token, and the grammaticalized function of *going (to)* and *have (to)* in 4b all promote reduced phonological forms, but Erich resists the effects of linguistic environment on his speech.

This precisely enunciated speech style has semiotic connections to literacy: nerdy teenagers frequently used something akin to "reading style" (Labov 1972) even in their spontaneous conversations.[6] Indeed, nerdy students occasionally employed pronunciations based on spelling rather than speech, such as [folk] for *folk* and [hɔŋ kɔŋg] for *Hong Kong*, as well as noncustomary pronunciations of words they encountered in their extensive reading but had not heard uttered aloud: for example, Loden pronounced her pseudonym as [lɑdn̩] rather than the more usual [lodn̩]; the name came from a class assignment. Here again iconization is at work. Nerds' careful speech style approximates in the spoken channel the linguistic forms as they would be written (this is especially clear in the use of spelling pronunciation).

This iconic link between careful speech and reading, moreover, forms the basis of a secondary link between careful speech and intelligence, via the (ideological) indexical association of advanced literacy, extensive education, and high intelligence. And intelligence in turn was associated, at least by nerds, with independent thought: a refusal to go along with the crowd whether in fashion or in phonology. The iconicity between resisting phonological pressure and

resisting peer pressure is a shortcut through the chain of semiotic links already established. Erich invokes this association in Example 5, in which he explains why he thinks the term *sophisticated* applies to himself and his best friend, Micah:

5. Erich: We're not sophisticated in a bad sense, we just have uh much-we're much more advanc:ed (.) in terms of uh (.) (xxx) in terms of the our- our ways of perceiving things, at least (.) myself and Micah. <Mary: *What do you mean by that?*> We don't think- I don't think of anything in a no:rmal way:, <Mary: *Mm.*> like uh and I don't- I use much more, I don't know how to describe it. I don't use all the abbreviations for words? <Mary: *Hm.*> Like most people abbreviate- cut off half the words? For no particular reason? And I don't do that. hhh <Mary: *Like, do you have an example of that?*> Uh uh they they they they cut off the "g" on the end of "tripping" [trɪpɪŋ:] <Mary: *Mm. Right.*> (and end,) N apostrophe. It makes it makes no sense to me.

Erich connects sophistication, in its positive (i.e., non-trendy) sense, both to "advanced" and unconventional perspectives and to careful pronunciation. From the more elevated position that sophistication affords, the colloquial style of youth culture (and of U.S. culture more widely) simply "makes no sense." Here again Erich displays his rather clinical knowledge of slang even as he distances himself from it. His fastidious pronunciation of the slang word *tripping,* with a full superstandard [ŋ], is the linguistic equivalent of holding a particularly distasteful scientific specimen between thumb and forefinger for inspection before it is discarded. This blending of casual and formal language allows Erich to display knowledge without embracing the identity usually associated with such knowledge. Aware of my interest in language, Erich takes a researcherly analytic stance toward his own linguistic style.

SUPERSTANDARD GRAMMAR AND LEXIS

Related to the phonological formality of nerdy speech is its lexical formality. Nerds often chose formal-register polysyllabic variants of Greco-Latinate origin over more colloquial Germanic monosyllables, a long-standing stylistic distinction based on ideologies in the history of the English language. But where in Standard English these lexical items are associated with different registers, in superstandard English they were used across registers. Such lexical items therefore had the indexical effect of making speakers sound smart or learned. In Examples 6a and 6b, Erich discusses how he is different from other students at Bay City High:

6a. I just can't stand people who have all the outward signs of being an extremely stupid person.

6b. My observation is that other people think we're kind of foolish and crazy for the way we do things.

Erich's choice of the Latinate intensifier *extremely* and the nominalized form *observation* invests his discourse with a formal, literate tone; additionally, as in Example 5 both examples invoke a stance of scientific objectivity and detached empiricism, here achieved through such collocations as *all the outward signs* and *My observation is*. In Example 7 Claire takes a similar stance in responding to a question from me about what term she uses for male high-school students:

7. Claire: I-I-I tend to-to refer to (.) the whole (.) um Y chromosome (.) as a guy.

Claire's lexical choices are formal: *tend, refer*. And in invoking the register of biology (*the whole (.) um Y chromosome (.)*) she participates in the same nerdy practice of scientific discourse already exemplified by Erich. The deliberateness of Claire's choice is suggested by the brief pauses that bracket and highlight the term. Like Erich, Claire understands our interaction to be a shared intellectual enterprise, and she repeatedly demonstrates her ability to engage in the scientific discourse of research. Where her use of slang in Example 3 above showed a similar linguistic self-awareness, the effect of this awareness is quite different in each case. The hesitancy in the earlier example is not in evidence here. Instead, the pauses preceding and following the phrase *Y chromosome* operate like quotation marks, not only emphasizing the term but also displaying Claire's consciousness of its markedness. Her utterance thus also illustrates the process of erasure: in highlighting her use of superstandard lexis, she implies the existence of an unmarked (standard) norm. It is at such moments that nerdiness moves from practice to performance, a move that is partly explicable in light of Claire's identity change-in-progress.

Undoubtedly, my role as a researcher triggered this analytic style in some students, and in fact all the teenagers I interviewed engaged in style-shifting to some degree, as compared with their interactions with their friends. However, although all the teenagers I interviewed adjusted their speech to the situation, only those who engaged in other nerdy practices, and often adopted the nerd label as well, used superstandard English. Moreover, such teenagers employed this style even in interaction with their friends, a practice that I witnessed among no other teenagers.

HYPERWHITENESS AND THE REJECTION OF COOL

By distancing themselves from their cool white peers, nerds at Bay City High School created an even greater distance between themselves and their cool black peers. Although nerds did not necessarily understand their linguistic and other social practices in particularly racialized terms, these practices could take on racialized meaning in the context of the ideological black-white dichotomy that shaped whiteness for European American students at Bay City

High. Nerdy teenagers' deliberate avoidance of slang, for example, indexically displayed their remoteness from the trends not only of white youth culture but of black youth culture as well, since African American slang was a primary source of European American slang. While this was not necessarily an intended consequence, Example 1 provides evidence that nerds defined themselves in opposition to both coolness and blackness. Bob first utters the word *blood* (a term used by many African American boys at Bay City High) with stereotyped African American Vernacular English phonology and exaggerated intonation: [bləd]. Her marking of AAVE speakers in this example expresses the ideological distance between her identity and that of African American youth. Her return to her normal pronunciation in the second utterance of this word ([blʌd]) coincides with her attempt to provide a nonslang definition for the term. With this switch, coolness and blackness are recursively linked to each other and separated from the world of nerds.

Likewise, if the use of superstandard English worked to separate nerdy teenagers from their trendy white counterparts who generally spoke a more colloquial variety of Standard English, it also enforced a division between white nerds and most black students at Bay City High, who tended to use AAVE as their primary linguistic variety. The colloquial Standard English favored by cool white teenagers elided to some extent the structural differences between itself and AAVE (thereby allowing them a greater linguistic claim to coolness). Superstandard English, however, reinforced this racialized linguistic divide by exaggerating and highlighting the semiotic elements of Standard English that distinguish it from nonstandard forms of African American English.

Nerdy performances of intellectual ability also produced racialized difference, as suggested by Signithia Fordham's (1996) ethnographic study of academically successful students in a black high school. Fordham notes that some high-achieving African American students were accused by their black peers of "acting white" precisely because of their intellectual performance. This charge was often accompanied by the pejorative epithet *brainiac*, a term that, as Fordham makes clear, is racialized as black in much the same way that the analogous but not synonymous term *nerd* is racialized as white (1996:361, n. 2). At its most negative, the term *brainiac* refers to an African American whose display of intellectual ability indicates a capitulation to European American cultural values. To avoid being labeled *brainiacs,* black students in Fordham's study often hid or downplayed their academic accomplishments and demonstrated their engagement with the concerns of African American youth culture. By contrast, nerdy white teenagers at Bay City High presented themselves as fully engaged in academic endeavors and other intellectual work and showed their indifference toward the youth culture that surrounded them.[7] Such practices constituted a counterhegemonic erasure of the devaluation of academic achievement, but they also erased recognition of accomplished black (and white) students who chose not to openly display their abilities.

Through the use of superstandard English and the semiotic work it performed, nerds at Bay City High were classifiable not simply as white but as hyperwhite. As the most extreme form of whiteness, nerds might be expected to be the best—that is, most unmarked—example of that racial category. But it was precisely the hyperwhiteness of nerds that marked them as atypically white. In U.S. culture generally, the ideological norm of whiteness needs blackness to operate, not only to establish an Other against which to measure itself, but to provide cultural forms for whiteness to appropriate and re-racialize. As groundbreaking scholarship in other disciplines has shown (e.g., Lott 1993; Roediger 1991; Rogin 1996), whiteness is separated from blackness in ideology but inextricable from it in practice. White nerds at Bay City High violated this practice by refusing to appropriate African American cultural and linguistic forms.

Besides expressing their distance from African Americans symbolically and implicitly through linguistic and other social practices, some nerdy students also explicitly stated this ideology of identity. Thus Christine in Example 8 provides an overt statement that African American students are at best useful to know, but only as protection against other African Americans (see also Bucholtz 1999):

8. <In response to my question about whether she knows people in the "hip-hop crowd," a term she takes to mean "black students.">
   Christine: Well I know them.
                I know (.) I know some people.
                Which helps to alleviate situations sometimes.

Such sentiments insert a racialized subtext into the linguistic practices and ideologies that separated nerds from African American youth language and culture. Nerds' dismissal of black cultural practices often led them to discount the possibility of friendship with black students. In this sense, nerdy teenagers' social freedom in rejecting normative youth identities was constrained by their acceptance of normative, ideologically rooted views of their African American schoolmates.

The adoption of a cultural identity that could be read as hyperwhite did not guarantee, however, that nerds promoted what were viewed as "white" interests. During the time I was conducting fieldwork, a great deal of political debate in Bay City centered on the dismantling of affirmative action in California's higher education system. Erich was among the Bay City High School students who organized large-scale protests against these measures; meanwhile, many European American students who drew heavily upon African American youth language and culture did not participate. The wholehearted, or even halfhearted, appropriation of black cultural forms did not ensure that trend-conscious white teenagers would also adopt a political perspective that was sensitive to African American concerns. By the same token, the rejection of the identity associated with trendy white youth as it emerged from and reworked African American cultural practices did not necessarily entail that nerds were similarly disengaged from the politics of race. In challenging dominant ideologies of youth culture, nerds both reinscribed and revised prevailing models of whiteness.

CONCLUSION

White nerds inhabited an ambiguous racial position at Bay City High: they were the whitest group but not the prototypical representatives of whiteness. It is likewise difficult to disambiguate nerds' relationship to white domination. In refusing to exercise the racial privilege upon which white youth cultures are founded, nerds may be viewed as traitors to whiteness. But engaging in nerdy practices may itself be a form of white privilege, since these practices were not as readily available to teenagers of color and the consequences of their use more severe. The use of superstandard English is thus both a rejection of the cool white local norm and an investment in a wider institutional and cultural norm. This ambivalence toward normative practice is evident in Erich's discourse: he uses "normal" language rather than slang, but he does not "think of anything in a normal way." In the first use, he aligns himself with "normalness" and against trendiness; in the second use, he disaligns himself from both "normalness" and trendiness. These two valences of *normal* are akin to the two valences of whiteness in nerd identity: nerds at Bay City High were not normal because they were too normal, not (unmarkedly) white because they were too white.

In other words, the linguistic and other social practices by which nerds were culturally marked with respect to other, cooler, white students, also caused them to be racially marked with respect to both blacks and whites. While the semiotic processes of iconization, fractal recursivity, and erasure allowed nerds to challenge local ideologies based on subcultural identity, these same processes also imposed a set of racial ideologies on both nerds and their cooler counterparts, black and white. Thus although the marked hyperwhiteness of nerds undermines the racial project of whiteness as a normative and unmarked construct, it may also shore up racial ideologies of difference and division.

Notes

I am grateful to Karen Brodkin, John Clark, Alessandro Duranti, Sara Trechter, and two anonymous reviewers for comments and suggestions. All remaining weaknesses are my own responsibility.

1. Although, as I discuss below, nerds and similar identities exist in other racialized groups,... my focus is solely on white nerds. Some of the speakers I discuss identify as Jewish to varying degrees, but while many Jews understand themselves to be racially marked by their ethnicity (Modan 2001), hence "not quite white," these teenagers did not discuss their ethnicity in similar terms. It appears that in the Bay City High School context ethnicity was less salient than a racialized cultural style. However, Brodkin (1998:31) points to the pattern, early in the twentieth century, of Jewish academic achievement in higher education, "a setting where disparagement of intellectual pursuits and the gentleman C were badges of distinction." Hence

there may be a historical white ideology linking Jewishness and nerdiness, although such an ideology was not operative at Bay City High, except through ironic exploitation by Jews themselves.

2. While it may be argued that nerds participate in their own version of youth culture rather than rejecting it altogether, the practices associated with nerdiness are not primarily associated with youth nor do they perform an age-based identity in the same way as the practices associated with (dominant) youth culture.

3. All names and identifying information have been changed. Speakers chose their own pseudonyms.

4. I use the terms *superstandard* and *supercorrect* to distinguish between true hypercorrect language use (that is, use that violates a rule of descriptive grammar) and strict adherence to prescriptive grammatical rules accompanied by the use of other formal language features. As discussed below, however, hypercorrection is often part of superstandard English.

5. Transcription conventions are as follows: a period indicates falling intonation; a question mark indicates rising intonation; a comma indicates fall-rise intonation; a hyphen indicates a self-interruption that breaks the intonation unit; a dash indicates a self-interruption that breaks a word; between words, a hyphen indicates rapid speech; a (.) indicates a pause of less than one-tenth of a second; ellipsis indicates deleted text; (xxx) indicates unintelligible speech; hhh indicates laughter; angled brackets indicate transcriber comments or turns that are not the focus of analysis; and phonetic transcription appears in square brackets.

6. The resistance to assimilation processes does not, of course, have a single social meaning. In other contexts, researchers have found that some gay men may also use careful articulation (Campbell-Kibler et al. 2001; Walters cited in Barrett 1997:192) without any apparent association with bookishness. In fact, it is quite unlikely that careful articulation has only a single meaning even for nerds.

7. It is important to note, however, that contrary to the claims of conservative commentators like John McWhorter (2000), African American students do not show any less enthusiasm for school—and in fact may show more—than European Americans (see Voelkl 1997).

References

Barrett, Rusty. 1997. The "Homo-Genius" Speech Community. *In* Queerly Phrased: Language, Gender, and Sexuality. Anna Livia and Kira Hall, eds. pp. 181–201. New York: Oxford University Press.

Bauman, Richard, and Charles L. Briggs. 2000. Language Philosophy as Language Ideology: John Locke and Johann Gottfried Herder. *In* Regimes of Language: Ideologies, Polities, and Identities. Paul V. Kroskrity, ed. pp. 139–204. Santa Fe, NM: School of American Research Press.

Brodkin, Karen. 1998. How Jews Became White Folks and What That Says about Race in America. New Brunswick, NJ: Rutgers University Press.

Bucholtz, Mary. 1998. Geek the Girl: Language, Femininity, and Female Nerds. *In* Gender and Belief Systems: Proceedings of the Fourth Berkeley Women and Language

Conference. Natasha Warner, Jocelyn Ahlers, Leela Bilmes, Monica Oliver, Suzanne Wertheim, and Melinda Chen, eds. pp. 119–131. Berkeley, CA: Berkeley Women and Language Group.

——. 1999a. "Why Be Normal?": Language and Identity Practices in a Community of Nerd Girls. Language in Society 28(2): 203–223.

——. 1999b. You da Man: Narrating the Racial Other in the Linguistic Production of White Masculinity. Journal of Sociolinguistics 3(4): 443–460.

Campbell-Kibler, Kathryn, Robert J. Podesva, and Sarah J. Roberts. 2001. Sharing Resources and Indexing Meanings in the Production of Gay Styles. *In* Language and Sexuality: Contesting Meaning in Theory and Practice. Kathryn Campbell-Kibler, Robert J. Podesva, Sarah J. Roberts, and Andrew Wong, eds. Stanford, CA: CSLI Press.

Carter, Ronald. 1999. Standard Grammars, Spoken Grammars: Some Educational Implications. *In* Standard English: The Widening Debate. Tony Bex and Richard J. Watts, eds. pp. 149–166. London: Routledge.

Cheshire, Jenny. 1999. Spoken Standard English. *In* Standard English: The Widening Debate. Tony Bex and Richard J. Watts, eds. pp. 129–148. London: Routledge.

Chun, Elaine W. 2001. The Construction of White, Black, and Korean American Identities through African American Vernacular English. Journal of Linguistic Anthropology 11 (1): 52–64.

Crowley, Tony. 1989. Standard English and the Politics of Language. Urbana: University of Illinois Press.

Ervin-Tripp, Susan. 1973. The Structure of Communicative Choice. *In* Language Acquisition and Communicative Choice. Anwar S. Dil, ed. pp. 302–373. Stanford, CA: Stanford University Press.

Fordham, Signithia. 1996. Blacked Out: Dilemmas of Race, Identity, and Success at Capital High. Chicago: University of Chicago Press.

Hartigan, John, Jr. 1999. Racial Situations: Class Predicaments of Whiteness in Detroit. Princeton, NJ: Princeton University Press.

Irvine, Judith T. 2001. "Style" as Distinctiveness: The Culture and Ideology of Linguistic Differentiation. *In* Style and Sociolinguistic Variation. John R. Rickford and Penelope Eckert, eds. Cambridge: Cambridge University Press.

Kiesling, Scott. 2001. Stances of Whiteness and Hegemony in Fraternity Men's Discourse. Journal of Linguistic Anthropology 11 (1): 101–115.

Labov, William. 1972. The Isolation of Contextual Styles. *In* Sociolinguistic Patterns. pp. 70–109. Philadelphia: University of Pennsylvania Press.

Lhamon, W. T. 1990. Deliberate Speed: The Origins of a Cultural Style in the American 1950s. Washington, DC: Smithsonian Institution Press.

Lippi-Green, Rosina. 1997. English with an Accent: Language, Ideology, and Discrimination in the United States. New York: Routledge.

Lott, Eric. 1993. Love and Theft: Blackface Minstrelsy and the American Working Class. New York: Oxford University Press.

McWhorter, John H. 2000. Losing the Race: Self-Sabotage in Black America. New York: Free Press.

Milroy, James, and Lesley Milroy. 1999. Authority in Language: Investigating Standard English. 3rd ed. London: Routledge.

Modan, Gabriella. 2001. White, Whole Wheat, Rye: Jews and Ethnic Categorization in Washington, D.C. Journal of Linguistic Anthropology 11 (1): 116–130.

Morgan, Marcyliena. 1998. More than a Mood or an Attitude: Discourse and Verbal Genre in African American Culture. *In* The Structure of African American English. Salikoko Mufwene, John R. Rickford, Guy Bailey, and John Baugh, eds. pp. 251–281. New York: Routledge.

Roediger, David R. 1991. The Wages of Whiteness: Race and the Making of the American Working Class. London: Verso.

Rogin, Michael. 1996. Blackface, White Noise: Jewish Immigrants in the Hollywood Melting Pot. Berkeley: University of California Press.

Rose, Tricia. 1994. Black Noise: Rap Music and Black Culture in Contemporary America. Hanover, NH: Wesleyan University Press/University Press of New England.

Silverstein, Michael. 1996. Monoglot "Standard" in America: Standardization and Metaphors of Linguistic Hegemony. *In* The Matrix of Language: Contemporary Linguistic Anthropology. Don Brenneis and Ronald K. S. Macaulay, eds. pp. 284–306. Boulder, CO: Westview Press.

Solomon, R. Patrick. 1988. Black Cultural Forms in Schools: A Cross National Comparison. *In* Class, Race, and Gender in American Education. Lois Weis, ed. pp. 249–265. New York: SUNY Press.

Trubetzkoy, Nicholas. 1969. Principles of Phonology. Berkeley: University of California Press.

Voelkl, Kristin E. 1997. Identification with School. American Journal of Education 105(3): 294–318.

Post-reading Questions / Activities

- Did your high school and does your college have the social category of *nerd*? Did people in this category speak as do the students Bucholtz describes?
- Observe college students belonging to different social groups and assign their language, generally, to the categories "nonstandard," "standard," and "superstandard." Is there agreement among your fellow students about whose speech belongs in what categories? Why do you think this is the case?

Vocabulary

AAVE	marked, markedness	slang
hypercorrect	phonology, phonological	standard
iconization	pragmatic	superstandard
language ideology	prescription, prescriptive	token
lexical	register	
lexis	semiotic	

Suggested Further Reading

Eckert, Penelope. 1989. *Jocks and Burnouts: Social Categories and Identity in the High School.* New York and London: Teachers College, Columbia University.

Frankenberg, Ruth. 1993. *White Women, Race Matters: The Social Construction of Whiteness.* Minneapolis: University of Minnesota Press.

Milroy, James, and Lesley Milroy. 1999. *Authority in Language: Investigating Standard English.* 3d ed. London: Routledge.

Roediger, David R. 1999. *The Wages of Whiteness: Race and the Making of the American Working Class.* London: Verso.

CHAPTER 29

Language Ideology and Racial Inequality
Competing Functions of Spanish in an Anglo-Owned Mexican Restaurant

Rusty Barrett
(2006)

Identity—like other symbolic behavior—takes on meaning through contrast. People often construct ideas about the others with whom they frequently interact, though such ideas may not be held consciously. These ideas, or better, ideologies, bring with them notions of relative value and power.

In 1995 Jane Hill wrote an article in American Anthropologist *called "Language, Race, and White Public Space," in which she introduced the idea of "Mock Spanish." This is the notion that Spanish is associated in many Anglos' minds with laziness, with lack of education, and with humor. Speakers pretend to speak Spanish, flaunting their miserable accents, in a way that emphasizes their privilege as white.*

Rusty Barrett explores this ideology, as well as other aspects of ethnic and linguistic identity, in the setting of a single Anglo-owned Mexican restaurant in Texas. Barrett spent three years working and observing at this restaurant, mostly as a bartender. Observing interactions between workers, mostly Spanish-speaking, and managers, mostly English-speaking, permitted him to see how inequalities were enacted and carried out in this workplace, a microcosm of the larger forces in the United States. Many settings in the world have similar interactions between migrants and the dominant group, where language serves as a carrier of social meaning and difference.

Who is responsible for misunderstanding in an interaction? Responsibility falls on two potentially different actors: the person who caused it to happen, and the person who must deal with the consequences. According to Barrett, it is the inadequate Spanish used by managers that tends to cause lack of comprehension, but it is the workers who are left having to cope with incomplete or incomprehensible instructions. The way each group regards the other is not usually flattering or even sympathetic, and we can see this enacted in the minute-by-minute interactions at this probably typical restaurant. Indeed John Gumperz demonstrated something similar in his 1982 work on "crosstalk" where South Asian restaurant workers' falling question intonation was interpreted by native British speakers as rude though for them it was a normal intonation.

Interethnic interactions do not inevitably lead to friendship, understanding, or assimilation. Barrett's microanalysis of such interactions shows us the many forces at play.

Reading Questions

- What are the linguistic backgrounds, generally, of the kitchen versus wait staff at the restaurant Barrett studied? How do these differences correlate with social status?
- Barrett distinguishes between "Mock Spanish" and "actual Spanish." How does he differentiate them? Do you think this distinction is clear?

Rusty Barrett, "Language Ideology and Racial Inequality: Competing Functions of Spanish in an Anglo-Owned Mexican Restaurant." *Language in Society* 35 (2006): 163–204. Reprinted with the permission of Cambridge University Press.

- What are some of the linguistic peculiarities of the managers' Mock Spanish?
- What kinds of misunderstandings resulted from "language barriers"? What kinds of barriers were there?
- What benefits did the Spanish speakers derive from speaking Spanish?

This [chapter] examines the ways in which language ideology influences interactions between monolingual Spanish-speaking workers and Anglo (U.S. English speakers of European ancestry) managers and workers in a Mexican restaurant in Texas. Because of the widespread acceptability of "grossly non-standard and ungrammatical" Mock Spanish (Hill 1998:682), Anglo directives in Spanish (or in English with Mock Spanish elements) are often misinterpreted by Spanish speakers. The Anglos' disregard for producing grammatical (or even understandable) forms in Spanish shifts the communicative burden almost entirely to the Spanish speaker, who is often left with insufficient semantic content for interpreting Anglo speech. Anglo managers typically do not question whether their limited use of Spanish is sufficient for communicative success, and Anglos typically assume that the Spanish speakers are responsible for incidents resulting from miscommunication. A directive that fails (in that the requested act is done incorrectly or not done at all) is almost always interpreted on the basis of racist stereotypes of Spanish speakers as lazy, indignant, uncooperative, illiterate, or unintelligent. The Anglo use of Spanish marginalizes Spanish speakers within interactions, demonstrating a general disregard for Spanish speakers as cultural actors. The Anglo use of Mock Spanish to index a particular Anglo ethnic stance diminishes the ability of Spanish to serve a communicative function. The ideology of Mock Spanish reinforces racial inequality by restricting the agency of Latino workers.

In contrast, Spanish-speaking employees often use Spanish as a tool of solidarity and resistance. The fact that Anglos pay little attention to what is said in Spanish allows the Latino workers to use Spanish as a means of controlling resources in the restaurant. The lack of attention to Spanish also makes it possible for Spanish speakers to talk openly about (and sometimes mock) Anglo workers and managers, even when the referent is able to hear what is being said. Although Anglo uses of Spanish may be seen as ways of limiting the agency of Spanish speakers, Latino workers use Spanish to develop an alternative linguistic market in which individual agency may be asserted in different ways.

Hill 1998 argues that language ideology plays a role in delineating "white public space" through the use of varieties such as Mock Spanish (Hill 1993, 1995). In Mock Spanish, Anglo speakers incorporate Spanish words into otherwise English discourse to "create a jocular or pejorative 'key'" (Hill 1998:682). Hill (1998:682–83) lists the following strategies found in Mock Spanish:

Semantic pejoration of Spanish words—the use of positive or neutral Spanish words in humorous

or negative contexts (e.g., *nada* to mean "less than nothing," *peso* to convey "cheap")

Mock Spanish euphemism—the use of obscene or scatological Spanish words in place of English equivalents (e.g., the use of *cojones*)

The use of Spanish grammatical elements—the addition of the "Spanish" suffix *+o* to nouns and the use of the definite article *el* (e.g., *el cheapo*)

Hyperanglicization—parodic pronunciations and orthographic representations that reflect an exaggerated English phonology (e.g. *Fleas Navidad* on a Christmas card).

These strategies of Mock Spanish are used in Anglo speech designed for Anglo audiences and typically index racist stereotypes of Latinos. Although Mock Spanish usually carries a negative message, speakers of Mock Spanish are likely to view their use of Spanish as indexing positive personal qualities:

> Mock Spanish accomplishes the "elevation of whiteness" in two ways: first, through directly indexing valuable and congenial personal qualities of speakers, but importantly, also by the same type of indirect indexicality that is the source of its negative and racializing messages. It is through indirect indexicality that using Mock Spanish constructs "White public space," an arena in which linguistic disorder on the part of Whites is rendered invisible and normative, while the linguistic behavior of historically Spanish-speaking populations is highly visible and the object of constant monitoring. (Hill 1998:684)

In the context of a linguistic marketplace where Spanish is undervalued, Anglo use of Mock Spanish in interactions with Latinos serves as a "strategy of condescension" (Bourdieu 1991). Because Spanish is racialized to be an iconic marker of Latino ethnic identity (cf. Urciuoli 1996:15–40), the presence of any Spanish (even grossly distorted or obscene Spanish) indexes an acknowledgment of the racial difference in an interaction. Although the use of Mock Spanish often does little more than index the race of a Latino interlocutor, Anglos may interpret the use of any Spanish at all as an index of egalitarian attitudes toward Latinos and, by extension, general sympathy with minority groups. Speakers of Mock Spanish may thus produce offensive racialized meanings while simultaneously interpreting their utterances as a reflection of an open-minded (explicitly nonracist) point of view.

In the interactions presented [here], the language ideology of Mock Spanish leads to inequality in the communicative burden between native and nonnative speakers of English (Lippi-Green 1997, Lindeman 2002, Perkins &

Milroy 1997). While Spanish speakers must carefully monitor their use of both Spanish and English to ensure that they will be listened to, Anglo English speakers regularly produce ungrammatical and offensive forms of Spanish with no concern for how this Spanish might be perceived by actual Spanish speakers (cf. Hill 1993, 1995, 1998).

Mock Spanish as Linguistic Appropriation

Hill's groundbreaking work on Mock Spanish has inspired linguists to pay closer attention to Mock varieties (cf. Ronkin & Karn 1999, Mesthrie 2002, Chun 2004). All of these Mock varieties have certain common traits. They all reduce the grammar of the mocked variety to a stereotyped representation of the language. Mock varieties also index racist ideologies and reinscribe racist stereotypes, operating as forms of symbolic revalorization (Woolard & Schieffelin 1994, Walters 1995), in which attitudes toward particular language varieties stand in for (proscribed) expressions of racial or ethnic prejudice. Mock Ebonics (Ronkin & Karn 1999), for example, is typically used to reproduce racist humor directed against "speakers of Ebonics" rather than "African Americans." The racist nature of Mock Ebonics and Mock Asian (Chun 2004) is fairly transparent. The use of Mock Asian forms such as *ching-chong-ching-chong* (Chun 2004) to an Asian American is likely to be understood as a form of hate speech. The racist nature of Mock Spanish is covert, however, so that Anglos typically see their use of it as humorous, indexing a positive social identity (Hill 1998:683).

Despite its name, Mock Spanish may be better understood as an example of appropriation and not generally a form of overt mocking. Although Hill compares Mock Spanish to the crossover of words from African American English (AAE) into White English, she claims that the two cases are quite different. In actual usage, however, Mock Spanish is in many ways much closer to AAE crossover than to other Mock varieties. For example, Hill notes that Mock Spanish may be used in discourse unrelated to race and in speech to apparent Spanish speakers (1998:684). While Mock Ebonics and Mock Asian are overtly mocking racial caricatures, Mock Spanish patterns more like AAE crossover in that its context-of-occurrence is largely unrestricted. For example, white speakers may just as well say *Whassup?* to an apparent speaker of AAE as they would say *¿Que pasa?* to an apparent speaker of Spanish.

The label (or misnomer) "Mock Spanish" obscures the importance of Anglo Spanish as a form of linguistic appropriation. Hill recognizes the affinity between white appropriation of AAE and Mock Spanish, but she argues that AAE and White English are so "thoroughly entwined" that white usage of AAE is often indeterminate (1998:685). Words from AAE are readily borrowed into white usage, quickly losing their indexical association with speakers of AAE (cf. Smitherman 1994; Morgan 2001, 2002; Bucholtz 2004). Mock Spanish forms, however, are easily recognized as "Spanish" and maintain their indexical association with

Spanish speakers. This difference is quite important in understanding both forms of appropriation, but the distinction might also simply result from the fact that AAE crossover is a form of dialect borrowing, while Mock Spanish involves borrowing from another language. Hill's focus on the difference between the two forms of appropriation fails to highlight their numerous similarities.

The affinity between these two forms of appropriation can be illustrated with Hill's example of the use of Mock Spanish in the film *Terminator II: Judgment Day*. In teaching the Terminator "the way people talk," the child John Connor mixes Mock Spanish with other forms of slang, including the AAE crossover *to chill*:

(1) From *Terminator II: Judgment Day* (Cameron & Wisher 1991)
    John Connor: You gotta listen to the way people talk. You don't say "affirmative" or some shit like that. You say, "No problemo." And if someone comes off to you with an attitude, you say "Eat me." And if you want to shine them on it's "Hasta la vista, baby."
    Terminator: Hasta la vista, baby.
    John Connor: Yea, "Later dickwad." And if someone gets upset, you say "Chill out."

The phrase *chill out* is a fairly recent (i.e., probably not indeterminate in 1991) appropriation from AAE (cf. Smitherman 1994:78). In the Terminator's crash course in language socialization, Mock Spanish is linked both to AAE crossover and to more general "slang" forms such as *Eat me*.

Bucholtz 2004 argues that young white speakers see their use of AAE as the introduction of new slang forms, and not as something like second-dialect acquisition. The slang dictionary at urbandictionary.com (cf. Bucholtz 2004), which invites individuals to submit examples of slang, contains numerous examples of both AAE and Spanish appropriations. Spanish words submitted as slang include Mock Spanish standards such as *nada, hasta la vista*, and *cojones* as well as examples such as *chica* 'girl', *hombre* 'man', and *madre* 'mother'.[1] Eble (2004:376) defines slang as "deliberate alternative vocabulary that sends social signals," noting that slang vocabulary "rarely refers to meanings that the ordinary vocabulary does not have words to express" (2004:377). AAE crossover terms and Mock Spanish may both serve the same functions as general slang vocabulary. Appropriated terms serve as alternatives to "regular" vocabulary that may be used to index social affect. Thus, it is not surprising that speakers who visit urbandictionary.com freely submit forms from both AAE and Spanish as examples of what they see as "slang."

Bucholtz demonstrates that for some young white speakers, the simple addition of the article *da* to a noun may create a new slang form. Lexical entries submitted to urbandictionary.com include an abundance of *da*-formations, including *da club, da band, da fuck, da cheese,* and *da sex*. The *da* is adopted from a stereotype of the AAE pronunciation of *the* with an initial voiced stop and generalized from appropriated forms such as *da man* or *da bomb*. This use of *da* is identical to the use of the article *el* in Mock Spanish forms like *el cheapo*; indeed, the slang entries at urbandictionary.com include numerous cases of *el-* formations, many with the additional *+o* suffix. Examples include *el asso bandito*, *el pervert*, *el hobo*, *el homo*, *el bitcho*, and *el bastard* ("more of a bastard than the normal bastard"). In all these examples, the addition of a racially marked definite article (*da* or *el*) creates what white speakers understand as a new, alternative slang noun. As with AAE, the ideology of Spanish as colloquial or "slangy" licenses Anglo norms for the use of appropriated forms....

Chalupatown Restaurant[2]

Chalupatown is an Anglo-owned Mexican restaurant in Texas. The restaurant seats approximately 200 dining customers with a bar/waiting area that seats an additional 100 customers. Chalupatown is a successful restaurant with a clientele which is overwhelmingly middle-class and Anglo. My research at Chalupatown was conducted over the course of three years, when I worked there full-time—primarily as a bartender and occasionally as a server. The data were collected during the third year, after I had finished my Ph.D. and continued working in the restaurant while searching for an academic position.

Lindquist (2002, 2004) argues that bartenders are naturally occurring ethnographers because of their status as participant-observers in the social life surrounding the bar itself. That is, bartenders are simultaneously central to and removed from the social action of the surrounding bar (Lindquist 2002:300). A bartender holds an integral position in the culture of the bar and is central to interactions between customers. However, because bartenders are not actual customers, they maintain "outsider" status in relation to customers involved in bar culture. The position of restaurant bartenders is somewhat different from the position described by Lindquist of working in a bar. Restaurant bartenders are responsible for making drinks both for customers at the bar and for servers waiting on customers dining in the restaurant. The layout of Chalupatown included two bars, one for serving drinking customers and another for filling orders from servers. The back server bar was connected to a small wait station that connected the bar and the kitchen. Tickets for drink orders from servers would print out in the back bar, where the bartender would prepare the drinks and place them on the counter for servers to pick up. Because the bartender making drinks for servers worked right next to the wait station, interactions between servers and the bartender were quite frequent. During busy times, tickets would usually print continuously and servers frequently waited by the bar (either at the counter where drinks were given out or in the wait station) for their orders to be filled. The social relationship of the bartender working in the back bar was thus similar to that described by Lindquist, except that the interactions were with servers rather than with customers. Because the bar was some distance from the majority of customers, servers frequently used the area to hold discussions about their customers or activities occurring elsewhere in the restaurant.

Bartenders were also responsible for retrieving necessary supplies (liquor, carbon dioxide tanks, fruit for garnishing drinks, etc.) from the kitchen and storerooms to ensure that both bars were fully stocked. The bartender working the day shift performed prep work for the night shift bartenders, such as slicing fruit to garnish drinks, conducting inventory, and restocking beer and liquor. All the items that the daytime bartender required were in a storeroom that could be reached only by passing through the kitchen. During day shifts, there were very few drink orders or bar customers, so the bartender spent a large part of the day working in the storeroom. Because the daytime bartender spent a lot of time in the back part of the restaurant, interactions during these shifts were primarily with the kitchen staff rather than with the servers.

During the three years that I worked at Chalupatown, I alternated positions but primarily worked in the back (server) bar at night and during day shifts. I thus had many more interactions with both servers and kitchen workers than with actual bar customers. Because the day bartender spent a large part of the day in the back of the restaurant, I regularly observed interactions between managers and kitchen workers. After obtaining permission to conduct research from the restaurant's highest-ranking manager, I began collecting examples of Anglo Spanish. The initial motivation for this research was to examine the grammatical structure of Spanish-English alternations in the speech of Anglo workers and managers. It became clear, however, that the ethnographic aspects of Anglo Spanish were much more interesting than their linguistic structure, and I began collecting ethnographic notes in addition to recording instances of Anglo Spanish.

I transcribed written notices in the restaurant, and transcribed and collected tickets for food orders. Because of the difficulties of using recording equipment in a restaurant setting and the brief, fleeting nature of many of the interactions, I recorded verbal directives and ethnographic notes by hand. Employees were expected to carry a notepad and pen at all times, so it was usually possible to transcribe interactions as they occurred or immediately after. Other workers were aware that I was conducting research, and other Anglo workers would sometimes tease me for taking notes or ask me not to write down something that they had said. This [chapter] examines these interactions in terms of the ethnography of speaking. The analysis is inherently both subjective and local. Although I take a close look at interactions in a single restaurant, my experiences in other restaurants and discussions with workers from a variety of other restaurants outside Texas suggest that the sort of interactions found at Chalupatown are not unique. The choice to focus on data where issues of language and race are particularly salient ignores the majority of intraethnic interactions in the restaurant. Because of the focus on data involving issues of race, a number of the examples may be highly offensive.

The kitchen workers were evenly divided between workers originally from Guatemala and immigrants from Mexico. Because I had regular contact with the kitchen workers and was able to communicate with them in Spanish, I became close friends with a number of them (for which I was frequently ridiculed by Anglo co-workers). My position in the restaurant was unique in that I was an "in-group" participant in social networks of both servers and kitchen workers. I was, however, simultaneously "out-group" for both groups of workers. My friendships with Spanish-speaking employees made me an outsider for some Anglo workers, who would tease me for knowing the names of songs played in the kitchen, for spending time on the "wrong side" of town, and for socializing with Spanish speakers outside of work. As an Anglo I was also an outsider among the Latino kitchen workers, who joked about my ethnic status. Because of my outsider status in the kitchen, workers frequently asked me for favors that would require English or familiarity with American bureaucracy, such as obtaining identification cards, opening bank accounts, or making calls to help in searching for apartments.

During this research, the restaurant maintained around 105 employees, including about 45 kitchen workers and about 45 wait staff workers, with 10 managers. The numbers fluctuated continually owing to a very high employee turnover rate (common in restaurant work). The turnover was so frequent that most of the employees worked in the restaurant for only a few months or even less. All the kitchen workers were Spanish-speaking or bilingual first-generation immigrants from Mexico or Guatemala. The wait staff was overwhelmingly Anglo. The number of first-generation

Mexican servers ranged from zero to two, while the number of monolingual English-speaking Mexican American servers never rose above five. Managers were also predominantly Anglo. During the first two years of this research, there were two Mexican American (bilingual) managers, although both no longer worked in the restaurant during the third year. Tables 1 and 2 show the approximate breakdown of kitchen and wait staff at Chalupatown.[3]

In both wait staff and kitchen staff, employees in lower-paying positions have the opportunity to be promoted. Hosts may become servers and servers may become managers. Dishwashers may be promoted to busers and busers may be promoted to prep cooks, who in turn may be promoted to line cooks. Because more senior employees in higher positions had experience with other jobs in the restaurant, they were frequently used as a resource for newer employees. However, because managers were promoted from the wait staff (but never from kitchen staff), several Anglo managers were not entirely familiar with the regular work responsibilities of members of the kitchen staff. This lack of knowledge often contributed to problems that arose in interactions between kitchen workers and managers, particularly in cases where the manager was not sure of the usual procedure for completing a particular task.

Despite the relatively even numbers of kitchen and wait staff employees, differences in work responsibilities resulted in an uneven distribution between the two groups during the actual course of the workday. Table 3 shows the approximate number of employees in each job during the course of an average weekday.

Table 1. Kitchen Staff at Chalupatown (order reflects relative status)

Job Title	Primary Responsibilities	Approximate Number
Line cooks	Preparing food as it is ordered, cleaning line kitchen	14 (1 female, 2 bilinguals)
Prep cooks	Preparing food for line, making salsa, tamales, and other items that are prepared in advance, cleaning prep kitchen	8 (all male, 1 bilingual)
Tortilla makers	Making tortillas and heating tortillas as they are ordered	3 (all female)
Busers	Clearing tables, cleaning seating area and restrooms, maintaining salsa bar and drink stations	12 (all male)
Dishwashers	Washing and stocking dishes, unloading and stocking food deliveries, squeezing orange juice by hand, occasional work with prep cooks	8 (all male)

Table 2. Wait Staff at Chalupatown (order reflects relative status)

Job Title	Primary Responsibilities	Approximate Number*
Manager	Overseeing daily operation, scheduling, inventory, and sales reports; checking server and bartender daily reports and making alterations to server tickets (voids, discounts, etc.)	10 (4 male, 3 bilingual)
Server	Serving customers, making tea and coffee, conducting side work (filling salt shakers, sweeping, etc.)	30 (14 male, 2 bilingual)
Bartender	Serving customers, filling drink orders, stocking and cleaning bar area	9 (2 female, 1 bilingual)
Host	Seating customers, maintaining waitlist, side work (cleaning menus, etc.)	6 (2 male)

*The numbers are approximate due to regular fluctuations resulting from employee turnover.

Table 3. Number of Workers in Each Position over the Course of a Day

	Primarily English-Speaking Employees				Primarily Spanish-Speaking Employees				
Time	Manager	Host	Bar	Server	Line	Bus	Dish	Prep	Tortilla
6–9 A.M.	1		1		2		2	3	1
10 A.M.	2		1	2	4	1	2	4	1
11 A.M.	2	1	1	4	5	3	2	4	1
12 P.M.	2	3	1	11	5	4	2	3	1
1 P.M.	2	3	1	11	5	4	2	3	1
2–4 P.M.	2	1	2	3	5	4	2	3	1
5 P.M.	2	3	2	7	6	5	2		2
6 P.M.	2	3	3	14	8	5	3		2
7–9 P.M.	2	3	3	14	8	5	3		2
10 P.M.	2	2	2	7	8	5	3		1
11 P.M.	2		2	5	6	5	3		
12 A.M.	2		1	2	4	5	3		

Table 4. Number of Employees Speaking Each Language over the Course of a Workday

Time	Spanish	English
6–9 A.M.	8	2
10 A.M.	12	5
11 A.M.	15	8
12 P.M.	15	17
1 P.M.	15	17
2–4 P.M.	15	8
5 P.M.	15	14
6 P.M.	18	22
7–9 P.M.	18	22
10 P.M.	17	13
11 P.M.	14	9
12 A.M.	12	5

Prep cooks and dishwashers were required in the morning before the restaurant had actually opened, and line cooks, busers, and dishwashers were needed after it had closed. In contrast, the majority of the wait staff worked only during the heavy business hours of lunch and dinner. Because of the different times required for performing different tasks, the presence of Spanish-speaking versus English-speaking employees fluctuated over the course of a day. Table 4 collapses the various job categories in Table 3 in order to highlight the fluctuations in the Spanish: English ratio.

During the lunch and dinner periods, English-speaking employees slightly outnumbered Spanish-speaking employees. At other times, the workplace was predominantly Spanish-speaking. Interactions varied throughout the day as well. The highest rate of verbal directives between managers and Spanish-speaking employees occurred during the morning hours. During the hours before the lunch rush, Spanish-speaking employees were responsible for a more diverse set of tasks, such as cleaning the restaurant, squeezing orange juice, making *masa* (dough) for tortillas, checking inventory, receiving deliveries, slicing meats and

vegetables, and cooking large quantities of beans and rice. Because these tasks were often shuffled back and forth to accommodate specific needs (such as the arrival of deliveries), morning managers needed to use frequent verbal directives to ensure that each of these diverse tasks would be completed. During the lunch and dinner rushes, the primary form of directives was food orders sent to the kitchen by a computerized ordering system. Verbal directives certainly occurred during these periods, but they were restricted primarily to solving specific problems (incorrect orders, running out of a particular food item, etc.). Thus, the majority of verbal directives in this study occurred during the hours before the restaurant officially opened, while the food orders obviously occurred during working hours.

Racism at Chalupatown

Despite the fact that the entire enterprise of Chalupatown was centered around Mexican culture and cuisine, racism (particularly toward Latinos) was fairly common among a relatively small subset of the restaurant's wait staff. Some (though definitely not the majority) of the Anglo servers regularly exchanged strongly racist evaluations of their customers. These evaluations often included open use of offensive racist pejoratives. For example, one server complained to another that he was not receiving good tips because he had been repeatedly given "bad tables" by the host. Because of an ongoing dispute between the two, the server felt that the host was intentionally seating minority customers in his section to prevent him from making good tips. He complained to another server, "You would not believe the tables I've had today—Look, I made a list: four tables of beaners, two tables of niggers, and one table of deaf-mutes." My reaction to overhearing this resulted in an apology for using offensive language followed by several days in which various servers made repeated jokes and negative comments about my "hypersensitivity." The fact that such racist banter was tolerated by some of the servers and managers reflects the lack of concern about racism among the Chalupatown staff.

For these particular servers, keeping track of the ethnic background of their customers was viewed as a valid way to gain a sense of how much tip money they were making, with the implicit assumption that the more white customers one had, the higher his or her tips would be. Because their racist attitudes influenced the service they provided minority customers, their expectations of small tips were usually fulfilled. This group of Anglo servers regularly complained when given a table of Latino customers and consciously provided Latino customers with inferior service because of the racist assumption that Latino customers don't tip well. When the inferior service resulted in a small tip, this was seen as justification for inferior treatment itself, rather than as the actual result of providing poor service. Given that the customers were overwhelmingly Anglo, these servers felt they could afford to let service to Latino customers slide and make up the income by focusing on Anglo customers.

One server ultimately realized that she—not the race of her customers—was the cause of the low tips, and that her racist attitude was not in her own interest. She and I were scheduled to work the same shift as servers in adjacent sections of the restaurant. She arrived late, so I was given a table in her section. When she arrived, I apologized for taking her table and offered to have the manager transfer the ticket so that she could be their server. When she saw that the table was filled with a large Latino family, she said, "No way. You can have them. In fact, I'm giving you *all* my beaners today." Throughout the day she told the hosts to seat Latino customers in my section rather than hers, assuming she would increase her tips by giving me the "low-tipping" Latino customers and keeping the "high-tipping" Anglo customers for herself. At the end of the day the amount of my tips was substantially higher than what she had earned. She had a reputation as one of the highest-earning waitresses in the restaurant, and having been "out-tipped" was something of an embarrassment for her, especially since she had told several other servers that she was sabotaging my tips. A couple of weeks later, she thanked me for showing her that she had been wrong, saying, "If you're nice to them, they tip you really well. Now I just pretend not to hate them."

There were also occasional expressions of racist attitudes by some of the managerial staff, although these were much less common and less likely to be expressed openly, and they rarely included the use of pejoratives. One manager frequently had parties at her house that were initially open to the entire restaurant staff, although they were primarily attended by servers and other managers. The first time I attended one of the parties, I happened to bring several Spanish-speaking co-workers. From this point on, the parties stopped being open to all employees and became "invitation-only." After realizing that I knew the parties were continuing, the manager apologized for not inviting me, saying that it was because I regularly socialized with Spanish-speaking co-workers and she "didn't feel comfortable having them in her house." I was told that I was actually welcome at her parties in the future as long as I agreed not to bring any of the kitchen workers with me. The racialized nature of managerial attitudes toward the workers is reflected in the following interaction, which occurred when I came to pick up my paycheck.

(2) Manager: Oh, your check isn't in this pile, this is the *brown* pile?
    Me: They're divided that way?
    Manager: Well, you know, kitchen and wait staff.

Rather than refer to the kitchen staff in terms of the division of labor (the actual reason for two sets of checks), the manager referred to the stack of kitchen checks as the "brown pile." This incident is typical of the way in which the kitchen staff was viewed as a racialized Other by much of the Anglo staff. Managers and servers frequently referred to kitchen employees with phrases such as "that one" or "those two" rather than with personal pronouns such as "him" or "them." Many servers did not even seem to know the names of Spanish-speaking employees, and they would regularly ask bilinguals for the names of cooks and busers they were working with. Often, the question would be phrased as "What's that one there called?" rather than "What's his name?" or "What's that guy's name?" The use of "that one" dehumanizes the referent, similar to the use of animal metaphors in public discourse about Latinos discussed by Santa Ana 1999, 2002.

Racist assumptions were common among the restaurant's customers as well. One Chicano server (a native English speaker) repeatedly found that customers were hesitant to interact with him directly. Occasionally clients would express doubt that he was their actual server (despite his having introduced himself as such) and repeat their requests to an Anglo co-worker, explaining that they weren't sure that he was actually their "waiter." After repeatedly being taken for a buser rather than a server, he quit his job at Chalupatown (less than a month after starting) to take a job in another restaurant with more Latino servers and customers.

Despite the prevalence of such attitudes, neither the servers nor managers ever expressed the view that the restaurant was a "racist" environment. The owners often provided helpful services to Spanish-speaking workers, such as offering interest-free loans to long-time employees and helping with legal and medical matters. In organizing work-related events, the managerial staff always tried to convey a sense of inclusiveness, posting notices of events such as holiday parties or company picnics in both English and Spanish. Because they offered employee services that were absent in most restaurants, the treatment of Spanish-speaking workers at Chalupatown was in many ways much better than in other Anglo-owned restaurants. For the most part, the managerial staff (including the owners) saw themselves as open-minded and accepting toward Latino employees and did not feel that white racism was a problem in their establishment. If the owners did hear racist comments from Anglo workers, they were usually quick to chastise them. There was no overt attempt at discrimination, and racism was not discussed at meetings between workers and management. If racism was an issue, it was usually expressed in terms of Latino workers' attitudes toward whites. The segregated nature of the staff (with almost entirely Anglo wait staff and entirely Latino kitchen staff) was explained as being necessary and efficient, because the Latino workers were uncooperative and unwilling to work closely with English-speaking whites. This type of projection is typical in the discourse of color-blind racism (Bonilla-Silva & Forman 2000, Bonilla-Silva 2002), in which racist ideologies are reproduced in discourse that is outwardly anti-racist.

ANGLO USE OF SPANISH AT CHALUPATOWN

The menu at Chalupatown included a number of Mock Spanish phrases, such as "not your *ordinario* hard-shell tacos," "blended with *fruita fresca*" (cf. Spanish *fruta* 'fruit') and "big enough for a *macho* man!"[4] The menu even featured the gratuitous use of inverted exclamation marks on English phrases, as in "¡You'll love it!" The use of Mock Spanish at Chalupatown extended well beyond the menu, however. In many of the interactions at Chalupatown, Anglo speakers used Mock Spanish when communicating with Spanish-speaking employees. Although some Anglos simply issued directives in English, many used Spanish words embedded into otherwise English sentences, as in "You need a sharper *cuchillo*" ('knife').

At Chalupatown, ways of using Spanish were iconic markers of ethnic identity, with the use of Mock Spanish indexing a particular Anglo identity and the use of actual Spanish indexing Latino identity. It was common to comment on deviations from this racialized view of Spanish, and the ethnic authenticity of bilinguals was openly questioned by both Latinos and Anglos. One kitchen worker who had gained fluency in English was often singled out as "one of us"—"acceptable" to spend time with outside of work (e.g., being invited to parties held by servers). Similarly, I was told that I was a "burrito" (explained to me as being "white on the outside but pure beaner on the inside") for maintaining close friendships with Spanish-speaking co-workers.

The iconicity (Gal & Irvine 2000) of Spanish as an index of Latino identity is certainly not unique to Chalupatown (cf. Urciuoli 1996:35–37). Despite the fact that there were more Anglos able to speak Spanish than Latinos able to speak English, the communicative burden was implicitly a unidirectional accommodation to English. When I began working in the restaurant, I was told that I was "lucky" to speak Spanish because "they can't talk to us." The inverse ("we can't talk to them") was never expressed.

Although Anglos generally ignored conversations in Spanish, they regularly expressed suspicion about Spanish speakers that were directed to Anglo listeners, and exchanges between Spanish speakers were often interpreted as intentionally secretive (cf. Haviland 2003). It was commonly assumed that Spanish speakers were either saying something bad about a white co-worker, were doing something "under the table," or were giving one another preferential treatment. This suspicion moved beyond language use, so that kitchen employees were often suspected as being responsible for unexplained problems in the restaurant, such as missing food and liquor or a rise in food costs.[5] During a widely discussed attempt to reduce rising food costs, a handwritten sign was posted reminding servers that they were not allowed to take anything from the kitchen unless it had already been entered in the computer and a ticket had been printed:

(3) The kitchen cannot fill an order without a ticket. No exceptions—<u>EVEN IF YOU SPEAK SPANISH</u>!!

The phrase *even if you speak Spanish!!* was underlined three times and highlighted in yellow in addition to being written in all capital letters. Although there were only two native Spanish-speaking servers employed in the restaurant at the time, the manager writing the sign made language a specific issue as if to suggest (wrongly) that the problem with food costs was largely caused by the kitchen staff's showing favoritism toward other Spanish-speaking workers by allowing them to take food without placing an order for it.

Suspicion about interactions in Spanish and asking for names were the only contexts in which Anglo servers consistently sought out the help of bilingual employees. This generally occurred when servers were concerned that they were the subject of Spanish conversations and may have been insulted or sexually harassed. English speakers frequently sought help from a bilingual in order to learn a derogatory phrase that could be used as a retort. English-speaking co-workers often asked me how to say things like "Fuck off!" or "I'm gonna cut your dick off!" (I was, however, never asked how to say something like "How was your day off?") ... At Chalupatown, the use of bilinguals to facilitate confrontational language and translate obscenities was not restricted to potential cases of supposed "victimization" in Spanish. Although bilinguals were rarely used to translate directives that arose in the regular course of work, they were frequently sought for help in making reprimands and overt expressions of anger. For example, one manager who was firing an employee instructed a bilingual, "Tell him to get the fuck out of my restaurant and to never come back and I want you to translate it just like that!"

The Structure of Spanish-English Alternation in Anglo Speech

As noted above, my initial motivation for collecting data was to study the grammatical structure of Anglo code-switching at Chalupatown. The structure of alternations in Anglo speech is distinctly different from that of those found in studies of code-switching by native Spanish-English bilinguals.... [Examples (4) and (5) omitted.]

Although Anglo managers and servers might occasionally produce directives entirely in Spanish, directives were more typically given either entirely in English or in a mix of English and Spanish. Most use of Spanish by Anglos in the restaurant involved the substitution of single Spanish morphemes into otherwise English sentences, as in the following examples:

(6) There's *agua* ['water'] on the *piso* ['floor'].
(7) Did you *limpia* the *baño*?
    (*limpia* 'clean' 3rd singular present or adjective; *baño* 'bathroom')
(8) Why is this still *sucio* ['dirty']?
(9) Can you *ayuda* with these boxes?
    (*ayuda* 'help' 3rd singular present or noun)

Although Anglo speakers used Spanish often, the syntactic structure of these utterances was consistently English. The syntactic structure of Spanish was never involved. Anglo use of Spanish almost always involved cases of "nonce loans" (Poplack et al. 1988) or "insertions" (Muysken 2000) of Spanish constituents into English sentences.

The absence of Spanish grammatical structure in Anglo code-switching might lead one to assume that these utterances result from a lack of competence in Spanish. While it is clear that many of the Anglo speakers were not fluent speakers of Spanish, most of them had enough competence to produce many of these directives in Spanish. In cases of extreme urgency, Anglo speakers would often use sentences that were entirely in Spanish. The use of actual Spanish by Anglos was most common when in emergency situations or as a last resort when miscommunication had become an obvious problem. The following interaction took place after a prep cook cut his hand on the meat slicer. The manager is opening the first aid kit to pull out a bandage while another employee brings a car around to take the cook to the emergency clinic. Following the manager's instructions, the cook is holding his hand above his shoulder in a towel. The cook had lowered his hand several times and the manager repeatedly asked him to keep his hand up (a pattern that continued after this interaction):

(10) Manager (to cook):   *Hay que dejar la mano arriba.*
                           'You have to keep your hand up.'

     (cook lowers hand again)
     Manager: *¡Hay que dejar la mano arriba!*
                           'You have to keep your hand up!'

Manager (to Rusty):   Tell him he needs to keep his hand up.
Rusty: *Dice que–*
                       'She says that—'
Cook: —OK, OK (lifts arm)

Here the manager uses Spanish syntactic constructions that are quite distinct from English grammar. The construction *hay que* 'it is necessary that' has a null subject where English would generally use a personal pronoun. If the manager had been using only English grammar one might expect something like *tu necesitas* 'you need to' rather than an impersonal construction like *hay que*. The manager also correctly uses the definite article *la* with the noun *mano* (hand) where English would use a possessive pronoun (*your hand*). The correct use of the feminine *la* rather than the masculine *el* with the noun *mano* avoids another pitfall of L2 Spanish speakers, who may mistakenly use the masculine article under the assumption that all nouns ending in [o] have masculine gender. The (incorrect) use of *su mano* is extremely common in Anglo Spanish; even the restrooms at Chalupatown had the typical Mock Spanish *Lava sus manos* sign found throughout the Southwest (Peñalosa 1981, Hill 1998). The manager was at least fluent enough in Spanish to produce syntactic constructions that often pose difficulties for English monolinguals using Spanish as a second language. When the cook returned to work the next day, the same manager asked him "How is your *mano*?"—returning to the nonce borrowing pattern typical of Anglo Spanish. Although a lack of competence might explain some examples of Anglo nonce borrowings, in many cases the absence of Spanish grammar does not result from a lack of fluency, but rather reflects the absence of any attempt actually to speak Spanish.

The absence of Spanish syntax in Anglo speech at Chalupatown is similar to other forms of linguistic appropriation, which typically involve a greatly reduced (or entirely absent) grammatical structure of the source language. Actual Spanish grammar is virtually nonexistent in Mock Spanish, where the only productive grammatical processes seem to be the addition of +o to English nouns and the addition of the article *el*. Of course, the affixation of +o is not actually a rule for Spanish (actual Spanish nouns end in a wide range of sounds). Instead, the rule is specific to Mock Spanish. In an examination of Spanish textbooks written for Anglo employers, Erard 1996 also found that Spanish grammar is often greatly reduced or ignored in Anglo speech. For example, the authors of *Farm and Ranch Spanish* choose only to introduce the formal personal pronoun *Usted*, ignoring the familiar pronoun *tú* and its associated verb forms (Erard 1996:314), erasing the potential for indexing a position of familiarity with Spanish speakers. The general irrelevance of Spanish grammar for Anglo speakers reflects an ideology in which Spanish speakers themselves are viewed as inconsequential (cf. Santa Ana

2002:2–3). The erasure (Gal & Irvine 2000) of Spanish syntactic structure reflects a racial ideology involving erasure of Latinos themselves (cf. Perea 1995).

Anglo Spanish serves as an example of what Zentella 1996 has called the process of "chiquitification" of Spanish and Spanish speakers. Zentella defines "chiquitification" as a process which "diminishes the complexity of the languages and cultures of the more than 22 million Latinos who reside in the U.S." (1996:1). She argues that the ideology of chiquitification fuels discrimination and Hispanophobia. The difficulties Spanish-speakers at Chalupatown face when confronted with a chiquitified Spanish demonstrate the powerful impact of chiquitification in the everyday lives of Spanish-speakers.

Anglo Spanish as Mock Spanish

That Anglo use of Spanish is often simply Mock Spanish is evident in the exchange between a server and a bartender in example (11) below. The interaction occurs in a wait station, a small room with doorways on three sides that connects the kitchen, bar, and serving area. The area is only about four feet across, so that it is possible to conduct conversations across the room (such as between the bar and the kitchen). Because the area contains many items essential to servers (chips, soda machines, tea and coffee, an ice bin, and a register), the wait station is continuously busy with numerous workers passing back and forth between parts of the workplace. The server is standing in the wait station filling glasses at the soda machine as the bartender is returning from the restroom. As the bartender passes through the wait station to the bar, the server stops and asks him to have the buser refill the ice bin.

(11) Server: Will you ask ⟨Luis⟩ to refill the ice bin?
      Bartender: OK…How do you say "ice"?
      Server: I don't know? Ice-o? (both laugh)
      Bartender   (to buser who is passing through the wait station): *Mas* ice-*o, por favor.*
      Buser: *¿Qué?*
                    'What?'
[The server and bartender both laugh. The buser turns to Rusty, tilts back his head, and turns his hands up to indicate that he wants an explanation.]
      Rusty: (to buser) *No quiere nada.*
                    'He doesn't want anything.'
[Buser exits the wait station.]
      Bartender: Rusty, how do you say "ice"?
      Rusty: *hielo* ([ïjelo])
      Bartender: (moving back into the bar area) What?
      Rusty: *hielo.*
      Bartender: Yellow?
      Rusty: No, **hiii**-*jielo*
      Bartender: *hielo?* ([ïjelo])
      Rusty: Yea
      Bartender: I'll just say "yellow." That's close enough, right?

      Bartender: (back to the server): Just say "yellow"— like the color.

Example (11) reflects the common practice among Anglo servers of avoiding directives to Spanish employees by passing them off to other employees, particularly those who are newer, younger, or lower-status (i.e., not necessarily based on their potential competence in Spanish). In this example, the server's choice to pass the directive off to the bartender may result from the face-threatening nature of this specific request. Refilling the ice bin is not the buser's responsibility, and the server is basically trying to trick the bartender into convincing the buser to perform what should be the server's own job responsibility (hence my response to the buser). As a fairly new employee, the bartender was unaware that the job was the server's responsibility and became angry when I explained the situation later.

In this example, the speakers immediately resort to Mock Spanish when discussing how to communicate to a Spanish speaker. The first example, *mas ice-o*, involves the use of Spanish grammatical elements on English words (the addition of +*o* to an English noun). Immediately upon learning (and correctly pronouncing) the Spanish word, the bartender turns to hyperanglicization (*yellow*). Although the other bartender asks me if *yellow* is *close enough* to be understood as *hielo*, he instructs the server to *just say yellow* before I have a chance to respond. The Mock Spanish nonce forms are quite funny to the speakers, and both the server and bartender laugh throughout and after the exchange. Here the Spanish does not serve to facilitate communication with the Spanish-speaking employee; it does little more than index the racial difference between the buser and the servers themselves. The Spanish is entirely for the benefit of the Anglo speakers' own amusement, and the actual Spanish speaker is quite marginal to the interaction despite the fact that it revolves around an attempt to communicate with him. Spanish simply serves to index a particular Anglo understanding of social affect and humor, but it does not actually serve the function of facilitating communication with Spanish speakers (see discussion below).

The widespread use of Spanish obscenities noted earlier is another affinity between Anglo Spanish at Chalupatown and the mass-media productions of Mock Spanish described by Hill. Spanish expletives occurred both as substitutes for English obscenities and in combination with English expletives. Several English male monolinguals frequently boasted about their ability to express obscenities accurately in Spanish. These male servers repeatedly produced Spanish obscenities as an attempt at humor. A few male servers would regularly approach monolingual Spanish-speaking males with no other purpose than to utter highly offensive Spanish words in isolation. One server in particular would persistently accost male Spanish-speaking employees and yell isolated Spanish obscenities referring to female anatomy. These outbursts were usually prompted by the presence of a female customer he found attractive somewhere in the restaurant. However, the woman in question was rarely (if ever) near enough to be recognized as a contextual factor, so his outbursts seemed to occur for no reason at all. The Spanish speakers would occasionally react with laughter, but more often simply roll their eyes or shake their heads. Among other Anglos, the word *caca* 'shit' was the most common Spanish obscenity. Managers would regularly use *caca* in directives such as "Why is there *caca* on the floor?" (referring to trash that has spilled). Thus, common uses of Spanish at Chalupatown reflected stereotypical forms of Mock Spanish both in terms of their English-centered structure and in their negative indexical associations.

Use of Directives at Chalupatown

Verbal Directives. The Anglo managers at Chalupatown had distinct individual responses to the problem of communicating with Spanish-speaking employees, depending on individual stances toward Latino co-workers. Two of the Anglo managers knew enough Spanish to produce directives that were understandable in Spanish. Both these managers recognized that racism was a problem in the restaurant, something most other managers denied. In sharp contrast, two managers who openly expressed racist attitudes both used only English in interactions with Spanish speakers, with the exception of a few select Spanish words that were common knowledge among all employees (e.g., *mesa, agua, queso*). Regardless of whether they were speaking English or Spanish, Anglo speakers would often produce the English items with exaggerated nonnative phonology (e.g. [tʃíikin] or [tʃíips]) but produced anglicized forms of the Spanish items (e.g. [kʰéjsow] for *queso*). Spanish speakers used unmodified Spanish phonology for both the English and Spanish words.

The managers using "pure" English typically produced directives containing elements of "foreigner talk" (Ferguson 1975, 1981). Foreigner talk is a register that speakers use in attempts to communicate when they assume that an interlocutor does not know the speaker's language. Features of foreigner talk used by Anglo workers at Chalupatown included exaggerated gestures and facial expressions, speaking at higher amplitude, exaggerated pronunciation, and syntactic reduction. Frequently, Anglo speakers would use an exaggerated Mock Spanish accent when communicating with Spanish-speaking co-workers—for example, the phrase "MORE CHIPS" with the second word produced [tʃíips], accompanied by the gesture of pointing at the empty chip container. As with the use of Mock Spanish, the use of exaggerated nonnative pronunciation reproduced a negative racial stereotype for Anglo amusement.

The effectiveness of these directives was limited to a few specific contexts. Only one of the managers regularly sought out bilingual workers to translate directives to the kitchen staff. It is probably not coincidental that this particular manager grew up in Europe, was a native trilingual, and had a very positive attitude toward multilingualism.

The predominant means of issuing directives was used by managers with some knowledge of Spanish and involved utterances with primarily English content, with occasional words and (more rarely) phrases in Spanish. The amount of Spanish content varied, but it was sometimes insufficient for conveying meaning to a monolingual Spanish speaker. The phonology of these switches was always hyperanglicized, as in [hæblɑɪ] for *hablar* and [tɛlejfownow] for *telefono* in the following example:

(12) Manager: Could you *hablar* ⟨Juan⟩ *por telefono* and see if he can *trabajo*?
　　　　hablar 'to speak'; *por telefono* 'by phone';
　　　　trabajo 'work' (1st person singular present or noun)
　　　　'Could you talk (to) Juan by telephone and see if he can work?'

Although directives of this type were quite frequent, the managers seemed to recognize that they were often unintelligible to monolingual Spanish speakers. In the following example, the manager openly admits that the directive was not understood:

(13) Manager:　Did you go psst psst with the *manguera* ['hose?']
　　　Employee:　*Sí, sí.* ['Yes, yes']
　　　Manager:　Did you put *bolsas* ['bags'] in your *basura* ['garbage'] cans?
　　　Employee:　*Sí, sí.*
　　　Manager:　(to Rusty, working nearby): He didn't understand a thing I said. It takes them a while to get used to that. The scary thing is eventually they start to know what I'm saying.

It is assumed that Spanish-speaking employees will eventually "get used to" receiving directives that they cannot understand. Despite recognizing that directives were not always understood, managers typically blamed failure to follow a given directive on the Spanish-speaking employee. In the following example, a manager blames the failure on the "laziness" of the Spanish-speaking employee rather than on miscommunication, despite the fact that the directive contained only three words in Spanish, none of which is particularly helpful for determining the meaning of the sentence:

(14) Manager:　You have to finish *todo eso, porque* I have other things to do.
　　　　todo eso, 'all this'; *porque* 'because'
　　　Manager:　(later to Anglo employee): Did you see that? He didn't finish that—he didn't do what I told him!
　　　Rusty:　Maybe he didn't understand you.
　　　Manager:　Oh, he understood me all right, he's just lazy.

Having been told only 'all this' and 'because' in Spanish, the employee was left without sufficient information to comprehend the directive; it could be equally interpreted as 'I'll finish all of this because you have other things to do'. Nonetheless, when the directive was not followed, the manager accused the employee of being lazy.

These verbal directives maintain their performative effect as directives. Spanish speakers recognize that they are expected to perform some task. However, the referential function of the directives often fails because of the limited Spanish content. Spanish speakers are thus left in a situation where they must complete directives they may not fully understand (see below). The actions of Spanish speakers are evaluated as if the failure to fulfill directives were a willful act rather than a failure to understand....

Written Notices for Employees. Written notices posted for employees were much more likely to be entirely in Spanish, as opposed to the predominantly English verbal directives. The notices were sometimes written out by hand but more often prepared using a computer. Translations were either written out by managers themselves (often after consulting a bilingual) or obtained by using machine translation programs available over the Internet. Bilinguals were more likely to be consulted in the production of written notices than in the case of verbal directives. In cases where a bilingual was used, the translation was often orally transmitted, resulting in numerous changes when it was written down by the monolingual English speaker. The written notices typically contained sufficient Spanish for comprehension but displayed very little regard for actual Spanish grammar. For example, the written notice below (a reminder about daylight savings time) contains a mix of accurate and ungrammatical language:

(15) recuerden cambiar la hora a su relog el sabado en la
      noche
      cuando sean las 12:00 P.M. seran las 11:00 P.M.
      'remember to change the hour on your clock Saturday
      night
      when it is 12:00 P.M., it will be 11:00 P.M.'

In this case, the manager consulted with a bilingual speaker before printing out the final version of the notice. These consultations were cursory, usually just intended to check for the comprehensibility of particular words or phrases. Thus, the final version of the notice contains several errors despite the input of a native speaker (e.g., *a su relog* for *del reloj*, *en la noche* for *por la noche*). Notices prepared in consultation with bilinguals often contained grammatical forms not typically used by the managers themselves. For example, the notice about time change contains a fairly sophisticated use of the subjunctive and future tenses (*cuando sean las 12:00 P.M. seran las 11:00 P.M.*) that would not normally occur in the spoken Spanish of any of the Anglo managers.

The only time I was asked to check a translation, I was explicitly told not to worry about whether the grammar and spelling were correct, but only to verify that the notice would be understandable to a monolingual Spanish speaker. I was told that the use of "correct" Spanish was unnecessary because "most of them can't read anyway." This explanation surfaced repeatedly both as a justification for disregarding the grammatical rules of Spanish and as an explanation for misunderstandings in the transmission of kitchen orders (see below).

The managers and owners regularly (and incorrectly) asserted that the majority of the kitchen staff was illiterate. Although it would make sense to assume that a person with supposedly limited literacy skills would be more likely to understand written language if it were actually grammatical, the managers assumed that because the workers didn't regularly use formal standard Spanish, it was acceptable to address them in language that was highly nonstandard and irregular. This view persisted despite the fact that employees regularly corrected the ungrammatical Spanish in written notices, as in the example below:

(16)		
Original Spanish text	Corrections made by employees (<u>**underlined**</u> **in bold**)	English translation
Junta obligataria para todas las personas, de la cosina, la preparacion, los trastes, tortillas, los que limpian mesas. Tienen que venir a una de las juntas que abra.	Junta obligataria para todas las personas, de la <u>cocina</u>, la prepara<u>cíon</u>, los trastes, tortillas, los que limpian mesas. Tienen que venir a una de las juntas que <u>habrá</u>.	Obligatory meeting for all of the people, of the kitchen, the preparation, the dishes, tortillas, those that clean tables. You (pl) must come to one of the meetings that *might open* (fixed by employee to "will occur")

As posted, the verb in the second sentence of the posting (*abra*) was written without the initial ⟨h⟩ and without the accent on the final vowel. The written form is the present tense subjunctive of *abrir* 'to open' rather than the (intended) future form of *haber* 'to do'. The employee's correction restores the intended semantic content in addition to correcting spelling errors. Although the verb was corrected by a Spanish-speaking worker, this particular nonstandard orthography was actually used by some of the workers themselves. For example, the only notice written by the workers themselves contains exactly the same error:

(17)

TODOS ESTAN INVITADOS	EVERYONE IS INVITED
AL GRAN JUEGO DE FUDBOL	TO THE BIG SOCCER GAME
QUE SE LLEVARA ACABO	THAT WILL TAKE PLACE ON
EL DIA 4 DE JULIO	THE 4TH OF JULY
A LAS 9 DE LA MAÑANA	AT 9 IN THE MORNING
EN EL PARQUE DE ⟨NOMBRE⟩.	IN ⟨NAME⟩ PARK
JUGARAN LOS CREMAS DE	THE CREAM OF
GUATEMALA Y LOS HUELE MOLE	GUATEMALA WILL
DE MEXICO. NO FALTES. **ABRA**	PLAY THE MOLE [sauce]-
MUCHA CERVEZA Y ANTOJITOS.	SMELLING
QUE GANE EL MEJOR.	MEXICANS. DON'T MISS IT.
	THERE
	WILL BE A LOT OF BEER
	AND SNACKS.
	MAY THE BEST TEAM WIN.

Written notices posted by managers also contained sporadic inclusions of English content words with no regard for whether the employees would know what the English words actually meant, as in the examples below (note also that *necesito* is spelled incorrectly in the second example despite the fact that the correct spelling is closer to the English cognate "necessary"):

(18) Hay muchos cambios   'There are many changes in
     en *schedule*.   *schedule*.'
(19) Nesisito un ~~busboy~~   'I need a ~~busboy~~ dishwasher
     dishwasher
     Domingo Jan 2nd P.M.   Sunday Jan 2nd P.M.'

The most striking difference between Spanish and English notices posted at Chalupatown was that English notices were almost always mitigated in some way, while Spanish notices were more direct. Typically, English notices included an explanation for a particular directive, particularly in cases in which the workers might react negatively to the directive itself:

(20) Due to the very "high cost" of avacados [sic], they are no longer available to staff who eat free meals. This includes guacamole. Employees who pay ½ price may continue to have guacamole and avacado.
(21) PLEASE, DO NOT PLACE <u>ANY</u> OBJECTS <u>BEHIND</u> THE REGISTERS. (…because there are a lot of electrical wire thingys back there. Don't touch.) Thank you.

In example (20), the directive against eating avocados is accompanied by a justification (the price of avocados). The quotes around "high cost" seem to mark emphasis. Like the Spanish-speaking employees, English-speaking workers regularly corrected such errors on the notices themselves, often adding negative comments about the management. In example (21), the directive against placing objects behind registers also comes with an explanation. The informal tone of the justification (*electrical thingys*) and the inclusion of *thank you* further mitigate the directive. While nonstandard English marks familiarity, nonstandard Spanish serves to maintain social distance.

In contrast, Spanish-language notices were very direct and rarely included justification or explanations; they sometimes went so far as to include threats. An example is a notice that appeared during the "toilet paper war" between management and employees. There were often problems with the plumbing at Chalupatown, particularly in the restrooms. Overflowing toilets were common, especially on weekends when the restaurant was extremely busy. The busers regularly had to deal with these floods by manually unclogging the toilets and cleaning the water and excrement from the bathroom floor. Because the toilet was a continual problem, many of the Spanish-speaking workers put used toilet paper on the floor rather than placing it directly in the toilet and contributing to another flood. This follows the practice in most parts of Mexico and Central America, where the plumbing cannot operate properly when paper is flushed down the toilet. Many of the Mexican and Guatemalan workers maintained this practice in their own homes, placing a waste basket beside the toilet to collect paper rather than flushing it. Although the management was aware of this practice, they did not want waste baskets beside the toilets and were upset by customer complaints about piles of used toilet paper on the floor.

The managers first attempted to resolve the problem by selectively directing busers to not leave paper on the floor and asking them to spread the word to other Spanish-speaking employees. When the busers were told to let other employees know to flush their paper, they responded by explaining the problem with the plumbing and asking for the toilet to be fixed in order to accommodate flushed paper. The requests for repairs were ignored, and the verbal directives failed to resolve the problem. The management then posted the following written notice:

(22) Haga usted el favor de tirar el papel santario adentro de la taza de el excusado no en el piso. SU TRABAJO PELIGRA.

'Do the favor of throwing the sanitary paper inside of the bowl of the toilet not on the floor. YOUR JOB IS IN DANGER.'

In addition to the predictable grammatical errors (e.g., *de el* for *del*), the notice is somewhat overstated. The most direct way to make this directive would be simply to say, "Don't throw toilet paper on the floor" ("*No tire Usted papel higénico al suelo*"). The highly explicit and threatening nature of the notice contrasts sharply with the mitigated English notices and reflects the assumption that Spanish-speaking employees have a general problem with comprehending directives and require overly explicit directions accompanied by threats. It also places responsibility for the problem entirely with the workers themselves, ignoring the fact that the workers were acting in what they saw as the best interest of the restaurant by attempting to avoid overflowing toilets. The notice was not successful in stopping the appearance of toilet paper on the restroom floor. Because the owners had no plans to repair the plumbing and hence expected the busers to continue to clean flooded restrooms regularly, the kitchen workers were offended that their side of the problem had not been addressed. The threatening tone of the notice only complicated matters, and an employee tore the notice down after a few days. Eventually the managers held a meeting for all kitchen workers specifically to deal with the toilet paper problem. In the course of the meeting, the management finally agreed to bring in a plumber, and both problems (flooded restrooms and paper on the floor) were eventually resolved. The "toilet paper war" could have been resolved easily by responding to the busers' initial requests for plumbing repairs. The busers' recommendations were not taken seriously (or perhaps even listened to) until the situation had become something of a crisis.

Because native speakers were often consulted in their production, written notices were more likely to succeed in terms of both their directive function and their referential function; that is, they were more likely to be understood than were verbal directives. However, the disregard for Spanish grammar indexes a negative evaluation of Spanish and Spanish speakers. The chiquitification of Spanish sets up unequal relationships between participants in an interaction. The disregard for Spanish grammar was typically accompanied by a disregard for Spanish speakers as cultural actors....

LATINO USE OF SPANISH AT CHALUPATOWN

Fulfilling Directives One Doesn't Understand

Because failure to respond to directives was usually blamed on the Spanish-speaking employee, repeated failure to respond properly could lead to losing one's job. Asking for clarification often resulted in reprimand from the manager, and so some employees asked for more explicit or clearer instructions only as a last resort. Reprimands ranged from verbal admonishment to being fired. Failure to fulfill a directive typically resulted in scolding from a manager, but repeated failures to comply (or a single serious failure) could result in being "written up" or losing one's job.

Spanish-speaking employees had several mechanisms for coping with the continual demand to follow directives they did not understand. These strategies included extensive training, seeking clarification from more senior Spanish-speaking employees, and seeking the help of a bilingual.

Spanish-speaking employees took a very careful approach to employee training. Training of English-speaking employees usually consisted of one day of "shadowing" the trainer, followed by a day in which the trainee would do the majority of work under the trainer's supervision. Tasks of sporadic or rare occurrence (such as servers' placing specially modified food orders or bartenders' changing the carbon dioxide tanks for soft drinks) were usually not covered during the training of English-speaking employees. It was generally understood that when such needs arose, the employee could simply ask a manager for instructions. In contrast, the Spanish-speaking employees recognized that newly trained employees would need to know about ALL possible tasks (including relatively rare ones) because it was likely that they would never receive clear instructions from managers. Because of this difference in access to information, the initial training for Spanish speakers included details concerning locations for storing utensils and putting away shipments, including things that were rarely used.

In cases where a manager's directive involved something that hadn't been covered in training, employees would usually seek clarification from a more senior Spanish-speaking employee. Because most of the cooks had previously worked as dishwashers or busers, they were often familiar enough with other jobs in the restaurant to help the newer employee determine the meaning of a particular directive. In these cases, the newer employee would explain his limited understanding of a directive and request elaboration. Managers would sometimes use kitchenware or tools as a visual aid when giving verbal directives, and newer employees would simply carry the tool to a more senior employee and ask, "What am I supposed to do with this?" This means of seeking advice was the most common response to interpreting directives involving tasks that had not been covered in training.

Employees faced with directives they did not understand would also ask for help from a bilingual co-worker if one were readily available. In cases of very rare or highly specific directives, other monolingual employees often were also unable to interpret a particular directive, and looking for a bilingual was the employee's only option before returning to the manager and possibly facing a reprimand. Monolingual Spanish-speaking employees would typically try to remember the English content of directives in order to be able to ask a bilingual to translate a particular word or phrase so they could fully understand the directive in question. For example, I had the following interaction with a buser trying to interpret a directive—which must have been something like "We need more soap in the *baño*"—without knowing the English word *soap* (having heard English [sowp] as [su:p]).

(25) Buser: *¿Que quiere decir "soup"* [su:p] *?*
'What does "soup" mean?'

Rusty: *"Caldo" o "sopa"*
'"Caldo" or "sopa"'

Buser: *No...* [pause] *es algo que se pone en el baño.*
'No...it's something that goes in the restroom.'

Rusty: *Ah, "soap"—quiere decir "jabón."*
'Ah, "soap"—it means "jabón."'

On occasions when the Spanish-speaking employee could not remember the English content of a directive or when the directive had absolutely no retrievable Spanish content, even bilingual co-workers were unable to help. In these cases, the Spanish-speaking employee was only able to ask very general questions, such as "What does she want me to do?" These cases were most likely to result in the Spanish-speaking employee's returning to the manager for clarification. Employees were aware that a longer time spent trying to understand a directive would result in being scolded for not having fulfilled the directive promptly. Occasionally, employees would ask a bilingual to go to the manager directly and explain that the Spanish speaker did not know what was expected of him. Even if the bilingual were willing to intervene, this did not mean that a reprimand was always avoided: The manager would sometimes scold the employee both for not fulfilling the directive and for interrupting the bilingual's regular work.

Spanish as a Marker of Solidarity

The majority of Anglo workers did not generally pay attention to conversations between Spanish speakers in which no Anglos were involved. Latino workers were thus able to vent frustrations and negative assessments of co-workers fairly openly. Discussions about issues of racism, exceptionally rare in English, were quite common in Spanish. English-language discussions about race almost universally involved stereotyped assessments of customers or negative attitudes toward Latino co-workers. In contrast, Spanish-language discussions often dealt with racist attitudes of individual English-speaking workers or the general problem of racism in the restaurant.

Spanish-speaking workers would regularly discuss which co-workers were seen as *racistas* 'racists' and which were *buena gente* 'good people'. These discussions were generally framed as a mechanism for improving working conditions by alerting co-workers to avoid potential problems by avoiding interactions with potential *racistas*. Discussions of the possible racist attitudes of individual co-workers, especially managers, allowed workers to warn one another in order to avoid problematic interactions that might result in arguments. Because it was generally recognized that requests made to a *racista* were unlikely to be fulfilled, these discussions improved workplace efficiency by alerting workers to which Anglo co-workers were cooperative and which were more likely to complicate interactions because of their racist attitudes (cf. Lindeman 2002). New workers were often highly conscious of the *racista* and *buena gente* categories, frequently asking about different co-workers in order to learn which ones were best avoided.

Anglo co-workers most widely recognized as *racistas* were those who had repeatedly reprimanded or yelled at Spanish-speaking workers for minor infractions, particularly those that would typically go unmentioned if committed by an English-speaking worker. As is often the case with managers who are viewed as mean or unfair, employees would alert one another when the manager was present in the workplace. It should be noted that the two most prominent *racistas* were also negatively viewed by Anglo employees, suggesting that a more generally abrasive personality could contribute to the perception of one as *racista*.

Neither group of employees, Anglo nor Latino, generally knew the names of all the co-workers from the other group. Anglo workers did not generally talk about or interact with specific Latino employees enough to learn their names. In contrast, Spanish-speaking employees generally developed Spanish nicknames for many of the Anglo employees. This may be partially due to the difference in job duties. A server makes requests to the kitchen as a whole, while kitchen workers fill requests for specific servers. A server would not generally know who was preparing his or her order, but kitchen workers would know exactly which servers placed each order they prepared. Some of the nicknames referred to an individual's disposition or personality, such as *La Loca* 'the Crazy Woman' or *El Joto* 'the Fag' (offensive). More typically, they referred to an individual's physical characteristics, like *Pelón* 'Baldy', *La Gordita* 'the Chubby Woman', or *Nalgona* 'the Woman with a Big Butt' (offensive). Because nicknames were most common for Anglos who did not interact with Latino co-workers, most Anglos referred to by nicknames did not realize that they even had them.

Nicknames were regularly used to discuss *racista* co-workers openly in Spanish even when the manager in question was present. One manager who was relatively short in stature was nicknamed *Culerín* 'Little Asshole' (offensive). Another manager who frequently came to work high and took breaks to smoke marijuana behind the building was nicknamed *El Chinito* 'the Little Chinese Man' because he always kept his eyes squinted under the bright lights of the kitchen.

Although Anglo fears of Spanish being used in insults were generally exaggerated, Spanish-speaking employees would sometimes conduct negative appraisals of an Anglo co-worker in the co-worker's presence. Sometimes, mocking comments in Spanish would be directly addressed to an Anglo worker with the knowledge that the addressee was unlikely to understand what was being said.

Bilingual workers would also use code-switching to exploit the pragmatic potential of Spanish (cf. Valdés 1981). Switching into Spanish in a conversation with monolingual English-speaking participants might be used to exclude Anglos from the conversation. In the following example, the server Carmen (one of the two bilingual servers) uses Spanish to taunt the manager Culerín by hinting that he is the topic of the Spanish conversation. Culerín is managing the bar and thus has supervision over me, but not over Carmen. When the interaction begins, I am preparing drinks for servers and Carmen approaches to see if her order is ready. She begins talking about Culerín in Spanish while he is not present, but continues talking about him (to me in Spanish) after he approaches and attempts to enter into the conversation.

(26) Server: *¿Tienes muchos tickets?*
                'Do you have a lot of tickets?'
      Rusty: *No. Estoy haciendo lo tuyo.*
                'No, I'm making your [order now].'
      Server: *¿Estas trabajando con Culerín?*
                'You're working with Culerín?'
      Rusty: *'¿Cuando no?'*
                'As always', literally 'When not?'
      [Culerín approaches.]
      Culerín: How's everything going back here?
      Rusty: Fine.
      Culerín: ⟨Caaarmen!⟩ How you doing?
      Server: I'm fine.
      Server: [to Rusty] *Le odio.*
                'I hate him.'
      Rusty: *'¿Quien?'*
                'Who?'
      Server: [points with her head directly at Culerín]
                *Él. Tu **jefe**.* [laughs]
                *Le **odio**.*
                'Him. Your **boss. I hate** him.'
      Rusty: *Pues, yo tambien.*
                'Well, me too.'
      Culerín: OK you two. Break it up. We've got work to do.
      Server: [loading drinks onto her tray] ***Todos** le odian.*
                '**Everybody** hates him.'
      Culerín: OK, ⟨Carmen⟩, get back to work. You have customers.
      Server: See, that's why.

After a minimal phatic response to Culerín in English (*I'm fine*), Carmen returns to Spanish, telling me that she hates Culerín even though he has tried to start a conversation with her in English. When I ask whom she is referring to, she points her head at Culerín and says *él* (3rd singular pronoun). Carmen raises her voice and adds emphatic pitch accent when she says *él* and *tu jefe*, both Spanish phrases Culerín is likely to understand. Culerín begins by trying to initiate a friendly conversation with Carmen in English, but quickly moves to a managerial stance. Culerín's reaction, telling us to stop talking and return to work, suggests that he has gotten the hint. His reaction is understandable, since directly telling us not to talk about him in Spanish might convey insecurity or paranoia on his part.

After Carmen continues in Spanish, Culerín tries again to halt the Spanish conversation by telling her again to return to work, despite the fact that he is technically not her supervisor. Servers regularly complained about the fact that Culerín would try to tell them what to do even when he had no supervisory power over them. Carmen switches into English for her final comment to me, *see, that's why*, referring to the fact that Culerín has overstepped his job duties by acting like her boss. The switch into English as she walks away makes it fairly clear that Culerín was indeed the topic of our Spanish conversation without giving him an opportunity to respond.

Here Carmen is able to turn the tables and use Spanish in order to restrict the agency of Culerín. She drops hints about the referential meaning so that Culerín may recognize that he is the topic of the conversation. Because the conversation is in Spanish, Culerín is unable openly to express evaluation of the interaction or defend himself. He resorts to a position of relative power by taking a managerial stance in an attempt to end the conversation altogether.

Sometimes, mocking comments in Spanish would be directly addressed to an Anglo worker with the knowledge that the addressee was unlikely to catch all of what was being said. Most of the time, humor at the expense of Anglo co-workers went entirely unnoticed. On one occasion, a manager who was having a particularly bad hair day told me that she had been receiving compliments from the kitchen staff. She said, "The cooks told me I looked really pretty today. They said they liked my hair." Somewhat bewildered, given the state of her hair, I simply said "That's nice" and remained silent. After a short pause, the manager asked, "Hey, what does *escoba* ['broom'] mean?" Clearly she had not understood the sarcastic nature of the cooks' compliments. Thus, although the irrelevance of Spanish for managers made work more difficult for Spanish speakers, it also made it possible openly to vent frustrations and criticisms without sparking reprimands from managers.

Spanish as a Tool of Resistance

Anglo language ideology at Chalupatown constrained the agency of the Latino workers in English-dominated contexts, but the Anglo disregard for Spanish also made it possible for Latino workers to use Spanish to develop an alternative linguistic market. Although kitchen workers had control over very few resources in the restaurant, the Anglo disregard allowed kitchen workers to use Spanish to exert control over the limited resources available to them. Because the owners were concerned about theft by employees, many of the resources workers required to perform their jobs were kept in locked cabinets that could be opened only by a manager. Servers would regularly hide resources such as pens, credit card trays, and aprons to make sure that they could get them without help from a manager. For bartenders, hosts, and kitchen workers, garbage bags were the most difficult resource to obtain.

Although garbage bags were mostly used by busers and cooks, bartenders and hosts required them as well. Garbage bags were most needed toward the end of a shift, when managers were usually extremely busy and unlikely to stop and unlock the cabinet containing garbage bags. As it could take up to half an hour just to find a manager willing to open the cabinet, garbage bags took on great value for the workers who needed them. Some managers would occasionally give out an entire roll at once, since opening the cabinet repeatedly while trying to close the restaurant was impractical. Others would never give out more than one or two bags at a time. Because one never knew when the chance to get more bags would come around, workers would hoard garbage bags and hide them from other employees. I was actually told about the importance of hiding surplus garbage bags as part of my initial training as a bartender. Disputes over garbage bags were a regular occurrence, and workers would regularly change the secret location of their bags to keep them from being taken by other workers.

Because busers used many more bags than other employees, managers were more likely to fulfill their requests for an entire roll. Busers working day shifts would often save bags for those working at night and let them know where they were hidden. Busers were able to maintain the largest garbage bag stockpile in the restaurant and would usually share the location with other Spanish-speaking workers. Because I often worked shifts that overlapped with morning and evening buser schedules, the morning busers would often tell me the location of garbage bags (in Spanish) so that I could inform the busers working the night shift. Spanish speakers thus had better access to bags than English speakers and were less likely to end up in conflicts when they needed a bag. The option of simply asking where the bags were located was not available to other bartenders who did not speak Spanish regularly (i.e., those who used Spanish only for requests and directives). The busers would sometimes tease bartenders in Spanish rather than tell them where the bags were. For example, another bartender in search of bags once told me, "The bags are in the *escondidas*, wherever that is" (*escondidas* 'hidden', feminine plural).

Bartenders were often told they could leave as soon as the garbage had been taken out. If there were no bags, this might mean that the bartender would leave work late simply because of the time wasted searching for bags. If a bartender became frustrated trying to find bags, the access afforded by speaking Spanish took on real value, because busers would sometimes insist that bartenders give beer to all the kitchen workers in exchange for a few garbage bags.

Because of the division of labor along racial lines, Latino workers also had more direct access to food within the restaurant. At Chalupatown, servers could order food at half price, while bartenders, hosts, and kitchen workers received one free meal for each shift that they worked (excluding several of the higher-priced menu items). Because the Latino employees worked in the kitchen, they could prepare whatever they wanted with the ingredients available, while Anglo employees usually had to order from the menu. During periods when business was relatively slow, the cooks would sometimes prepare a large amount of a special dish for all of the kitchen workers. Word would spread around the restaurant in Spanish, so that the cooks could get an idea of how much food to prepare. The Anglo workers tired of eating off the same menu five days a week would often complain, "Why can't we get that?" When two of my Anglo co-workers realized that I was regularly asked if I wanted a serving, they asked if I could help "get them on the list."

Spanish also provided different access to food because of interactions with the delivery drivers for produce companies. The drivers all spoke Spanish and would sometimes leave gifts of fruit for the kitchen staff. Sometimes drivers or employees themselves would bring pastries for other workers. In the summer, the produce driver would leave a watermelon once every week or two. A group of Anglo servers once took the watermelon for a party to which kitchen workers were not invited. After this, the kitchen staff began to hide the watermelon in the cooler. As with specially prepared dishes, news that the watermelon was about to be cut or that pastries were available would spread through the restaurant in Spanish, making it unlikely that Anglos would be able to partake. Although the resources involved were fairly petty items like garbage bags and watermelons, kitchen workers were able to use Spanish to control the resources that were available to them.

Pretending Not to Understand

Another way in which Spanish allowed for resistance in the workplace was the possibility of pretending not to understand a directive. Because Anglo employees typically made little effort to make themselves understood in Spanish, Latino workers generally had that option. This strategy was not widely used and would not be effective in many cases owing to an assumption of comprehension by managers (cf. ex. 14 above). Contrary to the assumption of Anglo managers, Spanish-speaking workers would rarely if ever use this strategy to avoid their actual work responsibilities. Pretending not to understand was most frequently used to avoid conflict in cases where an Anglo employee asked a kitchen worker to violate workplace rules. Some of the Anglo employees would regularly try to get kitchen workers to perform tasks for them, as in the example of refilling the

ice bin. For several weeks, some Anglo servers would pay busers extra money to perform what should have been the servers' own side work (e.g., sweeping their section, refilling salt and pepper shakers). This practice was prohibited after the managers were forced to stay late one night, waiting for two busers to perform the side work ten different servers had paid them to do. Other examples in which servers might make special requests include asking for food items without ringing them in on the register, requesting larger helpings, and asking busers to pour water and tea for customers. In these cases, pretending not to understand was a viable strategy because the Anglo employees were aware that they were asking a co-worker to break the rules and would not generally press the issue. Although Anglos typically assumed that kitchen workers pretended not to understand a wide range of directives, this strategy was actually used most frequently in cases where Anglos were both trying to exploit Spanish-speaking co-workers and violating workplace rules. Pretending not to understand blocked Anglo attempts to assert control over the actions of Spanish-speaking employees, but it also reinforced the Anglo perception that Spanish speakers understood English more than they let on.

CONCLUSION: COMPETING FUNCTIONS OF SPANISH

Another Anglo bartender was telling me his reasons for quitting his job at Chalupatown and looking for other work. We worked together quite often and were good friends. He explained that the environment at Chalupatown was increasingly stressful for him, and that he had fallen into a deep depression and just couldn't take it anymore. I certainly understood, but as I came to have fewer and fewer Anglo co-workers I could talk to, I didn't want him to leave. "But see," he told me, "you speak Spanish well enough to escape. You can walk into the kitchen and talk to those guys for five minutes and remind yourself that the entire planet isn't populated with assholes. I don't speak Spanish that well. I don't have anywhere else to go." Although his comment reflects the central role of language in constructing social space within the restaurant, it is overly simplistic. The Anglo workers were not simply "assholes" or even "racists." Indeed, most of the Anglo managers presented themselves as explicitly ANTI-racist. The Anglo use of Spanish reproduces the prevalent norm for using Spanish to project a particular Anglo identity. In interactions with Spanish speakers, this Anglo appropriation of Spanish reproduces contexts of racial inequality, even though the use of Mock Spanish may not be consciously intended as racist.

The Spanish elements in Anglo directives may be fairly arbitrary (as in "You have to finish *todo eso*") so that they provide little help in actually conveying the information the directive requires. However, there are certainly some cases where the Spanish words would be helpful in conveying meaning. Saying that there is "*agua* on the *piso*" would certainly convey more information than "water on the floor."

Some Spanish is better than none at all.[6] Yet if the intent of including Spanish was actually to convey directives to Spanish speakers, one would expect the managers to utilize Spanish to the full extent of their competence and actually form Spanish sentences.

Although Anglo speakers had some knowledge of Spanish grammar, they rarely utilized this knowledge when communicating with a monolingual Spanish speaker. The intent behind this limited use of Spanish seems to be the same motivations Hill associates with some speakers of Mock Spanish: an attempt to convey congeniality and open-mindedness. Hill (1998:683) views Mock Spanish as part of Cmiel's (1990) "middling style," or "a way for elites to display democratic and egalitarian sensibilities by incorporating colloquial and even slangy speech." This "congeniality" is constructed through indexing racist stereotypes of Spanish speakers, however, and it is very Anglocentric.

Although the language ideology of Anglo workers restricted the ability of Spanish speakers to perform their job duties, the Anglo disregard for Spanish made it possible for employees to develop an alternative Spanish linguistic market. Spanish served as a means to provide crucial information both within and outside the workplace, and as an outlet for discussing the racial attitudes of Anglo co-workers. Kitchen workers were able to use Spanish to control the few resources available to them. The Anglo disregard for Spanish also made it possible for kitchen workers to claim a communication failure in order to opt out of conversations in which Anglos made overt attempts to exploit their Latino co-workers.

The Anglo use of Mock Spanish in interactions with Latino workers at Chalupatown is not particularly different from Hill's examples of its use in Anglo–Anglo discourse. There is no accommodation to Spanish speakers. Anglo Spanish marks racial difference through self-directed humor associated with an assumption of racial superiority. Mock Spanish does not generally facilitate communication of referential meaning, and the Anglo side of the communicative burden may involve nothing more than demonstrating recognition of the racial difference inherent in a particular interaction.

For Anglo speakers, the use of Spanish indexes AFFECTIVE STANCE (Ochs 1996:411). Ochs argues that social identities are constructed by varying indexical displays of stance across different situations (1996:424). The use of Spanish by Anglo speakers attempts to entail a context in which Anglo speakers project a social identity that includes an awareness of Spanish and a recognition that one is interacting with a Spanish speaker. Given the iconic relationship between Spanish and race, Anglos often interpret the full use of actual Spanish—speaking Spanish rather than inserting Spanish words into English—as an indexical sign that conveys solidarity with Spanish speakers (hence my being labeled a "burrito"). By using a little Spanish rather than full Spanish, Anglo speakers may be attempting to index a sympathetic stance toward Latinos without actually indexing a position of equality or solidarity. This is,

of course, an entirely Anglocentric view of the functions of Spanish.

For native Spanish speakers, the use of Spanish nonce borrowings in English does not index positive social affect but is simply interpreted as a poor effort at speaking Spanish. Spanish-speaking workers typically attributed Anglo Spanish either to a lack of speaker competence or to an unwillingness actually to speak Spanish. Occasionally, kitchen workers would complain about receiving incomprehensible directives from Anglos they knew spoke enough Spanish to make themselves understood. The structure of Anglo Spanish ignores the Spanish-speaking listener's ability to comprehend in favor of using Spanish primarily to exploit Anglo understandings of the indexical functions of Spanish....

Because Anglos use Spanish primarily for its presumed ability to index positive social stance, the ability of Spanish to serve its basic communicative function is diminished. The resulting limitations on the use of Spanish leave Spanish-speaking workers with a diminished ability to participate fully in interactions with Anglos. This interactional limitation constrains the agency of Spanish speakers. The ability for one's actions to affect others (and oneself) is diminished because the Spanish speaker does not have access to information that is vital to the evaluation of his or her actions. The language ideology of Mock Spanish serves directly to enact systematic conditions of racial inequality....

Language ideology both reflects and enacts racial inequalities. In Anglo–Anglo interactions, Mock Spanish may function as a form of symbolic revalorization, reproducing derogatory racial portrayals of Latinos for Anglo amusement. When used in interactions with Spanish speakers, Mock Spanish serves to exclude Spanish speakers from interactions in which they should be active participants. The failure to listen to the needs of Latinos and the failure earnestly to attempt to communicate with Spanish speakers are not forms of symbolic revalorization, but are basic components of racial subordination. The ideology of Mock Spanish is not simply a media tool for reproducing negative stereotypes of Latinos, it is a basic component in the maintenance of racial inequality in the United States.

Notes

I am greatly indebted to the restaurant workers who shared their experiences and opinions with me. For helpful discussions and comments, I would like to thank Eriko Atagi, Mary Bucholtz, Elaine Chun, Erin Debenport, Jane Hill, Jennifer Palmer, Robin Queen, Otto Santa Ana, Teresa Satterfield, Keith Walters, Albert Zapata, and an anonymous reviewer.

1. All examples from http://www.urbandictionary.com. Entries change regularly over time. The examples here were present on the website as of October 24, 2004.

2. "Chalupatown" and all other names [here] are pseudonyms.

3. The numbers are approximate because of fluctuations resulting from frequent employee turnover.

4. Menu quotes have been slightly altered to maintain anonymity.

5. Food cost (not actual food prices) refers to the ratio of money spent on food to the income from food orders. A rise in food costs implies that food is leaving the restaurant at a higher rate, either through larger portions, failure to ring in items, or employee theft.

6. For example, a Spanish-speaking friend working at a restaurant in Michigan was simply given a photocopy of fairly complex English instructions for operating an industrial dishwasher with the assumption that he could find someone to translate it for him.

References

Bonilla-Silva, Eduardo (2002). The linguistics of color-blind racism: How to talk nasty about Blacks without sounding "racist." *Critical Sociology* 28:41–64.

———, & Forman, Tyrone (2000). "I'm not racist, but...": Mapping White college students' racial ideology in the United States. *Discourse and Society* 11:50–85.

Bourdieu, Pierre (1991). *Language and symbolic power.* John B. Thompson (ed.), Gino Raymond & Matthew Adamson (trans.). Cambridge, MA: Harvard University Press.

Bucholtz, Mary (2004). The appropriation of African American Vernacular English as European American youth slang. Paper presented at New Ways of Analyzing Variation (NWAV) 33, University of Michigan, Ann Arbor.

Cameron, James, & Wisher, William, Jr. (1991). *Terminator II: Judgment Day* (James Cameron, director). Tri Star Pictures.

Chun, Elaine (2004). Ideologies of legitimate mockery: Margaret Cho's revoicings of Mock Asian. *Pragmatics* 14:263–89.

Cmiel, Kenneth (1990). *Democratic eloquence.* New York: Morrow.

Eble, Connie (2004). Slang. In Edward Finegan & John R. Rickford (eds.), *Language in the USA: Themes for the twenty-first century*, 375–86. New York: Cambridge University Press.

Erard, Michael (1996). Models of Spanish and Spanish speakers in the political economy of Anglo Spanish. In Alice Chu et al. (eds.), *SALSA IV: Proceedings of the Fourth Annual Symposium about Language and Society—Austin.*

Ferguson, Charles (1975). Toward a characterization of English foreigner talk. *Anthropological Linguistics* 17:1–14.

——— (1981). "Foreigner talk" as the name of a simplified register. *International Journal of the Sociology of Language* 28:9–18.

Gal, Susan, & Irvine, Judith (2000). Language ideology and linguistic differentiation. In Paul Kroskrity (ed.), *Regimes of language*, 35–84. Santa Fe, NM: School of American Research Press.

Haviland, John B. (2003). Ideologies of language: Some reflections on language and U.S. law. *American Anthropologist* 105:764–74.

Hill, Jane H. (1993). Is it really "No Problemo"? In Robin Queen and Rusty Barrett (eds.), *SALSA I: Proceedings of the First Annual Symposium about Language and Society—Austin. Texas Linguistic Forum* 33:1–12.

——— (1995). Mock Spanish: A site for the indexical reproduction of racism in American English. Originally posted at University of Chicago Lang-cult site: http://www.cs.uchicago.edu/discussions/l-c.

——— (1998). Language, race and white public space. *American Anthropologist* 100:680–89.

Lindeman, Stephanie (2002). Listening with an attitude: A model of native-speaker comprehension of non-native speakers in the United States. *Language in Society* 31:419–41.

Lindquist, Julie (2002). *A place to stand: Politics and persuasion in a working-class bar.* New York: Oxford University Press.

——— (2004). Class identity and the politics of dissent: The culture of argument in a Chicago neighborhood bar. In Marcia Farr (ed.), *Ethnolinguistic Chicago: Language and literacy in the city's neighborhoods.* Mahwah, NJ: Erlbaum.

Lippi-Green. Rosina (1997). *English with an accent: Language, ideology, and discrimination in the United States.* London: Routledge.

Mesthrie, Rajend (2002). Mock languages and symbolic power: The South African radio series *Applesammy and Naidoo. World Englishes* 21:99–112.

Morgan, Marcyliena (2001). "Nuthin' but a G thang": Grammar and language ideology in Hip Hop identity. In Sonja Lanehart (ed.), *Sociocultural and historical contexts of African American Vernacular English*, 187–210. Amsterdam: John Benjamins. [Reprinted in this volume, Chapter 27.]

——— (2002). *Language, discourse, and power in African American culture.* New York: Cambridge University Press.

Muysken, Pieter (2000). *Bilingual speech.* Cambridge: Cambridge University Press.

Ochs, Elinor (1996). Linguistic resources for socializing humanity. In John J. Gumperz & Stephen C. Levinson (eds.), *Rethinking linguistic relativity*, 407–37. Cambridge: Cambridge University Press.

Perea, Juan (1995). Los olvidados: On the making of invisible people. *New York University Law Review* 70:965–91.

Perkins, Lisa, & Milroy, Lesley (1997). Sharing the communicative burden: A conversation-analytic account of aphasic/non-aphasic interaction. *Multilingua* 16:199–215.

Peñalosa, Fernando (1981). *Chicano sociolinguistics.* Rowley, MA: Newbury House.

Poplack, Shana, Sankoff, David, & Miller, Christopher (1988). The social correlates and linguistic processes of lexical borrowing and assimilation. *Linguistics* 26:47–104.

Ronkin, Maggie, & Karn, Helen E. (1999). Mock Ebonics: Linguistic racism in parodies of Ebonics on the Internet. *Journal of Sociolinguistics* 3:360–80.

Santa Ana, Otto (1999). "Like an animal I was treated": Anti-immigrant metaphor in U.S. public discourse. *Discourse and Society* 10:191–224.

——— (2002). *Brown tide rising: Metaphors of Latinos in contemporary American public discourse.* Austin: University of Texas Press.

Smitherman, Geneva (1994). *Black talk: Words and phrases from the hood to the amen corner.* Boston & New York: Houghton Mifflin.

Urciuoli, Bonnie (1996). *Exposing prejudice: Puerto Rican experiences of language, race, and class.* Boulder, CO: Westview Press.

Valdés, Guadalupe (1981). Code-switching as deliberate verbal strategy: A microanalysis of direct and indirect requests among bilingual Chicano speakers. In Richard P. Durán (ed.), *Latino language and communicative behavior*, 95–108. Norwood, NJ: Ablex.

Walters, Keith (1995). Contesting representations of African American Language. In Risako Ide et al. (eds.), *SALSA III: Proceedings of the Third Annual Symposium about Language and Society—Austin, Texas Linguistics Forum* 36:137–51. Austin: University of Texas Department of Linguistics.

Woolard, Kathryn A., & Schieffelin, Bambi (1994). Language ideology. *Annual Review of Anthropology* 23:55–82.

Zentella, Ana Celia (1996). The "Chiquitification" of U.S. Latinos and their languages, or: Why we need an anthropolitical linguistics. In Risako Ide et al. (eds), *SALSA III: Proceedings of the Third Annual Symposium about Language and Society—Austin, Texas Linguistics Forum* 36:1–18.

Post-reading Questions / Activities

- Why would someone (an English speaker) who actually knows quite a bit of Spanish choose to use incorrect Spanish or English with Spanish words inserted? Is there a remedy for the underlying attitude?
- How did Barrett's position as a worker affect his observations? Could a pure researcher have learned as much as he did? What other methods might someone use to study these issues?
- Might there be a solution to the tensions evident in a restaurant such as the one described in this chapter? What would it be?
- Observe interactions in an ethnic restaurant. Are there clear differences in the identities of different workers? What role does language play?
- How might interactions be different at, say, a French or Italian restaurant? A Chinese restaurant? What accounts for these differences?

Vocabulary

AAE	"foreigner talk"	Mock Spanish
bound morpheme	free morpheme	morpheme
code switching	hyperanglicize	nonce borrowing
directive	interlocutor	register
ethnographer	language ideology	slang
ethnography of speaking	linguistic marketplace	

Suggested Further Reading

Gumperz, John J. 1982. "Interethnic Communication." *Discourse Strategies,* pp. 172–203. Cambridge: Cambridge University Press.

Hill, Jane H. 1998. "Language, Race, and White Public Space." *American Anthropologist* 100: 680–689.

Urciuoli, Bonnie. 1996. *Exposing Prejudice: Puerto Rican Experiences of Language, Race, and Class.* Boulder, CO: Westview Press.

CHAPTER 30

"Women's Language" or "Powerless Language"?

William M. O'Barr and Bowman K. Atkins

(1998 [1980])

William O'Barr and Bowman Atkins set about to test the hypothesis that there were absolute differences in the ways women and men talk, looking in particular at the ways witnesses speak and are spoken to during trials.

There has been a lot of research on linguistic interactions in various institutions, such as law, medicine, and schools. In each institution, individuals play particular roles, which always have linguistic dimensions. Sometimes they reflect broader social roles and sometimes they are particular to that setting.

O'Barr and Atkins summarize Robin Lakoff's findings about the features of women's language, features that have intuitive power. They find that in some cases their data corresponded quite well to Lakoff's, but in other cases there were significant differences. This then led them to suggest an alternative explanation for the features they found.

Reading Questions

- What advice do trial practice manuals give about special treatment for women?
- Which features of "women's language" did O'Barr and Atkins find used by women? By men? Under what circumstances? How did O'Barr and Atkins explain their findings?

The understanding of language and sex in American culture has progressed far beyond Robin Lakoff's influential and provocative essays on "women's language" written only a few years ago (Lakoff 1975). The rapid development of knowledge in what had been so significantly an ignored and overlooked area owes much to both the development of sociolinguistic interest in general and to the woman's movement in particular. But as a recent review of anthropological studies about women pointed out, this interest has grown so quickly and studies proliferated so fast that there is frequently little or no cross-referencing of mutually supportive studies and equally little attempt to reconcile conflicting interpretations of women's roles (Quinn 1977). A similar critique of the literature on language and sex would no doubt reveal many of the same problems. But in one sense, these are not problems—they are marks of a rapidly developing field of inquiry, of vitality, and of saliency of the topic.

Our interest in language and sex was sharpened by Lakoff's essays. Indeed, her work was for us—as it was for

many others—a jumping off point. But unlike some other studies, ours was not primarily an attempt to understand language and sex differences. Rather, the major goal of our recent research has been the study of language variation in a specific institutional context—the American trial courtroom—and sex-related differences were one of the kinds of variation which current sociolinguistic issues led us to consider. Our interest was further kindled by the discovery that trial practice manuals (how-to-do-it books by successful trial lawyers and law professors) often had special sections on how female witnesses behave differently from males and thus special kinds of treatment they require.

In this paper, we describe our study of how women (and men) talk in court. The research we report here is part of a 30-month study of language variation in trial courtrooms which has included both ethnographic and experimental components. It is the thesis of this study that so-called women's language is in large part a language of powerlessness, a condition that can apply to men as well as women. That a complex of such features should have been called "women's language" in the first place reflects the generally powerless position of many women in American society, a point recognized but not developed extensively by Lakoff (1975: 7–8). Careful examination in one institutional setting of the

William M. O'Barr and Bowman K. Atkins. "'Women's Language' or 'Powerless Language'?" In *Language and Gender: A Reader*, ed. by Jennifer Coates. Oxford: Blackwell, 1998, pp. 377–387.

features which were identified as constituting "women's language" has shown clearly that such features are simply not patterned along sex lines. Moreover, the features do not, in a strict sense, constitute a *style* or *register* since there is not perfect co-variation.

[This chapter proceeds] as follows: first, it examines the phenomenon of "women's language" in the institutional context of a court of law; second, it shows that the features of "women's language" are not restricted to women and therefore suggests renaming the concept "powerless" language due to its close association with persons having low social power and often relatively little previous experience in the courtroom setting; [...] and finally, it calls for a refinement of our studies to distinguish powerless language features from others which may in fact be found primarily in women's speech.

How to Handle Women in Court— Some Advice from Lawyers

One of the means which we used in our study of courtroom language to identify specific language variables for detailed study was information provided to us in interviews with practicing lawyers. More useful, however, were *trial practice manuals*—books written by experienced lawyers which attempt to discuss systematically successful methods and tactics for conducting trials. Typically, little effort is devoted to teaching and developing trial practice skills in the course of a legal education. Rather it is expected that they will be acquired through personal experimentation, through watching and modeling one's behavior after successful senior lawyers, and through reading the advice contained in such manuals. Those who write trial practice manuals are experienced members of the legal profession who are reporting on both their own experiences and the generally accepted folklore within the profession. In all these situations, the basis for claims about what works or what does not tends to be the general success of those who give advice or serve as models—judged primarily by whether they win their cases most of the time.

One kind of advice which struck us in reading through several of these manuals was that pertaining to the special treatment which should be accorded women. The manuals which discuss special treatment for women tend to offer similar advice regarding female witnesses. Readers are instructed to behave generally the same toward women as men, but to note that, in certain matters or situations, women require some special considerations. Some of this advice includes the following:

1. *Be especially courteous to women.* ("Even when jurors share the cross-examiner's reaction that the female witness on the stand is dishonest or otherwise undeserving individually, at least some of the jurors are likely to think it improper for the attorney to decline to extend the courtesies customarily extended to women.") (Keeton 1973: 149.)

2. *Avoid making women cry.* ("Jurors, along with others, may be inclined to forgive and forget transgressions under the influence of sympathy provoked by the genuine tears of a female witness." "A crying woman does your case no good.") (Keeton 1973: 149; Bailey and Rothblatt 1971: 190.)

3. *Women behave differently from men and this can sometimes be used to advantage.* ("Women are contrary witnesses. They hate to say yes.... A woman's desire to avoid the obvious answer will lead her right into your real objective—contradicting the testimony of previous prosecution witnesses. Women, like children, are prone to exaggeration; they generally have poor memories as to previous fabrications and exaggerations. They also are stubborn. You will have difficulty trying to induce them to qualify their testimony. Rather, it might be easier to induce them to exaggerate and cause their testimony to appear incredible. An intelligent woman will very often be evasive. She will avoid making a direct answer to a damaging question. Keep after her until you get a direct answer—but always be the gentleman.") (Bailey and Rothblatt 1971: 190–1.)

These comments about women's behavior in court and their likely consequences in the trial process further raised our interest in studying the speech behavior of women in court. Having been told by Lakoff that women do speak differently from men, we interpreted these trial practice authors as saying that at least some of these differences can be consequential in the trial process. Thus, one of the kinds of variation which we sought to examine when we began to observe and tape record courtroom speech was patterns unique to either women or men. We did not know what we would find, so we started out by using Lakoff's discussion of "women's language" as a guide.

Briefly, what Lakoff had proposed was that women's speech varies from men's in several significant ways. Although she provides no firm listing of the major features of what she terms "women's language" (hereafter referred to...as WL), we noted the following features, said to occur in high frequency among women, and used these as a baseline for our investigation of sex-related speech patterns in court.

1 *Hedges.* ("It's sort of hot in here."; "I'd kind of like to go."; "I guess..."; "It seems like..."; and so on.)

2 *(Super)polite forms.* ("I'd really appreciate it if..."; "Would you please open the door, if you don't mind?"; and so on.)

3 *Tag questions.* ("John is here, isn't he?" instead of "Is John here?"; and so on.)

4 *Speaking in italics.* (Intonational emphasis equivalent to underlining words in written language; emphatic *so* or *very* and so on.)

5 *Empty adjectives.* (*Divine; charming; cute; sweet; adorable; lovely;* and so on.)

6 *Hypercorrect grammar and pronunciation.* (Bookish grammar; more formal enunciation.)

7 *Lack of a sense of humor.* (Women said to be poor joke tellers and to frequently "miss the point" in jokes told by men.)

8 *Direct quotations.* (Use of direct quotations instead of paraphrases.)

9 *Special lexicon.* (In domains like colors where words like *magenta, chartreuse,* and so on are typically used only by women.)

10 *Question intonation in declarative contexts.* (For example, in response to the question, "When will dinner be ready?", an answer like "Around 6 o'clock?", as though seeking approval and asking whether that time will be okay.)

WHAT WE FOUND

During the summer of 1974, we recorded over 150 hours of trials in a North Carolina superior criminal court. Although almost all of the lawyers we observed were males, the sex distribution of witnesses was more nearly equal. On looking for the speech patterns described by Lakoff, we quickly discovered some women who spoke in the described manner. The only major discrepancies between Lakoff's description and our findings were in features which the specific context of the courtroom rendered inappropriate, for example, *tag questions* (because witnesses typically answer rather than ask questions) and *joking* (because there is little humor in a courtroom, we did not have occasion to observe the specifically female patterns of humor to which she referred).

In addition to our early finding that some women approximate the model described by Lakoff, we also were quick to note that there was considerable variation in the degree to which women exhibited these characteristics. Since our observations were limited to about ten weeks of trials during which we were able to observe a variety of cases in terms of offense (ranging from traffic cases, drug possession, robbery, manslaughter, to rape) and length (from a few hours to almost five days), we believe that our observations cover a reasonably good cross-section of the kinds of trials, and hence witnesses, handled by this type of court. Yet, ten weeks is not enough to produce a very large number of witnesses. Even a single witness may spend several hours testifying. In addition, the court spends much time selecting jurors, hearing summation remarks, giving jury instructions, and handling administrative matters. Thus, when looking at patterns of how different women talk in court, we are in a better position to deal with the range of variation we observed than to attempt any precise frequency counts of persons falling into various categories. Thus, we will concentrate our efforts here on describing the range and complement this with some non-statistical impressions regarding frequency.

Our observations show a continuum of use of the features described by Lakoff.[1] We were initially at a loss to explain why some women should speak more or less as Lakoff had described and why others should use only a few of these features. We will deal with our interpretation of these findings later, but first let us examine some points along the continuum from high to low.

A. Mrs. W,[2] a witness in a case involving the death of her neighbor in an automobile accident, is an extreme example of a person speaking WL in her testimony. She used nearly every feature described by Lakoff and certainly all those which are appropriate in the courtroom context. Her speech contains a high frequency of *intensifiers* ("*very* close friends," "*quite* ill," and so on often with intonation emphasis); *hedges* (frequent use of "you know," "sort of like," "maybe just a little bit," "let's see," and so on); *empty adjectives* ("this *very* kind policeman"); and other similar features. The first example below is typical of her speech and shows the types of intensifiers and hedges she commonly uses.[3] (To understand what her speech *might* be like without these features, example (2) is a rewritten version of her answers with the WL features eliminated.)

(1) L. State whether or not, Mrs. W, you were acquainted with or knew the late Mrs. E. D.
   W. Quite well.
   L. What was the nature of your acquaintance with her?
   W. Well, we were, uh, very close friends. Uh, she was even sort of like a mother to me.

(2) L. State whether or not, Mrs. W, you were acquainted with or knew the late Mrs. E. D.
   W. Yes, I did.
   L. What was the nature of your acquaintance with her?
   W. We were close friends. She was like a mother to me.

Table 1 summarizes the frequency of several features attributed to WL by Lakoff. Calculated as a ratio of WL forms for each answer, this witness's speech contains 1.14—among the highest incidences we observed.

B. The speech of Mrs. N, a witness in a case involving her father's arrest, shows fewer WL features. Her ratio of features for each answer drops to .84. Her testimony contains instances of both WL and a more assertive speech style. Frequently, her speech is punctuated with responses like: "He, see, he thought it was more-or-less me rather than the police officer." Yet it also contains many more straightforward and assertive passages than are found in A's speech. In example (3), for instance, Mrs. N is anything but passive. She turns questions back on the lawyer and even interrupts him. Example (4) illustrates the ambivalence of this speaker's style better. Note how she moves quickly to qualify—in WL—an otherwise assertive response.

(3) L.   All right. I ask you if your husband hasn't beaten him up in the last week?
    W.   Yes, and do you know why?
    L.   Well, I…
    W.   Another gun episode.
    L.   Another gun episode?
    W.   Yessiree.

(4) L.   You've had a controversy going with him for a long time, haven't you?
    W.   Ask why—I mean not because I'm just his daughter.

C.   The speech of Dr. H, a pathologist who testifies as an expert witness, exhibits fewer features of WL than either of the other two women. Her speech contains the lowest incidence of WL features among the female witnesses whose speech we analyzed. Dr. H's ratio of WL features is .18 for each answer. Her responses tend to be straightforward, with little hesitancy, few hedges, a noticeable lack of intensifiers, and so on. (See Table 1.) Typical of her speech is example (5) in which she explains some of her findings in a pathological examination.

(5) L.   And had the heart not been functioning, in other words, had the heart been stopped, there would have been no blood to have come from that region?
    W.   It may leak down depending on the position of the body after death. But the presence of blood in the alveoli indicates that some active respiratory action had to take place.

What all of this shows is the fact that some women speak in the way Lakoff described, employing many features of WL, while others are far away on the continuum of possible and appropriate styles for the courtroom. Before discussing the reasons which may lie behind this variation in the language used by women in court, we first examine an equally interesting finding which emerged from our investigation of male speech in court.

We also found men who exhibit WL characteristics in their courtroom testimony. To illustrate this, we examine the speech of three male witnesses which varies along a continuum of high to low incidence of WL features.

D.   Mr. W exhibits many but not all of Lakoff's WL features.[4] Some of those which he does employ, like intensifiers, for example, occur in especially high frequency—among the highest observed among all speakers, whether male or female. His ratio of WL features for each answer is 1.39, actually higher than individual A. Example (6), while an extreme instance of Mr. W's use of WL features, does illustrate the degree to which features attributed to women are in fact present in high frequency in the speech of some men.

Table 1. Frequency Distribution of Women's Language Features[a] in the Speech of Six Witnesses in a Trial Courtroom

	Women			Men		
	A	B	C	D	E	F
Intensifiers[b]	16	0	0	21	2	1
Hedges[c]	19	2	3	2	5	0
Hesitation forms[d]	52	20	13	26	27	11
W asks L questions[e]	2	0	0	0	0	0
Gestures[f]	2	0	0	0	0	0
Polite forms[g]	9	0	2	2	0	1
Sir[h]	2	0	6	32	13	11
Quotes[i]	1	5	0	0	0	0
Total (all powerless forms)	103	27	24	85	47	24
No. answers in interview	90	32	136	61	73	52
Ratio (no. powerless forms for each answer)	1.14	0.84	0.18	1.39	0.64	0.46

[a]The particular features chosen for inclusion in this table were selected because of their saliency and frequency of occurrence. Not included here are features of WL which either do not occur in court or ones which we had difficulty operationalizing and coding. *Based on direct examinations only.*

[b]Forms which increase or emphasize the force of assertion such as *very, definitely, very definitely, surely, such a,* and so on.

[c]Forms which reduce the force of assertion allowing for exceptions or avoiding rigid commitments such as *sort of, a little, kind of,* and so on.

[d]Pause fillers such as *uh, um, ah,* and "meaningless" particles such as *oh, well, let's see, now, so, you see,* and so on.

[e]Use of question intonation in response to lawyer's questions, including rising intonation in normally declarative contexts (for example, "thirty?, thirty-five?") and questions asked by witness of lawyer like "Which way do you go…?"

[f]Spoken indications of direction such as *over there,* and so on.

[g]Include *please, thank you,* and so on. Use of *sir* counted separately due to its high frequency.

[h]Assumed to be an indication of more polite speech.

[i]Not typically allowed in court under restrictions on hearsay which restrict the situations under which a witness may tell what someone else said.

Source: Original data.

(6) L. And you saw, you observed what?

W. Well, after I heard—I can't really, I can't definitely state whether the brakes or the lights came first, but I rotated my head slightly to the right, and looked directly behind Mr. Z, and I saw reflections of lights, and uh, very, very, very instantaneously after that, I heard a very, very loud explosion—from my standpoint of view it would have been an implosion because everything was forced outward, like this, like a grenade thrown into a room. And, uh, it was, it was terrifically loud.

E. Mr. N, more toward the low-frequency end of the continuum of male speakers, shows some WL features. His ratio of features for each answer is .64, comparable to individual B. Example (7) shows an instance of passages from the testimony of this speaker in which there are few WL features. Example (8), by comparison, shows the same hedging in a way characteristic of WL. His speech falls between the highest and lowest incidences of WL features we observed among males.

(7) L. After you looked back and saw the back of the ambulance, what did you do?

W. After I realized that my patient and my attendant were thrown from the vehicle, uh, which I assumed, I radioed in for help to the dispatcher, tell her that we had been in an accident and, uh, my patient and attendant were thrown from the vehicle and I didn't know the extent of their injury at the time, to hurry up and send help.

(8) L. Did you form any conclusion about what her problem was at the time you were there?

W. I felt that she had, uh, might have had a sort of heart attack.

F. Officer G, among the males lowest in WL features, virtually lacks all features tabulated in Table 1 except for hesitancy and using *sir*. His ratio of WL forms for each answer is .46. Example (9) shows how this speaker handles the lack of certainty in a more authoritative manner than by beginning his answer with "I guess...". His no-nonsense, straightforward manner is illustrated well by example (10), in which a technical answer is given in a style comparable to that of individual C.

(9) L. Approximately how many times have you testified in court?

W. It would only have to be a guess, but it's three or four, five, six hundred times. Probably more.

(10) L. You say that you found blood of group O?

W. The blood in the vial, in the layman's term, is positive, Rh positive. Technically referred to as a capital r, sub o, little r.

Taken together these findings suggest that the so-called women's language is neither characteristic of all women nor limited only to women. A similar continuum of WL features (high to low) is found among speakers of both sexes. These findings suggest that the sex of a speaker is insufficient to explain incidence of WL features, and that we must look elsewhere for an explanation of this variation.

Once we had realized that WL features were distributed in such a manner, we began to examine the data for other factors which might be associated with a high or low incidence of the features in question. First, we noted that we were able to find *more* women toward the high end of the continuum. Next, we noted that all the women who were aberrant (that is, who used relatively few WL features) had something in common—an unusually high social status. Like Dr. H, they were typically well-educated, professional women of middle-class background. A corresponding pattern was noted among the aberrant men (that is, those high in WL features). Like Mr. W, they tended to be men who held either subordinate, lower-status jobs or were unemployed. Housewives were high in WL features while middle-class males were low in these features. In addition to social status in the society at large, another factor associated with low incidence of WL is previous courtroom experience. Both individuals C and F testify frequently in court as expert witnesses, that is, as witnesses who testify on the basis of their professional expertise. However, it should be noted that not all persons who speak with few WL features have had extensive courtroom experience. The point we wish to emphasize is that a powerful position may derive from either social standing in the larger society and/or status accorded by the court. We carefully observed these patterns and found them to hold generally.[5] For some individuals whom we had observed in the courtroom, we analyzed their speech in detail in order to tabulate the frequency of the WL features as shown in Table 1. A little more about the background of the persons we have described will illustrate the sort of pattern we observed.

A   is a married woman, about 55 years old, who is a housewife.

B   is married, but younger, about 35 years old. From her testimony, there is no information that she works outside her home.

C   is a pathologist in a local hospital. She is 35–40 years old. There is no indication from content of her responses or from the way she was addressed (always *Dr.*) of her marital status. She has testified in court as a pathologist on many occasions.

D   is an ambulance attendant, rather inexperienced in his job, at which he has worked for less than 6 months. Age around 30. Marital status unknown.

E   is D's supervisor. He drives the ambulance, supervises emergency treatment, and gives instructions to D. He has worked at his job longer than D and has had more experience. Age about 30–35; marital status unknown.

F   is an experienced member of the local police force. He has testified in court frequently. Age 35–40; marital status unknown.

"Women's Language" or "Powerless Language"?

In the previous section, we presented data which indicate that the variation in WL features may be related more to social powerlessness than to sex. We have presented both observational data and some statistics to show that this style is not simply or even primarily a sex-related pattern. We did, however, find it related to sex in that more women tend to be high in WL features while more men tend to be low in these same features. The speech patterns of three men and three women were examined. For each sex, the individuals varied from social statuses with relatively low power to more power (for women: housewife to doctor; for men: subordinate job to one with a high degree of independence of action). Experience may also be an important factor, for those whom we observed speaking with few WL features seemed more comfortable in the courtroom and with the content of their testimony. Associated with increasing shifts in social power and experience were corresponding decreases in frequency of WL features. These six cases were selected for detailed analysis because they were representative of the sorts of women and men who served as witnesses in the trials we observed in 1974. Based on this evidence, we would suggest that the phenomenon described by Lakoff would be better termed *powerless language*, a term which is more descriptive of the particular features involved, of the social status of those who speak in this manner, and one which does not link it unnecessarily to the sex of a speaker.

Further, we would suggest that the tendency for more women to speak powerless language and for men to speak less of it is due, at least in part, to the greater tendency of women to occupy relatively powerless social positions. What we have observed is a reflection in their speech behavior of their social status. Similarly, for men, a greater tendency to use the more powerful variant (which we will term *powerful language*) may be linked to the fact that men much more often tend to occupy relatively powerful positions in society.

Conclusion

In this study, we have attempted to argue that our data from studying male–female language patterns in trial courtrooms suggest that Lakoff's concept of "'woman's' language" is in need of modification. Our findings show that, in one particular context at least, not all women exhibit a high frequency of WL features and that some men do. We have argued that instead of being primarily sex-linked, a high incidence of some or all of these features appears to be more closely related to social position in the larger society and/or the specific context of the courtroom. Hence, we have suggested a re-naming of the phenomenon as "powerless language." What has previously been referred to as "women's language" is perhaps better thought of as a composite of features of powerless language (which can but need not be a characteristic of the speech of either women or men) and of some other features which may be more restricted to women's domains.

Thus, Lakoff's discussion of "women's language" confounds at least two different patterns of variation. Although our title suggests a dichotomy between "women's language" and "powerless language," these two patterns undoubtedly interact. It could well be that to speak like the powerless is not only typical of women because of the all-too-frequent powerless social position of many American women, but is also part of the cultural meaning of speaking "like a woman." Gender meanings draw on other social meanings; analyses that focus on sex in isolation from the social positions of women and men can thus tell us little about the meaning of "women's language" in society and culture.

Notes

The research reported here was supported by a National Science Foundation Law and Social Science Program Grant (No. GS-42742), William M. O'Barr, principal investigator. The authors wish to thank especially these other members of the research team for their advice and assistance: John Conley, Marilyn Endriss, Bonnie Erickson, Bruce Johnson, Debbie Mercer, Michael Porter, Lawrence Rosen, William Schmidheiser, and Laurens Walker. In addition, the cooperation of the Durham County, North Carolina, Superior Court is gratefully acknowledged.

1. Actually each feature should be treated as a separate continuum since there is not perfect co-variation. For convenience, we discuss the variation as a single continuum of possibilities. However, it should be kept in mind that a high frequency of occurrence of one particular feature may not necessarily be associated with a high frequency of another.

2. Names have been changed and indicated by a letter only in order to preserve the anonymity of witnesses. However, the forms of address used in the court are retained.

3. These examples are taken from both the direct and cross examinations of the witnesses, although Table 1 uses data only from direct examinations. Examples were chosen to point out clearly the differences in style. However, it must be noted that the cross examination is potentially a more powerless situation for the witness.

4. This speaker did not use some of the intonational features that we had noted among women having high frequencies of WL features in their speech.

5. We do not wish to make more of this pattern than our data are able to support, but we suggest that our grounds for these claims are at least as good as Lakoff's. Lakoff's basis for her description of features constituting WL are her own speech, speech of her friends and acquaintances, and patterns of use in the mass media.

References

Bailey, F. Lee and Rothblatt, Henry B. (1971) *Successful Techniques for Criminal Trials*. Rochester, NY: Lawyers Cooperative Publishing Co.

Keeton, Robert E. (1973) *Trial Tactics and Methods*. Boston: Little, Brown.

Lakoff, Robin (1975) *Language and Woman's Place*. New York: Harper & Row.

Quinn, Naomi (1977) "Anthropological studies of women's status." *Annual Review of Anthropology*, 6, 181–225.

Post-reading Questions / Activities

- Does the list of features of "women's language" seem plausible to you? Why or why not? Would you change this list? How?
- Where besides a courtroom might you expect to find evidence of "powerless language," and which groups would be likely to use the features of powerless language?
- O'Barr and Atkins wrote this article based on research conducted in the 1970s. Since that time, there has been considerable social change, including some change in gender roles. Gain permission to record at a trial, analyze the data using the features in O'Barr and Atkins's analysis, and compare the similarities and differences between their results and yours. Alternatively, you could analyze trial scenes on television or in movies. This would convey people's stereotypes about courtroom behavior, rather than actual behavior.

Vocabulary

hedge   style
register   tag question

Suggested Further Reading

Bucholtz, Mary, A. C. Liang, and Laurel A. Sutton, eds. 1999. *Reinventing Identities: The Gendered Self in Discourse*. New York: Oxford University Press.

Cameron, Deborah. 1992. *Feminism and Linguistic Theory*. 2d ed. London: Routledge.

———, and Jennifer Coates, eds. 1988. *Women in Their Speech Communities: New Perspectives on Language and Sex*. London: Longman.

Coates, Jennifer, ed. 1998. *Language and Gender: A Reader*. Malden, MA: Blackwell.

Eckert, Penelope, and Sally McConnell-Ginet. 1992. "Think Practically and Look Locally: Language and Gender as Community-Based Practice." *Annual Review of Anthropology* 21: 461–490.

———, and ———. 2003. *Language and Gender*. Cambridge: Cambridge University Press.

Graddol, David, and Joan Swann. 1989. *Gender Voices*. Oxford: Blackwell.

Hall, Kira, and Mary Bucholtz, eds. 1995. *Gender Articulated: Language and the Socially Constructed Self*. New York and London: Oxford University Press.

Holmes, Janet. 1995. *Women, Men, and Politeness*. London and New York: Longman.

Lakoff, Robin Tolmach. 1975. *Language and Woman's Place*. New York: Harper & Row.

———. 2004. *Language and Woman's Place: Text and Commentaries*. Revised and expanded edition, edited by Mary Bucholtz. Oxford and New York: Oxford University Press.

Ochs, Elinor. 1991. "Indexing Gender." In *Rethinking Context*, edited by Alessandro Duranti and Charles Goodwin, pp. 335–358. Cambridge: Cambridge University Press.

Philips, Susan U., Susan Steele, and Christine Tanz, eds. 1987. *Language, Gender, and Sex in Comparative Perspective*. Cambridge: Cambridge University Press.

Romaine, Suzanne. 1999. *Communicating Gender*. Mahwah, NJ: Erlbaum.

Tannen, Deborah. 1990. *You Just Don't Understand: Women and Men in Conversation*. New York: Ballantine Books.

Thorne, Barrie, and Nancy Henley, eds. 1975. *Language and Sex: Difference and Dominance*. Rowley, MA: Newbury House.

———, Cheris Kramarae, and Nancy Henley, eds. 1983. *Language, Gender, and Society*. Rowley, MA: Newbury House.

CHAPTER 31

Women Talk Too Much

Janet Holmes

(1998)

It is common for analysts to assume that the amount *of talk someone produces is a measure of power. When someone speaks, she or he has* the floor, *and the attention of others. People with less power are often, like mythical children, quiet unless spoken to.*

At the same time, unwanted talk by another is regarded as annoying, something that cannot be avoided but has not been solicited.

It has been a common belief in many cultures that women are simply the talkative ones. And that their talkativeness is improper and annoying.

The first generation of students of women's language believed, in contrast, that women were often silenced because they were not given the right to speak.

Eventually, when scholars began to study the actual occurrence of speaking, they realized that situations have to be divided into those in which women were speaking with other women, those in which women were speaking in private with men, and those in which women were speaking publicly in mixed groups. For quite some time the general belief was that when women spoke with other women or privately with men, they dominated the conversation, but that women were more reticent to speak publicly in mixed groups. (This forms some of the basis of arguments for gender-segregated classrooms.)

In this chapter, Janet Holmes reviews the myth that women talk too much, showing the dominance of men in mixed-gender settings.

A recent study (Mehl et al. 2007) had college students wear tape recorders. It showed that women and men speak about the same amount during a day, even if they each spoke more in some settings and less in others. As with most human activity, though, there is an enormous range of behavior, and the greatest differences occur within any group rather than between groups.

Reading Questions

- What are the different associations between talk in public (including classrooms) and talk in private? Do they serve different functions?
- What does Holmes mean by "social confidence"? Who has more of it, and why?
- What is Holmes's conclusion about how much women talk, compared to men? How does Holmes explain her findings?

Do women talk more than men? Proverbs and sayings in many languages express the view that women are always talking:

> Women's tongues are like lambs' tails—they are never still.—English

> The North Sea will sooner be found wanting in water than a woman at a loss for words.—Jutlandic

> The woman with active hands and feet, marry her, but the woman with overactive mouth, leave well alone.—Maori

Some suggest that while women talk, men are silent patient listeners.

> When both husband and wife wear pants it is not difficult to tell them apart—he is the one who is listening.—American

> Nothing is so unnatural as a talkative man or a quiet woman.—Scottish

Janet Holmes, "Women Talk Too Much." In *Language Myths*, ed. Laurie Bauer and Peter Trudgill. London: Penguin, 1998, pp. 41–49.

Others indicate that women's talk is not valued but is rather considered noisy, irritating prattle:

> Where there are women and geese there's noise.—Japanese

Indeed, there is a Japanese character which consists of three instances of the character for the concept 'woman' and which translates as 'noisy'! My favourite proverb, because it attributes not noise but rather power to the woman speaker is this Chinese one:

> The tongue is the sword of a woman and she never lets it become rusty.

So what are the facts? Do women dominate the talking time? Do men struggle to get a word in edgewise, as the stereotype suggests?

The Evidence

Despite the widespread belief that women talk more than men, most of the available evidence suggests just the opposite. When women and men are together, it is the men who talk most. Two Canadian researchers, Deborah James and Janice Drakich, reviewed sixty-three studies which examined the amount of talk used by American women and men in different contexts. Women talked more than men in only two studies.

In New Zealand, too, research suggests that men generally dominate the talking time. Margaret Franken compared the amount of talk used by female and male "experts" assisting a female TV host to interview well-known public figures. In a situation where each of three interviewers was entitled to a third of the interviewers' talking time, the men took more than half on every occasion.

I found the same pattern analysing the number of questions asked by participants in one hundred public seminars. In all but seven, men dominated the discussion time. Where the numbers of women and men present were about the same, men asked almost two-thirds of the questions during the discussion. Clearly women were not talking more than men in these contexts.

Even when they hold influential positions, women sometimes find it hard to contribute as much as men to a discussion. A British company appointed four women and four men to the eight most highly paid management positions. The managing director commented that the men often patronized the women and tended to dominate meetings:

> I had a meeting with a [female] sales manager and three of my [male] directors once…it took about two hours. She only spoke once and one of my fellow directors cut across her and said "What Anne is trying to say Roger is…" and I think that about sums it up. He knew better than Anne what she was trying to say, and she never got anything said.

There is abundant evidence that this pattern starts early. Many researchers have compared the relative amounts that girls and boys contribute to classroom talk. In a wide range of communities, from kindergarten through primary, secondary, and tertiary education, the same pattern recurs—males dominate classroom talk. So on this evidence we must conclude that the stereotype of the garrulous woman reflects sexist prejudice rather than objective reality.

Looking for an Explanation

Why is the reality so different from the myth? To answer this question, we need to go beyond broad generalizations and look more carefully at the patterns identified. Although some teachers claim that boys are "by nature more spirited and less disciplined," there is no evidence to suggest that males are biologically programmed to talk more than females. It is much more likely that the explanation involves social factors.

What Is the Purpose of the Talk?

One relevant clue is the fact that talk serves different functions in different contexts. Formal public talk is often aimed at informing people or persuading them to agree to a particular point of view (e.g., political speeches, television debates, radio interviews, public lectures, etc.). Public talk is often undertaken by people who wish to claim or confirm some degree of public status. Effective talk in public and in the media can enhance your social status—as politicians and other public performers know well. Getting and holding the floor is regarded as desirable, and competition for the floor in such contexts is common. (There is also some risk, of course, since a poor performance can be damaging.)

Classroom research suggests that more talk is associated with higher social status or power. Many studies have shown that teachers (regardless of their gender) tend to talk for about two-thirds of the available time. But the boys dominate the relatively small share of the talking time that remains for pupils. In this context, where talk is clearly valued, it appears that the person with most status has the right to talk most. The boys may therefore be asserting a claim to higher status than the girls by appropriating the majority of the time left for pupil talk.

The way women and men behave in formal meetings and seminars provides further support for this explanation. Evidence collected by American, British, and New Zealand researchers shows that men dominate the talking time in committee meetings, staff meetings, seminars, and task-oriented decision-making groups. If you are sceptical, use a stopwatch to time the amount of talk contributed by women and men at political and community meetings you attend. This explanation proposes that men talk more than women in public, formal contexts because they perceive participating and verbally contributing in such contexts as an activity which enhances their status, and men seem to be more concerned with asserting status and power than women are.

By contrast, in more private contexts, talk usually serves interpersonal functions. The purpose of informal or intimate talk is not so much status enhancement as establishing or maintaining social contact with others, making social connections, developing and reinforcing friendships and intimate relationships. Interestingly, the few studies which have investigated informal talk have found that there are fewer differences in the amount contributed by women and men in these contexts (though men still talked more in nearly a third of the informal studies reviewed by Deborah James and Janice Drakich). Women, it seems, are willing to talk more in relaxed social contexts, especially where the talk functions to develop and maintain social relationships.

Another piece of evidence that supports this interpretation is the *kind* of talk women and men contribute in mixed-sex discussions. Researchers analysing the functions of different utterances have found that men tend to contribute more information and opinions, while women contribute more agreeing, supportive talk, more of the kind of talk that encourages others to contribute. So men's talk tends to be more referential or informative, while women's talk is more supportive and facilitative.

Overall, then, women seem to use talk to develop personal relationships and maintain family connections and friendships more often than to make claims to status or to directly influence others in public contexts. Of course, there are exceptions, as Margaret Thatcher, Benazir Bhutto, and Jenny Shipley demonstrate. But, until recently, many women seem not to have perceived themselves as appropriate contributors to public, formal talk.

In New Zealand we identified another context where women contributed more talk than men. Interviewing people to collect samples of talk for linguistic analysis, we found that women were much more likely than men (especially young men) to be willing to talk to us at length. For example, Miriam Meyerhoff asked a group of ten young people to describe a picture to a female and to a male interviewer. It was made quite clear to the interviewees that the more speech they produced the better. In this situation, the women contributed significantly more speech than the men, both to the male and to the female interviewer.

In the private but semi-formal context of an interview, then, women contributed more talk than men. Talk in this context could not be seen as enhancing the status of the people interviewed. The interviewers were young people with no influence over the interviewees. The explanation for the results seems to be that the women were being more cooperative than the men in a context where more talk was explicitly sought by the interviewer.

Social Confidence

If you know a lot about a particular topic, you are generally more likely to be willing to contribute to a discussion about it. So familiarity or expertise can also affect the amount a person contributes to a particular discussion. In one interesting study the researcher supplied particular people with extra information, making them the "experts" on the topic to be discussed. Regardless of gender, these "experts" talked more in the subsequent discussions than their uninformed conversational partners (though male "experts" still used more talking time in conversation with uninformed women than female "experts" did with uninformed men).

Looking at people's contributions to the discussion section of seminars, I found a similar effect from expertise or topic familiarity. Women were more likely to ask questions and make comments when the topic was one they could claim expert knowledge about. In a small seminar on the current state of the economy, for instance, several women economists who had been invited to attend contributed to the discussion, making this one of the very few seminars where women's contributions exceeded men's.

Another study compared the relative amount of talk of spouses. Men dominated the conversations between couples with traditional gender roles and expectations, but when the women were associated with a feminist organization they tended to talk more than their husbands. So feminist women were more likely to challenge traditional gender roles in interaction.

It seems possible that both these factors—expert status and feminist philosophy—have the effect of developing women's social confidence. This explanation also fits with the fact that women tend to talk more with close friends and family, when women are in the majority, and also when they are explicitly invited to talk (in an interview, for example).

PERCEPTIONS AND IMPLICATIONS

If social confidence explains the greater contributions of women in some social contexts, it is worth asking why girls in school tend to contribute less than boys. Why should they feel unconfident in the classroom? Here is the answer which one sixteen-year-old gave:

> Sometimes I feel like saying that I disagree, that there are other ways of looking at it, but where would that get me? My teacher thinks I'm showing off, and the boys jeer. But if I pretend I don't understand, it's very different. The teacher is sympathetic and the boys are helpful. They really respond if they can show YOU how it is done, but there's nothing but "aggro" if you give any signs of showing THEM how it is done.

Talking in class is often perceived as "showing off," especially if it is girl-talk. Until recently, girls have preferred to keep a low profile rather than attract negative attention.

Teachers are often unaware of the gender distribution of talk in their classrooms. They usually consider that they give equal amounts of attention to girls and boys, and it is only when they make a tape recording that they realize that boys are dominating the interactions. Dale Spender, an Australian feminist who has been a strong advocate of female rights in this area, noted that teachers who tried to restore the balance by deliberately "favouring" the girls were astounded to find that despite their efforts they continued to devote more time to the boys in their classrooms. Another study reported that a male science teacher who managed to create an atmosphere in which girls and boys contributed more equally to discussion felt that he was devoting 90 per cent of his attention to the girls. And so did his male pupils. They complained vociferously that the girls were getting too much talking time.

In other public contexts, too, such as seminars and debates, when women and men are deliberately given an equal amount of the highly valued talking time, there is often a perception that they are getting more than their fair share. Dale Spender explains this as follows:

> The talkativeness of women has been gauged in comparison not with men but with *silence*. Women have not been judged on the grounds of whether they talk more than men, but of whether they talk more than silent women.

In other words, if women talk at all, this may be perceived as "too much" by men who expect them to provide a silent, decorative background in many social contexts. This may sound outrageous, but think about how you react when precocious children dominate the talk at an adult party. As women begin to make inroads into formerly "male" domains such as business and professional contexts, we should not be surprised to find that their contributions are not always perceived positively or even accurately.

CONCLUSION

We have now reached the conclusion that the question "Do women talk more than men?" can't be answered with a straight "yes" or "no." The answer is rather, "It all depends." It depends on many different factors, including the social context in which the talk is taking place, the kind of talk involved and the relative social confidence of the speakers, which is affected by such things as their social roles (e.g.,

teacher, host, interviewee, wife) and their familiarity with the topic.

It appears that men generally talk more in formal, public contexts where informative and persuasive talk is highly valued, and where talk is generally the prerogative of those with some societal status and has the potential for increasing that status. Women, on the other hand, are more likely to contribute in private, informal interactions, where talk more often functions to maintain relationships, and in other situations where for various reasons they feel socially confident.

Finally, and most radically, we might question the assumption that more talk is always a good thing. "Silence is golden," says the proverb, and there are certainly contexts in all cultures where silence is more appropriate than talk, where words are regarded as inadequate vehicles for feelings, or where keeping silent is an expression of appreciation or respect. Sometimes it is the silent participants who are the powerful players. In some contexts the strong silent male is an admired stereotype. However, while this is true, it must be recognized that talk is very highly valued in western culture. It seems likely, then, that as long as holding the floor is equated with influence, the complexities of whether women or men talk most will continue to be a matter for debate.

Sources and Further Reading

For more detailed information including more details about the examples discussed, see the following sources: Deborah James and Janice Drakich, "Understanding gender differences in amount of talk" in *Gender and Conversational Interaction*, Deborah Tannen (ed.) (Oxford: Oxford University Press, 1993, pp. 281–312); Janet Holmes, *Women, Men and Politeness* (London: Longman, 1995, chs. 2 and 6); Dale Spender, *Man Made Language* (London: Routledge & Kegan Paul, 1980); and Dale Spender and Elizabeth Sarah (eds.), *Learning to Lose* (London: The Women's Press, 1982).

Post-reading Questions / Activities

- How would you explain teachers' perceptions about how much time they are devoting to boys and girls, in contrast to the actual time recorded?
- Observe two different classrooms. Count the number of male and female students. Count the number of turns had by each gender. Are the numbers of turns proportional to the numbers of speakers? How can you account for any discrepancy? Does the teacher's gender play a role? What? Then conduct a similar measure of the length of turn of each speaker and see if there are any correlations with gender.

Vocabulary

floor

Suggested Further Reading

Bucholtz, Mary, A. C. Liang, and Laurel A. Sutton, eds. 1999. *Reinventing Identities: The Gendered Self in Discourse*. New York: Oxford University Press.

Cameron, Deborah. 1992. *Feminism and Linguistic Theory*. 2d ed. London: Routledge.

——, and Jennifer Coates, eds. 1988. *Women in Their Speech Communities: New Perspectives on Language and Sex*. London: Longman.

Coates, Jennifer, ed. 1998. *Language and Gender: A Reader*. Malden, MA: Blackwell.

Eckert, Penelope, and Sally McConnell-Ginet. 1992. "Think Practically and Look Locally: Language and Gender as Community-Based Practice." *Annual Review of Anthropology* 21: 461–490.

——, and ——. 2003. *Language and Gender*. Cambridge: Cambridge University Press.

Goodwin, Marjorie Harness. 1990. *He Said–She Said: Talk as Social Organization Among Black Children*. Bloomington: Indiana University Press.

Graddol, David, and Joan Swann. 1989. *Gender Voices*. Oxford: Blackwell.

Hall, Kira, and Mary Bucholtz, eds. 1995. *Gender Articulated: Language and the Socially Constructed Self*. New York and London: Oxford University Press.

Holmes, Janet. 1995. *Women, Men, and Politeness*. London and New York: Longman.

Ide, Sachiko, and Naomi Hanaska McGloin, eds. 1990. *Aspects of Japanese Women's Language*. Tokyo: Kurosio Publishers.

Inoue, Miyako. 2006. *Vicarious Language: Gender and Linguistic Modernity in Japan*. Berkeley and Los Angeles: University of California Press.

Irvine, Judith T. 1979. "Formality and Informality in Communicative Events." *American Anthropologist* 81 (4): 773–790.

Johnson, Sally, and Ulrike Hanna Meinhof, eds. 1997. *Language and Masculinity*. Oxford: Blackwell.

Lakoff, Robin Tolmach. 1975. *Language and Woman's Place*. New York: Harper and Row.

——. 2004. *Language and Woman's Place: Text and Commentaries*. Revised and expanded edition, edited by Mary Bucholtz. Oxford and New York: Oxford University Press.

Mehl, Matthias R., et al. 2007. "Are Women Really More Talkative Than Men?" *Science* 317 (July 6): 82.

Mori, Kyoko. 1997. *Polite Lies: On Being a Woman Caught Between Cultures*. New York: Henry Holt & Co.

Ochs, Elinor. 1991. "Indexing Gender." In *Rethinking Context*, edited by Alessandro Duranti and Charles Goodwin, pp. 335–358. Cambridge: Cambridge University Press.

Philips, Susan U., Susan Steele, and Christine Tanz, eds. 1987. *Language, Gender, and Sex in Comparative Perspective*. Cambridge: Cambridge University Press.

Romaine, Suzanne. 1999. *Communicating Gender*. Mahwah, NJ: Erlbaum.

Smith, Janet Shibamoto 1985. *Japanese Women's Language*. New York: Academic Press.

Tannen, Deborah. 1990. *You Just Don't Understand: Women and Men in Conversation*. New York: Ballantine Books.

Thorne, Barrie, and Nancy Henley, eds. 1975. *Language and Sex: Difference and Dominance*. Rowley, MA: Newbury House.

——, Cheris Kramarae, and Nancy Henley, eds. 1983. *Language, Gender, and Society*. Rowley, MA: Newbury House.

CHAPTER 32

Power and the Language of Men

Scott Fabius Kiesling
(1997)

Researchers on language, gender, and society have shown that many features of language can be explained by power asymmetries: who has the right to control the floor, who is considered to be higher in status, who performs "action that modifies action." Though we can generalize and say that "men have more power than women," it is clearly not true that all *men have more power than* all *women.*

Rather than make vague statements about power, Kiesling and many other analysts have delved into the details of language-in-use, or discourse *(adjective,* discursive*), looking at the kinds of words people use, their tone, the flavor of vocabulary, their pacing, and much more. Many of the broader generalizations people make derive from the interactive details, even though we are often unaware of many of them.*

In his analysis of language in a college fraternity, Kiesling uses notation from conversational analysis, *which tries to convey in a transcript as many details of an interaction as are relevant. (No transcript can ever convey* all *details.) Punctuation is not according to grammar, but according to what people actually said and how they said it. While it may seem that many of the speakers Kiesling quotes fumble, repeat themselves, and are not consistent in their sentence structures, this is typical of all informal speech. The kind of well-crafted sentences that some fluid speakers can produce are not the norm in ordinary conversation. In fact, in this chapter the speakers are generally speaking one at a time because they are participating in a meeting with rules for regulating speakers. In ordinary talk, people often overlap with one another, making a much messier (and more complex) transcript and reality. Kiesling includes, at the end of his article, the conventions for the transcription, rather like the legend for a map.*

Reading Questions

- What are the types of power that Kiesling analyzes? Which are the most powerful, and why? How is power connected to roles?
- Why are fraternities (and sororities) ideal places in which to study language and society? What other similar settings can you think of that would similarly show important social features?
- Which aspects of the fraternity Kiesling studied are hierarchical?
- How is masculinity—or at least men's identities—enacted through the speech event depicted here?

Power is usually cited as the most important factor when discussing the ways in which men's identities are constructed.[1] For example, in "Men, inexpressiveness, and power," Jack Sattel argues that: "the starting point for understanding masculinity lies, not in its contrast with femininity, but in the asymmetric dominance and prestige which accrues to males in this society" (1983, p. 119). In this chapter, I aim to show how issues of power and dominance as they relate to male identities are more complex than previously suggested. I will provide examples of some of the discursive strategies used by individual men in order to create and demonstrate power, showing how each man adopts a

Scott Fabius Kiesling, "Power and the Language of Men." In *Language and Masculinity*, ed. Sally Johnson and Ulrike Hanna Meinhof. Oxford, UK: Blackwell, 1997, pp. 65–85.

unique and personal approach when doing so. In particular, I will demonstrate how sequentiality and activity type must be taken into account when exploring the construction of men's identities through language.

It cannot be denied that men have more power than women in modern Western society. Men still dominate the upper echelons of government and business, and women continue to perform most of the unpaid labour of housework and child care. In addition, women still frequently earn less than men for comparable work, and professions dominated by women are less valued monetarily than those dominated by men (see Hewlett, 1986). Along with the freedom brought by power, however, comes the expectation (or requirement) that a man will somehow embody this power in his identity. This expectation is by no means as restrictive as those which obtain where women's identities are concerned; when a man constructs a powerful identity, it is usually connected in some way to "real" power. Thus, the expectation of a "powerful" identity for men is not symmetrical to the expectation of a "powerless" identity for women, since a man's powerful identity is *rewarded* (with power), whereas a woman's non-powerless identity may be *punished*.

Following Sattel's suggestion, therefore, I take the power of men as a starting point for investigating how men construct their identities through language; I unpack the concept, describe different kinds of power, and show how these work with specific regard to four individual men.

My analysis is based on data gathered during a continuing ethnographic study of a fraternity in the United States. A fraternity is an all-male social club at a university, in which membership is selective. Typically, the fraternity becomes the central organization around which members structure their college lives, especially socially. It is a "community of practice" (Eckert and McConnell-Ginet, 1992), defined sharply from the rest of the university through various means—initiation rituals, secret ceremonies, and exclusive social events. Cynthia McLemore (1991) has worked on intonation in the female counterpart to the fraternity—the sorority. She showed that this type of community is ideal for studying language and society, especially the language of society's privileged members, because it is an intensely social, well-defined community, and its activities are based primarily on talk (e.g., meetings and parties). In addition, fraternities exhibit processes typical of other social groups more intensely: entrance into the community is carefully guarded, its members change completely every four years, and yet it manages to retain a unique history and ideology. Finally, fraternities are important to study because they prepare their members for the world of work after college. By analysing the strategies that men learn in fraternities, we can therefore gain insights into how men acquire, construct, and reproduce certain social practices in anticipation of dominance over others in later life.

In this chapter, I will explore how the fraternity's ideology and the immediate speech situation work together to constrain the members' identities. I use the term "constrain," rather than "affect" or "determine," because identity construction is, to some extent, a creative endeavour. In theory, the men are free to create any identity they want, but in practice, they are pushed (and push themselves) towards identities which do not challenge the perceived values of the fraternity or of dominant US society. Each man also has different discursive resources (e.g., storytelling ability, joking ability, a powerful structural role, a loud voice, etc.) in order to draw upon disparate types of power. And crucially, each member has his own personal history within the fraternity, which further constrains the kind of identity he can display at any given time. Each time he speaks, then, the man must produce an utterance (and posture, gaze, etc.) that satisfies these constraints as far as possible. At the same time, he must make the utterance coherent within each current speech situation.

Because I am focusing on power, I will begin by outlining the framework of power used in my analysis. I will then discuss the specific ideology of power at work in the fraternity in question, exploring, for example, the kinds of constraints which the community places on a member's presentation of self. Finally, I will analyse excerpts from my corpus in order to illustrate how men draw upon, and construct, different types of power through their use of language.

A FRAMEWORK FOR POWER

Before [a concept is applied] to any analysis, it should be well defined. When power is used as an explanation in sociolinguistic analyses, however, it is frequently undefined and unanalysed. Because I am taking power as the starting point for my work, I will briefly sketch the theoretical approach which is to be employed.

Following Foucault (1982), power is action that modifies action. The effect of this action need not be immediate, direct, or even real. So, for example, because power takes place in actions, it is exercised to the extent that people *believe* that they should perform an action because of another action. However, power is not something that individuals may suddenly pull out and use. It must be salient to the situation; the people being acted on must believe in it. Thus, illusions can be powerful motivators. People believe that they should act in certain ways with certain people because they feel that not acting in these ways would have serious consequences. The reasons for performing a given action might therefore seem irrational, such as the avoidance of embarrassment, or the appearance of foolishness or "weakness." But what constitutes a serious consequence is, in turn, dependent on the community in question and its own particular values. This means that any analysis exploring issues of power must be based on a primary analysis of the local community's values and its ideology.

Whilst this view of power is flexible, it lacks analytical force. At a practical level, therefore, I assume that people have power because they occupy roles—some so enduring as to seem eternal and necessary, some fleeting and unnoticed, and some newly created within specific interactions.

People place themselves in roles by using language because different ways of speaking are associated with such roles. A new role may be thrown together out of bits of others, and, in some cases, a single role may dominate a personality. But such roles can only really be discovered by analysing the discourse of community members, and by examining the community's formal and informal structures through ethnographic observation and interviewing.

On the basis of my own study, I have identified seven types of power processes from which local roles may be built: physical (coercive and ability), economic, knowledge, structural, nurturant, demeanour, and ideological. I distinguish between two types of physical power: *coercive physical power* is the power of the mugger, while *ability physical power* is an action made possible by physical ability or skill. *Economic power* is the process that rewards one action (e.g., labour) with the possibility of another action (e.g., purchasing goods). *Knowledge power* is the process of gaining knowledge in order to perform an action. *Structural power* is the power of a place within a structure, classically (but not necessarily) a hierarchy. *Nurturant power* is the process of helping another, as in teaching or feeding. *Demeanour power* is the power of solidarity: moral authority, being liked, being "a good guy." The process of demeanour is not normally addressed by views of power, because the actions in this type of power act on emotions. Thus a person exhibits demeanour power when others feel happy, entertained, involved, respectful, etc.

But it is the ideological process which is the most important. This is a "defining process," because individuals evaluate the other types of power processes through the ideological process. This defining process—which I will refer to as *ideological power*—ratifies certain traits as powerful, and determines which of the other processes are available (i.e., identifies the roles in the community). Within each of the other processes, ideological power identifies what is, and what is not, powerful. Thus, ideological power is the process of power whereby ways of thinking about the world are naturalized into a community's behaviour.

Each of the seven types of power outlined is not isolated from the others, but all are closely connected to form what Foucault refers to as: "a net-like organization [...] something which circulates, or rather (as) something which only functions in the form of a chain" (1980, p. 98). In this way, an ideology such as the competitive, hierarchical, group ideology frequently identified as typical of all-male interaction is likely to affect the way in which men structure their groups, change their demeanour, and learn disciplines. Men may be inclined to form hierarchical communities, act in ways that always seem competitive, and see education and work as a competition. The success with which they learn to think and act in these ways will, in turn, affect their ability to use economic, structural, physical, knowledge, and demeanour processes of power.

Power is therefore a way of viewing local practices globally: an etic framework filled in by emic values. Power in this view (as a role focused on—or created in—a community-defined structure) is similar to concepts of footing and alignment (see Goffman, 1981). However, by using the framework I have outlined, we can identify the types of roles which are available and created vis-à-vis power. As a consequence, we will not be limited to analyses using broad, universal categories. Moreover, we can approach some comparability across communities by looking at the ways in which different communities deal with similar ideologies of power, and similar communities deal with different ideologies of power.

"IDEOLOGY POWER" IN A FRATERNITY

In the light of the framework I have outlined, I need to discuss the ideology of the fraternity in question before analysing how power works in the fraternity's discourse. The way a man presents himself within a fraternity is of ultimate importance because he becomes a member of and gains status in the fraternity by projecting the right kind of identity.

Gaining membership to a fraternity is contingent upon successfully negotiating the process of "rush," which is not unlike courtship. In this process, current members meet prospective members (known as "rushes") at organized social functions; they also socialize informally, for example, by talking in dormitory rooms. Prospective members gauge whether they want to be a part of the fraternity, and current members consider whether they want to invite the prospective members to join. The rushes selected by the current members are then offered an invitation for membership, and can accept or reject the "bid," as the offer is known. Once they have accepted a bid, the rushes become probationary members, or "pledges." During the "pledge period," which lasts for six to eight weeks, pledges learn the fraternity's traditions, and pledge education activities take place in unofficial secret ceremonies, which are similar to military "boot camps." Pledges are treated as second-class citizens, subordinating their autonomy and identities to the fraternity as an institution, and to individual older "brothers," as members are called. Pledges "earn respect" and the privilege to become members themselves. They also learn the fraternity's customs, traditions, and oral history. During this time, a strong bond tends to form between so-called pledge brothers, who are members of the same "pledge class," because of their common adversity as second-class citizens.

The pledge period culminates in initiation, a formal clandestine ceremony where the secrets, rights, and responsibilities of membership are imparted. However, the newly initiated brother—known by the acronym "nib"—is still inexperienced in the eyes of the fraternity. He lacks knowledge and past accomplishments in order to prove that he will function well in a fraternity office. In the social sphere, nibs normally follow the older brothers' lead, show respect to them, and defer to their judgement. But nibs still have more latitude here than in the fraternity's "business" sphere, which will be discussed below. As a brother becomes older, he has a chance to prove himself by performing services for the fraternity. Also, simply by becoming older, he gains the respect of younger 'generations' of members.

In the fraternity I studied for over a year, which I will call Gamma Chi Phi (ΓΧΦ), almost all of the men were Caucasian. Out of fifty-seven members, one was Korean-American, and four were Arab-American. Most were of college age (17–22 years old); three alumni members were in their late twenties. By comparison, the university as a whole is 88 percent Caucasian, 10 percent Asian, and 6 percent African-American.

I was able to gain entry into this fraternity because, as an undergraduate, I was a member of the same national fraternity. I first contacted the national fraternity to describe my project, attending several meetings of the steering committee, the National Council. Once I had chosen the local chapter, I contacted the president of that chapter (whom I had met previously at the National Council meeting), and described the project to him in detail in a letter. I told him that I was interested in studying interaction among men, and that I would be observing and audio-tape-recording, as well as conducting interviews with members. He then asked the members for permission to allow me to go ahead with my research at a general meeting of the fraternity, and the members approved. I was permitted to attend any function and visit any individual member. I was also allowed to attend secret ritual ceremonies, but not to tape the ceremonial portion of the ritual activities. The names of the fraternity and all members are aliases.

At ΓΧΦ, there is an overt distinction between the formal, governing sphere of the fraternity, on the one hand, and the social sphere, on the other. However, the border between the two is fuzzy; older, office-holding members tend to associate together, and personality plays a large role in deciding who is elected into fraternity offices. Nonetheless, the ideological organization is the same throughout the fraternity, and can best be described as hierarchic.[2]

The hierarchical nature of the fraternity is already evident in the stages of acquiring membership outlined above. First, because only certain men are accepted into membership, the fraternity experience begins by valuing one identity over another. In ΓΧΦ, demeanour and physical power are highly valued. If someone is rich, caring, or gets good grades, he is not more likely to be offered membership. The current members value skill at playing sports[3]—so a prospective member who played baseball in high school will be highly respected because he can help the fraternity win at intramural softball. Demeanour power is, however, most important in terms of gaining membership.[4] Members told me in interviews that the main reason they joined was because they thought the fraternity was "a good group of guys"; similarly, bids are offered because a prospective member seems like "a good guy."

But what is "a good guy"? Members themselves had difficulty defining this characteristic. For them, a good guy would seem to be someone who others enjoy being with, and someone who would appear to exemplify the members' own ideology. Thus, it may be someone who tells funny stories, or who is the subject of funny stories. Because of the hierarchic, competitive ideology of the organization, a man who acts strong, competitive, and quick is valued. Friendship and community is shown through what seems like competitive talk filled with insults, boasts, orders, and embarrassing jokes and stories. A "good guy" is someone who exemplifies powerful, competitive traits in all spheres: he works hard, gets things accomplished, is seen as a leader, and is verbally skilled in the "competitive cooperative" style through which the men build solidarity. By selecting only men with certain characteristics, the fraternity creates a hierarchy between its members and outsiders (although non-members are also ranked).

Once access to the fraternity has been gained, there is still an implicit hierarchy evident in all stages of membership. The pledges begin their fraternity experience by being treated as unknowledgeable, childlike servants, and even when the pledges become full members, they are still not valued as highly as older members. Usually, only after at least one year of membership does a man have the power to affect, through his own actions, the actions of the fraternity and its members. When attempting to influence the fraternity in this way, ability and demeanour power are highly valued, along with knowledge power. This is especially evident during elections, for example, where members evaluate candidates' work ethic, experience, personality, and skills.

Thus, the main constraint that the men place on each other is to present a competitive, successful, confident identity. The fraternity ideology also values hard work, especially work that promotes the good of the group. In this way, members are taught to protect and care for each other.

DATA ANALYSIS: POWER AND IDENTITY IN PRACTICE

In this section, I will explore how four men employ different discursive means in order to construct powerful identities. The excerpts I analyse come from an election meeting involving the entire fraternity membership. Ordinary meetings are held every Sunday evening in a campus classroom, but elections are held only once a year, usually in the autumn.

Because they are speaking in a meeting, the four men in question have much at stake. Initially, they must show that they have the authority to speak. But because their identities are on public display in the business sphere, the men are more constrained than usual by the competitive, hierarchic ideology of the fraternity. Through the varying employment of mitigation, mood, pronoun use, and personal experience, these members orient themselves towards different processes of power. The processes they draw upon are consistent with the identities that they have constructed previously in the fraternity, but are nevertheless specific to the time of speaking.

The excerpts I analyse are taken from a discussion during elections for the office of chapter correspondent, whose job it is to communicate with the national fraternity through letters published in the fraternity's national magazine. The position traditionally goes to a younger member because it requires little experience or knowledge of how the fraternity works. After the four candidates—Kurt, Ritchie, Mullin, and Ernie—give their speeches, they leave the room so that other members can discuss the candidates' strengths and weaknesses. The four members I shall focus on are Darter, Speed, Ram, and Mack.

Darter

The first speaker I consider is Darter, a newly initiated brother. He no doubt still feels deferential to those men who, until a few weeks ago, had almost total control over his life. Although he was the president of the pledge class, and is recognized as a possible future leader of the fraternity, he is not in a position to exercise demeanour or structural power because he is a nib, and does not hold a high position. In his comments, the first he has made in the elections, Darter bases his argument on his knowledge of the candidates' abilities. Two of the candidates are his pledge brothers, Ritchie and Ernie. Kim is Korean-American; Speed is an older brother.

Excerpt 1

48 DARTER: Um *Ri:tchie* may come off like he's really like a dumb ass
49   and everything but uh
50   he's like one of the smartest people
51   I know y'know
52   I went to high school with him
53   and he was like ranked *fifth* in our class.
54   and he can he can write like rea:lly well
55 KIM: He's
56   *A:sian* man, what do you expect?
57 SPEED: (sarcastic) Is he really?
58 DARTER: I mean he he *types* like unbelievably
59   …quick. um I just think this would be a good position for him
60   to hold because he's a really good writer,
61   I mean I've read a lot of papers of his.

Because he is young and a new brother, Darter does not normally speak in meetings. But in this comment Darter draws from his specialized knowledge—his high school friendship with Ritchie—to assert his right to speak. He begins by acknowledging the identity that Ritchie has in the fraternity (line 48).[5] Darter then contrasts this identity with the identity he remembers from high school (lines 50–4). He then states his position: "I just think this would be a good position for him to hold." He mitigates his statement through the use of "I just think," which suggests his opinion is not very valuable. By using "I think" and the conditional "would," he frames his statement as a suggestion, rather than a fact (e.g., "this is a good position for him"). Instead of simply making this more direct statement, he includes a dependent clause that explicitly highlights his reasoning ("because he's a really good writer"), which is implicit from his statements in lines 50–4. (I show below that the older brothers do not need to provide this kind of justification.) Darter then emphasizes

once again how he knows that Ritchie is a good writer. He thus explicitly justifies his support for Ritchie through his knowledge of the latter's writing abilities. His power is therefore not based on his demeanour or position in the fraternity, but on knowledge, which he is careful to highlight extensively. He presents himself as holding information important to the debate, but as unsure of its worth.

Speed

The next speaker I introduce is Speed, a third-year member. Of the four men I am considering, he speaks next in the meeting. His statement is short and to the point.

Excerpt 2

83 MICK: Speed.
84 SPEED: Ri:tchie. I like Ritchie 'cause he's smart
85   and he probably writes really good too:
86   so let him do it dude.

Speed at first does not justify his statement. He merely states Ritchie's name. Then he notes that Ritchie is smart and (extrapolating from line 84) that Ritchie is capable of doing the job. His short statement indicates that for him the choice, based on Ritchie's ability, is simple. It is just a matter of "letting him do it." In addition, by first only uttering Ritchie's name, Speed implies that members should be swayed by the mere fact that he is for Ritchie.

Ram

Ram presents his powerful identity in a different way. An older brother, he has just finished a year as treasurer. He creates a fatherly, "wise elder" identity through his comment:

Excerpt 3

119 Ram: um I'd like to endorse David here, surprisingly
120   I mean the kid—
121   I don't want to see him fall into another—
122   and I'm not saying that he would
123   Kevin Fierst type thing,
124   I think we need to make him—
125   we need to strongly involve him *now*
126   I think he's pretty serious about it, y'know
127   and with a little guidance I mean he'll do a fine job.

Ram creates a powerful identity by putting himself in the role of a person with age and experience: he refers to David as "the kid," and he shows off his knowledge of past members of the fraternity (Kevin Fierst was a member who dropped out of school because of substance abuse problems). He further highlights his position through his use of the phrase "with a little guidance," suggesting that he is qualified to give that guidance. He also shows concern for David ("I don't want to see him fall into another…Kevin Fierst type thing"), which suggests a fatherly position. Thus, he draws on the part of the fraternity ideology that stresses "looking out for" another brother. Finally, he also uses the device of speaking on behalf of the fraternity ("we need to strongly involve him now"), although he mitigates his statement more than Mack, in the next section, by embedding it in "I think."

Mack

Contrast Darter's and Speed's comments with those made by Mack, a fourth-year member, who was Darter's pledge educator (in charge of the programme and activities during the pledge period). Mack affects actions through his demeanour, using little mitigation in his statements, and through the imperative mood. Mick is the president, Pencil is the graduate advisor.

Excerpt 4

```
184  MICK:     Mack.
185  MACK:     Okay…
186            This is it…
187            Somebody said something about =
188  PENCIL:              =Again, we need to reorganize (?).
189  MACK:     yeah somebody's—
190            we need to look at what we have left here,
191            and there are certain positions
192            that everybody fits into perfectly.
193            Ernie does not fit into this: (0.1)
194            I'm not sure where Ernie fits in just yet.
195  ?:        historian
196  MACK:     but I: a:m afraid that we are going to waste uh
197            one of the few brains left. in someplace that
              that
198            uh historian has potentially been a
199            non-existent position. uh I think for a couple
200            semesters yahoo took some pictures,
201  PENCIL:   We're talking about chapter correspondent now
202  MACK:     what's that? I know
203  PENCIL:   and he can hold both positions
204  MACK:     I understand that. (0.3)
205            But he won't.
206            (0.5)
207            I see—I see Kurt—I see Kurt—I see Kurt—
208  PENCIL:   Then talk about chapter correspondent.
209            point of order.
210  ?:        we have we have four left.
211  PENCIL:   point of order.
212  MACK:     I see Kurt as chapter correspondent.
213            not Ritchie damn it.
```

Mack begins by serving notice that his word is gospel: "This is it." It is unmitigated and imperative. Unlike Darter, Mack does not justify his statement at all. This non-mitigation and non-justification presents a role of someone who can make a proclamation—someone with power. In line 190, he emphasizes this view by instructing the members on how to go about making a decision ("We need to look at what we have left"). He does this by using the first person plural

subject without any hedges (or "I think," as Darter does), and by using "need" instead of "should." Contrast his statement with what might be termed its "opposite": Mack might have said "I think we should look at what's left." By using a bald imperative, then, Mack implicitly puts himself in a role of structural power. However, Mack is not constructing a new place for himself in the fraternity, but continuing in a carefully constructed role: that of the elder, wise, behind-the-scenes manipulator. In an interview, he indicated this manipulator role was the one he seeks for himself. Although he has held few fraternity offices, he goes to other members before elections, and suggests that they run for certain positions, then makes comments in their favour during elections.

Mack was also the pledge educator for the newly initiated brothers, which may affect his comments in two ways. First, he has had a position of supreme authority over the new members until recently—he was their teacher and "drill sergeant"—so that they perceive him as an authority within the fraternity. Second, he can claim to know the new members better than any other member (except perhaps the new members themselves). Thus, he can claim to be qualified to make these pronouncements. He can use his structural and demeanour power to influence the new members, many of whom will vote in the election, and he can employ his knowledge power to influence older brothers.

Mack also demonstrates his role by where he sits in the classroom in which the meeting is held. Older members sit on the right-hand side of the room, and Mack sits as far to the right as possible. Darter, in contrast, sits on the "younger" left-hand side, towards the middle (the extreme left-hand side is empty). Mack's cadence is also significant. Though not evident in the transcript, he speaks with a slow, pause-filled cadence that gives the impression of thoughtfulness and wisdom, while Darter speaks very quickly.

Mack continues to use unmitigated, authority-laden devices throughout his comments. In lines 191–4, he sets up a system in which each member has his place, and Mack knows who belongs where. He presents his statements as axiomatic truths by using "there are" without any indication that he is actually voicing a personal opinion. Had he used modality markers, such as "may," he would be implying that members can decide the issue for themselves. Instead, he leaves no room for doubt. In line 196, he presents himself as advisor to the fraternity ("I am afraid"). In contrast, instead of using these devices to speak for the collective in a leader-like role, he might have said something like "I think Ritchie is overqualified for this position." It is unclear where his argument is going from line 197 forward, because he stops his sentence, and begins to discuss the historian position. It looks as if he planned to highlight his age, by discussing the past worth of the historian position in lines 198–200 ("historian has potentially been a non-existent position"). Pencil then argues with him about discussing one position at a time (lines 201–11), which prompts Mack to finish his statement. Mack ends by simply stating that he "sees" Kurt as correspondent, again without any justification (in fact, with less justification than at the beginning of his comments). This construction, "I see," is used by other brothers to create a similar air of authority, as though the speaker were a visionary, who speaks with the wisdom of the ages.

Thus, there is a large difference between the way in which the older brothers and a younger brother present themselves. The older brother has a position of experience and respect that he can implicitly draw upon, while the younger brother, lacking this structural and demeanour power, is explicit about his reasoning to sway votes in his direction. While both are under similar general pressures to present a "powerful" identity, each has different resources and solves the problem in his own way.

Speed

Now contrast Mack and Ram's remarks with a later comment by Speed. After Mack speaks, other older members have taken up the discussion of finding offices for the newly initiated brothers. Speed responds to this trend, and returns to his utilitarian theme. Speed's comments are given in a hurried, shouting voice, as if he is angry.

Excerpt 5

```
245  SPEED:  All right look.
246          first of all, you guys need to realize we do not
247          ha:ve to ne- necessarily make a:ll the new
248          brothers, put them in positions right away.
249          a lot of the new brothers already have positions.
250          they can get elected next year or next semester.
251          there are some positions that are semesterly.
252          we don't have to make sure that every one of
                them
253          has a position. they need time to learn and
                grow–
254          it's better that//they're– that they're=
255  ?:     I need an assistant
256  SPEED:  =shut the fuck up.
257          it's better that they're–
258          that they're almost like I was with Tex.
259          I was Tex's like little bitch boy ... graduate
260          affairs, and I learned a lot more there,
261          than I would if I got stuck in some leadership
262          role, so fuck 'em,
263          I don't care if any of 'em don't get a position.
264          but I'm telling you right now,
265          I think Ritchie should do it because like Kim
266          said, people are gonna read this shit,
267          Kurt might get ha:mmered and write some
                shitty..
268          fuckin' letter, Ernie can't write,
269          fuckin' Mullin already has a position,
270          so put Ritchie in there,
271          and stop fuckin' trying to.. set everybody up in
272          a position. Christ.
273  MICK:   Alex.
274  SPEED:  I:'d like one
275          (laughter)
```

Speed is an older brother, but he has created an adversarial identity in the fraternity, resisting those in formal offices. He relies on a different presentation of power, one that sets him up in opposition to others. Even though he is a third-year member, he always sits on the "non-powerful" left-hand side, in the back of the room, thus showing his contempt for the fraternity hierarchy. Speed's argumentative identity is evident in this speech, but he uses some of the same linguistic devices as Mack. Like Mack, Speed uses the imperative. He begins by saying "All right look," which is similar in tone to Mack's "This is it." In line 246, Speed states that "you guys need to realize," which is similar to Mack's "we need to look at what we have left." Speed then shows his knowledge of the fraternity, continuing in an imperative mood, saying "we don't have to make sure that every one of them has a position," which contrasts with Mack's "we need to look at what we have left here."

Speed then draws on his personal experience (as Ram did) in the fraternity for an example in lines 259–62 (notably in a low position— "I was Tex's like little bitch boy"). This statement disparages "leadership positions," and implicitly the organizational structure of the fraternity. Next, he uses an aggravated, bold statement to show his indifference to the brothers' aspirations in lines 262–3 ("so fuck 'em ..."). Speed then again presents a utilitarian argument for voting for Ritchie by pointing out why other candidates are unqualified (lines 264–70). In line 264, he uses a pedagogic tone similar to Mack's ("I'm telling you right now"). Note that this rhetoric is consistent with his argumentative, impatient identity: he sums up each person quickly, with aggravation and profanity. Then, at the very end (line 274), he injects some self-directed humour. Throughout the elections, he has been unable to get elected, and this has become a running joke. When he says "I'd like one," he adds to his demeanour with a joke making fun of himself. Ending with a joke is a common device used by the members in these comments; it builds demeanour power by easing the tedium that accompanies the election meetings.

Thus Speed, while staying within the constraints of the hierarchic fraternity ideology, manages to construct an identity that appears to reject the manipulative structural power used by some of the older brothers. He accomplishes his identity by focusing on the value of competing against a structure of power; rebellion and independence are consistent with the fraternity's competitive ideology. He also focuses on the need to do what is best for the group by highlighting why Ritchie is best qualified for the position. Thus, Speed, Mack, and Ram, while using similar linguistic devices to convince the members and present their identities, nevertheless construct very different identities. Because he is younger, Darter, on the other hand, has different constraints on the identity he presents in the meeting. He does not have a demeanour or structural power process working in his favour, so the problem presented to him—of creating an identity consistent with the fraternity ideology—is much different than the problem presented to Speed, Mack, and Ram. Darter must create a means of influencing voting (an action that will affect other actions) without any prior history of being able to do so. He must also construct a role for himself that fits within the constraints of being a nib, but nevertheless convinces people to vote for his favoured candidate. Darter therefore draws on his specialized knowledge of the candidate.

It is important to notice also that Speed was genuinely impatient with the discussion at the time of his second statement, as seen by a comparison of his two utterances. In the first statement, he simply says why Ritchie is qualified for the position. In the second, however, he is arguing *against* other members—especially Mack—as much as *for* Ritchie, in addition to arguing about the progress of the debate generally. This place in the discussion (he is nearly the last speaker) sets up a context in which he can position himself as the defender of ability power over structural power for its own sake. In other words, he can make clear his dislike of voting members into structural positions without any clear functional reason for doing so. This secondary argument was not possible in Speed's first comments because none of the older members had suggested considering all the new members, and what offices they should occupy. His identity construction in the second statement therefore shows the situated, sequence-dependent nature of identity.

Speed also exhibited this adversarial identity in an interview, however. The semester before the interview, Speed had been the pledge educator, but was ousted because of what he sees as his "independence":

Excerpt 6

```
1  SCOTT:  Did you keep it ((the pledge period)) the way
2          you had it?
3  SPEED:  I tried to, man, but they wouldn't let me so:
4          I had to I had to succumb to their rules
5          th th– th– they got all pissed off at me and tried
           to take my
6          position away from me and all that shit,
7          man. (1.0) Bunch a dicks.
```

Speed's independence shows through in this excerpt when he says "I had to succumb to their rules." Speed also sees that he lost his position because he didn't follow the dominant ideology, but evaluates that ideology—or its proponents—negatively ("Bunch a dicks"). Thus, Excerpt 6 provides more evidence for an ideological clash between Speed's alleged independence, and the fraternity's expectation of sacrifice in return for structural power.

All the men discussed create powerful identities, but they each use disparate strategies in order to achieve a different kind of power. Differences can be seen in how the men orient themselves to various features of the fraternity ideology. Most appeal to what will be best for the fraternity. Darter and Speed focus on the ideology of being

rewarded for ability. They both argue that Ritchie is simply the most qualified candidate, and voting for him will benefit the fraternity the most. They therefore appeal to the part of the ideology that puts the group before the individual. Ram also appeals to this value, but in another way. He argues that the fraternity will lose Kurt if they don't involve him in it. Mack, however, focuses on the fraternity's hierarchical nature; for him, some jobs are more important than others, and must be "assigned" to more important members. Thus, he wants Ritchie to have a job other than chapter correspondent. Mack also sees his own role as that of manipulator, and uses his structural position of age to put members in the offices that he "sees" for them. Finally, Speed fights against this focus on structural power.

The elections are very important to the members. They care deeply about the fraternity and its future. Who they elect very much affects what happens in the fraternity. In addition, the outcomes affect their own power within the fraternity and, even more important perhaps, their ability to affect the actions of others in the future.[6]

DISCUSSION

I have thus shown how four men employ both similar and varied discursive devices in order to construct a particular kind of identity, given certain constraints on that identity. All four manage to present some kind of identity valued by the competitive, hierarchic fraternity ideology. Darter had to justify his statements overtly. Ram created a fatherly image. Mack spoke with a voice of the elder. Speed "resisted" the dominance of structural power over ability, and the good of the fraternity and its members over trying to control every detail of the fraternity's future. While being men in a fraternity affected their language in similar ways, their individual solutions in time and space were unique. It is worth pointing out, however, that I have only had sufficient space to consider one speech activity here; in fact, the men's identities vary even more when other speech activities are analysed.

Sociolinguists often group people together based on criteria external to the community, and focus on how people of certain groups use language in a similar way. Generalizations about men and women are among the most common. But within these generalizations we find many variations. Within the fraternity community, for example, we can group older members together, because they tend to use less mitigation and justification and, more importantly, because age is one way the members group themselves. Clearly, then, it is essential, when considering the language of men, to explore how gender is mediated by age, status, and so on, in the same way that this has been necessary when analysing the speech of women. But even grouping Speed, Ram, and Mack together as elder members of the fraternity ignores their very different individual presentations of self.

Meaningful generalizations are, however, still possible and necessary. We can still say that, in some general sense, many men in the United States construct powerful, competitively oriented identities. Moreover, due to the ideology of difference in US society, the motivation for men to construct these identities is of a different nature than for women, and the outcomes for "resistance" are different for each of the two sexes. Men who construct the "preferred" gender identity are rewarded with power, while women are not rewarded in the same sense when they construct the identity that society "prefers" for their gender. In fact, a "powerless" identity that many researchers have shown to be the "preferred" identity for a North American woman could actually be seen as punishing women. Real resistance to the gender order, for instance a "powerful female" identity or a "powerless male" identity, may have similar consequences. But many men arguably have little motivation for such resistance. Speed, for example, appears to be resisting "the establishment," but he is nevertheless using that "resistance" as an alternative way of constructing a powerful, individualistic identity that is ultimately ratified by the fraternity ideology.

The way in which the fraternity men create different yet powerful identities suggests that particular roles, such as workplace and family roles, may be the specifics that make up what people idealize as "masculinity" and "femininity." The men discussed here adopt elements of archetypal male roles: loyal friend, concerned father, wise elder, pragmatic individualist. In addition, two of the men identify *themselves* as having the identities they present in the election.

As Sattel (1983) points out, many men are expected to take on positions of leadership. But the direction of the indexing of men's identities and leadership is not clear; we might also say that society expects leadership positions to be held by men. Work such as Bonnie McElhinny's (1993) study of female police officers in Pittsburgh similarly highlights the importance of work and family roles in society's view of masculinity and femininity. Further research is needed in this area to learn more about such roles and their relationship to the construction of gender. In my research, I plan to return to the fraternity to test whether new members take on the same kinds of roles as older members who have left. Does Darter become a "wise elder," a "concerned father figure," an "impatient individualist"? Or does he create an entirely new role, or a combination of all?

CONCLUSION

In this chapter, I have explored the way in which the identities of four fraternity members are constructed through interaction in an election meeting. My findings have, however, a number of implications for work on language and gender in more general terms. For example, I have shown how the four men construct their own identities, drawing upon both the same, and different, types of power processes through the language they use. Thus, although all the men manage to evoke some type of power with their language, it would be extremely difficult to draw specific conclusions on the types of linguistic structures (e.g., tag-questions, hedging, etc.) used by men "as a group" on the basis of my data since their usage is highly contextualized....

Transcription Conventions

Turn-taking

//	Bounds simultaneous speech.
=	Connects two utterances that were produced with noticeably less transition time between them than usual.
(number)	Silences timed in tenths of seconds.
(.)	Noticeable silence less than 0.2 second.
#	Bounds passage said very quickly.

Sound Production

^	Falsetto.
TEXT	Upper-case letters indicate noticeably loud volume.
*	Indicates noticeably low volume, placed around the soft words.
text	Italics indicate emphatic delivery (volume and/or pitch).
–	Indicates that the sound that precedes it is cut off, stopped suddenly and sharply.
:	Indicates that the sound that precedes it is prolonged.
'	Indicates a slight intonational rise.
?	Indicates a sharp intonational rise.

Breathiness, Laughter, Comments

h	An audible outbreath.
'h	An audible inbreath.
he, ha	Laughter.
(text)	Transcript enclosed in single parentheses indicates uncertain hearing.
((comment))	Double parentheses enclose transcriber's comments.

Notes

1. I have chosen the term "men's identities," rather than "masculinity," for several reasons. First, "masculinity" is not a neutral term; it connotes a single stereotype of male identity, for example, John Wayne and Arnold Schwarzenegger in their movie roles. However, the majority of men in Western culture do not present themselves as copies of these movie heroes (Kessler and McKenna, 1978; Segal, 1990). Some men even contradict this view of men's identities. Thus, masculinity, as I use the term, is but one possible (idealized) type of male identity. Similarly, that there is no "natural," single identity to which men aspire is an important point; hence, I use the plural "identities." Men's (and women's) identities are constructed, negotiated, and changing, but they are also constrained by social structures that value some types of identities over others. Furthermore, I use the term "men" rather than "male" or "masculine" in order to highlight the fact that the identity is a social as opposed to biological construction; it is gender, not sex. "Identity" is an intersection between a social presentation of self, and a psychological understanding of that self.

2. This hierarchic ideology is similar to Connell's characterization of hegemonic masculinity (1987, 1995).

3. Interest in sports, of course, is also connected to competition; in this case, the desire is to be the best fraternity on campus in intramural sports.

4. The fact that demeanour is of primary importance in the fraternity supports its inclusion as a type of power, and not something other than power.

5. Line numbers match those from a complete transcript.

6. Ritchie won the election.

References

Connell, R. W. 1987. *Gender and Power*. Stanford, CA: Stanford University Press.

———. 1995. *Masculinities*. Oxford: Polity Press.

Eckert, Penelope and McConnell-Ginet, Sally 1992: Think practically and look locally: language and gender as community-based practice. *Annual Review of Anthropology* 21, 461-90.

Foucault, Michel 1980: *Power/Knowledge: Selected Interviews and Other Writings*. New York: Pantheon Books.

———. 1982: The subject and power. *Critical Inquiry* 8, 777-95.

Goffman, Erving 1981: *Forms of Talk*. Philadelphia: University of Pennsylvania Press.

Hewlett, Sylvia Ann 1986: *A Lesser Life: The Myth of Women's Liberation in America*. New York: Warner Books.

Kessler, S. and McKenna, W. 1978: *Gender: an Ethnomethodological Approach*. New York: John Wiley & Sons.

McElhinny, Bonnie 1993: We all wear the blue: language, gender and police work. Unpublished Ph.D. dissertation. Stanford, CA: Stanford University.

McLemore, Cynthia 1991: The pragmatic interpretation of English intonation: sorority speech. Unpublished Ph.D. dissertation. Austin: University of Texas at Austin.

Sattel, Jack 1983: Men, inexpressiveness and power. In B. Thorne, C. Kramarae and N. Henley (eds.), *Language, Gender and Society*. Cambridge, MA: Newbury House, 119-24.

Segal, L. 1990: *Slow Motion: Changing Masculinities, Changing Men*. London: Virago.

Post-reading Questions / Activities

- What does it mean that identity has to be constructed? How is language involved in the construction of identity?
- Why is masculinity especially connected to competition and power? Might this assumption differ among men of different ages?
- Record a gathering of men and analyze its discourse, following the model in Kiesling's chapter. Do your observations support or refute Kiesling's? In what ways?

Vocabulary

community of practice	discursive	etic
discourse	emic	mitigate

Suggested Further Reading

Bucholtz, Mary, A. C. Liang, and Laurel A. Sutton, eds. 1999. *Reinventing Identities: The Gendered Self in Discourse*. New York: Oxford University Press.

Coates, Jennifer, ed. 1998. *Language and Gender: A Reader*. Malden, MA: Blackwell.

Eckert, Penelope, and Sally McConnell-Ginet. 1992. "Think Practically and Look Locally: Language and Gender as Community-Based Practice." *Annual Review of Anthropology* 21: 461–490.

———, and ———. 2003. *Language and Gender*. Cambridge: Cambridge University Press.

Goodwin, Marjorie Harness. 1990. *He Said–She Said: Talk as Social Organization Among Black Children*. Bloomington: Indiana University Press.

Graddol, David, and Joan Swann. 1989. *Gender Voices*. Oxford: Blackwell.

Hall, Kira, and Mary Bucholtz, eds. 1995. *Gender Articulated: Language and the Socially Constructed Self*. New York and London: Oxford University Press.

Holmes, Janet. 1995. *Women, Men, and Politeness*. London and New York: Longman.

Inoue, Miyako. 2006. *Vicarious Language: Gender and Linguistic Modernity in Japan*. Berkeley and Los Angeles: University of California Press.

Johnson, Sally, and Ulrike Hanna Meinhof, eds. 1997. *Language and Masculinity*. Oxford: Blackwell.

Ochs, Elinor. 1991. "Indexing Gender." In *Rethinking Context*, edited by Alessandro Duranti and Charles Goodwin, pp. 335–358. Cambridge: Cambridge University Press.

Philips, Susan U., Susan Steele, and Christine Tanz, eds. 1987. *Language, Gender, and Sex in Comparative Perspective*. Cambridge: Cambridge University Press.

Romaine, Suzanne. 1999. *Communicating Gender*. Mahwah, NJ: Erlbaum.

Tannen, Deborah. 1990. *You Just Don't Understand: Women and Men in Conversation*. New York: Ballantine Books.

Thorne, Barrie, and Nancy Henley, eds. 1975. *Language and Sex: Difference and Dominance*. Rowley, MA: Newbury House.

———, Cheris Kramarae, and Nancy Henley, eds. 1983. *Language, Gender, and Society*. Rowley, MA: Newbury House.

CHAPTER 33

Performing Gender Identity
Young Men's Talk and the Construction
of Heterosexual Masculinity

Deborah Cameron
(1997)

People in every society have ideas, or ideologies, about the ways men and women are supposed to act, and about how they talk. There are also ideas about what kind of talk is valued, whether it is talk that conveys information or talk that furthers a relationship (see Chapter 34 and Unit 6). Along with gender roles are ideas about sexuality. In the United States, masculinity is associated with heterosexuality.

Using Judith Butler's idea of performativity, *in which humans enact gender through activity rather than simply reiterating something previously given, Deborah Cameron analyzes part of a conversation recorded by a student in one of her classes, pointing out ways that easy equation of "rapport" with women is inadequate for understanding all the ways gender is performed. Rather, speakers draw on linguistic resources available to all as members of many communities to accomplish certain aims in certain circumstances.*

Reading Questions

- What does Cameron observe in the conversation Danny recorded that Danny had overlooked? How does she explain his partial understanding of the conversation?
- What is the difference between "rapport talk" and "raport talk"? Which is typically associated with women? Which does Cameron see in this conversation, and how does she explain it?
- What do the five men talk about, besides wine, women, and sports, and how do they do it?
- Why does Cameron say that the conversation is "not only *about* masculinity, it is a sustained performance *of* masculinity"? Why does she insist that the conversation is not in a "feminine" conversational style, despite its resemblance to many conversations among women?
- What is the point of the antigay content of this conversation?

———•———

In 1990, a 21-year-old student in a language and gender class I was teaching at a college in the southern U.S. tape-recorded a sequence of casual conversation among five men; himself and four friends. This young man, whom I will call "Danny,"[1] had decided to investigate whether the informal talk of male friends would bear out generalizations about "men's talk" that are often encountered in discussions of gender differences in conversational style—for example that it is competitive,

Deborah Cameron, "Performing Gender Identity: Young Men's Talk and the Construction of Heterosexual Masculinity." In Sally Johnson and Ulrike Hanna Meinhof, eds., *Language and Masculinity.* Oxford: Blackwell, 1997, pp. 47–64.

hierarchically organized, centres on "impersonal" topics and the exchange of information, and foregrounds speech genres such as joking, trading insults, and sports statistics....

Danny reported that the stereotype of all-male interaction was borne out by the data he recorded. He gave his paper the title "Wine, women, and sports." Yet although I could agree that the data did contain the stereotypical features he reported, the more I looked at it, the more I saw other things in it too. Danny's analysis was not inaccurate, his conclusions were not unwarranted, but his description of the data was (in both senses) *partial*: it was shaped by expectations that caused some things to leap out of the record as "significant," while other things went unremarked.

I am interested in the possibility that Danny's selective reading of his data was not just the understandable error of an inexperienced analyst. Analysis is never done without preconceptions, we can never be absolutely non-selective in our observations, and where the object of observation and analysis has to do with gender it is extraordinarily difficult to subdue certain expectations.

One might speculate, for example, on why the vignettes of "typical" masculine and feminine behaviour presented in popular books like Deborah Tannen's *You Just Don't Understand* (1990) are so often apprehended as immediately *recognizable*.[2] Is it because we have actually witnessed these scenarios occurring in real life, or is it because we can so readily supply the cultural script that makes them meaningful and "typical"? One argument for the latter possibility is that if you *reverse* the genders in Tannen's anecdotes, it is still possible to supply a script which makes sense of the alleged gender difference. For example, Tannen remarks on men's reluctance to ask for directions while driving, and attributes it to men's greater concern for status (asking for help suggests helplessness). But if, as an experiment, you tell people it is women rather than men who are more reluctant to ask for directions, they will have no difficulty coming up with a different and equally plausible explanation—for instance that the reluctance reflects a typically feminine desire to avoid imposing on others, or perhaps a well-founded fear of stopping to talk to strangers.[3]

What this suggests is that the behaviour of men and women, whatever its substance may happen to be in any specific instance, is invariably read through a more general discourse on gender difference itself. That discourse is subsequently invoked to *explain* the pattern of gender differentiation in people's behaviour; whereas it might be more enlightening to say the discourse *constructs* the differentiation, makes it visible *as* differentiation.

I want to propose that conversationalists themselves often do the same thing I have just suggested analysts do. Analysts construct stories about other people's behaviour, with a view to making it exemplify certain patterns of gender difference; conversationalists construct stories about themselves and others, with a view to performing certain kinds of gender identity.

IDENTITY AND PERFORMATIVITY

In 1990, the philosopher Judith Butler published an influential book called *Gender Trouble: Feminism and the Subversion of Identity*. Butler's essay is a postmodernist reconceptualization of gender, and it makes use of a concept familiar to linguists and discourse analysts from speech-act theory: *performativity*. For Butler, gender is *performative*—in her suggestive phrase "constituting the identity it is purported to be." Just as J. L. Austin (1962) maintained that illocutions like "I promise" do not describe a pre-existing state of affairs but actually bring one into being, so Butler claims that "feminine" and "masculine" are not what we are, nor traits we *have*, but effects we produce by way of particular things we *do*: "Gender is the repeated stylization of the body, a set of repeated acts within a rigid regulatory frame which congeal over time to produce the appearance of substance, of a 'natural' kind of being" (p. 33).

This extends the traditional feminist account whereby gender is socially constructed rather than "natural," famously expressed in Simone de Beauvoir's dictum that "one is not born, but rather becomes a woman." Butler is saying that "becoming a woman" (or a man) is not something you accomplish once and for all at an early stage of life. Gender has constantly to be reaffirmed and publicly displayed by repeatedly performing particular acts in accordance with the cultural norms (themselves historically and socially constructed, and consequently variable) which define "masculinity" and "femininity."

This "performative" model sheds an interesting light on the phenomenon of gendered *speech*. Speech too is a "repeated stylization of the body"; the "masculine" and "feminine" styles of talking identified by researchers might be thought of as the "congealed" result of repeated acts by social actors who are striving to constitute themselves as "proper" men and women. Whereas sociolinguistics traditionally assumes that people talk the way they do because of who they (already) are, the postmodernist approach suggests that people are who they are because of (among other things) the way they talk. This shifts the focus away from a simple cataloguing of differences between men and women to a subtler and more complex inquiry into how people use linguistic resources to produce gender differentiation. It also obliges us to attend to the "rigid regulatory frame" within which people must make their choices—the norms that define what kinds of language are possible, intelligible, and appropriate resources for performing masculinity or femininity.

A further advantage of this approach is that it acknowledges the instability and variability of gender identities, and therefore of the behaviour in which those identities are performed. While Judith Butler rightly insists that gender is regulated and policed by rather rigid social norms, she does not reduce men and women to automata, programmed by their early socialization to repeat forever the appropriate gendered behaviour, but treats them as conscious agents who may—albeit often at some social cost—engage in acts of transgression, subversion, and resistance. As active producers rather than passive reproducers of gendered behaviour, men and women may use their awareness of the gendered meanings that attach to particular ways of speaking and acting to produce a variety of effects. This is important, because few, if any, analysts of data on men's and women's speech would maintain that the differences are as clear-cut and invariant as one might gather from such oft-cited dichotomies as "competitive/cooperative" and "report talk/rapport talk." People *do* perform gender differently in different contexts, and do sometimes behave in ways we would normally associate with the "other" gender. The conversation to which we now turn is a notable case in point.

THE CONVERSATION: WINE, WOMEN, SPORTS,... AND OTHER MEN

The five men who took part in the conversation, and to whom I will give the pseudonyms Al, Bryan, Carl, Danny, and Ed, were demographically a homogeneous group: white, middle-class American suburbanites aged 21, who attended the same university and belonged to the same social network on campus. This particular conversation occurred in the context of one of their commonest shared leisure activities: watching sports at home on television.

Throughout the period covered by the tape-recording there is a basketball game on screen, and participants regularly make reference to what is going on in the game. Sometimes these references are just brief interpolated comments, which do not disrupt the flow of ongoing talk on some other topic; sometimes they lead to extended discussion. At all times, however, it is a legitimate conversational move to comment on the basketball game. The student who collected the data drew attention to the status of sport as a resource for talk available to North American men of all classes and racial/ethnic groups, to strangers as well as friends, suggesting that "sports talk" is a typically "masculine" conversational genre in the U.S., something all culturally competent males know how to do.

But "sports talk" is by no means the only kind of talk being done. The men also recount the events of their day—what classes they had and how these went; they discuss mundane details of their domestic arrangements, such as who is going to pick up groceries; there is a debate about the merits of a certain kind of wine; there are a couple of longer narratives, notably one about an incident when two men sharing a room each invited a girlfriend back without their roommate's knowledge—and discovered this at the most embarrassing moment possible. Danny's title "Wine, women, and sports" is accurate insofar as all these subjects are discussed at some length.

When one examines the data, however, it becomes clear there is one very significant omission in Danny's title. Apart from basketball, the single most prominent theme in the recorded conversation, as measured by the amount of time devoted to it, is "gossip": discussion of several persons not present but known to the participants, with a strong focus on critically examining these individuals' appearance, dress, social behaviour, and sexual mores. Like the conversationalists themselves, the individuals under discussion are all men. Unlike the conversationalists, however, the individuals under discussion are identified as "gay."

The topic of "gays" is raised by Ed, only a few seconds in to the tape-recorded conversation:

ED: Mugsy Bogues (.) my name is Lloyd Gompers I am a homosexual (.) you know what the (.) I saw the new Remnant I should have grabbed you know the title? Like the head thing?

"Mugsy Bogues" (the name of a basketball player) is an acknowledgement of the previous turn, which concerned the on-screen game. Ed's next comment appears off-topic, but he immediately supplies a rationale for it, explaining that he "saw the new Remnant"—The Remnant being a deliberately provocative right-wing campus newspaper whose main story that week had been an attack on the "Gay Ball," a dance sponsored by the college's Gay Society.

The next few turns are devoted to establishing a shared view of the Gay Ball and of homosexuality generally. Three of the men, Al, Bryan, and Ed, are actively involved in this exchange. A typical sequence is the following:

AL: gays=
ED: =gays w[hy? that's what it should read [gays why?
BRYAN: [gays]   [I know]

What is being established as "shared" here is a view of gays as alien [that is, the group defines itself as heterosexual and puzzled by homosexuality ("gays, why?"), and also to some extent comical]. Danny comments at one point, "it's hilarious," and Ed caps the sequence discussing the Gay Ball with the witticism:

ED: the question is who wears the boutonnière and who wears the corsage, flip for it? or do they both just wear flowers coz they're fruits

It is at this point that Danny introduces the theme that will dominate the conversation for some time: gossip about individual men who are said to be gay. Referring to the only other man in his language and gender glass, Danny begins

DANNY: My boy Ronnie was uh speaking up on the male perspective today (.) way too much

The section following this contribution is structured around a series of references to other "gay" individuals known to the participants as classmates. Bryan mentions "the most effeminate guy I've ever met" and "that really gay guy in our Age of Revolution class." Ed remarks that "you have never seen more homos than we have in our class. Homos, dykes, homos, dykes, everybody is a homo or a dyke." He then focuses on a "fat, queer, goofy guy...[who's] as gay as night" [sic], and on a "blond hair, snide little queer weird shit," who is further described as a "butt pirate." Some of these references, but not all, initiate an extended discussion of the individual concerned. The content of these discussions will bear closer examination.

"The Antithesis of Man"

One of the things I initially found most puzzling about the whole "gays" sequence was that the group's criteria for categorizing people as gay appeared to have little to do with those people's known or suspected sexual preferences or practices. The terms "butt pirate" and "butt cutter" were used, but surprisingly seldom; it was unclear to me that the individuals referred to really were homosexual, and in one case where I actually knew the subject of discussion, I seriously doubted it.

Most puzzling is an exchange between Bryan and Ed about the class where "everybody is a homo or a dyke," in which they complain that "four homos" are continually "hitting on" [making sexual overtures to] one of the women, described as "the ugliest-ass bitch in the history of the world." One might have thought that a defining feature of a "homo" would be his lack of interest in "hitting on" women. Yet no one seems aware of any contradiction in this exchange.

I think this is because the deviance indicated for this group by the term "gay" is not so much *sexual* deviance as *gender* deviance. Being "gay" means failing to measure up to the group's standards of masculinity or femininity. This is why it makes sense to call someone "*really* gay": unlike same- versus- other-sex preference, conformity to gender norms can be a matter of degree. It is also why hitting on an "ugly-ass bitch" can be classed as "homosexual" behaviour—proper masculinity requires that the object of public sexual interest be not just female, but minimally attractive.

Applied by the group to men, "gay" refers in particular to insufficiently masculine appearance, clothing, and speech. To illustrate this I will reproduce a longer sequence of conversation about the "really gay guy in our Age of Revolution class," which ends with Ed declaring: "he's the antithesis of man."

BRYAN: uh you know that really gay guy in our Age of Revolution class who sits in front of us? he wore shorts again, by the way, it's like 42 degrees out he wore shorts again [laughter] [Ed: That guy] it's like a speedo, he wears a speedo to class (.) he's got incredibly skinny legs [Ed: it's worse] you know=

ED: =you know
like those shorts women volleyball players wear? it's like those (.) it's l[ike

BRYAN: [you know what's even more ridicu[lous? When
ED: [French cut
spandex]

BRYAN: you wear those shorts and like a parka on...
(5 lines omitted)

BRYAN: he's either got some condition that he's got to like have his legs exposed at all times or else he's got really good legs=

ED: =he's probably he'[s like
CARL: [he really likes

BRYAN: =he
ED: =he's like at home combing his leg hairs=
CARL: his legs=

BRYAN: he doesn't have any leg hair though=   [yes and oh
ED: =he real[ly likes

ED: his legs=
AL: =very long very white and very skinny

BRYAN: those ridiculous Reeboks that are always (indeciph) and goofy white socks always striped=
[tube socks
ED: =that's [right

ED: he's the antithesis of man

In order to demonstrate that certain individuals are "the antithesis of man," the group engages in a kind of conversation that might well strike us as the antithesis of "men's talk." It is unlike the "wine, women, and sports" stereotype of men's talk—indeed, rather closer to the stereotype of "women's talk"—in various ways, some obvious, and some less so.

The obvious ways in which this sequence resembles conventional notions of "women's talk" concern its purpose and subject-matter. This is talk about people, not things, and "rapport talk" rather than "report talk"—the main point is clearly not to exchange information. It is "gossip," and serves one of the most common purposes of gossip, namely affirming the solidarity of an in-group by constructing absent others as an out-group, whose behaviour is minutely examined and found wanting.

The specific subjects on which the talk dwells are conventionally "feminine" ones: clothing and bodily appearance. The men are caught up in a contradiction: their criticism of the "gays" centres on their unmanly interest in displaying their bodies, and the inappropriate garments they choose for this purpose (bathing costumes worn to class, shorts worn in cold weather with parkas which render the effect ludicrous, clothing which resembles the outfits of "women volleyball players"). The implication is that real men just pull on their jeans and leave it at that. But in order to pursue this line of criticism, the conversationalists themselves must show an acute awareness of such "unmanly" concerns as styles and materials. ("French cut spandex," "tube socks"), what kind of clothes go together, and which men have "good legs." They are impelled, paradoxically, to talk about men's bodies as a way of demonstrating their own total lack of sexual interest in those bodies.

The less obvious ways in which this conversation departs from stereotypical notions of "men's talk" concern its *formal* features. Analyses of men's and women's speech style are commonly organized around a series of global oppositions, e.g., men's talk is "competitive," whereas women's is "cooperative"; men talk to gain "status," whereas women talk to forge "intimacy" and "connection"; men do "report talk" and women "rapport talk." Analysts working with these oppositions typically identify certain formal or organizational features of talk as markers of "competition" and "cooperation," etc. The analyst then examines which kinds of features predominate in a set of conversational data, and how they are being used.

In the following discussion, I too will make use of the conventional oppositions as tools for describing data, but I will be trying to build up an argument that their use is problematic. The problem is not merely that the men in my data fail to fit their gender stereotype perfectly. More importantly, I think it is often the stereotype itself that underpins analytic judgements that a certain form is cooperative rather than competitive, or that people are seeking status rather than connection in their talk. As I observed about Deborah Tannen's vignettes, many instances of behaviour will support either interpretation, or both; we use the speaker's gender, and our beliefs about what sort of behaviour makes sense for members of that gender, to rule some interpretations in and others out.

Cooperation

Various scholars, notably Jennifer Coates (1989), have remarked on the "cooperative" nature of informal talk among female friends, drawing attention to a number of linguistic features which are prominent in data on all-female groups. Some of these, like hedging and the use of epistemic modals, are signs of attention to others' face, aimed at minimizing conflict and securing agreement [cf. Holmes 2006]. Others, such as latching of turns, simultaneous speech where this is not interpreted by participants as a violation of turn-taking rights (cf. Edelsky 1981), and the repetition or recycling of lexical items and phrases across turns, are signals that a conversation is a "joint production": that participants are building on one another's contributions so that ideas are felt to be group property rather than the property of a single speaker.

On these criteria, the conversation here must be judged as highly cooperative. For example, in the extract reproduced above, a strikingly large number of turns (around half) begin with "you know" and/or contain the marker "like" ("you know like those shorts women volleyball players wear?"). The functions of these items (especially "like") in younger Americans' English are complex and multiple, and may include the cooperative, mitigating/face-protecting functions that Coates and Janet Holmes (1984) associate with hedging. Even where they are not clearly hedges, however, in this interaction they function in ways that relate to the building of group involvement and consensus. They often seem to mark information as "given" within the group's discourse (that is, "you know," "like," "X" presupposes that the addressee is indeed familiar with X); "you know" has the kind of hearer-orientated affective function (taking others into account or inviting their agreement) which Holmes attributes to certain tag questions; while "like" in addition seems to function for these speakers as a marker of high involvement. It appears most frequently at moments when the interactants are, by other criteria such as intonation, pitch, loudness, speech rate, incidence of simultaneous speech, and of "strong" or taboo language, noticeably excited, such as the following:

ED: he's I mean he **like** a real artsy fartsy fag he's **like** (indeciph) he's so gay he's got this **like** really high voice and wire rim glasses and he sits next to the ugliest-ass bitch in the history of the world

ED: [and
BRYAN: [and they're all hitting on her too, **like** four

ED: [I know it's **like** four homos hitting on her
BRYAN: guys [hitting on her

It is also noticeable throughout the long extract reproduced earlier how much latching and simultaneous speech there is, as compared to other forms of turn transition involving either short or long pauses and gaps, or interruptions which silence the interruptee. Latching—turn transition without pause or overlap—is often taken as a mark of cooperation because in order to latch a turn so precisely onto the preceding turn, the speaker has to attend closely to others' contributions.

The last part of the reproduced extract, discussing the "really gay" guy's legs, is an excellent example of jointly produced discourse, as the speakers cooperate to build a detailed picture of the legs and what is worn on them, a picture which overall could not be attributed to any single speaker. This sequence contains many instances of latching, repetition of one speaker's words by another speaker (Ed recycles Carl's whole turn, "he really likes his legs," with added emphasis), and it also contains something that is relatively rare in the conversation as a whole, repeated tokens of hearer support like "yes" and "that's right."[4]

There are, then, points of resemblance worth remarking on between these men's talk and similar talk among women as reported by previous studies. The question does arise, however, whether this male conversation has the other important hallmark of women's gossip, namely an egalitarian or non-hierarchical organization of the floor.

Competition

In purely quantitative terms, this conversation cannot be said to be egalitarian. The extracts reproduced so far are representative of the whole insofar as they show Ed and Bryan as the dominant speakers, while Al and Carl contribute fewer and shorter turns (Danny is variable; there are sequences where he contributes very little, but when he talks he often contributes turns as long as Ed's and Bryan's, and he also initiates topics). Evidence thus exists to support an argument that there is a hierarchy in this conversation, and there is competition, particularly between the two dominant speakers, Bryan and Ed (and to a lesser extent Ed and Danny). Let us pursue this by looking more closely at Ed's behaviour.

Ed introduces the topic of homosexuality, and initially attempts to keep "ownership" of it. He cuts off Danny's first remark on the subject with a reference to *The Remnant*: "what was the article? cause you know they bashed them they were like." At this point Danny interrupts: it is clearly an interruption because in this context the preferred interpretation of "like" is quotative—Ed is about to repeat what the gay-bashing article in *The Remnant* said. In addition to interrupting so that Ed falls silent, Danny contradicts Ed, saying "they didn't actually (.) cut into them big." A little later on during the discussion of the Gay Ball, Ed makes use of a common competitive strategy, the joke or witty remark which "caps" other contributions (the "flowers and fruits" joke quoted above). This, however, elicits no laughter, no matching jokes, and indeed no take-up of any kind. It is followed by a pause and a change of direction if not of subject, as Danny begins the gossip that will dominate talk for several minutes.

This immediately elicits a matching contribution from Bryan. As he and Danny talk, Ed makes two unsuccessful attempts to regain the floor. One, where he utters the prefatory remark "I'm gonna be very honest," is simply ignored. His second strategy is to ask (about the person Bryan and Danny are discussing) "what's this guy's last name?" First Bryan asks him to repeat the question, then Danny replies "I don't know what the hell it is."

A similar pattern is seen in the long extract reproduced above, where Ed makes two attempts to interrupt Bryan's first turn ("That guy" and "it's worse"), neither of which succeeds. He gets the floor eventually by using the "you know, like" strategy. And from that point, Ed does orient more to the norms of joint production; he overlaps others to produce simultaneous speech but does not interrupt; he produces more latched turns, recyclings, and support tokens.

So far I have been arguing that even if the speakers, or some of them, compete, they are basically engaged in a collaborative and solidary enterprise (reinforcing the bonds within the group by denigrating people outside it), an activity in which all speakers participate, even if some are more active than others. Therefore I have drawn attention to the presence of "cooperative" features, and have argued that more extreme forms of hierarchical and competitive behaviour are not rewarded by the group. I could, indeed, have argued that by the end, Ed and Bryan are not so much "competing"—after all, their contributions are not antagonistic to one another but tend to reinforce one another—as engaging in a version of the "joint production of discourse."

Yet the data might also support a different analysis in which Ed and Bryan are simply *using* the collaborative enterprise of putting down gay men as an occasion to engage in verbal duelling where points are scored—against fellow group members rather than against the absent gay men—by dominating the floor and coming up with more and more extravagant put-downs. In this alternative analysis, Ed does not so much modify his behaviour as "lose" his duel with Bryan. "Joint production" or "verbal duelling"—how do we decide?

Deconstructing Oppositions

One response to the problem of competing interpretations raised above might be that the opposition I have been working with—"competitive" versus "cooperative" behaviour—is inherently problematic, particularly if one is taken to exclude the other. Conversation can and usually does contain both cooperative and competitive elements: one could argue [along with Grice (1975)] that talk must by definition involve a certain minimum of cooperation, and also that there will usually be some degree of competition among speakers, if not for the floor itself then for the attention or the approval of others (see also Hewitt 1997).

The global competitive/cooperative opposition also encourages the lumping together under one heading or the other of things that could in principle be distinguished. "Cooperation" might refer to agreement on the aims of talk, respect for other speakers' right, or support for their contributions; but there is not always perfect co-occurrence among these aspects, and the presence of any one of them need not rule out a "competitive" element. Participants in a conversation or other speech event may compete with each other and at the same time be pursuing a shared project or common agenda (as in ritual insult sessions); they may be in severe disagreement but punctiliously observant of one

another's speaking rights (as in a formal debate, say); they may be overtly supportive, and at the same time covertly hoping to score points for their supportiveness.

This last point is strangely overlooked in some discussions of women's talk. Women who pay solicitous attention to one another's face are often said to be seeking connection or good social relations *rather than* status; yet one could surely argue that attending to others' face and attending to one's own are not mutually exclusive here. The "egalitarian" norms of female friendship groups are, like all norms, to some degree coercive: the rewards and punishments precisely concern one's status within the group (among women, however, this status is called "popularity" rather than "dominance"). A woman may gain status by displaying the correct degree of concern for others, and lose status by displaying too little concern for others and too much for herself. Arguably, it is gender-stereotyping that causes us to miss or minimize the status-seeking element in women friends' talk, and the connection-making dimension of men's.

HOW TO DO GENDER WITH LANGUAGE

I hope it will be clear by now that my intention in analysing male gossip is not to suggest that the young men involved have adopted a "feminine" conversational style. On the contrary, the main theoretical point I want to make concerns the folly of making any such claim. To characterize the conversation I have been considering as "feminine" on the basis that it bears a significant resemblance to conversations among women friends would be to miss the most important point about it, that it is not only *about* masculinity, it is a sustained performance *of* masculinity. What is important in gendering talk is the "performative gender work" the talk is doing; its role in constituting people as gendered subjects.

To put matters in these terms is not to deny that there may be an empirically observable association between a certain genre or style of speech and speakers of a particular gender. In practice this is undeniable. But we do need to ask: in virtue of what does the association hold? Can we give an account that will not be vitiated by cases where it does *not* hold? For it seems to me that conversations like the one I have analysed leave, say, Deborah Tannen's contention that men do not do "women's talk," because they simply *do not know how*, looking lame and unconvincing. If men rarely engage in a certain kind of talk, an explanation is called for; but if they do engage in it even very occasionally, an explanation in terms of pure ignorance will not do.

I suggest the following explanation. Men and women do not live on different planets, but are members of cultures in which a large amount of discourse about gender is constantly circulating. They do not only learn, and then mechanically reproduce, ways of speaking "appropriate" to their own sex; they learn a much broader set of gendered meanings that attach in rather complex ways to different ways of speaking, and they produce their own behaviour in the light of those meanings.

This behaviour will vary. Even the individual who is most unambiguously committed to traditional notions of gender has a range of possible gender identities to draw on. Performing masculinity or femininity "appropriately" cannot mean giving exactly the same performance regardless of the circumstances. It may involve different strategies in mixed and single-sex company, in private and in public settings, in the various social positions (parent, lover, professional, friend) that someone might regularly occupy in the course of everyday life.

Since gender is a relational term, and the minimal requirement for "being a man" is "not being a woman," we may find that in many circumstances, men are under pressure to constitute themselves as masculine linguistically by avoiding forms of talk whose primary association is with women/femininity. But this is not invariant, which begs the question: Under what circumstances does the contrast with women lose its salience as a constraint on men's behaviour? When can men do so-called feminine talk without threatening their constitution as men? Are there cases when it might actually be to their advantage to do this?

WHEN AND WHY DO MEN GOSSIP?

Many researchers have reported that both sexes engage in gossip, since its social functions (like affirming group solidarity and serving as an unofficial conduit for information) are of universal relevance, but its cultural meaning (for us) is undeniably "feminine." Therefore we might expect to find most men avoiding it, or disguising it as something else, especially in mixed settings where they are concerned to mark their difference from women (see Johnson and Finlay 1997). In the conversation discussed above, however, there are no women for the men to differentiate themselves from; whereas *there is* the perceived danger that so often accompanies western male homosociality: homosexuality. Under these circumstances perhaps it becomes acceptable to transgress one gender norm ("men don't gossip, gossip is for girls") in order to affirm what in this context is a more important norm ("men in all-male groups must unambiguously display their heterosexual orientation").

In these speakers' understanding of gender, gay men, like women, provide a contrast group against whom masculinity can be defined. This principle of contrast seems to set limits on the permissibility of gossip for these young men. Although they discuss other men besides the "gays"—professional basketball players—they could not be said to gossip about them. They talk about the players' skills and their records, not their appearance, personal lives, or sexual activities. Since the men admire the basketball players, identifying *with* them rather than *against* them, such talk would border dangerously on what for them is obviously taboo: desire for other men.

Ironically, it seems likely that the despised gay men are the *only* men about whom these male friends can legitimately talk among themselves in such intimate

terms without compromsing the heterosexual masculinity they are so anxious to display—though in a different context, say with their girlfriends, they might be able to discuss the basketball players differently. The presence of a woman, especially a heterosexual partner, displaces the dread spectre of homosexuality, and makes other kinds of talk possible; though by the same token her presence might make certain kinds of talk that take place among men impossible. What counts as acceptable talk for men is a complex matter in which all kinds of contextual variables play a part.

In this context—a private conversation among male friends—it could be argued that to gossip, either about your sexual exploits with women or about the repulsiveness of gay men (these speakers do both), is not just one way, but the most appropriate way to display heterosexual masculinity. In another context (in public, or with a larger and less close-knit group of men), the same objective might well be pursued through explicitly agonistic strategies, such as yelling abuse at women or gays in the street, or exchanging sexist and homophobic jokes. *Both* strategies could be said to do performative gender work: in terms of what they do for the speakers involved, one is not more "masculine" than the other, they simply belong to different settings in which heterosexual masculinity may (or must) be put on display.

CONCLUSION

I hope that my discussion of the conversation I have analysed makes the point that it is unhelpful for linguists to continue to use models of gendered speech which imply that masculinity and femininity are monolithic constructs, automatically giving rise to predictable (and utterly different) patterns of verbal interaction. At the same time, I hope it might make us think twice about the sort of analysis that implicitly seeks the meaning (and sometimes the *value*) of an interaction among men or women primarily in the style, rather than the substance, of what is said. For although, as I noted earlier in relation to Judith Butler's work, it is possible for men and women to performatively subvert or resist the prevailing codes of gender, there can surely be no convincing argument that this is what Danny and his friends are doing. Their conversation is animated by entirely traditional anxieties about being seen at all times as red-blooded heterosexual males: not women and not queers. Their skill as performers does not alter the fact that what they perform is the same old gendered script.

Transcription Conventions

=	latching
[	turn onset overlaps previous turn
[]	turn is completely contained within another speaker's turn
?	rising intonation on utterance
(.)	short pause
(indeciph)	indecipherable speech
italics	emphatic stress on italicized item

Notes

1. Because the student concerned is one of the speakers in the conversation I analyse, and the nature of the conversation makes it desirable to conceal participants' identities (indeed, this was one of the conditions on which the data were collected and subsequently passed on to me), I will not give his real name here, but I want to acknowledge his generosity in making his recording and transcript available to me, and to thank him for a number of insights I gained by discussing the data with him as well as by reading his paper. I am also grateful to the other young men who participated. All their names, and the names of other people they mention, have been changed, and all pseudonyms used are (I hope) entirely fictitious.

2. I base this assessment of reader response on my own research with readers of Tannen's book (see Cameron 1995: Chapter 5), on non-scholarly reviews of the book, and on reader studies of popular self-help generally (e.g., Lichterman 1992; Simonds 1992).

3. I am indebted to Penelope Eckert for describing this "thought experiment," which she has used in her own teaching (though the specific details of the example are not an exact rendition of Eckert's observations).

4. It is a rather consistent research finding that men use such minimal responses significantly less often than women, and in this respect the present data conform to expectations—there are very few minimal responses of any kind. I would argue, however, that active listenership, involvement, and support are not *absent* in the talk of this group; they are marked by other means such as high levels of latching/simultaneous speech, lexical recycling, and the use of *like*.

References

Austin, J. L. (1962) *How To Do Things with Words*, 2d ed. Ed. by J. O. Urmson and Marina Sbisa. Cambridge, MA: Harvard University Press.

Butler, J. (1990) *Gender Trouble: Feminism and the Subversion of Identity*, New York: Routledge.

Cameron, D. (1995) *Verbal Hygiene*, London: Routledge.

Coates, J. (1989) "Gossip revisited: language in all-female groups" in Coates, J. and Cameron, D. (eds.) *Women in their Speech Communities*, Harlow: Longman, 94–121.

Edelsky, C. (1981) "Who's got the floor?" *Language in Society* 10 (3): 383–422.

Grice, (1975) "Logic and conversation" in Coler, P. and Morgan, J. L. (eds.) *Syntax and Semantics*, volume 3, New York: Academic Press, 41–58.

Hewitt, R. (1997) "'Box-out' and 'Taxing'" in Johnson, S. and Meinhof, U. H. (eds.) *Language and Masculinity*, Oxford: Blackwell, 27–46.

Holmes, J. (1984) "Hedging your bets and sitting on the fence: some evidence for hedges as support structures," *Te Reo* 27: 47–62.

Holmes, J. (2006 [1995]) "Women, men, and politeness: agreeable and disagreeable responses," in Jaworski, A. and Couplard, N. (eds.) *The Discourse Reader*, 2d ed., London and New York: Routledge, 324–31.

Johnson, S. and Finlay, F. (1997) "Do men gossip? An analysis of football talk on television," in Johnson, S. and Meinhof, U. H. (eds.) *Language and Masculinity*, Oxford: Blackwell, 130–43.

Lichterman, P. (1992) "Self-help reading as a thin culture," *Media, Culture and Society* 14: 421–47.

Simonds, W. (1992) *Women and Self-Help Culture: Reading Between the Lines*, New Brunswick, NJ: Rutgers University Press.

Tannen, D. (1990) *You Just Don't Understand: Women and Men in Conversation*, New York: Ballantine Books.

Post-reading Questions / Activities

- What can we learn from a close look at the details of conversation that would not be evident from listening to a conversation? What special tools are needed?
- What are the functions of gossip? Is gossip gendered?
- What does Cameron mean when she contrasts the traditional assumption of sociolinguistics that "people talk the way they do because of who they (already) are," with the assumption of postmodernists, that "people are who they are because of (among other things) the way they talk"? What would be the implications of such a viewpoint for social analysis?
- Record a conversation among friends. Transcribe it carefully, omitting names of speakers. Have someone else read it. Is it possible to determine the speakers' genders? How?

Vocabulary

face	latching	quotative
hedging	mitigating	tag question
joint production	performativity	turn

Suggested Further Reading

Bucholtz, Mary, A. C. Liang, and Laurel A. Sutton, eds. 1999. *Reinventing Identities: The Gendered Self in Discourse*. New York: Oxford University Press.

Butler, Judith. 1990. *Gender Trouble: Feminism and the Subversion of Identity*. New York: Routledge.

Coates, Jennifer, ed. 1998. *Language and Gender: A Reader*. Malden, MA: Blackwell.

Eckert, Penelope, and Sally McConnell-Ginet. 1992. "Think Practically and Look Locally: Language and Gender as Community-Based Practice." *Annual Review of Anthropology* 21: 461–490.

———, and ———. 2003. *Language and Gender*. Cambridge: Cambridge University Press.

Goodwin, Marjorie Harness. 1990. *He Said–She Said: Talk as Social Organization Among Black Children*. Bloomington: Indiana University Press.

Graddol, David, and Joan Swann. 1989. *Gender Voices*. Oxford: Blackwell.

Hall, Kira, and Mary Bucholtz, eds. 1995. *Gender Articulated: Language and the Socially Constructed Self*. New York and London: Oxford University Press.

Holmes, Janet. 1995. *Women, Men, and Politeness*. London and New York: Longman.

Inoue, Miyako. 2006. *Vicarious Language: Gender and Linguistic Modernity in Japan*. Berkeley and Los Angeles: University of California Press.

Johnson, Sally, and Ulrike Hanna Meinhof, eds. 1997. *Language and Masculinity*. Oxford: Blackwell.

Ochs, Elinor. 1991. "Indexing Gender." In *Rethinking Context*, edited by Alessandro Duranti and Charles Goodwin, pp. 335–358. Cambridge: Cambridge University Press.

Philips, Susan U., Susan Steele, and Christine Tanz, eds. 1987. *Language, Gender, and Sex in Comparative Perspective*. Cambridge: Cambridge University Press.

Romaine, Suzanne. 1999. *Communicating Gender*. Mahwah, NJ: Erlbaum.

Tannen, Deborah. 1990. *You Just Don't Understand: Women and Men in Conversation*. New York: Ballantine Books.

Thorne, Barrie, and Nancy Henley, eds. 1975. *Language and Sex: Difference and Dominance*. Rowley, MA: Newbury House.

———, Cheris Kramarae, and Nancy Henley, eds. 1983. *Language, Gender, and Society*. Rowley, MA: Newbury House.

CHAPTER 34

Norm-Makers, Norm-Breakers
Uses of Speech by Men and Women in a Malagasy Community

Elinor Keenan (Ochs)

(1974)

It is often the case that information about language use in societies other than one's own can illuminate both the other social practices and those from home. Anthropologists and linguists have investigated language use by women and men in a variety of social settings throughout the world. One society that has much to offer is Japan, where explicit "women's language" contrasts consciously and ideologically with (unmarked) men's language. Recent studies show that this distinction is not as absolute as the ideology holds. In any case, this is different from many "Western" societies in which the construction of gendered language is different.

Other places that often illuminate the range of gender roles include Papua New Guinea and Oceania, favorite anthropological sites. Elinor Keenan's chapter here describes the language ideology in a particular hamlet in Madagascar, where people speak a Malayo-Polynesian language. The values regarding language are held very strictly, and moral judgments follow from people's overt following of norms. In this context, those who break the norms of proper language use are evaluated morally. Practice, however, does not always follow ideology, and not everyone in a particular setting shares norms of practice.

Reading Questions

- What are *kabary* and *resaka*? When is each of them expected to be used? Who are the typical speakers of each?
- What are the two types of requests in this hamlet? Which type may be denied? Which type obligates the hearer?
- What does Keenan mean by saying that women are norm-breakers?
- What is the connection between respect and indirect speech? How does this intersect with gender?

THE COMMUNITY

Namoizamanga is a hamlet composed of twenty-four households, situated in the southern central plateau of Madagascar. This area is generally referred to as *Vakinankaratra*,[1] meaning 'broken by the Ankaratra'. The Ankaratra Mountains do in fact form a natural boundary in the north. They separate this area somewhat from other parts of the central plateau area. This separation has sociological significance in

that the people of this community and communities nearby identify themselves as Vakinankaratra. The present generation recognize an historical link with the dominant plateau group, the Merina, but choose a separate social identity.

A partial explanation for this parochialism lies in the nature of the ties which brought these people formerly in contact. In the late eighteenth century and into the nineteenth century, people of the Vakinankaratra were conquered by the Merina and brought north as slaves. When the French abolished ownership of slaves and the existence of a slave class (*andevo*), many slaves moved back into the traditional homeland of their ancestors. A villager speaks of this time with great difficulty and embarassment. The people know themselves to be former *andevo* and are known by others to be such, but the term itself is almost never used. To address or refer to someone as *andevo* is a grave insult.

Elinor Keenan (Ochs), "Norm-Makers, Norm-Breakers: Uses of Speech by Men and Women in a Malagasy Community," in *Explorations in the Ethnography of Speaking*, 2d ed., edited by Richard Bauman and Joel Sherzer. New York: Cambridge University Press, 1989 [1974], pp. 125–143. Reprinted with the permission of Cambridge University Press.

Genealogical reckoning is shallow, typically going back two to three generations. With some exceptions, local histories begin with the settling of ancestors into these villages in the early part of this century.

Within the village, fixed distinctions in social status are few. All members of a community (who are part of a household) are considered *havana* (kinsmen). Those outside the community are *vahiny* (guests, strangers). Within the *havana* group, those adults who have taken a spouse, especially those with children, are considered to be *ray-aman-dreny* (elders; literally 'father-and-mother') of the community. A respected adult without spouse or children can be a *ray-aman-dreny*, but the status typically implies these qualifications. Decisions which affect a family or the community are usually handled by these *ray-aman-dreny*. Traditionally, village leadership is not fixed with any one particular individual.

Superimposed on this communal framework is a hierarchy of government officials who represent the national political party in power. These officials collect taxes, regulate elections, and act as general liaisons between the government and the people in their sphere of authority. These officials are referred to by French terms: *chef d'hameau* (head of a hamlet), *chef de village* (head of those hamlets which compose an official village), *chef de quartier* (head of those villages which compose a quartier), and so on.

LINGUISTIC REPERTOIRE
OF THE COMMUNITY

The language spoken throughout Madagascar, in various dialects, is Malagasy. It is a verb-first, subject-final language belonging to the Western Malayo-Polynesian subfamily of languages. The people of Namoizamanga speak the major dialect of the island, *Merina*. French is taught in local schools but few villagers, and no adults, speak fluently. Nonetheless sets of French terms may be employed to communicate specific information in particular activities. For example, French directional terms are used almost exclusively in giving orders to cows (see Bloch 1998). We will see below that this specific use of French can be understood in terms of the speech norms we shall present.

There are two major modes of speech use distinguished by the villagers. First, there is *resaka*. This term refers to *teny-an-dava'andro* (everyday speaking). *Resaka* is also characterized as *teny tsotra* (simple talk). The specific kinds of speech behavior covered by the term *resaka* are numerous. *Tafatafa* (gossip), *fiarahabana* (greetings), *fangatahana* (requests), *fiantsoana* (calling out), *fierana* (consultations), *dinika* (discussion), *mitapatap'ahitra* (examine closely; literally 'to break grass'), for example, are *resaka*.

Resaka contrasts with *kabary*, which refers both to ceremonial speech situations and to the highly stylized mode of speech which characterizes such situations. *Kabary* speech is governed by a series of well-known rules which concern the sequencing and content of particular speeches. *Kabary* is characteristic of formal speech situations. *Fanambadiana* (marriages), *fandevenana* (burials), *famadihana* (ancestral bone-turnings), *famorana* (circumcisions), for example, use a specific *kabary* as part of the ritual. But any situation can become "ceremonial" if one chooses to use the *kabary* format, as in for example the expression of gratitude by guest to host, or in the expression of sympathy in visiting mourners or the ill.

We consider *resaka* and *kabary* to be contrastive speech uses of the same generality. This consideration is based on comparison of these terms in unsolicited speech of the villagers themselves. In particular, these two modes of speech usage are frequently contrasted with each other by speechmakers. The contrast appears in that part of a *kabary* in which the speechmaker is expected to convey his inability, unworthiness as a speechmaker. He does this frequently by claiming that his words are not *kabary* but *resaka*.

AVOIDANCE OF DIRECT AFFRONT
AS A SOCIAL NORM

Status as a Norm

Particular uses of speech by a villager are constrained to some extent by notions of what is expected behavior in particular situations. For example, in the Vakinankaratra, one is expected (in many social situations) to avoid open and direct confrontation with another. One is expected not to affront another, not to put an individual in an uncomfortable or unpleasant situation. It is this sort of expected behavior which I am considering as a behavioral norm, relative to particular situations.

When one conducts oneself in violation of these expectations, as in directly confronting another, the action is censured by other villagers. For example, children who confront strangers (*vahiny*) by making direct demands of them are reprimanded by their mothers or elder siblings. An adult who insults (*manevateva*) another openly is ignored by those sympathetic to the injured party. In one case for example, a family who had offended other members of the village with direct insults was physically cut off from most village social life. The footpath running between their house and the rest of the village was blocked. Sisal shrubs were placed across the passage. No member of the village helped the family with rice-planting, whereas normally groups of men and groups of women from each household cooperatively worked each other's fields.

Another form of public censure is to speak of offensive conduct as causing *henatra* (shame). One who has caused *henatra* is thought to *mangalabaraka* (to steal honor) from one's family or community. One who has caused *henatra* is the center of much gossip (*tafatafa*). One strives not to bring *henatra* upon himself or other individuals, and one way to reduce the risk of *henatra* is to act in ways which support the norm of non-confrontation.

Expression of the Non-confrontation Norm in Speech Interaction

Affront can result from a number of interpersonal actions: catching an individual off-guard, unexpectedly, is an affronting action, for example. Thus, in Namoizamanga, to enter another's house without any warning is always inappropriate. If the callers are *havana* (kinsmen or neighbors), they shout *haody*, which signals to those inside the house that they are about to receive visitors. Those inside respond to this signal by saying *mandrosoa* (enter!). This exchange confirms that those inside the house are, in principle, ready to receive the callers. Such an exchange allows those inside the house a moment of preparation to rise from their beds, dress, stop eating, or the like. On the other hand, if the guests are not *havana*, they may in addition send a messenger ahead to ascertain whether or not these others can receive them. It is highly offensive then to catch one unawares, as this may put him in a disadvantaged position.

Equally inappropriate is an open and direct expression of anger or disagreement. Physical fighting among adults is almost non-existent. Small boys have mock fights, but these are always playful, never angry. Typically anger or disapproval is not directed toward the relevant person or persons. Rather, each side tells sympathetic associates of their sentiments, and these sentiments are then made known to the other side by intermediaries. Disputes then are often resolved by intermediaries, such as local elders or persons in the area known to be *mpanao fihavanana* (restorers of relationships). These persons are invited by some person associated with both sides to resolve the dispute.

We should note also that the censuring behavior referred to above is subject to the norm of non-confrontation. Thus, with one important exception to be discussed below, censure is not communicated directly and openly to an adult violator of a norm.

Similarly criticism levelled by speechmakers at each other during *kabary* performances is also subject to the non-confrontation norm. Many *kabary* performances involve at least two speechmakers (*mpikabary*) who engage in a ritualized dialogue which varies according to the nature of the occasion. Usually the second speaker or group of speakers represents the listener group to whom the first speaker addresses himself. The second speaker normally affirms his (his group's) support for and solidarity with the first speaker and his group. However, there are occasions when the second speechmaker wishes to criticize the first one. For example, if the first has made some error in the sequence of speech acts which constitute the *kabary* or has given some incorrect information, the second speechmaker will usually point this out. In so doing he enhances his status as one knowledgeable in matters of the *kabary*. Thus the *kabary* functions on two levels at once. On one level, it is concerned with the ritual at hand: marriage request, funeral, circumcision. And on a second level it is a forum displaying the skill and knowledge of the speakers. An able speechmaker excels by revealing an intimate acquaintance with *kabary* format and with the range of proverbs (*ohabolana*) and traditional sayings (*hainteny*) associated with the particular event.

One way of expressing expertise is to dispute some aspect of the *kabary* handled by the other speechmaker. But the expression of disagreement must be done delicately. It must be shown that an error has been made, but it must not be shown too bluntly or explicitly. The second speechmaker must avoid confronting the first with explicit criticism. In fact, if the second speechmaker were to directly confront the first he would bring *henatra* upon himself and his group. On the other hand, the more subtly the criticism is couched, the greater his status as speechmaker becomes. So, rather than making explicit verbal attacks, the speechmaker makes use of a number of stylistic techniques. First, he softens the negative intent of his remarks by prefacing them with compliments. For example:

> Thank you very much, sir. The first part of your talk has already been received in peace and happiness. I am in accordance and agreement with you on this, sir. You were given permission to speak and what you said gave me courage and strength. You said things skillfully but not pretentiously. You originate words but also recognize what is traditional. But as for myself I am not an originator of words at all but a borrower. I am more comfortable carrying the spade and basket. You, on the other hand, have smoothed out all faults in the speech; you have woven the holes together. You have shown respect to the elders and respect to the young as well. This is finished. But... (Criticism begins.)

Second, criticisms are usually not simply stated but rather alluded to. Proverbs, poetry, traditional expressions are all brought in to reveal bit by bit the direction of the utterance. The same kind of proverbs, poetry, and traditional expressions are used over and over again for these purposes, so that the other speechmaker knows exactly what is being implied by each stylistic device. For example, a criticism might typically begin with the proverb *Atao hady voamangan'Ikirijavola ka potsika amin'ny amboamasony* (Done like Ikirijavola digging sweet potatoes: the digging stick jabbed straight into a potato eye). This proverb refers to a similar behavior performed by the other speaker. It implies that the other speaker has rushed into the *kabary* too swiftly and too abruptly. Like Ikirijavola who has spoiled the sweet potato, the other speaker has mishandled some part of the *kabary*. The proper way of digging sweet potatoes calls for a careful loosening of the earth which surrounds the root. And the proper way of performing a *kabary* calls for a careful treatment of each *kabary* segment. If such a criticism were uttered in all its explicitness, the other speechmaker and his group would take offense. They might choose to leave rather than bear this loss of face. In making use of a more allusive frame, the speechmaker not only displays his knowledge and skill, he also allows the *kabary* to continue and maintains the flow of communication between the two groups.

Accusations (*fiampangana*, or more usually *manome tsiny* [give guilt]) are another form of speech behavior subject to this norm in that they are rarely made in an explicit and open manner. Typically suspicions are communicated in conversation and gossip, but explicit accusations are rare. One is not even directly accused when, as they say, one is caught *tratra am-body omby* (caught in the act; LIT 'caught on the back of the cow'). Thus one is rarely held accountable for having done something wrong as others hesitate to confront that person with that information.

The hesitation to commit oneself explicitly to an idea or opinion is itself an important behavioral norm in this community. One is noncommittal for fear that an action openly advocated might have consequences that would have to be borne alone. One avoids accusation because one does not wish to be responsible for providing that information. If the wrongdoer is to be pointed out, the rest of the community must share the responsibility for the act, and they must share any guilt that may result. One speechmaker gave this account of what occurs in such situations:

> Even if someone was caught in the act of doing something wrong, then you cannot directly point at this person to dishonor him directly. You must use special expressions or go about it in a roundabout way. But if by chance there are people who demand that this wrongdoer be pointed out directly, then the speaker must say directly in the *kabary* who the person is. But because he must speak directly the speaker must ask the people to lift all guilt from him (*aza tsiny*). If there is someone in the audience who wants to know more, who doesn't understand, then he may respond during a break in the talk, "It is not clear to us, sir. It is hard to distinguish the domestic cat from the wild cat. They are the same whether calico or yellow or grey. And if it is the wild cat who steals the chicken, we cannot tell him from the others. The wild cat steals the chicken but the domestic cat gets its tail cut off. So point directly to the wild cat."

In general then one avoids confronting another with negative or unpleasant information. Disputes, criticisms, accusations are typically not straightforward. Disputes are often carried through mediators. Criticisms are veiled in metaphor. Accusations are left imprecise, unless the group is willing to share responsibility for the act of accusation. Direct affront indicates a lowering or absence of respect on the part of the affronter. In public situations, however, show of respect is expected. And, in formal public situations such as the *kabary* performance, it is obligatory. Every speechmaker interviewed stressed the importance of respect:

> In the *kabary*, it is not good to speak directly. If you speak directly the *kabary* is a *kabarin-jaza* (child's *kabary*) and there is no respect and honor.

> Speakers are not afraid to explain to one another, to answer with wisdom. But the censurer must be careful not to dishonor or mock or lower in public that speaker, because this was *fady* (taboo) for our ancestors.

A *kabary* which blames, disgraces is not a *kabary fankasitrahana* (*kabary* of agreement) but a *kabary fankahalana* (*kabary* of hatred). And the audience leaves. "This is a *kabary ratsy* (bad *kabary*)," they say.

Direct affront, then, risks censure of others. Directness is associated with the ways of children and with things contrary to tradition. A speechmaker who affronts may be left without an audience. His status as speechmaker is lowered. Direct affront can bring *henatra* and possibly *tsiny* (guilt). These considerations help to explain the general hesitation to openly accuse, criticize, or dispute.

The norm of avoidance of explicit and direct affront underlies other speech acts as well. The speech acts of *fandidiana* (ordering) and *fangatahana* (asking), for example, are affected. These speech acts are particular sorts of interpersonal directives (my terminology): they are used to get someone to do something. The use of an interpersonal directive creates an active confrontation situation. The person directed (ordered, asked) is confronted with having to comply with the directive or with having to reject it. And the director (orderer, asker) is confronted with the possibility that his authority to direct will not be acknowledged. A directive which is too explicit may affront the person directed. An explicit rejection of the directive may affront the director.

We consider *fandidiana* (ordering) and the ways the possibility of affront can be reduced.

First, the order is typically softened by a number of verbal niceties. The order is typically preceded by the word *mba* (please). It is typically followed by the word *kely*, usually translated as 'small' but here just a softening word which reduces the harshness of the speech act. These verbal softeners convey respect to the person ordered. In so doing, they transform the order into a more egalitarian type of encounter where personal affront is less likely.

A more important way in which the orderer shapes the speech act of *fandidiana* is in the handling of imperatives. Orders are frequently formed by imperatives. What is interesting is that the speaker has a choice of three distinct forms of imperative to use: the active imperative, the passive imperative, and the circumstantial imperative.

These imperative forms correspond to the three verb voices in Malagasy. The active and passive voices operate much the same as in Indo-European languages. The passive voice takes some object of the active sentence and makes it a superficial subject. The third verb voice, the circumstantial, operates in much the same way. The circumstantial voice makes a superficial subject out of a constituent which refers to some circumstance—place, time, instrument, etc.—of the action. Thus, the active declarative sentence:

Manasa ny lamba amin'ny savony <u>Rasoa</u>.
'Rasoa is washing the clothes with the soap.'
(LIT washes the clothes with the soap Rasoa.)

becomes in the passive voice:

Sasan-dRasoa amin'ny savony ny <u>lamba</u>.
'The clothes are washed by Rasoa with the soap.'
(LIT washed by Rasoa with the soap the clothes.)

The direct object of the active sentence is moved to subject position (indicated by underlining), and the verb form is modified. In the circumstantial voice, the instrumental constituent of the active is moved to subject position, and its case marker (*amin'ny*) is dropped. Again the verb form is modified:

Anasan-dRasoa ny lamba ny <u>savony</u>.
'The soap is used by Rasoa to wash the clothes.'
(LIT washes Rasoa the clothes the soap.)

The three forms of imperative operate in a similar fashion. In the active imperative:

Manasá ny lamba amin'ny savony.
'Wash the clothes with the soap.'

the person addressed ('you' in this example) is the subject. In the passive imperative:

Sasao ny lamba amin'ny savony.
'Have the clothes washed with the soap.'
(LIT have washed the clothes with the soap.)

it is the object of the active order 'the clothes' which is the subject. Likewise, the circumstantial imperative makes the instrumental complement 'the soap' the subject of the order:

Anasao lamba ny savony.
'The soap is to be used to wash clothes.'
(LIT have-washed-with clothes the soap.)

But although these three forms of imperative are available to the speaker, they are not used with equal ease in ordering. In cases where all three are grammatically possible, the speaker prefers to use the passive or the circumstantial voice. (This preference holds for declaratives as well.) The active imperative differs from both the passive and circumstantial in that the person ordered is the subject of the utterance. In the passive and circumstantial imperative, on the other hand, emphasis is withdrawn from the person ordered by making some other aspect of the order the subject. Thus the passive imperative topicalizes the object of the action—*what* is to be done rather than *who* is to do it. And the circumstantial imperative stresses the instrument or place or person for whom the action is to be accomplished rather than who is to accomplish the action.

To use the active imperative where it is grammatically possible to use the passive or circumstantial causes affront. The active imperative is considered harsh and abrupt, without respect. It is the socially marked form of imperative. The passive and circumstantial forms of imperative convey greater deference and are normally more appropriate in giving orders to persons. They avoid stressing the person ordered and, in so doing, reduce the risk of an unsuccessful, unpleasant social encounter.

A third way of mitigating an order lies in the interesting syntactic possibility Malagasy affords of focusing on some particular part of the action ordered. Syntactically the focus operation relates (1) and (2) below:

(1) *Narian' i John   ny fotsy.*
    'The white ones were thrown out by John.'
    (LIT: thrown out by John the white.)
(2) *Ny fotsy   no narian' i John.*
    'It was the white (ones) that were thrown out by John.'

The semantic effect of moving the constituent *ny fotsy* (the white ones) to the front and inserting the abstract particle *no* is exactly that indicated by its English translation. That is, in the focused sentence, (2), it is the information in the phrase 'the white ones' which is most prominent; it is only that information which can be naturally questioned or denied. That is, the question *Ny fotsy ve no narian'i John?* (Was it the white ones that John threw out?) questions only the identity of the objects thrown out, not whether there were any. Similarly *Tsy ny fotsy no narian'i John* (It wasn't the white ones that were thrown out by John) still implies that John threw out something—it only denies that the things thrown out were the white ones. Notice however that if we question or deny sentence (1) we are not permitted to infer that John threw out something. For example *Tsy narian'i John ny fotsy* (The white ones were not thrown out by John) leaves open the possibility that John did not throw out anything at all. Thus focusing on a part of a sentence raises that information to the level of explicit assertion and relegates the rest to the level of presupposition. . . .

What is interesting in Malagasy is that this focus operation applies also to imperatives. Thus in addition to the unmarked passive imperative is much less accessible to questioning and denial.
Ario ny fotsy (roughly: have the white ones thrown out) we find *Ny fotsy no ario* (roughly: it's the white ones which are to be thrown out [by you]). The latter order differs in meaning from the former in essentially the same way as the focused declarative (2) differs from the unfocused one (1). Specifically the focused order basically presupposes that something is to be thrown out and asserts that it is the white things.

Thus in focused orders, the speaker focuses on some aspect of the action ordered—such as the object which will be affected by the order or some circumstance of the ordered action—rather than the order itself. The order is taken for granted, that is, presupposed, and the immediate issue in the utterance is the identity of the objects affected by the order. In this way, the speaker can give an order with minimum stress on the fact that it is an order which he is giving. Through the use of the focus operation the speaker is able to shift the attention of the listeners away from the fact that the utterance is an order. This provides the addressee with the option of failing to execute the order by calling into question the identity of the objects rather than by refusing to execute the order. That is, one might naturally respond to *Ny fotsy no ario* (it's the white ones you're to throw out) by questioning *Ny fotsy sa ny mainty?* (The white ones, or the black ones?). Thus, since the identity of the object to be thrown out has been made the issue, it is possible to 'disagree' with an order without actually refusing to execute it—and thus without directly challenging the authority of the orderer or explicitly asserting one's own power.

The risk of affront through direct confrontation is minimized in *fangatahana* (askings) as well. To understand the operation of this norm in this speech act, we must break it down into at least two unnamed modes of use. These two modes are distinguished on the basis of the social category of the asker and the one asked and on the nature of the service or property asked for. One mode of asking applies to situations in which the asker and one asked are *havana* (kinsmen) and in which what is being asked for is some ordinary minor service (expected of *havana*) or some ordinary, not uncommon piece of property, such as tobacco or hair grease. Let us call this category of things asked for category A. A second mode of asking applies to more than one social category and to more than one goods and services category. First of all, it applies to all *fangatahana* in which the asker and asked are *vahiny* (non-kinsmen) regardless of the goods and services asked for. Secondly, it applies to *fangatahana* between *havana* where the good or service asked for is not minor or ordinary or automatically expected of *havana*. Let us call this category of things category B. For example, a *havana* asking to borrow another's plough or wagon would use this mode of *fangatahana*. This second mode of use then applies to *vahiny* for category A or B things and to *havana* for category B things only.

	Vahiny	*Havana*
Mode 1	—	A
Mode 2	A or B	B

These two modes of use differ in the degree to which the one asked is obligated to comply with the directive. *Havana* asked for category A goods and services are obligated to comply. They must provide these goods and services, provided they are in a position to. This obligation is a basic behavioral expression of the *havana* relationship. Another verbal expression of the *havana* relationship is the greeting which one *havana* gives another when entering his or her house: *Inona no masaka?* (What's cooking?) This expression is taken as a demand for a cooked meal, in particular, for rice. Close *havana* have the right to this food. Many times there is no cooked food in the house, and the visitor does not really expect to eat. He demands just out of form, to emphasize the kind of tie which exists between them. Similarly, a *havana* expects another *havana* to provide him or her with tobacco or sweets or other goods which belong to this category. This kind of obligation is not expected among *vahiny*, however, nor among *havana* for category B goods and services.

Where a strong obligation to comply with the directive does not exist, the person asked is thought to be in a superior position relative to the asker; the one asked has the right

to refuse the asker. This difference in status is well understood by speechmakers, who are often put in the position of asking for things in public *kabary*. In every *kabary*, the speechmaker asks for the blessing and support of the audience, permission to speak, guilt to be lifted, and so on. And in these parts of every *kabary*, the speechmaker stresses his inferiority in an elaborate manner.

> When I ask for the guilt and blame to be lifted from me (for standing here before you), I am not an originator of words but a preserver only of tradition, a successor to my father by accident. And not only this, I am like a small cricket, not master of the tall plant or able to perch on the tip of the tall plant like the *sopanga* cricket, but my destiny is to stay on the ground because I am the *tsimbotry* cricket, an orphan with no ancestors. I am not the prince of birds, the *railovy*, but the *tsikirity* bird who trails behind in the flock, for I am not an originator of words but a borrower and a preserver of tradition and by accident replace others. So I ask for the guilt and taboo to be lifted, respected gentlemen and all those facing (me) at this moment.

One *kabary* is a *fangatahana* in itself. That is the *kabary vody ondry*, the marriage request. The askers are the boy's family and those asked are the girl's family, and the marriage of the girl to the boy is what is asked for. The *kabary* itself is an elaborate expression of the second mode of *fangatahana*, where the speaker for the boy's family is considered to be much lower than that of the speaker for the girl's family. A speechmaker made these comments to me concerning this relationship:

> You should use *teny malemy* (soft words) when you make requests. You shouldn't be like a boaster or person on the same level as the other. It is our *fomba*, custom, to think of requesters, in this case, the boy's family, as lower than the requested, for example, the elders of the girl's family. Even if the girl's speaker is unskilled, you must put yourself in a lower position and appear to lose the *kabary* (that is, to appear less knowledgeable) to give honor to the girl's side of the family.

In the second mode of *fangatahana*, then, the one asked has in principle the option of refusing to comply. In the first mode, the one asked is rather obligated to comply. The risk of affront to the asker is much higher in the second mode than in the first because of this option. That is, a *havana* who asks another *havana* for a category A item is not risking loss of face. He knows the other must comply if possible. On the other hand, where rejection is a possibility as in the second mode of *fangatahana*, affront is also a possibility. Given this, the asker acts in ways which minimize the risk of personal affront. In particular, the asker avoids directly confronting the one asked with having to comply with the directive or having to reject it. He avoids putting the one asked on the spot.

First, direct affront is avoided in this mode of *fangatahana*, which I shall call the request mode, in that the request is often not presented by the actual requester(s) but by a stand-in who represents the actual requester(s). This is formalized in request *kabary* where speechmakers are employed to represent others. This arrangement does not place the actual requester and the one requested in a direct relationship. The actual requester is saved from any possible affront which could result from the request.

Second, the request mode is typically formulated and presented in a veiled manner. The asker does not make it explicit that he is requesting some object or service from the other. Rather, that which is desired is alluded to in the conversational context. Often a request is signaled by an abrupt change in conversational topic. The new topic moves the speaker or speakers to make reference to what is desired from the listener(s). Young boys suddenly speak of a journey to be made that evening and describe the blackness of the night and their lack of candles. Women will chatter about the poor quality of Malagasy soap in relation to European soap in my presence. Men will moan over the shortage of funds for a particular project. The host or listener is expected to pick up these cues and satisfy the request.

A consequence of this format is that neither the requester nor the requestee is committed to a particular action. That is, in alluding to, rather than openly specifying the thing requested, the requester does not commit himself to making the request and is not so open to the rebuff of having the request denied. He may intend the utterance to be taken as a request, but he does not make this explicit.

This lack of commitment, of course, allows the person requested the same option. He is not obligated to recognize the utterance as a request. He may choose just how he wishes to define the activity and need not commit himself to any response at all. Thus the party to whom the request is directed is not forced to deny the request (if that is his intention) and, in so doing, cause great loss of face on both sides. The allusive format, then, enables the one requested to deny the request (by "misinterpreting" it) without affront.

Where the risk of affront is minimal, as in the first mode of *fangatahana*, these constraints do not exist. The asking is relatively direct and explicit, and there are no stand-in requesters. *Havana* are able to ask for category A items in this manner because compliance, if possible, is assured. The asker is not faced with a possible loss of face or rebuff. The one asked may only grudgingly give up tobacco from the market but he does give in to the *fangatahana*. Where affront is a risk, then, *fangatahana* are inexplicit and indirectly presented (mode 2). Where affront is not a risk or is a minimal risk, *fangatahana* are straightforward.

WOMEN AS NORM-BREAKERS

According to the norm, one avoids putting another individual in an uncomfortable or unpleasant position, where loss of face could result. One shows respect to the other by avoiding this type of confrontation. Women, however, do not appear to operate according to these community ground rules for speaking. In particular they are associated with the direct and open expression of anger towards others. Their social behavior contrasts sharply with men in this respect. Men tend not to express their sentiments openly. They admire others who use language subtly. They behave in public in such a way as to promote interpersonal ease. In short, they avoid creating unpleasant face-to-face encounters. Women, on the other hand, tend to speak in a more straightforward manner. They express feelings of anger or criticism directly to the relevant party. Both men and women agree that women have *lavalela*, a long tongue.

Men acknowledge this difference in the speechways of men and women. They consider the use of speech by men to be more skillful than that by women. What is not acknowledged is that men often make use of this difference. In other words, men often use women to confront others with some unpleasant information. Women communicate sentiments which men share but dislike expressing. Men are associated with the maintenance of good communication in a relationship, and women are associated with the expression of socially damaging information. In one instance, for example, the young boys of the village played ball against the side of a newly whitewashed house. They chipped off patches of color. The landlord returned, observed this situation but after an entire day in the village, said only, "If you don't patch that, things might not go well between us." The next day he returned with his wife. As she approached the village, she accosted the first person she saw (which happened to be the eldest man in the village) with accusations. She told everyone within hearing range of their anger and just what must be done to repair the wall. This outburst caused a great deal of grumbling and unpleasant feelings among the villagers. But the outburst was almost expected. It was not a shocking encounter as it came from the wife and not the landlord himself. Such a display of anger is permissible, perhaps even appropriate, because it is initiated by a woman.

In another instance, the oldest man in the village acquired a wife without consulting other kinsmen in his village. Without a word, the old man conducted the woman into his house. A week went by and no one said anything to him or his woman. Then, as the old man passed in front of a gathering of women one morning, they let loose their criticism of his behavior. He looked down, made excuses, and exhibited signs of discomfort. Then, one of the other village men approached and began to talk of some trivial topic, as if he had been totally unaware of the scene which had just passed. The other man marked his entrance with a change of topic. He refused to be associated with the behavior of the women, even though he agreed with their opinions. Women relieve some social pressure in this way, for after these episodes generally nothing more is said. But women can never be *mpanao fihavanana* (restorers of relationships) because they are thought to lack subtlety and sensitivity and because they are associated with communication of negative information.

In fact, women are associated with direct speech, and they are used by men wherever this manner is useful. A man and woman are walking along the side of a road. It is the woman who waves down our car and asks if they might have a ride. And it is the woman who asks for information such as: Where are you going? Where have you been? How much did that cost? All of these speech acts put the addressee on the spot. All are potentially affronting situations.

It is in part because women are more straightforward that they are the ones who sell village produce in the markets, and the ones who buy the everyday necessities in the markets. Buying and selling is a confrontation situation as bargaining is the norm and as the seller has to declare an initial price. The seller commits himself to wanting to sell by virtue of his position. Women are not afraid to confront the buyer or seller with their opinions as to what the price ought to be. They bargain in an expeditious and straightforward manner. Men bargain as well, but their manner is more subtle and ornate. The encounter is much more elaborate; it can sometimes be a show, where others gather round to watch the proceedings. And, rather than lose face, the buyer will frequently walk away from the last given price and later send a young boy back to buy the item. In this way, both the buyer and seller have avoided an unpleasant confrontation. This kind of bargaining is typical of that between men. But this kind of bargaining does not put as many coins in the pocket as do the more rapid transactions between women. Men sell typically those items which have a more or less fixed price. For example, they sell all the meat in the market. Women tend to sell the more bargainable items such as vegetables and fruit. Sometimes these stalls are manned by a husband and wife. But it is typically the wife who bargains and the man who weighs the items and collects the money. Men pride themselves on their ability to bargain skillfully, but they leave the majority of bargaining encounters to their women.

Women use one kind of power and men another. Women initiate speech encounters which men shy away from. They are the ones who primarily reprimand children. They discuss in detail the shameful behavior of others in daily gossip and speak openly of those who *mangala-baraka*, steal honor away from the family. They are associated with direct criticism and haggling in markets. They are able to put others on the spot, to confront others with possibly offensive information where men cannot or prefer not. Women tend to be direct and open in manner. Men tend to conduct themselves with discretion and subtlety. Women dominate situations where directness is called for. Men, on the other hand, dominate situations where indirectness is desirable.

Indirectness as Ideal Style

Indirectness is desirable wherever respect is called for, and affront is to be avoided. In particular, it is desirable in all *kabary* (ceremonial speech situations). As mentioned before, the *kabary* performance is a formal dialogue between speechmakers representing different groups, for example, the hosts of a particular ceremony and those who have come to participate, or, as in the marriage request, the family of the girl and the family of the boy. Each speechmaker answers the

other. That is, the first speechmaker completes one part of the *kabary* and the second speechmaker responds. The first speechmaker does not proceed without the support of the second speechmaker and the group he represents. Thus, a good deal of the *kabary* is spent eliciting the approval and support of the other group and affirming this support. For example, in the opening parts of a major *kabary*, the speechmaker asks for the blessing of the audience and they answer:

> *Mahaleova! Mahazaka! Andriamatoa o! Tsy ho solafaka, tsy ho tafintohina fa dia: mahavita soa aman-tsara.*

> Go ahead! Be able! Not to slip, not to bump into things, but to finish good and well.

Furthermore, the speechmaker stresses unity of both groups by making frequent reference to *isika mianankavy* (we family [inclusive of addressee]). Often reference to the inclusive *isika* will occur two or three times in one passage:

> *Dia misaotra an'Andriamanitra isika mianankavy, nohon'ny fanomezany tombon'andro antsika rehetra izao, ka tratry izao fotoana anankiray izay nokendrentsika mianankavy izao.*

> Then *we family* thank God for the gift of a tranquil day for *us all* at this time so one time has arrived now which was envisioned by *us family*.

Support and unity cannot be achieved where respect is not shown by the speechmaker. And the major way in which respect is expressed is by using indirect speech. A speechmaker who speaks directly, bluntly, affronts his audience. This effect is recognized by speechmakers, and they often make use of traditional sayings relevant to this behavior in the *kabary* itself. For example:

> *Tonga eto aminareo mianankavy izahay. Tsy mirodorodo toa omby manga, fa mitaitsika toa vorom-potsy, mandeha mora toa akanga diso an'Andringitra, ary mandeha miandana toy ny akoho hamonjy lapa.*

> We come here to you family. Not stampeding like wild bulls but approaching softly like a white bird and slowly, proceeding carefully like a lost pigeon and proceeding slowly like a chicken to reach the palace.

To speak indirectly is to speak with skill. Men and women alike consider indirect speech to be more difficult to produce than direct speech. Most villagers can tell you that one who speaks well *manolana teny* (twists words). In *kabary*, a good speechmaker *miolaka* (winds in and out). The meaning of the utterance becomes clear gradually as the speaker alludes to the intent in a number of ways. This style of speech use is referred to in a number of proverbs often used by the villagers, for example:

> *Toy ny manoto, ka mamerina in-droa manan'antitra.*

> Like paint, one returns twice and makes it darker.

Each time a speechmaker alludes to the subject matter, the richer the meaning of that subject becomes. A good speechmaker can return to a subject in many ways. He is able to use proverbs (*ohabolana*), traditional sayings (*hainteny*), and elaborate metaphors to this end. One measures his ability in terms of this kind of richness. Speech which is used in this manner is *tsara lahatra* (well arranged). Speech which is simple and direct is *teny bango tokana* (speech of a single braid), that is, unsophisticated speech.

Men alone are considered to be able speechmakers. Even in everyday *resaka*, they are associated with the style of speaking required for the *kabary*: their requests are typically delayed and inexplicit, accusations imprecise, and criticisms subtle. They conduct themselves so as to minimize loss of face in a social situation. As women are associated with quite the opposite kind of behavior, they are in general considered unsuitable as speechmakers. The one exception to this is the *kabary* given by a woman of a boy's family to women of a girl's family in arranging for a marriage. The *kabary* is short and relatively simple, however, and many times it is replaced by simple *resaka*. Furthermore, it is a *kabary* to be heard by women only: "When the mother of the boy speaks, it is only the women who listen. It is not right if there are men there," commented one speechmaker.

Woman are considered able in handling everyday interactions within the village. The people with whom they interact most frequently are other women of the village and children. In fact, women with their young children form a semi-autonomous group within the village. They work together in the fields, and they relax together around the rice-mortars in the village courtyards. They have a more intimate relationship with one another than do men with each other or do men with women. (An exception to this generalization is the intimacy shown in joking relationships such as those which obtain between brothers-in-law, brother- and sister-in-law, and so on [M. Bloch, personal communication].) They use intimate terms of address and talk about intimate subjects: dysentery, intestinal worms, menstruation, malformed babies, sexual relations outside marriage. They are able to invade each other's personal space (Goffman 1971) in a way that would be taboo among most adult men. They dig into each other's hair looking for fleas. They look underneath a pregnant woman's dress to peek at the bands applied by the midwife to her womb. They bathe together in streams. Within this group, intimacy and directness is the norm.

Kabary, on the other hand, typically involve more than one village. They establish settings where people *tsy mifankazatra* (not accustomed to one another) interact—distant *havana* (kinsmen) and *vahiny* (strangers). Within this group, respect and indirectness are the norms.

We have, then, on the one hand, directness associated with women and children, and on the other hand, indirectness associated with men and intervillage situations. But directness and indirectness have further association. Indirectness is considered to be *fomban'ny ntaolo* (the way of one's ancestors). The use of *teny miolaka* (winding speech) represents to the villager a set of social attitudes held in the past, where respect and love for one another were always displayed. It is the traditional Malagasy speechway. The use

of direct speech, such as that of women and that of "askings" between kinsmen, is associated with a loss of tradition, with contemporary mores. It is felt that today people speak directly because they do not value interpersonal relationships:

> The people today speak more directly than the ancestors. The people before took care to preserve relationships. Today people just say directly the faults of others, challenge the other. The ancestors could not answer like that. They made circles around the idea. Today few young people like the *kabary* and proverbs and traditional sayings. They don't like Malagasy language but foreign languages. Children are afraid of being beneath another child in knowledge of French or math. It is like our speechways were lost.... The government should give an examination, make everyone learn these Malagasy ways and the ways of mutual respect. (Speechmaker at Loharano)

As indicated in this quote, the change in speech use is thought to be due in part to the influence of European languages, in particular of French. Children learn foreign languages in school and they forget traditional speechways—this sentiment is expressed by many elders. The contrast in speech use for Europeans and for Malagasy is evident in urban contexts, where both interact in commercial settings. In these settings, the Malagasy must conform to the more direct, European-style service encounters. For the average villager from the countryside, these encounters are not always successful. For the European or European-trained Malagasy, these encounters are irritating and time-consuming. Some large business firms, in fact, recognize the difference in interactional style to the extent that particular employees are delegated to handle encounters with rural Malagasy. But further, Malagasy are expected to handle service encounters with Europeans in town markets, where *they* are the vendors and Europeans form part of the clientele. It is appropriate, then, that women rather than men are recruited from the village to confront the European buyer. Directness and matter-of-factness are characteristic of both.

This final association of directness with the use of European languages helps to explain an important exception in the use of speech by men. There is one consistent situation in which men do not conform to the ideal style of indirect speech. When giving orders to cows, men speak in a terse and abrupt manner (Bloch 1998 [1971].) But what is interesting is that these orders are couched in French rather than Malagasy. In particular, the French directional terms *à gauche!* and *à droite!* are used. There exists an equivalent set of directional terms in Malagasy. We must ask, then, why French is selected. At least a partial answer can be gained from this analysis, for the contexts in which men address cows necessitate immediate and direct action. For example, many tasks in cultivation are accomplished with cows. And in these contexts allusive speech is not effective. It is consistent with this analysis that men should choose to use French in such moments. Furthermore, animals occupy a low status. They are not approached with respect. The direct use of speech by men expresses this relationship (see also Bloch 1998 [1971]).

Indirectness	Directness
Men	*Women*
Skilled speech	*Unsophisticated speech*
Traditional speech ways	*Contemporary speech ways*
Malagasy language	*European languages*

We have presented a norm and an ideal speech style. Men tend to conduct themselves in public in accordance with the norm. Women tend to operate outside this norm. Further, the speech of men is thought (by men and women) to come closer to the ideal use of speech than the speech of women. Where subtlety and delicacy are required in social situations, men are recruited—witness the *kabary*. Where directness and explicitness are desirable in social situations, women are recruited.

References

Bloch, M. 1998 [1971]. *Why do Malagasy cows speak French?* In *How We Think They Think: Anthropological Approaches to Cognition, Memory, and Literacy.* Boulder, CO: Westview Press.

Goffman, E. 1971. *Relations in Public.* New York: Basic Books.

Post-reading Questions / Activities

- How would you characterize the overall interactions in the Malagasy village Keenan describes? Is this familiar or unfamiliar to you?
- If men use women to convey unpleasant information, are men complicit in these interchanges? If it is understood that women will do the "dirty work" of interaction, is it appropriate to characterize the entire village as aiming to avoid confrontation?
- Does your own society have gender norms for directness and indirection, or for skilled speech-making? For commercial transactions? How do they compare with those in this chapter?

Vocabulary

circumstantial voice	face	linguistic repertoire
directive	*kabary*	*resaka*

Suggested Further Reading

Bloch, Maurice. 1989. *Ritual, History, and Power: Selected Papers in Anthropology.* London and Atlantic Highlands, NJ: Athlone Press.

Brown, Penelope, and Stephen C. Levinson. 1987. *Politeness: Some Universals in Language Usage.* Cambridge: Cambridge University Press.

Holmes, Janet. 1995. *Women, Men, and Politeness.* London and New York: Longman.

Ochs, Elinor. 1991. "Indexing Gender." In *Rethinking Context*, edited by Alessandro Duranti and Charles Goodwin, pp. 335–358. Cambridge: Cambridge University Press.

Philips, Susan U., Susan Steele, and Christine Tanz, eds. 1987. *Language, Gender, and Sex in Comparative Perspective.* Cambridge: Cambridge University Press.

Romaine, Suzanne. 1999. *Communicating Gender.* Mahwah, NJ: Erlbaum.

PART III

Language as Social Action

Language has structure; language creates the human race; language operates to create, enforce, and perform our various identities. But language does many more things than that. Since J. L. Austin published his striking *How to Do Things with Words*, philosophers of language, linguists, and anthropologists have busily established some of the many ways humans make use of language in carrying out the specific activities of their lives. This focus on action has developed in a number of different directions, some of which are introduced in this part of the book.

In contrast to a *referential* view of language, in which language conveys information ("says something") or an *indexical* view of language, in which language conveys social identities, focus on how language *does* things is called a *pragmatic* view of language. That is, it focuses on consequences and effects of language in context.

Austin's and the latter Wittgenstein's new way of regarding language drew attention to many of the performative aspects of language or "language games." In works from this perspective, terms used include "performance," "emergence," and "action." The study of discourse and performance emerged in the 1980s as folklorists, linguists, and anthropologists began to study complex forms of language use in their contexts. One prominent pursuit in this was the study of what had previously been called "folklore" but began to be called "verbal art"; the new field of "ethnopoetics" was formed.

Units of analysis were necessarily much larger than sentences, and a variety of creative approaches were invented to understand "discourse." In discourse analysis, there is always a focus on details of conversation (conversational analysis is the most prominent subset of discourse analysis) with a concomitant consideration of the broader context without which it took place.

Beyond art, however, this study also showed how thoroughly political every aspect of performance was. Power was the newest ingredient in the study of language.

Some of the many topics investigated from this perspective include language socialization (how children are socialized into and through language), religious ritual (in which language is often seen as having efficacy), emotion (in which language is seen to create emotion), politics and power (in which language creates and reinforces power differences), and healing (in which language is often seen as bringing about improvements in health). In all such studies, language has to be looked at in its full social and cultural context. It cannot be dissociated from the conditions in which it is used, because the *meaning* lies in its use, not in a combination of dictionary and grammar. Here we find a breathtaking range of human uses of language throughout the world.

The final topic here is that of language ideology. This involves what the uses of language are for its speakers: how they see language functioning, what kinds of language they see as more desirable or even more beautiful, and where language should and should not be used. These aspects of language have been studied increasingly in the decades since the term was first widely used in the 1990s.

Suggested Further Reading

Abu-Lughod, Lila. 1986. *Veiled Sentiments: Honor and Poetry in a Bedouin Society*. Berkeley: University of California Press.

———, and Catherine Lutz, eds. 1990. *Language and the Politics of Emotion*. Cambridge: Cambridge University Press.

Briggs, Charles. 1986. *Learning How to Ask: A Sociolinguistic Appraisal of the Role of the Interview in Social Science Research*. Cambridge: Cambridge University Press.

Brown, Penelope, and Stephen C. Levinson. 1987. *Politeness: Some Universals in Language Usage*. Cambridge: Cambridge University Press.

Feld, Steven. 1982. *Sound and Sentiment: Birds, Weeping, Poetics, and Song in Kaluli Expression*. Philadelphia: University of Pennsylvania Press.

Grice, Paul. 1989. *Studies in the Way of Words*. Cambridge, MA: Harvard University Press.

Keenan, Elinor Ochs. 1976. "The Universality of Conversational Postulates." *Language in Society* 5 (1): 67–80.

Lutz, Catherine A. 1988. *Unnatural Emotions: Everyday Sentiments on a Micronesian Atoll and Their Challenge to Western Theory*. Chicago: University of Chicago Press.

Malinowski, Bronislaw. 1923. "The Problem of Meaning in Primitive Languages." In *The Meaning of Meaning*, edited by C. K. Ogden and I. A. Richards. New York: Harcourt, Brace.

———. 1935. *Coral Gardens and Their Magic: A Study of the Methods of Tilling the Soil and of Agricultural Rites in the Trobriand Islands*. New York: American Book Company.

———. 1948. *Magic, Science, and Religion, and Other Essays*. Boston: Beacon Press.

Rosaldo, Michelle Z. 1982. "The Things We Do with Words: Ilongot Speech Acts and Speech Act Theory in Philosophy." *Language in Society* 11: 203–235.

Searle, John R. 1969. *Speech Acts: An Essay in the Philosophy of Language*. Cambridge: Cambridge University Press.

UNIT 5

DISCOURSE, PERFORMANCE, AND RITUAL

Language, treated as social action, focuses on the ways people accomplish things by means of language; in Austin's terms, we perform actions rather than simply reporting on them. The context of use is always relevant, since words used have an effect on the world in which they are spoken.

This tradition extends back also to the pioneering anthropologist Bronislaw Malinowski, who noted that in the Trobriand Islands of Papua New Guinea, people often used language for reasons quite different from that of conveying information, which is known as the *referential* function of language.

Other fascinating things people do with language, not included here because of space limitations, include all the ways language is used in religion—for supplication, for exorcism, to testify to things seen—in emotion, in politics, and in every facet of life. In such studies, the veracity of language is often secondary to the effectiveness of language-in-use.

Suggested Further Reading

Abrahams, Roger D. 1983. *The Man-of-Words in the West Indies: Performance and the Emergence of Creole Culture.* Baltimore: Johns Hopkins University Press.

Bauman, Richard, and Charles L. Briggs. 1990. "Poetics and Performance as Critical Perspectives on Language and Social Life." *Annual Review of Anthropology* 19: 59–88.

Bloch, Maurice, ed. 1975. *Political Language and Oratory in Traditional Society.* London: Academic Press.

Duranti, Alessandro. 1994. *From Grammar to Politics: Linguistic Anthropology in a Western Samoan Village.* Berkeley: University of California Press.

Hymes, Dell. 1975. "Breakthrough into Performance." In *Folklore: Performance and Communication*, edited by D. Ben-Amos and K. S. Goldstein, pp. 11–74. The Hague: Mouton.

———. 1981. *"In Vain I Tried to Tell You": Essays in Native American Ethnopoetics.* Philadelphia: University of Pennsylvania Press.

Keating, Elizabeth. 1998. *Power Sharing: Language, Rank, Gender, and Social Space in Pohnpei, Micronesia.* New York: Oxford University Press.

Sherzer, Joel. 2002. *Speech Play and Verbal Art.* Austin: University of Texas Dress.

Tambiah, S. J. 1979. *A Performative Approach to Ritual.* Proceedings of the British Academy 65. London: Oxford University Press.

Tedlock, Dennis. 1983. *The Spoken Word and the Work of Interpretation.* Philadelphia: University of Pennsylvania Press.

CHAPTER 35

How to Do Things with Words

J. L. Austin
(1962)

Philosophers of language such as Bertrand Russell worked hard to explain how language derived its meaning, aiming to describe it like mathematics or formal logic. They looked principally at the grammar and the logical operators that linked words such as nouns and verbs. What was critical was to determine its "truth value," since its primary function seemed to be to convey factual information.

J. L. Austin followed a different path. Known as an ordinary language philosopher, he looked at the actual acts people performed in ordinary life by means of language. Thus, what was most important was what happened through use of language, or what language does, rather than what language means. He is considered the founder of Speech Act Theory, and also influential in the development of the pragmatics branch of linguistics, both very rich sources of inspiration for the study of language.

This chapter is the first of the twelve chapters in his book How to Do Things with Words, *originally a series of lectures given at Harvard University in 1955. Although Austin is not the first to note that looking at sentences simply for their "truth value" is not adequate to account for every use of language, he put it extremely clearly, using ordinary, everyday examples.*

In later chapters in the book Austin distinguishes the locutionary act *(what people say) from the* illocutionary act *(what people intend) and the* perlocutionary force *(what results from the utterance). Though he initially applied this analysis principally to what he names in this chapter the* performative utterance—*that special kind of sentence that accomplishes something in the world like christening a ship, using the present-tense form of a verb and potentially using the word* hereby—*he later made clear that in some sense all language is performative. This was a revolution in the study of language, and we are all its beneficiaries.*

Reading Questions

- What kinds of sentences do philosophers usually analyze?
- What examples does Austin give of "constatives" and of "performatives"? What is each type of utterance for?
- Why can't performatives be true or false?
- Are there some utterances that *must* be made for an action to take place? What examples can you think of?

What I shall have to say here is neither difficult nor contentious; the only merit I should like to claim for it is that of being true, at least in parts. The phenomenon to be discussed is very widespread and obvious, and it cannot fail to have been already noticed, at least here and there, by others. Yet I have not found attention paid to it specifically.

Reprinted by permission of the publisher from *How to Do Things with Words* by John L. Austin, edited by J. O. Urmson and Marina Sbisa, pp. 1–11, Cambridge, MA.: Harvard University Press, Copyright © 1972, 1975 by the President and Fellows of Harvard College.

It was for too long the assumption of philosophers that the business of a 'statement' can only be to 'describe' some state of affairs, or to 'state some fact', which it must do either truly or falsely. Grammarians, indeed, have regularly pointed out that not all 'sentences' are (used in making) statements: there are, traditionally, besides (grammarians') statements, also questions and exclamations, and sentences expressing commands or wishes or concessions. And doubtless philosophers have not intended to deny this, despite some loose use of 'sentence' for 'statement'. Doubtless, too, both grammarians and philosophers have been aware that it is by no means easy to distinguish even questions, commands, and so on from statements by means of the few and jejune grammatical marks available, such as word order, mood, and the like: though perhaps it has not been usual to dwell on the difficulties which this fact obviously raises. For how do we decide which is which? What are the limits and definitions of each?

But now in recent years, many things which would once have been accepted without question as 'statements' by both philosophers and grammarians have been scrutinized with new care. This scrutiny arose somewhat indirectly—at least in philosophy. First came the view, not always formulated without unfortunate dogmatism, that a statement (of fact) ought to be 'verifiable', and this led to the view that many 'statements' are only what may be called pseudo-statements. First and most obviously, many 'statements' were shown to be, as KANT perhaps first argued systematically, strictly nonsense, despite an unexceptionable grammatical form: and the continual discovery of fresh types of nonsense, unsystematic though their classification and mysterious though their explanation is too often allowed to remain, has done on the whole nothing but good. Yet we, that is, even philosophers, set some limits to the amount of nonsense that we are prepared to admit we talk: so that it was natural to go on to ask, as a second stage, whether many apparent pseudo-statements really set out to be 'statements' at all. It has come to be commonly held that many utterances which look like statements are either not intended at all, or only intended in part, to record or impart straightforward information about the facts: for example, 'ethical propositions' are perhaps intended, solely or partly, to evince emotion or to prescribe conduct or to influence it in special ways. Here too KANT was among the pioneers. We very often also use utterances in ways beyond the scope at least of traditional grammar. It has come to be seen that many specially perplexing words embedded in apparently descriptive statements do not serve to indicate some specially odd additional feature in the reality reported, but to indicate (not to report) the circumstances in which the statement is made or reservations to which it is subject or the way in which it is to be taken and the like. To overlook these possibilities in the way once common is called the 'descriptive' fallacy; but perhaps this is not a good name, as 'descriptive' itself is special. Not all true or false statements are descriptions, and for this reason I prefer to use the word 'constative'. Along these lines it has by now been shown piecemeal, or at least made to look likely, that many traditional philosophical perplexities have arisen through a mistake—the mistake of taking as straightforward statements of fact utterances which are *either* (in interesting non-grammatical ways) nonsensical *or else* intended as something quite different.

Whatever we may think of any particular one of these views and suggestions, and however much we may deplore the initial confusion into which philosophical doctrine and method have been plunged, it cannot be doubted that they are producing a revolution in philosophy. If anyone wishes to call it the greatest and most salutary in its history, this is not, if you come to think of it, a large claim. It is not surprising that beginnings have been piecemeal, with *parti pris*, and for extraneous aims; this is common with revolutions.

PRELIMINARY ISOLATION OF THE PERFORMATIVE[2]

The type of utterance we are to consider here is not, of course, in general a type of nonsense; though misuse of it can, as we shall see, engender rather special varieties of 'nonsense'. Rather, it is one of our second class—the masqueraders. But it does not by any means necessarily masquerade as a statement of fact, descriptive or constative. Yet it does quite commonly do so, and that, oddly enough, when it assumes its most explicit form. Grammarians have not, I believe, seen through this 'disguise', and philosophers only at best incidentally.[3] It will be convenient, therefore, to study it first in this misleading form, in order to bring out its characteristics by contrasting them with those of the statement of fact which it apes.

We shall take, then, for our first examples some utterances which can fall into no hitherto recognized *grammatical* category save that of 'statement', which are not nonsense, and which contain none of those verbal danger-signals which philosophers have by now detected or think they have detected (curious words like 'good' or 'all', suspect auxiliaries like 'ought' or 'can', and dubious constructions like the hypothetical): all will have, as it happens, humdrum verbs in the first person singular present indicative active.[4] Utterances can be found, satisfying these conditions, yet such that

A. they do not 'describe' or 'report' or constate anything at all, are not 'true or false'; and

B. the uttering of the sentence is, or is a part of, the doing of an action, which again would not *normally* be described as, or as 'just', saying something.

This is far from being as paradoxical as it may sound or as I have meanly been trying to make it sound: indeed, the examples now to be given will be disappointing.
Examples: *Not describing the act; they are the act itself*

(E. *a*) 'I do (sc. take this woman to be my lawful wedded wife)'—as uttered in the course of the marriage ceremony.[5]

(E. *b*) 'I name this ship the *Queen Elizabeth*'—as uttered when smashing the bottle against the stem.

(E. *c*) 'I give and bequeath my watch to my brother'—as occurring in a will.

(E. *d*) 'I bet you sixpence it will rain tomorrow.'

In these examples it seems clear that to utter the sentence (in, of course, the appropriate circumstances) is not to *describe* my doing of what I should be said in so uttering to be doing[6] or to state that I am doing it: it is to do it. None of the utterances cited is either true or false: I assert this as obvious and do not argue it. It needs argument no more than that 'damn' is not true or false: it may be that the utterance 'serves to inform you'—but that is quite different. To name the ship *is* to say (in the appropriate circumstances) the words 'I name, &c.'. When I say, before the registrar or altar, &c., 'I do', I am not reporting on a marriage: I am indulging in it.

What are we to call a sentence or an utterance of this type?[7] I propose to call it a *performative sentence* or a performative utterance, or, for short, 'a performative'. The term 'performative' will be used in a variety of cognate ways and constructions, much as the term 'imperative' is.[8] The name is derived, of course, from 'perform', the usual verb with the noun 'action': it indicates that the issuing of the utterance is the performing of an action—it is not normally thought of as just saying something.

A number of other terms may suggest themselves, each of which would suitably cover this or that wider or narrower class of performatives: for example, many performatives are *contractual* ('I bet') or *declaratory* ('I declare war') utterances. But no term in current use that I know of is nearly wide enough to cover them all. One technical term that comes nearest to what we need is perhaps 'operative', as it is used strictly by lawyers in referring to that part, i.e., those clauses, of an instrument which serves to effect the transaction (conveyance or what not) which is its main object, whereas the rest of the document merely 'recites' the circumstances in which the transaction is to be effected.[9] But 'operative' has other meanings, and indeed is often used nowadays to mean little more than 'important'. I have preferred a new word, to which, though its etymology is not irrelevant, we shall perhaps not be so ready to attach some preconceived meaning.

CAN SAYING MAKE IT SO?

Are we then to say things like this:

'To marry is to say a few words', or
'Betting is simply saying something'?

Such a doctrine sounds odd or even flippant at first, but with sufficient safeguards it may become not odd at all.

A sound initial objection to them may be this; and it is not without some importance. In very many cases it is possible to perform an act of exactly the same kind *not* by uttering words, whether written or spoken, but in some other way. For example, I may in some places effect marriage by cohabiting, or I may bet with a totalisator machine by putting a coin in a slot. We should then, perhaps, convert the propositions above, and put it that 'to say a few certain words is to marry' or 'to marry is, in some cases, simply to say a few words' or 'simply to say a certain something is to bet'.

But probably the real reason why such remarks sound dangerous lies in another obvious fact,…which is this. The uttering of the words is, indeed, usually a, or even *the*, leading incident in the performance of the act (of betting or what not), the performance of which is also the object of the utterance, but it is far from being usually, even if it is ever, the *sole* thing necessary if the act is to be deemed to have been performed. Speaking generally, it is always necessary that the *circumstances* in which the words are uttered should be in some way, or ways, *appropriate*, and it is very commonly necessary that either the speaker himself or other persons should *also* perform certain *other* actions, whether 'physical' or 'mental' actions or even acts of uttering further words. Thus, for naming the ship, it

is essential that I should be the person appointed to name her, for (Christian) marrying, it is essential that I should not be already married with a wife living, sane and undivorced, and so on: for a bet to have been made, it is generally necessary for the offer of the bet to have been accepted by a taker (who must have done something, such as to say 'Done'), and it is hardly a gift if I *say* 'I give it you' but never hand it over.

So far, well and good. The action may be performed in ways other than by a performative utterance, and in any case the circumstances, including other actions, must be appropriate. But we may, in objecting, have something totally different, and this time quite mistaken, in mind, especially when we think of some of the more awe-inspiring performatives such as 'I promise to…'. Surely the words must be spoken 'seriously' and so as to be taken 'seriously'? This is, though vague, true enough in general—it is an important commonplace in discussing the purport of any utterance whatsoever. I must not be joking, for example, nor writing a poem. But we are apt to have a feeling that their being serious consists in their being uttered as (merely) the outward and visible sign, for convenience or other record or for information, of an inward and spiritual act: from which it is but a short step to go on to believe or to assume without realizing that for many purposes the outward utterance is a description, *true or false*, of the occurrence of the inward performance. The classic expression of this idea is to be found in the *Hippolytus* (1. 612), where Hippolytus says

ἡ γλῶσσ' ὀμώμοχ', ἡ δέ φρὴν ἀνωμοτός,

i.e., 'my tongue swore to, but my heart (or mind or other backstage artiste) did not'.[10] Thus 'I promise to…' obliges me—puts on record my spiritual assumption of a spiritual shackle.

It is gratifying to observe in this very example how excess of profundity, or rather solemnity, at once paves the way for immodality. For one who says 'Promising is not merely a matter of uttering words! It is an inward and spiritual act!' is apt to appear as a solid moralist standing out against a generation of superficial theorizers: we see him as he sees himself, surveying the invisible depths of ethical space, with all the distinction of a specialist in the *sui generis*. Yet he provides Hippolytus with a let-out, the bigamist with an excuse for his 'I do' and the welsher with a defence for his 'I bet'. Accuracy and morality alike are on the side of the plain saying that *our word is our bond*.

If we exclude such fictitious inward acts as this, can we suppose that any of the other things which certainly are normally required to accompany an utterance such as 'I promise that…' or 'I do (take this woman…)' are in fact described by it, and consequently do by their presence make it true or by their absence make it false? Well, taking the latter first, we shall next consider what we actually do say about the utterance concerned when one or another of its normal concomitants is *absent*. In no case do we say that the utterance was false but rather that the utterance—or rather the *act*,[11] e.g., the promise—was void, or given in bad faith, or not implemented, or the like. In the particular case of promising, as with many other performatives, it is appropriate that the person uttering the promise should have a certain intention, viz., here to keep his word: and perhaps of all concomitants this looks the most suitable to be that which 'I promise' does describe or record. Do we not actually, when such intention is absent, speak of a 'false' promise? Yet so to speak is *not* to say that the utterance 'I promise that...' is false, in the sense that though he states that he does, he doesn't, or that though he describes he misdescribes—misreports. For he *does* promise: the promise here is not even *void*, though it is given *in bad faith*. His utterance is perhaps misleading, probably deceitful, and doubtless wrong, but it is not a lie or a misstatement. At most we might make out a case for saying that it implies or insinuates a falsehood or a misstatement (to the effect that he does intend to do something): but that is a very different matter. Moreover, we do not speak of a false bet or a false christening; and that we *do* speak of a false promise need commit us no more than the fact that we speak of a false move. 'False' is not necessarily used of statements only.

Notes

1. It is, of course, not really correct that a sentence ever *is* a statement: rather, it is *used* in *making a statement*, and the statement itself is a 'logical construction' out of the makings of statements.

2. Everything said in these sections is provisional, and subject to revision in the light of later sections.

3. Of all people, jurists should be best aware of the true state of affairs. Perhaps some now are. Yet they will succumb to their own timorous fiction, that a statement of 'the law' is a statement of fact.

4. Not without design: they are all 'explicit' performatives, and of that prepotent class later called 'exercitives'.

5. [Austin realized that the expression 'I do' is not used in the marriage ceremony too late to correct his mistake. We have let it remain in the text as it is philosophically unimportant that it is a mistake *J.O. Urmson,* ed.]

6. Still less anything that I have already done or have yet to do.

7. 'Sentences' form a class of 'utterances', which class is to be defined, so far as I am concerned, grammatically, though I doubt if the definition has yet been given satisfactorily. With performative utterances are contrasted, for example and essentially, 'constative' utterances: to issue a constative utterance (i.e., to utter it with a historical reference) is to make a statement. To issue a performative utterance is, for example, to make a bet. See further below on 'illocutions'.

8. Formerly I used 'performatory': but 'performative' is to be preferred as shorter, less ugly, more tractable, and more traditional in formation.

9. I owe this observation to Professor H. L. A. Hart.

10. But I do not mean to rule out all the offstage performers—the lights men, the stage manager, even the prompter; I am objecting only to certain officious understudies, who would duplicate the play.

11. We deliberately avoid distinguishing these, precisely because the distinction is not in point.

Post-Reading Questions / Activities

- What is the difference between looking at language as *utterances* and looking at language as *sentences*? How would you have to study language following these two different approaches?
- If the important thing about performatives is that they accomplish something in the world, is it the case that speaking always makes things happen? Why or why not? Can you declare yourself ruler of a kingdom? Can you christen a ship by smashing a bottle of Champagne over the prow and declaring the vessel christened?
- Do utterances have a single function? How can you determine it?
- Keep track of all the ways people are using language (their goals, the effects) for an hour. How often are people attempting to make referential statements, and how often are they doing something different? Could you create a list of those functions? Do you think this would be a finite list? Why or why not?

Vocabulary

constative	statement
performative	utterance

Suggested Further Reading

Austin, John L. 1975 [1962]. *How to Do Things With Words,* 2d ed. Cambridge, MA: Harvard University Press.

Rosaldo, Michelle Z. 1982. "The Things We Do with Words: Ilongot Speech Acts and Speech Act Theory in Philosophy." *Language in Society* 11: 203–235.

Searle, John R. 1969. *Speech Acts: An Essay in the Philosophy of Language.* Cambridge: Cambridge University Press.

CHAPTER 36

Kuna Curing and Magic
Counseling the Spirits

Joel Sherzer
(1983)

Throughout the world, anthropologists have recorded and analyzed what Malinowski called "magic, science, and religion"—aspects of life that in the contemporary technologically advanced world people often wish to separate clearly. Curing and medicine are other topics often associated with those three. What is magic? How can we distinguish it from science? From medicine? And how do all of them work? In all societies, there are ritual dimensions to curing, whether the consultation is followed by a prescription in North America or by the elaborate ceremonies of shamans in Peru or southeast Asia. Language plays various roles in such curing.

This chapter presents one section of Joel Sherzer's book Kuna Ways of Speaking, *a detailed examination of all the ways Kuna Indians in San Blas, Panama, use their language. This comes from an approach to language known as the "ethnography of speaking," in which all aspects of language were taken into account: who says what to whom, in what way, and what happens as a result of that speaking. This approach was introduced by Dell Hymes and John Gumperz, and the contributions of Richard Bauman and Sherzer and others made it a productive way to study language.*

Sherzer has written extensively about the Kuna (also sometimes spelled Cuna) and other Native American groups, also writing important works on verbal art and discourse. The chapter here focuses on an island referred to by the villagers as Mulatuppu, less than an hour from Panama City, with 1,626 inhabitants (1970 census) densely inhabiting neatly arranged houses. Sherzer explains his book's goal very clearly: "It is my aim to enter their world through speaking, not just because the Kuna dedicate a vast amount of time to talk, which they do, but because their world is perceived, conceived, and especially organized and controlled by means of language and speech."

Three distinct ritual traditions, each associated with linguistic varieties and styles, are political, curing and magic, and puberty rituals. In the preceding chapter, Sherzer had introduced language used in public and political gatherings, or the "gathering house." The chapter presented here focuses on the ways language is used in curing and magic, sometimes explicitly contrasting with that of other genres. All transcripts are taken from naturally occurring events that Sherzer recorded.

Reading Questions

- How do Kuna bring about curing? What gives plants and other curative objects their power?
- Sherzer distinguishes between primary and secondary contexts of *ikarkana* (ways, texts) spoken or chanted by the "*ikar* knower," or specialist. What are those different contexts?

Joel Sherzer, "Curing and Magic: Counseling the Spirits." *Kuna Ways of Speaking: An Ethnographic Perspective.* Austin: University of Texas Press, 1983, pp. 110–138.

- Sherzer says that while the *ikarkana* are theoretically fixed and unchanging, they actually have some variation. What kinds of variation does he identify and why do they occur?
- What is parallelism? In what part of the language of *ikarkana* is it found?

Unlike curing and magic in other societies, in particular many North and South American Indian groups, Kuna curing and magic involve no drugs, no trances, and no spectacular tricks or sleight of hand. Rather, Kuna magical actions are achieved solely by means of verbal communication between humans and spirits. According to Kuna belief, there is a world of spirits which underlies and animates the concrete world of humans, plants, animals, and objects. The spirits behave in every way just like real, living Kuna. Their family and social organization is Kuna. Their needs and desires, such as eating and drinking, are expressed and satisfied according to Kuna practice. And, like all Kuna, they have a great appreciation for verbal artistry and verbal play. There are spirits of good and spirits of evil. Both are controlled by means of a set of *ikarkana* (ways, texts) which are addressed by *ikar wismalat* (*ikar* knowers) directly to them. *Ikarkana* are used for curing, disease prevention, advising and counseling medicine, acquiring special abilities, in certain rites of passage, and, in general, for magical control of the spirit world.

Kuna curing and magical events share with events of the *onmakket neka* (gathering house) a focus on language and speech. It is through language and speech that medicine becomes effective, the spirits of good are put to work, and the spirits of evil are neutralized and disarmed. At the same time, the use of language and speech in magic is significantly different from that in 'gathering house' ritual. Curing and magic constitute a separate ritual tradition from that of the 'gathering house,' with regard to social organization, setting, linguistic variety, and the overall structure of events.

There is no Kuna word for magic, just as there is no Kuna word for politics, or religion, or law. I use the term magic here, following anthropological tradition, to refer to the causation of supernatural actions by means of special power. For the Kuna the special power is verbal—communication with spirits through the performance of *ikarkana*. While *ikarkana* are used primarily for curing and disease prevention, they are also used more generally in order to cause or insure the occurrence of a wide variety of actions. For this reason I stress a close association between curing and magic throughout this chapter.

Curing Events

When a Kuna woman, man, or child is ill, a member of the family is sent to a *nele* (seer), who decides what the cause of the sickness is and what cure is needed. Through her or his ability to communicate with the spirits, the 'seer' is able to determine what the patient's problem is. If the cure involves actual medicine, this medicine must be acquired from an *inatulet* (medicinal specialist), who also serves as a diagnostician in the absence of a 'seer.' The 'medicinal specialist' gathers plants of medicinal value from the nearby jungle. Before giving these plants to the patient's family, he counsels them in order to activate them and give them life; that is, he transforms the plants into usable medicine. This activation process is carried out by directly addressing the spirits of the plants and telling them what they need to know in order to carry out their work.

In addition to the administration of physical medicine, curing, especially of serious diseases, often involves the performance of appropriate *ikarkana*. An *ikar* is performed by an 'ikar knower' for the benefit of the sick person but addressed directly to the spirit world, in the form of a box of *suar nuchukana* (stick dolls), the representatives of the spirits of good, whose role it is to counter the evil spirits causing the disease. The sick person lies in a hammock in his or her house, and the 'ikar knower' sits alongside on a bench. Under the hammock is the box of 'stick dolls,' as well as a pot of burning hot peppers and burning hot cacao, also used to fight off disease.

The 'ikar knower' makes no physical gestures during the performance. He stares vaguely into space and, from time to time, smokes tobacco in his pipe. Others in the house either go about their usual business or sit beside the sick person and the 'ikar knower.' The 'ikar knower' performs the long (typically one hour or more) *ikar* in the late afternoon or early evening, after he has finished his other work for the day; he then leaves the house of the patient. He carries his walking stick and wears beads, signs of his role, and sometimes a tie. Performance of a curing *ikar* is usually repeated on four successive days.

THE TYPOLOGY OF *IKARKANA*

Curing and Disease Prevention

There are a variety of diseases or infirmities for which a particular named *ikar* is used. Most common is *kapur ikar* (the way of the hot pepper), used in the curing of high fever and diseases accompanied by high fever. Another is *kurkin ikar* (the way of the hat), used in curing headaches. Others are *muu ikar* (the way of birth), used in difficult childbirths; *aplis wiloet ikar* (the way of blood strengthening), used to augment the blood; *serkan ikar* (the way of the deceased persons), used to avoid having nightmares about dead spirits; *purwa ikar* (the way of the wind), used against epilepsy; *nika ikar* (the way of strength), used to give the patient strength; *nia ikar* (the way of the devil), used for mentally deranged persons; *akkwanele ikar* (the way of the magic stone), used to return a lost soul to the body of the patient; and *tala kannoet ikar* (the way of eye strength), used to improve the sight of the patient.

Immediately related to the *ikarkana* used in curing diseases is another set, used in the prevention of disease or other evils. According to Kuna belief, some people are likely to succumb to certain diseases or are marked to fall prey to certain calamities. Some of these proclivities can be noted by the midwives at the birth of a child; they inform the child's family so that it can have the appropriate medicine and *ikar* administered.

'Seers,' because of their great mental powers, are subject to headaches; the performance of *nele kurkin ikar* (the way of the seer's hat) prevents them from getting such headaches. *Ukkunakpe ikar* (the way of the rattlesnake) is performed for individuals who have a propensity to be bitten by snakes, in order to prevent this from happening. The rattlesnake is counseled to attack other snakes and thus protect the marked individual. Also used against snakes is *wekko ikar* (the way of the hawk)—the hawk eats snakes and in this *ikar* it is counseled to do just that. *Purpa oteket ikar* (the way of the bringing down of the soul), also called *tampoet ikar* (the way of the cooling off), is performed for children so that they do not die, especially when other children have died in the same family or when the child in question keeps getting sick. *Pinnuwar olaet ikar* (the way of the felling of the *pinnuwala* [*Anacardium* species] tree), also called *suar olaet ikar* (the way of the felling of the tree) or *mortup okwaet ikar* (the way of the changing of the clothesline), is performed next to felled trees, where disease-causing spirits are located. In this *ikar* the spirits of good are counseled to in turn counsel the evil spirits residing in the tree to move to another tree. If the evil spirits do not move, they become angry and dangerous.

No doubt the most spectacular of the *ikarkana* involved in curing and disease prevention is that used for the mass exorcism of evil spirits. This *ikar* is called *apsoket ikar* (the way of the mass curer) or *ukkurwala ikar* (the way of the balsa wood). Its performer is called an *apsoket*; his title is derived from the verb *apsoke* (to converse). In this *ikar*, the 'mass curer' converses with both good and evil spirits in order to defeat the evil spirits. The whole event is called *nek apsoket* (mass-curing ritual, literally to converse with the place), place having the sense of the world, the environment, and conditions in general, ultimately referring to the spirits who inhabit the world and its environment and cause conditions. It is also called *nekuet* (smoking the surroundings), which refers to the smoking of tobacco by members of the community who participate in the ritual; this smoking is an essential feature of the efficacy of the exorcism.

The 'mass curer' is the most respected of all medicinal and curing '*ikar* knowers.' 'The way of the mass curer' is extremely long and takes many years to learn. Furthermore, it is used not for the benefit of a single individual but, rather, for the well-being of an entire community. All the aspects of ordinary curing rituals are more elaborate in the 'mass-curing ritual.' The entire community is present in the 'gathering house,' in which this *ikar* is performed. It lasts for eight days, beginning each day in the late afternoon and continuing until midnight. Enormous balsa wood figures

are brought into the 'gathering house' and placed against the benches of the *arkarkana* (spokesmen); these are large versions of the 'stick doll' representatives of the spirits of good which are used in all curing events.

From the center of the 'gathering house' the 'mass curer' addresses these figures in his *ikar*, while the other members of the community sit silently and smoke tobacco, literally smoking out the evil spirits. Large quantities of cacao, hot peppers, and other medicine are also burned as part of the smoking-out process. All members of the community (not just the ritual performer, as in ordinary curing ceremonies) must refrain from sexual relations during the entire eight-day period. Quiet is maintained during the daytime and the village is under strict quarantine—no outsiders are allowed in. The 'mass-curing ritual' is used to cure whole communities of epidemics, to clear new lands of dangerous sicknesses in preparation for habitation and farming, and generally to rid an area of disease, danger, and evil.[1]

'Medicine Counsels'

Intimately related to the curing and prevention of disease is *ina uanaet* (medicine counsel), a set of *ikarkana* used to advise and counsel various types of medicine in order to activate them and render them effective. Certain objects in nature—for example, plants in the nearby mainland jungle—are inherently of medicinal value.[2] Nonetheless, in order to be effective, to be given life, these potential medicines must be told how to carry out their cure. This is precisely what occurs in 'medicine counsel' when the 'medicinal specialist' addresses the spirits of these plants directly. 'Medicine counsel' is performed in the jungle, at the moment of the cutting of the particular plant, and/or later on, in the home of the 'medicinal specialist.' The 'medicinal specialist' either sits or stands, with the medicine he is addressing placed directly in front of him. In addition to plants, such objects as pieces of glass, sticks, stones, phonograph needles, old shoes, or bars of soap can become medicinally effective if counseled. So while medicine is effective because of a combination of internal medicinal properties and power rendered through language, it is the verbal 'counsel' which is ultimately supreme, since without it nothing is effective and with it anything can become effective.

'Medicine counsels' are performed frequently and relatively publicly. They are typically performed by the 'medicinal specialist' when he returns from his morning's work in the jungle. Many men have some knowledge of traditional medicine so that, even when they go to the jungle primarily for the purpose of farming or cutting wood, they often bring some medicine back with them. As a result, if you wander through a Kuna village at midday, through the bamboo walls of many houses you will hear the voices of men performing 'medicine counsel' to their just gathered medicine. These voices are often mingled with other voices and noises—the preparation of midday meals, children playing after their morning session at school, ordinary conversations, and radios.

There are various 'medicine counsels,' depending on what the medicine is to be used for and where it comes from. *Muu ina uanaet* (birth medicine counsel) advises medicine used in childbirth. *Ina pukkip ikar* (the way of much medicine), performed in the home of a sick person, counsels all the medicine in the jungle to come to the patient's aid. *Ina ulukanki* (medicine in the trunks) counsels a whole medicinal laboratory; it is performed either in the home of the 'medicinal specialist,' in front of his collection of medicine, or in the home of a sick person. *Ina tiikinet ikar* (the way of the medicine in the water) counsels the medicine located at the bottom of a river.

Abilities (particularly in hunting) relate to economic concerns.

The Acquisition of Abilities

Another set of *ikarkana* is performed for the purpose of enabling one to acquire particular abilities or achieve particular goals. *Pisep ikar* (the way of the basil) is performed for the benefit of a man who wants to become a great hunter or is about to set out on a particular hunting expedition. This man makes a potion out of basil and other fragrant plants; then 'the way of the basil' is performed to the potion by a 'knower,' who addresses the spirit of the plant directly and explains to it what animals will be hunted. The hunter then bathes in this perfume and, as a result, becomes fragrantly attractive to animals, who fall in love with him and approach him, enabling him to kill them. During the period of the efficacy of the potion, the hunter is not permitted to have sexual relations;[3] the interdiction of sex is characteristic of all the *ikarkana* discussed here and is an aspect of their magical power. Also used in hunting is *yauk ikar* (the way of the sea turtle), performed to a potion which is used in the hunting of these turtles. *Ikarkana* such as 'the way of the basil' and 'the way of the sea turtle' are directly related to economic concerns. There are always a need and a demand for meat within San Blas. A number of years ago, there was a great demand for sea turtles, since their shells were being purchased for very high prices. These shells often reached Japan, where they were used to make frames for eyeglasses. At that time many men were asking to have 'the way of the sea turtle' performed for them or were learning it themselves. Still another *ikar* performed to a potion is *mutup ikar* (the way of birth string); in this case, bathing in the advised potion makes a man attractive to women.

Other *ikarkana* are used for the acquisition of other types of abilities. An example is *neloet ikar* (the way of seeing), which is performed for 'seers' while they are still children, in order to develop their potentially extraordinary mental abilities.

Rites of Passage

There are *ikarkana* whose role is to assure passage through stages in the Kuna life cycle. Many of these focus on young girls and women. For example when a girl is two or three years old, a hole is pierced in her nose, and from that moment she begins to wear a gold nose ring (Kuna women wear nose rings throughout their lives). In order to assist in the nose-piercing process, *ikko ikar* (the way of the needle) is performed.

Other *ikarkana* are directly involved in girls' puberty rites and in the preparation and consumption of *inna*, an alcoholic beverage, during these rites. Several days before the rites and associated festivities begin, the men and women of the village communally prepare the *inna*, under the supervision of a specialist. After its preparation, *inna sopet ikar* (the way of the making of *inna*) is performed to render the drink stronger. It is performed by the *inna sopet* (*inna* maker) and is addressed to the spirit of the *inna*. Another *inna*-related *ikar* is *wipoet ikar* (the way of sobering up), used during puberty rites by an extremely inebriated individual in order to sober up. Other *ikarkana* are performed for the benefit of various objects and persons involved in the events which occur during the girls' puberty rites....

Two *ikarkana* are performed after a death to assure proper travel to and through the afterworld. The very long *masar ikar* (the way of the bamboo cane) is addressed by a 'knower' to the spirit of cane while the corpse lies at home; it is continued during the trip to the cemetery and at the cemetery. It assures safe passage into and through all parts of the afterworld. *Orpatte ikar* (the way of the golden elevator) aids passage to the afterworld. Like all *ikarkana*, these must be paid for. However, the family of the deceased individual does not always have the means or the desire to pay for the performance of such a long and expensive *ikar* as 'the way of the bamboo cane.' Part of the expense often involves bringing a specialist from another village, sometimes rather distant, since there are relatively few 'knowers' of this *ikar* in San Blas.

Magical Control

A very interesting set of *ikarkana* is related to the carrying out of magiclike feats, such as grabbing a dangerous snake, holding a hot iron harpoon, or surrounding oneself with bees without being attacked by them. The addressees of these *ikarkana* are the spirits of the objects to be controlled—the snake, harpoon, or bees. However, such controlling activities are often carried out, not by performing the longer *ikar*, but by either intoning or thinking a short charmlike incantation called a *sekretto*, which is associated with the particular *ikar* and magical act. The *sekretto* is the 'secret' of or the key to the object.

There is a large set of such 'secrets.' Some have to do with controlling—touching or being near—otherwise dangerous animals or objects, such as bees, wasps, scorpions, spiders, vipers, poisonous ants, or hot harpoons. Others can cause extraordinary events to occur, such as water not draining through the holes of a sieve or a rattle bursting open by itself. Some are used in the curing of sick individuals, such as persons who have fainted or who have tumors or boils. Some are used to achieve success in certain activities, such as attracting women or hunting. Finally, some are used by certain individuals for protection in the afterworld. Thus, if a man has had sexual relations with the *iet* (haircutter) at girls' puberty rites, he will want to know the *tisla sekretto* (the scissors secret), in order to prevent giant scissors from cutting him in the afterworld. 'Medicinal specialists' must know the medicine 'secret' in order to cross a lake of medicine in the afterworld.

'Secrets' are in a linguistic variety quite distinct from that of the *ikar*. In fact, 'secrets' are not really in any particular linguistic variety at all. Rather, they are combinations of words from various languages—Kuna (modern and archaic), Choco, English, Spanish, and Latin. They have no referential content but evoke a mystical magic through their rhymes and rhythms. I cite a few lines here for illustrative purposes but do not present a complete example, because of the incantations' very secretive position within Kuna genres of speaking.

> santa lusia e pasato.
> kona leche.
> pita se kayó.
> wes pasarió.
> paitera amen.

Sounds and sound oppositions are manipulated, almost playfully, as in the following lines.

> elis elis ihelis.
> iklesia iklasia.
> matté mattéus.
> temones teppottes.

'Secrets' are intended to inform the spirit of the object in question that the performer knows its origin and is therefore able to control it. Understanding Kuna magical control requires paying attention to the relationship among *ikarkana*, 'secrets', and another verbal genre, *purpa* (soul).[4] Associated with almost every *ikar* is a 'soul', a relatively short text in everyday though somewhat esoteric Kuna. The 'soul' describes the origin of the object to be controlled by the *ikar* in explicit terms and is an essential aspect of the learning of an *ikar*. The choice of whether to use an *ikar*, a 'soul', or a 'secret' on a particular occasion depends on the circumstances or activity involved and on what a particular specialist happens to know. For most diseases and disease prevention, it is most common to use the long *ikar*. For ailments which require quicker, more direct results, 'souls' are used. For the control of such objects as bees and snakes, where a rapid magical demonstration of power is called for, the short 'secret' might be employed.

It is interesting to ask why there exist long *ikarkana* for the magical control of objects when short 'secrets' would seem to suffice and in fact are sometimes used in the actual magical act. However, the long *ikarkana* are always an important element in the process of controlling objects and spirits—they are a reminder of the power the '*ikar* knower' has over them, including the fact that he can also control them with 'secrets'. These *ikarkana* are also part of the knowledge of the specialist, necessary to his work, and are learned only after hard study. But *ikarkana* are also pleasurable verbally in and for themselves. They can be performed for the enjoyment and benefit of the 'knower' himself or for his family or friends and are appreciated for their aesthetic qualities, even if some of the listeners understand little of the referential content. Spirits as well appreciate the verbal artistry of these *ikarkana* and in part follow the directions of the performer because of the pleasure they derive from this verbal play and poetry.

Becoming an expert and specialist in a particular area of Kuna curing and magic—curing fever, preventing snakebite, aiding women in childbirth, or benefiting hunters—thus involves learning a complex of verbal skills and the traditions associated with them. This complex includes a set of related *ikarkana*, a set of 'souls,' and a set of 'secrets.' The more of this verbal complex a specialist knows and performs, the greater his prestige and renown.

CONTEXTS FOR THE PERFORMANCE OF *IKARKANA*

It is characteristic of all *ikarkana* (but not 'souls' or 'secrets') that they are performed in a variety of contexts, in addition to the primary one of curing, preventing disease, improving abilities, or magical control. These other, secondary contexts include the practicing of an *ikar* by a 'knower,' the learning and teaching of an *ikar*, and the chanting of an *ikar* for the pleasure of the 'knower' and his human and spirit listeners during certain festivities (especially those associated with girls' puberty rites). On all these occasions, performers are usually said to *namakke* (chant) the *ikar* rather than *sunmakke* (speak) it—the latter is the appropriate way to perform *ikarkana* in their primary context for their primary function. There are ambiguities in this distinction, however, in that each performer has his own style of both *namakke* and *sunmakke*, depending on whom he learned the *ikar* from.

One distinguisher between performances in the principal primary context and performances in secondary contexts is the tightening of the larynx in secondary contexts, resulting in a voice quality considered to be aesthetically pleasing. The 'knower' begins these secondary performances of an *ikar* with the words *wai sae*, which tightens the larynx. The Kuna show a certain lack of agreement concerning the *namakke-sunmakke* distinction, generally using *namakke* to label secondary contexts but alternating between *namakke* and *sunmakke* for the labeling of primary performances, which are definitely tuneful and melodic. This contrasts with the chanting of *saklakana* (chiefs) in the 'gathering house,' which is consistently called *namakke*.

When chanted for practice or for the personal pleasure of the 'knower,' *ikarkana* are performed in his home or that of a member of his family, usually late at night after the evening 'gathering' or even while this 'gathering' is taking place, if the 'knower' does not attend. Learning and teaching are carried out in the house of the 'knower' at night. The process is as follows. The teacher first performs the *ikar* completely. Then the student learns it by a line-by-line repetition. When the student becomes more familiar with the text, he begins the session by performing the *ikar* himself. The teacher corrects the student when he makes mistakes....

During the festivities associated with girls' puberty rites, 'knowers' perform *ikarkana* either in the *inna neka* (*inna* house) or in a private home. These are not official parts of the ritual....Rather, they are one of a number of pleasurable activities that people engage in while drinking *inna* and other alcoholic beverages. The performer, usually quite drunk himself, sits surrounded by other men, equally drunk, who listen. Performer and audience, as well as spirits, enjoy the event immensely. Members of the audience often provide a bottle of rum to consume during the performance—this willingness to spend money indicates the degree to which the verbal art is appreciated.

These secondary purposes or contexts for the performance of *ikarkana* are of great significance in Kuna society and should not be viewed as marginal in any sense. Obviously the performance of *ikarkana* in learning and teaching is the process by which they are passed on from generation to generation. But performing for practice and personal pleasure is also important. And, while the Kuna clearly enjoy *ikarkana* for purely aesthetic reasons, there are other motivations and functions for such performances as well. This is most evident with regard to *ikarkana* which are rarely used for their primary purpose or are performed for their primary purpose in a place where they cannot be heard. It may be, as in the case of 'the way of the devil,' used for mentally deranged individuals, that it has been some time since anyone had the disease or, as in the case of 'the way of birth,' used for difficulty in childbirth, that outsiders are not permitted to be present when it is performed or, as in the case of 'the way of the bamboo cane,' used to guide a dead person's soul into and through the afterworld, that it has been a while since anyone died who left a family willing to pay for the performance. Thus how can an '*ikar* knower' remind members of his community that he is indeed a specialist in a particular *ikar*? The best way is to perform the *ikar* in secondary contexts.

An illustrative example is Manuel Campos, a now deceased Mulatuppu '*ikar* knower' who was the only person in his large village who knew 'the way of the bamboo cane.' He would often practice it at night on evenings when men were talking in the 'gathering house.' Of his many relatives' homes, he would often select that of a daughter who lived near the 'gathering house.' Thus, as they talked, the men could hear the booming voice of Campos practicing 'the way of the bamboo cane' for hours at a time. Who could deny that he indeed knew it, that he fully deserved the credit and respect associated with it?

Ikar Structure and Content

Since the purpose of *ikarkana* is to counsel and control representatives of the spirit world, their various themes or topics can be seen as subservient to that purpose. At the same time, they have a narrative structure in their own right.

One frequent *ikar* theme is the description of the conception and birth of the object to be controlled; this description may be quite graphic, as in 'the way of birth' or 'the way of the basil.' The actual labeling of the body parts and acts involved in conception and birth is in a vocabulary particular to the *ikar*. If the words have meanings in everyday Kuna which are different from the meanings they have in the *ikar*, the result is metaphorical, achieved at the intersection of two linguistic varieties. Here is the description of the birth of the plant in 'the way of the basil.'

> Inapiseptili [the spirit name of the plant] in the golden box
> is moving.
> In the golden box is moving.
> Inapiseptili in the golden box is swinging from side to side.
> In the golden box is swinging from side to side.
> Inapiseptili in the golden box is trembling.
> In the golden box is trembling.
> Inapiseptili in the golden box is palpitating.
> In the golden box is palpitating.
> Inapiseptili in the golden box is making a noise.
> In the golden box is making a noise.
> Inapiseptili in the golden box is shooting out.
> In the golden box is shooting out.[5]

On the other hand, the *ikar* might merely state that the '*ikar* knower' is acquainted with the object and its parts, its origin and its 'secret.' It is understood, especially by the spirit of the object, to which the *ikar* is addressed, that this knowledge involves detailed understanding of conception and birth. An example is *pulu ikar* (the way of the wasp), used to attract and control wasps.

> The specialist knows your secret origin.
> The specialist says.[6]

Nakpe ikar (the way of the snake), used to grab a dangerous snake and raise it into the air, first announces that the '*ikar* knower' is in complete control of knowledge about the snake's origin.

> Machi Oloaktikunappinele [the spirit name of the snake] calls [to the specialist].
> 'How well do you know the abode of my origin?'
> Machi Oloaktikunappi calls.
> The specialist counsels Machi Oloaktikunappi.
> 'Indeed [I] already know the abode of your origin.
> Indeed [I] have come to play in the abode of your origin.
> Indeed I have come to encircle the abode of your origin.'

This same *ikar* then lists, in a series of parallel lines, all the parts of the snake, thus enabling the '*ikar* knower' to display his anatomical knowledge about the snake's origin.

> The specialist says.
> 'Indeed how your lips were placed on.

The specialist knows well.'
The specialist says.
The specialist says.
'How your chin was put in place.
How your lower chin was formed.
The specialist knows well.'
The specialist says.
Indeed the specialist says.
'How your pupils were formed.
The specialist knows well.'
The specialist says.
The specialist says.
'How the point of your tongue was put in place.
The specialist knows well.'
The specialist says.
He counsels Machi Oloaktikunappi.
Indeed the specialist [says].
'How your golden arrow [fangs] was put in place.
How your golden arrow was buried in.
The specialist knows well.'
The specialist says.[7]

There is a great deal of secrecy and taboo surrounding conception and birth among the Kuna, this being the most sensitive of all topics for them; thus there is power in knowledge about this area. The intersection of taboo and power with regard to knowledge of and speaking about conception and birth is deeply embedded in Kuna beliefs and practices, from the most everyday to the most ritual and magical. There is an interdiction on talk about conception and birth in everyday interaction, especially in the presence of children. This is an area of vocabulary in which euphemisms abound. At the same time, by revealing to a spirit in an *ikar* that he knows its origin (that is, its conception and birth), an '*ikar* knower' is able to control it.

Some *ikarkana* contain taxonomies of plants or animals—of the objects whose spirits are addressed in the *ikar*. These taxonomies, at times rather long and complicated, are usually in the special lexicon of the linguistic variety of the spirits and of curing and magical *ikarkana*. The presentation of these taxonomies is related to the highly parallelistic structure of *ikarkana*. It is also intimately associated with the statement of the origin of the object to be controlled in that it shows the place of the object in nature, its origin and essence, in truly structural terms. Taxonomies are either localized in a particular portion of an *ikar* or dispersed throughout as a recurrent theme.

A taxonomy of hot peppers appears in 'the way of the hot pepper', used in calming high fever. The spirits of these peppers are called into action in the fight against disease; fifty-five parallel stanzas are used to name fifty-five plants.

The specialist is calling.
He is calling to the mountains.
He is calling the spirits.
Nele Pinaisepa Nele [hot pepper].
Ulu Sankwali Nele [*sankwa*-type pepper].
Ulu Tipyana Nele [toasted pepper].
Ulu Opirpa Nele [ground pepper].

Upikkwa Nele [well-ground pepper].
Alakkwa Nele [almost ground pepper].[8]

This taxonomy includes pepper types as they are found in nature as well as types that have been transformed by human action.

In 'the way of the basil', the spirits of a taxonomy of fragrant plants are addressed. The hunter bathes in a potion made of these plants so that animals fall in love with him and are attracted to him. The spirits of the plants are named in a set of parallel lines, each of which ends and thus punctuates a parallel stanza.[9]

Pisep, I am advising you…
Achueryala, I am advising you…
Kokke, I am advising you…
Nopar, I am advising you…
Aksar, I am advising you…
Pakla, I am advising you…

The spirits of the plants are provided with a taxonomy of animals to be hunted. These animals are of two types, *tulekala* (walking) and *ullukka* (flying). This animal taxonomy is presented in a set of parallel lines, each of which opens a parallel stanza.

The specialist's hat makes noise like a *tulekala yaya* [an agouti]…
The specialist's hat makes noise like a *tulekala manikwillosakpia* [a collared peccary]…
The specialist's hat makes noise like a *tulekala punayai* [a white-lipped peccary]…
The specialist's hat makes noise like a *tulekala ukkusalu ekwilamakkatola* [a tapir]…
The specialist's hat makes noise like a *tulekala narwalipe* [a rabbit]…
The specialist's hat makes noise like a *tulekala tukkwa* [a squirrel]…
The specialist's hat makes noise like a *ullukka sitoni* [a curassow]…
The specialist's hat makes noise like a *ullukka kwami kwami* [a wild bird]…
The specialist's hat makes noise like a *ullukka mormolipe* [a wild bird]…
The specialist's hat makes noise like a *ullukka kokorkwana* [a wild bird]…[10]

In addition to those of plants and animals, there are other taxonomies. For example, a taxonomy of directions occurs in a version of 'the way of the basil', performed by a different '*ikar* knower.'

Your branches are pointing to where the sun rises.
Your branches are pointing to where the sun sets.
Your branches are pointing to where the sun is highest.
Your branches are pointing to where the sun rises halfway.[11]

Another topic or theme of these *ikarkana* is the detailed description of the day-to-day life of the objects being addressed. Since these objects, especially animals, have spirits with social organizations and daily activities identical to those of humans, these texts provide fascinating insights into the Kuna perception of their own daily round of activities—sleeping, waking up, drinking, eating, hunting, and conversing with family and friends. In 'the way of the rattlesnake,' used as protection against dangerous snakes, the rattlesnake gets ready to go hunting while, just as happens every morning as real Kuna farmers and hunters go off to the mainland jungle to work, his wife prepares a beverage for him.

> Puna Inakunipyaisop [the spirit name of Rattlesnake's wife] responds [to Rattlesnake].
> 'You are going hunting for me,' she says.
> 'I will prepare your beverage for you.'
> The wife says.
> She lights the fire.
> She turns the firewood.
> In the fireplace the fire begins.
> The fire burns brightly.
> On top of the fire she places a pot.
> Inside the pot she places the fruit.
> She lowers the liquid [to the fire].
> The liquid begins to boil.[12]

Some *ikarkana* depict in detail Kuna cultural activities which are associated with the object being addressed and the functions of the *ikar*. 'The way of the bamboo cane,' used to guide the soul of the deceased, describes in great and gory detail the sickness, death, funeral, and passage to the afterworld of an individual. In the following passage the patient, in the final moments of his life, converses with his family. He is surrounded by his wife and female relatives, who have already begun their *poe* (tuneful weeping) for him. They will continue their 'tuneful weeping' after his death. This *ikar* reflects such basic Kuna concerns as the ability of 'medicinal specialists' to care for the sick and the inheritance of the property of the deceased. It is noteworthy that the concerns and conflicts of everyday life are expressed in a fixed, ritual text in an esoteric language.

> The patient says.
> 'The medicinal specialists cannot help me.'
> The patient's wife says.
> 'It is very serious; he is going to die.'
> The relatives speak.
> The female relatives say.
> 'There is much medicine under the hammock.
> Cups of medicine are lined up.
> There are many cups of medicine.'
> The patient cannot speak.
> The patient is very congested.
> His throat makes a rasping noise.
> The patient's mouth tastes bitter.
> He has no taste in his mouth.
> The patient's tongue is pale.
> His tongue is white.
> The patient's eyes are weak.
> His eyes flutter.
> He does not open his eyes.

> The patient says his last words.
> 'I left you enough.'
> The patient says his last words.
> 'I planted enough for you.
> After my death you will take care of it.
> I planted enough coconuts for you.
> After my death you will take care of them.'[13]

In 'the way of the making of *inna*,' used to render the alcoholic beverage consumed at girls' puberty rites stronger, all activities—personal, cultural, and social—relating to the preparation of the beverage are described in detail. Here the Kuna perception of their own activities is reflected in the depiction of Kuna actors in a narration addressed to spirits.

> The *inna*-making specialist awakens.
> The cock crows.
> The owners of the *inna* [members of the community] are making a lot of noise.
> There is much commotion.
> The owners of the *inna* are grinding sugarcane.
> The *inna*-making specialist calls his group together.
> He calls his assistants together.
> He calls his *inna* tasters together.
> His wife says.
> 'Let us change clothes, blouses, pants.
> We will go to the river to bathe.'
> They go to the river to bathe.
> They stand up in the river.
> The water makes waves.
> The water really makes waves.
> The water is splashing.
> The water is gushing.
> The river sardines leave their smell in their hair.[14]

Some *ikarkana* narrate mythic struggles, epic battles between opposing forces, as in war. In these struggles between the spirits of good and the spirits of evil, the spirits of good eventually win out, simultaneously eliminating the patient's disease. Here is a portion of 'the way of the balsa wood,' used to exorcise evil spirits in the 'mass-curing ritual.'

> The balsa wood spirit leaders are climbing.
> They have all of their equipment.
> The balsa wood spirit leaders are climbing.
> They are at the mouth of the Opakki River.
> They fill the *inna* house.
> They stuff the *inna* house.
> The spirits are ready to fight.
> The balsa wood spirit speaks.
> 'You are going to the place of evil spirits.'

In these battles, the physical characteristics and clothing of the spirits are described.

> The balsa wood spirit leaders are massing.
> The balsa wood spirit leaders are marching.
> Their golden hats are almost touching each other.
> Indeed their golden hats are almost touching each other.

The balsa wood spirit leaders are marching.
The balsa wood spirits' golden shoes are almost touching
each other.
Indeed their golden shoes are almost touching each other.
The balsa wood spirit leaders are marching.
Through the streets of the people.

Conversations among good spirits and between good and evil spirits are quoted. In fact, what is involved are more trickster-type foolery and conversational chicanery than actual gory battles. The spirits of good utilize such ploys as including in their ranks a drunken spirit (made from 'drunk wood') who, because of his inebriated state, fights furiously.

The balsa wood spirit leader speaks.
'Friend drunk wood spirit.
Do not worry so much.'
The balsa wood spirit leader speaks.
'We will place friend drunk wood spirit in the rear' [to
back up the ranks with his attack].
The balsa wood spirit says.
'For the good of human people.
To eliminate evil spirits.
Let us examine everything well.
Let us clear out everything.
To the sixth level underground.
Let us dig.
I say.'
The balsa wood spirit leaders descend.
To the first level underground the balsa wood spirit
leaders descend.
The evil spirit boat owners speak.
'For what reason have you entered my house?'
The balsa wood spirit responds to the evil spirit
boat owners.
'My people have many sicknesses.'[15]

Finally, *ikarkana* can be viewed as 'counsel' to objects and especially to spirits on how to behave, on what to do in order to carry out the biddings of the performer, the specialist 'knower,' and this fact is repeated over and over, addressed directly to the spirits.

The specialist counsels Machi Oloaktikunappi [the spirit
name of the snake].[16]
The specialist is again counseling Puna Olosemaktili [the
spirit name of the wasp].[17]

Curing and magical *ikarkana* consist of a series of themes, topics, and episodes which are strung together. While a primary characteristic of these *ikarkana* is that they are putatively fixed or unchangeable in form, and thus must be learned by rote memorization, there is some variation. Depending on the particular origins of the disease or on the particular object of several possible objects to be controlled, choices are made in the selection of topics or themes. In 'the way of the basil,' for example, verses relevant to the particular animal the hunter is desirous of killing or to a combination of these are chosen. *Ikarkana* can also be made longer or shorter, according to the selection of appropriate episodes and themes. Once the selection has been made, however, the '*ikar* knower' proceeds according to a line-by-line, fixed text. This is quite different from the chanting and speaking of 'chiefs' and other political leaders in the 'gathering house,' in which a theme or an idea is taken as a point of departure and then elaborated in a fresh, spontaneous way.

Parallelism

A pervasive feature of the structure of curing and magical *ikarkana* is parallelism—the patterned repetition of sounds, forms, and meanings. Many types of parallelism are found; in every *ikar* certain crucial lines are repeated identically or almost identically throughout the text, punctuating it and marking the boundaries of sections within it.[18] In 'the way of the snake,' for example, used to enable a specialist to grab a dangerous snake, the snake's spirit is continually reminded that the '*ikar* knower' is advising it. Likewise, in 'the way of the cooling off,' used to cool and calm a feverish patient, the medicine spirits are repeatedly told to cool off the patient's spirit.

Adjacent lines of *ikarkana* are linked by various types of parallelism. Two or more lines may be identical, with the exception of the deletion of a single word, as in 'the way of the basil.'[19]

Inapiseptili in the golden box is moving.
In the golden box is moving.[20]

Two or more lines may differ in nonreferential morphemes (in addition to the possible deletion of a word), as in 'the way of the snake.'

The specialist is sharpening [*nuptulu-makke-kwichiye*] his
little knife.
Is sharpening [*nuptulu-sae-kwichiye*] his little knife.

Notice that the verb stem formative *makke* of the first line is replaced by the verb stem formative *sae* of the next line.

Two or more lines may be identical except for the replacement of a single word, the two or more words having slightly different meanings within the same semantic field. Here are several examples of paired lines from 'the way of the snake.'

He is cutting small bushes.
He is clearing small bushes.

The specialist moves a little.
The specialist advances.

His [the snake's] hooks open and close.
His [the snake's] hooks open and close repeatedly.[21]

Here are two examples of series of such parallel lines from *nakrus ikar* (the way of the cross), used to scare away the devil.

The specialist is calling you.
The specialist is naming you.
The specialist is listing you.

The leaders are carrying the silver crosses.
The leaders are walking with the silver crosses.
The leaders are turning around with the silver crosses.

The leaders are moving their hands with the silver crosses.
The leaders are moving their hands rapidly with the silver
    crosses.
The leaders are holding the silver crosses.
The leaders are making signs with the silver crosses.[22]

The result of this type of parallelism is a slow-moving narration which advances by slight changes in referential content, added to repeated information. Extreme attention is paid to minute and precise detail.

Sometimes the pattern underlying the parallel structure involves not a single sentence or line but, rather, an entire set of lines, a verse, or a stanza, a frame which is repeated over and over with changes in one or more words. For example, in 'the way of the cooling off', the patient's illness is described as follows.

Our child has a feverish spirit.
We must cool off his spirit for him.
We must really cool off his spirit.

Our child has feverish blood.
His blood is very feverish.
We must cool off his blood for him.
We must really cool off his blood.

Our child has feverish skin.
His skin is very feverish.
We must cool off his skin for him.
We must really cool off his skin.

Our child has a feverish body.
His body is very feverish.
We must cool off his body for him.
We must really cool off his body.

Our child has a feverish head.
His head is very feverish.
We must cool off his head for him.
We must really cool off his head.

Our child has feverish hair.
His hair is very feverish.
We must cool off his hair for him.
We must really cool off his hair.[23]

Each of these examples involves a quite similar process, namely, the projection of a paradigm or taxonomy onto a fixed verse structure or frame. In addition to this poetic function,[24] clearly an aspect of these *ikarkana* and appreciated as such by the Kuna, the process of projecting paradigms and taxonomies onto fixed verse structures has other functions. Since it is important for these *ikarkana* to be long, length being a major aspect of their magical power, such projection enables one to generate a long text or portion of a text. Since '*ikar* knowers' have to memorize these texts, the taxonomy is related to the memorization process. That is, the memorization process involves the learning of the taxonomy together with the fixed verse pattern. And, since the *ikar* is learned line by line as a text and not, as might be expected given its underlying structure, in two parts—taxonomy plus fixed verse pattern—it is

an interesting question whether the taxonomy helps one learn and remember the *ikar* or whether the *ikar* helps one learn and remember the taxonomy or both.[25]

The parallelistic structure of curing and magical *ikarkana* is found at all levels, from the most macro—repetition of whole verse and stanza patterns—to the most micro—repetition of words and morphemes. The result is an overlapping intersection of various parallelistic patterns. An excellent example is provided by the opening of 'the way of the basil', in which the plant's birth is described.

Inapiseptili olouluti tulalemaiye.
            olouluti tulallemaiye.
Inapiseptili olouluti sikkirmakkemaiye.
            olouluti sikkirmakmamaiye.
Inapiseptili olouluti wawanmakkemaiye.
            olouluti wawanmakmainaye.
Inapiseptili olouluti aktutumakkemaiye.
            olouluti aktutulemainaye.
Inapiseptili olouluti kollomakkemaiye.
            olouluti kollomakmainaye.
Inapiseptili olouluti mummurmakkemaiye.
            olouluti mummurmakmainaye.

Inapiseptili in the golden box is moving.
            In the golden box is moving.
Inapiseptili in the golden box is swinging from side to side.
            In the golden box is swinging from side to side.
Inapiseptili in the golden box is trembling.
            In the golden box is trembling.
Inapiseptili in the golden box is palpitating.
            In the golden box is palpitating.
Inapiseptili in the golden box is making a noise.
            In the golden box is making a noise.
Inapiseptili in the golden box is shooting out.
            In the golden box is shooting out.[26]

If this text is represented as a series of the following symbols, the overlapping patterns of parallelism become much more striking.

a: Inapiseptili
b: golden box
c, d, e, f, g, h: various verb stems
W, w: *makke, mak*: verb stem formative endings
x: *mai*: verbal suffix, 'in the process of, in a horizontal position'
y: *nae*: verbal suffix, 'go to a location'
z: *ye*: verbal suffix, 'optative, emphatic'

The text can now be rewritten as follows.

```
a b c     x    z
  b c     x    z
a b d W x      z
  b d w x x z
a b e W x      z
  b e w x y z
a b f W x      z
```

```
b  f     x  y  z
a  b  g  W  x     z
   b  g  w  x  y  z
a  b  h  W  x     z
   b  h  w  x  y  z
```

Figurative Language and Speech

As in the chanting and speaking of the 'gathering house,' curing and magical *ikarkana* contain instances of figurative and metaphorical speech. But in these *ikarkana*, as distinct from those of the 'gathering house,' the metaphors are fixed; they are not elaborated, manipulated, or individually developed by the performer. Furthermore, they are, with a few exceptions, completely different from those of the 'gathering house.' The figurative language of curing and magical *ikarkana* can be approached in two ways. The first way is lexical. There are words in curing and related *ikarkana* which exist in colloquial Kuna as well but which in the *ikarkana* have distinct, derived, figurative meanings. Table 1 lists some examples.

At times a single word in the colloquial language is used with distinct meanings in different *ikarkana*. For example, *mola* (shirt or blouse in colloquial Kuna) signifies leaves in 'the way of the hot pepper' and skin in 'the way of the cooling off.' From a sociolinguistic point of view, these examples are part of the special lexical system of the 'stick doll' linguistic variety....

Second, the figurative speech found in curing and magical *ikarkana* occurs in the form of whole descriptive passages which are to be understood as symbolic representations or as statements of analogous relationships between the spirit and the physical world. Thus the description of the movements of the plant in 'the way of the basil' represents the actual birth of the spirit of this plant. The description of the house of *muu* in 'the way of birth' is to be understood as a simultaneous description of the body of the childbearing woman and a real spirit house.[27]

While figurative-metaphorical language is clearly an aspect of Kuna curing and magical *ikarkana*, it is not as crucial to the functioning of these *ikarkana* as it is in 'gathering house' discourse, where metaphors are creatively adapted and manipulated. Thus Kuna magical language cannot be productively analyzed by focusing exclusively on metaphors

Table 1. Figurative Vocabulary in Curing and Magical *Ikarkana*

Word	Meaning in *Ikar*	Colloquial Meaning
kurkin	brainpower	hat
inna ipet	Kuna person	owner of the *inna*
urwetule	evil spirit, sickness	angry person
alulukwale	red	firelike
ansuelu	fangs of snake	hook
siku	fangs of snake	arrow
puti	fangs of snake	blowgun
kole	to speak	to call

and metaphorical relationships, as Tambiah has analyzed Trobriand magical language, Rosaldo Ilongot magical language, or Howe Kuna 'gathering house' language.[28]

WHAT MAKES CURING AND MAGIC WORK

In describing the Kuna system of curing and the related magical control of spirits and objects, I have focused on the verbal properties of curing and magical *ikarkana*. It is also useful to ask what makes the system effective, what makes it work. The Kuna share with other American Indian societies the existence of curing specialists who perform their duties by means of communication with the spirit world. But whereas in many of these societies, especially in tropical forest South America, specialists make extensive use of drugs and induced trances, the Kuna employ neither. Rather, the spirit world is controlled solely by means of the performance of *ikarkana* by their specialists, the 'ikar knowers.'

One way in which the *ikarkana* are conceived is as an *apsoket* (conversation) between the 'knower' and the spirits. The name of the most spectacular of all these *ikarkana*, that of mass curing and the exorcising of evil spirits, is derived from the word *apsoket*. The *ikarkana* are also 'counsel,' explicit directions on how to carry out the bidding of the performer. In this 'counsel,' the performer speaks directly to the spirits in their own language. He demonstrates intimate knowledge of them by describing their origin, their home, their various names, the parts of their bodies, and their daily activities. Having convinced them in this way that he knows them, the specialist is able to control them. This is achieved by describing and narrating a series of events. Because of this narration and simultaneous with it, the events described occur in the spirit world.[29] As a result of the performance of the *ikar*, the spirits then bring about the desired result in the physical world—the calming of a fever, the disappearance of a headache, a successful hunt, or the grabbing of a snake. Verbal control is magical control.

Kuna magic involves no abracadabra, hocus-pocus, unintelligibility, or weirdness, as Malinowski thought should be everywhere characteristic of magic.[30] Although not understood by noninitiates, curing and magical *ikarkana* are definitely understood by spirits and are clearly intelligible in the sense that they can be analyzed phoneme by phoneme, morpheme by morpheme, word by word, line by line, verse by verse, and stanza by stanza. In these *ikarkana*, grammar, rhetoric, speech play, poetry, and magic intersect. In the verbal mediation among humans, nature, and the world of spirits, grammar becomes poetry and poetry becomes magic.

This is how the *ikarkana* work with regard to interaction between the 'ikar knower' and the spirit or object. What about Kuna individuals and Kuna society more generally? How does Kuna curing work psychologically and sociologically? Those who are not 'ikar knowers' do not generally understand the *ikarkana*, which in any case are not addressed to them. Yet they have ample opportunity to see and hear them performed, either in actual curing, whether for their own benefit or for that of friends or members of their family, or in the learning, teaching, or practicing by 'ikar knowers' or students. So the existence, efficacy, verbal artistry, and general importance of these *ikarkana* are constantly brought to public attention. And, while ordinary Kuna may not understand an *ikar* in absolute detail, they are quite aware of its purpose and general structure. And to varying degrees they understand some of the *ikar*, ranging from a few words here and there to whole passages.

Thus, the psychological efficacy of *ikarkana* depends on individuals' knowledge of and belief in the general features of the process rather than on a comprehension of its minute referential and symbolic details. Furthermore, the repetitive, incantatory, and euphonic nature of these *ikarkana* renders them mentally relaxing. Performed by a specialist in whom the patient has the utmost confidence and combined with the administration of actual medicine, the *ikarkana* usually prove to be quite effective. Thus Lévi-Strauss' interesting analysis of a Kuna curing text is both wrong and right. Lévi-Strauss is incorrect in his assumption that the patient understands the language and symbolism of the text. But he is no doubt correct in the more abstract sense that the patient's general knowledge of the nature of the text and how it works is psychologically effective.[31]

So, while the Kuna curing and magical system is the specialty of certain ritualists, it is also a public affair, a constant part of Kuna life for all to see, appreciate, and respect. And since for the most part it does not contradict but complements the changing world—with its new diseases, medicines, and hospitals—it is quite adaptable.

VARIATION AND ADAPTATION

Given that *ikarkana* are passed on by rote memorization from teacher to student, they constitute a most traditional aspect of Kuna life. Viewed in this way, Kuna curing and magical events seem to contrast with events of the 'gathering house' with regard to flexibility and adaptability. And to a certain degree this is true. The most striking aspect of 'gathering house' chanting as well as speaking is their focus on creative adaptation, on the ability of individuals—'chiefs' and followers, women and men, young and old—to perform verbally for long periods of time, on the spot, with no preparation, taking a theme, an idea, or a metaphor and developing it to make it fit the particular issue at hand. In curing and magical *ikarkana*, on the other hand, the texts appropriate for particular diseases or other purposes are putatively fixed, and the 'ikar knowers' make changes, really choices, in these fixed texts only according to the origin of the disease or the particular goal of the *ikar*.

Nevertheless, as is characteristic of Kuna life in general and speaking in particular, there is room for change and adaptation within the tradition of continuity. This is possible because of variations (both in the approach to disease and related matters and in the existence of differing traditions of the same *ikar*), conflicts, new situations, and a generally eclectic attitude on the part of the Kuna.

Varying approaches to curing can cause differences of opinion. A particularly good example has to do with snakebite. This is a very sensitive area in that the Kuna are agriculturalists and the jungle mainland is populated by a number of very dangerous snakes. There are curing specialists who believe that in the treatment of snakebites, because evil spirits abound, the entire village must be involved. In extreme cases this might mean the prohibition of work in the jungle and the prohibition of noise in the village, especially at night. Radios are silenced, people are told to walk barefoot, and 'gatherings' are either canceled or held in a whisper; no chanting is permitted. Other specialists, however, disagree. They hold that if a curing specialist is adequately trained, if he is truly an expert, he should be able to cure a snakebite victim rapidly without the need to disrupt village life—medicine, *ikarkana*, and 'secrets' should suffice.

These differences can lead to conflict, especially when the principal exponents of the different approaches live in the same village. Just such a situation occurred in 1970 in Mulatuppu, when the village gave a scholarship to a respected curing specialist, Olowitinappi, to permit him to study snakebite medicine with a renowned expert in a distant village.... Just after his departure, a man was bitten by a snake on his evening hunting trip to the jungle. The victim was placed in the care of another curing specialist, who insisted on the village-wide measures described above. When the patient did not get better, there was considerable tension on the island. Evening 'gatherings' heatedly (though in a whisper) debated whether the methods were effective. Some men argued that, when Olowitinappi returned, he would be able to handle such cases without all the village-wide fuss. Finally, the man's family decided to take him to a missionary-run hospital in another village, six hours away by motorboat.

The case of the snakebite victim is a good illustration of the role of variation in the Kuna curing system. On the one hand, variation is a source of conflict, both between individual specialists and between factions within the community. On the other hand, both variation and conflict provide opportunities for change and adaptation. And both relate to empirical reality—the important fact that sometimes cures do not work. Another case provides a useful illustration.

In March of 1979, Armando, a Mulatuppu 'chief' and an active political leader in the eastern region of San Blas, fell seriously ill. His friend Richards was called on to perform 'the way of the hat' for him. Richards is a respected curing specialist who often publicly affirms his abilities, especially claiming that he is the best performer of an *ikar* on the island or that his version is the best. At the same time, other versions of 'the way of the hat' are known in Sasartii-Mulatuppu; in fact, [they are] commonly known. While each version is, from an official point of view, equally effective, there is always the possibility that on a particular occasion one version or one performer might be more successful than another.[32] The performance of long *ikarkana* such as 'the way of the hat' is, furthermore, time-consuming and tiring. It was thus decided that

Richards and another 'medicinal specialist' and 'knower,' Mastayans, would alternate performing the *ikar* on successive afternoons. In this way, potential conflict between the two respected specialists, while not necessarily avoided, was channeled into a cooperative, if nonetheless competitive, medical team. As it turned out, Armando was slow to recover, his illness became the subject of a 'gathering house' discussion, and it was decided that he should go to the local government-run hospital. The argument was that, while the Kuna approach is effective, it takes longer than Panamanian medicine; since it was important for Armando to resume his official duties and responsibilities as soon as possible, it was best that he go to the hospital. Armando was thus cured by an effective combination of native Kuna specialists and a modern Panamanian hospital, all potentially in conflict with one another.

A good example of variation and especially adaptation which functions to maintain tradition within the Kuna curing system is 'medicine counsel.' This set of *ikarkana* is used not only for traditional Kuna medicine but for any object or substance which is to be used as medicine. It is the 'medicine counsel' which renders the medicinal potential inherent in an object effective and gives it life, by explaining to it how to go about its work. This openness with regard to the class of medicine and its relationship to 'medicine counsels' makes it possible to accept and welcome non-Kuna, western medicine. From the Kuna point of view, it is quite possible for there to be medicine other than the plants that 'medicinal specialists' gather in the jungle; many objects are potentially medicinal. The skill of the 'medicinal specialist' consists not only in knowing what plants have medicinal value but in being able to counsel them and thus empower them. Similarly, the *ikarkana* used in the curing of disease are not in opposition to the medicine which is also used in the cure—they are complementary. The *ikar* advises the spirits of good to struggle against the spirits of evil. The *ikar* and the medicine work together. The more the patients have going for them, the better. So a cure can be effective by using Kuna medicine, Kuna *ikarkana*, and non-Kuna medicine, all at the same time. This is something which the Kuna understand perfectly well but outsiders have trouble grasping. An incident is representative of this situation.

Recently a hospital was built on the mainland near Mulatuppu. After it began operating, the Panamanian minister of health visited it to see how things were working out. He was greeted by a local 'chief,' to whom he made long speeches explaining how lucky the Indians were to have a government which built them schools and hospitals, supplied them with medicine, and so on, so that they could progress. The 'chief' responded that he agreed and that his people were most thankful. The minister of health then took off in his goverment helicopter, in time to have lunch in the capital. The 'chief' set off on his typical morning chore, gathering medicine in the jungle—he is also a respected 'medicinal specialist' in the community.

There are also various ways in which new *ikarkana* can develop, if the need arises. And needs do arise—new diseases occur, old diseases get harder to cure, and people need new skills. Although *ikarkana* are primarily transmitted through teaching, there is another way as well. Certain specialists, especially 'seers,' can learn *ikarkana* in their dreams. In such dreams, the 'stick doll' representatives of the spirit world or *serkan* (deceased persons) teach the 'seer' the *ikar*. The 'seer' is then capable of teaching it to others, who become 'knowers' as well. It is because the *ikarkana* are in their language and are in their realm of knowledge that the spirit representatives are able to teach them to 'seers'. But, while these *ikarkana* are traditional in theme, form, and content, they can be new, either new versions of existing *ikarkana* or totally new.[33] They might thus be effective in ways that old *ikarkana* no longer are.

The learning of *ikarkana* in dreams is not always believed or accepted by all members of the community. Specialists who have learned their *ikarkana* by the long, tedious, and difficult method of apprenticing themselves to a teacher are particularly skeptical. It is in moments of crisis especially that representatives of the spirit world tend to appear in the dreams not only of 'seers' but of other village leaders and ritual specialists as well, in order to comment on and criticize aspects of Kuna life and behavior and to propose solutions to village problems.

Thus curing and magic can be seen as an essentially traditional aspect of Kuna life, involving a set of ritual specialists, a secretive, somewhat archaic language, and a set of *ikarkana* passed on from 'knowers' to their students. These *ikarkana* derive their efficacy from the belief that the spirits of good and evil can be controlled when properly advised, in their language with the appropriate memorized text. At the same time, the system is not frozen. There are openness and adaptability; there is always the possibility for change and development in order to meet new situations and new problems in the context of tradition.

Notes

1. For a fuller analysis of the 'mass-curing ritual', see Howe (1976).

2. These objects acquired their potential medicinal value as a result of a previous 'counsel', the one they received from God at the world's beginning. I am indebted to James Howe for calling this to my attention.

3. If the performer even thinks about women while chanting, he will attract women instead of animals.

4. There is some terminological overlap here. The 'souls' are at times also referred to as 'secrets.'

5. Portion of 'the way of the basil', performed by Pranki Pilos of Mulatuppu.

6. Portion of 'the way of the wasp', performed by Pranki Pilos of Mulatuppu.

7. Portion of 'the way of the snake', performed by Pranki Pilos of Mulatuppu.

8. Portion of 'the way of the hot pepper,' performed by Nipakkinya of Mulatuppu.

9. The use of the term stanza, like line and verse, for Kuna poetic-discourse units is adapted from Hymes (1977), which discusses Chinookan narrative structure.

10. Portion of 'the way of the basil,' performed by Pranki Pilos of Mulatuppu.

11. Portion of 'the way of the basil,' performed by Olowitinappi of Mulatuppu.

12. Portion of 'the way of the rattlesnake,' performed by Olowitinappi of Mulatuppu.

13. Portion of 'the way of the bamboo cane,' performed by Manuel Campos of Mulatuppu.

14. Portion of 'the way of the making of *inna*,' performed by Mastaletat of Mulatuppu.

15. Portion of 'the way of the balsa wood,' performed by Pranki Pilos of Mulatuppu.

16. From 'the way of the snake,' performed by Pranki Pilos of Mulatuppu.

17. From 'the way of the wasp,' performed by Pranki Pilos of Mulatuppu.

18. I include identical repetition as a type of parallelism here—although other students of parallelism might not—because of its role in the overall parallelistic patterning and structuring of Kuna magical *ikarkana*.

19. Here and elsewhere in this section, certain lines are indented in order to illustrate the parallelistic patterns. The blank spaces left by the indentations should *not* be interpreted to signify silences or other units of performance or structure.

20. From 'the way of the basil,' performed by Pranki Pilos of Mulatuppu.

21. From 'the way of the snake,' performed by Pranki Pilos of Mulatuppu.

22. Portion of 'the way of the cross,' performed by Mastayans of Mulatuppu.

23. Portion of 'the way of the cooling off,' performed by Pranki Pilos of Mulatuppu.

24. See Jakobson (1960), in which poetry is defined as the projection of paradigmatic axes onto syntagmatic axes.

25. I am grateful to Dennis Tedlock for pointing out this interesting issue. On preliterate oral memorization systems, see Goody (1977) and Yates (1966).

26. Portion of 'the way of the basil,' performed by Pranki Pilos of Mulatuppu.

27. Chapin (1983) argues convincingly that the descriptions contained in the *ikarkana* are to be taken both literally (as actually occurring in the spirit world) and figuratively (as metaphors for the real, physical world).

28. See Howe (1977), Rosaldo (1975), and Tambiah (1968).

29. Kuna magical *ikarkana* are thus performative in the sense of Austin (1965), in that they not only describe actions or events but, through their correct (memorized) narration, actually cause them to occur. 'Gathering house' discourse, by contrast, is exhortative rather than performative.

30. See Malinowski (1935).

31. See Chapin (1976) and Lévi-Strauss (1949).

32. Smith, a respected Mulatuppu '*ikar* knower,' knows two versions of 'the way of birth,' used to alleviate difficult childbirths. One version is longer than the other; Smith considers this longer version to be more powerful and effective. He learned the two versions from two different teachers in two different villages. The longer version cost him more money to learn.

33. These *ikarkana* are in fact new, but according to Kuna doctrine they are old. They have existed in the spirit world but were locally unknown. I am indebted to James Howe for pointing this out.

References

Austin, J. L. 1965. *How to Do Things with Words*. New York: Oxford University Press.

Chapin, Macpherson 1976. *Muu ikala*: Cuna birth ceremony. In Philip Young and James Howe (eds.), *Ritual and Symbol in Native Central America*, pp. 57–65. University of Oregon Anthropological Papers 9.

———. 1983. Curing among the San Blas Kuna of Panama. Ph.D. dissertation. University of Arizona.

Goody, Jack 1977. *The Domestication of the Savage Mind*. Cambridge, Cambridge University Press.

Howe, James 1976. Smoking out the spirits: A Cuna exorcism. In Philip Young and James Howe (eds.), *Ritual and Symbol in Native Central America*, pp. 67–76. University of Oregon Anthropological Papers 9.

———. 1977. Carrying the village: Cuna political metaphors. In J. David Sapir and J. Christopher Crocker (eds.), *The Social Use of Metaphor*, pp. 132–163. Philadelphia: University of Pennsylvania Press.

Hymes, Dell 1977. Discovering oral performance and measured verse in American Indian narrative. *New Literary History* 8: 431–457.

Jakobson, Roman 1960. Closing statement: Linguistics and poetics. In Thomas A. Sebeok (ed.), *Style in Language*, pp. 350–377. Cambridge, MA.: MIT Press.

Lévi-Strauss, Claude 1949. L'efficacité symbolique. *Revue de l'Histoire des Religions* 135: 5–27.

Malinowski, Bronislaw 1935. *Coral Gardens and Their Magic*. Vol. 2: *The Language of Magic and Gardening*. London: Allen and Unwin.

Rosaldo, Michelle 1975. It's all uphill: The creative metaphors of Ilongot magical spells. In Mary Sanches and Ben G. Blount (eds.), *Sociocultural Dimensions of Language Use*, pp. 177–203. New York: Academic Press.

Tambiah, S. J. 1968. The magical power of words. *Man* 3: 175–208.

Yates, Frances 1966. *The Art of Memory*. Chicago: University of Chicago Press.

Post-Reading Questions / Activities

- Look at one of the narrations carefully. What is its function? When is it spoken? What are the linguistic structures that order it? Discuss their parallelism.
- How would you characterize the way Kuna think of the relationship between language and curing? Is this entirely unfamiliar to you? Why?
- Compare curing systems in a number of societies. How do people in those societies explain what happens to make curing happen? Why does Sherzer disagree with Malinowski's characterization of magic?

Vocabulary

ikarkana: (Kuna) ways, texts

Suggested Further Reading

Bauman, Richard, and Joel Sherzer, eds. 1989 [1974]. *Explorations in the Ethnography of Speaking*. Cambridge and New York: Cambridge University Press.

Evans-Pritchard, E. E. 1937. *Witchcraft, Oracles and Magic Among the Azande*. Oxford: Clarendon Press.

Feld, Steven. 1982. *Sound and Sentiment: Birds, Weeping, Poetics, and Song in Kaluli Expression*. Philadelphia: University of Pennsylvania Press.

Gumperz, John J., and Dell Hymes, eds. 1986 [1972]. *Directions in Sociolinguistics: The Ethnography of Communication*. Oxford: Blackwell.

Lévi-Strauss, Claude. 1963a. "The Effectiveness of Symbols." In *Structural Anthropology*, translated by Claire Jacobson and Brooke Grundfest Schoepf. New York: Basic Books, pp. 186–205.

————. 1963b. "The Sorcerer and His Magic." In *Structural Anthropology*, translated by Claire Jacobson and Brooke Grundfest Schoepf. New York: Basic Books, pp. 167–185.

Malinowski, Bronislaw. 1923. "The Problem of Meaning in Primitive Languages." In *The Meaning of Meaning*, edited by C. K. Ogden and I. A. Richards. New York: Harcourt, Brace.

————. 1935. *Coral Gardens and Their Magic: A Study of the Methods of Tilling the Soil and of Agricultural Rites in the Trobriand Islands*. New York: American Book Company.

————. 1948. *Magic, Science, and Religion, and Other Essays*. Boston: Beacon Press.

Sherzer, Joel. 1983. *Kuna Ways of Speaking: An Ethnographic Perspective*. Austin: University of Texas Press.

————, and Regna Darnell. 1986 [1972]. "Outline Guide for the Ethnographic Study of Speech Use." In *Directions in Sociolinguistics: The Ethnography of Communication*. Edited by John J. Gumperz and Dell Hymes. Oxford: Blackwell, pp. 548–554.

Tambiah, S. J. 1968. "The Magical Power of Words." *Man* 3: 175–208.

A rich website that includes recordings of Kuna discourse, performances, and other information is: The Archive of the Indigenous Languages of Latin America. http://ailla.utexas.org.

CHAPTER 37

Naming Practices and the Power of Words in China

Susan D. Blum

(1997)

Kinship or family relations have been at the center of anthropological research for more than a century. How people are related, and then how they act once they are related, as well as variations in human views of relationships, are an unendingly fascinating topic. The research on property among Iroquois of the influential nineteenth-century anthropologist Lewis Henry Morgan depended largely on his understanding of the responsibilities that accompanied kin relations. This led, ultimately, to his seeking information about kinship terms worldwide, and to both his Systems of Consanguinity and Affinity of the Human Family *and to his systematizing work,* Ancient Society, *which undergirded almost a century of anthropological studies.*

Key to our understanding of human relations are the terms we use for and with those relations, whether we use what we would consider names or the commonly used kinship terms.

In terms of naming, we might wish to distinguish reference (how we refer to someone) and address (how we address someone). The terms used are rather different. Further, in many cases we have a variety of relationships with people, and can choose how to make use of one or another in a given case.

This article argues that rather than naming being a single once-and-for-all affair of choosing a name for a baby, naming as practice occurs daily in all social interactions in China. It points out that relationships are constructed, in part, through the choice of title or form of address used at a particular moment in a particular interaction. Moreover, these utterances are too important to be left to the whims of young children, so children are shown, exactly, how to address the important people in their lives. Despite an egalitarian ideology that governed China during its most radical and revolutionary years, there was never a challenge to the idea that relationships are frequently unequal. The term comrade (tongzhi) *which was proposed to replace virtually all social titles waned; it is now used for gay partners.*

Reading Questions

- What is meant by "naming practices"? How are such practices observed? What considerations are made when people engage in naming practices?
- Who has the responsibility in a relationship for uttering the proper naming term? How do people know what name to use with someone else?
- Why is inequality not considered anathema to participants in the Chinese naming system?
- Why are kin terms often preferred to personal names?

Susan D. Blum, "Naming Practices and the Power of Words in China." *Language in Society* 26 (3) (1997): 357–379.

> Nets are for catching fish; after one gets the fish, one forgets the net. Traps are for catching rabbits; after one gets the rabbit, one forgets the trap. Words are for getting meaning; after one gets the meaning, one forgets the words. Where can I find people who have forgotten words, and have a word with them?
>
> (ZHUĀNGZI, *chap. 26*)

Names are often regarded as one-time labels fixed to solid objects, useful for identifying them but without any real substance or inherent interest. Philosophers of language, anthropologists, linguists, and ordinary people have often been drawn to the topic, each with their own idea of the origins of names: Adam created them in the Judeo-Christian tradition; the mythical sage-emperor Fúxī discovered the Eight Trigrams (*bā guà*) that developed into characters in one version of the Chinese myth; "society" creates them in a sociological interpretation; a child's parents select names in a commonsense explanation. Contemporary structural linguists, from Saussure on, write of the arbitrariness of the sign (but see Benveniste 1966b, Friedrich 1979). Most assume the primacy of the thing/object/signified, and the subsequence of the label/name/signifier. The underlying ontology of a split between substance and surface appears in much analysis of language (see Derrida 1982 for a critique of this position), and in mainstream anthropological considerations of language use. When the distance between word and object appears collapsed, practices revolving around language are often termed "magical"—notwithstanding almost a century of critique of the category of magic as opposed, say, to science (Malinowski 1935, 1948, O'Keefe 1982).

[Here] I analyze a wide range of practices revolving around naming in a very well-known society: China. I use the term "naming" as the superordinate category, within which I include the categories of "proper names," "kinship terms," and pronouns.[1] The ambiguity of the term "naming" between a nominal and a verbal reading emphasizes that this is an active set of practices rather than a static system.

In the process I hope to demonstrate an alternative approach to conceptualizing naming practices and indeed language use in general, while explaining some specific features of Chinese language use. Chinese naming practices reveal a view of the Chinese person as thoroughly embedded in a world of speakers and hearers whose relationships to each other and the world are constituted through speaking certain terms, and where sound, object, and name are in some important senses combined. I will show further that what accounts for the success of a language act is not that it springs spontaneously from an emotion-filled, intention-driven, sincere individual, as might be presumed in the West, but that it demonstrates respect through willingness to be educated by others—often by rehearsal through verbatim routines, which function also as a sort of three-way negotiation of place in the hierarchy. Language acts in China are seen as continuous with other sorts of action rather than as belonging to a separate domain. As such, they are managed as other behavior is, and socialized as other forms of social practice are—through imitation and direct

repetition. Finally, I will show that solidarity is built through affectionate affirmation of hierarchy, and that hierarchy is often seen as involving no contradiction to affection.

The Chinese term *míng* 'name' refers to both proper and common names, including people's names; in political philosophy, it often refers to public or social roles. The most famous discussion of the importance of appropriate naming is in the *Analects* of Confucius (3rd century B.C.E.) with its discussion of *zhèng míng*, usually translated 'rectification of names' (Waley 1938:171, D. C. Lau 1979:118, Huáng 1990). Throughout the Warring States period (5th through 3rd centuries B.C.E.) political philosophers contemplated the proper way to conduct moral and effective government. Correct naming was the proper method for *rú*-ists ("Confucians") and Legalists. Other philosophical schools, including those of the Logicians and Daoists, were more playful. Thus Zhuāngzi argued (Guō 1983:944) that one could forget a name once one attained the thing to which it referred; and that before language there was a real world, so the linguistic distinctions over which people fought so hard were really beside the point (see Guō 1983, Hansen 1992:291, and cf. Granet 1934, Munro 1969, Hansen 1983, Graham 1989, Makeham 1994).

The importance of personal naming also is visible throughout imperial China. Reign periods were segments of emperors' rules that had propitious names; a single ruler could have several different reign periods, changing the names of the periods to change the fortunes of the empire. Emperors' personal names were powerful, tabooed both during life and after death. If their names contained ordinary syllables, like *guāng* 'glorious', that word had to be replaced in all written texts.

Public figures had names that were public currency. By the Sòng dynasty (960–1279), writers commonly selected *zì* 'style names' or *hào* 'courtesy names' that indicated something about their character that they wished to have known, or about their biography. Sū Shì, for instance, selected his style name as Dōngpō 'Eastern Slope'; a famous dish is known as "Dongpo's soup" after a recipe he described in an essay. The Míng philosopher Wáng Shǒurén's selection of his style name, Yángmíng 'bright yang-ness', indicates the centrality of illumination to his thought. Ever since, the name Yángmíng is widely known to refer to that thinker. The mountain just north of Taibei, Yángmíng Shān, is named for him.

Philosophical ruminations about the nature of naming pervade China's intellectual history. In recent years, Mao insisted that what counted was practice, rather than idealism and intellectual work. Nevertheless, the 20th century focus has been on selecting appropriate names for individuals.

Are they "enemies of the people"? What kind of "contradiction" (i.e., conflict) exists in a particular case? Assigning roles has been a central activity of contemporary China; those who stray have to be 'rectified' (*zhèng*), using the term of the Warring States thinkers, though in this case it is the PERSON who most critically must be rectified, not the name. Crimes are assigned to appropriate categories such as disagreement, or counter-revolution. Clearly, the place of naming has had significant ramifications for much of public life throughout China's long history. However, the remainder of this [discussion] does not refer to philosophical writings on names, but rather attempts to account for patterns in observable naming behavior.

The analysis here focuses on the contemporary mainland of China, and on the political economic circumstances that surround the use of language. I add material reported for other Chinese societies, especially Taiwan, when this helps explain naming practices I have observed. This account is based in part on fieldwork conducted in Kunming, capital of Yunnan province in southwest China, as well as other stays in the People's Republic of China (PRC) and Taiwan over the course of the last 14 years, and on other written analyses of naming practices in China. I also sent a general inquiry out on the Internet in 1996 over the H-ASIA network, soliciting comments on contemporary PRC naming practices and speculating about a possible return of more "traditional" practices.

I begin with a routine which I have observed hundreds of times,[2] and which goes something like this. In the presence of C (father's father), A (parent) prompts B (child) to speak:

A (parent):	*Jiào "yéye."*	Say "Grandfather."
B (child):	*Yéye.*	Grandfather.
	or	
A (parent):	*Jiào "yéye zàijiàn."*	Say "Goodbye grandfather."
B (child):	*Yéye zàijiàn.*	Goodbye grandfather.

Jiào 'call', meaning both 'address someone as' and 'utter', opens the routine, signaling that what follows is to be repeated verbatim. The intonation of the repeated phrase is often fairly flat, not enthusiastic—because, I believe, what matters is not the heartfelt depth of the utterance, but the mere fact of its being stated. It is also meaningful not merely because it gauges the child's knowledge, but because it evokes compliance and produces the desired object: the spoken kinship term. Such routines, for greetings and partings in particular, are common in Chinese communities and persist into the child's adulthood, when it is no longer caregivers but the all-important *zhōngjiānrén* 'middle-person, intermediary' who gives these instructions. The importance of knowing and UTTERING the proper kinship term is illustrated by the ubiquity of these routines. I will place this example in the context of other possible forms of address and reference, accounting for the importance of the utterance of kinship terms by juniors through their ability to invoke prototypes of relationships.

KINSHIP TERMS

Kinship terms are the ultimate expression of solidarity. Many anthropologists who have written about "classificatory" kinship (Morgan 1871, Schneider 1984, Trautmann 1987) have shown that, in some societies, all persons are assigned the nearest kinship term in order to create a meaningfully populated world (cf. Witherspoon 1977:88, Kondo 1990:11–26, Chagnon 1992).[3] Even strange outsiders like anthropologists are often assigned to one group or another (Bell 1993:18–21), permitting persons in small communities to have an identity. This has been referred to rather problematically as "fictive" kinship. In the case of anthropologists who look vastly different from those among whom they work, it is easy enough to recognize the fictitious nature of the relationship; but calling native terms "fictive" suggests that only the anthropologist's system reflects "reality"—a reality where "blood" relations are paramount—while those participating are somehow simple-minded and ignorant of the real state of affairs (see Bowen 1964:64, 74, 75).

Chinese kinship was a general problem in anthropology for a time; even Kroeber wrote an analysis of it (1933). The Chinese kinship terms are often considered classificatory, of the "bifurcate-collateral" type (Kroeber 1952:192). Friends and patrilateral cousins call one another by sibling terms, e.g., *mèimei* 'Younger sister'; friends of the family are called "Aunt" and "Uncle," while older women on the street are called *pópo* 'Grandmother'.

Yet considering kinship relations to be emergent in interaction, rather than reflected or expressed by use of kinship terms, clarifies our opening puzzle: only by speaking the terms does the relationship emerge (Mannheim & Tedlock 1995:8). Prototypes of the expression-construction are viewed daily; rare is the family drama on television that does not end with some scene like that of a tearful child murmuring "Mama, Ma" as her mother dies, moves away on the train, or walks off. Movies and TV dramas are filled with dialog that may consist of little more than the exchange of kinship terms—and these evoke sobs from audiences. The use of such terms in address is mandatory for the closest relationships; it is preferable for medium-distance ones; and it is usable even with strangers, such as old women from whom one wishes to ask directions. The use of pronouns, which is quite common in many languages for addressing people of all different classes, has rather limited scope in China, in contrast to kinship terms. In fact, it is often considered insulting and impudent to use a pronoun. But kinship terms may be too intimate in some cases, and a junior may use a proper title instead.

In most cases lexical reciprocity exists, an automatic pair of relationships signaled by kinship terms and by some titles: *Māma* 'mother' implies *háizi* 'child', *gēge* 'older brother' implies *dìdi* 'younger brother' or *mèimei* 'younger sister', *lǎo X* 'elder/superior surname-X' implies *xiǎo Y* 'younger/inferior surname-Y', *pópo* 'grandmother' implies *sūnzi/sūnnǚ* 'grandson/granddaughter', *lǎoshi* 'teacher' implies *xuésheng* 'student'. But reciprocity does not mean actual symmetry;

a senior can use the junior's name, but the junior can only use the proper (kinship) term. The kinship terms referring to the junior are rarely used in address, except sometimes in melodrama (Chao 1956:237). THUS IT FALLS TO THE JUNIOR TO NAME THE RELATIONSHIP AND ASSENT TO THE HIERARCHY. The junior must desire seniors with whom to maintain solid, affectionate relationships; and these are by nature, in the Chinese case, hierarchical. Reminiscent of the Japanese notion of *amae*, affectionate dependence of a junior on a senior (Doi 1971), children's earliest experiences include the willing act of naming their seniors.

In contrast to the way FACE is usually regarded, the junior in a close relationship confers face on the senior, especially before a third party. Indeed, the prototypical case described above of addressing others—visible throughout the life cycle in China—involves at least three participants.

For children, a parent—often a mother, but also possibly another caregiver—initiates the exchange. The child does her part, and the elder kinsperson receives the utterance as a kind of gift. Teachers similarly remind their young students to address visitors; *Āyí shūshu zàijiàn!* 'Goodbye, aunt(s) (*āyí*) and uncle(s) (*shūshu*)!' In the traditional literature on speech act theory and linguistic analysis, the prototypical exchange is of two equal partners (but see Goffman [1979] 1981a:129–30); in China, however, it seems to be a hierarchy of three graded participants, seeking to determine places for themselves vis-à-vis one another. Animators of authors' words speaking to a third person are seen as in no way less "authentic" or "genuine" than someone speaking alone and from the heart. Here the contrast with a generalized Western linguistic ideology is sharp: the intention or originality of an utterance is much less central than mastery of a form through practice.

Failures occur not when the junior somehow doesn't mean what is said, but rather when the term is not uttered. When a child refuses to perform—a rare occurrence in my experience—there is often much consternation on the part of the parent. The person who should have been named may say *Méi guānxi, tā hái xiǎo* 'It doesn't matter, s/he's young.' But learning to be a full person presupposes mastery of this kinship-naming routine. This hierarchical, familial relationship is the ultimate endpoint of solidarity, in which a kinship term MUST BE UTTERED to acknowledge, illustrate, and create the desired relationship.

The same principle is visible when a young woman marries into a family. The essential transformative moment occurs—not, as in the US, in an overt performative statement *I do* [agree to be and am hereby married]—but when she speaks the kinship terms appropriate for a husband and wife to use. She becomes a wife by uttering the terms for his relatives. The film *Small Happiness* (Hinton 1984) has a memorable scene where a young bride in North China is forced to *kètóu* (kneel and bow her head, preferably by knocking it on the ground) as her husband's relative reads the kinship terms of the husband's relatives; she protests and resists. This is often seen as an educational ritual in which the bride LEARNS the terms; but it may also be regarded as performative. While the resistance seems somewhat stylized, that does not necessarily make it less genuine.[5] The likely explanation is that the sudden incorporation into a husband's family through the use of these kinship terms is painful and undesired. She has no genuine bond with these new affines; but by acquiescing to the terms, she is agreeing that such bonds will inevitably develop and the behavior associated with the terms will be produced—and she is assenting to enter a world in which she has little power. Concomitantly, the bonds with her natal family will weaken.[6]

Changing a title can change the relationship. Topley (1974:246–47) describes a certain diagnosis of incompatible horoscopes, accompanying physical symptoms of a culture-bound ailment in the Canton delta, similar to what Western pediatricians call "failure to thrive." This ailment is explained as stemming from a problematic relationship, a lack of bonding, between a mother and child. One cure is to change the term that the child uses for her mother:

> There is no real solution if such a child remains with its mother, but one could try to redefine the problem, adjusting the role to the behavior rather than behavior to the role. By changing the term of address, one suggests that the mother is not really the mother. The child is taught to call her either *a- tse*, "elder sister," *a-so*, "brother's wife," or *a-naai*, "wet- nurse"…I was told that when the term of address was modified, the child should not really treat its mother as elder sister or brother's wife, but the mother need not feel so bad if the child who did not call her mother was difficult to control.

The terms chosen as replacement indicate close relationships which are not as difficult as that between mother and child. This is said to modify the bad feelings the mother has if her child treats her poorly, not as a mother should properly be treated; it is more acceptable for a greater degree of indifference in a relationship between older sibling and younger sibling than between mother and child. The names—here, kinship terms—are not merely descriptive, but potent. They are inevitably hierarchical; selection is made among alternative forms of hierarchy that are nonetheless intimate and affectionate.

Socialization of children in China, as in many societies, includes much attention to the proper use of naming practices, as the above example suggests. But by contrast with many societies, the routine in which a third party clarifies the forms of address that should be used by the other two participants is not limited to childhood. It is not something that is supposed to be internalized and mastered, and thereafter volunteered by the two participants. The presence of a third party is presumed as the default case. After describing other forms of naming, I will return to this point.

NICKNAMES

Within a family and outside most official contexts, and before entering school, children are known by and addressed almost exclusively with nicknames. So-called *xiǎomíng* 'small names' or *nǎimíng* 'milk names' are often (in Mandarin) reduplicated syllables from a child's formal personal name, thus Chén Qīngzhū 'dark pearl' might be called Zhūzhu. (In Taiwanese—also called Fujianese, Hokkien, Southern Min, or Minnanhua—they are often prefaced by *a-*, and then one syllable of a child's personal name is used: Qīngzhū would be addressed as Āzhū.) These are the names by which a child is called at home by elders, and sometimes by all the family members. R. Watson 1986 and Farris 1988 have shown that adult women may have only such small names, which blur the boundary between proper and common nouns, e.g., *xiǎomèi* 'little sister' or *sānmèi* 'third daughter'. Farris shows how marked many of the terms referring to women are, even when words referring to women have related terms referring to men. But these are only loosely related pairs. Those referring to women often suggest sexuality and depravity, e.g., *biǎozi* 'prostitute, bitch'; in contrast, the insulting term for males is *biǎozi yǎngde* 'raised by a bitch' or *biǎozi érzi* 'son of a bitch' (Farris, 293–95). Alice Murong Pu Lin (1988) has a story titled "Grandmother Had No Name," which dealt with exactly this matter: her grandmother was known only as "wife of Li," and even Lin's mother did not know her own mother's name (she knew her only by the local term meaning Mom, *Muma*, p. 14). Kingston (1975:3–16) writes of an unmarried aunt who violated the family honor by having a child out of wedlock, and who was thereafter never referred to; her existence was presumed erased, her name never uttered.

Those at the lower end of the economic ladder, like women, may have no real formal name, or names that verge into mere designation (Alleton 1993:173, 205–8). Nicknames are sometimes recorded by officials sent to record the names of the illiterate villagers under their jurisdiction, but at their limit they may simply be kinship terms.

In contrast, upper-class men have often had a multitude of names—courtesy names, pen names, studio names, style names. They have also been certain of their "real" names. In Chinese traditional times (which were far from unitary), men of the elite classes often selected names for themselves to correspond to given attributes of their (desired) character, and these were included in their biographies as pen names.[7] Though this practice is in some ways obsolete, people in public life often change their names to reflect attitudes toward the world. The well-known political figure Dèng Xiǎopíng is unofficially reported to have had the original name Kàn Zégāo; his five children all use his adopted surname Dèng (Hsu 1982:351).[8] The 20th century writers Lǔ Xùn (born Zhōu Shùrén [J. Lau & H. Goldblatt 1995:xxxii]), Bā Jīn (Lǐ Fèigān [Lau & Goldblatt 1995:xxv]), Lǎo Shě (born Shū Qìngchūn [Lau & Goldblatt 1995:xxx]), and Máo Dùn (born Shěn Yànbīng [Lau & Goldblatt 1995:xxxiii]) all selected these as their public names—sometimes called Party names. The tightness of fit that many Westerners often claim to exist (or wish to exist) between their unitary individual essence and name appears more malleable for people in China. The more manipulation on the part of the name-holder, the higher the status.

Ordinary people's names, in contrast, appear to vary, and it is impossible to draw boundaries between types of naming practices. If some kinship terms become nicknames which are then recorded as formal names—or if people adopt politically fashionable names that give an impression of revolutionary ardor, and then pass them on to their children—then it is necessary to include within a single analysis all these naming practices. In a sense there is a single "system" or universe that includes social and occupational titles, pronouns, introductions, status, nicknames, and multiple names. Indeed, only now we arrive at "proper" names.

"PROPER" NAMES

Names are fascinating to people in China. They are discussed avidly and frequently, and have been written about voluminously. Hansen argues (1992, 4n.) that names (*míng*) rather than sentences are central to all Chinese philosophy—and that this fact distinguishes the Chinese approach to reality, which is more important than a theory of truth. Proper names in China have been dealt with in great detail by Alleton 1993, following earlier treatments by Chao 1956, Sung 1979, 1981, Liu 1981, R. Watson 1986, Wáng 1988, Zhào 1988, Chén 1990, and Erbaugh 1993. I will not repeat this information here, except to state that parents and grandparents (usually) select infants' names according to a given set of criteria: they should be auspicious; they are viewed as governing the child's fate in some ways; they should harmonize with the time, and often the place, of the child's birth; they may be changed if, through illness or misfortune, a diagnosis of mismatch with the name is made; they may indicate membership in a generation in a family of intellectuals; they may be female names which typically come from a much reduced and stereotypical stock, compared to that for male names; they may reflect changes in naming styles resulting from various political and intellectual trends.

However, what most analysts skim over is the very role of naming: after the first bestowing of a personal name, many other things are still done with names. People are accustomed to being addressed and referred to by an assortment of names, and they do not necessarily retain any of them as their "real" name or as the one that they feel reflects their identity. A friend in Kunming told me that though "her name" in Mandarin was Zhào Hóngdá, everyone called her Xiǎohóng ([Xiaohom] in Kunming dialect); to her, both dialect versions were acceptable. Another friend, a member of a minority group, had one "proper" name in her native Yi language, another in Kunming dialect, still another in Standard Mandarin; engaged to a foreign man who did not speak much Chinese, she had an English name ("Priscilla") by which he called her; most other foreigners called her with *xiǎo* (little) and her surname. Which one is her name? All of them, in a way. And there are other variants as well: her family called her by a familiar name at home, and school friends by yet another.

Personal names play very little role in the actual exchanges of everyday life, though they are often included in introductions (they do sit, baldly, on identification cards in the PRC, Taiwan, Hong Kong, and Singapore.)[10] When two people of approximately equal status and some education meet, in the absence of a mutual acquaintance who can perform the introduction, one person may say something like "I am Yang Jihua." The interlocutor will respond with a query about the characters constituting the name, since there are so many homophones in Chinese and the names may be made of virtually any words that are not inauspicious (Alleton 1993:21–32). But this will occur only with virtual equals: students in the same class, friends of friends, etc. In most other circumstances, a *zhōngjiānrén* 'middle-person, intermediary' will perform the introductions, which are followed by attempts to work out the relationships and settle on the proper title. This replicates the prototypical routine described at the beginning of this [chapter], where there are necessarily three participants and where the junior must utter the proper terms for the ensuing relationship:

A:	*Zhèiwèi shi Jì Chǎngzhǎng.*	This distinguished person (C) is Factory-head Ji.
B:	*Jì Chǎngzhǎng.*	(Repeating the surname and title)
C:	*Nǐ hǎo.*	Hello.

Repetition of the surname *Ji* with the title *Chǎngzhǎng* constitutes acknowledgment of the introduction and acceptance of this title; C's moving on to a greeting demonstrates that the relationships have been properly cared for. A person who will be called by a name that indicates speaker's superiority to that person, such as an employee, will be introduced by full name, and called either by full name or by a diminutive and the surname: *Xiǎo Wáng*, comparable to English use of surname alone (especially British: *Jones*).

A:	*Zhè shì Wáng Shěn.*	This is Wáng Shěn.
B:	*Xiǎo Wáng.*	[I am acknowledging you as] Wang (i.e., Hello).
C:	*Jì Chǎngzhǎng hǎo.*	Hello Factory-head (Mr.) Ji.

Assenting to the forms of address, each person utters them for the first time. The junior has the obligation to utter the form of naming, but is expected to say nothing else. In negotiating a new relationship, the participants will sometimes dispute the terms gently—the senior or superior perhaps reluctant to accept the honor and responsibility that follow greater distance. A young woman might say *Gūmā* 'Older aunt', and the older woman say *Jiào wǒ āyí* 'Call me āyí (younger aunt)'. Such struggles seem at first glance to be attempts to diminish any sense of hierarchy, but I suggest that we view it rather as an attempt to diminish the distance while retaining the hierarchy. The recipient of the correction tries to maintain the original greater distance, but only with difficulty. The names are murmured, rather than spoken in the same volume as other exchanges—thus marking this part of the exchange, the FRAME (Goffman 1981b: 174–78), conducted in metalinguistic terms about what will be said in the future, as a separate piece of discourse. It will be altered

only with great difficulty in the future.[11] In our putative prototypical case, the goal was to agree about participants' relative position and statement of these terms; but especially with "fictive" kinship, the positions are often unclear and require negotiation.

Instruction and guidance about these matters is often desired, but not forced. Children, but not only children, rely on others to help them figure out which term and which relationship is appropriate. In a novel about a Cantonese family in San Francisco's Chinatown, Fae Myenne Ng's protagonist (the native-born daughter of immigrants) describes her discomfort at being alone with her mother's new husband—not because of any sense of danger, but because she doesn't know how to address him: "This is what I'd worried about all through the bus ride up here: What to call him after they married. I expected Mah to give me instructions, but she didn't, and now Leon and I were alone" (Ng 1993:186). Though it is possible for a junior to ask directly *Wǒ zěnme jiào nǐ?* or *Wǒ zěnme chēnghu nǐ?* 'How do I address you?'— a metalinguistic act that occurs with great regularity—it is greatly preferable for a third person to give the instructions.

In China as elsewhere, one can disparage people by calling them by a lesser term than expected; or one can try to oblige others by calling them by an "undeserved" higher term. One can also flatter through choice of naming practice, and these strategies are often considered very carefully by adults. Jianying Zha, a writer born in China who came to the US as a young woman, returned to China as an adult to try to grasp and describe the contemporary climate. She reports deliberately choosing a title desired by her interlocutor in order to gain entry into a particular informant's good graces:

> I call her "Teacher Bei," instead of "Aunt Bei" as Chinese normally call somebody her age, because of a warning from the friend who introduced us: It is very important, he said, to make her feel that she belongs to the educated class and is someone with culture. Teacher Bei was so pleased by our visit and got to talking so much that she skipped her nap and made a big pot of tea. (Zha 1995:25)

Here the speaker is quite conscious of the flattery, but its effectiveness is nonetheless clear. Note too the inclusion in this brief discussion of "the friend who introduced us"; he had conferred with Zha about the proper way to address "Teacher Bei."

In a story by the contemporary author Zhāng Jié, a very calculating, middle-aged Communist party member named Yue meets a former classmate and current colleague while out jogging. He chooses his naming practices deliberately as well, but to bolster his own position, not to flatter his acquaintance:

> He caught up with Little Duan. They had called him "little" in college because he was the youngest in the class. Though he was growing bald now, Yue still addressed him this way. Since becoming section chief he had taken to prefacing the names of many of his subordinates with

"little." Apart from sounding fatherly, it also conveyed his own seniority. (Zhang 1986:65)

These two had been classmates (*tóngxué*) and hence had a relationship institutionalized as egalitarian. (This is something like age-mates in some African societies, though without the ritual rites of passage that are so anthropologically famous.) Classmates spend their entire time at the school together, moving from subject to subject while remaining in their classroom—a room for which they are responsible. Even in higher education, entering students take the same subjects, study together, graduate together, and often marry one another. (Indeed, the closeness of classmates is known as an unparalleled opportunity for young people of the opposite sex to meet. The many people in the countryside who leave school well before marriageable age, often after fifth grade—at age 12 or so—are aware of the fact that they have few opportunities to meet appropriate partners, and they rely on introductions from mutual acquaintances to succeed in setting up a marriage.)

Students at the same school but in different years are also *tóngxué*, but are clearly distinguished as in the class above (*xuéxiōng* 'older-brother student' and *xuéjiě* 'older-sister student') or the class below (*xuédì* 'younger-brother student' and *xuémèi* 'younger-sister student'), in contrast to *tóngbān tóngxué* 'classmates of the same class'.

Classmates keep in touch throughout their lives, having reunions whenever possible and helping one another through difficulties. During my last visit to China (1994), one of my husband's former students learned that we were there after a three-year absence, and on almost no notice—in a day—assembled a group of eight or so classmates who were now scattered throughout the city of Kunming. They had all graduated, a few were engaged (one is now married), and several had gone home to rural locations, but most kept track of one another. This is the most egalitarian relationship that a Chinese person encounters, and it also takes place in the setting most likely to include frequent hearing of people's full personal names. Hence classmates are likely to know one another's full names, and sometimes even to use them. As Chao points out (1956:239, 1968:514) spouses may even use these names to address one another, especially in certain circumstances: when a wife addresses her husband, before they have children and begin to use teknonyms, if the personal name is monosyllabic and thus bound, and if they met as classmates and grew accustomed to hearing and using the combination of surname with personal name. Clearly, these conditions are rarely all met, and other forms of naming are much more common. As in the vignette quoted above, we see that other forms of address may even be employed among classmates: some are selected as superior, others as junior.

This nuanced way of addressing even the most equal of people in China helps explain what might be seen as puzzling to Western linguists in China: avoidance of pronouns. While it might seem desirable to use pronouns for their social neutrality, I argue that this neutrality is precisely what

is UNDESIRABLE, indeed insupportable, to those who insist on maintaining strict hierarchy. This is most true when referring to exalted others, particularly in their presence.

PRONOUNS

Pronouns are names in the sense that they "stand in for names." We all know of the familiarity and slight insult used when a husband says, without antecedent, *She won't let me go to the game*. It is somewhat different when a student says of a professor, *She gave me a C on my paper*, without ever mentioning a "real name." (I think it reflects a desire to challenge the power of the professor, a challenge that would not be voiced in her presence.) Chinese pronouns are fascinating, especially when we bring in the written evidence of the last 2,000 years. They have varied from period to period, and in the present vary greatly among dialects (Chao 1956:240, Norman 1988:182, 190, 196, 203, 205, 208, 220, 223, 227, 234). Plural markers are fairly recent, and number does not have the importance that it has in English and other Indo-European languages. Only animate, human nouns may even be distinguished with a plural marker; but they may also be left unmarked. Pronouns are the only obligatory location for plural/singular distinctions, and this distinction is felt rather more loosely than in English; even pronouns can be considered neutral between singular and plural in some cases (e.g., *nín*; see below). Elsewhere I have treated Chinese pronouns in reference to ethnic groups (Blum 1994a, 1994b:296–310, 1998), showing that those groups that are seen as equivalent agents to Han speakers are more likely to be referred to in the 3rd person plural (*tāmen*), while those that are non-individuated and known as a type are more likely to be referred to in the singular (*ta*).

Still, pronouns are used more commonly in Chinese than, say, in Japanese (Hendry 1993, Bachnik & Quinn 1994) or in Javanese (Errington 1985, 1988); see also P. Brown & S. Levinson 1987. In some areas in North China, 1st person plural pronouns can be distinguished by inclusive and exclusive varieties (*zámen* 'we the people involved in this conversation' vs. *wǒmen* 'I and some people not now present'). A 2nd person polite pronoun (*nín*) is said to be unmarked for number—quite unlike the Indo-European pronouns for politeness, which seem to have come from the plural (R. Brown & A. Gilman 1960). Use of *nín* has increased steadily over the past decade, as the norms governing deference have increased and egalitarian ideals have been less enforced. (On pronouns see also Benveniste 1966a, Friedrich 1972, P. Brown & S. Levinson 1987, Urban 1996: 28–65.)

But use of pronouns is commonly seen as neutral with respect to hierarchy and relationship; and within the entire naming system, it is believed to confer little meaning. So it ends up conveying the meaning of LACK of respect; ultimately one flatters by using a title in place of a pronoun: *Lǎoshī shénme shíhou dào wǒmen zhèr lái?* 'When will the teacher come to our house?', which can only be translated as "When will [you] come to our home?"—though there is no literal "you" (*nǐ/nín*). Again, *Xiānsheng de shūfa wànshì wúxiǔ* 'Master's/Teacher's calligraphy will not fade for ten thousand generations'—i.e., "Your calligraphy, Teacher/Master, will endure through the generations." One uses names and forms of address in a manner identical to reference, as if honoring the addressee by speaking to a third person—which recalls the suggestion made earlier that prototypical interactions in China involve three parties.

Young (1994:149–52) demonstrates how employees can threaten the face of employers by publicly performing functions that are supposed to be to the credit of the superior. What is crucial here is the observation of a third person. Similarly, Kipnis (1995:126–27), following the suggestion of one of his consultants, shows how face requires the participation of three people. Without too great a divergence into the topic of "face," I invoke these two authors' works to demonstrate how interwoven the notion of threesomes is with naming.[12]

So how can we understand the significance of Chinese naming practices in the context of Chinese culture and in the context of the anthropological concern with naming in general? Individual psychological identity appears not to be critical; but factors such as face, where other participants must be considered, are essential. In this sense language can be seen as continuous with other forms of social action. To understand this fully, we must consider how words in general function in Chinese culture.

THE POWER OF WORDS

The act of naming events (with "common," not "proper" names) is regarded as powerful in China, as in many other cultures. Taboos against "bad luck" words are well known (Sung 1979), especially on otherwise happy (but liminal and dangerous) occasions—e.g., New Year (see Lu Hsun [1924] 1972:130) or weddings. One avoids saying words that sound like *sǐ* 'die', in order to avoid a bad beginning of the year (Sung 1979:24); and on all occasions one tries to avoid giving gifts that could be counted as *sì* 'four' (stems of flowers, apples, etc.) because of the similarity of sound (disregarding tone) with *sǐ*. Words and the objects of the events to which they refer are intimately connected; this extends to homophones of such words, and to the objects to which the homophones refer.

Many "traditional" ritual practices involve the use of objects of which the "name" (common noun) is auspicious:[13] *zǎozi* 'dates' are eaten at weddings to encourage the early coming of sons (*zǎo* 'early', *zǐ* 'son'); *chángmiàn* 'long noodles' are homophonous with 'long life'; *yú* 'fish' is homophonous with 'surplus', so banquets end with fish so that one can say *Niánniáan chī yú* 'Eat fish/have surplus every year'. This is rather different from the sort of magical power usually attributed to words (Frazer [1890] 1981:9–12, Malinowski [1935] 1978: 52–62, Tambiah 1968, O'Keefe 1982:39–56), in which either a metaphoric or metonymic relationship is seen as accounting for the efficacy of words in ritual. Here it is a demonstration of the continuum of language and object:

when one utters a word, it (and its homophones) are psychologically and actually present; when one focuses on an object, its names and homophones are also present.[14]

These matters may not be left to whim; children are not allowed to make grave mistakes in these practices. (Others have pointed out that the general style of socializing children in China is intolerant of experimentation, and hence of error. Children are shown the proper procedure and are rehearsed in it, but only when they have become competent to learn. Children walk, for instance, at an average age older than in the US.) Recall that even adult children are told *Jiào Wáng Shūshu* 'Call him (younger) uncle Wang' when meeting a new adult. Emotions are not what is primarily being indexed; rather, respect for proper authority and form, demonstrated through mastery of the proper words, demonstrates the speaker's sincere desire to be guided by teachers (Blum 1996) and an eagerness to define hierarchy properly. The critical factor is not emotional (Potter 1988, Abu-Lughod & Lutz 1990); the power of words is that they invoke prototypes which then guide people's actions. This is the key to understanding Chinese naming practices.

CHINESE NAMING PRACTICES

Treatments of naming in China usually focus on proper names (Chao 1956, Sung 1979, 1981, R. Watson 1986, Alleton 1993), though all mention the rarity of their use (Alleton 201–4). What has not been discussed in much detail is the strategic way in which speakers select from among their options for various purposes in particular contexts. Liu 1981 and Chao 1956 describe certain linguistic aspects of forms of address, especially kinship terms. Chao gives a chart with choices that should cover every social or linguistic situation, but his discussion is limited to the semantic and social meanings of terms—and it describes usage from his youth in China in the early 20th century. I suggest that cultural meanings can be grasped only if we situate naming in a broader context that includes the ontology of language—a consideration of the nature of language in the Chinese world, and what language is seen as being able to do.

Given structures of meaning and status, individuals employ means at their disposal to create/enforce relationships at every turn. In Japan (Bachnik & Quinn 1994) and Java (Errington 1985, 1988, Siegel 1986:15–33), a speaker cannot evade commitment to one social level or another; in China, the choice about which name to use (or not) commits one to a particular position. There is no neutrality; relationship and status are evident at all times. This is common throughout virtually all non-egalitarian societies; what varies is the particular means through which the principle is effected, and the homologies with other aspects of the culture.

In traditional Chinese domestic religious practice, now being revived to some degree in the mainland of China (see Siu 1989, Feuchtwang 1992, Dean 1993), the ontological categories of living and dead, human and godlike intersect with the otherwise vital ones of female and male, adult and child, married and unmarried, educated and illiterate, senior and junior, kin and stranger. Ghosts discovered to be powerful sometimes get renamed and are worshipped as gods (Harrell 1974), while gods retain their names until they fade completely from memory. Ancestors too may be forgotten; but unlike strangers, they have once been named. Ghosts are the spiritual counterpart to strangers, the undesirable element in the well-researched triad of god, ghost, and ancestor—corresponding to officials, strangers, and kin (see Jordan 1972, Ahern 1973, 1981, A. Wolf 1974a, Feuchtwang 1992). Ghosts are blamed for all manner of ailment, and are feared. Ancestors for whom proper rituals are not maintained can be ghosts, as when a woman commits suicide in a family well (Kingston 1975:1–16, M. Wolf 1975, Spence 1978, Tan 1989). Kinship relations are disturbed by the death's occurrence in an unnatural and undesirable way; and the person is then often left unnamed, as if no longer in the family. Such improper death results in taboo of the name: powerful but silenced.

Like ghosts, strangers can easily pass in the street, and can negotiate use of space without verbal interaction. The difference between words used and words not used, between silence and speaking (Becker 1984:136, Tannen & Saville-Troike 1985), is a basic aspect of discourse that must be described for each society. There may be words to name those encountered, even if these words are unuttered. Strangers may be referred to or addressed or both or neither. Chinese public life, especially urban life, involves daily contact with countless strangers. Most are ignored and unaddressed.

CONCLUSION

Words that name people also name and thus create relationships among speakers, hearer(s), and persons named. The relative statuses of all three, if all are present, is an important factor in determining which term will be used. Considerations of closeness sometimes override those of distance: closeness can be part of distance if it is generational or conventional. Unlike Americans, who usually seek the most egalitarian forms of address (*Professor Jones? Is it okay if I call you Linda?*), Chinese usually seek to be told about their status relative to one another through the help of a mutual acquaintance, and they do so throughout their lives.

A common cultural prototype in China is of the benevolent (paternalistic?) older kin who takes care of the younger ones, who reciprocate with affection, later in life with care, and finally (traditionally) with the performance of ritual remembrances ("ancestor worship"). Invocation of the kinship term calls up images of the prototype for speaker and hearer, reminding all of the full potential for practice implied by the term. But speakers do not always have the right to use close kinship terms, and relationships do not always fall into kinship patterns. However, prototypical relationships may still be hierarchical, such as that of employer and employee. Clearly, hierarchy does not impede formation of close attachments; the literature on politeness, however,

tends to portray a world of instrumental manipulators of limited goods.[15] I have suggested [here] that in China, even when speaking with and of one's closest intimates, choices may be made about the term that embodies the proper relationship, which may be one of hierarchy, but not distance. The maintenance of face can be signaled and granted by selecting intimate terms, and in fact requires this labeling for the relationship to be forged. Silently knowing how one feels is not expected to be adequate; nor does one speak volumes about relationships (*I love you so much…*). Affection is conveyed through the naming patterns over which one has control; and the socialization of children into this mastery is a powerful way in which they learn to be persons among others.

I have examined the role of language, and especially naming, in the face-to-face interactions of everyday Chinese life; names are one element to be deployed in strategies of giving, withholding, and exchanging face. I have shown that face is bestowed through naming practices, and that this can operate in terms of solidarity (which is not the same as equality) as well as authority. This occurs in some cases through the utterance of certain terms which have the power to affect the world. I have also explained some of the principles underlying the choice of particular terms, from the available font of naming possibilities, in particular situations—showing that reliance on prototypical relationships allows speakers to employ selected terms, in anticipation that the relationship will embody features common to that prototype. But intention and emotion are not especially important here. I have shown further that naming practices reveal distinctions among what may be said, what may not be said, and what must be said, in monitoring the delicate balance of self and world.

What we often refer to as "language," easily and casually, designates diverse entities. Words are imbued with different sorts of qualities in different cultures. Language may be seen as separate from other social practices, or as isomorphic with them, or as contradictory. It may be seen as ideally expressing the speaker's innermost thoughts, or it may be seen as exemplifying the speaker's knowledge of what is expected on certain occasions and in certain contexts. It can be performative (Austin 1962) or descriptive of the state of affairs of the world (but see Kripke 1980, Rosaldo 1982). It can be, and usually is, a source of social information about identities of many sorts: gender, age, status, occupation, and ethnic identity (Li 1994). In some areas, language is seen as efficacious (Tambiah 1968); in others, it is superfluous (Bauman 1983); in many societies, it is dangerous (Favret-Saada 1977, Wagner 1978). Writing of this plethora of ways in which language is viewed, Woolard & Schieffelin (1994:55) have defined "language ideology" as the often explicit "notions of how communication works as a social process." I have discussed [here] one aspect of Chinese language-in-use—naming—as a preliminary contribution to a broader explicit understanding of the diverse ways in which language functions in social life.

Notes

This research relies in part on observations made while I conducted fieldwork for my dissertation during the 1990–91 academic year under the auspices of the Committee on Scholarly Communication with the People's Republic of China (National Academy of Sciences), now the Committee on Scholarly Communication with China. I thank Norma Diamond, Sergei Kan, Donald Munro, Bruce Mannheim, Haun Saussy, Sara Davis, and Lionel Jensen for reading drafts of this article in its various incarnations. William Bright and two reviewers for *Language in Society* made invaluable suggestions; it is not their fault if I did not follow all of them. Sara Davis also helped with enthusiastic bibliographic and other assistance, thanks to support from Greg Possehl and the Department of Anthropology at the University of Pennsylvania; H-ASIA subscribers responded to my request for current information about naming practices. I am grateful to the Department of Asian Studies at the University of Texas (Austin) and the Center for East Asian Studies at the University of Pennsylvania for opportunities to present material related to this article.

1. Social and occupational titles and on-the-spot terms should also be included, but in the interest of brevity I have omitted them here.

2. Yunnan province borders Burma, Laos, and Vietnam, as well as Guizhou and Sichuan provinces and the autonomous areas of Tibet and Guangxi. It is ethnically quite diverse: Yunnan counts 24 officially recognized ethnic minority groups among its inhabitants. Its capital city, Kunming, has also been home to many migrations of the majority Han Chinese from elsewhere in China; hence its linguistic stock is quite diverse. *Kūnmínghuà* 'Kunming dialect' is a variant of southwest Mandarin, somewhat similar to Sichuan dialects. Other Chinese dialects in the province, all termed *Hànhuà* 'language of the Han,' are similar enough to be intelligible to natives of Kunming, but distinctive enough to be (it is claimed) identifiable. Most ethnic minorities have languages associated with them, though not all members of those groups speak "their" language. *Pǔtōnghuà*, Standard Mandarin, is found in official and formal contexts, though when spoken by natives of the area it usually carries a "southern accent." Migrants from northern areas sometimes retain their more standard pronunciation, which may be perceived as odd by Yunnan natives (see Blum 1994b:150–78).

   My general argument about strategies reflects my observations in Yunnan; but I believe that many of the principles can be observed elsewhere, at least among Han Chinese in the People's Republic. Regional variation among Han Chinese causes less variation in underlying principles than do factors such as social status and gender, among others, in particular situations.

   The question of the speech community intersects with that of the national community. Claims about essential cultural homogeneity in China (Cohen 1994, Tu Wei-ming 1994a, etc.) and in other Chinese societies (Erbaugh 1995) sit alongside predictions that China will soon unravel (Friedman 1994). Practices like those described here must be considered when any such conclusions are drawn. How prevalent are these practices—at least the underlying principles? It is possible that, in addition to the unification provided by the use of a single script and the ideology of unity accompanying it, China is unified by certain pragmatic principles. I welcome comments from researchers in other areas of China who can support or refute notions of the uniformity of pragmatics in the nation-state. Comments from scholars in China would be especially welcome.

3. See Urban (1996:99–133) for a fresh account of the history of the term "classificatory," and of the offhand way in which Morgan announced that he had "discovered" classificatory kinship—as if it were a solid object available to be picked up and put in a backpack.

4. The model of a prototype that is psychologically present is a useful one; but like all models, it is a construct of analysts (see Lakoff 1987, Quinn & Holland 1987, MacLaury 1991).

5. See Urban 1988 on ritual laments and Johnson 1988 on funeral laments. Emotion in these cases is inseparable from its expression.

6. There is little anthropological treatment of wedding ceremonies with the degree of detail necessary to draw conclusions about this moment; one wishes for a conference and volume akin to that for death ritual (see J. Watson & E. Rawski 1988). See M. Wolf 1978 for discussion of the good wife's infrequent contact with her natal family, and Judd 1989 for a correction of the view that women severed ties with their natal families upon marriage.

7. Many famous people are remembered principally in terms of their studio names (Sū Dōngpō rather than Sū Shì, Pú Sōnglíng). Wáng Shǒurén, the Ming philosopher, took "Yángmíng" as his style name, and it now refers to him even without his surname. Zhōngshān, Sun Yat-sen's style name pronounced in Mandarin, is another case.

8. Huà Guófēng, Mao's immediate successor, is unofficially reported to have been born Su Zhu, and his children are reported to retain his natal name of Su (cf. Hsu 1982: 351–52). Mao's wife Jiāng Qīng was reported to have been born Li Zhongjin (Snow 1968:459), Li Jin (Witke 1977:45), Luan Shumeng (Chung & Miller 1968:12), Lǐ Yúnhè (Bartke 1981:576), or Lǐ Nà (Wang Jie, p.c.) She took the name Lán Píng as a film actress, and later took Jiāng Qīng as her Party name. Most Chinese sources fail to give the original names for many people, such as Huà or Jiāng Qīng, while English-language sources fail to provide tonal marks for the romanized names. It is more common for English-language sources to inquire into the original names, while Chinese-language sources tend to retain the name that was used after a person became well known.

9. See He Liyi (1993:121–27) and Miller (1993:7) for descriptions of naming among the Bai minority. The Bai, one of Yunnan's dominant ethnic minorities, rely on chance to select the bestower of a child's name on his or her full-month birthday. Miller reports being asked to select a child's name, and feeling a tremendous degree of undesired responsibility for this stranger's child.

10. Thanks to a reviewer for *Language in Society* for pointing out this obvious but unremarked point.

11. Chao (1956:224, 225, 237) describes meeting an illustrious person of superior age, but equal status: the speaker chooses to use the courtesy name with title, knowing that in the future the title may be dropped. It would be more difficult to move from a formal name and title to the bald courtesy name. These elaborate social considerations are no longer part of Chinese etiquette, to my knowledge—and certainly were never part of common folks' practices. However, in responses to an inquiry I made over the Internet, several people reported a significant

increase in the use of the personal name during the last two or three years, often with a title but without the surname.

12. Face in China and face in general have been treated extensively. It is often, as Kipnis 1995 points out, a virtual "fetish" of Chineseness, with even theoretical treatments returning to classic sources on China (Hu 1944, Martin Yang 1945, Goffman 1967:5–6). Face has been central in the extensive literature on politeness (P. Brown & S. Levinson 1987) and is one aspect of the person discussed in the literature on personhood (Goffman 1967, Geertz 1973, Mauss 1985). It is somewhat surprising, however, to notice how seldom issues of face have surfaced in recent accounts of the anthropology of the self and the person. This may be because of the American folk ideology of the self which privileges interior experience over practice and surface; however, see Potter 1988, Abu-Lughod & Lutz 1990, Wikan 1995.

Negative and positive face—the desire to be left alone, the desire to be acknowledged for achievement—and their involvement in politeness are often treated as clustering around poles of power and solidarity, but these factors are not always easy to sort out. Kinship relations are solidary and yet hierarchical, as many feminist analysts have pointed out (Collier & Yanagisako 1987); but intimacy, affection, and respect are intermingled most evidently within family relations. A degree of pleasure may be derived from uttering a kinship term, or being called by a kinship term, because one gains "face" from it. However, another source of pleasure comes from performing scripts—acting in accord with a prototype of kinship relations—in which the relationship is enforced and in some sense created by the utterance or invocation of the proper term.

Children can give face to their parents through achievements, just as they can lose face for them through misdeeds. There is a sense in which the face of a family is shared by all its members. Thus Daniel (1984, chaps. 2 and 3), writing about India, describes the substance of a *jati* being shared by its members in Tamil Nadu, and indeed by the very soil of its homeland. *Jati* is usually translated as 'caste' but is more accurately described as an endogamous, ranked, localized, corporate group.

Face is prototypically involved in two types of cases: first, instrumental public relations, where factors of power and status must be considered (see Hu 1944, Martin Yang 1945, Mayfair Yang 1994, Kipnis 1995), and second, intimate relations within the family, where affective factors must also be considered (see Potter 1988, Jankowiak 1993)—but not necessarily egalitarian relations. In fact, relations in the family are, according to predominant Chinese ideology, all hierarchical.

13. See Siu 1989 on the transformation of the meaning of traditional practices despite continuity of form; and see Dean 1993. The question of cultural continuity alongside "modernity," socialism, or nationalism is in many ways a central one in anthropology now. Siu argues in a Saussurean way (like Sahlins 1981) that a "traditional" practice in a changed context has an entirely different meaning (value) than it had in the past. Pemberton 1994 makes basically the same point about the use of "tradition" in New Order Indonesia.

14. Ahern 1979 writes that her informants in Taiwan explained similar actions as expressing wishes, rather than as actually capable of bringing about changes in the world. She terms these "weak illocutionary acts," in contrast to the more literal reading of them as illocutionary acts.

15. A reviewer of this article pointed out that "hierarchy is often equated with hegemonic discourse, and hegemonic discourse is universally disvalued" in our "social scientific climate." I think this is true, and it is an important example of how the cultural values of social scientists affect our analysis of other cultures.

References

Abu-Lughod, Lila, & Lutz, Catherine A. (1990). Introduction: Emotion, discourse, and the politics of everyday life. In Catherine A. Lutz & Lila Abu-Lughod (eds.), *Language and the politics of emotion*, 1–23. Cambridge & New York: Cambridge University Press.

Ahern, Emily Martin (1973). *The cult of the dead in a Chinese village*. Stanford, CA: Stanford University Press.

———. (1979). The problem of efficacy: Strong and weak illocutionary acts. *Man* 14:1–17.

———. (1981). *Chinese ritual and politics*. Cambridge & New York: Cambridge University Press.

Alford, Richard D. (1988). *Naming and identity: A cross-cultural study of personal naming practices*. New Haven: HRAF Press.

Alleton, Viviane (1993). *Les Chinois et la passion des noms*. Paris: Aubier.

Austin, John L. (1962). *How to do things with words*. Cambridge, MA: Harvard University Press.

Bachnik, Jane M., & Quinn, Charles J., Jr. (1994). *Situated meaning: Inside and outside in Japanese self, society, and language*. Princeton, NJ: Princeton University Press.

Bartke, Wolfgang (1981). *Who's who in the PRC*. Hamburg: Institute of Asian Affairs.

Bauman, Richard (1983). *Let your words be few: Symbolism of speaking and silence among seventeenth-century Quakers*. Cambridge & New York: Cambridge University Press.

Becker, Alton L. (1984). Biography of a sentence: A Burmese proverb. In Edward Bruner & A. L. Becker (eds.), *Text, play, and story*, 135–55. Washington, DC: American Ethonological Society.

Bell, Diane (1993). *Daughters of the dreaming*. 2d ed. Minneapolis: University of Minnesota Press.

Benveniste, Emile (1966a). La nature des pronoms. In his *Problèmes de linguistique générale* 1:251–57. Paris: Gallimard. [Translated by Mary Elizabeth Meek as The nature of pronouns, in *Problems in general linguistics*, 217–22. Coral Gables, FL: University of Miami Press, 1971.]

———. (1966b). Nature du signe linguistique. In his *Problèmes de linguistique générale* 1:49–55. Paris: Gallimard. [Translated by Mary Elizabeth Meek as The nature of the linguistic sign, in *Problems in general linguistics*, 43–48. Coral Gables, FL: University of Miami Press, 1971.]

Blum, Susan D. (1994a). Constructing a "Chinese" identity in the modern nation-state. Paper presented at the annual meeting of the Association for Asian Studies, Boston.

———. (1994b). *Han and the Chinese other: The language of identity and difference in Southwest China*. Dissertation, University of Michigan, Ann Arbor.

Blum, Susan D. (1996). The power of words in China. Paper presented at the Center for East Asian Studies, University of Pennsylvania, Philadelphia, February 2.

——. (1998). Pearls on the string of the Chinese nation: Pronouns, plurals, and prototypes in talk about identities. *Michigan Discussions in Anthropology*, 13: 207–237.

Bowen, Elenore Smith [Laura Bohannan] (1964). *Return to laughter: An anthropological novel.* New York: Doubleday.

Brown, Penelope, & Levinson, Stephen C. (1987). *Politeness.* Cambridge & New York: Cambridge University Press. [Originally published in 1978.]

Brown, Roger, & Gilman, Albert (1960). The pronouns of power and solidarity. In Thomas A. Sebeok (ed.), *Style in language*, 253–76. Cambridge, MA: MIT Press.

Chagnon, Napoleon (1992). *Yanomamo.* 4th ed. Fort Worth, TX: Harcourt Brace Jovanovich.

Chao, Yuan-ren (1956). Chinese terms of address. *Language* 32:212–41.

——. (1968). *A grammar of spoken Chinese.* Berkeley: University of California Press.

Chén Ruìjùn (1990). Xìngmíngxué qǐguān [A glance at naming]. *Dōngxiàng* 6:551.

Chung Hua-min, & Miller, Arthur C. (1968). *Madame Mao: A profile of Chiang Ch'ing.* Hong Kong: Union Research Institute.

Cohen, Myron L. (1994). Being Chinese: The peripheralization of traditional identity. In Tu Weiming (ed.), 88–108.

Collier, Jane Fishburne, & Yanagisako, Sylvia Junko (1987), eds. *Gender and kinship: Essays toward a unified analysis.* Stanford, CA: Stanford University Press.

Daniel, E. Valentine (1984). *Fluid signs: Being a person the Tamil way.* Berkeley: University of California Press.

Dean, Kenneth (1993). *Taoist ritual and popular cults of Southeast China.* Princeton, NJ: Princeton University Press.

Derrida, Jacques (1982). White mythology: Metaphor in the text of philosophy. In his *Margins of philosophy,* 207–71. Chicago: University of Chicago Press.

Doi, Takeo (1971). *Amae no koozoo.* Tokyo: Koobundoo Ltd. [Translated by John Bester as *The anatomy of dependence.* Tokyo: Kodansha, 1973.]

Erbaugh, Mary S. (1993). The making of modern Chinese: Language and power in modern China. MS.

——. (1995). Southern Chinese dialects as a medium for reconciliation within Greater China. *Language in Society* 24:79–94.

Errington, J. Joseph (1985). *Language and social change in Java: Linguistic reflexes of modernization in a traditional royal polity.* Athens: Ohio University Center for International Studies.

——. (1988). *Structure and style in Javanese: A semiotic view of linguistic etiquette.* Philadelphia: University of Pennsylvania Press.

Farris, Catherine S. (1988). Gender and grammar in Chinese, with implications for language universals. *Modern China* 14:277–308.

Favret-Saada, Jeanne (1977). *Les mots, la mort, les sorts.* Paris: Gallimard. [Translated by Catherine Cullen as *Deadly words: Witchcraft in the bocage.* Cambridge & New York: Cambridge University Press, 1980.]

Feuchtwang, Stephan (1992). *The Imperial metaphor: Popular religion in China.* London: Routledge.

Frazer, James G. (1890). *The golden bough: A study in magic and religion.* Abridged ed. New York: Macmillan. [Reprinted 1981.]

Friedman, Edward (1994). Reconstructing China's national identity: A southern alternative to Mao-era anti-imperialist nationalism. *Journal of Asian Studies* 53:67–91.

Friedrich, Paul (1972). Social context and semantic feature: The Russian pronominal usage. In John J. Gumperz & Dell Hymes (eds.), *Directions in sociolinguistics: The ethnography of communication,* 270–300. New York: Holt, Rinehart & Winston.

——. (1979). The symbol and its relative non-arbitrariness. In his *Language, context, and the imagination,* 1–61. Stanford, CA: Stanford University Press.

Geertz, Clifford (1973). Person, time, and conduct in Bali. In his *Interpretation of cultures,* 360–411. New York: Basic Books.

Goffman, Erving (1967). On face-work: An analysis of ritual elements in social interaction. In his *Interaction ritual: Essays on face-to-face behavior,* 5–45. New York: Pantheon.

——. (1979). Footing. *Semiotica* 25:1–29. [Reprinted in Goffman 1981a:124–57.]

——. (1981a). *Forms of talk.* Philadelphia: University of Pennsylvania Press.

——. (1981b). The lecture. In Goffman 1981a:160–96.

Graham, Angus (1989). *Disputers of the Tao: Philosophical argument in Ancient China.* La Salle, IL: Open Court.

Granet, Marcel (1934). *La pensée chinoise.* Paris: Albin Michel.

Guō Qìngfān (1983), ed. *Zhuāngzi Jíshì* [Annotated Zhuāngzi]. (Sìbù Kānyào.) Táiběi: Hànjīng wénhuà shìyè.

Hansen, Chad (1983). *Language and logic in ancient China.* Ann Arbor: University of Michigan Press.

——. (1992). *A Daoist theory of Chinese thought: A philosophical interpretation.* Oxford & New York: Oxford University Press.

Harrell, Stevan A. (1974). When a ghost becomes a god. In Arthur P. Wolf (ed.), 193–206.

He Liyi (1993). *Mr. China's son: A villager's life.* Boulder, CO: Westview Press.

Hendry, Joy (1993). *Wrapping culture: Politeness, presentation, and power in Japan and other societies.* Oxford: Clarendon Press.

Hinton, Carma (1984), director. *Small happiness: Women of a Chinese village* (film). Long Bow Productions. Produced by Richard Gordon, Kathy Kline, and Daniel Sipe. Distributed by New Day Films, Wayne, NJ.

Hsu, R. S-W. (1982). Personal and family names. In Brian Hook (ed.), *The Cambridge Encyclopedia of China,*

351–52. Cambridge & New York: Cambridge University Press.

Hu, Hsien Chin (1944). Chinese concepts of face. *American Anthropologist* 46:45–64.

Huáng Kǎn (1990), ed. Lùnyǔ Zhùsù [Critical commentaries on the Analects]. (Shísānjīng zhùsù.) Shanghai: Gǔjí chūbǎnshè.

Jankowiak, William R. (1993). *Sex, death, and hierarchy in a Chinese city: An anthropological account.* New York: Columbia University Press.

Johnson, Elizabeth L. (1988). Grieving for the dead, grieving for the living: Funeral laments of Hakka women. In Watson & Rawski (eds.), 135–63.

Jordan, David K. (1972). *Gods, ghosts, and ancestors: Folk religion in a Taiwanese village.* Berkeley: University of California Press.

Judd, Ellen R. (1989). *Niangjia:* Chinese women and their natal families. *Journal of Asian Studies* 48:525–44.

Kingston, Maxine Hong (1975). *The woman warrior: Memoirs of a girlhood among ghosts.* New York: Vintage.

Kipnis, Andrew (1995). "Face": An adaptable discourse of social surfaces. *Positions: East Asia Cultures Critique* 3:119–48.

Kondo, Dorinne K. (1990). *Crafting selves: Power, gender, and discourses of identity in a Japanese workplace.* Chicago: University of Chicago Press.

Kripke, Saul A. (1980). *Naming and necessity.* Cambridge, MA: Harvard University Press.

Kroeber, Alfred L. (1933). Process in the Chinese kinship system. *American Anthropologist* 35:151–57. [Condensed and reprinted in his *The nature of culture,* 190–95. Chicago: University of Chicago Press, 1952.]

Lakoff, George (1987). *Women, fire, and dangerous things: What categories reveal about the mind.* Chicago: University of Chicago Press.

Lau, Dim Cheuk (1979), trans. *The Analects.* Harmondsworth: Penguin Books.

Lau, Joseph S. M., & Goldblatt, Howard (1995), eds. *The Columbia anthology of modern Chinese literature.* New York: Columbia University Press.

Li Wei (1994). *Three generations, two languages, one family.* Clevedon, UK: Multilingual Matters.

Lin, Alice Murong Pu (1988). *Grandmother had no name.* San Francisco: China Books.

Liu, Charles A. (1981). Chinese kinship terms as forms of address. *Journal of the Chinese Language Teachers Association* 16:35–45.

Lu Hsun (1924). The New Year's sacrifice. Translated in *Selected stories of Lu Hsun,* trans. by Yang Hsien-yi & Gladys Yang, 125–43. Beijing: Foreign Languages Press, 1972.

MacLaury, Robert E. (1991). Prototypes revisited. *Annual Review of Anthropology* 20:55–74.

Makeham, John (1994). *Name and actuality in early Chinese thought.* Albany: State University of New York Press.

Malinowski, Bronislaw (1935). *Coral gardens and their magic.* New York: American Book Co. [Reprinted, New York: Dover, 1978.]

———. (1948). *Magic, science and religion, and other essays.* Boston: Beacon. [Reprinted, Garden City, NY: Doubleday, 1954.]

Malkolkin, Anna (1992). *Name, hero, icon: Semiotics of nationalism through heroic biography.* Berlin: Mouton de Gruyter.

Mannheim, Bruce, & Tedlock, Dennis (1995). Introduction. In D. Tedlock & B. Mannheim (eds.), *The dialogic emergence of culture,* 1–32. Urbana: University of Illinois Press.

Mauss, Marcel (1985). A category of the human mind: The notion of person; the notion of self. In Michael Carrithers et al. (eds.), *The category of the person: Anthropology, philosophy, history,* 1–25. Cambridge & New York: Cambridge University Press. [Originally published in 1938.]

Miller, Lucien (1993). The ethnic chameleon: Bakhtin and the Bai. Paper presented at the International Society for the Comparative Study of Civilizations, Scranton, PA.

Morgan, Lewis Henry (1871). *Systems of consanguinity and affinity of the human family.* Washington, DC: Smithsonian Institution.

Munro, Donald J. (1969). *The concept of man in early China.* Stanford, CA: Stanford University Press.

Ng, Fae Myenne (1993). *Bone.* New York: Hyperion.

Norman, Jerry (1988). *Chinese.* Cambridge & New York: Cambridge University Press.

O'Keefe, Daniel Lawrence (1982). *Stolen lightning: The social theory of magic.* New York: Continuum.

Pemberton, John (1994). *On the subject of "Java."* Ithaca, NY: Cornell University Press.

Potter, Sulamith Heins (1988). The cultural construction of emotion in rural Chinese social life. *Ethos* 16:181–208.

Quinn, Naomi, & Holland, Dorothy (1987). Culture and cognition. In D. Holland & N. Quinn (eds.), *Cultural models in language and thought,* 3–40. Cambridge & New York: Cambridge University Press.

Rosaldo, Michelle (1982). The things we do with words: Ilongot speech acts and speech act theory in philosophy. *Language in Society* 11:203–37.

Sahlins, Marshall (1981). *Historical metaphors and mythical realities: Structure in the early history of the Sandwich Islands Kingdom.* Ann Arbor: University of Michigan Press.

Schneider, David M. (1984). *A critique of the study of kinship.* Ann Arbor: University of Michigan Press.

Siegel, James T. (1986). *Solo in the new order: Language and hierarchy in an Indonesian city.* Princeton, NJ: Princeton University Press.

Siu, Helen F. (1989). *Agents and victims in South China: Accomplices in rural revolution.* New Haven, CT: Yale University Press.

Snow, Edgar (1968). *Red star over China.* New York: Grove Press.

Spence, Jonathan D. (1978). *The death of Woman Wang.* New York: Viking Press.

Sung, Margaret M. Y. (1979). Chinese language and culture: A study of homonyms, lucky words, and taboos. *Journal of Chinese Linguistics* 7:15–30.

———. (1981). Chinese personal naming. *Journal of the Chinese Language Teachers Association* 16:67–90.

Tambiah, Stanley J. (1968). The magical power of words. *Man* 3:175–208.

Tan, Amy (1989). *The Joy Luck Club.* New York: Ballantine Books.

Tannen, Deborah, & Saville-Troike, Muriel (1985), eds. *Perspectives on silence.* Norwood, NJ: Ablex.

Topley, Marjorie (1974). Cosmic antagonisms: A mother–child syndrome. In A.P. Wolf (ed.), 233–49.

Trautmann, Thomas R. (1987). *Lewis Henry Morgan and the invention of kinship.* Berkeley: University of California Press.

Tu Wei-ming (1994a). Cultural China: The periphery as the center. In Tu Wei-ming (ed.), 1–34.

———. (1994b), ed. *The living tree: The changing meaning of being Chinese today.* Stanford, CA: Stanford University Press.

Urban, Greg (1988). Ritual wailing in Amerindian Brazil. *American Anthropologist* 90:385–400.

———. (1996). *Metaphysical community: The interplay of the senses and the intellect.* Austin: University of Texas Press.

Wagner, Roy (1978). *Lethal speech: Daribi myth as symbolic obviation.* Ithaca, NY: Cornell University Press.

Waley, Arthur (1938), trans. *The Analects of Confucius.* London: Allen & Unwin. [Reprinted, New York: Vintage, 1967.]

Wáng Quàngēn (1988). *Huáxià Xìngmíng Miànmiàn Guān* [A comprehensive look at Chinese names]. Nánníng: Guǎngxī rénmín chūbǎnshè.

Watson, James L., & Rawski, Evelyn S. (1988), eds. *Death ritual in late imperial and modern China.* Berkeley: University of California Press.

Watson, Rubie S. (1986). The named and the nameless: Gender and person in Chinese society. *American Ethnologist* 13:619–31.

Wikan, Unni (1995). The self in a world of urgency and necessity. *Ethos* 23:259–85.

Witherspoon, Gary (1977). *Language and art in the Navajo universe.* Ann Arbor: University of Michigan Press.

Witke, Roxane (1977). *Comrade Chiang Ch'ing* [Jiang Qing]. Boston: Little Brown.

Wolf, Arthur P. (1974a). Gods, ghosts, and ancestors. In A. P. Wolf (ed.), 131–82.

———. (1974b), ed. *Religion and ritual in Chinese society.* Stanford, CA: Stanford University Press.

Wolf, Margery (1975). Women and suicide in China. In M. Wolf & R. Witke (eds.), 111–41.

———. (1978). Child training and the Chinese family. In A. P. Wolf (ed.), 221–46.

———, & Witke, Roxane (1975), eds. *Women in Chinese society.* Stanford, CA: Stanford University Press.

Woolard, Kathryn A., & Schieffelin, Bambi B. (1994). Language ideology. *Annual Review of Anthropology* 23:55–82.

Yang, Martin C. (1945). *A Chinese village.* New York: Columbia University Press.

Yang, Mayfair Mei-hui (1994). *Gifts, favors, and banquets: The art of social relationships in China.* Ithaca, NY: Cornell University Press.

Young, Linda W. L. (1994). *Crosstalk and culture in Sino-American communication.* Cambridge & New York: Cambridge University Press.

Zha, Jianying (1995). *China pop: How soap operas, tabloids, and bestsellers are transforming a culture.* New York: New Press.

Zhang Jie (1986). The time is not yet ripe. Trans. by Gladys Yang. In *Love must not be forgotten*, 63–77. San Francisco: China Books.

Zhào Ruìmín (1988). *Xìngmíng yú Zhōngguó Wénhuà* [Names and Chinese culture]. Chóngqìng: Hǎinán rénmín chūbǎnshè.

Post-reading Questions / Activities

- This article emphasizes that performance is more important than how the speaker feels about the utterance. How do you regard what you say? Is it your own choice? Are you coerced by others' expectations to say what you do?
- Discuss the suggestion made here that a prototypical exchange in China involves three parties rather than two.
- Keep track for an hour or two of all the ways you and people around you interact, jotting down the ways people address one another (by nickname, title, first name, etc.). What kinds of equalities and inequalities can you observe through these interactions? Would changing the form of address change the relationship?

Vocabulary

amae (Japanese)	metalinguistic
classificatory kinship	metaphoric
common name	metonymic
face	ontology of language
fictive kinship	proper name
interlocutor	teknonym
marked	unmarked

Suggested Further Reading

Abu-Lughod, Lila. 1986. *Veiled Sentiments: Honor and Poetry in a Bedouin Society*. Berkeley: University of California Press.

———, and Catherine Lutz, eds. 1990. *Language and the Politics of Emotion*. Cambridge: Cambridge University Press.

Austin, John L. 1975 [1962]. *How to Do Things With Words*, 2d ed. Cambridge, MA: Harvard University Press.

Blum, Susan D. 2007. *Lies That Bind: Chinese Truth, Other Truths*. Lanham, MD: Rowman and Littlefield.

Briggs, Charles. 1986. *Learning How to Ask: A Sociolinguistic Appraisal of the Role of the Interview in Social Science Research*. Cambridge: Cambridge University Press.

Brown, Penelope, and Stephen C. Levinson. 1987. *Politeness: Some Universals in Language Usage*. Cambridge: Cambridge University Press.

Grice, Paul. 1989. *Studies in the Way of Words*. Cambridge, MA: Harvard University Press.

Keenan, Elinor Ochs. 1976. "The Universality of Conversational Postulates." *Language in Society* 5 (1): 67–80.

Lutz, Catherine A. 1988. *Unnatural Emotions: Everyday Sentiments on a Micronesian Atoll and Their Challenge to Western Theory*. Chicago: University of Chicago Press.

Malinowski, Bronislaw. 1923. "The Problem of Meaning in Primitive Languages." In *The Meaning of Meaning*, edited by C. K. Ogden and I. A. Richards. New York: Harcourt, Brace.

Rosaldo, Michelle Z. 1982. "The Things We Do with Words: Ilongot Speech Acts and Speech Act Theory in Philosophy." *Language in Society* 11: 203–235.

Searle, John R. 1969. *Speech Acts: An Essay in the Philosophy of Language*. Cambridge: Cambridge University Press.

CHAPTER 38

Amen and Hallelujah Preaching
Discourse Functions in African American Sermons

Cheryl Wharry
(2003)

African American society has often been said to be characterized by its orality, something derived from the African societies from which most slaves were taken. In this chapter, Cheryl Wharry examines specific discourse markers in one genre of African American communication: the sermon. She is quick to point out that such sermons must be perceived as spontaneous and spoken, even if a written text exists to prompt the speaker, because the sermons must be "open to the direction of the 'Spirit'."

Wharry looks at discourse markers, such as Amen *and* Hallelujah, *in the sermons of three male and three female evangelists. She distinguishes the purposes of these discourse markers as follows:*

- *Textual boundary: as in the end of a topic (much like the end of a paragraph or section in writing)*
- *Call for response*
- *Spiritual filler*
- *Rhythmic marker*
- *Multiple roles*

Fillers are words or phrases (like um, you know, I mean *in English) that permit the speaker time to reflect and prepare the next phrases, though they can also be habits and have other meanings as well. Spoken language is characterized by a great deal of incompleteness, false starts, redundancy, all of which must be processed by listeners who are also, often, attending to other matters at the same time. All this is dispreferred in writing and in some genres that build from writing, such as formal lectures, which make them much more difficult to process aurally than ordinary speech.*

The contrast with ordinary speech is prominent in the sermons and preaching discussed here. Spirituality pervades the sermon, even down to what preachers do when they can't think of the next word in their spontaneous delivery.

Reading Questions

- How did Wharry carry out her research? What are the benefits of this kind of study? What are its limitations?
- On what basis does Wharry claim that African American society is oral?
- How do members of Black congregations indicate disapproval of a sermon? How do they indicate approval?
- What are the differences between African American secular and spiritual discourse styles?

●━━━━━━━━━━━━━━━━━━━━━━━━━━━━━━●

Many discourse analysts have explored the genres of conversation and lecture and the roles of markers within

Cheryl Wharry, "Amen and Hallelujah Preaching: Discourse Functions in African American Sermons." *Language in Society* (2003) 32: 203–25. Reprinted with the permission of Cambridge University Press.

these genres; however, few studies exist on the identification and function of specific socially constructed discourse markers (DMs) in the SERMON genre. The few studies that have taken discourse approaches to sermon analysis typically have analyzed seminary-trained White preachers. These studies, particularly those of Smith 1993 and Zeil 1991, have made excellent contributions to our understanding of gender-linked differences in sermon delivery and in audience perception of those sermons. Still lacking, though, are studies that analyze DMs in African American sermons and that consider both textual and cultural influences on the roles of DMs.

Although such specific studies are lacking in the literatures of discourse and of African American culture, a number of studies have explored the broader topic of African cultural survivals in traditional Black churches. Some of these retentions have a direct connection to the performance of African American sermons.

Work on cultural "survivals" or "retentions" primarily addresses the question of whether people who are forcefully taken away from their countries leave elements of their culture behind as well, or whether they hold strongly to their native cultural practices. Herskovitz's (1958) seminal work on African cultural survivals in the United States includes call-response and ritual-like dancing as examples of African retentions in Black American churches. Similarly, Lincoln 1974 argues that Blacks brought their religion with them from Africa, and that later they "accepted the white man's religion, but they haven't always practiced it in the white man's way. It became the black man's purpose…to shape, to fashion, to recreate the religion offered to him by the Christian slave master, to remold it nearer to his own heart's desire, nearer to his own peculiar needs" (quoted in Mitchell 1970:6). Suggesting that slaves and their descendants were not stripped entirely of their African religious heritage, many researchers have illuminated similarities between African American religious practices and West African rituals (Robert 1972, Barrett 1974, Mitchell 1975, Daniel & Smitherman 1976, Smitherman 1986, 2000, Simpson 1978, Raboteau 1978, Blassingame 1979, Jules-Rosette 1980, Sernett 1985, Twining 1985, Pitts 1986, 1989).

If West African cultural retentions do exist among African Americans, it would be difficult and erroneous to discuss any aspect of the Black church without mentioning orality. Traditional West Africans and African Americans have been described as having a strong oral culture (Edwards & Seinkewicz 1991). In his work on American sermons from the time of the Pilgrims to Martin Luther King, Jr., Warner 1999 claims that American sermons have a written foundation. What makes this claim problematic is the generalization that "American sermons" are all similar in this way. Traditional African American sermons are typically NOT first written and do not command their value in the context of WRITTEN LITERATURE. They do not conform to the criterion of being initially "reduced" (a word that might be selected by those who find orality more meaningful than literacy in their communities) to the written word. Because of the multiple cultural functions of the spoken word, African Americans have tended to value oral performance much more highly than do cultures that are closer to the literate end of the literacy-orality continuum. The traditional African American sermon is no exception. Although preachers may choose to write their sermons first, if they wish their delivery of the sermon to be accepted within traditional Black churches, the

sermon must have at least the APPEARANCE of not having been finished beforehand; the Black preaching event should be constructed by both congregation and preacher, and it should be open to the direction of the "Spirit."

Edwards and Seinkewicz (1991) highlight the following specific features that all oral cultures tend to share: audience plays a central role in all performances; different audiences have different ways of expressing their approval or disapproval of the speaker; referential structure is used to unite audience and performer and to create dialogue between the two; distinct textual features of rhyme, tempo, pitch, and formulaic language are present; and aesthetic strategic elements such as elaboration, exaggeration, and metaphor are evident. That description is applicable in all particulars to the African American preaching event, but the emphasis on unity between audience and performer is especially noteworthy because the idea of a jointly produced sermon tends to influence linguistic choices and to distinguish traditional Black churches. Specifically, if preachers and congregations prefer that the sermon not be a monologue but that pulpit and congregation both participate, verbal and nonverbal discourse markers should reflect this preference in the same way that DMs in lectures and conversation can reveal information about the roles of participants in those discourse genres.

That African American preaching reflects an oral heritage is well documented (Abrahams 1970, 1976, Mitchell 1970, Smitherman 1986, 2000, Dundes 1981, Kochman 1981, Erickson 1984, Pitts 1986, 1989). African American preaching, the most prominent and longstanding discourse event (performance) in traditional African American churches, generally can be evaluated according to how well the performers (preacher AND congregation) meet the criteria of oral tradition. Smitherman 1986 says that the dialogue between preacher and congregation ("call-response"), which begins with the preacher responding to a prior call from God to preach, serves to unify the preacher with his or her audience. In fact, personal communication and observation suggest that Black preachers who do not get congregational responses (e.g., *Amen, Das right, you sho' 'nuff preachin'*), will feel a sense of separation from the audience. Either they have "lost" the congregation by speaking "above their heads" or by boring them, or they are presenting material with which the audience totally disagrees. Silence in traditional Black churches is generally not viewed as indicative of a mesmerized or attentive audience; instead, it typically carries negative connotations. This call-response format used to unify participants is evident not only in the preaching event but also in most other African American Vernacular English (AAVE) speech events. Informal observations and personal interviews with Black preachers show that many traditional African American preachers, when speaking to audiences who do not use call-response, do not feel "at home" and may be uncomfortable with delivering sermons in those contexts. This discomfort exists because, in most Black churches, the audience's responses actually assist in the formation of spontaneous sermons, a combined effort of preacher and congregation.

Structure allows for spontaneity.

Mitchell's (1970) and Davis's (1987) works on African American sermons have been useful in describing general components of a Black sermon framework. Mitchell's much-quoted work identifies two major principles crucial to Black preaching: (i) The gospel must be presented in the language and culture of the people, the vernacular; and (ii) the gospel preached must speak to contemporary people and their needs (as was the case with Black spirituals). Mitchell claims that it is impossible to provide an outline for the Black sermon, given the individuality, imagination, and spontaneity of Black preaching; he focuses instead on describing such aspects as cultural context, reasons for use of Black English in sermons, and descriptions of a sermon's climax.

Davis (1987), in contrast, gives a detailed description of the overall structure of the African American sermon as a narrative event. He identifies five major components of traditional Black sermons: (i) Preacher tells the congregation that the sermon was provided by God; (ii) preacher identifies the theme, followed by a Bible quotation; (iii) preacher interprets the scripture literally and then broadly; (iv) each unit of the sermon contains a secular-versus-sacred conflict and moves between concrete and abstract; (v) closure is absent, and the sermon is left open-ended (1987:67–90).

Both Mitchell's general descriptive features and Davis's broad outline appear to hold true for most traditional Black sermons; still, the context within which all these components are displayed tends to be one of the oral-tradition call-response format. The sermons can be viewed as a structured stretch of discourse with room for individuality or relative creativity. Davis 1987 refutes Rosenberg's (1970) claim that Black preaching's spontaneity results from the African American folk preacher "subordinate[ing] everything he has to say to the demands of meter." Generally speaking, Rosenberg argues that Black preachers arrange all their sermons to create a musical effect.

In contrast, Davis believes that, while Black sermons appear to have uniform meter, the lengths of sermon lines vary widely. Sermon lines are irregular (made rhythmic through emphatic repetition, dramatic pause, etc.), and the most important characteristic of the African American sermonic formula is groups of lines shaped around a central theme. Theme (with irregularity and/or contrasts), not meter, is what primarily provides cohesion in African American sermons. Clearly, Black sermons are not confined to metrical demands, and both unifying theme and rhythm in a call-response format are key descriptors of the Black sermon; spontaneity exists within a specific order, or form.

Pawley's (1992) discussion of the paradoxical role of speech formula in the creative use of language is applicable to this aspect of Black preaching:

> In the production of extended discourse, formulas are essential building blocks: ready-made units which free speakers and hearers from the task of attending consciously to each word. Thus freed, they are able to focus on the larger structure and sense of the discourse, or nuances of wording or sound. In speech, as elsewhere, people prefer their novelty to come highly structured, in the form of familiar themes. Formulaic constructions provide schemas for saying new things without breaking conventions of idiomaticity and good style—something that grammar alone does not do. (1992:23)

This notion of formulaic construction in general discourse is applicable to Black preaching in that participants expect both STRUCTURE (e.g., call-response format, verbal mention of God's having authored the sermon, indication of theme and related scripture, secular/sacred conflicts, sermon elevation or climax) and FREEDOM to allow individuality and to welcome the spontaneity of the "Holy Ghost" (spirit of God). In his work on transcendence and the Holy Spirit in African American gospel, Hinson 2000 highlights the connection between elevated delivery styles and supernatural empowerment in sanctified churches:

> This perceived connection finds its most telling confirmation in sermons, where this same heightened style often emerges after the point of "elevation," when preachers are said to start receiving ideas and words from on high. Again the voice eases from a conversational to a poetic mode. Again the words pattern themselves into short, cadenced phrases. And again these phrases assume a distinctly melodic lilt, taking on tonal contours that lend the whole a chant-like character. In the sermon, these features emerge markedly when the preacher moves into "high gear" and the Spirit is said to take greater control of the preaching voice. At this same time, the Spirit often makes itself manifest in a variety of other ways. Preachers cry out; deacons weep; mothers leap into the holy dance. Once again, speech style and signs of the Spirit coincide. (2000:71)

Hinson's description is a perfect example of a survival of African oral tradition in the U.S., and also of the importance of individuality of expression within the culturally defined framework and formula of the African American sermon. The point of elevation of which Hinson speaks does not tend to occur at the beginning of the sermon; as with other discourse genres, there is a preferred order. The preacher and congregation must first be spiritually and physically prepared for this part of the sermon to occur. The "spirit" does not tend to make its presence known in places where it is not welcome. Hence, this usually occurs AFTER prayer and scripture have been presented. Linguistically, it occurs AFTER a gradual rise in intonation and volume.

Previous research on the traditional African American sermon has primarily highlighted its connection to the African oral tradition of call-response and the notion of an oral formula that shapes the general sermon but allows room for individuality of expression. Like other forms of spoken discourse, the sermon genre has specific, definable patterns. Even irregularity of sermon lines can be viewed as a pattern; the absence of line regularity is a significant distinguishable characteristic of the Black sermon in the same way that back-channeling, continuous floor-holding changes, and absence of immediate feedback are distinguishable features of traditional lectures as contrasted with conversation.

Research on components of the lecture and conversation discourse genres and of boundaries that divide them have shown that, although specific characteristics help to distinguish lecture from conversation, there is often some overlap; discourse analysts have identified this as "fuzzy boundaries" of discourse genres. In a study of therapeutic discourse—the type of discourse used in psychotherapy sessions—Ferrara (1994) proposes a seven-part model that, she states, can be used to differentiate conversation (or "the unmarked form of discourse") from other types of discourse. She includes in this model such features as RECIPROCALITY (knowledge that participants will share the floor by negotiation) and PARITY (agreement among participants to share power equally). Conversation is characterized by negotiation for the floor, interchanging of turns, spontaneity, and verbal participation by two or more participants; lecture typically does not share those characteristics. Dudley-Evans & Johns (1981), however, identify several different STYLES of lecture (reading, conversational, and performance styles); the conversational style could suggest that the boundaries between lecture and conversation may not be as clear-cut as often believed. That is, it is not necessarily the case that all lectures are devoid of features typically found in conversation, such as floor sharing and negotiation.

Not only have discourse analysts studied characteristics of these two genres as a whole; many have also examined a number of discourse markers within the two genres and have shown that linguistic utterances previously viewed as insignificant often play important roles in production and comprehension of texts. Schiffrin (1988) highlights multiple functions of markers such as *well* and *you know* in conversation. Chaudron & Richards (1986) shed light on different functions of micro- and macro-markers as aids in the comprehension of lectures.

The African American sermon is an interesting genre for linguistic analysis for two reasons. The first is the strong sociolinguistic connection between African and African American cultural norms and specific linguistic features that typically appear almost exclusively in church settings; and second, from a discourse analysis perspective, this genre also provides an excellent example of the "fuzzy boundaries" of genres more broadly. The African American sermon has features both similar to and different from those found in lecture and conversation, and these features are primarily linked to and perhaps shaped by a distinctly African American emphasis on oral tradition that is expected in traditional Black church services. Specifically, shorter utterances within the larger African American sermon reveal both structured and spontaneous culturally shaped discourse.

Most references to such shorter religious formulaic expressions as *Amen* concern expressions the congregation utters as a part of call-response. Smitherman (2000) illustrates this well: "In the sacred style, the minister is urged on by the congregation's *Amen's*, *That's right*, *Reverend's*, or *Preach Reverend's*. One also hears occasional *Take your time's* when

the preacher is initiating his sermon, the congregation desiring to savor every little [bit] of this good message they bout to hear" (2000:64). What has not been examined is PREACHERS' use of such expressions and the role(s) that their use of them plays in sermon performance. Focusing particularly on discourse functions of markers in sermons preached in traditional Black churches, this study highlights a genre that is underexamined from a discourse perspective and its specific discourse markers that have not been fully analyzed; it also shows the import of both textual and cultural analysis for comprehension of roles discourse markers can play.

The primary question examined in this study is whether call-response is the sole function of traditional Black preachers' utterances of specific religious formulaic expressions (e.g., *Amen, Hallelujah, Praise God*), or whether these expressions also have other discourse-marking functions. I hypothesize that although the preacher may utter such expressions as *Say Amen* that appear on the surface to have a call-response function (preacher directly and specifically soliciting a congregational response), we cannot assume that the illocutionary force, or speaker's intention, is solely that of a call for congregational response. To comprehend fully the function(s) of such expressions, we must consider both text and cultural analysis. Call-response is certainly evident in traditional African American sermons, but preachers' specific utterances that initially APPEAR to observers to elicit a response may in actuality serve some other function within the preaching discourse. I will use both significant consideration of African American church cultural norms and textual analysis to determine what the functions of these utterances are.

METHOD

The discourse community discussed in this study includes six preachers and congregations representing a traditional African American worship style that includes such West African cultural survivals as call-response, shouting, "holy dancing," and speaking in tongues, along with sermon characteristics described by Davis (1987) (preacher's indication of "message sent from God," literal and broad scripture interpretation, secular vs. sacred conflict, moves between concrete and abstract) and by Mitchell (1970) (use of vernacular, connections to contemporary needs, spontaneity and individuality in performance, climax). Instead of focusing on one denomination, I selected independent nondenominational churches with preachers and members who had backgrounds in different denominations, but all with a common "traditional Black worship" thread; the most common backgrounds included Pentecostal Holiness, Church of God in Christ (COGIC), and Baptist. The primary reason the pastors had left these denominations had little or nothing to do with the style of worship; that was typically maintained in their independent churches. Reasons for leaving tended to center on a desire for freedom from standard hierarchies or on preachers' "call from God" to establish a church or churches through which their God-given visions could be realized without hindrance from denominational authorities who might not "see" the same vision. The six churches also represented different regions of the U.S., again with the common bond of "traditional Black church" format and style; cities included Los Angeles and Oakland (California), Salisbury (Maryland), Jacksonville (Florida), and Memphis (Tennessee). Three preachers were female (two pastors and one "evangelist"[1]), and three were male pastors. All the preachers were older than fifty, and all had more than ten years of preaching experience.

Before collecting tape-recorded sermons preached in these churches, I participated in numerous services and compared those experiences with my childhood experience and knowledge of the culture (my mother was an evangelist, and my stepfather an apostle/pastor/evangelist, in the types of churches described in the study). I conducted informal interviews with preachers and church members to solidify my understanding of the community. (For detailed descriptions of my personal experiences and of interviews with pastors, see Wharry 1996.) I then selected six sermons (60–90 minutes in length) that had been previously audiotaped. Since it was common practice for the services to be tape-recorded so people could hear the sermons again or so that members who missed the service could listen to the message, the preachers were aware that they were being recorded, but they were not aware that their sermons would later be analyzed by a researcher.

I then transcribed the sermons according to intonational units, identified each instance of the formulaic expressions (*Amen, Hallelujah, Praise God*, etc.) used, and examined the textual (e.g., preceding and following text) and situational (e.g., audience participation) context of the expressions. A major reason for the selection of the *Amen* and *Hallelujah* kinds of expressions is that these are often associated with call-response functions (expressions used by the audience as back-channeling cues for the preacher), but preachers use them in their sermons as well. Mentions in earlier studies of a preacher using these expressions often view this as a call for the audience to respond verbally (e.g., *Amen church, Somebody say Amen*). As discussed previously, these preachers' utterances may or may not actually have a call-response function, and if they do, this may not be their sole function. Another initial response to observing these utterances could be to label them as verbal or pause fillers; however, preliminary observations of the situational context and more specific textual analysis could suggest that these expressions have functions other than call for response or pause filler.

RESULTS

Although the primary goal of this study was to explore discourse functions of utterances, one immediate observation was that gender-linked differences appeared to exist in the degree of variety of formulaic expressions used. Female preachers were likely to produce a greater number of different tokens, while male preachers tended to stick with one

expression. Further analysis of this and other gender-linked differences in Black preaching will be explored in a separate study.

General results of the functions of expressions examined show that the TEXTUAL BOUNDARY MARKER was the most frequently occurring function (77 out of 112 cases, or 69% of the cases examined, had this function). All of the tokens (*Amen, Hallelujah, Praise, Glory, Bless* ...) functioned at least four times as textual boundary markers (see Table 1). This function was divided into three subcategories: text type change, topic/subtopic boundary, and topic continuity. Only 1 of the 112 tokens identified in the sermons had a call-response function (see Table 2).

A second significant function appeared on the surface to be simply as verbal filler, but these expressions actually functioned not only to give preachers time to think about their next statements or to fill space while members of the congregation were "caught up in the Spirit." Here, preachers' choice of religious formulaic expressions instead of such secular and typical pause fillers as *uh* suggests a function of maintaining spiritual discourse during these moments. These markers, labeled SPIRITUAL DISCOURSE MAINTENANCE markers, represent 21% (23 out of the 112) of the formulaic expressions examined.

RHYTHMIC MARKERS, a third function that represents 10 of the 112 markers identified, reinforce the importance of preachers' establishing a rhythmic balance both within the sermon itself (as an individual performer) and with the audience (as a co-performer). This function, perhaps more than others, shows the importance of discourse community knowledge for comprehension of the roles formulaic expressions can have.

The least common function of sermonic formulaic expressions was CALL-RESPONSE. Even though we might expect more of these expressions to function in this way, in my data only once did a preacher use expressions like *Will you say Amen?* or *Amen?* for the purpose of eliciting a congregational response.

Overall results suggest that religious formulaic expressions in traditional African American sermons tend to function primarily as textual boundary markers, but they can also have three other qualitatively significant roles. Though less frequent, all these assist in making the sermon performance characteristically African American.

The following section includes explanations and examples of the aforementioned roles: textual boundary markers, spiritual discourse maintenance markers, rhythmic markers, and call-response marker. Preachers' utterances, with formulaic expressions set in bold, are written in lines according to intonation units. Instances of members of the congregation responding in a call-response manner are indicated in parentheses as "congregational response" because, in most cases there was not one single, uniform response; different members of the congregation tended to use different expressions simultaneously. In a separate work, I will explore individual members of the congregation and their response preferences (e.g., *you sho nuff preachin* vs.

Table 1. Raw Frequencies of Expressions by Role

	Textual Boundary	Call for Response	Spiritual Filler	Rhythmic Marker	Multiple Roles	T
Amen	28	1	12	1	1	43
Hallelujah	16	0	2	5	0	23
Yeah Lord/Hey God	4	0	0	0	0	4
Praise	4	0	6	0	0	10
Thank	12	0	1	4	0	17
Glory	5	0	1	0	0	6
Bless	4	0	1	0	0	5
Mercy	4	0	0	0	0	4
Total	77	1	23	10	1	112

Table 2. Frequencies and Percentages of Roles for Combined Expressions

	Raw Frequency	Percentage of Expressions Functioning in Indicated Roles
Textual boundary	77	69
Call for response	1	1
Spiritual filler	23	21
Rhythmic marker	10	8
Multiple roles	1	1
Total	112	100

alright now vs. *Glory!* vs. *Amen preacher* vs. simply standing with hands on hips and head nodding while saying nothing). This may reveal interesting information about the role of linguistic individuality (verbal and nonverbal) within the larger group context. Because of the present study's emphasis on the PREACHER's use of formulaic expressions, those are highlighted. General observations suggest that even though different audience members choose different expressions to express their agreement with the preacher, the varied utterances serve a similar purpose that allows for joint production of the preaching performance.

Textual Boundary Markers

Items placed in the textual boundary category included markers of (i) text type changes (changes or moves from one text type or speech event to another; e.g., narration to evaluation, constructed speech to statement of proposition, scripture reference to personal experience); (ii) topic or subtopic boundary (changes from one discourse topic to another; e.g., change from talking about legalism in the church to speaking about having riches); and (iii) topic continuity (used for returns to previously introduced topics after a digression). Although there are differences among the three markers identified, they share a role of signaling change within the text.

Following are examples of the three types of textual boundary markers.

(1) *Text type change*
none of us today,
that I know of,
is in jail! (congregational responses)

Lord have mercy, (congregational response)
..so we shouldn't bc:,
in prison,
in our mind.

Although the preacher continues with the "prison" subtopic introduced earlier in the text, **Lord have mercy** appears between a literal presentation of *jail* and a figurative or abstract concept of *prison in our mind*. The preacher clearly has not uttered this expression to elicit a response, since the congregation has already responded. This textual boundary is reinforced by the short pause and *so*. Even if one argues that the preacher may have used this utterance to extend time for formulation of following words (a verbal filler role), an explanation of why he uses this utterance at this point in the discourse can be based on the change that takes place—the move to the abstract. If there is any call for response here, it is the preacher's statement that nobody in the congregation is in jail, coupled with his change in intonation. When it is time for the change from the literal *jail* to the abstract *prison in our mind*, the preacher is not doing this alone; the congregation is actively participating, with anticipation that the preacher will make this point personally relevant.

Example (2) is a similar case of formulaic expression functioning as a marker of text type change:

(2) ...to be restored in the spirit.
..a spi:ritual restoration.
..a spi:ritual revival.
..a spi:ritual resurrection.
..a spi:ritual refreshing. (congregational responses)
..a spi:ritual revitalization. (congregational responses)
..Praise God.

from theoretical to a specific example

..a spi:ritual rejuvenation. (congregational responses)
..Thank you Lord. (congregational responses)
..Glory to God. (congregational responses)
..Hallelujah.
..the word "restoration" comes from the word "restore",
..which means turn ba:ck,
o:r,
to rebuild.

What is perhaps most notable about this excerpt is the preacher's effective use of lexical and phonological repetition (alliteration); the "spiritual r…" unit is similar to units Tannen (1989) selected from orations by Martin Luther King, Jr., and Jesse Jackson as exemplary involvement strategies used in oratory. The focus here, though, is on the placement and function of formulaic expressions in the text. There is a noticeable difference between what precedes the *Thank you Lord, Glory to God, Hallelujah* string of utterances and what follows. Not only is there a move from synonymous statement of the preacher's sermon topic to definition; in addition, the sound (especially the rhythm) of her "spiritual r…" unit is strikingly different from the *word "restoration"* section. With the definition section, the preacher decreases speech volume, congregational responses temporarily cease, and a less heightened emotional atmosphere is created. This change is introduced by the three formulaic expressions along with phonological prominence.

Items in the "text type change" category do not signal major changes in the topic or subtopic of the sermons examined, even though this is the most common type of textual boundary marker for conversations. Instead, this kind of discourse marker signals a change from one speech event to another. The next section explains the better-known "topic boundary marker" function.

Topic Boundary

Examples (3–4) show formulaic expressions appearing not between different textual types but between different discourse topics or subtopics:

(3) you say "well this is mind over
matter".
no this is the word of Go:d,
over matter. (congregational response)
..this is the words of God over the problem.
this is u:sing the words of Go:d,
over the negative.
this is using the word of Go:d,
over..**Amen** the strategy and the tricks
of the enemy. (congregational response)
…**Amen.** (congregational response)
…so then,
…as a person with blood pressure says,

The second **Amen** in (3) appears just after the preacher has completed a *this is…word of God* unit with high congregational involvement. The end of this unit is signaled by

lowered volume, a long pause, **Amen**, a following pause, and *so then*. This is not a change in the larger sermon topic but a change in the speaker's subtopic, from the theoretical *using the word of God* to his specific example of a person with high blood pressure who uses *the word* to get healed.

A second example of subtopic boundary marker shows an even stronger content contrast. In (4), the speaker sets up a contrast between Black legalistic churches and White charismatic (more lenient) churches, and places **Thank you Jesus** at the boundary between the two groups being contrasted:

(4) …I look good 'cause I don' covered
up a few things.
(congregational response)
…and y'all gonna put me in hell,
you ain't gon' put me in hell behind
that foolishness.
(congregational response)
I ain't goin' to hell behind that.
(congregational response)
Thank you Jesus. (congregational response)
you go right over,
and I'm gon' preach it,
and I I don't mean to put nobody—
—down,
but you go to Morris Cerullo's—
—meetings,
you go to uh uh Marilyn Hickey's—
—meetings,
you go to any of these meetings,
you know who's sitting up there?
thousands of you:r people.
(congregational response)
…and I don' went to see them,
for myself. (congregational response)
..and you know who's writing checks—
—for five hundred dollars,
and a thousand dollars?
and supporting they ministry?
..yo:ur people. (congregational response)
…and they be there with pants on,
they be there with lipstick on,
they be there everything on,
but you know what,
cancer's being healed,
(congregational responses through next seven intonation
units)
high blood pressure being,
all kind of miracles is being—
—wrought,
'cause they up there talking about—
—nothing but the po:wer!
of the living God!

Black Churches

→ *(Boundary)*

White Churches

In the unit preceding the preacher's **Thank you Jesus**, she complains about Black church members judging people for wearing makeup. What follows the expression is a strong contrast to the legalistic attitudes and behaviors of Black church members; she discusses both the different way that Blacks behave when they attend White churches (as opposed to their behavior at their own churches) and the absence of legalism at the White churches visited. She says that there are miracles at some White churches even though they "be there with pants on, they be there with lipstick on, they be there [with] everything on."

The topic boundary marker signals a change from one discourse (sermon) topic or subtopic to another topic not previously occurring in the current discourse. The following section provides examples of a third type of textual boundary marker, the "topic continuity" marker.

Topic Continuity

The previous two types of textual boundary markers (text-type change and topic boundary) are similar to the third, topic continuity, in that all three function to signal textual change: however, topic continuity suggests a return to something previously mentioned in the text. In (5), the preacher utters a formulaic expression after a diversion and before a return to the topic that appeared before the diversion:

(5) ..now there are two points in—
  —the Bible,
  that are very important,
  in your understanding.
  I don't wanna preach.
  I said "God shall I preach or—teach?"
  God says.. "you just open your—
  —mou:th." (congregational response)
  ...I don't wanna preach.
  ..I wanna tal:k
  ...**Amen**.
  ...listen.
  ...uh,
  ..there are two points,

[handwritten: Must get back after "metalanguage" / talking about his own sermon]

Beginning with the fourth line in (5), the preacher creates a diversion by using metalanguage: He comments about his delivery of the sermon. Earlier in the sermon, the preacher had produced several units of talk with high volume and pitch. He now wants to *calm down* a bit and just *teach*, but after his constructed speech of his talk with God, the congregation gives praise again. It must have been *you just open your mou:th* that triggered a response. After the praise, the preacher says again that he doesn't want to preach but that he wants to teach instead. This is followed by a pause and *Amen*. After *Amen*, other signals of textual change appear (e.g., pause and *listen*). This is not a topic change, though, because he is just repeating the point he mentioned at the beginning of this unit (i.e., there are two points), before the diversion. An interesting note about this preacher's mention of his struggle to teach and to resist preaching is that, for most congregation members like those in this study, sermon discourse that lacks a high level of rhythmic intensity and sounds like "lectures" is not classified as "real preachin'";

that kind of discourse, for them, lacks an important spiritual dimension and is classified as "teaching" (something "unsaved folks" do). See Wharry 1996 for a detailed discussion of interview results on the teaching/preaching distinction.

In (6), a formulaic expression appears before a return to a topic and after a related subtopic:

(6) ..and the scripture teaches,
  that there is power,
  ..the power to get you over,
  ...**Amen**.
  and get you through your valley.
  ..power,
  to restore your health.
  ..power,
  to bring success. .and the blessings—
  —of God into your life.
  ..power to turn your situation—
  -around.
  ...and it is all in the power of the—
  —words that can come out of your—
  —mouth.
  ..o:r,
  ..on the other hand,
  power to cast you down to the lowest—
  —hell.
  power to impoverish you,
  power to send you to an early and a—
  —premature grave.
  power to rob you of the blessings—
  —and the privileges of sonship.
  and,
  uh **Amen** association with Christ. *[handwritten: used to break up this line.]*
  power to bind you,
  power to curse you,
  power to defeat you,
  a:ll in the power of the to:ngue.
  (congregational response)
  ...**Somebody say Amen**.
  (congregational response)
  ...words! (congregational response)
  ...words. (congregational response)

The first two expressions in (6) appear to function as fillers, with the first *Amen* appearing as the preacher is trying to set up what will be a very effective rhythmic *power* series and the second appearing at a place in the *power* series after an intonation unit considerably longer than other units in the series. *Somebody say Amen* is clearly different from the first two formulaic expressions in this excerpt. It appears immediately after the preacher finishes his *power to* unit and before a return to an emphasis on *words*, mentioned 15 lines earlier and previously in the sermon. Although this expression may appear to be a call for response if viewed out of context, looking at both the congregational expressions preceding it (suggesting no need to call for a response) and the falling intonation of the utterance suggests a different function. *Somebody say Amen*, along with pause and intonation changes, signals a return to a previous lexical theme. The preacher clearly was not asking people to "say Amen"; people were already participating verbally during this part of the sermon. Instead, he uses this expression to signal that he is leaving the subtopic of power and returning to his previous emphasis on words.

Spiritual Discourse Maintenance Marker

Examples (7–8) illustrate a role that may initially appear as a verbal filler role. Holmes & Stubbe (1995) claim that this is one of the more simplistic functions of pragmatic devices. While they agree that utterances previously identified by some linguists as verbal fillers or as hedges may have the suggested functions of allowing time for verbal planning or of creating a hedging effect (suggesting insecurity of disempowered groups), Holmes & Stubbe claim that closer contextual analysis of these expressions (e.g., *you know, I mean, sort of*) reveals a greater and more complex range of meanings.

The results of this study support Holmes & Stubbe's claim regarding range of meanings for expressions that appear to be used to allow time for planning utterances. Although a number of preachers' sermonic *Amens* may have a space-filling function, their choice of words is significant. In the specific context of African American sermonic discourse, that only 21% of such expressions seem to function in this manner is not quantitatively significant. Qualitatively, however, these occurrences are remarkably significant in that preachers choose to select "religious-sounding" expressions to be consistent with the preaching context in places where, in secular settings, they might use *uh* or other fillers. To maintain the spiritual atmosphere and not disrupt the continuity of the sermon and flow of the Spirit, preachers tend to use fewer "secular" verbal fillers. Because of their double function as both fillers and maintainers of the spiritual environment, these expressions have been labeled SPIR-ITUAL DISCOURSE MAINTENANCE FILLERS.

In (7), the preacher uses both and interrupts two secular verbal fillers with *Amen*:

(7) ...God wrote his fi:rst word to—
    —mankind,
    in stone.
    ..he didn't write it on paper,
    he didn't write it on (?),
    he didn't write it on anything that—
    —was transitory,
    that could fade away,
    that could be uh,
    ..**Amen** uh,
    ..smudged over,
    but he wrote it on sto:ne.

In the latter part of this excerpt, the preacher appears to be searching for words. It was not unusual that formulaic expressions that did not appear at textual boundaries and were not elicitations of audience responses were accompanied by *uh*. It appears that the inclusion of *Amen* lessens the appearance of the preacher's having moved out of the spiritual; his **Amen** seems to suggest that even though he may need time to *get his words together*, he is not relying totally on the secular self but is still in the spiritual realm. Although this expression is surrounded by other hesitation markers (i.e., *uh*), this is not a requirement for the spiritual maintenance filler role.

In some cases, as in (8), a religious formulaic expression may be used instead of *uh* to replace a pause or to shorten the length of pause:

(8) ...this is the word of God over the—
    —pro:blem.
    this is using the word of Go:d,
    over the negative.
    this is using the word of Go:d,
    over..**Amen** the strategy and the—
    —tricks,
    of the e:nemy. (congregational responses)

Here the formulaic expression is preceded by a pause and followed immediately, without pause, by the rest of the intonation unit members. It would not seem strange if this speaker had used *uh* here instead of **Amen**. Using **Amen** helps the preacher to avoid a noticeably long pause that might disrupt the flow of his sermon. Also, since the expectations of this particular discourse community include spiritual or religious language, using **Amen** or similar expressions instead of *uh* or other nonreligious fillers helps the preacher to seem more "together."

Although the function of spiritual discourse maintenance fillers is viewed as qualitatively significant (Table 2), for no preacher in the study did more than 40% of expressions examined function as fillers alone (Table 3). As stated previously, the textual boundary marker functions were by far the most quantitatively significant.

Rhythmic Marker

Another discourse function identified appeared on a surface level to be a verbal filler as well, but upon further examination of both textual and situational context, it seems clearly to function in an interestingly different manner. Preachers may use the rhythmic marker, or enhancer, function either to strengthen the rhythm of a set of utterances or to keep themselves in tune with what the audience is doing by letting the intonation pattern match the flow of the service. In the latter sense, the preacher is responding to the audience. Although the use of formulaic expressions as rhythmic markers was evident in only two of the six sermons, the significance of this marker lies in textual-cultural connections and, more specifically, points to a function that may have genre implications. Davis (1987) has shown that African American sermons have irregular lines that are made rhythmic by such devices as dramatic pause and repetition. The results of my study show that formulaic expressions are also used to aid in the establishment of that rhythm.

Table 3. Preachers' Percentages of Roles for All Expressions Combined

	Textual Boundary	Call for Response	Spiritual Filler	Rhythmic Marker	Multiple Roles	T
Preacher #1	65	0	20	15	0	100
Preacher #2	50	5	40	0	5	100
Preacher #3	70	0	0	30	0	100
Preacher #4	85	0	10	5	0	100
Preacher #5	60	0	40	0	0	100
Preacher #6	92	0	8	0	0	100

In (9), **_Hallelujah_** is used as a rhythmic enhancer; these strategically placed expressions appear in a climactic part of the sermon. They are used in places where some preachers might take audible and rhythmic breaths throughout the most intense passages. Although these too could be classified as verbal fillers, the purpose of filling the pauses is strikingly different. The use of these expressions in this unit is by no means simplistic. The preacher ("performer" comes to mind here) is catching his breath in a rather rhythmic way that actually enhances the high emotional level of the preaching event; he is not just tired and in need of taking a breath, nor does he appear to be searching for words:

(9) . . . some of our mi:nds,
    are so narrow. (congregational response)
    to fee:l,
    that Go:d,
    only have,
    yo:ur people,
    (congregational responses follow each of the following intonational units in this section)
    as being,
    his church.
    Hallelujah.
    Je:sus,
    suffered too lo:ng,
    Hallelujah.
    to die for a few people.
    Thank you Lord.
    He die:d,
    That the whole wo:rld,
    would have an opportunity,
    to be saved.
    but what he sai:d,
    Hallelujah,
    he sai:d,
    Hallelujah,
    he said to Peter.
    Hallelujah.
    fee:d,
    my lamb.

In (10), another type of rhythmic marker is identified, but this one could be labeled more specifically as a "flow gauger" rather than as an "enhancer" (as in 9). As a rhythmic marker, the formulaic expressions used tell us something about the rhythm of the utterances or signal prominent

rhythmic activity. This use shows the speaker's greater attention to the audience's behavior rather than an intentional creative performance strategy. Furthermore, this function is one that appears to work perfectly with African American sermon performance styles:

(10) I want you to. . speak to me,
     and God said "they're fighting—
     —battles that are already won.
     (congregational responses begin and gradually lessen in intensity throughout the next four intonation units)
     . . . Tha:nk you Jesus.
     . . . Tha:nk you Jesus.
     . . . Tha:nk you Jesus.
     . . Thank you Lo:rd.   _textual boundary._
     . . . And so, (much higher pitch)
     . . we find today. . that,
     the spirit of God is,
     show:in us the way.

As the congregation "goes up in praise" when hearing _fighting battles already won_, the preacher uses the formulaic expressions highlighted above. Interesting to note is that the fourth token (**_Thank you Lo:rd_**) has intonational and lexical changes. Instead of stressing **_Tha:nk_**, the first word in the formulaic expression unit, he places emphasis on the last word and changes from **_Jesus_** to **_Lord_**. The **_Tha:nk you Jesus_** expressions appear to be functioning to show the verbally active audience that the preacher is "with them"; complete silence on the part of the preacher might have weakened his perceived support of the congregational praise. He is essentially following the audience's lead. The preacher's intonational and lexical changes with the fourth token (**_Thank you Lo:rd_**) have a different function, though: This phonologically prominent formulaic expression is not a rhythmic marker, but seems to function as a textual boundary (specifically, topic continuity) along with the following _and so_. It signals a move from praise and a return to the sermon topic.

Unlike the textual boundary marker and spiritual filler functions, the rhythmic marker role is clearly tied to performance (in an oral-tradition sense). As discussed by Wharry (1996, chap. 3), one of the important criteria for good African American preaching is that the preacher be a good "performer"; it is important that the preacher not "lecture" or "teach," but "preach." This role is not likely to appear in conversation (except in AAVE conversations) or lecture (but cf.

Dudley-Evans & Johns (1981) on the performance style of lecture).

Although the rhythmic marker function is a perfect example of a discourse marker strongly connected with traditional African American culture, the predominant call-response format seen in traditional Black churches is displayed in the overall service and in congregational responses, but it is infrequently a function of the preacher's formulaic expressions.

Call-and-Response Marker

As stated previously, the call-and-response function is the label applied to formulaic expressions used by a preacher to elicit a response from the audience. Only one of the 112 expressions in the study functioned mainly as a call for congregational response:

(11) . . we try to understand everything
(congregational response)
. . and there's some things in this life,
that you just absolutely not gonna—
—understand.
. . . Will you say Amen? (congregational response)
. . . there are some things that you're not—
—gonna understand,
. . you will just have to,
. . believe it,
. . and,
. . do it. (congregational response)

Although the preacher received responses to his statement about people trying to understand everything, there were no responses to the following line, which is really the main point. The speaker pauses and then says, with question intonation, **Will you say Amen?** This gets a response, and the preacher repeats the main point. An important note is that there were other cases of expressions with **Say Amen** that did not function as calls for audience response, illustrated in (12):

(12) . . . the scripture says,
. . life and death,
. . are in the to:ngue.
. . either one.
. . either one.
. . life,
. . or death,
. . are in the tongue
. . . Will you say Amen? *no response.*
. . I recently read,
. . about a doctor,
. . who to:ld one of his patients,
. . that she needed,
. . an operation

In this example, **Will you say Amen?** is not functioning as a request for action (response), and the congregation understands that; they do not give a response here. This is the

beginning of the preacher's sermon, and he is not really desiring *Amens* yet. Instead, he is using this utterance to signal a change from scripture reference to exemplary personal experience, a textual boundary marker function.

A similar example of an utterance that appears on the surface to be a call for response but that functions differently is the following:

(13) . . . most people offer absolutely no: resistance,
when the enemy comes in like a flood,
they accept whate:ver,
the devil brings,
against them and into their lives,
. . and they offer no resistance. (congregational responses)
. . . Say Amen
. . . I want you to kno:w,
that when we realize the power of wo:rds,
. . and the power of a positive confession,
the power of a positive acknowledgment,
. . things are going to begin to happen,
. . in. . our. . lives.

In this excerpt, also from near the beginning of a sermon, **Say Amen** signals a contrast between negative (not resisting the devil) and positive (recognizing the power of words and using positive confessions to cause great things to occur in our lives). This formulaic expression functions not as a call for response but as a textual boundary marker.

That only one formulaic expression functioned as a call for response does not suggest a lack of importance for call-response in African American sermons. Instead, this may indicate that the preacher has other strategies for "calling." Most often, the preachers in this study appeared to rely more on phonological prominence; the congregation is well attuned to the preacher's rhythm and can interact accordingly, without the need for a direct call to say *Amen*.

CONCLUSION

Findings show that multiple functions exist for religious formulaic expressions in African American sermons, and that identification of these roles requires both textual and discourse community knowledge. Knowing that *Somebody say Amen* is not necessarily a call for response requires contextual analysis, just as the identification of the rhythmic marker function requires an understanding of the importance of oral-tradition "performance" in African American discourse communities. The use of *Amen, Praise God,* and similar expressions as spiritual maintenance fillers is connected with the importance of "sounding spiritual" and the strong preaching/teaching distinction in this particular religious discourse community. That is, to preach a good traditional African American sermon, the preacher and congregation must display oral-tradition features (some of which are aided and/or represented by formulaic expressions). Although such features as call-response and establishment of rhythm connect the African American preaching style with secular AAVE styles, the "spiritual" language distinguishes them. In addition, the call-response and rhythmic marker functions point to the African American sermon as a discourse genre that crosses the boundaries of conversation and lecture. Like participants in conversation, the preacher and congregation jointly produce the sermon, and both use socially constructed DMs in that production. Like a lecturer the preacher is still clearly in charge and has the power to change or support the flow of the church service by using a variety of verbal strategies (e.g., "flow gauger" rhythmic markers). Clearly, the most common function of *Amens* was to signal textual boundaries (69%). This again points to a similar function of "sounding spiritual" while performing a different function—in this case, alerting the congregation to coming changes in discourse topic or returns to previous discourse. Preachers could choose to use more secular cohesive markers (e.g., *on the other hand, in contrast, however*), but although these mark boundaries, they do not reinforce the spiritual tone of sermonic discourse as do religious formulaic expressions such as *Amen* and *Hallelujah*.

Note

I would like to thank Jane H. Hill and an anonymous reviewer for critical suggestions, thought-provoking questions, and encouraging comments on earlier drafts of this article. I would also like to thank Carol Lynn Moder for invaluable suggestions and support during the development of the doctoral dissertation upon which this article is based. I am especially grateful to the preachers and church members whose lives and expressions make this work possible.

1. An "evangelist" is a preacher whose primary ministry involves traveling to different churches to preach, unlike pastors, whose main ministry usually involves providing spiritual leadership and preaching at one home or local church.

TRANSCRIPTION CONVENTIONS (MODIFIED BY EDITOR FROM TANNEN, CHAPTER 25)

…half-second pause. Each dot represents another half-second of pause

. sentence-final falling intonation

, clause-final intonation (more to come)

! excited intonation

: lengthened vowel sound

bold indicates text that is analyzed in the chapter

(congregational response[s]) indicates the congregation providing some audible response

References

Abrahams, Roger (1970). *Deep down in the jungle: Negro narrative folklore from the streets of Philadelphia*. Chicago: Aldine Press.

Abrahams, Roger (1976). *Talking black*. Rowley, MA: Newbury House.

Baer, Hans, & Singer, Merrill (1992). *African American religion in the twentieth century: Varieties of protest and accommodation*. Knoxville: University of Tennessee Press.

Barrett, Leonard (1974). *Soul-force: African heritage in Afro-American religion*. Garden City, NY: Anchor Books.

Baugh, John (1983). *Black street speech: Its history, structure, and survival*. Austin: University of Texas Press.

Blassingame, John W. (1979). *The slave community: Plantation life in the antebellum South*. New York: Oxford University Press.

Chaudron, Craig, & Richards, Jack C. (1986). The effect of discourse markers on the comprehension of lectures. *Applied Linguistics* 7:113–127.

Daniel, Jack L., & Smitherman, Geneva (1976). "How I got ovah": Communication dynamics in the Black community. *Quarterly Journal of Speech* (February):26–39.

Davis, Gerald (1987). *I got the world in me and I can sing it, you know*. Philadelphia: University of Pennsylvania Press.

Dudley-Evans, Tony, & Johns, Alana (1981). A team teaching approach to lecture comprehension for overseas students. In *The teaching of listening comprehension*. (ELT Documents Special, pp. 30–46). London: British Council.

Dundes, Alan (1981). *The evil eye: A folklore casebook*. New York: Garland Publishers.

Edwards, Viv, & Seinkewicz, Thomas J. (1991). *Oral cultures past and present: Rappin and Homer*. Oxford: Blackwell.

Erickson, Millard J. (1984). *Christian Theology*. Grand Rapids, MI: Baker Book House.

Ferrara, Kathleen (1994). *Therapeutic ways with words*. New York: Oxford University Press.

Frazier, E. F. (1964). *The Negro church in America*. New York: Holt, Rinehart & Winston.

Herskovits, Melville J. (1958). *The myth of the Negro past*. Boston: Beacon Press.

Hinson, Glenn (2000). *Fire in my bones: Transcendence and the Holy Spirit in African American gospel*. Philadelphia: University of Pennsylvania Press.

Holmes, Janet, & Stubbe, Maria (1995). You know, eh, and other "exasperating expressions": An analysis of social and stylistic variation in the use of pragmatic devices in a sample of New Zealand English. *Language and Communication* 15(1):63–88.

Jules-Rosette, Bennetta (1980). Creative spirituality from Africa to America: Cross-cultural influences in contemporary religious forms. *Western Journal of Black Studies* 4:273–285.

Kochman, Thomas (1981). *Black and White styles in conflict*. Chicago: University of Chicago Press.

Lincoln, Charles Eric (1974). *The Black experience in religion*. Garden City, NY: Anchor Books.

Mitchell, Henry (1970). *Black preaching*. Philadelphia: Lippincott Publishers.

Mitchell, Henry (1975). *Black belief*. San Francisco: Harper & Row.

Pawley, Andrew (1992). Formulaic speech. In W. Bright (ed.), *Oxford International Encyclopedia of Linguistics*, vol. 2, 22–25. New York: Oxford University Press.

Pipes, William H. (1951). *Say Amen, brother! Old time Negro preaching: A study in American frustration*. New York: William Frederick.

Pitts, Walter (1986). *Linguistic variation as a function of ritual frames in the Afro-Baptist Church in central Texas*. Dissertation, University of Texas, Austin.

Pitts, Walter (1989). West African poetics in the black preaching style. *American Speech* 64:137–149.

Raboteau, Albert J. (1978). *Slave religion*. New York: Oxford University Press.

Robert, Charles Edwin (1972). *Negro civilization in the South*. Black Heritage Library Collection: Ayer Publishers.

Rosenberg, Bruce (1970). *The art of the American folk preacher*. New York: Oxford University Press.

Schiffrin, Deborah (1988). *Discourse markers*. New York: Cambridge University Press.

Sernett, Milton D. (1985). *Afro-American religious history: A documentary witness*. Durham, NC: Duke University Press.

Simpson, George Eaton (1978). *Black religions in the New World*. New York: Columbia University Press.

Smith, Frances (1993). The pulpit and woman's place: Gender and framing of the exegetical self in sermon performance. In Deborah Tannen (ed.), *Framing in discourse*, 146–175. New York: Oxford University Press.

Smitherman, Geneva (1986 [1977]). *Talkin and testifyin: The language of Black America*. Boston: Houghton Mifflin.

Smitherman, Geneva (2000). *Talkin that talk: Language, culture, and education in African America*. New York: Routledge.

Tannen, Deborah (1989). *Talking voices: Repetition, dialogue, and imagery in conversational discourse*. New York: Cambridge University Press.

Twining, Mary Arnold (1985). Movement and dance on the sea islands. *Journal of Black Studies* 15: 463–479.

Warner, Michael (1999). *American sermons: From Pilgrims to Martin Luther King Jr.* Washington, DC: Library of Congress.

Wharry, Cheryl (1996). *I'm gonna preach it, amen: Discourse functions of formulaic expressions in African American sermons*. Dissertation, Oklahoma State University, Stillwater.

Zeil, Catherine Agnes (1991). *Mother-tongue/father-tongue: Gender-linked differences in language use and their influence on the perceived authority of the preacher*. Dissertation, Princeton Theological Seminary.

Post-reading Questions / Activities

- How can such small words as *Amen* have such impressive functions? Look carefully at several of the sermons transcribed here. Read them out loud. Can you see exactly the claims that Wharry is making?
- What discourse markers might you find in other American subcultures, or other cultures around the world? How do they function? How can you figure out their functions? Can you just ask the speakers?
- Observe two religious services and record the discourse markers used in each. Compare and explain them. Then observe another kind of speech situation (lecture, political speech). How are the discourse markers similar and different between the two types of speech events?
- How does audience participation (what Wharry mentions as "congregational response") work? Do you see a pattern that you could analyze? What does it mean to say that "Like participants in conversation, the preacher and congregation jointly produce the sermon"?

Vocabulary

AAVE	floor
back-channel cues	formulaic expression
call-response	genre
cultural survivals	hedge
discourse analysis	hesitation marker
discourse analysts	illocutionary force
discourse markers	orality
filler	token

Suggested Further Reading

Abrahams, Roger D. 1974. "Black Talking on the Street." In *Explorations in the Ethnography of Speaking*, edited by Richard Bauman and Joel Sherzer, pp. 240–262. Cambridge: Cambridge University Press.

———. 1983. *The Man-of-Words in the West Indies: Performance and the Emergence of Creole Culture*. Baltimore: Johns Hopkins University Press.

Baugh, John. 1983. *Black Street Speech: Its History, Structure, and Survival*. Austin: University of Texas Press.

Bauman, Richard, and Charles L. Briggs. 1990. "Poetics and Performance as Critical Perspectives on Language and Social Life." *Annual Review of Anthropology* 19: 59–88.

Bloch, Maurice, ed. 1975. *Political Language and Oratory in Traditional Society*. London: Academic Press.

Duranti, Alessandro. 1994. *From Grammar to Politics: Linguistic Anthropology in a Western Samoan Village*. Berkeley: University of California Press.

Hymes, Dell. 1975. "Breakthrough into Performance." In *Folklore: Performance and Communication*, edited by D. Ben-Amos and K. S. Goldstein, pp. 11–74. The Hague: Mouton.

———. 1981. *"In Vain I Tried to Tell You": Essays in Native American Ethnopoetics*. Philadelphia: University of Pennsylvania Press.

Labov, William. 1972. *Language in the Inner City: Studies in the Black English Vernacular*. Philadelphia: University of Pennsylvania Press.

Morgan, Marcyeliena. 2002. *Language, Discourse, and Power in African American Culture*. Cambridge: Cambridge University Press.

Rickford, John R., and Russell J. Rickford. 2000. *Spoken Soul: The Story of Black English*. New York: Wiley.

Smitherman, Geneva. 1977. *Talkin and Testifyin: The Language of Black America*. Boston: Houghton Mifflin.

———. 1994. *Black Talk: Words and Phrases from the Hood to the Amen Corner*. Boston: Houghton Mifflin.

Tedlock, Dennis. 1983. *The Spoken Word and the Work of Interpretation*. Philadelphia: University of Pennsylvania Press.

CHAPTER 39

Courtroom Questioning as a Culturally Situated Persuasive Genre of Talk

Yanrong Chang

(2004)

Institutions such as law and medicine operate within a broad cultural context but may have specific features unique to those spheres (cf. Chapter 30). When we think about questions in court, we often think of them as designed to turn up certain kinds of information (demonstrating a general tendency to foreground the referential function of language, or its purpose in providing information).

Yanrong Chang points out, however, that questioning (as an embodied act, rather than being seen strictly in terms of isolated questions) may have rather different purposes. In Chinese court proceedings, prosecuting attorneys are attempting to get confessions and admissions of guilt (which is assumed), rather than to provide an opportunity for a defendant to be exonerated. (By far the majority of cases end in conviction in China.) This reminds us that legal systems are not universal, but rather that they partake of the social assumptions that guide them.

Many of the cases excerpted in this chapter revolve around bribery, or what the Chinese consider corruption. The line between gift and bribe is notoriously thin, and those giving or receiving sums that call for reciprocity may claim that they were simply giving or receiving a gift.

Questions and answers, together, form what Schegloff called an adjacency pair, *a twofold set of utterances by two people in conversation that belong together. (Another example would be compliments and their responses: "That's a beautiful skirt." "Thanks." or "I got it at Filene's Basement for six dollars 10 years ago!") Adjacency pairs have expected components, and are made up of a* first pair-part *and a* second pair-part. *The wrong second pair-part (SPP) can be seen as indicating disrespect, confrontation, or some other social gaffe.*

Further, power is implicit in every adjacency pair. The questioner has the power to control the topic, the timing, and the switch from one line of questioning to another; to accept an answer or persist in the same question; and to make accusations.

Members of societies with different legal traditions may find these snippets of courtroom discourse discomfiting. Such reactions are worth examining as data in their own right.

Reading Questions

- What are declaratives, interrogative yes/no questions, interrogative wh-questions, requestions, and imperatives, and what does Chang mean that this list is "in the order of descending coerciveness"? How do questions coerce?
- What are some of the functions of questioning in the courtroom transcripts Chang provides?

From Yanrong Chang, "Courtroom Questioning as a Culturally Situated Persuasive Genre of Talk." *Discourse and Society* (2004) 15 (6), 705–722, by permission of Sage Publications Ltd.

- How do legal systems, the questioning tactics they use, and the assumptions underlying them differ in different societies?
- In many cases in the transcripts given, questions are repeated. Why is this done?
- What are legitimate and what are illegitimate questions? What kind do you see here?

Questioning takes on culture-specific forms and has culture-specific functions. This is a study of questioning in Chinese criminal courtrooms. Questioning in Chinese criminal courtrooms is not to obtain information; rather, it is to persuade. Patterns of questioning are used to extract confessions or remorse from defendants. After a brief literature review and a discussion of data collection and data analysis, these patterns of questioning are described and their persuasive dimensions explored.

Courtroom Questioning: A review of the Literature

Two interconnected foci characterize the existing body of literature on questioning as a type of legal discourse: the typologies and functions of questions (Danet and Kermish, 1978; Danet et al., 1980). Questions play a coercive function by constraining the responses elicited (Danet and Kermish, 1978; Danet et al., 1980; Dunstan, 1980). In the order of descending coerciveness, five types of questions are identified by Danet et al. (1980): (i) declaratives, (ii) interrogative yes/no questions, (iii) interrogative wh-questions, (iv) requestions,[1] and (v) imperatives. Besides the coercive function, questions also function as means to obtain information[2] (Danet and Kermish, 1978), to weaken and rebut witnesses' testimonies (Danet et al., 1980; Drew, 1990), or to enact social status and authority (Philips, 1984).

Current questioning research in the legal context has three limitations: (i) it has generally been examined outside its sociocultural context; (ii) it has mostly been studied as single utterances (i.e., questions), rather than as sequences of talk (i.e., questioning); and (iii) it has been approached mainly from a legal or sociolinguistic perspective and has never been investigated from a communicative perspective. To remedy these limitations, this study will explore, using a communicative approach, questioning as sequences of talk in its sociocultural context.

Data Collection and Analysis

The data used in this study consist of (i) four videotaped criminal trials that have been shown on public television in China in recent years; (ii) direct observations and field notes of five criminal trials in an Intermediary Court in Cangzhou City, Hebei Province; and (iii) interviews with 10 lay people and four legal professionals. The direct observations and interviews were conducted during a 3-month field trip to China in the summer of 2001.

The domain analysis method (Spradley, 1980) is used to identify cultural domains—participants, types of questions, questioning sequences, etc., whereas discourse analysis[3]

enables the description of patterns of questioning in criminal courtrooms and analysis of the underlying cultural meaning system of criminal trials in China.

The following information concerning a trial is included in square brackets at the beginning of each extract: the name of the case, its nature (e.g. criminal [CRT]), its source (video [V] or observation [P]), and the year in which the trial happened. Notations for the four criminal trials used for our analysis are:

BC.CRT.P.2001: Bribery Case
IK1.CRT.V.1999: Intentional Killing 1
IK2.CRT.V.1997: Intentional Killing 2
FV.CRT.V.1999: Family Violence

Notation Marks

Q: questioners (Presiding Judge [PJ] or Public Prosecutor [PP])
A: respondents (Defendants [D])

Questioning Discourse as Persuasion

Observable in Chinese criminal courtrooms are distinct patterns of questioning: (i) repeating key questions, (ii) invalidating excuses or accounts, (iii) asking unanswerable questions, (iv) supplying answers, and (v) paraphrasing or restating defendants' responses. A close examination of these patterns shows that they are used to help the court extract a confession or remorse from defendants as they transform questioning into an intermingled process of accusing, invalidating, and shaming defendants.

Let Me Repeat! Persuasion Through Repetition

Some questions are repeated constantly by the presiding judge or prosecutor. On closer inspection, these repeated questions are invariably those to which the expected responses will lead to the confession of guilt (see Extract 1).

Extract 1 [BC.CRT.P.2001]

01 Q: (*Calm voice and moderate volume*) As the public prosecutor asked just now,
02   what was your purpose of sending the money (to the director)?
03 A: (*Inaudible response; head bent*)
04 → Q: (*Louder*) But you still didn't tell us the purpose of your sending the money.
05 A: (*Silence; head bent*)

06 → Q: *(Even louder and harsher)* It's because without his help you couldn't get the
07   project, so you gave him ¥20,000 in order to get the project, wasn't it?
08 A: *(Unclear response; head bent)*
09 → Q: *(Impatient and lower in voice)* What function do you think the director played
10   in the project, positive or negative?
11 A: *(Inaudible)*
12 → Q: *(Shouting)* Don't answer that! I asked you whether (the full name of the bribed)
13   played a positive role or a negative role in the project?
14 A: *(Silence)*
15 → Q: *(Impatiently and angrily)* But I didn't ask you that. I only asked you what type
16   of role (the full name of the bribed) played.

This questioning sequence happens between the presiding judge and the defendant, a male in his 30s who has been accused of bribing a leader. As indicated in the transcript, the presiding judge talks loudly, powerfully, and fiercely. In contrast, the defendant talks in a drawn-out manner with such an extremely low voice and unclear articulation that it quite often becomes inaudible. Such sharp paralinguistic contrast between the questioner (i.e., the presiding judge or prosecutor) and defendant is also apparent in other trials. It enacts the power difference between the two parties in Chinese culture.

In Extract 1, the presiding judge repeats his questions five times. He starts by asking the defendant about the purpose of sending the money to the director in ll. 01–02 in a calm voice. The defendant makes some inaudible response, which is discounted as the right answer by the presiding judge in l. 04. At the same time, the presiding judge criticizes the defendant for not providing the right answer through his tone of voice. The defendant gives a silent response in l. 05 which provokes the presiding judge to repeat his question in a different form in ll. 06–07: instead of asking the defendant to tell the purpose of sending the money, he supplies the 'correct' answer himself and asks only for confirmation from the defendant. When that also fails, the presiding judge becomes even more impatient and angry, as indicated by his increased volume and harsher tone. He reformulates his question in ll. 09–10 by shifting the focus onto the role the 'bribed' played in the defendant getting the project, which is repeated twice in ll. 12–13 and 15–16.

The persuasive intent on the part of the presiding judge is obvious. In order to obtain the expected answer, he not only repeats his questions, but he also repeats them using strategies. There is a transition from an open-ended question (ll. 01–02) to a closed yes/no question (ll. 06–07) and eventually to a question with a completely different, yet relevant, focus (ll. 09–10). By shifting the focus of the questioning from the defendant's act to another party's role, the presiding judge is

trying to reduce the apparent psychological burden of the defendant—it seems he is not asked to describe his own crime but that of others—and thus facilitates the defendant's confession.

Despite the repeated efforts by the questioners, defendants in Chinese criminal trials refuse to comply. Their persistent denial coupled with the questioners' insistence on obtaining a confession result in extended question–answer sequences in Chinese criminal courtrooms.

DON'T TRY TO DENY! PERSUASION THROUGH INVALIDATING SEQUENCES

Analysis reveals three sets of inferential rules[4] that are invoked by the presiding judge or prosecutor during questioning in order to invalidate defendants' excuses. These are: (i) heuristic rules (or common sense rules), (ii) moral or cultural rules,[5] and (iii) factual or evidential rules.

Invalidating Rules I. Do You Lack Common Sense?

One way to render defendants' accounts invalid is to transform them into nonsense. To accomplish this, the presiding judge or prosecutor resorts to heuristic or common sense knowledge. Extract 2 provides an example of questioning in which the presiding judge appeals to one heuristic rule.

Extract 2 [BC.CRT.P.2001]

01 Q: Who was the money left with?
02 A: It was left with my wife.
03 Q: What did they say when they left the money with your wife?
04 A: They said nothing.
05 → Q: *(Loud)* How could that be possible, bringing money without saying anything?

In l. 03, the presiding judge asks the defendant to describe the verbal interaction between his wife and the 'briber', which might reveal the 'real' motive behind the act of sending the money. Yet, the defendant claims that the 'briber' did not say anything, which is immediately invalidated in l. 05 by the presiding judge who appeals to a common sense rule of social interaction: people should explain why they have sent money to someone else's home before leaving. Because this is a commonly shared norm of interaction, it casts doubt on and revokes the defendant's response. At the same time, the invalidating question in l. 05, coupled with the disbelieving tone of the presiding judge, shames the defendant by implying that he either is lying or lacks common sense. Hence, heuristic rules persuade through a dual process of norming and shaming.

In Extract 3, the prosecutor also evokes one heuristic rule of behavior in rendering the defendant's accounts questionable.

Extract 3 [BC.CRT.P.2001]

01 Q: Whence did the grateful feeling come?

02 A: *(Silence)*

03 → Q: If it were indeed as what you said, why didn't you give the money to

04   anybody else? Do you think this is reasonable that you gave money to

05   somebody for nothing? (*Harsh and denouncing tone*) You must confess this

06   honestly! When someone asked you to send the money to the director, you

07   simply didn't think about anything?

08 A: *(Silence)*

In the bribery case, all three defendants stuck to the account that the money was sent out of gratitude. The prosecutor in Extract 3 resorts to a list of heuristic rules in his questions from ll. 03 to 07: (i) if one sends money to someone else out of gratitude, then he or she will do this to anybody, not merely to leaders; (ii) one gives someone money for some personal purposes; and (iii) when one follows others' directions, he or she will think about why. A bald-on-record face-threatening act (Brown and Levinson, 1987), the fusillade of heuristic-rule-laden questions uttered in a harsh and denouncing tone shames the defendant as it directly challenges his common sense and calls his character into question.

Invalidating Rules II. Do You Lack Moral Sense?

Besides heuristic rules, cultural or moral standards are also resorted to by the prosecutor or presiding judge in order to invalidate defendants' excuses or accounts. Moral rules are more coercive in that they perform three functions at the same time: invalidating, shaming, and criticizing.

Extract 4 [FV.CRT.V.1999]

01 Q: Just now both the public prosecutor and the defense lawyer have asked you

02   about one question, that is, the purpose of taking the iron rod. You said you

03   only wanted to vent your anger?

04 A: *(Confidently)* Yes.

05 → Q: (*Harsh & critical tone*) When would you think you had sufficiently vented your

06   anger?

07 A: *(Rapidly)* I didn't think that much at that time. I only wanted to beat him.

08 → Q: (*Loudly and slowly*) That is to say, you beat (the victim) without any restraint.

09   You would stop only when you had fully vented your anger, right?

10 A: (*Low voice and rapidly*) I didn't think that much.

The defendant in this case was a woman in her late 30s or early 40s who was accused of killing her husband. The presiding judge in Extract 4 is questioning her about the purpose of carrying an iron rod with her to the bedroom in the morning. The question in ll. 02–03, "You said you only wanted to vent your anger?" which is a question in the form of a reported speech, indicates that the questioner does not believe its validity and, what is more, it signals the importance that this account be invalidated in order to convince the defendant of her guilt. The defendant sounds very sure of her account (l. 04). Then in ll. 05–06 the presiding judge shifts the focus onto something quite different: assuming that it is true that the defendant only wanted to vent her anger, he asks, "When would you think you had sufficiently vented your anger?" The way he asks this question conveys to the defendant that he is not actually seeking any specific information; rather, he is criticizing her for her behavior. His disapproval and criticism are further enacted through his questions in ll. 08–09 in which he invokes one moral rule: as a human being, one should be humane. Hence, in this sequence of questioning, the defendant is portrayed as an irrational, selfish, and relentless wife, who lacks moral sense (e.g., beating her husband ruthlessly and persistently) and thus should feel ashamed of herself. In reaction to such a moral accusation, the defendant cannot find any other excuses but keeps saying, "I didn't think that much" in ll. 07 and 10, though she was very confident earlier in the interaction (l. 04).

Thus, through evoking moral or cultural rules in questioning, the prosecutor or the presiding judge invalidates defendants' accounts or excuses, accuses them of immoral acts, and shames them accordingly.

Invalidating Rules III. Don't You See the Evidence?

Apart from appealing to heuristic and cultural/moral rules to invalidate defendants' accounts, the prosecutor or presiding judge also resorts to factual or evidential rules. Researchers and scholars have examined the coercive power of legal language in contrast to ordinary language in courtrooms. According to O'Barr and Conley (1991), the American court system values the deductive narrative structure that highlights legal rules, supporting evidence, and concise presentation of relevant facts to a case. Most lay litigants, however, prefer narrating chronologically, describing everyday life details, stressing emotions, etc., which is inductive in nature. Owing to the imbalanced use of legal discourse by legal professionals (e.g., attorneys, judges, prosecutors, etc.) and lay people (e.g., litigants), lay litigants were greatly dissatisfied with the American court system. In addition, speech style was also identified as a potential means of injustice. O'Barr (1982) concluded that judicial decision-making was affected by speech styles in the courtroom: powerful speech style, the preferred courtroom language style, correlated with high credibility, thus favorable decisions.

The imbalanced use of legal discourse is also evident in Chinese criminal courts. Whereas the prosecutor or presiding judge uses legal logic, defendants tend to account for their behaviors by using everyday logic. Consequently, defendants' accounts are easily nullified when the prosecutor or presiding judge resorts to legal rules. For example, one legal rule in China is "let evidence and facts speak." In criminal trials, the presiding judge routinely announces to the court evaluations of the pieces of evidence and facts presented, i.e., what is confirmed by the court and why, as well as what is rejected and the reasons for the rejection. This legal rule is so powerful that once something is credited as "evidence or fact" it becomes undisputable. However, if one's account does not qualify as legally defined evidence or fact, even if it makes perfect sense according to everyday logic, it is easily disputed as invalid by the court. The evidential rule is invoked in Extract 5 to revoke the defendant's account.

Extract 5 [IK1.CRT.V.1999]

01   Q: Defendant xxx, next I'm going to ask you several questions. After you got to

02   the market, why did you kill people with your knife?

03   A: At that time I was thinking of taking revenge against my boss. I wasn't bent

04   on killing other people.

05 → Q: You wanted to take revenge against your boss. But were the people killed by

06   you your boss whom you wanted to revenge against?

07   A: No, they were not.

The defendant in Extract 5 is a young man in his early 20s. He was accused of killing people—all women and small children—at a market, using a knife. As killing, especially the killing of women and children who are considered weak and thus need protection, is absolutely intolerable and unforgivable in Chinese culture, the prosecutor and presiding judge used an extremely loud and denouncing tone throughout the trial. This trial was shown on public television, and it was named "*Lansha Wugu, Tianli Nanrong*" (literally, killing the innocent, a crime against nature), which was charged with negative emotions (e.g., hatred, indignation, disgust, etc.).

In Extract 5, the defendant is asked to account for his criminal acts in l. 02. In ll. 03–04, he tries to exonerate himself by framing (Goffman, 1974, 1981) the incidence in terms of revenging his boss rather than intentional killing. This account is nullified as groundless when the presiding judge resorts to the evidential rule in ll. 05–06 by asking the defendant whether the people he killed were his boss and to which the defendant replies, "No" (l. 07). In ll. 05–06 the presiding judge is also appealing to one cultural/moral rule, which is enhanced through his denouncing tone of voice, that is, no one should kill or injure innocent others. What is more, his denouncing tone indicates that the real purpose of questioning is not to obtain any specific information, but to accuse the defendant of his criminal acts.

In Extract 6, the everyday logic that the defendant uses is counteracted by the legal logic that is invoked in the prosecutor's questioning.

Extract 6 [FV.CRT.V.1999]

01   Q: What was your purpose of bringing that iron rod with you?

02   A: I took the iron rod in order to protect myself.

03 → Q: When you entered the room, (the victim) was arranging pillows and other stuff

04   on bed and didn't attack you. Then from what were you protecting yourself?

05   A: He was going to suffocate me to death once in bed.

06 → Q: What I'm asking you now is when you entered the room with an iron rod in

07   hand he was arranging stuff on bed and had no intention to attack you.

08   A: I didn't think that much. I only wanted to beat him with the iron rod to vent

09   my grievances.

As analyzed in Extract 4, one of the key questions in the trial entitled "Family Violence" is the motive behind the defendant's carrying an iron rod with her to the bedroom in the morning. In Extract 6, the prosecutor once again brings up the same question in l. 01. This time the defendant provides a different account—to protect herself (l. 02). Although this account is reasonable from ordinary everyday logic, it is groundless from a legal perspective, which is appealed to in the questioning in ll. 03–05 when the prosecutor points out that the victim had no intention of attacking her at that moment. In response to this rebuff, the defendant comes up with an explanation for her legally unreasonable behavior: the victim had made an attempt to kill her in bed in the past (l. 05). Though, once again, this explanation makes sense according to everyday logic, it is not supported by legal logic which defines self-defense as the act of self-protection when one's life is threatened "here and now." The prosecutor restates his question in ll. 07–09, stressing that the victim was not engaging in any attacking behavior at that very moment. Unable to combat the powerful legal logic, and after her two accounts have been completely invalidated, the defendant finds herself reiterating her old excuse, "I didn't think that much. I only wanted to beat him with the iron rod to vent my grievances" (ll. 10–11). Unfortunately, as shown in Extract 4, that account has already been nullified by the presiding judge who transforms her act into a morally detestable one.

Sometimes defendants' accounts are easily invalidated when the prosecutor or presiding judge asks directly for evidence, which quite often the defendant cannot supply immediately. Extract 7 provides such an example.

Extract 7 [IK2.CRT.V.1997]

01   Q: Why on earth did you cut xxx?

02   A: First she cheated ¥20,000 from me. Secondly, she tried to drive me away.

03   Thirdly, she refused to give me one cent.

04 → Q: You gave xxx ¥20,000. Is there any evidence? Who can prove that you did?

05 A: This question, this question is hard to answer. Any
         family life is like this; who
06   tells other people when he gives his wife money?

The defendant in this case was a poorly educated elderly man in his 60s and he was accused of killing his wife (or more accurately cohabitee) using a cutting knife. One of the key questions, "Why did you cut xxx?" was asked repeatedly throughout the trial. In Extract 7, the prosecutor asks the question in l. 01. The defendant provides three accounts in ll. 02–03: (i) the victim cheated him out of ¥20,000 (roughly US $3000); (ii) the victim drove him away; and (iii) the victim refused to give him any money. Two of the accounts are ignored by the prosecutor as she only questions the second account in l. 04 where she asks the defendant to supply evidence or a witness. The defendant is baffled, as indicated by his stuttering at the beginning of l. 05, and counterattacks the prosecutor by resorting to a heuristic rule—when a husband gives his wife money, he does not go and tell others about it. However, the heuristic rule loses its persuasive force when it is used by the socially and culturally stigmatized to revoke the argument of the more powerful party.

PERSUASION THROUGH UNANSWERABLE QUESTIONS

Lakoff (1973) defined appropriate questions as being characterized by two features: (i) the speaker does not know the answer but really wants to (sincerity); and (ii) the speaker has a reason to believe that the hearer knows the answer. Lakoff's definition reflects the perceived function of questions, that is, to get information. Given this assumption, questions will be deemed unanswerable if, for example, the questioner is perceived as knowing the answer to the question he or she is asking (i.e., he or she is not seeking specific information); or the questioner asks a question that he or she knows that the respondent does not have the answer to; or the questioner constructs questions in a way (verbally and nonverbally) that baffles or cognitively debilitates the respondent.

Unanswerable questions or inappropriate questions are not allowed in American courtrooms as the attorneys will immediately raise verbal objections. However, in Chinese criminal courtrooms, verbal objections are virtually nonexistent. The tolerance of any type of question asked in any manner grants the questioner (i.e., the prosecutors or presiding judge) more power, which facilitates their persuasive attempts.

Unanswerable Questions I. Double-Barreled Questions

Sometimes people ask more than one question at a time (i.e., double-barreled questions). When questions are asked in a certain way (nonverbally), they become unanswerable. In Chinese criminal courtrooms, double-barreled questions are uttered in a negative tone (e.g., harsh, denouncing,

disapproving, or impatient) with no perceivable pause between them. Consequently, defendants respond with silence,[6] indicating that they perceive the questions as statements conveying criticism or denunciation rather than requests for information. Extract 8 provides such an example:

Extract 8 [BC.CRT.P.2001]

01 Q: (*Rapidly and in a critical tone*) Did you sign your
        name on the contract?
02   (*Almost no pause*) Who gave you that ¥20,000?
03 A: (*Silence*)
04 Q: (*Loudly and angrily*) Why do you think they gave
        you ¥20,000?
05 A: (*Inaudible*)

The prosecutor asks two questions—an interrogative yes–no question and an interrogative wh-question—one immediately after the other in ll. 01–02. His tone indicates anger and criticism. The defendant makes a silent response in l. 03, showing his perceived knowledge that the prosecutor is not seeking specific information. That perception is further confirmed when the prosecutor, without waiting for answers to his first two questions, throws in a third question in l. 04 which is an attributional wh-question and which asks about something completely different from the previous two. By asking "Why do you think *they* gave you ¥20,000?" he implies, through his use of "they" and the "why-question," that he already has the answers to the previous two questions.

In Extract 9, the prosecutor asks three questions in immediate succession in a denouncing tone, which brings no response from the defendant.

Extract 9 [BC.CRT.P.2001]

01 Q: In order to get this project, did you need some
        personal connections? A[7] (*angry*
02   *and denouncing tone*) You said you sent him money
        out of gratitude? What were
03   you grateful for?
04 A: (*Silence*).

Unanswerable Questions II. Shaming Questions

As an integral part of criminal trials in China, shaming punishes defendants through humiliation and debasement, to use Karp's (1998) terms. To shame defendants, the prosecutor or presiding judge uses (i) competence-challenging questions, (ii) accusatory questions, and (iii) meta-questions.

Can you answer my question?

Competence-challenging questions belittle defendants and make them feel debased. In Extract 10, the presiding judge asks whether the defendant has the ability to answer his question.

Extract 10 [BC.CRT.P.2001]

01 Q: I asked you what role (the full name of the briber) played, positive or negative.
02 → Can you answer the question? Can you answer it?
03 A: (*Silence*)
04 → Q: (*Louder voice*) Can you answer this question? Can or cannot?
05 A: (*Silence*)
06 → Q: (*In stern voice*) Can you answer it? Positive or negative?
07 A: (*Silence*)

In Extract 10, the presiding judge repeats his question, "Can you answer the question?" three times in ll. 02, 04, and 06. That the defendant does not respond with either "Yes, I can" or "No, I cannot" shows that these questions are used to shame and criticize the defendant for not confessing.

Then why did you…?

Accusatory questions are used to criticize defendants. Those criticisms are direct and strong enough to make defendants feel ashamed.

Extract 11 [BC.CRT.P.2001]

01 Q: Also, the public prosecutor wants to remind you. Here is what you confessed at
02 the police station before: Question: "Why did (full name of one of the bribers)
03 give you ¥20,000?" Answer: "(Full name of one briber) asked (full name of the
04 other briber) to send it to me. At that time I thought it was out of gratitude to
04 me." Was that true?
06 A: (*Inaudible. The defendant seems to deny that it was true.*)
07 → Q: Then why did you confess that way?
08 A: (*Silence*)

Extract 12 [BC.CRT.P.2001]

01 Q: Then did you keep that ¥20,000?
02 A: Yes.
03 → Q: If you were not clear about the purpose of the money, then why did you still
04 keep it? Why didn't you send it back?
05 A: (With a long pause, the defendant replies in a very low voice) It's been a long
06 time, besides… (*inaudible*)

In Extracts 11 and 12, the prosecutor expresses his disapproval with the defendant's past behavior by asking two accusatory questions in l. 07 and ll. 03 and 04, respectively. In l. 07 in Extract 11, the prosecutor is actually criticizing or accusing the defendant for being dishonest, which is a shameful act in Chinese culture. The questions in Extract 12 are criticizing the defendant, a Communist Party member and a leader, for his lack of self-restraint and self-discipline.

Being publicly criticized is such a tremendous face-damaging act for the defendant that he tries to defend himself (ll. 05–06) in vain.

This question is or does not…

Meta-questions are questions that make comments on other questions, for example, characterizing the difficulty level of a question or its nature. When a question is described as easy and yet no prompt answer is given, the respondent is implicitly or subtly criticized and shamed: either they are being dishonest (a criticism of their character) or they are incompetent. Such shaming and criticizing meta-questions abound in the bribery trial. The following are some examples.

Extract 13 [BC.CRT.P.2001]

01 Q: What function do you think the director has played in the project?
02 A: (*Inaudible. A significant pause*)
03 → Q: (The defendant's full name), this does not require much thinking, right?
04 A: (*Silence*)

Extract 14 [BC.CRT.P.2001]

01 Q: What function do you think the director played in the project, positive or
02 negative?
03 A: (*Inaudible*)
04 → Q: This question is not complicated, nor is it hard to answer, since it doesn't
05 require any calculation.
06 A: (*Inaudible*)

Through public humiliation and debasement by means of questioning, the prosecutor and presiding judge inflict feelings of shame/guilt on defendants. Shaming messages have been found to have an impact on individuals' esteem (see, e.g., Planalp et al., 2000). According to Messner and Buckrop (2000), feelings of shame/guilt can be so strong that they cause chaotic mental states that sometimes drive people to suicide as an agentic action to restore order. In this way, shaming questioning facilitates persuasion in Chinese criminal courtrooms in that it creates a chaotic state in defendants who will seek any means to restore order and yet the only agentic action they can take seems to be confession and remorse for their crimes.[8]

LET ME ANSWER IT FOR YOU! PERSUASION THROUGH ANSWERING ONE'S OWN QUESTIONS

When repeated efforts in obtaining the expected answer fail, the prosecutor or presiding judge answers their own questions, evidencing defendants' guilt, and asks defendants to make a verbal confirmation. As in Extract 1, the prosecutor provides an answer to his question, "What was your purpose of sending the money?" by saying, "It's because without his help you couldn't get the project, so you gave him ¥20,000 in order to get the project, wasn't it?" Supplying the answer to one's own question betrays one's insincerity in asking that question, as well as the questioner's hidden agenda. In Chinese criminal courtrooms, it is used as a means to elicit a confession. Extract 15 provides another example.

Excerpt 15 [BC.CRT.P.2001]

01 → Q1: (*Loud*) Why do you think they gave you ¥20,000?
02   A: (*In a low voice*) Maybe out of gratitude.
03   Q1: (*Loud and angry*) Besides gratitude, what other reasons do you think there are?
04   A: (*In an even lower voice*) I'm not clear.
05   Q1: (*Loud and impatient*) There must be other reasons besides gratitude?
06   A: (*Inaudible*)
07   Q1: (*In a serious tone*) Defendant xxx, the public prosecutor wants to remind you,
08   this is an open trial today, that is to say, the court wants to give you a last
09   chance. In a word, (we) hope that you tell the truth (*shi shi qiu shi*) and confess
10   what happened before, honestly. So why do you think that they gave you
11   ¥20,000?
12   A: (*Slowly and in a low voice*) Nothing more than gratitude.
13   Q1: (*Shouting*) Gratitude. What else besides gratitude? And why were they
14   grateful to you? (*As the public prosecutor uttered these words, his tone of*
15   *voice got harsher. This leads to silence from the defendant.*)
16   Q2: (*To the defendant*) the public prosecutor has asked you a question. "Yes" or
17   "no." Say it. What's difficult about that?
18   A: (*Inaudible*)
19 → Q1: It's simply because they wanted you to offer them some advantage. Were
20   there such factors involved?
21   A: There might be such factors, but it is unclear which side gets the advantage.
22   Q1: Then did they give you any money before this happened?
23   A: No.
24   Q1: Now explain why the other person gave you ¥15,000?
25   A: (*Inaudible*)
26 → Q1: How did you spend the money?
27   A: (*Inaudible*)
28 → Q1: It has all been used personally for yourself, right?
29   A: (*Silence*)
30 → Q1: Then what about the other ¥20,000?
31   A: (*Inaudible*)
32 → Q1: It has also been used for yourself, right?

33   A: Yes.
34   Q1: The public prosecutor rests his case.

In Extract 15, the prosecutor asks in l. 01, "Why do you think they gave you [the money]?" to which the defendant responded, "Maybe out of gratitude" in l. 02. The prosecutor is dissatisfied with the response and presses for other reasons in ll. 03, 07, and 10–11. Before he asks the question in ll. 10–11, he admonishes and instructs the defendant to take advantage of the opportunity that the court has provided him by telling the truth in order to obtain a lighter punishment. This "action projection," to use Schegloff's (1990) term, is to make sure that the defendant will answer in the expected manner. However, the defendant insists, "nothing more than gratitude" in l. 12, which provokes another round of questioning by the prosecutor, who makes it clear that he will not take this response as the answer to his question. The defendant keeps silent and the presiding judge intercedes in ll. 16–17 asking the defendant to provide a response. Yet, the defendant supplies another "dispreferred SPP"[9] (Schegloff, 1990). As a result, the prosecutor gives the answer himself in ll. 19–20, "It's simply because they wanted you to offer them some advantage. Were there such factors involved?" The defendant's ambiguous response in l. 21 is taken as a confirmation, signaling the end of one adjacency pair, as the prosecutor moves onto a different question in l. 22.

The prosecutor supplies answers to two more questions he asks. In l. 26 he asks, "How did you spend the money?" and answers in l. 28, "It's all been used personally for yourself, right?" To his question in l. 30, "Then what about the other ¥20,000?" he answers, "It has also been used for yourself, right?" in l. 32. Once the defendant makes a confirmative response in l. 33, which signals the voluntary confession, the prosecutor calls an end to the interrogation. This questioning sequence shows that supplying answers to his own questions is one strategic move by the prosecutor to obtain the admission of guilt from the defendant.

IS THAT WHAT YOU SAID/MEANT? PERSUASION THROUGH PARAPHRASING

In the trials observed there are instances when the prosecutor or the presiding judge paraphrases or restates defendants' responses. A careful examination shows that whenever paraphrasing or restatement occurs, defendants' criminal acts are spotlighted. A dramatization of defendants' crimes is created through selective paraphrasing or restatement.

Extract 16 [FV.CRT.V.1999]

01   Q: Why didn't you attempt to rescue (the victim)?
02   A: I did think of rescuing him, but I came from *Xinjiang*[10] and was alone here. All
03   his family members live here so I was afraid that his family were going to take
04   revenge against me.

05 → Q: That is to say, you didn't intend to rescue (the victim) when you saw him in
06   such a dangerous condition, right?
07   A: No (ambiguous reply—unclear whether she was
denying or admitting). I didn't
08   think that much.

The prosecutor's presumed knowledge that the defendant didn't intend to rescue the victim is woven into his question in l. 01 where he is actually accusing the defendant of not intending to rescue the victim. The defendant tries to deny that, but her use of the "but" clause immediately signals a denial of the expectations built by the preceding sentence, namely, she wanted to rescue him (Tannen, 1978). Hence, the prosecutor ignores what she says after "but" but restates her response in l. 05. Not only does the prosecutor delete the latter part of her response, but he also adds his own interpretation, "So you didn't intend to rescue him *when you saw him in such a dangerous condition?*" (emphasis added). Consequently, through the prosecutor's paraphrasing, the circumstance becomes more serious in nature and the defendant's acts become more intolerable: she did not intend to rescue someone who was in a very dangerous condition. In this way, the enormity of the defendant's crime is dramatized.

Questioning as a Culturally Situated Persuasive Genre of Talk

So far, my analysis shows that questioning discourse is a persuasive process of obtaining a confession from defendants in Chinese criminal courts. To achieve the persuasive goal, the prosecutor and presiding judge use various patterns of questioning such as repeating key questions, invalidating sequences, asking unanswerable questions, answering their own questions, and paraphrasing the defendants' responses in order to dramatize.

The sequential structure of the questioning discourse accounts for its rhetorical functions. As an adjacency pair, a question must be paired with an answer. Such an interactive rule legitimizes persistent efforts from the questioner in order to obtain the expected answer, resulting in an extended sequence of questioning–answering (Schegloff, 1990). Besides the interactive structural rule, the questioning discourse enacts and generates power differences between the questioner and the respondent in that the former is in a leading position (Sacks, 1992). As a leader, the questioner controls the contents and direction of interactions for their purposes.

In Chinese criminal courtrooms, the questioning discourse permits the prosecutor or presiding judge to control and extend the questioning sequences as much as necessary to extract the desired response, namely, a confession, from defendants. Defendants, by contrast, are interactively required to make responses to the questions asked. Any responses they provide that are not confessions are invalidated. At the same time, defendants are greatly shamed

or criticized, which creates the impression that there is no other choice but to confess in order to stop the questioning process.

The questioning discourse performs its rhetorical functions in specific social and cultural contexts. To put it another way, it is a culturally situated genre of persuasive talk. Questioners must also be granted social or cultural power in order for them to exercise the communicative power embodied in their roles as questioners. The questioners in Chinese criminal courtrooms (i.e., the presiding judge and prosecutor) enjoy supreme power and authority in Chinese society. As a result, they can exercise fully their interactive power as questioners to accuse, humiliate, and attack their moral senses in order to elicit confession or remorse. In a culture such as the US, in which defendants are socially considered equal to the questioners, such patterns of rhetorical use of questioning may be deemed inappropriate.

Questioning Discourse as a Cultural Form of Punishment

Defendants in Chinese criminal courtrooms are put in a disadvantageous position both interactively and socioculturally. The questioning discourse exercises its power of punishment mainly by invocation of the cultural notion of shame that is considered one of the most severe types of discursive punishments in Chinese culture (Hu, 1944). In addition, because morality is highly valued in Chinese culture, accusing people—in public—of having done something immoral is another serious discursive punishment for them (Miller et al., 1996, 1997). As a form of discursive punishment, the questioning discourse also helps achieve another cultural function, that is, to forestall crime in Chinese society. Rooted in the traditional Confucian belief that criminal acts are learned rather than the result of an innate predisposition is a cultural belief that people become criminals because of an inadequate education and exposure to bad influences. Crimes can thus be prevented by educating the public about lawful behaviors (Yu, 1998). Chinese criminal trials are used to deter the public from committing crimes through the threat of punishment, both discursively as a result of punitive questioning, and judicially as a result of sentencing. Seeing defendants penalized in both ways is both a deterrent and instructive to the public who are likely to circumvent potential punishment by behaving in legally acceptable ways. Courtroom trials, many of which are purposely shown live on Chinese TV, thus serve a double educative and persuasive function in Chinese society.

Notes

An earlier version of this article was presented at the annual conference of the International Communication Association, San Diego, California, May 2003. The author would like to thank Dr. Steve Duck, Dr. Gerry Philipsen, and Dr. Roger Shuy for their valuable comments on earlier versions of this article. As this article was developed on the basis of my doctoral dissertation, thanks also go to my dissertation committee members, in particular, Dr. Kristine Fitch, the chair of the committee.

1. Requestions are questions that convey two meanings at the same time—a request and a question. An example of requestion is "Can you describe...?" Requestions are categorized as noncoercive by Danet et al. (1980).

2. This view has been criticized by Dunstan (1980), who observed that most questions were not for information and it was written in trial manuals that in cross-examination one should never ask any questions for which one does not have an answer.

3. For a summary of the use of discourse analysis methods in the legal context, see Shuy (2001).

4. The term "referential rules" was borrowed from Gronbeck (1982).

5. The pervasive use of moral accusations and common sense expectations in Chinese criminal courtrooms contrasts strongly with questioning in American courtrooms which revolves mainly around facts. This difference can be explained in at least two ways, the premise of defendants as being guilty versus innocent before trials in the two cultures; and the pedagogical function of criminal trials in China.

6. In American courtrooms, silence is not tolerated even when it is virtually impossible to give a yes/no answer. However, silence by defendants is acceptable in Chinese criminal courtrooms. Such a difference reflects that the purpose of courtroom questioning in China is not to obtain information as it is in American courts. To obtain specific information, a verbal response is crucial. However, for the purpose of convincing defendants of their crimes, silence is fine as it shows that defendants are there listening, though their verbal confession is necessary. So silence is considered to indicate participation in Chinese criminal courtrooms.

7. A Chinese particle expressing curiosity, anger, or indignation.

8. In recent years, there have been discussions of the effectiveness of using shaming as one form of punishment for criminals and delinquents (see, e.g., Braithwaite, 2000; Garvey, 1998; Kahan and Posner, 1999; Karp, 1998; Makkai and Braithwaite, 1994; Scheff, 1988; Vagg, 1998). According to Karp (1998), shaming resorted to normative standards rather than legal standards and the power of sanction depended on the threat of social exclusion, which went against American cultural ethos of individualism. Neither did it fit in with a collectivistic ideology as it excluded individuals from the community (Vagg, 1998).

9. According to Schegloff (1990), an adjacency pair consists of two parts, the first pair part (FPP) and the second pair part (SPP). For example, question–answer is an adjacency pair that is composed of question as FPP and answer as SPP.

10. *Xinjiang* is a minority ethnic autonomous region located in the northwestern part of China, which is far away from *Hebei* province where the defendant in this case lived.

References

Braithwaite, J. (2000) "Shame and Criminal Justice," *Canadian Journal of Criminology,* July: 281–98.

Brown, P. and Levinson, S. (1987) *Politeness: Some Universals in Language Usage.* Cambridge: Cambridge University Press.

Danet, B. and Kermish, N. (1978) "Courtroom Questioning: A Sociolinguistic Perspective," in L. Massery II (ed.) *Psychology and Persuasion in Advocacy,* pp. 413–41. Washington, DC: The Association of Trial Lawyers of America.

Danet, B., Hoffman, K., Kermish, N., Rafn, H., and Stayman, D. (1980) "An Ethnography of Questioning in the Courtroom," in *Colloquium on New Ways of Analyzing Variation in English,* 5th ed., pp. 222–34. Washington, DC: Georgetown University Press.

Drew, P. (1990) "Strategies in the Contest Between Lawyer and Witness in Cross-Examination," in J. L. A. Walker (ed.) *Language in the Judicial Process,* pp. 39–64. New York: Plenum Press.

Dunstan, R. (1980) "Context for Coercion: Analyzing Properties of Courtroom 'Questions,'" *British Journal of Law and Society 7:* 61–77.

Garvey, S. P. (1998) "Can Shaming Punishments Educate?" *University of Chicago Law Review 65:* 733–94.

Goffman, E. (1974) *Frame Analysis.* New York: Harper & Row.

Goffman, E. (1981) "Footing," in *Forms of Talk,* pp. 124–59, Philadelphia: University of Pennsylvania Press.

Gronbeck, B. (1982) "On Classes of Inference and Force," in R. E. McKerrow (ed.) *Explorations in Rhetoric: Studies in Honor of Douglas Ehninger,* pp. 85–106. Glenview, IL: Scott, Foresman.

Hu, H. C. (1944) "The Chinese Concepts of 'Face,'" *American Anthropology 46:* 45–64.

Kahan, D. M. and Posner, E. (1999) "Shaming White-Collar Criminals: A Proposal for Reform of the Federal Sentencing Guidelines," *Journal of Law and Economics 42(1):* 365–91.

Karp, D. R. (1998) "The Judicial and Judicious Use of Shame Penalties," *Crime and Delinquency 44:* 277–94.

Lakoff, R. (1973) "Questionable Answers and Answerable Questions," in B. B. Kachru, R. B. Lees, Y. Malkiel, A. Pietrangeli, and S. Saporta (eds.) *Issues in Linguistics: Papers in Honor of Henry and Renée Kahane,* pp. 453–67. Urbana: University of Illinois Press.

Makkai, T. and Braithwaite, J. (1994) "Reintegrative Shaming and Compliance with Regulatory Standards," *Criminology 32:* 361–85.

Messner, B. A. and Buckrop, J. J. (2000) "Restoring Order: Interpreting Suicide Through a Burkean Lens," *Communication Quarterly 48(1):* 1–18.

Miller, P., Fung, H. and Mintz, J. (1996) "Self-Construction Through Narrative Practices: A Chinese and American Comparison of Early Socialization," *Ethos 24:* 237–80.

Miller, P., Wiley, A., Fung, H., and Liang, C. (1997) "Personal Storytelling as a Medium of Socialization in Chinese and American Families," *Child Development 68:* 557–68.

O'Barr, W., and Conley, J. (1991) "Litigant Satisfaction Versus Legal Adequacy in Small Claims Court Narratives," in D. R. Papke (ed.) *Narrative and the Legal Discourse:*

A Reader in Storytelling and the Law, pp. 65–89. Liverpool: Deborah Charles.

O'Barr, W. M. (1982) *Linguistic Evidence: Language, Power, and Strategy in the Courtroom.* New York: Academic Press.

Planalp, S., Hafen, S., and Adkins, D. (2000) "Messages of Shame and Guilt," *Communication Yearbook* 23: 1–65.

Philips, S. U. (1984) "The Social Organization of Questions and Answers in Courtroom Discourse: A Study of Changes of Plea in an Arizona Court," *Text* 4(1–3): 225–48.

Sacks, H. (1992) *Lectures on Conversation.* Oxford: Blackwell.

Scheff, T. J. (1988) "Shame and Conformity: The Deference–Emotion System," *American Sociological Review* 53(3): 395–406.

Schegloff, E. A. (1990) "On the Organization of Sequences as a Source of 'Coherence' in Talk-in-Interaction," in B. Dorval (ed.) *Conversational Organization and its Development,* pp. 51–77. Norwood, NJ: Ablex.

Shuy, R. (2001) "Discourse Analysis in the Legal Context," in D. Schiffrin, D. Tannen, and H. Hamilton (eds.) *Handbook of Discourse Analysis,* pp. 437–52. Oxford: Blackwell.

Spradley, J. (1980) *Participant Observation.* New York: Holt, Rinehart & Winston.

Tannen, D. (1978) "The Effect of Expectations on Conversation," *Discourse Processes* 1: 203–9.

Vagg, J. (1998) "Delinquency and Shame: Data from Hong Kong," *British Journal of Criminology* 38: 247–64.

Yu, R. (1998) *RuJia fa sixiang tonglun: Guanxi* [Confucian Legal Thoughts: Guanxi]. Renmin: Renmin Publishing.

Post-reading Questions / Activities

- Examine one of the excerpts closely. Look at the ways power permeates the interaction. Are there turns in the interaction where alternative replies might have been possible?
- If questioners, as in Extract 1, reject defendants' answers, why must this exchange continue to occur? What would be an acceptable answer to the questions?
- Observe questioning for an hour (perhaps in a classroom, restaurant, or other setting). Alternatively, record an interaction. Or, analyze a courtroom scene from a film. What functions does the questioning serve? How do they compare to what Chang describes?
- If different institutions have different purposes and logics, how might questioning in a different institution—medicine, education, government—function? Consider, for example, a psychologist's consultation or a teacher-student interaction.

Vocabulary

adjacency pair
bald-on-record face-threatening act
discourse analysis

paralinguistic
SPP

Suggested Further Reading

Peerenboom, R. P. 2002. *China's Long March Toward Rule of Law.* Cambridge and New York: Cambridge University Press.

Philips, Susan Urmston. 1998. *Ideology in the Language of Judges: How Judges Practice Law, Politics, and Courtroom Control.* New York and Oxford: Oxford University Press.

CHAPTER 40

The Internet and Relationships

Daniel Miller and Don Slater

(2000)

Daniel Miller is one of the foremost ethnographers of material life—that is, of the ways humans and things interact and mutually constitute—create—each other. His interests have turned in recent years to electronic media as another form of materiality and technology. He views technology not as independent and forcing changes on otherwise passive social life but as brought selectively and in particular ways by particular people into particular societies. There is no unitary "Internet," only the Internet as used by Trinidadians (Trinis) or by Indians or by Japanese. (A recent book by Miller and Heather Horst looks at the cell phone in Jamaica.)

This study examines how Trinidadians in Trinidad and in Diaspora—dispersed from their place of origin—use the Internet and what it means to them. Using ethnographic methods, Miller and Don Slater seek to understand how the Internet is integrated into people's everyday lives.

Bronislaw Malinowski, a Polish anthropologist inadvertently stuck in the remote Trobriand Islands of New Guinea during the First World War, pointed out that people in "primitive societies" use language not only to communicate substantive information but also to maintain relationships. He termed the latter function of language phatic communion, *and subsequent anthropologists, sociologists, and linguists have demonstrated how much of all communication is for the purpose of sustaining a connection among people ("Looks like rain, doesn't it?" "How 'bout them Cubs?"). The centrality of relationships is evident in gift-giving, as shown by Marcel Mauss and Malinowski's study of the Kula ring, a series of exchanges that seem to have little economic function at all. From these studies, it appears that much human communicative activity is intended to serve relationships. But people use them in subtle ways; not all relationships are equal.*

Reading Questions

- What are some of the different ways men and women use chatting and other functions of the Internet?
- How does Internet use vary by the age of its users?
- How do Trinis distinguish more and less important relations?
- What are some of the uses of the Internet?

A recent advertising campaign for a British beer company proclaimed that real men go out to the pub and relate to females, not just to emails. It reflected a widespread assumption (shared by some academics) that the Internet generates a culture of "nerds" who substitute virtual relationships for "real" ones, a charge that is inadequately met by the opposite argument that virtual relationships are themselves real. The

opposition of real and virtual in both cases completely misses the complexity and diversity of relationships that people may pursue through the communicative media that they embed in their ongoing social lives. The point is made clearly by thinking back historically to the times when "old (media) technologies were new" (Marvin 1988). Worries about the reality of telephone or telegraph relationships and their impact on "real" (i.e., face-to-face ones) may have been rampant at the time of their introduction (Stein 1999), but it is no surprise that the bulk of present-day telephone advertising can take it for granted that the telephone is widely accepted as a means of enhancing and developing relationships, not for replacing them. Where public concern re-emerges—as with the introduction of mobile phones—it is articulated in far less global, far more contextualized terms.

Hence, we will pursue the present discussion as if the Internet technologies were older, reflecting the alacrity with which Trinidadians have indeed embedded them in relationships, ignoring the issue of "real" versus "virtual." This is particularly evident in looking at the family, especially the Diaspora family, with which we begin. The second section examines the use of the Internet in friendships, including those that develop into love and marriage, and the third section deals with the immediate spaces in which Internet use and relationships take place, using as examples our studies of cybercafés and of Internet use amongst schoolchildren. Finally, in the conclusion some of this evidence will be considered in terms of the history and theory of Trinidadian society.

FROM DIASPORA FAMILY
TO INTERNET FAMILY

Prior to the arrival of the Internet, the family was indeed under threat as the core institution of social life in Trinidad. The Caribbean family is highly distinctive, as is indicated by the anthropological literature discussed in the conclusion to this chapter. Most anthropological accounts have been conservative in emphasizing continuities or a well-established normativity in expectations about the family. To understand the use of the Internet, however, we need to focus on a radical disruption that has been of huge importance for more than a generation: the impact of widespread Caribbean emigration on the Trinidadian family (see Basch, Glick Schiller, and Szanton Blanc 1994; Chamberlain 1998; Ho 1991). Migration from Trinidad has been very extensive, even if it has not matched other Caribbean contexts where the majority of those who identify with an island now live abroad (e.g., Olwig 1993). Miller (1994: 21) found in his earlier survey that in the majority of families at least one member at the nuclear level (that is either parents, siblings, or children) was living abroad. Therefore the following discussion of the use of the Internet by diasporic families[1] actually applies to the vast majority of Trinidadian families overall.

Email was taken up readily as an intuitive, pleasurable, effective, and above all inexpensive way not only for families to be in touch, but to be in touch on an intimate, regular, day-to-day basis that conforms to commonly held expectations of what being a parent, child, or family entails. It appeared as an obvious way of realizing familial roles and responsibilities that had been ruptured by Diaspora, and even of reactivating familial ties that had fallen into abeyance. Email contrasted on the one hand with letter-writing, which was seen as proverbially problematic to Trinis (perhaps the most common generalization people made during fieldwork was that "Trinidadians hate writing letters") and stymied by what was regarded as an inefficient postal service. In practice letter-writing was important to some of those living in the UK, but they were a minority.

On the other hand, while the phone has dominated contact amongst family members it was viewed as inordinately expensive. It tended to be associated with less frequent use and therefore with a very different temporality, appropriate for the exchange of news rather than casual communication. Telephones were also considered to be more suitable than email for special occasions and lifetime events such as births, marriages, deaths, and other rites of passage, but as far too expensive for enacting what are held to be the more "Trini" forms of communication, involving liming, banter, and ole talk, which were pleasurably performed through email and chat (as discussed in [Miller and Slater, 2000,] Chapter 4), where time could flow more naturally without an eye on the phone bill. But this connects to a wider sense of why email and chat could so easily serve the purposes of re-establishing normal or normative family relations: conversation could be mundane, everyday, intimate in a household way, in both style and content. Internet communication could shift contact from once a month to three times a week. This was sufficient to turn these into quite different types of relationship, because of the sense of the present it allowed. Email could allow constant, taken-for-granted communication, engaged in without great thought. It was informal or playful in style, and filled with everyday trivia (what we had for dinner, or bought at the shop, or who said what to whom) or with nothing much at all except a sharing of each other's "voices." Email could also encompass the exchange of mundane "objects" such as scanned photos, addresses of websites the other might like, jokes found online and forwarded to a family member with the thought—clearly expressed by informants—of bringing a familiar smile to the other's face. Indeed, it was rare for people to talk about email without a smile.

This use of email extended into the hugely popular practice of sending each other e-greetings or virtual postcards (as well as electronic flowers and chocolates). This applied to many relationships besides family ones. Websites offering greeting card services were amongst the most frequently visited by Trinidadians, who invested a lot of time in finding ones that were animated, multimedia, or simply unusual, often sentimental. This use of cards was interesting not only as an extension of a long Trini tradition, but also in making explicit the latent sense that an email was in some ways itself a gift, though one that could be offered at any time, not merely special occasions. And yet it demanded a response, and therefore created the conditions for sustaining relationships through reciprocity (see Carrier 1995; Mauss 1954).

Approximately half the Trinidadians we contacted in the UK primarily used the Internet for such mundane and constant email contact with their families. Given the nature of the Diaspora this could as well be family living outside Trinidad as within. If only one side of the family had online access they often exerted considerable pressure on the other end of the family also to go online, in some cases buying and sending the equipment. For example, several older people came into one of our ethnographic sites (a little shop with an online computer) brandishing letters from relatives abroad instructing them to set up an email account, and giving their own address. Someone in the shop (sometimes one of us) would help them register on a web-based email site. The ability to engage in routine contact through the Internet had two primary effects: the first was to re-establish the kinds of family contact that would have existed in a non-Diaspora context and the second was sometimes to actually expand the family as a viable unit of sociality. Ann-Marie may exemplify the first point. Perhaps the important relationship that emerges in Trinidadian discussions of the family is mother–daughter relations, and the sundering of these in the Diaspora family had often been a cause of anxiety, especially for the mothers. But with the Internet Ann-Marie reports the following norms of contact:

Q: So your mother emails you every day? What kinds of things does she talk about?
A: Nag.
Q: What kinds of things does she nag you about?
A: Motherly things—like eat properly, dress well and she checks out everyday the weather in London. And she would say all right you are going to have a little bit of sun next week. And then she will talk about whatever she has done.... My dad is not into it at all, you will not get a letter from him at all. But Mummy she is home and she got time to sit down.
Q: How long has she been doing this for?
A: For a year. She likes to know everything that is going on so she can tell you how to take your vitamins and how to do this. It is almost as if you are talking all the time because she is always giving advice, she would do a paragraph at a time.

Others who reported such regular connections with parents revealed how this re-constructed the common ambivalence of living together as a family. For example a UK-based student noted on the one hand:

> By speaking to my family every week, I do feel that they still have quite a strong hold on me. I feel that they do need to know where I am and what I'm doing. For instance I wanted to quit my Ph.D. about 6 months ago. I felt that I needed to consult them as it was common that I did when it came to big decisions. They were not very happy about the decision and used the guilt factor to make me continue. I'm still doing the Ph.D.

On the other hand a moment later she notes: "I do feel that it's keeping them close and despite differences in opinions at times, I don't feel alone here in England knowing that I could contact them at any time." Just as when people are actually living together within a household, parents could be regarded as oppressive and constraining, but this co-existed with the sense that one had returned—thanks to the Internet—to the security and support of this fundamental family relationship. It was also not uncommon for the relationship to work the other way around, so that a Trinidadian parent who had left her or his child in Trinidad used the Internet to continue to provide support to their children, though in most cases returning at times when more support was required, such as exam-taking. The Internet assuaged some of the problems and sense of guilt of leaving the children behind, since it made possible a new mediated parenting.

The impact of the Internet is not restricted to the nuclear family. In the case of the extended family, and in particular in relationships between cousins, there is the possibility not only of repairing the rupture caused by emigration, but also long-term relationships between cousins are made viable in a way they had not been before. For example George has settled in the UK for many years, but keeps in contact through the Internet:

A: The only person I [am in] contact with in Trinidad is my cousin. Every weekend Saturday five P.M. in UK time we hook up and have a little chat.... We speak for about three hours. All my aunts and cousins and everybody coming down. They want to speak to this one, that one. I will call my cousins and they will come to him. They are of the same household. But everyone will speak. Some of my cousins who can't afford PCs in Trinidad will come on weekends and have a little chat.
Q: So you are quite close with that family?
A: Yes. What we do as well is that all of the cousins, I got most of my cousins as well in Canada, we do link up together on weekends and all of us have a little family reunion every week. It's just an hour. Just a family thing.

As in this case it was common for an online relative to then communicate news to other relatives who are not online. Group cousin chatting could also take place through chat sites: "I met six of them and we chatted. We were on the chat site for about three hours on a Sunday. It was quite good though—everybody use a different colour." As well as this collective sense of family, cousins were also very often the "friends" one confided in, confidants for discussing intimate problems such as reactions to the death of a relative. Equally for those in Trinidad the most common use of the Internet for contacting people abroad was related to aunts, uncles, and cousins. Of course not every cousin turns out to be a natural friend. As a UK-based Trinidadian noted: "Stephen would send email, but he has got a weird sense of pornographic humour, I do not reply. I don't even open the attachment because I did once and I said O God! He sent about a hundred disgusting jokes."

In general Trinidadians found that their "cousinhood" is now viable as a much larger phenomenon, bringing back into the fold relatives that would not otherwise have been included. Discovery of a cousin in New York they had not heard from in ten years would re-create the relationship, or on returning for Carnival they might meet a cousin settled in Japan who had also returned to Trinidad. They would then exchange email addresses and strike up the relationship on their return to their respective homes. It is possible that these contacts will decline as the cousins grow up, just as one would expect in the conventional developmental cycle of the domestic group. It is also possible that one result of the Internet will be a longer maintenance of such relationships, since the factors that often break up "cousinhoods," such as moving away, will no longer have the same effect. However, the time depth of our study is too shallow for confident predictions.

The possibilities for actually expanding the family were most dramatically illustrated by George:

A: Both my parents split up twenty-eight years ago. I had contact with my Mom but I never had contact with my Dad. Twenty-eight years and I never [knew] what he look like, I never knew where he was, what he did, or anything. And through the Internet I decided, I saw these search engines. So I was going to fiddle around and see to try and get a world-wide one, which there wasn't. Then I thought America is the biggest country on the Internet. I'll try a search there. I came up with nothing. I then tried one in Canada, and half an hour later I came up with twenty-five names and I thought every week I would send out one letter and see what happens. So the first name I pick from the list and four days later, about four o'clock in the morning the phone rang, and it was my Dad. He couldn't believe it himself, I couldn't believe it too. I thought it was a joke or something. But what happened about this letter I send out. I sent a photo of me and I send a photo of him. His wife phones me back, and that caused a bit of problem there.

Q: She never knew…?

A: She never knew if I existed. That was a shock to her.

Q: So he is in Canada?

A: He is in Canada. He phones me every two weeks.

Q: So he phoned you first to check it out?

A: She phoned me and she thought it was a joke as well. Because she is looking at my photo and she is looking at his photo and she is saying to me where did you get this photo from? This is my son and this is his Dad. I said no, it isn't. That's me and that's my Dad and she thought it was a hoax and I thought she was a hoax as well.

Q: Did you ever meet?

A: We met last year. One of my brothers or sisters were suppose to come but financially they weren't able to. I think I am going to make an effort go across to them actually.

Internet use by the elderly is more rarely encountered but is perhaps an important pointer to the future. One example was a widow who seemed to have lost much of her reason for living when her husband died. In order to keep in touch with a particularly close grandchild who had gone abroad, she was persuaded to educate herself in Internet use. Subsequently she contacted many other relatives abroad and in Trinidad, and has taken to the net to such a degree that the younger members of her family swear it has given her "a new lease of life." This might offer a partial resolution to the increasingly common problem of elderly people who had previously tended to live in the homes of their descendants but are now being encouraged to live by themselves: the Internet keeps the new physical separation but in some other respects can keep them in the heart of family life. However, this is currently rare, and there are worries that the effective family might become restricted to those that are online, which would particularly exclude the elderly. On the other hand, a UK Trini noted that although the Internet tended to determine which of his cousins he continues to be close to, it would in no way affect the close personal relationship he has with his grandmother, who happens not to be online.

FRIENDS AND PARTNERS

In contrast to family relationships, friendships, acquaintances, and chat partners point to less well-defined relationships that can be more ambiguous when pursued online. Establishing their character and status as relationships may need more reflection, since they may take novel forms that have to be assessed in terms of new normative concepts of friendship. Moreover, in addition to being a means for pursuing established relationships (school friends, boy- and girlfriends, colleagues), the Internet—particularly chat and ICQ—routinely opens up the possibility of engaging online with people from anywhere in the world whom one has not and probably will not meet face-to-face; and these contacts are likely to be made through interests or even through random meetings and coincidences.

The situation is made more complicated by the dynamics of Internet mediation. People tend to experience the Internet as a battery of related but separate possibilities for pursuing relationships, which they assemble in different ways according to their particular preferences. One individual who has his own personal website abhors the use of chatlines and makes all his new friendships through signing the guestbooks of personal web-pages that happen to appeal to him. He will make a comment about that website, and hope for a reply from which further contact can ensue. Another uses chat but hates using email, while a third only uses email and extends his range of contacts by being put in touch with friends of his current email friends. Sometimes this is just conservatism; an individual is "taught" one method, takes to it, and is resistant to alternatives. A UK Trini suggested that he continued to phone friends where the relationship predates the Internet, but emails those who have become friends through the Internet, though this was a rare distinction.

Chat and ICQ, however, are the Internet media that were most fashionable in pursuing relationships, and ones that corresponded more to what we have called "expansive potential" than to the "expansive realization" that marked family relationships. Especially for the young within Trinidad, Internet chat and ICQ marked their entry into an expanded possibility of new encounters, including immediate, unexpected, and volatile styles of encounter. Chat can be used as a straightforward extension of pre-existing relationships, or of ones related to the immediate locale (as with the schoolchildren discussed below), or it can be a vehicle for developing relationships that were initially made on ICQ itself. Or it can be a mixture, as in the case of one teenage informant who carried with him a list of fifty ICQ friends, most of them from other parts of Trinidad but all first encountered online, some of whom he then met offline, some not. ICQ software includes the ability to make lists of ICQ contacts and categorize them as one wishes (e.g., home versus away, work versus personal), a feature that recognizes the desire to be flexible in ordering, or even separating out, the variety of possible relationships.

In fact, many people claimed that they only put a very few people on their lists. This generally indicates that people make strong distinctions about which relationships are valuable and therefore should be closely integrated into their online activities, and which are not. This distinction—which we encountered across many observations and interviews—was closely tied to the issue of time, of dividing online relationships between those considered short, casual, and "light" and those that are more serious, enduring, and emotionally weighty. This tallied very closely with Slater's (1998) previous observations of "trading sexpics on IRC": chat comprises a larger number of short-term casual encounters, which can be exciting, interesting, boring, or lunatic, but are treated as relatively weightless as relationships. They may be valued and sought for many reasons, but they are in a different category from the serious relationships into which a very few of them will develop, which are characterized by the kinds of trust, investment, and intimacy that are only possible over a longer term: "Every time you go online, you'll always find some crazy fool out there, talking rubbish…there for theirself, just to be on the net, that's all they're there for. You talk shit to them and that's about it but you don't take them on, you don't get down to anything. With a long-standing relationship you talk to them for *loooooooong*, [i.e.] you start to share stuff between each other." In Trini chat, just as in the chat studied by Slater, "long term" is not necessarily all that long in comparison to offline relationships of a similar seriousness. Because of the dynamic character of these social settings and because of their intensity, three months is very good going, but this might mean three months of spending as many hours of the day as possible locked into the highly internalized modality of chat. This intensity also means that chat very much takes place in the moment: people frequently talk about current relationships as if they were several years rather than weeks old, while earlier similar relationships are all but forgotten.

Short-term encounters of a largely random nature are primarily a form of mutual entertainment. Their essential characteristic—that the other person could turn out to be more or less anyone, and one can never know—already gives it something of the *frisson* of gambling. In addition it commonly has the additional *frisson* of sexual banter. While this is no difference in principle from non-Trini chat (again see Slater 1998) the role of flirtation and sexual language in Trini culture (see…Yelvington 1996; [Miller and Slater 2000, Chapter 4]) gives it a very particular salience for Trinis who use it. While some users will talk to same-sex others, most readily admit that almost all their chat is with opposite-sex others (reflecting a pervasive assumption of heterosexuality offline).

For example a man notes he chats to: "Mostly women! The only time I would chat to men is when I want information on music, games, and stuff. When I want to download something from the Net and they might know where it is." Once a partner has been located then the encounter sets up a challenge where there is relatively little to lose, given the cover of anonymity, but much to be gained:

> Yes, you learn a lot from them, especially the different types of expression for stuff.…It's like when you go on, the first time, uh talking to a female over the Net, it's kind a like if you meet a female on the street, uh tackling her. You're not seeing what she looks like unless you have video conferencing, but she sounds good. What she said really catches your attention and you're able to hold that attention. It's kinda like a thrill, the longer you could talk to this person, keep them excited as well as they keep you excited and sometimes the things they say to you, well.…It surprised me the first time. After a while I started to get used to it.

Quite apart from this art of banter, at which Trinis know they are particularly proficient, for many users the experience of playful sexuality is clearly a major part of the pay-off of the time spent online, even if some of the stories are apocryphal:

> There was one time we actually got a girl sent us twelve different video clippings of her while she was talking and then she started to take off her clothes. She stopped when she reached half way. And I bet you it was real. There are chances it might not have been real but it was fun. It's like you being able to do what you want and knowing that the person doesn't have to know who you are, because you could never meet them at all.

For women, in particular, however, there is the problem that Trinidadian forms of sexual banter can be quite different from many of the societies of those they are chatting with, so the scope for being misconstrued is endless. A girl who went by the "nick" Miss Sexy simply could not see why she kept having such problems:

> I know, it does: it simply does attract a lot of people, because basically most of them come on and say "what your name goes with, why are you calling yourself Miss Sexy?" and I simply tell them, that to me, I'm very beautiful and to me, I think I'm sexy, but it's nothing more than that. Most of them think I want to do stuff. I simply said, no my name is not Miss Sexy, just my nickname 'cause I'm friendly, I'm kind-hearted and understanding. Basically I want to chat with them, and there where the conversation goes they find I'm intelligent and what they think I was with my nickname is not what I am.

While sex dominated, there are other concerns in short-term chat. These include simply the interest in each new person. For example, "every time I go on ICQ it's somebody new, something new, some different story, some guy claims he's having family problems or with some woman, this sort of thing. Each time I get ICQ it is a unique story." There is also a kind of mediated but personal tourism, where the interest is in meeting people from different countries and learning about the countries. The implications for Trinidadian identity are discussed in [Miller and Slater (2000, chapter 4)]. More female chatters seem to follow this route, and they often seem particularly interested in interleaving it with discussions about personal problems such as dealing with their parents. The result confirms for them the general sense that "underneath our differences we are all the same," so that an aura of global sentimentality can be one product of these kinds of encounter.

Given the "lightness" of these short-term encounters, when did Trinidadians ascribe them "weight"? We [have] argued...that "virtuality" needs to be treated as a social accomplishment rather than an analytical assumption, that we need to understand when, why, and how particular people come to treat online relationships as "real" or not. Slater has previously argued that, in the apparently extremely disembedded context of "sexpics trading on IRC," this was crucially related to the ways in which one could establish sufficient trust in the authenticity of the other to warrant the risk of investing in them emotionally, and that this was related to the persistence of the other's online presence over time, as well as to ways in which they could be "embodied" through encountering them through additional media.

Similar dynamics were clearly at play in Trinidadian chat relationships, and a range of social and technical possibilities were used to sort out which relationships mattered and how they should be conducted. Firstly, just as with email in a family context, there was a great stress on sharing a mundane life with the other both on- and offline. That is to say, people could spend a great deal of very intense time chatting online, over the course of which they felt that the other had a clear idea of their daily lives, thoughts, and attitudes. One informant, Jason, had some unusually long-lasting relationships (one of over two years' duration), which he placed at the same level as face-to-face relationships on the basis that they knew him well, were stitched into his everyday life and had been tried and tested over time by a variety of means:

A: Yeah I would say I take them seriously. 'Cos they ask me, how ya going today? They knew when my baby was born. They all got the news that my baby was born—send cards of congratulations, everything. When I go online they say, how's ya baby going today? What's she doing da? It's like regular people, regular conversations....they're just a part of your friendship group: you still consider them the way you consider the friends who you see everyday.
Q: They feel part of your everyday life?
A: Yeah—also part of your everyday life, 'cos basically I get an email from them every day, chat with them every day....

This sharing of mundane life included everyday exchanges of electronic jokes, pictures, e-greetings and postcards, electronic boxes of chocolates and bouquets of flowers that people scoured the net to find for their friends. Sites for e-greetings were amongst those most commonly visited by Trinidadians, and are offered by Trinidadian companies and found on Trinidadian portal sites. These new electronic gifts are indeed new material forms that constitute relationships in new ways: that is to say, they should be treated seriously as mediations or material culture (Jaffe 1999). Virtual postcards, as noted, extend to the Internet the immense and long-term popularity of such cards in Trinidadian society generally. However, in going online, postcards have now slipped out of their previous more formal frame of being used for marked events and special occasions. They have become a regular means for maintaining general contact, acquiring—like email—the informality of a gesture or spontaneous moment of acknowledging the other. Moreover, people seek out cards with animations, music, or other such accompaniments so that they can also feel they are part of a "coolhunt," and they accept the gift of cool (one teenager talked with zest about the recent receipt of: "the frog in the blender swimming, and he's insulting you and you have to press each knob on the blender and in the end, it just blend him up...cool!").

Stitching the other into a shared everyday world rapidly extends to the sharing of intimacies, problems, perspectives, and values, so that you not only feel that the other really knows you, and vice versa, but also that they [are] reliably "there for you" as a persistent and embodied ethical other.

Q: How much do you value a [long-term] relationship like that; how real does it feel?
A: You have to think about how well you know the person, what you talk about, things like that....we exchange ideas about what's going on [in] her life and what's going on in my life, and we put together what we think about it and how it should be and how it shouldn't be. We learn from each other.
Q: So part of being a real relationship is getting into real issues?
A: Real issues, yeah. Because I tell her what's up with me and she tells me what's with her. I know her family, what's going on with her. How she handles going to school and her family, being with them. Her mum is separated from her Dad so she tells me how different her life is from living with her Dad from living with her mum 'cos I'm the same, I'm living with my Dad and I told her about it.
Q: You feel she understands you and shares your values? You trust it?
A: Yes, everything, yes.

People could describe this sharing in nearly therapeutic terms, as in the case of one woman who actually was a counsellor and transferred her listening skills and values to ICQ.

This intimacy can be treated and treasured as something that is largely detached from offline consequences and costs and at the same time differentiated from "the usual stupidness" of casual chat encounters. Although we encountered almost no talk that corresponded to cyberutopian expectations about a radical break between offline and online identities, Jason talked about his serious online relationships through a notion of "just communicating":

A: Sometimes it's more meaningful, right, 'cos they know you're not taking them on any other level but the mind, it's like a kinda brain-to-brain kinda thing…yeah, just communicating, looking out for each other. Talking, being friends, without the hangups.
Q: So there's almost something pure about it?
A: Yeah, yeah [he agrees with that]. That's the exact term: there is something pure about it.

The nature of the "impurities" from which his serious chat relations released him in order to be treated as "real" relationships were quite clear:

A: Even though we try not to be, we all have our prejudices, right, and there will be people who automatically on sight you see them and you categorize them. On the Internet it is not like that. Right. Especially the chat sites or whatever: you actually see into people's minds, their personalities, right there.
Q: But you can be wrong about people, taken in by them?
A: If you're stupid, yeah. You are what you type. Especially the way people type in the chat groups you could actually get a hint of their accents, of the way they speak, everything from the way they type, the word structures, everything. You got good feeling for people. And you know if they are lying, hands down—'cos a lot of them saying, "well I am 5'11", the usual stupidness. But when you get, like you meet people seriously, and ya talking to them, it's a whole different level. You don't consider what they look like, whatever: it's a mind-to-mind contact kind of thing. It's entirely different, and you actually find yourself making a good few friends online. 'Cos I got four or five people that I can really kick with regularly. And I just met them over the net.

Jason—like most people who take seriously any online relationship—felt he had reliable strategies and instincts for assessing these relationships. In fact he was pragmatic in sorting out the real—trustworthy, serious, weighty—relationships, and therefore in deciding where to place his trust:

But the way I'm made up, I always give everybody, no matter who, right, that comes into my space and touch my life, they always get a chance to screw me up—but they only get one chance to screw me up. You tell me this and you say this is the truth, I take it as ok. But when you're online and you're getting to learn somebody you do proceed with a little more caution. In this case you can see somebody's eyes and you know—well yeah, he lying to me, or—he pulling a fast one. Online you track what they say—me, I track what they say. The trust comes from normal banter, because when you first meet somebody online you're usually talking some stupidness or the other. You're not really into anything serious. Most of the times it's a lot easier to trust someone online because

they can't hurt you as much as someone who you trust face to face.

Finally, Jason not only sorted the light from the heavy relationships, but he placed them in quite different ethical universes of responsibility and commitment. As we have argued previously, the issue here is in no sense a distinction between the "real" and the "virtual," but rather the ways in which Jason chose to frame online relationships as significant and what consequences he then attached to them:

The thing is when they say stuff, say in the general chat rooms, etc., stuff is said, whatever goes. But when you're on a one-on-one with somebody, and [when] you get past the bullshit and the jokes, people really reveal a lot of their soul to you. And you are entrusted to keep what you have there as sacred property, 'cos they share a piece of theirselves with you. And if you sharing you expect that they return the sentiment, and they do.

Whereas Jason tended to see chat relationships as a potentially very pure form of what he valued in offline relationships, a surprising number of people framed special chat relationships as very literal forms of the most conventional primary relationships. They talked to us of boyfriends or girlfriends or even fiancées who turned out to be entirely online correspondents living in another part of the world. In an even more surprising number of cases we could confirm that these relationships, formed through random chat encounters, had in fact been pursued into serious offline encounters, including living together or marrying. For example, in one family visited, the daughter, a university student, had met a Buddhist from Brazil online. The relationship developed, and the Brazilian twice visited Trinidad; but finally the religious divide from the staunchly Catholic daughter proved too great a barrier to a permanent relationship. While the daughter has since fallen in love with a Trinidadian, she has also managed to develop a sufficiently deep friendship with a Danish male that he also planned to visit her in Trinidad. So common is this kind of occurrence that we would predict that for the young the tradition of anonymous tourism may increasingly be replaced by holidays being taken on the basis of a previous long-term Internet-based friendship.

Serious relationships and indeed marriage developed from online meetings. These can be framed in quite diverse ways, as could be seen in the case of several relationships within one family. The mother had actually married an American whom she originally met online. However, she still not only expressed worry about the online relationships that her children were concurrently developing, but also doubted the reality and seriousness of their relationships as opposed to hers. She pointed out that although there were several months of purely online communication before she met her husband face to face, she did not and would not characterize it as friendship, let alone as developing on to love, until they had actually met in person. It was not "real," and there was too much possibility for deception. In this and other respects, such as her distaste at the very idea of cybersex, she clearly distanced her own actions from her children's, who fell in love and got serious without meeting the persons concerned. A further irony here was that her children's practice was condemned mainly on the basis of her own ideals, that a couple should live together before marriage. It seemed in talking to her own children separately that one of them had internalized his mother's strictures and was clear that the eight-month relationship he had had online was only to be understood within the confines of the medium. It was also clear that his brother and sister were much less constrained or influenced by her scepticism, and saw their online relationships in terms of love and possible marriage. This is a clear example of the different ways in which people can construct or assess the "virtual"; not as an assumed property of Internet relations but as a criterion by which they understand them.

On the same day and at the same cybercafé at which these interviews were conducted, an 18-year-old girl had just announced to us that she was getting engaged to a man in Australia whom she had never met, on the basis of almost daily ICQ contact supplemented by occasional phone calls to him and to his parents. As one of the company pointed out, it is "mostly girls and those who are rather sheltered at home. You know they have problems, they don't agree with their parents, and they are looking for getting out of the house and maybe out of the country." It was implicit that this remark particularly applied to Indian girls living in the local villages. As in this case, such relationships could be unusually public in their development. Another large group reported eagerly awaiting the first visit to Trinidad of one of their friend's ICQ correspondents from Dominica, and their delight when the couple subsequently married.

Sometimes these relationships start as unintended consequences of short-term random chats, with conversations about their respective countries and common popular culture leading to an exchange of photographs, and then a mixture of flirting and discussing personal problems. In most such cases the Trinidadians have a clear normative model of how such relationships should develop, and a rich language to describe this. Their correspondents are commonly accused of being too *maco* (nosy) or too *fass* (fast); they give one the horrors and fail to keep cool. In short Trinidadians do not like people who come on too fast and too strong. Many users had stories about dropping people from chat-lists because they were incapable of taking things at the pace the Trinis wanted. On the other hand there are some who go online with the specific intention of looking for long-term rather than short-term relationships, which they expressly state on the information forms attached to their names on ICQ. Since already many Trinidadians know of others who have found partners this way, the Internet has quickly become a specific option for those in search of love, with the additional implication of leaving for another country through marriage. This is a possibility that many Trinidadians, young and old, view with what might be termed an interested ambivalence. Another option is to establish long-term online relationships without either partner's having any particular expectation of this ever turning into a face-to-face relationship.

Once established, these relationships can have many of the characteristics of any other long-term relationships. When those involved discuss them, often with rich details about quarrels and making up and issues of different degrees of commitment, it is very hard to discern any tangible difference from their discussion of offline relationships. When a woman storms into the room in a fury of "God that man drives me to...," the man in question may be in the room she has just stepped out of; but equally he may be on the screen in that room. Sometimes there is an online version of a common offline scenario. For example, one woman noted that: "I have this boyfriend and I caught him sweet-talking somebody else in a next chat room. I dumped him. I don't remember her name, but I found him out. Well, I tell him it's over. I stop talking to him."

This implies that those involved do not perceive as problematic what to outsiders might be the "obvious" constraints of online romance. This is important not only in new relationships with those living abroad, but also to ongoing relationships between Trinidadians. Internet use in respect of long-term friendships follows a similar pattern to that with relatives: partly recovery, partly maintenance, partly expansion. Indeed, there is a close similarity in the use of the Internet to "repair" the specific problem of relationships that would have been sundered when one partner went abroad to study and the other remained at home. A common speculation was that a particular relationship would have subsequently broken up, but thanks to the Internet was maintained until the couple could be together again. It was very common for those who had not gone online while at school to purchase a first computer or to go to a cybercafé when their school friends went abroad to study or work. So here the Internet comes across as the saving of such relationships. For example, a married couple had known each other since they were 15, but had had to spend three years apart, as she was in the UK and he remained in Trinidad. During this time they would email every day, and go on a chat line every 2 or 3 days. As they noted this was: "Fantastic. It was more effective than a phone call. It was harder to say goodbye than when I was on the phone. Strange enough, it was as good as actually sitting down and talking to the person. When you are on the phone you just don't get that sort of...; probably because we write and that sort of triggers off all the emotions. We get more time to think, I guess."

This was a rare statement; most couples wanted to complement their online chat with telephone calls, and ideally with visits. This was a clear difference from short-term use, where the other is viewed specifically as an online correspondent. But for long-term relationships the medium does not define the partner; rather, it is merely the means by which the partner is encountered. Some users never seem to be that comfortable with chat and email as a means to express deep emotions; but it is striking that most users have quickly taken these new media for granted as entirely appropriate for expressing emotions, running the gamut of love, anger, jealousy, guilt, and intimacy. This is evident not only from discussing online relationships, but also from watching people online getting riled by but also intensely involved in their communications, or waiting around in agitation (particularly at cybercafés) when there is a technical problem that delays them from finding out if the significant he/she has left a message.

Chat and ICQ lend themselves to floating and unstable populations; ICQ encounters are commonly fleeting. However within the institutional facilities created to make chat possible there are provisions for photographic and personal archives and message boards, which may be used to support relationships in a more enduring, visible, and material form. A more formal and perhaps more socially consequential example of this would be the lists of alumni posted on their websites by some of the prestige schools. These often list names, email addresses, websites, and graduation years of any school graduates who are online. This was clearly a significant resource for a body of alumni that largely disperses to further studies around the globe immediately on graduation. There remains a strong sense of "old boy" and "old girl" affinity with their "alma mater" fostered by the schools. Perhaps the most conspicuous example of this Diaspora effect was Fatima College. Because of its long-term association with computer and Internet teaching, this school seemed to have a presence on the Internet well beyond its relative size. As well as the alumni listed on its own site, there is a separate website developed in Canada. Broken down by current place of residence, this reveals the following spread of ex-students, which in turns explains the immediate significance of the Internet: USA 170; Trinidad and Tobago 148; Canada 87; UK 13; country not entered 10; Jamaica 3; together with 2 each for Australia, Grenada, Scotland, and Venezuela and 1 each for Bermuda, Botswana, Brazil, Denmark, Ireland, Japan, and Switzerland.

The significance of such lists goes beyond renewing friendships. Simply by hyperlinking between the websites of all these graduates, the Internet comes both to represent and to replicate a key aspect of Trinidadian social structure. The Internet not only maps it but plays a part in reproducing it through the practical interconnections it enables. Some of our research developed by following such links and email addresses, which have become an effective means of tracing the Trini elite.

PLACES OF SOCIALITY

In so far as Internet studies have shifted their gaze from what happens online, they have started to investigate the micro-sociological contexts of Internet use, such as cybercafés or domestic spaces (Crang, Crang, and May 1999; Furlong 1995; Wakeford 1999). The immediate social locations of Internet use both frame and set limits on the kinds of relationships that take place through them. For example, workplace access could range from minimal to extensive, and from extremely liberal attitudes to personal use to a restrictive, "business use only" policy. Hence some people could treat their office as a place for pursuing family contacts on behalf of their entire household, for chatting, and even for cybersex; others could not relate workplace access to any kind of sociality.

Just as important as the impact of social spaces on the way relationships were pursued through the Internet was their impact on relationships around the computer. Two places of sociality that brought out quite different possibilities for relationships were cybercafés and secondary schools.

Cybercafés

The global usage of cybercafés is diverse, as Rao (1999) has noted. In Trinidad, they were largely unstable and in most cases unprofitable enterprises. They were generally either adjuncts to other businesses (computer sales or maintenance, private IT courses) or on the verge of transforming into other businesses (webdesign and Internet technologies). They also ranged from scams (one charged people TT$5 for each email sent or received) to dynamic community centres.

In the event, we were able to visit six operating cybercafés, each of which was very different in style and in the kinds of sociality it generated. For example, of the two in which we spent a good deal of our research time, Café A had a strong emphasis on an informal and convivial ambience. There was always music, loud conversation, bustling activity. It was also literally a cybercafé, in that it served food and drink. The eight computers were placed along the outside walls of the main rooms so that anyone sitting at the spare tables in the centre could see what was going on at the monitors. It was a very public space and a friendly liming spot. This reflected the personality and strong beliefs of the couple who owned it, especially the husband, who was regarded by many users as a kind of father-figure, who calmly dispensed advice, support, and encouragement, as well as keeping both order and excitement. He combined entrepreneurialism and nationalism in typical Trini measure (see [Miller and Slater, 2000, Chapter 4]), doing his utmost to develop his users' Internet expertise and enterprise. He also gathered about himself talented and enthusiastic young people who could use the facilities to develop commercial projects in webdesign and programming.

The second cybercafé—B—was an adjunct to a computer retail business that also had an extensive programme of computer courses. This was distinctly a business premises, with white and undecorated walls. Partly for teaching purposes, the computers were sited in three different rooms, and within them machines were positioned to give much privacy to the user. There was no area for general liming, and the consumption of food and drink was forbidden. Despite the different style, the social ambience was very friendly and supportive, but this was entirely due to a core of employees, their relatives, and some regulars.

In each case there were probably a majority of people who used the spaces as individuals, without much apparent connection to the cafés as institutions beyond finding them more or less congenial. This included people stopping by to check their email or research a particular topic or just surf or chat for a while. The population was mainly, but not exclusively, young. They related to the staff mainly for technical support and help in using software.

On the other hand, both places had a core of one or two dozen regulars who came in very frequently and spent a lot of time there. One person we knew seemed to live there, chatting non-stop to her cyber-fiancé in Australia, to a degree that staff expressed some concern to us. Hourly charges were laxly enforced, and in some cases the most regular visitors paid for little of their online time, but in return helped the employees sort out "newbies" and generally added to the ambience of the place. Even though Café B had little in the way of atmosphere, and certainly did not put itself forward as a liming spot, regular users still strongly identified with it, and another cybercafé noted that most of their Christmas decorations were put up by users. Café A went much further. A few people said that they came there even though they had online computers at home or work; others hung out after school with no apparent desire to use a computer at all: "Nearly every day after work I come up here, even if is not to use the PC, if I buy something from the cybercafé downstairs and I'll come up and eat, or just chill. People come up here to study too. It does be a real nice lime."

Sociality comprised a wider variety of collective uses of the space than simply hanging out. At this point, the styles of the two places diverged more markedly. A lot of the activity in cybercafé B was oriented to chat. Partly because of the privacy afforded by the room and monitor arrangements, people could both pursue their own activities and at the same time form small groups, sharing their experiences. This might mean that regular users found their on- and offline worlds merging in interesting ways: for example, they might pass chat friends on to each other, or gather round a screen as a chat progressed. The girl mentioned above, recently engaged to a man in Australia, encouraged him to find Australian girls who would chat to a boy she had come to know at the café. Equally his interests in certain games led him to make friends both with café regulars and with some online contacts. Often young users would want to make sure there were friends around to appreciate some sexual adventure or the excited danger of encountering a hacker online. Regulars would rush over to a friend's screen to take over their keyboard and latch on to some event, in between juggling half a dozen open windows and conversations on their own machine.

The private spaces possible in Café B (especially, but not exclusively, its "back room") also allowed looking at pornography, alone or in groups (pornography was banned at Café A, because of the public view of all monitors rather than for reasons of principled disapproval). For example, a group of gay Trinidadians collectively used the back room to look at sexual material—an important opportunity in Trinidad, which has tended to be highly homophobic. The staff are clearly aware of the pornographic material being used, and

themselves suggested that this represented some 70 per cent of all usage (we felt this was an exaggeration, although some users claimed the same figure); but their concern was primarily to ensure that such activities be carried out in privacy and not be directly exposed to chance encounters with schoolchildren and others who would be offended. Our observations would then certainly support Wakeford (1999: 188–94) in noting the importance of spatial order within the cybercafé to understanding the kinds of interaction that take place there.

Coming into the café as a group generally tended to have an impact on machine use, creating the bravado for illicit activities. In addition to porn, this might include schoolchildren who would impress each other with their ability to work as hackers. Another example was:

> Sometimes me and my friend will come as a group and just sit at a computer and go into ICQ and just diss everybody and get thrown out from the chat room. Well, we just like to interfere with people. Like harmless, just embarrass, just jump in, listen to a particular conversation and then we chose this one and decide that we going to harass this one. Out of kicks and then everybody just get involved. Only as a group, until we got banned, restricted, eventually: got kicked out a couple of times, then we got banned.

Sociality in Café A was rather different. As opposed to the groups huddled around monitors in Café B, people were either liming at the tables or engaged in more purposeful (but still sociable and pleasurable) development of their skills or projects. There was a great emphasis on helping each other learn ever more ambitious skills and on projects. Finally, and rather unusually for Trinidad, where computer game culture is not as important to Internet use as in North America and Europe, there were a number of people at Café A, many of them core staff and regulars, who were heavily into networked games such as Quake. There were occasional all-nighters, and some investment of time in downloading the paraphernalia of Quake clans.

One final case of cybercafé sociality that indicates how unexpected the relationships formed around the Internet can be: a cybercafé recently opened up in an up-market mall by a young woman turned into a kind of virtual crèche. She started by offering basic training in Internet use to younger children and found that not only did the children love it, but their mothers loved leaving them there, in safety and worthy educational pursuits, while they shopped for several hours. One particularly wealthy family regularly left their son there with his personal bodyguard, and both would play for hours.

Secondary Schools

One of the traumas of Trinidadian life is the common entrance exam, which separates children between the more prestigious Church-founded secondary schools and the ordinary government schools. The striking difference between the two was that the Internet had already become an integral part of school culture for students of the prestige schools. This was as much a reflection of the fact that they tended to come from wealthier families with Internet access at home as from the much improved online facilities at school (clearly evident in their school websites,...). [As indicated in Miller and Slater (2000)] Chapter 2, provision for boys and for girls was radically unequal, though this did not seem to make the Internet any less of a feature for girls' school culture or schoolwork, at least at the schools we visited. Home use was more equal, with several individuals and groups suggesting a figure of around a third of schoolchildren having online access at home, though those without access might come and use the computers of those with. Schoolchildren with online computers at home tended to receive 5 to 20 emails a week. There was much sharing of online culture, with people forwarding jokes and cards but also friends to each other. Chat and ICQ were very common for younger children. One noted how she had stopped using ICQ, since she had found it so addictive during the four months she had used it. For boys music was the most common use after chat and ICQ, followed by email, and then porn, with rather less use for sports and games.

Perhaps in schools more than anywhere else one has a sense of the Internet as something that already has a history, and also a relationship to the school as a life course. For example, there is the sense of a pre-ICQ phase or a pre-personal webpage phase. There is already the expectation amongst school-children that members of a certain school form would go through a phase of heavy involvement in Internet pornography or cybersex, but that by the next school year this was already seen as immature and not really cool. In one year children might come into school and call each other by their ICQ nicks instead of their real names; but again this would be scorned by the more senior year. As one pupil put it: "Some get out of the phase faster than others, others are still into it. They are the minority. The other forms are in it right now. When we were in lab in Computer Science everybody had their own porno section. I had 300 pictures, a friend had about 400 pictures. Now if you go back only the lower forms have their porno sections. The school doesn't really know."

Schoolchildren constituted one of the only groups that extensively exploited the Internet for socializing with other Trinidadians in Trinidad. One example of this was the extension of playground gossip and interaction. ICQ seemed to have replaced the telephone as the privileged medium for continuing school conversations after school, letting each other know about or comment on events that day, in the privacy of their one-to-one chat. Already the patterns of spitefulness, cliquishness, sentimentality, and making-up that are familiar genres offline were finding their online equivalents. Also there was the concomitant rise of the particularly Trinidadian sense of bacchanal and *commess* (disorder caused by gossip). For example schoolgirls relished the story of a boy who published gossip about his friends on his personal website. News of this event spread quickly, so that they too had

visited the site. During the one week before the boy's mother closed the site down, it had been hacked—we were told—by some of those concerned to publish counter-accusations about the website author. Another story concerned a boy watching a screen with his girlfriend while gossip about this girlfriend was being relayed. A more direct relationship was established in San Fernando, where there is a concentration of secondary schools. Many pupils used an IRC-based chat room where they tended to congregate online, especially on Friday nights continuing through into the morning hours while the parents were asleep. They also arranged to meet occasionally for a group lime at the food court of the local mall. Email and ICQ might also be used to plan a weekend lime or other gathering.

The Internet was also providing schoolchildren with a major conduit to offline relationships. Chat was seen as an ideal precursor to dating, since both boys and girls could be less reticent and feel their way towards a relationship while staying relatively anonymous:

> "Before, the girls are shy kind of way, so it would take a fellow to go over and meet a girl and talk. But with ICQ it's easier. You speaking to them like you know them kind of thing, before you actually know them. And when you meet you already know them." Another boy noted of a friend: "He met her on one of the open chat lines and then he met her in real. They going strong now, haven't had a fight yet. It's a good way of meeting girls. It's easier than walking up to someone and talking."

Internet content becomes common school culture as easily as television programmes such as *South Park*. In the morning people would report new sites or software. The Internet could be used to constitute the non-school sociality of children, as: "A place to get away from school, that's what the Internet is for my class. They look at it as liming on the net. They are all in one big chat room and lime." But this was the least academic class in the year. For most students the relationship between the Internet and school culture clearly integrated both sociality and also educational activities, such as sharing Internet resources for schoolwork. One group of schoolgirls laughed at our adult naivety when we discussed using books for essay-writing, since they pointed out the great store of previously written essays existing on the Internet that could be mined as the basis for their own essays. They all claimed that they themselves (of course) only ever used ideas and snippets of these essays, but that others in their class had submitted entire essays taken from the web without as yet ever being caught out by the teachers. One group did suggest, however, that their teachers were asking more obscure questions in subjects such as literature partly in response to the threat of their pupils' merely presenting public-domain essays. Books and libraries were seen as passé: according to the girls, even teachers accepted the inability to find information online as a reasonable excuse for not handing in a homework project.

Almost all these children will at least investigate the possibility of further education abroad through researching the net; indeed throughout Trinidadian society this has become a far more frequent use of the Internet than pursuits such as sports and games. This was confirmed by inspection of many "histories" recorded on web-browsers in cybercafés. At Fatima College around half the students were expected to take SAT exams for US colleges, of whom around half were expected to obtain full scholarships to prestigious universities in the US. The evidence from the alumni lists on the school websites suggest this is not unrealistic. The schools themselves clearly recognized that Internet skills were becoming an integral part of general education. Some were quite liberal in opening up their banks of computers to after-school use, even when finding on occasion that a schoolchild was still online when they returned for school the next morning! Fatima funded its computer laboratories partly through putting on annual courses for the public. IT remains integral to the social relations of its alumni.

The personal websites of schoolchildren are themselves clear expressions of school culture. They also make far more inventive use of the technology than even the most expensive commercial sites. "Maria's So Called Life," with the address "sullengirl," has words like "pathetic" and "wasting away" that come and go within a frame. Instead of the simple "about me" found in most personal websites (see [Miller and Slater, 2000] Chapter 4), this one states "Stuff on me, WARNING!—Before you proceed to waste your time by reading this page I should warn you…it SUCKS!!! I don't know why I'm doing this really, guess it's because I have a lot of time on my hands." Sullengirl thereby illustrates the effectiveness of a website in conveying the typical sense of the teenager as alienated: even visually, she mainly appears on the site as an alien. Other teenage sites also present themselves as stupid and pathetic and tell us how they really shouldn't be working on this site one week before taking their examinations but….

What is impressive is not just the sheer dynamics and creativity of these sites, but the techniques they use to entrap surfers and draw them in. For example,…one site [brilliantly] exploits a conventional form of computer link to suck in the passing surfer. The crucial factor in all these sites seems to be not just the ability to attract surfers but also to engage in the act of exchange represented by the (usually mutual) signing of their guestbooks. It is this that attests to the fame/name of the website creator, and is analogous to the circles of exchange that create the name and fame of those who transact Kula (Munn 1986). Surfers are drawn to share the offerings of the site, for example their jokes, their MP3s, their friends, or their links to other sites as long as they sign the guestbook and attest thereby to the fame of the creator.

The Internet was also at the centre of school cultures of heroes and outlaws that focused on technical feats and knowledge, generally possessed by boys (this was not confined to schools, but certainly prevalent there). While some of this involved relationships formed between technically proficient boys who were developing small website businesses or helping manage school IT facilities, the thrilling stuff involved various kinds of organized outlawry, often

mythological, directed against school or each other. One school had allowed a highly skilled 15-year-old to develop their website and other computer facilities for the school. The fact that the same pupil was reputed to then hack into the system at will led to a subsequent parting of ways. All the students had a repertoire of stories about master hackers and hacking feats, of particularly devastating viruses and ingenious "trojans" that could take control over anyone's computer. It was hard to confirm any of these stories, and many of them were pretty outlandish (the shared ultimate ideal was for some schoolboy to hack into the Trinidadian banking system); but it was clear that reports of such exploits were a guaranteed addition to peer status. As one 15-year-old put it:

> Normally they brag about how good they are at hacking, or blowing up somebody's system, shutting them down. Some instances—they are true. People that [say] they do it to come back and talk about it. They does be real vex. They quarrel a lot. Why you do me that? They have this fella, he left school now, he was in form five with us, he could shut down somebody even on the net, or disconnect, he's real good.

Hacking involved competitive bravado between the boys. By contrast, a 15-year-old schoolgirl noted that girls would commonly send viruses to each other, often in the belief that they were already victims of a virus sent by the girl in question. Girls would come to school also moaning about how their computer had been messed up and how they would wreak revenge on the girl they believed had sent the virus. Again, the mix of truth and lore is both undecidable and revealing of school culture, but the comment that "this is their mentality" strongly suggested that the stereotypes that are developing about how schoolgirls and schoolboys respectively use their skills closely follow older gender stereotypes.

Continuities

Much of the first half of this chapter could have been written under the rubric of kinship studies. At first glance the material appears very different from what one might expect to encounter in kinship studies; but we want to suggest that there may be much more continuity here than meets the eye. This becomes more apparent when it is recognized that the relationships discussed throughout this chapter are, like kinship itself, an idiom for the expression of core Trinidadian values. The central argument of Miller 1994 was that there existed a historical logic that could confer on Trinidad a vanguard position in arguments about the nature of modernity. It was suggested that the relevant values—termed there "transience" and "transcendence"—were historically first developed and expressed through the idiom of kinship. After the oil boom of the 1970s the same contradiction in values was also expressed through the meanings given to the objects of mass consumption, perhaps now through the medium of the Internet.

The key author for understanding the distinctive character of West Indian kinship is R. T. Smith (1988, 1995). Trinidad had equivalent norms of kinship to those Smith describes for Jamaica, although they have recently moved closer to international norms and ideologies as a result of affluence and cosmopolitan aspirations. Smith (1988: 49) found that Jamaicans typically recognized a large number of people as relatives (a mean of 284 in 51 cases). As in Trinidad, these became a kind of potential network rather than, as in other countries, a series of concentric circles representing decreasing degrees of contact and obligation. Closeness or affection is almost an independent variable one establishes with some kin but not with others. Connections with kin are rather less tied to a sense of obligation based on relative closeness of blood than would be true elsewhere. As a potential network these connections grow in particular ways. For example, in Trinidad the birth of a baby signifies the creation of new bonds irrespective of the continued presence of the baby's father. This relative separation between a sense of connection and a sense of obligation may be understood in part as an act of resistance to historical pressure from groups such as the Church to develop more institutionalized norms of kin. For example, there was resistance to marriage prior to demonstrating the ability to have children and most especially the ability to own and run a house.

Instead, kinship included a strong element of pragmatism. One might be only vaguely aware that a particular relative lived in a locality until the decision to send one's son to school in that area, in which case that relative's house becomes the obvious place for him to live. Similarly if one wanted to extend a business link to a new region. The same applied to affection in general. Cousins were more like a pool of potential close relations; but only through mutual attraction does a very close friendship develop with one particular cousin. So what mattered was not the distance between any two relatives, but rather the realization of particular pragmatic and affective relations out of a pool of possible relationships. Even in the practice of sexuality there is a stress on the mutual act of exchange, for example of giving one's labour in clearing the yard of one's sexual partner as part of mutual recognition of the relationship. There is also an antipathy to forms of marriage in which partners can take each other for granted in providing either sex or labour.

In effect kinship represents a potential pool of people, while circumstances are allowed to determine whether or not there develops a bond of affection or whether or not a relative becomes an important node in solving some logistical problem. In Miller 1994 (pp. 168–93) it was argued that all of this expresses the value of transience, in which institutions are prevented from limiting the sense of freedom and voluntarism basic to what are seen as authentic relationships. Its roots in the particular history of the region are therefore clear.

Such a perspective is very different from the "baggage" that usually comes with terms such as "community" and "family" if used as models for Internet use. Usually such terms tend to assume a commonalty of sentiment in which community as a symbol and focus of commitment transcends the relations that constitute it. If, however, West Indian kinship of this transient variety is taken as the model for Internet use, other possibilities arise. The first analogy is found in the way people use the Internet to create networks. One common concern is simply to expand the number of people one knows or knows of. Once one has had a communication with them it could in future be extended if that were mutually desired. This evolution occurs through a number of different routes. These include creating networks of potential correspondents, for example through contacting distant kin on the Internet, developing a list of "nicks" on one's ICQ link, or signing a website's guestlist. A prime example of this would be the "de Trini Lime," an ICQ list that grew as we were doing fieldwork to 2,215 people. The only criteria that mattered as far as most people were concerned were that the other person on the lime was a genuine Trini and then also usually that they were of the opposite sex.

As in the transient family, one finds with Internet relationships that larger appeals to sentiment or obligation on the basis of nearness or proximity often have little authority. Rather, there is a large pool of potential contacts that can be realized for either or both of two main reasons, one being to create bonds of affection, sometimes including deep intimacy and acts of confession. The other is to engage in mutual communication in order to fulfil some largely pragmatic and perhaps fortuitous need, such as a common desire for computer games cheats, though such a need might also be represented by something one might think of as more personal. Many of the random chat links are based around discussions of such things as how to deal with nagging parents or teachers, or persistent ex-boyfriends.

As a result the presence of the correspondent cannot be taken for granted. It follows that there is a constant need to recreate the mutuality of the relationship. This works for both short- and long-term relationships. As some young men noted in trying cybersex, they simply had to show more sensitivity and concern for the pleasure of their female partners than they had in offline sex, since otherwise their partners would just leave them standing (as it were). So, as in transient kinship, Internet relationships are more dyadic, voluntaristic, and based on the continuity of their re-constitution through constant acts of exchange. This is not to say that the relationships are more superficial or less normative or lacking in the possibility of affection; but rather it makes these compatible with using relationships to objectify a project of freedom as a central value of modernity. This argument thereby exemplifies the dynamics of normative freedom as discussed in [Miller and Slater, 2000,] Chapter 1.

The final point is that contrary to expectations such uses of the Internet are not to be opposed to "traditional" forms of relationship and especially kinship (Castells 1998: 340–51). In this case, by contrast, such attributes would make the Internet strongly continuous with those values that were developed first in kinship and later through the experience of mass consumption (see Miller 1994: Chapter 5). So while it is too early to know to what degree these Trinidadian uses of the Internet are highly specific, if they are, there will be a local historical trajectory that might help us account for that specificity. Once again there may be elective affinities at play; but most importantly, the argument suggests that the relationships outlined here cannot be assumed to be mere creatures of the Internet developed in opposition to or replacement of something else called "traditional kinship."

Conclusions

The evidence in this chapter suggests that online and offline worlds penetrate each other deeply and in complex ways, whether people are using the Internet to realize older concepts of identity or to pursue new modes of sociality. With respect to the family, the Internet is used largely to roll back changes that were dissolving some family relations. It is used to bring people back to what they think of as "proper" family life. As such it is a prime example of…the expansive realization. Chat and ICQ can further new kinds of social contact, which then have to be assessed and related to a normative sense of what a "real" relationship is. They may also be reframed as, or even literally lead to, the most traditional forms of sociality, such as marriage. Apparently quite mundane new media, such as virtual postcards, can both transform older gifting practices and materially re-constitute the relationships in which they are embedded. Spaces of sociality emerge around Internet use in cybercafés and schools, with their own norms and variations based on a complex interweaving of online and offline worlds, frequently more significant in their intensification of offline rather than online relationships, or in the way they integrate the two.

Virtuality, [see Miller and Slater, 2000, Chapter 1] is unhelpful or even misleading as a point of departure in sorting out this complexity. Ethnographically, it is at best a special case that emerged in Jason's valuation of "just communicating" in chat relationships—yet even he did not use the term "virtual." Rather he stressed that the value of these relationships hinged on the way in which they were stitched into his everyday life, exemplified in their knowledge and participation in his family life. Similarly, although it is tempting to treat the alumni lists of prestige schools as a kind of virtual social structure, they evidently arose from and maintained an intricate relationship with a quite conventional sense of social structure, and had an eminently practical function in reproducing that structure, alongside other modes of formal and informal practices (for example, careers, travel, and business contacts).

…[These] conclusions are tied to local circumstances. It need not follow that ICQ will necessarily have the same consequence for another society or Diaspora. The "elective affinity" by which a particular Internet technology can be developed to enhance a particular genre of relationships is highly contextualized. Indeed, it was suggested at the end that there may be strong continuities with earlier forms of kinship, partly because both kinship and the Internet are being employed as idioms to express particular values that connect with what we have termed normative freedom. To try and separate our material into the "real" and the "virtual" would thus seem to us to lose almost everything that can be learnt from studying relationship on and through the Internet.

Note

1. The term Diaspora here is used to include not only Trinidadian families that live overseas but also families that are split between residence in Trinidad and overseas. Obviously this does not accord with the usual definition of the term Diaspora, but we feel the text would lose rather than gain clarity by trying to specify the degree of transnationalism in each case. With respect to the issue of Internet use we are concerned with all situations where some members of a family that was once from Trinidad now live outside Trinidad. It would also seem to be pedantic to try to be too precise about the semantics of migration, since most accounts show just how fluid identities and residence can often be for Caribbean migrants (e.g., Basch, Glick Schiller, and Szanton Blanc 1994; Chamberlain 1998).

References

Basch, L., Glick Schiller, N., and Szanton Blanc, C. 1994. *Nations Unbound*. Amsterdam: Gordon & Breach.

Carrier, J. 1995. *Gifts and Commodities*. London: Routledge.

Castells, M. 1998. *End of Millennium*. Oxford: Blackwell.

Chamberlain, M. 1998. *Caribbean Migration: Globalised Identities*. London: Routledge.

Crang, M., Crang, P., and May, J. 1999. *Virtual Geographies*. London: Routledge.

Furlong, R. 1995. There's No Place like Home, in M. Lister (ed.), *The Photographic Image in Digital Culture*. London: Routledge.

Ho, C. 1991. *Salt-Water Trinis: Afro-Trinidadian Immigrant Networks and Non-Assimilation in Los Angeles*. New York: AMS Press.

Jaffe, A. 1999. Packaged Sentiments. The Social Meaning of Greeting Cards. *Journal of Material Culture* 4: 115–41.

Marvin, C. 1988. *When Old Technologies Were New*. New York: Oxford University Press.

Mauss, M. 1954. *The Gift*. London: Cohen and West.

Miller, D. 1994. *Modernity: An Ethnographic Approach*. Oxford: Berg.

Miller, D., and Slater, D. 2000. *The Internet: An Ethnographic Approach*. Oxford and New York: Berg.

Munn, N. 1986. *The Fame of Gawa*. Cambridge: Cambridge University Press.

Olwig, K. F. 1993. *Global Culture, Island Identity: Continuity and Change in the Afro-Caribbean Community of Nevis*. Chur, Switzerland: Harwood.

Rao, M. 1999. Bringing the Net to the Masses: Cybercafes in Latin America. *Cybersociology* 4 22/04/99 http://www.cybersoc.com/magazine.

Slater, D. 1998. Trading Sexpics on IRC: Embodiment and Authenticity on the Internet. *Body and Society* 4 (4).

Smith, R. T. 1988. *Kinship and Class in the West Indies*. Cambridge: Cambridge University Press.

Smith, R. T. 1995. *The Matrifocal Family*. London: Routledge.

Stein, J. 1999. The Telephone: Its Social Shaping and Public Negotiation in Late Nineteenth- and Early Twentieth-century London. In M. Crang, P. Crang, and J. May (ed.), *Virtual Geographies*, pp. 44–62. London: Routledge.

Wakeford, N. 1999. Gender and the Landscapes of Computing in an Internet Café. In M. Crang, P. Crang, and J. May (eds.), *Virtual Geographies*, pp. 178–201. London: Routledge.

Yelvington, K. 1996. Flirting in the Factory. *Journal of the Royal Anthropological Institute* 2: 313–33.

Post-reading Questions / Activities

- How does Miller and Slater's account of Trinidadian Internet use compare with your own?
- Miller and Slater wrote before the rise of social networking websites such as Facebook. Discuss how Facebook, MySpace, and other sites work and why they are popular. Does your analysis contradict or support the conclusions of Miller and Slater?
- Keep a record for a week of the uses to which you put the Internet. Note especially which people you contact or are contacted by, how much time you spend with each, what the form of your communication is, and the purpose or function of each particular exchange. Do you see an overall pattern to your Internet use?
- Do you think that the Internet has fundamentally transformed human relationships? Are relationships mediated by technology fundamentally different from face-to-face relationships? Support your answer.

Vocabulary

crèche	kula
Diaspora, diasporic	lime, liming
ICQ	mediated

Suggested Further Reading

Baron, Naomi S. 2008. *Always on: Language in an Online and Mobile World*. Oxford and New York: Oxford University Press.

Crystal, David. 2006. *Language and the Internet*. 2d ed. Cambridge: Cambridge University Press.

Horst, Heather A., and Daniel Miller. 2006. *The Cell Phone: An Anthropology of Communication*. Oxford and New York: Berg.

Ito, Mizuko, Daisuke Okabe, and Misa Matsuda, eds. 2005. *Personal, Portable, Pedestrian: Mobile Phones in Japanese Life*. Cambridge, MA, and London: MIT Press.

Malinowski, Bronislaw. 1922. *Argonauts of the Western Pacific*. London: G. Routledge and Sons.

———. 1923. "The Problem of Meaning in Primitive Languages." In *The Meaning of Meaning*, edited by C. K. Ogden and I. A. Richards. New York: Harcourt, Brace.

Mauss, Marcel. 1954. *The Gift: Forms and Functions of Archaic Exchange*. Translated by Ian Cunnison. London: Coehn and West.

Miller, Daniel, and Don Slater. 2000. *The Internet: An Ethnographic Approach*. Oxford and New York: Berg.

UNIT 6

Language Ideology

As occasionally happens in intellectual matters, the concept *language ideology* named something that anthropologists, linguists, and other analysts of language had been aware of for some time: different values are placed on various aspects of language at different times and in different places. We see it as early as in Malinowski's "The Problem of Meaning in Primitive Languages," in much work on the ethnography of speaking [including in Joel Sherzer and Regna Darnell's "Outline Guide for the Ethnographic Study of Speech Use" (especially the section on "Attitudes Toward the Use of Speech")], and in a good portion of the work of Michael Silverstein. When Kathryn Woolard and Bambi Schieffelin gave a name to this approach to the understanding of language in 1994, they unleashed a new creative energy in this study (see also Schieffelin, Woolard, and Kroskrity 1998, Kroskrity 2000). This links the subtle analysis that we can achieve of looking at how people regard the very nature of language with notions of power and politics, conveyed by the term *ideology* (in contrast to *idea*).

Writing on language ideology is very broad and very rich. Elsewhere in this book we have also seen it applied to norms of direction and indirection (Chapter 34), to attitudes toward hip-hop music and identity (Chapter 27), and to the meanings of Spanish in the context of Anglo-Mexican interactions (Chapter 29). The term is now used in studies of gender, multilingualism, language policy, language standardization, prejudice, language shift, language socialization, and many more topics.

Suggested Further Reading

Bauman, Richard, and Joel Sherzer, eds. 1989 [1974]. *Explorations in the Ethnography of Speaking.* 2d ed. Cambridge: Cambridge University Press.

Gumperz, John J., and Dell Hymes, eds. 1986 [1972]. *Directions in Sociolinguistics: The Ethnography of Communication.* Oxford: Blackwell.

Kroskrity, Paul V., ed. 2000. *Regimes of Language: Ideologies, Polities, and Identities.* Santa Fe, NM: School of American Research Press.

Malinowski, Bronislaw. 1923. "The Problem of Meaning in Primitive Languages." In *The Meaning of Meaning,* edited by C. K. Ogden and I. A. Richards. New York: Harcourt, Brace.

Ryan, Ellen Bouchard, and Howard Giles, eds. 1982. *Attitudes Towards Language Variation: Social and Applied Contexts.* London: Edward Arnold.

Schieffelin, Bambi B., Kathryn A. Woolard, and Paul V. Kroskrity, eds. 1998. *Language Ideologies: Practice and Theory.* New York and Oxford: Oxford University Press.

Sherzer, Joel, and Regna Darnell. 1986 [1972]. "Outline Guide for the Ethnographic Study of Speech Use." In *Directions in Sociolinguistics: The Ethnography of Communication,* edited by John J. Gumperz and Dell Hymes, pp. 548–554. Oxford: Blackwell.

Silverstein, Michael. 1979. "Language Structure and Linguistic Ideology." In *The Elements: A Parasession on Linguistic Units and Levels,* edited by Paul R. Clyne, William F. Hanks, and Carol L. Hofbauer, pp. 193–247. Chicago: Chicago Linguistic Society.

———. 1998. "The Uses and Utility of Ideology: A Commentary." In *Language Ideologies: Practice and Theory,* edited by Bambi B. Schieffelin, Kathryn A. Woolard, and Paul V. Kroskrity, pp. 123–145. New York: Oxford University Press.

———, and Greg Urban, eds. 1996. *Natural Histories of Discourse.* Chicago and London: University of Chicago Press.

Woolard, Kathryn A., and Bambi B. Schieffelin. 1994. "Language Ideology." *Annual Review of Anthropology* 23: 55–82.

CHAPTER 41

Anger, Gender, Language Shift, and the Politics of Revelation in a Papua New Guinean Village

Don Kulick

(1998)

The New Guinea landmass is the world's second largest island. It contains Papua New Guinea and Irian Jaya, part of Indonesia. Papua New Guinea is sparsely populated, but among its 5.4 million people, more than 800 languages are spoken. (Ethnologue gives the figure of 820, but it is notoriously difficult to divide up languages, and most of these are unstudied.) Many of the languages of Papua New Guinea have fewer than 500 speakers.

Papua New Guinea (PNG) has three official languages: English, Tok Pisin (a creole), and Hiri Motu. Many of the smaller, local varieties are endangered, as villagers shift their language use to one of the three lingua francas. In this chapter, Don Kulick connects the shift to Tok Pisin in one village to other aspects of language ideology, including the wide assumption that people don't say what they mean! He does so by connecting gender, anger, and language, all revolving around people's goals for development through Christianity. Here language ideology is connected to the ideology of many other aspects of people's lives in a quintessentially anthropological web.

Reading Questions

- What are Gapun ideas about language? How do they regard knowledge? Why is it potentially lethal? What do they see as the relations between language and knowledge?
- How do Gapun villagers regard anger?
- What is a *kros*? Who performs *kros*es, and on what occasions? What is oratory? Who performs it, and on what occasions? How does the difference between *kros* and oratory contribute to the shift from the local language (Taiap) to the lingua franca (Tok Pisin)?
- What do anger and gender have to do with the shift to Tok Pisin?

In a number of recent publications, Catherine Lutz (1986, 1990) has explored the network of associations in Western culture that link women with emotion, which in most cases is overtly devalued. A contrasting situation is described by Bambi Schieffelin (1990), E. L. Schieffelin (1976, 1985), and Steven Feld (1990), all of whom argue that among the Kaluli people of Papua New Guinea, it is *males* who are "stereotypically culturally constructed as the emotional gender" (Feld 1990:262) and that this emotionality is encouraged and strongly valued in a wide variety of ritual and mundane contexts. Studies like these, as well as many others by anthropologists (e.g., articles in Lutz and Abu-Lughod 1990, Bloch and Parry 1982, Watson-Gegeo and White 1990, White and Kirkpatrick 1985), have shown that in probably all communities throughout the world, the expression of affect is engendered and that, therefore, in Catherine Lutz's words, "any discourse on emotion is also, at least implicitly, a discourse on gender" (Lutz 1990:69; see also Ochs 1988:177–83, 215–16).

Because both emotion and gender are indexed and expressed in large measure through language, we can augment Lutz's generalization with the observation that discourses on emotion and gender are also bound up with discourses, or ideologies, of language (Ochs 1992:341). We can, furthermore, expect that at certain periods in the history of a language and its speakers, the links that exist

Don Kulick, "Anger, Gender, Language Shift, and the Politics of Revelation in a Papua New Guinean Village." In *Language Ideologies: Practice and Theory*, ed by Bambi B. Schieffelin, Kathryn A. Woolard, and Paul V. Kroskrity. Oxford and New York: Oxford University Press, 1998, pp. 87–102.

among discourses on affect, gender, and language may come to salience and work to compel speakers to engage in linguistic practices that may result in changes in the language itself.

Michael Silverstein has drawn attention to this type of process in his discussion of the Quaker challenge to the seventeenth-century English system of distance and deference (Silverstein 1985). Silverstein argues that two factors were decisive in the shift from a pronominal system signaling deference and intimacy (through the second-person ye/you–thee/thou opposition) to one in which those affects were no longer encoded grammatically. The first factor was an emergent yet widespread idea about the value of "plain English" as a means of both signifying opposition to traditional knowledge and authority and directly apprehending religious and scientific "truth." The second was Quaker applications of this idea in their everyday speech practices and in their rhetoric about language. Quakers defied contemporary sociolinguistic norms by refusing to use the polite deference (ye/you) forms when addressing others, partly because English scriptural prose used the familiar thee/thou forms and partly because they felt that the ye/you forms contradicted their religious doctrine that all people were equal before God. Quaker usage was in this sense "explicitly subversive," as well as being "societally shocking [and] insulting" (1985:249) to non-Quaker interlocutors, who spoke to the Friends with the polite 'you', only to be answered with the familiar 'thou'. A situation thus arose in which:

> Friends [i.e., Quakers] use symmetric T [thee/thou], and hence others had to avoid it, lest they be mistaken for members of the sect; Friends avoid symmetric Y [ye/you], and hence others must use only it. Consequently, a new system emerges, in which societal norms abandon T decisively as usage indexing speaker as Quaker and take up the invariant usage of Y. A STRUCTURAL OR FORMAL change in the norms of English has been affected. (1985:251; capitals in original)

Silverstein summarizes and generalizes this process as follows:

> Ideological rationalization [can] engage . . . with language at and through an intersection of structural form and indexical usage, producing tension in the highly charged "metaphoricization" of indexical meanings and forms. The resolution of this tension seems to move the very structural system into new configurations, generally unforeseen by the users of the language. (1985:252)

I draw attention to this analysis by Silverstein because in this chapter I focus on a similar, though much more far-reaching, process of ideological and linguistic change that is under way in a small village (population ca. 110) in Papua New Guinea called Gapun.[1] Gapun is located about 10 kilometers from the northern coast of Papua New Guinea, roughly midway between the lower Sepik and the Ramu rivers. It is a relatively isolated village, and the villagers are self-supporting through a combination of swidden agricul-

ture, hunting, and sago processing. Despite their isolation and their consequently low level of participation in cash cropping or other money-generating projects, the villagers of Gapun are very keen to 'develop' (kamap), and thinking about how this might happen occupies a great deal of their time. The villagers have been nominally Roman Catholic since the late 1940s, and their hopes for development are pinned in elaborate ways on Christianity and on the imminent second coming of Christ.

In Gapun, a language shift is currently under way from the village vernacular—a Papuan language called Taiap—to Tok Pisin, the creole language that has become Papua New Guinea's most widely spoken national language. Children are no longer learning the vernacular, and when I last visited the village in 1991, no one under fourteen years of age actively commanded it. The reasons behind this shift are complex and many-stranded, but here I focus on what I see as one of the most central reasons behind the shift—namely, links that exist in village discourses among gender, the expression of anger, and particular ideologies of language that see language as indexical of sociability and the ability to handle knowledge.

Two specific speech genres invoke these links very clearly for the villagers. The first is a kind of dramatic public display of anger that occurs virtually daily in the village. The word by which the villagers most commonly call this speech genre is a Tok Pisin word, kros, which literally means 'anger' (in the village vernacular, the name is _pwapǝŋgar nam_,[2] literally 'angry talk'). Kroses are considered by Gapuners—both men and women—to be stereotypically feminine expressive modes.

The second speech genre I discuss is called 'men's house talk' (_ambagaiŋa nam_). This talk is oratory, by men, that occurs inside or in the immediate vicinity of one of the men's houses in the village. Unlike kroses, which foreground and proclaim anger, men's house talk is not always and explicitly concerned with anger as such. However, a central structuring characteristic of men's oratories is a concern to downplay conflict and reframe disputes so that everyone appears to be content and harmonious. On certain occasions, such as during meetings called to help heal a sick person, anger is made an explicit topic of discussion, and men are urged to "expose" their anger and "reveal" their complaints.[3]

In my discussion of kroses and oratories, I concentrate on the ways in which discourses of gender, affect, and language are mutually reinforcing and sustained through specific linguistic practices. Ultimately, my point is that those discourses, and the practices that constitute and inform them, are nowadays invoked by villagers to position women and men in different and opposing relationships to those institutions and values that everyone in the village agrees are important: namely, Christianity, modernity, and civilization. This positioning constitutes the kind of "tension" to which Silverstein refers in the preceding quotation. And as he suggests, the resolution of the tension is moving the linguistic situation itself into new, unforeseen configurations, ones that in this case are resulting in the demise of the village vernacular itself.

LANGUAGE IDEOLOGY AND KNOWLEDGE

A basic tenet of Gapun villagers' language ideology is that speakers do not normally say what they mean. That is, unlike much Western philosphical tradition and unlike the values generally associated with contemporary middle classes, which view language as a "transparent window to truths both formulable and communicable in it" (Silverstein 1985:248; see also Reddy 1979), villagers in Gapun interpret speakers' words neither as a reflection of their inner state nor as an accurate representation of their opinions on a matter. In fact, the general assumption is that language 'hides' (*haitim*/*ambu*-) meanings that the speaker either cannot or will not state openly. Consequently, interpretation in the village is geared toward getting "behind" or "inside" or "underneath" the words actually used in speech.

The realizations and consequences of this linguistic ideology have been discussed in earlier work on Gapun with relation to literacy (Kulick and Stroud 1990), language socialization (Kulick 1992:223–47) and codeswitching (Stroud 1992). In those works, Christopher Stroud and I have examined the villagers' ideas about language by embedding them in local notions of personhood that make it very risky to appear too blunt or demanding. Here, I foreground a complementary consideration that is mentioned but not elaborated in those earlier analyses: in addition to being linked to and reinforced by conceptions of personhood and sociability, village language ideology is also related to particular village ideas about the nature and consequences of knowledge.

In Gapun, a great number of forms of knowledge consistently carry with them associations of danger. All those forms of knowledge that were traditionally valued—such as knowledge of healing chants, knowledge of certain myths, knowledge of the men's *tambaran* cult and of special skills such as yam planting or wood-carving—are bound up with hazard. Knowledge about any facet of the *tambaran* cult, for example, is believed to have the power to cause the deaths of women and noninitiated boys who might somehow acquire such knowledge. Even initiated men must carefully guard their knowledge of the cult secrets, for to reveal them to the noninitiated would cause the cult deities to murder the speaker. Magic chants, even benevolent ones, link their knower to ancestral spirits or men's cult deities that may act entirely on their own to bring harm to anyone who displeases the knower, even if the knower does not wish this. Overhearing certain myths is viewed as having the potential to cause sickness, and uttering secret names may cause environmental disturbances, or even death, for large numbers of people. Even private knowledge is fraught with danger. Unlike some Melanesian societies, such as the Sepik River Avatip, where knowledge appears to be dangerous only to the extent that it is made public (Harrison 1990:102), in Gapun even the private discovery of knowledge is enough to put the knower in danger. On one occasion, for example, a senior man explained to me that he had repeatedly tried and finally managed to re-create, on a fan he was weaving,

a specific mythologically important pattern that he recalled seeing as a boy. "Nobody taught me to weave the design," he told me. "I exposed (*kamapim*) it in my thoughts." This exposure, however, apparently angered the ancestral ghost-owners of the design, who retaliated by inflicting the old man with a serious illness.

This kind of understanding of knowledge makes possessing it and imparting it a somewhat risky business. Knowledge is valuable, but it is also—and this, of course, is part of what constitutes its value—potentially lethal. It must be handled, passed on, and made public in very delicate ways. Anthropologists working in Papua New Guinea have noted that this kind of orientation to knowledge seems very widespread throughout the area. They have also noted that practices of knowledge throughout Melanesia tend to pivot around an oscillation between concealment and revelation. At certain times and under certain conditions, knowledge of sensitive matters—say, of cult secrets (Barth 1987) or clan wealth (Strathern 1979:249)—is revealed to initiates or trading partners. But such knowledge, once revealed, is almost immediately hidden away again, and, furthermore, it frequently carries with it an implicit tag (made explicit in subsequent revelations) that the revelation disclosed only part of, or perhaps even a false impression of what there is to know.

Gapun villagers' language ideology, which privileges ambiguity, hidden meanings, and meanings construed by listeners rather than those conveyed by speakers, provides them with ways to traffic in knowledge without putting themselves or their interlocutors in too much danger. By oscillating between "inside" talk and "outside" talk (Stroud 1992:147), by making deliberately ambiguous, self-contradictory statements (Kulick 1992:127–31), by pressing into service specific structural features such as codeswitching (Stroud 1992) and diminutives (Kulick and Stroud 1993), and by deploying discursive features such as repetition and dissociation (Kulick 1992:127–36), speakers in Gapun manage to reveal, discuss, and circulate knowledge even as they conceal it and thereby gingerly sidestep many of the potentially fatal consequences that stark, unmitigated knowledge is known to have.

ANGER

Anger enters this discussion as a singularly inflamed object of knowledge. In village discourses on emotion and knowledge, anger in adults is always linked to danger. If anger is not voiced or acted on, it will, villagers explain, remain in the stomach (the seat of emotions) and 'rot' (*sting*/*pisimb*-). The putrification of anger may mobilize the ancestral spirits associated with the aggrieved person, and these may cause harm to whomever provoked anger in that person. Alternatively, rotting anger may "give bad thoughts" to the aggrieved, driving them to seek out the services of a sorcerer, who will be paid to murder the object of the anger.

If anger is voiced or acted on, there is a risk that its expression will provoke the wrath of the ancestral spirits associated with the person who is abused or attacked. Abusing or attacking another person may also drive that person to a sorcerer. So, no matter how it is ultimately dealt with, anger is dangerous. People in Gapun die from anger. Village deaths (all of which are held to be caused by sorcery) are almost inevitably accounted for at least in part by recalling past arguments or fights that the deceased or his or her close family members or matrilineal relatives had with other people.

Anger (*kros/pwap-*) is one of the relatively few affects that villagers regularly speak about and attribute to themselves and others (the other affects that feature in village discourse are shame [*sem/maikar-*], concern and sadness [*wari/punat-*], dissatisfaction [*les/mnda-*], and fear [*pret/rɛw-*]). Of these emotions, anger and dissatisfaction are seen as the earliest and most basic. They are tied to a dimension of personhood that the villagers call *hed* in Tok Pisin and *kɔkir* in the vernacular. Both these words mean 'head'. Each individual, the villagers maintain, has *hed*. By this, they mean that each individual has a basic and volatile sense of personal will and autonomy. The concept of *hed* in Gapun signifies egoism, selfishness, and maverick individualism. It denotes emotional bristliness and defiant, antisocial behavior, and it is roundly condemned in village rhetoric.

For the villagers, one of the embodiments of *hed*, of this volatile dimension of personhood, is small children. Babies and toddlers in Gapun are routinely said to be, and treated as if they were, continually dissatisfied and angry. A child cooing softly on its mother's lap may suddenly be shaken lightly and asked "Ai! What are you mad about? Ah?!" (*Ai! Yu belhat long wanem samting? Ah?!*). Likewise, a mother who sees her eight-month-old daughter reaching out toward a dog lying beside her will comment, "Look, she's mad (*kros*) now, she wants to hit the dog," and she will raise the baby's hand onto the dog's fur, telling the child, "That's it, hit it! Hit it!" One of the clearest indications of how villagers view the affective state of children is in the first words they attribute to them. In the village, a child's first word is generally held to be *ɔki*, which is a vernacular word meaning, approximately, "I'm getting out of here." Attributed to infants as young as two months, this word encapsulates the adult belief that babies "do what they want" (*bihainim laik bilong ol yet*) and go where they want to go regardless of the wishes of others. The two words that villagers consider to rapidly follow *ɔki* also underscore the notion of a baby as a gruff, independent individualist with a "strong" *hed*. These are the Taiap words *mnda* (I'm sick of this) and *aiata* (stop it).

In the villagers' view of the socialization process, children should come to understand that *hed* and the display of anger and dissatisfaction that typifies it must be suppressed (*daunim*). The expectation is that, as they mature, children will curtail their expressions of anger, that they will begin to accept and accommodate others, that they will share with others and conduct themselves "quietly" (*isi/tɔwer*). Anger, in this cultural understanding, in addition to being fraught

with danger, is also seen as childish and immature. Although it is explicitly recognized to be a central component of all people, it is one that adults should do their best to suppress and conceal.

Unfortunately, however, people do become angry at the actions of other people: other people who steal betelnut, who neglect to collect firewood for the evening meal, who forget to return a borrowed item, who engage in extramarital affairs, who talk behind people's backs, and so on. Villagers have developed a number of ways of dealing with the anger they see as being provoked in them, including destroying their own possessions and outright fighting (Kulick 1992:50–52). The single most common way in which anger is conveyed, however, is through the village speech genre known as a *kros*.

PROCLAIMING ANGER IN A *KROS*

The best way to give an impression of the general tenor of *kroses* in Gapun is to briefly examine an extract from one that was recorded and transcribed in June 1991. This is a *kros* between two sisters who live next door to each other. It arose because for several weeks the younger sister, a woman in her thirties named Sake, had been complaining loudly about the fact that children who played in the area near her house littered the ground with coffee beans, which they shot at each other and at pigs through bamboo tubes. One afternoon, Sake caught her sister's ten-year-old son red-handed as he stood shooting coffee beans at pigs underneath her house. She chased him and shouted at him and threatened him. At one point during her tirade at the boy, Sake asked him in a loud voice: "Does your mother come and clean up around here?!" (the answer, Sake knew, was no). Hearing this rhetorical question from inside her house, the boy's mother, a woman in her forties named Erapo, began yelling at Sake. Sake strode into her own house and responded with full force. This segment occurs about five minutes into the shouting match:

SAKE	<u>No good rotten big black hole!</u>
ERAPO	Smelly cunt bloody bastard!
SAKE	<u>I was talking to Erapo</u> [sarcastic]. I was talking good about the rubbish [i.e., the coffee beans], Erapo gets up and swears at me. Fucking cunt-hole bastard you!
ERAPO	This hole of yours ⌈( )
SAKE	⌊Rotten! Your dirty cunt is <u>a big black hole</u>. Bastard. <u>Black guts! What is she, what is Erapo talking to me about, *kros*-ing me about, swearing at me for?! Ah?! Erapo [you have] a rotten black hole!</u>
	[one utterance distraction]
SAKE	<u>Catfish cunt! Erapo has a black cunthole! A black cunthole Erapo! Erapo has a huge black cunthole! Erapo has an enormous black cunthole! Satan fucks you all the time, Satan is fucking you Erapo! Erapo! Satan is fucking you</u>

really good! Your cunt is sagging like loose mud
on a riverbank. Catfish cunt!

This is a typical Gapun *kros*. It exhibits many of the conventions that characterize the speech genre, such as the spatial placement of the speakers inside their respective houses, vituperative insults and gross vulgarity, loud voices shouted out over the village, and harsh, explicitly confrontational accusations of wrongdoing. As the *kros* continues, the insults that the women exchange become interwoven with direct threats, and Sake, especially, repeatedly challenges Erapo to come down from her house so that Sake can "beat her till she shits."

*Kros*es in Gapun are gendered speech genres that are associated with and almost inevitably enunciated by women.[4] Whenever Sake or some other woman has a loud *kros*, those village men not directly involved in some way make clucking sounds of recognition, shake their heads disparagingly, and mutter knowingly that "this kind of rubbish talk is the habit of women, it's their way" (*desela kain rabis tok em we bilong ol meri, pasin bilong ol*). Women are collectively held by village men to be more *bikhed* (willful, big-headed) than men. In ways similar to those in most Melanesian societies, women in Gapun are associated with individualism, atomicity, and antisocial behavior. Traditionally, men, through their common residence in the men's house and through their perpetual preparations for and acting out of funerary feasts, initiation rites, and war raids, represented and embodied cooperation and society. The collective actions of men were considered the 'bones' (*bun/ning*) of society. The actions of women, even though these were sometimes collective in nature (Kulick 1992:286, n. 7), do not appear to have been accorded the same type of cultural significance as those of men, and women were and continue to be represented as divisive troublemakers whose selfish actions constantly threaten the solid, manly group. Echoing a statement heard all over New Guinea, village men sometimes remind one another that "we fight over women"; that is, we would not fight if there were no women. Women, with their anger, their *kros*es, and their unwillingness to "suppress" their *hed*s, are the root of all conflicts.

Individual women in Gapun do not share this view of themselves as destructive troublemakers. Women who have *kros*es do not interpret their own behavior in reference to the stereotype. When Sake, for example, has a *kros*, she does not consider that she is being divisive; she is legitimately defending herself and her rights from some violation and attack. When another woman has a *kros*, however, Sake is often quick to sniff that the woman is "a woman who always gets angry for no reason" (*meri bilong kros nating nating*).

The existence of a culturally elaborated stereotype of women as quarrelsome means that such a role is available for any woman to act out, however. And as a stereotypically female role, it is unattractive for men. Men in the village like to pretend that they have no conflicts with others, and they dismiss *kros*es as *samting bilong ol meri/naŋɔma ɔrak* (what women do). The village stereotype of what represents ideal male behavior puts pressure on the men to be more sociable,

generous, dignified, and temperate than their wives, who are expected to fly off the handle and have a *kros* at the slightest excuse. In most cases, in a manner remarkably similar to that described by Elinor Ochs ([1974] 1989:137–38) for Madagascar, a married man is able to uphold this stereotype and simultaneously announce infringements by simply informing his wife about some slight or infraction that he has been subjected to (such as someone's failure to return a borrowed axe or shovel). The wife can usually be counted on to take it from there, and in doing so she reinforces the stereotype of quarrelsome, loud-mouthed women. Even on those occasions when a man publicly *belhat* (gets angry, shouts), the anger is usually directed at his wife or close female relatives. Public arguments thus almost inevitably involve women at some level. Both men and women blame (other) women for making trouble, for not being able to contain their anger, and for "showing *hed*" (see also Goldman 1986:236, Nash 1987:105, Harrison 1990:162).

CONCEALING ANGER IN THE MEN'S HOUSE

In very marked contrast to women's *kros*es, oratories in the men's house are occasions on which men in Gapun engage in speeches that downplay tension, smooth over disagreement, and stress consensus in the village. Oratories occur whenever meetings are called in the men's house: to announce the need for labor to clear overgrown paths or repair rotten footbridges; to work out the arrangements that have to be made for funerary feasts; to discern the meaning of messages and news items that villagers bring back with them from their travels to other villages or to the Marienberg mission station; to arrange to help a village man and his wife in some task that requires a number of laborers, such as carrying house posts, roofing a house, or clearing the forest to plant a garden; or to discuss any number of other public issues.

Because they are so strongly associated with the men's house, oratories, by definition, are male discourses. Only men in Gapun are considered to orate. There is no rule or explicit consensus in the village that women cannot orate, and there are a few strong-willed women in Gapun who do occasionally speak in public gatherings that concern both men and women. Women's speeches contain many of the same rhetorical features, such as repetition, that are predominant in oratories, but they differ importantly in that they are much briefer than most men's speeches (which usually last about ten to fifteen minutes but which can go on for up to forty-five minutes), and they never contain any of the particular formulaic tags that the men use to mark their speech as oratorical. Furthermore, women, who are not allowed inside the men's house, obviously cannot speak from there, and so their contributions to a discussion have a peripheral character that is underscored by their spatial placement. Because of factors like these, women who make short speeches at public gatherings are not considered to be orating; they are, rather, "complaining."

Usually, anger is not an explicit topic of discussion in contexts dominated by oratorical speechmaking. Quite the opposite. Skillful orators draw on a wide variety of paralinguistic cues (e.g., speakers are called and assembled under the same roof), metalinguistic cues (e.g., speakers address their talk directly to a general public and use politeness markers to assume and relinquish the floor), and linguistic cues (e.g., there is a marked preference for speakers to use diminutives in order to downplay their own status and talk, and oratories are characterized by supportive repetition from listeners). All these semiotic devices are drawn on to pointedly ignore and downplay the tensions that infect daily life in the village and to promote an illusion that everyone is in agreement and that there really is no anger and consequently no conflict at all. In creating this illusion and bringing the villagers together in this way, orators demonstrate for others their own social awareness and skills, even as they work to create a context in which others can demonstrate their sociability by listening and contributing to the buildup of the consensus by repeating and agreeing.

Sometimes, however, village men focus explicitly on anger, and there are contexts in which they spend much time and talk urging one another to 'expose' (*autim*/<u>*arɔni*</u> <u>*gur-*</u>) their anger, to 'break it open' (*brukim*/<u>*kra-*</u>), to 'reveal' (*kamapim*/<u>*mamanj-*</u>) it. This kind of speechmaking occurs whenever somebody in the village is struck down by a serious illness that people conclude is being caused by ancestral spirits. When this happens, men gather together in a men's house and talk about conflicts. When everybody who wants to talk has had a turn, senior men invoke the village ancestors and call on them to stop causing the sickness. Everybody present in the men's house then dips his forefinger in a glass of water, which is subsequently used to wash the sick person. The idea behind this procedure is that the men in this context embody both themselves and their ancestral spirits, and by first "revealing" their anger and then dipping their forefingers in the water, they "cool" the anger that is causing sickness in the afflicted person.

The following text is extracted from a meeting in the men's house, attended by all village men, called to effect a cure for the author of this paper, who in June 1991 became afflicted with disabling pains that the villagers, on hearing the symptoms, immediately identified as "a sickness of the ground" (i.e., a sickness caused by village ancestral spirits). Note how anger is talked about here.

MONE   Whoever feels that something isn't right, all right expose it. It's like we're breaking open the talk now. It isn't good if this [anger] remains in our stomachs, because he [i.e., Don] will suffer. We have to expose all the little talk.

KAWRI   <u>Yeah.</u>

MONE   Like yesterday too I talked about doing work for him [Mone means that yesterday he exhorted the villagers to get to work building a house for me. Work on this house had been progressing extremely slowly, because even though the

villagers had volunteered to build it for me, they found themselves unwilling to work together due to various village conflicts]. We were all lazy [and therefore did no work yesterday]. Or maybe we have some worries, or maybe we're tired of doing work, or maybe we're just tired for no reason, or like that.

KRUNI   That's it.

MONE   All right we're gonna reveal all these little worries: "This man said something to me and so I'm unwilling to work," this kind of thing. All right, when we've finished talking we'll/or we'll talk about the spirits of the village, of the men's house, OK, and we'll put our fingers in the water all right Don will/we'll hold Don's pain, wash it in the water of our talk. Like just try it. It's not this [i.e., a sickness caused by a village spirit], it's a [white man's] sickness he's got, he'll go to the hospital.

KRUNI   At the hospital it'll finish. We'll try it our way [first].

MONE   <u>There's no talk</u> [i.e., no dissension]. Like we can/ maybe we don't have any talk, or maybe we can talk about the spirits of the village, we don't think that something is as it should be/we can talk about work or about something that is amongst us giving illness to him, all right we'll talk straight about that. Talk straight and put fingers in the water.

Later, toward the end of this session, after several men had revealed "little" irritations or conflicts that they were involved in or had heard about, the talk is summarized like this:

KEM   We're gonna hold the water and rub his pain. <u>These things</u>, there's not plenty of complaints.

SAIR   <u>No.</u>

ANDON   <u>There's no</u> complaints.

KEM   <u>Our</u> ⌈ -<u>little talk, that's</u> it.

KAWI   ⌊ -little crumbs of <u>talk.</u>

KEM   <u>We're making it.</u>

The aspect of this talk to which I wish to draw attention is the way in which anger, even though it is explicitly spoken about here, is consistently embedded in speech characterized by hedges ("maybe we don't have any talk"), the presentation of alternative positions ("or maybe we're just tired for no reason," "it's a [white man's] sickness he's got"), and specific denials that the anger the men are supposed to be exposing is in fact anger at all. Choruses like the one here, in which several men hasten to agree with one another that there are no complaints, occur throughout meetings like this, and they become particularly insistent whenever somebody actually does "expose" a happening or occurrence that caused them to feel anger.

At one point during this meeting, for example, a senior man "revealed" that the men present were reluctant to work on my house because they were angry at Allan, my adoptive village "father." The anger, it was pointed out, stemmed from the fact that Allan and his wife had moved into my previous, communally built, house when I completed my original fieldwork and left the village in 1987. The couple made this move in defiance of received village opinion, and the other villagers now accused Allan and his wife of "ruining" that previous house. Every person present at this meeting was acutely aware of the truth of this senior man's "revelation," because in private villagers routinely expressed bitter resentment toward Allan and his wife for having moved into the house. In the men's house, though, the revelation was handled in the following way:

KEM	All right, you all gave up on poor Allan, he's by himself [i.e., working on building my new house by himself]. You all have this thought, I know, you can't cover it up it, we're showing Christian belief here. It's not anger (*kros*), it's like you're talking straight. OK, and you hold the water now and <u>the spirit will go inside it. It's like that.</u>
ANDON	<u>Is it</u> anger? [rhetorical question]
KRUNI	<u>It isn't</u> anger.
MARAME	There's no anger, it's talk.
MONE	<u>Yes.</u>

One of the most significant ways in which men's public talk about anger differs from women's is in this kind of cooperative recontextualizing work, where speakers weave together their words to reframe anger as not-anger, and where they sometimes even go so far as to congratulate themselves on talking about anger as a way of 'showing Christian belief' (*autim Bilip*). I interpret this kind of supportive discursive interaction between men to be a linguistic manifestation of the village orientation to knowledge as something that in many cases is safely revealed only if it is somehow subsequently reconcealed.

And that is the main point. One of the most significant differences between women's *kros*es and men's oratories—and the difference that seems to evoke the greatest degree of discomfort in villagers—is not so much that female speakers publicize anger. In many ways this is, in fact, commendable, since villagers agree that it is much better to express anger than to let it remain unexposed and rotting in one's stomach (indeed, the public exposure of anger is the whole purpose of the kind of gatherings in the men's house just discussed). What is unacceptable and dangerous about *kros*es is that

women complete only half the discursive equation. Women reveal anger without subsequently reconcealing it. They expose anger and leave it uncovered, where it is thought to act like a throbbing, hot lightning rod of unleashed dissension, pulling sorcery, sickness, and death into the village.

Women's linguistic practices for dealing with anger are in almost every way inversions of men's practices. In addition to exposing anger without hiding it again, women's *kros*es emanate from inside or nearby private dwelling houses. Men's oratories, on the other hand, occur in or near the communal men's house. *Kros*es are organized as competing monologues. In oratories, the people being orated at are free to contribute sympathetic interjections throughout the speech and follow the orator by producing a speech or a summation in which they "give support" to the orator. *Kros*es are dramatic declarations of self-display in which speakers assert themselves and their personal autonomy by broadcasting throughout the village that these have been violated. Oratories are characterized by self-effacement; speakers repeatedly remind their listeners in polite, muted tones that they only have "little crumbs of talk" or "a little worry" to draw to everyone's attention. *Kros*es are meant to shame a specific, named person or a specific unknown, unnamed culprit. Oratories are intended to generalize and address people as members of a group; even in those cases where the topic of an oratory is some sort of transgression committed by some specific person, blame is inevitably diffused and generalized, and listeners are reminded that others in the village (though not necessarily they themselves) are just as lazy or uncooperative or big-headed as the (always unnamed) individual(s) who committed the transgression. For both men and women, *kros*es are associated with (other) women and divisiveness. Oratories, on the other hand, are seen as concrete evidence that men in Gapun really are more placid, consensus oriented, sociable, and reasonable than their tempestuous, forever bickering wives (Table 1).

LANGUAGE SHIFT

In the ways I have outlined, we can consider anger as a kind of locus where ideologies of language, gender, and affect all converge, creating in that convergence a discursive space in which gender stereotypes are both imagined and acted out. In large measure because of their linguistic practices for publicly dealing with anger, men in Gapun are credited by everyone with greater knowledge about how to handle

Table 1. Summary of Contrastive Features of *Kros*es and Oratories

*Kros*es	Oratories
Enunciated by women	Enunciated by men
Emanate from individual houses	Emanate from communal men's house
Vulgarity	Politeness
Self-display	Self-effacement
Competing overlapping monologues	Supportive serial monologues
Reveal anger	Reveal anger only to reconceal it again
Address intravillage affairs	Link village affairs to outside world
Vernacular language (Taiap) predominates	National language (Tok Pisin) predominates

knowledge, as it were. By exposing anger even as they deny it and conceal it, men present themselves, and are understood by others, as providing and embodying a protective buffer against the ravages that naked anger is known to be able to summon forth. Women, by contrast, brazenly expose anger but subsequently do nothing to mitigate the negative consequences that may be generated by this exposure. This particular linguistic practice of handling anger has become representative of "what women do," and it permits the maintenance of a stereotype that demeans women as childish, destructive, and irresponsible.

Although there are differences, this situation in many ways parallels Silverstein's example of the sociolinguistics of seventeenth-century British society, discussed at the beginning of this chapter. In the case of both Quakers in Britain and women in Gapun, a specific group of people comes to be symbolized in meaningful ways through their linguistic practices. Once this symbolic bond becomes marked, it becomes important for people who do not wish to be identified with that group (non-Quakers in Britain and men in Gapun, as well as individual women in the village who do not wish to be negatively labeled by others) to begin avoiding the type of verbal behavior that is seen as indexical of the group. Thus, non-Quakers avoided the familiar second-person address forms, and men in Gapun avoid *kroses*. The question that arises now is the one with which I began…: namely, how is the convergence of anger, gender, and the politics of revelation working to produce a tension in Gapun such that the linguistic situation of the village is moving toward new configurations?

The answer to that question lies in the ideology and practice associated with the two languages that villagers use in their day-to-day talk. Basically, the situation is one in which the vernacular language, Taiap, is nowadays associated with tradition, the land, the local concept of *hed*, and women. Tok Pisin, on the other hand, has come to be bound up with modern processes and phenomena. Tok Pisin is tied to Christianity, white people, money, and schooling; significantly, it is also tied to men and those affective stances that are seen to characterize them.

These associative networks are frequently made explicit in men's house talk. At some point during each meeting in the men's house, no matter what the original reason for the meeting happened to be, somebody will inevitably make a speech in Tok Pisin extolling Christian ideals, reaffirming the value of education, devaluing the ways of the ancestors, and urging the villagers, and specifically the village women, to suppress their anger and stop their fighting so that everybody can "come up" (*kamap* 'change, develop'). The men's house has thus become an important arena in which individual men can publicly assert their familiarity with the modern world by reminding others that the Catholic Church, school, "Papua New Guinea," and *bisnis* (cash-generating enterprises) have altered the nature of village relationships and must be accorded a central role in village life. In making those assertions, Gapun men are able to substantiate their claims to knowledge about the modern world by choosing to orate primarily in the language through which that world is understood to be constituted—that is, Tok Pisin (cf. Sankoff 1980:44). Angry women employ what amounts to a similar discursive strategy in their public speeches. They substantiate their dissatisfaction and foreground their claims to having been violated and impinged on by choosing to announce those claims primarily in the language through which affective discourse is constituted—that is, the village vernacular, Taiap.

Those practices and the ideas that inform them are moving the village vernacular toward extinction. Powered by its links with women and the associations bound up with stereotypes of them, it seems likely that the Taiap language itself will increasingly come to be associated with negatively valued aspects of life, such as affective excess, discursive irresponsibility, and dangerous knowledge. This process is already well under way and is evidenced by villagers who sometimes pointedly refuse to speak their vernacular among themselves in order to prove that they are not "hiding" talk (e.g., during periods of millenarian activity or during sensitive meetings with people from other villages) or by village children who understand purposeful parental switches from Tok Pisin into the vernacular as conveying disapproval and anger (Kulick 1992:217).

Like the particular linguistic forms that became connected with seventeenth-century Quakers in Britain, it seems probable that the Taiap language itself will eventually be abandoned. The main relevance of this in the context of…language ideology is that what we see in Gapun is the way in which particular linguistic practices reinforce and are reinforced by particular ideas that exist in a community about language, affect, gender, and the relationships among those phenomena. By speaking in particular ways, women and men in Gapun activate complex webs of associations that link a wide array of discourses. So women in their *kroses* are not only spitting curses, and men in their oratories are not only making dispassionate, measured speeches that smooth over conflicts in the village. By using language in the specific ways they do, speakers embody and re-create salient stereotypes about what women and men are, they engender affect, and they position themselves in socially meaningful ways in relation to Christianity, civilization, and the modern world.

One of the contributions that I believe this example from Gapun can make to our discussions of language ideology is the reminder that language ideologies seem never to be solely about language—they are always about entangled clusters of phenomena, and they encompass and are bound up with aspects of culture like gender, and expression, and being "civilized." Furthermore, this inherently snarled and delicately layered nature of language ideology can provide colonial discourses of Christianity and modernity with numerous sites of entry into local practices and understandings, as well as with ample possibilities to penetrate and, as has happened in Gapun, enmesh themselves with both linguistic practices and local ideas about gender, affect, and language.

Notes

I am grateful to my colleague Christopher Stroud; to Michael Silverstein, who was my discussant at the invited session "Language Ideologies: Theory and Practice," organized by Paul Kroskrity, Bambi Schieffelin, and Kit Woolard at the Ninetieth Meeting of the American Anthropological Association, Chicago, November 1991; and to all the participants in that session who commented on an earlier version of this paper.

1. Fieldwork in Gapun was carried out during fifteen months in 1986–87, and for two months in 1991. Fieldwork in 1986–87 was financed by the Swedish Agency for Research Cooperation with Developing Countries (SAREC) and the Swedish Council for Research in the Humanities and Social Sciences (HSFR). Fieldwork in 1991 was conducted as part of a postdoctoral fellowship at the Department of Linguistics, Research School of Pacific Studies, Australian National University, and was financed by that department.

2. Throughout this text, words that are underlined and italicized are vernacular language words. Words that are only italicized are Tok Pisin words. In addition, the following transcription conventions are used in the examples:

    ( )   unintelligible utterance
    [overlapping utterances
    /   self-interruption or false start

    Notes on situational context and nonverbal action are given in square brackets [ ] in the body of the transcripts.

3. See also my discussion of oratorical harangues in Kulick 1992:139–47.

4. Those men known throughout the village as ones who sometimes have *kroses* are men who are either old widowers or divorced middle-aged men. That is, they are men without access to a woman's voice. Kulick 1993 is a much more detailed anaysis of gender and *kroses*.

References

Barth, Fredrik. 1987. *Cosmologies in the Making*. Cambridge: Cambridge University Press.

Bloch, Maurice, and Jonathan Parry, eds. 1982. *Death and the Regeneration of Life*. Cambridge: Cambridge University Press.

Feld, Steven. 1990. *Sound and Sentiment: Birds, Weeping, Poetics and Song in Kaluli Expression*, 2d ed. Philadelphia: University of Pennsylvania Press.

Goldman, Laurence. 1986. The Presentational Style of Women in Huli Disputes. *Pacific Linguistics* 24:213–289.

Harrison, Simon. 1990. *Stealing People's Names: History and Politics in a Sepik River Cosmology*. Cambridge: Cambridge University Press.

Kulick, Don. 1992. *Language Shift and Cultural Reproduction: Socialization, Self, and Syncretism in a Papua New Guinean Village*. New York: Cambridge University Press.

———. 1993. Speaking as a Woman: Structure and Gender in Domestic Arguments in a Papua New Guinean Village. *Cultural Anthropology* 8(4):510–541.

———, and Christopher Stroud. 1990. Christianity, Cargo, and Ideas of Self: Patterns of Literacy in a Papua New Guinean Village. *Man* 25:286–303.

———, and ———. 1993. Conceptions and Uses of Literacy in a Papua New Guinean Village. In *Cross-Cultural Approaches to Literacy*, ed. Brian Street, pp. 30–61. Cambridge: Cambridge University Press.

Lutz, Catherine. 1986. Emotion, Thought, and Estrangement: Emotion as a Cultural Category. *Cultural Anthropology* 1:405–436.

———. 1990. Engendered Emotion: Gender, Power, and the Rhetoric of Emotional Control in American Discourse. In *Language and the Politics of Emotion*, ed. Catherine Lutz and Lila Abu-Lughod, pp. 69–91. Cambridge: Cambridge University Press.

———, and Lila Abu-Lughod, eds. 1990. *Language and the Politics of Emotion*. Cambridge: Cambridge University Press.

Nash, Jill. 1987. Gender Attributes and Equality: Men's Strength and Women's Talk Among the Nagovisi. In *Dealing with Inequality: Analysing Gender Relations in Melanesia and Beyond*, ed. Marilyn Strathern, pp. 150–173. Cambridge: Cambridge University Press.

Ochs, Elinor. 1988. *Culture and Language Development: Language Acquisition and Language Socialization in a Samoan Village*. New York: Cambridge University Press.

———. 1992. Indexing Gender. In *Rethinking Context: Language as an Interactive Phenomenon*, ed. Alessandro Duranti and Charles Goodwin, pp. 335–358. New York: Cambridge University Press.

Ochs [Keenan], Elinor. [1974] 1989. Norm-makers, Norm-breakers: Uses of Speech by Men and Women in a Malagasy Community. In *Explorations in the Ethnography of Speaking*, ed. Richard Bauman and Joel Sherzer, pp. 125–143. Cambridge: Cambridge University Press. [Reprinted as Chapter 34 in this volume.]

Reddy, Michael. 1979. The Conduit Metaphor—A Case of Frame Conflict in Our Language about Language. In *Metaphor and Thought*, ed. A. Ortony, pp. 284–324. Cambridge: Cambridge University Press.

Sankoff, Gillian. [1971] 1980. Language Use in Multilingual Societies: Some Alternate Approaches. In *The Social Life of Language*, pp. 29–46. Philadelphia: University of Pennsylvania Press.

Schieffelin, Bambi. 1990. *The Give and Take of Everyday Life: Language Socialization of Kaluli Children*. New York: Cambridge University Press.

Schieffelin, Edward L. 1976. *The Sorrow of the Lonely and the Burning of the Dancers*. New York: St. Martin's.

———. 1985. The Cultural Analysis of Depressive Affect: An Example from New Guinea. In *Culture and Depression: Studies in the Anthropology and Cross-cultural Psychiatry of Affect and Disorder*, ed. Arthur Kleinman and Byron Good, pp. 103–133. Berkeley: University of California Press.

Silverstein, Michael. 1985. Language and the Culture of Gender: At the Intersection of Structure, Usage, and Ideology.

In *Semiotic Mediation: Sociocultural and Psychological Perspectives*, ed. Elizabeth Mertz and Richard J. Parmentier, pp. 219–259. New York: Academic Press.

Strathern, Marilyn. 1979. The Self in Self-Decoration. *Oceania* 49(4):241–257.

Stroud, Christopher. 1992. The Problem of Intention and Meaning in Code-switching. *Text* 12(1):127–155.

Watson-Gegeo, Karen Ann, and Geoffery M. White, eds. 1990. *Disentangling: Conflict Discourse in Pacific Societies.* Stanford, CA: Stanford University Press.

White, Geoffery M., and James Kirkpatrick, eds. 1985. *Person, Self, and Experience: Exploring Pacific Ethnopsychologies.* Berkeley: University of California Press.

Post-reading Questions / Activities

- How do you usually think of emotion? What do you think of as the relationship between emotion and language?
- How do you usually think of language? Do you assume that people should and can "say what they mean"?
- In your culture, is strong emotion (stereotypically) associated with one gender?
- Examine your reactions to the angry exchanges recorded here. What linguistic ideological assumptions do you think explain your reaction?

Vocabulary

affect	language shift
discursive	metalinguistic
hedge	paralinguistic
kros	swidden agriculture

Suggested Further Reading

Kulick, Don. 1992. *Language Shift and Cultural Reproduction: Socialization, Self, and Syncretism in a Papua New Guinean Village.* New York: Cambridge University Press.

Sankoff, Gillian. 1980. *The Social Life of Language.* Philadelphia: University of Pennsylvania Press.

Summer Institute of Linguistics (SIL International). 2006. "PNG Language Resources." http://www.sil.org/pacific/png/index.asp.

CHAPTER 42

Accent, Standard Language Ideology, and Discriminatory Pretext in the Courts

Rosina Lippi-Green
(1994)

The idea of a "standard" language is powerful. It allows us to evaluate people on the basis of their speech, sorting them into speakers of the standard and speakers of a nonstandard variant of the language. Of course, a standard is essentially arbitrary. In many settings there is not any actual variety that meets the standard. But the ideology of a standard language may nonetheless endure. Indeed, discrimination of people on the basis of their perceived distance from the standard is widespread.

The concept of "accent" does not exist in linguistics, because there is no such thing as speech without some characteristics. What ordinary people mean by "accent" is usually just how different someone else's way of talking is from the listener's own speech or from an idealized character-free variety.

Reading Questions

- How has accent discrimination been intertwined with other forms of discrimination?
- What are the employers' reasons for not hiring, not promoting, or firing employees with "accents"?
- In what institutions does Lippi-Green see the perpetuation of a standard-language ideology?
- What does Lippi-Green mean that "the communicative burden [is] distributed between speakers and audience"? When is this more true and when does it not entirely apply?

> The stranger within my gate,
> He may be true or kind,
> But he does not talk my talk—
> I cannot feel his mind.
> I see the face and the eye and the mouth,
> But not the soul behind.
> The men of my own stock,
> They may do ill or well,
> But they tell the lies I am wonted to,
> They are used to the lies I tell;
> And we do not need interpreters
> When we go to buy and sell.
> RUDYARD KIPLING

In 1965, at the age of 29, Sulochana Mandhare left her home in Maharashtra, India, and came to the United States. At that point in her life, Ms. Mandhare—a native speaker of Marathi—had been studying English for almost 20 years.

Ms. Mandhare is soft-spoken; she speaks an English which is characterized by full vowels in unstressed syllables, distinctive intonation patterns, aspirated fricatives, and a lack of distinction between initial /v/ and /w/. She is an

Rosina Lippi-Green, "Accent, Standard Language Ideology, and Discriminatory Pretext in the Courts." *Language in Society* 23 (1994): 163–198. Notes have been edited and renumbered. Reprinted with the permission of Cambridge University Press.

intelligent and articulate woman, and she tells her story in a clear and completely comprehensible language.

After some time in the U.S., Ms. Mandhare relates, she decided to continue her education. She had arrived with undergraduate degrees in both liberal arts and education; but she returned to school, and in 1972 completed a master's degree in education at New Orleans's Loyola University. In 1979 she was certified as a school librarian after completing a program at Nichols State University. After working for one year as an elementary school librarian, Ms. Mandhare applied for and was given a job as a librarian at a school serving kindergarten through second grade in the Lafargue, Louisiana, school district, for the 1980–81 school year.

Ms. Mandhare speaks of that year as a happy and successful one. Her responsibilities were to oversee the small library, read stories to the children, and introduce them to using the resources; she enjoyed this work. Therefore, when in April 1981 she was told that her contract would not be renewed because of her "heavy accent, speech patterns, and grammar problems"—in spite of her excellent skills as a librarian (*Mandhare* 1985:240–41)—she was stunned and angry.[1] She investigated her options; and because she understood that the U.S. Civil Rights Act prohibits discrimination by national origin in the workplace, she filed suit. This civil action was decided in Ms. Mandhare's favor, but the decision was reversed by the U.S. Court of Appeals in favor of the school board.[2]

Ms. Mandhare's case, and others like hers, are important because they provide real-life examples of many phenomena which have long been of interest to linguists. There is a body of work on the processes involved when listeners evaluate speakers (Lambert et al. 1960, Carranza & Ryan 1975, Rickford 1985), on social stereotyping based on language (Lambert 1967, Giles & Ryan 1982), on the psychological processes involved in speech accommodation (Giles 1984, Giles & Coupland 1991), on the cognitive processes which structure collaboration in discourse (Clark & Wilkes-Gibbs 1986), and on language-focused discrimination (Labov 1969, Giles 1971, Kalin & Rayko 1978, Milroy & Milroy 1985, Rickford & Traugott 1985). More recently, there has developed a body of work on the relationship among institutionalized power constructs, ideology, and language (Thompson 1984, Kress 1985, Fairclough 1989). But in spite of such extensive inquiry, many areas remain unexplored. One such area is the range of ways in which *accent* is defined, and how it is put to use.

Accent is used by phoneticians to discuss pitch or stress, or by orthographers to refer to specific diacritics. More generally, however, the term is used as a loosely defined reference to sets of distinctive differences over geographic or social space, most usually phonological and intonation features. In the case of second language learning, accent may refer to the carryover of native language phonology and intonation into a target language.

One of the first, and sometimes most difficult, lessons for a linguist in training is the abandonment of subjective evaluations. In the pursuit of knowledge about the structure and function of language, heavily influenced by scientific method, *belief* has no place; it can serve only to obscure the process of discovery. Linguists proceed on the assumption that all naturally occurring languages, whether or not they have a literate tradition, are equally functional and have the same potential to develop further functions as necessary; there has been no evidence in the many years of inquiry to disprove this basic thesis. Linguists further differentiate language from speech, speech from communication, and fluency from communicative competence. (Like accent, *fluency* is a general term without technical definition.) The crucial concept of communicative competence is defined as the ability to use and interpret language in a stylistically and culturally appropriate manner. This moves far beyond the set of phonological and intonation features which bundled together may be marked as accent.

The general public, however, does not make such distinctions. For most people, accent is a dustbin category: it includes all the technical meanings, and a more general and subjective one: accent is how *the other* speaks. It is the first diagnostic for identification of geographic or social outsiders. For a native of the north side of Chicago—a cab driver, elementary school teacher, or district judge—all the following "have an accent": people from southern Indiana, Georgia, Brooklyn, England, or South Africa; the native speaker of African American English Vernacular who lives down the street or west of the Loop; the co-worker from Jamaica; and the man selling papers on the corner whose Guatemalan phonology and intonation shine through into his English. No distinction is made between pidgin or creole, socially or geographically based variation, native or nonnative language: they are all just accents, which may be described as adenoidal, barbarous, broad, cute, distinct, educated, flat, foreign, funny, guttural, harsh, heavy, lilting, nasal, posh, provincial, quaint, rough, rustic, sing-song, strong, and uneducated (McArthur 1992:10). The subjective nature of these qualifiers is clear.

Much of linguistic variation is structured around social identity. Linguists know this, but nonlinguists know it too, and act on it: accent becomes both manner and means for exclusion. The fact is, however, that when people reject an accent, they also reject the identity of the person speaking: his or her race, ethnic heritage, national origin, regional affiliation, or economic class.[3] Thus the concept of accent, so all-encompassing in the mind of the public, is a powerful one which needs to be investigated.

In the remainder of this [discussion], my goal is to illustrate the nature and some of the repercussions of accent discrimination. In the process, I hope to demonstrate that accent—particularly when associated with racial, ethnic, or cultural minorities—is most likely to pose a barrier to effective communication when two elements are lacking. The first element is a basic level of communicative competence on the part of the speaker, *independent* of L1 phonology and intonation. The second element, even more important but far more difficult to assess, is the listener's goodwill. Without that goodwill, the speaker's command of the language, i.e., his or her degree of communicative competence, is irrelevant. Prejudiced listeners cannot hear what a person has to say, because accent, as a mirror of social identity and a litmus test for exclusion, is more important.

After a more general discussion of background issues, the examination of accent discrimination, referred to here more specifically as *language-trait focused* (LTF) discrimination, is limited because of space considerations to the workplace and the courts. More generally this is the beginning of an exploration of why so many of us continue to use linguistic traits to rationalize and justify discrimination of all kinds—and to tolerate such discrimination, even when it is directed toward ourselves.

STANDARD LANGUAGE IDEOLOGY

In matters of language history, structure, function, and standardization, the average individual is, for the most part, simultaneously uninformed and highly opinionated. When asked directly about language use, most people will draw a very solid basic distinction of "standard" (proper, correct) English vs. everything else. If asked for a more exacting definition, most will not be able to provide it, or will couch it in terms of salient features of nonmainstream language varieties: "Proper English is having your subjects and verbs agree"; "Why can't they see that the word is spelled *a-s-k*, not *a-x*?"; "[kwɔ fi]—that sounds so ignorant."

LTF discrimination stems primarily from the acceptance of a *standard language ideology* (a term coined by Milroy & Milroy 1985). The definition used here is: a bias toward an abstracted, idealized, homogeneous spoken language which is imposed from above, and which takes as its model the written language. The most salient feature is the goal of suppression of variation of all kinds.[4]

What is the source of the standard language (SL) ideology? How is it "imposed from above"? Who is responsible for its propagation?[5]

SL ideology is part of a greater power construct, a set of social practices on which people depend without close analysis of underlying assumptions. In a thought-provoking discussion of the relationship between language and social power, Fairclough (1989:33) points out that this institutionalization of behaviors which originate with the dominant bloc (an alliance of those who see their interests as tied to capital and capitalism) functions to keep separate the powered and the disempowered:

> Ideological power, the power to project one's practices as universal and "common sense," is a significant complement to economic and political power, and of particular significance here because it is exercised in discourse.... There are...in gross terms two ways in which those who have power can exercise it and keep it: through coercing others to go along with them, with the ultimate sanctions of physical violence or death; or through winning others' consent to, or at least acquiescence in, their possession of exercise of power. In short, through *coercion* or *consent*.

The SL ideology is one route, and a major one, to establishing consent. There are four immediately identifiable proponents of SL ideology, all of which are part of the "dominant bloc": the educational system, the news media, the entertainment industry, and what has been generally referred to as corporate America. At the end of this [discussion], I argue for adding the judicial system to this list.

The Educational System and Standard Language Ideology

Much of what the American educational system teaches children about language is factually incorrect; in this it is thorough, consistent, and successful across social and economic boundaries. The phenomenon has been observed by others:

> It is a tribute to our educational system that the overwhelming majority of Americans have been instilled with a rocklike conviction that certain linguistic forms are correct, while others are wrong. Even those Americans who are uncertain about precisely which forms are correct are usually confident that to find the answer they need only look the matter up in the right book or consult the proper authority. (Burling 1973:130)

These are strong statements, but they are easily verified. Everyone has anecdotes about language arts instruction from their elementary school education, but stronger evidence is available in a wide range of texts written for teachers and children. The underlying message is clear in each of the following examples.[6]

(a) A direct link between "nonstandard" language and lack of logic and clarity, with blurring of the written/spoken boundaries:

Almost any sentence or sentence fragment may be acceptable in casual conversation. In more formal speaking and writing, however, nonstandard grammar is rarely acceptable. We need to know how to speak and write in complete, grammatical sentences that convey our thoughts clearly to others. (Ragno et al. 1987:T22)

(b) There is one correct way to speak and write English:

[This series of textbooks] focuses on grammar study, listening and speaking skills, and correct usage. (Strickland 1983:T21)

(c) Overt authoritarianism:

Practice saying the following combinations of words. Avoid slurring any sounds, such as *whacha* for *what do you*.... *Whip* is pronounced *hwip*, not *wip*...pronounce the following troublesome words correctly. Consult the dictionary if you are in doubt...Twenty-five words often misspelled because of faulty pronunciation: *busy, which, since, history*.... (John et al. 1975:28–9)[7]

SL ideology is found at work not just in textbooks and language arts instruction classrooms, but also in school administration. In 1987, the Board of Education of Hawaii put forth a proposed policy on "Standard English and Oral Communication," which would have outlawed Hawaiian Creole English (HCE) in the schools. A survey of 986 graduating seniors, conducted by a Honolulu newspaper, indicates how well many of those students were indoctrinated in the SL ideology, and serves as an illustration of the ideology's close relationship to issues of race and economics.

> Whereas only 26 percent of the private school students surveyed felt that HCE use should be allowed in school, 54 percent of the public school students supported this idea...Comments ranged from "Pidgin English fosters illiteracy," "Pidgin is a lazy way to talk; it promotes backward thinking," and "Correct English will get you anywhere" to the polar opposites of "Banning pidgin would violate our freedom of speech," "Pidgin is a natural language," and "It's our way to make Hawaii different from anywhere else in the United States." (Verploegen 1988, as cited by Sato 1991:654)

...

Are there no examples of educators with more informed and enlightened approaches to diversity in language? teachers who strive to teach children to read and write, and at the same time respect the sanctity of the home language and social identity? teachers who question underlying assumptions, and who do not automatically contribute to the propagation of the current power distribution? Of course there are. Take for example Mary Berger of Columbia College in Chicago—who, as an English teacher, "teaches standard style to augment, not replace, dialect" (Warren 1993:2). The *Chicago Tribune* found Ms. Berger's methods so remarkable that they ran an article on her approach, and highlighted her classroom practice of "[not] scold[ing] her black students...when they said 'ax', rather than 'ask'...."

For the most part, however, teachers are bound by the standard language ideology. For example, almost exactly 15 years after the controversial *King* case was decided in Ann Arbor, parents of African American middle school students complained to the school board about a teacher who allegedly had been ridiculing Black students for using their home language, specifically for saying *ax* instead of *ask* (Windsor 1993:C1, C3).[8]

Standard language ideology is a basic construct of our elementary and secondary schools' approach to language and philosophy of education. The schools provide the first exposure to SL ideology, but the indoctrination process does not stop when the students are dismissed.

The Media and the Standard Language Ideology

The media—and by this is usually meant national broadcasting institutions—have taken on the job of defending the "national culture" (Cormack 1993: 102–3), which means the propagation of a homogeneous nation-state, in which everyone must assimilate or be marginalized. As part of this process, the print and broadcast news media and the entertainment industry take on the job of reinforcing SL ideology on a daily basis.[9]...

More usually, complaints about language use are tucked away as an afterthought, but the underlying message is clear: there is a right and a wrong way to talk, and it is perfectly acceptable, even judicious, to censor and punish those who do not conform:

> Residents of Brooklyn, New York, have long been known—and sometimes mocked—for their heavy accents. Ginny Most reports on a group of students who are trying to learn to talk right—or should I say *correctly*.
>
> [G.M.]: Some people have a funny way of saying what flows under the Brooklyn Bridge...[Student]: "*wata*—it's so ugly."...(*CNN Headline News,* March 12, 1993)

> Ungrammatical street talk by black professional athletes, and other blacks in public professions such as the music industry, has come to be accepted...The dilemma is that it doesn't make much difference for the black professional athletes, etc., who talk this way—they're wealthy men who are going to live well off their bodily skills no matter if they can talk at all, much less correctly...(Bob Greene's sports column, *Chicago Tribune,* December 3, 1979)[10]

> We like Hahn, 34, who was born in South Korea and whose positions on controlling growth are much like our own. Unfortunately, we think his heavy accent and somewhat limited contacts would make it difficult for him to be a councilman. ("For Santa Clara County," *San Jose Mercury News,* October 18, 1988, as cited in Matsuda 1991:1346)

> [Oprah] is an image. So is Jesse Jackson.... They can effectively articulate with subject and verb agreement. And if it had not been for God who gives us the wisdom—we have to attribute this to God—to know how to sound, to articulate and to know how to use subject-verb agreements, we wouldn't be where we are today. (Toni Tucker, African-American talk show host, as audience member on "Black English," *Oprah Winfrey Show,* November 19, 1987)

> Gov. Clinton, you attended Oxford University in England and Yale Law School in the Ivy League, two of the finest institutions of learning in the world. So how come you still talk like a hillbilly? (Mike Royko's syndicated "Opinion" column, *Ann Arbor News,* October 11, 1992)[11]

The media claim that the intention is not to make news, but report it, and that they do not intend to serve as an agent of social change or an enforcer of norms. Of course, this line is crossed repeatedly by the media, simply by virtue of the topics chosen for reporting. In bringing to the public's attention the boom in accent-reduction schools, and by slanting the tone of their reports toward an idealized standard, the media become complicit in the process of discrimination.

The SL ideology is introduced by the schools; it is vigorously promoted by the media, and (as is shown in the next sections) is further institutionalized by the corporate sector. Thus it is not surprising that many individuals do not recognize the fact that, for spoken language, variation is systematic, structured, and inherent, and that the *national standard* is an abstraction. What *is* surprising, even deeply disturbing, is the way that many individuals—though they consider themselves democratic, even-handed, and free of prejudice—hold tenaciously to a standard ideology which attempts to justify restriction of individuality and rejection of the *other*.

LTF discrimination can be found everywhere in our daily lives. In fact, such behavior is so commonly accepted, so widely perceived as appropriate, that it must be seen as the last widely open backdoor to discrimination.

LTF DISCRIMINATION AND THE CIVIL RIGHTS ACT

Some types of LTF discrimination have been illegal *in the workplace* since 1964, when Title VII of the Civil Rights Act of 1964 (42 United States Code §§2000e-2000e-17 [1982]) was passed into law.[12]

Title VII provides recourse for workers who are discriminated against on the basis of race, color, religion, sex, or national origin.[13] However, it was not until 1980 that the Equal Employment Opportunity Commission (EEOC), a body created by Title VII, directly addressed trait-based discrimination.[14] In their *Guidelines on discrimination because of national origin,* revised on a regular basis, the EEOC currently defines national origin discrimination: "…broadly as including, but not limited to, the denial of equal employment opportunity because of an individual's, or his or her ancestor's place of origin; or because an individual has the *physical, cultural or linguistic characteristics* of a national origin group" (Federal Register 1988, ¶1606.1; emphasis added). The spirit of the law is clear: an employer may not reject a job candidate, or fire or refuse to promote an employee, because that employee externalizes in some way an allegiance to another culture.

In the case of racial discrimination, "It is clearly forbidden by Title VII to refuse on racial grounds to hire someone because your customers or clients do not like his race" (Matsuda 1991:1376, fn. 169). Similarly, a qualified person may not be rejected on the basis of linguistic traits that the employer or the employer's customers find esthetically objectionable. In contrast to racial discrimination, however, an employer has some latitude in matters of language:[15] "an adverse employment decision may be predicated upon an individual's accent when—but only when—it interferes materially with job performance" (Civil Rights Act of 1964, §701 et seq., 42 U.S.C.A. §2000e et seq.).[16]

Title VII is very limited in its scope. Under the law as it currently stands, discrimination on the basis of *regional* origination is not covered. An accent must be directly traceable to a specific national origin to be eligible for Title VII protection.

Raj Gupta, attorney counsel to the commissioner of the EEOC, states (p.c.) that some forces within the EEOC would like to see the definition of LTF–national origin discrimination made more comprehensive. So, in his example, a person from Appalachia would have recourse under Title VII because the features of Appalachian are directly traceable to a number of dialects in Great Britain.[17]

The Legal Process

Alleged LTF–national origin discrimination cases usually begin when an individual files a complaint with the EEOC (or a similar agency on a state or local level). The employee may then file a civil action in the trial courts, in which he or she claims that civil liberties, as set out in the federal statutes known as the Civil Rights Act of 1964, have been violated. In some instances, these cases are brought to the courts not by the individual or group of individuals with the same complaint, but by a private agency acting for the injured party, such as the American Civil Liberties Union (ACLU), or by a government agency, such as the EEOC. This action may be initiated at the state level, as many states have adopted civil liberties legislation patterned on the federal statutes.[18]

An individual claiming LTF discrimination must first prove a prima facie case of disparate treatment, in four steps: (a) establishment of identifiable national origin; (b) proof of application for a job for which he or she was qualified, and for which the employer was seeking applicants; (c) evidence that the applicant was rejected in spite of adequate qualifications; and (d) evidence that, after such rejection, the job remained open, and the employer continued to seek applicants with the plaintiff's qualifications. After a prima facie case has been established, the burden shifts to the employer to rebut presumption of discrimination by articulating some legitimate, non-discriminatory reason for the action. If the employer does this, the burden shifts back to the plaintiff, to show that the purported reason for the action was pretext for invidious discrimination. The plaintiff can show the employer's pretext directly, by demonstrating that the employer was more likely motivated by discriminatory reasons; or indirectly, by showing that the proffered reason is unworthy of credence (Civil Rights Act of 1964, §701 et seq., 42 U.S.C.A. §2000e et seq.).

DISCRIMINATION IN THE WORKPLACE

In an excellent study of language and discrimination in the workplace in Great Britain, Roberts et al. 1992 provided numerous examples of discrimination focused on language, and directed toward ethnic and racial minorities. No such systematic and well-documented study exists for workers in the U.S., although this is an area of great importance. The evidence of discrimination provided here is limited to specific instances which have found their way into the legal system.

Table 1 provides a breakdown of 25 LTF–national origin discrimination cases heard in the federal and state courts and by the EEOC since 1972, with exceptions as noted. Further excluded or missing are cases which concerned the

Table 1.　Distribution of 25 LTF Discrimination Cases in the Courts/EEOC Hearings, by Plaintiff's National Origin

Plaintiff's National Origin	No. Cases Filed	Court Found for*	
		Plaintiff	Defendant
Asia, Pacific Rim			
Philippines: Lubitz, Fragante, Carino	3	1	2
Vietnam: Tran	1	0	1
China: Ang, Hou	2	0	2
India: Duddey, Mandhare, Patel	3	1	1
Cambodia: Xieng	1	1	0
Korea: Park	1	1	0
Subtotal	11	4	6
Caribbean/West Indies			
Dominican Republic: Meijia	1	0	1
Haiti: Stephen	1	0	1
Cuba: Rodriguez	1	0	1
Subtotal	3	0	3
Central/South America			
Venezuela: Dercach	1	0	1
Bolivia: Ipina	1	0	1
Subtotal	2	0	2
Eastern Europe			
Armenia: Vartivarian	1	0	1
Poland: Berke	1	1	0
Ukraine: Staruch	1	0	1
Subtotal	3	1	2
Africa			
Nigeria: Dabor	1	0	1
Liberia: Andrews	1	0	0
Ghana: Kpodo	1	0	0
Subtotal	3	0	1
Other			
African-American: Sparks, Edwards	2	2	0
Hawaiian Creole: Kahakua	1	0	1
Subtotal	3	2	1
Totals	25	7	15

*Discrepancy in some of the totals is due to the fact that one case (Patel) was settled out of court; two others had not yet been decided (Andrews, Kpodo) at the time of this writing.

English-only question (e.g., *H. Garcia*) and cases in which LTF discrimination played a minimal role in the plaintiff's arguments (*C. Garcia, Bell,* and many others). In some of the cases included, both racial and national origin discrimination were at issue. In most of the cases, accent, language use, and communication figured prominently in the testimony, argumentation, discussion, and final opinion.[19]

How widespread is LTF discrimination? The General Accounting Office of the United States Government (GAO GGD 90–62 Employer Sanctions, 27) conducted a carefully designed statistical study of a stratified random sample of employers nationwide, and reported that 10% of their sample, or 461,000 companies employing millions of persons, openly if naïvely admit that they "discriminated on the basis of a person's foreign appearance or accent" (ibid., 38). In hiring audits, specifically designed to detect discrimination on the basis of accent (telephone inquiries about advertised jobs), such discrimination was found to be prevalent (ibid.).[20] This type of behavior was documented again in *Carroll,* when an employment agency receptionist was directed by her manager to screen all persons inquiring over the telephone: to those who did not "speak right," the job was closed. The receptionist was also told to make notations about the caller's speech and accent (*Carroll,* 1173).

There are a number of possible reasons for the low number of documented cases. Employers who discriminate may do so in a nonblatant way; the persons discriminated against may be so accustomed to this treatment that they no longer react; if they are aware of the treatment, they may not know that they have legal recourse, or how to pursue it; complaints may be handled internally, and resolved before litigation becomes necessary. Of course, many people discriminated against on the basis of language may not find anything surprising or wrong about that fact. This is, after all, not the only society in the world that promotes a standard language ideology....

Once cornered in a courtroom, what do the employers offer by way of excuses? The approaches taken by defendants range from the naïvely and openly discriminatory to the subtle.

In offering examples of Mr. Dercach's communication problems, Mr. Moser explained that workers would ask Mr. Dercach what he wanted them to do, and then simply walk away, unable to understand. Mr. Moser refused to attribute such incidents to Mr. Dercach's accent, but offered no other explanation. He said they just couldn't understand him "like normal people with normal language." (*Dercach*, 899)

After listening to the transmission described by Dispatcher Mixon as *jargon*,…Rodriguez claims that during [a telephone] conversation Sgt. McElligat told him to "speak English like in Queens, New Jersey, not Little Havana." Sgt. McElligat testified that he could not recall ever having talked to Rodriguez. (*Rodriguez*, LEXIS)

Managerial level employee Linda Sincoff told Xieng he was not being promoted because he could not speak "American." (*Xieng*, Appeal Court Opinion, 5)

…the complainant's supervisor had removed her because of concern about the effect of her accent on the "image" of the IRS, not any lack in either communication or technical abilities. (*Park*, EEOC press release dated June 8, 1988)

…the ability to speak clearly is one of the most important skills…we felt the applicants selected would be better able to work in our office because of their communication skills. (*Fragante* 1989:598)[21]

So the court has before it a plaintiff who claims that his or her basic civil liberties have been violated, and an employer who claims the right to make appropriate business decisions. How do courts handle this conflict? What factors, legal and otherwise, play a role in the decision-making process?…

In some cases one must assume that a plaintiff may claim LTF discrimination when in fact none has taken place. Or there may be clear evidence of LTF discrimination which the court overlooks because there is, in addition, a bona fide reason to deny employment. In *Dercach*, the court felt that blatant LTF discrimination could not mitigate the fact that the plaintiff, while hardworking and knowledgeable, was illiterate. Because the job required close work with a written code book, and the ability to write multiple reports on a weekly basis, the court found for the defendant.

The courts have stated that "there is nothing improper about an employer making an honest assessment of the oral communications skills of a candidate for a job when such skills are reasonably related to job performance" (*Fragante* 1989:596–7). Matsuda 1991 calls this the *doctrinal puzzle of accent and antidiscrimination law*: Title VII disallows discrimination on the basis of accent when it correlates to national origin, but it allows employers to discriminate on the basis of job ability. Employers claim that "accent" impedes communication, and thereby poses a valid basis for rejection; Matsuda found that the courts are especially receptive to this argument (1348 ff.).[22]…

But how can the courts distinguish an *admissible* business judgment, based on business necessity or personal preference, from *inadmissible* considerations, based on race or national origin? Is it simply a matter of presentation of the right arguments by the employer? Cutler 1985

has pointed out that employers are favorably predisposed to potential employees who are "like" them, and less disposed toward potential employees who are "unlike" them. Because the courts fail to recognize this fact, and refuse to reject the validity of the personal preference rationale, "Title VII becomes a statute which, at best, coerces job applicants to assimilate and, at worst, keeps them jobless" (1985:1166)….

STANDARD LANGUAGE IDEOLOGY IN THE COURTROOM

The opinions put out by the courts display a range of approaches toward communication and accent. One assumes that the courts are unbiased, and sometimes there is evidence of that.

Accent and national origin are obviously inextricably intertwined in many cases. It would therefore be an easy refuge in this context for an employer unlawfully discriminating against someone based on national origin to state falsely that it was not the person's national origin that cause the employment or promotion problem, but the candidate's inability to measure up to the communications skills demanded by the job. We encourage a very searching look by the [trial] courts at such a claim. (*Fragante* 1989:596)

Testimony of both Plaintiff's and Defendants' witnesses have convinced the Court that the Plaintiff's accent was a major factor in the Defendants' evaluation of his supervisory abilities…a trait related to national origin must be of an immutable nature in order to come within Title VII protections…An accent would appear to approach that sort of immutable characteristic…(*Carino*, 1336–7)

Plaintiff's accent did not interfere materially with his job performance, nor would it have interfered materially with his job performance…if he had been promoted…(*Xieng*, Supreme Court Opinion, 2)

But at the same time, and sometimes *in the same cases*, it is clear that the courts are willing to depend on their own often factually incorrect understanding of language issues.

Fragante argues the district court erred in considering "listener prejudice" as a legitimate, nondiscriminatory reason for failing to hire. We find, however, that the district court did not determine [that] Defendants refused to hire Fragante on the basis that some listeners would "turn off" a Filipino accent. The district court after trial noted that: "Fragante, in fact, has a difficult manner of pronunciation…." (*Fragante* 1989:597)

The judge discounted the testimony of the linguist who stated that Hawaiian Creole pronunciation is not incorrect, rather it is one of the many varieties of pronunciation of standard English. *The linguist, the judge stated, was not an expert in speech.*

(Matsuda 1991:1345–6, including quotations from *Kahakua* 1987:22–3, emphasis added)[23]

...

The judges who wrote these opinions are willing to depend on their own expertise in matters of language in a way they would never presume to in matters of genetics or mechanical engineering or psychology. In *Kahakua*, the judge heard testimony of expert witnesses, and then chose to give credence to that witness whose testimony most closely matched his own personal opinions on matters of language use. In none of these cases was there any attempt to assess the communication demands of the job in a nonprejudicial way, and *intelligibility* was a matter of opinion only.

How do some plaintiffs manage to win? *Xieng* provides an example of a successful case.

Phanna Xieng is a Cambodian-American who worked for Peoples National Bank of Washington. Mr. Xieng was repeatedly denied a promotion although he had an excellent work history, high marks in his reviews, and for an extended period had been filling in on the very position for which he was applying. There were documented comments from his superiors concerning his accent as the primary stumbling block to his promotion. In this case, the court could not overlook the fact that Mr. Xieng could carry out the job he claimed he could do, in spite of his accent, precisely because *he had already been performing well at the job*. It might seem that being on the inside—already employed by the defendant—would provide an employee with a valid LTF discrimination complaint with some strong evidence; but there are many other cases of denied promotion which were not so successful as *Xieng*....

Education-Related Cases

I consider here four cases in which educators sued their respective schools or school systems for racial and/or LTF-national origin discrimination:

(a) *Sparks*: an African-American who was dismissed from her job as a school teacher.
(b) *Hou*: a native of China and professor of mathematics who was refused promotion.
(c) *Edwards*: an African-American whose teaching contract was not renewed.
(d) *Mandhare*: a native of India who was denied reappointment to her position as a librarian at a K–2 school.

Ms. Sparks and Ms. Edwards won their cases; Ms. Mandhare won at trial court but lost on appeal; Dr. Hou lost his case.

Academic institutions were meant to be included within the scope of Title VII; nevertheless, the "trend in many courts has been to exercise minimal scrutiny of college and university employment practices, due, in large part, to the subjective factors on which many academic employment decisions are based" (*Hou,* 1546). They will intercede, but seem to do so with considerable forbearance for the opinions put forth by school administration. In addition, the courts have shown reluctance to reverse administrative decisions (ibid., 1958).

This deference for academic decision making was the downfall of *Hou*. The judge pointed out:

> The issue of accent in a foreign-born person of another race is a concededly delicate subject when it becomes part of peer or student evaluations, since many people are prejudiced against those with accents. (*Hou*, 1547)

The judge went on to approve the loophole used by the institution.

> We find that comments about Dr. Hou's accent, when made, were directed toward the legitimate issue of his teaching effectiveness. Teaching effectiveness, as the testimony at trial indicated, is an elusive concept.... Teaching effectiveness does, however, include the ability to communicate the content of a discipline, a quality which should be carefully evaluated at any college or university. (ibid.)

There was never any discussion of appropriate, nonprejudicial assessment of Dr. Hou's communicative competence or intelligibility. The defense depended *exclusively* on anecdotal evidence provided by the defendant, and this satisfied the court.

> [The college records showed that] he is at a decided disadvantage in the classroom because of his natural accent...he has a difficult time overcoming this handicap. The obvious grammatical errors on his application attest to his communication problems...(*Hou*, 1547).

The question must be, then, why other education cases prevailed where *Hou* could not. I consider *Sparks* and *Edwards* before a discussion of *Mandhare*.

Sparks and *Edwards* were built primarily on racial discrimination. In many pages of correspondence on the matter of Ms. Sparks's dismissal, the school administrator (Mr. Griffin) commented only once on the language issue: "Mrs. Sparks has a language problem. She cannot help the negro dialect, but it is certainly bad for the children to be subjected to it all day" (*Sparks*, 437). In *Edwards*, the discussion of language use is limited to general comments: "The plaintiff's contract was not renewed allegedly because of complaints received from parents and students....Several complaints concerned students' alleged inability to understand the plaintiff's 'black accent'" (*Edwards*, LEXIS).

In both these cases, the opinions indicate that the heart of the matter was racial discrimination. In other words, if the accent issue had never been raised in *Sparks* or *Edwards*, these plaintiffs would still have won. This was fortunate for the courts, as it relieved them of the trouble of dealing with the matter of language and accent. In discussing the LTF discrimination portion of *Sparks*, the court limited its comments to one short footnote: "With no disposition to be unkind, we question, based on the spelling and composition of the two letters...the ability of Mr. Griffin to diagnose a 'language-problem'" (*Sparks*, 442). The letters written by Mr. Griffin regarding the dismissal of Ms.

Sparks, to which the court referred, were in fact poorly written, and contained many spelling and/or typographical errors. Nevertheless, the court is clearly uncomfortable in chiding an educator (in this case, an administrator with advanced degrees) in matters of language use: "with no disposition to be unkind." More importantly, the court never addressed the *content* of Mr. Griffin's complaint—Ms. Sparks's "negro dialect" and its appropriateness for the classroom; it addressed only the superintendent's qualifications to make judgments on that dialect, *given his poor letter-writing skills....*

The court neatly sidestepped the "concededly delicate subject" of LTF discrimination for *Edwards* as well: "The district court stated in its opinion that it was 'apparent' that the plaintiff could be easily understood and that there was no evidence the plaintiff made grammatical errors rendering her speech difficult to understand." In these two cases, the schools were deservedly punished for racial discrimination; for LTF discrimination, they were slapped on the wrist.

I return now to the *Mandhare* case, with which I began. Earlier it was established that Ms. Mandhare's contract as a school librarian was not renewed after that first year because her duties were thought to be compromised by her heavy accent, specifically because her "problems with speech and grammar made it difficult for her to be understood by students and teachers...plaintiff would do an excellent job at a school where her speech, grammar and story telling would not be so critical" (*Mandhare* 1985:238).

The official published summary of the case indicates that Ms. Mandhare then met with the Superintendent of Schools, and on the advice of her supervisor requested a transfer to Thibodaux Junior High School, as a librarian.[24] The school board refused to reappoint Ms. Mandhare to this requested new position; testimony revealed that, in their private and public deliberations, Ms. Mandhare's foreignness and accent were discussed.

The trial court was very firm in this case: Ms. Mandhare had been discriminated against, and must prevail. However, the school's initial decision that the plaintiff could not teach young children because of her "heavy accent and speech patterns and grammar problems [which] prevented her from effectively communicating with primary school students" (ibid.) *was never questioned*. The court took this claim on faith, and instead stated:

> Defendant's contention that its legitimate reason for plaintiff's termination or non-appointment was that she had a communication problem because of her accent which prevented her from effectively communicating with primary school students is a feigned contention. Plaintiff was not being considered for a position which would require such communication. She was to be appointed librarian at a Junior High School, a position for which it was established that she was eminently qualified.

It is important to remember that in this case, as in every other case discussed, no effort was made to make an objective assessment of the communication skills required for the job, the plaintiff's speech, the quality of her interaction with children, or her intelligibility. The administrators found the plaintiff's accent difficult; they decided not to reappoint her to her job in the grade school. This alone would have made them the focus of the court's scrutiny (although not necessarily to the plaintiff's favor). However, they redeemed themselves in the court's eyes: they praised the plaintiff's industry and skill, and they went out of their way to locate a position in a school where her accent would *neither offend nor inconvenience*. The court could then focus on the school board, which refused to give the plaintiff this new job. The validity of the initial firing was never challenged. Thus everyone (except the school board) was happy: the administrators were left intact as arbiters of the SL ideology, and were lionized for their largesse; the court was not forced to challenge those educators on the factual basis for their decisions about appropriate language; and Ms. Mandhare was to be reinstated as a librarian, in a junior high school.

The question remains: Were Ms. Mandhare's civil rights protected? Were her best interests really served? Put more controversially, if Ms. Mandhare had been forbidden to ride a public bus, and challenged that restriction, should she then have been pleased to be offered alternate transportation in the form of a bicycle, a Mercedes-Benz—or another, different but equally functioning, bus?

Ms. Mandhare did not really want the transfer to another school in a school district which had treated her so badly; she wanted back pay, which she did not get. Whether or not she would have been satisfied with the new position was never established, because the trial court decision was reversed by the U.S. Court of Appeals for the Fifth Circuit:

> The district court's determination that the Board had intentionally discriminated against Mandhare is clearly erroneous. The court focused on the wrong issue. It premised its conclusion on the Board's refusal to follow LeBlanc's recommendation that Mandhare be transferred to a junior high librarian position. That was not the issue as framed by the unamended pleadings and pre-trial order. Mandhare's action asserted discrimination in the Board's refusal to reemploy her as elementary school librarian, not their failure to create and transfer her to a junior high position. (*Mandhare* 1986:5)

The terrible irony of this reversal should be clear: Ms. Mandhare was originally protesting her *dismissal* on the basis of LTF–national origin discrimination; the judge in that first case chose not to deal with the delicate issue, but to bypass it completely by focusing on the possibility of a position in another school. This gave the appeal court an out, which it took. The appeal court accused the trial court of focusing on the wrong issue; and *on that basis*, it reversed the decision.

In the end, both courts were satisfied to let the school administrators and school board exclude on the basis of accent. In the analogy previously cited, the first court offered Ms. Mandhare a Mercedes-Benz when all she wanted to do was ride the bus. The appeal court said that the trial court had been wrong to offer Ms. Mandhare a Mercedes-Benz that did not exist and that no one was obliged to buy for her; it did not even question why she had been forced off the bus in the first place, and it certainly did not offer her the opportunity to get back on, or compensate her for her trouble.

The appeal court filed the reversal on May 2, 1986, six years after Ms. Mandhare was denied renewal. The failure of the American judicial system caused her untold emotional anguish and financial difficulty, and was detrimental to her health. Today she works as librarian for a private school in her home town of Thibodaux, but she will carry this experience with her for the rest of her life.

...

ACCENT AND COMMUNICATION

Employers present to the courts a model of communication in the workplace which has three main points:

(a) Good communication skills are necessary for job X.
(b) Accent Y impedes communication.
(c) The applicant speaks with accent Y.
(d) Conclusion: The applicant does not possess a basic skill necessary for job X.

A first criticism of this model must address the overly simplistic characterization of communication, in which the listener is relieved of any responsibility in the communicative act, and the full burden is put directly on the speaker. Herbert Clark has developed a cognitive model of the communicative act (Clark & Wilkes-Gibbs 1986, Clark & Schaefer 1989) which is based on a principle of mutual responsibility, in which participants in a conversation collaborate in the establishment of new information. This involves complicated processes of repair, expansion, and replacement in iterative fashion until both parties are satisfied: "Many purposes in conversation...change moment by moment as the two people tolerate more or less uncertainty about the listener's understanding of the speaker's references. The heavier burden usually falls on the listener, since she is in the best position to assess her own comprehension" (Clark & Wilkes-Gibbs 1986:34). This contrasts markedly with the employer's version of communication, in which the speaker (the person with the accent) carries the majority of responsibility in the communicative act.

The whole concept of units of conversation in which two partners work toward mutual comprehension assumes a certain state of mind on the part of the participants. Work in accommodation theory suggests that a complex interplay of linguistic and psychological factors will establish the predisposition to understand. Thus Thakerar et al. 1982 conducted a series of empirical tests to examine accommodation behavior. They were not working directly with "accented" speech, but their findings are generally typical of such studies, which verify something known intuitively: listeners and speakers will work harder to find a communicative middle ground and foster mutual intelligibility when they are motivated, socially and psychologically, to do so. Conversely, when the speaker perceives that the act of accommodating

or assimilating linguistically may bring more disadvantages than advantages, in in-group terms, he or she may diverge even farther from the language of the listener.[25]

Roberts et al. 1992 (RDJ) point to the larger social context of language comprehensibility in the workplace, and demonstrate "how native speakers' assumption that they have the right to dominate and control, and the way that this is reinforced by the worker's lack of ability to negotiate the right to be heard, affect the detailed processes of routine interactions and their outcomes" (1992:35). All this work points to two crucial concepts not included in the employer's model of communication in the workplace. First, *Linguistic competence on the part of the employee, taken alone, is insufficient for successful communication.* Degree of accentedness, whether from L1 interference, or a socially or geographically marked language variety, cannot predict the level of an individual's communicative competence. In fact, communicative competence can often be so high as to compensate for strong L1 interference. RDJ provide an excellent example of this, in which an Asian factory worker tries to negotiate with his supervisor to obtain work for his son. The supervisor is at first unwilling to help, but the worker negotiates past the supervisor's reluctance. In their commentary on the exchange, RDJ (1992:40–1) point out that, in spite of strong interference from the native language, the worker shows several positive qualities.

(a) He is sensitive to context, using an appropriate discourse convention to set the scene.
(b) He is focused, and able to keep relevant topics "on stage."
(c) He is able to compensate for and repair communicative difficulties: "For example, when there is a confusion over 'first' and 'fast,' he reformulates..."

[Worker]:   Boy say I not working on the fast.
[Supervisor]: Not working on the first?
[Worker]:   On the fast Ramadan you know.

(d) He is in touch with cultural differences, and is able to negotiate the supervisor out of "a gatekeeping role."[26]

A second crucial concept is that *the burden of communication is shared, on every level, by both participants.* If one accepts that good communication skills are necessary for job X, without further definition of those skills, one must still question the employer's claim that accent Y impedes communication. In fact, it is not necessarily the accent which is the problem, but negative subjective evaluation on the part of the listener. It has been shown, in cases such as *Dercach*, that lack of goodwill can be as much of an obstacle to understanding, if not more.

Matsuda (1991:1369 ff.) has pointed out the fact that no consistent, disinterested, fair procedures exist to verify these claims, and that development of such a protocol is imperative. This would provide an objective way to establish employment situations in which accent really is more likely to pose a valid obstacle. Thus claims made by the employer about the effect of accent on job performance would be subject to scrutiny that moves beyond the subjective and anecdotal. Of course, such measures are important precisely because accent, in the general sense that has been used here, can sometimes be an impediment to communication, even when all parties involved in the communicative act are willing, and even eager, to understand.

In Matsuda's scheme, the full communicative burden might be placed on the speaker if (a) the consequences of miscommunication are grave; (b) the job is primarily oral in nature; (c) the setting is stressful, and time is of the essence; or (d) interaction is contextless, and restricted to one-time exchanges. Of course, this list could, and probably must, be expanded and revised. For example, there seems to be no real reason to take together the conditions of context and amount of contact; in fact, one can think of cases in which the context is indirect (over the telephone) but not limited to one-time exchanges (a dispatcher speaking to the same truck drivers many times every day). There are many communicative situations where the burden is not distributed evenly because the power and solidarity factors between speakers interfere (e.g., doctor/patient interactions); all these variables must be taken into account. In addition, the variables of stress and time need further definition and clarification.

When all four of her conditions are met (as in the case of a 911 operator), Matsuda suggests that the speaker's accent should then be evaluated in an unbiased, consistent way to determine degree of intelligibility—possibly by means of matched-guise testing. This is thought to be one way to ascertain whether or not the candidate is intelligible to the pool of relevant, nonprejudiced listeners. Obviously, the construction of an appropriate matched-guise protocol would be a challenging task, and one that the courts are clearly neither able nor willing to take on at present.

In other cases where only one or two of these conditions are met, there is room and opportunity for goodwill and accommodation, and it is reasonable to expect that the burden be distributed between speaker and audience. Here Matsuda draws heavily on legislation such as the Physical Disabilities Act, where reasonable accommodation is a major factor....

Kalin et al. 1979 conducted an experiment in which students were asked to play the role of personnel consultant, matching taped voices of applicants with jobs characterized as "high" and "low" status. The "applicants" spoke with a variety of ethnic accents. For the highest status job, the students ranked the applicants in the following order: English, German, South Asian, West Indian. This order was exactly reversed for the lowest status job.

Many of these students will go out into the work force, and will someday become involved in the hiring process. They will continue to confuse their valid concern that employees be able to communicate effectively with the political and social complexities of accent. They will first judge individuals not on how logically or clearly they talk about themselves, their goals, and their abilities, but instead on the rhythms of their speech—rhythms which are linked to skin color, economic resources, or homeland. They will exclude and discriminate on the basis of language because they have been taught, by example, that language is sufficient and appropriate justification for this behavior. They will continue to *hear* with an accent: the accent of the intolerant, empowered mainstream.

THE LINGUIST'S CONTRIBUTION

If ideology is most effective when its workings are least visible (Fairclough 1989:85) then the first step must be to *make visible* the link between the enforcement of SL ideology and social domination. The educational system is the obvious point of departure, but that system is itself part of the dominant bloc. Given the way schools, the broadcast and print media, the entertainment industry, and employers work together to promote an SL ideology, the education of the public is both a lonely and a difficult task, but certainly not an impossible one.

Beyond education, linguists have hard-won knowledge to offer which would be of some assistance in the difficult questions faced in matters of language policy. That knowledge is often not sought; and if sought, it may be summarily rejected; but in either case, it is often hotly resented. Nevertheless, there are good reasons to persevere, beyond the fact that the kind of linguistic dilettantism demonstrated here is damaging to our professional pride. This type of behavior causes real harm to real individuals, and it deserves our attention....

Xieng provides an interesting illustration of the status of linguistics in the courts. There was no expert testimony at all on the pivotal matter, which was the employer's claim that Mr. Xieng's accent was too strong and impeded communication. However, a psychiatrist was called, who then argued and convinced the court that there did exist a "causal relationship between the [employer's] national origin discrimination and Xieng's severe emotional distress and depression" (*Xieng* 1991:A13).

Psychologists ask themselves a two-part question to determine the quality of their forensic contributions: (a) Can we answer questions with reasonable accuracy? (b) Can we help the judge and jury reach a more accurate conclusion than would otherwise be possible (Faust & Ziskin 1988:31)? That is, does the subject lie beyond the knowledge and experience of the average layperson? Can the expert give information without invading the province of the jury by expressing a conclusion as to the ultimate issue?

For most of the cases presented here, a list of questions could have been presented to linguists which would have met both these basic criteria. Questions about the process of standardization, differences between spoken and written language varieties, cultural differences in discourse style and structure which may cause processing difficulties, second language acquisition and accent, subconscious social evaluation of active variation, and change over time and space could be answered with reasonable accuracy. We *could* provide the judge and the jury with information and knowledge beyond that of the average layperson. But the issue is this: we cannot make them *want* that information, no matter how factually correct or how strongly supported by empirical evidence....

CONCLUSIONS

There are many people who must cope, day by day, with LTF discrimination. Some of them have other currencies—political and economic power, social pre-eminence, artistic excellence, academic achievement—which they can use to offset the disadvantages of accent, and to disarm the prejudiced listener. Most listeners, no matter how overtly negative and hostile, would be hard pressed to turn away and ignore Ann Richard, Jesse Jackson or Ed Koch, Cesar Chavez or Derek Wolcott, Butros Butros Ghali or Liu Xiaobo, Rigoberta Menchu, Benazir Bhutto or Corazon Aquino, if the opportunity for discussion presented itself.[27]

Of course, most people who do not speak the language of the mainstream do not have such extraordinary resources. There are many of them: since 1961, over 15 million persons have legally immigrated into the United States (U.S. INS 1992:11). Many times that number of citizens, born in the U.S., speak with a regional accent that is not fashionable, or are native speakers of a variety of English which is directly linked to race, ethnicity, or income. In a time when multiculturalism and diversity are held up as ideals, one might think that a standard language ideology would give way to a more realistic and tolerant approach to language use. Unfortunately, there is little evidence of this. LTF discrimination is a widespread problem which permeates much of our day-to-day existence. It is the site on which racism and ethnocentrism are institutionalized.

...

Notes

I am thankful to the following persons for their encouragement and for many insightful comments on drafts of this article: Joe Salmons, Pamela Moss, Lesley and James Milroy, Jackie Macaulay, Deborah Keller-Cohen, Ann Ruggles Gere, Bill Green, Raj K. Gupta, Arnetha Ball, Dennis Baron, and Roger Shuy. I also thank Raj Gupta of the Equal Employment Opportunity Commission for his helpfulness in supplying original source material. In addition, I must point out the importance of work by Mari Matsuda 1991 and Stephen Cutler 1985; these articles gave me the start I needed to explore the legal side of this issue. I am grateful to all these persons for their help, but I retain sole responsibility for the contents of this article.

1. Court case citations are abbreviated as follows: *Mandhare v. W. S. Lafargue Elementary School, the Lafourche Parish School Board, Parish of Lafourche* appear in the text as *Mandhare*. This material originates from opinions, briefs, *Findings of Fact*, and other legal documents associated with each case. In the case of Mandhare, interviews with the plaintiff are also cited. Complete references are given at the end of this article.

2. Later...I explore in greater detail the reasoning of the courts, and their interpretation of matters regarding language use and prescription in *Mandhare*.

3. Many basic concepts in sociolinguistics have been challenged for their lack of theoretical cohesiveness within a more general theory of sociology. The concepts which have come under close scrutiny include such giants as *social class, status, prestige,* and *gender*. As such terms come into discussion, I will outline my working definitions. In the case of the concepts *class* and *status*, I follow sociologists Bell & Newby (1971:218 ff.): class refers to *economic* resources, whereas status is reserved for the determination of *what is achieved* with economic resources.

4. Crucial here is the distinction between spoken and written forms of language. Because the written word was developed and exists to convey decontextualized information over time and space, standardization is necessary and appropriate. The problem at hand has come about because of a blurring between the written/spoken boundary; the written language has acquired dominance in the minds of speakers, so that goals appropriate for the written language are generalized to speaking, and the written word is adopted as a model for all language.

5. The history of standardization is a long and complex one. It has been treated extensively elsewhere (see, e.g., the excellent presentation of these issues in Milroy & Milroy 1985 and Bailey 1991).

6. Space does not permit a long discussion of the development of SL ideology in the schools, which was clearly well established at the beginning of the century. In 1911, J. Forbes Robertson addressed the Indiana Association of Teachers of English: "There are three causes of this poor English. They are ignorance, affectation, and indifference...one of the most important points to remember in the correct articulation and pronunciation of words is to give the vowels their correct sound" (Robertson 1911:5).

7. One such dictionary might be the *Oxford English Dictionary*, with the following prescriptive definition of *accent*: "the mode of utterance peculiar to an individual, locality, or nation....This utterance consists mainly in a prevailing quality of tone, or in a peculiar alteration of pitch, but may include mispronunciation of vowels or consonants, misplacing of stress, and misinflection of a sentence. The locality of a speaker is generally marked by this kind of accent."

8. On May 17, 1978, Judge Charles Joiner handed down a decision, in *Martin Luther King Elementary School Children v. The Michigan Board of Education and the Ann Arbor School District Board*, which directed the School Board to train teachers on the basis of "existing knowledge" regarding language use and variation; the existence and structure of Black English Vernacular; and the necessary skills to teach the plaintiffs, who were native speakers of BEV, how to read (see Chambers 1983 for detailed discussions of the *King* case).

9. In entertainment, linguistic stereotypes have long been a stock-in-trade. Dialect was used to draw character in Chaucer, and can be followed to the present time. In broadcast and film entertainment, the use of linguistic stereotypes mirrors the evolution of national fears and obsessions: Japanese and German characters in Disney cartoons during the Second World War, Russian spy characters in children's cartoons in the 1950s and 1960s, Arab characters in the era of hostilities with Iran and Iraq. More general stereotyping is also prevalent in television programming and movies: situation comedies (*Beverly Hillbillies, I Love Lucy, Sanford and Son, All in the Family*) and animated films (*Jungle Book, Dumbo*) provide numerous examples. The 1993 film *Falling Down* provides a disturbing example. In that film, a middle-class worker, portrayed as beleaguered by inner-city life, loses his temper with an irascible convenience store clerk. The episode begins when the protagonist, D-Fens (played by Michael Douglas), asks the price of an item. The following is from the script:

The proprietor, a middle-aged Asian, reads a Korean newspaper.... The Asian has a heavy accent...

Asian: Eighdy fie sen.
D-Fens: What?
Asian: Eighdy fie sen.
D-Fens: I can't understand you...I'm not paying eight-five cents for a stinking soda. I'll give you a quarter. You give me seventy "fie" cents back for the phone...What is a fie? There's a "V" in the word. Fie-vuh. Don't they have "v's" in China?
Asian: Not Chinese, I am Korean.
D-Fens: Whatever. What difference does that make? You come over here and take my money and you don't even have the grace to learn to speak my language...

Here, the clerk's accent—and the Korean clerk—are portrayed as negative elements of urban life.

10. For a more lucid discussion of the issues raised in this column, see Raspberry 1990.

11. Headlines alone are often revealing: "Black English is silly" (*Chicago Sun-Times*, July 10, 1979); "Hush mah mouth! Some in South try to lose the drawl; 'accent reduction' becomes a big bidness in Atlanta; searchin' for the lost 'G'" (*Wall Street Journal*, December 13, 1991); "Proper English, Yes; but Educationalists, No" (*New York Times*, September 18, 1989); "Twangy Guy Next Door Ousts the Professionals" (*Marketing*, January 13, 1992); "Lose that Thick Accent to Gain Career Ground" (*Wall Street Journal*, January 4, 1990); "Most officials don't talk li' dat these days" (*Honolulu Advertiser*, September 29, 1987, cited in Sato 1991).

12. Title VII is specific to employment issues; the legislation and court cases here cannot be applied to any other arena, e.g., education.

13. Companies employing less than 15 workers are not bound by these statutes.

14. Discrimination is a matter of law:

the effect of a statute or established practice which confers particular privileges on a class arbitrarily selected from a large number of persons, all of whom stand in the same relation to the privileges granted and between whom and those not favored no reasonable distinction can be found. (*Black's Law Dictionary*, 1991:323)

15. The discussion here excludes the very crucial "English Only" controversy, and the more general issues surrounding bilingualism. Those topics have been covered in great depth by Crawford 1992 and Baron 1990.

16. Under §703(e) of Title VII, an employer may defend his or her actions on the basis of national origin (a) "by demonstrating the 'business necessity' of the disputed employment practice—i.e., by showing the practice 'to be necessary to safe and efficient job performance' (Cutler 1985:1168, fn. 20); or (b) by establishing a bona fide occupational qualification (BFOQ) (ibid.). The BFOQ is the more difficult case for the employer. The path taken depends on which of two different theories of liability is used: *disparate treatment*, in which proof of discriminatory intent is crucial, requires a BFOQ defense; for *disparate impact*, in which such proof is not required, the employer must establish only business necessity: "The Plaintiff makes out a prima facie case by showing that the employer's selection device has a substantially adverse impact on his protected group...it remains open to the Plaintiff to show that 'other...selection devices, without a similarly undesirable...effect, would also serve the employer's legitimate interest[s]'" (ibid., 1169).

17. Of course the problems of associating specific regional or social dialects with specific foreign origins would be tremendous. Joe Salmons (p.c.) has brought to my attention work by Dillard 1992 which outlines the considerable difficulties of even identifying any salient features specific to Appalachian English (but see also Wolfram & Christian 1976 and Christian 1988, which provide evidence that these difficulties can be overcome).

18. The EEOC reviews complaints; if they find a violation has taken place, they may take on the case, and file suit for the employee against the employer. Raj Gupta of the EEOC estimates that the EEOC prosecutes 70% of such cases; in the other 30%, they may or may not grant a Notice of Right to Sue. Lack of such Notice does not prohibit the employee from proceeding; the right to pursue such matters in the courts is sacrosanct. Thus the Notice of Right to Sue is primarily an indication to the employee of the strength of the case. For employees of federal government agencies, the EEOC conducts the hearing, which is empowered by Title VII to hear discrimination cases; if they find for the plaintiff, they can order remedies. The federal agencies can appeal only to the EEOC.

19. Tracking down and documenting these cases was a matter of many hours in the University of Michigan Law Library. Certainly, cases have been excluded by oversight: there are no summary statistics kept by the EEOC, and no central logging system for these cases. Many cases are not summarized for publication. Thus no guarantee can be made of thoroughness of representation. The search for cases included in this article was concluded in May 1993.

20. This GAO study was conducted in response to a series of inquiries from Congress on the effect of the 1986 immigration laws. Not all the GAO's findings were clear or interpretable, especially in the matter of specifically accent-based discrimination. The report outlines a number of reasons for this, having to do with sampling and design questions.

21. Matsuda 1991 provides a thorough overview of the *Fragante* and *Kahakua* cases.

22. Dr. Jacqueline Macaulay, an attorney with a Ph.D. in social psychology, deals with family, employment, and civil rights cases; she has pointed out to me (p.c.) that the courts seem to be functioning on the basis of some "phantom legislature" which has mandated that a certain form of English is "Standard" and "unaccented."

23. It seems that three distinct kinds of expert witnesses testify in these trials: linguists (e.g., Charlene Sato of the University of Hawaii testified in *Kahakua*), speech pathologists, and "speech consultants." This last class is the most troublesome one, composed of those who teach "accent reduction" classes, or otherwise have a vested interest in the official commendation of a "standard English." Some judges, especially the judge who heard *Kahakua*, are very receptive to arguments of this kind.

24. Ms. Mandhare tells a very different story. In a phone interview, she indicated that her first year at the K–2 school was also the principal's first year, and that he openly admitted he had prom-

ised her job as librarian to someone else. He asked her to request a transfer, which she did not wish to do. After this episode, he told her in a one-on-one meeting that she had a "very heavy accent," although it had never been made an issue previously, and she had had no complaints from children or teachers.

25. This has been stated more simply (and admittedly in an anecdotal way) by persons who daily depend on accommodation. Joy Cherian, Commissioner of the EEOC, has commented: "I myself speak with a foreign accent. My colleagues sometimes have to listen to me more carefully simply to fully understand what I am saying. Perhaps that makes for better communication between us" (EEOC PR, June 8, 1988).

26. Fairclough (1989:47) defines a gatekeeping encounter as follows:

> encounters such as a job interview in which a "gatekeeper" who generally belongs to the societally dominant cultural grouping controls an encounter which determines whether someone gets a job, or gets access to some other valued objective. In contemporary Britain, for example [as in the preceding passage], it is mainly white middle-class people who act as gatekeepers in encounters with members of the various ethnic (and cultural) minorities of Asian, West Indian, African, etc., origin.

27. Jesse Jackson (African-American religious and political leader), Ed Koch (former mayor and native of New York), Derek Wolcott (West Indian poet, awarded 1992 Nobel Prize for Literature), Butros Butros Ghali (Egyptian former secretary-general of the United Nations), Liu Xiaobo (Chinese student activist and dissident, jailed after Tiananmen), Rigoberta Menchu (Guatemalan Mayan Indian, awarded 1992 Nobel Peace Prize), Corazon Aquino (former president of the Philippines).

References

COURT CASES CITED WITH SOURCES

Note: LEXIS is a computerized legal document search and retrieval service.

Andrews 1992. George W. Andrews v. Cartex Corporation. Civil Action No. 91–7109. 1992 U.S. District Court. Source: LEXIS 11468.

Ang 1991. Ignatius G. Ang v. The Procter & Gamble Company. Source: Federal Reporter (2d) 932:540; LEXIS 8993; Fair Employment Practices Cases (BNA) 55:1666; Employment Practices Decisions (CCH) 56:40732.

Bell 1984. Bell v. Home Life Insurance Company. Source: Federal Supplement 596:1549.

Berke 1980. Rozalia Berke v. Ohio Department of Public Welfare. Source: Federal Reporter (2d) 628:980–81.

Carino 1981. Donaciano Carino v. Regents of the University of Oklahoma. Source: Federal Reporter (2d) 750:815; Fair Employment Practices Cases (BNA) 25:1332.

Carroll 1989. Doritt Carroll v. Elliott Personnel Services. Source: Fair Employment Practices Cases (BNA) 51:1173; Employment Practice Decisions (CCH) 52:39508.

Casas 1983. Casas v. First American Bank. Source: Fair Employment Practices Cases (BNA) 31:1479.

Dabor 1991. E.G. Dabor v. Dayton Power & Light Company. Source: LEXIS 2402.

Dercach 1987. Anthony Dercach v. Indiana Department of Highways. Source: Fair Employment Practice Cases (BNA) 45:899; LEXIS 13413.

Duddey 1989. John Duddey v. David S. Ruder, Chairman Securities & Exchange Commission, EEOC No. 05890115. Source: EEOC materials and press releases.

Edwards 1978. Violet B. Edwards v. Gladewater Independent School District. Source: Federal Reporter (2d) 572:496; Fair Employment Practices Cases (BNA) 21:1374; Employment Practices Decisions (CCH) 16:8288.

Garcia, C. 1978. Christobal Garcia et al. v. Victoria Independent School District et al. Source: Employment Practices Decisions (CCH) Vol. 17, Para. 8.544, S.D. Texas.

Garcia, H. 1980. Hector Garcia v. Alton V. W. Gloor et al. Source: Federal Reporter (2d) 618:264, Fair Employment Practices (BNA) 22:1403.

Fragrante 1987. Fragrante v. City and County of Honolulu. Source: Federal Supplement 699:1429–32.

Fragante 1989. Fragante v. City and County of Honolulu. Source: Federal Reporter (2d) 888:591, 594–95; Matsuda 1991.

Hou 1983. Hou v. Pennsylvania Department of Education. Source: Federal Supplement 573:1539–49.

Ipina 1988. Jorge M. Ipina v. State of Michigan Department of Management and Budget. Source: Federal Supplement 699:132; LEXIS 15381.

Kahakua 1987a. Kahakua v. Friday. Source: Federal Reporter (2d) 876:896.

Kahakua 1987b. Kahakua v. Hallgren, No. 86–0434. District Hawaii. Source: Matsuda 1991 (no published opinion or summaries).

King 1978. The Martin Luther King Junior Elementary School Children v. The Michigan Board of Education, the Michigan Superintendent of Public Instruction, and the Ann Arbor School District Board, Civil Action No. 77–71861, U.S. District Court, Eastern District of Michigan, Southern Division. Source: Memorandum Opinion and Order of Charles W. Joiner (reproduced in Chambers 1983).

Kpodo pending. EEOC v. Madison Hotel Corporation, Civil Action No. 92–718 A, Eastern District Virginia, Alexandria Division. Source: EEOC materials.

Lubitz 1992. John R. Lubitz v. H. Lawrence Garrett, III, Secretary of the Department of the Navy. Source: Federal Reporter (2d) 962:7; LEXIS 17272.

Mandhare 1985. Sulochana Mandhare v. W. S. LaFargue Elementary School, the Lafourche Parish School Board, Parish of Lafourche. Source: Federal Supplement 605:238; Fair Employment Practices Cases (BNA) 37:1611; Federal Reporter (2d) 788:1563; Fair Employment Practices Cases (BNA) 41:64; Fair Employment Practices Cases (BNA) 42:1014; LEXIS; interview with S. Mandhare, 29 March 1993.

Mandhare 1986. Sulochana Mandhare v. W. S. LaFargue Elementary School, the Lafourche Parish School Board, Parish of Lafourche. Source: Unpublished opinion of Chief Judge Clark, U.S. Court of Appeals, Fifth Circuit, No. 85–3212.

Meijia 1978. Meijia v. New York Sheraton Hotel. Source: Federal Supplement 459:375–77.

Park 1988. Kee Y. Park v. James A. Baker III, Secretary of the Treasury, EEOC No. 05870646. Source: EEOC materials.

Patel 1992. U.S. Equal Employment Commission v. Eiki International, Inc. U.S. District Court for the Central District of California. Source: EEOC materials; telephone interview with R. Gupta; EEOC; newspaper reports.

Rodriguez 1989. Bernardino Rodriguez v. City of Hialeah. Source: Federal Supplement 716:1425; LEXIS 4616.

Sparks 1972. Sparks v. Griffin. Source: Federal Reporter (2d) 460:433–36, note 1.

Staruch 1992. Staruch v. U.S. Bureau of Information. Source: EEOC Opinion.

Stephen 1989. Stephen v. PGA Sheraton Resort, Ltd. Source: Federal Reporter (2d) 873:276, 280–81.

Tran 1983. Tran v. City of Houston. Source: Fair Employment Practices Cases (BNA) 35:471.

Vartivarian 1991. Angel K. Vartivarian v. Golden Rule Insurance Company. United States District Court for the Northern District of Illinois, Eastern Division, No. 88 C 1269. Source: LEXIS 6558.

Xieng 1991. Phanna K. Xieng et al. v. Peoples National Bank of Washington. Source: Federal Reporter (2d) 821:520; Washington State Appeals Court Opinion; *Findings of Fact* WL 269877.

Xieng 1992. Phanna K. Xieng and Bathou Xieng, husband and wife v. Peoples National Bank of Washington. Source: Washington State Supreme Court opinion dated January 21 1993 (No. 59064–8).

OTHER REFERENCES

Bailey, Richard (1991). *Images of English. A cultural history of the language.* Ann Arbor: University of Michigan Press.

Baron, Dennis (1990). *The English-Only question: An official language for Americans?* New Haven: Yale University Press.

Bell, Colin, & Newby, Howard (1971). *Community studies: An introduction to the sociology of the local community.* London: Allen & Unwin. (2nd rev. ed., 1982.)

Black's (1991). *Black's law dictionary,* abridged 6th ed. St. Paul, MN: West.

Burling, Robbins (1973). *English in black and white.* New York: Holt, Rinehart & Winston.

Carranza, Michael A., & Ryan, Ellen B. (1975). Evaluative reactions of adolescents toward speakers of standard English and Mexican American accented English. *International Journal of the Sociology of Language* 8:3–102.

Chambers, John W., Jr., ed. (1983). *Black English: Educational equity and the law.* Ann Arbor, MI: Karoma.

Christian, Donna (1988). *Variation and change in geographically isolated communities: Appalachian English and Ozark English.* Tuscaloosa: University of Alabama Press.

Clark, Herbert H., & Schaefer, Edward F. (1989). Contributing to discourse. *Cognitive Science* 13:259–94.

Clark, Herbert H., & Wilkes-Gibbs, Deanna (1986). Referring as a collaborative process. *Cognition* 22:1–39.

Cormack, Mike (1993). Problems of minority language broadcasting: Gaelic in Scotland. *European Journal of Communication* 8:101–17.

Crawford, James (1992). *Hold your tongue: Bilingualism and the politics of English Only.* Reading, MA: Addison-Wesley.

Cutler, Stephen (1985). A trait-based approach to national origin discrimination. *Yale Law Journal* 94:1164–81.

Dillard, J. L. (1992). *History of American English.* London: Longman.

Eisenstein, Miriam (1983). Native reactions to non-native speech: A review of empirical research. *Studies in Second Language Acquisition* 5:160–76.

Fairclough, Norman (1989). *Language and power.* London: Longman.

Faust, David, & Ziskin, Jay (1988). The expert witness in psychology and psychiatry. *Science* 241:31–5.

Federal Register (1988). *Guidelines on discrimination because of national origin.* Vol. 45, No. 250, Part VI. Washington, DC: U.S. Equal Employment Opportunity Commission, Rules and Regulations.

Giles, Howard (1971). Ethnocentrism and the evaluation of accented speech. *British Journal of Social and Clinical Psychology* 10:187–88.

——. (1984). *The dynamics of speech accommodation.* Berlin: Mouton.

——, & Coupland, J., eds. (1991). *Contexts of accommodation: Developments in applied sociolinguistics.* Cambridge & New York: Cambridge University Press.

——, & Ryan, Ellen B. (1982). Prolegomena for developing a social psychological theory of language attitudes. In E. B. Ryan & H. Giles (eds.), *Attitudes toward language variation: Social and applied contexts,* 208–23. London: Arnold.

John, Mellie; Yates, Paulene; & DeLancy, Edward (1975). *The New Building Better English.* 4th ed. Vol. 9: *Text and grammar handbook.* Evanston, IL: Harper & Row.

Kalin, Rudolf, & Rayko, Donald S. (1978). Discrimination in evaluative judgments against foreign-accented job candidates. *Psychological Reports* 43:1203–9.

——; ——; & Love, N. (1979). The perception and evaluation of job candidates with four different ethnic accents. In Howard Giles et al. (eds.), *Social psychology and language,* 197–202. London: Pergamon.

Kress, Gunther R. (1985). *Linguistic processes in sociocultural practice.* 2d ed. Oxford & New York: Oxford University Press.

Labov, William (1969). The logic of non-standard English. *Georgetown Monographs on Language and Linguistics* 22:1–22.

Lambert, Wallace E. (1967). The social psychology of bilingualism. *Journal of Social Issues* 23:91–109.

——; Hodgson, R.; Gardner, R. C.; & Sillenbaum, S. (1960). Evaluational reactions to spoken languages. *Journal of Abnormal and Social Psychology* 60:44–51.

Matsuda, Mari J. (1991). Voice of America: Accent, antidiscrimination law, and a jurisprudence for the last reconstruction. *Yale Law Journal* 100:1329–1407.

McArthur, Tom, ed. (1992). *The Oxford companion to the English language.* Oxford & New York: Oxford University Press.

Milroy, James (1989). On the concept of prestige in sociolinguistic argumentation. *York Papers in Linguistics* 13:215–26.

Milroy, James, & Milroy, Lesley (1985). *Authority in language: Investigating language prescription and standardisation.* London: Routledge. (2nd rev. ed., 1992.)

Ragno, Nancy; Toth, Marian; & Gray, Betty (1987). *Silver Burdett English: Teacher's edition 5.* Morristown, NJ: Silver Burdett.

Raspberry, William (1990). What it means to be Black. In Paul Eschholz et al. (eds.), *Language awareness*, 5th ed., 269–72. [Originally published in the *Washington Post*, 1985.]

Rickford, John (1985). Standard and non-standard language attitudes in a creole continuum. In Nessa Wolfson & Joan Manes (eds.), *Language of inequality*, 145–60. Berlin: Mouton.

———, & Traugott, Elizabeth Closs (1985). Symbol of powerlessness and degeneracy, or symbol of solidarity and truth? Paradoxical attitudes toward pidgins and creoles. In Sidney Greenbaum (ed.), *The English language today*, 252–61. Oxford: Pergamon Press.

Roberts, Celia; Davies, Evelyn; & Jupp, Tom (1992). *Language and discrimination: A study of communication in multiethnic workplaces.* London: Longman.

Robertson, J. Forbes (1911). Pronunciation. In *Proceedings of the Indiana Association of Teachers of English*. Bloomington: Indiana University Press.

Sato, Charlene J. (1991). Sociolinguistic variation and language attitudes in Hawaii. In Jenny Cheshire (ed.), *English around the world: Sociolinguistic perspectives*, 647–63. Cambridge & New York: Cambridge University Press.

Shuy, Roger (1993). *Language crimes: The use and abuse of language evidence in the courtroom*. Oxford: Blackwell.

Strickland, Dorothy (1983). *Language for daily use: Teacher's edition, Level 3*. New York: Harcourt Brace Jovanovich.

Thakerar, Jitendra N.; Giles, Howard; & Cheshire, Jenny (1982). Psychological and linguistic parameters of speech accommodation theory. In Colin Fraser & Klaus R. Scherer (eds.), *Advances in the social psychology of language*, 205–55. Cambridge & New York: Cambridge University Press.

Thompson, John B. (1984). *Studies in the theory of ideology*. Cambridge: Polity.

U.S. Immigration and Naturalization Service (1992). *Statistical yearbook*. Washington, DC.

Verploegen, H. (1988). Pidgin in classroom stirs spirited debate by seniors. *Honolulu Star-Bulletin*, June 1, pp. A1, A8.

Warren, James (1993). English vs. English. *Chicago Tribune*, January 17, 1993. Tempo, p. 2, Zone C, Sunday Watch.

Windsor, Patricia (1993). Clague teacher's remarks show bias, black parents charge. *Ann Arbor News*, April 22, 1993, pp. C1, C3.

Wolfram, Walt, & Christian, Donna (1976). *Appalachian speech*. Arlington, VA: Center for Applied Linguistics.

Post-reading Questions / Activities

- The issue of what constitutes an impediment to job performance is vexing. If people bring a lack of what Lippi-Green calls "goodwill" to an encounter, they are more likely to find a speaker "unintelligible." How might the courts weigh employees' and employers' rights?
- Do you think that hiring, say, teachers whose speech has features of regional accents is problematic? When do you find "accent" important and when is it irrelevant?
- Interview five people about their views of what kind of language is "standard." Make sure there is some variety among them: age, gender, region, ethnicity, social class, and so on. Are their views homogeneous? What accounts for the overlaps, and what accounts for the differences?

Vocabulary

accent	L2
aspirated	LTF
code switching	matched-guise test
communicative competence	phonology, phonological
fricatives	prescriptive
intonation	SL
L1	standard
L1 interference	target language

Suggested Further Reading

Lippi-Green, Rosina. 1997. *English with an Accent: Language, Ideology, and Discrimination in the United States.* London: Routledge.

Milroy, James, and Lesley Milroy. 1985. *Authority in Language: Investigating Standard English.* 3rd ed. London and New York: Routledge.

CHAPTER 43

Orality
Another Language Ideology
Laura Polich
(2000)

Laura Polich uses the notion of language ideology—*a taken-for-granted belief about language and power relations—to challenge the dominance of orality, the notion that language is fundamentally oral. In Unit 1 we saw scholars grappling over the question of which aspect of language was central to defining it, and that only some of them focused on its oral or spoken nature. Polich argues that the anthropological and linguistic focus on spoken* language as fundamental is a kind of language ideology, *favoring what she calls* orality. *This makes sign languages odd, marked, not normal, and somehow not "real" language.*

In contrast, for quite some time in the United States, scholars and the public have recognized that sign languages are real languages. Indeed, American Sign Language is often taught at colleges throughout the United States as a foreign language, along with Spanish and Russian. Sign languages are not intuitive, inborn gestures; they are rule-governed systems that have conventions and even dialects.

Polich shows through her field experiences how pervasive the ideology of orality is in Nicaragua, with a deaf community only about twenty years old. For instance, at parties at the Deaf Association, music is played and adults—even deaf adults—are expected to dance to it while attempting to break the piñata. This shows that the pressure of social expectations developed among the hearing community are not challenged by the deaf community there. Households where children can both sign with their parents and speak are regarded as "sad" by others, because there is no talking. Since sign language is not a translation of a spoken language but rather an entirely different system of grammar and vocabulary, signing of songs does not usually yield coinciding of words from sung to signed. For the Nicaraguan national anthem, a one-to-one translation has been encouraged so that the songs end simultaneously, again showing the dominance of the oral version.

Reading Questions

- What evidence does Polich present about the taken-for-granted equivalence of language and speech?
- Why does Polich challenge the dominance of the ideology of orality, given that 99% of the world's languages are spoken?
- Why are the terms *sordo/sorda* 'deaf' preferable to the Nicaraguan deaf community, rather than the commonly used terms *sordomudo/sordomuda* 'deaf-mute' or *mudo/muda* 'mute'? How does Polich use this in her claims about a language ideology of orality?
- How do Nicaraguans look at silence?

Laura Polich, "Orality: Another Language Ideology." *Texas Linguistic Forum (Proceedings of the seventh annual Symposium About Language and Society—Austin)* 43 (2000): 189–199.

- How do deaf adults dance?
- What are some of the ways in which there is a mismatch between speaking people's and signing people's expectations?

LANGUAGE IDEOLOGIES

Language ideologies are taken-for-granted frames of reference about language that users employ as they perform social interaction, and which shape how language use is interpreted. In 1994, two prominent linguistic anthropologists, Kathryn Woolard and Bambi Schieffelin, wrote a summary article for the *Annual Review of Anthropology* on the topic of Language Ideology. In 1998, they, along with Paul Kroskrity, edited a book-length collection of articles on the subject, including an expanded and updated version of the previous summary article. In these works, the authors mention that issues as diverse as the evolution of language structures, the organization of language events, acts or styles, the interpretation of language contact and conflict, as well as the manipulation or preservation of languages are areas ripe for the the study of language or linguistic ideologies.

While Woolard and Schieffelin's omnibus survey and the later book of articles have both striven to be comprehensive, there is, however, one language ideology which has received little, if any, attention, although it is omnipresent in daily life. Orality is another language ideology, and one that deserves serious attention when taken-for-granted frames of reference regarding language are considered.

ORALITY

By orality, I refer to the presumption that, at their core, languages are oral, and as a corollary, that an oral language is more language-like, more "real" than a non-oral language. For the majority of written history, language has been identified with its physical manifestation (cf. Bloomfield, as quoted in Joseph 1990:57), and the belief that language IS speech has been widespread. Western philosophers from the time of Socrates have debated whether humans who do not have access to speech could be considered language users, and typically they concluded their ruminations in the negative (Scouten 1984).

Beginning in the middle of the [twentieth] century, however, under the influence of Noam Chomsky and colleagues, the thesis that language is better identified with its underlying rule system rather than with its physical signal came to gain adherents. It is now commonly accepted, at least in academia, that language can be manifest through multiple modalities (oral, visual, tactual) and is not restricted to the oral/aural modality. How slow has been the spread of this notion from academia to practical application can be gauged from the fact that it was only last year (1998) that the American Speech, Language and Hearing Association announced that it was changing the name of its journal from *Journal of Speech and Hearing Research (JSHR)* to *Journal of Speech, Language & Hearing Research (JSLHR)* in view of the now commonly accepted fact that language is separate from speech (ASHA 1998). When the

association began in the 1920s, and the journal was founded, the two were assumed to be synonymous. Only … forty years after the theoretical basis was laid for distinguishing speech from language [had] the bureaucratic wheels turned enough to make that distinction official in the journal's name.

Many academic writers who are quite aware that language and speech are in no way co-terminous, still operate within the orality paradigm. I am certain that Woolard and Schieffelin, for example, understand that not all languages are oral. Yet what is interesting is that within their omnibus review which includes 329 articles and books, not one refers to a non-oral language. Is this because non-oral languages are not beset by the ideological problems that Woolard and Schieffelin identify for oral languages? Probably not. The commentary and descriptions used by the authors are, however, written within an oral paradigm. Woolard and Schieffelin throughout the review equate language with speech: "…our topic is ideologies *of* language [italics theirs]…There is as much cultural variation in ideas about speech as there is in speech forms themselves" (55). Or later, in introducing studies of prescriptivism: "Notions of better or worse speech have been claimed to exist in every linguistic community…" (69). Speech and language throughout the discussion are treated as equivalent. The omnibus review is one influenced by the ideology of orality.

In the "common sense" views of language held by most laypeople, orality is a fundamental ideology. Georges Gusdorf (1965) articulates this taken-for-granted frame of reference when he clearly identifies oral language with human language, and finds any other modality to be an unacceptable attempt at an imitation:

> Nothing is more significant…than the situation of man deprived of vocal communication with others….Deaf-mutes used to be reduced to a kind of idiocy, a vegetable existence, at least until the day when someone discovered the means of re-establishing in indirect ways the communication they lack. By being given speech, they were made human beings….It would seem that gestures, attitudes, and all kinds of mimicry are only corollaries of the voice. Speaking is the principal dimension of expression. To take speech away is to make of human reality a kind of silent and absurd film. (94)

Gusdorf here illustrates bluntly an ideology that commonly influences actions, but which is rarely so explicitly or condescendingly articulated. It is certainly not surprising, given the fact that 99% of the human population uses oral languages, to find orality permeating our language interactions, but it is a bias that has consequences for those who rely upon non-oral languages. The extent and effects of this ideology really only began to be clarified when we look at the world of persons who are deaf, the main users of non-oral languages.

ORALITY IN NICARAGUA

Nicaragua is one country in which orality is a pervasive linguistic ideology, and I will draw upon examples I collected in my fieldwork there in 1997 to illustrate my point. I do not single out Nicaragua because I believe that country is unusual in its adherence to orality. I submit, rather, that Nicaragua is prototypical of many contemporary societies in respect to the scope and ubiquity of that ideology. As I did the research for my doctoral dissertation in Nicaragua (Polich 1998) I had the opportunity to collect various ethnographic examples while my mind was concentrated upon the everyday lives of deaf persons and their role in society. The force of orality is perhaps a little more obvious in Nicaragua because the deaf community there does not have a history anywhere as long as the various deaf communities in other areas, such as the United States or France. The first deaf community in Nicaragua formed only about twenty years ago.

The Importance of Speech

In Nicaragua, speaking is a socially-salient characteristic, as anyone who has worked with the deaf soon finds out. When I first began my fieldwork, sensitive to the very negative connotations that the cognates "*mudo*/mute" have in Spanish and English, I avoided both, as well as the terms "*sordomudo*/deaf-mute." The preferred term in the Deaf Association in Managua was *sordo* (deaf), the typical manner in which deaf people in Nicaragua self-identify.[1] But this delicacy of language was not very useful when dealing with the general public. On more than one occasion, I arrived at an approximate location[2] where I had been told a deaf person lived only to find my query denied: *Por acaso, no conoce Ud. la casa donde vive una mujer sorda? No, señora, por aquí no vive ninguna sorda* (By any chance, do you not know where the deaf woman lives? No, ma'am, nobody deaf lives around here). Perplexed, I would recheck the directions, retrace my steps, only to find that I was more or less in the right location. I asked other people. They, too, denied any *personas sordas*. Finally, someone noticing that I was foreign, would try to interpret my question more meaningfully: "Well, there *is* the mute woman (*la mudita*) who lives in that house," pointing across the street. And, in time, I swallowed my political correctness, and learned that if *sordo/sorda* brought a negative reply, to repeat the question using *sordomudo/sordomuda*, or even *mudo/muda*. Or to attach an explanation when using *sordo/sorda*:...*donde vive una sorda, Ud. sabe, una persona que no habla* (...where a deaf woman lives, you know, a person who doesn't talk). My success rate at locating deaf people improved immensely.

How unintelligible speech or poor quality speech is related to hearing loss was not in the past, and probably is still not, clear to many laypeople. The mother of a daughter with a profound hearing loss told me that she grew up in an area where a man known as *El Mudo* (the Mute) sold bread door-to-door. Like all the ambulant vendors of Nicaragua, he had his chant that he would call out from the street, and prospective clients would come to their doors if they wanted to buy. *El Mudo's* characteristic mispronunciation of "bread" and whatever else he sold was well known to the persons on his route. "I never thought of him as deaf and no one else ever mentioned such a thing to me either," this mother told me. "I always just thought he didn't know how to talk. That is what we all commented on. It is only now that I have my own daughter that I recognize the vocal characteristics that go along with deafness. He was certainly deaf, but I heard him go by every day for fifteen years and it never occurred to me."

On one occasion, I accompanied three adult deaf persons in Tipitapa to the homes of deaf children for the express purpose of inviting the children and their parents to an activity at the home of one of the deaf leaders in the town. We had very specific addresses, and my deaf companions were excellent guides. Arriving in the general vicinity, I was the designated speaker: *Andamos buscando la casa de un niño sordomudo que vive por aquí. Nos puede indicar la casa?* (We're looking for the house of a deaf child who lives around here. Can you show us which house it is?) A man in his 30s was sitting on the porch, and he shook his head: *No, por aquí no vive ningún sordomudo* (No, there is no deaf-mute who lives around here). We re-consulted our directions, but again, we were where we were supposed to be. *La maestra de la escuela nos ha dicho que por aquí vive un niño que no oye bien y no habla claramente. No lo conoce?* (The teacher at school told us that there was a boy who lived around here who doesn't hear well and doesn't speak clearly. Don't you know him?) *Ahhhh! Sí, sí, sí. Están hablando de mí hijo. Es cierto que era sordomudo, pero ya se superó. Ya habla.* (Ohhh. Yes, yes, yes. You're talking about my son. It's true that he used to be a deaf-mute, but he has overcome that. He talks now.)

The father invited us in. The eight-year-old boy was out playing, and the father sent a sibling to fetch him. When he arrived, the father urged him to talk to me to show off his precious speech, which evidently saved him from the category of "deaf-mute." The boy was barely intelligible, and from the father's description, had an oral vocabulary of perhaps thirty words, mostly the names of relatives and food items and clothing. He lipread a similar amount. The family had participated periodically in an oral language development program sponsored by a well-known not-for-profit institution, but the distance and transportation costs made it difficult to keep up with the program, and the father noted that although the son had at least attained speech, he did not seem to be improving very much now. While I was talking with the father, my companions naturally began a conversation with the boy in Nicaraguan Sign Language [NSL]. His facility with that language, which he was learning at the special education school, was in advance of his oral skills, and it was evident even to a non-signer, such as his father. Watching the four signers laugh at each others' jokes, and observing how his son was animatedly telling the adults about his family and where he played, the father turned to me: *Y esas mímicas—solo los mudos pueden aprender comunicarse así?* (And those gestures—can only mutes learn to communicate like that?) No, I told him, hearing people can learn the language too.

I've learned some. I told him what his son was talking about, and some of the adults' replies. He responded:

> *Me gustaría aprender así. Casí no tenemos manera de comunicarnos con el niño. Es bien difícil. Antes cuando estaba más chiquito, era mejor, pero ya en cuanto que va creciendo, se dificulta la situación.* (I would like to learn that. We almost have no way to communicate with the boy. It is hard. Before when he was small, it was better, but now as he grows bigger, the situation gets more and more difficult.)

These examples illustrate the importance that is given to talking in Nicaragua. The characteristic that typical Nicaraguans notice is not how well one hears, but how well one speaks. The deaf boy's father's remarks are particularly interesting in that he was very proud that his son had a small, but oral, vocabulary. This amount of speech, he hoped, placed the child in a different category (*ya se superó* "he has overcome that") even though communication in the home was basically non-functional. Within the ideology of orality, some speech, any speech, is better than no speech.

The Importance of Sound

Anyone who has spent much time in Nicaragua, a tropical country with little air-conditioning, knows that large portions of life are lived either outdoors, or with all the windows open. This means being bathed in sound from dawn to dusk, and often longer. Radios blare loudly, televisions are played non-stop, ambulant vendors hawk every imaginable item in voices meant to penetrate the depths of any house. Traffic noise is mixed with the jingling bells of the ice-cream vendors, at the same time that evangelicals sing hymns amplified through speakers five feet high, and trucks with huge speakers cruise slowly up and down the streets announcing funerals, vegetable sales, or when the water is expected to be turned off for repairs. Sound, constant sound, is integral to Nicaraguan life. And when Nicaraguans imagine life without sound, as they imagine life must be for the deaf, they are jarred by the deprivation they believe it represents.

I went one evening to the house of a deaf secretary, Fatima Maria, one of the few persons truly bilingual in Nicaraguan Sign Language and in Spanish. This woman lived with her mother and two daughters, whom she supported on her single salary. My conversations at her home were always oral in order to include her mother, who had never learned to sign. That evening I mentioned that I had visited a deaf family who lived very close—both parents were profoundly deaf, and only signed, and they had two hearing children, one five and one two years old. The five-year-old daughter was, as many children her age brought up in such a home, fluent in speech and fluent in signing. Fatima Maria's mother, a woman probably seventy years old, turned to me and said:

> *¡Ah, que lástima me da ese caso! He visto la niña con su mamá cuando van para hacer compras. La niña tiene que hablar porque ¡la mamá no habla nada! Pero cuando pienso en que triste tiene que ser esa casa, con tanto silencio, me da ganas de llorar. Y la niña, cierto que le va a afectar mentalmente, ¡viviendo en un ambiente tan triste!* (Oh, how sad that case is! I have seen that child with her mother when they go out shopping. She has to talk, because her mother doesn't say a word. But when I think of how sad it must be in that house, with so much silence, it just makes me want to cry. And it is probably going to affect the child mentally, living in such a sad atmosphere!)

I honestly didn't know what to say to this mother who had lived in the closest of proximity to a deaf person and her friends for the past 48 years, and yet remained convinced that the lack of speech meant the lack of language. The house in which the little girl was growing up was in no way *triste* (sad), but was alive with conversation, none of it oral.

Orality at the Deaf Association

Orality has a deep impact upon behavior at the Deaf Association in Managua also. In other parts of the world, in more established deaf communities where orality is perhaps less pervasive, one notices that many social customs have been adapted to visual, as opposed to oral, needs. In mainstream American society, it is common to excuse oneself verbally when passing in front of another person. It is just as important to do the same in mainstream Nicaragua. When one must pass in front of persons engaged in an oral conversation, one mumbles "*con permiso*" (excuse me) and one of the speakers waves one on through usually without interrupting the conversation.

Now, signed conversations are easier to carry out if the two participants stand farther apart than is typical for two oral conversational participants (Siple 1994). It is not uncommon for two signers to stand on opposite sides of a hallway and converse. When a third party needs to pass the signers, etiquette among users of American Sign Language, for example, calls for simply walking swiftly "through the conversation" without distracting the signers to excuse oneself, or at the most, signing "excuse me" as one walks through the conversation as quickly as possible. This provides the least amount of disruption, and a person who hesitates before walking through such a conversation, forcing the participants to stop and give eye contact before the intruder signs "excuse me" and walks through, is considered gauche. But in the Deaf Association in Managua, great emphasis is placed upon not walking in front of any person, without first gaining eye contact, signing "excuse me,"[3] and waiting for the person in front of whom one needs to walk to give permission, usually with a wave of the hand. This interrupts completely any signed conversation to which it is applied.

What is happening here is that the social *mores* of the mainstream hearing society, based upon usages adapted to oral communication, are being used in the Deaf Association without adaptation, where adaptation would make them more functional. Thus, even the Deaf Association is influenced by the ideology of orality which pervades Nicaraguan society.

Music is another component of the background of sound and orality that is typical in Nicaragua. No celebration is complete without music and dancing. And this includes celebrations at the Deaf Association, where many, if not most, of the participants, do not hear the music at all. All of the parties for special occasions, from the presentation of the Nicaraguan Sign Language Dictionary, to the Mother's Day celebration, to birthday parties, to *las Fiestas Patrias* (Independence Day celebration) that I witnessed at the Deaf Association involved music. The deaf danced just as much as the hearing, the only difference being that the profoundly deaf would have to watch someone with full or partial hearing to know when the music began or when it stopped.

In Nicaragua, piñatas are not just for children. Adult parties may also include a piñata, but the role of the piñata is very different. Children spend their time attempting to break the piñata, but for adults, especially adult women, the turn at being blindfolded is an opportunity to show off one's dancing ability. Typically, an adult woman will be blindfolded, given a stick, turned around to disorient her, and the music will be turned on. She will make one quick swipe with the stick, then dance in place to the music for a few minutes, take another swipe, dance again, until her turn is up. I never saw an adult woman seriously attempt to break a piñata. My point here, is that at parties at the Deaf Association, the piñata is considered obligatory, as is the dancing to the music during the various turns. This means that adults who cannot hear the music, willingly take their turn to be blindfolded, which effectively cuts off any visual cues about the music (which they might get from watching a hearing person move in rhythm to the music, etc.) and dance in place for the usual five or so minutes, until they are tapped on the shoulder to indicate that their turn is up. This dancing display takes place within a paradigm of aurally-based social interaction, and is related to the pervasive paradigm of orality.

Linguistic issues do provide sources of conflict and debate among the present Nicaraguan deaf community, even though Nicaraguan Sign Language is less than twenty years old. Exactly what constitutes the sign language that the deaf community in Nicaragua will use is not settled. All of the issues of language contact, linguistic purism, and prescriptivism are being confronted now by the community. What should be considered a dialectal variation versus what should be treated as a non-standard (and thus treated as "wrong") sign are topics that surface every day. Access to the sign language for most deaf children is through schooling, but the linguistic models in the schools are teachers who are not fluent, in fact, usually not even competent, signers. Most teachers believe that Nicaraguan Sign Language is deficient because it does not mark nouns for gender or verbs for person. In the past seven years in which signing has become more widespread in the Special Education schools, the teachers have agitated for more incorporation of Spanish grammar into the sign language. In some instances, these requests are ignored, but in others, the deaf community assents.

The acquiescence in this regard is illustrated in the standardization of the signed version of the Nicaraguan National Anthem which I witnessed in 1997. The Nicaraguan National Anthem is a poem set to music, as are most anthems. The arrangement of the words is based upon oral aesthetic principles, and much of its drama is provided by the imposing martial music that accompanies the lyrics. The music, naturally, is not available to most deaf Nicaraguans, so the emotional effect for deaf persons of participating in the performance of the National Anthem would depend upon interpretation of the poetic effect of the lyrics. This can be done in Nicaraguan Sign Language, but it requires a bit of study since the meaning of the metaphors and allusions is not clear from a quick read-through. At a Mother's Day celebration in San Marcos I did observe the National Anthem signed as a visual poetic performance by a young man while a scratchy recording of the music (to which he was oblivious) played in the background.

The difficulty is that when signed this way, the signing does not coincide with the words which any hearing people are supposed to be singing or with the music to which the words are supposed to fit. This means that at any official ceremony the signing and the singing would not be coordinated. The decision, therefore, was evidently made by the sign language teachers at the Deaf Association in Managua (who are, themselves, deaf) to decree that the National Anthem would henceforth be signed in what is essentially "Sign-Supported Spanish" or signs in Spanish word order with an attempt made to equate the signs and the words on a one-to-one basis.[4] Articles (e.g., *de, a*) which do not exist in Nicaraguan Sign Language are added by fingerspelling. Short Spanish words, which would be incorporated into facial grammar if included at all in the signing, are spelled out. Similes, metaphors, or idioms are translated literally rather than signed for their conceptual meaning (e.g., *la voz del cañón*, signed as "the voice of the cannon," instead of "warfare"). The revised signed version mirrors perfectly the Spanish version.

The problem is that the resulting performance has little, if any, meaning to someone who cannot understand the Spanish version, and for Spanish at that level of difficulty (poetry) that means the majority, if not all, of the deaf community. The "singing"/signing of the National Anthem at ceremonies, then, becomes a rote performance in which there is an arbitrary sequence of signs, which is unintelligible to anyone relying only upon the signing, and understandable only to someone who can go from the signs back to the meaning of the original Spanish. This privileges the oral language over the non-oral language to the point of obliterating any meaning for the non-oral performance. And, in this case, it was a decision made by the users of the non-oral language. The orally-sung anthem is here interpreted as more "real" than a signed translation of the poem, so that it is therefore more important to synchronize one's hands to units of the oral text than to produce a linguistically comprehensible message.

In the same vein, the publication of the Nicaraguan Sign Language dictionary in 1997 through funding by the Swedish Deaf Association was an action generally interpreted as a reification of Nicaraguan Sign Language, and a statement by the Deaf Association that Nicaraguan Sign Language was just as much a true language as any other sign language, and just as deserving of respect. But contradictions remain. The dictionary, for instance, does not include the sign for *gallo pinto* (and there is one), a mixture of rice and red beans which the majority of Nicaraguans eat at least once, if not three times a day, but it does include the signs for *ostrich* (178) and *kangaroo* (26), words I never heard occur spontaneously in my ten months of fieldwork in Nicaragua, but which are included in other "real" dictionaries, which the editors of the Nicaraguan Sign Language Dictionary evidently consulted as models.

Thus, even though the deaf in Nicaragua through the formation and activities of the Deaf Association are asserting an alternate social agency, one which allows them to be societal members through the use of a non-oral language, these members are still immersed in an oral society and in a linguistic ideology of orality. They are willing, at times, to compromise their historically-young and highly-prized non-oral language for the trade-off of participation in typical societal ceremonies. Their assertion of an alternate non-oral agency thus, is only in its preliminary stages, and is, at this point, still timid.

WHY MENTION THE IDEOLOGY OF ORALITY?

Since 99% of human languages appear to be oral languages, it may seem trivial and nit-picking to point out that orality is another language ideology. The parallel I would make is that for many years any discomfort with the sexist ideology inherent in the generic use of masculine pronouns was also considered trivial and nit-picking (Cameron 1990). But studies such as those of Inge Broverman (1970, as cited in Minnich 1989:278) ultimately pointed out that the use of pronouns in this way (along with other linguistic markers of the ideology of sexism) was not neutral or without consequence, but resulted in an identification of the normal "man" with normal "human." Thus:

> ...[this left] a woman with the option of being a "normal" woman and therefore an "abnormal" human, or a "normal" human and therefore an "abnormal" woman. The real thing is the male (white, heterosexual, usually Euro-American). The rest of us are deviants from the norm, are kinds of humans to their assumed central humanity, and are, therefore, at best subtopics of knowledge. When the part defines itself as the whole, the rest of us...have to fight to be seen as the same as...[those of] the defining center, in order to be considered "real." (Minnich 1989:278)

Orality and the Deaf

In a speaking world, a person who is deaf is always at a distinct disadvantage. Even those who attain very competent oral language retain a distinctive "deaf" voice quality (Tucker 1995; Kisor 1990). In a study of intelligibility, Sims, Gottermeier, and Walter (1980) found that only 28% of the profoundly hearing-impaired (i.e., deaf) students they studied attained a "functional" speaking ability. Native mastery would imply not only a functional speaking ability in all situations, but also a speaking voice that did not call attention to itself, as well as mastery in the use and understanding of all of the supraseg-

mentals (most of which are neither auditorally nor visually available to deaf persons). Thus, speech is a medium which is nearly impossible for deaf persons to master to a native ("does-not-call-attention-to-itself") level, and deaf persons in a speaking world always function at a disadvantage to hearing people who *do* have access to full mastery of oral language, and who are the ones judging what level of competence a particular deaf person has reached or when.

And their non-mastery is a factor used against persons who are deaf. In a study of the relationship between intelligibility and attributed characteristics, normally-hearing subjects rated speakers with less-intelligible voices as less intelligent and less socially competent (Blood, Blood, and Danhauer 1978).

Thus, when orality reigns as the presumed, unquestioned language ideology, persons who are deaf find that speech is identified with human language, and that speaking is identified with being human (cf. Gusdorf, 1965), and this leaves them with only paltry choices. If they choose oral language, they are measured and found wanting in what is considered a quintessentially human characteristic. They are then not-quite-full humans. But if they embrace non-oral language (in which they *do* have the potential to attain native fluency), they are still relegated to being "abnormal" humans because human language is identified with oral language.

As with most language ideologies, this choice is, basically, one with power implications, and it impacts mainly persons who are deaf. As Bourdieu has pointed out (1991), linguistic competence is not a matter of simply producing possible utterances. "The competence adequate to produce sentences that are likely to be understood may be quite inadequate to produce sentences that are likely to be *listened to*..." (55) [emphasis in original]. Life within the ideology of orality is not a trivial matter for persons who are deaf. It is for this reason that I take this opportunity to point out...the presence of orality as another language ideology. It is transparent to many, probably no more noticeable than the air that humans breathe, but for a certain segment of the population—those who rely upon non-oral languages—orality is an ideology with ominous implications.

Notes

1. The sign they used is also cognate to the sign in American Sign Language: an index finger pointing first to the mouth and then to the ear.

2. There is no general system of street addresses in Nicaragua. Addresses consist of the naming of a landmark, and then the approximate distance from the landmark. They are always ambiguous. One arrives in the general area and then asks passers-by or residents to point out specific houses. For example, my address in Nicaragua was "from the Sinsa Hardware store, one and one-half blocks to the east." If one had wanted to find me, it would have been necessary to follow those directions and then ask passers-by or residents "Do you know which is the house in which the *gringa* (North-American) lives?"

3. A flat B-hand rubbed in a circular motion on the back of the opposite hand. This is not an ASL cognate.

4. Note also that, under most circumstances, it will only be persons who have access to both codes who will notice the discrepancy. The deaf never begin to sign the anthem until they receive a signal that a musical recording has begun to play or they see hearing people's mouths move. Most hearing persons would only note a non-synchrony if the signing continued after the music had stopped. Thus, only a very small number of persons with some competence in both languages are able to judge whether there is synchonization of the Spanish words with NSL signs or not. Those who would notice are mainly hearing teachers of the deaf, particularly those who want NSL to mirror Spanish. But the argument for the primacy of the oral words evidently convinced the deaf leaders, for it was they who formulated and decreed the synchronization.

References

Asociación Nacional de Sordos de Nicaragua (ANSNIC). 1997. *Diccionario del Idioma de Señas de Nicaragua.* Managua: Copy Fast, S.A.

ASHA Leader. 1998. Journal to Change Name. July 28:2.

Blood, G., I. Blood, and J. Danhauer. 1978. Listener's impressions of normal-hearing and hearing-impaired children. *Journal of Communication Disorders* 11:513–518.

Bourdieu, Pierre. 1991. *Language and Symbolic Power.* Cambridge: Polity Press.

Cameron, Deborah. 1990. Demythologizing sociolinguistics: Why language does not reflect society. In *Ideologies of Language,* J. Joseph and T. Taylor (eds.). London: Routledge. 79–93.

Gusdorf, G. 1965. *Speaking (La Parole).* Chicago: Northwestern University Press.

Joseph, J. 1990. Ideologizing Saussure: Bloomfield's and Chomsky's readings of the *Cours de Linguistique Générale.* In *Ideologies of Language,* J. Joseph and T. Taylor (eds.). London: Routledge. 51–78.

Kisor, H. 1990. *What's That Pig Outdoors?: A Memoir of Deafness.* New York: Hill & Wang.

Minnich, E. 1989. From the circle of the elite to the world of the whole: Education, equality, and excellence. In *Educating the Majority: Women Challenge Tradition in Higher Education,* C. Pearson, D. Shavlik, and J. Touchton (eds.). New York: Macmillan Publishing Company. 277–293.

Polich, Laura. 1998. Social agency and deaf communities: A Nicaraguan case study. Ph.D. Dissertation, The University of Texas at Austin.

Schieffelin, Bambi, Kathryn Woolard, and Paul Kroskrity. 1998. *Language Ideologies: Practice and Theory.* New York: Oxford University Press.

Scouten, E. 1984. *Turning Points in the Education of Deaf People.* Danville, IL: The Interstate Printers and Publishers, Inc.

Sims, D., L. Gottermeier, and G. Walter. 1980. Factors contributing to the development of intelligible speech among prelingually deaf persons. *American Annals of the Deaf* 125:374–381.

Siple, L. 1994. Cultural patterns of deaf people. *International Journal of Intercultural Relations* 18:345–367.

Tucker, B. 1995. *The Feel of Silence.* Philadelphia: Temple University Press.

Woolard, Kathryn, and Bambi Schieffelin. 1994. Language ideology. *Annual Review of Anthropology* 23:55–82.

Post-reading Questions / Activities

- How is the essence of language different if we no longer regard speech as the essential part of it? What *does* Polich regard as the essential ingredient of language?
- Compare Polich's argument with Hockett's design features (Chapter 2). How would the design features differ if what he was describing was sign language?
- Look in newspapers for the ways sign language is spoken of in the popular media. Do you observe the tendencies that Polich points out?

Vocabulary

ASL	orality
cognate	prescriptivism
dialectal	suprasegmentals
NSL	

Suggested Furthert Reading

Klima, Edward S., and Ursula Bellugi. 1979. *The Signs of Language.* Cambridge, MA: Harvard University Press.

Meier, Richard P., Kearsy Cormier, and David Quinto-Pozos, eds., with the assistance of Adrianne Cheek, Heather Knapp, and Christian Rathmann. 2002. *Modality and Structure in Signed and Spoken Languages.* Cambridge and New York: Cambridge University Press.

Monaghan, Leila Frances. 2007. *Many Ways to Be Deaf: International Variation in Deaf Communities.* Washington, DC: Gallaudet University Press.

CHAPTER 44

Let Your Words Be Few
Speaking and Silence in Quaker Ideology

Richard Bauman
(1983)

We often think of culture as belonging more or less to a country: "Chinese culture," "Italian culture," "Mexican culture," even though we all know that countries contain many subgroups, each with their own ways of acting and valuing. Sometimes people can deliberately, intentionally, set themselves apart from a group within which they otherwise share many traits. The Quakers in seventeenth-century England did just that, and language played a central role in their self-conscious separateness.

Quakers refused many of the social niceties that are uttered simply to improve relationships. Like most European languages, originally English had a respectful pronoun, you/ye, and an informal pronoun, thou/thee. The Quakers despised social hierarchy, such as that expressed by having two second-person pronouns. Thus they rejected the formal, second-person pronoun, you, in favor of the familiar and more equal, thou. To differentiate themselves from the unpopular Quakers, mainstream society adopted the pronoun that Quakers rejected, you. (For the story of how the formal outlived the informal, see Brown and Gilman 1960.)

Also, Quakers, as Richard Bauman shows here, did not feel any obligation to speak at all. Silence was perfectly acceptable in a variety of contexts, including worship services ("meeting").

Regarding language as ideally a vehicle for expressing true, God-given insights, and only for this (in contrast to "carnal speaking"), Quakers regarded talk as something created for the purpose of expressing God's truths. (This idea is shared by others, including St. Augustine.) Anything said for the purpose of flattering other people, or just for social reasons, was regarded as a distortion of the real purpose of language. Hence, only when these truths needed expression should a person speak. At all other times, silence was reasonable and admirable.

Here we can see an explicit ideology of silence and speech, at odds with the broader cultural ideology held by others in the society.

Reading Questions

- What is "carnal speaking"?
- What are the reasons the Quakers advocated silence? Was there a place for speaking at all? Who has a right to speak?
- What is "Truth" for early Quakers? How is it transmitted?
- What is "plain speech"? How did Quakers regard life in society, and how is this connected to their view of speech?
- Why does Bauman consider speaking and silence to be "key symbols"?

———————————————————

For the seventeenth-century Quakers, in common with all Christians, the crucifixion was a key symbolic frame of

Richard Bauman, "Let Your Words Be Few: Speaking and Silence in Quaker Ideology." From *Let Your Words Be Few: Symbolism of Speaking and Silence among Seventeenth-Century Quakers.* Cambridge: Cambridge University Press, 1983, pp. 20-31.

reference, a metaphorical model that organized and served as a standard for both the interpretation of history and the direction of human action. But the crucifixion, as the central symbol of Christianity, has been saturated throughout its history with a multitude of significances, any of which may be selected out and highlighted as semantically and operationally central by a given Christian sect or denomination and used as a base from which to generate further active meanings. Two elements of the crucifixion symbol that served the early Quakers in this way were the doctrine of salvation through suffering—*No Cross, No Crown* as Penn stated it in his famous work (1865)—and the related symbolic opposition between the flesh and the spirit.

As Barbour has pointed out (1964:144), the Quaker contrast between the flesh and the spirit did not carry with it the otherworldly ascetic's extreme renunciation of the former, of man's "natural," earthly existence (cf. Weber 1958: 193–194n); nor, as we shall see, did Quaker belief and practice rest on a simple dualistic contrast between the two. It is clear, however, that the early Quakers considered the perfection of the spirit to be the chief end of human existence and the life of the flesh, if not subordinated to this spiritual mission, to be dangerous and corrupting. The proper relation between the two was implicit in the metaphor of crucifixion: As Christ's sacrificial suffering on the cross made possible mankind's spiritual redemption, so the taking up of the cross by every person—the sacrifice of the earthly will—was the means of attaining spiritual salvation for each individual Christian. "If…ye quench the spirit, and join to the flesh, and be servants of it," wrote George Fox, "then ye are judged and tormented by the spirit; but if ye join to the spirit and serve God in it, ye have liberty and victory over the flesh and its works. Therefore keep in the daily cross, the power of God, by which ye may witness all that to be crucified which is contrary to the will of God, and which shall not come into his kingdom" (1952:18). The Quakers saw themselves as having been "brought forth in the cross; in a contradiction to the ways, worships, fashions, and customs of this world…that so no flesh might glory before God" (Penn [1694]:42).

For the early Quakers, speaking was basically a faculty of the natural man, of the flesh. Fox experienced early in his life the realization that "the people of the world," those who were joined to the flesh and servants of it, "have mouths full of deceit and changeable words" (1952:2).

It is not that languages or speaking were seen as inherently evil. Mankind's earthly existence might be difficult, a time of testing and suffering that must be borne on the way to everlasting salvation, but while on earth one did have to live in society and communicate about earthly matters with others, and "natural" speaking was the legitimate means of doing so: "Natural languages…may be serviceable for natural uses, natural transactions in civil affairs betwixt nation and nation, man and man" (Howgill 1676:491). Again, it is not that speaking could not be turned to the service of spiritual salvation, for…the early Quakers were known as irrepressible talkers in the service of their religion, and preaching and praying were essential elements of their religious practice. Rather, speaking in the service of the spirit had to derive in a special way from a proper spiritual source, and "carnal talk" (Fox 1952:12), talk that did not stem from that spiritual source, was inadequate to comprehend spiritual truth, the service of which was the most important business of man

on earth. More than that, carnal talk was dangerous; even as a youth, Fox records, he "was afraid of all carnal talk and talkers, for I could see nothing but corruptions, and the life lay under the burden of corruptions" (1952:12). It is in this context that we must interpret Farnsworth's injunctions that "fleshly speaking is an unprofitable action, and is altogether useless in point of salvation and worship of God" (1663:14), and Howgill's further observation that "although there may be languages, and each have an interpretation and a signification, they are all short to declare the life, the immeasurable being of eternal life" (1676:134). At the foundation of these principles was the powerfully resonant awareness that natural languages came into being at Babel and that only by regaining the "state in which Adam was before he fell" could one comprehend the eternal and "divine Word of wisdom" (Fox 1952:27).

If carnal speaking, as a faculty of the natural man, is inadequate for the attainment of the desired spiritual condition, which are the proper behavioral means by which this condition may be attained? For the Quakers, one of the most fundamental means was *silence*. Silence was very close to the center of seventeenth-century Quaker doctrine and practice, and much of our effort in this work will be devoted to the exploration of its complex range of meanings and implications for action. For now, however, we must begin with the meaning of silence in its most immediate and open sense, as the refraining from outward speaking: "Let all flesh be silent before the Lord, amongst you; cease from a multitude of words…cease from those discourses that draw the mind from an inward, deep sense of the invisible, immutable power of the Lord God Almighty" (Marshall 1844:128). The further dimensions of Marshall's injunction will emerge in the course of our further explication of Quaker belief and practice, but this much at least should be clear: Silence demands a limitation on speaking, though not necessarily a full rejection of it.

But the principle of silence extended far beyond the curtailment of speaking in a literal sense. Outward speaking, as "carnal" activity, became a type case for all fleshly activity, for as some of our earlier quotations from Fox make clear, an excessive reliance on carnal speaking was one of the principal symptoms for the early Quakers of all that was corrupt in the world around them. Accordingly, silence, as the cessation of outward speaking, became a metaphor for the suppression of all joining to the flesh: "Seeing all our joys, pleasures, profits, or other things delightful to the flesh, to be but vanity and vexation, we become silent thereunto, not answering to obey the lusts of the carnal mind" (Britten 1660:6). Insofar as natural, fleshly activity is activity done in one's own will, it is antithetical to the suppression of the earthly self and subjection to God's will that are necessary to the attainment of a proper spiritual state.

Silence, in its broader sense, demands the suppression of self and of self-will. Barclay makes this clear in his *Apology*: "As there can be nothing more opposite to the natural will and wisdom of man than this silent waiting upon God, so neither can it be obtained, nor rightly comprehended by man, but as he layeth down his own wisdom and will, so as to be content to be thoroughly subject to God" (1831, 2:353). Silence as self-sacrifice in a most immediate sense, the sacrifice of self-will through suppression of the earthly self, was one means of reenacting the crucifixion, of "taking up the cross," and thus of attaining the proper state of spiritual grace.

With the salvation of one's soul dependent, at least in part, on silence, and speaking susceptible to fleshly corruption, it is not surprising that the early Quakers, notwithstanding their recognition of the necessity of social speaking during man's sojourn on earth, manifested, like many of their contemporaries (Fraser 1977:31), a pronounced distrust of speaking and a concern to keep it to a minimum. Time and again, throughout the early period of Quakerism, we encounter injunctions such as those of William Dewsbury—"All take heed of many words, at all times let them be few" (1689:175–176)—or Edward Burrough—"It's better to speak little, than to utter multitude of vain words" (1660:11–12). The implications and consequences of this moral requirement to "let your words be few" (Ecclesiastes 5:2) ramify throughout the communicative system of Quakerism, and its importance as a principle and concern cannot be overstressed.

For one thing, the proliferation of words carried with it the danger of distracting one from the spirit through too great an engagement in worldly affairs. As early as 1652, Farnsworth cautioned that it would "draw your minds out above the cross, to live in words" (in Barclay 1841:355). William Bayly gave fuller voice to the same concern in 1664, adding a caution against the temptations of asserting self-will in speaking by loudness, forwardness, or hastiness of speech, and identifying the devil as the source of all idle words and willful speaking:

> Take heed of discourse among yourselves which are unnecessary; for the enemy hath a secret end to effect among such things, to draw out your minds from the living sense of the precious, tender seed of God in you....So my dear friends, be very careful, and let your words be few....And take heed of loudness, forwardness, or hastiness of speech in all your discourse about the things of this world. (1830:288)

Warnings such as these were repeated throughout the period (see, e.g., Marshall 1844:57), often grounded in the biblical text from Matthew 12:36: "But I say unto you, that every idle word that men shall speak, they shall give account thereof in the day of judgment." Idle words, to be more specific, are "words out of their service and place,...out of the truth," according to Fox (1657:9); "own words," words "not in the life," according to William Smith (1663:15, 18).

Singled out for special condemnation, as we might expect in a radical puritan movement, was talk for its own sake, for the carnal pleasure it afforded. All forms of speech play and verbal art were to be rejected as the idlest of idle and corrupt speaking, all "wicked singing, and idle jesting, and foolish laughter" (Symonds 1656:4), all "foolish jesting, and tales and stories" (Parnel 1675:37; see also Taylor 1661:7). Appropriate, unadorned, minimal speech was called, in the idiom

of the period, "plain speech": "Plainness of speech all dwell in...and few words" (Camm and Audland 1689:286). The Quaker plain speech was an instance of the tendency on the part of many religious movements to adopt a cultural style "dominated by the cultural idiom of indigence," as Turner has observed (1974:267). "Plain speech" subsequently came to designate primarily those Quaker speech conventions that were most visible and distinctive vis-à-vis the speaking of others, such as their pronominal usage and names for the days of the week and the months of the year..., but the original impulse extended across all Quaker speaking, creating a morally defined speech style for the Friends. This speech style was appropriately accompanied by a characteristic demeanor: "Our words were few and savoury...our countenances grave, and deportment weighty" (Marshall 1844:39; cf. Bayly 1830:212; Ellwood 1906:15, 40, 91).

Silence, for the Quakers, was not an end in itself, but a means to the attainment of the defining spiritual experience of early Quakerism, the direct personal experience of the spirit of God within oneself. Birthright membership in the Society of Friends was adopted in 1737, but up to that point membership in the Quaker fellowship had to be achieved, and this could be done only by undergoing a particular kind of religious experience.

The doctrine of the indwelling spirit of God in everyone was distinctive to the Quakers among the religious sects and denominations of the period. The most common metaphor employed by the Quakers for this indwelling spirit of God was—and has remained—the Inward Light.

Writing in 1658, Edward Burrough, one of the most effective of the early Quaker tract writers at systematizing Quaker doctrine for public presentation, outlined the source, nature, and worship of the Inward Light in particularly clear terms in his introductory "Epistle to the Reader" of Fox's *Great Mystery of the Great Whore Unfolded* (Fox 1831, vol. 3). "God," Burrough tells us, "had given to us, every one of us in particular, a light from himself shining in our hearts and consciences; which light, Christ his son, the saviour of the world, had lighted every man withal." The primitive church lived in the knowledge and experience of that Light, but the subsequent history of religion, in the Quaker view, was one of centuries of corruption and decline, in which the Light was obscured by the idolatry, superstition, and formalism of the Catholic church.

In their own day, however, God had brought the Quakers forth "to know and understand, and see perfectly" that his Light was to be found shining within them,

> and by it, in us, we came to know good from evil, right from wrong, and whatsoever is of God, and according to him, from what is of the devil, and what was contrary to God in motion, word, and works. And this light gave us to discern between truth and error, between every false and right way, and it perfectly discovered to us the true state of all things. (Burrough 1658:12)

The Light metaphor, drawing on the light imagery of the New Testament—Christ, the Word, as "the true Light, which lighteth every man that cometh into the world" (John 1:9)—and perhaps colored also by hermetic philosophy, conveys a sense of God's luster and brilliance and of his spirit as a beacon, but it says little of the substance of his message to man or how it is *communicated*. For this, the Quakers resorted to a second metaphor, shifting from the visual to the verbal, the spirit of God within as the *voice* of God, God the *speaker*: "the small still voice, moving in man Godwards" (Marshall 1844:89). Fox frequently referred to God as speaker: "God is become the speaker again, that was the first speaker in Paradise, God hath spoken to us by his Son. Here do people come to hear his voice from Heaven" (see Fox 1972:8–9; Graves 1972:212). Indeed, Barclay, in his *Apology*, the major systematic exposition of Quaker belief and practice during our period, identifies God the speaker as the very object of Quaker faith: "The object of this faith is the promise, word, or testimony of God, speaking in the mind. Hence it hath been generally affirmed, that the object of faith is…God speaking" (1831, 2:34).

To say that the voice of God within is a "still" one is to underscore the need for man to be in a state of spiritual silence in order to hear it. It is a voice that "speaks to our spiritual, and not our bodily ear" (Barclay 1831, 2:36). Although a direct personal communion with God speaking within was the core religious experience of early Quakerism, the experience that made one a Quaker, the religious duties of the early Quakers were far from limited to a silent waiting upon this small still voice. Again, although outward speaking in one's own will about worldly matters was distrusted at best and dangerous at worst, there remained a central and vital place for properly motivated *religious* speaking, both for spiritual edification among Friends and for advancing God's cause in the world. Indeed,…the frequently expressed caution to Friends to "let your words be few" in worldly matters did not hold in the same way for religious talk.

Here again, the voice of God the speaker was the measure of appropriateness and power, for God spoke not only *within* the Quakers, but *through* them. Taking up in their own day an apostolic mission, they accepted Jesus' charge to his first apostles, including his injunction that "it is not ye that speak, but the spirit of your father which speaketh in you" (Matthew 10:20).

Richard Farnsworth articulated the relationship between the experience of the voice within and outward speaking in God's service in these terms:

> And as the bodies of men and women subjected unto and guided by the spirit of God are the temple of God; therefore the spirit of God may speak in and through them; and as the Lord is the teacher of his people he may be the speaker in them and through them…and he may make use of them, and speak in them and through them, according to his own good will and pleasure. (1663:15)

This prophetic giving of voice to the Word of God speaking within one, properly done, was not only legitimate, but necessary (Camm and Audland 1689:293); though outward, it was in polar contrast to "carnal talk." It was, rather, "the pure language, which disquiets the birth born of the flesh" (Fox 1657:7).

The Quaker belief in the voice of God speaking within those who were attentive to the Inward Light was the basis of a major doctrinal difference between the Quakers and others of their day, including other Puritan groups and the Church of England alike. For the latter, the Scriptures were *the* Word of God, given once and for all—revelation was a closed account. The Quakers, however, hearing the voice of God speaking in them and through them, knew the account was far from closed. God's "immediate speaking never ceased in any age" (Barclay 1831, 2:32). For them, the Scriptures were rather the tangible reports of the Word of God that was in those who spoke and recorded them (Fox 1831, 3:611), an important record of God's earlier messages to men, and thus serviceable as a guide and a standard, but no more intrinsically valid than the Word of God within themselves, continuously revealed (Bayly 1830:180–181; Farnsworth 1656:3–4). The physical written record that was the Bible could not in itself be *the* Word of God, for "the Word of God is like unto himself, spiritual…and therefore cannot be heard or read with the natural external senses, as the Scriptures can" (Barclay 1831, 1:155; Fox 1831, 3:611).

One additional term that was part of the Quaker paradigm of the Inward Light, the Voice of God, and the Word, was the *Truth*. In many contexts the terms were synonymous and interchangeable: A Quaker minister might just as well exhort his or her hearers to "dwell in the Light" or "live in the Truth," or a tract writer define one in terms of the other (e.g., Penington 1863:501). And certainly, as the speakers of the pure language (Zephaniah, 3:9), the Quakers were bound to *truthfulness*: "The remnant of Israel shall not…speak lies; neither shall a deceitful tongue be found in their mouth" (Zephaniah 3:13). "Truth," however, tended to be the term of choice in referring to the true, valid (Quaker) religious *way* in its outward, communicable aspect, as in Fox's exhortation to "live in the life of truth, and let the truth speak in all things" (1831, 7:192).

Fox's words are also suggestive in another respect. By saying "let the truth speak in all things," Fox makes speaking the primary channel by which Truth is to be communicated. But how does Truth speak in all things? And what is the relationship between living in the life of Truth and letting Truth speak in all things? Fox's words are really the expression of a broader Quaker folk theory of symbolic action in which speaking as a means of communication is metaphorically extended to communication by other forms of behavior and action. Both the primacy of speaking and its metaphorical extension are captured with vigor and economy in Fox's famous exhortation from Pardshaw Crag in 1652: "Let your lives speak." Moreover, communication of (religious) Truth is perhaps the primary function of human social life; on another occasion, Fox urged the Quakers to live in such a way "that…your conversations, lives, practices, and tongues may preach to all people, and answer the good, just, and righteous principle of God in them all" (1831, 7:191).

There are really two dimensions of the communicative process discussed here: the "preaching" of the Truth by word and deed, and the means by which that preaching is rendered effective. To this point, I have been dealing with early

Quaker belief concerning the *production* of speech; Fox's statement takes us over into conceptions of the rhetorical process and the hearer's response. Here again, as might be expected, the Inward Light, the "religious principle of God in...all," is the key.

The Quaker doctrine of the Inward Light was universal in its scope; the Holy Spirit shone in every person—Quaker or non-Quaker, Christian or pagan—lighted by Jesus Christ. Such was the spiritual state of mankind, however, that the Light shone unrecognized and unheeded by most, obscured by the corruption of empty and formal religion and the life of the flesh. Nevertheless, by virtue of the presence of the Light within, every person was potentially responsive to the Truth: "Truth hath an honour in the hearts of people that are not Friends" (Fox 1952:341).

If Friends themselves were attentive to the Light within themselves, and spoke or acted according to its leadings, their behavior would arouse the spirit of God in those who witnessed it, provided they were ready to receive the Truth, because the spirit was everywhere unitary and identical. It was not necessary to belabor, threaten, cajole, or reason people into belief or persuasion, but simply to "bear the testimony of the Lord as we have received it from him," in the confidence that the spirit of Truth within the hearer would respond to it (Furly 1663:i). "Words that come from the life will go to the life," wrote Farnsworth, "and raise up that which is pure in one another" (Barclay 1841:355). God's words did not suffer from the communicative defects of natural language.

Again and again, one finds the early Quakers employing such phrases as "to that in your consciences do I speak, which changeth not" (Anon. 1654:14); "to the Light in all your consciences I speak, which will let you see whose servants you are" (Audland 1655:22); "to that of God in you I speak" (Fox 1831, 7:29); or "let that of God in you answer these things" (Burrough 1658:23). The rhetorical model was clearly recognized and acted upon as a frame of communicative reference. The confidence of the early Friends in the power of the Light as a communicative channel was tellingly expressed in Burrough's challenge to the world to acknowledge the power of the Quaker mission: "And do not they preach in the power of God, and reach to your consciences, when you hear them? And doth not the light in you answer that they speak the truth?" (1658:24).

This same confidence accounts for those instances in which Friends seem to have relied on a capacity for xenoglossia (Samarin 1972:109–115) to communicate the Truth across the barrier of natural languages, as in the case of the two missionaries who were found in Paris in January of 1657, "half-starved with cold and hunger, and said that 'they were ambassadors from the Lord to the Duke of Savoy...they despaired not of the gift of tongues, and the Lord had told them they should have success'" (Braithwaite 1955:416). Fox himself recounts in his journal how "there was a young man convinced in Scarborough town whilst I was in prison, the bailiff's son: and he came to dispute and spoke Hebrew to me and I spoke in Welsh to him

and bid him fear God, who after became a pretty Friend" (1952:505).

This rhetorical model I have outlined obtained in all Quaker communication, for all purposes, whether explicitly sacred or secular. Here, for example, is Thomas Ellwood's account of his proposal of marriage to his future wife: "I used not many words to her, but I felt a divine power went along with the words, and fixed the matter expressed by them so fast in her breast, that...she could not shut it out" (1906:214). Or Charles Marshall's advice to those engaged in trade: "After you have put a price on your commodities, which is equal, as you can sell them, then if the persons you are dealing with multiply words, stand you silent in the fear, dread and awe of God; and this will answer the witness of God in them you are dealing with" (1844:57). Indeed, if your own spiritual power was strong enough, communication could be effected without the overt intention of sending any message at all. Fox recorded in his journal concerning his passage in 1654 from Swarthmoor to Lancaster: "And so through many towns, and felt I answered the witness of God in all people, though I spoke not a word" (1952:177).

The rhetorical stakes were highest, of course, in the effort to bring people into the Quaker fold, to "convince" them of the Truth by turning them inward to the Light. Convincement was the culmination of the rhetorical process in religious discourse with non-Friends. Most commonly, the term "convincement" was employed for the full conversion experience, but some Friends drew a distinction between convincement and conversion, as in Dewsbury's critical observation: "Many [are] convinced that are not converted" (1689:319). This suggests the possibility that some could feel the Light within themselves respond to the Truth, but resist or refuse outright to follow it through to full spiritual submission to its leadings. Others, clearly, required time before they were fully ready to take up the cross, though the process was begun when they felt the first inward response to the Truth (e.g., Ellwood 1906).

Convincement was the most powerful experience of their lives for the early Quakers and figures prominently in the spiritual journals of the period. A typical example is Stephen Crisp, convinced by the young James Parnel in 1655: "When I saw this man, being but a youth, and knew not the power nor spirit that was in him, I thought to withstand him...but I quickly came to feel the spirit of sound judgment was in him, and the witness of God arose in me, and testified to his judgment, and signified I must own it" (1822:27).

Some Quaker ministers were noted for their special sensitivity to the spiritual state and responsiveness of others, thus enhancing their rhetorical power still further. But this sensitivity was also seen in terms of the spiritual/rhetorical link between the Light within themselves and the others. To cite just one of many possible examples, it was recorded of Robert Withers, an early Quaker minister in Pardshaw, Cumberland, that "several was convinced by him, for his service was to speak to particular persons, he having the spirit of discerning by which he could read the states and conditions of many" (Penney 1907:36). One often sees in the early Quaker journals the phrase, "he spoke to my condition," to describe the hearer's sense of the striking personal relevance of a Friend's message, seen as a confirmation on both sides of the power of communication in Truth. When spiritual communication was taking place, the channel was felt to be open in both directions, and the speaker could sense the responsiveness of others to his message. George Whitehead records of another Friend, William Barber:

> I first met him…at Diss in Norfolk, and declared the Truth to him and some others present…William was very tenderly affected, and broken into tears; and his spirit bowed and humbled, though he had been a great man and captain in the army: Truth was near in him, and I felt him hear it; and my heart was open and tender toward him, in the love of Christ. (1832, 1:57)

* * * *

Let me attempt to draw together in synthetic fashion some of the principal elements making up the symbolic complex of speaking and silence in early Quaker ideology. I use ideology here, after Geertz and Burke, to designate a symbol system that is a guide for understanding and behavior (Geertz 1973:218, 220), that names the structures of situations in such a way that the attitude expressed toward them is one of commitment (Geertz 1973:231).

Many historians of modern Christianity have observed that the emergence of Protestantism was accompanied by a progressive interiorization of the word (see, e.g., Ong 1967:262–286), as intermediary symbols, rituals, and functionaries that stood between the individual and the experience of the Word of God were stripped away from religious practice. Mary Douglas sees this in anthropological terms as part of a more general process that marks an alienation from current social values:

> A denunciation not only of irrelevant rituals, but of ritualism as such; exaltation of the inner experience and denigration of its standardized expressions; preference for intuitive and instant forms of knowledge; rejection of mediating institutions, rejection of any tendency to allow habit to provide the basis of a new symbolic system. (1973:40)

Though not written specifically about the early Quakers, Douglas's description could hardly apply more closely to their mission and ideology.

In these terms, Quakerism may be seen as a carrying of the Protestant tendency to its logical extreme. The spirit of Christ, for whom Christian tradition already made available the symbolic identification as the Word of God—the Son as "the primary 'utterance' of the Father" (Ong 1967:185)—was located *within* the individual. God spoke his Word anew within the soul of every person, doing away with virtually all mediating agencies in the ultimate exaltation of inner experience. The experience of God speaking within was the spiritual core of Quakerism.

As this most important act of speaking took place inwardly and was spiritual, it required that one refrain from speaking that was outward and carnal. Hence the motivation toward silence in Quaker ideology, consistent too with the alienation from current social values; as Susan Sontag has observed: "Behind the appeals for silence lies the wish for a perceptual and cultural clean slate" (1969:17). It is important to emphasize, though, that the resultant outward silence did not represent a complete cessation of speaking or its polar opposite. It involved rather a shifting of the locus and character of religious speaking from outward, human speech to the inward spiritual speaking of God.

By making the speaking of God within man the core religious experience of their movement, the Quakers elevated speaking and silence to an especially high degree of symbolic centrality and importance. Victor Turner has suggested that iconoclastic religions, by eliminating iconic symbols, place ever greater stress on the Word (1975:155). Again, the early Quakers carried this tendency close to its extreme among contemporary radical puritan sects by the symbolic weight they attached to speaking and silence.

But speaking is a potentially problematic symbolic resource for religious purposes. When the speaker is God, speaking can represent the vehicle and essence of spiritual Truth. Under the best of conditions, in Quaker belief, that Truth might be communicated—within individuals, and even between them—without outward speaking. However, in a world that was seen to be just emerging from a long period of spiritual degeneration, and in which all people were manifestly *not* attuned to the voice of God within them, outward speaking might be seen as necessary to bear a public witness for God and to help others reach to the Light within them. The problem was that outward speaking was basically a human faculty, susceptible to the impulses of fleshly will and the service of fleshly indulgence. How could this be controlled against?

One means of control was to make outward speech in the service of religion the giving of voice to *God's* Word, speaking *through* man.… The notion of silence may continue to apply here by metaphorical extension: When outward speaking represented a giving of voice to God speaking through man, a silence of the flesh and self-will could continue to prevail. For the rest, however, it was best to neutralize the susceptibility of speaking to carnal impulse by minimizing speaking as much as possible: "Let your words be few."

To be sure, speaking was not the only element of the human condition subject to carnal impulse. Indeed, all of life on earth was seen as susceptible to natural indulgence and therefore to be kept under control in the conduct of the godly life. Here is where the key symbols of speaking and silence were drawn upon by the Quakers for metaphorical extension beyond their primary verbal referents. Accordingly, speaking became a metaphor for all human action—"let your lives speak"—which was thereby encompassed by the same moral rules that governed verbal activity, that is, the stripping away of superfluity and carnal indulgence and the maintenance of a "silence" of the flesh in all things.

Notwithstanding the symbolic extension of speaking and silence beyond the verbal, the centrality of these symbols in Quaker ideology made for an especially heightened awareness of verbal activities and forms on the part of the early Friends and the elevation of speaking into a cultural focus....

References

Anon. 1654. *The Glorie of the Lord Arising*. London.

Audland, John. 1655. *The Innocent Delivered Out of the Snare*. London.

Barbour, Hugh. 1964. *The Quakers in Puritan England*. New Haven: Yale University Press.

Barclay, A. R. 1841. *Letters, &c. of Early Friends*. London.

Barclay, Robert. 1831. *Truth Triumphant*. 3 vols. Philadelphia.

Bayly, William. 1830. *A Collection of the Several Writings of... William Bayly*. Philadelphia and New York.

Braithwaite, William C. 1955. *The Beginnings of Quakerism*. 2d ed. Cambridge: Cambridge University Press.

Britten, William. 1660. *Silent Meeting, a Wonder to the World*. London.

Burrough, Edward. 1658. Epistle to the Reader. In George Fox. *The Works of George Fox*, vol. 3. Philadelphia, 1831.

———. 1660. *A Vindication of the People of God, Called Quakers*. London.

Camm, John, and Audland, John. 1689. *The Memory of the Righteous Revived*. London.

Crisp, Stephen. 1822. *The Christian Experiences... and Writings of... Stephen Crisp*. Philadelphia.

Dewsbury, William. 1689. *The Faithful Testimony of... William Dewsbury*. London.

Douglas, Mary. 1973. *Natural Symbols*. New York: Random House (Vintage Books).

Ellwood, Thomas. 1906. *The History of the Life of Thomas Ellwood*. S. Graveson, ed. London: Headley Brothers.

Farnsworth, Richard. 1656. *The Priests' Ignorance and Contrary-Walkings to the Scriptures*. London.

———. 1663. *The Spirit of God Speaking in the Temple of God*. London.

Fox, George. 1657. *Concerning Good-Morrow and Good-Even...* London.

———. 1831. *The Works of George Fox*. 8 vols. Philadelphia.

———. 1952. *The Journal of George Fox*. Rev. ed. by John L. Nickalls. Cambridge: Cambridge University Press.

———. 1972. *Narrative Papers of George Fox*. Henry J. Cadbury, ed. Richmond, IN: Friends United Press.

Fraser, Russel. 1977. *The Language of Adam*. New York: Columbia University Press.

Furly, Benjamin. 1663. *The World's Honour Detected*. London.

Geertz, Clifford. 1973. Ideology as a Cultural System. In *The Interpretation of Cultures*. New York: Basic Books.

Graves, Michael P. 1972. The Rhetoric of the Inward Light: An Examination of Extant Sermons Delivered by Early Quakers 1671–1700. Ph.D. diss., University of Southern California.

Howgill, Francis. 1676. *The Dawnings of the Gospel Day*. London.

Marshall, Charles. 1844. *The Journal of Charles Marshall*. London.

Ong, Walter. 1967. *The Presence of the Word*. New York: Simon & Schuster.

Parnel, James. 1675. *A Collection of the Several Writings [of] James Parnel*. N.p.

Penington, Isaac. 1863. *The Works of Isaac Penington*. 4 vols. Philadelphia.

Penn, William. [1694]. *The Rise and Progress of the People Called Quakers*. Philadelphia: Friends Book Store.

———. 1865. *No Cross, No Crown*. Philadelphia.

Penney, Norman. 1907. *First Publishers of Truth*. London: Friends Historical Society.

Samarin, William J. 1972. *Tongues of Men and Angels*. New York: Macmillan.

Smith, William. 1663. *The Work of God's Power in Man*. London.

Sontag, Susan. 1969. The Aesthetics of Silence. In *Styles of Radical Will*. New York: Farrar, Straus.

Symonds, Thomas. 1656. *The Voyce of the Just Uttered*. N.p.

Taylor, Thomas. [1661]. *A Faithful Warning to Outside Professors*. N.p.

Turner, Victor. 1974. *Dramas, Fields and Metaphors*. Ithaca, NY: Cornell University Press.

———. 1975. Symbolic Studies. In *Annual Review of Anthropology*, vol. 4. Bernard J. Siegel, ed. Palo Alto, CA: Annual Reviews.

Weber, Max. 1958. *The Protestant Ethic and the Spirit of Capitalism*. New York: Scribner.

Whitehead, George. 1832. *Memoirs of George Whitehead*. 2 vols. Philadelphia.

Post-reading Questions / Activities

- How is Quakerism "a carrying of the Protestant tendency to its logical extreme"? What is the role of the individual, in contrast to that of the group?
- Quaker views (ideology) of language stemmed from their views of humankind in general. Try to identify your fundamental views of language, including speech and silence. Can you connect them to your views of humankind?

- What are some of the meanings of silence in your experience? How do you know what someone *means* when the person doesn't say it?
- Observe the alternation of silence and speech at a religious ceremony. Observe it in another setting (a classroom, a chat with friends, a film, a therapy session). How is silence used? What is supposed to happen during it? Is it successful?

Vocabulary

pronominal   xenoglossia

Suggested Further Reading

Bauman, Richard. 1983. *Let Your Words Be Few: Symbolism of Speaking and Silence among Seventeenth-Century Quakers.* Cambridge: Cambridge University Press.

Brown, Roger, and Albert Gilman. 1960. "The Pronouns of Power and Solidarity." In *Style in Language*, edited by Thomas A. Sebeok. Cambridge, MA: The MIT Press, pp. 253–276.

Tannen, Deborah, and Muriel Saville-Troike, eds. 1985. *Perspectives on Silence.* Norwood, NJ: Ablex.

CHAPTER 45

"To Give Up on Words"
Silence in Western Apache Culture

Keith H. Basso
(1970)

Stereotypes of others are part and parcel of human experience. Not all stereotypes are entirely erroneous; there is often a kernel of truth behind them, though stereotypes often make it seem unnecessary to understand the context or nuances surrounding a mysterious way of doing things.

Keith Basso has been interpreting Apache culture since the 1960s, shattering stereotypes or explaining reasons that might lie behind them. In this case he examines some of the circumstances under which Western Apache may remain silent. Using the ethnography of speaking approach pioneered by Dell Hymes, Basso focuses on the function of silence, in appropriate settings, rather than on the form. (And, as he says so succinctly, "the form of silence is always the same.")

Basso gives six types of situation in which he has observed restraint from speech. He discusses the reasons for silence with local people, usually at a later time, coming up with a fairly powerful reason in each of these cases. He ends with a more synthetic generalization that accounts for all six cases, suggesting that this might or might not explain silence in other cultures.

Reading Questions

- What are the circumstances in which Apaches refrain from speech? Would you do the same in some of these situations? For the same or different reasons?
- What is the unifying reason for the Apache to remain silent?
- Why is the stereotype of Indian silence misleading?

It is not the case that a man who is silent says nothing.
Anonymous

I

Anyone who has read about American Indians has probably encountered statements which impute to them a strong predilection for keeping silent or, as one writer has put it, "a fierce reluctance to speak except when absolutely necessary." In the popular literature, where this characterization is particularly widespread, it is commonly portrayed as the outgrowth of such dubious causes as "instinctive dignity," "an impoverished language," or, perhaps worst of all, the Indians'

Keith H. Basso, "'To Give Up on Words': Silence in Western Apache Culture." *Southwestern Journal of Anthropology* (1970) 26 (3): 213–230. Notes have been renumbered and edited.

"lack of personal warmth." Although statements of this sort are plainly erroneous and dangerously misleading, it is noteworthy that professional anthropologists have made few attempts to correct them. Traditionally, ethnographers and linguists have paid little attention to cultural interpretations given to silence or, equally important, to the types of social contexts in which it regularly occurs.

This study investigates certain aspects of silence in the culture of the Western Apache of east-central Arizona. After considering some of the theoretical issues involved, I will briefly describe a number of situations—recurrent in Western Apache society—in which one or more of the participants typically refrain from speech for lengthy periods of time.[1] This is accompanied by a discussion of how such acts of silence are interpreted and why they are encouraged and deemed appropriate. I conclude by advancing an hypothesis that accounts for the reasons that the Western Apache refrain from speaking when they do, and I suggest that, with proper testing, this hypothesis may be shown to have relevance to silence behavior in other cultures.

II

A basic finding of sociolinguistics is that, although both language and language usage are structured, it is the latter which responds most sensitively to extra-linguistic influences (Hymes 1962, 1964; Ervin-Tripp 1964, 1967; Gumperz 1964; Slobin 1967). Accordingly, a number of recent studies have addressed themselves to the problem of how factors in the social environment of speech events delimit the range and condition the selection of message forms (cf. Brown and Gilman 1960; Conklin 1959; Ervin-Tripp 1964, 1967; Frake 1964; Friedrich 1966; Gumperz 1961, 1964; Martin 1964). These studies may be viewed as taking the now familiar position that verbal communication is fundamentally a decision-making process in which, initially, a speaker, having elected to speak, selects from among a repertoire of available codes that which is most appropriately suited to the situation at hand. Once a code has been selected, the speaker picks a suitable channel of transmission and then, finally, makes a choice from a set of referentially equivalent expressions within the code. The intelligibility of the expression he chooses will, of course, be subject to grammatical constraints. But its acceptability will not. Rules for the selection of linguistic alternates operate on features of the social environment and are commensurate with rules governing the conduct of face-to-face interaction. As such, they are properly conceptualized as lying outside the structure of language itself.

It follows from this that for a stranger to communicate appropriately with the members of an unfamiliar society it is not enough that he learn to formulate messages intelligibly. Something else is needed: a knowledge of what kinds of codes, channels, and expressions to use in what kinds of situations and to what kinds of people—as Hymes (1964) has termed it, an "ethnography of communication."

There is considerable evidence to suggest that extra-linguistic factors influence not only the use of speech but its actual occurrence as well. In our own culture, for example, remarks such as "Don't you know when to keep quiet?" "Don't talk until you're introduced," and "Remember now, no talking in church" all point to the fact that an individual's decision to speak may be directly contingent upon the character of his surroundings. Few of us would maintain that "silence is golden" for all people at all times. But we feel that silence is a virtue for some people some of the time, and we encourage children on the road to cultural competence to act accordingly.

Although the form of silence is always the same, the function of a specific act of silence—that is, its interpretation by and effect upon other people—will vary according to the social context in which it occurs. For example, if I choose to keep silent in the chambers of a Justice of the Supreme Court, my action is likely to be interpreted as a sign of politeness or respect. On the other hand, if I refrain from speaking to an established friend or colleague, I am apt to be accused of rudeness or harboring a grudge. In one instance, my behavior is judged by others to be "correct" or "fitting"; in the other, it is criticized as being "out of line."

The point, I think, is fairly obvious. For a stranger entering an alien society, a knowledge of when *not* to speak may be as basic to the production of culturally acceptable behavior as a knowledge of what to say. It stands to reason, then, that an adequate ethnography of communication should not confine itself exclusively to the analysis of choice within verbal repertoires. It should also, as Hymes (1962, 1964) has suggested, specify those conditions under which the members of the society regularly decide to refrain from verbal behavior altogether.

III

The research on which this [work] is based was conducted over a period of sixteen months (1964–1969) in the Western Apache settlement of Cibecue, which is located near the center of the Fort Apache Indian Reservation in east-central Arizona. Cibecue's 800 residents participate in an unstable economy that combines subsistence agriculture, cattle-raising, sporadic wage-earning, and Government subsidies in the form of welfare checks and social security benefits. Unemployment is a serious problem, and substandard living conditions are widespread.

Although Reservation life has precipitated far-reaching changes in the composition and geographical distribution of Western Apache social groups, consanguineal kinship—real and imputed—remains the single most powerful force in the establishment and regulation of interpersonal relationships (Kaut 1957; Basso 1970). The focus of domestic activity is the individual "camp," or *gową́ą́*. This term labels both the occupants and the location of a single dwelling or, as is more apt to be the case, several dwellings built within a few feet of each other. The majority of *gową́ą́* in Cibecue are occupied by nuclear families. The next largest residential unit is the *gotáá* (camp cluster), which is a group of spatially localized *gową́ą́*, each having at least one adult member who is related by ties of matrilineal kinship to persons living in all the others. An intricate system of exogamous clans serves to extend kinship relationships beyond the *gową́ą́* and *gotáá* and facilitates concerted action in projects, most notably the presentation of ceremonials, requiring large amounts of manpower. Despite the presence in Cibecue of a variety of Anglo missionaries and a dwindling number of medicine men, diagnostic and curing rituals, as well as the girls' puberty ceremonial, continue to be performed with regularity (Basso 1966, 1970). Witchcraft persists in undiluted form (Basso 1969).

IV

Of the many broad categories of events, or scenes, that comprise the daily round of Western Apache life, I shall deal here only with those that are coterminous with what Goffman (1961, 1964) has termed "focused gatherings" or "encounters." The concept *situation,* in keeping with established usage, will refer inclusively to the location of such a gathering, its physical setting, its point in time, the standing behavior patterns that accompany it, and the social attributes of the persons involved (Hymes 1962, 1964; Ervin-Tripp 1964, 1967).

In what follows, however, I will be mainly concerned with the roles and statuses of participants. The reason for this is that the critical factor in the Apache's decision to speak or keep silent seems always to be the nature of his relationships to other people. To be sure, other features of the situation are significant, but apparently only to the extent that they influence the perception of status and role.[2] What this implies, of course, is that roles and statuses are not fixed attributes. Although they may be depicted as such in a static model (and often with good reason), they are appraised and acted upon in particular social contexts and, as a result, subject to redefinition and variation.[3] With this in mind, let us now turn our attention to the Western Apache and the types of situations in which, as one of my informants put it, "it is right to give up on words."

V

1. "Meeting strangers" (*nda dòhwáá'iłtsééda*). The term, *nda,* labels categories at two levels of contrast. At the most general level, it designates any person—Apache or non-Apache—who, prior to an initial meeting, has never been seen and therefore cannot be identified. In addition, the term is used to refer to Apaches who, though previously seen and known by some external criteria such as clan affiliation or personal name, have never been engaged in face-to-face interaction. The latter category, which is more restricted than the first, typically includes individuals who live on the adjacent San Carlos Reservation, in Fort Apache settlements geographically removed from Cibecue, and those who fall into the category *kii dòhandáágo* (non-kinsmen). In all cases, "strangers" are separated by social distance. And in all cases it is considered appropriate, when encountering them for the first time, to refrain from speaking.

The type of situation described as "meeting strangers" (*nda dòhwáá'iłtsééda*) can take place in any number of different physical settings. However, it occurs most frequently in the context of events such as fairs and rodeos, which, owing to the large number of people in attendance, offer unusual opportunities for chance encounters. In large gatherings, the lack of verbal communication between strangers is apt to go unnoticed, but in smaller groups it becomes quite conspicuous. The following incident, involving two strangers who found themselves part of a four-man round-up crew, serves as a good example.

My informant, who was also a member of the crew, recalled the following episode:

> One time, I was with A, B, and X down at Gleason Flat, working cattle. That man, X, was from East Fork [a community nearly 40 miles from Cibecue] where B's wife was from. But he didn't know A, never knew him before, I guess. First day, I worked with X. At night, when we camped, we talked with B, but X and A didn't say anything to each other. Same way, second day. Same way, third. Then, at night on fourth day, we were sitting by the fire. Still, X and A didn't talk. Then A said, "Well, I know there is a stranger to me here, but I've been watching him and I know he is all right." After that, X and A talked a lot.... Those two men didn't know each other, so they took it easy at first.

As this incident suggests, the Western Apache do not feel compelled to "introduce" persons who are unknown to each other. Eventually, it is assumed, strangers will begin to speak. However, this is a decision that is properly left to the individuals involved, and no attempt is made to hasten it. Outside help in the form of introductions or other verbal routines is viewed as presumptuous and unnecessary.

Strangers who are quick to launch into conversation are frequently eyed with undisguised suspicion. A typical reaction to such individuals is that they "want something," that is, their willingness to violate convention is attributed to some urgent need which is likely to result in requests for money, labor, or transportation. Another common reaction to talkative strangers is that they are drunk.

If the stranger is an Anglo, it is usually assumed that he "wants to teach us something" (i.e., give orders or instructions) or that he "wants to make friends in a hurry." The latter response is especially revealing, since Western Apaches are extremely reluctant to be hurried into friendships—with Anglos or each other. Their verbal reticence with strangers is directly related to the conviction that the establishment of social relationships is a serious matter that calls for caution, careful judgment, and plenty of time.

2. "Courting" (*líígoláá*). During the initial stages of courtship, young men and women go without speaking for conspicuous lengths of time. Courting may occur in a wide variety of settings—practically anywhere, in fact—and at virtually any time of the day or night, but it is most readily observable at large public gatherings such as ceremonials, wakes, and rodeos. At these events, "sweethearts" (*zééde*) may stand or sit (sometimes holding hands) for as long as an hour without exchanging a word. I am told by adult informants that the young people's reluctance to speak may become even more pronounced in situations where they find themselves alone.

Apaches who have just begun to court attribute their silence to "intense shyness" (*'isté*) and a feeling of acute "self-consciousness" (*dàyéézi'*) which, they claim, stems from their lack of familiarity with one another. More specifically, they complain of "not knowing what to do" in each other's presence and of the fear that whatever they say, no matter how well thought out in advance, will sound "dumb" or "stupid."[4]

One informant, a youth 17 years old, commented as follows:

> It's hard to talk with your sweetheart at first. She doesn't know you and won't know what to say. It's the same way towards her. You don't know how to talk yet...so you get very bashful. That makes it sometimes so you don't say anything. So you just go around together and don't talk. At first, it's better that way. Then, after a while, when you know each other, you aren't shy anymore and can talk good.

The Western Apache draw an equation between the ease and frequency with which a young couple talks and how well they know each other. Thus, it is expected that after several months of steady companionship sweethearts will start to have lengthy conversations. Earlier in their relationship, however, protracted discussions may be openly discouraged. This is especially true for girls, who are informed by their mothers and older sisters that silence in courtship is a sign of modesty and that an eagerness to speak betrays previous experience with men. In extreme cases, they add, it may be interpreted as a willingness to engage in sexual relations. Said one woman, aged 32:

> This way I have talked to my daughter. "Take it easy when boys come around this camp and want you to go somewhere with them. When they talk to you, just listen at first. Maybe you won't know what to say. So don't talk about just anything. If you talk with those boys right away, then they will know you know all about them. They will think you've been with many boys before, and they will start talking about that."

3. "Children, coming home" (čəgəše nakáii). The Western Apache lexeme iltá'inatsáá (reunion) is used to describe encounters between an individual who has returned home after a long absence and his relatives and friends. The most common type of reunion, čəgəše nakáii (children, coming home), involves boarding school students and their parents. It occurs in late May or early in June, and its setting is usually a trading post or school, where parents congregate to await the arrival of buses bringing the children home. As the latter disembark and locate their parents in the crowd, one anticipates a flurry of verbal greetings. Typically, however, there are few or none at all. Indeed, it is not unusual for parents and child to go without speaking for as long as 15 minutes.

When the silence is broken, it is almost always the child who breaks it. His parents listen attentively to everything he says but speak hardly at all themselves. This pattern persists even after the family has reached the privacy of its camp, and two or three days may pass before the child's parents seek to engage him in sustained conversation.

According to my informants, the silence of Western Apache parents at (and after) reunions with their children is ultimately predicated on the possibility that the latter have been adversely affected by their experiences away from home. Uppermost is the fear that, as a result of protracted exposure to Anglo attitudes and values, the children have come to view their parents as ignorant, old-fashioned, and no longer deserving of respect. One of my most thoughtful and articulate informants commented on the problem as follows:

> You just can't tell about those children after they've been with White men for a long time. They get their minds turned around sometimes...they forget where they come from and get ashamed when they come home because their parents and relatives are poor. They forget how to act with these Apaches and get mad easy. They walk around all night and get into fights. They don't stay at home.
>
> At school, some of them learn to want to be White men, so they come back and try to act that way. But we are still Apaches! So we don't know them anymore, and it is like we never knew them. It is hard to talk to them when they are like that.

Apache parents openly admit that, initially, children who have been away to school seem distant and unfamiliar. They have grown older, of course, and their physical appearance may have changed. But more fundamental is the concern that they have acquired new ideas and expectations which will alter their behavior in unpredictable ways. No matter how pressing this concern may be, however, it is considered inappropriate to directly interrogate a child after his arrival home. Instead, parents anticipate that within a short time he will begin to divulge information about himself that will enable them to determine in what ways, if any, his views and attitudes have changed. This, the Apache say, is why children do practically all the talking in the hours following a reunion, and their parents remain unusually silent.

Said one man, the father of two children who had recently returned from boarding school in Utah:

> Yes, it's right that we didn't talk much to them when they came back, my wife and me. They were away for a long time, and we didn't know how they would like it, being home. So we waited. Right away, they started to tell stories about what they did. Pretty soon we could tell they liked it, being back. That made us feel good. So it was easy to talk to them again. It was like they were before they went away.

4. "Getting cussed out" (šiłditéé). This lexeme is used to describe any situation in which one individual, angered and enraged, shouts insults and criticisms at another. Although the object of such invective is in most cases the person or persons who provoked it, this is not always the case, because an Apache who is truly beside himself with rage is likely to vent his feelings on anyone whom he sees or who happens to be within range of his voice. Consequently, "getting cussed out" may involve large numbers of people who are totally innocent of the charges being hurled against them.

But whether they are innocent or not, their response to the situation is the same. They refrain from speech.

Like the types of situations we have discussed thus far, "getting cussed out" can occur in a wide variety of physical settings: at ceremonial dance grounds and trading posts, inside and outside wickiups and houses, on food-gathering expeditions and shopping trips—in short, wherever and whenever individuals lose control of their tempers and lash out verbally at persons nearby.

Although "getting cussed out" is basically free of setting-imposed restrictions, the Western Apache fear it most at gatherings where alcohol is being consumed. My informants observed that especially at "drinking parties" (*dá'idlą́ą́*), where there is much rough joking and ostensibly mock criticism, it is easy for well-intentioned remarks to be misconstrued as insults. Provoked in this way, persons who are intoxicated may become hostile and launch into explosive tirades, often with no warning at all.

The silence of Apaches who are "getting cussed out" is consistently explained in reference to the belief that individuals who are "enraged" (*has˙kéé*) are also irrational or "crazy" (*bìné'idįį*). In this condition, it is said, they "forget who they are" and become oblivious to what they say or do. Concomitantly, they lose all concern for the consequences of their actions on other people. In a word, they are dangerous. Said one informant:

> When people get mad they get crazy. Then they start yelling and saying bad things. Some say they are going to kill somebody for what he has done. Some keep it up that way for a long time, maybe walk from camp to camp, real angry, yelling, crazy like that. They keep it up for a long time, some do.
>
> People like that don't know what they are saying, so you can't tell about them. When you see someone like that, just walk away. If he yells at you, let him say whatever he wants to. Let him say anything. Maybe he doesn't mean it. But he doesn't know that. He will be crazy, and he could try to kill you.

Another Apache said:

> When someone gets mad at you and starts yelling, then just don't do anything to make him get worse. Don't try to quiet him down because he won't know why you're doing it. If you try to do that, he may just get worse and try to hurt you.

As the last of these statements implies, the Western Apache operate on the assumption that enraged persons—because they are temporarily "crazy"—are difficult to reason with. Indeed, there is a widely held belief that attempts at mollification will serve to intensify anger, thus increasing the chances of physical violence. The appropriate strategy when "getting cussed out" is to do nothing, to avoid any action that will attract attention to oneself. Since speaking accomplishes just the opposite, the use of silence is strongly advised.

5. "Being with people who are sad" (*nde dòbíłgòzóóda bigą́ą́*). Although the Western Apache phrase that labels this situation has no precise equivalent in English, it refers quite specifically to gatherings in which an individual finds himself in the company of someone whose spouse or kinsman has recently died. Distinct from wakes and burials, which follow immediately after a death, "being with people who are sad" is most likely to occur several weeks later. At this time, close relatives of the deceased emerge from a period of intense mourning (during which they rarely venture beyond the limits of their camps) and start to resume their normal activities within the community. To persons anxious to convey their sympathies, this is interpreted as a sign that visitors will be welcomed and, if possible, provided with food and drink. To those less solicitous, it means that unplanned encounters with the bereaved must be anticipated and prepared for.

"Being with people who are sad" can occur on a footpath, in a camp, at church, or in a trading post; but whatever the setting—and regardless of whether it is the result of a planned visit or an accidental meeting—the situation is marked by a minimum of speech. Queried about this, my informants volunteered three types of explanations. The first is that persons "who are sad" are so burdened with "intense grief" (*dółgozóóda*) that speaking requires of them an unusual amount of physical effort. It is courteous and considerate, therefore, not to attempt to engage them in conversation.

A second native explanation is that in situations of this sort verbal communication is basically unnecessary. Everyone is familiar with what has happened, and talking about it, even for the purpose of conveying solace and sympathy, would only reinforce and augment the sadness felt by those who were close to the deceased. Again, for reasons of courtesy, this is something to be avoided.

The third explanation is rooted in the belief that "intense grief," like intense rage, produces changes in the personality of the individual who experiences it. As evidence for this, the Western Apache cite numerous instances in which the emotional strain of dealing with death, coupled with an overwhelming sense of irrevocable personal loss, has caused persons who were formerly mild and even-tempered to become abusive, hostile, and physically violent.

> That old woman, X, who lives across Cibecue Creek, one time her first husband died. After that she cried all the time, for a long time. Then, I guess she got mean because everyone said she drank a lot and got into fights. Even with her close relatives, she did like that for a long time. She was too sad for her husband. That's what made her like that; it made her lose her mind.
>
> My father was like that when his wife died. He just stayed home all the time and wouldn't go anywhere. He didn't talk to any of his relatives or children. He just said, "I'm hungry. Cook for me." That's all. He stayed that way for a long time. His mind was not with us. He was still with his wife.
>
> My uncle died in 1941. His wife sure went crazy right away after that. Two days after they buried the body,

we went over there and stayed with those people who had been left alone. My aunt got mad at us. She said, "Why do you come over here? You can't bring my husband back. I can take care of myself and those others in my camp, so why don't you go home." She sure was mad that time, too sad for someone who died. She didn't know what she was saying because in about one week she came to our camp and said, "My relatives, I'm all right now. When you came to help me, I had too much sadness and my mind was no good. I said bad words to you. But now I am all right and I know what I am doing."

As these statements indicate, the Western Apache assume that a person suffering from "intense grief" is likely to be disturbed and unstable. Even though he may appear outwardly composed, they say, there is always the possibility that he is emotionally upset and therefore unusually prone to volatile outbursts. Apaches acknowledge that such an individual might welcome conversation in the context of "being with people who are sad," but, on the other hand, they fear it might prove incendiary. Under these conditions, which resemble those in Situation No. 4, it is considered both expedient and appropriate to keep silent.

6. "Being with someone for whom they sing" (*nde bìdádìs-tááha bìgą́´ą´*). The last type of situation to be described is restricted to a small number of physical locations and is more directly influenced by temporal factors than any of the situations we have discussed so far. "Being with someone for whom they sing" takes place only in the context of "curing ceremonials" (*gòjˇitáł; èdotáł*). These events begin early at night and come to a close shortly before dawn the following day. In the late fall and throughout the winter, curing ceremonials are held inside the patient's wickiup or house. In the spring and summer, they are located outside, at some open place near the patient's camp or at specially designated dance grounds where group rituals of all kinds are regularly performed.

Prior to the start of a curing ceremonial, all persons in attendance may feel free to talk with the patient; indeed, because he is so much a focus of concern, it is expected that friends and relatives will seek him out to offer encouragement and support. Conversation breaks off, however, when the patient is informed that the ceremonial is about to begin, and it ceases entirely when the presiding medicine man commences to chant. From this point on, until the completion of the final chant next morning, it is inappropriate for anyone except the medicine man (and, if he has them, his aides) to speak to the patient.[5]

In order to appreciate the explanation Apaches give for this prescription, we must briefly discuss the concept of "supernatural power" (*diyí´*) and describe some of the effects it is believed to have on persons at whom it is directed. Elsewhere (Basso 1969:30) I have defined "power" as follows:

The term *diyí´* refers to one or all of a set of abstract and invisible forces which are said to derive from certain classes of animals, plants, minerals, meteorological phenomena, and mythological figures within the Western Apache universe. Any of the various powers may be acquired by man and, if properly handled, used for a variety of purposes.

A power that has been antagonized by disrespectful behavior towards its source may retaliate by causing the offender to become sick. "Power-caused illnesses" (*kásit ídiyí´ bìł*) are properly treated with curing ceremonials in which one or more medicine men, using chants and various items of ritual paraphernalia, attempt to neutralize the sickness-causing power with powers of their own.

Roughly two-thirds of my informants assert that a medicine man's power actually enters the body of the patient; others maintain that it simply closes in and envelops him. In any case, all agree that the patient is brought into intimate contact with a potent supernatural force which elevates him to a condition labeled *gòdiyó´* (sacred, holy).

The term *gòdiyó´* may also be translated as "potentially harmful" and, in this sense, is regularly used to describe classes of objects (including all sources of power) that are surrounded with taboos. In keeping with the semantics of *gòdiyó´*, the Western Apache explain that, besides making patients holy, power makes them potentially harmful. And it is this transformation, they explain, that is basically responsible for the cessation of verbal communication during curing ceremonials.

Said one informant:

When they start singing for someone like that, he sort of goes away with what the medicine man is working with (i.e., power). Sometimes people they sing for don't know you, even after it (the curing ceremonial) is over. They get holy, and you shouldn't try to talk to them when they are like that…it's best to leave them alone.

Another informant made similar comments:

When they sing for someone, what happens is like this: that man they sing for doesn't know why he is sick or which way to go. So the medicine man has to show him and work on him. That is when he gets holy, and that makes him go off somewhere in his mind, so you should stay away from him.

Because Apaches undergoing ceremonial treatment are perceived as having been changed by power into something different from their normal selves, they are regarded with caution and apprehension. Their newly acquired status places them in close proximity to the supernatural and, as such, carries with it a very real element of danger and uncertainty. These conditions combine to make "being with someone for whom they sing" a situation in which speech is considered disrespectful and, if not exactly harmful, at least potentially hazardous.

VI

Although the types of situations described above differ from one another in obvious ways, I will argue in what follows that the underlying determinants of silence are in each case basically the same. Specifically, I will attempt to defend the hypothesis that keeping silent in Western Apache culture is associated with social situations in which participants perceive their relationships vis-à-vis one another to be ambiguous and/or unpredictable.

Let us begin with the observation that, in all the situations we have described, *silence is defined as appropriate with respect to a specific individual or individuals.* In other words, the use of speech is not directly curtailed by the setting of a situation nor by the physical activities that accompany it but, rather, by the perceived social and psychological attributes of at least one focal participant.

It may also be observed that, in each type of situation, *the status of the focal participant is marked by ambiguity*— either because he is unfamiliar to other participants in the situation or because, owing to some recent event, a status he formerly held has been changed or is in a process of transition.

Thus, in Situation No. 1, persons who earlier considered themselves "strangers" move towards some other relationship, perhaps "friend" (*šìdikéé*), perhaps "enemy" (*šikédndíí*). In Situation No. 2, young people who have had relatively limited exposure to one another attempt to adjust to the new and intimate status of "sweetheart." These two situations are similar in that the focal participants have little or no prior knowledge of each other. Their social identities are not as yet clearly defined, and their expectations, lacking the foundation of previous experience, are poorly developed.

Situation No. 3 is somewhat different. Although the participants—parents and their children—are well known to each other, their relationship has been seriously interrupted by the latter's prolonged absence from home. This, combined with the possibility that recent experiences at school have altered the children's attitudes, introduces a definite element of unfamiliarity and doubt. Situation No. 3 is not characterized by the absence of role expectations but by the participants' perception that those already in existence may be outmoded and in need of revision.

Status ambiguity is present in Situation No. 4 because a focal participant is enraged and, as a result, considered "crazy." Until he returns to a more rational condition, others in the situation have no way of predicting how he will behave. Situation No. 5 is similar in that the personality of a focal participant is seen to have undergone a marked shift which makes his actions more difficult to anticipate. In both situations, the status of focal participants is uncertain because of real or imagined changes in their psychological makeup.

In Situation No. 6, a focal participant is ritually transformed from an essentially neutral state to one which is contextually defined as "potentially harmful." Ambiguity and apprehension accompany this transition, and, as in Situations No. 4 and 5, established patterns of interaction must be waived until the focal participant reverts to a less threatening condition.

This discussion points up a third feature characteristic of all situations: *the ambiguous status of focal participants is accompanied either by the absence or suspension of established role expectations.* In every instance, non-focal participants (i.e., those who refrain from speech) are either uncertain of how the focal participant will behave towards them or, conversely, how they should behave towards him. Stated in the simplest way possible, their roles become blurred with the result that established expectations—if they exist—lose their relevance as guidelines for social action and must be temporarily discarded or abruptly modified.

We are now in a position to expand upon our initial hypothesis and make it more explicit.

1. In Western Apache culture, the absence of verbal communication is associated with social situations in which the status of focal participants is ambiguous.
2. Under these conditions, fixed role expectations lose their applicability and the illusion of predictability in social interaction is lost.
3. To sum up and reiterate: keeping silent among the Western Apache is a response to uncertainty and unpredictability in social relations.

VII

The question remains to what extent the foregoing hypothesis helps to account for silence behavior in other cultures. Unfortunately, it is impossible at the present time to provide anything approaching a conclusive answer. Standard ethnographies contain very little information about the circumstances under which verbal communication is discouraged, and it is only within the past few years that problems of this sort have engaged the attention of sociolinguists. The result is that adequate cross-cultural data are almost completely lacking.

As a first step towards the elimination of this deficiency, an attempt is now being made to investigate the occurrence and interpretation of silence in other Indian societies of the American Southwest. Our findings at this early stage, though neither fully representative nor sufficiently comprehensive, are extremely suggestive. By way of illustration, I quote below from portions of a preliminary report prepared by Priscilla Mowrer (1970), herself a Navajo, who inquired into the situational features of Navajo silence behavior in the vicinity of Tuba City on the Navajo Reservation in east-central Arizona.

I. *Silence and Courting:* Navajo youngsters of opposite sexes just getting to know one another say nothing, except to sit close together and maybe hold hands.... In public, they may try not to let on that they are interested in each other, but in private it is another matter. If the girl is at a gathering where the boy is also present, she may go off by herself. Falling in step, the boy will generally follow. They may just walk around or find some place to sit down. But, at first, they will not say anything to each other.

II. *Silence and Long Absent Relatives:* When a male or female relative returns home after being gone for six months or more, he (or she) is first greeted with a handshake. If the returnee is male, the female greeter may embrace him and cry—the male, meanwhile, will remain dry-eyed and silent.

III. *Silence and Anger:* The Navajo tend to remain silent when being shouted at by a drunk or angered individual because that particular individual is considered temporarily insane. To speak to such an individual, the Navajo believe, just tends to make the situation worse.... People remain silent because they believe that the individual is not himself, that he may have been witched, and is not responsible for the change in his behavior.

IV. *Silent Mourning:* Navajos speak very little when mourning the death of a relative.... The Navajo mourn and cry together in pairs. Men will embrace one another and cry together. Women, however, will hold one another's hands and cry together.

V. *Silence and the Ceremonial Patient:* The Navajo consider it wrong to talk to a person being sung over. The only people who talk to the patient are the medicine man and a female relative (or male relative if the patient is male) who is in charge of food preparation. The only time the patient speaks openly is when the medicine man asks her (or him) to pray along with him.

These observations suggest that striking similarities may exist between the types of social contexts in which Navajos and Western Apaches refrain from speech. If this impression is confirmed by further research, it will lend obvious cross-cultural support to the hypothesis advanced above. But regardless of the final outcome, the situational determinants of silence seem eminently deserving of further study. For as we become better informed about the types of contextual variables that mitigate against the use of verbal codes, we should also learn more about those variables that encourage and promote them.

Notes

At different times during the period extending from 1964–1969 the research on which this paper is based was supported by U. S. P. H. S. Grant MH-12691-01, a grant from the American Philosophical Society, and funds from the Doris Duke Oral History Project at the Arizona State Museum. I am pleased to acknowledge this support. I would also like to express my gratitude to the following scholars for commenting upon an earlier draft: Y. R. Chao, Harold C. Conklin, Roy G. D'Andrade, Charles O. Frake, Paul Friedrich, John Gumperz, Kenneth Hale, Harry Hoijer, Dell Hymes, Stanley Newman, David M. Schneider, Joel Sherzer, and Paul Turner. Although the final version gained much from their criticisms and suggestions, responsibility for its present form and content rests solely with the author. A preliminary version of this paper was presented to the Annual Meeting of the American Anthropological Association in New Orleans, Lousiana, November 1969.

1. The situations described [here] are not the only ones in which the Western Apache refrain from speech. There is a second set—not considered here because my data are incomplete—in which silence appears to occur as a gesture of respect, usually to persons in positions of authority. A third set, very poorly understood, involves ritual specialists who claim they must keep silent at certain points during the preparation of ceremonial paraphernalia.

2. Recent work in the sociology of interaction, most notably by Goffman (1963) and Garfinkel (1967), has led to the suggestion that social relationships are everywhere the major determinants of verbal behavior. In this case, as Gumperz (1967) makes clear, it becomes methodologically unsound to treat the various components of communicative events as independent variables. Gumperz (1967) has presented a hierarchical model, sensitive to dependency, in which components are seen as stages in the communication process. Each stage serves as the input for the next. The basic stage, i.e., the initial input, is "social identities or statuses." For further details see Slobin 1967:131–134.

3. I would like to stress that the emphasis placed on social relations is fully in keeping with the Western Apache interpretation of their own behavior. When my informants were asked to explain why they or someone else was silent on a particular occasion, they invariably did so in terms of *who* was present at the time.

4. Among the Western Apache, rules of exogamy discourage courtship between members of the same clans (*kii àɫhánigo*) and so-called "related" clans (*kii*), with the result that sweethearts are almost always "non-matrilineal kinsmen" (*dòhwàkíída*). Compared to "matrilineal kinsmen" (*kii*), such individuals have fewer opportunities during childhood to establish close personal relationships and thus, when courtship begins, have relatively little knowledge of each other. It is not surprising, therefore, that their behavior is similar to that accorded strangers.

5. I have witnessed over 75 curing ceremonials since 1961 and have seen this rule violated only 6 times. On 4 occasions, drunks were at fault. In the other 2 cases, the patient fell asleep and had to be awakened.

References

Basso, Keith H. 1966. *The Gift of Changing Woman.* Bureau of American Ethnology, bulletin 196.

——. 1969. *Western Apache Witchcraft.* Anthropological Papers of the University of Arizona, no. 15.

——. 1970. *The Cibecue Apache.* New York: Holt, Rinehart & Winston.

Brown, R. W., and Albert Gilman. 1960. "The Pronouns of Power and Solidarity," in *Style in Language* (ed. by T. Sebeok), pp. 253–276. Cambridge: The Technology Press of Massachusetts Institute of Technology.

Conklin, Harold C. 1959. Linguistic Play in Its Cultural Context. *Language* 35:631–636.

Ervin-Tripp, Susan. 1964. "An Analysis of the Interaction of Language, Topic, and Listener," in *The Ethnography of Communication* (ed. by J. J. Gumperz and D. Hymes), pp. 86–102. *American Anthropologist*, Special Publication, vol. 66, no. 6, part 2.

Ervin-Tripp, Susan. 1967. *Sociolinguistics.* Language-Behavior Research Laboratory, Working Paper no. 3. Berkeley: University of California.

Frake, Charles O. 1964. "How to Ask for a Drink in Subanun," in *The Ethnography of Communication* (ed. by J. J. Gumperz and D. Hymes), pp. 127–132. *American Anthropologist*, Special Publication, vol. 66, no. 6, part 2.

Friedrich, P. 1966. "Structural Implications of Russian Pronominal Usage," in *Sociolinguistics* (ed. by W. Bright), pp. 214–253. The Hague: Mouton.

Garfinkel, H. 1967. *Studies in Ethnomethodology.* Englewood Cliffs, NJ: Prentice-Hall.

Goffman, E. 1961. *Encounters: Two Studies in the Sociology of Interaction.* Indianapolis: Bobbs-Merrill Co.

———. 1963. *Behavior in Public Places.* Glencoe, IL: Free Press.

———. 1964. "The Neglected Situation," in *The Ethnography of Communication* (ed. by J. J. Gumperz and D. Hymes), pp. 133–136. *American Anthropologist*, Special Publication, vol. 66, no. 6, part 2.

Gumperz, John J. 1961. Speech Variation and the Study of Indian Civilization. *American Anthropologist* 63: 976–988.

———. 1964. "Linguistic and Social Interaction in Two Communities," in *The Ethnography of Communication* (ed. by J. J. Gumperz and D. Hymes), pp. 137–153.

American Anthropologist, Special Publication, vol. 66, no. 6, part 2.

———. 1967. "The Social Setting of Linguistic Behavior," in *A Field Manual for Cross-Cultural Study of the Acquisition of Communicative Competence (Second Draft)* (ed. by D. I. Slobin), pp. 129–134. Berkeley: University of California.

Hymes, Dell. 1962. "The Ethnography of Speaking," in *Anthropology and Human Behavior* (ed. by T. Gladwin and W. C. Sturtevant), pp. 13–53. Washington, DC: The Anthropological Society of Washington.

———. 1964. "Introduction: Toward Ethnographies of Communication," in *The Ethnography of Communication* (ed. by J. J. Gumperz and D. Hymes), pp. 1–34. *American Anthropologist*, Special Publication, vol. 66, no. 6, part 2.

Kaut, Charles R. 1957. *The Western Apache Clan System: Its Origins and Development.* University of New Mexico Publications in Anthropology, no. 9.

Martin, Samuel. 1964. "Speech Levels in Japan and Korea," in *Language in Culture and Society* (ed. by D. Hymes), pp. 407–415. New York: Harper & Row.

Mowrer, Priscilla. 1970. Notes on Navajo Silence Behavior. MS, University of Arizona.

Slobin, Dan I. (ed.). 1967. *A Field Manual for Cross-Cultural Study of the Acquisition of Communicative Competence (Second Draft).* Berkeley: University of California.

Post-reading Questions / Activities

- Compare Basso's explanation of Apache silence with Bauman's treatment of Quaker silence. Does silence mean the same thing? Does it come from the same values?
- What are some of the assumptions you tend to make when someone doesn't speak?
- When are you comfortable and when uncomfortable with silence? On what does this difference depend?
- Are you familiar with cultural prescriptions about the proper time to speak and the proper time to remain silent? Collect slogans and clichés about this. Then observe actual behavior and see what caveats must be made about silence.

Vocabulary

consanguineal kinship
ethnography of communication
exogamous clans
extralinguistic

informant
lexeme
matrilineal kinship
taboo

Suggested Further Reading

Basso, Keith H. 1986 [1970]. *The Cibecue Apache.* Prospect Heights, IL: Waveland Press.

———. 1979. *Portraits of the "Whiteman": Linguistic Play and Cultural Symbols Among the Western Apache.* Cambridge and New York: Cambridge University Press.

Gumperz, John J., and Dell Hymes, eds. 1986. *Directions in Sociolinguistics: The Ethnography of Communication.* Oxford: Blackwell.

Tannen, Deborah, and Muriel Saville-Troike, eds. 1985. *Perspectives on Silence.* Norwood, NJ: Ablex.

GLOSSARY

Note: Many of these terms have multiple meanings, and quite a few have been the subject of lengthy discussion or controversy. Some have been invented by or associated with particular individuals, whose names are provided. These definitions are intended to aid you in understanding the chapter in which the terms appear in this book.

AAE: African American English

AAVE: African American Vernacular English

aboriginal: from Latin, *ab origine*, there from the beginning; "native" or indigenous

absolute coordinate system: a frame of reference for describing the locations of objects in a geocentric way (e.g., "The house is south of the mountain.")

accent (nontechnical term): a set of features of pronunciation associated with a particular geographic location or a social group

additive multilingualism: a kind of multilingualism in which new languages are added while original languages are retained

adjacency pair: two utterances that belong together (e.g., "Thank you." "You're welcome.")

affect: conscious experience of feeling

affix: something added to a word, such as a prefix or suffix

affricate: a class of sound that stops the flow of air and then continues with friction in the same position, such as the initial sound in *chop*

alphabetic writing: a system of writing in which symbols refer to contrastive sound units (phonemes)

alternate sign languages: sign languages used in addition to another, usually spoken, language

amae (Japanese): a sense of dependence and love felt by the junior in a relationship

analog: a system in which elements may grade infinitely

anglophone: describing areas or persons that use English

animate: a class of words that refer to living things

arbitrariness: See *arbitrary*

arbitrary: related by convention and rules, not by natural necessity, bond, or connection; unmotivated

ASL: American Sign Language

aspect: a characteristic of verbs that conveys a sense of whether the action is complete or incomplete, ongoing or punctual

aspirated: producing air on pronunciation

autonomous: independent, as grammar from cognition

back-channel cues: active feedback from the "listener" in a conversation

bald on-record face-threatening act (FTA): unmitigated, openly stated verbal action that can be construed as threatening the hearer's face (see also *face*)

behaviorism: a psychological theory that sees all human behavior (including thought) as learned; associated with the idea of the mind as "blank slate"

bidialectalism: use of two variants (dialects) of the "same" language

bilingual education: education in two languages simultaneously

binocular: using two eyes for depth perception

bipedalism: walking upright, on two legs

blending: a form of linguistic productivity that combines elements of more than one call or utterance

blending systems: linguistic systems in which combinations of elements result in properties taking on aspects of all elements

borrowing: use of terms from one language in another

bound morpheme: a morpheme that cannot be used in isolation (see also *morpheme*)

call-response: a system of communication in which one person's utterances expect a voiced response

call system: nonlinguistic communicative repertoire of animals (including humans)

cardinal numbers: numbers that count things

caste (India): a class in a hereditary system of social classes

circumstantial voice: a sentence construction in which a constituent (place, time, instrument, etc.) is made into the subject of the action

classificatory kinship: a kinship system that combines individuals from what are considered "different categories" into a single category

closed-call system: a communicative system in which there are a fixed number of calls

code switching, code-switching: use of more than one identifiable linguistic code in a single stretch of discourse

cognate: describing terms in two languages related by genetic relationship and having the same meaning

cognitive sciences: fields of study devoted to the study of cognition; sometimes used in the singular as an interdisciplinary field colonial language: language used by the colonial rulers

common name: a noun referring to a thing

communicative competence: the ability to use and comprehend appropriate language

community of practice: a group of people who interact for a shared purpose, often producing shared modes of communication (coined by Jean Lave and Etienne Wenger)

comparative method (of historical linguistics): a method of reconstructing a parent language by comparing lexical items and phonological systems of descendant languages

consanguineal kinship: relationships by "blood" or descent

consonantal writing system: a system of writing in which symbols refer only to consonants

constative: a statement that conveys information; an utterance that can be judged true or false

constituent structure: the property of language that combines medium-sized groups of words into units

conversational implicature: a term coined by Paul Grice to indicate the work done by conversational partners to interpret the underlying functions and meanings of utterances as consistent with his overall "cooperative principle" despite apparent violations of this principle

copula: a verb that links a subject and predicate; in English it is the verb *to be*

crèche: child care center

creole: a language evolved from the pidgin formed through the interaction of speakers of unrelated languages; a creole takes on some characteristics of each of its donor languages and has regular syntax and vocabulary

cultural survivals: cultural traits that endure past their original function

CVCV: consonant vowel consonant vowel

deference: respect conveyed through interaction (this usage often attributed to Erving Goffman)

deictic: an expression that depends on context of use for interpretation (like English *here* or *I*)

deixis: the property of languages to "point to" proximity or distance, or to derive meaning from context

description, descriptive grammar or linguistics: analysis that describes the actual usage of language users

design features: the analytic components of a communicative system (Charles Hockett)

diachronic: across time

dialect: a variety of a language

dialectal: related to Dialects

Diaspora: the dispersal of a population from its original home territory

diasporic: related to Diaspora

digital: a system in which elements are discrete, with absolute distinctions

diglossia: a situation in which an H ("high") and an L ("low") language coexist in a speech community and are used for complementary functions

directive: an utterance or action that makes someone else do something

discourse: a unit of language above the level of the sentence

discourse analysis, discourse analysts: a field of study that looks at language in its social context; analysis of language above the level of the sentence. One kind of discourse analysis is conversational analysis.

discourse markers: units in a stretch of discourse that have communicative functions

discrete, discreteness: divided, distinct, noncontinuous (said, for example, of speech sounds)

discursive: related to discourse

displacement: the ability to refer to things outside the immediate situation, often removed in time and space from the moment of utterance

double articulation: another term for *duality of patterning*

duality of patterning: the property of smaller meaningless elements combining at a higher level to create meaning

emic: from the participant's point of view; derived from *phonemic* (Kenneth Pike)

endangered language: a language likely to become extinct

endoglossic: describing languages coming from within a society

English-immersion: an approach to teaching English as a new language that puts learners immediately into a setting in which only English is used

ethnographer: someone who investigates culture through participant observation

ethnography: a study of a particular setting, using participant observation; or, an account of such a study

ethnography of communication: an approach to the study of language in society that looks at who says what to whom in what way, incorporating social, cultural, and linguistic dimensions of particular speech events; also called *ethnography of speaking* (Dell Hymes, John Gumperz)

ethnography of speaking: an approach to the study of language in society that looks at who says what to whom in what way, incorporating social, cultural, and linguistic dimensions of particular speech events; also called *ethnography of communication* (Dell Hymes, John Gumperz)

etic: from an outsider's point of view; derived from *phonetic* (Kenneth Pike)

exogamous clans: clans that do not marry each other's members

exogamy: marriage outside a group

exoglossic: describing languages coming from outside a society

extragenetic: outside genetic transmission (usually through cultural transmission)

extralinguistic: outside language

face: reputation, honor, dignity, prestige, value in the eyes of others

featural writing system: a system of writing in which symbols refer to the distinctive phonological features of sounds

fictive kinship: a relationship expressed through the idiom of kinship, though without actual kin relations

filler: expressions that fill time while the speaker thinks about what to say next

floor: the right to speak and be listened to

"foreigner talk": a particular register in which people address those who are not native speakers of a language

formulaic expression: a fixed expression

francophone: describing areas or people that use French

free morpheme: a morpheme that can stand alone (see also *morpheme*)

fricatives: a class of sounds with "friction" but not complete closure, like the first sound in *ship.*

GAE: General American English

gender: a class of words; this can be masculine, feminine, neuter, animate, etc.

generative grammar: a theory of language that looks at the ways novel sentences are generated through rules for movement and combination (Noam Chomsky)

genre: a style of a particular communicative variety with recognizable form and function

gesticulation: waving arms and hands accompanying speech

gesture-call: a system of communication that has a number of gestures combined with vocalizations

grammar: a code or rules for combining words

grapholect: a type of writing that transcends the differences among "dialects" of its users

HE: Hispanized English

hedge, hedging: a verbal form that makes a stance less clear or firm

heritable, heritability: the quality of traits' variation stemming from genes

hesitation marker: verbal time fillers, such as English *um*

hominid, hominin: erect, bipedal members of the Hominidae primate family. The human lineage emerges from the hominin (or hominids).

hominoid: apes and humans

homophones: words with the same pronunciation

hyperanglicize: to exaggerate the English pronunciation of a foreign word

hypercorrect: beyond correct; using a formal form in a situation where a more casual one may be expected

iconic signs: signs that resemble their referent

iconicity: the trait of signs resembling the concept to which they refer

iconization: a perceived relationship in which the language is seen as resembling its speaker

ICQ ("I Seek You"): computer programs and interfaces for the purposes of interacting; principally Instant Messaging and chatting

ideographic writing: see *logographic writing*

ikarkana (Kuna): ways, texts

illocutionary force: the intended effect of an utterance (J. L. Austin)

immediacy: the quality of acting in the present and responding to stimuli actually there

inanimate: not alive

inflected: a category of languages that indicate grammatical relations through inflections

inflection: elements added to base words to provide information about relationships, time, and other grammatical or semantic features

informant: a participant in a culture consulted by an ethnographer

innate: inborn

interference: deviation from standard patterns in a language, resulting from multilingual individuals' knowledge of other languages

interlocutor: a partner in a conversation

intersentential code switching: code switching at sentence or clause boundaries

intonation: rhythm, stress, and pitch changes accompanying ordinary speech

intrasentential (intra-sentential) code switching: code switching within a sentence boundary

intrinsic coordinate system: a frame of reference for describing the locations of objects in an object-centered way (e.g., "The house is in front of the school.")

isolating: describing a category of languages that indicate grammatical relations by the use and position of particular words

joint production: a view of human culture that sees all participants involved in creating exchanges

kabary: formal or ceremonial speech among Malagasy speakers

Kiswahili: Swahili, an African lingua franca

kros (Tok Pisin): 'angry'

Kula: a set of exchanges linking people throughout the Trobriand Islands

L1: a native language

L1 interference: features of a person's native language being used inappropriately in a second language

L2: a language learned beyond childhood; a second language

language contact: a situation in which speech communities with different languages interact frequently

language endangerment: a situation in which a language is at risk of dying

language ideology: ideas about language held by people in a particular society

language loss: the decrease in the viability of a language or languages

language maintenance: ongoing use of an earlier-learned language after a new one has been learned

language mixing: use of more than one language within the same utterance

language planning: study and implementation of policies with regard to language, often institutionally

language policy: legislation and regulation regarding language

language revitalization: effort to increase language use of an endangered language, especially in younger speakers

language revival: bringing back to full use a language that has been moribund

language shift: change in dominant language

latch: no pause before turn taking

latching: turn transition without pause or overlap

lexeme: word

lexical: having to do with words

lexical item: a word

lexicon: a mental dictionary; the collection of words in a language

lexis: lexicon

lime, liming: Trinidadian term for spontaneous, leisurely group meetings and participation in them

lingua franca: a language spoken across a region, often learned by people whose mother tongues differ, in order to foster communication across language boundaries

linguistic determinism: the notion that language determines people's thought

linguistic insecurity: difference between the speaker's own speech and judgment of "correct" speech

linguistic marketplace: the entire range of linguistic resources

linguistic repertoire: the range of linguistic resources of a person or community

linguistic security: fit between a person's perception of standard and perception of their own speech

literacy: the ability to read and write (often imprecise)

loan word: use of a word from one language in another

logographic writing: a system of writing in which each symbol represents a word

LTF: language-trait focused

Machiavellian intelligence hypothesis: see *social intelligence theory*

manual language: a language involving use of the hands rather than speech

manual: using the hands

marked, markedness: atypical, not the default case; having to be indicated by some particular mark; for example, in English the singular is unmarked, and the plural tends to be marked, as in *car - cars*

matched-guise test: a test of attitudes toward languages in which bilingual speakers are recorded and listeners are asked to evaluate them; the listeners do not realize that the speakers have two "guises"

matrilineal kinship: relationships through the female line

MC: middle class

mediated: going through an intermediary

metalinguistic: relating to language about language

metaphor, metaphoric: expression of one thing in terms of another

metaphorical concept: linguistic expressions that structure thought by conceiving of one thing in terms of another

metaphorical code switching: code switching done because of an association between a code and a topic, a stance, a feeling, or something related to a particular code within a single conversation

metonym, metonymic: a figure of speech in which a part stands for a whole or a feature stands for something associated with it, as in *the crown* for *the ruler*

mitigate, mitigating: softening, reducing the impact

Mock Spanish: a genre of speech in which apparently Spanish usage is employed

modular: describing a system with components that can occupy particular places in a structure

monosyllabic: made of one syllable

moribund language: a language no longer being learned by children as a mother tongue

morpheme: the smallest meaningful element in language

morphology: study of morphemes

morphophonemic: related to the interaction between morphemes and phonology, or sounds and meaningful units

mother tongue: the language spoken earliest and at home

mutually intelligible: able to be understood by speakers of both varieties

nativism: a view of human features as innate

Neanderthal, Neandertal: *Homo sapiens neanderthalensis* (according to some scholars; others call it its own species): a hominid living about 200,000 to 30,000 years ago in Europe, western Asia, and northern Africa

negative face: honoring people by giving them options

network analysis: study of regular social interactions among individuals

nonce borrowing: a word borrowed into a language just on a particular occasion

NSL: Nicaraguan Sign Language

NSPRS: Nonstandard Puerto Rican Spanish

number: the grammatical feature in some languages that distinguishes singular and plural, and sometimes other categories such as dual

official language: a language used for administrative and national communication

ontology of language: a view of the nature of language; see also *language ideology*

oralism: advocacy of teaching the deaf to speak

orality: a primary orientation through speech; the presumption that languages are, at their core, oral

ordinals: numbers that order things (e.g., English *first, second*, etc.)

orthographic: from spelling

orthography: writing system

overlap: to speak simultaneously; also a noun referring to this phenomenon

paralinguistic: related to elements in addition to words said (including intonation, volume, etc.)

paralinguistics: aspects of language in addition to words said (including intonation, volume, etc.)

performative: a type of utterance that performs an action (J. L. Austin)

performativity: a theory of human culture in which meanings and identities emerge from performance (Judith Butler)

philology, philological: the study of the origins of languages, sometimes as they appear in literature

phoneme: the smallest unit of sound that makes a difference in meaning (e.g., the initial sounds of *bat* and *pat*)

phonemic: related to the meaningful sound contrasts in a language

phonemic writing: a system of writing in which symbols refer to consonants and vowels

phonological: relating to the sound pattern in a language

phonological variables: aspects of the sound pattern that vary systematically

phonology: the study of the systematic sound pattern of a particular language

phrase structure: the structure of the syntactic constituents of sentences

pictographic: describing writing that conveys meanings through images that call words to mind

pidgin: the rudimentary, possibly unstable, form of language produced out of necessity for communication by people whose native languages differ

plasticity: the capacity of the brain to change

plurality: the grammatical quality of number beyond one

politeness: principles of human linguistic interaction that gives face to others

pongid: the family of apes that includes gorillas, chimpanzees, and orangutans

positive face: honoring people by showing enthusiasm or sharing

postvocalic: following a vowel

pragmatic: relating to context and use

PRE: Puerto Rican English

preconsonantal: before a consonant

prescription, prescriptive, prescriptive grammar, prescriptivism: describing analysis or attitudes that tells people how their language should be

primary orality: the orality of people unfamiliar with writing or literacy

primary sign languages: sign languages used as the main form of communication

primate: an order of mammals with binocular vision, the ability to grasp, and a large brain; this includes humans, apes, and monkeys

productivity: the capacity to say things that have never been said before

pronominal: related to pronouns

proper name: a unique or limited term by which to identify individuals

proto: the original, hypothesized earlier form of a language

proto-Indo-European: the hypothetical original language of which the descendents are other living (and extinct) languages in Europe and South Asia

quotable gestures: conventional hand and other gestures that must be learned; also called *emblems*

quotable vocalizations: conventional expressions that are not words, such as *m-hm* or *uh-oh*

quotative: introducing a quotation

rebus: representation of words through images or symbols which, when pronounced, sound like those words, such as *ICU* for *I see you*, or a combination of phonetic and logographic elements, such as *gr8* for *great*

receptive trilingualism (multilingualism): a form of trilingualism (multilingualism) in which all parties understand all languages but are active in using only one or two

recursion: the quality of being able to be repeatedly applied

recursive: able to be repeatedly applied, as in recursive grammatical rules

register: a more-or-less consistent version of a language that is used in a professional, social, or other setting or context

relative coordinate system: a frame of reference for describing the locations of objects in a viewpoint-dependent way (e.g., "The map is to the right of the car keys.")

resaka: informal, everyday speech among Malagasy speakers

rhetoric: public speaking, oratory (in the classic, Greek sense)

rhotics: /r/ and related sounds

SAE: usually Standard American English; for Whorf, Standard Average European

schwa: an unstressed vowel, such as the two last vowels pronounced in the word *vegetable*

SEC: socioeconomic class

secondary orality: the orality of people in technologically developed societies

secondary sign: a sign that refers to another semiotic system

semantic: relating to meaning

semantic extension: emphasizing one aspect of an English word, extending or changing its focus

semantic inversion: reversing customary meaning; for example, a word in AAE having the opposite to its meaning in GAE

semanticity: the quality of conveying meaning through utterances

semiology: the science of the study of signs; more commonly called *semiotics*

semiotic: related to signs and meaning

semiotics: the science of the study of signs

sign: something that points to something else

sign language: a language using hand shapes, arms, and face

signified: the "meaning" of a sign

signifier: the outside appearance of a sign

"Simple Nativism": the view that all major properties of language are dictated by inbuilt mental apparatus (see Chapter 12 by Levinson)

Sinitic: related to the family of Chinese languages

situational code switching: code switching done because of a set of activities or speakers associated with a particular code

SL: standard language

slang: a set of terms associated with a particular social group and context

social intelligence theory: the theory that what separates primates from all other animals is the complexity of their social relationships

social stratification: levels of social differentiation with evaluative differentiation

sociolinguistics: a branch of linguistics that investigates the relationships between linguistic and social factors

speech community: a group of people who use a particular language to communicate with one another

SPP: second pair-part (in a two-part exchange or *adjacency pair* [q.v.]) (Harvey Sacks)

SPRS: Standard Puerto Rican Spanish

stable bilingualism: a situation in which two languages coexist with complementary functions

stable multilingualism: a situation in which several languages coexist with complementary functions

standard, standard language: a language variety defined as the correct version against which other varieties are measured

standardization: the process by which a particular linguistic variety becomes established as the standard

statement: an utterance that provides information or facts

stop: a class of sounds that stops the flow of air, such as the two consonants in *tad*

style, conversational: the paralinguistic and discursive aspects of speech: pitch, amplitude, intonation, voice quality, lexical and syntactic choice, rate of speech and turn taking; what is said; how discourse cohesion is achieved

superlaryngeal vocal tract: the part of the vocal tract above the larynx

superstandard: a linguistic variety that surpasses the prescriptive norm established by the standard language or is used in situations where a less formal variety would be expected

suprasegmentals: aspects of utterances above the level of phonemes, such as pitch, tone, or stress

swidden agriculture: slash-and-burn agriculture; fields are burned to provide nutrients in ash

syllabary: a collection of written syllables, each symbol referring to a syllable

syllabic writing: a system of writing in which symbols refer to syllables

synchronic: at a given moment in time

syntax: the order of items in an utterance

synthetic: describing a category of languages that indicate grammatical relations by internal transformations within words

taboo: something powerful, often with strict prohibitions in some circumstances or for some individuals or classes

tag question: a question appended to an utterance, as in *She's a top-notch researcher, isn't she?*.

target language: the language being learned

teknonym: a term of address indicating parenthood or grandparenthood, named for the child, as in *Rachel's mother*

tense: a characteristic of verbs indicating temporal relationships

token: an instance of a linguistic type or term

topic: the subject of an utterance or conversation

traditional transmission: the passing on of knowledge through contact with people in society

triglossia: a situation in which three languages coexist with complementary functions

Trobriand Islands: a collection of islands in Papua New Guinea, made famous in anthropology through the pioneering work of Bronislaw Malinowski and studied subsequently by many others

turn: an instance of having the floor in a conversation

turn taking: alternation of turns

UMC: upper middle class

unmarked: the default or typical case (as singular versus plural)

utterance: something said, of any length or quality

variety: any distinctive spoken, written, printed, electronic, or other aspect of a language

vehicular languages: languages used for inter ethnic communication

vernacular: sometimes refers to a nonstandard variety of a language

vernacular languages: languages used within ethnic communities

vernacularization: the adoption of an indigenous language as the official language

visual-manual: the mode or channel of signed languages

vocal-auditory: the mode or channel of spoken languages

voice: the characteristic of a sound in terms of vibration or lack of vibration of the vocal cords

voiced: involving vibration of the vocal cords, as in the initial consonant of *zoo*

voiceless: without the vibration of the vocal cords, as in the initial consonant of *soon*

WC: working class

Whorfianism: shorthand expression for the approach to the relationship between language and thought associated with Benjamin Lee Whorf; also called linguistic relativity

xenoglossia: a speech situation in which individuals speak to one another in different languages

INDEX